W9-BRZ-132

Corporate Financial Management

Corporate Financial Management

RAYMOND P. KENT
Professor of Finance and Business Economics
University of Notre Dame

1969
Third Edition

Richard D. Irwin, Inc., Homewood, Illinois
Irwin-Dorsey Limited, Nobleton, Ontario

Third Edition

First Printing, March, 1969

Library of Congress Catalog Card No. 69–15545
Printed in the United States of America

To

Claudia

Ray

Claudia Marie

and Bob

PREFACE

For this third edition of my textbook, I have greatly expanded the treatment of the theory and techniques of capital budgeting and have added a new chapter on the cost of capital. In the matter of capital budgeting, I give particular emphasis to the problem of choosing among the variety of expansion projects which, for the typical corporation, compete for funds, including a detailed examination of the analytical methods of measuring prospective payback and profitability as means for judgments. In this examination, mathematical procedures are treated, I think, clearly and comprehensively, with extensive illustrations, and with new sets of present-value tables for reference in relation to the exposition and for students' use in the solution of problems. In the matter of cost of capital, I stress the importance of its relationship to estimates of profitability, the theory and mathematical techniques of its estimation, its complexities as a concept, and the limitations of theory and techniques. In all other chapters of the new edition, I have tried to bring all materials thoroughly up to date. This updating means citation of the latest available data on various kinds of developments, the revision of tabular material, many new references to recent corporate actions for illustration, references to changes in laws and their effects, taking note of amendments to tax legislation and their probable influence upon corporate practices, and the revision of illustrative material to reflect changes in tax rates and tax treatment. But even more important, I think, is the updating of materials to give a proper place to recent extraordinary developments in corporate practices, such as the voluminous exchanges of securities in the accelerating merger movement, the flood of convertible securities, and the important new role for guaranteed obligations in the financing of operations abroad. Finally, I have thoroughly reworked most of the end-of-the-chapter questions, many of which I have striven to state in ways that invite discussion, and have presented end-of-the-chapter problems entirely changed—of new types, in some instances, but changed in content in all instances.

In this third edition, I continue to emphasize the managerial point of view—explaining the theories that business managers ought to know about for good decision making; presenting facts, problems, and the circumstances of laws, taxes, competition, and so on, as business managers are likely to evaluate them; describing the kinds of records, reports, and techniques that they should have available; and analyzing practices and developments as evidences of decisions arrived at and policies adopted. At the same time, I try to maintain a fair balance between the "internal" concerns of decision makers in the day-to-day financial management of their enterprises, and their "external" concerns as in borrowing and repaying loans and designing and floating security issues. Recent developments have surely proved that the "external" concerns hardly deserve to be played down (because of their relative rarity, as some have said)—developments such as the feverish scramble for both short-term and long-term funds in recent periods of tight money, the constant search of many corporations for favorable opportunities for "acquisitions" by way of merger, the new design and the resurrection of old designs of security features to fit shifts in investor interests, and the turning on of the stock-certificate printing press by many corporations to provide a substitute for money for the buying up of the properties of other corporations.

Although it is obviously my opinion that the sequence of topics in the textbook is a logical one for courses bearing such descriptive titles as "Corporation Finance" and "Business Finance," instructors who prefer a different order of presentation for their courses should have no great difficulty in adapting the book to serve their requirements. Such adaptation should be especially easy for those who prefer to take up the means of financing rather early in the course and to leave asset management till later. This can be done by going direct from Chapter 6 to Chapter 11 or to Chapter 15, as one may choose. Since financial management is simultaneously asset management and liability-and-equity management, it would not seem to matter greatly which aspect of this dual focus is treated first. At any rate, the chapters on financing (Chapters 15 through 34) are quite comprehensible as a unit without an earlier investigation of asset management. Instructors will find, too, I think, that the book is adaptable for courses of either one or two semesters. It should not require an undue amount of hurrying to cover the whole book in a single semester, while a more intensive treatment of most of the topics covered will surely be possible in two-semester courses. In one-semester courses, some instructors may decide that some of the topics should be passed over lightly or omitted so that more time can be spent on others; and in two-semester offerings, some may decide that the textbook should be supplemented with readings, cases, or problems (in addition to those I supply), or some combination of these.

I am most pleased to have this opportunity to express my great appreciation to all the generous people whose advice and criticism have served to make this book better than it otherwise would have been. As all the effort that went into the first two editions continues to be reflected in this third edition, I remain deeply indebted to all who helped me with the earlier editions, especially Professor Hubert H. Frisinger of the University of Toledo; Professor LeClair H. Eells, for long a most esteemed colleague at the University of Notre Dame; Professor Stanley W. Preston of Louisiana State University; the late Professor Karl A. Boedecker of Michigan State University; Professor Sergei Dobrovolsky of Wayne State University; Professor Edward E. Edwards of Indiana University; Professor Donald M. Halley of Tulane University; Professor Harold W. Stevenson of the University of Minnesota; and Professor James O. Horrigan of the University of New Hampshire. For most helpful criticism and advice aimed especially at improvements for this third edition, I am greatly indebted to Professor Henry J. Guithues of St. Louis University for his detailed criticism of the second (revised) edition and for his many good recommendations; and to my Notre Dame colleagues, especially Professor Bernard J. Kilbride, Professor Paul F. Conway, and Professor Eells for their ever-encouraging support of my efforts, many enlightening discussions, and numerous valuable suggestions. I find it most pleasant, also, to be able to express sincere appreciation to the many professors at many colleges and universities who have given me, in briefer comments and suggestions, the benefits of their experience in using the first two editions. Finally, Claudia my wife always helps in innumerable ways most patiently and graciously—to her my debt is forever greatest.

Notre Dame, Indiana RAYMOND P. KENT
February, 1969

TABLE OF CONTENTS

Part V. Financial Structure

Part VI. Financing with Common Stock

Part VII. Financing with Preferred Stock

Part VIII. Financing with Retained Earnings

Part IX. Financing with Bonds

Part X. Financing without Securities

Index

Part I

FINANCE AND THE BUSINESS CORPORATION

chapter 1

THE FIELD OF CORPORATION FINANCE

INTRODUCTION

Like all other things that bear the label *finance* or *financial*, corporation finance has to do with money. As a field of study, it embraces all the theories, procedures, institutions, instruments, problems, and policies that are involved in the acquisition and use of money by business corporations.

Business corporations seek to acquire many kinds of assets, and the money holdings of the typical corporation at most times represent only a minor fraction of its total assets; nevertheless, the quest for land, buildings, machinery, equipment, inventories, and other kinds of assets usually starts out as a quest for money. Because money is the generally accepted medium of exchange, it is the one kind of asset that is readily convertible into all other kinds. Thus business corporations want to acquire money so that it can be used to buy productive facilities.

Business Corporations

Business corporations, with whose financial activities the study of corporation finance is concerned, constitute just one of several classes of corporations that operate in the United States—a very large class, but far from being all-inclusive. Such a corporation is a distinct entity or personality created by the federal or a state government as a means by which people can pool their resources to carry on some kind of business activity for the purpose of deriving profits that they alone have the right to share in.

It is the profit motive of the business corporation—or, perhaps one should say more accurately, the profit motive of its stockholders—that distinguishes it from other classes of corporations; and it is its status as a distinct entity or personality that distinguishes it from other forms of business enterprise.

As thus differentiated, a very large majority of business corporations are created or chartered by the state governments, since the federal government charters only a few.

Other Classes of Corporations

Stockholders make contributions to the assets of business corporations in the expectation of receiving dividends in proportion to the respective amounts of their contributions; and, as indicated, they do not expect anybody who is not a stockholder to share in the dividends, no matter how worthy or needy he may be. Other kinds of corporations are operated in the expectation or hope that their income will exceed their expenses, but without expectation that any excess of income will be shared as dividends by any class or group, regardless of its responsibility for success or failure. Thus, *public corporations*, including chiefly incorporated city governments and school districts, will simply use excess revenues of a given year to pay off accumulated debts or to carry on their regular operations in the following year. One does not expect the excess to be distributed as dividends to the citizens who can be regarded as the stockholders or members of these municipal corporations.

A state government that derives profits from the operations of an incorporated system of liquor stores in which it has sole ownership, or a city government that obtains profits as owner of a separately incorporated waterworks or bus line—such enterprises are classified as *public proprietary corporations*—is expected to devote this income to police and fire protection, education, highway building and maintenance, and other public functions, or perhaps to the expansion of the proprietary enterprises themselves. It is not, in any case, expected to pay pro rata cash dividends to the citizens of the state or the city.

Likewise, corporations organized for religious, educational, charitable, and scientific purposes are expected to devote directly to these purposes any income they currently receive in excess of current expenditures. The Red Cross does not distribute dividends to its members—that is, the people who make contributions to it—even though in some years it may have more revenue than it expends on its great work of philanthropy. Corporations that have objectives of the kinds just mentioned are classified as *private nonprofit corporations;* they are described as "private" to distinguish them from public (governmental) entities and enterprises, and as "nonprofit" because no net income or profit is payable to their members, regardless of the size of the excess of current income over current expenditures.

Enterprises described as *cooperative corporations* have primary objectives such as helping their members to cut production or distribution costs by means of mass buying and selling or the joint use of certain kinds of facilities. Though such corporations may pay moderate dividends on the basis of stockholdings, most of their distributions of "profits" to members are generally made proportional to the total value of goods each member has brought from them, the quantity of his output he has sold through them, or the extent to which he has used their facilities. Accordingly, the distributions are chiefly rebates on fees and charges paid by members, rather than shares in net income.

In our analysis of the materials of corporation finance, therefore, we will ignore the financial activities of public corporations, public proprietary corporations, private nonprofit corporations, and cooperative corporations. Some of these—particularly the public proprietary corporations and the cooperatives—may be business enterprises in every aspect but profit motive, and the others may be strongly advised to employ "sound business methods" in managing their affairs; nevertheless, their policies and procedures in matters of finance tend to be quite different from those of business corporations.

PROFIT ORIENTED

Special Position of Financial Institutions

In the study of corporation finance, it is also customary to ignore the activities of commercial banks, savings banks, and other financial institutions insofar as these activities have to do with their own procedures in acquiring money. Though most financial institutions are incorporated and have as their primary objective the earning of profits for the benefit of their stockholders, their distinctive arrangements for acquiring money give them a character decidedly different from that of manufacturing, mercantile, and other such subclasses of business corporations. The fact that our Federal Reserve and commercial banks have the capacity *to create money* puts them in a position quite unlike that of other business corporations. Likewise, the receiving of deposits makes the money-acquiring processes of some other classes of financial institutions far different from those of nonfinancial business corporations.

But the use to which money is put by financial institutions is a matter of very great interest in the study of corporation finance, because these institutions are the most important suppliers of money to nonfinancial business corporations. Hence, we will give close attention to the activities of financial institutions, not primarily from the standpoint of how they run their affairs—this constitutes much of the material in the separate field of study called *money and banking*—but with emphasis on how they serve all other kinds of business corporations in providing money in a wide variety of circumstances and on the basis of terms and conditions of great diversity.

Operating Areas of Business Corporations

Because our study excludes the financial activities of public, private nonprofit, and cooperative corporations, as well as the money-acquiring procedures of financial institutions, one should not conclude that the field of corporation finance is a decidedly limited one. Quite the contrary. Materials of almost endless variety as they concern tens of thousands of operating corporations remain available for study, so that the student is faced with the task, not of seeking topics worthy of analysis, but of sifting through the abundant materials to discover those that are truly important.

We find, indeed, that corporation finance is concerned with the finance functions of almost 1.031 million business corporations, which:

1. Operate in all areas of manufacturing, mining, and contract construction.
2. Provide transportation, communication, and other public utility services, such as railroads, airlines, truck and bus lines, telephone companies, television and radio broadcasting companies, and electric power and gas companies.
3. Engage in wholesale and retail trade, which includes incorporated food stores, department stores, restaurants, automobile agencies, and gasoline filling stations.
4. Provide many kinds of professional and personal services such as incorporated engineering firms, employment agencies, hotels, motels, theaters, barber shops and beauty parlors, and laundries and dry-cleaning establishments.

Types of Corp

A breakdown of the number of corporations functioning in these areas as indicated by federal income tax returns filed for fiscal years ending between July 1, 1965, and June 30, 1966, is presented in Table 1–1.

TABLE 1–1
Number and Industrial Classsification of Business Corporations, 1965–66*

Industrial Classification	*Number*
Agriculture, forestry, and fisheries	27,582
Mining	13,326
Contract construction	113,403
Manufacturing	186,613
Public utilities	59,846
Wholesale and retail trade	441,538
Services	188,284
Total	1,030,592

*Based on federal income tax returns filed by "active" corporations for fiscal years ending between July 1, 1965, and June 30, 1966. Also, for this period 389,634 returns were filed by corporations engaged in finance, insurance, and real estate, and 7,380 returns by corporations the nature of whose business was not allocable. In addition, returns filed by "inactive" corporations—defined as those reporting no item of income or deduction—numbered 66,120.

SOURCE: U.S. Treasury Department, Internal Revenue Service, *Statistics of Income, 1965—Preliminary: Corporation Income Tax Returns* (Washington, D.C.: U.S. Government Printing Office, 1967), pp. 2, 14–18.

Other Forms of Business Enterprise

The status of business corporations as distinct entities or personalities distinguishes them from other forms of business enterprise. As an entity or personality, a business corporation is a being quite separate from the persons who organize it, its stockholders, and its managers. If three men decide to establish a business enterprise and have it incorporated, a fourth entity, or person, comes into existence the moment the state issues a charter to them.[1] As a person created by the action of the state government, the new corporation has power: to buy and sell goods; to own land, buildings, machinery, and other equipment; to hire employees; to bring lawsuits; and so on—all in its own name as if it were itself a human being.

In contrast to this, a proprietorship is a business carried on by a single individual in his own name. A proprietor may give his enterprise a resounding title such as the "Imperial Manufacturing Company," but this action does not endow the enterprise with existence or being apart from his own. Similarly, three men who establish a general partnership are not confronted by a fourth being coming into existence by action of the state; as individual human beings, and in their own names, the partners buy and sell goods, hold land, buildings, and other property, hire labor, and engage in other kinds of activities. Other less common forms of business enterprise are also generally lacking in status as legal entities or personalities. Among these are business trusts, joint stock companies, limited partnerships, mining partnerships, partnership associations, and joint ventures. In a few states, the business trust has gained a position comparable to the legal-entity status of a corporation; nevertheless, the remaining states generally refuse to recognize such an enterprise as a distinct person or entity. Thus, a business trust that enjoys what amounts to legal-entity status in one state is likely to be treated as a partnership by other states into which it may want to expand its business activities. On the other hand, all states recognize and honor the business corporation's status as a legal entity without regard to charter origin. New York, for example, treats as persons business corporations established in the other 49 states; likewise, each of the 49 treats as persons corporations chartered by New York.

[1]The organizers of a corporation (or their attorneys) draw up articles of incorporation, setting out details as to its structure and purposes. These are submitted to a designated state official, usually the secretary of state, who, if he finds them in proper order, authorizes the carrying on of business according to the terms of the articles *and* the state's corporation laws. This authorization may be said to be the corporation's charter. These matters are taken up in detail in Chapter 3. As mentioned earlier, the federal government charters only a few business corporations; it largely limits its chartering to financial institutions such as national banks, federal savings and loan associations, and federal credit unions.

Corporation Finance and Business Finance

Just as corporation finance as a field of study avoids treating the financial policies and activities of certain classes of corporations, such as public corporations and private nonprofit corporations, so also does it give no direct attention to the finance functions of the noncorporate forms of business enterprise as mentioned in the preceding paragraph. Here again, however, the student should avoid the conclusion that the field of corporation finance is an unduly restricted one. Much of the subject matter of corporation finance is directly and precisely applicable to the financial activities of all kinds of private profit-seeking enterprises, and not to those of business corporations only. Therefore, although the term *business finance* is often used to describe a field of study somewhat broader than corporation finance one should realize that a good knowledge of corporation finance provides a broad grasp of the theories that are applied, the procedures and instruments used, the institutions employed, the problems faced, and the varieties of policies that are adopted in connection with the finance functions of all forms of business enterprise.

The following are but a few examples of the financial phenomena that are much the same for all kinds of business enterprises, regardless of their form.

1. The general scope of finance functions.
2. The circular flow of cash.
3. The adoption of sound asset-management policies.
4. Budgetary procedures.
5. Decisions on what amounts of money can be safely borrowed.
6. Selection of lending institutions to which applications for loans will be made.
7. Settling on the kinds and terms of loans.
8. Deciding what proportion of profits can be safely withdrawn by owners for their personal use.

Other similarities abound. A mortgage bond issue of a corporation closely compares with the mortgage debt of any other kind of borrower, and a promissory note given to a lender by a corporate borrower is likely to be indistinguishable in form from that given by, say, a proprietor or the members of a partnership. Again, the certificates of beneficial interest issued by business trusts are quite similar to stock certificates issued by corporations; indeed, certificates of beneficial interest are often referred to simply as "stock." In a word, then, corporation finance may be thought of as a subdivision of business finance, but it is a very large subdivision, encompassing much of the business finance field.

THE MATERIALS OF CORPORATION FINANCE

Although the remainder of this textbook is dedicated to an analysis of the theories, procedures, institutions, instruments, problems, and policies of corporation finance, it should be advantageous to have a preliminary view of these materials. Such a preliminary view should help the student to see the interrelationships among the materials as they are taken up in connection with specific topics in subsequent chapters—to help him to see how the parts fit into the whole picture.

Theories or Principles

Because a business corporation is simultaneously a creature of the state and a private profit-seeking enterprise, it is surrounded with both legal theories and economic and accounting theories. Some principles of corporation finance, therefore, are largely if not exclusively legal; others have their origin in economics and accounting; and still others blend ideas that originate in the law on the one hand and in economics and accounting on the other.

The legal theory that most strongly influences the financial policies and practices of business corporations has already been indicated, namely, that the corporation is a distinct entity having a life apart from the lives of its organizers, stockholders, managers, and other employees. Closely related to this are legal theories that: (1) a business corporation owns its own property; (2) only stockholders, as such, are the owners of a corporation; (3) the stockholders, though owning the corporation, do not own its assets; and (4) bondholders, as creditors, have no ownership rights. Upon other legal theories are based the respective managerial rights of stockholders and boards of directors, the ranking of rights between common stockholders and preferred stockholders, and the liability of stockholders who buy stock at a discount. Still other legal theories indicate the rights of creditors, how rights vary between secured and unsecured creditors, and the order in which creditors' claims will be met through the liquidation of a corporation's assets if it is unable to meet them in the ordinary course of business.

Most of the economic theories that find a place in the principles of corporation finance are inseparable from accounting theories—it is virtually impossible to say where one of these areas of thought leaves off and the other begins as they apply to corporation finance. At any rate, it can be said that economic and accounting theories, in a kind of partnership, indicate what are reasonable proportions between stockholders' equity and debt in the financial structures of corporations, relate the value of corporations' assets to their earning power, and distinguish between the asset values of corporations as going concerns and the sum of the market values of the separate items that make up the assets. Other theories of this joint classification may justify write-ups and write-downs in asset values as carried on the books, indicate the appropriate ways to treat items of extraordinary expense and income, and serve as criteria for the proper management of the surplus accounts. Likewise, we encounter theories about when and how expansion of the scale of business operations by the individual corporation is justified, as well as theories about why corporations run into financial difficulties.

Both legal and economic and accounting theories are applicable to questions involving dividend payments. Legal theory indicates in what circumstances boards of directors may declare dividends without themselves incurring liability; economic and accounting theory supplies the pros and cons of dividend declaration from the standpoint of expediency—from the standpoint, one may say, of trying to balance the long-run welfare of the corporation with the immediate interests of its stockholders. Again, both legal theory and economic and accounting theory come into play—and sometimes into conflict—in the determination of what outlays of cash are properly to be treated as current operating expenses and what are to be treated as acquisitions of assets to be charged off to expense over a period of years. The managers of a business corporation may be inclined to treat certain outlays as current expenses, but whether they may deduct such outlays from income in computing the corporation's federal income tax liability depends on the legal theories of deductible expenses as incorporated in the federal tax legislation.

Procedures

Procedures employed in the performance of the finance functions of business corporations are, again, both legal and economic. Aside from promotional activities in planning new corporations, the legal procedures come first; it is necessary, first of all, to get the enterprise firmly established as a creature of the state. This requires filing articles of incorporation with the appropriate official of the state from which a charter is desired, as well as taking certain additional actions the law requires. Later on, other legal procedures may be necessary, as when the corporation wants to change the provisions of its original articles, to qualify new security issues for sale within the state or in interstate commerce, or, perhaps, to merge with another corporation. At all times, certain other procedures will be governed, at least in part, by stipulations of pertinent laws, such as procedures for calling and holding stockholders' and directors' meetings, choosing directors, and counting votes.

Economic or business procedures in corporation finance include:

1. Forecasting of cash flows.
2. Controlling cash receipts and disbursements.

3. Safeguarding and temporarily investing cash balances.
4. Keeping records and making reports.
5. Offering new issues of securities to present stockholders.
6. Making arrangements with investment bankers for underwriting new securities issues.
7. Negotiating with commercial banks and other direct lenders.
8. Listing securities on the stock exchanges.
9. Making provisions for the retirement of securities already outstanding.

Many of these procedures require a high degree of managerial skill, while others, such as supervising cash receipts and disbursements, record-keeping, handling transfers of stocks and bonds, and paying dividends on stock and interest and principal on bonds, tend to be quite mechanical.

Institutions

The principal institution dealt with in the study of corporation finance is obviously the business corporation itself. Other institutions are treated because they provide financial assistance to business corporations, supply certain kinds of clerical aids that relieve them of burdensome details, or regulate some kinds of corporate financial activities.

Institutions that provide financial assistance to corporations are chiefly, of course, the various kinds of financial institutions. Some of these, such as the investment banking houses, serve corporations by helping them to sell their securities to the public. Others grant loans to them direct; these include commercial banks, commercial finance companies, and sales finance companies. Still others, such as the stock exchanges and brokerage houses, contribute to the attractiveness of new security issues by providing market facilities for those already outstanding. Finally, institutional investors are important because they buy large quantities of corporate securities without necessarily entering into any kind of direct negotiations with the corporations that issue the securities. Institutional investors include life insurance companies, trust companies, the trust departments of commercial banks, investment companies, and pension and endowment funds.

Trust companies and the trust departments of commercial banks are significant for a second reason: they help corporations with the clerical details of managing their security issues. In this regard, they serve as transfer agents and registrars of stock issues, indenture trustees for bond issues, and paying agents for dividends and other kinds of cash distributions.

Institutions that have the power to regulate specific phases of corporate financial activities are governmental agencies. Some of these, such as the Interstate Commerce Commission and many of the state public service commissions, have authority to approve or reject financing projects proposed by the corporations subject to their jurisdiction. Others, including the federal Securities and Exchange Commission and the state securities commissions, have the authority to prevent the sale of security issues that have not been properly qualified for sale in accordance with the respective federal and state laws. A final group, including trustees in bankruptcy, may entirely supplant corporation managements, at least temporarily, in the determination of financial policies.

Instruments

As corporation financial policy is strongly influenced by the provisions of certain kinds of laws, these laws must be allotted an important place as instruments for study. Laws that have significant prescriptions with respect to corporation finance include:

1. Corporation codes of the various states, on whose basis corporations are formed, have their charters amended, merge or consolidate with other corporations, and are dissolved.
2. Laws that give government agencies authority to regulate the security issues of certain kinds of corporations, especially corporations that provide transportation, communication, and other public utility services.
3. Laws that require the registration of security issues, security dealers, and stock exchanges.
4. Laws that provide for the reorganization of corporations.
5. Laws that establish procedures for recording liens, obtaining judgments, and initiating foreclosure actions.
6. Laws that give the quality of negotiability to promissory notes, bonds, stock certificates, and certain other documents.

Many kinds of instruments are used in the issuance of stock and in the exercise of stockholders' rights. These include stock certificate books, stockholders' ledgers, stock purchase warrants, registration statements, prospectuses, proxy statements, and proxy forms. Likewise, borrowing calls into use many different kinds of instruments, whether the borrowing is done through the sale of bond issues or by means of loans obtained direct from banking institutions. Such instruments include bond certificates, bond coupons, indentures, authentication forms, registration statements, prospectuses, promissory notes, underwriting contracts, and term-loan agreements.

Also highly significant in both the study and practice of corporation finance are cash and capital budgets (and other kinds of budgets, as well) as instruments for forecasting cash flows, and balance sheets, statements of manufacturing costs, income statements, statements of sources and applications of funds, and other reports that indicate the results of operations. All such budgets, statements, and reports are of great importance as "tools" of financial management.

Problems and Policies

The kinds of problems dealt with in corporation finance, as a field of study, are largely identical with those actually faced in the financial management of business corporations. They all involve a search for the best ways of applying theories or principles, with the help of existing institutions, and with the use of suitable instruments, to attain specific goals. As so described, they are necessarily of a bewildering variety and of many degrees of complexity. Only a small sampling of these problems need be mentioned here.

1. Setting maximum and minimum levels within which corporation managements will seek to maintain their cash holdings.
2. Deciding what to do with temporary excessive holdings of cash.
3. Deciding whether or not to sell on a credit or deferred-payment basis.
4. Selecting advantageous inventory valuation methods.
5. Choosing between the purchase and lease of plant and machinery.
6. Selecting favorable depreciation-charging methods.
7. Deciding whether in certain instances the cost of additional assets should be met by further investment by stockholders or through the expansion of debt.
8. Determining whether, in given circumstances, preferred stock should be issued rather than additional common stock.
9. Deciding to what extent earnings should be retained and to what extent used for cash dividends.
10. Finding a workable relationship between the respective amounts of long- and short-term debt.
11. Selecting channels through which securities will be sold or loans will be sought.
12. Fixing terms and features of security issues to enhance their marketability.
13. Adjusting asset values when they appear to be out of proper relationship with earning power.
14. Selecting appropriate policies for the retirement of debt.
15. Meeting the extraordinary kinds of difficulties that are occasioned by recessions and depressions in general business activity.

Identity in the scope of the problems of corporation finance, as a field of study, and the problems of financial management in operating corporations does not necessarily mean that students of finance and corporation managers must agree on solutions to specific problems. As a rule, in adopting policies—which are, after all, solutions to problems, as actually selected—corporation managers strive toward the goal of maximizing the strength and profitability of their enterprises. But what appears to a corporation management to be a good policy may really be a bad one from the standpoint of the welfare of society as a whole. Accordingly, the student of finance must seek solutions and support policies that, at least, are not harmful to the general welfare, and that, desirably, make a positive contribution to it. He may find it imperative to condemn as unethical or antisocial certain kinds of policies that some corporate managements adopt and implement. On the other hand, corporate managers who are aware of their social responsibilities, and who are willing to give these responsibilities proper weight in their decision making, can generally be expected to adopt policies that can be fully approved by the impartial student.

IMPORTANCE OF CORPORATION FINANCE

Dominance of the Corporation

The importance of corporation finance is proportional, one may say, to the tremendous productivity of the very business corporations it is concerned with. Everyone is aware of the vast flow of goods that comes annually from the factories, workshops, stores, and warehouses owned and operated by corporations—a flow that contributes greatly toward satisfying high standards of living and assuring national well-being in a material sense. Such a flow of output must be financed: corporations must raise money to add to their equipment, to meet their payrolls, and to cover other costs incurred in preparing goods for the market. Men and machines may stand idle, despite a strong market demand for the goods they could produce, if the corporations that hire the men and own the machines do not have enough money to put these factors of production to work. Bottlenecks in the production stream due to a lack of adequate means of financing are thus possible in addition to those that exist because of a lack of physical facilities and skilled manpower of particular kinds.

Of the total of more than 8 million private nonfarm business enterprises in operation in the United States, only approximately one sixth are corporations.[2] But though corporations are far outnumbered by proprietorships and partnerships combined in business as a whole, they outnumber proprietorships and partnerships in some areas of business, as in many sectors of manufacturing and in some phases of transportation and other public utility services. The dominance of the corporation in manufacturing—in number of establishments, num-

[2]Based upon the number of business firms filing federal income tax returns for fiscal years ending between July 1, 1965, and June 30, 1966. As indicated in Table 1–1 and its footnote, the number of active corporations outside the agriculture, forestry, and fisheries industries was 1,400,024, and separately reported as operating outside these industries were 5,853,200 proprietorships and 786,433 partnerships, for a total number of 8,039,657 nonfarm business enterprises. Corporations, therefore, accounted for about 17.4 percent of this total. In addition to the source cited in Table 1–1, see U.S. Treasury Department, Internal Revenue Service, *Statistics of Income, 1965—Preliminary: U.S. Business Tax Returns* (Washington, D.C.: U.S. Government Printing Office, 1967), pp. 1–2.

ber of employees, size of payrolls, and value added in manufacturing operations—is indicated by the Bureau of the Census data presented in Table 1–2.

TABLE 1–2
Comparative Position of Corporations in Manufacturing in 1963
(Employees in thousands; dollar amounts in millions)

Forms of Enterprise	*Number of Establishments*	*Number of Employees*	*Salaries and Wages*	*Value Added in Manufacture*
Corporations	176,190	15,245	$89,357	$184,100
Proprietorships	99,174	536	2,033	3,916
Partnerships	27,677	334	1,340	2,726
Other	3,576	120	559	1,361
Total	306,617	16,235	$93,289	$192,103

SOURCE: U.S. Department of Commerce, Bureau of the Census, *Summary and Subject Statistics* (*Census of Manufactures, 1963*, Vol. 1) (Washington, D.C.: U.S. Government Printing Office, 1966), pp. 3–5.

Even where outnumbered, moreover, corporations tend to dominate in volume and value of output, number of employees, and size of payrolls, except in a few fields such as agriculture and some of the personal service areas. The field of retail trade, for example, is usually regarded as being one especially suitable for unincorporated enterprises; yet, data for the year 1963 as presented in Table 1–3 indicate that corporations accounted for 61.9 percent of the retail sales and 69.8 percent of the total retail payroll of that year, even though they owned only 21 percent of the retail outlets then in operation. It is noteworthy, moreover, that a larger number of corporations operate in the area of retail trade than in any other major field of business activity.

TABLE 1–3
Comparative Position of Corporations in Retail Trade in 1963
(Dollar amounts in millions)

Forms of Enterprise	*Number of Establishments*	*Sales**	*Salaries and Wages**
Proprietorships	1,124,583	$ 65,738	$ 5,862
Corporations	359,409	151,093	19,293
Partnerships	210,694	23,873	2,182
Cooperatives	6,480	2,097	180
Other	6,765	1,400	114
Total	1,707,931	$244,202	$27,632

*Items do not add exactly to total because of rounding.
SOURCE: U.S. Department of Commerce, Bureau of the Census, *Retail Trade—Summary Statistics* (*Census of Business, 1963*, Vol. 1) (Washington, D.C.: U.S. Government Printing Office, 1966). Part 1, pp. 3–5.

The overall dominance of business corporations in productive operations is demonstrated by the size of their contribution to the national income, that is, total payments to the factors of production for their respective contributions to output. In 1967, the corporate share amounted to $368 billion out of total contributions of private businesses of $552 billion.[3] Despite their minority in numbers, therefore, business corporations far exceed in production all other forms of private enterprise combined.

Large and Small Corporations

Almost all large business enterprises, regardless of their fields of operation, are incorporated, but this does not mean that corporation finance as a field of study has to do solely with big business. Though some kinds of business activity are unquestionably concentrated in a few giant corporations, the average corporation, like the average proprietorship and the average partnership, is a relatively small undertaking. Referring to a further breakdown of the 1965–66 income tax data presented in Table 1–4, we find that of a total of 1,427,606 corporations that filed tax returns no fewer than 618,166 had total assets individually of less than $50,000. Two quick computations show, moreover, that 1,339,587 corporations had total assets individually of less than $1 million, and that all but 24,945 had total assets individually of less than $5 million. Thus, a very large majority

TABLE 1–4
Number, Assets, and Net Income of Business Corporations, by Size of Total Assets, 1965–66*

Size of Total Assets (in Thousands)	*Number of Tax Returns*	*Total Assets (in Millions)*†	*Net Income (in Millions)*
Under $50‡	618,166	$ 10,657	$ 461
50 under 100	233,206	16,746	786
100 under 250	277,922	44,351	2,440
250 under 500	137,307	48,235	2,370
500 under 1,000	72,986	50,425	2,718
1,000 under 5,000	63,074	131,164	6,501
5,000 under 10,000	10,978	76,746	2,955
10,000 under 25,000	7,617	118,048	3,948
25,000 under 50,000	2,892	100,270	3,582
50,000 under 100,000	1,537	106,779	4,017
100,000 under 250,000	1,092	167,091	7,476
250,000 or more	829	865,838	36,943
Total	1,427,606	$1,736,349	$74,197

*All active corporations filing federal income tax returns for fiscal years ending between July 1, 1965, and June 30, 1966. Unlike Table 1–1, therefore, this table includes data for corporations in finance, insurance, and real estate, and for those whose business was not allocable by industry.

†Items do not add exactly to total because of rounding.

‡Including corporations with assets at zero or not reported.

SOURCE: U.S. Treasury Department, Internal Revenue Service, *Statistics of Income, 1965—Preliminary: Corporation Income Tax Returns* (Washington, D.C.: U.S. Government Printing Office, 1967), p. 19.

[3]*Survey of Current Business*, June, 1968, pp. 4–5.

of corporations are small or, at most, only moderately large. All of this, of course, does not gainsay the vast role of the giants. Of great significance is the fact that only 829 corporations in the top-size group had asset holdings of $865,838 million out of a total for all corporations of $1,736,349 million, equal to 49.9 percent, and net profits of $36,943 million out of a total of $74,197 million, equal to 49.8 percent.

Most appropriately, therefore, corporation finance must be concerned with the finance functions of corporations of all sizes—large, intermediate, and small. That is the point of view of this textbook. Nevertheless, one must not assume that there are great differences in the character of the financial activities of corporations of the different size groups, aside from the amount of money involved in specific kinds of transactions. Most corporations start out as small enterprises, but from the beginning they face financial problems much like those simultaneously facing large corporations that have been operating for many years, and much like those that they themselves will continue to encounter as they grow older and larger. Although the amounts of money involved in corporate affairs may vary enormously depending on the size of corporations, the character of financial problems tends to be much the same for all corporations regardless of size; they may thus be said to differ in degree but not in kind.

QUESTIONS

1. What is the scope of corporation finance as a field of study? Is there any significant difference between corporation finance and business finance? Explain.

2. How are business corporations distinguished from public corporations, public proprietary corporations, private nonprofit corporations, and cooperative corporations? Which of the latter group most closely resemble business corporations? Explain.

3. Cite by name a corporation or two of each of the five classes mentioned in the preceding question.

4. Why are financial institutions treated in a special way in studies in corporation finance?

5. What is meant by the description of business corporations as "entities" or "personalities"? Does this description apply also to the other classes of corporations mentioned in question 2? Does it apply to proprietorships and partnerships? Why or why not?

6. Why are the theories or principles of corporation finance said to have both legal and economic aspects? Give examples.

7. Aside from the business corporation itself, what three classes of institutions are important in the study of corporation finance? Why are they said to be important?

8. Discuss the reasonableness of the proposition that policies are "solutions to problems, as actually selected."

9. Why is the idea of "social responsibility" introduced in this chapter? Does it really belong here? Discuss.

10. What evidence is there for the claim that the business corporation is the dominant form of business organization in the United States?

PROBLEMS

1. As measured by value added by manufacture, what do the data of Table 1–2 indicate about the size of the average manufacturing corporation by comparison with the average proprietorship and partnership engaged in manufacturing?

2. What does Table 1–3 reveal about the average levels of (*a*) corporate sales and (*b*) wages and salaries in retail trade by comparison with average levels for proprietorships and partnerships?

3. From the totals of Table 1–4, compute to three decimal places the average rate of net income earned by American corporations in 1965–66 in relation to their assets.

4. From the data of Table 1–4, compute to three decimal places the rates of net income earned in relation to total assets by corporations that had assets between $50,000 and $100,000, between $500,000 and $1 million, between $5 million and $10 million, and between $50 million and $100 million. What pattern of relationship, if any, do these rates reveal about the size of corporations and their profitability?

chapter 2

THE BUSINESS CORPORATION

CHOICE OF THE FORM OF ORGANIZATION

People who establish business enterprises generally have full freedom in choosing the form of organization they will use, whether the proprietorship, the general partnership, the corporation, or one of the less common forms mentioned in the preceding chapter. Likewise, those who are already operating businesses of particular forms are usually quite free to change these forms. A proprietor may decide that it would be advantageous to take in several additional investors as partners; or the members of a partnership may conclude that the incorporation of their firm would be beneficial; or the stockholders of a corporation may decide that it would be helpful to reorganize as a partnership.

Why are decisions of these kinds made? Why is one form of organization selected in preference to others? The answer to these questions must surely be that enterprisers select the form of organization that they think will serve them best. They see certain advantages in the use of a given form of organization not present at all or to the same degree in other forms; likewise, they probably recognize certain disadvantages peculiar to it. The matter of selection is purely relative: the form of organization that will serve best in a given situation may be quite inappropriate in other circumstances.

Advantages and disadvantages in the use of specific forms of organization are largely financial in character—having to do with ease in acquiring money from owners and prospective owners, whether few or many, ease in borrowing, credit standing, expenses incurred in getting organized, the burden of taxation, and so on. The very selection of a form of organization puts it to use, as a financing instrument. Hence, the business corporation described in the preceding chapter as the principal institution with which corporation finance deals might also have been described as, in and of itself, an important instrument of finance.

No attempt will be made in the following pages to present an exhaustive list of the advantages and disadvantages of each of the various forms of organization. Since our study is devoted to corporation finance, it should suffice to confine our attention to the advantages and disadvantages of the corporate form of organization. Reference will be made here and there to certain advantages and disadvantages of the proprietorship and the general partnership, but the objective of these references will be to point up the position of the corporation rather than to give a well-rounded account of the features of these other forms of enterprise. At the same time, reference to the limited partnership, the joint stock company, the business trust, and other relatively rare forms of organization will generally be avoided, as such reference would probably be more confusing than enlightening. In any case, such forms are decidedly of limited importance in the totality of business.

ADVANTAGES OF THE CORPORATE FORM OF ORGANIZATION

Limited Liability of Stockholders

Nature of Limited Liability. The principle that a stockholder in a business corporation risks only the amount of money that he has actually invested in it, and not his entire wealth, is an outstanding reason for the attractiveness of the corporate form of organization. Innumerable investors who would be unwilling to participate as owners in partnerships tend to have an entirely different attitude toward the purchase of corporate stock. The "limited liability" of a corporation's stockholders, as contrasted with the unlimited liability of sole proprietors and members of general partnerships for the debts of their enterprises, is the point that makes the difference. For example, a person may invest $2,000 in the stock of a corporation with the thought: "I can afford to lose this sum"; but he may shy away from investing the same amount in a partnership, thinking: "If things go badly, I may lose every cent I have, including my home, as all my property could be seized in satisfaction of the debts of the partnership."

In a strict sense, the stockholders of a corporation are not liable at all for its debts. This fact follows from the position of a corporation as a legal entity. As an entity or person, the corporation makes its own contracts, including those whereby it incurs obligations to make payments, and it alone is responsible for fulfilling them. People who enter into contracts with corporations are expected to know the nature of this exclusive corporate responsibility. Such responsibility means that any and all of the corporation's assets may be seized to satisfy creditors' claims if they are not satisfied by cash payments in the ordinary course of business. Thus, assets contributed by the stockholders, as well as those the creditors themselves have supplied, may be seized; it is in this sense, then, that the stockholders are said to be limitedly liable for a corporation's debts. They may not get back what they invested, since it may have to be used to pay off the creditors. But personal assets of the stockholders—property they have not invested in the corporation—are generally quite beyond the reach of its creditors.

Such a limitation on the liability of stockholders remains in effect regardless of the amount of losses creditors may suffer. A bankrupt corporation may have sufficient assets to pay off creditors' claims at a rate of only 20 or 30 cents on the dollar, yet the stockholders have no legal responsibility whatsoever to ease the creditors' losses. The stockholders may still be wealthy despite the loss of the full value of their investment in the corporation, and the creditors may be men of quite limited means; nevertheless, the doctrine of limited liability prevents the stockholder from being burdened with an obligation to the creditor.

Limited Liability in Large Corporations. Large enterprises, in particular, are likely to find the limited liability feature of the corporate form of organization indispensable; in fact, one can say that in most instances enterprises have been able to grow to large and even giant sizes only because they were able to incorporate and thus give their stockholders the protection of limited liability. Large incorporated enterprises are able to offer their stock issues to thousands of individual and institutional investors with full assurances that the buyer risks only the amount of his investment. Many investors thus approached are able to spare only a few hundred dollars, and many others not more than a thousand or two; but whether the amount available for investment is large or small no investor is repelled by fear of loss of personal wealth *not invested* in the enterprise.

Indeed, any investor might be called foolhardy, regardless of the amount of his wealth and the prestige of the firm he invests in, should he be willing to participate as an owner in a large enterprise without the protection of limited liability. Imagine one's becoming unlimitedly liable for all the debts of an enterprise of the size of the United States Steel Corporation or of the Westinghouse Electric Corporation on account of an investment in it of, say, $1,000!

Limited Liability in Small Corporations. Even for smaller enterprises, the limited liability feature can be decidedly attractive. If the organizers of a relatively small enterprise anticipate a need of offering stock to many prospective buyers—expecting, probably, to get from each buyer only a moderate sum—they can hardly hope for success unless they are able to provide the protection of the limited liability feature. A wealthy capitalist might be willing to back the venture by participating as an owner to the extent of a few thousand dollars, but he would be unlikely to participate should he have to assume full personal responsibility for its debts.

On the other hand, the limited liability feature may not mean much to a small group who are pooling their own funds in a business venture and who have no expectation of making an outside appeal for proprietary funds. If they have minimal personal assets outside the business, they are likely to see little difference between limited and unlimited liability: they can hardly lose much beyond what they have actually invested. Or if they have a substantial amount of nonbusiness assets, they may decide that the best way to protect these assets is to transfer title to their wives, to their children, or perhaps to trust estates. Another consideration is that they may think it futile to try to escape unlimited liability by incorporating when by the terms of contracts creditors can, in effect, reestablish it. Thus, the principal stockholders of a small close[1] corporation may be told by a banker that he will grant it loans only if they cosign or endorse its promissory notes.

Divisibility of Ownership

Flexibility in Stock Issues. The stock of a business corporation may be described as *shares of ownership* in it. It is an instrument of marvelous flexibility. Stock issues can be tailored to provide attractions to prospective investors of varying means, interests, and temperaments. It can be given a value of many hundreds of dollars or of only a few cents—or, indeed, of a fraction of a cent. The organizers of a corporation who want to raise, say, \$100,000 by a sale of stock may decide on an issue of 1,000 shares of \$100 par value, of 10,000 shares of \$10 par value, of 100,000 shares of \$1 par value, or of 1,000, 000 shares of a par value of 10 cents, depending on the class of people to whom they will make their sales appeal.

So flexible, indeed, are stock issues that the shares need not be given a value at all at the time they are authorized in a corporation's charter. Such no-par stock, as it is called, may be sold from time to time at varying prices, depending on the changing market situation. Again, flexibility is such that the features of issues can be readily

[1]A *close* corporation is one whose entire outstanding stock is owned by a single individual, the members of a family, or some other small group. The stock is closely held—that is, it has but few owners. On the other hand, an *open* corporation is one whose stock is widely distributed, so that anybody who wants to buy some can usually find somebody else who is willing to sell. Sometimes, open corporations are described as "public" corporations, but this use of the term is confusing, because city governments, other municipal corporations, and government proprietary corporations are also classified as public corporations.

changed; our states are most liberal in permitting changes. A corporation that originally provided for an issue of no-par stock may subsequently have its articles of incorporation amended to give the stock a par value; or if it originally issued stock of a par value of $10 it can have its articles changes to give the stock a value of $5; or if it originally provided for an issue of 10,000 shares of a given value it can have the articles changed to permit it to issue an additional 10,000 or 20,000 shares of the same or a different par value.

Still further flexibility is imparted to stock in that it can be issued in different classes; in this way, holders of stock of the different classes can be given varying rights to dividends, participation in management, participation in assets in case of dissolution, and so on. Many corporations put out both common and preferred stocks. And if two classes of stock should be insufficient to tap the potential market, arrangements can be made for the issuance of two or more classes of common and two or more classes of preferred, each with different rankings according to the terms of the articles of incorporation.

Divisibility and Limited Liability. The extraordinary divisibility of stock, as an advantage of the corporate form of organization, must be recognized as being closely tied in with the limited liability feature of corporate enterprise. Without this tie-in, divisibility may not be considered as an advantage at all. It would be rather ridiculous for a corporation to provide for the issuance of thousands of shares valued at a few cents or a few dollars each if there were no prospects that people would be willing to buy such small slices of ownership. The prospects would surely be quite slim if the prospective buyers could not be promised the protection of limited liability.

In this regard, it is pertinent to observe that, legally, ownership interests in partnerships are just as divisible as are those in corporations. There is nothing in the laws pertaining to partnerships to prevent the sale of ownership interests of 1/10,000 or 1/100,000. But, practically, people would not ordinarily be willing to buy such interests since they would, at the same time, assume full liability for partnership debts. Nor would members of existing partnerships be willing to accord to people having minute interests the full power to enter into contracts on behalf of their partnerships—which is, indeed, one of the rights of any full-fledged partner.

Transferability of Shares

Corporations have a financing advantage over the proprietorship and partnership in that through the sale of stock they are often able to attract investors' funds on a temporary basis. Stock has no date of maturity, which states when the principal or face value is repayable, but absence of a maturity date does not mean that the typical investor expects to hold stock for his entire lifetime and then bequeath it to his heirs. He may think of it simply as a short-term asset, to be disposed of when he needs money for some other purpose. The more strongly he has this attitude, the more willing is he likely to be to buy stock as a means of using his money temporarily to earn income. He buys today in the expectation of being able to sell next year, and he may actually be able to sell next year because somebody else may be willing to buy at that time in the expectation of being able to resell in, say, six months.[2]

Advantage accrues to the corporation because it gets its money in the original sale of its stock issues, *and its assets and life are not affected by subsequent transfers of that stock,* no matter what their number and frequency may be. The original buyer of the stock holds it for, perhaps, three years and then sells it, and the new owner holds it for three months, and the next buyer holds it for only three weeks. But the corporation is affected only by the first transaction, since it has no obligation to redeem the stock—that is, to use its assets to buy it back. Nobody disputes the right of the selling stockholder to thus sever his interests in the corporation. Nobody suggests that a lawsuit for damages should be brought because of his withdrawal. Nobody claims that the person who buys the stock someone else is selllng has no right to become a stockholder.

The situation in a partnership is quite different from this. A person would not ordinarily become a member of a partnership on a temporary basis, for his withdrawal would cause a dissolution of the partnership! As the ownership interest of a withdrawing partner must generally be paid off out of partnership assets, this payment may make it impossible for the remaining partners to carry on. At the least, their business operations are likely to be seriously disrupted by a withdrawal. In some instances, it is true, an outsider may be willing to buy our the interest of the withdrawing partner, but finding such a person does not necessarily solve the problem. Brown may be willing to buy out Green's interest in the partnership of Grey, Black, and Green, but this requires more than an agreement between Brown and Green. According to the doctrine of *delectus personae*, people who form partnerships have the right to decide who their partners will be—partners cannot be forced on them. Green cannot make Brown a partner simply by selling his interest to him. Brown must be accepted by Grey and Black; if they are not willing to accept him, and if Green still insists on withdrawing, he must be paid off, presumably out of

---

[2]All this is not meant to imply that corporate stockholders can always sell their shares at what they would consider fair prices. It is often virtually impossible or at least extremely difficult to find buyers for shares in close corporations. Even for stockholdings in corporations whose shares are widely held, possibilities of getting a fair price depend on whether or not the stocks are listed on prominent stock exchanges, the scope of investor interests in them, the tempo of business activity in the industries in which the corporations operate and in the economy as a whole, and other factors.

the partnership assets. If Grey and Black cannot be forced to accept Brown as a partner, neither can they force Green to remain as a partner when he no longer wishes to remain. Of course, if he has specifically agreed to maintain his position as a partner for a given period of years, and if he decides to withdraw before the expiration of that period, Grey and Black may have grounds to sue him for damages.

Independent Life of the Corporation

The corporation enjoys a most important advantage in having a life quite independent of those of its stockholders, directors, and officers. Because it is a distinct entity, it can go on living for as long as the state that creates it says it can; and as a being "invisible, intangible, and existing only in contemplation of law,"[3] it need not have its life related in any way to the lives of human beings. The fact is that the organizers of business corporations can generally get perpetual charters simply for the asking. Only a few states do not issue perpetual charters, and even these few permit the stated term of life to be quite a long one; they provide also for easy amendment to charters so that a corporate life that is approaching expiration can be extended by an additional generous grant of years. Thus, corporate longevity is always possible, either by way of perpetual life from the beginning or by a ready process of rejuvenation.

By contrast, general partnerships are seriously limited in attractiveness, since their continued existence is so closely dependent on the lives of their owners as human beings. People may refuse to become partners in business concerns, despite high confidence in the integrity and abilities of the people with whom they would be associated, because they realize that any partnership may be suddenly terminated by the death, insanity, bankruptcy, or other legal incompetence of one or more of the partners, or simply because one of the partners decides that he must withdraw. At the very time that a partnership

[3]The corporation was so described by Chief Justice Marshall in his celebrated opinion in the *Dartmouth College* case. His full statement was as follows: "A corporation is an artificial being, invisible, intangible, and existing only in contemplation of law. Being the mere creature of law, it possesses only those properties which the charter of its creation confers upon it, either expressly, or as incidental to its very existence. These are such as are supposed best calculated to effect the object for which it was created. Among the most important are immortality, and, if the expression may be allowed, individuality; properties by which a perpetual succession of many persons are considered as the same, and may act as a single individual. They enable a corporation to manage its own affairs, and to hold property without the perplexing intricacies, the hazardous and endless necessity, of perpetual conveyances for the purpose of transmitting it from hand to hand. It is chiefly for the purpose of clothing bodies of men, in succession, with these qualities and capacities, that corporations were invented, and are in use. By these means, a perpetual succession of individuals are capable of acting for the promotion of the particular object, like one immortal being." *Dartmouth College* v. *Woodward,* 4 Wheaton 518 (1819).

may be moving along most successfully, operations may be disrupted and the whole outlook changed because it becomes necessary to pay off the interest of a partner to his executor if he dies, to his commission or guardian if he goes insane, to the trustee if he goes bankrupt, or to the man himself if he wants to withdraw. Prospective creditors, too, may be quite reluctant to grant loans or to sell on account to partnerships whose early demise, for reasons of the kinds indicated, they anticipate. Though they would have claims against the assets of the partnership superior to those of the owners, they might want to avoid the delays and difficulties of estate settlement, court proceedings, and the like.

In the corporation, a person may become a stockholder with full assurance that his coming will not disturb its operations in any way; that his going, if he decides to sell his stock later on, likewise will cause no disturbance; and that the comings and goings of other stockholders will similarly be free of unsettling effects. He knows that, should certain stockholders die, become insane or bankrupt, or suffer other legal disabilities, their stock would be taken over temporarily by executors, guardians, or trustees, and that, depending on circumstances, these new holders would sooner or later turn it over to heirs or sell it in the market—all these events would have no effects on the life of the corporation. He may expect, moreover, that banks and other lenders and suppliers of merchandise will be quite willing to extend credit to the corporation because they need not fear having their claims held up pending legal proceedings such as settlement of decedents' estates and handling of the affairs of bankrupts.

Independence of life is especially important for larger enterprises. In many of our largest corporations, hundreds of shares of stock are exchanged between departing stockholders and arriving stockholders every business day; yet, such transfers simply require, one may say, a few clerical operations, and not a ripple in the life of the corporation and its current activities results. In small corporations, on the other hand, certain transfers of stock may have profound effects on business operations, even though there is no legal impact on the life of the corporation. The death of a principal stockholder who has also been the president and general manager of a corporation may truly be as disrupting to its operations as the death of a partner in the case of a partnership.

Satisfactory Credit Standing

Because the owners of proprietorships and partnerships are unlimitedly liable for the obligations of their enterprises, while the stockholders of corporations have only limited liability for corporate obligations, one may expect the proprietorships and partnerships to have high preference in obtaining loans, in buying goods on account, and in incurring debts in other ways. Nevertheless, the limited liability feature of corporations apparently does not detract from their position as debtors and prospective debtors; indeed, the access of corporations of given sizes to credit appears to be somewhat better than that of proprietorships and partnerships of comparable size groupings.

The following may be cited as probable reasons why the credit standing of proprietorships and partnerships is not superior to that of corporations.

1. A very large proportion of the assets of proprietors and partners are their business assets, so that they have little outside their businesses to back up their unlimited liability.
2. Many creditors are convinced that the seizure of personal assets, such as homes, household furniture, and the family automobile, is a poor means of enforcing business claims.
3. Creditors are fully aware that proprietors and partners can put their nonbusiness assets in the names of their wives or children or set up trusts to hold them, thus effectively removing them from seizure for the satisfaction of business debts.

On the other side of the picture, one reason the credit standing of corporations may not be weakened because of limited liability is that prospective creditors have ways of nullifying it. For example, a commercial bank may agree to grant a loan to a corporation only on condition that its principal stockholder or stockholders endorse the corporation's promissory note. In this way, should the corporation fail to meet its obligations, the private property of these stockholders would be subject to seizure to satisfy the bank's claims.

Representative Government

The operation of business corporations on the basis of a system of representative government has both advantageous and disadvantageous aspects. Representative government in the corporation means that the stockholders, even though they are the owners of the enterprise, do not determine operating policies, negotiate specific kinds of purchase and sales contracts, hire employees, and so on, but choose directors who have the power to do these things. The stockholders occupy a position somewhat like that of American citizens who elect representatives to Congress, to state legislatures, and to city councils—representatives who, rather than the citizens themselves, have the power to enact laws. But there the parallel ends, for American citizens, as voters, also choose governmental executives, from the President down to township officials, whereas in a business corporation it is normally the function of directors to choose the executive officers.

At any rate, once directors and officers have been chosen, prospective creditors, in particular, can find clear lines of authority and can determine definitely whether or not certain officers have the power to negotiate specific kinds of contracts. For transactions between a corporation and a commercial bank, for example, the bank is likely to stipulate that before a deposit account is opened, checks are drawn, or loans are granted, the board of directors of the corporation must adopt and submit a resolution authorizing the opening of the account and specifically designating which of its officers have the right to sign checks, to borrow money in its name, and to pledge its property as collateral security for loans.

No one would question the right of a proprietor to borrow money or to buy on account in his own name for the benefit of his business, but in transactions with partnerships, creditors may get themselves into family quarrels they would rather avoid. The members of a partnership may agree among themselves that only partner X has the right to buy materials and supplies, but partner Y, thinking that quick action must be taken to get the advantage of some bargain, may sign some purchase contracts in violation of the agreement. Partnership law holds that each partner is a principal in the sense of having capacity to enter into contracts binding the partnership as long as they are related to partnership business. Accordingly, partner Y binds the partnership, and the supplier from whom he buys gets a valid claim. Nevertheless, there may be many delays and difficulties as the supplier tries to obtain payment, occasioned by the warring that may be going on among the partners as a result of partner Y's failure to live up to his agreement.

It is possible that prospective investors will shy away from the corporation because of its representative form of government. Realizing that the corporate stockholder risks his money but gets only an indirect right to management—that is, by choosing directors who make the actual decisions—these investors may decide not to buy corporate stock. On the whole, however, we are so accustomed to representative government in political affairs that we are inclined to accept it in corporate affairs without hesitation. Indeed, a major criticism of the corporate form of organization from the standpoint of social welfare is that many stockholders fail to exercise the rights of participation in management that they *do* possess—that they ignore calls to stockholders' meetings, cast no ballots for directors, and pass up opportunities to vote on issues that the directors actually present to them for decision.

DISADVANTAGES OF THE CORPORATE FORM OF ORGANIZATION

Burdens on Establishment

Often cited as a disadvantage of the corporate form of organization are the expenses and difficulties of getting started. But these are, at most, a minor disadvantage; certainly, their financial burdens are of modest proportions. Seeing that the procedure of incorporation as set out in the state law is followed through carefully (so that the right of the enterprise to carry on business activities as a corporation and to enjoy the advantages of the legal-entity status will never be questioned) usually requires the services of competent attorneys. But the formation of any other kind of enterprise in which two or more persons are to be associated as owners, whether a general partnership, a limited partnership, a business trust, or some other form, should be guided just as carefully by competent attorneys. The establishment of a general partnership on the basis of an oral contract, or on the basis of a contract written by the partners themselves, is often a dangerous thing. As many as possible of the questions of rights and responsibilities that are likely to come up later should be anticipated, and governing provisions concerning them should be clearly written down. Foresight of this kind in the establishment of a partnership, no less than care required in the establishment of a corporation, generally calls for the assistance of legal counsel.

Aside from attorneys' fees, the most important items of expense ordinarily incurred in the establishment of a corporation are the fees and organization taxes that must be paid to the government of the state in which the corporation is chartered. In no state are these prohibitive; rarely, indeed, would the organizers of a business enterprise decide to forgo the advantages of the corporate form simply to avoid these costs. Filing fees, as a rule, do not exceed $50. In a few instances, the organization tax is also established as a set amount, as Arizona's $25, but most states provide for a variable tax related to the amount of stock that the new corporation is authorized to issue. Connecticut, for example, levies its organization tax at the rate of 1 cent per share of authorized capital stock, with a minimum tax of $50. In some states, the rate structure is regressive, that is, the rate is lower for certain larger batches of stock than for smaller amounts; such a rate structure in a given state serves as an invitation to larger corporations to make that state their home. Thus, the state of Delaware, which has been an extremely popular state for incorporations, has an organization tax on par-value stock of 10 cents for each $1,000 of stock up to $2 million, 5 cents for each $1,000 on amounts of stock between $2 million and $20 million, and 2 cents for each $1,000 on amounts over $20 million. A Delaware corporation that has an authorized stock issue of $10 million would accordingly pay a tax of $600—certainly not a great burden for a corporation of that size.

Other special kinds of expenses incurred by corporations on organization include the costs of forms used in applying for the charter, stock certificate books, minute books, and forms for the stockholders' ledger. But legal stationers carry materials of these kinds designed for general use, and their charges are quite moderate. Greater expense

is incurred, of course, if the organizers of a corporation decide that they want something distinctive—for example, a specially engraved stock certificate form.

Government Regulation

More important than the expense and difficulty of getting started as a disadvantage of the corporate form of organization are the government regulations to which corporations are subjected. Here, reference is made to special kinds of regulations that usually apply only to corporations and not to the broad rules that apply to all kinds of business enterprises, or to all kinds in a given industry. The special regulations may be classified as follows: (1) those of the state of incorporation prescribing specific procedures for certain kinds of actions, (2) those pertaining to qualification to do business in states other than the state of incorporation, and (3) those requiring reports and authorizing investigations.

Prescribed Procedures. State laws require certain formalities in the procedures of the corporations they charter, especially for actions taken by the stockholders, the choice and service of directors, and changes in the scope of operations.

The state laws uniformly provide that there must be an annual meeting of the stockholders, and they go on to stipulate how and when notice of this meeting and of special meetings must be given, in what circumstances notice of meetings may be waived, what constitutes a quorum, what business may be taken up at a meeting with or without notice, how votes are to be counted, and so on. They require that a record of actions taken at stockholders' and directors' meetings —minutes—be kept. They usually designate the minimum number of directors a corporation may have, frequently set down certain qualifications for directors, and designate what the term of office of directors shall be. Likewise, they have provisions concerning the removal of incompetent directors, quorums for directors' meetings, and the filling of board vacancies between the annual meetings of the stockholders. Provisions such as these are not difficult to observe, of course, but they are restrictions on freedom of action of kinds that the members of partnerships do not have to worry about. For the small close corporation in which the same few people are simultaneously stockholders, directors, and officers, such provisions are likely to be condemned as requiring a lot of red tape.

If the directors of a business corporation want to change its name, its authorized stock issues, the duration of its life, the scope of its operations, or anything else provided for in its articles of incorporation, they cannot do so by simply voting the change and having the stockholders approve it. They must draw up articles of amendment, have the stockholders approve them, submit them to the secretary of state or other designated state official, pay filing fees—and additional taxes, if the authorized stock is being increased—obtain from the state official a certificate of amendment or some similar document, and file a copy of the articles of amendment with the county recorder. The members of a partnership, on the other hand, may take comparable actions entirely on their own volition, without need of any legal procedures as here described.

Entrance to Other States. Although a corporation is legally recognized as a person, it is not a citizen of the state in which it is incorporated or of the United States. It does not enjoy, therefore, the protection of the provision of the Fourteenth Amendment to the Constitution, which says: "No State shall make or enforce any law which shall abridge the privileges or immunities of citizens of the United States."[4] Accordingly, any state government may forbid corporations chartered by other states to do business within its borders, or it may place restrictions on their activities such as it does not place on corporations that it itself charters. Proprietors and the members of partnerships, on the other hand, cannot be so excluded or restricted; if they are "born or naturalized in the United States," they are citizens of the state in which they reside and of the United States, thus getting the protection of the provision quoted above.

In this regard, each of our state governments classifies corporations operating within its borders as *domestic*, *foreign*, and *alien* corporations. To it, a domestic corporation is one that it itself has chartered; a foreign corporation is one chartered by another state; and an alien corporation is one chartered by a foreign country. Thus, a Delaware corporation is a domestic cororation in the purview of the state of Delaware, but it is classified as a foreign corporation in each of the other states it operates in. Likewise, a corporation chartered in Canada would be classified as an alien corporation in all our states. In certain circumstances, then, a state can exclude or restrict the activities of foreign and alien corporations as thus classified.

Nevertheless, the state governments may not restrict the operations of foreign and alien corporations in interstate and international commerce. Under the Constitution, Congress has the power to regulate interstate and international commerce, and it is a well-established doctrine that the states may not take any action that would place unreasonable burdens on this commerce. Always an important question, therefore, is the distinction between intrastate and interstate commerce—between what constitutes doing business in a given state and what represents doing business across state lines. The distinction is by no means clear, but some rules have been enunciated by the courts for guidance. The following are samples of these rules. A corporation is said to be doing business in a foreign state if:

[4]Section 1.

1. It owns real estate or maintains a sales office there.
2. It sells through agents who have power to enter into contracts without reference to the home office.
3. It sells things that must be installed by its employees.
4. It stores goods in warehouses in the foreign state preparatory to sale.
5. It buys goods there and stores them temporarily, pending shipment to the home state.

If a corporation can avoid circumstances of these kinds in its transactions with firms and individuals in other states, its operations generally qualify as interstate in character; as such, they are not subject to the restrictive regulations of the other states.

Although state governments have the power to restrict, and even to exclude, the intrastate activities of foreign corporations, they rarely do so. Each state observes a policy of reciprocity, freely permitting foreign corporations to come in to do business in the expectation that other states will freely permit entrance to its chartered corporations. The expectation is fully justified, for the system of reciprocity is now nationwide in scope. Nevertheless, entrance to a foreign state is not without legal complexities, and the red tape involved is clearly burdensome to corporations. To obtain a license or "certificate of authority" to do business in the foreign state, a corporation must generally file with it a certified copy of its articles of incorporation and designate an agent resident within the state on whom legal papers can be served—the state wants to be able to reach the corporation through the agent if it cannot do so directly. In connection with this filing requirement, a fee must be paid, and usually a tax based more or less arbitrarily on the proportion of the corporation's assets to be employed in the foreign state, as determined by the use of a prescribed formula.[5]

The filing and tax-paying procedure must be followed through for each foreign state where a corporation wants to enter to do business. Further, foreign states must usually be notified of important changes in a corporation's organization and scope of operations—changes such as those that necessitate the amendment of its articles of incorporation in the home state. For a corporation that wants to do business in many states, obtaining certificates of authority and filing notices of subsequent changes may be a considerable burden. Proprietorships and partnerships, to repeat, are subject to no such requirements.

The failure of a corporation to obtain a certificate of authority in a

[5]Like organization taxes, entrance taxes levied on foreign corporations are technically based on capital stock—the proportion of a corporation's capital stock to be used in the foreign state. But corporations do not "use" their capital stock anywhere, since stock simply represents shares of ownership that belong to the stockholders. By most formulas, therefore, the amount of capital stock "used" in the respective states is determined on the basis of assets held or to be held therein in relation to total assets.

foreign state where it does business means that it will have no standing in the courts of that state in bringing lawsuits, as for the enforcement of contracts. In some states, moreover, the corporation and its agents are subject to fines.

Reports and Investigations. Government regulation places a further burden on corporations in requiring them to file annual reports and in making them subject to certain kinds of investigations. Each state usually requires annual reports of its own chartered corporations as well as of foreign corporations doing business within its borders. A corporation that operates in many states may have a sizable burden in turning out the required reports, because the prescribed content differs rather widely from state to state. As a rule, the individual report is not difficult to prepare, as the data required are not comprehensive; on the other hand, some states require the disclosure of information that the managers of business enterprises may prefer to keep secret. For many years, for example, the only definitive information that the public had about the assets and liabilities of the Ford Motor Company was that revealed in its annual report required by the Commonwealth of Massachusetts.

Investigations to which corporations are subject are chiefly examinations to determine whether taxes are being paid in the proper amounts. Tax collectors generally have powers to inquire into the affairs of all classes of taxpayers, but, because corporations must pay several special kinds of taxes, they are likely to be visited more often by tax investigators than are unincorporated enterprises and individuals. In some instances, moreover, a corporation's records may be subject to inspection to determine the payment or nonpayment of certain taxes not levied on the corporation itself. This applies particularly to stock transfer taxes imposed by a few of the states, including New York. Tax investigators may want to look at the stock certificate books to see that the transfer stamps in the proper amounts have been appropriately attached.

Taxes on Corporations

Although a few managers of business enterprises probably decide against incorporation because of the expenses and difficulties of starting, and many to avoid the kinds of government regulation just described, most of those who decide against incorporation, it is surely safe to say, do so because they wish to avoid certain special kinds of taxes that are levied on corporations by both the federal and state governments. Corporations must pay their share of taxes that are imposed on all persons, or on all businesses, or on all businesses that operate in particular industries, such as property taxes, manufacturers' excise taxes, retail sales taxes, business license taxes, and gross income taxes, but they are also singled out for additional levies that individuals and enterprises of other forms[6] are not called on to pay. The additional tax burden of annual state-imposed franchise taxes on corporations varies from trifling to substantial amounts, but large or small it is an expense of operation that unincorporated businesses are not required to meet. The degree of burden of state-imposed corporation income taxes depends on whether or not the state also has an individual income tax and on how corporate dividends are treated in individual tax returns. And the degree of burden of the federal corporation income tax—heaviest, by far, of all corporation taxes—depends on many things, including the size of the corporation's income, the size of stockholders' income from sources other than the corporation (this is important, of course, because, as everybody knows, the federal government also has a steeply graduated individual income tax), the extent to which stockholders can withdraw corporate income in the form of salaries, and the proportion of income they want the corporation to retain for expansion.

Always, therefore, to be considered most carefully in arriving at decisions whether or not to incorporate is an estimation of what incorporation would cost in the way of special taxes—in additions to the tax bill beyond what unincorporated businesses must pay. In some instances, the decision to incorporate is a foregone conclusion. This is true of enterprises that have or expect to have many owners (stockholders). These enterprises must be able to offer their owners the privilege of limited liability, regardless of the price in taxes they must pay for it. In other instances, the prospective tax bill clearly exceeds a reasonable price for the advantages of the corporate form, so that incorporation must be quickly ruled out. But in between are many situations when it is most difficult to determine whether corporate tax bills plus the other disadvantages we have discussed outweigh or are outweighed by the advantages corporations enjoy. Obviously, such situations call for prolonged study before decisions are arrived at—study not only of the present circumstances but also of prospects of future changes in tax legislation. Finally, in some situations—undoubtedly the most interesting of all—owners of business enterprises can reduce their overall tax obligations by incorporating. For those who find themselves in this position, the special taxing of corporations turns out to be an advantage of the corporate form rather than a disadvantage!

State Taxation

Annual Franchise or Capital Stock Taxes. Approximately three fourths of the states impose on corporations an annual tax related to

[6]Unless such enterprises are recognized as being so similar to corporations that they are treated as corporations for tax purposes. Thus, business trusts are required to pay federal corporation income taxes.

stock issues variously called a franchise tax, a capital stock tax, a license fee, a privilege tax, or a corporation fee. This tax is levied on both domestic and foreign corporations; it is usually based on outstanding capital stock, although some states use as a base authorized capital stock, some use authorized or outstanding stock plus all or a portion of the surplus accounts, and at least one or two use stock plus surplus plus debt. The usual procedure is to tax only that proportion of capital stock that can be allocated to the individual taxing state, the allocation being made in terms of tangible property held in the state in relation to total tangible property or, in some instances, in terms of both tangible property and gross sales within and without the state. Although a state may constitutionally tax the entire capital stock of domestic corporations, it usually chooses not to do so, in order not to made itself unattractive for incorporations; thus, its procedure of allocation applies to both domestic and foreign corporations.

Pennsylvania's tax of 0.5 percent ($5 per $1,000) is applied to the actual cash value of capital stock "used in the state," that is, allocated as indicated above. Delaware—always to be mentioned in view of its popularity as a state of incorporation—has a series of flat charges graduated up to $55 for 10,000 shares of authorized stock, with $27.50 the charge for each additional 10,000 shares; it also stipulates that the tax may not be less than $10 or more than $100,000. Michigan charges 0.5 percent on capital stock and surplus allocated to the state, with a minimum of $10. Colorado's charge ranges from $10 on corporations with authorized capital stock up to $50,000 to $250 on those with authorized capital stock of $1 million or more; and Florida has a regressive schedule that runs from $20 on corporations with capital stock not exceeding $10,000 to $2,000 on those that have capital stock of more than $2 million.

State Net Income Taxes. Some states levy on corporations an annual net income tax in addition to an annual capital stock tax; some levy an annual net income tax in lieu of a capital stock tax; and some have neither of these two kinds of taxes. (The last-named group, however, usually has some modest fee, from $1 to $10, to be paid when the annual corporate report is filed.) In all, about 40 states have corporation net income taxes in their tax structures.

Most states that have corporation net income taxes levy a flat rate on the taxable income regardless of amount; the most common rate is 5 percent. The lowest rate charged at the present time is Missouri's 2 percent, and the highest is Minnesota's 8.5 percent. A few states have progressive rate schedule—that is, the higher brackets of income are taxed at higher rates than are the lower brackets. Thus, North Dakota has a rate schedule running from 3 percent on the first $3,000 of income to 6 percent on income in excess of $15,000.

According to accepted constitutional principles, a state may tax the entire net income of domestic corporations, but only that portion of the income of foreign corporations that is derived from doing business within its borders. However, only Alabama and Louisiana tax the entire net income of domestic corporations; other states choose not to do so lest they be bypassed by people seeking corporate charters. Taxing only income derived within the state, whether that of domestic or that of foreign corporations, requires some basis of allocation, and the states take care of this in various ways. In the overall situation, most corporate income is allocated to individual states on the basis of prescribed formulas by which two, three, or more dollar-value factors are used to distinguish in-state income from out-of-state income. Some states, however, require the keeping of specific accounting records to distinguish in-state income when the nature of corporate operations makes this feasible, and others accept income reports on the basis of such records as substitutes for formula applications. Many stipulate that certain items of income must be reported as in-state income while providing for the allocation of the balance of income on formula bases, and some prescribe different formulas for different areas of business operations. The most commonly used allocation formula—often called the Massachusetts formula—is this:

$$\frac{\dfrac{\text{Tangible property within the state}}{\text{Total tangible property}} + \dfrac{\text{Gross sales within the state}}{\text{Total gross sales}} + \dfrac{\text{Payroll within the state}}{\text{Total payroll}}}{3} = \text{Proportion of total taxable by the state}$$

Thus, a corporation that has one fourth of its (owned and rented) property, one fifth of its gross sales, and one tenth of its payroll within a state that uses this formula would have 11/60 of its net income subject to taxation by that state. Because of variations in the formulas used, the total net income upon which a corporation may be taxed in combination by all the states in which it does business may be more or less than the amount of its true net income. This fact indicates an important need of a uniform formula for use throughout the country.

Federal Corporation Income Tax

Relation to Individual Income Taxes. Because the federal government taxes corporate net income at the high (normal tax) rate of 22 percent on the first $25,000 and at the much higher (normal plus surtax) rate of 48 percent on all amounts in excess of $25,000,[7] and

[7]Basic rates in effect in the year 1968 with the surtax rate, of course, at 26 percent. (Thus, the individual corporation was said to have a surtax exemption of $25,000.) A tax measure adopted in June, 1968, imposed a surcharge of 10 percent to be added to corporate tax bills as determined by application of the

because dividends paid by corporations are included in the income of the stockholders to be taxed again in the individual income tax structure (with only a moderate exclusion[8]), incorporation would appear to be an extremely expensive way of carrying on business operations. The double taxation of corporate income—as corporate income and again as dividends distributed to stockholders—would seem to be an unconscionable burden. But the entire income of proprietors and partners from their businesses is taxed as individual income in the year derived, and the rates of the individual income tax run from 14 percent on the first $1,000 of income to 70 percent on that portion of income that exceeds $200,000.[9] Stockholders in corporations do not pay individual income taxes on that portion of corporation earnings *which the corporations do not pay out as dividends;* hence, it may turn out to be advantageous to have business income taxed at the corporate rates if by this means the amount of income taxable as individual income can be substantially reduced.

Accordingly, organizers of new business enterprises must carefully estimate the relative tax burdens that will fall on the owners should they operate as proprietors or partners on the one hand or as corporate stockholders on the other. Indeed, continuing analysis of relative tax burdens is appropriate for businesses already in operation, for changing circumstances may make it advantageous to incorporate proprietorships and partnerships or, contrariwise, to surrender corporate charters and to continue business as proprietorships and partnerships. Estimates and analyses of these kinds are most difficult. Not only must there be comparisons on the basis of present corporate and individual tax rates, but consideration also must be given to possible or probable rate changes in the future. Moreover, certain provisions of the income tax legislation complicate the analysis. Among these are provisions that:

1. Permit corporations to deduct as expenses "reasonable" salaries paid to stockholders who are also officers or employees in other capacities.

---

basic normal and surtax rates. The surcharge was made retroactive to January 1, 1968, and was scheduled to expire as of June 30, 1969.

[8]Dividends received up to $100 may be excluded from the taxpayer's taxable income. If both husband and wife received dividends and if they file a joint tax return, up to $100 may be excluded for each, but one spouse may not take the unused exclusion of the other.

[9]Basic rates in effect in the year 1968 for married persons filing joint returns with their spouses. For single individuals and for married persons not filing joint returns, the range of basic 1968 rates was from 14 percent on the first $500 of income to 70 percent on income in excess of $100,000. As referred to in footnote 7, the surcharge of 10 percent was also made applicable in 1968 to individual tax bills as determined by application of the basic rates (with some exceptions for people who have very low tax liabilities at the basic rates). For individuals, it was made retroactive to April 1, 1968, and was scheduled to remain in effect only until the end of June, 1969.

2. Allow corporate deductions for:
   a) Contributions to pension and profit-sharing plans for employee-stockholders.[10]
   b) Premiums on group life insurance policies protecting their families as beneficiaries.
   c) Certain kinds of death benefit payments to their families.
   d) Medical insurance premiums as well as specific medical expenses and up to $100 a week for living expenses for employee-stockholders absent from work because of sickness or injury (such payments are not includable in the stockholders' individual income subject to tax).
3. Recognize certain kinds of payments as deductible expenses for corporations but not for other forms of business organizations.

Position of Stockholders Who Have Moderate Incomes. Payment of federal corporation income taxes almost always works to the disadvantage of stockholders who have moderate incomes. Let us suppose, for example, that a corporation's before-tax income attributable to the shares held by a small stockholder is $800, that it pays tax on this income of, let us say, $384,[11] and that it gives the remaining $416 to the stockholder as a dividend. Suppose, further, that the stockholder's income from other sources is $8,000, that his allowable deductions for certain kinds of expenses amount to $900, that he is married and has two children, and that he files an individual tax return jointly with his wife. At the rates in effect in the year 1968, his individual income tax would amount to $813,[12] and this plus the $384 of tax paid by the corporation would make his total tax bill $1,197. Were he, however, to receive $800 as a share in partnership profits rather than as a dividend on corporate stock, his total tax bill would be only $905.[13]

---

[10] These deductions are allowed for such payments on behalf of any employees, but here, of course, attention is confined to employees who are also stockholders.

[11] It may be assumed that the corporation's net income is far in excess of $25,000, so that its tax rate on total income is quite close to 48 percent. (This illustration and those that follow on corporate tax liabilities ignore the 10 percent surcharge added in 1968, as referred to in footnote 7.)

[12] In this and the following illustrations of individual income taxes, allowance is made for the exclusion of $100 of dividends from taxable income as referred to in footnote 8, but the 10 percent surcharge on individual taxes added in 1968, referred to in footnote 9, is ignored.

[13] The very important question of tax shifting and incidence is ignored in this illustration and in those that follow. One could argue that the corporation might have been able to raise the selling prices of its goods to cover all or a portion of its income tax liabilities. In that circumstance, its customers, rather than its stockholders, or in addition to its stockholders, would be bearing all or a portion of the corporate income tax levies. Assuming the complete shiftability of the tax, its repeal in a fully competitive situation should have resulted in a lowering of selling prices by the amount of the tax, so that the profit distributable to the stockholder of the illustration would still have been only $416. In that case, however, one could hardly say that the stockholder's tax bill included anything in addition to his individual tax of $813. But such an assumption would logically require one to consider also the possibilities of shifting the individual income tax on the

Position of Stockholders Who Have Large Incomes. Stockholders who have relatively large incomes can be benefited or hurt by having income taxed as corporate income, depending on the amounts of dividends their corporations distribute from the profits that remain after payment of the tax. To illustrate, let us suppose that Mr. Green is one of three partners who are analyzing the pros and cons of incorporation. The partners have been sharing profits equally, and Green's share has been averaging $200,000 a year. He is married, has two children, and files individual income tax returns jointly with his wife who has no separate income. Assuming that he has $4,000 of allowable deductions and no income from other sources, and applying 1968 tax rates, his individual income tax comes to $106,564. The partners anticipate that should they incorporate the profits of the enterprise would continue to average $600,000, and they expect to allow themselves salaries of $20,000 each—salaries they have every reason to believe the Internal Revenue Service would allow as a deductible expense to the corporation as reasonable compensation for their managerial services. The tax on the corporation's net profit of $540,000, after deduction of the salaries, would be $252,700, and Green's share of this would be $84,233. His individual income tax on the salary, with allowance for the deductible expenses of $4,000 and personal exemptions for himself, his wife, and his children, would come to $2,660. Thus, his total tax bill, corporate and individual, would be $86,893—an amount $19,671 less than his tax bill as a partner. Such a prospective tax saving would appear to make incorporation highly desirable, but the full amount of the saving would be enjoyed only if the partners agreed that as stockholders their salaries of $20,000 would be quite enough for living expenses and that all other earnings after corporate taxes would be left with the corporation. Should they, at the other extreme, decide that they would want to take out as dividends all corporate earnings after taxes, they would quickly conclude that incorporation would be most undesirable, for their combined corporation and individual tax bill would be unconscionably high. Mr. Green's individual tax on his $20,000 salary and dividends of $95,767 (one third of the corporation's profit of $540,000 reduced by corporation income taxes of $252,700) would be $50,926. This sum plus his $84,233 share of the corporate taxes would bring his total tax obligations to $135,159. Of course, the partners might agree that as directors of the proposed corporation they would allow themselves dividends that at the maximum would not make their tax liability greater than it would be were they being

partnership profits. Unfortunately, little is known conclusively of the extent to which taxes on the profits of corporations and other businesses are shifted; hence, business managers, in considering income taxation in relation to the merits and demerits of the corporate form, are likely to disregard the possibilities of shifting in making comparisons of the kinds illustrated in the text.

taxed as partners. Dividends to Green of about $46,500 would make his total federal taxes approximately equal to the $106,564 individual tax paid on his $200,000 share of partnership income.

Further Considerations. One thing that Mr. Green, his partners, and all other people coping with comparable problems would want to be sure of is that they could justify as reasonable whatever salaries they wished to allow themselves as corporate employees. The Internal Revenue Service must be satisfied that salaries are in keeping with the value of services rendered; if not so satisfied, it may disallow all or part of them as a deductible corporation expense.

Another point that must be kept in mind by those who weigh the respective tax advantages and disadvantages of operating as proprietorships and partnerships on the one hand or as corporations on the other is that corporate managements must be in a position to defend themselves if accused by the Internal Revenue Service of retaining earnings to enable stockholders to avoid the individual income taxes they would have to pay if the earnings were distributed as dividends. Under Sections 531–537 of the Internal Revenue Code, a corporation is permitted to accumulate $100,000 of earnings without question, but further "accumulated taxable income" in any year becomes subject to a special additional tax of 27.5 percent on the first $100,000 and 38.5 percent on any amount over $100,000 if it is determined (probably in proceedings before the Tax Court) that the income was, indeed, accumulated to avoid individual income taxes.

A third consideration is that corporation dividends paid in any year are subject to individual income taxes, even though they represent accumulations of past years. Accordingly, it would not be wise for Mr. Green and his fellow stockholders to forgo dividends for, say, five years, and then to take out in the sixth year all the earnings thus accumulated. In general, therefore, when foregoing dividends in favor of corporate expansion stockholders plan to make the plowing-under permanent. Usually, they expect the value of their stock to rise in some close relationship to the accumulation of earnings. This enables them to have their reward, if they want it, by selling all or a portion of their stock and thereby realizing a capital gain. The pleasant aspect of this procedure is that net long-term capital gains are taxed in the individual income tax structure at rates not exceeding 25 percent rather than at the steeply progressive rates on ordinary income, which, as mentioned above, run as high as 70 percent.[14] Perhaps even better, stockholders may plan to allow the corporate earnings accumulate (and, of course, their potential capital gains) until the time of death.

---

[14]The general rule is that only 50 percent of net long-term capital gains (after the deduction of net short-term capital losses, if any) are recognized as taxable income, and that the taxpayer may choose to have this portion of the long-term gain taxable at the ordinary rates of the individual income tax or at the special

In this way, individual income taxes on retained corporate earnings as well as capital gains taxes on increases in the value of stocks are completely avoided.

In a different direction, the partners would also want to consider the possible tax advantages of establishing several corporations to take over the partnership assets. If the partnership had been manufacturing several products, each in a separate plant, or if it had been operating a chain of retail stores, each plant or store might be separately incorporated. From the tax standpoint, the objective would be to establish such a number of corporations as would ensure that none would have net taxable income in excess of $25,000. In this way, all the net income of the several corporations would be taxed at 28 percent,[15] and none of it would get into the 48 percent bracket, as in the illustration. Aside from the tax aspects of the move, moreover, the partners might see a great advantage in limiting their risks of loss. Should one of the separate corporations fail, its creditors could seize its assets in satisfaction of their claims, but the assets of the remaining corporations would be beyond their reach. Another advantage might be that each plant or store could be more efficiently managed if owned and operated by a separate corporate entity.

Treatment of Small Corporations as Partnerships. Considering the quite significant advantages of the corporate form of organization on the one hand and possible great disadvantages of the double taxation of corporate income on the other, business proprietors would seem to be especially favored should they be permitted to incorporate while paying income taxes as if their businesses were proprietorships or partnerships. Under the federal Internal Revenue Code, indeed, such a privilege has been granted by Congress to what it classifies as "small business corporations"—the term *small* refers to the number of stockholders and not to dollar-and-cents figures, such as value of assets or amount of income.

To qualify as a small business corporation, a corporation must have only one class of stock (that is, only common stock), not more than 10 individual stockholders (among whom estates may be included), and no stockholder who is a nonresident alien. It cannot qualify if more than 80 percent of its gross receipts are derived from sources outside

---

capital gains rate of 50 percent. If the special rate is chosen, the maximum tax is obviously 25 percent *of the gain iteslf* (.50 × .50).

A long-term capital gain is one derived from sales or exchanges of stocks, bonds, and other capital assets, as defined in the law, held for periods of more than six months. Short-term gains, derived from sales or exchanges of capital assets held for six months or less, are taxed at the ordinary rates of the individual income tax to the extent that they are not offset by short-term capital losses and net long-term capital losses.

[15]Note that the privilege of getting a surtax exemption for each corporation of the controlled group would cost a penalty of 6 percentage points added to the normal tax rate of 22 percent.

the United States, nor if its gross receipts from royalties, rents, dividends, interest, annuities, and gains from sales or exchanges of stock or securities exceed 20 percent of its total gross receipts. All stockholders must consent to the election to have their corporation treated as a partnership for tax purposes. The election means that the stockholders must report in their individual income tax returns for each year their respective shares of corporate net income earned in that year, whether or not received as dividends. The corporation, accordingly, pays no tax on its income, regardless of the amounts distributed as dividends or retained.

An election can be revoked should the stockholders of a small business corporation find the special tax arrangement no longer advantageous. Like an election itself, a revocation requires the consent of all stockholders. If made in the first month of a taxable year, it can be applied to that year; if made later, it becomes effective for the following taxable year. Revocation also occurs automatically if the enterprise no longer qualifies as a small business corporation—if it adds a stockholder who does not consent to the prior election, if it gets more than 10 stockholders, if a nonresident alien becomes a stockholder, if more than 80 percent of its gross receipts in any year are derived from foreign sources, and so on.

That the privilege of electing to be taxed as a small business corporation is an attractive one is indicated by the fact that out of approximately 1,428 million income tax and information returns the Internal Revenue Service received from active corporations for fiscal years ending between July 1, 1965, and June 30, 1966, about 174,000 were information returns filed by small corporations that were taking advantage of the privilege.[16]

Future Taxes

In weighing the attractions and burdens of incorporation, organizers and owners of business enterprises are well advised to consider not only tax statutes currently in force but also the possibilities of changes therein. It has already been mentioned that possible changes in federal corporation income tax rates must be considered, but the same advice is applicable for all kinds of special taxes levied on corporations. A consideration of equal importance is the likelihood that varieties of taxes not currently on the statute books will be imposed. Surmises here may be chiefly concerned with what Congress may decide to do, as federal taxes affecting business enterprise tend to be much heavier than those imposed by the states.

Forecasts may well be based on what has happened in the past.

---

[16]U.S. Treasury Department, Internal Revenue Service, *Statistics of Income, 1965—Preliminary: Corporation Income Tax Returns* (Washington, D.C.: U.S. Government Printing Office, 1967), p. 1.

Thus, it is pertinent to observe that wars almost invariably bring new taxes, as well as increases in the rates of old ones, and it is surely not by chance that corporations are often singled out to bear certain kinds of additional burdens. In view of our adoption of such a tax in 1918, 1940, and 1950, the levying of an excess-profits tax on corporations can surely be anticipated for the period of any future war of considerable magnitude. In the matter of wartime levies, the federal capital stock tax adopted in 1917 and not repealed until 1925 also deserves mention, as does the addition in 1968 of a 10 percent surcharge to tax obligations, with much uncertainty about its duration. But circumstances unrelated to war sometimes give rise to new or refurbished taxes on corporations. Among these, we may recall the interrelated capital stock and declared-value excess-profits taxes in effect from 1934 to 1945, and the much-condemned undistributed-profits tax in effect from 1936 to 1938.

QUESTIONS

1. In what sense is it said that the stockholders of a business corporation are only limitedly liable for its debts? Is the corporation itself only limitedly liable? Explain.

2. Is there any relationship between the doctrine of the corporation as a distinct legal entity and the doctrine of limited liability? Explain.

3. Why is the doctrine of limited liability likely to be less significant for small corporations than for large ones?

4. What is a close corporation? An open corporation? A public corporation?

5. In what respects is corporate stock flexible as a financing instrument? Cannot ownership interests in partnerships be made equally flexible and with equal advantage? Explain.

6. Of what advantage to corporate stockholders is the easy transferability of their shares? Explain whether or not shares of ownership in partnerships are transferable with equal ease.

7. How does the life of a corporation differ from that of a partnership? In terms of life, which of these two forms of organization has the principal advantages?

8. How can one account for the fact that the credit standing of corporations does not seem to be weakened because of the limited liability of stockholders?

9. In what sense does the concept of representative government apply to the operations of business corporations? Is this advantageous for the stockholders? Discuss.

10. What are the principal burdens in establishing corporations? Do these burdens explain why there are many more proprietorships and partnerships than business corporations in the United States? Discuss.

11. To what extent can a corporation chartered in a given state operate

in interstate commerce? In what circumstances can it do business in other states? Why is this distinction important for corporations but not for partnerships?

12. From the standpoint of any given state, what are domestic corporations? Foreign corporations? Alien corporations?

13. In addition to organization and entrance taxes, what are the two kinds of taxes most commonly imposed on corporations by state governments? In general terms, how burdensome are these taxes?

14. Assuming that the federal corporation income tax is not shifted, why is it likely to be especially burdensome to stockholders who have moderate incomes? In what circumstances can it work to the advantage of stockholders who have large incomes?

15. Explain why each of the following is an important factor in determining the stockholders' burden of the federal corporation income tax: size of corporate income, size of the stockholders' income from sources other than dividends, amount of dividends distributed, salaries paid to stockholders as officers, and special treatment of long-term capital gains in the federal tax laws.

16. If a small business corporation elects to have its income taxed by the federal government as if it were a partnership, how and when is the income actually taxed?

PROBLEMS

1. What organization tax would a Connecticut corporation pay on an authorized issue of 100,000 shares of stock of $20 par value? 100,000 shares of $40 par value? 100,000 no-par shares?

2. What organization tax would a Delaware corporation pay on an authorized issue of 10,000 shares of $20 par value? 500,000 shares of $5 par value? 500,000 shares of $50 par value?

3. What annual franchise tax would a corporation pay to the state of Michigan on $3 million of capital stock and surplus allocated to that state?

4. What annual franchise tax would a corporation pay to the state of Delaware on allocated capital stock amounting to 60,000 shares of $10 par value? 600,000 shares of $25 par value?

5. State Y levies an annual corporation income tax of 5 percent on corporate income allocated to it on the basis of the Massachusetts formula. In a certain year, the sales of the ABX Corporation in state Y amounted to $2 million out of total sales of $12 million; its payroll in state Y amounted to $600,000 and its total payroll to $3 million; the value of its tangible property located in state Y amounted to $1 million, while its total tangible property was valued at $2 million. Its total net income was $900,000. What was the amount of its income tax liability to state Y?

6. At the basic federal corporation income tax rates in effect in the year 1968, as mentioned in this chapter, what would be the tax liability of a corporation with net taxable income of $10,000? $100,000? $1 million? For these three amounts of income, what would be the tax liability with the addition of the surcharge referred to in footnote 7 on pages 36–37?

chapter 3

THE FORMATION OF BUSINESS CORPORATIONS

It is easy to form a business corporation. The states are most generous in granting corporate charters; in their general incorporation statutes or codes, they have outlined simple procedures whereby charters can be obtained quickly and conveniently. In most states, the secretary of state or some subordinate official in his department has the authority to issue charters, but whoever the official is, or whatever the department he may be located in, he is generally able to exercise his authority purely as a matter of clerical routine.

An attractive aspect of incorporation is that the secretaries of state or other officials do not have power to pass on the merits of the business ventures for which charters are sought—the legislatures have not given these officials the right to sit in judgment on the proposed incorporations that come before them. They do not reject applications on the grounds that the incorporators and proposed directors have had insufficient managerial experience, that they are starting out with too little money to accomplish what they propose to do, or that they want to enter a field of enterprise in which competition is already much too keen. All that the officials are concerned with is to see that the requirements of the law are fulfilled and that the prescribed fees and taxes are paid. If these conditions are met, they have no choice but to issue the charters applied for. In our day, free enterprise thus means not only freedom to establish new enterprises and free access to markets, but also ready access to corporate charters.

Only when applicants for charters propose to carry on businesses that our states, under their police powers, choose to regulate closely in the public interest do the state officials with whom applications are filed have the authority to reject them. Such businesses usually include: railroads, streetcar and bus lines, and certain other classes of enterprises in the transportation field; electric, gas, and water companies; commercial and savings banks; savings and loan associations; credit unions; and insurance companies. Applications for charters for businesses of these kinds customarily bypass the secretaries of state and go direct to other officials who already have regulatory jurisdiction in the respective fields, as the superintendents of banking, the secretaries of insurance, and the public service commissions.

PROCEDURE OF INCORPORATION

Taking Subscriptions to Stock

The first step in the establishment of a business corporation is the taking of subscriptions to the stock that it will issue. The states are extremely easygoing in their requirements here, ordinarily stipulating that subscriptions of $1,000 or $2,000 must be obtained before the application for a charter is filed, and that at least half the amount so stipulated must be paid in before the corporation begins business.

Nevertheless, the promoters of a new corporate organization are likely to pay little attention to the minimum subscription requirements of the state law. If, for example, they anticipate that to get started on a strong footing their enterprise, will need a stockholders' investment of $100,000, they would be acting rather foolishly were they to proceed with the incorporation on accumulating subscriptions of only $1,000 or $2,000. Indeed, many proposed ventures stop at this point. The refusal of relatives, friends, and acquaintances to subscribe a sufficient amount disillusions the promoters, and they reluctantly abandon their projects—and their dreams!

Adequate subscriptions to the stock of proposed corporations, on the other hand, may be obtained almost instantaneously. This is especially true of the incorporation of firms already well established as unincorporated businesses. Thus, the members of a partnership may reach a decision to incorporate, with the dominant figure among them saying something like this: "We have made approximately equal contributions to the partnership's assets, and we have been sharing profits and losses equally. We will establish a corporation, have it take over the partnership assets at their present book values, and have it issue us equal blocks of stock of the same total value." In such circumstances, assuming the quick agreement of the other partners, the subscription books are opened and closed simultaneously.

Subscribers' Meeting

When stock has been subscribed in an amount sufficient to promise success in getting a new corporate venture started, a meeting of the subscribers is held. The principal purpose of the meeting is to choose incorporators who will have the responsibility of carrying through the procedure of incorporation as prescribed by the state law. The incorporators draw up and sign the articles of incorporation (with the advice and aid of competent attorneys, it is to be expected), submit them to the secretary of state, pay the required fees and taxes, and take care of whatever other details the law may require.

The state laws generally provide that there must be not fewer than three incorporators, that they must be natural persons—which means that corporations, as *legal* persons, cannot serve as incorporators of other corporations—and that they must be at least 21 years of age. In most states, there is the further stipulation that some number or proportion of the incorporators must be citizens of the United States, and some go on to provide that some number or proportion must be residents of the state to which the application for a charter is being made.

Some states stipulate that the original board of directors shall be elected at the subscribers' meeting; in others, the choice of directors is deferred until a meeting of the stockholders to be held after the charter has been granted.

Very often, the subscribers name themselves as the incorporators, and also, if it is appropriate to do so at the time of the subscribers' meeting, as the first board of directors. Because most corporations start as small ventures involving only a few persons, such persons, or most of them, can usually be expected to serve in all capacities—that is, first as subscribers and incorporators, and subsequently as stockholders, directors, and officers.

Articles of Incorporation

The document that most concerns the incorporators is known in some states as the "articles of incorporation" and in others as the "certificate of incorporation." Throughout this textbook, the term "articles of incorporation" is used exclusively; hence the student should note that the articles discussed in the next few pages and referred to elsewhere may be a certificate in his home state or in some other state whose law he may examine.

The articles of incorporation are of major importance in the life of a business corporation. When the secretary of state accepts and approves the articles as having been properly prepared, the new corporate entity is authorized to carry on business in accordance with the terms of the selfsame articles and in accordance with the terms of the state law under which they have been filed and approved. The state law gives every corporation established under it certain broad powers that need not be mentioned in the articles, and it likewise places on it certain responsibilites and limitations, whether or not they are mentioned in the articles. Thus, it may be said that the powers, responsibilities, and restrictions provided for in the state law, coupled with the provisions contained in a corporation's articles, constitute its *charter*. When it is said, therefore, that a corporation may do this or that according to the terms of its charter, what is meant is that the action is in accordance with either the provisions of the state law or those of its own articles.

The states require that certain details be specifically set out in the articles of incorporation (see Figure 3–1); other details, they provide, may be included or excluded at the discretion of the incorporators. Let us, first of all, consider what is required.

Name. The name of the proposed corporation must be stated in the articles. Many states prescribe that the name must include a word such as *corporation, incorporated*, or *limited*, or an abbreviation of one of these words, so that everybody will know that the enterprise is a corporation and that the liability of its stockholders for its debts is limited. Other states, however, are not so precise in their requirements, so that it may be impossible to determine from the names used by business enterprises organized in these states whether or not they are corporations. Another common prescription is that the name must not be identical with or confusingly similar to that of another domestic corporation already in operation or to that of a foreign corporation already authorized to do business in the state. Moreover, the name must not include words suggesting that the corporation has powers that it does not or cannot have. Thus, the South Bend Banking Corporation would not be an acceptable name for a manufacturing company.

There is much in a name. So the Securities and Exchange Commission found in its comprehensive special study of the securities markets published in 1963. Referring to the many hot issues of common stocks floated by corporations in certain glamour industries in the period 1959–61, the SEC reported:

> Some companies with prosaic names were rechristened in order to give the impression, correct or not, that they had some connection with electronics, in much the same way as Hollywood starlets are renamed and glamorized to satisfy the public's craving for romance. Monumental Engineering Corp. became Astrotherm Corp.; North Shore Name Plate Corp. became Anodyne Corp.; Iresco, Inc., became Aero Space Electronics, Inc.; Safety Tower Ladder Co., Inc., which manufactures safety belts and attachments, became Air Space Devices, Inc. A representative of American Orbitronics Corp. told prospective customers, "I'm told the name alone is worth $5 a share in this crazy market."[1]

Purposes. The incorporators must be especially careful in stating the purposes or objects of the proposed corporation. As a general rule, a corporation can undertake only such kinds of business activities as

[1]Securities and Exchange Commission, *Report of Special Study of the Securities Markets* (House Doc. No. 95, Pt. 1, 88th Cong., 1st sess. [Washington, D.C.: U.S. Government Printing Office, 1963]), p. 498.

FIGURE 3–1

Form of Articles of Incorporation (New Jersey)

FORM 2

(R. S. 14:2–3, 4)

CERTIFICATE OF INCORPORATION

OF THE

This is to Certify, That we ....

....

do hereby associate ourselves into a corporation, under and by virtue of Title 14 of the Revised Statutes, and do severally agree to take the number of shares of capital stock set opposite our respective names.

(a) The name of the corporation is

....

(b) The location of the principal office in this State is at No. .... Street, in the .... of .... County of ....

(c) The name of the agent therein and in charge thereof, upon whom process against this corporation may be served, is ....

(d) The objects for which this corporation is formed are ....

....

The corporation shall also have power to conduct its business in all its branches, have one or more offices, and unlimitedly to hold, purchase, mortgage and convey real and personal property in any State, Territory or colony of the United States and in any foreign country or place.

(e) The total authorized capital stock of this corporation is .... dollars, divided into .... shares of a par value of .... dollars each.

(f) The names and post-office address of the incorporators and the number of shares subscribed for by each, the aggregate of which ($ ....) is the amount of capital stock with which this company will commence business, are as follows:

Name.	Post-Office Address.	Number of Shares.

(g) The period of existence of this corporation is unlimited.

In Witness Whereof, we have hereunto set our hands and seals the .... day of .... A. D., One thousand nine hundred and ....

....(L. S.)
....(L. S.)
....(L. S.)

Signed, sealed and delivered in the presence of

....

STATE OF } ss.
COUNTY OF .... }

Be it Remembered, That on this .... day of ...., A. D. nineteen hundred and .... before me, a ...., personally appeared ....
whom I am satisfied are the persons named in and who executed the foregoing certificate, and I having first made known to them the contents thereof, they did each acknowledge that they signed, sealed and delivered the same as their voluntary act and deed, for the uses and purposes therein expressed.

are specifically described in its articles as the purposes or objects for which it is formed. It is particularly important that narrow definitions of purposes be avoided; if not avoided, an enlargement of the corporation's scope of operations may necessitate the red tape of formally amending the articles (a procedure to be discussed later in this chapter).

The importance of the statement of purposes or objects was illustrated by changes of rather dramatic proportions made in 1963 in the articles of incorporation of the Curtis Publishing Company, publisher of the *Saturday Evening Post*, the *Ladies' Home Journal*, and other popular magazines. Before the changes, its statement of purposes was this: "Manufacturing, printing, and publishing newspapers, periodicals, magazines and books and materials necessary therefor." In the amendment, however, several further sweeping statements of purposes were added, including the following.

> (3) The prosecution and improvement of the business and arts of communication including the creation, construction, installation, servicing and operation of communications systems of every type and kind, throughout the world and interspace and the sending and receiving of communications of every nature and kind.
>
> (4) The purchase, sale, leasing, merchandising and distribution of articles of commerce of every nature and kind.
>
> (5) The creation, purchase, sale and dissemination of advertising material and services of every nature and kind.
>
> * * * * *
>
> (7) The development, exploitation, sale and leasing, of timber and mineral resources of every nature and kind.[2]

In a similar fashion, the Youngstown Sheet & Tube Company amended its articles of incorporation early in 1968 to escape the restrictions of a statement of purposes narrowly confining its business activities to basic iron and steel and products of iron and steel.

On the other hand, every kind of action the corporation may or must take to achieve its stated purposes need not be listed in detail in the articles. Most kinds of actions will be readily recognized by courts as incidental to its stated purposes or implied by the very fact that the corporation is a business enterprise. When, for example, the stated purpose is to manufacture and sell certain kinds of appliances or "appliances of every nature and kind," it is not necessary for the incorporators to state in the articles that the corporation shall have as purposes the buying of raw materials, the hiring of labor, the placing of advertising in this or that medium, the borrowing of money from banks, the issuing of bonds, and so on.

---

[2]*Notice of Annual Meeting and Proxy Statement,* March 8, 1963, pp. 6, 13.

A broad statement of purposes enables the stockholders, directors, and officers of a corporation to extend its scope of activities freely without fear that actions in new directions will be adjudged *ultra vires.* Acts *ultra vires* are those outside the stated purposes of the corporation and beyond the powers incidental thereto. In some states, a corporation has no standing in the courts in trying to enforce contracts found to be *ultra vires.* The other parties to the contracts will not be required to fulfill their obligations if they can prove to the satisfaction of a court that in entering the contracts the corporation has attempted to do something beyond its powers. Yet, the corporation itself is not likely to be permitted to avoid its obligations under existing contracts, even if it can prove that it was acting beyond its powers in entering them. Moreover, stockholders may seek injunctions to prevent their corporations from carrying on what they regard as *ultra vires* functions, and they may sue directors personally for losses incurred because of alleged *ultra vires* acts. The attorney general of the state, too, may go to court to obtain injunctions to prevent corporate acts alleged to be *ultra vires;* indeed, he may initiate proceedings for the dissolution of corporations on the grounds that they persist in committing such acts. Such legal difficulties are likely to originate, of course, only when the statement of purposes in the articles of incorporation is narrow or ambiguous. Although, therefore, directors may successfully defend themselves and their corporations in legal proceedings of the kinds referred to, it would surely be far better to avoid the threat of such litigation in the first place by a broad, clear statement of purposes.

Principal Office and Resident Agent. A state should be able at all times to reach its corporate creatures to serve legal papers, to assess taxes, to make inquiries, and to transact other kinds of public business —hence the requirement for a principal office within the state and a resident agent. In most instances, the incorporators designate as the principal office what will be that truly, and name the president of the proposed corporation as its resident agent.

However, the designation of *any* office and agent, as long as they are located within the state, will usually satisfy the legal stipulation. An attorney or trust institution, for example, may be named as resident agent and his or its office designated as the corporation's principal office. Such an arrangement is common when most of a corporation's plants and sales and administrative offices are (or are expected to be) located outside the state of incorporation. According to *The Wall Street Journal:*

As a result, a major service company like Corp. Trust represents more than 20,000 corporations at its unobstrusive quarters on the 12th floor of an office building . . . in Wilmington. Corp. Trust has so many clients that its secretaries often have to check their records to determine whom they represent.[3]

In states where personal property owned by corporations is taxed at the places where their principal offices are located, small cities and villages where tax rates are relatively low may be selected for the location of such offices. For example, the borough of Flemington, New Jersey, with a population of 3,232 reported in the 1960 census, is the location of the principal office of the $15.2 billion Standard Oil Company (New Jersey)!

Life. With few exceptions, our states authorize perpetual charters for corporations. Some provide that the life of every corporation chartered will be perpetual unless the incorporators state a specific term of years in the articles of incorporation; in these states, therefore, nothing need be said in the articles about the life or duration of the corporation if perpetual existence is wanted or is acceptable. In the few states that do not grant perpetual charters, a term of years must obviously be specified in the articles; and in all other states, of course, the articles must designate either perpetual life or a term of years, whichever may be desired.

In states where perpetual corporate life is generously made available, incorporators almost always accept it for their enterprises. Even if the purposes of the corporation are expected to be fulfilled in a few years, perpetual life is the source of no inconvenience. It is as easy to wind up the affairs and effect the dissolution of a corporation having perpetual life as to terminate the life of one having, according to the duration stated in its articles, only a few months or years remaining. Because incorporators tend always to anticipate that something will turn up to justify the continued operation of their corporations—even those that start out with short-term objectives—they want to make unnecessary a later amendment of the articles to extend the corporate life.

Stock Issues. At the minimum, the corporation laws require the incorporators to state in the articles whether the corporation will issue only one class of stock or two or more classes, how many shares of the single class or of the several classes will be authorized, whether or not the stock will have a par value, what the par value will be, and the amount that must be paid in on stock subscriptions before the corporation will commence business. For the amount that must be paid in before business starts, the laws, as indicated above, stipulate some modest minimum sum, such as $500 or $1,000.

As a general rule, if more than one class of stock is to be authorized, such as common and preferred, or common and two or more classes of preferred, the incorporators have the choice of including in the articles "the designation of each class and a statement of the preferences,

[3]Midwest Edition, April 16, 1968, p. 4.

qualifications, limitations, restrictions, and the special or relative rights in respect of the shares of each class,"[4] or of stating that the board of directors shall have power to fix these details from time to time before shares of the respective classes are issued. Likewise, the articles may provide for the issuance of a given class of stock in series, and the details may be included in the articles, or there may be inserted a statement that the board of directors shall have power to determine these details from time to time. For example, a corporation may have only one class of preferred stock, but it may reserve the right to issue from time to time blocks with differing dividend rates, voting powers, and other features.

If power to establish the details of different classes or series of stock is reserved to the board of directors, subsequent action by the directors in the exercise of this power must be taken by the adoption of formal resolutions. Copies of these resolutions must be filed with the secretary of state and usually with a designated county official in the county where the corporation's principal office is located—that is, the principal office as designated in the articles. The idea is that a complete public record of the details of a corporation's stock should be available for examination by anyone interested in the corporation, such as persons who may want to buy some of the stock and prospective creditors. The public record is also useful, of course, in the levying of taxes on the corporation, especially the annual franchise tax if the state has one.

Directors and Incorporators. Provisions in the articles concerning the board of directors may generally be quite brief; in some states, indeed, nothing need be said in the articles about the board. About all that needs to be indicated in the states that require a statement is the number of directors the corporation will have or a permitted range in the number of directors, as not fewer than 5 nor more than 10. In almost all states, the minimum number permitted is three.

Obviously, the names and addresses of the incorporators must be included in the articles, since it is they who are the applicants for the charter. In some states, each incorporator must indicate the number of shares of stock for which he has subscribed; in others, the law has no such requirement.

Other Provisions. So much for the provisions that the state laws in one way or another require to be included in the articles of incorporation. If the incorporators so choose, additional details about the organization and government of the corporation may be included, provided only that such details do not run counter to the provisions of the laws. For example, the law of New Jersey authorizes inclusion in the articles of:

> . . . any provision, consistent with law, which the incorporators may

[4]State of Illinois, *The Business Corporation Act*, sec. 47–7.

choose to insert, for the management of the business and the conduct of the affairs of the corporation, and any provision creating, defining, limiting and regulating the powers of the corporation, its directors and stockholders or any class of stockholders.[5]

The common practice, nevertheless, is to keep out of the articles all kinds of provisions not specifically required. Additional details about organization and government can be much better placed in the bylaws of the corporation (to be described briefly below) where they can be amended from time to time as the changing circumstances of the corporation may require. Altering details set out in the articles generally requires the formal process of amendment, whereas changing the bylaws can be effected with much less formality and fuss.

Filing the Articles

After the articles of incorporation have been properly drawn, the requisite number of copies are filed with the secretary of state (or such other official as the state may have designated) and the prescribed fees and taxes are paid. When the secretary of state approves the articles as being in conformity with the state law, the existence of the corporation begins. The approval is indicated in various ways. In some states, the secretary simply notifies the incorporators of his approval. In others, he issues a certificate of incorporation, which is a specific authorization to the corporation to carry on business in accordance with the provisions of its articles and the state law—in substance, this is the "charter" as that term was defined earlier in this chapter. In still others, the secretary returns a copy of the articles duly certified.

A further filing requirement laid down in the state laws is that for placing a copy of the articles of incorporation on record in the office of a county official in the county where the corporation's principal office, as designated in the articles, is located. This official is variously the county clerk, the recorder of deeds, or the prothonotary.

Organization Meetings

Stockholders' Meeting. Following approval of a corporation's articles by the secretary of state, meetings of the stockholders and the original board of directors are generally in order, although, as indicated in the second paragraph following, a meeting of the stockholders at this time may be unnecessary. If the stockholders have a meeting, it is ordinarily held for the purpose of drawing up and approving bylaws and electing the first board of directors. The bylaws may be described as a body of internal legislation for the government of the corporation. They must not have any provisions in conflict with the articles of incorporation or the state corporation laws, although they

---

[5]State of New Jersey, *The General Corporation Law*, chap. 2, sec. 14:2-3.

may limit the exercise of powers granted in the articles and laws. Accordingly, they may be said to be supplementary to the laws and articles, containing details not prescribed in or forbidden by the laws, and not thought to be convenient for insertion in the articles.

Covered in the bylaws are:

1. Time and place of the annual meeting of the stockholders, giving of notice of such meetings, what constitutes a quorum, who presides, method of voting, whether or not cumulative voting is permitted,[6] use of proxies, and calling of special meetings.
2. Number, qualifications, and compensation of the directors; the time and place of directors' meetings; what number of directors constitutes a quorum; and the method of filling vacancies in the board.
3. Designation of the titles of the principal officers, as president, vice president, secretary, and treasurer; general scope of their duties; their scale of compensation; and whether or not they are to be bonded.
4. Procedures for the issuance and transfer of stock and the keeping of records of the stockholders.
5. Provisions for the control of the corporation's cash and valuable papers, and for the safeguarding of its property of other kinds.
6. Limitations on the amount of its indebtedness and on the pledging of its property for the security of its obligations.
7. Provisions designating the procedure for amending the bylaws.

---

[6]Cumulative voting is designed to give proportional representation on the board of directors to whatever factions may exist among the stockholders, so that each faction will be in a position to promote its views and protect its interests. In cumulative voting, each stockholder has votes equal to the number of shares he owns times the number of directors to be elected, and he may cast this "cumulated" total for a single candidate or distribute it among two or more candidates. Suppose, for example, that the majority faction among the stockholders of a corporation holds 7,500 of its 10,000 shares and the minority faction the remaining 2,500 shares, and that 9 directors are to be elected. In ordinary voting, the majority would cast 7,500 votes for its slate of 9 candidates, and it would thus win all the places on the board since the minority could not cast more than 2,500 votes for any candidate. In cumulative voting, on the other hand, the minority with 22,500 votes could cast, say, 11,250 votes for each of two candidates, and the majority could not possibly defeat these two candidates and win all 9 places on the board, no matter how it might divide up its 67,500 votes. In fact, 9,001 votes would be required to choose 1 director, as determined by the following formula:

$$\frac{\text{Total votes available (90,000)}}{\text{Number of directors to be elected (9)} + 1} + 1 = 9{,}001$$

Accordingly, the majority could be sure of seven places but not eight or nine, and the minority could be sure of two places but not three or four. Should the minority try to get more than its proportional representation by casting, say, 5,625 votes for each of 4 candidates, it would probably be frozen out completely, since the majority could cast 7,500 votes for each of 9 candidates. For cumulative voting to be successful in providing proportional representation, therefore, each faction must know its strength and concentrate or spread its votes in keeping with this knowledge.

In some states, the corporation laws confer on the directors the power to adopt, amend, and repeal bylaws, unless the power is reserved to the stockholders in the articles of incorporation; many others authorize a delegation of the power to the directors by specific provision in the articles of incorporation. Theoretically, the principal function of bylaws is to protect the interests of the stockholders as owners of a corporation; hence, giving directors the right to adopt, amend, and repeal these rules of internal government is illogical. Because, however, bylaws adopted by directors are subject to amendment, repeal, or replacement by action of the stockholders taken at annual or special meetings, the stockholders continue to have the final authority. At any rate, if the directors have powers with respect to the bylaws, and if the stockholders are satisfied to let them exercise these powers, no questions pertaining to the bylaws need to be taken up at the organization meeting of the stockholders. Indeed, the stockholders need have no organization meeting at all if the directors are to take care of the bylaws and if the first board itself was chosen by the subscribers at their earlier meeting.

Directors' Meeting. First in the order of business at the directors' organization meeting is the adoption of the bylaws if that job falls within their province. Next comes the choice of the officers and other key personnel, the fixing of lines of authority, the allocation of duties and responsibilities, and the setting of a scale of salaries if not already set out in the bylaws. Finally, the directors adopt an official seal, which is to be placed on reports to the state, stock certificates, and other documents requiring a seal. These actions must be taken to complete the organization of the corporation, and they constitute, as it were, the agenda of the organization meeting; however, the directors may continue, if they wish, with what could be called a regular business meeting. Indeed, they may be quite anxious to go ahead with the discussion and ratification of many pending contracts having to do with the actual launching of business operations.

General Corporate Powers

Important to the careers of business corporations are the general powers conferred on them by the state corporation laws. These powers may be exercised even though not mentioned in the articles and regardless of what the stated purposes of the individual corporations may be. They tend toward uniformity from state to state, although one must always be on the lookout for exceptions. As extensively revised in 1967, the general powers granted by the state of Delaware are stated as follows.

Every corporation created under this chapter shall have power to—

(1) Have perpetual succession by its corporate name, unless a limited period of duration is stated in its certificate of incorporation;

(2) Sue and be sued in all courts and participate, as a party or otherwise, in any judicial, administrative, arbitrative or other proceeding, in its corporate name;

(3) Have a corporate seal, which may be altered at pleasure, and use the same by causing it or a facsimile thereof to be impressed or affixed or in any other manner reproduced;

(4) Purchase, receive, take by grant, gift, devise, bequest or otherwise, lease, or otherwise acquire, own, hold, improve, employ, use and otherwise deal in and with real or personal property, or any interest therein, wherever situated, and to sell, convey, lease, exchange, transfer or otherwise dispose of, or mortgage or pledge, all or any of its property and assets, or any interest therein, wherever situated;

(5) Appoint such officers and agents as the business of the corporation requires and to pay or otherwise provide for them suitable compensation;

(6) Adopt, amend, and repeal by-laws;

(7) Wind up and dissolve itself in the manner provided in this chapter;

(8) Conduct its business, carry on its operations, and have offices and exercise its powers within or without this State;

(9) Make donations for the public welfare or for charitable, scientific or educational purposes, and in time of war or other national emergency in aid thereof;

(10) Be an incorporator, promoter, or manager of other corporations of any type or kind;

(11) Participate with others in any corporation, partnership, limited partnership, joint venture, or other association of any kind, or in any transaction, undertaking or arrangement which the participating corporation would have power to conduct by itself, whether or not such participation involves sharing or delegation of control with or to others.

(12) In time of war or other national emergency, to do any lawful business in aid thereof, notwithstanding the business or purposes set forth in its certificate of incorporation, at the request or direction of any apparently authorized governmental authority;

(13) Make contracts, including contracts of guaranty and suretyship, incur liabilities, borrow money at such rates of interest as the corporation may determine, issue its notes, bonds and other obligations, and secure any of its obligations by mortgage, pledge or other encumbrances of all or any of its property, franchises and income;

(14) Lend money for its corporate purposes, invest and reinvest its funds, and take, hold and deal with real and personal property as security for the payment of funds so loaned or invested;

(15) Pay pensions and establish and carry out pension, profit sharing, stock option, stock purchase, stock bonus, retirement, benefit, incentive and compensation plans, trusts and provisions for any or all of its directors, officers, and employees, and for any or all of the directors, officers, and employees of its subsidiaries;

(16) Provide insurance for its benefit on the life of any of its directors, officers, or employees, or on the life of any stockholder for the purpose of acquiring at his death shares of its stock owned by such stockholder.[7]

---

[7]State of Delaware, *General Corporation Law*, sec. 122.

Beyond such a general grant of powers, the states provide that their corporations will have such additional powers as are necessary or convenient for the accomplishment of their stated purposes. For example, Illinois sets out this type of provision: "To have and exercise all powers necessary or convenient to effect any or all of the purposes for which the corporation is formed."[8]

AMENDING THE ARTICLES

Need of Amendments

Any lack of foresight on the part of the incorporators or their attorneys in drawing up articles of incorporation does not mean that a corporation will be straitjacketed throughout its life; as far as legal procedure goes, it is as easy to amend the articles as to have them approved in the first place. As a practical matter, however, it is usually much easier for a handful of incorporators to agree on the details of the articles than to later get the approval of the requisite number of stockholders for amendments. All the more is this likely to be true, of course, if at the time amendments are proposed there are many stockholders, and if the proposals for amendment are of a controversial nature. It behooves incorporators, therefore, to proceed with such care that they can be reasonably sure that amendments, aside from those involving stock authorizations, will not be necessary for many years.

Only in the matter of stock issues is it likely that amendment from time to time will be anticipated as a desirable step. Many of the states, as we have seen, base their organization taxes on the authorized stock issues, rather than on the amount of stock to be issued immediately. In such states, therefore, tax liabilities of this kind can be minimized by limiting the authorized stock issues to an amount not in excess of what will probably be issued in the first few years of operation.[9]

Amending Procedure

The ordinary procedure for amending the articles begins with the adoption by the board of directors of a resolution setting forth a careful statement of the proposed amendment. The resolution is then submitted to the stockholders for their approval. This may be done at the regular annual meeting of the stockholders or at a special meeting called at any time. Depending on the state law and provisions in the articles themselves, an affirmative vote of stockholders who own a majority or two thirds or some other proportion of the stock "repre-

[8]State of Illinois, *The Business Corporation Act*, sec. 5(p).

[9]In various situations, however, stockholders' interests may be best served if boards of directors have substantial amounts of authorized stock available for immediate issuance without need of an approval vote of the stockholders. For a discussion of this matter, see pp. 524–25.

sented at the meeting and entitled to vote" is necessary for approval.

On approval by the stockholders, articles of amendment are drawn up and are submitted to the secretary of state in duplicate or triplicate, as the law may require, together with the inevitable filing fee, and with a payment for taxes if the amendment calls for an increase in the authorized stock. The secretary may issue a certificate of amendment or indicate his approval in whatever other way the law provides for; at any rate, approval by the secretary, as for the original articles, has the effect of putting into force the change desired. There is also a requirement for filing a copy of the articles of amendment with an official of the county where the principal office of the corporation is situated.

CHOOSING THE STATE OF INCORPORATION

Location of Properties and Business Activities

Because most corporations are small at the time of their establishment, the great majority are incorporated in the states where their promoters reside. The promoters expect to locate their plants, stores, or other properties entirely within the borders of their home states, and they anticipate that all or almost all their business activities, for many years or perhaps permanently, will be similarly confined. There may be little prospect of their doing business in other states. Almost as a matter of course, they plan from the beginning to send their papers to Springfield, Albany, Atlanta, Harrisburg, Sacramento, and so on, because they reside in the states whose capitals these cities are. In most instances, they probably do not even consider that they could get a charter in another state as easily, or almost as easily, as in the home state. Those promoters of small, localized corporations who do consider this possibility are likely to reject it quickly, thinking of the additional red tape of having to obtain a certificate of authority from the state of residence, and of the continuing obligation to pay taxes and to file reports in both the chartering state and the state of residence.

Shopping around among several states to find the one that appears to offer most advantages for incorporation is thus likely to be of interest only to larger enterprises. The members of a partnership already doing business in many states would be likely to analyze most carefully the advantageous and disadvantageous aspects of these states should they decide to incorporate. They might even select a state in which very little or none of their business was being transacted should they be convinced of the preponderance of its advantages. Likewise, the managers of a corporation that has grown large and has extended its operations into several or many states may be more or less constantly on the lookout for advantages to be gained by giving up the corporation's charter in the state of original incorporation and obtaining a new one in another state. For example, a major reason given for the move of Textron Inc. from Rhode Island to Delaware in October, 1967, was that under Delaware law the directors could set the dividend rate, convertibility provisions, and other features of preferred stock issues to be offered to stockholders of other corporations in merger bids, whereas under Rhode Island law it would be necessary to call stockholders' meetings to vote on such matters.

In many instances, indeed, plans for mergers and consolidations present new opportunities for analyzing the merits and demerits of charters as granted by different states. If corporation A chartered in Maryland and corporation B chartered in Ohio—each doing business in several states—are to be combined, it may be decided that the most advantageous arrangement would be to have a new corporation, corporation C, chartered in Delaware to take over A and B.

When circumstances appear to make shopping around advisable, advantages and disadvantages are usually thought of in terms of three things: (1) taxation, (2) the stability of the corporation laws, and (3) the liberality of these laws.

Taxation

The burden of special corporate taxes is of great importance in deciding whether or not a business should be incorporated. This we have already seen. It is of much less importance in choosing the state of incorporation, although still worthy of study. A major reason for this reduced importance is that the heaviest tax levies placed on corporations are those of the federal government, and such taxes are payable, of course, regardless of the state of incorporation—or even the country of incorporation.[10] Another reason is that the states that levy annual franchise and corporate income taxes impose them on foreign corporations as well as on domestic ones.

Nevertheless, some tax economies are possible by judicious choice of the state of incorporation. States that place relatively high organization taxes on total authorized stock are likely to be avoided. Also likely to be quite unattractive are states that annually tax the entire net income of their domestic corporations. Finally, an analysis of the formulas by which states allocate their annual franchise and net income taxes may reveal that the selection of a particular state for incorporation may minimize the total burden of these taxes. For ex-

[10]Alien corporations pay federal corporation income taxes on that portion of their income that is derived within the United States, its territories, and dependencies. Certain credits against the tax liability are allowed for taxes paid to foreign governments, but such credits obviously do not reduce the total tax bill. Nevertheless, certain arrangements have been available from time to time whereby incorporation in foreign countries has been a means of considerable tax savings. Witness the use of Bermuda corporations and the registry of American-owned tankers under the flags of Liberia and Panama.

ample, substantial tax saving was given as a reason for United States Steel Corporation and Botany Industries Inc. switches from New Jersey to Delaware in 1967.

Stability of Corporation Laws

A corporate charter is of the nature of a contract between the corporation and the state that grants it. But the states reserve the right to change the terms of the contract unilaterally, that is, to change their corporation laws without asking their corporate creatures for permission to do so. The greater the possibility, therefore, that a state will significantly change its laws from time to time, the less attractive it is as a source of charters. Especially do promoters think it wise to avoid states whose laws lack clearly stated provisions concerning one or more important aspects of corporate organization, government, and powers, as well as states whose laws have ambiguous or conflicting provisions.

A comprehensive body of court decisions in which the corporation laws have been thoroughly analyzed and interpreted may be also said to be a source of stability. It is always disturbing and sometimes quite upsetting to corporate policies to have a court declare a provision of the corporation laws void because of a conflict with the state constitution. Similarly upsetting may be a court decision that the legislature meant thus and so when it enacted a certain feature of the law, while corporate managements had always thought that the legislature meant something quite different. A consistent line of many court decisions is likely to be found in a state that has already chartered many thousands of corporations, and this very fact surely contributes further to its popularity. Thus, *The Wall Street Journal* quotes an unnamed attorney of Wilmington, Delaware: "A lawyer has a pretty good idea of what the courts will say here in a given situation. In some states, you don't know what the courts will do."[11]

Liberality of Corporation Laws

Of outstanding importance to larger enterprises seeking the most favorable state for incorporation is the comparative liberality of the corporate laws of the various states. The more generous the grant of powers and privileges to corporations and the fewer the restrictions placed on them, the greater is the liberality of the laws said to be. Few would question the common sense of promoters in seeking liberality as thus described!

Liberality for Directors. A phase of liberality that is especially sought is the concentration of corporate powers in the board of directors. Directors like to be in a position to make almost all kinds

[11]Midwest Edition, April 16, 1968, p. 4.

of decisions without having to go continually to the stockholders for a new grant of powers or for approval of actions they propose to take. Liberality of this kind is found in provisions of corporations laws that: (1) specifically place in the directors the power to adopt, amend, and repeal bylaws; (2) permit them to change the number of directors and to fill vacancies occurring between annual meetings of the stockholders; (3) and authorize staggered terms for the directors, with only one half, one third, or one fourth coming up for election each year, so that it is difficult for a faction among the stockholders opposed to the incumbent board to gain control. Liberal provisions are also found with respect to the capacity of directors to manage stock issues, to issue stock in exchange for property and services, and to declare dividends. Numbered among liberal provisions of these kinds are those:

1. Permitting articles of incorporation to authorize the directors to put out additional batches of stock from time to time and to determine what classes of stock such issues will be, what rights and preferences they will have, and so on.
2. Giving directors wide discretion in the valuation of property and services for which stock is given, and relieving them of liability for overgenerous valuations except in cases of proven bad faith or fraud.
3. Permitting the directors to allocate to the surplus accounts portions of the proceeds of the sale of no-par stock.
4. Allowing the payment of dividends out of sources of surplus other than net profits on operations, such as premiums received in the original sale of stock and surplus put on the books as a result of write-ups in the value of assets.
5. Permitting the payment of dividends out of current profits, even though deficits of earlier years have not been made good.

Liberality favoring the directors may also be said to exist in state laws that provide that holders of simple majorities of the stock may approve proposals of the directors requiring stockholder approval rather than, say, majorities of two thirds or three fourths.

Other Liberal Features. Other features of corporation laws generally described as liberal, though not directly involving the directors, include the following:

1. Permission to hold annual and special meetings of the stockholders outside the state of incorporation.
2. The granting of wide powers to corporations to buy and sell property, their own stock previously issued, and the stocks of other corporations.
3. Permission to issue nonvoting stocks and stocks lacking the preemptive right (that is, the ordinary right of stockholders to get the first chance to buy additional issues in proportion to their existing holdings).

4. Power to issue par-value stock at a discount without liability accruing to the subscribing stockholders or to the directors for the amount of the discount.
5. Annual report requirements calling for minimal information.

In almost all states, recent trends of legislation having to do with the chartering and operations of corporations have been rather strongly in the direction of liberality. Thus, comparisons of state corporation laws on the basis of their degrees of liberality, though still of importance, are not nearly so important as in times past when some states were known as charter-mongering states. Such states were so called because they had deliberately adopted liberal laws to attract incorporations at a time when the laws of other states were relatively strict. At the present time, one seldom hears references to charter-mongering states; one is more likely to hear allusions to a few states as being strict, the implication being that all others are liberal in varying degrees.

QUESTIONS

1. Our states are reluctant to issue corporate charters, and applications are often rejected on the grounds that the applicants are not qualified to operate businesses in the corporate form. Is this proposition true or false? Discuss.

2. From the standpoint of state requirements generally, how much of the stock of a proposed corporation must be subscribed before it qualifies for a charter? How much must be paid in for stock before it may begin business?

3. In the formation of a new corporation, what work is done by the incorporators? How are they chosen?

4. Since, as a rule, natural persons only are qualified to serve as incorporators, how has it been possible for many corporations to establish subsidiary corporations?

5. What are the articles of incorporation of a corporation? What is the relationship between a corporation's articles and its charter?

6. In the preparation of articles of incorporation for a new corporation, why is it especially important to formulate the statement of its objects or purposes with great care?

7. What details about a corporation's authorized stock issues must be given in its articles of incorporation? About its life or duration?

8. What kinds of operating powers do corporations have, even though not specifically stated in their articles of incorporation?

9. What kinds of rules are included in a corporation's bylaws? How are the powers to adopt, amend, and repeal bylaws shared between boards of directors and stockholders? Who has the final word?

10. What is the procedure for amending a corporation's articles of incorporation? For what reasons might corporations want to amend their articles?

11. As a criterion for determining from what states corporate charters will be sought, how important is location of properties and principal business activities? How important is taxation?

12. On what basis are the corporation laws of some states classified as being liberal?

PROBLEM

The articles of incorporation of Dempsey & Benton, Inc., provide that its board of directors shall have nine members to be elected annually and that cumulative voting is permitted in their election. The corporation has outstanding 400,000 shares of stock, and a minority group wants to be sure to get its full proportional representation on the board by concentrating its votes cumulatively on the maximum number of candidates it can be certain to elect. How many candidates should the group nominate if the members of the group own 75,000 shares? 150,000 shares? 190,000 shares?

PROJECT

Obtain a copy of the general corporation law of your home state and compare its provisions, item by item, with the general description of the features of such laws in this chapter. For class discussion, note especially in what details the provisions of the law of your state differ from the description in this chapter. (In most states, the general corporation law is supplied in pamphlet form free of charge by the secretary of state. In some states, a small charge, such as $1, is made. At any rate, the student should find it enlightening to check general statements in reference to corporations as made throughout this textbook against the specific provision of the corporation law of his own state.)

Part II

FINANCE FUNCTIONS AND CASH FLOWS

chapter 4

FINANCE FUNCTIONS

Although financial questions are importantly involved in decisions whether or not to incorporate, choices as to the states in which charters will be sought, decisions about what stock issues articles of incorporation should provide for, and so on, it can be said that the responsibilities of corporate financial managers come into being only when the process of organization has been completed. Before that, decisions are in the hands of organizers and promoters who may or may not subsequently become the financial managers. It is the objective of the present chapter, therefore, to analyze in a broad way the duties and powers of corporate financial managers—as a preliminary to the more detailed treatment in the remainder of this textbook. Our immediate task is twofold: (1) to examine what may be called the *finance functions* of business corporations (and, really, of all kinds of business enterprises), and (2) to study the lines of authority and responsibility in corporations for the fulfillment of these functions.

THE SCOPE OF THE FINANCE FUNCTIONS

It is often said that all the operations of business enterprises can be classified as falling within three areas—production, marketing, and finance. No great difficulty is ordinarily encountered in deciding what are production and marketing functions, but the scope of the finance functions cannot be so readily distinguished. The reason for this uncertainty about the scope of the finance functions is that it is quite impossible, in most instances, to divorce financial considerations from production and marketing goals, decisions, and operations. Almost all kinds of actions in the area of production and marketing directly, or at least indirectly, involve the acquisition and use of money. The determination of factory employment policies clearly comes within the purview of production, but employment requires the payment of wages and salaries and social security taxes, and it is likely to call also for the provision of certain classes of fringe benefits. Where, then, is the separation between the production function of setting employment policies and the finance function of providing means of meeting the costs of employment? All the more is the point of separation hard to find when it is realized that the finance function in the matter of employment is not simply one of looking for money once employment policies have been set; it is one of helping to decide what employment policies are feasible, given the financial position of the business enterprise and its access to additional sources of funds. The determination of advertising policies—deciding what products to advertise, settling on the content of advertising material, selecting the mediums to be used, and so on—is surely a marketing function, but advertising requires outlays of cash and necessarily, therefore, involves finance. How can one say where the marketing function of establishing advertising policies ends and where begin the finance functions of determining what advertising budget is financially sound and of actually providing the money for it?

In truth, the questions raised have no clear-cut answers. The finance functions having to do with the acquisition and use of money are there, but their limits cannot be clearly marked out for the general run of businesses. The limits vary in innumerable ways, depending on the dissimilar positions of individual enterprises. A corporation that finds itself in a tight financial position, with limited cash resources and limited access to additional cash, must surely give financial considerations dominant weight; that is, it must try to devise production and marketing policies in keeping with its strained circumstances. On the other hand, the managers of a corporation that has access to a plentiful supply of cash can doubtless feel free to study a wide range of possibilities in deciding on production and marketing policies, expecting to be able to easily devise financial policies to fit their production and marketing decisions.

Although it is difficult to set limits to the finance functions, the functions themselves can be readily classified and described. They are of two kinds, and they may be called, respectively, *executive* finance functions and *incidental* finance functions. Executive finance functions require great skill—a high order of administrative ability—in planning and execution; the incidental functions are concerned with routine work, chiefly clerical, necessary to carry into effect financial decisions at the executive level.

The executive finance functions are the following.

1. Establishing asset management policies.
2. Determining the allocation of net profits.
3. Estimating cash flows and requirements.
4. Controlling the flow of cash.

5. Deciding on needs and sources of new outside financing.
6. Carrying on negotiations for new outside financing.
7. Checking on financial performance.

This listing is not necessarily in the order of priority—priority in the sense of importance, or priority in the sense of timing decisions. Each executive finance function is important, and decisions and actions concerning most of them must be made or less simultaneously. All are closely interrelated, so that a change in decisions in one category is likely to require changes in decisions in some or all the others.

For example, cash flows cannot be estimated until asset management and profit allocation policies have been at least tentatively determined; yet, the determination of these policies depends in a very important way on estimates of the inflow of cash in the ordinary course of business, together with estimates of the amount of cash that can be raised through new outside financing. As used in studies in corporation finance, the term *financing* means the acquisition of cash or other assets by incurring debts, by sales of additional stock, or by retaining net profits and the cash throw-offs from charges for depreciation, depletion, and amortization.[1] Incurring debts and selling additional stock to acquire assets are often described as means of outside or external financing, while retaining profits and cash throw-offs is described as internal financing. In a similar way, decisions about the payment of cash dividends to the stockholders—a matter obviously having to do with the allocation of net profits—must be tied in with acceptable asset management policies, and properly related to estimates of cash flows and requirements and a consideration of sources of new outside financing.

The incidental finance functions are as follows.

1. Supervision of cash receipts and disbursements and the safeguarding of cash balances.
2. Custody and safeguarding of securities, insurance policies, and other valuable papers.
3. Taking care of the mechanical details of new outside financing.
4. Record-keeping and reporting.

Executive Finance Functions

Establishing Asset Management Policies. All finance functions are concerned with the management of cash—with the control of the cash flows of the individual enterprise. Cash requirements can be estimated and arrangements can be made to take care of them only if the financial managers know quite definitely how cash will be used as it is acquired by the enterprise. Outstandingly, this means that they

[1]Why cash throw-offs are recognized as sources of assets is explained in Chapter 6. See pp. 118–19.

must know how much cash will be tied up in the various kinds of noncash assets. Thus, the establishment of sound and consistent asset management policies is an indispensable prerequisite to successful financial management.

The financial managers themselves must participate in determining asset management policies. Their special knowledge of the cash flow processes, the possibilities of slowdowns and speedups in the ordinary inflows and outflows of cash on account of changing business conditions, the sources of new financing, the prevailing terms and conditions of new financing, and so on, should be invaluable in asset planning. Were they to have no such authority, plans prepared by others for the acquisition of assets might often be quite unrealistic in view of the enterprise's financial position and prospects.

The relationship of asset management policies to financial management can be readily understood if reference is made to the kinds of questions that must be answered before policy decisions are finally reached. Consider questions such as the following. What will be the inventory policy of the enterprise? Will it buy stocks of goods for resale, or will it be able to obtain them on a consignment basis? What are the minimum varieties and quantities of goods that it must have on hand at all times to serve its customers adequately? Will it buy goods in extraordinary quantities in anticipation of price increases? Will it attempt to sell slow-moving goods by substantial price cuts? Will it sell for cash or on account? If it sells on account, will it allow a cash discount for early payment? What rate of discount will it allow? If it needs additional facilities, will it buy these outright or seek to rent them? If it buys them outright, will it pay cash in full at once, or will it be able to arrange payment on an installment basis over a period of months or years? If it rents them, will it be required to make a large initial rental payment?

The determination of asset management policies, it should be added, includes decision making about the kinds and coverages of insurance that an enterprise will carry—an area of decision making in which financial managers are ordinarily expected to be much more competent than production and marketing executives. The enterprise's stake in inventories, buildings, and other facilities is protected against losses due to fire, windstorm, and other hazards if insurance coverages of the proper kinds are obtained. The enterprise is likewise protected against drains from its assets due to embezzlement, robbery, damages to be paid on account of injuries to its employees and the public, and so on, when it carries surety bonds on employees who handle cash and securities, robbery insurance, workmen's compensation insurance, public liability insurance, and the like.

The role of financial managers in trying to reach answers to questions of the kinds listed above and in planning an adequate program of insurance coverages—their role, that is, in establishing asset management policies—cannot ordinarily be an exclusive one. Production managers can be expected to insist on their right to participate in making decisions concerning the carrying of inventories of raw materials and factory supplies, employment policies, and the purchase or renting of factory machinery and equipment. Marketing executives, likewise, must participate in decisions involving the carrying of inventories of finished goods, advertising policies, and customer credit policies. Once again, therefore, we come to the conclusion that there is no exact way of determining where financial management leaves off and production and marketing management begins. The individual enterprise must seek, therefore, to establish lines of authority in such a manner that every decision will be based on a careful balancing of production, marketing, and finance considerations.

Determining the Allocation of Net Profits. The typical corporation may be said to have three choices in the allocation of whatever net profits it has after the payment of income taxes: (1) to pay dividends to the stockholders as a return on their investment, (2) to make distributions to people other than the stockholders, as in employee profit-sharing plans, and (3) to retain them for the expansion of assets. The second alternative is ordinarily made on a long-range basis, so that once an employee profit-sharing plan, for example, has been adopted as a fringe benefit it continues annually to be apportioned a percentage of the net profits as a matter of contract or as a matter of fixed policy. Whether or not, therefore, a corporation has an allocation of the second kind, its continuing free choices in the use of net profits generally involve only the other two alternatives—payment of dividends and acquisition of additional assets.

It may appear that the acquisition alternative is by far the more important, since a corporation cannot continue to operate profitably without an adequate supply of productive assets, and since the stockholders' interests are necessarily served in assuring this capacity for continued profitable operation. Nevertheless, dividend policy cannot be based simply on a standing decision to distribute to the stockholders whatever cash is left after all likely and possible cash needs in the business have been allowed for. If that were the basis of policy, all too often no dividends would be paid, for corporate managements tend always to have in mind expansion plans sufficiently broad to absorb all cash that is likely to become available. On the contrary, corporate managements must realize that dividend policies have important bearings on prospects of additional sales of stock as a means of raising cash, on credit standing, which determines capacity to buy on account and to borrow money, and, indeed, on their own prospects of continuing to hold their jobs.

The determination of dividend policies is almost exclusively a finance function. Only because dividend payments reduce the amount of cash available for other purposes are production and marketing executives inclined to be interested; their interest, therefore, is likely to be much less keen than in the determination of asset management policies. Accordingly, the financial managers are much more likely to have the final word in decisions on dividends than in asset management decisions.

Cash Requirements and Flows: Estimation and Control. A prime responsibility of financial management is to see that an adequate cash supply is on hand at the proper times for asset acquisition and for making allocations of net profits, as in dividend payments, and in making appropriations, as for employee profit-sharing plans. (Meeting all kinds of current operating expenses, it is important to emphasize, is simply a process of acquiring assets; likewise, paying off liabilities is ordinarily the discharge of obligations for assets already acquired. Therefore, when one speaks of a need of cash for the acquisition of assets one necessarily allows for the use of cash for paying operating expenses and meeting maturing liabilities.) A failure of the financial managers to provide cash in adequate amounts at the proper times must at least impede the smooth flow of operations, and, of course, it may result in grave embarrassment.

As a rule, the financial managers must look to the ordinary day-to-day operations of their corporations as the source of the principal volume of inflowing cash. For most businesses, this inflow comes from sales, either at the time of sale or at a later time if goods or services are sold on a deferred-payment basis. In most instances, likewise, cash requirements are closely related to the volume of sales. It is clear, then, that asset management and profit allocation policies must be closely tied in with the anticipated level of sales; and it is equally clear that the responsibility for providing cash in the proper amounts at the proper times requires forecasting. It is not enough to forecast the year's collections from sales and the year's cash requirements on the basis of expected sales, for such forecasts reveal little about the timing of cash inflows and outflows. Financial embarrassment may result from a lack of coordination in the inflows and outflows, even though, in annual totals, cash receipts may substantially exceed cash disbursements. Thus, forecasts must ordinarily be put on the basis of monthly expectations within the longer period of, say, a year. Often, indeed, it is advantageous to use periods shorter than a month for the estimates, especially in forecasts for the immediate future. Needless to say, forecasts must make allowance for anticipated inflows of cash from sources other than sales, as well as for outflows other than those required for meeting the expected level of sales.

By means of forecasting, the financial managers ought to be able to judge rather closely how much cash will be coming in and going out from month to month, or perhaps from week to week. They will realize, of course, that since cash flows depend on the volume of operations much of them will not be strictly controllable by decisions that the managers may make. Nevertheless, they will know that timing of the flows can be at least moderately altered by certain kinds of decisions, such as decisions to concentrate advertising campaigns or to offer goods at reduced prices in certain months, to modify inventory accumulation policies, or to change dividend payment practices by paying dividends, say, semiannually rather than quarterly. On the basis of the forecasts, too, the financial managers may anticipate a need of borrowing during some period in the course of the year when, as the forecasts indicate, cash inflows from ordinary operations will be quite insufficient to meet cash requirements, and they may, accordingly, take immediate steps to arrange for loans. Or they may anticipate having excess supplies of cash in certain periods, and they may make immediate plans for the temporary investment of these excess funds.

Deciding on Needs and Sources of New Outside Financing. As just indicated, on the basis of their forecasts of the volume of operations the financial managers may have to plan on borrowing as a means of supplementing cash flowing from these operations. As noted earlier, such borrowing would be described as a means of financing. Two of the principal means of outside financing are the sale of additional stock and all kinds of borrowing, including borrowing from commerical banks and other financial institutions and the flotation of bond issues.

That financing plans require foresight also was pointed out. On the basis of their forecasts of the inflow and outflow of cash in the ordinary course of operations, the financial managers should be able to judge rather closely the time when additional funds from outside sources will be needed, how long they will be needed, and from what sources the means of repayment (in the case of borrowing) are to be derived. The financial managers would hardly be acting competently if they woke up to a realization of a need of additional funds only when the cash account had been almost exhausted.

Not only must the financial managers foresee financing requirements, they must select the means of meeting them. In this regard, a distinction must usually be made between short-term requirements that turn up again and again year after year, in much the same pattern, and long-term requirements. The distinction is important for two reasons: (1) it tends to indicate the nature of the requirements, and (2) it suggests what are likely to be the best sources of the funds needed.

Short-term requirements usually result from unevenness in the inflow and outflow of cash on account of the very nature of business operations. Production requiring large outlays may be heavily concentrated in one period of the year, whereas sales may be concentrated in a later period; thus, cash disbursements for production in the earlier period may require temporary borrowing, to be repaid out of the later cash inflows from sales. Financing of this kind is often planned for on a continuing basis, as by making and annually renewing arrangements for lines of credit at commercial banks or with sales finance companies.

Long-term requirements, on the other hand, most commonly arise because of programs for substantial expansion in the scope of operations. Additional plant, machinery and equipment, and other facilities may be needed to meet an expected long-range expansion in sales, and, typically, cash inflows from ordinary operations are quite inadequate to take care of both the expansion of facilities and continued outlays required for day-to-day activities. Commercial banks, sales finance companies, and other lenders that supply short-term funds may also be willing to provide some longer-term funds, and the financial managers may not need to go beyond them in getting the cash needed for expansion. On the other hand, for various reasons they may prefer to go to the stockholders and ask them to buy additional stock, or to institutions such as investment banking firms and life insurance companies, which concentrate on providing long-term money.

Carrying on Negotiations for New Outside Financing. When decisions that outside financing must be undertaken have been made, the financial managers have the responsibility to arrange for it. As noted above, short-term financing requirements are often arranged for on a continuing basis, as in the establishment of lines of credit at commercial banks. Commercial banks are distinguished from all other classes of financial institutions in that they alone receive deposits of the public subject to repayment on demand on the written orders of the depositors. By its very nature, therefore, a commercial bank offers checking account facilities to its customers.[2] A line of credit is a commitment of a lender to a borrower to advance funds up to a designated amount at any time within a specified period that the borrower may want them. At the time the line of credit is arranged, there is usually an agreement on the maturity of the loans that may be granted and whether such loans are to be secured or unsecured. The interest rate the borrower is to pay may also be stipulated, although the determination of the interest rate may be deferred until the time the funds are actually called for. Even a continuing arrangement of this kind, however, requires negotiations. As lines of credit are ordinarily held open for not more than a year, it is necessary to an-

[2]For a brief statement on the importance of the commercial banks in our economy, see pp. 841–43.

nually reopen negotiations for the renewal of the lines. To keep a line open, the borrower generally is also required to file periodic financial statements with the lender, so that he may be assured that the credit standing of the borrower is not deteriorating in any significant way.[3]

When corporations need to borrow only sporadically for short-term purposes, they are unlikely to have lines of credit already set up. Accordingly, when loans are applied for, delays in getting the funds are to be expected because of the compiling and analysis of credit information by prospective lenders. Thus, the beginning of negotiations well before money is actually needed is important; so, once again, foresight is to be emphasized.

Negotiations and the completion of arrangements for long-term financing usually require much more time than does the working out of arrangements for short-term borrowing, so that advance planning is all the more important. Procedures for the issuance of additional stock and for the issuance of bonds, in particular, are generally complex and time-consuming. The financial managers of a corporation do not decide on a long-term financing project one week and carry it through the following week. Such a project may require several months for negotiations and for working out procedures in meticulous detail.

Checking on Financial Performance. Much attention in financial management must be given to checking on performance. Especially important is observing day-to-day cash inflows and outflows to see how close to the forecasts they are proceeding. Nobody expects the actual results of operations to be exactly as predicted, and the likelihood of moderate divergences between actual results and those forecast should have already been allowed for in any sound forecasting procedure. The occurrence of moderate divergences, therefore, should not be the source of any surprise nor of any need of a sudden change in plans. However, when actual results turn out to be far different from what was anticipated, drastic changes in financial planning are likely to be necessary. The new situation must be analyzed to determine what changes in the financial plans must be immediately instituted, and all estimates about future developments must be thoroughly recast.

Checking on performance also requires a looking back to operating periods that have come to an end in order to evaluate the wisdom and efficiency of the financial planning of these periods. A time shortly

[3]It is customary to require balance sheets and income statements. The requirement may be for monthly, quarterly, semiannual, or annual statements, depending on the size of the line of credit, the nature of the borrower's business, his usual practices in preparing statements, and other factors. Lenders frequently stipulate that, at least once a year, statements prepared by certified public accountants must be submitted. For a discussion of the nature of balance sheets, see p. 94, and of income statements, pp. 101–2. For a further discussion of lines of credit as arranged with commercial banks, see pp. 845–48.

after the end of the year when all results of operations are known is a good time for such an evaluation. A reconsideration of the *wisdom* of completed financial plans is especially important. While a net profit at approximately the level forecast may have been derived, such a reconsideration may indicate that the profit would have been substantially larger if certain policies had not been adopted at all or had been materially modified. Or it may indicate that certain outside means of financing actually selected were inferior to others that could have been chosen—that, for example, intermediate-term rather than short-term loans should have been sought. As for checking the efficiency of financial planning, perhaps cash inflows and outflows were nicely coordinated in the course of the year, but still not according to the pattern of expectations. Expenditures of certain kinds may have been much greater than had been anticipated, but no difficulties may have been encountered because cash inflows from sales were also much greater than anticipated. Or it may be that while some expenditures were much greater others were much less than the forecasts indicated. Reasons for substantial variations of these kinds must be sought, and judgments must be arrived at concerning whether or not the actual state of affairs could better have been anticipated had different forecasting principles and techniques been used. All of which means that analyses of what has happened (analyses *ex post* they may be called if one wants to use an elegant term) should be of great value in improving the standards, techniques, and procedures of financial control.

7

Incidental Finance Functions

The incidental finance functions follow from the exercise of the executive finance functions. They chiefly involve all the paper work that must be done to provide the facts and materials for efficient financial control. They usually require a great amount of time, often much more than is required for the executive functions. Deciding on a need of new financing and the form it should take, for example, may require only a few hours of discussion among the financial managers. But the clerical work involved in, say, an offering of additional stock to the present stockholders may require many days of work by numerous employees—work in preparing and sending out notices of the offering, filling in and sending out subscription warrants, keeping a record of these, receiving and recording subscriptions, and subsequently sending out and keeping a record of the stock certificates themselves. On the other hand, the incidental finance functions are, for the most part, of a routine, repetitive character, so that they require only a moderate amount of supervision by the financial managers. The financial managers need only to set up rules of procedure, select forms to be used, participate in establishing standards for the employment of competent personnel, and, once again, check on performance to see that the rules are observed and the forms properly used.

Supervision of Cash Transactions and Custody of Cash Balances. All assets of a business corporation must be protected in the most careful ways possible, but the protection of cash is almost invariably the particular responsibility of the financial managers. Protective provisions for cash receipts and balances include the following.

1. Careful selection of commercial banks as depositaries, and filing with each a resolution of the board of directors, stating specifically how the deposit account or accounts are to be handled—who may make deposits, how deposits are to be segregated (as when the corporation plans to have two or more accounts at the same bank, such as a general account and a payroll account), and what signature or combination of signatures are required on checks drawn on the accounts.
2. Measures for the safeguarding of coin, paper money, and checks coming into the corporation's possession, and for the bonding of employees who handle these items.
3. Requirements such as that all cash and cash items (chiefly checks) must be deposited in the bank or placed in its night depository on the day received.
4. Placing of responsibility for the custody and replenishment of the petty cash funds set up for making small disbursements in paper money and coin.
5. Rules of internal check, such as the rule that employees who handle cash and cash items must have no access whatsoever to the accounting records—a safeguard designed to reduce temptations toward embezzlement on the part of employees who may hope to cover up defalcations by fictitious entries on the books.

The protective supervision of cash disbursements goes somewhat beyond the measures for safeguarding cash already referred to. Here, the basic idea is that each disbursement must be made only on proper authorization, whether it is made by check drawn on the bank or from the petty cash funds. Invoices and other bills must be carefully checked for prices, extensions, and footings, and, even more importantly, there must be assurance in every instance that materials and services billed for were actually received. A rule commonly applied is that officers who are given power to authorize payments should not also have the capacity to sign checks or have custody of the petty cash funds. The rule of requiring two signatures on each check, as that of the president or a vice president in addition to that of the treasurer or an assistant treasurer, is also a means of safeguarding against improper payments. Still a third rule is that requiring the prompt entry of every payment in the accounting records, and the frequent auditing of these records to ensure that payments are being made only in accordance with authorizations.

Custody and Safeguarding of Valuable Papers. The custody of all kinds of papers and documents evidencing the ownership of property and property rights of various kinds is also generally a responsibility of the financial managers, and protective rules for safeguarding these instruments must ordinarily be regarded as essential as for cash. The papers and documents include:

1. Obligations of the United States Treasury, in which many corporations temporarily invest idle cash, accumulated during slack periods or to meet liabilities coming due at specific times, such as federal income tax payments.
2. Life insurance policies, when corporations observe the rather common custom of insuring the lives of principal officers, naming themselves, of course, as beneficiaries.
3. Other insurance policies that cover the many kinds of hazards against which corporate managements decide protection is needed, such as the risk of destruction of buildings and equipment by fire, windstorms, and explosions; the risks of injuries to employees; and the risks of injuries to other persons or their property.
4. Promissory notes received from customers.
5. Securities of other enterprises, such as stock in subsidiary corporations.
6. Deeds and certificates of title insurance.
7. Stock certificate books and unissued bond certificates, if these are not in the possession of transfer agents and indenture trustees, respectively.[4]

Decisions to invest in treasury obligations or in the securities of other enterprises, to carry insurance of certain kinds and amounts, to accept promissory notes from customers under certain terms and conditions, and so on, fall within the province of the executive finance functions—obviously, these are asset management decisions. Hence, the work of custody and safeguarding referred to is, once again, the routine kind of activity that originates in connection with or follows on the exercise of the executive functions.

The examples given above of the rules and procedures adopted to protect cash should readily suggest the kinds of parallel actions that must be taken to safeguard valuable papers and documents. Suffice it to say that any lack of care in the adoption of protective measures or any lack of rigor in their enforcement reflects most unfavorably on the competence of the financial managers.

Taking Care of Mechanical Details of Outside Financing. Deciding on new outside financing, negotiating with prospective stock buyers or lenders, working out the details of loan contracts, the signing of contracts, arrangements when required for the pledge of prop-

---

[4]For a discussion of the functions of transfer agents, see p. 409; of indenture trustees, pp. 680–83.

erty, and signing documents to effect the pledges—all these kinds of activities clearly come within the purview of the executive functions. But when actions such as these have been taken, much work often remains to be done, especially for the issuance of bonds or of additional stock. However, most of the additional work is of a routine, clerical character; it can be delegated to clerical employees, with a need only of proper direction and continued supervision to see that it is properly done.

Clerical work related to new stock issues has already been briefly described. That connected with bond issues includes checking bond forms for omissions, misstatements, and typographical errors as they are delivered for proofreading by the printer; checking the serial numbers of the bonds to be sure they are all in order and all accounted for; and examination of all bonds before delivery to be sure they have the proper signatures and bear the corporate seal.

Much clerical work, moreover, is often required to keep up with stocks and bonds already outstanding. A principal source of such work is the need of making transfers. Mr. Black who has a certificate for 50 shares of stock wants to sell 20 of his shares to Mr. Brown. Black endorses the certificate to this effect and turns it in to the corporation, and the corporation must cancel it and issue two new certificates—one for 30 shares to Black and one for 20 shares to Brown. Likewise, bondholders may want to sell bonds registered in their names on the books of the corporation, exchange coupon or bearer bonds for registered ones or vice versa, or exchange bonds of one denomination for others of a different denomination.

The clerical work involved in issuing stocks and bonds and in taking care of subsequent transactions in them often becomes so voluminous, especially in larger corporations, that trust companies and the trust departments of commercial banks are hired to take over. The corporate financial managers expect it to be much more economical to hire out the work than to maintain a permanent staff of employees to do it; nevertheless, they continue to have responsibility to see that the trust institutions do the work competently.

Record-Keeping and Reporting. If all the finance functions, as reviewed in the preceding pages, are to be fulfilled creditably, accurate accounting records must at all times be available to the financial managers, and accurate reports drawn from the records must be forthcoming at convenient intervals. Accounting records and reports, we are often told, are management tools of outstanding importance. This does not necessarily mean that the financial officers must have direct responsibility for keeping records and drawing off reports. At the least, however, they must be in a position to insist on the assembly and reporting of such kinds of information as they find indispensable for the fulfillment of their duties. They should have authority to prescribe new forms for records and reports, and especially to order extensions in the scope of the data to be assembled, if the accounting system already in use is deficient in these respects.

Actually, however, most corporations place the financial officers in a position where they have only themselves to blame if records and reports are inadequate; they do this by assigning to them jurisdiction over the accounting department and its activities. The accounting department is most commonly found in the office of the treasurer or the controller—officers who ordinarily have at least moderate authority with respect to some or all the finance functions already analyzed. Indeed, in the absence of information to the contrary, on looking at the roster of officers of a given corporation one usually takes for granted that either its treasurer or its controller (if it uses both these designations) must be its chief accounting officer; at the same time, one concludes that he probably has additional functions specifically in the area of finance.

The preparation and interpretation of reports drawn from the accounting records often require a high order of executive ability—in the sense, as always, of ability to make significant decisions. Therefore, although, the discussion in this section has been largely confined to operations of a clerical character one must allow for the fact that the principal financial officers of a corporation may devote much time and exercise meticulous care in working over the details of reports of certain kinds. This is almost surely true of the federal income tax return, other statements and reports required by taxing authorities, reports to regulatory authorities such as the Securities and Exchange Commission, and annual and other reports to the stockholders. It is often true also of other varieties of financial reports aside from those designed solely for internal use.

THE FINANCIAL MANAGERS

In the foregoing description of the finance functions of business corporations, frequent references were made to the financial managers. Who are these people? What positions do they hold in the typical business corporation? In truth, we cannot be very sure about the answers to these questions. We cannot point out an officer who has a title such as treasurer and say that he is the principal financial officer, that his subordinates are thus and so, and that his powers and responsibilities include this and that. As we look closely at the setups of individual corporations, we find that in some the treasurer is indeed the principal financial officer, with broad powers of decision making, but we also find that in others his functions seem to make him only a chief clerk, and that in many others his role fits in at various levels between these two extremes. The lines of authority concerning the finance functions are scattered around in American corporations in a bewildering variety of ways, and things are often not what they seem to be. Thus, the production manager of one corporation may be truly its chief financial officer in the sense that he generally has the final word when financial decisions are made; in another, it may be the sales manager; in another, the vice president for finance; in another, the chairman of the board of directors; in another, the chairman of the executive committee of the board of directors; and in many others, as one might well expect, the president.

One fact about which we can be reasonably sure is that most of the powers of financial management, as most of other corporate powers, reside in the board of directors. The corporation laws of the states are unanimous in saying so. Thus, the law of New York states that "the business of a corporation shall be managed by its board of directors,"[5] and the law of Illinois puts it this way: "The business and affairs of a corporation shall be managed by a board of directors."[6] We can also be reasonably sure that officers who have designations such as treasurer and controller will have responsibility for some of the finance functions, although not necessarily the more important ones. Beyond this, our area of certainty is, indeed, severely limited. Let us, however, look at the status of the financial managers in as orderly a fashion as the situation permits.

THE BOARD OF DIRECTORS

Limitations on Directors' Powers

Although the powers of financial management of a corporation tend to be concentrated in its board of directors, powers held by the board are not absolute. They are limited by the provisions of corporation laws, the stipulations of the corporation's own bylaws, and legal rules of directors' responsibility.

Statutory Limitations. Most important among the limiting provisions of the corporation laws are those that give the stockholders the power to elect and remove directors. In a sense, then, the stockholders have the ultimate powers of management; if they are not satisfied with what the directors do, they can replace them with others who are more likely to perform according to their wishes. Ultimate control in the stockholders is often absolute in corporations that have a limited number of stockholders, and especially in those that have a handful who own a sufficient number of voting shares to give them a decisive voice. In a corporation with thousands of stockholders, on the other hand, the replacement of an inefficient or unpopular board may be long delayed. Though stockholders who own

[5]State of New York, *Business Corporation Law,* art. 7, sec. 701.
[6]State of Illinois, *The Business Corporation Act,* sec. 33.

a majority of the voting shares may be quite dissatisfied with the policies of the incumbent board, they may not, individually, realize the extent to which their fellow stockholders share their dissatisfaction. Thus, they may make no effort to combine in an annual meeting to effect a change. In such circumstances, an inefficient or unpopular board may succeed in being virtually self-perpetuating.

Other statutory restrictions on the powers of boards of directors include requirements for the submission of certain kinds of proposals to the stockholders for their approval. Here again, of course, the stockholders may be said to have the ultimate power of decision making. Typical among proposals that must be submitted for stockholder approval are those for the amendment of the articles of incorporation to permit additional issues of stock or to change the features of stock already outstanding, for amendments to the articles for other reasons, for the merger of the corporation with others, and for the sale of all or almost all of the assets.

Limitations in the Bylaws. In their right to adopt, amend, and repeal bylaws, the stockholders have a continuing means of limiting the exercise of power by the board of directors.[7] As examples, the directors may be restricted in their capacity to borrow money in the name of the corporation, to pledge its property as security for loans, and to fix the level of salaries to be paid to the officers. Directors' powers may also be limited somewhat by provisions of bylaws that stipulate in some detail the powers and duties of the president, vice president, and other officers. The directors may want to delegate some of these stipulated powers to officers other than those designated. Nevertheless, this kind of limitation is not likely to be a serious handicap, since the directors generally have the right to choose officers and remove them at will. Hence, the officers can be moved around so that delegated powers of management will be where the directors want them to be.

Legal Rules of Directors' Responsibility. The exercise of managerial powers by the board of directors is also limited by the very nature of their position. Elected to protect and promote the interests of the stockholders, the directors accept a kind of fiduciary responsibility. Whatever their personal interests may be, they must always act in good faith to advance the welfare of the corporation and its stockholders as they make all kinds of managerial decisions. They must not seek to advance their own interests to the detriment of those of the stockholders, as when making contracts with other firms in which they participate as owners. They must not spend the corpora-

[7] It was explained in the preceding chapter that although this right may be given to the board of directors by the state law or in the articles of incorporation, the stockholders retain power to alter or repeal bylaws adopted by the directors, as well as to adopt other bylaws of their own choosing.

tion's money or use its property wastefully, as in the payment of lavish salaries or fees to friends and relations who do little for the corporation to merit such payments. On behalf of the corporation and all its stockholders, any stockholder may bring lawsuits for damages against directors on grounds that they are dissipating the corporation's assets to advance their personal interests or that they are otherwise mismanaging its affairs. Additionally, he may ask the court to remove the accused directors.

Dominance of Directors

Although it is wise to take account of limitations on the powers of boards of directors, we must recognize, nevertheless, that the board remains as the chief repository of corporate powers. Even when the directors must go to the stockholders for the approval of certain proposals, they usually have their way. They are able to present their proposals in the most favorable light, well buttressed with data and arguments carefully selected to prove their point, and the stockholders—especially when they are numbered in the hundreds or thousands—are not likely to be prepared to present a strong opposing collection of data and arguments. Very large numbers of the stockholders of larger corporations, in particular, are often described as being apathetic in the sense that they will readily assent to what the directors do and want to do as long as the corporation is making fair profits and they are receiving reasonable dividends.

Delegation of Powers

But saying that the board of directors is the chief repository of corporate powers does not mean that the board meticulously exercises all the powers with which it is endowed. As boards ordinarily meet not oftener than once a month, they must delegate to the officers quite extensive authority to make decisions concerning the multitude of transactions and problems that come up for consideration every day. Were it necessary for the officers to run to the board for advance approval of every proposed decision of significance, the corporation would be quickly reduced to a state of impotence. Some boards, it is true, try to keep close contact with the officers by setting up, from among their own members, one or more committees. In matters that concern a specific committee, those directors involved are expected to develop a much more extensive knowledge and handling competence than can be expected of the other directors. Moreover, since a committee usually consists of only three or four directors, it can be much more quickly called together for consultation on pressing problems than can the whole board. If there is only one committee, it is usually called the executive committee; if there is more than one, there is still likely to be an executive committee, and others may be, for example, a finance committee, a production committee, a sales committee, and a personnel committee.

The usefulness of committees is customarily greatly enhanced by a rule that whatever a committee approves within its special jurisdiction will, as a matter of course, be ratified by the whole board at its next meeting. Thus, quick action can often be taken when the officers, in their individual capacities, are unwilling to take responsibility for making certain decisions or are lacking in delegated authority to make them. The use of committees, however, does not eliminate the need of delegating extensive decision-making authority to the officers; although committees may be more accessible to the officers than is the whole board, a need of the officers to consult frequently with the respective committees would seriously slow down the pace of corporate activity. Accordingly, only extraordinary matters, rather than those of daily routine, are reserved for submission to committees or to the board itself.

Basic Responsibilities

A board of directors must be careful to avoid extreme generosity in delegating authority, either to its own committees or to the officers. Overgenerous delegations of authority may be the grounds for stockholders' suits charging the directors with gross negligence or mismanagement—especially so, of course, if decisions made by committees and officers, however well intentioned, result in losses. Too generous delegations to officers may be particularly dangerous, since the officers are not selected by the stockholders nor are they directly responsible to them, whereas the directors are so selected and are so responsible. Even committees composed of directors cannot be given sweeping powers without danger to the full board. It is a well-established principle of corporation law that directors hold and exercise power only collectively—that is, as a board. This means, in effect, that the individual director, as a director, enjoys managerial authority only when at regular or special meetings he participates with his fellow board members in arriving at decisions.

All of which indicates that the board of directors of a business corporation has certain basic responsibilities that cannot be delegated without danger of charges of gross negligence or mismanagement. These may be listed as follows.

1. Determination of major operating policies.
2. Approval or disapproval of extraordinary contracts.
3. Appointment of officers and the supervision of their work.
4. Determination of the time and amount of dividend payments.

Major Operating Policies. Major operating policies are those likely to have a very important bearing on the corporation's success or failure. Each of the following would surely be a most important policy decision whose responsibility the directors could hardly avoid.

1. To add an important line of new products, or to drop important items already being produced.
2. To spend large sums of money for the automation of certain factory processes.
3. To transform selling channels, as by closing retail outlets and substituting sales through jobbers and wholesalers.
4. To adopt a comprehensive financial plan—that is to say, a budget[8]—for the coming year.
5. To borrow money by the flotation of a bond issue.
6. To call an outstanding bond issue for redemption.
7. To effect a large-scale expansion of operations.
8. To inaugurate a system of paid vacations for employees.

On the other hand, the directors probably would not be accused of neglect of duty if they were to delegate rather complete power to the production manager to make from time to time such piecemeal changes in factory layout as he might find convenient; to the sales manager to drop wholesalers from the corporation's preferred list and to add others, as he might see fit; or to the advertising manager to vary the amounts of money to be spent on each of the advertising mediums, while keeping within the limits of the total budgeted expenditure.

Extraordinary Contracts. In the course of any business day, the typical corporation enters into scores of contracts—and many corporations into hundreds and thousands. Every time a sale or purchase is made, or an employee is hired, or a service is arranged for, a contract comes into being. It quickly becomes apparent, therefore, that the board of directors of a corporation could not possibly be responsible for the specific approval or disapproval of the mass of contracts it enters. This kind of responsibility extends only to contracts of extraordinary significance.

Should the directors decide, for example, that the factory facilities must be expanded to meet a growing demand for the corporation's products, they might delegate to certain officers the tasks of seeking a factory site; having specifications for the building, machinery, and equipment drawn up; and negotiating with landowners, building contractors, and machinery manufacturers on prices, terms of payment, delivery dates, and so on. But the directors would surely recognize it to be their duty to review the officers' findings; consider alternative courses of action; study the details of tentative contracts for the purchase of land, erection of the building, and purchase of the machinery and equipment; and, finally, give specific approval to these contracts or reject them.

---

[8]For a discussion of budgets and budgetary principles and procedures, see pp. 242–315.

Appointment and Supervision of Officers. Because the directors, by the very nature of the corporate setup, must delegate much authority to the officers, they have the duty of exercising reasonable skill and prudence in the selection of the officers and the supervision of their work. Officers are removable at will by the directors; hence, they can be held strictly accountable for their stewardship. The directors would be hard put to find excuses were they to permit incompetent officers to remain long in their positions. Supervising the work of the officers requires much more than simply having them report back the results of extraordinary assignments, as in the foregoing illustration of planning for factory expansion. Supervision requires continual evaluations of officers' performance in handling the ordinary day-to-day tasks of administration assigned to them. Helpful to such evaluations are requirements that the officers report frequently to the board on their activities and decisions. Also helpful is a continuous audit of the books and records of the corporation—indicated by the rule of many corporations that the auditor always reports direct to the board—as are periodic audits made by firms of certified public accountants.

Dividend Policies. The authority of the directors to decide what dividends, if any, will be paid to the stockholders is sometimes described as an inalienable right; this means that the directors cannot give away the power without grave danger of personal liability, even should they be willing to do so. The right surely cannot be delegated to any officer. Even the stockholders, who are the owners of the corporation, cannot determine dividend policies. They may place in the bylaws certain restrictions on the payment of dividends, such as establishing upper limits, but they have no authority to order the payment of dividends of a given amount. Only by choosing directors who will surely accede to their wishes about dividend payments can the stockholders be said to have power with respect to dividend policies.

Legal Qualifications

The corporation laws of the states are not at all strict in setting down legal qualifications for directors. One rule that in well-nigh universal is that a corporation must have not fewer than three directors. Approximately one third of the states stipulate that directors must be stockholders, but this is not a difficult requirement, as the ownership of one share usually suffices. Thus, the owner of all the stock of a corporation needs only to donate or sell a qualifying share to each of the people he wants to elect as directors. Some states require that all or some proportion of the directors be residents. Such a requirement is not ordinarily a source of difficulty, although it can be for a corporation whose principal operations are concentrated in places distant from the state in which its charter was obtained.

The usual term of office for directors is one year, although many states permit the election of directors for longer terms on a staggered basis, with only one half, one third, or one fourth of the directors coming up for election each year. An advantage claimed for election on a staggered basis is that the holdover directors can keep to the operating policies already in effect while newly elected directors are getting their bearings, but this mode of election turns out to be disadvantageous to the stockholders when they want to oust a board for the very reason that they do not like its existing operating policies.

Practical Situations

In the management of corporations, as in life generally, activities do not always proceed according to rules, and appearances are often deceiving. The corporation laws may be quite clear in granting broad powers to the directors, and legal rules of directors' responsibility may indicate a need of great caution in delegations of their powers. Yet, we must allow for the many instances in which powers actually reside where they do not seem to belong and responsibilities are taken lightly by those on whom they are supposed to devolve.

Especially in small corporations are we often likely to find theory and practice rather far apart. A stockholder who owns, say, 90 percent of the voting stock of a corporation of moderate size is likely to have no difficulty in getting the directors to adopt the major operating policies he proposes, to choose as officers the persons he recommends, to approve the contracts he thinks should be approved and to reject those he does not like, and even to declare the dividends that he thinks should be paid. Such a stockholder may issue numerous orders to the officers, and they are not likely to refuse to obey on the grounds that they are employees of the corporation and not his employees. Such a stockholder might choose not to be a member of the board of directors or to serve as an officer; yet, all the corporate powers could surely be said to be his.

In the small corporation, too, informality is often the order of the day. All the stockholders may be simultaneously directors and officers. As they expect to elect themselves directors year after year, they may decide there is not much sense in having an annual meeting of the stockholders. Since they are engaged in active day-to-day management in their capacity as officers, they may see little of value in formal directors' meetings. Should a stockholder-director-officer run into a problem of unusual difficulty, he might buttonhole each of his colleagues, discuss the problem, get some advice, and make a decision—all without a specific counting of yeas and nays and the entry of a vote in the minutes book.

FINANCIAL OFFICERS

The Treasurer

In almost every corporation, the treasurer, as may be inferred from his title, has significant functions as a finance officer. Nevertheless, he may not be the corporation's chief finance officer in the sense of having final authority to make important decisions or of being most influential in advising the board of directors in its decision making. In many corporations of all sizes, but particularly in the smaller ones, he is an officer of this description, but in many others, particularly in the very large ones, his position, power, and influence are clearly subordinated.

At the least, jurisdiction over the incidental finance functions tends to be concentrated in the treasurer.

1. He ordinarily has custody of all the cash resources, owned securities, insurance policies, and other valuable papers.
2. He is responsible for all cash receipts and for their prompt deposit in the banks with which the corporation has accounts.
3. He supervises all cash disbursements, usually having the duty of signing (or cosigning with another officer) all checks issued.
4. He takes care of the technical details of borrowing from banks and other lenders.
5. He has responsibility for obtaining surety bonds on all employees whose positions warrant this kind of insurance protection.

Very often the treasurer is charged with the duty of preparing financial reports for the use of the directors and other officers, for submission to the stockholders, for supplying information to banks and other lenders, and for filing with governmental agencies. Closely related to this duty is that of preparing and filing tax returns with federal, state, and local taxing authorities. When responsibility for the preparation of reports and tax returns is placed in the treasurer, he is likely also to have jurisdiction over the accounting department; thus, he may have responsibility for the assembly and maintenance of the records from which the reports and tax returns are derived. The preparation of budgets, whereby the scope of future operations is estimated and planed for, is often, too, a duty of the treasurer. In many cases, however, the treasurer's responsibility extends only to cash and capital budgets,[9] and all other tasks of budgeting are assigned to other officers.

The treasurers of many corporations prepare and disburse what is called the confidential payroll; in some, all payroll administration is a

---

[9]The principles and procedures of cash and capital budget preparation and use are discussed in detail in Chapters 11–13.

function of the treasurer's office. A confidential payroll is so called because it comprises the salaries of the corporation's executives—information that, it is thought, ought not to be disclosed to payroll clerks and other employees of the payroll department. In many corporations, too, the treasurer is in charge of credits and collections; that is, he decides which customers will be permitted to buy on account and the maximum credit each will be allowed, and he supervises collections from them.

The Controller

Many large corporations, and quite a few of medium size as well, have controllers in addition to treasurers. In almost all instances when there is both a treasurer and a controller, the controller assumes responsibility for all or almost all varieties of record-keeping and for the preparation of financial statements and other reports based on the records. He is thus generally recognized as a corporation's chief accounting officer. His position as such makes it feasible for him, rather than the treasurer, to prepare tax returns and to work up the budget and check performance in accordance with it. It is often regarded as appropriate, however, to leave with the treasurer responsibility for the preparation and supervision of the cash budget as well as for the budgeting of additions to long-term assets such as machinery and equipment. In many instances, payroll matters are transferred from the treasurer's department to that of the controller, and in some the controller is given jurisdiction over credits and collections.

Many corporations give their controllers the authority to pass on and approve all disbursements before payment is actually made by the treasurers. Such an arrangement may be simply one aspect of a system of internal check designed to safeguard a corporation's assets, and particularly its cash resources.

Other Finance Officers

If the treasurer of a corporation has only limited authority to make day-to-day financial decisions and only limited access to the board of directors to advise it on financial matters of major importance, much broader capacities of these two kinds are almost surely to be found in an officer of superior rank. This officer is most likely to be the president. One ordinarily expects the president of a corporation to have broad powers of decision making, always subject, of course, to the policies laid down by the board of directors. Probably, most corporation presidents feel that they have both the abilities and the duty to take the leading role in making decisions, whether they have to do with production or marketing or finance.

It is by no means uncommon, however, for a corporation president to acknowledge that he is a production man or a marketing man and that, accordingly, he has little knowledge of the intricacies of finance or competence to grapple with them. Such a president may be quite satisfied to let the treasurer play the role of principal financial officer, or, perhaps, to assign it to an executive vice president or to a vice president for finance. A notable development of recent years has been, indeed, the multiplication of corporate officers bearing titles such as vice president for finance—officers who usually have authority over treasurers and controllers simultaneously, and who often have very great influence in the determination of financial policies.

It often happens, however, that presidents, executive vice presidents, and vice presidents for finance, though designated as the principal financial officers of their respective corporations, and though having all confidence in their abilities to serve well in that capacity, find their authority and influence in matters of finance to be much less than that of the chairmen of their boards of directors, the chairmen of the executive or finance committees of their boards, or even two or three chairmen of such descriptions.

QUESTIONS

1. Why is it difficult to draw clear lines of distinction between the finance functions of business enterprises and their production and marketing functions?

2. On what basis is a distinction made between executive finance functions and incidental finance functions?

3. What is the scope of asset management as a finance function? Why is the determination of insurance programs included within the scope of this function?

4. Is profit allocation so difficult and time-consuming that it deserves classification as a separate finance function? Explain.

5. In the forecasting of cash flows, why does major emphasis fall on the anticipated level of sales?

6. What is financing? What is the distinction between internal and external financing?

7. By what procedure do the financial managers of a business enterprise determine when and how much outside financing is needed? How do they determine whether this financing should be short term or long term?

8. What kinds of negotiations are necessary for outside financing? How much time do they require?

9. What is meant by "checking on financial performance" as a finance function? Should not this be included among the incidental finance functions rather than with the executive functions? Discuss.

10. Support or attack this proposition: Since the incidental finance functions chiefly involve paper work that can be performed by clerical employees, the finance officers need to devote very little time and attention to them.

11. Give several examples of rules commonly observed for the safeguarding of cash balances. Mention several classes of valuable papers it is important to protect.

12. What four areas of decision making are said to be basic responsibilities of corporate boards of directors?

13. In what respects are the powers of boards of directors limited by state corporation laws? In what respects can they be limited by corporations' own bylaws?

14. To what extent, if at all, do boards of directors run into the danger of stockholders' lawsuits for damages when they delegate to officers powers to make decisions? To board committees? Discuss.

15. Why is it sometimes difficult to determine who are the principal finance officers of given business corporations?

chapter 5

THE FLOW OF CASH

To understand the nature of the problems involved in the determination of asset management and dividend policies, and in the fulfillment of the other executive finance functions described in Chapter 4, one must have a good knowledge of the processes whereby, in the typical business enterprise, cash is constantly being converted into various kinds of noncash assets, and these, in turn, are constantly being reconverted into cash. An examination of these processes is the purpose of Chapters 5 and 6.

CURRENT AND FIXED ASSETS

The conversion of cash into some kinds of noncash assets and their reconversion into cash take place in a short period of time. Assets that move in such a short cycle are called *current assets*. Current assets are said to comprise cash itself and all other kinds of assets that will be converted into it in the ordinary course of business within one year. Aside from cash, therefore, current assets generally include inventories of goods to be processed and sold, accounts receivable or claims on customers for goods sold to them, other short-term receivables, short-term holdings of investment securities, and certain kinds of items called prepaid expenses and deferred charges.

But the conversion of cash into noncash assets and their reconversion may also be an intermediate- or long-term process. The longer cycle is said to involve *fixed assets*, including buildings, factory machinery and equipment, store and office fixtures, delivery equipment, mineral deposits, standing timber, patents, and franchises. In keeping with the definition of current assets in terms of a year, fixed assets may be described in a negative sense as those assets that will not be *completely* converted into cash in the ordinary course of business within one year. It is recognized that most kinds of fixed assets are gradually being converted into cash, but that, as indicated, the overall process of conversion requires more than a year; often, indeed, it requires a long period of years. The managers of a business enterprise may expect to sell for cash within three or four months all the goods held in their inventory at the beginning of that period, so that inventory is, without question, a current asset. But they may expect to recover the cost of their store fixtures only within a period of 20 years, so that this asset must be classified as fixed. The cost of fixed assets is recovered by means of charges for depreciation, depletion, and amortization, about which more will be said later in this chapter.

THE CIRCULATION OF CURRENT ASSETS

The constant movement of cash into noncash current assets and their reconversion into cash is often described as the circular process; accordingly, current assets are frequently called circulating assets. To see how the circular process works, let us consider what goes on in a manufacturing firm. For this purpose, we may assume that a new corporation, the ABC Manufacturing Corporation, has just completed its organization and is getting ready for actual manufacturing operations.

Original Position

Transaction 1. To set the stage for these operations, let us further assume that stock of a par value of $450,000 was exchanged for fixed assets of various kinds and values, and that stock of a par value of $550,000 was sold for that amount of cash. Although this transaction does not involve the circulation of current assets, we may keep track of it by calling it Transaction 1.

With the stage thus set, we may want to see what the position of the corporation is just before it launches its manufacturing operations. A picture of this position can best be shown by means of a *balance sheet.* With names and values assigned to the fixed assets acquired, such a balance sheet would be as follows:

Balance Sheet 1

ABC MANUFACTURING CORPORATION

BALANCE SHEET

Date

Assets			*Liabilities and Equity*	
Current assets:			Stockholders' equity:	
Cash		$ 550,000	Common stock	$1,000,000
Fixed assets:				
Land	$ 25,000			
Building	120,000			
Machinery and equipment	280,000			
Delivery equipment	14,000			
Office fixtures	11,000	450,000		
Total Assets		$1,000,000	Total Liabilities and Equity	$1,000,000

Balance sheets constitute a class of *financial statement* of outstanding importance and of widespread use throughout the business world. Such a statement is designed to reveal the financial position of an enterprise at the close of business on the day indicated in its heading. As the transactions of each day have the effect of changing a firm's financial position, one day's balance sheet is no longer true or accurate at the close of the following business day. A balance sheet is simple in conception; there is nothing mysterious about it. On one side are listed all the assets an enterprise owns, with their assigned values, and on the other side are listed the sources of these assets in type and amount. The sources consist of obligations to creditors, termed *liabilities*, and the book value of the owners' investment, variously called *equity*, *net worth*, *capital*, or *interests* of the owners of the enterprise.[1] Every asset must have come from some source; hence, the total of assets and the total of liabilities and equity must always be equal. The balance sheet must always balance! In Balance Sheet 1 of the ABC Manufacturing Corporation, therefore, we see that the sale of common stock was the source of all the assets listed there.

Cash to Inventories

Transaction 2. After acquiring the necessary fixed assets, the ABC Manufacturing Corporation spends $125,000 in buying raw materials, $10,000 for factory supplies, and $1,000 for office supplies. Thus, the process of circulation begins, and the current asset position of the corporation is changed. The altered position can be shown in a new balance sheet, as follows (the fixed asset section and the liability side are omitted, since the transaction does not affect them).

Balance Sheet 2 (in part)

Current assets		
Cash		$414,000
Inventories:		
Raw materials	$125,000	
Factory supplies	10,000	
Office supplies	1,000	136,000
Total Current Assets		$550,000

Transaction 3. Next, labor is hired to work on the raw materials (direct labor), and other factory personnel is assigned to tasks that do not involve direct work on raw materials (supervision and indirect labor). Raw materials that cost $90,000 go immediately into the productive process, workers whose labor is classified as direct receive wages of $58,000, and supervisory and other factory workers

[1]Sometimes, the term *liabilities* is used to include owners' equity as well as obligations to creditors, but confusion is avoided when its use is limited to creditors.

are paid salaries and wages totaling $22,000. A total of $30,000 is paid in cash in meeting various factory overhead expenses, such as the cost of power, light, heat, and maintenance and repairs of the building and machinery, and factory supplies worth $750 are used up. Finally, a charge is made to factory expense for the estimated cost of the wear and tear on the factory building and equipment on account of operations to date. This charge for *depreciation*, as it is called, is $650 for the building and $3,400 for the machinery and equipment. All these developments produce changes in the financial position of the ABC Manufacturing Corporation, and this altered position can be shown in a new balance sheet, as follows (the cost of raw materials used and all other costs incurred to date are reflected in an inventory of goods in process).

Balance Sheet 3

ABC MANUFACTURING CORPORATION

BALANCE SHEET

Date

Assets			*Liabilities and Equity*	
Current assets:			Stockholders' equity:	
Cash		$ 304,000	Common stock	$1,000,000
Inventories:				
Raw materials	$ 35,000			
Goods in process	204,800			
Factory supplies	9,250			
Office supplies	1,000	250,050		
Total Current Assets		$ 554,050		
Fixed assets:				
Land		25,000		
Building	$120,000			
Less: Allowance for depreciation	650	119,350		
Machinery and equipment	$280,000			
Less: Allowance for depreciation	3,400	276,600		
Delivery equipment		14,000		
Office fixtures		11,000		
Total Fixed Assets		$ 445,950		
Total Assets		$1,000,000	Total Liabilities and Equity	$1,000,000

Transaction 4. Of the total inventory of goods in process shown in the foregoing balance sheet, goods valued at $179,000 are completed in the following period. To bring these goods to a state of completion, direct labor is expended on them at a cost of $80,000,

and other expenses are allocated to them as follows: supervision and indirect labor, $30,000; out-of-pocket overhead expenses, $40,000; factory supplies used, $800; depreciation of building, $500; and depreciation of machinery and equipment, $2,000. Additional expenses are allocated to uncompleted goods in process as follows: direct labor, $8,000; supervision and indirect labor, $3,000; out-of-pocket overhead expenses, $4,000; factory supplies used, $80; depreciation of building, $50; and depreciation of machinery and equipment, $200. All these operations produce further changes in the financial position of the ABC Manufacturing Corporation, and its new status is shown in a balance sheet as follows.

Balance Sheet 4

ABC MANUFACTURING CORPORATION

BALANCE SHEET

Date

Assets			*Liabilities and Equity*	
Current assets:			Stockholders' equity:	
Cash		$ 139,000	Common stock	$1,000,000
Inventories:				
Raw materials	$ 35,000			
Goods in process	41,130			
Finished goods	332,300			
Factory supplies	8,370			
Office supplies	1,000	417,800		
Total Current Assets		$ 556,800		
Fixed assets:				
Land		25,000		
Building	$120,000			
Less: Allowance for depreciation	1,200	118,800		
Machinery and equipment	$280,000			
Less: Allowance for depreciation	5,600	274,400		
Delivery equipment		14,000		
Office fixtures		11,000		
Total Fixed Assets		$ 443,200		
Total Assets		$1,000,000	Total Liabilities and Equity	$1,000,000

Although the foregoing balance sheet would reveal to the financial managers of the ABC Manufacturing Corporation how it stood on the completion of the transactions described up to this point, they might well want to know how changes in the corporation's position were brought about—how, in other words, the corporation moved from the position revealed in Balance Sheet 1 to that revealed in Balance Sheet 4. To provide this information, the accountants would prepare a second kind of financial statement of great importance in the business world, namely, a statement of the costs of goods manufactured. Such a statement is designed to show the scope of manufacturing operations in dollar terms *over a period of time*, whereas the balance sheet shows the financial position at the close of business on a designated day. As a summary of the manufacturing operations of the ABC Manufacturing Corporation, the statement would be as follows.

ABC MANUFACTURING CORPORATION

STATEMENT OF COST OF GOODS MANUFACTURED

For the Period—

Raw materials:		
Purchases	$125,000	
Less: Inventory, end of period	35,000	$ 90,000
Direct labor		146,000
Manufacturing expenses:		
Indirect labor and supervision	$ 55,000	
Power, light, heat, etc,	74,000	
Factory supplies used	1,630	
Depreciation of factory building	1,200	
Depreciation of machinery and equipment	5,600	137,430
		$373,430
Less: Goods in process, end of period		41,130
Cost of Finished Goods Manufactured		$332,300

At a glance, therefore, the financial managers could see:

1. The value of raw materials acquired during the period, how much had been used, and how much remained unused at the end of the period.
2. What had been the total costs of direct labor, other factory personnel, and the various kinds of out-of-pocket overhead expenses.
3. The value of factory supplies used.
4. What had been charged for depreciation of the factory building and equipment.
5. The respective values of goods completed during the period and goods remaining uncompleted at the end of the period.

Inventories to Receivables

Transaction 5. From its finished goods inventory, the ABC Manufacturing Corporation sells goods valued at $250,000. The selling price is $300,000, and the customers buy on account, which means, of course, that they do not pay the purchase price immediately but merely incur an obligation to pay it within the period of credit allowed by the corporation. The full difference between the value of the goods sold and the selling price is not profit, for the ABC Manufacturing Corporation incures various kinds of selling and administrative expenses in addition to its manufacturing expenses. Let us assume, therefore, that selling expenses, including salesmen's salaries, advertising, and such out-of-pocket delivery expenses as gasoline and truck maintenance and repair, amount to $14,000; and that administrative expenses, including salaries and wages, maintenance of office equipment, and light and heat, amount to $7,500. In addition, there should undoubtedly be charges to expense for the estimated depreciation of the delivery equipment and the office fixtures on account of their use up to date; these charges we may assume to be $1,100 and $275, respectively. Furthermore, the corporation's officers anticipate that in view of the collection experience of other firms in the same line of business not all the claims on customers will be collected in full. They estimate that such uncollectible accounts will amount to 0.5 percent of the sales figure; accordingly, they consider the amount of this estimate, $1,500, as an additional expense of operation—an expense generally labeled "bad debts." The officers also anticipate that their collections from customers will be somewhat reduced on account of discounts allowed for early payment. Such discounts, like the allowance for bad debts, represent an offset to gross sales income. Nevertheless, it is customary to take up discounts as an expense when payments less the discounts are received, rather than to charge an expense account in advance on the basis of an estimate of what discounts will be taken. A final assumption is that office supplies of a value of $225 have been used up in taking care of transactions to date.

However, even after all these expenses have been accounted for as deductions against the income from sales (in addition to the cost of finished goods sold), the balance is not clear profit for the corporation. Its liability for income taxes must also be taken into consideration. We may assume that the state or states in which the corporation derives its income have no income taxes, so that only the federal income tax applies here. On the basis, then, of the corporation's indicated net profit *before taxes* of $25,400, it would anticipate having to pay a federal income tax of $5,692.[2]

All these elements of Transaction 4 would place the ABC Manufacturing Corporation in a new financial position, as indicated in Balance Sheet 5.

Analysis of Balance Sheet 5. Balance Sheet 5, unlike the ones preceding it, shows an increase in total assets, as well as changes

[2]Applying the basic tax rates in effect for the year 1968, that is, 22 percent on the first $25,000 of taxable income and 48 percent on taxable income in excess of $25,000, and ignoring the surcharge of 10 percent adopted in June, 1968, but scheduled to expire at the end of June, 1969.

on the liability side. The increase in total assets is explained, of course, by the fact that the claims on customers, recorded as accounts receivable, exceed by $25,400 the cost of goods sold and the expenses of selling and administration.

Balance Sheet 5

ABC MANUFACTURING CORPORATION

BALANCE SHEET

Date

Assets		
Current assets:		
Cash		$ 117,500
Accounts receivable	$300,000	
Less: Reserve for bad debts	1,500	298,500
Inventories		
Raw materials	$ 35,000	
Goods in process	41,130	
Finished goods	82,300	
Factory supplies	8,370	
Office supplies	775	167,575
Total Current Assets		$ 583,575
Fixed assets:		
Land		25,000
Building	$120,000	
Less: Allowance for depreciation	1,200	118,800
Machinery and equipment	$280,000	
Less: Allowance for depreciation	5,600	274,400
Delivery equipment	$ 14,000	
Less: Allowance for depreciation	1,100	12,900
Office fixtures	$ 11,000	
Less: Allowance for depreciation	275	10,725
Total Fixed Assets		$ 441,825
Total Assets		$1,025,400

Liabilities and Equity		
Current liabilities:		
Estimated liability for federal income tax		$ 5,692
Stockholders' equity:		
Common stock	$1,000,000	
Surplus	19,708	1,019,708
Total Liabilities and Equity		$1,025,400

The sources of assets, as noted earlier, are shown on the liability side of a balance sheet. As we look at the asset side, we may say: "These are the things that the corporation owns." And as we look at the liability side, we may say: "It is from these sources that the assets came." In the case of the ABC Manufacturing Corporation, we could say that of the total assets of $1,025,400 shown in Balance Sheet 5 the stockholders supplied assets of a value of $1,019,708, and that the federal government supplied assets of a value of $5,692! Since the federal government could insist on collecting its taxes on the profits of business enterprises as soon as derived, its willingness to wait for collection until some future tax payment data means that it temporarily leaves assets with the enterprises. So it is with all kinds of liability and equity items: creditors and owners contribute to an enterprise assets that they leave for short or long periods. All the assets are contributed by somebody: this, to repeat, is the reason balance sheets must always balance—the total of the assets must always be equal to the total of the liabilities and equity.

Liabilities and the stockholders' equity can be looked on, not only as sources of assets, but also as claims on the assets. But the moment we shift our point of view from liabilities and equity as sources to their role as claims, we hasten to emphasize the distinction between the claims of creditors and those of owners. One of the most important facts of business life is that creditors must generally be paid when obligations to them come due; if not, the debtor enterprise may quickly find itself in serious difficulties. On the other hand, owners, such as the stockholders of a corporation, are much more moderate in their demands for payment. Only if they vote the liquidation of their corporation do they expect—or, rather, hope—that their claims will be paid in full. Otherwise, they usually expect to enforce their claims only to the extent of getting a reasonable dividend from time to time, and are quite satisfied to leave in the corporation indefinitely the bulk of the assets they have contributed. Indeed, even in enforcing claims for dividends, their success, as we saw in Chapter 4, depends on decisions of the board of directors rather than on their own wishes.

Because creditors are so much more insistent on the satisfaction of their claims than are the stockholders, it is usually found desirable to classify creditors' claims as to time of payment. The financial managers must be ever anxious to meet these claims as they fall due, but obviously they will tend to be much more anxious about claims coming due in a few weeks or months than about those whose due dates are much more remote. Accordingly, creditors' claims, like assets, are classified as *current* and *fixed*. Current liabilities are those payable in the ordinary course of business (almost invariably in cash) within one year, and fixed liabilities are those payable in the ordinary course of business beyond one year. In this way, the definitions of current and fixed liabilities parallel the definitions of current and fixed assets.

A final observation about the details of Balance Sheet 5. The student will notice that the net profit on sales after the deduction of the estimated liability for federal income taxes was placed in an account called "surplus" on the liability side under the equity heading. As shown in a corporation's balance sheet, every equity item stands for a stockholders' contribution to the assets; hence, the entry in the surplus account in Balance Sheet 5 indicates that the stockholders of the ABC Manufacturing Corporation have increased their contribution to assets beyond the amount of their original investment in its common stock. The corporation earned a profit on the stockholders' investment, and that investment is therefore increased. The increase in the investment remains, of course, so long as it is not offset by the payment of dividends to the stockholders or by subsequent losses. As long as the profit is not disturbed, therefore, the surplus account must remain to show that the additional investment is there. Surplus is nothing more or less than this. It is not something put into a balance sheet to make it balance. All assets, liabilities, and equity items must be placed in the balance sheet if it is to balance, and surplus is simply one of the equity items. One must be especially careful not to confuse surplus and cash. Because surplus appears on the liability side of balance sheets, *it can never be cash,* nor can it be said to represent a certain amount of cash as shown on the asset side. Some corporations have large surplus accounts and little cash; others have large amounts of cash and little surplus. Thus, we inevitably come back to saying that surplus simply represents a contribution by the stockholders to assets over and above the par or stated value of their stock. Since surplus is an equity item, it may also be described as a claim of the stockholders on the assets; nevertheless, it is an undifferentiated claim —it is not a claim on any specific asset. Indeed, this is the general status of all the liabilities and equity items shown in a balance sheet. The claims of creditors extend indiscriminately to *all* the assets, regardless of what they may have contributed individually,[3] and owners' interests or claims likewise extend to all the assets, regardless of what may have been done with their money as originally invested or as accumulated through profits.

Income Statement. Just as a statement of cost of goods manufactured was found useful in indicating how the ABC Manufacturing Corporation moved from its position as shown in Balance Sheet 1 to that shown in Balance Sheet 4, so also can an income statement—a third kind of financial statement of major importance—be used to reveal why the corporation's position shifted from that of Balance Sheet 4 to that of Balance Sheet 5. Such a statement (really, in this instance, a résumé of Transaction 5) would be drawn up as follows.

[3]It is possible, however, to give preferred claims against certain assets by specifically pledging them to secure obligations owing to one or more of the creditors.

ABC MANUFACTURING CORPORATION

INCOME STATEMENT

For the Period

Sales		$300,000
Less: Cost of goods sold:		
Cost of finished goods manufactured	$332,300	
Less: Inventory, end of period	82,300	250,000
Gross profit on sales		$ 50,000
Less: Selling and administrative expenses:		
Salesmen's salaries, advertising, etc.	$ 14,000	
Office wages, light and heat, etc.	7,500	
Depreciation of delivery equipment	1,100	
Depreciation of office fixtures	275	
Office supplies used	225	
Bad debts	1,500	24,600
Net profit before federal income tax		$ 25,400
Less: Estimated liability for federal income tax		5,692
Net Profit to Surplus		$ 19,708

Thus, the financial managers would be able to see:

1. How the accounts receivable of $300,000 came into being.
2. Why, however, they are carried at less than the full amount of sales on account of the allowance for bad debts.
3. Why the inventories of finished goods and office supplies were reduced.
4. Why cash was reduced on account of the payment of expenses.
5. Why the values of the delivery equipment and office fixtures were written down.
6. Why a tax obligation was set up as a liability.
7. Why there was an increase in the equity accounts equal to the net profit after the provision for federal income tax.

Receivables to Cash

Transaction 6. Completion of our illustration of the circulation of current assets requires only, as a final step, the collection of cash from customers as payments on their obligations for goods purchased. Let us assume that the ABC Manufacturing Corporation allows 1 percent discount on accounts paid within 10 days of the date of invoices, and that most of the customers take advantage of this inducement toward prompt payment by remitting $217,800 to settle obligations totaling $220,000. On the asset side of the corporation's balance sheet, only the cash and accounts receivable accounts are affected by this transaction. On the liability side, the federal income tax obligation and the surplus account are affected by the sales discounts of $2,200, which, of course, must be accounted for as a further expense of operation. The new position of these affected accounts would be as follows.

Balance Sheet 6 (in part)

Current assets:			Current liabilities:	
Cash		$335,300	Estimated liability for	
Accounts receivable	$80,000		federal income tax	$ 5,104
Less: Reserve for			Stockholders' equity:	
bad debts	1,500	78,500	Surplus	18,096

Continuity in the Circular Flow

For the sake of simplicity, the foregoing illustration was presented in steps to bring out the details of the movement of cash to inventories, inventories to receivables, and receivables back to cash. Actually, of course, businesses as a rule do not undertake one kind of operation in one time interval, another kind in a second time interval, and still another kind in a third. All the movements tend to be continuous and constantly overlapping. On any day, an enterprise is likely to be buying raw materials and supplies, using direct and indirect labor in the factory, meeting many kinds of cash expenses, completing goods that have been in process, putting additional raw materials into process, making sales, and collecting from customers on account of sales made earlier. As cash comes in from collections, it may be rather quickly spent in buying additional materials and supplies, in meeting the payroll, and in meeting other kinds of expenses. In terms of the illustration, the financial managers of the ABC Manufacturing Corporation might expect never again to have a cash balance equal to the $550,000 with which they began the circular process among the current assets. Thus, the estimation of cash requirements and the control of the flow of cash, as executive finance functions, are greatly complicated by the limitless variations that are possible in the timing of cash inflows and outflows.

For reasons of simplicity, also, the balance sheets, the statement of the cost of goods manufactured, and the income statement used in connection with the illustration were presented at points in the discussion where, it appeared, their significance would be most appreciated. In actual business practice, it is customary to have such statements prepared on the basis of an established time schedule, as monthly, quarterly, semiannually, or, at the very least, annually. The balance sheet of an operating business will show the effects on its financial position of numerous transactions rather than the effects of a handful of transactions, as in the illustrative balance sheets. Its statement of the cost of goods manufactured and income statement will report the volume of operations for a month or other specific period of time, rather than the scope of one or a few transactions, as in the illustration.

It should be mentioned also that many kinds of complications in addition to variations in the timing of cash inflows and outflows were ignored in the presentation of the illustration. But we shall consider some of the more important of these in Chapter 6. For the moment, however, we may conclude our preliminary discussion of cash flows by analyzing what happens to fixed assets.

FIXED ASSETS AND THE FLOW OF CASH

Like noncash current assets, most of the fixed assets owned by business firms are involved in a process of conversion into cash. The reduction in the value of these assets that comes about through their use, wear and tear, the action of the elements, exhaustion, or the mere passage of time is periodically charged as an expense of operations. This expense, like all other expenses, the business enterprise expects to be able to cover in the selling prices of its goods or services. If the enterprise succeeds in covering it, it gets cash either immediately or at a later time (as it makes collections on its accounts receivable) equal to the estimated reduction in value. How this works we have already seen in the effects of the depreciation charges of the ABC Manufacturing Corporation. Its illustrative balance sheets indicate how fixed assets gradually become current assets. In comparing Balance Sheets 1 and 3, one sees in 3 a reduction in the total value of the fixed assets from $450,000 to $445,950—a reduction equal to the depreciation charges of $4,050—and one sees an increase in the total amount of current assets of $4,050—an increase reflected in the inventory of goods in process on account of the taking up of depreciation as an expense.

The conversion of fixed assets into current assets, and ultimately into cash, is a relatively slow process; by definition, it requires more than a year. Otherwise, there would be no need of a separate classification of fixed assets. Obviously, however, the process is one of varying degrees of speed—or, perhaps one should say, of slowness. For some kinds of fixed assets, the process is a very slow one, indeed, as for factory and office buildings; for others, it is relatively rapid, as for delivery equipment and certain kinds of machines and machine tools. (Tools whose life does not extend beyond one year are customarily classified as "factor supplies" among the current assets rather than as "machinery and equipment" among the fixed assets.) Some kinds of fixed assets are regarded as not being used up at all; such assets do not participate in the process of conversion into cash. This is true chiefly of the land on which factory and office buildings are erected, but it is also true of such fixed assets as stocks of subsidiary corporations held by their parents and franchises of perpetual duration.

Depending on the nature of different classes of assets, estimated reductions in their values, to be charged as current expenses of operation, are described as depreciation, depletion, and amortization.

Depreciation

Depreciation is a reduction in the value of fixed assets due to wear and tear in use and the action of the elements. Only physical assets, such as buildings, machinery and equipment, store fixtures, and office fixtures, can depreciate; considering the sense in which the term is used, it is impossible for intangible assets to depreciate.[4]

Present-day charges for depreciation almost invariably include an allowance for what is called ordinary obsolescence. An asset becomes obsolete when because of technological developments or shifts in demand for products it is no longer wise to continue it in use. Machines become obsolete—and some of them rather quickly—because other machines that can do the job much more efficiently have been developed. A new machine may be expected to have a useful life of 20 years in the sense that it would continue in good working order throughout that period. But its owners, considering the speed at which technological changes are taking place in their industry, may estimate that after, say, 10 years it will have to be replaced by a much more efficient machine—one yet to be invented or developed. They would think of the machine as having *for them* a useful life of only 10 years rather than 20, and they would want to recover its cost through depreciation charges in the shorter period.

In accounting for depreciation, then, the idea is to periodically write down the value of the depreciable asset during its useful life—as limited or reduced to allow for ordinary obsolescence—so that when the time comes for replacement the value remaining on the books will not exceed the scrap, secondhand, or trade-in value, as the case may be. These write-downs are charged as current expenses of operations to be recovered in the selling prices of goods and services. Were a firm to ignore the steady decline in the value of its depreciable assets and therefore fail to charge depreciation as an expense of operation, it would obviously be overstating its profits or understating its losses.

The effect of charging of depreciation as a current expense to be recovered in the selling prices of goods and services is that the enterprise gradually sells its fixed assets to the people who buy its products. When we buy an electric refrigerator, for example, we are not likely to think of ourselves as buying minute portions of the manufacturer's buildings, machinery and equipment, office fixtures, and other de-

---

[4]Although the federal Internal Revenue Code has provisions concerned with the depreciation of intangible assets such as patents and copyrights, economists and business analysts generally prefer the term *amortization* as used subsequently in the text.

preciable assets. In effect, however, we do buy minute amounts of these things when the price we pay is sufficient to cover depreciation charges in addition to all other costs. Thus, depreciable assets really move toward conversion into cash, but, as has been indicated, the movement is generally much slower than for noncash current assets.

Depletion

In careful usage, the term *depletion* is applied only to the exhaustion of natural resources. Depletion is the reduction in the value of land as coal or ore is mined, as oil is pumped, as timber is cut, and as other such exhaustive operations are performed. If a corporation were to invest $5 million in a tract of land containing an estimated 5 million tons of ore of a certain kind, the value of the land would obviously decline by $1 with every ton of ore mined.[5] To operate profitably, the corporation would surely have to cover this cost of $1 per unit, plus all its other expenses, and plus a markup in the selling price of its output.

In the development of wasting assets—a term often applied to natural resources subject to depletion—the output, in effect, becomes an inventory of the producing firm; once again, therefore, we have the gradual movement of a fixed asset into the current classification. And of course, the inventory, in turn, continues the movement in the direction of cash as it is disposed of in sales to customers.

Amortization

Amortization is a loss in the value of fixed assets occurring by reason of the mere passing of time. It is an attribute of certain kinds of intangible fixed assets, such as patents, copyrights, and limited-term franchises. Whatever investment is made in intangible assets of these kinds must presumably be recovered during the period of their respective lives. As with depreciation and depletion, therefore, it is appropriate to make periodic charges to expense accounts so that the investment will be gradually recovered in the selling prices of the related goods or services.

If money invested in intangible assets of the kinds mentioned is to be fully recovered through sales, the periodic charge to amortization expense must be based on a realistic estimate of the income-producing life of the asset rather than on a term arbitrarily fixed by legislation or by the decree of a governmental body. Should a corporation, for example, spend $500,000 in research and experimentation in the development of a new product for which it obtains a patent, it might be most unwise to write off only one seventeenth of this value each year

[5]Assuming, of course, that the land would have no value for other purposes after all the ore had been removed.

simply because the federal government gives patent rights for 17 years. If it were reasonably estimated that the popularity of the patented article would not extend for more than four years, then it would be appropriate to write off $125,000 of the patent value each year.

QUESTIONS

1. What kinds of assets owned by a business enterprise are classified as current assets? As fixed assets? What is the principal test or rule for distinguishing between these two classes of assets?

2. Why are current assets described as "circulating assets"? Do fixed assets also circulate? Explain.

3. What are the two principal sources of a firm's assets? What is the relationship between total assets and total sources of assets?

4. In what sense can the sources of a firm's assets be said to be claims against its assets? Why are these claims said to be undifferentiated? Why is it important to distinguish between liabilities as claims and equity as claims?

5. What kinds of creditors' claims are classified as current liabilities? As fixed liabilities? For a given creditor's claim, could there ever be a shift in this classification? Explain.

6. What kinds of items are contained in the balance sheet of a business enterprise? Why must a balance sheet always be in balance?

7. What kinds of information are presented in a firm's income statement? What is its relationship, if any, to the firm's balance sheet?

8. Does it make sense to say that a business firm acquires assets by incurring expenses? Discuss.

9. What is the nature of surplus as it appears in a corporation's balance sheet? How is it related, if at all, to the corporation's cash balance? Its total assets? Its other equity accounts?

10. What is depreciation? Why is it treated as an expense? What is its relationship to obsolescence?

11. Explain the proposition that, in effect, firms gradually convert fixed assets into current assets through their depreciation charges.

12. What kinds of assets are subject to depletion and amortization? Could a given asset be simultaneously subject to both depletion and amortization? Why or why not?

PROBLEM

At the beginning and end of September, 19xx, the inventories of Cooke & Lessing, Inc. were as follows.

	Beginning	*End*
Raw materials	$335,000	$289,000
Goods in process	540,000	492,000
Finished goods	568,000	603,600
Factory supplies	12,620	12,200
Office supplies	1,550	1,700

The corporation's transactions during the month were as follows.

Sales	$2,820,000
Purchases of raw materials	622,000
Labor costs:	
Factory direct labor	770,000
Factory indirect labor and supervision	245,000
Salesmen and truck drivers	138,000
Administrative	162,000
Factory supplies purchased	7,500
Office supplies purchased	730
Sundry factory expenses	273,000
Sundry selling expenses	135,000
Sundry administrative expenses	78,700

Charges for depreciation and bad debts were made at the end of the month as follows.

Depreciation, factory building	3,410
Depreciation, factory machinery and equipment	6,220
Depreciation, delivery equipment	4,830
Depreciation, office equipment	490
Bad debts	8,150

For the month of September, 19xx, prepare a statement of cost of goods manufactured and an income statement for Cooke & Lessing, Inc. Assume that the federal income tax rate applicable to the September net profit is 48 percent.

chapter 6

FURTHER ASPECTS OF CASH FLOWS

In the illustration of the operations of the ABC Manufacturing Corporation presented in Chapter 5, complicating details were avoided as far as possible so that the main course of the circular flow of cash could be made to stand out clearly. It now becomes necessary to look at some of the circumstances in the actual operations of businesses that result in modifications of cash inflows and outflows—that make cash flows vary from a relatively simple course such as that of the illustration. An examination of these circumstances is important, because they are the sources of most of the problems with which the financial managers of business enterprises must cope in establishing asset management policies and in working toward other kinds of decisions.

The continuous overlapping of activities requiring cash payments and those producing cash receipts was briefly considered in Chapter 5. Other kinds of circumstances that give rise to complications in cash flows may be grouped as follows: (1) the prepayment and deferment of income and expenses; (2) breaks in the circular flow through additions and withdrawals of cash; (3) differences in the scope of business activities; and (4) general business developments of a cyclical kind.

PREPAYMENTS AND DEFERMENTS

The cash requirements of a business enterprise are increased by prepayment of expenses and by deferment of the realization of income in cash; its cash requirements are reduced by incurring expenses on a deferred-payment basis and by the receipt of cash as advance realization of income. Prepayments and deferments that cause an increase in cash requirements may be said to slow down the flow of cash; those that result in a decrease in cash requirements may be said to speed up the flow of cash. Were a firm to operate entirely on a cash basis, selling each day for cash all goods bought that day for resale, and meeting by immediate cash payments all operating expenses, including the cost of the goods purchased, it could manage a given volume of operations with a much smaller cash investment than could a second firm that carried a large inventory over from day to day and sold on account. The circular flow of cash would be completed daily for the first firm, but it would require a much longer period for the second firm.

Included in the illustration of the operations of the ABC Manufacturing Corporation in Chapter 5 were examples of the prepayment of expenses in its purchases of raw materials, factory supplies, and office supplies; an example of the deferment of the realization of income in its sales on account; and an example of the incurring of an expense on a deferred-payment basis in its liability for federal income tax. Examples such as these deserve further examination. Moreover, we must look at some others to get a well-rounded picture of the effects of prepayments and deferments.

Investment in Inventories

When a manufacturing firm buys raw materials and pays for them before it sells the finished goods in which they are incorporated, it prepays expenses. The same is true of a mercantile firm that buys finished goods and pays for them some time before it sells them to its customers. Such prepayments, of course, are extremely common. Firms hold inventories for weeks and months awaiting sale—inventories for which full payment has been made. While the inventories are being held, they may properly be classified as current assets and be shown as such in balance sheets, but when they are sold they are transferred to expense accounts, being treated in much the same way as other manufacturing, selling, and administrative expenses.

Cash is released from inventories as cash sales are made or as collections are made from accounts receivable, but the typical firm that deals in tangible products must be constantly replenishing its inventories. If the firm is to continue to efficiently serve its customers, it cannot permit its inventories to fall below some minimum limit. It must *permanently* tie up cash in inventories at this minimum level. At certain times in the course of the year, inventories may be much larger than the minimum required, but the additional cash absorbed in inventories is there only temporarily, as it is released when the inventories are sold down toward the minimum. Not so, however, with cash absorbed in inventories at the minimum level, for, by definition, its release would make it impossible for the firm to efficiently serve its customers.

If, for example, inventories worth not less than $100,000 must always be carried by a certain firm if it is to give its customers good service, its financial managers may as well decide that cash of that amount has been put permanently beyond reach—forever unavailable for other purposes. The composition of the inventories would change, probably daily, but the inventories as a prepaid expense (or, alternatively, in the balance sheet sense, as a current asset) would permanently dam up $100,000 of cash.

Prepayment of Other Expenses

The prepayment of any expense has effects on the circular flow of cash similar to those resulting from investment in inventories; it slows this flow, or, to put the proposition in its alternative form, it increases cash requirements. To see why this is so, we may analyze the transaction of the ABC Manufacturing Corporation in buying office supplies. The corporation immediately spent $1,000 for such supplies, yet it is reasonable to assume that they would not all be used up for several months. Suppose that supplies worth $100 were consumed in the first month. At the end of that month, then, the corporation would have a prepaid expense of $900, damming up $900 of cash. Had the corporation decided to buy, in the beginning, only enough supplies for the one month, its expenditure would have been only $100 instead of $1,000, and it would have had $900 of cash available for other uses. To put it differently, it could have managed to get along with $900 less of cash. Indeed, had it decided to operate its office on a hand-to-mouth basis, it might have needed only about $4, say, to buy each day the office supplies needed for that day! All of which does not mean that the managers of the ABC Manufacturing Corporation were unwise to invest $1,000 in office supplies, for tying up cash of this amount may have been justified by lower prices for quantity purchases and, even more importantly, on grounds of convenience.

Premiums paid to insurance companies for protection against property losses on account of fire, windstorm, and other hazards represent another very common kind of prepaid expense. Such premiums are almost invariably payable in advance, and the insurance companies encourage prepayment for two, three, or more years by providing lower yearly rates for longer-term policies than for one-year policies. Other examples of prepaid expenses are advances to employees against wages and salaries yet to be earned and advance payments to suppliers for merchandise to be delivered later.

Carrying Accounts Receivable

The realization of income in cash is obviously deferred when a firm sells goods to its customers on account—that is, when it gives them a certain period of time beyond the date of sale in which to make payment. The firm's circular flow of cash is necessarily slowed, depending on the length of the credit period allowed.

Alternatively, once again, we can say that the cash requirements of a firm selling on account are increased. In a manufacturing firm, for example, money is spent in buying materials and supplies, in paying labor, and in meeting other manufacturing, selling, and administrative expenses, but it is not recouped as soon as goods are sold. Cash must be available to make the necessary outlays, but it is not immediately forthcoming from customers to continue these outlays.

One may object, however, that any increase in cash requirements because of selling on account must be, in most instances, a short-run requirement, perhaps of not more than 30 or 60 days, perhaps of not more than 10 days if cash discounts for early payment are allowed. But such an objection is not valid. The contrary is true: the carrying of accounts receivable, like the carrying of inventories, tends to *permanently* absorb or tie up cash. While it is true that individual accounts are paid off in short periods of time, these are constantly replaced by others as long as the firm continues to sell on account. Thus, there will be a permanent absorption of cash in accounts receivable related to the minimum amounts these accounts fall to. As with inventories, the amount of cash absorbed in accounts receivable will often be well in excess of the minimum; but it can hardly be less than this if the firm is to continue to satisfy those customers who want to buy on account and who can qualify on the basis of credit standing.

One should observe that the amount of cash absorbed in accounts receivable is not the amount of the receivables but is related to it. This is so because claims on customers include a firm's markups or profit margin—a factor that requires no outlay of cash by the firm. If, for example, a firm produces goods at a total cost of $25,000 and sells them on account for $30,000, cash absorbed in accounts receivable obviously amounts to the smaller of these figures.

Acquisition of Goods and Supplies on Account

While spending cash for inventories, the prepaying of other expenses, and the carrying of accounts receivable absorb cash—slow down its flow—obtaining goods and supplies on a deferred-payment basis conserves cash or, in other words, reduces the need of it. The creditors who await payment for goods and supplies furnished serve as a new or additional source of assets, as is indicated by the appearance of the obligations owing to them as accounts payable, classified in the balance sheet as a current liability. It is true that the individual obligations that constitute these accounts must be paid within the allowed credit periods (and paid scrupulously if the debtor firm is to preserve a good credit rating), but these obligations tend to be constantly replaced by others as additional purchase on account are effected. For the typical business enterprise, therefore, accounts payable represent a permanent source of assets—a permanent means of reducing cash requirements—as measured by the minimum amount they fall to over the years, and a temporary source as measured by amounts in excess of the minimum.

For illustration, we may refer again to the transactions of the ABC Manufacturing Corporation. Had the corporation in Transaction 2 bought its raw materials and factory and office supplies on account, the current sections of Balance Sheet 2 would have appeared as follows.

Current assets:			Current liabilities:	
Cash		$550,000	Accounts payable	$136,000
Inventories:				
Raw materials	$125,000			
Factory supplies	10,000			
Office supplies	1,000	136,000		
Total Current Assets		$686,000		

Thus, the corporation would have had current assets of $136,000 in excess of the total disclosed in the original Balance Sheet 2, and obviously the trade creditors would have been the suppliers of these additional assets—a fact indicated by the entry for accounts payable on the liability side. (As was explained in Chapter 5, one could also say that the trade creditors would have had a claim against the assets of the corporation to the amount of $136,000, but it is to be repeated that this would have been a claim against all the assets—an undifferentiated claim—and not simply a claim against the raw materials and supplies they actually would have sold to the corporation.)

By this point, the observing student may have concluded that the author has got himself into a tight spot. Earlier, he said that cash requirements are increased through investment in inventories, and now he says that cash requirements are reduced when goods and supplies are bought on account. But authors should always be able to get out of tight spots. In this instance, that apparently can be done by observing that the *net* effect on cash requirements and cash flows depends on timing of the resale of inventoried goods and timing of the payment to the trade creditors. When a business enterprise buys goods on account, it obviously does not thereby tie up any money in inventories; it is the creditors who supply the additional goods. The enterprise's cash requirements are not increased, and its flow of cash is not slowed in any way. But should it pay off the creditors before reselling the goods and collecting payment from the buyers, it would cause cash to be absorbed in the inventories. On the other hand, should it sell the inventoried goods for cash some days or weeks before the due dates of its obligations to the trade creditors, not only would it not tie up cash in inventories but it also would have the creditors supplying it with cash that could be used for other purposes. For most businesses, however, the value of the inventories at any time usually exceeds the amount of trade accounts payable, so that the excess roughly measures in each case how much of a firm's cash has been absorbed in inventories.[1]

Accrued Wages

It is customary for most businesses to pay payrolls only every week or every two weeks, and sometimes, particularly salaries, only monthly. Moreover, payrolls are often deferred to give the payroll department adequate time to make them up, as when the payroll to be paid at the middle or end of this week covers wages earned last week. The employees of an enterprise, therefore, make a net contribution to its assets equal to the amount of the unpaid wages. They provide the enterprise with asset-building services, one might say, and they do not make immediate demands for payment. Such a contribution reduces the cash requirements of the employing firm. Furthermore, this reduction in cash requirements has elements of permanence. If the firm's unpaid wages never amount to less than a certain sum, the employees make a permanent contribution to its assets of that amount, releasing an equivalent amount of cash for other uses. And, of course, the employees make additional temporary contributions to assets to the extent that unpaid wages from time to time exceed the minimum.

To refer once again to the transactions of the ABC Manufacturing Corporation, as presented in Chapter 5, let us suppose that $6,000 of the wages and salaries earned by its employees had not been paid at the time of preparation of Balance Sheet 3. As a result, the corporation's assets at that time would have been $6,000 greater, the addition being attributable to the employees' contribution. Accordingly, the current sections of the balance sheet would have appeared as follows.

Current assets:			Current liabilities:	
Cash		$310,000	Accrued wages	$6,000
Inventories:				
Raw materials	$ 35,000			
Goods in process	204,800			
Factory supplies	9,250			
Office supplies	1,000	250,050		
Total Current Assets		$560,050		

[1]The measure is ordinarily an inexact one because of differences in the methods of valuing inventories. If, for example, inventories appear in a balance sheet at values less than cost, the excess of these values over the amount of trade accounts payable shown in the same balance sheet obviously does not measure in any accurate way how much cash the inventories have absorbed. For a discussion of inventory valuation methods and their effects, see, pp. 165–70.

Other Deferred Payments

Many other kinds of expenses that do not require immediate cash payments are incurred by business enterprises. The expenses go into the building of noncash assets, but, temporarily at least, the enterprises do not have to use cash equivalent to the value of these additions. Cash is conserved: at least temporarily, it can be used in other directions.

In addition to trade creditors and employees, therefore, electric power companies, water companies, telephone and telegraph companies, repairmen, firms that provide professional services, and many other service institutions contribute to the assets of the business enterprises to which they sell their services. Daily use is made of these services—and resulting accretions to the assets of the business enterprises, therefore, take place—but the suppliers of the services are generally willing to await payment for some days or even weeks after they have submitted their respective statements or bills.

In a similar way, by deferring the collection of taxes governmental bodies make temporary contributions to the noncash assets of the enterprises on which the taxes are levied. Taxes add to assets no less than do all other kinds of expenses, in the sense that they are properly includable in the valuation of goods to be sold; yet, such additions to noncash assets do not have to be matched with cash outlays until the tax payment dates arrive. In Chapter 5, we saw how this works with the federal corporation income tax. It works in much the same way with other kinds of taxes—federal, state, and local. Thus, the liability for state and local property taxes may be said to come into existence on the date of assessment, but the state and local governments generally establish tax payment dates some months beyond the dates of assessment.

It is of interest to observe that governmental bodies provide business firms with an additional source of cash when they call on them to act as tax collectors. Although tax monies acquired in this capacity do not constitute business expenses, their effects on assets are much the same as if they were expenses. If, for example, a firm adds a federal excise tax or a state sales tax to the selling price of its goods, it is in a position to use for business purposes the tax monies collected from its customers until the time they must be paid over to the taxing government. Likewise, a portion of the assets contributed by employees through their unpaid labor service comes to represent a government contribution through the deduction from payrolls of federal withholding and social security taxes. Thus, should a firm's unpaid payroll amount to $10,000, and should $800 of this represent personal income taxes of the employees withheld, and $225 represent deductions for social security taxes, the employees could be said to be making a contribution to the firm's assets of $8,975, and the federal government a contribution of $1,025. Many managers of business enterprises, nevertheless, are not at all pleased to have tax collection duties thrust on them. They generally feel that the expenses of bookkeeping and reporting far outweigh the advantages of the temporary use of tax funds.

Unearned Income

The receiving of cash income in advance of the sale of goods or the performance of services obviously reduces a need of cash from other sources; it may also be said to speed the flow of cash. Cash income is received in advance much more commonly by financial institutions and transportation firms than by enterprises engaged in manufacturing and selling tangible products. Examples include the receipt of premiums by insurance companies for protection of lives and property to be provided in the ensuing year or period of years, and the advance sale of tickets for passenger transportation by railroads, airlines, bus lines, and other transportation companies.

Sometimes, customers of manufacturing companies made advance payments to cover at least part of the cost of goods to be produced for them, most often when the goods must be specially designed. The federal government has been especially liberal in making advance payments to producers of military equipment and supplies. During World War II, many manufacturers were able to produce war materials only because the Treasury's advance payments gave them the means to do so. Moreover, the government's policy of making advance payments continues at the present time—in keeping, one might say, with its huge military budgets. As of December 31, 1967, for example, American corporations were reported as having liabilities for advances and prepayments from the federal government totaling $5.8 billion.[2]

BREAKS IN THE CIRCULAR FLOW

When one speaks of the circular flow of current assets, one has in mind, as we have seen, the spending of cash for inventory and in meeting other varieties of operating expenses (all these are included in the value of goods offered for sale), the conversion of these goods into cash as sales are made or as collections are made on accounts receivable, the respending of this cash for additional inventory and in meeting additional operating expenses, and so on continuously. But it is clear that the managers of business enterprises can decide from time to time to remove cash from the circular process, and that, likewise, they can decide now and then to pump additional cash into it.

[2]Securities and Exchange Commission, *Statistical Bulletin*, May, 1968, p. 24.

This is the meaning of "breaks" in the circular flow of current assets to be considered in this section.

In corporations, the most common reasons for the removal of cash from the circular process are the payment of dividends to stockholders, the repayment of borrowings, and the purchase of fixed assets. Less common reasons include the use of cash to buy out other businesses and to pay off portions of the stockholders' investment, as in the retirement of preferred stock. The only significant reason for adding to the amount of cash in the circular process is to make possible an expansion in current operations—to enable the corporation to expand its inventories, meet a larger volume of operating expenses, and carry a larger quantity of accounts receivable. The cash added chiefly comes from borrowing and the sale of additional stock, although other sources may be occasionally available, as, for example, the sale of fixed assets or donations from stockholders. In many cases, of course, the drawing in of additional cash and its use occur outside the circular process, as when a corporation borrows from one financial institution to repay loans owing to another, or floats a bond issue to raise money to expand its holdings of fixed assets.

If the amount of cash already in the circular process is in excess of what is needed to continue it, the financial managers obviously have no great problem in drawing off the excess and devoting it to other uses. Likewise, they have no serious problem if additional cash is needed to expand current operations and it is readily forthcoming from lenders or stockholders. On the other hand, a corporation's problems relative to breaks may be quite difficult—and even at times insolvable—when, for example, cash is sorely needed for the expansion of current operations and it cannot readily be obtained from lenders or from the sale of additional stock, or when there is an acute need to replace or add to fixed assets and cash cannot be withdrawn from the circular process or readily obtained from outside. Whether or not such problems are easy or difficult depends largely on two factors: (1) the corporation's profit or loss experience, and (2) its rate of expansion. Let us see how these factors apply in a variety of situations.

Profitable Corporations Not Expanding

Corporations that consistently operate at a profit while having no occasion or intention to expand the scale of their operations must tend constantly to build up an excess supply of cash in their circular processes. Without loss of efficiency or profit-making potentialities, this excess cash can be readily withdrawn for the payment of dividends, for the repayment of debts, for the replacement of fixed assets, or for other purposes. The tasks of their financial managers are likely to be not at all nerve-racking.

With each complete movement of the circular flow, such a corporation will have a *cash throw-off* equal to the amount of its profit (before the deduction of income taxes) plus the amount of its bookkeeping charges for depreciation, depletion, and amortization. Assume that a manufacturing corporation produces goods at a total cost of $448,000 and sells them for $500,000. Included in the total cost of $448,000 are the costs of raw materials, direct labor, manufacturing overhead, selling, and administration of $410,000—cash outlays for all these must be made sooner or later, depending on prepayments and deferments—depreciation charges of $35,000, and an allowance for bad debts of $3,000. If the corporation collects from its customers $497,000 (indicating that its estimate of bad debts was correct, and assuming that it allows its customers no discounts for prompt payment), it will have $87,000 of cash in excess of what it currently spent in producing the goods sold. To put the matter in more significant terms, it will have $87,000 of cash in excess of what it needs to maintain production at the existing level. Thus, the corporation's cash throw-off is $87,000—an amount equal to its profit of $52,000 plus the depreciation charge of $35,000.

Of the cash throw-off of $87,000, the financial managers of this corporation would probably retain or invest in short-term securities $18,460 to enable it to pay, when due, the federal income tax on its profit.[3] They might also decide to temporarily invest in high-quality securities an amount equal to the depreciation charge, $35,000, to accumulate a fund to be used to replace the fixed assets at the expiration of their useful lives. Indeed, they might decide to invest more than this, should they expect the replacements to cost more than did the fixed assets already held. On the other hand, should replacement requirements not be expected to materialize for several years, they might decide to use the money in the meantime for other purposes, as for the repayment of debt. The balance of the cash throw-off—that portion not allocated for the payment of income taxes and for the replacement of fixed assets—would be freely disposable at the discretion of the financial managers. Probably a goodly amount would be allocated for the payment of dividends to the stockholders, and the remainder for such purposes as the repayment of debt or the retirement of preferred stock.

A pleasant aspect of the position of the corporation in the foregoing illustration—assuming its continued operation at the existing level and continued success in selling—is that a cash throw-off of approximately $87,000 would become available on the completion of each

[3]Computed at the basic tax rates in effect for the year 1968, that is, 22 percent on the first $25,000 of taxable income and 48 percent on taxable income in excess of $25,000, and ignoring the surcharge of 10 percent adopted in June, 1968, but scheduled to expire at the end of June, 1969. It is assumed that the states in which the corporation derives its income have no corporation income taxes.

round of the circular process. The exact amount of cash becoming available for withdrawal within any period would depend on the effects of prepayments and deferments of income and expenses. Nevertheless, it can be said that *eventually* in connection with each circuit approximately $87,000 of cash could be withdrawn without reducing the efficiency or profitability of the corporation's productive operations. Needless to say, the cash throw-off could vary, too, because of changes in the profit margins. For example, the corporation might not be able to increase its selling prices to absorb increases in costs; thus it might remain profitable, but at a reduced level. The financial managers might, therefore, have some rather difficult problems to cope with—but surely not nearly so difficult as those of corporations that operate in the red or that need to expand at a rapid rate.

Break-Even Corporations Not Expanding

Assuming no occasion or wish to expand the scale of operations, the financial managers of corporations that are able only to break even in their operations will be in a position to withdraw cash from the circular process. Although the gross income of a break-even corporation is, by definition, only sufficient to cover all its operating costs, including charges for depreciation, depletion and amortization, with each circuit it should have a cash throw-off equal to these charges. These cash throw-offs would most likely be accumulated for the replacement of fixed assets, probably by means of temporary investment in high-quality securities. If, then, the cost of replacing the assets turned out to be no greater than their original cost, the corporation could continue to operate without financial embarrassment for a period of many years or even of many decades. The situation would not be a happy one for the stockholders, since the corporation would have no profits out of which dividends could be paid. Accordingly, they might decide to liquidate the corporation to recover as much as possible from their profitless investment, but at any rate the threat to its life would not come from an inability to meet operating expenses or to pay off maturing liabilities.

Suppose, for example, that the corporation of the illustration given above were able to sell its output for only $448,000, of which it is able to collect only $445,000 because $3,000 of the accounts receivable turn out to be uncollectible. It could continue with the existing level of operations by the expenditure of $410,000 for materials, labor, and other out-of-pocket operating expenses, and it would have the remaining $35,000, equal to the charges for depreciation, available for withdrawal from the circular process.

Loss Corporations Not Expanding

Any corporation able to sell its goods at prices high enough to cover its out-of-pocket costs for materials, labor, and operating expenses plus some portion of its changes for depreciation, depletion, and amortization will have cash throw-offs equal to the amounts by which the last three charges are covered. If such a corporation has no occasion or wish to expand, it ought to be able to continue in operation without financial embarrassment, except embarrassment in the sense of not being able to pay dividends, until such time that the fixed assets must be replaced. Should the corporation of our illustration be able to sell its goods for only $425,000 and to collect only $422,000 from its customers, it would be covering its depreciation charges to the extent of $12,000, and this, of course, would be the amount of each cash throw-off. While such a sum would doubtless prove to be quite inadequate for the replacement of the fixed assets, it could be withdrawn with each round of the circular process without interfering with current operations at the existing level.

Instead of a cash throw-off, there is a cash deficit with each round of the circular process for any corporation that is unable to sell its goods at prices high enough to cover its out-of-pocket costs. Such a corporation is likely to quickly encounter serious financial difficulties. If it is to continue the current scale of operations, it must repeatedly pump money into the circular process—with each round, an amount approximately equal to the cash deficit. Likewise, it must look outside for new sources of cash for the replacement of fixed assets when that becomes necessary. Its prospects must be poor, indeed, for lenders are not to be expected to risk their money on such a losing venture, nor are stockholders likely to be willing to add more funds to an investment that has already become most unattractive to them.

Expanding Corporations

Profitable corporations that are rapidly expanding the scale of their operations are likely to find their cash throw-offs quite insufficient to meet all their requirements. The problem facing their financial managers is not one of deciding what to do with the throw-offs but of finding ways to supplement them from outside sources. They may decide to trim dividends to the bone or to omit them entirely—not necessarily a wise decision—so that all or almost all the profits after provision for income taxes can be devoted to the expansion of current operations. Likewise, they would probably decide to devote to the same drive for expansion the portion of the cash throw-offs attributable to depreciation, depletion, and amortization charges—assuming, of course, no immediate need for the replacement of fixed assets.

In many instances, however, an expansion of current operations—we may also call it an expansion in the volume of the circular flow—is impossible unless there is also an expansion in the volume of fixed assets. Hence, the rapidly expanding corporation is most unlikely to be able to meet out of its cash throw-offs a need both to expand the size of the circular flow and the volume of its fixed assets. Accordingly, it will probably find it necessary to go to outside sources in a quest for funds. Its profit experience and its growth potentialities, of course, should make it attractive to lenders and, if it has not been extremely niggardly in its dividend policies, to present and prospective stockholders as well.

In break-even and loss corporations that want to expand, breaks in the circular flow will surely involve additions to cash rather than withdrawals if additions can be arranged for. The financial managers of such corporations will doubtless look everywhere for new sources of cash, although they may not succeed in finding them. In most instances of this kind, the financial managers find themselves in a vicious circle. The very reason their corporations have been operating at or below the break-even point is that they have not been able to reach a volume of production and sales that would put them in a profitable position; yet, their very lack of profitability tends to make lenders look on them as questionable risks, and to make stockholders and prospective stockholders shy away from buying additional issues of their stock. Expanding the scale of operations would make possible a spreading of fixed and semivariable overhead expenses over a larger quantity of produced goods, thereby reducing costs of production per unit of output; yet, the money to make possible the expansion may be difficult to come by. Cash throw-offs, representing the portion of depreciation, depletion, and amortization charges that is covered by sales proceeds, may be quite inadequate to finance expansion of the scope that is needed—and especially so, of course, if the expansion requires both an increase in the size of the circular flow and additions to fixed assets.

THE SCOPE OF BUSINESS ACTIVITIES

Patterns of cash flow—and, therefore, of cash requirements—differ greatly among business enterprises according to the nature of their respective operations, the seasonality and secular trend of these operations, and the competitive situation in which each business finds itself.

Nature of Operations

For an understanding of variations in cash-flow patterns related to the nature of operations, let us compare the positions of manufacturing and mercantile firms.

Manufacturing Firms. As a rule, the circular processes of manufacturing enterprises are slower than those of firms engaged in mercantile operations or in providing services; hence, the cash requirements of manufacturing establishments are generally higher *for a given volume of total sales.* Manufacturing operations are time-consuming—

sometimes long drawn out, especially if goods in process must be aged—and selling the finished product may require as much time for a manufacturer as for a merchant. Thus, the circular flow of the manufacturer who sells on account spans three time intervals—the time required for manufacturing, the time required for selling, and

FIGURE 6–1
Cash Flows of a Manufacturing Firm

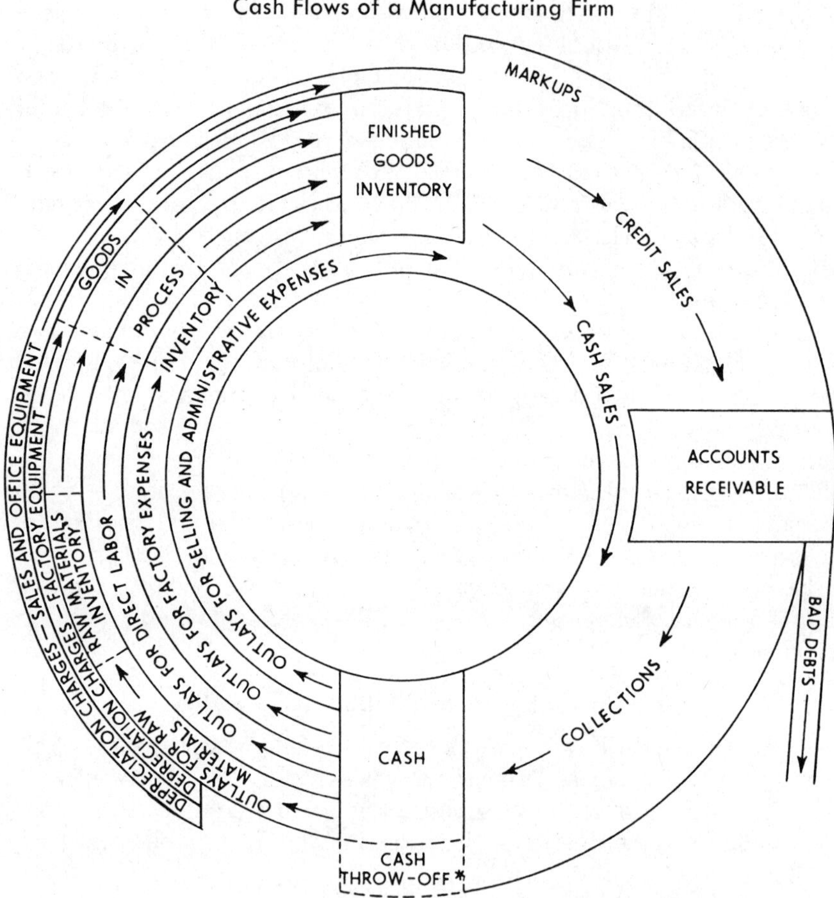

*Equal to the sum of net profit before income taxes and depreciation charges; available for income tax payments, dividends, expansion in the volume of the circular process, investment in fixed assets, repayment of debt, and so on.

the time required for the collection of payments from customers—while that of a merchant who sells on account spans only the second and third of these intervals. To put the comparison on a different basis, one may say that the manufacturer who sells on account must invest in raw materials, goods-in-process, and finished goods inventories and in accounts receivable, whereas the merchant who sells on account has only to invest in finished goods and accounts receivable. Difference in the circular flows of manufacturing firms and mercantile firms, both types selling on account, can be seen by a comparison of Figures 6–1 and 6–2.

FIGURE 6–2
Cash Flows of a Mercantile Firm

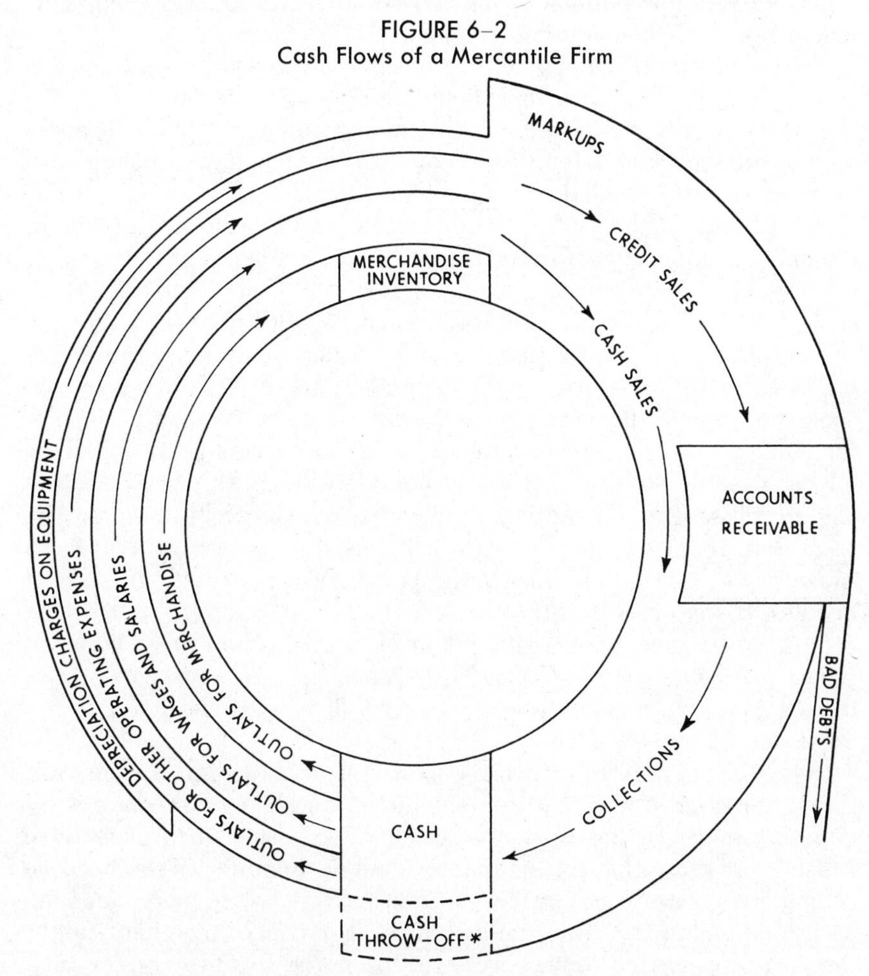

*Equal to the sum of net profit before income taxes and depreciation charges; available for income tax payments, dividends, expansion in the volume of the circular process, investment in fixed assets, repayment of debt, and so on.

Among manufacturing enterprises themselves, important differences in the circular flow occur because of very wide variations in the time required to turn out finished products. The flow must necessarily be slow—cash requirements must be relatively high for a given volume of sales—when goods in process must be aged for months or even years, as in the tobacco and distilling businesses, or when much time is needed to complete all the multifarious details of turning out the completed product, as in shipbuilding. On the other hand, manufacturers able to complete within a few hours or days the total productive process because of assembly-line methods or because the productive process, by its very nature, is a simple one may complete their circular flows much more rapidly than do the merchants to whom they sell their finished products.

Although it is the preponderant policy of American manufacturers to sell their goods on account, some are able to speed up the circular flow of their current assets by selling on a cash basis. Thus, our automobile producers have long been noted for their policy of selling only on the basis of immediate cash payment.

Mercantile Firms. As with manufacturers, wide variations in circular flows occur among mercantile establishments on account of the myriad varieties of the products they sell. Some kinds of goods, such as fresh fruits and vegetables, must be sold quickly if they are to be sold at all; others, such as most kinds of apparel, move less quickly but by no means slowly; and still others, such as household tools and many other kinds of hardware, move rather slowly. Therefore, much attention is given to inventory turnovers as an indicator of the speed or slowness of circular flows in different kinds of mercantile establishments. Inventory turnover is computed by dividing the total cost of sales for a year or other period of time by the average inventory (at cost) held during the period. To effect a given volume of sales, therefore, a firm that has an annual turnover of 2 must have a much larger average investment in inventories than one whose annual turnover is, say, 5. To put this proposition in alternative form, once again, the circular flow of the first firm must be much slower than that of the second.[4]

A significant way by which mercantile firms can control their cash flows, and therby alter the amount of their cash requirements, is by choosing to sell or not to sell on account. As a rule, such firms have much more discretion in this matter than do manufacturers, because selling on account is not nearly so universal a policy in merchandising as in manufacturing. In some instances, it is true, a merchant might lose many of his customers were he to choose to sell only for cash while all his competitors were selling on account. In many mercantile lines, however, it appears that the choice can be rather freely made. Witness the operation, side by side, of independent grocers who sell on account and chain stores that insist on a cash-and-carry basis.

Seasonality and Secular Trend

Seasonality. Wide variations in the cash flows of business enterprises occur not only because of the almost limitless diversity of their

[4]For a further discussion of inventory turnover and its significance, see pp. 160–64.

products, they also occur because of seasonal swings in production and selling. A firm that is able to produce or sell at close to a constant rate throughout the year will be likely, of course, to have a smoothly moving cash flow; its cash requirements will tend to be uniform from month to month. On the other hand, a firm whose operations are characterized by wide seasonal fluctuations will necessarily have a very jerky kind of circular flow. This will be evidenced by a large throw-off of cash at certain times, and at others a pressing need to pump into the circular process much additional cash.

Seasonality in business activity—and in cash flows and requirements—may result from the behavior of either supply or demand; although it is probably true that much more seasonality results from variations in demand than from variations in supply. Natural forces are often accountable for variations in supply. For example, processors of frozen foods and canners must concentrate their productive activities at the times when nature provides her harvests, and steel companies that are dependent on the Mesabi Range must stock up their inventories of iron ore before the lake routes freeze over. Nature also has much to do with variations in demand, as one can readily see by considering the many kinds of goods sold in great quantities in wintertime but only in driblets, if at all, in the summertime, and the many kinds whose seasonal performance is the opposite. Custom, too, causes variations in demand. The custom of gift-giving at Christmastime results in December sales for many mercantile establishments far out of line with average monthly sales for the year.

Processors of frozen foods and canners must tie up extraordinary sums of money in their inventories at harvest times; their stocks must be sufficient to meet demand until the time of the next pack. They cannot escape the seasonal pattern in these operations, although they may try to even out their production by adding product lines with different seasonal patterns. Grocers who sell frozen foods, on the other hand, may not be much bothered by the seasonal pattern of the supply of such foods, since they can buy from month to month in accordance with seasonal changes in demand. Indeed, manufacturers are generally much more burdened by seasonal fluctuations in both supply and demand than are merchants. Manufacturers must ordinarily accept the burden of accumulating large inventories of seasonal goods for the very reason that merchants refuse to accept such burdens.

Secular Trend. The secular trend of an industry is its long-run tendency to expand, contract, or remain stable in volume of output, regardless of short-run fluctuations of a seasonal, cyclical, or random character. (Cyclical fluctuations will be discussed below; random fluctuations are short-lived changes in the volume of business activity due to such events as strikes, destructive storms, and temporary shortages of raw materials.) Industries that have expanding secular trends are often described as growth industries. Happily, we have many of them, including electric power and electronics, chemicals, synthetic fibers, plastics, aerospace research and development, and recreation equipment. Industries that have a contracting secular trend are, fortunately, much fewer in number and importance. They include street railways; railroads in certain aspects of their operations, such as long-distance passenger traffic and track mileage; and some branches of the textile industry.

Growth industries tend to be chronically short of cash. Though they may be enormously profitable, profits after income taxes and dividends are likely to be most inadequate to meet the constantly recurring needs to add to both noncash current assets and fixed assets to take advantage of ever-expanding markets. Therefore, they must continually be on the lookout for new outside sources of cash for the development of their productive facilities. In industries subject to secular decline, by contrast, the individual firms, especially if they continue to operate profitably despite decreasing volume, are likely to have substantial cash throw-offs that can be safely withdrawn from the circular process. Such firms can be expected to reject as most unwise all suggestions for the investment of available cash throw-offs in existing kinds of fixed facilities. However, investments in other kinds of facilities may be judged sound and desirable, as when prospects are attractive for adding new expanding lines to take up the slack in the declining lines. In the absence of opportunities to take on new lines, the financial managers of firms in declining industries are most likely to use cash throw-offs in the payment of liquidating dividends to the stockholders as a procedure of gradually retiring their investment and gradually withdrawing from business operations.

Competitive Situation

On many occasions, the managers of business firms must adopt policies they do not like simply because their competitors have decided to adopt these policies. A comfortably situated manufacturer or merchant may take on additional product lines or develop new service facilities in the expectation of gaining a competitive advantage. He may expect his competitors to imitate his innovation, but he may hope to have succeeded in weaning away some of their customers before they have developed comparable facilities. As indicated, the competing firms may dislike the innovation, but their managers may quickly decide that they have no choice but to follow along. These firms may not be nearly so comfortably fixed as the innovator; they may, indeed, be extremely short of cash. Thus, they may be forced to look for new sources of cash for a kind of expansion hitherto regarded as outside their normal area of operation.

Where competition is not keen, the financial managers of business enterprises may find it possible to conserve cash by changing operating policies long in effect. A manufacturer may drop product lines on which he had been only breaking even, thereby making possible a reduction of his cash investment in inventories and, assuming that he sells on account, in accounts receivable. Or he may drop such lines in order to expand others on which he has substantial margins of profit. Similarly, a merchant who has been selling on account may reduce his cash requirements—speed up the circular process—by making a decision to sell henceforth only on a basis of cash on delivery.

BUSINESS CYCLE

The great majority of business firms experience alternative waves of expansion and contraction, which we know as the business cycle. Our business history clearly shows that such waves have been going on since early in the 19th century, and that each period of expansion or contraction and its succeeding period of movement in the opposite direction has lasted longer than 1 year but not more than 12 years. Thus, the business cycle is a kind of fluctuation in business activity different from seasonal fluctuations, which recur annually according to a distinct pattern, and different from the secular trend, which, as was indicated above, is a long-term tendency—usually in terms of decades—in a given direction. For example:

Severe contraction—the Depression—of 1929–33.
Postwar expansion period of 1946–48.
Contraction period—recession—from late 1948 to late 1949.
Expansion period—prosperity—from late 1949 to summer, 1953.
Contraction—recession—from summer, 1953, to late summer, 1954.
Expansion to summer, 1957.
Contraction to spring, 1958.
Expansion to spring, 1960.
Contraction to February, 1961.
Expansion continuing to as late as the summer of 1968, but with some slowdowns and faltering, as in the period from late fall, 1966, to early fall, 1967.

Cyclical Patterns

Cyclical movements in total business activity pose many problems for the financial managers of business concerns. The managers of firms in growth industries, continually on the lookout for cash to finance expansion, find their cash requirements even more pressing in periods of general business expansion. However, even they are likely to enjoy—that does not seem to be the proper word!—some respite from these pressures in times of general business contraction. Managers of firms in declining industries, by contrast, may be delighted with increasing sales in periods of cyclical expansion—they may begin to hope that their industry is no longer declining. But in periods of cyclical contraction, they may think that decline is ending in death as sales fall off to an extraordinary degree. In a similar way, a merchant whose sales have a distinct seasonal pattern may know that his December volume always tends to be about 80 percent above average monthly sales. But in a period of general business expansion, the average may be in the vicinity of $2 million and the December sales around $3.6 million, whereas in a period of contraction the average may be approximately $1 million and the December volume around $1.8 million. Obviously, it would be possible for him to make serious mistakes in accumulating inventory for the December market (and for other months as well, of course), perhaps understocking in periods of cyclical expansion so that customers must be turned away unsatisfied, and perhaps overstocking in periods of cyclical contraction so that the cash flow would be slowed in an extraordinary way because much of the inventory fails to move.

While it is generally true that cash needs become most pressing for most kinds of businesses in periods of cyclical expansion, pressures of this kind are also often experienced in periods of contraction. Inventories become slow-moving, yet the trade creditors who supplied them, the employees, and the suppliers of services must be paid. From what source does the money come to meet these obligations? Likewise, accounts receivable tend to become slow. Even customers of hitherto high credit repute, finding themselves pinched, ask for extensions of the credit period, and delays in collections are experienced whether or not extensions are granted. In this way, forecasts of collections from accounts receivable as a means of meeting a firm's own obligations may turn out to be seriously in error.

Shifts in the Price Level

Often extremely important as sources of difficulty for the financial managers of business enterprises are the price changes that take place in the course of the business cycle. The tendency is for most kinds of prices to rise in periods of general business expansion and to fall in periods of general business contraction. In some periods of expansion, the rise in prices is rapid and substantial—a development described as inflation—and in some periods of contraction the fall in prices is also rapid and substantial—then it is described as deflation. Price developments of an inflationary or deflationary degree can be expected to pose problems of greater difficulty for financial managers than those engendered by price changes of a slower or more moderate kind.

Even if all prices were to change in equal proportions in the same direction in a given period, financial problems growing out of the price developments would not be eliminated. In a period of rising prices, for example, the typical firm needs more cash even if its volume of operations is no greater than before the price rise began. In such a period, the same volume of operations requires higher cash outlays for inventories, labor, and other kinds of services, and if goods are being sold on a credit basis, accounts receivable also absorb more cash. A need to replace fixed assets adds to the difficulties, since their cost at higher prices cannot be met out of cash throw-offs resulting from depreciation charges on the lower-cost assets to be replaced. On the other hand, equal proportional increases in prices of all classes would mean increases in the amount of profits. Accordingly, the larger cash requirements for current assets, or for both current and fixed assets, might be met, at least in part, from this source.

Actually, of course, all kinds of prices do not change proportionally in a given direction in periods of general business expansion and contraction. Some prices do not change at all; some move in the same direction as the general movement, although not to the same degree, and often more slowly or more rapidly; and others even move in the direction opposite that of the general movement. Such a diversity of price changes has the effect of easing the financial problems of some business firms while intensifying those of others. A firm that is able to raise its selling prices by a greater amount than that by which its total costs increase in a period of rising prices tends to have its problems eased. Like any other firm, it must increase its cash outlays to maintain the same level of operations, but its increased margin of profit may yield sufficient additional cash for this purpose—perhaps more than a sufficient amount. Conversely, a firm that is unable to increase its selling prices by an amount to match increases in its costs has its difficulties multiplied. It must step up its cash outlays to maintain a given volume of operations while, simultaneously, its cash throw-offs on account of profits are reduced.

QUESTIONS

1. How does investment in inventories affect the cash requirements of business enterprises? Does it matter whether or not the inventoried goods are bought on account? Explain.

2. In what sense do business firms tie up cash permanently in inventories and accounts receivable?

3. Even though a firm's operations are not expanding, its cash needs are likely to expand in periods of rising prices. Is this proposition true or false? Explain.

4. Explain how it is possible for accounts payable to trade suppliers to be a source of cash for operations other than inventory acquisitions.

5. In what sense do the employees of business firms make permanent contributions to the firms' assets and thereby reduce their need of cash?

6. Is it not rather ridiculous to claim that governments, in the process

of levying and collecting taxes, make contributions to the assets of business firms? Discuss.

7. Why is the cash required to carry accounts receivable related to their dollar amount rather than equal to this amount exactly?

8. What is the nature of cash throw-offs? What do they amount to for a corporation that operates at a profit? For one that breaks even? For one that operates at a loss?

9. How often do the cash throw-offs of a firm occur?

10. What kinds of financial difficulties, if any, are likely to be encountered by break-even corporations that have no need to expand operations? By break-even corporations that must expand operations if they are to become profitable?

11. For equal volumes of sales, why do manufacturing firms generally have cash needs greater than those of mercantile firms?

12. Distinguish between supply and demand forces as causes of seasonality in business activity and cash flows. Why do these forces tend to affect manufacturers more severely than merchants?

13. What is the nature of the secular trend in given lines of business activity? How does it influence the cash requirements of individual enterprises?

14. Explain how the cash needs of individual firms are likely to be affected by differing competitive situations in their respective industries.

15. What is a business cycle? When does it occur? How long does it last? What effects does it have on the cash needs of business firms?

Part III

ASSET MANAGEMENT

chapter 7

THE MANAGEMENT OF CASH AND SHORT-TERM INVESTMENTS

We now have in mind:

1. The processes by which cash flows in and out of individual business firms.
2. How cash movements—and therefore cash requirements—are affected by prepayments and deferments of income and expenses, seasonal patterns of operation, the forces of secular growth and decline, competitive factors, and cyclical developments in general business activity.
3. How cash requirements vary according to the nature of operations, as, for example, between manufacturing and mercantile enterprises.
4. How cash throw-offs become available.

So we are prepared to turn our attention to a detailed study of the use of cash in the acquisition and maintenance of the more important kinds of business assets. How cash is to be so used depends on the asset management policies that the directors and officers of individual enterprises decide on. Hence, our investigation of the use of cash will be an investigation of asset management policies, as presented in this chapter and the next three chapters.

At the outset, it is well to repeat[1] that the payment of all kinds of business operating expenses is really a procedure of acquiring assets. This is clearly seen in factory operations, where the costs of raw materials, direct labor, and overhead expenses find their way into the valuation of inventories of goods in process and finished goods. But it is no less true of selling and administrative expenses. Business firms expect to cover all such expenses in the selling prices of their products; hence they are, by implication, also included in the valuation of

[1]See p. 72.

inventories of finished goods, whether such goods are produced by the firms themselves or are bought for resale. One should not lose sight of this essential fact, even though in accounting statements selling and administrative expenses are not shown as being included in inventories or in accounts receivable. Making payments for advertising, delivery costs, or office salaries is just as much an acquisition of assets as is buying factory, store, or office equipment. It follows, therefore, that business managers must be as careful in controlling expenses as they are in the formulation and execution of policies that are concerned with the acquisition and maintenance of things specifically labeled as assets.

ASSET MANAGEMENT IN GENERAL

Considering the diversity of the scope of operations among our millions of business firms, the many varieties of their seasonal patterns, the varied influences of secular growth and decline, the diverse effects of cyclical developments in general business activity, the wide differences in the degrees of competition among firms and industries, and variations among firms in their access to new sources of cash, it is patently impossible to formulate a set of asset management rules or policies that would be good for all businesses at all times. Indeed, a most reasonable conclusion is that asset management policies that are good for a given firm at a given time may be quite bad for another at that time, as well as for the firm itself at other times when surrounding circumstances have changed.

Accordingly, our study of asset management policies must be confined to an analysis of the principal theories the financial manager should know about and the principal problems he is likely to encounter in arriving at decisions about the best uses of cash in investment in the various classes of assets. Our interest must be devoted basically to the kinds of materials the financial manager has to work with rather than to an attempt to tell him what is the best thing he can do in given circumstances. We will find it especially desirable to give attention to alternative policies among which financial managers may choose, for policy determination is usually not a discovery of ideal solutions to problems but one of compromise, as when we say that we can have more of one thing if we are satisfied to get along with less of another.

Conservation of Cash

Although it is impossible to formulate a set of asset management policies of universal applicability, one policy or rule that appears to be unanimously accepted is that cash must be conserved. Few businesses, even the wealthiest, have sufficient cash to do all the things they want to do. Financial managers, therefore, must be constantly on the lookout for ways to reduce cash requirements—to economize in its use. Whether it is better to buy or to rent equipment, to expand one class of assets rather than another, to use cash for expansion or to pay dividends—problems such as these arise because available cash is limited in amount and must be used sparingly. Another way of looking at the rule of conservation of cash is to say that, because cash is expensive it ought to be acquired and used with caution. In the case of corporations, cash can be acquired from stockholders on a continuing basis ordinarily only if there are good prospects that they will be rewarded through the distribution of reasonable dividends. Cash can be acquired from lenders only on the basis of an obligation to pay interest and an obligation to repay the principal of loans. The interest is an additional expense of operation in any case. Moreover, either the principal or the interest obligation can turn out to be a most expensive one, in the sense that it may threaten the very existence of the corporation should difficulty in meeting it result from an inept use of the cash.

Statistics of Corporate Assets

Before we take up a detailed analysis of what the financial managers of corporations may decide in the formulation of asset management policies, we should find it worthwhile to look at what they have actually been doing. Their decisions are revealed (but in part only, of course) in the actual distributions of assets as disclosed in their balance sheets. Excellent statistics of corporate asset distributions, as compiled from balance sheets submitted with federal income tax returns, are published annually by the Internal Revenue Service of the Treasury Department. In Table 7–1, for fiscal years ending between July 1, 1964, and June 30, 1965, data of this kind are presented for broad industrial groups of corporations and their total (with some exceptions as noted in a footnote to the table).[2]

The relationships indicated by these figures can be taken as being reasonably definitive. Shifts in the position of particular assets in relation to one another and to the respective totals can be expected to take place from year to year; yet, one has no reason to expect a pronounced shifting in any short period of years, except, perhaps, between periods of high prosperity and depression of considerable severity. But the data probably underemphasize the importance of inventories and possibly accounts receivable, and accordingly over-

[2]One can consult the *Statistics of Income* reports of the Treasury for the data of subgroups within the broad classifications. For example, within the retail trade classification will be found separate data for corporations in each of the following business areas: foods; general merchandise; apparel and accessories; furniture, home furnishings, and equipment; automotive dealers and gasoline stations; eating and drinking places; building materials, hardware, and farm equipment; and miscellaneous retail stores.

TABLE 7–1

Classes of Assets of Business Corporations in 1964–65*
(Dollar amounts in millions)

Classes of Assets	Agriculture, Forestry, Fisheries		Mining		Contract Construction		Manufacturing		Public Utilities		Wholesale Trade		Retail Trade		Services		All Groups†	
	Amount	Per-cent	Amount	Per-cent	Amount	Per-cent	Amount	Per-cent	Amount	Per-cent	Amount	Per-cent	Amount	Per-cent	Amount	Per-cent	Amount	Per-cent
Cash	$ 359	5.6	$ 1,232	7.0	$ 2,356	10.1	$ 17,817	5.3	$ 4,023	2.3	$ 4,087	8.1	$ 5,132	8.4	$ 2,545	8.5	$ 37,551	5.4
Notes and accounts receivable	829	12.8	2,673	15.1	7,744	33.2	67,449	20.2	7,384	4.2	17,823	35.3	15,005	24.6	5,017	16.8	123,924	17.7
Inventories	697	10.8	939	5.3	3,013	12.9	68,108	20.3	3,471	2.0	14,864	29.5	19,569	32.1	1,546	5.2	112,207	16.1
Investments—government obligations	75	1.2	713	4.0	359	1.5	12,752	3.8	4,482	2.6	423	.8	447	.7	470	1.6	19,721	2.8
Other current assets	83	1.3	427	2.4	2,384	10.2	6,203	1.9	3,879	2.2	844	1.7	1,249	2.0	755	2.5	15,824	2.3
Other investments	807	12.5	2,239	12.6	1,744	7.5	40,735	12.2	8,480	4.8	4,560	9.0	4,039	6.6	3,282	11.0	65,886	9.4
Depreciable assets	1,918	29.7	6,226	35.1	3,983	17.1	102,285	30.5	138,416	79.1	5,480	10.9	11,641	19.1	12,820	42.8	282,769	40.5
Depletable assets	57	.9	2,112	11.9	59	.3	4,517	1.3	118	.1	209	.4	14	‡	30	.1	7,116	1.0
Land	1,406	21.8	336	1.9	732	3.1	5,176	1.5	1,407	.8	914	1.8	1,769	2.9	1,831	6.1	13,571	1.9
Intangible assets	3	‡	227	1.3	14	.1	1,445	.4	142	.1	55	.1	80	.1	160	.5	2,126	.3
Other assets	220	3.4	601	3.4	921	4.0	8,702	2.6	3,110	1.8	1,212	2.4	2,004	3.3	1,496	5.0	18,266	2.6
Total Current Assets	$2,043	31.7	$ 5,984	33.8	$15,856	67.9	$172,329	51.5	$ 23,239	13.3	$38,041	75.4	$41,402	67.9	$10,333	34.5	$309,227	44.3
Total fixed Assets	4,411	68.3	11,741	66.2	7,453	32.1	162,860	48.5	151,673	86.7	12,430	24.6	19,547	32.1	19,619	65.5	389,734	55.7
Total Assets	$6,453	100.0	$17,724	100.0	$23,309	100.0	$335,189	100.0	$174,913	100.0	$50,471	100.0	$60,949	100.0	$29,951	100.0	$698,959	100.0
Number of income tax returns	25,933		14,487		104,134		184,961		56,338		142,603		272,166		176,902		977,524	

*Active corporations filing federal income tax returns for fiscal years ending between July 1, 1964, and June 30, 1965, excluding corporations engaged in trade not allocated to wholesale or retail; in finance, insurance, and real estate; and in miscellaneous operations not classified as to industry. Receivables as reduced by reserves for bad debts, and depreciable and depletable assets as reduced by allowances for depreciation and depletion, respectively. Total current and fixed assets as computed by the author, classifying the first five items as current assets and the remainder as fixed assets. In some instances, vertical items do not add exactly to totals because of rounding. Percentages supplied by the author.

†With exceptions as indicated in preceding footnote.

‡Less than 0.05 percent.

SOURCE: U.S. Treasury Department, Internal Revenue Service, *Statistics of Income, 1964—U.S. Business Tax Returns* (Washington, D.C.: U.S. Government Printing Office, 1967). pp. 107–13.

emphasize the importance of cash and investment in government securities. These probabilities and possibilities must be recognized because many corporations select slack seasons for the ends of their fiscal years, so that the balance sheets that accompany their income tax returns necessarily reveal slack-season arrays of assets. These corporations want to minimize the burden of inventory-taking and valuation, and this is most feasible in slack seasons when the inventories are at or close to their lowest levels. In such periods, too, accounts receivable balances may be unusually low, because many customers have already paid for their purchases on account in preceding brisk periods.

Despite these cautionary remarks, the following relationships as indicated by the tabular data appear to be noteworthy.

1. A division between current and fixed assets in the totality of corporations only moderately favoring the fixed.
2. The substantial holdings of cash and government securities (mostly short term, one presumes) by all industrial groups except public utilities.
3. The very high proportions of current assets in the construction and wholesale and retail trade groups.
4. The very high proportion of fixed assets in the public utility group as well as the relatively high proportion in mining and among the service corporations.
5. The position of inventories as the largest current asset in the manufacturing and retail trade groups.
6. The extraordinarily high proportion of receivables to total assets in the construction industry and in wholesale trade, its very low level among public utilities, and its substantial level in all other groups.
7. The wide divergence of the pattern of asset distribution of public utilities from that of each of the other groups, as well as from that of the overall totals.

CASH

It may appear that a corporation's cash position must depend on all its asset management policies—that it must be the resultant of all the decisions concerning investment in noncash assets, borrowing, payment of dividends, and so on. Nevertheless, certain policies with respect to cash balances themselves must be formulated—policies, one may say, not immediately related to other kinds of asset management decisions. Such purely cash policies include all the rules established for the protection of cash while it is in a corporation's possession (rules of the kinds briefly discussed in Chapter 4), together with the standards set for minimum and maximum cash balances, precautions exercised to avoid the special federal tax on "unreasonable accumulations of surplus," and rules for the investment of cash temporarily in excess supply.

Minimum Balances

The financial managers of most corporations set a figure below which they do not want cash balances to fall at any time except in periods of emergency. The idea is that no matter how large cash outlays must be at certain times or in certain circumstances, except for emergencies, cash in excess of the established minimum should be available to meet these outlays, so that the minimum need not be encroached on.

Emergencies. As indicated, the possible occurrence of emergencies is a reason for setting a standard of minimum balances, although, as we shall see later, it is not the only reason. The most common kind of emergency planned for is an extraordinary slowing down of the cash inflow from normal sources during periods when customary outlays must continue to be made. In a period of business recession, the sales volume may fall off both sharply and suddenly, and many accounts receivable, hitherto judged to be of high quality, may turn out to be slow; yet, the corporation's obligations to make current cash payments may not be appreciably diminished. For minimum balance standards, therefore, financial managers often set levels of cash holdings that would enable their corporations to meet the normal outflow for a period of two or three weeks, or a month, or perhaps as long as two months, even should the normal inflow of cash from operations come to a complete halt.

Credit Standing with Trade Creditors. A second reason financial managers decide to have at all times, except in emergencies, cash balances not less than stimulated sums is to maintain their corporations' credit standings with trade creditors. As a matter of course, a corporation will take advantage of opportunities to buy goods and supplies on account, but suppliers do not, as a matter of course, sell on account to every corporation that asks for such accommodations. The suppliers' decisions to sell or not to sell on account will be based on analyses of a prospective buyer's credit position. In other words, they will evaluate his position to determine whether or not he has or will have the capacity to pay within the allowed credit period. Because suppliers are almost always short-term creditors, they are inclined to concentrate attention on the buyer's *working capital position*. Working capital is defined as the net difference between the total of a firm's current assets and the total of its current liabilities. Its working capital position is, accordingly, the total array of the kinds and amounts of its current assets and the kinds and amounts of its current liabilities. This array is important to the trade supplier because the goods sold will be added to the buyer's current assets, and his claim for payment will be added to the buyer's current liabilities.

In analyzing a prospective buyer's working capital position, the trade supplier will unquestionably give particular attention to cash holdings. Suppose, for example, that Corporations A and B have working capital positions as follows.

CORPORATION A

Current assets:		Current liabilities:	
Cash	$ 5,000	Accounts payable	$40,000
Accounts receivable	60,000	Accrued wages	5,000
Inventories	75,000	Other accrued expenses	15,000
Total Current Assets	$140,000	Total Current Liabilities	$60,000

CORPORATION B

Current assets:		Current liabilities:	
Cash	$ 25,000	Accounts payable	$40,000
Accounts receivable	40,000	Accrued wages	5,000
Inventories	75,000	Other accrued expenses	15,000
Total Current Assets	$140,000	Total Current Liabilities	$60,000

Suppose, further, that each of these corporations wants to buy $20,000 worth of goods on account from a certain supplier. It may appear, at first glance, that both corporations are equally creditworthy: they have equal amounts of current assets and current liabilities, so that the dollar amounts of their working capital are likewise equal. But the supplier would not be satisfied with first glances. He would surely notice that Corporation A could pay off only 8⅓ percent of its existing current liabilities out of its cash resources, and only 6¼ percent should a liability to him of $20,000 be added; whereas Corporation B could pay off 41⅔ percent of its existing current liabilities, and 31¼ percent were a liability of $20,000 to be added. Though he might not reject A's application for credit, surely he would be much less inclined to grant it (aside from other considerations) than to grant that of B.

For the sole purpose of making their working capital positions look better, some corporations (as well as business enterprises of other legal forms) at times borrow money before submitting their balance sheets to prospective trade creditors. Any action that is specifically designed to improve the look of the working capital position for credit purposes, but does not actually strengthen that position, is often described as window dressing. A short-term loan does not increase the amount of a firm's working capital, since it adds equal amounts to current assets and current liabilities, but the augmentation of the cash account tends to make the firm's situation look more favorable. Had Corporation A of the foregoing illustration borrowed, say, $10,000 from a commercial bank, the current section of its balance sheet (disregarding whatever discount the bank might have charged) would have appeared as follows.

CORPORATION A

Current assets:		Current liabilities:	
Cash	$ 15,000	Accounts payable	$40,000
Accounts receivable	60,000	Notes payable	10,000
Inventories	75,000	Accrued wages	5,000
		Other accrued expenses	15,000
Total Current Assets	$150,000	Total Current Liabilities	$70,000

In this way, the corporation would have had cash equal to 21³⁄₇ percent of its current liabilities even as increased by the obligation to the lending bank, and equal to 16⅔ percent were a further liability of $20,000 to the supplier to be added.

Good Bank Relations. Maintaining good relations with the commercial banks from which they borrow is a third reason why business enterprises establish standards for minimum cash balances. Commercial bankers preach the doctrine that their lending capacity comes chiefly from the deposits left with them by customers rather than from the capital accounts of their stockholders, and that firms that want to borrow should contribute to this lending capacity by leaving substantial deposit balances with them. Bankers are especially devoted to this doctrine in times of tight money—that is, when the volume of acceptable loan applications exceeds their capacity to lend. In such periods, they are likely to be generous in granting loans to firms that customarily maintain sizable deposit balances, and to be rather niggardly toward firms not so qualifying, assuming that they are willing to do anything at all for them.

Often too, particularly in periods of tight money, commercial banks stipulate in loan contracts that *while the loan is outstanding* the borrower must not let his deposit balance fall below some percentage of the loan, perhaps 10 or 15 percent, or perhaps as much as 20 percent. Such compensatory balances undoubtedly enable banks to individually grant larger volumes of loans than otherwise would be possible[3]—to take care of a larger number of their customers—and give them interest income at higher rates than the rates stated in the loan contracts. For the borrower, however, there are commensurate burdens in his inability to use the entire proceeds of the loan and in the pay-

[3]But the lending capacity of the commercial banking system as a whole is not thereby increased, since that depends on the amount of the system's own cash (primary) reserves. Thus, the fact that an individual bank is able to increase its lending capacity by the enforcement of a compensatory balance rule means that the lending capacity of other banks is held to a level below what it otherwise would tend to be.

ment of a higher rate of interest than the named rate on the portion of the proceeds that he is actually permitted to use. In setting standards for their cash balances, at any rate, the financial managers of business enterprises must obviously give attention to bankers' attitudes toward deposit balances, as indicated both in their preachments and in their actual demands for compensatory balances in connection with loan contracts.

Although maintenance of substantial cash balances with commercial banks to qualify for loans, or in relation to loans already obtained, appears to work a hardship on firms that borrow, there is usually a savings factor to be considered. Most banks levy service charges on each depositor measured in relation to the volume of clerical operations involved in handling his account. The charges are assessed at a few cents for each item handled—for checks and other cash items deposited in an account, checks drawn on the account, deposit slips, checks certified, and promissory notes taken for collection—and at quantity rates on the amount of paper money and coin deposited. But the banks generally reduce total service charges as thus computed by giving the customer a credit in proportion to his average deposit balance, the idea being that because customers' deposits contribute to the banks' earning capacity they can afford to allow them free services in proportion to these deposits. Accordingly, the financial managers of business firms may conclude that their deposit balances pay their way by reducing or eliminating bank service charges that otherwise would be assessed.

Minimum Standards in Periods of Tight Money. In periods of tight money, financial managers face strong temptations to relax whatever standards for minimum cash balances they have previously maintained. This is so because such periods are generally characterized by high levels of business activity.[4] As their sales expand, many firms find that additional cash requirements tend to exceed by far the throw-offs becoming available through the circular process. As workers are added to payrolls and as, perhaps, wage rates are increased, more money must be made available; inventories must be expanded, probably at higher prices; and more money must be tied up in accounts receivable. In such circumstances, every effort must be made to use cash as efficiently as possible, and holding idle balances, in keeping with an established standard, may not appear to be a very efficient way of doing things. Financial managers may even conclude that the prompt use of all their cash will preclude a need to borrow, so that they can afford to ignore bankers' preachments and compensatory

---

[4]Historically, the principal exceptions have been periods of tight money occasioned by financial crises in depressions, as in 1893, 1907, and 1932–33.

balance rules. Borrowing at the high rates of interest that usually prevail in periods of tight money while holding idle cash balances may look like an unsound policy.

Nevertheless, arguments for holding to the established cash standards appear to be much stronger than those for relaxation. These include the need of maintaining credit standing with trade suppliers at a time when dependence on them is presumably growing, the possibility of needing to borrow after cash balances have been exhausted and of finding nobody willing to lend, and, most important of all, the possibility that business activity will abruptly turn downward, perhaps causing the very kind of emergency for which minimum standards are primarily designed.

Maximum Balances

The financial managers of many establishments have no occasion to worry about setting upper limits to their cash balances. They are well pleased if they succeed in having only sufficient cash to meet requirements for current outlays plus the amounts of the minimums they have established. But many firms tend to accumulate cash far beyond what they need for current outlays and to satisfy minimum balance standards. For many, the accumulations are purely temporary ones, so that no difficult problem of cash management arises. This is particularly true of the accumulations that take place in the slack seasons of businesses whose operations fluctuate substantially each year according to seasonal patterns. All that is required is the holding of the excess cash or its temporary investment in high-quality, short-term securities until needed for the more active seasons. Other enterprises, however, tend to chronically accumulate excess cash; these are generally highly successful enterprises, large and small, that are not expanding at a fast pace, if they are expanding at all. Their cash throw-offs, after allowing for the continuance of the circular process, the replacement of fixed assets, the payment of income taxes, and the distribution of generous dividends to the stockholders, constantly tend to pile up funds well beyond the minimum standards. What should be done with these funds?

In seeking an answer to this question, the financial managers should not lose sight of the fact that cash is an expensive asset and that, as always, the rule of cash conservation should be applied. Idle funds are expensive in the sense that if they cannot be used profitably in a given business they are likely to be usable profitably elsewhere; hence, income possibilities are probably being lost as long as the funds continue to be held idle. If there is every assurance that a corporation's working capital position would be quite strong without such funds, and if there is no reasonable opportunity to use them profitably in expanding operations, they should unquestionably be distributed to the stockholders. To give the stockholders the opportunity to dispose of the cash as they might choose would surely be more fitting than to have the directors substitute their own choice, such as investing the excess money in securities of unrelated corporations.

However, the financial managers of corporations that enjoy strong cash positions are inclined to be quite generous in their estimates of cash requirements. Minimum balances that might be needed for emergencies are likely to be very generously estimated, and the concept of emergency itself is likely to be expanded to cover many kinds of possibilities not ordinarily envisaged when that term is employed. Thus, the financial managers may think of the convenience of having large amounts of ready cash available should inventions and innovations make necessary a transformation of operating facilities and procedures, should opportunities arise for buying out competing firms on favorable terms, or should a general business depression of unusual severity develop. It may be that the financial managers would be quite right in so thinking. At any rate, recent trends, as seen particularly in large corporations, have been in the direction of the accumulation of cash balances and holdings of short-term, high-quality investments well beyond what appears to be necessary for quite safe working capital positions.

The holding of cash and short-term investments in amounts in excess of reasonable requirements is often criticized as tending to weaken the sense of responsibility of business managers. If liberal dividends are already being paid to the stockholders, the managers may feel that their principal obligation to the stockholders has been fulfilled; accordingly, they may think themselves at liberty to use the remaining excess cash in trying out new projects. Their vigilance in seeking ways to cut costs may be greatly reduced. Indeed, they may be quite extravagant in replacing fixed assets that have many years of useful life remaining, in furnishing their own office quarters, in wining and dining customers and prospective customers, and so on. On the other hand, net profit as *a rate of return on total assets* tends to be reduced if cash (or any other asset) is superabundant. Hence, the managers, realizing that their stewardship may be judged by a comparison of this rate of return with that of other corporations, may prefer to pass on excess cash to the stockholders rather than to use it extravagantly.

Cash Holdings and Special Taxation

Directly related to the determination of policies for maximum cash balances is a need to exercise precautions to avoid taxation according to the terms of Sections 531–537 of the federal Internal Revenue Code. As was pointed out in Chapter 2, this legislation places a special tax on corporations found to be unreasonably accumulating surplus to enable stockholders to avoid the high rates of the individual income tax. Although much of the burden of proving that a given corporation is unreasonably retaining income for the purpose of tax avoidance falls on the Internal Revenue Service, the holding of cash and short-term investments[5] well in excess of the corporation's current or prospective needs for regular operations would surely be strong evidence of such a purpose. A corporation that has large amounts of excess cash and large accumulating surplus balances but only vague ideas about future expansion would be likely to find itself in a vulnerable position.

One must remember, of course, that there is no typically close relationship between the size of a corporation's cash account and the size of its surplus account or accounts. A corporation that has large amounts of cash and little surplus cannot be reached by the provisions of Sections 531–537. Such a corporation may be one in a declining industry; the conditions of these were examined in Chapter 6. On the other hand, a corporation that has what appears to be excess amounts of cash as well as a large surplus account may have real difficulty in trying to refute charges of unreasonably accumulating surplus.

Investment of Excess Cash

A most remarkable development of the past 15 years, roughly speaking, has been the ever-increasing attention given by many corporate managements—especially the managements of large corporations—to the short-term investment of idle cash. The treasurers of many corporations have been hailed for their astuteness in controlling their corporations' money position, as they have constantly sought to pick up a few dollars of interest income by investing idle cash for three or four days, or as they have chosen one kind of investment security rather than another to gain an interest rate differential of perhaps one fourth of a percentage point. Although the amount of interest to be earned on each dollar of a weekend investment may seem to be infinitesimal, interest earned in a year can amount to a tidy supplement to income from sales if the investments of very short term involve many hundreds of thousands or millions of dollars and if the transactions can be repeated frequently in the course of the year. After all, each year has 52 weekends and some have 53! A government securities dealer has remarked: "Some financial men earn more by investing idle corporate cash over a weekend than some operating divisions can earn in a week."[6]

---

[5]Although we are interested here chiefly in excessive holdings of cash or its alternative, short-term, high-quality securities, heavy investment in stocks or long-term bonds unrelated to the investing corporation's purposes, as indicated in its articles of incorporation, might also be taken as evidence of unreasonable accumulation of surplus.

[6]*The New York Times*, June 15, 1963, p. 27.

Corporate treasurers who think along the lines suggested above generally have the attitude that while minimum cash balances must constantly be planned for, substantial portions of them from time to time can safely take forms other than cash itself. They are encouraged to invest portions of these balances even for a few days because of the widespread availability of short-term investment outlets of virtually riskless character—outlets to be discussed in the following pages.

Other corporate treasurers—perhaps they could be said to be more conservative—are inclined to argue that the bother of investing for a few days portions of what are supposed to be minimum cash balances is not compensated for by the interest earned. But they readily agree that there can be no excuse for the idleness of funds held for tax payments to be disbursed in a month or two, for meeting a sinking-fund payment on a bond issue due in a month or two, or for other such outlays of some degree of remoteness. Similarly, almost all treasurers would surely agree that temporary investment is imperative for cash accumulated by seasonal enterprises during their slack periods, as well as for that being assembled by any enterprise for the future expansion of the scale of its operations. A corporation, for example, may sell additional stock or float a bond issue to finance the acquisition of additional fixed assets, but a considerable period of time may be expected to elapse between the date when the proceeds of the sale of the securities will be received and the date on which payment for the fixed assets must be made. The wisdom of bridging the two dates by the temporary investment of the cash could hardly be questioned.

SHORT-TERM INVESTMENTS

To put temporarily idle cash to work in earning interest, the financial managers of business corporations generally choose among short-term obligations of the federal Treasury, certain additional kinds of short-term paper of very high quality, time deposits in commercial banks, and, especially in smaller corporations, share accounts in savings and loan associations. They conclude that their choice must be in the direction of something that is as good as cash in the sense of safety and, of course, has the additional advantage of providing a return. The watchword is that safety must never be sacrificed for income.

Credit Risk and Money Rate Risk

Safety in the short-term investment of funds means two things—namely, the avoidance of credit risks and the avoidance of what is called money rate risk or interest rate risk. Credit risk is determined by the capacity of debtors to meet their obligations, while money rate risk develops from fluctuations in the market prices of obligations due to changes in the structure of interest rates. Thus, we usually say that obligations of the Treasury are entirely free of credit risk, for nobody doubts the federal government's capacity to pay off its obligations at their face value at maturity. But the market prices of Treasury obligations fluctuate, which indicates that they are by no means free of money rate risk. Fluctuations in the market prices of Treasury obligations occur, not because of anything that the Treasury does or does not do; they fluctuate, as was indicated, simply because the structure of market rates of interest changes from time to time. Treasury notes that have several years to run to maturity and bear interest at 5 percent will surely fall below par value in market price if market rates of interest rise, as would be evidenced, for example, were the Treasury to put out at par a new issue of notes with the same maturity but bearing interest at 5½ percent. If investors could buy at par a security of a certain quality and maturity paying 5½ percent, they would be most unwilling to pay par value for one of identical quality and maturity paying only 5 percent; thus, the 5 percent note would fall below par value to a level where the return on the two note issues would be equalized![7]

If investment securities must be sold at prices less than the purchase prices due to a rise in market rates of interest between the dates of purchase and resale, the losses are as hard to take as would be those resulting from the inability of debtors to pay at maturity the full amounts of their obligations. For this reason, in seeking investment outlets for idle cash corporate managers must be as zealous in avoiding money rate risks as they are in avoiding credit risks. They can avoid credit risks by buying only securities of the highest quality, such as Treasury obligations, but how can they avoid money rate risks? The answer is by concentrating in short-term obligations. Money rate risk is a function of time to maturity—in other words, the longer the time to maturity, the greater this risk. Thus, should the applicable market rate of interest rise from 5 percent to 5½ percent, a 5 percent obligation that had three months to run to maturity would fall in market price only from par to 99.86, whereas one that had 20 years to run would fall from par to 93.98.

Treasury Obligations

Treasury bills are the most popular medium for the temporary investment of business corporations' excess cash. Because these instruments are obligations of the federal government, they are devoid of credit risk, and because they invariably have maturities of not more than one year, money rate risk is slight. In view of the large size of our national debt, these instruments are available in abundant quantities, and the typical corporation has little difficulty in buying a suf-

[7]The equalization would come about because though the investor would be paying less than par value for the 5 percent note he would receive not only interest at 5 percent on the par value but also the par value itself as principal at maturity.

ficient amount to satisfy its requirements. At the end of February, 1968, for example, $72.9 billion of bills were outstanding, and for the same date the Treasury estimated holdings of bills by corporations other than the Federal Reserve banks and other financial institutions at $4,015 million, and their holdings of other federal obligations maturing within one year at $1,370 million. By contrast, holdings of these corporations in Treasury obligations maturing beyond one year were estimated at only $1,204 million.[8]

Bills. Two issues of bills are sold every week by the Treasury; they are offered broadside to all who may want to enter subscriptions by filing the prescribed forms at the Federal Reserve banks. The usual maturity for one issue is 91 days and for the other 182 days. In the early summer of 1968, the weekly sales of 91-day bills amounted at par value to approximately $1.6 billion, and sales of the 182-day bills were approximately $1.1 billion. In ordinary circumstances, the proceeds of the bill sales of any week are simply used by the Treasury to pay off the issue of 91-day bills sold 13 weeks earlier and the issue of 182-day bills sold 26 weeks earlier. In some periods, however, the Treasury gets new money by stepping up the amount of its weekly offerings, because it thereby takes in more than enough to pay off the earlier issues. The Treasury also makes regular monthly offerings of bills maturing in one year, and in some years it puts out special issues of tax anticipation bills, which run for periods of varying lengths since they are slated to mature on or close to important tax payment dates, such as the following March 15 or June 15. The Treasury's practice of issuing tax anticipation bills recognizes the popular corporation policy of early accumulation of cash to pay income taxes; hence, it taps this tax money in advance by means of its special offerings.

Business corporations, as well as other classes of buyers, can enter subscriptions for bills of the various issues with the Federal Reserve banks of their respective districts. Bills are sold to the highest bidders among those entering subscriptions, and are redeemed at maturity at par value. The bills do not bear interest on their face; hence, the bid price indicates the interest rate on the basis of which the subscriber is willing to buy. For example, if a corporation bids 98.750 for a quantity of 91-day bills, it indicates that it expects to earn in the period of 91 days $1.25 on each amount of $98.75 of its investment, which adds up to a rate of interest per annum of approximately 5 percent. To encourage the entry of subscriptions by corporations and other investors who do not want to make guesses about what the level of acceptable bids will be, the Treasury provides that subscriptions up to stipulated amounts, such as $200,000 for 91-day bills and $100,000 for 182-day bills, may be entered by prospective buyers

---

[8]*Federal Reserve Bulletin,* May, 1968, pp. A–38, A–39.

without the designation of bid prices. Bills to cover such subscriptions are then supplied by the Treasury at a price equal to the average of the accepted bids.

Many corporations invest in bills as well as in other classes of Treasury obligations without entering subscriptions at the Federal Reserve banks. There exists for all kinds of Treasury marketable obligations a broad, well-organized market in which a large volume of transactions takes place daily. Accordingly, a corporation can buy already outstanding Treasury obligations directly or indirectly from dealers. The existence of excellent market facilities, is of course, an important reason investment in Treasury obligations is popular among corporations. A corporation need not hold such securities till maturity if it requires cash earlier; it can simply sell them to a dealer.

Certificates. For many years before 1964, a means regularly employed by the Treasury for short-term borrowing was the issuance of certificates of indebtedness, which had maturities ranging upward from six months but never exceeding one year, and which bore interest at rates designated by the Treasury at the time of offering. Since 1964, however, the Treasury has depended very little on certificates for its short-term borrowing; it has apparently preferred its one-year bills as a substitute. When available, at any rate, certificates are as attractive for the investment of temporary excess holdings of corporate cash as other short-term Treasury obligations. Outstanding issues can be bought through banks and other dealers and brokers, and subscriptions may be entered at the Federal Reserve banks for new issues if and when offered by the Treasury.

Notes and Bonds. Two additional classes of marketable obligations issued by the Treasury are its notes and bonds. Notes are intermediate-term obligations, generally having maturities between three and seven years. Bonds are classified as long-term obligations, usually having maturities of more than 10 years and as long as 40 years, although a few issues of recent years have had maturities between 5 and 10 years. Treasury notes and bonds that are closely approaching their maturity dates have the same qualities as bills and certificates—that is, a total lack of credit risk and only a slight degree of money rate risk. Corporations, therefore, can invest in them as safely as in bills and certificates.

Corporations that are accumulating funds for intermediate- and long-term purposes, such as plant expansion to be undertaken several years hence, often invest such funds in Treasury notes and bonds that have maturities close to the time the money will be needed for the expansion projects. As the Treasury will surely pay off these obligations at par at maturity, the corporations can ignore interim fluctuations in their market prices—fluctuations likely, of course, to be much wider than those for bills and certificates.[9] On the other hand, a corporation would be ill-advised to invest cash needed in a few months in notes and bonds that have several years to run to maturity, because declines in market value due to rising rates of interest might wipe out, or more than wipe out, the interest earned on such securities. On June 28, 1968, for example, notes of the Treasury's 4¾ percent issue due in February, 1972, were selling in the market at 96⅞, and bonds of the 2½ percent issue due in December, 1972, were selling at 89 13/16.[10]

Other Short-Term Investment Paper

Other instruments or paper both readily available and attractive for the short-term investment of excess corporate cash include obligations of state and local governments, maturing bonds of high-rated business corporations, promissory notes of finance companies and other business enterprises, and time certificates of deposit issued by commercial banks (to be discussed separately below). Additionally, some large corporations are in a position to lend excess funds to dealers in government securities.

Although many of the debt instruments of state and local governments of high credit ratings outstanding at any time have maturities too lengthy to preclude money rate risk, others are short term as issued, and still others are issues or portions of issues that, though originally intermediate or long term, are closely approaching their maturity dates. At any rate, the popularity of state and local issues among corporate treasurers was indicated by estimated nonfinancial business corporation holdings of $5.1 billion at the end of 1967, as reported by the Federal Reserve authorities.[11] Always a special advantage of investment in such issues is the exemption from federal income taxes of interest earned on them.

The rates of interest that can be earned by short-term investment in the maturing bonds of high-rated business corporations are often better than can be gained for equal periods of time on Treasury obligations and obligations of state and local governments, even with the government tax-exemption feature. However, the available

---

[9]Technically, the accumulation of cash for an intermediate- or long-term objective takes the funds or the securities in which they may be invested out of the current asset classification. It is logical, therefore, to show the funds or securities, as the case may be, among the fixed assets in the corporation's balance sheet.

[10]Aubrey G. Lanston & Co., Inc., *Comparative Yields of United States Treasury Securities*, July 1, 1968, p. 2.

[11]Board of Governors of the Federal Reserve System, *Flow of Funds Accounts 1945–1967* (Washington, D.C., 1968), p. 174A.

evidence does not indicate any widespread preference for the corporate issues for this or any other reason.

Much more popular with many corporate treasurers who are inclined to invest in business rather than government paper are the promissory notes sold broadside by sales and consumer finance companies and other enterprises as means of short-term borrowing.[12] The large finance companies sell the notes through their own facilities, but the smaller companies as well as enterprises in other industrial areas usually depend on the services of specialized dealers who buy issues in bulk and then retail them to their customers. In a dealer's list of offerings, a corporate treasurer can usually find notes of qualities and maturities to meet his requirements, and he can get what he wants even more facilely in dealing with the large finance companies that market their own notes. Such a company will generally issue a note for any sum a corporation wants to advance temporarily, bearing interest at a publicly announced rate, and for any maturity requested from three days to nine months. Thus, it offers an opportunity for precisely tailored investment, including weekend arrangements.

Short-term investments by way of loans to government securities dealers usually take the form of repurchase agreements whereby the dealer sells the corporation a block of government securities at a designated price, at the same time obligating himself to buy back the selfsame securities at an agreed on time at a slightly higher price. In effect, the transaction is a loan. The government securities serve as collateral, and the differential in prices is the interest paid by the dealer and earned by the corporation.

Bank Time Deposits

Many corporations transfer temporarily idle cash balances from their demand deposit or checking accounts with the commercial banks to time deposit accounts with the same institutions. This is done because the banks are forbidden by law to pay interest on checking accounts, but they do pay interest on time accounts. The banks may be asked to carry the time deposit balances as open accounts, which are comparable to individuals' savings accounts although not usually classified as such in government regulations. Or they may be asked to issue certificates of deposit. A certificate of deposit (CD) is made payable "to the order of" the corporate depositor or to the "bearer"—whichever way the corporation wants it—and it stipulates that payment of the face amount plus interest

---

[12]Such promissory notes are generally known as open-market commercial paper, or simply commercial paper. In Chapter 33, their characteristics, marketing, and use are examined in greater detail from the standpoint of the issuers as borrowers. See pp. 857–59.

at a designated rate shall be made by the bank on a specified day on surrender of the certificate.

As an outlet for idle corporate money, bank time deposits, especially in the form of CD's, have grown mightily in popularity since the early 1960's. For many years, smaller business firms and firms of intermediate sizes had made extensive use of open accounts and CD's as means of earning a return on temporarily idle money, but the financial managers of large corporations showed relatively little interest in bank time accounts. Beginning in 1961, however, the attitude of the large corporations shifted markedly. Many metropolitan banks urged their large corporate customers to put their idle funds in CD's, and certain securities dealers helped out by announcing that they would provide market facilities for buying and selling outstanding CD's.

Further promoting the use of CD's were repeated actions of the Board of Governors of the Federal Reserve System and the Federal Deposit Insurance Corporation in raising the levels of interest rates that member banks and insured banks, respectively, were authorized to pay on time accounts. Their special favoring of CD's of large face amounts (most likely, of course, to be issued to large corporations) was indicated by maximum authorized rates in effect in June, 1968. On CD's of $100,000 face amount or more with maturities from 30 to 59 days, the rate was 5½ percent; from 60 to 89 days, 5¾ percent; from 90 to 179 days, 6 percent; and 180 days or over, 6¼ percent. But the rate was only 5 percent on CD's of less than $100,000 face amount (regardless of maturity) and on open accounts payable in 90 days or more, and only 4 percent on savings accounts and open accounts payable in 30 to 89 days.[13]

Against the background of such developments, the financial managers of many large corporations often find that they can earn higher rates of interest on CD's of large face amounts than on Treasury obligations and other investments of equal amounts and comparable maturities. That they channel much cash in this direction is continually indicated by the outstanding CD's as reported by large commercial banks[14] to the Federal Reserve authorities. For example, the report of May 29, 1968, disclosed outstanding CD's of $100,000 or more face amount individually totaling $19.5 billion, of which $12.1 billion had been issued to "individuals, partnerships, and corporations"[15]—chiefly nonfinancial business corporations, one may

---

[13]*Federal Reserve Bulletin*, June, 1968, p. A–11.

[14]These are large banks located in all sections of the country that voluntarily make weekly reports of their assets and liabilities, so that, among other things, the Federal Reserve authorities will have a means for quickly judging the course of financial developments.

[15]*Ibid.*, p. A–29.

assume. Even when they expect to need their money in, say, two or three months, corporations frequently find it advantageous to take out CD's that have maturities of 180 days or more. When they want to recover their money for operations, they are able to sell their CD's to dealers at prices yielding them rates of return materially higher than they would have got by originally investing in CD's or other paper maturing in two or three months.

The compensatory balance rules of commercial banks, related to outstanding loans as discussed earlier in this chapter, ordinarily are not satisfied by the holding of balances in time deposit open accounts and CD's. Nevertheless, the typical banker will surely recognize time balances as a source of funds for loans, and will, accordingly, take them into consideration in deciding how much he can afford to lend to his corporate customers. Likewise, it is not customary to give credit against service charges on the basis of balances held in open accounts and CD's, so that a corporation that has only a moderate balance in its checking account may be required to pay service charges for the activity in that account, even though it is simultaneously carrying relatively large amounts as time balances.

Share Accounts in Savings and Loan Associations

Often, the managers of smaller corporations prefer to invest temporarily idle cash in the shares of savings and loan associations. Such associations are chartered by both federal and state governments. Their principal operations are the sale of their shares to accumulate funds, and the lending of these funds for the construction of residential property, the purchase of existing residential property, and the repair and modernization of such property.

Investment in the shares of savings and loan associations is attractive in many cities and towns because the associations located there pay on their share accounts higher rates of interest (usually called dividends) than the commercial banks of the same localities pay on time deposits.[16] Moreover, most of the associations have their accounts insured by the Federal Savings and Loan Insurance Corporation to the amount of $15,000 individually, thereby matching the Federal Deposit Insurance Corporation insurance provided by most commercial banks on deposit accounts up to $15,000.

A possible disadvantage of share accounts is that the savings and

[16]Differentials of one half percentage point or more in favor of the savings and loan associations used to obtain in almost all localities. In recent years, however, the situation has become a mixed one, with the commercial banks of some communities paying as much as or more than associations, at least on some classes of their time accounts. Changes in the competitive climate between the two kinds of financial institutions have been attributable chiefly to the tight money developments that originated in 1966 and to dissimilar rate regulations of government supervisory authorities.

loan associations do not have an absolute obligation to meet withdrawal demands at specified times or within specified periods following the receipt of shareholders' requests. Payments must be made to meet withdrawal demands only as money becomes available, whereas commercial banks' failures to meet withdrawal demands according to the terms of contracts with depositors mark the defaulting banks as insolvent and therefore subject to reorganization or liquidation by federal or state supervisors.

However, most savings and loan associations are required by law to hold cash and other liquid assets equal to stipulated percentages of their share accounts, and associations that are members of the Federal Home Loan Bank System—a substantial majority of all associations, and almost all of the larger ones—can generally borrow freely from the home loan banks when money is needed to meet withdrawal demands of holders of share accounts. Indeed, the associations insured by the Federal Savings and Loan Insurance Corporation pridefully advertise that at no time since 1934, when the insurance system was established, has an insured association invoked the privilege of meeting withdrawal demands on a delayed rotation basis Accordingly, most holders of share accounts, including corporations look on their balances in these accounts as being as readily accessible as balances in time accounts with commercial banks.

QUESTIONS

1. Is not the incurring of operating expenses a source of liabilities and possible losses rather than a procedure of acquiring assets, as is claimed in the text? Discuss.

2. Is it not an exaggeration to claim that the financial managers of great corporations such as General Motors seek to conserve cash—to economize in its use? Discuss.

3. Why is it likely that the published balance sheets of many corporat tions understate the importance of inventories and accounts receivable? If this is so, the importance of what kinds of assets is likely to be overstated?

4. In which industrial areas are current assets much larger in amount than fixed assets, and in which areas are fixed assets much larger in amount than current assets? In which areas are inventories especially large amonthe current assets? Accounts receivable?

5. Why should a firm's cash balance be of particular interest to trade suppliers in deciding whether or not to sell to it on account?

6. What is the relationship between a firm's cash holdings and its access to commercial banks for loans and services?

7. What is working capital? In evaluating a firm's working capital position, why is it insufficient to determine simply the ratio of its current assets to its current liabilities?

8. Support or attack this proposition: The typical corporation should set a level above which it does not want its total holdings of cash and short-term, high-quality investments to go.

9. If a firm has excess cash that will not be needed for, say, a week, and if it uses it to buy short-term, high-quality investment paper, may this paper be reasonably regarded as part of the firm's cash balance? Discuss.

10. Why is investment in long-term Treasury obligations, despite their high quality, unsuitable for corporate funds that will be needed for operations within a few months?

11. What are the four types of marketable obligations of the Treasury? How do they differ among one another?

12. Why do corporate treasurers often choose to invest temporarily idle money in short-term obligations of state and local governments rather than in short-term Treasury obligations?

13. How can one account for the popularity of certificates of deposit (CD's) issued by commercial banks as means for investing corporate cash temporarily in excess supply?

14. With respect to safety, ease of withdrawal, and rate of return, how do share accounts in savings and loan associations compare with bank time deposits as investment outlets for excess corporate cash?

PROBLEMS

1. If a Treasury 5 percent note is selling in the market at 102, would a buyer who holds the note to maturity earn more or less than 5 percent on the amount of his investment? Explain. What, if anything, would the price of 102 indicate about the maturity of the note? A price of 98?

2. If a person buys a Treasury 2½ percent bond at its current market price and holds it to maturity, he will earn 5 percent a year. Is the market price above or below 100? Explain. From the figures given, is it possible to judge how far above or below 100 the market price is? Explain.

3. Assume that a corporate treasurer's bid of 97.375 for $2 million of 182-day Treasury bills is accepted and that the corporation holds the bills to maturity. What rate of interest per annum will it have earned?

4. A corporate treasurer makes a weekend investment of $10 million for 4 days in a finance company's commercial paper paying interest at 6 percent per annum. What is the amount of interest income earned? (Make the computation on the basis of a 360-day year—that is, on the basis of ordinary interest.)

chapter 8

THE MANAGEMENT OF INVENTORIES

IMPORTANCE OF INVENTORIES

The statistics presented in Chapter 7 showed inventories to be outstandingly important among the assets of corporations engaged in manufacturing, wholesale trade, and retail trade, and of minor importance only for public utilities, service corporations, and corporations engaged in mining and quarrying. For the majority of American corporations, therefore, inventory management policies are of major significance. This is emphasized even more by the fact that manufacturing and mercantile corporations constituted 61 percent of the number, and held 64 percent of the total assets, of the corporations whose balance sheets were summarized in Table 7–1.

It is true, of course, that considerable variation in the importance of inventories in asset structures exists among manufacturing and mercantile corporations. This is shown in Table 8–1, in which inventory figures for the subgroups of manufacturing and retail trade corporations as percentages of total assets are presented. Noteworthy in the manufacturing classification is the extremely high percentage of inventory investment in tobacco manufactures, and the quite high percentages in the subgroups designated "apparel and other fabricated textile products," "leather and leather products," and "transportation equipment except motor vehicles," as well as the relatively low percentages in the subgroups designated "petroleum refining and related industries" and "printing, publishing, and allied industries." Noteworthy in the retail trade classification are the high percentages of inventory investment for corporations selling automobiles and gasoline, apparel and accessories, and building materials, hardware, and farm equipment, as contrasted with the low percentage for corporations that operate eating and drinking places. In all instances, however, one should keep in mind the probable understatement of the average level of inventory investment. As was pointed out in Chapter 7, many corporations close their fiscal years, and prepare their tax returns with accompanying balance sheets, in slack seasons when inventories can be expected to be at or near their lowest annual levels.

TABLE 8-1
Investment in Inventories in Relation to Total Assets in Manufacturing and Retail Trade, 1965-66
(Dollar amounts in millions)

Business Classification	*Inventories*	*Total Assets*	*Percentage of Total Assets*
Manufacturing:			
Food and kindred products	$ 7,321	$ 32,548	22.5
Tobacco manufactures	2,681	4,038	66.4
Textile mill products	3,055	10,999	27.8
Apparel and other fabricated textile products	2,873	7,895	36.4
Lumber and wood products	1,452	7,916	18.3
Furniture and fixtures	1,003	3,401	29.5
Paper and allied products	1,803	13,297	13.6
Printing, publishing, and allied industries	1,486	13,363	11.1
Chemicals and allied products	5,805	33,827	17.2
Petroleum refining and related industries	3,913	58,924	6.6
Rubber and miscellaneous plastic products	1,757	7,420	23.7
Leather and leather products	798	2,500	31.9
Stone, clay, and glass products	1,729	11,783	14.7
Primary metal industries	6,572	34,802	18.9
Fabricated metal products, except machinery and transportation equipment	4,758	17,411	27.3
Machinery, except electrical	8,776	29,421	29.8
Electrical machinery, equipment, and supplies	6,284	22,737	27.6
Motor vehicles and motor vehicle equipment	5,713	34,585	16.5
Transportation equipment, except motor vehicles	5,429	13,760	39.5
Scientific instruments, photographic equipment, watches and clocks	1,654	6,766	24.4
Miscellaneous, including ordnance and accessories	1,341	5,052	26.5
Manufacturing not allocable	32	136	23.5
Total Manufacturing	$76,234*	$372,583*	20.5
Retail trade:			
Building materials, hardware, and farm equipment stores	$ 2,184	$ 5,953	36.7
General merchandise stores	5,905	21,855	27.0
Food stores	2,557	8,044	31.8
Automotive dealers and gasoline service stations	5,393	11,618	46.4
Apparel and accessory stores	1,891	4,722	40.0
Furniture, home furnishings, and equipment stores	1,610	4,698	34.3
Eating and drinking places	238	3,625	6.6
Miscellaneous retail stores	2,738	7,804	35.1
Retail trade not allocable	25	55	45.5
Total Retail Trade	$22,541	$ 68,375*	33.0

*Items do not add exactly to totals because of rounding.
SOURCE: U.S. Treasury Department, Internal Revenue Service, *Statistics of Income, 1965—Preliminary: Corporation Income Tax Returns* (Washington, D.C.: U.S. Government Printing Office, 1967), pp. 14-17. (Percentages supplied by the author.)

It is apparent, therefore, that for most manufacturing and mercantile corporations—and for many others as well—the formulation and execution of sound inventory management policies must be a managerial responsibility of the highest rank. It is often said that more firms fail because of inept inventory management than for any other reason. The managerial objective must be the avoidance of overinvestment and underinvestment in inventories—a proposition that appears to indicate that there must be some right amount of inventory investment for maximizing profits. But while it is easy to indicate the harmfulness of overinvestment and underinvestment, it is often difficult to recognize overinvestment and underinvestment in actual situations. It is difficult, in other words, for the managers of the individual enterprise to set an inventory volume that will surely be the right amount.

Evils of Overinvestment

The most obvious evil that results from overinvestment in inventories is that the erring firm is likely to find itself short of cash for other purposes, such as the payment of maturing liabilities, the carrying of accounts receivable, and the expansion of fixed assets. Instead of generating its own funds for these purposes, as may be possible with a better-designed inventory program, such a firm is likely to find it necessary to increase its borrowings, thereby adding to its overhead expenses by way of interest costs.

Excessive quantities of goods in inventories require storage space. Facilities that could be better used for other purposes may have to be used for storage, or, indeed, additional facilities may have to be bought, erected, or rented. Costs of handling, inspection, and accounting are increased. Since insurance charges and personal property taxes are based on the value of property, they go up.

For some kinds of goods held in inventories, losses through shrinkage and spoilage may increase substantially; for others there may be increased danger of theft; and for still others goods may become obsolete because of changes in customers' preferences. For almost all kinds of goods, there is the further danger of declines in supply prices, so that the overinvesting firm may find itself with a high-cost inventory at a time when its competitors are carrying on their operations with goods purchased more recently at lower prices.

Consequences of Underinvestment

A firm that is unduly niggardly in its inventory investment policy is likely to lose customers. Customers of a mercantile firm in this position may go elsewhere because they cannot find on its shelves a sufficient variety of goods of a given line to make a reasonable selection or because they are precluded from one-stop shopping for the reason that it does not carry a sufficient variety of lines. Customers of a manufacturing firm similarly situated may turn away because of what they consider unreasonable delays in the delivery of goods ordered.

Besides having difficulty in holding customers' goodwill, manufacturing firms with inadequate inventory investment are likely to be burdened with many unnecessary costs of operation. Shortages of raw materials may bring temporary shutdowns, with many kinds of overhead expenses continuing to accumulate during the periods of idleness. Labor costs, too, tend to mount, perhaps as a result of slowdowns whereby the workers try to stretch out the limited supplies of raw materials to make them last as long as possible, and perhaps through labor turnover as dissatisfied workers quit their jobs to seek employment elsewhere.

A firm with inadequate inventories, moreover, is at the mercy of rising prices. Lack of foresight in the accumulation of inventories in times of plentiful supply and relatively low prices may result in substantial increases in costs of goods manufactured or in costs of goods sold. It is hard enough to take increased supply prices due to rising costs incurred by the suppliers, but all the greater is the burden if unforseen shortages enable the suppliers to sharply mark up their prices. Even in the absence of price increases due to rising costs or shortages, hand-to-mouth stocking of inventories is often expensive in increased transportation costs. Firms faced with a lack of goods to maintain manufacturing or selling operations may see no alternative to having new supplies delivered by faster, but more expensive, means of transportation, such as choosing express shipments in place of freight, or air freight in place of rail freight.

Right Amount of Inventory Investment

So great is the diversity among firms in the role that inventories play in the earning of profits, and so complex are the circumstances that must bear on the decisions of the individual firm, that one must quickly confess the impossibility of formulating a set of rules or standards whereby the rightness of the inventory policies of business enterprises can be determined. No two firms will be faced with an identical set of circumstances in consideration of which decisions must be made. What, therefore, is right for one firm may be wrong for another, and what is right for a given firm at a certain time will not necessarily continue to be right for it at another time. Nevertheless, certain observations about the determination of good inventory policies can be made.

In the first place, overinvestment and underinvestment in inventories cannot be recognized simply by their size. A firm that has a very large inventory—much larger relatively than those of its competitors—will be in a most favorable position if supply prices are rising or if shortages in supply are developing. Its managers, therefore, would deserve great praise as being wiser than those of the competing firms. Likewise, an extraordinarily small inventory at certain times may indicate great astuteness of financial managers in foreseeing the coming of a business recession with declining prices or a shift in consumer preferences to goods of other kinds.

Inventory policies must be expected to differ markedly among businesses according to the nature of their activities. Typically, for a given volume of sales, manufacturing concerns must have larger inventories than mercantile firms, since in addition to holding finished goods for sale manufacturers must also have inventories of raw materials and goods in process. Manufacturing firms that carry through time-consuming processes from remote raw material stages to highly complex finished goods stages will surely have much greater investment in inventories—given a certain volume of sales—than those that buy finished parts and simply assemble some final product. Mercantile firms that sell things that can be classified as daily necessities, such as many kinds of foods, will almost invariably have smaller inventories in relation to sales than those that sell articles that the average customer buys only once or twice in a lifetime, such as many items of household furniture.

Location is also an important factor in the determination of sound inventory policies—location both of sources of supply and of sales outlets. For example, a firm that is dependent on foreign sources of supply for its principal raw materials will ordinarily find it necessary to carry a much larger inventory in relation to sales than one whose suppliers are located in the same country. The same is true for an eastern firm whose chief sources of supply are located on the West Coast as compared with one whose suppliers are located in the same community. In a similar way, a firm that establishes branch warehouses at various points throughout the country may find it desirable to carry complete lines of goods at each of them. It will be likely, therefore, to have a total inventory much larger in relation to sales than will a firm that makes all its deliveries from a single warehouse. In recent years, indeed, many firms have been seeking inventory economies by replacing numerous warehouses, each serving a relatively small marketing area, with "distribution centers" that supply much wider areas.

Closely related to location as a determinant of inventory management policies is the speed of deliveries of goods both inward and outward. This depends on the availability of the different kinds of transportation facilities as well as on the varying competence of the carriers available. Speed in delivery also depends on the reliability of suppliers. Inventory trimming may be possible for a firm that can depend on its suppliers to dispatch goods quickly on receiving orders, whereas it is not likely to be feasible for one whose suppliers are erratic in their treatment of orders.

Other important factors that account for widely diverse inventory policies (although not always justifying diversity) are:

1. Great variations among businesses in the seasonality of their operations, both in sources of supply and in customer demand.
2. Judgments about the future course of general business activity, such as anticipations of cyclical expansion with rising prices or of cyclical contractions with falling prices.
3. Special situations arising because of firms' positions in growth or declining industries.
4. Peculiar competitive situations whereby, for example, firms must add certain lines of goods for no better reason than that their competitors have decided to add them.

All these factors were discussed in Chapter 6 as causes of variations in cash flows; therefore, at this time a further detailed analysis is unnecessary. Suffice it to say that since inventories constitute the most important single asset of many manufacturing and most mercantile enterprises, modifications in cash flows brought about by the factors mentioned must largely involve the tying up of additional cash in expanded inventories or the release of cash as inventories are reduced.

INVENTORY TURNOVER

Although the formulation of a set of policies that ought to be right for the generality of businesses at all times may be impossible, a means of testing the reasonableness of inventory investment at a given level is available and widely used. This is the computation of inventory turnovers. The computation of turnovers is, at best, a very rough method of testing, and serious errors can result if in arriving at judgments turnover figures are accorded greater weight than they deserve—if turnover ratios, in other words, are used routinely or mechanically in judging inventory investment policies without analyses of the complex circumstances that bear on policy formulation in the individual firm. Nevertheless, turnover ratios have proved themselves to be of great worth in innumerable instances.

Computation of Turnovers

The inventory turnover of a firm for a given period of time can be computed by the solution of either of the following two formulas:

$$\text{Inventory turnover} = \frac{\text{Cost of goods sold}}{\text{Average inventory at cost}}$$

$$\text{Inventory turnover} = \frac{\text{Net sales}}{\text{Average inventory at selling prices}}$$

It is immaterial whether the one or the other of these formulas is used, as the result should be approximately the same for both. Most firms value their inventories on a cost basis, although, as we shall see in the subsequent discussion of inventory valuation, "cost" may actually be "cost or market, whichever is lower." Some firms, however, find use of the second formula more convenient. Department stores, for example, customarily value their inventories at selling prices, using the so-called retail method for this purpose.

For greatest accuracy in the computation of inventory turnovers, monthly inventories should ordinarily be used; this is especially desirable if the size of inventories fluctuates substantially in the course of the year. Average inventory for a year, then, is the sum of the opening inventory and the inventory at the end of every month, this total to be divided by 13. Many firms, as we have seen, operate on the basis of a fiscal year other than the calendar year for the very reason that they want their yearly operations to conclude at a time when inventories are at or near their lowest level. This arrangement makes possible appreciable economies in the work of inventory-taking and valuation. For a firm in this position, however, a turnover ratio computed on the basis of the average of opening and closing inventories would be much higher than one computed on the basis of an average of monthly inventories; accordingly, it would be quite misleading.

Interpretation of Turnover Ratios

An inventory turnover ratio standing by itself means absolutely nothing. To say that the turnover of a particular firm is, say, 5 indicates nothing about the wisdom of its inventory management policies. To give meaning to a turnover figure, one must compare it with other such figures. Most fruitful are comparisons with a firm's turnover ratios computed for other periods and comparisons with those of other firms operating in the same area of business activity—that is to say, with the ratios of one's competitors. If a firm's turnover ratio in the year just ended is 5, whereas in the preceding year it was 5½, and in the year before that it was 6, strong evidence of growing deficiencies in inventory management is brought out—not conclusive evidence, by any means, but sufficient, certainly, to warrant a thoroughgoing analysis of the situation. Likewise, if a firm's turnover ratio in the year just ended is 5, while those of principal competitors are, say, 6, 6½, and 7, respectively, an investigation of the causes of what appears to be a record of poor performance would surely be in order.

Out-of-Line Ratios on the Low Side. If a firm's inventory turnover ratio declines from year to year, or if for any year its ratio is materially less than those of competing enterprises, there is justification for suspicion that serious mistakes have been made in inventory management. The likelihood of overinvestment in inventories is especially to be considered. Thus, if the cost of goods sold of each of two firms is $500,000, and if one has average inventories of $60,000 while the other has average inventories of $80,000—their ratios being, respectively, of course, 8⅓ and 6¼—the evidence is strong that the second firm is carrying larger inventories than it needs to carry to properly serve its customers.

Overinvestment here might mean simply that the second firm has overstocked goods of proper qualities and kinds that it will eventually sell at satisfactory prices. Another possibility, however, is that the firm has been caught with an unusual amount of slow-moving goods, so that it may not have excessive quantities of other kinds of goods that move more speedily. Still another possibility is that the inventory of the second firm includes large quantities of shopworn or obsolescent goods on which its managers are reluctant to acknowledge losses, as would be done by a drastic cutting of selling prices to move them.

Out-of-Line Ratios on the High Side. Rising inventory turnover ratios and ratios higher than those of competing firms are usually accepted, at first glance, as being indicative of good inventory management. If, in a certain year, each of two corporations sells for $600,000 goods that cost $400,000, and if the first carries an average inventory of $80,000 while the second carries one of $100,000, the first corporation has a gross profit *as a rate of return* on its average investment in inventory of 250 percent, whereas the second has a rate of return of only 200 percent. Should the two corporations incur about the same amount of operating expenses, as might well be expected, the first would likewise have a much more favorable rate of net profit (assuming, as seems reasonable, that the investment of the stockholders of the first corporation would be $20,000 less than that of the second). One can well understand, therefore, why managers of business firms tend to take pride in turnover ratios that are high in comparison with those of earlier years and with those of other firms. Indeed, the maximization of turnover is often considered to be the principal objective of inventory management policies.

Need of Caution in Analysis. Nevertheless, a comparison of turnover ratios can easily lead to unsound conclusions. Comparative ratios, standing alone, can never wisely te taken as proof that inventory management has been good or bad. When ratios are found to be out of line, praise for or blame on the makers of policy must be withheld until the reasons for the out-of-line result have been sought and found. For one thing, inventory ratios vary according to the methods of inventory valuation used—a topic to be discussed later in this chapter—and especially if the methods of valuation are changed. A relatively low ratio may result from the heavy stocking of inventory in anticipation of price increases. Should the price increases actually come about, the managers would surely be deserving of praise rather than blame. Or a low ratio may result from a stabilization of production—that is, the spreading out of productive operations over the year, as by a manufacturing firm whose sales are heavily concentrated in a few months.

Moreover, a relatively high turnover ratio may not really be an indicator of favorable results and prospects. It may indicate a serious underinvestment in inventories. Surely there would be strong evidence of this if while a firm's turnover rate is rising its sales are falling off or are expanding at a slower rate than the rates of other firms. A loss of customers because of inability to show them complete lines or to make prompt deliveries could hardly be regarded as a favorable development.

Stabilization of Production and Inventory Turnover. The need of exercising great care in the interpretation of comparative inventory turnover ratios can be emphasized by considering the position of a manufacturing corporation that wants to stabilize its productive activities even though its sales are largely concentrated in a few months of the year. Let us assume that the corporation's sales in the months from January through September (in terms of cost of goods sold) are uniform at $20,000 a month, and that in October, November, and December they reach the high level of $80,000 a month. To adequately serve its customers, the corporation must have at the beginning of each month from January to September inventories of raw materials, goods in process, and finished goods of $40,000, and at the beginning of October, November, and December inventories of these three kinds totaling $100,000. Accordingly, the corporation has the choice of (1) limiting the scale of its manufacturing operations in the period from the beginning of December to the end of August, and then stepping it up mightily in September, October, and November, or (2) trying to even out production through the year. If it takes the first course, its inventory turnover ratio will be 7.8 (cost of goods sold of $420,000 divided by average inventory of $53,846, the second figure being the sum of 10 inventories at $40,000 and 3 at $100,000 divided by 13). If it takes the second course, the ratio will be only 3.6, as is shown in the table and computation on page 164.

Were the corporation to shift from the first course in one year to the second course in the following year, an injudicious observer might condemn the management for the sharp drop in its inventory turnover ratio from 7.8 to 3.6. Would this condemnation have any merit? Definitely not from the point of view of public welfare, for the stabilization of employment in seasonal industries is an important social goal. From the standpoint of the profit-seeking interests of the stockholders, moreover, the condemnation would probably not be justified, for stabilization of production very often results in increased net profits, and not the contrary. It is true that the corporation would incur increased costs of carrying a much larger average inventory—costs of storage facilities, handling, accounting, insurance, personal property taxes and, possibly, spoilage, shrinkage, and theft. It might have to borrow money for investment in the inventories, thus incurring an additional interest expense. However, labor costs and overhead expenses per unit of output might well be materially reduced. With stabilized production, the corporation could offer full-time regular employment to all its personnel. It would thus be able to avoid the annual costs of recruiting and training a short-term labor force on

Month	*Production (At cost)*	*Cost of Goods Sold*	*Inventory at End of Month*
			$ 55,000*
January	$ 35,000	$ 20,000	70,000
February	35,000	20,000	85,000
March	35,000	20,000	100,000
April	35,000	20,000	115,000
May	35,000	20,000	130,000
June	35,000	20,000	145,000
July	35,000	20,000	160,000
August	35,000	20,000	175,000
September	35,000	20,000	190,000
October	35,000	80,000	145,000
November	35,000	80,000	100,000
December	35,000	80,000	55,000
Total	$420,000	$420,000	$1,525,000
Average inventory			$117,308

$$\frac{\$420,000}{\$117,308} = 3.6 \text{ turnovers}$$

*Inventory at the end of the preceding year.

the approach of the peak period, and possibly payments for overtime during that period. A year-around labor force, furthermore, would probably be much more competent and loyal than that portion of one brought in only on a temporary basis. In the matter of overhead expenses, the corporation would no longer accumulate expenses in connection with idle facilities, such as insurance, maintenance, and property taxes. Indeed, with operations stabilized throughout the year the corporation would almost surely be able to get along with a much smaller aggregate of facilities. Accordingly, the increased investment in inventories might be offset in whole or in part, or more than offset, by a reduction of investment in fixed assets.

INVENTORY VALUATION

Relation to Turnover Ratios

It was mentioned above that inventory turnover ratios vary according to the method of inventory valuation used, and especially if the valuation method is changed from one year to another. If, for example, a firm values its inventories at cost at a time when market prices are declining, it will have a lower turnover ratio than will a firm that in the same circumstances values its inventories at market. (One should observe that market or market price in inventory valuation means the price at which goods in the inventory could be replaced at the time of inventory taking.)

Let us suppose that each of two firms, Corporations A and B, has an inventory of 30,000 units valued at $1 per unit at the beginning of a certain month, that in the course of the month each buys 50,000 units at a price of $1 per unit, and that at the end of the month each has 20,000 units remaining in its inventory. A values its inventory at cost, and B at cost or market, whichever is lower. Let us assume that at the end of the month market is 90 cents per unit. The computation of the respective turnovers, then, would be as follows.

	Corporation A	*Corporation B*
Cost of goods sold:		
Inventory, beginning of month.......	$30,000	$30,000
Purchases..........................	50,000	50,000
Goods available for sale.............	$80,000	$80,000
Less: Inventory, end of month......	20,000	18,000
Cost of goods sold..............	$60,000	$62,000
Inventory turnovers:		

$$\text{Corporation A: } \frac{60,000}{\frac{30,000 + 20,000}{2}} = 2.40$$

$$\text{Corporation B: } \frac{62,000}{\frac{30,000 + 18,000}{2}} = 2.58$$

Relation to Profits and Income Taxes

The effects of different methods of inventory valuation on turnover ratios are significant, but much more important are their effects on the amount of profits recognized and, consequently, on the amount of income tax liabilities. These more important effects can be understood if we carry the foregoing illustration a step further. We may assume that the sales of 60,000 units of each of the corporations were made at a price of $1.40 a unit. Accordingly, Corporation A would recognize a gross profit on sales of $24,000, whereas Corporation B's gross profit on sales would be placed at $22,000. Assuming that the two corporations incurred the same amount of operating expenses, A would have a net profit $2,000 greater than that of B. Because the federal taxing authorities permit business firms to select whatever method of inventory valuation they wish (as long as it is "reasonable," it is used consistently from year to year, and it is changed, if at all, only with the permission of the Internal Revenue Service), A would have $2,000 more of taxable income than B. With federal corporation income tax rates prevailing at 22 percent on the first $25,000 of taxable income and at 48 percent on amounts in excess of $25,000,[1] A's inventory valuation method would obviously be working to its disadvantage.

It is to be noted, too, that after the deduction of federal tax liabilities Corporation A would have more net profit available for dividends than would Corporation B. It might be pleasant for the directors of A to be able to report a higher net profit after taxes than its competitor; however, A's stockholders might expect to receive a larger amount of cash dividends. If, therefore, the directors of A were inclined to be generous in the distribution of dividends, they would face two cash drains in relation to the $2,000—one in the direction of the federal Treasury and one in the direction of the stockholders in cash dividends.

Considerations in the Selection of Inventory Valuation Methods

As a rule, the financial managers of business enterprises seek a method of inventory valuation that will result in the lowest possible amounts of gross and net profits and that will, at the same time, be acceptable to the federal taxing authorities as reasonable for the computation of income tax liabilities. This does not mean that the financial managers seek to understate their profits. Rather, it means that they go along with the oft-stated principle of conservative accounting that all losses should be accounted for but that profits should not be taken up till actually earned. Indeed, at the time a given method of inventory valuation is used it is quite impossible to say whether it results in an understatement or overstatement of profits; a final conclusion about this can only be reached subsequently as the inventoried goods are sold. At the time of inventory-taking, therefore, as much as can be said is that one method results in higher or lower profits *at that time* than do other methods.

Avoidance of Income Taxes. The avoidance of federal and state income taxes—especially federal, of course—is doubtless the principal reason that the financial managers of business enterprises seek the inventory valuation methods that will result in profit figures of the lowest possible levels. While it may appear that taxes avoided in one year will have to be paid in subsequent years, it does not always work out that way. If, for example, the long-term trend of prices is upward, as it has been in the United States since 1933, the use of the last-in,

[1]Basic rates in effect in 1968. Tax legislation adopted in June of that year added a surcharge of 10 percent to corporate tax obligations as determined by the basic rates. The surcharge was made retroactive to the beginning of the year but was scheduled to expire at the end of June, 1969.

first-out method of inventory valuation (lifo) may result in a net decrease in tax liabilities that will never be offset.

Furthermore, even if taxes avoided in one year must be made up in a subsequent year, corporate managers are generally pleased with the deferment. Cash saved from current tax payments can be temporarily used for expanded operations, and expanded operations will be likely to increase the corporations' capacity to pay taxes in future years. For a variety of reasons, corporate managers are doubtless inclined to think that improvements in their corporations' positions from year to year will make tax payments in future years less burdensome than they would be at the moment. And there is always the hope that tax rates in the future will be lower than at present.

Avoidance of Demands for Increased Dividends. A second reason for the choice of inventory valuation methods that result in the lowest possible profit figures is the avoidance of pressures on corporate directors to raise the levels of cash dividends paid to the stockholders. In ordinary circumstances, the higher a corporation's profits, the greater are the stockholders' expectations for generous dividends—expectations to which the directors must surely give consideration in almost any circumstances, but especially if they were voted their directoships by narrow margins. If the directors would prefer to use available cash to the greatest extent possible for expansion rather than for increases in cash dividends, it must seem wise to them to hold down, by whatever means possible, the amount of profits reported—means that include a careful choosing among inventory valuation methods.

Some justification for directors' attitudes toward tax and dividend payments, as just described, is found in the fact that a corporation's *cash position* is not improved by the use of an inventory valuation method that results in higher reported profits than do other methods, nor is that position impaired by the use of a method that results in lower reported profits. In the illustration given on pages 165–66, there was no indication that Corporation A had a cash throw-off exceeding that of Corporation B, even though it was reporting a net profit exceeding that of B by $2,000. Since all aspects of the operations of the two corporations except their inventory valuation methods were described as identical, it would be reasonable to assume that cash collections on account of sales, cash payments to trade suppliers, and cash payments to meet operating expenses were also identical. If this were so, Corporation A would be in no better position to pay income taxes and dividends than Corporation B.

Inventory Valuation Methods

The methods of inventory valuation most commonly used by American business enterprises are the following.

1. Specific identification.
2. First-in, first-out (fifo).
3. Last-in, first-out (lifo).
4. Average cost.

The specific identification method can be used conveniently when each item is clearly distinguishable as having been included in a particular purchase, as in the case of bulky items such as electric refrigerators, television sets, and suites of living room furniture. The other methods are used when various lots purchased from time to time are intermingled in such a way that the identity of each item, or bushel, or ton—whatever the measure may be—cannot be traced to a given purchase invoice.

In use of the first-in, first-out method, the inventory at the end of a period is considered as having goods most recently purchased—an application of the idea that the older stock is moved first. In the use of the last-in, first-out method, the closing inventory is considered as having goods most remotely purchased; thus, in many instances, the closing inventory will be assumed to contain all or much of the goods contained in the opening inventory. In the use of the average cost method, the closing inventory is considered as having an array of items in proportion to those contained in the opening inventory and in each of the purchases made in the course of the year or other period.

For the computation of taxable profits, the federal income tax authorities permit the use of any of these methods, provided that the method chosen is used consistently from year to year. Except for the last-in, first-out method, moreover, the taxpayer may choose to value his closing inventory either at cost or at cost or market, whichever is lower, provided, again, that he is consistent in using one alternative or the other.

Application of Inventory Valuation Methods: Illustrations. Depending on price changes currently going on, each of the methods of inventory valuation as well as each of the alternatives tends to give differing results. For a demonstration, a few simple figures will suffice. Suppose that a corporation had 4 items in its opening inventory valued at 65 cents each and that in the course of the year—a period of falling prices—it made purchases of individual items at prices in cents as follows: 64, 62, 59, 58, 56, 53, 51. We may further assume that the corporation has 3 items in its closing inventory, that the market (replacement) price at the time of inventory-taking is 50 cents, and that, for the specific identification method, the items in the closing inventory are those of the third, fourth, and fifth purchases. The corporation's closing inventory, then, may have any one of the following values, depending on the valuation method (or its alternative, if available) selected.

Valuation Method	*Cost*	*Cost or Market, Whichever Is Lower*
Specific identification	$1.73	$1.50
First-in, first-out	1.60	1.50
Last-in, first-out	1.95	
Average cost	1.808	1.50

To see how the variations in inventory values may work out in a period of rising prices, let us assume that the market (replacement) price at the end of the year was 77 cents, and that in the course of the year individual purchases were made as follows: 67, 68, 70, 72, 73, 74, 76. Assuming all other facts to be the same as in the first illustration, the corporation's closing inventory valuation might be any one of the following amounts.

Valuation Method	*Cost*	*Cost or Market, Whichever Is Lower*
Specific identification	$2.15	$2.15
First-in, first-out	2.23	2.23
Last-in, first-out	1.95	
Average cost	2.073	2.073

Effects of Use of Different Methods. When one reflects that differences in inventory values, as produced by the various methods of valuation, mean differences in cost of goods sold, gross and net profits, and income tax liabilities, one can see why care in the selection of the method to be used is important. It is true that if prices move upward and downward more or less persistently within a given range the advantage a particular method gives in one year or in a series of years is likely to be offset by a disadvantage in another year or series of years. But if price movements tend to persist in a given direction over a long period of time—something that has been characteristic of economic development in the United States—there is no doubt that a method can be selected that will give a corporation a long-term net advantage. The advantage of the use of the last-in, first-out method in a period of increasing prices has already been mentioned. Although the beginning of the long-term upward trend in prices that continues at the present time dates from 1933, it was not until 1939 that Congress specifically authorized the use of the last-in, first-out method. Since 1939, therefore, and particularly since the end of World War II, many business enterprises have received permission to switch to this method.

Aside from possibilities of cutting net income tax liabilities, the last-in, first-out method is said to give a truer picture of earning capacity than does, for example, the first-in, first-out method. In a period of rising prices, a corporation that uses the last-in, first-out method is likely to find its cost of goods sold rising at a rate close to the rate of rise in its sales income. This happens because it charges to cost of goods sold the prices paid for goods most recently purchased—purchased, that is, at the rising prices. On the other hand, a corporation using the first-in, first-out method is likely to find its cost of goods sold moving up at a rate slower than the rate of rise in sales income; this occurs because it charges to cost of sales goods purchased more remotely at lower prices. In a period of falling prices, likewise, the corporation that uses the last-in, first-out method again finds its cost of sales moving in close relationship with sales income, while the corporation that uses the first-in, first-out method appears to be selling earlier purchased high-priced goods at lower selling prices.

Rising prices and an expansion in business activity generally go hand in hand, making it possible for most enterprises to show good profits without need of such additions as would tend to result from the use of a particular inventory valuation method. Falling prices and a contraction in general business activity usually go together, producing a situation in which it is highly advantageous to be able to show profits, even if the profits are attributable to the use of a given inventory valuation method. Thus, the last-in, first-out method seems to have superiority in both directions. In other words, it tends to smooth out profits during the swings of the business cycle, holding them down somewhat in years of business expansion and preventing an exaggerated fall in years of business contraction.

INVENTORY ECONOMIES

Some business enterprises are able to economize in their investment in inventories by passing on to other firms some of the burdens of inventory accumulation. A lowering of its profit margin is the usual price that the economizing firm pays for the privilege of shifting burdens, since the firms that accept the burdens are willing to do so ordinarily only if they can do so profitably. However, a firm subject to strict limits on its access to cash may regard this price as not too much to pay; without opportunities for the shifting of inventory burdens, it may not be able to remain in business at all. Procedures of shifting include the following: (1) obtaining goods on consignment, (2) negotiating exclusive sales contracts, and (3) farming out certain kinds of manufacturing operations.

It is obvious that shifting the burdens of carrying inventories is only one among many possibilities for cutting investment in inventories and the costs of handling and distribution. However, shifting is directly related to the financial capacities of firms to carry inventories and, therefore, to financial management, while other possibilities for economies, though important to finance, fall principally within the purview of production and sales management. Interest in achieving economies of the sales classification has been especially strong in recent years; many corporate managements confess their long neglect of soaring distribution costs while concentrating on efforts to pare production costs. Evidence of strong interest in this avenue of inventory economies has been seen in the consolidation and automation of warehouses, closer inventory control through the use of electronic computers, the dropping of slow-moving goods from product lines, the elimination of numerous variants of basic models of given products (not the automobile industry for this one!), and, among retailers, the development of cooperative buying.

Consignments

When a firm receives goods on consignment, it does not get title to them, and it ordinarily has no obligation to make payment until it has sold them and collected from its customers. The firm (consignee) acts simply as an agent for the firm supplying the goods (consignor), and its compensation is really not a sales profit but a commission at a fixed rate on the selling price of the goods. The commission is likely to be less than would be the profit margin were it buying outright and selling from its own inventory—a fact illustrative of the price of burden shifting, as mentioned above. A moderate amount of cash is still needed by the consignee for what might be called inventory investment, as he usually meets out-of-pocket costs of freight and drayage, other handling, and perhaps advertising. Such expenses are chargeable against the consignor, and are reimbursed when payments are collected from customers. Assume, for example, that a consignee incurs $180 of expenses in acquiring and selling at $4,000 certain goods shipped to him on consignment. The consignor allows a commission of 20 percent on the selling price. After collecting from his customers, therefore, the consignee would remit $3,020 to the consignor—that is, $4,000 less his commission of $800 and less $180 to cover his expenses.

Outstanding among enterprises that obtain a substantial portion of their wares on a consignment basis are firms in the retail jewelry trade. Considering the high unit value of many of these wares, such as diamond rings and brooches, and considering the limited access to cash of small shop owners, many would be unable to carry reasonable selections were it necessary for them to buy their entire stocks outright.

Exclusive Sales Contracts

The carrying of inventories of finished goods pending sale is largely obviated by the negotiation of exclusive sales contracts whereby manufacturing firms agree to sell their entire output to other firms. As soon as goods have been completed, they can be delivered to the buying firm, and if the buyer has agreed to pay promptly, cash is quickly released for reinvestment in productive operations. Inventories of raw materials and goods in process must still be carried by the selling firm, although in some instances the buying firm even undertakes to supply the raw materials.

Exclusive sales contracts are numerous; they are the tie that binds thousands of supplier firms to great manufacturing corporations, as in the automobile industry. Each supplier may make only one or a few parts to be incorporated in the final product of the large corporation, but that firm, in turn, may have hundreds of different kinds of parts and subassemblies coming in from all directions.

Not only does the supplier firm economize in its need of cash for investment in finished goods inventories, it also eliminates almost all kinds of selling expenses. But an exclusive sales contract ties the fortunes of the supplier very closely to those of the buying firm. If sales of the buyer fall off, it has no choice but to reduce its purchases from the supplier, and the supplier, in turn, finds itself without a developed alternative market. Moreover, the managers of the buying firm, well aware as they must be of the dependence of the supplier, are likely to be shrewd bargainers in negotiations to fix the prices at which parts are to be delivered. They must be willing to allow the supplier firm a fair margin of profit if it is to be persuaded to continue the intercompany relationship; nevertheless, this margin may be considerably less than that of comparable firms selling in the open market.

Farming Out Manufacturing Operations

In many instances, the farming out of manufacturing operations is simply the other side of the exclusive sales contract. The supplying firm is able to economize in investment in finished goods inventories, but the large buying firm is able to reduce its investment in raw materials and goods in process—or, at least, to reduce the length of the period required for such investment. Aside from this, as indicated previously, the buying firm may be able to obtain parts and subassemblies at lower prices than would be charged in the open market.

But many firms, large and small, farm out manufacturing operations without thought of exclusive sales contracts. A substantial number of enterprises that are well known because of the popularity of their branded products carry on no manufacturing operations whatsoever—the products are really those of unidentified manufacturers. Such enterprises engage other firms to carry through the complete manufacturing processes, providing them with detailed specifications, and sometimes lending them special kinds of dies, tools, and machines on which the buying firms have patents. Some brands of great popularity are actually produced by several manufacturers; the product gets a single identity only when it receives the label of the buying firm. Hence, the buyer is essentially a selling organization.

In other cases, firms that farm out manufacturing operations also reserve some manufacturing functions for themselves. Participation by such firms in manufacturing is subject to wide variations. At one extreme are firms that depend on other manufacturers only to a small extent, so that their inventory economies tend to be quite small; and at the other extreme are firms that undertake only a relatively simple final assembly of parts and subassemblies manufactured elsewhere.

PURCHASE DISCOUNTS

A final topic for consideration in relation to inventory management policies is the proper treatment of discounts allowed for the prompt payment of invoices of raw materials, finished goods, and supplies. For example, a trade supplier may allow the buyer 30 days for the payment of a given invoice, but he may permit the buyer to take a discount of, say, 2 percent if he pays within 10 days. The terms of this transaction would be indicated 2/10 n/30; the n stands for net or the full amount of the obligation.

The accounting aspect of the treatment of discounts is easily disposed of: when discounts are taken, it matters little whether they are handled as reductions from the prices of goods bought or are entered in the income statement as "other" or "miscellaneous" income. Slight are the effects of these alternative modes of treatment on inventory turnover ratios and the amounts of gross and net profit.

Much more significant is the question of when business firms should take advantage of discounts offered by suppliers for prompt payment. If a firm has cash available for payment within the discount period, it obviously has the choice of so using it or of using it for some other business objective. Which use will be the most advantageous? If it does not have cash available, it may be in a position to borrow to meet the payment within the discount period. Here, the question of advantage turns on the relationship between the rate of discount allowed and the rate of interest the firm would have to pay on the borrowed money. Customarily, if stipulated at all, discount rates are set at levels to make them clearly attractive; hence, financial managers hold it to be a good rule that discounts should normally be taken, whether a firm's own funds or borrowed funds are to be used for this purpose. A related observation is, therefore, that a lack of cash and a lack of borrowing capacity to enable a firm to take advantage of desirable discounts is evidence of poor financial management!

Suppose, for example, that a firm has bought a shipment of goods for $10,000 on terms of 2/10 n/30, that it has no cash available for payment within 10 days, but that it expects to have $10,000 available at the end of the 30-day period. Should it simply forget about the discount? In ordinary circumstances, this would be unwise. Assume that on the 10th day the firm could obtain a bank loan of $9,800 repayable in 20 days with interest at 6 percent per annum. By borrowing and making payment to the supplier on that day, the firm would be earning the discount of $200, and this, reduced by the interest of $32.67 payable to the bank, would give it a net saving of $167.33. For the 20-day period, the firm would be earning net interest at a rate of 30.7 percent per annum on the prepayment of $9,800.

It is possible, however, for discount terms to be unattractive. If the terms of the invoice mentioned above were 1/10 n/120, the borrowing of $9,900 for 110 days at 6 percent per annum would cost $181.50 in interest, while the discount to be earned would amount to only $100. In periods of tight money, moreover, highly competent financial managers may decide to forgo quite generous purchase discounts in the belief that the limited supplies of cash, whether derived from operations or through borrowing, can be used more profitably in other directions. They may judge the scramble for hard-to-get cash to be the very reason for the offer of generous discount terms by their trade suppliers.

Aside from extraordinary situations, such as periods of tight money, the repeated failure of firms to take advantage of attractive discounts is widely regarded as an unfavorable reflection on their creditworthiness. Such a firm, therefore, both misses an income opportunity and suffers some impairment in its credit rating.

QUESTIONS

1. "More firms fail because of inept inventory management than for any other reason." Does not this assertion exaggerate the importance of inventories in business operations? Discuss.

2. How can the financial managers of business firms determine whether or not they are overinvesting in inventories? Underinvesting?

3. Why might a firm have the right amount of inventory investment, even though smaller inventories are carried by well-managed competing firms that have comparable sales volumes?

4. How are inventory ratios computed? What do they reveal individually? In comparison with other ratios of the same kind?

5. If the inventory turnover ratio of a given firm in a certain year is substantially less than those of competing firms, is this proof of the incompetence of its management? Is it proof if the same situation continues year after year? Discuss.

6. What are the probable economies of stabilized production that may more than offset the increased costs of carrying larger average inventories? Why is stabilized production described as desirable from the standpoint of public welfare?

7. Explain how the choice among methods of inventory valuation is likely to be influenced by federal income tax considerations.

8. In the valuation of inventories "at cost or market, whichever is lower," what does "market" mean? Is this the so-called retail method of valuing inventories? Explain.

9. Why is it claimed that the last-in, first-out method of inventory valuation gives a truer picture of operating results than other methods give? Is the claim realistic for periods of falling prices as well as periods of rising prices? Explain.

10. How does a consignment differ from a sale?

11. If one firm enters into a contract to sell its entire output to another, which firm gains the benefits of inventory economies, or do both have gains of this kind? Explain.

12. Why do credit analysts tend to look unfavorably on firms that fail to take advantage of discounts for early payment offered by sellers? Is this attitude always justified? Explain.

PROBLEMS

1. At the beginning of the year 19xx, the inventory of the Anton Sales Corporation amounted to $265,000 at cost, and at the end of the year to $325,000. During the year, additional estimates of inventory values, all at cost and all thought to be reasonably accurate, were made as follows: March 31, $480,000; June 30, $425,000; and September 30, $440,000. Anton's cost of goods sold for the year was $2,620,000. Compute its inventory turnover (*a*) using the opening and closing inventories, and (*b*) using all quarterly inventories. Which turnover ratio is the more realistic? Why?

2. At the beginning of the year 19xx, Farmer & Co., Inc. had on hand 200,000 units of a product in which it deals exclusively, valued at $1.30 per unit. During the year, it made successive purchases of the product at varying prices as follows: 400,000 units at $1.32, 300,000 units at $1.35, 200,000 units at $1.31. The inventory at the end of the year amounted to 240,000 units, and market at that time was $1.29 a unit. Net sales for the year amounted to $1,700,000.

Determine the corporation's gross profit on sales (net sales less cost of goods sold) on the basis of each of the following methods of inventory valuation:

a) Average cost—at cost.
b) Average cost—at the lower of cost or market.
c) First-in, first-out—at cost.
d) First-in, first-out—at the lower of cost or market.
e) Last-in, first-out—at cost.

3. The TWG Corporation has received bills from suppliers of $90,000 with terms of 2/20 n/60. It does not have sufficient cash to pay within 20 days, but it expects to be able to pay without difficulty in 60 days. It could, however, take the discount by obtaining a 40-day loan from its commercial bank on which the bank would charge 7 percent per annum at maturity. Should it do so? What would be the amount of its saving? What would this saving be as a rate of interest per annum on the amount of its early payment to the trade suppliers?

chapter 9

THE MANAGEMENT OF ACCOUNTS RECEIVABLE

CHOICE OF SELLING TERMS

Areas of Limited Choice

In many areas, business firms have little if any choice between selling for cash and selling on account. The policy of selling on account has become so firmly established in these areas that individual firms would place themselves in a position of severe competitive disadvantage were they to try to operate on a basis of cash selling. This is especially true in the majority of manufacturing industries, in the construction industry, and in wholesale trade, but it is also true in a goodly number of retail mercantile and service lines.

In fields of business enterprise where selling on account is a firmly established practice, the individual firm must be in a position to tie up cash—probably much of it continuously—in accounts receivable,[1] the amount depending, of course, on the volume of its sales and the terms of the credits granted. If it has the opportunity to increase the volume of its sales, it will ordinarily need additional cash, not only for the expansion of its inventories but also for carrying the expected expansion in the volume of its accounts receivable. Customers who increase the size of their orders and new customers will expect, as a matter of course, to be carried by the firm for the customary credit period. Inadequacy in the firm's access to cash, therefore, could be a serious obstacle to expanded sales and profits—much more so than for an enterprise that is in a position to sell for cash.

Areas of Broad Choice

In fields of business activity where the terms of sale are not stan-

[1]Unless it chooses a means of economizing in investment in receivables, as discussed in the concluding section of this chapter. See pp. 194–98.

dardized, as in many retail lines, the individual firm must weigh the relative advantages of selling for cash and selling on account. In such fields, the firm that sells on account is often thought to have a competitive advantage, since it may well be in a position to attract customers who prefer to pay cash in addition to those who prefer to buy on a deferred-payment basis. But an advantage of this kind is by no means assured. Moreover, such an advantage may be offset in whole or in part, or more than offset, by the burdens of credit selling.

As for the burdens of selling on account, probably the most obvious one is the need of additional cash for investment in accounts receivable—a burden that is measurable in terms of the interest or dividends that must be paid to acquire the cash. Also to be regarded as burdens are the costs of credit administration, including all the expenses of making credit investigations, maintaining files and accounting records concerning credit customers, and handling delinquencies. A third kind of burden results from bad-debt losses whereby the firm fails to collect from given customers all or portions of amounts due.

If to cover these additional costs a firm sells at prices higher than are charged by its cash-selling competitors, it may drive away prospective cash customers. Such people are likely to feel that they ought not to be made to bear costs of operation that are of no specific benefit to them. If, on the other hand, it sells at the same prices as its competitors, its expanded gross profits due to increased sales may be swallowed up, or more than swallowed up, by the burdens of credit selling referred to. In some cases, however, an expanded volume of sales at prices no higher than those of cash-selling competitors makes possible operating economies sufficient to cover all or a substantial proportion of the special costs of selling on account; thus, a firm that is able to develop such economies stands to gain material advantages by selling on account. In other instances, firms are able to add finance charges to the prices of goods sold to credit customers, so that their prices to cash customers need be no higher than those of competitors that sell only for cash.

All of which leads to the conclusion that where a choice of terms of sale is available it is not likely to be a clear-cut one. It must depend on a host of circumstances, each of which may be evaluated in different ways by different groups of business managers. In a given situation, the financial managers of some firms will be convinced that a policy of selling only for cash is bound to be the more profitable one, while the managers of others will be as strongly persuaded that the advantages of selling on account outweigh its disadvantages. This must be so, since we find some stores selling a given line of goods on a cash basis and others selling the same line on a credit basis operating in close proximity to one another.

Recent Developments

Whatever may be the choice in individual cases, postwar developments have been sharply toward increased selling on account. Evidence is strong that the financial managers of more and more businesses have been concluding that net profits can be expanded by the adoption of selling-on-account practices, the lengthening of credit periods, and the carrying of increased balances for individual customers. Typical of this evidence have been the go-now-pay-later arrangements for passenger transportation inaugurated by railroads and airlines, and the proliferation of credit cards issued by oil companies, hotels, commercial banks, and other enterprises.

The issuance of credit cards by commercial banks (reaching virtual flood proportions in 1966–67) has been especially significant in encouraging selling on account by merchants who formerly sold on a cash-and-carry basis and who find selling on account quite safe and convenient by arrangement with the card-issuing banks. In some cases, no doubt, the adoption or liberalization of credit policies has been a means of defending levels of profits already achieved rather than a move for their expansion; in other words, firms that would have preferred to continue to sell for cash have thought it necessary, in order to hold their customers, to fall into line with credit-selling competitors.

For business corporations in general, data published by the Securities and Exchange Commission throughout the post-World War II period have revealed a persistent, rapid expansion in the volume of outstanding accounts receivable. Even for a relatively short period, such as the six-year period from the end of 1961 to the end of 1967, for which current asset figures are presented in Table 9–1, the expansion in receivables of business corporations (with certain classes of financial institutions excluded) was both large in itself and far in excess of the dollar expansion in any other class of current assets.

TABLE 9–1
Current Assets of Business Corporations, 1961 and 1967*
(Dollar amounts in billions)

Current Assets	*Amounts Held December 31*		*Increases*	
	1961	*1967*	*Amount*	*Percentage*
Cash	$ 40.7	$ 52.0	$ 11.3	27.8
U.S. government securities	19.2	12.1	− 7.1	− 37.0
Accounts and notes receivable	136.7	216.9	80.2	58.7
Inventories	95.2	152.5	57.3	60.2
Other	12.9	26.6	13.7	106.2
Total	$304.6†	$460.1	$155.4	51.0

*Excluding banks, savings and loan associations, insurance companies, and investment companies.
†Items do not add exactly to total because of rounding.
SOURCE: Estimates of the Securities and Exchange Commission, as reported in *Federal Reserve Bulletin*, June, 1968, p. A-47. (Amounts and percentages of increase supplied by the author.)

CREDIT ADMINISTRATION

Allocation of Authority

For firms that decide to sell on account, the establishment of policies and the devising of procedures for credits and collections are necessarily matters of great importance. Aside from whatever decisions in these matters boards of directors may choose to make, they are generally thought to fall within the jurisdiction of the principal financial officers of enterprises, whether financial vice presidents, treasurers, controllers, or whoever else they may be. As a recognized asset management function of financial officers, indeed, the management of credits and collections is second only to the administration of cash and short-term investments. In the management of inventories and the various kinds of fixed assets, production and sales managers are often much more competent than the financial officers in shaping policies likely to prove most favorable. Accordingly, decisions about inventory and equipment requirements are often reached on the insistence of production and sales managers that "we must do this," and "we must buy that," so that financial managers are left only with an assignment to find the money. Most questions concerning accounts receivable, however, are not technical ones of production and selling; they are financial problems. Choosing which prospective customers will be allowed to buy on account is based on credit investigations, and such investigations are largely analyses of the financial positions of the prospective customers—a kind of work for which the financial officers should be well prepared. Deciding whether cash discounts shall be allowed for early payment is essentially a financial problem of weighing the advantage of a speedier flow of funds—a net reduction in cash requirements—against the obvious disadvantage of the discounts themselves as a financial cost. Similarly, deciding whether certain delinquent customers shall be pressed for payment or whether extensions of the credit period will be readily granted is a matter of comparing financial burdens—the cost of carrying accounts for lengthy periods as against the possibility of losing the patronage of customers who are pressed for payment.

All this does not mean that the sales executives should have nothing to say about credit policies and practices. The sales executives can be expected to contribute highly significant information about the position and prospects of present and prospective customers—kinds of information and observations that tend to improve the quality of credit analyses—and they surely should be in a position to oppose the adoption of credit standards they think would be unreasonably restrictive. Indeed, a conviction that financial officers tend to be overanxious about bad-debt losses has led a goodly minority of firms to place primary responsibility for credit administration in their sales managers. But the majority, though they may recognize tendencies toward undue strictness in their financial officers, appear to be convinced that in their anxiety to expand the volume of sales the sales executives tend to err even more seriously in the direction of laxity. The ideal solution here, as in most cases when conflicting interests must be reconciled, is doubtless the promotion of mutual respect and a spirit of cooperation. In the matter of credit administration, this should mean a close and harmonious working relationship among the financial and sales managers.

Credit Terms

Where selling on account is an established policy in a given field o industry, the individual firm often has as little discretion in deciding on the terms of its credit sales as it has, in the first place, in deciding whether or not to sell on account. The terms of credit, no less than the fact that credit will be granted, tend to become standardized. Any firm that might be tempted to liberalize its credit terms to attract customers from its competitors would probably reject the temptation rather quickly in the expectation that the competitors would promptly imitate its example, so that nobody would have a net gain in sales and all would be disadvantaged by the increased burdens in relation to their accounts receivable. Thus, managers usually must accept and apply as standard the existing practices concerning matters such as length of the credit period, availability of cash discounts, rate of such discounts, period within which they may be taken, and specially allowed deductions from customer remittances (as for local advertising of the seller's product to be undertaken by the customer). The determination of broad credit policies by the individual firms' managers is, therefore, not likely to be a difficult chore.

Far different is the situation of the managers of firms operating in areas where credit practices among competitors vary greatly. Such managers face the intricate problem of deciding precisely where they will put their firms—at one extreme with a rigorous cash-and-carry policy, at the other extreme with a policy of nothing down and a dollar a week, or, what is more likely in most instances, a point somewhere between these extremes. Because the range of possible selection is so wide, it must be difficult in virtually every case to determine what point or position is or would be the best one. Even after a position has been selected and maintained for a lengthy period, no easily applied criteria are available for judging if profits are thus maximized. There is always the possibility that moving to a position of less or more liberal credit granting would result in a net addition to profits. Yet, a firm's managers will ordinarily be reluctant to change policies to test these other positions because of the probably difficulty of retracing their steps should a change turn out to be a bad one in the sense of reduced profits. For example, a firm might not add much to its sales volume by extending its credit period from 30 to 60 days, but a return to a 30-day basis might lose some customers who before the change were quite satisfied with that basis.

Choosing Credit Customers. A decision by a business enterprise to sell on account does not obligate it to accept as credit customers all who may want to be so treated. Whether credit selling is an industry-wide practice or an independently determined policy, the individual firm must select its credit customers as carefully as it selects the varieties and qualities of the goods it includes in its inventories. Its objective must always be to choose customers from whom payment according to the terms of credit sales is reasonably assured, and to avoid those in relation to whom the risks of nonpayment are relatively high.

This does not mean that the typical firm that sells on account hopes to avoid bad-debt losses; its objective, rather, is to *minimize them in relation to its volume of sales*. The complete avoidance of bad-debt losses would ordinarily require a restriction of credit selling only to buyers of the strongest credit ratings. Hence, a substantial additional volume of sales to people not so highly rated—but most of whom would meet their obligations—would be sacrificed for the dubious record of having a perfect collection experience. If a firm can expand its net profit by $50,000 (before deductions for bad debts originating in the additional sales) by selling to a group of customers who have credit standings substantially inferior to the best, and if it thereby incurs bad-debt losses of $30,000, the net result would surely indicate the wisdom of the sales expansion. A record of low bad-debt losses may thus be indicative of a too-restrictive credit policy—of poor financial management rather than the reverse.

The risks that a firm can afford to take in its selection of credit customers depend on such circumstances as its margin of profit and the phase of the business cycle in which the sales take place. Other things being equal, a bad-debt loss of $100,000 would be a much bigger blow to a firm whose markup measured in terms of selling prices is 20 percent than it would be to one with a markup of, say 50 percent. The loss would wipe out the gross profit on $500,000 of sales of the first firm, but that on only $200,000 of sales of the second. As for the business cycle, the probabilities of collecting payments from customers of relatively poor credit standing are generally much better in its expansion phase than in the contraction phase; hence, more liberal selling to these people may be hazarded in periods of expansion. During periods of general business contraction, however, increased caution in selling on account, even to customers of hitherto excellent credit standing, may be advisable—something that would be out of the question in the expansion phase of the cycle.

Credit Limits. Deciding which prospective customers will and which will not be allowed to buy on credit requires something more than a mere placing of names in one category or the other. For each customer who is approved for credit, a maximum limit for the amount of his indebtedness at any time is usually also desirable. An analysis of the financial position of a customer may indicate that he should be able to meet obligations up to $10,000 without serious difficulty, but that he would be overextending himself should he take on an obligation to pay within a limited period of time, say, $12,000 or $14,000. For this customer, accordingly, the selling firm would be wise to set $10,000 as the maximum credit to be outstanding at any time.

For firms of the highest credit standing, sellers ordinarily set no limits—they are happy to sell on account as much as these firms are willing to take, always depending, however, on the sellers' own cash positions, that is, their capacity to carry the accounts. For other firms, the maximum limits are not necessarily the final word. When the seller, on the basis of repeated transactions, finds that the buyer meets his obligations within the prescribed limit faithfully and without apparent strain, he may move the limit upward by successive steps, perhaps rather substantially with each step. In other instances, though there may be no reason to lift limits on a permanent basis, special circumstances may occasionally justify going beyond them.

The setting of limits makes possible the handling of most sales on account on a routine basis. As long as a customer's orders are within his limit, and provided that his obligations already on the books are not past due, the orders can be filled without reference to the credit department for specific approvals. Only orders that go beyond the limits or have special problems involved need go to the credit manager and his staff for separate consideration.

Credit Periods. Among manufacturers and wholesalers, in particular, the time allowed to buyers to pay for goods purchased on account is usually tailored in relation to the period required for the buyers, in turn, to resell the goods and to collect payment for them. Thus, the buyer will not necessarily pay out of his existing means at the time of sale to him, but out of the proceeds of resales to his own customers. For this reason, credit terms on interbusiness sales of goods of rapid turnover, such as foodstuffs, are usually much shorter than for goods of relatively slow turnover, such as electrical appliances and furniture. Also, terms are often shorter on sales to firms that themselves sell for cash than they are to firms that sell on a deferred-payment basis. In a similar way, credit sales of goods to be devoted to the buyer's own use, such as industrial equipment, often call for shorter terms than those on sales to buyers for resale.

As a rule, firms selling on account tend to be somewhat less strict in insisting on payment within the prescribed credit period than they are with other conditions of the credits they grant. This does not mean that a well-managed firm will be lax in its collection policy; if it were, it could hardly be described as well managed. What is meant is that such a firm is likely to take prompt action to collect past-due accounts if extensions, for good reasons, have not been requested, but that it is likely to be rather generous in granting extensions when they are requested well in advance of due dates and the requests are well supported with evidence to justify them. At the very time of sale, moreover, such a firm will probably allow some customers terms longer than the usual ones if the customers are able to advance good reasons for special treatment. Many firms, indeed, deliberately take on a limited number of customers who are known to be slow pay; they conclude that the additional profits to be made on sales to these people will exceed the additional costs of carrying the receivables for longer periods as well as expanded collection expenses.

Sales Discounts. In Chapter 8, it was pointed out that buyers of goods should find it highly advantageous—except possibly in certain extraordinary situations such as periods of tight money—to take cash discounts allowed for prompt payment. But if the taking of discounts is advantageous to buyers, the granting of such discounts must ordinarily be disadvantageous to the sellers. If in taking cash discounts the buyer earns interest at a high rate—30.7 percent per annum in the illustration of Chapter 8—the seller necessarily pays interest at the same high rate on the money that his customers pay him ahead of time. It is a reasonable proposition, therefore, that sellers generally ought not to allow cash discounts unless the competitive situation has made the giving of discounts a standard practice.

When the seller has a choice in the matter, circumstances justifying cash discounts must be rare indeed. Allowing cash discounts should have little effect toward reducing bad debts. Customers who are able to pay within 10 days to earn a discount will surely pay within 30 or 60 days, or whatever the regular credit period may be, if they are not allowed a discount. People whose accounts are destined to turn out to be uncollectible will rarely have more capacity to pay if a discount is allowed than if not allowed. And, in the matter of high interest rates, a firm that needs money within 10 days from the date of certain sales ought to be able—in consideration of the good, collectible accounts on its books, if for no other reason—to find a financial institution willing to lend it the money at a rate per annum of, say, 5 or 6 percent. Only in periods of tight money is it possible that such a financial institution may not be found.

Notes and Drafts. In a few lines of business, such as the wholesale jewelry trade, the buyer on credit is customarily required to give the seller a promissory note in which a promise to pay the amount of the invoice at a designated time is specifically written out with the signature of the buyer. In a few others, the seller draws a draft on the buyer, ordering him to pay the amount of the invoice at a designated time, and the buyer is required to write the word "accepted," the date of acceptance, and his signature on the face of the instrument. In legal complexion, an accepted draft and a promissory note are much the same, for the acceptor of a draft, no less than the signer of a note, promises to make payment according to the terms of the instrument. For this reason, both notes and accepted drafts are usually shown among the current assets in the selling firm's balance sheet simply as "notes receivable"—a designation that distinguishes them from the more common "accounts receivable," which designates claims on customers not evidenced by notes or drafts.

By contrast with the use of book accounts for recording customers' obligations, the use of notes and drafts offers some advantages. For unpaid obligations that become the subjects of lawsuits, it may be somewhat easier, by producing customers' notes or accepted drafts, for sellers to prove their right to payment than it would be to prove it by means of book entries, invoices, and other such documents. If a seller wants to borrow from a commercial bank or other lender on the security of his receivables, he will surely find it more convenient to discount his holdings of notes and accepted drafts or to transfer them to the lender as collateral than to sell or pledge accounts receivable. Moreover, some debtors seem to feel a stronger compulsion to pay written obligations than oral ones. All the more is this to be expected when the note or draft of a debtor is made payable at the bank with which he ordinarily does business, for the dishonor of a note or draft presented through the bank for payment would undoubtedly injure his credit standing, not only with the trade creditor but also with the bank itself.

Despite these advantages of the use of notes and drafts, the vast majority of American firms that sell on a credit basis are quite satisfied to sell on open account—that is, by simply recording in ledger accounts customers' obligations to pay. Additionally, of course, they have invoices, copies of bills of lading, and other kinds of documents to prove the existence of obligations should disputes arise about their nature and amounts. In some cases, however, firms that do not use notes and drafts in the ordinary procedures of credit selling make use of them in handling delinquent accounts. A customer who does not pay within the allowed credit period may be granted an extension only if he agrees to sign a note specifically promising payment at the end of the extended period. The delinquent debtor may be required to make the note payable at his bank, but whether he is or is not so required, presentment of the note for payment through that bank is often thought a desirable procedure for putting additional pressure on him. A delinquent debtor who refuses to sign notes, or who refuses to cooperate with his creditor in other ways, may be prodded, nevertheless, if the creditor chooses to draw a draft on him for the amount of his unpaid obligation, and has it presented to him for payment by the bank with which he keeps his deposit account and from which, perhaps, he obtains loans. Although the draft, being simply an order to pay, adds nothing to the creditor's right to payment, the debtor may fear a loss of credit standing in the eyes of his bank should he fail to honor it.

Credit Investigation

Classifying prospective customers as acceptable or nonacceptable as credit risks and determining credit limits for the acceptable ones require a painstaking collection and analysis of many kinds of pertinent information about each applicant. Credit investigation is expensive, but the firm that tries to economize in its outlays for this purpose is likely to have resulting bad-debt losses far exceeding what it saves through its efforts toward expense cutting. In small, isolated transactions, to be sure, the costs of thoroughgoing credit investigations could hardly be justified; hence, such sales must be made, if at all, on the basis of rather scanty credit information. But for the general run of transactions, the assembly and analysis of comprehensive credit data, whatever it may cost, is indispensable.

Character, Capacity, and Capital. The objective of a credit investigation, it is often said, is a judgment of the character, capacity, and capital of the person or firm that applies for credit. On the basis of judgment by the three C's of credit, applications will be granted or denied, or it may be that sale on regular terms will be denied, but the door will be left open for the working out of some kind of special terms.

Character pertains to the integrity of the customer—his moral qualities. Does he have the intention of fulfilling his obligations? Will he made every effort to meet the obligation according to its terms? Or will he try to delay payment even though he is well able to pay within the allowed credit period? Will he demand reductions in his obligation by dishonest claims that goods were received in poor condition or that they were not exactly what he ordered? *Capacity* has to do with managerial ability. Does the customer have the knowledge, skill, and experience to properly run his business? Specifically, can he, within a reasonable time and with a reasonable profit, resell the goods bought on account, so that he will have the means to make payment within the allowed credit period? *Capital* is concerned with the customer's financial position—the existing relationship of his assets and liabilities. Does he have the facilities necessary for the operation of a successful business? Are these facilities conveniently located and intelligently arranged so that they can be used with a minimum of operating costs? What liabilities does the customer already have—their nature, amount, and terms? Which of these liabilities will have priority of payment over the obligation to the selling firm? Will the addition of an obligation to the selling firm make the customer's liabilities unreasonably high in relation to his own investment in the business?

Sources of Credit Information. To answer questions of the kinds just suggested—and many others of similar import—information is drawn from many sources. With repeat customers, much useful information can be drawn from the selling firm's own ledgers and files. Here is a record of how the customer has behaved in the past—whether he has customarily made payment within the discount period or the allowed credit period, or has permitted his account to become delinquent; whether he has shown restraint or has been unreasonable in making claims for damaged goods; whether he has attempted to deduct cash discounts long after expiration of the discount period; and whether he has been prompt or slothful in answering correspondence about credit problems.

Interviews with customers, both old and new, are usually considered an important means of acquiring credit data. The customer should know more about his business than anybody else, and the information that he supplies should be invaluable, assuming that he gives it both frankly and honestly. In many instances, however, only the salesmen of a credit-granting firm have personal contacts with the customer, and salesmen often resent being delegated the task of collecting credit information because they feel that it interferes with their primary goal of making sales. Many salesmen, indeed, are probably poorly equipped to judge what is or is not important from the standpoint of credit analysis—they may collect the wrong facts or put erroneous interpretations on the right ones. Thus, there is every good reason—except for the additional expense involved—for credit managers or members of their staffs to visit customers to make their own judgments. Field trips of credit men among customers have been increasing in popularity. It is being more and more widely recognized that personal relationships originating in direct contacts of credit men with customers give both a much better understanding of mutual problems. Such an understanding often makes possible the working out of difficult situations on a much friendlier and mutually satisfactory basis than otherwise would be possible.

The customer also provides information about himself by supplying financial statements—a balance sheet, an income statement, and, for a corporation, a statement of surplus and, desirably, a series of these over a period of years. Judgments about a customer's capital are largely based on an analysis of such statements. Various ratios computed from these statements are compared with similar ratios computed from earlier statements and with representative ratios computed for other firms in the same industry (as published, for example, by Dun & Bradstreet and by some trade associations). Such comparisons often reveal much about the position and prospects of the customer's business.

Additional credit information is obtained by correspondence with other sellers on account and banks and by drawing on the many facts and figures acculculated by credit-rating agencies and credit interchange bureaus. A new customer who wants to buy on account will be asked to supply the names of several other firms he buys from on that basis, as well as the name of the bank he does business with. The selling firm will ask these sources for whatever information they can reveal about the applicant's creditworthiness. Firms and banks thus approached for credit information are inclined to be rather generous in providing it—as long as they can feel that they are not revealing something confidential—since they hope to be treated generously, in turn, when they take this route to obtain information about their customers and prospective customers. Generally regarded as essential for any firm that sells a substantial volume of goods on account are subscriptions to the services of Dun & Bradstreet, which is a general credit-rating and credit-reporting agency, or of specialized agencies in certain business fields, such as the Jewelers Board of Trade and the Lumberman's Credit Association, Inc., and membership in local credit interchange bureaus affiliated with the National Association of Credit Management. Dun & Bradstreet provides its subscribers with its *Reference Book*, in which credit ratings are given to a large majority of firms operating in all lines of business in the United States and Canada. On specific request, it provides detailed reports on the affairs of individual firms (the subscription price varies, of course, according to the number of such reports requested). The specialized agencies supply similar services in their respective fields. Members of local credit interchange bureaus periodically turn into them information about their experiences with all their credit customers, and copies of these reports are filed with the central office of a national interchange system. From the central file, reports summarizing evaluations of individual firms as filed by their trade creditors can be drawn at the request of a local interchange bureau member.

Interpretation and Revision. Greater acumen and skill are required in analyzing credit data than in gathering it. The analyst must be able to pick out and assign appropriate weights to the facts that are most significant as indicators of a customer's position and prospects; this obviously means that he must have a sufficient sense of discrimination to recognize other facts as being relatively inconsequential. Especially must he avoid what may be called mechanical interpretations of a customer's position, as in the interpretation of rations computed from the customer's financial statements. Ratios of a given magnitude must not be regarded as absolute indicators of the strength or weakness of the customer's credit standing; they can have meaning only when evaluated in the light of surrounding circumstances. A careful analysis of the particular circumstances of a customer's operations may result in a favorable judgment on his creditworthiness, despite an out-of-line situation in his ratios as compared with those of other firms or with his own in preceding years.

No less important than original evaluations of customers' credit positions is their continual reevaluation, so that maximum limits can be increased as improvements are shown, or reduced or even canceled if deterioration is apparent. What may be a safe limit for a given customer in a period of expansion in general business activity may become quite unsafe in a period of general business contraction; and what may be a safe limit for a customer who is expanding his sales of a given type of goods may be quite unsafe if he is taking on new lines with which he has had little experience. In brief, credit administration requires constant vigilance to detect changes in circumstances and conditions that tend to make earlier evaluations of doubtful further usefulness.

Collection Policy

A thoroughgoing investigation of an applicant for credit and a continuing careful analysis of assembled data pertaining to him should have the very beneficial effect of keeping down the costs, difficulties, and possible loss of goodwill incident to efforts to collect payment on overdue accounts. Accordingly, a striving for economies in credit investigation and analysis may turn out to be shortsighted in that economies realized may be more than offset by additional costs incurred in prodding delinquent customers to meet their obligations, as well as by bad-debt losses. With competent credit management, expenses in collecting a substantial majority of a firm's accounts should be very small. This means that a goodly majority of the customers should be of such credit standing that they can be depended on always, or almost always, to pay in strict accordance with the terms allowed them.

But rare is the firm selling on account that has no collection problems. An extremely low incidence of delinquencies, indeed, would doubtless be indicative, in most instances, of too-strict credit standards—indicative of a neglect of sales possibilities on which profits probably would considerably exceed additional collection expenses and bad-debt losses. Many firms, as has been noted, deliberately choose to sell to firms known to be slow pay as well as to classes of customers of inferior credit standing among whom, on the average, a certain incidence of bad debts is expected.

But if sales on account are made to customers of slow-pay reputation and to others of inferior credit ratings, efforts must be made to collect from *all* these people. All have obligations to pay, and the hope is that all will pay. The expectation of an *average* number of delinquencies or an *average* bad-debt loss does not mean that this customer or that one is to be excused as a matter of course if he fails to pay on time or if he indicates his intention of not paying at all. Thus, collection policies must be as carefully devised and administered as are those concerned with credit investigation and analysis. For the slow-pay people, the objective generally is to collect as quickly as possible but with as much finesse as possible so that their goodwill can be preserved. For those with whom the likelihood of payment decreases with each passing day—because of their deteriorating financial position, for example—the objective ordinarily is to collect as quickly as possible, regardless of the preservation of goodwill.

In trying to collect overdue accounts, credit managers make varied uses of collection letters, telephone calls, telegrams, collection drafts, the services of attorneys and collection agencies, and lawsuits for judgments against delinquent customers. However, we need not attempt to review here the substance, logic, and priorities of these procedures. Suffice it is to say that in most instances the procedures can be made largely a matter of routine, but that, nevertheless, a study of the individual case often suggests departures from routine that can prove to be most beneficial.

Credit Insurance

Since the determination of a firm's insurance program is essentially a finance function, its financial managers are likely to be responsible for weighing the pros and cons of credit insurance as a means of reducing the risks of selling on account. Credit insurance is designed to give sellers protection against *abnormal* losses on their accounts receivable. Hence, a firm's financial managers must consider, on the one hand, the possibilities of abnormal losses and, on the other, the premiums charged for the protection that credit insurance provides. The protection of credit insurance probably would be attractive if:

1. A firm has a few accounts much larger than the average of its accounts.
2. A relatively small firm has only a few large accounts, any one of whose loss would seriously threaten the seller's solvency.
3. A firm's customers are largely concentrated in one locality or in an industry noted for rather violent cyclical fluctuations.
4. There is much uncertainty about the future course of general business activity.

Credit insurance policies can be obtained either for general coverage of accounts receivable or for the coverage of specific accounts. For the firm that has a few accounts much larger than the average, therefore, specific coverage for these large accounts may be regarded as adequate.

The usual general coverage policy provides that the insurance company will bear 90 percent of the loss on insured accounts, but with a deduction for what is called the primary loss on these accounts. The primary loss provision means that the insured firm will still bear normal losses incurred in selling on account, and the 90 percent provision means that it will also absorb a portion of abnormal losses in the role of coinsurer. To illustrate, let us assume that a certain firm in a given year has sales covered by credit insurance of $900,000, that its primary loss rate is stipulated in the insurance policy at .75 percent of credit sales, that the policy has a 10 percent coinsurance clause, and that its bad-debt losses on the year's sales actually turned out to be $25,000. Its claim against the insurance company would be determined as follows.

Losses on sales on insured accounts	$25,000
Less 10 percent for coinsurance	2,500
	$22,500
Less primary loss (.75% of $900,000)	6,750
Net claim on insurance company	$15,750

Obtaining credit insurance does not eliminate the need of careful credit and collection administration. The insurance companies do not insure accounts whose credit ratings (as published by Dun & Bradstreet and other rating agencies) fall below certain stipulated levels, nor do they insure portions of accounts in excess of the maximum limits that they prescribe. Necessarily, therefore, the insuring firm continues to take the full risk on sales to customers whose credit ratings are below the stipulated levels, as well as on sales in excess of the maximum limits prescribed by the insurance companies for customers with acceptable ratings.

TESTING ACCOUNTS RECEIVABLE MANAGEMENT

As means of evaluating the results of a firm's accounts receivable management policies—and, therefore, of judging the soundness of the policies—its financial managers may compute several kinds of ratios and call for the preparation of several kinds of reports. A brief survey of the more significant of these ratios and reports is appropriate at this time.

Ratio of Accounts Receivable to Daily Credit Sales

Probably most useful as a quick means of checking the effectiveness of credit and collection policies is the ratio of accounts receivable at the end of a month to the average daily credit sales of that month. Suppose, for example, that a firm's accounts receivable at the end of a certain 30-day month amount to $80,000 and that its average daily credit sales during the month were $2,000. The ratio is thus 40, indicating that on the average 40 days are required to collect on credit sales. Is this good or bad? The answer depends, of course, on the credit terms stipulated by the firm. If the firm sells on the basis of net payment in 30 days, with no discount allowed for earlier payment, the ratio would indicate a substantial volume of delinquencies, for about $20,000 of the account balances probably originated in sales of months preceding the present one.[2] If the firm allows a cash discount for payment within, say, 10 days, with the net amount due in 30 days, the ratio would be indicative of a much worse delinquency situation, since many of the buyers in the present month must have already paid to take advantage of the discount. If, on the other hand, the firm's terms call for net payment in 45 days, with no cash discount allowed for earlier payment, the ratio would indicate the possibility that no accounts are delinquent, and that, indeed, quite a few of the customers have paid well before expiration of the 45-day period.

As with almost any ratio, the usefulness of a ratio of accounts receivable to average daily credit sales is enhanced if it can be compared with similar ratios of other firms and with the same type of ratio for the firm itself computed for other periods. Unfortunately, published statements of other firms usually do not give details about monthly credit sales and monthly balances of accounts receivable, nor do credit-rating agencies and trade associations publish information of this kind. But a firm can certainly compare its own ratios as computed from month to month. Thus, in terms of the illustration just used, the situation is improving, whatever the credit terms of the firm may be, if in the preceding month the ratio was 42 and in the month before that, 45. Equally, it is deteriorating if in the preceding month the ratio was 39 and in the month before that, say, 37.

Aging Accounts Receivable

While the ratio of accounts receivable at the end of a month to the credit sales of that month serves as a quick means of testing, the financial managers of a business enterprise are likely to want details about the exact status of the accounts that are current (not past due) and those that are delinquent. For this purpose, a statement in which the accounts receivable are aged is most commonly used. A form of this statement, with a few illustrative entries, is presented as Figure 9–1.

---

[2]The amount would be probable because transactions do not necessarily take place evenly from day to day at the average rate.

Such a statement is especially useful in judging the effectiveness of credit and collection policies when it is compared with similar statements prepared for preceding months. For example, deterioration in the quality of the accounts receivable is indicated if the largest proportion of delinquencies reported this month are in the 31- to 60-day class, whereas last month only a small proportion were in this class and in longer-term classes. Comparison with aging statements of the same month in preceding years is also desirable, since certain seasonal factors affecting many of the firm's customers may account for a rise in the amount and length of delinquencies in the same month or group of months year after year. If expansions in the amounts and lengths of delinquencies in preceding years according to a seasonal pattern did not result in an unusual amount of bad-debt losses, a rise this year need not occasion undue anxiety.

FIGURE 9–1
Form for Aging Accounts Receivable

JAMES BATES & CO., INC.
Age of Accounts Receivable
September 30, 19—

				Overdue			
Customer	*Address*	*Total Balance*	*Current*	*1–30 Days*	*31–60 Days*	*61–90 Days*	*Over 90 Days*
Ames Corporation...	Chicago, Ill.	$ 6,285.20	$ 6,285.20				
Anderson & White...	Denver, Colo.	1,812.45			$1,812.45		
Atlas Sales Co.......	Sioux City, Ia.	850.00	700.00	$ 150.00			
Ballinger Corp......	Dallas, Tex.	5,212.90	5,212.90				
Bond & Drexel......	Detroit, Mich.	1,281.50				$ 623.20	$ 658.30
Total........		$286,175.19	$245,112.20	$23,189.50	$9,175.12	$5,283.12	$3,415.25

Delinquency Ratios

Monthly statements in which accounts receivable are aged provide data for the computation of various kinds of significant delinquency ratios. In terms of the totals presented in Figure 9–1, it is significant that total delinquencies at the end of September amounted to 14.3 percent of accounts receivable then, and that, in turn, delinquencies of 1 to 30 days amounted to 8.1 percent of accounts receivable, those of 31 to 60 days to 3.2 percent, those of 61 to 90 days to 1.8 percent, and those over 91 days to 1.2 percent. A comparison of ratios of this kind from month to month is often much more revealing of an improving or deteriorating situation than a comparison of the *amounts* of current balances and delinquencies, especially if the volume of credit sales and accounts receivable varies substantially throughout the year on account of seasonal factors. Suppose, for example, that the August aging statement of James Bates & Co., Inc. revealed a total of approximately $35,000 of balances 1 to 30 days past due. A comparison of that figure with the related figure of $23,189.50 in the

September statement might be taken as evidence of improvement. But if total accounts receivable at the end of August had amounted to approximately $500,000, the ratio of delinquencies in the 1- to 30-day class in that month would have been in the vicinity of 7 percent—obviously a more favorable ratio than that of September.

Often useful also are ratios of delinquencies to the credit sales of the months in which the delinquencies originated. Referring again to Figure 9–1, and assuming that James Bates & Co., Inc. sells on the basis of 30 days net, the balances 1 to 30 days past due must have originated in August, those 31 to 60 days past due, very largely in July, and so on. If, then, ratios of past-due balances to the credit sales of the originating months are found to be out of line with other similar ratios for other months or for the same months in other years, an investigation of the reasons for the deviations is immediately suggested.

Bad-Debt Ratios

Many business firms base judgments of the quality of their credit and collection policies, in part at least, on ratios of bad-debt charge-offs of a given period to the credit sales of that period. But such ratios must be used with caution. Whether or not they are significant depends on a firm's charge-off policy. If the firm delays for a year or more in writing off accounts eventually found to be uncollectible, the charge-offs of any year are obviously quite unrelated to the credit sales of that year. Similarly, it is patently illogical to relate to this year's credit sales an uncollectible account charged off, say, in April but originating in a sale made in December of last year.

Even when charge-offs are properly related to the year or periods in which the uncollectible accounts originated, judicious interpretation is necessary. If the ratio of bad debts to the related credit sales increases from year to year, and sales are not expanding significantly, growing laxity in credit administration is strongly indicated. But if the increase in the ratio is accompanied by rapidly expanding sales, it may simply reflect a policy of extending credit to additional classes of lower-rated customers in the expectation that earnings from the additional sales will exceed the increased incidence of bad debts. In this case, therefore, the bad-debt ratio must be considered in relation to changes in net profit; only on the basis of such a consideration can the wisdom of the new policy be determined. Again, bad-debt ratios declining from period to period, with sales decreasing or at least not expanding significantly, may be indicative of an unwise tightening of credit standards and terms; while declining ratios from period to period with sales rapidly expanding would be good evidence of a high degree of administrative efficiency.

Usually to be recommended is the keeping of a record of credit orders declined on account of unsatisfactory ratings of the would-be buyers. Studied in relation to bad-debt ratios, such a record may suggest certain conclusions deserving further investigation. For example, low bad-debt ratios for periods in which many orders were declined would, again, be indicative of excessive strictness in credit standards and terms; and, on the other hand, high bad-debt ratios in periods in which there were many refusals to sell on account would be evidence of incompetence in credit administration.

Collection Reports

A further means of checking upon the quality of a firm's credit and collection policies is the preparation of periodic reports to show what percentage of customers' balances on the books at the beginning of each period is collected during the period. For a firm whose credit period does not exceed 30 days, a monthly report is likely to be most useful; for one whose credit period falls between 30 and 60 days, a bimonthly report, and so on. In such a report, it is usually desirable, for purposes of comparison, to show the percentage collections of one or more preceding periods or of the "year to date," as well as those of the same months or periods of the preceding year. Changes in collection percentage points from period to period may also be shown to emphasize the comparison. The accounts themselves can be classified in various ways, but a classification on the same basis as in the aging statement, as illustrated in Figure 9–2, is likely to be especially useful in tying together the two kinds of data.

FIGURE 9–2
Collection Report

JAMES BATES & CO., INC.
Collections as Percentages of Opening Balances
For the Month of October, 19–

Classification	*Current Month*	*Preceding Month*	*Year to Date (Average)*	*Last Year*		*Net Change— Current Month Last Year to Current Month This Year*
				Same Month	*Year to Date (Average)*	
Current..........	92.6	93.3	91.9	88.2	87.7	+4.4
Past due:						
1–30 days.....	86.5	87.7	88.0	84.5	85.4	+2.0
31–60 days.....	63.8	67.9	65.2	59.3	61.3	+4.5
61–90 days.....	54.2	61.2	56.5	52.2	53.2	+2.0
Over 90 days...	45.7	43.3	42.8	38.7	40.1	+7.0

ECONOMIZING INVESTMENT IN ACCOUNTS RECEIVABLE

In some lines of business, it is possible for firms to sell substantial volumes of goods on a credit basis and yet to invest little or none of their own cash in carrying accounts receivable. One way this can be done is to have customers sign promissory notes, evidencing their obligations to pay, and then to sell these notes to financial institutions such as sales finance companies and commercial banks. A second way is to use the services of factors. Let us consider these procedures.

Sale of Customers' Notes

The procedure of taking and selling customers' notes is feasible chiefly in connection with sales of goods on an installment payment basis. It is especially prominent, therefore, in the sale of consumer durable goods, such as automobiles, electrical appliances for the home, household furniture, jewelry, and furs. But it has also long been common in the sale of machinery and other productive equipment to farmers, and in recent years it has rapidly grown in popularity in the sale of machinery and equipment to manufacturing companies.

Conditional Sales Contracts. The instrument most commonly used in effecting installment sales is the conditional sales contract. The installment buyer of an automobile, for example, signs a contract in which he promises to pay a specific sum of money monthly for a stipulated period, such as 24 or 30 months. The total of the installment payments thus promised is equal to the selling price of the automobile plus certain insurance and finance charges, and minus the down payment made at the time of purchase or the allowance for a used car traded in. The seller of the automobile—or his assignee if he sells the contract, such as to a financial institution—retains title to it until full payment of the installments has been made, and the contract provides that on such full payment the installment buyer becomes the owner. If the buyer defaults on the contract, he forfeits all payments made up to that time, and the seller or his assignee has the right to repossess the car.

Arrangements with Financial Institutions. In buying an installment sales contract from a dealer in automobiles or other durable goods, a sales finance company or commercial bank ordinarily pays him an amount equal or close to the unpaid balance of the selling price. Thus, with the down payment or the trade-in plus the payment received from the financial institution, the dealer is in a position much as if he had sold on a straight cash basis. In fact, he is exactly in this position, one may say, if he is able to sell the contract on a nonrecourse basis. This means that the financial institution gives up its right to proceed against the dealer to recover losses due to the installment buyer's default; it bears the loss should its advance to the dealer exceed its collections from the buyer plus whatever it can recover by repossessing and reselling the automobile or other good. However, buying installment contracts on a nonrecourse basis is not favored by the financial institutions. Only a few of the smaller sales finance companies, it appears, are willing to operate on this basis.

Sometimes, dealers sell their contracts on a full-recourse basis whereby they are contingently liable for the installment buyer's unpaid obligation. On such a basis, however, the dealer has the right to repossess the financed article and to recover by its resale as much of his loss as is possible. By far the most common procedure is for the dealer to sell his contracts on the basis of a repurchase agreement. On this basis, the dealer agrees to buy back the financed article from the financial institution for the amount of the installment buyer's unpaid obligation (adjusted downward for unearned finance charges and prepaid insurance premiums), *if it is possible for the financial institution to repossess it.* If an automobile, for example, has been confiscated by a government agency because it has been used for illegal purposes, or if it is beyond repossession because the installment buyer has skipped with it, the financial institution rather than the dealer bears such loss as is not covered by insurance.

Sale of Contracts versus Loans. It is not unreasonable to argue that a dealer who assigns installment contracts on a recourse or repurchase basis is really selling his goods on account, that he continues to carry accounts receivable, and that he is actually borrowing from the sales finance company or the commercial bank to carry these accounts receivable. It can be argued, in other words, that the dealer simply borrows to carry accounts receivable just as he might borrow for any other purpose.

Nevertheless, there are substantial differences between selling installment contracts and obtaining a loan, say, on the security of one's accounts receivable. On a loan, the dealer has a primary obligation to pay at a specific time; in a sale of contracts, he is only contingently obligated to pay—that is, only if the installment buyer does not pay. Most installment contracts are paid without a hitch, so that the dealer, one may say, has no further concern with these once they have been assigned to a financial institution. Even when defaults occur, the resale of the financed articles is often sufficient to meet the installment buyers' unpaid obligatlons. Again, the financial institutions see to it that financed goods are well protected by insurance—the premiums being paid by the installment buyers. Accordingly, if an automobile, for example, is demolished in a collision the loss falls chiefly on the insurance company rather than on the dealer. Still another common circumstance that eases a dealer's worries about his contingent liability is that most sales finance companies and commercial banks set aside individual loss reserves for the benefit of each dealer with whom they do business. To such a reserve is allocated a portion of the finance charge collected by the financial institution on the installment contracts assigned by the dealer. Thus, a dealer's own cash is encroached on by losses only when they exceed the amount accumulated in his loss reserve.

Factors' Services

Factors are specialized business organizations that are willing to assume full responsibility for the management of the accounts receivable of other enterprises. For their clients, as we may call those who use their services, they investigate the credit standings of prospective customers, approve sales to those of acceptable ratings, and undertake to make collections. In effect, they buy a client's accounts receivable as originating in approved sales, and on these they take the full risks of nonpayment. A factoring organization that has agreed to handle a client's receivables obligates itself to pay on a computed average due date all the accounts or invoices assigned to it within a given period, such as a month. The payment is the amount of the accounts reduced by such cash discounts as the client allows (whether or not the client's customers actually take these discounts[3]), whatever allowances have been made for returned goods, other similar allowances, and the amount of the factor's commission or fee. The factor's obligation is binding whether or not it has collected from the client's customers. If the client so wishes, the factor will provide cash in advance of the average due date. In this circumstance, the client receives in cash the amount of the receivables less the amount of the deductions indicated above[4] and less an additional interest charge measured by the number of days for which the advance is made.

If a client chooses to wait for payment until the average due date, it does not economize in its investment in accounts receivable. For the period from the date of sale to the average due date, it obviously has cash tied up on account of credit selling much as it would were it not using the factor's services. Nevertheless, it relieves itself of all expenses of credit and collection administration, and it avoids all risks of bad-debt losses since the factor buys the accounts without recourse. A factor's charges for these kinds of services depend on the types of goods the client sells, the volume of its sales, the average size of its invoices, and classes of its customers, their credit ratings, and other similar circumstances. Charges generally range from 0.75 percent to 1.5 percent on the volume of credit sales.[5]

However, the client can avoid investing cash in accounts receivable by indicating to the factor that it wants immediate payment as orders

---

[3]This rule applies because in computing average due dates the factor uses the earliest dates provided for in the terms of the individual sales. Thus, a sale on April 12 on terms of 2/10 n/60 would be considered due on April 22. By this arrangement, the factoring organization must use its own funds in making payment to the client if the client's customer does not pay within the 10-day period; but it is compensated by taking the cash discount for itself.

[4]Since the amount of allowances for returned merchandise, damages in transit, and the like cannot be known when the advance is given, the factor ordinarily retains a reserve equal to 5 to 10 percent of the face amount of the accounts. Any excess of the reserve over allowances as subsequently granted is later paid over to the client.

[5]Monroe R. Lazere (ed.), *Commercial Financing* (New York: The Ronald Press Company, 1968), p. 74.

are approved by the factor and as the goods are billed and delivered. For advance payment of this kind, as was indicated above, the factor charges interest for the period from the date of the advance payment to the average due date. Rates of interest generally range between 6 and 7 percent per annum. It should be observed that a client does not really obtain a loan from the factor by means of the arrangement just described; the client has no obligation to make any kind of repayment nor to make good on any accounts that turn out to be uncollectible. The interest is paid, therefore, simply as a means of having the advantage of present funds as against future funds—that is, as a means precisely of avoiding the investment of cash in accounts receivable.

Up to the early years of the present century, the services of factors were available almost exclusively to textile manufacturers, their sales agents, and converters, but since then a substantial broadening of the scope of their operations has taken place. The expansion was directed, first, to apparel manufacturers and wholesalers, but more recently factors' services have been made available to enterprises quite unrelated to the textile and apparel industries, including manufacturers, wholesalers, and distributors of furniture, electrical appliances, hardware, chemicals, cosmetics, paint, and paper products. Nevertheless, by far the greatest volume of accounts handled by factors continues to originate in the textile and apparel industries.

QUESTIONS

1. Compare the size and growth of the investment of corporations collectively in accounts receivable with their investment in inventories.
2. In what circumstances do business firms have a choice between selling for cash and selling on account?
3. When corporations have clear choices in deciding on terms of sale, what advantages can they gain by selling only for cash?
4. Why is the credits and collections function of business enterprises usually assigned to finance officers rather than to sales executives?
5. After a firm has decided to sell on account to meet competition, what additional kinds of decisions must it continue to make?
6. An important goal of credit administration is to minimize bad-debt losses. Is this proposition true or false? Discuss.
7. Discuss the pros and cons of allowing sales discounts as a means of persuading credit customers to make early payments.
8. In relation to credit sales, what use is made of promissory notes and commercial drafts?
9. On the basis of what kinds of factual information do credit managers judge the creditworthiness of customers and prospective customers? What are the principal sources of these facts?
10. Explain the meaning of character, capacity, and capital as criteria for credit judgments.

11. Explain the role of credit insurance as a means of protecting firms against bad-debt losses. How are coinsurance and primary loss provisions applied?

12. Explain how ratios of accounts receivable to credit sales can be used as means of testing the quality of firms' credit management.

13. What is the procedure of aging accounts receivable? What is such an analysis supposed to reveal?

14. What is a conditional sales contract? Why is the use of such contracts likely to be especially advantageous for firms that want to economize in their investment in accounts receivable?

15. Explain the procedure by which factoring organizations enable firms that sell on account to economize in their investment in accounts receivable.

PROBLEMS

1. In the year 19xx, the Seton Corporation had bad-debt losses of $20,000 on total credit sales of $550,000. Its policy of credit insurance provides protection against abnormal credit losses on total credit sales (all were within the limits allowed by the insurance company for each customer), has the 90 percent coinsurance clause, and sets 1 percent as Seton's ratio for primary loss. Determine the amount of Seton's claim for recovery against the insurance company.

2. The credit sales and charge-offs of bad debts of Antioch Sales, Inc. over a three-year period were as follows.

Year	*Credit Sales*	*Charge-offs*
19xx	$6,200,000	$35,000
19yy	5,800,000	33,000
19zz	6,100,000	37,000

Assuming that the charge-offs have been assigned to the years in which the related sales were made, even when they occurred later, what do the figures indicate about the quality of Antioch's credit management and, possibly, its improvement or deterioration?

3. Analyses of the accounts receivable of Lester and Lake, Inc. revealed the following percentages of accounts current and past due at the end of three successive months of the year 19xx.

	April	*May*	*June*
Current	78.6	83.5	81.5
Past due:			
1–30 days	9.5	10.6	4.2
31–60 days	6.3	2.3	9.8
61–90 days	4.8	3.4	1.3
Over 90 days	.8	.2	3.2

Assuming that the corporation's selling terms are net payment in 30 days, what do these figures indicate about the effectiveness of its credit and collection policies?

chapter 10

THE MANAGEMENT OF FIXED ASSETS

Sometimes, one hears or reads that current assets are the "lifeblood of industry"—a claim that seems to imply that current assets are much more important in business operations than are fixed assets. But trying to rank current and fixed assets in the order of importance is much like trying to decide which blade of a pair of scissors is the more important for cutting cloth. In the typical business enterprise, current and fixed assets must be combined in appropriate proportions for effective and profitable operations; one class of assets is no more dispensable than the other. A retail establishment that owns a large and well-selected inventory of goods would doubtless be most unhappily situated were it to lack facilities for the storage, display, and sale of these goods. Similarly, a manufacturing concern would surely be uncomfortable were it to have an excellent building and rows of machines well laid out, but lack raw materials and cash with which to pay wages and to meet other kinds of operating expenses. Therefore, only in the sense that current assets include cash—with which anything marketable, including fixed assets, can be bought, provided one has enough of it—can it be said that such assets are more important for business purposes than are fixed assets.

However, when a distinction is made between the *ownership* of assets and their *use* a further argument can be advanced for giving current assets a superior ranking. The typical enterprise owns all the current assets it employs in its operations, but enterprises collectively use fixed assets, worth many billions of dollars, that they do not own. Opportunities for renting land, buildings, machinery, and other fixed assets abound, in contrast with opportunities for acquiring current assets on a nonownership basis—for example, obtaining inventories on consignment. Thus, the financial managers of a business firm must ordinarily estimate cash requirements on a basis of needing to buy inventories, to carry receivables, and to meet current operating expenses, but they may simultaneously plan to avoid large outlays of cash for fixed assets in the expectation of being able to rent such facilities.

FIXED ASSET OWNERSHIP AND ACQUISITIONS

Post-World War II Record

Unfortunately, statistics of the value of fixed assets *used* by firms in the various industrial sectors are not available; hence, it is impossible, in any exact way, to rank these sectors according to the preponderance of fixed or current assets in their arrays of productive facilities. However, ownership data, such as those assembled in Table 7–1, page 136, give us a fair idea of the situation. A study of the figures presented there for holdings of land and other fixed assets indicates: (1) their outstanding position in public utility operations; (2) their quite substantial position in the operations of enterprises in agriculture, forestry, fisheries, mining, manufacturing, and service; and (3) their more moderate, but by no means inconsequential, position in contract construction and in wholesale and retail trade.

However, as indicators of the importance of fixed asset management in the affairs of business concerns, statistics of acquisitions in given periods of time tend to be more significant than statistics of ownership at specified times. Statistics of acquisitions are presented in Tables 10–1 and 10–2. Much has been heard of the great surge of business spending for facilities in the post-World War II period; its phenomenal character is surely proved by the figures of the two tables.

In Table 10–1 are presented estimates of the Board of Governors of the Federal Reserve System for corporate acquisitions of assets of the principal classes in the period 1946–67. Here, by comparison with acquisitions of other classes of assets the predominant position of plant and equipment acquisitions stands out clearly, amounting to the almost unbelievable sum of $714.6 billion in the 22-year period, and equal to 68.5 percent of total corporate asset acquisitions. This does not mean, of course, that a net expansion in the value of fixed asset holdings occurred at this level, since charges to depreciation during the period partially offset the additions to book value because of the acquisitions.[1] Nevertheless, the fact remains that corporations poured $714.6 billion into new plant and equipment, while allocating to the expansion of receivables only a little more than one fifth as much, and to the expansion of inventories only about one ninth as much.

---

[1]For the amount of corporate charges to depreciation in the post-World War II years, see Table 16–3, page 373.

That corporations were not alone in spending heavily for plant and equipment is indicated by a comparison of the grand totals in Tables 10–1 and 10–2, since the first records corporate spending and the second reports spending by "U.S. business" in general. However, this comparison is subject to distortion because of differences among the inclusions and exclusions in the two tables, as described in their footnotes. Accordingly, the greater significance of Table 10–2 is in its industrial breakdown, especially in its revelation of the outstanding role of manufacturing, "commercial and other," and public utility enterprises in plant and equipment acquisitions.

TABLE 10–1
Net Corporate Acquisitions of Assets, 1946–67*
(In billions of dollars)

Year	*Plant and Equipment*	*Inventories*	*Receivables*	*Liquid Assets*†	*Other Assets*	*Total*‡
1946	$ 12.0	$ 6.0	$ 4.3	$–4.6	$–.6	$ 17.0
1947	16.0	1.2	6.9	1.1	.5	25.7
1948	18.2	2.1	3.1	1.1	.5	25.0
1949	17.0	–1.7	– .4	3.1	.6	18.6
1950	19.3	4.8	12.6	4.4	.8	41.9
1951	21.4	8.6	4.4	2.9	.6	37.8
1952	22.2	2.2	4.5	.4	.4	29.7
1953	23.8	.8	– .5	1.9	.3	26.3
1954	23.6	–1.9	5.2	– .2	1.3	27.9
1955	26.6	4.9	12.1	5.2	2.6	51.4
1956	31.0	4.9	7.9	–4.2	3.5	43.1
1957	34.1	.6	2.8	– .1	2.6	40.0
1958	29.8	–2.5	8.4	2.5	3.9	42.1
1959	32.8	4.1	8.0	5.6	3.8	54.3
1960	36.1	3.0	6.5	–3.9	3.5	45.3
1961	35.5	1.5	10.1	3.5	4.4	55.0
1962	40.0	4.7	9.1	4.1	3.7	61.6
1963	42.3	4.3	9.2	4.3	5.6	65.8
1964	47.7	5.9	9.3	.8	2.9	66.6
1965	55.8	7.7	14.0	.8	8.8	87.1
1966	62.9	12.3	11.9	1.0	5.9	94.0
1967	66.5	4.8	8.0	1.9	6.4	87.6
Total	$714.6	$78.3	$157.4	$31.6	$62.0	$1,043.8
Percentage of grand total	68.5	7.5	15.1	3.0	5.9	100.0

*Excluding banks and other financial corporations and farm corporations.

†Consisting of paper money and coin, demand and time deposits, open-market commercial paper, and U.S. government securities.

‡In some instances, horizontal items do not add exactly to totals because of rounding.

Source: Board of Governors of the Federal Reserve System, *Flow of Funds Accounts 1945–1967* (Washington, D.C., 1968), pp. 35–36. (Totals and percentages supplied by the author.)

Ownership Policies and Problems

As they pertain to fixed assets, ownership problems and their solutions—solutions that appear as policy formulations—begin with decision making about whether or not to own at all. If opportunities to rent land, buildings, machinery and equipment, and other facilities abound, as we said earlier, decisions may be made in the direction of renting all or most of the fixed facilities that enterprise may need; then, ownership problems will be minimal, although some managerial problems will surely remain. Or decisions may go in the direction of economizing investment in fixed assets in other ways; some possibilities are described later in this chapter. If decisions are made in favor of ownership, many complex questions must be analyzed and answered, such as: What classes and proportions of needed fixed assets should be bought outright? When and from what sources

TABLE 10-2
Expenditures on New Plant and Equipment by U.S. Business, 1946-67
(In billions of dollars)

Year	*Manufacturing*	*Mining*	*Railroads*	*Other Transportation*	*Public Utilities*	*Communications*	*Commercial and Other**	*Total†*
1946	$ 6.8	$ .4	$ .6	$ .9	$ .8	$ .8	$ 4.5	$ 14.8
1947	8.7	.7	.9	1.3	1.5	1.4	6.1	20.6
1948	9.1	.9	1.3	1.3	2.5	1.7	5.2	22.1
1949	7.1	.8	1.4	.9	3.1	1.3	4.7	19.3
1950	7.5	.7	1.1	1.2	3.3	1.1	5.7	20.6
1951	10.9	.9	1.5	1.5	3.7	1.3	5.9	25.6
1952	11.6	1.0	1.4	1.5	3.9	1.5	5.6	26.5
1953	11.9	1.0	1.3	1.6	4.6	1.7	6.3	28.3
1954	11.0	1.0	.9	1.5	4.2	1.7	6.5	26.8
1955	11.4	1.0	.9	1.6	4.3	2.0	7.5	28.7
1956	15.0	1.2	1.2	1.7	4.9	2.7	8.4	35.1
1957	16.0	1.2	1.4	1.8	6.2	3.0	7.4	37.0
1958	11.4	.9	.8	1.5	6.1	2.6	7.2	30.5
1959	12.1	1.0	.9	2.0	5.7	2.7	8.2	32.5
1960	14.5	1.0	1.0	1.9	5.7	3.1	8.4	35.7
1961	13.7	1.0	.7	1.9	5.5	3.2	8.5	34.4
1962	14.7	1.1	.9	2.1	5.5	3.6	9.5	37.3
1963	15.7	1.0	1.1	1.9	5.7	3.8	10.0	39.2
1964	18.6	1.2	1.4	2.4	6.2	4.3	10.8	44.9
1965	22.5	1.3	1.7	2.8	6.9	4.9	11.8	52.0
1966	27.0	1.5	2.0	3.4	8.4	5.6	12.7	60.6
1967	26.7	1.4	1.5	3.9	9.9	5.9	12.3	61.7
Total	$303.9	$22.2	$25.9	$40.6	$108.6	$59.9	$173.2	$734.2
Percentage of grand total	41.4	3.0	3.5	5.5	14.8	8.2	23.6	100.0

*Including trade, service, finance, and construction.
†In some instances, horizontal items do not add exactly to totals because of rounding.
SOURCE: U.S. Department of Commerce, Office of Business Economics, *U.S. Income and Output* (Washington, D.C.: U.S. Government Printing Office, 1958), p. 193; and *Survey of Current Business*, various issues. (Vertical totals and percentages supplied by the author.)

should the buying be done? What limits should be assigned to the amounts of money to be invested in given groupings of assets? How are choices to be made among alternative investment proposals? And always closely related to questions such as these are problems of the availability of money and the costs that should be assigned to it. So complex, indeed, are many of these questions that a reasonably comprehensive treatment of them requires two chapters—Chapter 13 on capital budgeting and Chapter 14 on the cost of capital. In view of this later treatment, therefore, attention in the present chapter will be chiefly directed to problems and policies in the continuing management of fixed assets already acquired.

Financial problems related to fixed assets already owned continue as long as they are held. Some of these are routine in character—for example, providing cash on a continuing basis to keep the assets in a proper state of repair, to have them insured, and to pay property taxes on them. Cash to meet expenses such as these, as for other operating costs, is expected to be derived in the regular course of business out of the proceeds of sales. Often, however, additional cash must be provided to increase the productive potential of existing fixed assets—that is, for improvements and betterments. Expenditures for improvements and betterments—for example, the placement of partitions for the better utilization of office space or the addition of new kinds of appliances to machines to increase their capacities—do not simply conserve the existing values of assets; they increase these values.

The financial managers, moreover, must give careful thought to policies of charging depreciation to account for the gradual loss of value of fixed assets because of wear and tear and the action of the elements. Even though a firm's depreciation charges do not require current cash outlays, they do have important bearings on the profits it reports and the income taxes it must pay, and in many cases also on its dividend policies, its credit standing, the attractiveness of its stock, its property tax liabilities, and its pricing policies.

DEPRECIATION POLICY

Objectives in Charging Depreciation

The periodic charging of depreciation may be said to have two objectives: (1) to recognize as a current cost of operation the consumption of fixed assets in the normal course of business, and therefore to include this cost among the expenses of producing and selling; and (2) to retain in the business enterprise net asset values equal to the original values of the fixed assets. These two objectives are really so closely related as to be virtually identical; nevertheless, it may contribute to clarity to treat them separately.

Cost of Fixed Assets as Expense. In the illustrations presented in Chapter 5, we saw how depreciation charges are included among expenses of operation in the same way as are costs requiring current cash outlays. Indeed, total expenditures in the purchase of depreciable fixed assets could be immediately carried to expense accounts if their useful lives did not extend beyond one accounting period. Were a firm's accounting period, say, 20 years, and were it expected that all its original depreciable assets would wear out within that period, the firm could most conveniently charge the cost of the assets to an expense account and ignore the procedure of making a periodic charge for depreciation. Indeed, expenditures for small tools and other productive equipment expected to be short-lived are often treated exactly in this way. The cost of small tools, for example, is charged to an expense account, and at the end of the accounting period a deduction from this account is made for the value of tools still on hand, just as the inventory of office supplies at the end of the period is often deducted from the expense account for office supplies to arrive at the net expense for the period.

Only because what we call depreciable fixed assets are expected to have useful lives well beyond the ordinary accounting period of one year, therefore, are they treated differently from expenses. The services that are derived from direct and indirect labor and electric power are instantaneous; accordingly, there is no question that obligations incurred in obtaining these services are immediately chargeable as expenses of the current year. But the services to be derived from the use of a factory building may be expected to run for 40 years, so that it seems to be appropriate to set up its cost originally as an asset, and then to allocate a portion of this cost on some reasonable basis to each of the years of service. Such an allocation is, of course, the depreciation charge. Were the full cost of the building to be charged to an expense account in the year of acquisition, the profits of that year would be greatly understated, and those of each of the remaining 39 years overstated. And if, on the other hand, the cost were set up in an asset account and no annual depreciation charge taken, profits would be overstated in the first 39 years, and greatly understated in the 40th year, assuming that the valuelessness of the building were then recognized.

Retention of Net Asset Values. A second objective of charging depreciation, we say, is to retain in an enterprise net asset values equal to the original values of its fixed assets. How this works we saw in Chapter 6. We observed there that the cash throw-off with each circular flow of current assets is equal to profits (before income taxes) plus depreciation, and we noted that the depreciation charge has the effect of converting fixed assets into current assets. Since the portion of the throw-off attributable to depreciation is not income, no part of it should be paid to the government as taxes nor to the stockholders as dividends. Hence, it is retained in the business. A further illustration will show what happens. Suppose that a corporation begins business with assets and stockholders' equity as follows:

Assets		*Liabilities and Equity*	
Current assets	$500,000	Common stock	$900,000
Fixed assets	400,000		

Let us assume that the corporation's fixed assets are expected to have a useful life of 10 years and that their salvage value (trade-in, secondhand, or scrap value) at the end of that period is expected to be $50,000. If, therefore, the corporation charges depreciation on the straight-line basis, the annual charge will be $35,000. The corporation has, let us say, annual sales of $600,000, and annual out-of-pocket costs of operation of $480,000. Accordingly, its annual profit before income taxes but after deduction of the depreciation charge is $85,000. After the payment of income taxes, the entire remaining profit, let us say, is distributed as dividends to the stockholders. But the cash throw-off is $120,000, not $85,000; hence, at the end of the first year (assuming no further acquisitions of fixed assets), the balance sheet should look like this.

Assets			*Liabilities and Equity*	
Current assets......		$535,000	Common stock..............	$900,000
Fixed assets........	$400,000			
Less: Allowance				
for depreciation.	35,000	365,000		

And at the end of the tenth year (with the same assumptions), it should appear as follows:

Assets			*Liabilities and Equity*	
Current assets......		$850,000	Common stock..............	$900,000
Fixed assets........	$400,000			
Less: Allowance				
for depreciation.	350,000	50,000		

Thus, by appropriate depreciation policy the corporation will have conserved its assets. It will hold a total of assets at the end of the 10-year period equal to what it had in the beginning, although the composition of these assets will have changed.

Depreciation Charges and the Replacement of Fixed Assets

Nothing in the foregoing illustration indicates that the corporation would have sufficient *cash* to replace its fixed assets at the end of the 10-year period. It is true, of course, that the corporation might have set up a *replacement fund* by annually investing $35,000 in high-quality securities—that is, an amount equal to the cash throw-off on account of the annual depreciation charge. In this way, it might have had available for replacement purposes at the end of the 10-year period $350,000 plus the earnings on the fund. But if the corporation had had opportunities to expand sales during this period, it might have decided to use the annual cash throw-off of $35,000 to increase its inventories and accounts receivable. In this way, the firm would have had no more cash on hand at the end of the period than at the beginning; and it would be impossible to use inventories and accounts receivable as means of replacing the fixed assets. It would thus be necessary to look elsewhere for a new source of cash to effect the replacement.

The important fact that the foregoing discussion is designed to emphasize is that though the proper charging of depreciation conserves a firm's assets it does not automatically provide means to replace assets of the fixed classification. If goods are sold at prices high enough to cover all expenses of operation, including depreciation charges, there will be a cash throw-off equal to the depreciation charges, but the financial managers may decide to use this cash in many different ways. Unless they specifically set it aside, as by investment in securities, their capacity to replace fixed assets when they have outlived their usefulness is by no means assured.

Replacement at Higher Prices. Thinking of depreciation charges as providing means to replace fixed assets, many business executives argue that for income tax computations they ought to be permitted to deduct depreciation charges based on the replacement cost rather than on the original cost of such assets. The idea is that in or following periods of inflation, replacement assets of exactly the same qualities and capacities as the original ones will cost substantially more than did the original ones; thus, depreciation charges based on original cost must necessarily be inadequate for replacement. This plea has been much heard of in recent years, and understandably so since the trend of prices has been generally upward—sometimes sharply—since 1933.

Nevertheless, the federal tax authorities persistently reject this kind of plea as being unrealistic. It is their contention that taxable profits represent the difference between income and the costs incurred in deriving that income, and they hold that costs are to be measured by what has actually been spent in turning out products, not by what may have to be spent at some future time. The cost of labor is the bill for wages actually paid or accrued, and not what may have to be paid for wages next year. Accordingly, the tax authorities argue that the proper depreciation charge is the portion of the original cost that can reasonably be allocated to the current year, and not an allocation based on what may have to be paid for fixed assets at some future time.

Appropriations of Surplus for Replacement. Although the income tax regulations preclude for tax purposes the deduction of depreciation based on the prospective replacement cost of fixed assets, the financial managers of a business firm may nevertheless think it expedient to set up a fund to provide for higher cost replacements. To do this, they would doubtless place in the fund an amount equal to the cash throw-off from depreciation as actually charged, and add a further amount derived, it is likely, from the cash throw-off from profits. For the profits throw-off, they would restrict dividend payments to the stockholders and would appropriate for replacement purposes the profits thus withheld. In terms of the illustration given above, suppose that the corporation's managers expect the cost of replacing the fixed assets at the end of 10 years to be $650,000. They want to accumulate the difference between this sum and the expected salvage value of the existing fixed assets ($50,000)—that is, $600,000—and they estimate that cash contributions to the replacement fund of $47,000 annually, with interest to be earned on fund investments, will give them the amount aimed at. Of the annual cash throw-off from profits, they could take $12,000, add it to the throw-off of $35,000 on account of depreciation, and invest the combined sum of $47,000 in the replacement fund. Income tax liabilities, of course, would not be reduced by this allocation of $12,000, but dividends to the stockholders would necessarily be curtailed by that amount. At the end of the first year, then, the balance sheet of the corporation would appear as follows.

Assets			*Liabilities and Equity*	
Current assets......		$500,000	Stockholders' Equity:	
Fixed assets:			Common stock..............	$900,000
Machinery and equipment.....	$400,000		Surplus appropriated for replacement of fixed assets..............	12,000
Less: Allowance for depreciation.	35,000			
	$365,000			
Replacement fund.	47,000	412,000		
Total Assets..		$912,000	Total Equity..........	$912,000

It should be observed that the withholding of profits from dividend payments, like the charging of depreciation, results in no automatic provision for the replacement of fixed assets. Just as the cash throw-off provided by depreciation charges can be invested in inventories or accounts receivable, so also can that thrown off by profits not paid out as dividends. If cash for the replacement of fixed assets must be on hand at a given time, it must be specifically put aside for that purpose, unless, of course, there are expectations that it can be drawn in from outside, such as by borrowing or by the sale of additional stock. At any rate, cash thought to be temporarily invested in inventories and accounts receivable is likely to prove permanently thus invested—incapable of being pulled out at will for spending for fixed assets.

Application of Depreciation Theory

That properly allocated costs of depreciation, no less than the costs of labor, raw materials, and miscellaneous overhead items, ought to be recovered by a business establishment before profits are recognized is a theory beyond argument. But application of the theory is not an easy matter. Difficulties abound, even though one may be willing to concede that in keeping with the federal income tax regulations, depreciation should be based on original cost.

Estimation of Useful Lives. One difficulty is that of estimating the useful lives of the many different kinds of depreciable assets owned by operating businesses. The estimation of probable life is especially difficult in times of rapid technological development—something that seems to be a lasting and, for the most part, highly desirable feature of present-day civilization. Certain kinds of machines owned by a business enterprise may still be in excellent operating condition but may be quite useless, because public fancy has swung away from the product they were designed to turn out, or because newly invented machines of greater efficiency can turn out the product at much lower cost. In estimating the useful lives of depreciable assets, business managers are expected to make allowance for ordinary obsolescence—the normal probability, one might say, that useful lives will end some years before physical deterioration would render the assets unfit for efficient use. The income tax regulations permit taxpayers to allow for such ordinary obsolescence in determining what their deductible charges for depreciation should be, but allowance for extraordinary obsolescence is permitted only when the taxpayer is able to prove to the satisfaction of the tax authorities that specific actual or impending events will have the effect of substantially shortening the lives of machines and other assets as originally estimated.

The great influence of estimates of useful lives on the finances of business enterprises was clearly demonstrated after the Treasury published new guidelines for making these estimates in the summer of 1962—guidelines that, in effect, authorized the charging of depreciation on the basis of substantially shorter asset lives than had previously been permitted. As a result, many business managers immediately revised their estimates of useful lives downward, stepped up their depreciation charges, and thereby reduced their income tax liabilities; all this was revealed in tax returns. According to a survey reported by the Department of Commerce, in 1962 corporations increased depreciation charges by $2.4 billion on account of their adjustments to estimated asset lives, thereby reducing their tax bills for that year by approximately $1,250 million.[2]

Estimation of Salvage Values. A second difficulty arises from the need of estimating what will be the trade-in, secondhand, or scrap value of depreciable assets at the end of their estimated useful lives. Errors in estimating this value are ordinarily not so far-reaching in effect as are errors in estimating the duration of useful life, but they can be significant. In some cases, salvage values are often substantial,

---

[2]*Survey of Current Business*, July, 1963, p. 3.

as those for trade-in allowances for delivery trucks; in others, they are less than nothing, as when the cost of removal of old buildings exceeds the value of materials that can be salvaged. Technological developments can account for errors in estimating salvage values, no less than in estimating useful lives. At the time of acquisition of a particular kind of machine, for example, the managers of a firm may decide that it should have a good secondhand market eight years later when it will no longer be useful to the firm, but inventions and innovations in the meantime may have the effect of eliminating this secondhand market, causing the salvage value to fall to a level barely better than scrap value.

Selection of Method. Still a third difficulty is that of selecting the best method of allocating over the years of estimated useful life the total amount to be charged off as depreciation. Should equal annual charges be made? Should more be charged in the early years than in later years, or the reverse of this? Should the depreciation charges be related directly to output, with high charges, therefore, in years of high-level production and much smaller ones in years of low-level activity?

Such questions are important. Differences in methods of charging depreciation will usually mean differences from year to year in the amount of profits recognized and the size of income tax and property tax liabilities, and they may also account for variations in dividends, the selling prices of products, property insurance coverage and premiums, in the market behavior of corporate stocks, and credit standing—matters to which we will give attention a little later. Therefore, although total depreciation charges over the period of useful life may be identical, regardless of the method used, any method will tend to produce operating results and financial positions from year to year different from those that other methods would produce.

Effects of Varying Estimates of Useful Life: Illustration. Let us assume that three corporations, A, B, and C, have approximately identical complements of depreciable fixed assets acquired at a cost of $1.2 million, and that each earns annually $500,000 before deductions for depreciation and federal income taxes. We may also assume that there are no applicable state income taxes. Two further assumptions are that the managers of all three corporations decide that the fixed assets will have no salvage value at the expiration of their useful lives, and that they all choose to charge depreciation on the straight-line basis. But there agreement ends, for the managers have quite different opinions about the useful lives of the assets. The managers of Corporation A hit on eight years, and accordingly set the annual depreciation charge at $150,000. The managers of Corporation B are more—should we say?—pessimistic, thinking in terms of a useful life of six years, and therefore set the annual charge at $200,000. Corporation C's managers are decidedly optimistic, setting their sights on a useful life of 12 years with an annual depreciation charge of $100,000. In any of the early years, then, the results of operations of the three corporations would be as follows.

	A	*B*	*C*
Net profits before depreciation and federal income taxes	$500,000	$500,000	$500,000
Less depreciation	150,000	200,000	100,000
Net profits before federal income taxes	$350,000	$300,000	$400,000
Less federal income taxes*	161,500	137,500	185,500
Net profit to surplus	$188,500	$162,500	$214,500

*At 1968 rates but without the surcharge of 10 percent temporarily added in that year.

Now, let us make the further important assumption that the lives of the depreciable assets of all three corporations will actually turn out to be eight years, and that they will have no salvage value at the expiration of that period. Since Corporation A's estimate is the correct one (with the additional assumption that the straight-line method of charging depreciation is the most appropriate one for it), its annual depreciation charge, its determination of net profits, and its income tax payments must also be correct throughout the eight-year period. It is in a position to correctly judge the amount of property insurance it should carry from year to year, and it probably incurs property tax assessments in reasonable relation to the declining value of the assets. As the corporation's profits after income taxes are correctly reported, its directors presumably are not misled in making decisions about the distribution of dividends and the pricing of the corporation's products. Outsiders, it may also be presumed, are also saved from error in judging the creditworthiness of the corporation, as well as in judging the reasonableness of the market value of its stock.

For Corporation B, however, the overcharging of depreciation in the first six years of the lives of its depreciable assets results in distortions. Its directors may make unwise changes in operating policies—unwise because they are based on faulty information. The apparent lower earning capacity of B, in comparison with A and C, may bring adverse judgments on its directors and officers, and these may be reflected in declines in the market value of the corporation's stock and a lowering of its credit rating. The directors may decide to be less liberal than the directors of A in paying dividends—a decision that may also lead to a decline in the market value of its stock—and in an attempt to bring up the level of their net profits after income taxes they may also decide to raise the selling prices of their products. But this kind of action may only have the effect of driving customers to A and C. Conversely, some of the distortions appear to work to B's benefit—namely, a lower level of income tax payments than A's, probably a lower level of property tax assessments, and lower insurance premiums if insurance is carried on the basis of the book values of the fixed assets.

Nevertheless, the distortions do not work in the same direction for the full period of eight years; in the seventh and eighth years their effects tend to be reversed. In those years, it is no longer permissible to deduct depreciation for income tax purposes, since the assets have been fully depreciated; hence, net profits both before and after income taxes, and the income taxes themselves, are higher than those of A. Such a result may have a favorable influence on the market behavior of B's stock and on its credit rating, and B's directors may be inclined to step up the level of dividend distributions and, perhaps, to lower the selling prices of the corporation's products. On the other hand, reduction of the book value of the fixed assets to zero would probably not preclude continued property tax assessments nor, it is likely, a continued carrying of property insurance.

The position of Corporation C in the early years looks much better than that of either A or B. Although it must pay more federal income taxes than either of its fellows, its net profits after income taxes are still substantially better than theirs. Its directors may be rather generous in their dividend policies, and this may have a highly favorable effect on the market value of its stock and its credit rating. It may have more property taxes to pay if assessors give close attention to book values, but this is problematic since assessors in many localities are notoriously inefficient. It may be tempted to lower the selling prices of its products, feeling that it can afford to do this in view of its superior profit record. But the apparent advantages cited here do not last forever. The sad day of awakening comes, shall we say, at the end of the eighth year when C's managers finally realize that they have a group of useless fixed assets still valued on the books at $400,000. Charging off this remaining book value as a loss, assuming that the assets are removed to make place for new ones, would reduce profits for the year to zero (loss of $400,000 added to the regular depreciation charge of $100,000 against net income from sales of $500,000), and this would surely make for gloomy prospects for dividends, as well as for the market value of the corporation's stock and its credit standing.

The directors and officers of C may sincerely regret what now are recognized to have been overgenerous dividend payments of prior years, perhaps overpayments of property taxes and excessive property insurance coverage, and perhaps price cuts. In the eighth year, it is true, Corporation C apparently would have no federal income taxes to pay, but even about this we cannot be absolutely sure. The Internal Revenue Service may argue against the deductibility of all or a part of the loss of $400,000. The regulations say that profits and losses on the sale or removal of fixed assets are recognized as the difference between the selling price of the assets and their cost as reduced by depreciation allowed or *allowable*. The Internal Revenue

Service may contend that Corporation C did not take depreciation to the extent that it was "allowable."

Methods of Charging Depreciation: Illustration. In the foregoing illustration, our acceptance of $150,000 as the proper amount of the annual charge for depreciation was based on the explicit assumption that the straight-line method of charging depreciation was the most appropriate one. But there are many good arguments in support of other methods of allocating depreciation charges. Thus, while we can continue to say that with respect to the illustration the proper amount of depreciation must *average* $150,000 annually during the eight years, we could hardly insist that it must be exactly that amount each year. The managers of Corporation A might have decided that charging varying amounts from year to year though averaging $150,000 would represent a more appropriate way of handling the costs of exhaustion of fixed assets. Had they, therefore, selected a different method, effects from year to year on profits, income tax and property tax liabilities, property insurance coverage and premiums, dividend policies, market behavior of stock, credit rating, and pricing policies might have been somewhat different from those already described.

To see why some or all of these effects would be expected to vary in relation to the method of depreciation used, let us determine what the annual depreciation charges of Corporation A would have been had it used any of the three other popular methods, namely, the sum of the years' digits method, the fixed percentage of declining balance method,[3] and the production units method. For the last-named method, we may assume that the productive capacity of the fixed assets for the entire period of their useful lives was estimated at 2,400,000 units of product, so that the charge per unit of output was put at 50 cents. Depreciation charges on the basis of each of the three methods would have been as follows (the straight-line charges also being shown for purposes of comparison).

Year	Straight-Line Method 12½% per Year	Sum of the Years' Digits Method	Fixed Percentage of Declining Balance Method (25%)	Production Units Method	
				Units Produced	Depreciation Charge
1	$ 150,000	$ 266,667	$ 300,000	200,000	$ 100,000
2	150,000	233,333	225,000	250,000	125,000
3	150,000	200,000	168,750	300,000	150,000
4	150,000	166,667	126,563	350,000	175,000
5	150,000	133,333	94,922	400,000	200,000
6	150,000	100,000	71,191	340,000	170,000
7	150,000	66,667	53,394	290,000	145,000
8	150,000	33,333	40,045	270,000	135,000
Total	$1,200,000	$1,200,000	$1,079,865	2,400,000	$1,200,000

[3]Frequently called the double declining balance method—"double" because the maximum percentage rate permitted under the Internal Revenue Code is twice the straight-line rate, as subsequently mentioned in the text.

Although the first three of the four methods of charging depreciation illustrated here are doubtless the most popular in present-day use, the four do not exhaust the list of available procedures. For federal income tax accounting, the Internal Revenue Service permits the use of any reasonable method sanctioned by trade practices.

Computation. The mechanics of computing depreciation by the four methods used in the foregoing illustration deserve a few words of explanation. The annual charge by the straight-line procedure is found, of course, by subtracting the estimated salvage value (if any) from the cost of the asset and dividing the remainder by the estimated number of years of useful life.

In applying the sum of the years' digits method, one adds 1, 2, 3, 4, and so on, for as many years as is the estimate of the asset's useful life. This total becomes the denominator of a fraction whose successive annual numerators are the digits themselves, beginning with the largest and running down to 1. These successively smaller fractions are then multiplied, each in its annual turn, by the difference between original cost and salvage value. In the illustration, the sum of the digits 1 to 8 is 36. Accordingly, depreciation for the first year was taken at 8/36 of $1.2 million (no salvage value has been assumed), for the second year at 7/36, for the third year at 6/36, and so on. It would be possible, obviously, to run the fractions in the opposite direction, using a depreciation rate of 1/36 in the first year, 2/36 in the second year, and so on; but there is little evidence that this variation is actually used by American businesses.

In application of the fixed percentage of declining balance method, the fixed percentage is applied to the original cost of the asset to find the depreciation charge for the first year. This amount of depreciation is subtracted from the cost to arrive at a new base, to which the fixed percentage is applied to ascertain the depreciation charge for the second year. The base is then further reduced by the second depreciation charge, and for the third year the fixed percentage is applied against the new balance so found, and so on. For fixed assets that have estimated salvage values, the fixed percentage to be used can be determined by mathematical formula. It is the percentage that, as applied over the years, will have the effect of reducing the original value to the salvage value at the expiration of the period of useful life.[4] For assets that have no estimated salvage values, on the other hand, any relatively high fixed percentage could be used, for even a rate of 99 percent applied against the declining balances would never bring book values down to zero. In the illustration, nevertheless, the

---

[4]The formula is the following.

$$r = 1 - \sqrt[n]{\frac{\text{salvage value}}{\text{cost}}}$$

where r is the fixed percentage, and n the number of years of useful life. For ex-

fixed percentage placed at 25 percent was considered wholly realistic, because federal income tax regulations limit the fixed percentage to a maximum of not more than twice what would be the straight-line depreciation rate as determined without consideration of salvage value. (The fixed percentage has generally been limited to 1½ times what would be the straight-line rate for property acquired before January 1, 1954, as well as for *used* property acquired since then.)

To use the production units method, it is necessary to estimate the life of fixed assets, not in years, but in units of product they have the capacity to turn out before reaching a state of deterioration or ordinary obsolescence that would make their removal advisable. This estimate of total productive capacity is divided into the difference between cost and residual value to get a rate of depreciation per unit of output. Actual output in a year or other period of time is then multiplied by the computed rate to find the depreciation charge for that period. Sometimes, this method is rearranged, one may say, to make it a production hours method. The procedure is the same, except that the original estimate of useful life is in terms of the probable total hours of operation (as of machines) rather than in terms of probable total product.

Comparison of Methods. The substantial differences in the amounts of depreciation chargeable from year to year on the basis of the four methods of our illustration indicate that the selection of methods is a matter of considerable importance. The financial managers of business concerns must study the pros and cons of each method. When they consider the probable effects of their selection of methods on profits, income taxes, property taxes, pricing policies, and so on, they will doubtless conclude that decisions must be arrived at only after painstaking analysis.

A strong argument in favor of the sum of the years' digits and the fixed percentage of declining balance methods is that heavy charges for depreciation should be concentrated in the early years of useful life because expenses for repairs and maintenance are likely to be relatively small in those years. In this way, the costs of using depreciable fixed assets tend, at least roughly, to be equalized annually over the course of their lives. Although the Internal Revenue Service had recognized the two methods for many years, new interest in them was generated by liberalized provisions of the Revenue Act of 1954 specifically authorizing their use for *new* tangible depreciable assets ac-

---

ample, had a salvage value of $150,000 been assumed in the illustration, we could have substituted in the formula as follows.

$$r = 1 - \sqrt[8]{\frac{150{,}000}{1{,}200{,}000}}$$

Solving the formula would have given us a fixed percentage of 22.8894 percent.

quired after December 31, 1953. Observers have generally agreed that these provisions of the 1954 tax legislation initiated a strong swing in the direction of the two methods. A disadvantage of the fixed percentage of declining balance method is that it may result in total depreciation charges for the period of useful life somewhat less than determinable by other methods. The reason for this, indicated previously, is that the fixed percentage is limited by law to a maximum of twice what the rate of straight-line depreciation would be. But in ordinary circumstances, the disadvantage is not likely to be a serious one. In the illustration on page 213, the fixed assets would still have a book value of $120,135 at the end of the eighth year if they had been depreciated on the declining-balance basis, but were they really valueless at that time the corporation would be able to deduct the write-off of $120,135 in determining the amount of its taxable income.

An important advantage claimed for the production units or production hours method is that depreciation charges vary from year to year according to the volume of operations: in periods of low income these charges are low, and in periods of high income they are relatively high. Such a result should be promotive of stability in annual profits. An objection to this method is that depreciation—certainly in the sense of ordinary obsolescence—goes on as rapidly in periods of low production or idleness as in periods of high production. Moreover, the Internal Revenue Service has not shown much enthusiasm for this method, holding that it is impossible to arrive at reasonable estimates of the lifetime productive capacities of most kinds of fixed assets.

Undoubtedly, the straight-line method continues to be a highly popular means of computing depreciation charges, despite the concession of the Revenue Act of 1954 toward the sum of the years' digits and the declining-balance methods. The straight-line method has the outstanding merit of simplicity, it is easily understood and applied, and its use has generally been approved without question by the federal revenue authorities. Its principal weakness appears to be the placing of heavier burdens on later years in the sense that depreciation charges plus maintenance costs are almost sure to be heavier in those years than in the early years of useful life.

For one class of fixed assets, the financial managers of a business concern may judge one method of charging depreciation to be the best, and for other classes, other methods. They may pick and choose, perhaps coming to a decision to use two or three or even four or more methods, each for a different class of fixed assets. They may even adopt different methods for different asset units within a given class, such as using the straight-line method for some machines and the declining-balance method for others. Under federal tax regulations, at any rate, the taxpayer has no obligation to use a uniform method;

the requirements are only that the results of the methods chosen, whether one or more, are reasonable in the sense of precluding excessive charges against income, and that permission be obtained in advance (in most instances) for changes from one method to another.

Preference for Rapid Depreciation

A large majority of business managers doubtless prefer to charge off the value of depreciable fixed assets, via the depreciation route, at a rapid pace. They are inclined to underestimate periods of useful life as well as salvage values. They are likely to turn more and more to the sum of the years' digits and the fixed percentage of declining balance methods in order to further accelerate their depreciation charges. Inclinations of these kinds are strongest, of course, in periods of prosperity and rising prices, but they do not seriously weaken in periods of less active business so long as sales proceeds are sufficient to cover the depreciation charges together with all other expenses.

The fear that fixed assets will become obsolete much more quickly than the ordinary obsolescence component of depreciation charges allows for is probably the most compelling reason for preferences for speedy write-offs. In times of rapid technological advance, business managers in almost all fields of industry can hardly escape fears that within a short period of time inventions and innovations of a revolutionary character will make obsolete their well-equipped and efficient factories. Constantly, they and we are being told that the development of atomic power for peacetime use, the automation of industrial processes, and other innovations will work an industrial transformation of unprecedented scope.

A second reason for the acceleration of depreciation charges is that expenses for repairs and maintenance are generally low in the early years of the lives of fixed assets and tend to mount substantially in later years. Overall annual costs in the use of fixed assets, it is held, can be pushed in the direction of uniformity by coupling relatively high depreciation charges with the low costs of repairs and maintenance in the early years, and by joining relatively low charges for depreciation to the much higher expenses for repairs and maintenance in the later years.

Rising prices also encourage rapid write-offs. During periods when selling prices rise and depreciation and other fixed charges remain unchanged, profit margins generally expand. But business managers are inclined to look on the expansion in profit margins as largely illusory. Anticipating much higher prices for the replacement of their depreciable assets, they are likely to conclude that depreciation charges based on original cost, unless accelerated in some way, give a distorted view of profitability.

A further reason for a preference for rapid write-offs of fixed asset values is the conviction of many business managers that highly desirable replacements are unlikely to be opposed by fellow managers if much of the value of the assets to be replaced has already been written off. To understand this proposition, we may refer to the illustration on page 213. Suppose that at the end of the fifth year the production managers of Corporation A strongly advise the replacement of the machinery on the grounds that much more efficient machines are now available and that, accordingly, retention of the old machines will gravely weaken the corporation's competitive position. If the corporation had been using the straight-line method of charging depreciation, its write-offs to the end of the fifth year would have amounted to $750,000, but if, say, the sum of the years' digits method had been used, total write-offs would have amounted to $1 million. So the replacement would mean a loss on the old machines of $450,000 with the straight-line method but a loss of only $200,000 with the sum of the years' digits method (disregarding the possibility of a salvage value at the end of the fifth year, though none was anticipated for the end of the eighth year). Thus, the board of directors and top financial executives might be much more amenable to the production managers' recommendation if the smaller loss can be shown.

Preferences for rapid write-offs can be attributed, finally, to the high rates of federal corporation income taxes (as well as to the high individual income tax rates that apply to the profits derived by many owners of unincorporated businesses). High rates of income taxation undoubtedly promote a zealous and continuous effort on the part of taxpayers to try to take advantage of every possible expense deduction. Because depreciation charges are only estimated expenses, there is a natural tendency, one may say, to make the estimates as high as the Internal Revenue Service will allow. One can argue that the reduction in the tax bill this year because of high depreciation charges will be offset by higher tax liabilities in later years when depreciation charges must necessarily be lower. But it is not easy to convince the business manager that things will work out that way. In rebuttal, he may say that tax rates in later years may be lower than they are at the present time. And he may add that even if the rates are not reduced the advantage of a tax saving this year of a given amount is by no means offset by an additional tax liability of the same amount due some years hence, since in the intervening period he can use the amount of the saving in expanding the operations and the profits of his business.

CAPITALIZATION POLICY

Capitalization versus Expense

In the establishment of policies for fixed asset management, standards must be set to distinguish between expenditures that add to the value of fixed assets and those that simply keep these assets in good operating condition. Whether an expenditure is to be capitalized—that is, added to the value of the fixed asset, or charged to an expense account depends on its effects on the life and efficiency of the asset. Thus, we distinguish additions, replacements, and betterments as adding to the value of assets, from expenditures for repairs and maintenance as only sustaining the capacity of assets to remain in ordinary operation.

In the normal course of business activity, it is usually easy to recognize additions and replacements; rarely, therefore, are they confused with repairs and maintenance. Knocking out a wall of a factory building, joining thereto a new structure for additional operating space, and installing newly purchased machines in this space obviously represent additions to plant and equipment. Likewise, one is not likely to question placing in the fixed asset accounts the purchase price of new machines installed as replacements for old ones (provided, of course, that the book value of the old machines is removed as they are traded in, sold in the secondhand market, or scrapped).

But betterments—they are also called improvements—are often difficult to distinguish from repairs and maintenance. The customary standard for making the distinction is that betterments increase the productive capacity of fixed assets beyond their original capacity or extend their useful lives beyond the original estimates. Nevertheless, the standard is difficult to apply, chiefly because certain kinds of expenditures often have elements of both betterments and repairs and maintenance. The replacement of leaking iron pipe with new sections of the same kind of pipe is surely a repair, but if the replacement is made with copper pipe an element of betterment is obviously added. Similarly, the rewiring of burned-out motors is surely to be treated as a repair, but a betterment is involved if worn-out motors attached to certain kinds of machines are replaced with motors of higher horsepower rating. Appropriately, in most cases of these kinds where betterments are involved, a portion of the expenditures should be added to the asset accounts and the remaining portion should be charged to expense.

Consequences of Errors in Capitalization

If expenditures for additions, replacements, and betterments are charged immediately to expense accounts, the consequences are much the same as those that result from overcharging depreciation. If expenditures that should be charged as repairs and maintenance are added to asset accounts, the consequences are similar to those that result from undercharging depreciation. But things will tend to come out even in the long run. In the first case, expenses will be overstated in the current year but understated in subsequent years, since there will be no charges for depreciation on the additions, replacements, and betterments. In the second case, expenses will be understated in the first year, but in subsequent years the expenditures that should have been taken up as repairs and maintenance will be gradually charged off by way of depreciation deductions.

However, the consequences may be bad precisely because expenses, whether repairs and maintenance or depreciation, are not properly allocated in the years they belong to, and even though in the long run total charges to expense accounts may be the same as if no errors had been made. In a year when expenses are overstated—additions, replacements, and betterments charged to expense accounts—profits are reduced, and the directors may decide to reduce dividend payments. One or both of these results may cause a decline in the market value of the corporation's stock as well as some deterioration in its credit rating. The lowered rate of return on stockholders' investment may tempt the corporation's managers to raise the selling prices of its products, but this action may injure it competitively. On the other hand, there may be some consolation in lowered income tax and property tax liabilities. It is true that such advantages and disadvantages are likely to be reversed in later years as a result of a counterbalancing understatement of expenses, but this does not necessarily mean that the errors in capitalization policy will have no lasting harmful effects. The financial managers would be basing their decisions throughout on distorted data, and the possibilities are great that some of these decisions would thus be rendered unwise.

Tendencies toward Undercapitalization

The possibilities of serious distortions in the asset and income positions of corporations as a result of errors (whether deliberate or inadvertent) in the treatment of additions, replacements, betterments, repairs, and maintenance are substantially reduced by the vigilance of the federal income tax authorities. They can be expected to assess corporations for additional taxes when their returns indicate that expenditures that should have been added to assets were, instead, deducted as expenses, or when this information is subsequently revealed in tax audits of the corporations' books. If it is subjected to an additional assessment in this way, a corporation will surely take immediate steps to correct its own books—that is, by capitalizing the expenditures so that in subsequent years it will be permitted to write them off by way of depreciation charges.

But in many situations, especially in the matter of betterments, as we have seen, it is difficult to say precisely how much should be added to asset accounts and how much charged to expense accounts. In such doubtful situations, most corporate managements certainly favor charging expense for the maximum amount that will be permitted by the tax authorities. Allowable deductions are zealously sought in periods of high tax rates. At present federal income tax rates on corporations, any deduction produces a tax saving equal to 48 percent of the deduction, assuming the corporation to have remaining taxable income in excess of $25,000.[5] Although a deduction this year for expenditures related to fixed assets means smaller deductions or none at all in future years, it may be that tax rates will be lower later on. Regardless of possibilities of a lowering of rates, moreover, most corporate taxpayers are quite happy to defer tax payments, even though the total amounts to be paid over the years are not thereby reduced. They have a good theoretical reason for so choosing, since the present (discounted) value of a future tax payment is less than an immediate payment of the same amount.

Other reasons for favoring the immediate deduction of expenditures related to fixed assets to the maximum extent permitted by the federal tax authorities are similar to the reasons discussed previously for favoring accelerated depreciation. Accordingly, a brief restatement at this point should suffice. In periods of rising prices, corporate managers are inclined to look on increases in their profit margins as being largely illusory. The margins will come down again, they expect, when it becomes necessary to replace low-cost fixed assets with high-cost ones; hence, it is realistic to seek at once deductible expenditures that will hold down the profit figures. All the more is this reasonable, they are likely to conclude, because holding down the level of reported profits does not reduce the amount of cash throw-offs. Fear of extraordinary obsolescence—fear, that is, that depreciation charges with their allowance only for ordinary obsolescence are inadequate—also seems to make wise additional deductions, wherever they can be found, to supplement the depreciation charges. Replacement of fixed assets before expiration of their useful lives as originally estimated is also less likely to be impeded if the fixed asset accounts have not been substantially increased by outlays for betterments—if, in other words, it has been possible to charge at least a portion of such outlays to expense accounts at the time incurred. Finally, the expectation of increased expenses for the repair and maintenance of fixed assets as they grow older may seem to justify charging off as current expenses as many outlays as the law and regulations can be stretched to allow, even though some of these may have the complexion of betterments.

TESTING FIXED ASSET INVESTMENT POLICIES

Ratio of Fixed Assets to Net Sales

It has often been said that the ownership of expensive fixed assets is, in itself, of no advantage to business enterprises. The ownership is

---

[5]Ignoring the surcharge of 10 percent added to tax liabilities on a temporary basis in 1968.

justified only if a reasonable rate of return is earned on the expensive fixed assets. A firm that is able to develop a sales volume of $1.2 million while employing fixed assets worth $300,000 (together with current assets, of course) would normally be expected to be more profitable than one in the same line of business that has a sales volume of approximately the same figure but uses fixed assets worth $400,000.

In the light of this kind of reasoning, ratios of fixed assets to net sales are often computed as means of testing the soundness of fixed asset investment policies. Such a ratio is found by dividing the average investment in fixed assets by the net sales for the year. The sum of the investment as revealed in the accounting records at the beginning and end of the year divided by 2 usually suffices for the figure for average investment. However, it is customary to exclude fixed assets not used in the ordinary course of business—for example, a factory building that a manufacturing corporation rents to another manufacturer. Investment in fixed assets, it should be added, is the original value less all depreciation charged against the assets from the time of acquisition.

As thus computed, the ratio of fixed assets to sales indicates how many dollars or cents have been invested in fixed assets to produce one dollar of sales. In terms of the figures cited above, the first firm has an investment in fixed assets of 25 cents for each dollar of sales, whereas the second has an investment of 33⅓ cents. Fixed asset ratios of this kind show wide variations from industry to industry. In the railroad and public utility industries, a dollar or more of fixed assets is generally needed for each dollar of sales, but in most retail trade lines investment in fixed assets ordinarily amounts to only a minor fraction of the sales volume. In the heavy-goods manufacturing industries—basic iron and steel, machinery manufacture, the manufacture of transportation equipment, and so on—the ratio of fixed assets to sales tends to be relatively high in comparison with that of enterprises engaged in light manufacturing operations.

As with other ratios, ratios of fixed assets to net sales have little significance individually; only when they can be used for comparisons in like situations are they useful for testing purposes. But even comparisons in like situations must be interpreted with caution. That a given firm's ratio is out of line with those of earlier years, or with those being currently shown by competing firms, is ordinarily to be taken as proof of nothing. It simply indicates that an investigation ought to be made to account for the difference, with praise or blame to be withheld pending the results of the investigation. A competing firm may have a lower ratio because it rents much of its equipment. The firm that makes the analysis may have an extraordinarily high ratio on account of the installation of new kinds of laborsaving equipment; but the equipment, by making possible a substantial reduction in costs, may give it a strong position in meeting competition. In a similar way, ratios may differ from firm to firm because of differences in methods of charging depreciation. For the individual firm, ratios may decline from year to year for no reason other than that annual depreciation charges constantly reduce the book value of its fixed assets.

Ratio of Fixed Assets to Net Profits

Since the computation of ratios in relation to fixed assets is designed to test the profitability of investment in these assets, it appears that a ratio of such assets to net profits (before the deduction of income taxes) is a better testing device than the ratio to net sales. A ratio of fixed assets to sales ignores operating costs, but a ratio of fixed assets to net profits necessarily allows for differences in costs, since net profits are found by subtracting operating costs from sales income. If certain assets are excluded from the computation because they are not used in the ordinary course of business, logic requires that the net income derived from them be excluded from the figure for net profits. The profitability of these assets in relation to the net income they produce can then, of course, be separately judged.

The firm that installed new kinds of laborsaving machinery may have fixed assets of, say, $500,000 and annual sales of $1 million, whereas its principal competitor, lacking such machinery, may have an equal sales volume but total fixed assets of only $250,000. The undiscriminating analyst may hastily conclude that the first firm had overinvested in fixed assets, since it has 50 cents in fixed assets for every dollar of sales while the competitor's investment in fixed assets is only 25 cents per dollar of sales. But if the first firm's total operating expenses amount to $800,000 while those of the second amount to $950,000—the first figure is much lower than the second chiefly because of reduced labor costs—the first firm would appear to have invested wisely. The comparative ratios of fixed assets to net profits, $2.50 and $5, respectively, would thus tend to lead more directly to a sound conclusion than would a comparison of ratios of fixed assets to sales.

Ratios of Operating Assets to Net Sales and Net Profits

As a testing device, many analysts have preferred to use the ratio of total operating assets—that is, the total of both current and fixed assets used in the ordinary course of business—to net sales rather than the fixed assets to sales ratio. The operating-asset ratio is said to be superior because it indicates the efficiency with which a firm uses all its assets in generating a given sales volume, and not simply its fixed assets alone. But there appears to be no good argument for the exclusive use of one type of ratio or the other. Both types can easily be computed, and perhaps one will reveal information worthy of further analysis that the other does not reveal.

A ratio of operating assets to net sales suffers from the same defect as the fixed asset to sales ratio, since it ignores varying levels of operating expenses. For this reason, a ratio of operating assets to net profits should be more reliable as a testing device than a ratio to net sales.

ECONOMIZING INVESTMENT IN FIXED ASSETS

When limitations on the availability of cash make necessary a choice between current asset expansion and fixed asset expansion, it falls in most instances to the current. Such a preponderance of choices necessarily indicates businessmen's estimations of higher rates of return to be earned on additions to current assets than on additions to fixed assets. This attitude is strongly engendered, no doubt, by the abundance of opportunities to rent buildings, machinery, and other facilities contrasted with the dearth of opportunities of this kind in relation to current assets. For example, buildings and space in buildings are generally available for rent for a wide variety of uses in many localities, while relatively few trade suppliers are willing to provide inventory on a consignment basis. Moreover, the offering of great quantities of productive facilities of the fixed classification for rent means that rental charges tend to be held to moderate levels, while the refusal of most trade suppliers to deliver goods on consignment means that the few who are willing to do so can be strict in their terms.

Rental arrangements are, by far, the most common means of economizing investment in fixed assets—avoiding absorptions of cash that, in the judgment of business managers, can be better used in inventory investment or in other directions. However, renting is not the whole story, for, as will be explained subsequently, stabilizing production, farming out manufacturing operations, and contracting out for peak production loads are additional means of economy in fixed asset investment.

Leases

Certain classes of property, if they are to be acquired at all, must be obtained on a lease basis because the owners refuse to sell. This is true in prominent locations in many of our principal cities, where land sites are often made available on leases running for 50 years or more. The tenants put up imposing buildings, expecting to recover their value during the periods of the leases, since the contracts usually provide that improvements revert to the lessors at the expiration of the lease periods as originally set or as later extended.

Owners of patents on machinery have sometimes refused to sell the patented machines, making them available only on lease to other firms. For many years, for example, it was impossible to buy many kinds of shoe-manufacturing and shoe-repair equipment on which the United Shoe Machinery Corporation held patents, and users could not buy certain kinds of office equipment and machines produced by the International Business Machines Corporation. But proceedings of the federal government resulted in court orders to these companies to offer their products for sale to those who prefer to buy rather than to rent. Other owners of patents refuse to sell the patents themselves but willingly license other firms to produce the patented products. The producing firm usually pays a royalty per unit of output, which is a rental payment for use of an intangible fixed asset—the patent itself. As an example, many of the wonder drugs developed and patented by pharmaceutical firms in recent years have been produced and sold, with distinctive trade names, by other firms licensed by the discoverers.

By means of another kind of renal or royalty arrangement of outstanding importance, many enterprises in the extractive industries gain access to what may be called their raw materials. Although some mining and lumber companies own their own lands, a large number much prefer to gain access to mineral deposits and standing timber on the basis of royalty contracts. The owners of land are asked to grant mining and cutting rights in consideration of a royalty to be paid at a stated rate per unit of output or as a percentage of the value of the output. Such contracts usually provide for a minimum payment to be made annually whether or not extractive operations proceed. In this way, the landowner is assured an annual income during the term of the contract, even though the lessee may decide to defer development until a later time. By means of such contracts, the investment of the mining and lumber companies in fixed assets can generally be limited to machinery and equipment needed to drill wells, to sink shafts, to fell trees, and so on.

However, certain kinds of property are rarely made available for rental, especially highly specialized kinds such as factory buildings that require features, facilities, and layouts peculiarly designed for the manufacture of given lines of products but of little usefulness for other kinds of manufacturing operations. Owners of factory sites are unlikely to construct rental property of peculiar and intricate design because should the original tenant fail or for any other reason abandon the lease it would be impossible to attract a new one.

In between, of course, there are innumerable classes of property available on either a sale or a lease basis, so that enterprises that could use such property conveniently have a rent-or-buy choice. Such, obviously, is the situation in many localities for office buildings, store buildings, and warehouses; but it is also widely true for various kinds of factory, store, and office machinery and equipment, delivery trucks, and even automobiles for the use of salesmen. Equipment leasing especially has had a huge growth in recent years, as indicated by the establishment of many new leasing companies and leasing departments in financial institutions to specialize in buying equipment outright and renting it to users, and as typified by the widespread acquisition of computer facilities on the basis of lease contracts.

Popularity of Leases. Business firms whose access to cash is severely limited must of necessity, one may say, rent land and buildings and perhaps other kinds of property if they are to be able to carry an adequate amount of inventories and accounts receivable. Such is commonly the situation in enterprises newly or recently established. The owners can put only moderate amounts of money into these enterprises, additional funds cannot be attracted as by offerings of stock to outsiders, and the prospects of the enterprises from a credit standpoint are so uncertain that borrowing beyond modest limits is impossible.

Though they may not be so severely limited in the availability of cash well-established firms often also have occasions to weigh carefully the respective advantages and disadvantages of the ownership and rental of land, buildings, and other fixed assets. They may decide that the rate of return to be earned on investment in inventories and accounts receivable is likely to be substantially higher than that to be expected on investment in, say, land and buildings; hence, they choose to rent land and buildings and to direct their cash resources into inventory and accounts receivable. Although such firms may be in a position to finance all their present requirements for both fixed and current assets through borrowing or sales of additional stock, they may prefer to reserve these means of financing to take care of future current asset requirements expected to result from expansions in the volume of sales. Were they to issue stock or borrow at present to buy fixed assets, they might find it difficult later to put out still more stock or to increase their borrowings to carry larger inventories and larger amounts of accounts receivable without which expansions in the volume of sales could not be effected.

In many cases, too, the managers of business concerns conclude that they are well equipped and staffed to manufacture and sell, or simply to sell, certain kinds of products, but that they are not so well fixed for the management of real estate. They realize that landowners expect to earn net returns—perhaps substantial ones—out of the rentals they charge, but they conclude that the costs of ownership may turn out to be not much less than the rentals. Landowners are likely to be specialists in the management of real estate, knowing how to keep costs down—a fact reflected in the rents they charge—whereas the business firm, by inept real estate management or by taking on itself the costs of hiring specialists of its own, may find ownership to be quite expensive. Therefore, that landowners often enjoy substantial net incomes is no more a reason for a firm to decide to own its land and buildings than is the realization of profits by producers of raw materials a reason for a firm's decision to manufacture its own raw materials.

Even firms of the strongest credit standing—firms whose access to money, if not unlimited, is nevertheless very great—often find it wise to rent certain kinds of property rather than to own it. This is seen especially in the rental of office space in our principal cities. Many firms of this class decide that they must have their principal business offices in New York or Chicago or some other great city, but they are content to rent suites of offices, or perhaps whole floors or several floors, in buildings owned by others. From the standpoint of their access to cash, they could well afford to put up their own office buildings—as some do indeed—but their financial managers apparently conclude that the disadvantages of this would outweigh the advantages.

Construction for Tenants. The popularity of leases is enhanced by the willingness of many landowners to put up buildings designed to meet the requirements of given tenants. This arrangement is most common in the construction of store buildings for the occupancy of chain store organizations. Unlike many kinds of factories, the store buildings are not so highly specialized in design and layout that other merchants could not be attracted should the original tenants move out. Nevertheless, it is the contract with the original tenant that persuades the landowner to build. This contract generally assures the landowner of the recovery of his investment in the building as well as a reasonable annual net profit during the period of the original tenant's occupancy. On the basis of market research, the chain store organization picks out promising sites for new stores and agrees to sign leases of, perhaps, 20 years if the owners will put up buildings according to certain specifications. Loans for the construction can usually be obtained without difficulty from financial institutions, since principal and interest obligations to them will be more than covered by the rentals that the chain store organization agrees to pay. Similar leasing arrangements originate in the promotion of suburban shopping centers, which have had a phenomenal growth since the close of World War II. In this kind of arrangement, the promoters themselves usually take the initiative. Having obtained options to buy likely sites for shopping centers, they approach chain store and other mercantile enterprises with propositions to build facilities according to their specifications on the promise of long-term leases.

A long-term lease, on the basis of which a landowner consents to construct a building for the use of the tenant, will usually provide that all costs of maintenance and repair, insurance, and property taxes are to be borne by the tenant; thus the rental payment itself becomes, in effect, the landowner's straight recovery of the principal of his investment and before-tax profit. Needless to say, such a lease must be prepared with great care. It is important that the rights and responsibilities of both landowner and tenant be set out clearly and in detail, so that disputes and possibly litigation because of omissions or ambiguities will be avoided. Long-term leases often give the tenant the option of having the term extended for an additional period of years on expiration of the original term. Such provisions customarily prescribe a sharply reduced rental for the additional period, since by the end of the original term the landowner will have recovered the full amount of his investment in the building.

Of special interest among arrangements for construction for tenants in recent years have been lease contracts worked out between manufacturing corporations and city, county, and other units of local government. By this arrangement, the government unit puts out an issue of industrial revenue bonds and uses the proceeds to buy a factory site and to finance the construction of factory buildings and the purchase of machinery and equipment specified by the industrial corporation as lessee. The bonds are called industrial revenue issues because they are to be paid off, interest and principal, from the rentals to be paid by the industrial tenant and not from ordinary tax collections. With safety generally assured by the long-term obligation of the tenant corporation to pay rentals, the bonds have been especially attractive to investors because of the exemption of their interest payments from federal income taxes.

This exemption feature, indeed, made the government–tenant corporation arrangement especially popular in the 1966–68 period of extraordinarily high market rates of interest. By being able to borrow at relatively low rates of interest because of the tax-exemption feature, the local governments could offer lease contracts to corporations at relatively low rentals, and the corporations were doubly attracted by the low rentals and the opportunities to avoid tying up their own funds in new facilities. In the spring of 1968, for example, lease arrangements financed by bond issues of local governments were entered into by such prominent corporations as United States Steel, National Steel, Uniroyal, Hercules, Ashland Oil, Escanaba Paper, and Zenith Radio. However, in June, 1968, Congress adopted legislation to remove the tax-exemption feature from issues of industrial revenue bonds exceeding $1 million individually. This move was undoubtedly aimed at large corporations as tenants, since smaller enterprises could still be attracted by local governments with financing by way of tax-exempt bond issues of $1 million or less individually.

Sale-and-Leaseback. Similar in form and results to the arrangements just described is sale-and-leaseback, a procedure that has had its development almost entirely since the close of World War II. By this arrangement, business firms that already own land and buildings sell them to life insurance companies, college endowment funds, or pension trust funds, and then lease them back for terms of (usually) 20 years or more. Firms that operate department stores, especially chain organizations, have probably been most prominent in working out arrangements of this kind. In these transactions, the life insurance companies and other investors gain an advantage in finding new outlets for investment funds, and the mercantile establishments gain in being able to devote to inventories, accounts receivable, and current operating expenses the funds released by the sale of their properties. A further advantage derived by the mercantile firms is the deductibility of all expenses connected with the leases in the computation of federal income taxes. If a firm agrees to bear all expenses of insurance, property taxes, and maintenance, and to pay a rental over and above these costs, it may, as a rule, deduct all such items in determining its taxable income. If it were the owner of the property, it would still be permitted to deduct insurance, property taxes, and maintenance, but its average annual deductible charge for depreciation would surely be less than the amount of the rental. Especially significant among the reasons for the excess of the rental charge would doubtless be its inclusion of rent for the use of land, whereas in the case of ownership, land is not subject to deductions for depreciation. All this is not meant to imply that rental costs at a higher level than ownership costs are, in themselves, advantageous. It simply means that income tax saving from the higher amount of deductible expenses has the effect of reducing spreads between the two kinds of costs, so that excess rental costs after adjustment for the tax saving may appear to be a reasonable price to pay for the advantages of renting.

As with leases for which buildings are specially constructed for tenants, those originating in sale-and-leaseback arrangements usually give the tenants options to have the leases extended for additional periods or additional series of periods, for which the rental payments will be materially reduced. Since the investment institution is expected to recover the full amount of its investment with interest during the original period of a lease, some contracts have given the tenant at the expiration of this period the further option of buying back the property at what is often described as a nominal price. But the wisdom of such a provision is doubtful, since the Internal Revenue Service may hold the whole transaction to be an installment sale of the property by the investment institution to the mercantile company, or a long-term loan, with title to the property being held by the investment institution as security. In so holding, it would probably limit the deductibility of the rental payments to amounts equal to the interest costs involved and what it would consider reasonable charges for depreciation.

Term of Leases. While leases that originate in arrangements of the kinds described in the foregoing paragraphs are invariably long term, many storerooms, offices, and warehouses are rented for short periods—very frequently for periods not exceeding one year. As between long-term and short-term leases, advantages and disadvantages are pretty well mixed both for the landowner and the tenant.

For the landowner, a long-term lease is advantageous in assuring a steady return for a lengthy period of years, relieving him of worries about extended vacancies on the departure of given tenants and possibly, as indicated above, removing responsibilities for maintenance, insurance, property taxes, and so on, except for the responsibility, one may say, of making periodic inspections to see that the tenant is fulfilling his obligations in these directions. On the other hand, if the landowner contracts for a fixed rental it may turn out within a few years to be unreasonably low because of a rise in property values in the neighborhood or a substantial increase in the general level of prices.

For the tenant, a long-term lease is advantageous in establishing the right to continue operations at a given location for a lengthy period of years. Additionally, should rents for property in the neighborhood generally rise during the term of the lease, he might have the advantage of occupying much cheaper quarters than do his competitors. But the tenant is likely to be disadvantaged if he finds it impossible to develop a sales volume of the size originally anticipated—perhaps because of a deterioration of the neighborhood or the arrival of competing enterprises—or if the trend of rents turns out to be downward throughout the neighborhood during the period of the lease.

Short-term leases enable landowners to adjust their rents in step with changes in property values and price levels, and to get rid of tenants found to be unsatisfactory, but such leases burden them with more pressing responsibilities for the maintenance of their properties and, not infrequently, the task of seeking new tenants as others move out. For the tenant, in turn, short-term leases give freedom of movement when certain locations prove to be unsatisfactory, and they allow opportunity to press for reduced rentals when circumstances so warrant. In times of high-level business activity when buildings are relatively scarce, however, the short-term tenant, though fully satisfied with his rented facilities, may be forced to abandon them because of the landowner's demands for substantial increases in rental payments.

Rental Payments. Because short-term leases come up for renewal with relative frequency, they almost always provide for rental payments of fixed amounts. Many long-term leases likewise provide for fixed payments, but some stipulate varying payments, usually on the basis of the volume of sales. A lease that calls for variable payments ordinarily fixes a basic sum that is to be paid monthly, quarterly, or annually in good times and bad, with provision for an additional payment equal to a stipulated percentage of the sales volume. In this way, the landowner is assured a minimum income even in bad times, provided, of course, that the tenant remains solvent, and in good times he is in a position to share in the good fortunes of his tenant. The tenant, too, is likely to be quite satisfied with such an arrangement. The burden of rental payments is reduced as sales go down; yet, he is able to pay increased rents with ease when sales are booming.

Lease of Entire Assets. It is legally permissible for a business firm to lease all or almost all of its operating assets to another firm; thus, a tenant firm at one stroke, so to say, may come into possession of a wide variety of assets, perhaps of great values, with no outlay of cash and with only the obligation to be fully responsible for the maintenance of the assets as well as to pay a periodic rental. It is a principle of corporation law that a board of directors has no authority to lease the entire assets of the corporation they manage; hence, a lease of such scope must have the approval of the stockholders. Some state laws permit approval by a simple majority of the shares voted at a stockholders' meeting, provided that a quorum is represented, while others require larger majorities, such as two thirds or three fourths. On the other hand, the rule is that the directors of the corporation that wants to lease the entire assets of another enterprise can approve the lease without submitting it to the stockholders for their ratification.

In our day, the leasing of entire assets rarely occurs. Indeed, one can say that transactions of this kind have always been rare except in the railroad industry. In that industry, they have been of outstanding importance. Many of the great railroad systems—of the East, especially—have been largely built up by the combination of large numbers of leased lines. The Pennsylvania Railroad acquired most of its facilities west of Pittsburgh by leasing the entire assets of the old Pittsburgh, Fort Wayne, and Chicago and the Pittsburgh, Cincinnati, Chicago, and St. Louis, while the New York Central (merged with the Pennsylvania in February, 1968, as the present Penn Central Company) assembled most of its facilities in the same region by leasing the operating properties of the Cleveland, Cincinnati, Chicago, and St. Louis (the Big Four) and the Michigan Central.

The early leases of the entire assets of railroad companies, as negotiated chiefly in the last three decades of the 19th century, often ran for terms of 99 or 100 years, 250 years, 500 years, and up to 999 or 1,000 years. A few were perpetual. In view of such extremely long terms, a tenant company generally assumed all the current liabilities of a lessor, became guarantor of the principal and interest of the lessor's outstanding bonds, and took on itself an obligation to pay a dividend at a stipulated rate on the lessor's outstanding stock. The securities of the lessor, accordingly, came to be designated as "guaranteed bonds" and "guaranteed stock." Actually, then, the rental payments to be made by the tenant were the amounts needed to meet interest and principal requirements on the lessor's bonds and dividend requirements at the stipulated rate on its stock, with, perhaps, a small additional amount for the remaining operating expenses of the lessor. With such arrangements in force, a lessor company had, in effect, no remaining functions. It had to continue its existence as a party to the lease, but it tended to become a mere shell—a set of books, as has often been said.

Although lessor companies are still the legal owners of a moderate proportion of the aggregate railroad properties operated by other companies, the system companies have long since bought controlling stock interests in most of the railroads whose properties they orginally acquired by lease. In many instances, on gaining control or at some time thereafter the system companies merged the lessors with themselves, thus causing the lessors to pass out of existence as separate entities. In the remaining cases, the lessors have been continued in existence, and operations have ostensibly continued on a lease basis, but the position of the lessors as subsidiary corporations, though still merely sets of books, has been more significant than their position as owners of leased properties. When lessor corporations have been continued in existence, their bonds have been for the most part long since paid off, but those portions of their stocks not held by the system companies remain in the hands of investors as guaranteed stocks.

Installment Buying of Machinery and Equipment. Sometimes it is argued that business enterprises' purchase of machinery and equipment on installment payment contracts is much the same as leasing as a means of economizing investment in fixed assets. Since an installment purchase requires a much smaller immediate outlay of cash than would a cash purchase, there is no denying that, temporarily, the amount of cash absorbed in fixed assets is reduced. Likewise, some installment contracts—notably equipment trust contracts employed by railroads to acquire most of their locomotives and cars—specifically state that the periodic payments are rents for use of the equipment.

Nevertheless, there is a fundamental difference between a true lease and an installment payment contract. Under a true lease, the tenant is not in a process of buying the property. Regardless of the number and amount of payments he makes, he gets no closer to ownership than when he made the first payment. Under an installment payment contract, on the other hand, the acquirer of the property is really buying it. As he is ordinarily required to provide a substantial down payment, he makes an immediate investment of appreciable size. Much more importantly, however, the contract stipulates that when he has made the final installment payment, title to the property will be transferred to him.

We may conclude, therefore, that the acquisition of machinery and equipment on an installment payment basis is not a means of economizing investment in fixed assets, that it is, rather, a procedure of acquiring fixed assets on a credit basis. It is much the same as when a firm borrows money with which to buy fixed assets by a single payment. But borrowing money and obtaining goods on credit are means of financing—a subject we are not specifically concerned with in this chapter. For this reason, we may defer a consideration of installment buying to a later chapter.[6]

Stabilized Production

Economies in investment in fixed assets can usually be achieved by stabilizing or regularizing production—that is, by spreading it out as evenly as possible throughout the year. This is an important fact for business firms whose sales are heavily concentrated in one or two periods during the year. In Chapter 8, it was pointed out that the stabilization of production requires a much heavier investment in inventories than does production on a concentrated seasonal basis, and an illustration was presented to show why this is so. But it was argued there that reduced costs of training new employees, the greater efficiency of a satisfied work force, reduced investment in fixed assets, and other advantages may more than offset the disadvantage of the larger inventory investment.[7] In the present chapter, then, we have the occasion to stress reduction in investment in fixed assets as one such advantage.

A brief illustration should help. Let us suppose that a firm sells 20,000 units of output in each of the first 9 months of the year and 140,000 units in each of the last 3 months, and that $10 of investment in fixed assets is required for each unit of output per month. If the firm chooses to operate its productive facilities according to the seasonal pattern of its sales, and if it produces each month only a sufficient number of units to meet the sales of the following month, it will need an investment in fixed assets of $1.4 million. But if it decides to produce 50,000 units each month to meet its annual volume of sales of 600,000 units, stocking up excess units produced in the lean sales months to meet the large demand of the last three months of the year, it will need an investment in fixed assets of only $500,000. By way of the second alternative, the needed amount of additional investment in inventories may offset or more than offset the economy in fixed asset investment, but that does not necessarily argue the undesirability of this alternative. The financial managers must take into

[6]See pp. 874–76.
[7]See pp. 163–64.

consideration the relative costs of carrying fixed assets idle for much of the year—depreciation, maintenance, insurance, property taxes, and so on—and the costs of carrying what may be called idle inventory, with proper attention to advantages and disadvantages not directly related to investment, such as the reduction in labor turnover made possible by stabilization.

It should be observed that stabilization of production is much more readily attainable by industries whose seasonality results from variations in demand for their products than by those where supply factors account for the seasonality. When seasonality results from variations in the supply of raw materials—for example, in most branches of the canning industry—stabilized production is likely to be difficult to achieve, if not impossible. Indeed, industries whose raw materials are available only seasonally are likely to need disproportionately large investments in both fixed assets and inventories—adequate facilities to take care of the supplies quickly as they become available, such as perishable crops, and the finished goods themselves pending their gradual sale throughout the months until the next supply of raw materials becomes available. Nevertheless, a fair degree of stabilization is sometimes achieved by adding lines of products that can be turned out by using the same facilities that the original product lines require, but in the primary products' off seasons.

Farming Out Manufacturing Operations

Attention was also directed in Chapter 8 to the farming out of manufacturing operations as a means of economizing investment in inventories. Farming-out arrangements are also a means of economizing investment in fixed assets. The two kinds of economy tend always to go together. If a firm buys parts and subassemblies for its finished products instead of producing them itself it simultaneously avoids investment in inventories of raw materials needed for their production and in the machinery and other facilities that would otherwise be needed to turn them out.

The farming out of manufacturing operations is an extremely common procedure. The farming out is sometimes complete in the sense that selling firms perform no manufacturing functions whatsoever on the products they sell under their own brand names. Produced by manufacturing firms other than the sellers are many brands of notable reputation, such as the Coldspot line of home refrigeration equipment of Sears, Roebuck and the Signature line of Montgomery Ward. At the other extreme, the farming out may involve only some relatively insignificant parts of a firm's final product, and in between, of course, dependence on outside suppliers for parts and subassemblies is subject to a wide range of variations.

The farming out of manufacturing operations is often especially advisable for new firms. Such a firm is likely to have great difficulty in gathering all the money needed for a complete array of productive equipment, and it must give important weight to the possibility that its products will not have the market appeal expected. A failure to develop an adequate market would be bad enough, but the situation would clearly be much worse if this failure had to be followed up with a liquidation of a large amount of fixed assets. On the other hand, a supplying firm with idle capacity could probably be readily engaged to manufacture products according to the specifications of the new firm. It would have the advantage of at least a temporary expansion in its operations, and it could hardly envisage grave consequences in the event of a subsequent loss of the manufacturing contract because of the inability of the new firm to develop a market. As new firms grow in experience and build a steady demand for their goods, they may find it advisable to absorb more and more of the manufacturing functions, but with such experience and such a market situation they would surely be in a much better position to do so than originally. They could probably devote a substantial proportion of their profits to investment in factory facilities, and their access to loan funds would surely be much better than it had been earlier. Nevertheless, many of our largest and most successful business organizations find reasons to continue indefinitely farming-out arrangements.

Contracting Out for Peak Loads

In some instances, manufacturing companies whose sales patterns are distinctly seasonal find it possible to depend on other firms for assistance in taking care of peak requirements. Such a company may plan to carry on manufacturing operations at a stable pace throughout the year, producing enough monthly to meet sales requirements at the average level of the slack season but contracting with other firms to supply it with the additional output needed to meet the peak demand. A successful program of this kind makes possible economies in investment in both fixed assets and inventories. In terms of the illustration presented on page 233, the manufacturing company might decide to produce 40,000 units monthly throughout the year, but production at that level would leave it with a deficiency of 120,000 units needed for its three peak months. Accordingly, it would contract with another firm to supply 40,000 units for each of the three months of high-level sales.

QUESTIONS

1. Compare the investment of business corporations in new plant and equipment in the period since 1946 with their additions to inventories and accounts receivable. Does the huge excess of plant and equipment indicate that fixed assets are much more important than current assets? Discuss.

2. What justification is there for holding that the cost of fixed assets is

a business operating expense? If valid, does this proposition apply to all classes of fixed assets? Explain.

3. Why does the charging of depreciation have the effect of retaining in an enterprise net asset values equal to the original values of its depreciable fixed assets? Is this always the result? Why or why not?

4. If a firm charges depreciation in reasonable amounts during the useful lives of its fixed assets, it will have no financial difficulty in replacing them at the expiration of these lives. Is this proposition true or false? Discuss.

5. In what circumstances might it be advisable to appropriate surplus for the replacement of fixed assets? What would be the effect of the appropriation?

6. What are the principal sources of difficulty in determining how much depreciation a firm should charge periodically on its fixed assets?

7. Describe the techniques of computing depreciation by each of the following methods: straight line, sum of the years' digits, fixed percentage of declining balance, and production units.

8. Why are income tax considerations important in the selection of methods of charging depreciation? In this regard, what was the significance of the Treasury's new guidelines published in 1962?

9. Why do business managers generally favor rapid write-offs of the value of their fixed assets by way of depreciation charges?

10. Why is the distinction between repairs and maintenance, on the one hand, and additions and betterments, on the other, important in fixed asset management?

11. What is supposed to be revealed by ratios of fixed assets to sales and to net profits, and ratios of operating assets to net profits? What are the weaknesses of these ratios as means of judging performance?

12. How important is leasing as a means of economizing in investment in fixed assets? What classes of property are widely available for leasing or for use on a royalty basis?

13. For the tenant, what advantages do short-term leases have over long-term leases?

14. Describe the procedure of sale-and-leaseback. What advantage does the arrangement have for the seller-tenant and for the buyer-lessor?

15. If a firm that is subject to great seasonal fluctuations in the demand for its products decides to stabilize productive operations, how will this decision be likely to affect its investment in fixed assets?

PROBLEMS

1. About 5 years ago when the Paulson Manufacturing Corporation bought new machinery at a cost of $2.4 million, its managers estimated that the machines would have useful lives of 6 years and a salvage value of $600,000. As they wanted to charge off the machines on an accelerated basis, they decided to use the fixed percentage of declining balance basis for determining depreciation charges, and they selected the rate of 33⅓

percent without reference to salvage value, the maximum rate allowed by Treasury regulations in this instance. But now, in the fifth year, they realize that the usefulness of the machines will not last beyond the end of the year, and that they will then have a salvage value of only $300,000.

Assuming that combined federal and state income taxes applicable to Paulson's income during the 5-year period has been 50 percent, draw up a table to show by how much its taxable income and tax liabilities have been overstated, and its after-tax income has been understated during the 5-year period as a result of its faulty estimation of useful lives.

2. The firm of Mendall and Mossi, Inc. has just bought a group of machines at a cost of $6 million. Its managers estimate that the machines will have useful lives of 10 years and a salvage value of $600,000. They want to minimize income tax liabilities, especially for the next three years, and they ask you to draw up a table to show clearly whether they should choose the sum of the years' digits method or the fixed percentage of declining balance method for charging depreciation. (As restricted by Treasury regulations, the annual rate for the declining-balance method would be 20 percent, but with salvage value ignored.)

Part IV

BUDGETING, CONTROL, AND THE COST OF CAPITAL

chapter 11

CASH BUDGETING

For the successful management of a business enterprise's finances, something is needed in addition to a thorough knowledge of the circular flow of cash and the kinds of conditions and circumstances that affect it, as discussed in Chapters 5–7; sound decisions on asset management policies, as analyzed in Chapters 8–10; and, of course, a high order of managerial competence. A fourth ingredient must be added—*financial forecasting.* The financial managers of an enterprise must at all times be in a position to anticipate with reasonable closeness how much cash will flow in from month to month within a period of moderate length, such as a year, and what the cash requirements will be from month to month within the same period. Careful forecasts of cash flows make possible the avoidance of many difficulties and, indeed, serious financial embarrassment. Probable sources of difficulty can often be skirted or completely eliminated by appropriate prompt adjustments in operating policies. Forecasts indicate the limits within which the financial managers must make their decisions for the forecast period.

The determination of asset management policies, financial forecasting, and advance decisions to borrow or to sell additional stock, to repay debt or to retire stock, and to pay dividends at specific times—all these are phases of *financial planning,* without which no business can be operated efficiently. These phases of planning are obviously quite closely interrelated. If a forecast indicates, for example, that a shortage of cash will develop at a certain time within the coming year, immediate plans may be made to borrow or to sell additional stock to supplement the regular cash inflow from operations. If prospects are slim for thus supplementing the cash flow, certain changes in asset management policies may be decided on well in advance so that the threatened shortage of cash will not occur. Thus, the introduction of a new line of products or the purchase of additional factory facilities, as originally scheduled for the coming year, may have to be deferred to a later period. Again, a financial forecast may indicate that it would be quite convenient to distribute a cash dividend at certain times but not at others, or that any distribution of cash dividends within the year would subject the cash account to a dangerous strain.

Most important among the instruments used in financial forecasting are *budgets*. Many kinds of budgets are prepared by business firms, but those of particular interest to its financial managers are cash and capital (fixed asset) budgets. In this chapter and the next two, therefore, major attention will be directed to these two classes of budgets. Nevertheless, it should be helpful to begin the discussion with a broad view of budgets, budgetary systems, and budgetary control.

BUDGETS IN GENERAL

Nature of Budgets

As used by business enterprises, a budget is a detailed estimate in numerical terms of the scale of operations in some phase of activity in some future period. Budgets are always forecasts of future activity, as contrasted with statements of manufacturing costs, income statements, and other similar statements, which are reports on what has happened in the past. Budgets are detailed. All kinds of anticipated transactions within the area of activity surveyed must be separately accounted for, and, as a rule, the volume of each kind of transaction for each month or for some other series of short periods within the longer forecast period must be separately estimated. Budgets are prepared in numerical terms, although not necessarily in terms of dollars and cents. Manufacturing expense and selling expense budgets will surely be in terms of dollars and cents, but sales and production budgets, for example, may be in terms of units of production, and direct labor budgets in terms of hours of employment.

Budget Periods and Breakdowns

In business budgets, the forecast period is most commonly one year, with a monthly breakdown for that period. In some instances, the budget is made continuous by extending the forecast by one month as the end of each month of actual operations approaches. After a start has been made with a year's forecast, estimates for January of next year are added toward the end of January of this year, estimates for February of next year toward the end of February of this year, and so on; in this way, a forecast for a full year is always available. In other instances, monthly breakdowns are made for only three to six months, with quarterly figures for the remainder of the year, and in still others the breakdowns are in terms of weekly, biweekly, or 10-day periods for the months immediately ahead or possibly for the entire year. Obviously, many other variations are possible.

Some budgets are made on a long-range basis. Especially do business managers think it important to have a long view of requirements for additional buildings, machinery and equipment, and other fixed facilities, as in capital budgeting. Expenditures for research represent another area for which long-term forecasts are often thought desirable. For phases of activity such as these, budgets for 5 or 10 years or even for longer periods are commonly prepared. Accordingly, business managers are often able to discuss their long-range expansion plans with a surprising amount of detail about when and how various steps are to be taken.

Budgets as Instruments of Control

Although budgets were introduced above as devices for business planning, they must be recognized as being, in addition, important instruments of control. If properly prepared, they are estimates of what is reasonably attainable, not of what could be attained in the best possible circumstances. It is expected that strong efforts will be exerted to reach projected goals, but there is no expectation that superhuman powers will be available and that all contingencies will turn out favorably. Budgets are sound only if possibilities of unfavorable developments in general business activity and in the affairs of the firm itself, as well as expectations of favorable developments, are given proper weight.

If, therefore, budgets are forecasts of attainable results, responsibility for their achievement can be assigned to the production, sales, and financial executives. All the more is this true if, as is customary, these executives are given a large share of authority in deciding what the budgets are to contain with respect to the operations over which they have jurisdiction. In conferences at various managerial levels, the original estimates of what is reasonably attainable may be changed, but ordinarily only after the executives have agreed on the soundness of the substitute figures. Accordingly, only after the operating executives have had their say are the budgets approved by the board of directors as a plan of operation for the forecast period. Depending on their individual jurisdictions, therefore, the operating executives can be called on to give an account of their stewardship if the volume of sales turns out to be substantially less than budgeted, if production fails to keep pace with the volume called for in the budget, if direct labor hours substantially exceed the number forecast for the budgeted volume of output, if selling expenses are markedly greater than the budget figure for a certain level of activity, or if at certain times within the forecast year cash is not available to meet obligations as they come due.

Control through the use of budgets is often said to be based on analysis of variances. When actual results of operations are reasonably close to the budget estimates, there is a strong presumption that managerial authority is being exercised efficiently. Although there is no reason for complacency, in the sense of neglecting to seek means of further improvement, the outcome can hardly be other than praiseworthy. On the other hand, a substantial falling short of actual results from those projected always justifies a search for causes followed by a fixing of responsibility, unless, perhaps, the variances are found to have resulted from outside developments that could not have been foreseen.

Fixed and Variable Budgets

In the preparation of budgets, a single set of figures may be selected in the expectation that operations during the forecast period will be carried on at a given percentage of the firm's capacity. Budgets so prepared are described as *fixed budgets.* They have the advantages of simplicity and relative ease in assembly, but, due to unforeseeable developments the actual scale of operations may turn out to be materially different from what was forecast. In such circumstances, the budgets quickly lose effectiveness as instruments of control, and the operating executives, who are supposed to be achieving results as budgeted, lose their bearings. If, for example, the volume of sales in terms of units falls 10 percent below the budget figures this does not mean that manufacturing overhead expenses, selling expenses, and other classes of expenses will likewise be down by 10 percent. In consideration of the influence of fixed and semivariable costs,[1] such a result is not to be expected. During the forecast period, frequent revisions of the whole range of budget figures might be necessary, but this would prove that the budget itself had been, in the first place, a poor tool for planning.

To avoid difficulties of these kinds, many firms prefer to use *variable budgets* whereby separate sets of estimates, each for a different level of operations, are prepared. The primary set is based on the volume of sales actually expected in the forecast period, but also formulated at once are other sets based on sales volumes of other levels—5 percent above the primary estimates, 10 percent above, 5 percent below, 10 percent below, and so on. If, then, sales start out as anticipated, budgetary control will be based on the primary set of estimates, but if a few months later sales soar to a level 10 percent above anticipa-

---

[1]See pp. 250–51.

tions, the alternative budget already prepared for that level will become effective.

Budget Systems

It is probably safe to say that virtually every business manager, no matter how small his enterprise, does something in the way of budgeting—certainly in the sense of forecasting if not in the sense of control. He may put no figures on paper in an orderly way, but surely he reflects from time to time about what sales he is likely to make in the next few weeks or months, what volume of goods he will need to purchase or produce, how many employees he must have, how much cash he will be collecting from his customers, what his total outlays will be, and so on. Such a reflective procedure may be derided as hit-or-miss—one likely to lead to serious errors in decision making—but at least it is indicative of the fact that budgeting, in a broad sense, is a practice well-nigh universal.

As one moves from the hit-or-miss procedures of forecasting toward the most formal and elaborate budgetary systems, one encounters systems of many different scopes. Some firms are quite satisfied to confine their formal budgeting to the use of cash budgets. Some prepare capital budgets in addition to cash budgets. Some tend to concentrate their attention on sales and production budgets. Some give primary attention to the various kinds of expense budgets. Many business managers, particularly those in control of firms of small and medium sizes, shy away from the installation of formal budget systems to avoid the extra administrative costs involved, but they forget that intelligent planning and control by means of budgets should be a means of avoiding many costly mistakes.

A complete budget system includes a specific budget for each significant phase of operations and a master budget in which the key figures from the specific budgets are brought together. For a manufacturing corporation, the specific budgets ordinarily include the following:

1. A sales budget, containing a monthly breakdown of expected sales in terms of units of the various kinds of products, unit prices, gross sales (units times prices), and perhaps further breakdowns such as for geographical areas in which it is expected sales will be made.
2. A production budget, indicating what scale of manufacturing operations must be undertaken from month to month to meet the anticipated sales volume.
3. A materials budget, showing what raw materials must go into production monthly.
4. A direct labor budget, indicating the number of hours of employment, the wage rates, and the total wages of employees needed to turn out the products.

5. Manufacturing expense, selling expense, and administrative expense budgets, setting forth all the costs, other than material and direct labor costs, expected to be incurred in producing and selling output and in the general administration of the enterprise.
6. Budgets for miscellaneous income and expenses.

Related to these are:

1. Inventory budgets, setting out details about what kinds and quantities of raw materials must be on hand from month to month, the indicated size of monthly goods-in-process inventories, and the quantities and kinds of goods to be carried from month to month in the finished goods inventories.
2. An accounts receivable budget, showing estimates of monthly debits to customers' accounts for credit sales, estimated monthly collections, and estimated monthly balances of uncollected accounts.
3. An accounts payable budget, having comparable details.
4. Budgets for monthly accruals of income and expenses.
5. Both short-term and long-term capital budgets, indicating anticipated additions to machinery, equipment, and other fixed assets, as well as expected sales and junking of fixed facilities that will reach the ends of their useful lives during the forecast periods.
6. The cash budget, summarizing all the effects on cash flows and balances expected to result from the scale of operations indicated in the other budgets.

Supplementary budgets can be used to set out details that are avoided in the principal budgets to which they are related. For example, monthly advertising expenses can be carried as single figures in the selling expense budget, but a supplementary advertising budget can indicate what proportions of the appropriations for advertising are to be spent on the various media.

CASH BUDGETS

Scope of a Cash Budget

A cash budget is a detailed estimate for some future period of cash inflows from all sources, cash disbursements for all purposes, and the resulting cash balances. As in the construction of most of the other kinds of budgets, the usual forecast period of a cash budget is one year. For this period, a breakdown is provided in terms of weeks, months, or other brief segments. Always possible, of course, are modifications in budgetary procedures. When the outlook is very uncertain, the financial managers of an enterprise may have to be satisfied with a projection for only six months or, perhaps, for as little as three months. Likewise, when approaching periods in which cash is expected to be unusually tight the financial managers may want breakdowns on a weekly basis—or even on a daily basis—though they may ordinarily be satisfied with monthly breakdowns.

Cash Budgets and Income Statements

Considering the foregoing definition of a cash budget, one should readily conclude that it is not an income statement projected for a forthcoming period. On the basis of the information contained in sales, materials, direct labor, and other operating budgets, it is true, income statements for future periods can be projected. Such *pro forma* statements, as they are called, often have significant uses, but they have little to do with the control of cash. The purpose of a projected income statement is to account for all sources of income to be tapped and for all classes of expenses to be incurred in a given period, *whether or not the income will be realized in cash in the period and whether or not the expenses will be matched by cash payments.* The purpose of a cash budget is to account for all expected inflows of cash from income sources of the same or other periods or from such nonincome sources as borrowing and stock sales, and to account for all expected outflows of cash as payments of expenses accrued in prior periods, the forecast period, or subsequent periods (prepayments), or as payments not immediately related to expenses—e.g., the purchase of fixed assets or dividend distributions to the stockholders. Thus, a firm that projects for the coming year a net profit before income taxes of, say, $800,000, may simultaneously anticipate in its cash budget a net increase in cash of $1 million, or perhaps one of only $400,000 or $500,000, or perhaps a net decrease in cash of, say, $200,000.

How transactions affect cash budgets and pro forma income statements in different ways is indicated in Table 11–1. The sampling of transactions included should suffice to show why the results of operations as projected for a given period in an income statement can be far different from the projected net change in cash holdings expected to result from the cash transactions of the same period.

Construction of Cash Budgets

For a firm that has a complete system of budgetary control, the preparation of a cash budget is a relatively simple matter. Most of the information needed for it is contained in budgets that precede it in formulation. It is necessary only to transfer to the cash budget the details of monthly cash receipts as indicated in sales, accounts receivable, and miscellaneous income budgets, and details of monthly cash expenditures as found in the budgets for materials and direct labor, the various budgets for overhead and miscellaneous expenses, and the short-term capital budget. In some instances, of course, information contained in sales and other operating budgets must be adjusted for the cash budget, as when sales figures given in terms of units of product are translated into dollar-and-cents estimates by the application of probable selling prices. Moreover, details of probable

TABLE 11–1
Effects of Transactions upon Pro Forma Income Statement and Cash Budget

Transactions Anticipated in Forecast Period	*In Pro Forma Income Statement*	*In Cash Budget*
Collections on accounts receivable of past periods	Excluded	Included
Collections on current sales to customers	Included	Included
Current sales, payment to be made in subsequent periods	Included	Excluded
Payment of current expenses	Included	Included
Incurring of expenses chargeable to forecast period but to be paid subsequently	Included	Excluded
Prepayment of expenses chargeable to subsequent periods	Excluded	Included
Depreciation charges	Included	Excluded
Purchase of new fixed assets for cash	Excluded	Included
Purchase of new fixed assets, payment to be made in subsequent periods	Excluded	Excluded
Sale of old fixed assets for cash at price less than remaining ing book value	Loss included	Total sales price included
Borrowing from banks	Excluded	Included
Repayment of bank loans	Excluded	Included
Payment of cash dividends to stockholders	Usually included	Included

borrowing and repayment of loans, sales and retirements of stock, and payments of cash dividends must be inserted in the cash budget independently of the other budgets.

Even when a firm is satisfied to confine its system of budgetary control to cash and capital budgets, most of the information that would be contained in the kinds of operating budgets referred to above must, nevertheless, be assembled. Estimates of sales, collections, production, direct labor hours, and so on, must be as carefully made and broken down for weekly, monthly, or other periods as if full-fledged budgets for the various phases of operations were to be used. A failure to assemble careful estimates of any kind of transaction likely to cause significant amounts of cash to flow in or out would obviously detract from the reliability and usefulness of the cash budget itself.

Sales and Collections. Like budgeting in general, cash budgeting begins with the forecasting of sales; for the typical business, the whole scale of operations of all varieties must be planned in relation to the expected sales volume. But projected sales figures, even if in terms of dollars and cents, cannot be taken directly into the cash budget. The important question is what cash collections will be made on account of sales. In the first place, therefore, it is necessary to have separate estimates of cash sales and credit sales. Second, returns and allowances must be estimated, with separate figures for those to be credited to customers' accounts and those to be met by cash refunds. Third, the amount of cash discounts that customers will probably take must be judged. Finally, with these estimates available, the actual volume of collections from credit customers must be estimated. This must take into account customers' debit balances on the books at the beginning of the forecast period as well as those to be created by credit sales during the period. The allowed credit period and the likelihood of prompt payment through the allowance of cash discounts are of outstanding importance, of course, as determinants of month-to-month collections, but their influence on the timing of collections can ordinarily be gaged on the basis of customers' payment behavior in the past. Necessarily, however, due weight must be given to new circumstances that may tend to cause future alterations in this behavior.

Other Cash Income. For most businesses engaged in selling tangible products or services, cash receipts in the ordinary course of business from sources other than sales are of minor or negligible importance; nevertheless, if such sources obtain, estimates of how much cash they will bring in must be included in the cash budget. The problem of estimation is usually not a difficult one. Rentals, interest on short-term investments, and dividends on holdings of stock of other unaffiliated enterprises ought generally to be easily estimable. But some items may be quite difficult to estimate. For example, probable cash receipts from royalties may be an elusive figure, as when a firm has licensed others to manufacture a product under its patents with royalties to be measured in proportion to the output of the licensees. Although discounts on purchases are often treated as other income in income statements, the preferable procedure in cash budgets is to classify them as deductions from the cash that must be paid in the forecast period for materials and supplies.

In the preparation of cash budgets by corporations that own subsidiaries, little attention is ordinarily given to the cash dividends that the subsidiaries are likely to pay to the parent corporation in the course of the forecast period. Instead, the cash inflows and outflows of the subsidiaries are estimated as carefully as for the parent company itself, and these, with proper adjustments for intercorporate cash transactions, are consolidated with those of the parent. In this way, the cash prospects of the whole family of corporations, parent and subsidiaries, can be seen in a single consolidated budget.

Cash Payments for Raw Materials or Finished Goods. Estimates of the amount and timing of payments for raw materials or finished goods during a forecast period are, as a rule, closely related to the sales estimates, but the relationship is not necessarily a precise one. A decision to carry larger inventories, whether of raw materials, goods in process, or finished goods, would obviously call for purchases beyond what would be required to meet estimated sales; while a decision to cut inventories would make it possible to meet a portion of estimated sales out of inventory already held, thereby bringing purchase requirements for the forecast period below what they otherwise would be. At any rate, when production schedules and buying programs have been established—on the basis, one may say, of sales estimates and separate inventory policy decisions—the timing of purchases and of payments therefor are not likely to be difficult to estimate.

In estimating month-to-month payments for raw materials and finished goods, the financial officers of an enterprise must give due weight to circumstances similar to those to be weighed in estimating cash collections from sales. They must distinguish between cash purchases and purchases on account, estimate probable returns and allowances, consider the credit terms of the various suppliers from whom goods will be purchased, and anticipate prompt payment to take advantage of whatever cash discounts may be allowed. They must also anticipate paying suppliers on obligations standing on the books at the beginning of the forecast period, as well as postponing payment on obligations that will originate during the period but will not reach their due or discount dates by its end.

Direct Labor. Business enterprises that pay direct labor on piece-rate bases can estimate their direct labor wage bill by simply applying the piece rates to the units of output called for in the production budget, at the same time taking into account prospective additional wage costs in the form of social security taxes, paid holidays and vacations, payments into company pension funds, payments for overtime work, and such bonuses as may be prescribed by incentive systems in operation. Enterprises that pay hourly rates must estimate the number of direct labor hours of workers of various skills that will be required to turn out the units of product as scheduled in the production budget, multiply the hours so found by the respective hourly rates, and add in supplemental wage costs of the kinds referred to above.

In making their estimates, enterprises of both classes must weigh all possibilities of changes during the forecast period in wage rates, payroll tax rates, and the scale of payments for fringe benefits. Not to be overlooked, also, is that accrued wages on the books at the beginning of the forecast period will require early payments in cash, and that accrued wages on the books at the end of the period will not require cash payments until the following period.

Overhead Expenses. In considering problems of estimating what cash payments will have to be made in a forecast period in meeting manufacturing, selling, and administrative expenses, one might hastily conclude that the least difficulty ought to be encountered with respect to fixed expenses, such as property taxes, property insurance, some of the executive salaries, and certain kinds of charges for maintenance. By definition, an expense of this class can be expected to hold at a specific level whether the scale of operations is high or low or somewhere in between. But fixity in an expense item does not mean that it will not change from this year to next year; it simply implies that if a change takes place the new level will prevail, regardless of the scale of operations next year. Local governments may raise their property tax rates, and insurance companies their rates for property insurance. Or the forecasting firm may be planning additions to fixed assets, which will hardly escape the watchful eye of the property tax assessor and on which the firm will surely want to carry insurance. One must conclude, therefore, that great care must be used in forecasting payments to meet fixed overhead expenses, that difficulties in estimation can no more be avoided here than in forecasting variable and semivariable expenses.

As for variable expenses, ease in forecasting is suggested by the fact that such expenses, by definition, are expected to vary in proportion to production or sales. If a firm's unit sales next year are expected to be 10 percent less than this year, its packaging costs and salesmen's commissions, as well as some kinds of its delivery expenses, may also be expected to fall by approximately 10 percent. But difficulties cannot be wholly avoided; there are possibilities of future changes in prices and costs. If the selling prices of the firm's products are to be lowered with no change in the salesmen's commission rate, or if the commission rate is to be reduced, the fall in total commissions can hardly be expected to be proportional to the fall in unit sales. If the prices of supplies used in packaging the products are expected to fall, total costs of this kind can be expected to be down by more than 10 percent.

Difficulties in estimating semivariable expenses come from two directions: the different kinds of expenses of this group tend to have disproportional patterns of variation in relation to the scale of operations, and changes in prices and rates affect them no less than fixed and variable expenses. A forecast of a lowered sales volume may be coupled with budgetary provisions for a substantial increase in outlays for advertising, the implication being that without increased spending for advertising the decline in sales volume would be expected to be much more severe. At the same time, the total increase in the advertising budget may be required not only because of the decision for a more extended coverage but also because of expected increases in rates for, say, newspaper and magazine space. In a similar way, a reduction in production of 5 percent may be projected without any cut in the estimated compensation for the factory superintendent and foremen, while a projected cut of 10 percent may be coupled with an estimated reduction in factory supervisory expenses of more than that proportion in the expectation of lowered salary rates and the laying off of one or more of the foremen.

Prepayments and accruals, it should be apparent, also complicate the estimation of cash outlays for meeting overhead expenses in a forecast period. In one year, payments for property insurance may be negligible, because policies prepaid in prior years are still in force; but payments for this purpose in another year may be substantial because most of the policies then come up for renewal. Estimates of cash payments for office supplies in the forecast year may be quite small in consideration of the large quantity expected to be on hand and already paid for at the beginning of the year, while cash disbursements for factory supplies may be placed at a relatively high figure because of an expected low inventory at the beginning of the year. In a comparable way, a large expense for an extraordinary advertising campaign projected for the late months of the forecast year may not show up in the cash budget, as payment is expected to be deferred until the following year.

Other Expenses. In their income statements, many concerns present a grouping of expense items separate from (and following) their classifications of manufacturing, selling, and administrative expenses. Such a grouping is variously labeled as other, miscellaneous, financial, or nonoperating expenses, and it includes such items as interest expense, sales discounts, and expenses incurred in the maintenance of properties not employed in the ordinary operations of the business.

For cash budgeting, of course, cash outlays in connection with other expenses must be as carefully estimated as are those directly related to manufacturing, selling, and administration. With sales discounts, however, we have already seen that the better budgetary practice is to regard them as deductions from cash to be collected from customers rather than as disbursements. Only in relatively rare instances do customers remit in full and then ask for refunds for the discounts they forgot to take. Cash requirements for interest on debts already outstanding or to be contracted in the forecast year are ordinarily quite easy to estimate. All one needs to know is the amount of debt, the portion of the year it will be outstanding, and the rate or rates of interest already stipulated or expected to be stipulated.

ILLUSTRATIVE CASH BUDGET

The usefulness of cash budgets as instruments of financial planning and control can be demonstrated by the presentation and analysis of an illustrative budget of a manufacturing corporation. We may assume that in the fall of the year 19xx the managers of the Carver Manufacturing Corporation tackle the job of preparing the cash budget for the following year—that is, for the year 19yy. On the basis of developments in the year 19xx to date, they expect the financial position of the corporation at the end of that year to be as indicated in the pro forma balance sheet presented in Figure 11–1.

FIGURE 11-1
Carver Manufacturing Corporation
Balance Sheet
Projected for December 31, 19xx

Assets

Current Assets:			
Cash		$ 415,000	
Short-term Treasury obligations		350,000	
Accounts receivable	$195,000		
Less: Reserve for bad debts	8,000	187,000	
Accrued interest receivable		3,750	
Inventories:			
Raw materials	$110,000		
Goods in process	92,000		
Finished goods	158,000	360,000	
Prepaid expenses		56,000	
Total Current Assets			$1,371,750
Fixed Assets:			
Land		$ 38,000	
Factory building	$200,000		
Less: Allowance for depreciation	75,000	125,000	
Machinery and equipment	$900,000		
Less: Allowance for depreciation	240,000	660,000	
Delivery equipment	$ 12,000		
Less: Allowance for depreciation	4,000	8,000	
Office equipment	$ 10,000		
Less: Allowance for depreciation	4,000	6,000	
Total Fixed Assets			837,000
Total Assets			$2,208,750

Liabilities and Equity

Current Liabilities:		
Accounts payable	$ 65,500	
Accrued wages	30,000	
Accrued expenses	46,000	
Accrued taxes	42,000	
Total Current Liabilities		$ 183,500
Stockholders' Equity:		
Capital stock	$1,600,000	
Earned surplus	425,250	
Total Equity		2,025,250
Total Liabilities and Equity		$2,208,750

Assumptions

Aside from their assumptions about the financial position of the corporation at the end of the year 19xx, as indicated in the pro forma statement, the financial managers of the corporation have the following additional facts and estimates (among others) to take into consideration in the preparation of the cash budget.

1. It is expected that operations in the year 19yy will be at approximately 90 percent of capacity.

2. The corporation has a distinct seasonal pattern in its sales. The lows occur in January, February, and March, followed by a rapid expansion to peak levels in August, September, and October, and sharp falloffs in November and December.

3. The corporation sells to a few customers on a cash basis, but most of its sales are on account. Its terms for credit sales call for net payment in 30 days, and no cash discounts are allowed for earlier payment. Accordingly, collections on accounts receivable in any month very largely flow from the sales of the preceding month.

4. Despite the seasonal pattern of its sales, the corporation tries to stabilize production. It builds up its inventories in months of slack sales to be able to meet the requirements of the peak months.

5. The corporation has a seasonal problem also in its purchases of raw materials. The price situation makes a concentration of raw materials buying in the period from December through April highly advantageous. The corporation ordinarily continues to buy raw materials throughout the year, but in much smaller quantities in the other seven months.

6. In view of the seasonal pattern of its sales, the corporation steps up its expenditures for advertising and other promotional efforts in April, May, and June. (This indicates that the corporation is willing to accept the seasonal pattern of its sales. Were it to conclude that the seasonal pattern could be changed by its own efforts, it would be likely to concentrate its selling efforts in or before the off-season months.)

7. The corporation's standard for minimum cash balances is $265,000.

8. Accounting for the Treasury securities shown in the pro forma balance sheet were purchases of $200,000 at the end of September and $150,000 at the end of October, 19xx. In those months, cash was in excess supply, but it was recognized that the excess was only a temporary one; accordingly, the investment in short-term obligations was made in anticipation of a high level of cash needs in the early months of the year 19yy. (For the sake of simplicity, it is assumed that the securities were bought at par on the date of issue and that they pay interest at the rate of 5 percent per annum.)

9. The accrued taxes entered in the pro forma balance sheet are the estimated unpaid balance of federal income taxes projected for the year 19xx—a balance payable in equal installments on March 15 and June 15, 19yy.

10. For several years, the corporation has been paying cash dividends to its stockholders in January, April, July, and October, each equal to 1¼ percent of the $1,600,000 par value of its outstanding common stock.

Carver's Cash Budget

On the basis of anticipations of position at the beginning of the year 19yy, as indicated in the pro forma balance sheet, the additional facts and estimates just outlined, and all the various kinds of information to be drawn from sales, accounts receivable, raw materials, production, and other budgets, the financial managers of the Carver Manufacturing Corporation, we may assume, draw up a cash budget for the year 19yy of the form and content of Figure 11–2. This indicates what they anticipate in the way of cash inflows and outflows, as well as monthly cash balances if the enterprise operates, as expected, at close to 90 percent of capacity. Should their budgetary system be variable, they would draw up comparable cash budgets for operations at other levels related to capacity, as 80 percent, 85 percent, and 95 percent.

A few of the items included in the receipts and payments sections of the illustrative budget require explanation.

1. It is expected that a portion of the factory building not needed for the productive operations of the corporation will be rented to another manufacturer beginning in April at an annual rental of $20,000 payable quarterly in advance (line 4).

2. In anticipation of a substantial increase in the scale of operations in the year 19zz, the corporation plans to buy additional machinery at a cost of $150,000 in November, 19yy (line 24).

3. It is assumed that in inserting the entries for federal income tax payments in the year 19yy (line 18) Carver's financial managers had in mind the federal tax rates and rules in effect in 1967 and expected to continue through 1968. Accordingly, the $21,000 payment of federal income tax entered for March and $21,000 of the $32,000 entry for June are the estimates of amounts still to be due on 19xx (1967) income, and the April, September, and December payments of $11,000 together with $11,000 out of the June total of $32,000 are installments on their estimates of Carver's pay-as-you-go tax obligation on 19yy (1968) income. As indicated in Carver's projected income statement for 19yy (1968) presented in Chapter 12, page 271, it expected its tax liability to be $143,784, so that it would anticipate declaring a pay-as-you-go obligation probably rounded to $44,000 and have the 4 installment payments of $11,000 each entered in its cash budget.

Up to June, 1968, the Internal Revenue Code provided that a corporation that kept its books on a calendar-year basis (as we have assumed Carver's practice to be) was required to make a declaration of estimated income tax for the current year by April 15 if before the beginning of that month it anticipated that its total tax for the year would exceed $100,000. With such an expectation and having made the declaration, it was required to pay not less than 25 percent of the estimated tax in excess of $100,000 by April 15, not less than 50 per-

FIGURE 11–2

Carver Manufacturing Company Cash Budget for the Year 19yy

Line		January	February	March	April	May	June	July	August	September	October	November	December	Total
1	Cash receipts from operations:													
2	Cash sales	$ 20,000	$ 15,000	$ 10,000	$ 20,000	$ 30,000	$ 30,000	$ 25,000	$ 35,000	$ 50,000	$ 40,000	$ 25,000	$ 15,000	$ 315,000
3	Collections, accounts receivable	180,000	120,000	100,000	110,000	190,000	240,000	305,000	315,000	460,000	420,000	395,000	250,000	3,085,000
4	Rental income			5,000			5,000			5,000			5,000	20,000
5	Total	$200,000	$135,000	$115,000	$130,000	$220,000	$275,000	$330,000	$350,000	$515,000	$460,000	$420,000	$270,000	$3,420,000
6	Additional sources of cash:													
7	Sale of Treasury obligations		200,000	150,000										$ 350,000
8	Interest on Treasury obligations		3,500	2,700										6,200
9	Short-term loans				180,000	90,000								270,000
10	Total		$203,500	$152,700	$180,000	$ 90,000								$ 626,200
11	Total Cash Receipts	$200,000	$338,500	$267,700	$310,000	$310,000	$275,000	$330,000	$350,000	$515,000	$460,000	$420,000	$270,000	$4,046,200
12	Cash payments for operations:													
13	Raw materials	$ 89,000	$ 85,000	$ 79,000	$ 72,000	$ 65,000	$ 37,000	$ 28,000	$ 15,000	$ 11,000	$ 14,000	$ 17,000	$ 21,000	$ 533,000
14	Direct labor	80,000	74,000	82,000	78,000	81,000	77,000	78,000	81,000	75,000	79,000	74,000	71,000	930,000
15	Manufacturing expense	50,000	48,000	51,000	49,000	50,000	48,000	49,000	50,000	48,000	51,000	47,000	46,000	587,000
16	Selling expense	40,000	39,000	46,000	64,000	58,000	65,000	46,000	48,000	44,000	42,000	40,000	37,000	569,000
17	Administrative expense	36,000	37,000	40,000	37,000	38,000	43,000	37,000	34,000	36,000	40,000	42,000	49,000	469,000
18	Federal income tax			21,000	11,000		32,000			11,000			11,000	86,000
19	Total	$295,000	$283,000	$319,000	$311,000	$292,000	$302,000	$238,000	$228,000	$225,000	$226,000	$220,000	$235,000	$3,174,000
20	Additional cash payments:													
21	Dividends	20,000			20,000			20,000			20,000			80,000
22	Discount on loans				3,900	1,950								5,850
23	Repayment of loans								180,000	90,000				270,000
24	Purchase of fixed assets											150,000		150,000
25	Purchase of Treasury obligations									200,000	200,000			400,000
26	Total	$ 20,000			$ 23,900	$ 1,950		$ 20,000	$180,000	$290,000	$220,000	$150,000		$ 905,850
27	Total Cash Payments	$315,000	$283,000	$319,000	$334,900	$293,950	$302,000	$258,000	$408,000	$515,000	$446,000	$370,000	$235,000	$4,079,850
28	Net receipts or payments (−)	$−115,000	$ 55,500	$−51,300	$−24,900	$ 16,050	$−27,000	$ 72,000	$−58,000	$ 0	$ 14,000	$ 50,000	$ 35,000	$ −33,650
29	Balance, beginning of period	415,000	300,000	355,500	304,200	279,300	295,350	268,350	340,350	282,350	282,350	296,350	346,350	415,000
30	Balance, end of period	$300,000	$355,500	$304,200	$279,300	$295,350	$268,350	$340,350	$282,350	$282,350	$296,350	$346,350	$381,350	$ 381,350

cent by June 15, not less than 75 percent by September 15, and not less than the full amount in excess of $100,000 by December 15. The balance of its tax liability for the year as finally determined (including the $100,000 exempted from the declaration base, if actually earned) was then payable in equal installments on March 15 and June 15 of the following year.

The tax legislation of June, 1968, provided for a gradual reduction of the pay-as-you-go exemption of $100,000 and its virtual elimination in 10 years. For 1968, the exemption was reduced to $81,100, even though the calendar year was almost half gone at the time the legislation was adopted, and further large reductions were set for the next 4 years—for example, to $62,200 for 1970. It should be added that corporations do not necessarily escape pay-as-you-go obligations for a full year if their estimates of tax liability as of March 31 are equal to or less than the year's allowed exemption. If there is a later revised expectation that tax liability for the year will be above the exemption level, a declaration must be made and pay-as-you-go obligations paid on a speedup basis. If, for example, the declaration is filed on September 15, at least 50 percent of the estimated current year tax in excess of the exemption must be paid immediately and the balance by December 15.

Analysis

In setting up their cash budget for the year 19yy, the financial managers of Carver would doubtless first fill in the details of lines 2–5 and 13–19 to reflect cash flows and balances expected to result from ordinary operations. The planned expenditure of $150,000 for machinery in November would next be entered (line 24) as something definitely programmed and for which financing would appear to be assured. Then the dividend payments (line 21) would probably be entered on a tentative basis. Although such payments would be at the discretion of the board of directors, to be finally decided on at its meetings during the course of the year, the prospective profit for the year 19yy (as revealed in the pro forma income statement presented in Chapter 12) would seem to justify dividends at a rate at least as high as had been paid for several years. Moreover, the board's approval of the cash budget containing the tentative dividend figures would surely indicate its intention to continue dividends at the existing rate.

A preliminary computation of monthly cash balances on the basis of all the items of cash inflow and outflow referred to in the preceding paragraph would indicate that for the year as a whole the cash situation would be satisfactory, that without regard to the subsequent entries for the purchase and sale of securities, and borrowing and the repayment of loans, the cash balance at the end of the year would be larger by $16,000 than at the beginning. But it would be quickly observed that the seasonal pattern of the corporation's sales and collections and of its raw material buying would bring the cash balance at the end of February far below the minimum standard of $265,000 and would cause quite serious cash deficits in the period from March through August. Hence, the additional entries on lines 7–9. These entries indicate how Carver's financial managers plan to meet the extraordinary cash drains that will begin in February. In the fall of 19xx, they invested excess cash in short-term obligations of the federal Treasury, and lines 7 and 8 show that they plan to liquidate these securities in February and March. Presumably, also, they have established a line of credit at a commercial bank, as is indicated by the entries for short-term loans on line 9 for April and May (with entries for the anticipated discount on the loans separately entered on line 22). It is worth mentioning here, in passing, that the willingness of the commercial bank to grant the loans would surely be strengthened by a demonstration of the corporation's capacity to repay—a demonstration for which the cash budget itself would serve excellently.

With the very large cash requirements of the early months planned for, Carver's financial managers would observe that beginning in August cash inflows from sales and collections far exceeding outflows for ordinary operations would cause the cash balance to mount well above the minimum standard. For this reason, they plan to repay the bank loans in August and September, as indicated by the entries on line 23, and to invest in short-term Treasury securities the additional excess cash expected to be available in September and October, as shown on line 25.

Since the corporation tends to run toward cash shortages early in the year and, indeed, must borrow to avoid what would be quite serious shortages, one may suggest a deferment of the dividend payments to stockholders until later in the year when plenty of cash is expected to be available. Such a deferment would reduce the borrowing requirements of the corporation by $60,000; yet, in the closing months of the year the stockholders could still be given a dividend of $80,000 if that continued to be the overall level chosen by the directors. Nevertheless, there is no compelling reason why a corporation that is in debt or that must go into debt following the payment of a cash dividend should avoid dividend distributions. If that were the rule, many corporations that now pay regular quarterly dividends would never pay dividends at all! The presence or absence of debt is only one factor to be considered by a board of directors in deciding about dividend payments. Other factors are of equal or greater importance; these will be studied in Chapter 26.[2] With respect to our

---

[2]See especially pp. 650–57.

illustration, then, we may conclude that because they anticipate profits for the year well above the dividends entered in the cash budget, and because they see certain advantages in regular quarterly payments, the directors of the Carver Manufacturing Corporation are quite content to plan for dividend payments, even in months when cash requirements for operations are especially heavy.

QUESTIONS

1. What kinds of anticipations are included in the scope of financial forecasting?

2. When the general business outlook is uncertain, is not a firm's financial forecasting likely to be so far off from actual developments as to be of little value? Discuss.

3. What is the relationship between financial forecasting and budgeting?

4. What is a budget? A cash budget? A capital budget?

5. Budgets are prepared for periods of what length? How detailed can they reasonably be?

6. What justification is there for describing budgets as instruments of control?

7. What is the difference between a fixed budget and a variable budget? Which is likely to be the more useful? Why?

8. Give several examples of anticipated transactions that would be included in cash budgets but excluded from projected income statements and vice versa.

9. What relationship does a cash budget have to a sales budget? A production budget? A budget for direct labor?

10. What is the distinction among overhead expenses classified respectively as fixed, semivariable, and variable? Give examples of expenses of each type.

11. For estimating borrowing requirements and dividend-paying capacity for the coming year, would the financial managers of a business firm get any help from a cash budget? Explain.

PROBLEM

To show the effects of the following transactions of the Talcott Corporation on its cash flows and on its after-tax net income for the year 19yy, enter them in the proper columns of a table with these columnar headings:

Cash		Net Income	
Inflow	Outflow	Decrease	Increase

Cash sales for the year	$ 415,000
Credit sales for the year	6,845,000
Collections on credit sales for the year	6,310,000
Collections on credit sales of 19xx	482,000
Purchases of raw materials and supplies on account	3,450,000
Payments to suppliers on foregoing purchases	3,109,000
Payments to suppliers on goods bought in 19xx	286,000
Advance payments to suppliers on goods to be delivered in 19zz	30,000
Inventory of raw materials and supplies, 1/1/19yy	310,000
Inventory of raw materials and supplies, 12/31/19yy	345,000
Wage and salary charges for the year	1,750,000
Accrued payroll of 12/31/19xx paid in 19yy	38,000
Other payroll payments in 19yy	1,725,000
Accrued expenses of 12/31/19xx paid in 19yy	81,000
Other operating expense payments in 19yy	967,000
Additional operating expenses chargeable to 19yy to be paid in 19zz	63,000
Federal income tax paid in 19yy on 19xx income	140,000
Federal income tax paid in 19yy on estimated 19yy income	320,000
Additional estimated federal income tax on 19yy income to be paid in 19zz	86,530
Purchase of warehouse and equipment for cash:	
Warehouse	400,000
Equipment	200,000
Sale of discarded equipment for cash:	
Selling price	75,000
Book value	45,000
Depreciation chargeable to 19yy	285,000
Dividends declared in 19xx and paid in 19yy	50,000
Dividends declared and paid in 19yy	75,000
Dividends declared in 19yy to be paid in 19zz	60,000

From the totals of the four columns, determine Talcott's net increase or decrease in cash and its after-tax net income for the year 19yy.

(Further reference to this problem and its solution is made in the problem at the end of Chapter 12.)

chapter 12

BUDGETARY CONTROL OF CASH FLOWS

CASH BUDGETS AS CONTROL INSTRUMENTS

The usefulness of cash budgets as instruments of control should be quite apparent on the basis of the illustrative budget and its analysis as presented in the closing pages of Chapter 11. This usefulness can be all the more appreciated if one reflects on the difficulties that the financial managers of the Carver Manufacturing Corporation might encounter in the year 19yy were they to lack a forecast of expected cash flows and advance plans for adjustment to distortions in the flows. They could be certain that the cash account could be replenished by the sale of the short-term Treasury obligations; but control of the corporation's cash position beyond that would presumably be on a makeshift basis.

Assuming that cash flows on account of ordinary operations turned out to be quite close to the illustrative figures, and that the short-term Treasury obligations were actually sold in February and March, the financial managers would find cash beginning to fall well below the minimum standard in April. They might decide that it would be appropriate to borrow, but the amount to be borrowed and the probable time when repayment could be made would be matters of great uncertainty. If they had not already established a line of credit at a commercial bank, they might not be able to borrow at all. At least, there would be delays for the bank's credit investigation before the loan would be granted. Later in the year, as cash became more plentiful the financial managers might decide that they could start to repay the bank loans, but they would be uncertain about the speed at which repayment could be made. After the loans had been repaid, and cash continued to pile up, there would be further uncertainty about how quickly the excess cash ought to be invested in short-term securities. The question whether already available cash should be used to pay for the machinery bought in November, or whether some other source of cash should be tapped for this purpose, would also have to be decided on a makeshift basis. Meanwhile, the payment of quarterly dividends of $20,000 could hardly be judged as being reasonable or unreasonable, since an overall picture on which to base a judgment would be lacking.

Further Control Aspects in Terms of the Illustration

The problems of cash control faced by the financial officers of our illustrative corporation can be described as relatively easy ones. They could have been made more difficult by the use of a different set of illustrative figures or by changes in the assumptions on which the illustration was built. But whether problems are easy or difficult, the forecast of what is likely to happen to cash movements must surely be regarded as essential for *sound* solutions. How a cash budget can serve as a basis for different sets of decisions in keeping with different sets of anticipations may, accordingly, be described in terms of the illustrative cash budget of the Carver Manufacturing Corporation. Although we need not attempt to exhaust the possibilities, we can see how the details of lines 7–9 and 21–25 of the illustrative budget could be changed if circumstances were somewhat different from those originally assumed.

Alternatives in a Tight-Money Situation. Suppose, for example, that the commercial bank had notified the officers of the corporation that because of extreme tightness in its lending capacity it would have to reduce Carver's line of credit to, say, $150,000. The unavailability of approximately $120,000 that the bank would in ordinary circumstances be expected to supply would obviously be a matter of only temporary embarrassment, and would occur only in the year 19yy and not in every year. Accordingly, finding a temporary or short-run solution for the problem would appear to be a reasonable objective. The embarrassment would be temporary, of course, since the cash budget indicates that whatever amount the corporation must borrow can be paid back in August and September, and that cash tends to pile up excessively in the later months of the year.

It might be decided that the circumstances were of a sufficiently emergency character to justify permitting cash balances to fall below the minimum standard of $265,000. A survey of the end-of-the-month cash balances shown on line 30 of the illustrative budget indicates that the cut in the bank's line of credit could be balanced should the corporation be satisfied to let its cash balance fall as low as approximately $150,000. But justification for this move would by no means be clear; perhaps this emergency would not be important enough to excuse a weakening of the cash position. The tight-money situation that prompted the bank to cut the line of credit might be expected to also affect the corporation's customers, causing them to slow down in meeting their obligations. To conserve their own cash, moreover, the customers might postpone purchases; thus, the corporation's sales and collections, though not ultimately reduced from the total expected volume, might come in months later than originally anticipated. The delay in cash inflows would surely mean a reduction in the corporation's cash balances below $150,000. A further consideration is that periods of tight money often precede periods of general business recession whose emergency character, with reduced sales and delays in collections, can hardly be doubted.

Accordingly, Carver's financial managers might decide that though the minimum balance standard of $265,000 could be breached, this concession ought not to be relied on to make up the entire deficiency of $120,000 in bank loans. Perhaps a drop of $40,000 or $50,000 below the minimum standard should be the limit of the breach. Accordingly, other means of conserving cash or supplementing its inflow would have to be sought. In a close corporation, one or more of the stockholders might be willing to advance funds on a loan basis for a few months, but this would not be a likely solution for a large corporation with a wide scattering of stockholders unless one or a few had quite large interests. Another possible partial solution would be the deferment of dividends till late in the year. This would have the effect of conserving $60,000 of cash during the tight period, and with the temporary lowering of the minimum balance standard it might be expected to be sufficient to meet the difficulty. Another possibility would be to buy raw materials less aggressively in the early months of the year, although some penalty might have to be paid in higher prices later on. Again, purchase discounts could be forgone so that the corporation could hold on to its cash to the end of the credit periods stipulated by sellers of raw materials.

On the other hand, Carver's financial managers would not be likely to give much thought to more far-reaching solutions to what would be, or would appear to be, a temporary problem. They might be able to speed up the inflow of cash by granting discounts to their customers for early payment, but such a change in credit terms could not easily be limited to a few months only. Once the customers had been allowed discounts, they would be likely to anticipate their continued availability. In addition, the corporation might be in a position to borrow on a long-term basis as by a bond issue, but this would not appear to be a sound way of curing a cash deficiency of a few months in one year. The same could be said for an additional issue of stock. Although the stockholders might be willing to buy more stock, it would seem wiser to defer the use of this source of long-term money for some as yet unforeseen, long-term purpose, rather than to use it now for a purpose extremely short-term in character.

Long-Term Funds for Equipment. In the original illustration of the Carver Manufacturing Corporation in Chapter 11, a decision was made to use available cash to buy some new machines in November at a cost of $150,000. But with a change in assumptions, the decision might have gone in a different direction. Suppose that the expenditure was expected to be only the first of a series of heavy outlays to prepare the corporation for a substantial expansion in the level of its output. In that situation, a search for new intermediate- or long-term funds would seem to be in order. Though the corporation could spend $150,000 for equipment without seriously weakening its working capital position, it obviously could not continue to make a series of outlays of large amounts without danger. Accordingly, considering the overall expansion programmed in their long-term capital budget the financial managers might immediately decide to sell additional stock or to float a bond issue to meet the total cost of the machines plus all the other equipment expected to be acquired over a period of several years. However, it would apparently be reasonable to use present cash to the extent of $150,000 to take care of the first step in the expansion program, and later on to put out additional stock or a bond issue of sufficient size both to finance further fixed asset acquisitions and to replenish the $150,000 of cash taken from working capital.

All the more would a stock or bond issue appear to be advisable for financing the acquisition of equipment when additional cash requirements for the circular process are taken into consideration. A sizable expansion in the level of operations ordinarily requires not only additional fixed assets but also more current assets as well; more cash is needed for minimum balances, for absorption in inventories and accounts receivable, and for meeting day-to-day operating expenses. It might be expected that some of these additional requirements would be offset by increased buying of raw materials on account and increases in unpaid payrolls and unpaid (accrued) expenses of other kinds, but such sources of additional current assets could hardly be expected to carry the whole load. Accordingly, the need of additional cash for the circular process as well as for the purchase of fixed assets would have to be kept in mind. In the original Carver case, had the expansion program not been expected to go beyond the expenditure of $150,000 for machines the decision to use available cash to meet the expenditure might have been predicated on an assurance that the corporation's line of credit at the bank could be increased to meet increased cash requirements for current purposes. If, however, a quite costly expansion program were envisaged—with an expectation, therefore, that much cash would be needed both for the purchase of fixed assets and for the circular process—the financial managers of Carver might decide that they would not be able, or would not want, to rely on the bank for all the additional cash expected to be needed for the latter purpose. Hence, they would probably decide that a portion of the additional cash requirements for current asset expansion, as well as all the cash needed for fixed asset expansion, should be acquired on an intermediate- or long-term basis. Were this their decision, they would make their stock or bond issue big enough to cover both kinds of requirements.

Changing Circumstances during the Budget Period

The foregoing discussion was designed to indicate the usefulness of cash budgets as tools of financial planning regardless, one might say, of the nature of business conditions anticipated. We started out with a given set of circumstances as anticipated and described what the decisions of the financial managers might be in the light of these anticipations; then we varied the anticipated circumstances somewhat to show how the variations would be likely to require decisions of different kinds. But cash budgets are also useful as guides in meeting unexpected changes in circumstances that occur during the periods for which they are forecasts.

The most far-reaching change in circumstance likely to occur during a budget period, and to make actual operating results quite different from those anticipated, is an expansion or contraction in general business activity. Such a development may cause sales to rise well above or to fall well below the level that was forecast. In the Carver case, operations at 90 percent of capacity were anticipated for the year 19yy, but what if they had risen to 100 percent or fallen to 80 percent? Difficulties could hardly be avoided, but in a good budget system—one of variable budgets, as described in Chapter 11—they would have been anticipated and prospective solutions already worked out. The 80 percent budget or the 100 percent budget would become the financial plan for the year, and the 90 percent one would be discarded even though major attention originally centered on it.

But competent planners ought not to be so wide of the mark that sales would start out at a level requiring operations at 80 percent or 100 percent of capacity when they expected sales that would require a level of operations midway between these levels. What is more likely to happen, therefore, is that sales will proceed for a while as anticipated and then veer off, perhaps sharply, in one direction or the other. In other words, a rise or fall in business activity that occurred near the beginning of the budget year ought, as a rule, to have been anticipated and planned for, but the forecasters might readily be excused for not having foreseen that such a development would occur in, say, July or August. Unquestionably, there are difficulties in switching in midstream from a 90 percent budget to one at 80 percent or 100 percent, and all the more so if a gradual shift, perhaps over a period of two or three months, is appropriate. But the difficulties should be minor compared with what they would likely be were no budgets available. If a plan is available for meeting whatever financial problems a *full year* at a level of 80 percent or 100 percent of capacity would be expected to create, it should also be highly useful in indicating what should be done if operations for only three or four months are at one of those levels.

Sometimes, of course, things happen that have not been anticipated in any of the budgets, regardless of the number of levels of operation planned for. For example, suppose that in August the Carver Manufacturing Corporation were offered at a most attractive price a quantity of raw materials equal to the volume that it would ordinarily buy in the months from December through April. Were we to assume its cash position in August to be at least roughly as indicated in the illustrative budget of Chapter 11, and the raw materials to cost $360,000, important changes in the plans as set out in the budget would have to be made to take advantage of the offer. But the budget would enable Carver's managers to recognize rather quickly where the changes could be made, and it would assure them of the wisdom of the changes. The bank could be asked to extend the maturities of its loans, since it could be demonstrated by means of the budget that the delay in payment would be one of only a few months. The plan of investing in short-term securities in September and October would surely be revised, since the objective of much of this planned investment would have already been realized.

PERIODIC REPORTS FOR CONTROL

As operations move into and through the year or other period of time covered by a cash budget, the financial officers must be supplied with periodic reports to enable them to check the budgeted figures against actual developments. The essential purpose of this requirement is to indicate if and when and to what degree financial plans must be switched.

Daily Cash Reports

The preparation of daily cash reports is probably the most convenient means of maintaining a running comparison of actual cash flows with budget projections. Although cash budgets are not set up on a daily basis, and although the actual cash receipts and payments of any one day are not likely to be of any great significance, the observance of cash receipts and disbursements in the reports of several consecutive days will indicate whether or not the rate of flow is proceeding as expected. Moreover, the balance figures in the daily reports will indicate whether or not net inflows or outflows of the year to date have been close to the expected level. Such figures also indicate, of course, when borrowing under already arranged bank lines of credit should be effected, as well as when superabundant cash should be used to repay bank loans or to buy short-term investment securities.

A daily cash report is ordinarily a simple document. Aside from the heading and date, many such reports contain nothing more than the opening cash balance of the day, the cash receipts and disbursements of the day, and the closing balance. Some are expanded to give broad classes of receipts and payments, as in Figure 12–1, which is a format that the Carver Manufacturing Corporation may want to use. Sometimes, still more elaborate reports are made by adding to a form such as Figure 12–1 columns for the month to date and the year to date for the entry of the opening balances of the month and year,

FIGURE 12–1
Carver Manufacturing Corporation
Daily Cash Report
January 2, 19yy

Opening balance		$415,000
Receipts:		
Cash sales	$ 1,100	
Collections, accounts receivable	4,100	
Other—		
Total Receipts	$ 5,200	
Payments:		
Operations	9,600	
Other—		
Dividends	20,000	
Total Payments	$29,600	
Excess of receipts/*payments*		*24,400*
Closing Balance		$390,600

the cumulative amounts of receipts and disbursements by major classes, and the closing balances. However, it is probably better to reserve such details for monthly cash reports.

Monthly Cash Reports

Monthly cash reports are designed to bring together for comparison and analysis the major details of actual cash flows for the individual month and for the year to date, and those of the budget for the same periods. Such a report indicates to what extent cash receipts and payments for the month and for the year to date have exceeded or fallen short of projected receipts and payments. What is more, the specific items of receipts and payments in which principal variances have occurred stand out for special study.

A type of monthly report that would tie in with the budget system of the Carver Manufacturing Corporation is presented as Figure 12–2. It has been filled in with assumed receipts and payments for the month of February 19yy, and for the two months ending February 28. The report shows that in February receipts fell short of expectations by $8,000, and that payments exceeded expectations by $13,400, for a total deficiency in actual net receipts, by comparison with the budgeted figures, of $21,400. However, net receipts in January must have been higher than expected, since the year-to-date columns indicate that the cumulative deficiency for the two months amounts to only $3,100. The specific variances item by item, as revealed in the report, should be even more important than their totals in indicating to Carver's financial managers when and in what direction, if at all, changes in financial planning should be effected.

FIGURE 12–2
Carver Manufacturing Corporation
Monthly Cash Budget Report
For the Month of February, 19yy

	This Month			*Year to Date*		
	Actual	*Budget*	*Excess of Actual*	*Actual*	*Budget*	*Excess of Actual*
Cash receipts:						
Cash sales	$ 15,600	$ 15,000	$ 600	$ 39,200	$ 35,000	$4,200
Collections, accounts receivable	111,400	120,000	*8,600*	298,400	300,000	*1,600*
Rental income						
Sale of investments	200,000	200,000		200,000	200,000	
Interest income	3,500	3,500		3,500	3,500	
Short-term loans						
Long-term loans						
Other—						
Total	$330,500	$338,500	$ *8,000*	$541,100	$538,500	$2,600
Cash payments:						
Raw materials	$ 87,200	$ 85,000	$ 2,200	$179,100	$174,000	$5,100
Direct labor	76,200	74,000	2,200	156,500	154,000	2,500
Manufacturing expense	52,800	48,000	4,800	96,700	98,000	*1,300*
Selling expense	41,600	39,000	2,600	77,000	79,000	*2,000*
Administrative expense	38,600	37,000	1,600	74,400	73,000	1,400
Federal income tax						
Interest expense						
Dividends				20,000	20,000	
Fixed assets						
Repayment of loans						
Investment in securities						
Other—						
Total	$296,400	$283,000	$13,400	$603,700	$598,000	$5,700
Excess of actual receipts/*payments* over budget			*$21,400*			*$3,100*

Other Reports

While daily and monthly cash reports identical with or comparable to the kinds illustrated are the principal means of checking cash flows to insure the constant availability of adequate cash, it should not be inferred that they are the only classes of cash reports prepared by business firms. But other classes are generally concerned with the safeguarding of cash rather than with its availability. These include statements for the reconciliation of deposit balances as reported by banks with the cash balances shown in the accounting records, and reports on disbursements from and balances in petty cash funds.

Moreover, one should not infer that in attempting to control the flow of cash financial managers make decisions solely on the basis of cash reports. A judgment about a firm's cash position at a given time can be sound only if the person making the judgment knows what are its volume of accounts receivable, inventory position, obligations owing to trade creditors, accrued payroll, unpaid obligations for all kinds of accumulated expenses, and so on. In other words, he must know what the prospects are for cash inflows and outflows in the immediate future, not only on the basis of what was budgeted several months earlier but on the basis of *what has actually happened* in the immediate past to sales and purchases on account, the incurring of expenses on a deferred-payment basis, and so on. Accordingly, the financial managers must, as a rule, give as close attention to periodic reports of accounts receivable, inventories, accounts payable, payrolls, and the like, as they give to daily and monthly cash reports.

OPERATING STATEMENTS AS TOOLS OF CONTROL

Well-designed budget systems usually include a forecasting of the results of operations for the coming year in terms of income and expenses and net profit or loss, and well-designed accounting systems always provide for operating statements to show what the results of operations have actually been. Forecasts are made at least for the full year but often also for monthly, quarterly, or semiannual periods. Accounting statements that show the actual results of operations are a must for the full year but are most useful, too, when also prepared for monthly, quarterly, or semiannual periods. Operating statements of both the forecast and actual-results varieties are of major importance as tools of cash control, as the following discussion will show.

Projected Operating Statements and Changes in Plans

The primary financial objective of business operations is earning profits, and not simply insuring that the enterprise will have at all times enough cash to meet its maturing obligations. A cash budget drawn up by a corporation on the basis of preliminary operating plans for the coming year may show that its cash balance at the end of the year would be larger than the opening balance, but a projected or pro forma income statement may indicate that if the preliminary plans of operation are carried into effect the result will be a net loss. The prospects of a net loss on operations, as pictured in the pro forma statement, may lead to decisions for comprehensive changes in operating plans—changes aimed toward reducing expenses and increasing income or toward finding new sources of income. But such changes would doubtless require major alterations in the cash budget, probably introducing cash management problems of a much more difficult kind than had been anticipated in relation to the original plans.

All this does not imply that prospective profits can always be increased or losses eliminated by changes in operating plans. In many cases, an analysis of projected operating statements will, indeed, reveal defects in preliminary plans that can be corrected, but in many others the results estimated in projected statements will be quickly recognized as the best that can be hoped for. At any rate, the thing to be emphasized is that a favorable cash outlook is not enough; it must always be related to the outlook for profits and losses. In some instances, the profit prospects can be substantially improved without giving rise to insuperable difficulties in cash management. In others, projected cash flows and positions preclude material changes in operating plans, even though the changes would improve profit prospects. In still others, a compromise may appear to be the best solution—one recognizing that moderate changes in operating plans are compatible with the cash outlook.

Illustration. The reason that changes in cash balances as projected in cash budgets may differ widely from anticipated profits and losses was indicated in Chapter 11, in the discussion of differences in the contents of cash budgets and income statements.[1] For a further consideration of this matter and its significance, we may again refer to the affairs of the Carver Manufacturing Corporation. With its cash budget for the year 19yy before us (as presented in Chapter 11, page 256), let us examine its projected statement of cost of goods manufactured and income statement for the same year. We may assume that these two statements were set up as in Figures 12–3 and 12–4.

As we see at once, the projected increase in cash and its equivalent (in this instance, short-term marketable Treasury securities) is far different from the anticipated net profit on operations after allowance for federal income taxes. The cash budget reveals an expected decrease in cash from $415,000 to $381,350, but an increase in holdings of short-term securities from $350,000 to $400,000, for a net increase in cash and equivalent of $16,350. But the pro forma income statement,

---

[1]See pp. 247–248.

FIGURE 12–3
Carver Manufacturing Corporation
Statement of Cost of Goods Manufactured
Projected for the Year Ending December 31, 19yy

Raw materials:		
Inventory, January 1	$110,000	
Purchases	552,000	
	$662,000	
Less: Inventory, December 31	145,000	$ 517,000
Direct labor		937,000
Manufacturing expense:		
Depreciation—factory building	$ 5,000	
Depreciation—machinery and equipment	60,000	
All other	623,500	688,500
		$2,142,500
Add: Goods in process, January 1		92,000
		$2,234,500
Less: Goods in process, December 31		109,000
Cost of Goods Manufactured		$2,125,500

FIGURE 12–4
Carver Manufacturing Corporation
Income Statement
Projected for the Year Ending December 31, 19yy

Gross sales		$3,467,000
Less: Returns and allowances		69,000
Net sales		$3,398,000
Cost of goods sold:		
Finished goods inventory, January 1	$ 158,000	
Cost of goods manufactured	2,125,500	
	$2,283,500	
Less: Finished goods inventory, December 31	227,000	2,056,500
Gross profit on sales		$1,341,500
Selling and administrative expenses:		
Depreciation, delivery equipment	$ 2,000	
Depreciation, office equipment	500	
Bad debts	13,600	
Other selling expenses	551,000	
Other administrative expenses	463,000	1,030,100
Net profit on sales		$ 311,400
Other expense:		
Interest expense		5,850
		$ 305,550
Other income:		
Rental income	$ 16,667	
Interest income	6,650	
Purchase discounts	6,100	29,417
		$ 334,967
Estimated liability for federal income tax		143,784
Net Profit		$ 191,183

as supported by the statement of manufacturing costs, projects a net profit of $191,183 after the deduction of $143,784 for estimated federal income taxes.[2] If the net profit will be approximately $191,183, why will cash and its equivalent increase by only $16,350? The answer must be that some of the expense and income items entered in the operating statements are not reflected in the cash budget because of prepayments and deferments, and that some of the cash receipts and disbursements entered in the cash budget (in this instance, cash disbusements only) are not reflected in the operating statements. Outstanding among these differences are:

1. The expenditure of $150,000 for new machines shown as a payment in the cash budget but not taken up anywhere in the operating statements.
2. The total charges for depreciation of $67,500 in the operating statements not requiring a cash disbursement and therefore not shown in the cash budget.
3. The big deduction in the income statement of $143,784 for estimated federal income tax, whereas only $86,000 for income tax payments is entered among the disbursements in the cash budget.
4. The payment of cash dividends of $80,000 to the stockholders entered in the cash budget but ignored in the operating statements.[3]

Cash Budget Items Based on Projected Operating Statements

Apart from serving as a means of coordinating the profit- and cash-control objectives of business enterprises, projected operating statements yield certain kinds of information essential for sound cash budget policies. For the Carver Manufacturing Corporation, the entries for the quarterly federal income tax payments in its budget for the year 19yy could be based only on the total tax liability as computed in the projected income statement on the estimated net profit for the year. Again, the expectation that Carver's directors will vote the regular quarterly dividend of $20,000, as shown in the cash budget, would presumably have for its basis the level of anticipated

---

[2]Computed at the rates that Carver's managers would presumably have expected to be in effect in 19yy (1968)—22 percent on the first $25,000 of taxable income and 48 percent on the balance of taxable income—but with a deduction of $10,500 from the tax liability thus computed as an investment credit. The Internal Revenue Code allows a deduction equal to 7 percent of the amount of new investment in productive facilities of certain classes, provided that the deduction does not exceed the first $25,000 of taxable income plus one half of the remainder of taxable income. For Carver, the investment credit would be anticipated on the basis of the proposed outlay of $150,000 for new machinery and equipment in November, 19yy.

[3]A statement of sources and application of funds may be used to show the complete relationship between changes in cash and equivalent, on the one hand, and profits, tax liabilities and payments, prepayments and deferments, and other items, on the other. Such a statement is illustrated and discussed on pp. 279–83.

net profit after income taxes, as revealed in the pro forma income statement. And, finally, the decision to use cash already on hand in the amount of $150,000 to pay for the machines to be bought in November, as incicated in the cash budget, probably would be predicated also on the profit expectation as arrived at in the income statement. The payment of $150,000 would be recognized as not really being a drain from the circular process—from working capital—since all of it could be considered as coming from the cash throw-offs on account of depreciation and profits plowed under after provisions for the federal income tax and the payment of dividends.

One should not conclude, however, that information about cash receipts from sales and cash expenditures for operating expenses would be drawn from projected statements of manufacturing costs and income statements for inclusion, after proper adjustment, in the cash budget. As was indicated in Chapter 11, this sort of information is drawn from separate budgets for sales, accounts receivable, production, direct labor, inventories, manufacturing expenses, and so on. These detailed budgets provide the data for the construction of both the cash budget and the pro forma operating statements, and only certain special items of information that appear in the pro forma statements, as applied in the manner described in the preceding paragraph, lay the foundation for additional entries in the cash budget.

Current Operating Statements

As tools of cash control, current operating statements of actual results, as distinct from projected ones, supplement daily and monthly cash reports, as do reports of sales, inventories, accounts receivable, accounts payable, and accrued expenses. They are clearly supplementary because, in most instances, results shown in current operating statements substantially different from those forecast will have already been reflected in the daily and monthly cash reports. If from time to time the volume of sales or of manufacturing operations gets out of line from the levels forecast, the inflows and outflows of cash are likely to vary commensurately.

It is possible, however, for the cash flows to be proceeding much as was expected while out-of-line situations of harmful character are developing elsewhere. For example, raw materials may be purchased in the usual quantities at the prices anticipated and payments made to the suppliers at the appropriate times, but extraordinary amounts of spoilage in manufacturing operations may occur. This might be observed by a careful examination of periodic inventory reports or of specific spoilage reports, but it would surely be dramatized by the higher than expected manufacturing costs shown in a current statement of such costs and by the lower than expected profit as disclosed in a current income statement.

BALANCE SHEETS AS TOOLS OF CONTROL

It is most advantageous for the financial managers of business enterprises to have available for analysis forecasts of the financial position of their enterprise for various dates in the approaching year, as well as to have periodic reports on the actual financial position as the year progresses. Hence, projected or pro forma balance sheets are important as tools of planning, and current balance sheets are important as instruments of continuing control.

Projected Balance Sheets

Although the expected level of cash at the end of each month or quarter in the coming year can be picked up from the cash budget, the amount of accounts receivable from the receivables budget, the amount of inventories from the inventory budgets, the amount of current obligations from accounts payable, payroll, and accrued expense budgets, and so on, it is most convenient to bring these items together in one place as soon as the detailed budgets have been completed. This is done by the preparation of projected monthly or quarterly balance sheets. A projected balance sheet makes it possible to judge to what extent an enterprise's financial position will be strengthened or weakened as a result of its planned activities up to the date for which it is prepared.

Often, projected balance sheets reveal errors in planning or expectations not readily discoverable elsewhere. Because a projected balance sheet brings together all prospective assets and liabilities as of a given date, unsatisfactory groupings and relationships among groups can be readily seen. While working on the detailed separate budgets for the coming year, the financial managers of a corporation might make unrelated decisions for substantial spending in April for machinery and equipment and a substantial outlay to meet an installment on a long-term loan, and for large purchases of raw materials on account in May. No bar to these transactions in the two months might be indicated by the entry of the proposed cash disbursements in the cash budget, but a pro forma balance sheet for April 30 of the coming year might show that the corporation's working capital position would be gravely weakened by the proposed April transactions. Projected balance sheets for later months might reveal that the weakness in working capital would be temporary, but the financial managers would realize that it would be showing up starkly at the very time that the suppliers of raw materials would be asked to grant extraordinary credits. Rather than holding to plans that could lead to the embarrassment of having their requests for credit refused, the financial managers would surely be inclined to rearrange the timing of the three transactions.

In a similar way, corporate financial managers know that their reported balance sheets are analyzed by prospective lenders, stockholders, bondholders, prospective investors in their stocks and bonds, and others who have financial interests of one kind or another. Accordingly, they have good reason to switch to new plans if the effects of earlier tentative decisions, as reflected in pro forma balance sheets, would be likely to be judged adversely by competent analysts. The contents of an actual balance sheet to be published some months hence must be expected to be quite close to the projected one—otherwise, forecasting would be nonsensical. If, therefore, the projected statement looks weak, plans must be changed so that the balance sheet of actual position *will not look so* when the time for its publication comes.

Because analysts tend to place great weight on various ratios computed from balance sheet data, the financial managers of businesses should find it advisable to compute the same kinds of ratios with respect to the figures assembled in their projected balance sheets. This should enable them to see in what direction the judgments of the analysts are likely to go, and to prompt them to change plans should it appear that the judgments are likely to be adverse. Of significance, therefore, are ratios of the kinds discussed in earlier chapters—cash to current liabilities, accounts receivable to credit sales, cost of goods sold to average inventories, fixed assets to sales, operating assets to sales, and so on. Many other ratios can be computed, but we need not survey the list, nor need we rehash the significance, merits, and demerits of those considered earlier. But we should find it advantageous to give further consideration to the analysis of working capital position, since balance sheet analysts always emphasize that aspect of financial standing. The matter of working capital position was briefly discussed in Chapter 7, but attention there was given chiefly to the relationship of cash to current liabilities.

Working Capital Ratio. Although one may know very little about balance sheet analysis, one is likely to know that the working capital ratio is the most widely used of all analytical devices based on the balance sheet, that it is the ratio of total current assets to total current liabilities, and that a widely respected rule of thumb is that the ratio should be no weaker than 2 to 1.

The great popularity of the working capital ratio indicates that almost everybody who has occasion to analyze balance sheets, whether he is primarily interested in the short-term or the long-term outlook, knows that the outlook for any period of time can only be bleak for firms that are not currently *solvent*—that is, in a position to apparently meet obligations currently coming due and expected to come due in the near future. Cash need not be already available to meet all the current liabilities shown in a balance sheet; but there should be good prospects of an adequate short-term inflow, indicated by holdings of accounts receivable and inventories. For most kinds of enterprises, therefore, working capital analysis is an examination of the relationship between cash (and equivalent—that is, short-term Treasury obligations and other short-term high quality investments), accounts receivable reduced by the reserve for bad debts, and inventories, on the one hand, and the array of current liabilities, on the other.

It might appear that if the total of cash, accounts receivable, and inventories is equal to the total of current liabilities, solvency is assured, so that to look for a ratio in the vicinity of 2 to 1 is to expect too much. But creditors want a margin of protection. There may be delays in collecting on accounts receivable, and even greater delays in converting inventories into accounts receivable and, in turn, collecting on these accounts. But the liabilities must be paid when their due dates arrive, unless further deferments are specially arranged for. In looking at the situation from another angle, it may be said that short-term creditors think it would be most unreasonable for them to be the sole suppliers of a firm's current assets. Therefore, when they insist on a ratio such as 2 to 1 they say, in effect, that at least half of the current assets should be supplied by the stockholders. However, they may be satisfied if some or even all of this half is provided by long-term creditors, such as bondholders.

Nevertheless, a working capital ratio such as 2 to 1 should not be regarded as something sacred. In some lines of business, firms tend to consistently have ratios weaker than this without adverse judgment; in many others, stronger ratios are commonplace and often come to be generally expected. The intelligent analyst knows, moreover, that the ratio of the individual firm will vary from month to month or from quarter to quarter, sometimes quite materially, according to changing circumstances that have no great bearing on solvency. He will keep in mind, too, the possibility of window dressing[4] as a procedure to improve the appearance of working capital positions.

In sum, the financial managers of business enterprises want working capital positions as indicated in projected balance sheets to be in line with what is expected in their respective fields of business activity. Although an unfavorable projection is only an expectation, they would not want to aim for a situation they would not want to come about. All the more is this true if they expect to publish or to supply to creditors actual balance sheets for the dates for which the projections are made—hence the desirability of changing plans to make the projected balance sheets and, it is presumed, the actual balance sheets later on look as favorable as possible.

Acid Test. A second testing device for working capital position is

---

[4]See pp. 139–40.

known as the acid test or the quick ratio. It is the ratio of cash (and equivalent) and receivables, reduced by the reserve for bad debts, to the total of current liabilities. The application of the acid test to the working capital position of a firm is predicated on the obvious fact that inventories are a step further removed from cash than are accounts receivable, and on the idea, therefore, that short-term creditors ought to be able to expect payment from existing cash balances and collections from accounts receivable, and not have to depend on the liquidation of inventories. Hence 1 to 1 is often said to be a desirable standard for the acid test.

But, as with the working capital ratio itself, an acid-test standard such as 1 to 1 ought not to be worshipped as something sacred. Much depends on circumstances. A seasonal business that seeks to stabilize production will tend to have a weak acid-test ratio during its period of slack sales, but a much stronger one in its period of heavy selling. The earlier weak position, therefore, would have to be judged in relation to the market prospects for the firm's products in the later period.

In the use of projected balance sheets as tools of planning, at any rate, financial managers must surely keep in mind the widespread application of the acid test, and take steps to adjust policies should projections indicate that at certain times in the coming year this ratio, in the absence of the adjustments, would look quite unfavorable to prospective creditors and other analysts.

Illustration. To illustrate the use of working capital and acid-test ratios, we may refer once again to the affairs of the Carver Manufacturing Corporation. Its expected financial position at the end of the year 19xx was indicated in the balance sheet presented near the end of Chapter 11, page 253. In the matter of working capital, its projected situation would appear to be a most favorable one. The projected working capital ratio is 7.6 to 1 (total current assets of $1,371,-750 to total current liabilities of $183,500), and the acid test is 5.2 to 1 (total current assets of $955,750, after excluding inventories and prepaid expenses, to current liabilities of $183,500)—both far above the rule-of-thumb standards and, presumably, quite satisfactory on any other basis, considering all that we now know of the activities of our illustrative corporation.

But Carver's managers would be especially interested in what their financial and working capital positions are likely to be at the end of March, 19yy, since they expect to go to the bank to borrow money in April, and at the end of April since they expect to return to the bank for another loan in May. They want to be able to present favorable current balance sheets to the bankers at the appropriate times. For our purposes, however, it should suffice to consider only the projected situation at the end of March. Let us assume, then, that the pro forma balance sheet drawn up for that date is that presented in Figure 12–5.

FIGURE 12–5
Carver Manufacturing Corporation
Balance Sheet
Projected for March 31, 19yy

Assets

Current Assets:			
Cash		$ 293,200	
Accounts receivable	$128,300		
Less: Reserve for bad debts	9,200	119,100	
Inventories:			
Raw materials	$216,000		
Goods in process	132,000		
Finished goods	444,000	792,000	
Prepaid expenses		60,750	
Total Current Assets			$1,265,050
Fixed Assets:			
Land		$ 38,000	
Factory building	$200,000		
Less: Allowance for depreciation	76,250	123,750	
Machinery and equipment	$900,000		
Less: Allowance for depreciation	255,000	645,000	
Delivery equipment	$ 12,000		
Less: Allowance for depreciation	4,500	7,500	
Office equipment	$ 10,000		
Less: Allowance for depreciation	4,125	5,875	
Total Fixed Assets			820,125
Total Assets			$2,085,175

Liabilities and Equity

Current Liabilities:		
Accounts payable	$ 49,880	
Accrued wages	32,250	
Accrued expenses	60,250	
Accrued taxes	21,000	
Total Current Liabilities		$ 163,380
Deferred Credit:		
Rent received in advance		5,000
Stockholders' Equity:		
Capital stock	$1,600,000	
Earned surplus	316,795	
Total Equity		1,916,796
Total Liabilities and Equity		$2,085,175

Thus, the working capital ratio at the end of March is expected to be slightly stronger than at the end of December, at 7.7 to 1 (total current assets of $1,265,050 to total current liabilities of $163,380), but the acid-test ratio is expected to be down from 5.2 to 1 to 2.5 to 1 (total cash and net receivables of $412,300 to total current liabilities of $163,380). Nevertheless, Carver's officers would not be likely to regard the indicated deterioration in the acid-test ratio a serious matter. The ratio remains well above the rule-of-thumb standard, and the decline in the three-month period is defensible as something to be expected in a period of heavy inventory stocking by a seasonal enterprise that has a policy of stabilizing production.

Current Balance Sheets

As actual operations produce changes in the financial position of a business enterprise during the course of a year or other period of time, the net effects of these changes can be seen in balance sheets prepared from time to time. Just as planned programs of operation can be approved when projected balance sheets indicate that they will result in the maintenance of a favorable financial condition, so also can such programs continue to merit approval when current balance sheets indicate that a satisfactory financial position continues to be maintained. And just as changes in plans may be decided on because projected balance sheets disclose that without the changes an unsatisfactory financial position would result, so also may plans be changed in midstream when current balance sheets indicate that operations to date have resulted in a deteriorating financial position.

Thus, current balance sheets serve as important instruments of continuing control. Their significance as control instruments may seem to be all the greater when they are to be supplied to prospective creditors or otherwise published, but a lack of pressure for disclosure would rarely be a valid excuse for reduced emphasis on them. For example, the financial managers of a corporation that publishes a balance sheet and operating statements only annually must know that developments revealed in monthly and quarterly statements, though these are prepared only for internal use, must eventually be reflected in the annual published reports.

STATEMENTS OF SOURCES AND APPLICATIONS OF FUNDS

Often useful as an additional tool of financial management are *statements of sources and applications of funds*. Such a statement is essentially an explanation of changes in financial position as revealed in successive balance sheets. It can be used for projections to show why the financial position of an enterprise at the end of given future periods is expected to be different from that at earlier dates, and it may be used currently to explain what has actually caused changes in financial position between balance sheet dates.

The format of statements of sources and applications of funds differs widely, depending on the kinds of changes in financial position that the analyst wants to emphasize. Since, however, our interest is primarily in cash control, we may confine our attention to an illustrative statement designed to account for changes in cash balances between two balance sheet dates. We return to the question raised earlier in this chapter about why changes in holdings of cash and its equivalent may differ greatly from the amounts of profits or losses reported in operating statements. In the earlier discussion, the principal reasons for differences in the projections of the Carver Manufacturing Corporation for the year 19yy were stated, but now it is desirable to account for all reasons for differences, both major and minor—in other words, to show precisely how the total difference between changes in cash balances and the amount of profits is expected to come about in the year 19yy. In Chapter 11, page 253, we have the projected balance sheet for December 31, 19xx; we now need such a statement for December 31, 19yy. Therefore, in Figure 12–6 an assumed statement for the 19yy date is presented, and for convenience in comparison the earlier statement is repeated. Our explanation, then, would take the form of a statement of sources and applications of funds as set up in Figure 12–7.

Analysis

The statement shows that the amount of cash and equivalent, in the absence of applications, would be expected to increase by the full amount of the net profit before allowance for federal income tax and by much more besides, for a total of $460,800. The increments of cash and equivalent beyond the amount of the profit would be expected to come:

1. From the cash throw-off occasioned by depreciation charges amounting to $67,500.
2. Through a conservation of cash totaling $39,400 by the acquisition of raw materials, supplies, and services on account, as indicated by the entries for accounts payable, accrued wages, and accrued expenses.
3. Because credit customers are expected to pay $15,600 in excess of the amount of sales to them in the year, as indicated by the entry for the decrease in accounts receivable.
4. Because of the anticipated prepayment by Carver's tenant of $3,333 of rent.

But cash and equivalent are not expected to increase by $460,800, or by any sum near that figure, on account of anticipated uses or applications of cash during the coming year. It is anticipated that $80,000 will be paid to the stockholders as dividends, that $86,000 will be paid to the federal Treasury on account of income taxes, and that $150,000 of cash will be used in buying additional machinery. It is anticipated, moreover, that $121,000 of cash will be devoted to expanding inventories, and that payments of $7,000 will be made in

FIGURE 12-6
Carver Manufacturing Corporation
Balance Sheet
Projected for December 31, 19xx and 19yy

	19xx		*19yy*	
Assets				
Current Assets:				
Cash		$ 415,000		$ 381,350
Short-term Treasury obligations		350,000		400,000
Accounts receivable	$ 195,000		$ 186,400	
Less: Reserve for bad debts	8,000	187,000	15,000	171,400
Accrued interest receivable		3,750		4,200
Inventories:				
Raw materials	$ 110,000		$ 145,000	
Goods in process	92,000		109,000	
Finished goods	158,000	360,000	227,000	481,000
Prepaid expenses		56,000		63,000
Total Current Assets		$1,371,750		$1,500,950
Fixed Assets:				
Land		38,000		38,000
Factory building	$ 200,000		$ 200,000	
Less: Allowance for depreciation	75,000	125,000	80,000	120,000
Machinery and equipment	$ 900,000		$1,050,000	
Less: Allowance for depreciation	240,000	660,000	300,000	750,000
Delivery equipment	$ 12,000		$ 12,000	
Less: Allowance for depreciation	4,000	8,000	6,000	6,000
Office equipment	$ 10,000		$ 10,000	
Less: Allowance for depreciation	4,000	6,000	4,500	5,500
Total Fixed Assets		$ 837,000		$ 919,500
Total Assets		$2,208,750		$2,420,450
Liabilities and Equity				
Current Liabilities:				
Accounts payable	$ 65,500		$ 78,400	
Accrued wages	30,000		36,000	
Accrued expenses	46,000		66,500	
Accrued taxes	42,000		99,784	
Total Current Liabilities		$ 183,500		$ 280,684
Deferred Credit:				
Rent received in advance				3,333
Stockholders' Equity:				
Capital stock	$1,600,000		$1,600,000	
Earned surplus	425,250		536,433	
Total Equity		2,025,250		2,136,433
Total Liabilities and Equity		$2,208,750		$2,420,450

FIGURE 12–7
Carver Manufacturing Corporation
Statement of Sources and Applications of Funds
Projected for the Year 19yy

Cash and equivalent, January 1, 19yy	$765,000
(Cash, $415,000, short-term Treasury obligations, $350,000)	
Add sources of cash:	
Net profit before deduction of federal income tax	$334,967
Cash throw-off from depreciation	67,500
Increase in accounts payable	12,900
Increase in accrued wages	6,000
Increase in accrued expenses	20,500
Decrease in accounts receivable	15,600
Rent received in advance	3,333
	$460,800
Deduct applications of cash:	
Payment of dividends to stockholders	$ 80,000
Payment of federal income taxes	86,000
Purchase of machinery	150,000
Increase in inventories	121,000
Increase in prepaid expenses	7,000
Increase in accrued interest receivable	450
	$444,450
Net increase in cash and equivalent	$ 16,350
Cash and equivalent, December 31, 19yy	$781,350
(Cash, $381,350, short-term Treasury obligations, $400,000)	

the year 19yy for expense items chargeable to later years and, therefore, not to be deducted in computing the profit for 19yy. And, finally, it is anticipated that interest income in the amount of $450, though to be included in profit in the year 19yy, will not have been realized in cash by the end of that year.

Thus, projected applications come to a total of $444,450, and the deduction of this amount from the expected total of the sources leaves a net projected increase in cash and equivalent of only $16,350.

Suggested Uses

Although the preparation of statements of sources and applications of funds appears to be fully justified by their function as a managerial tool, some corporation executives, writers on finance, and accountants recommend putting them to other uses. It is their contention that stockholders, employees and their unions, solicitors of funds for charitable purposes, and others often misjudge corporations' capacities to pay dividends and wages, to give donations, and to make other kinds of cash outlays, because they look only at reported figures of corporate profits. Since, therefore, statements of sources and applications of funds—of the form used in our illustration—clearly show that profits and cash availability are not necessarily closely related, the recommendation is that such statements be included as a matter of course with annual reports to stockholders, among the documents to be considered in wage-bargaining negotiations, and wherever else publicity is given to the size of profits. That this recommendation is being well received by corporate managements is indicated by the ever-increasing number of corporations that include such statements in their published annual reports.

QUESTIONS

1. If a firm's sales were to fall off sharply as a result of a general business recession, what effect would this development have on the usefulness of its cash budget? Explain.

2. What kind of information is presented in daily and monthly cash reports? How do these reports tie in with budgetary cash control?

3. To what extent, if at all, are projected income statements and balance sheets sources of details to be incorporated in cash budgets?

4. Give several examples of probable future developments that are likely to be revealed by projected income statements and balance sheets rather than by cash budgets.

5. What is a working capital ratio? A quick ratio? What are such ratios supposed to reveal about a firm's financial position? Of what significance are they in forecasting?

6. As rules of thumb, what working capital and quick ratios are generally recognized as indicative of satisfactory financial position? Are these rules of thumb logical? Why or why not?

7. What is a statement of sources and applications of funds? As shown in such a statement, what are the typical corporation's principal sources of funds? Its principal applications?

8. How is the use of statements of sources and applications of funds related to cash budgeting?

PROBLEM

Using the solution to the problem presented at the end of Chapter 11, prepare an income statement for the Talcott Corporation for the year 19yy and a statement of sources and applications of funds (of the form of Figure 12–7 in this chapter) to account for the net increase or decrease in its cash balance as a result of the year's transactions. For the funds statement, assume that cash and equivalent amounted to $353,000 at the beginning of the year 19yy.

chapter 13

CAPITAL BUDGETING

Capital budgeting is primarily the planning and control of expenditures for tangible fixed assets, such as:

1. Replacement of machinery and equipment nearing the ends of their useful lives.
2. Acquisition of new facilities that have higher productive or labor-saving capacities than do existing facilities, and removal of the old facilities even though they are fully capable of performing as originally designed.
3. Acquisition of new buildings, and the enlargement and improvement of existing buildings.
4. Acquisition of additional machines and other facilities of the kinds already owned in anticipation of increased sales of present product lines.
5. Acquisition of new kinds of facilities needed for new product lines to be taken on.

Some corporate managements also include in their capital budgets planned expenditures for advertising campaigns and R.&D. (research and development), especially when these expenditures are expected to be of extraordinary size and duration, and even though relatively small proportions will go for tangible fixed assets. Some include planned expenditures to gain controlling interests in other corporations, so that in many instances they will, indeed, gain access to additional tangible assets, and sometimes to huge arrays. For many kinds of capital budgeting decisions, moreover, it is essential that the corporate planners give careful consideration to the expanded investment in current assets that will have to be made, in addition to the investment in fixed assets, in relation to expanded sales of existing products, the taking on of new product lines, and so on.

GENERAL ASPECTS OF CAPITAL BUDGETING

Scope of Capital Budgets

From the standpoint of the periods that plans are made for, capital budgets are of two kinds—annual and long term. Annual capital budgets are comparable to budgets for raw materials, direct labor, and the various classes of overhead expenses in that they set out for the coming year the anticipated costs to be incurred from month to month in the purchase of fixed assets. Like budgets of the kinds mentioned, therefore, they serve as a source from which details about expected monthly cash expenditures are drawn for inclusion in cash budgets. The use of annual capital budgets tends to be confined to relatively large enterprises that have great aggregations of fixed assets of many kinds, among which replacements must constantly be made, and to which additions are constantly required. Smaller concerns, as well as larger ones with limited amounts and varieties of fixed assets, can usually get along without annual capital budgets. Their long-term budgets provide details of projected fixed asset expenditures of the approaching year sufficient for the requirements of their cash budgets.

A long-term capital budget is a projection of expected expenditures for fixed assets for a period of years. Very often, the period covered is describable as "intermediate" more properly than as "long," since it may be as short as 3 years and only occasionally does it exceed 10 years. It is probable that five years is the most common planning period. Long-term capital budgets are useful for enterprises of all sizes, small and large, and they are of special importance to financial managers, because long-range financing plans must be closely related to them. Since it may be assumed that, typically, the details of annual capital budgets, where used, are picked up from the long-term ones, we may well confine our attention in the following paragraphs to the long term.

Basis of Long-Term Capital Budgets

As in preparing the many kinds of annual budgets, setting up a long-term capital budget begins with a forecast of sales. The longer the period of years for which sales forecasts can reasonably be made, the longer is the period that can be covered by a capital budget. A firm that has experienced an expansion in its sales volume at a steady rate over a period of many years, even though interrupted at times by recessions in general business activity, has a basis for a rather confident prediction of the pace at which it will have to expand output and the pace at which, therefore, it will have to augment its productive facilities in the next few years. This has generally been the situation for many firms engaged in the basic steel and aluminum industries; those that provide certain kinds of public utility services, such as water, electricity, and air transportation; and many that produce certain kinds of consumer goods, such as automobiles and some varieties of foodstuffs. On the contrary, the sales outlook for firms in some industries is often so cloudy that little can be done in the way of planning long-range expenditures for fixed assets. This appears to be especially true of most branches of the textile industry at the present time.

In the preparation of annual operating budgets, as we saw in Chapter 12, the sales forecast is followed up by the preparation of detailed budgets of the expected costs of production, selling, and administration. Something of the same kind must be done for the projection of fixed asset acquisitions. Although forecasts of operating costs for several years can hardly be expected to be as accurate as short-run projections, or even as accurate as the longer-run projections of sales, reliable estimations of future operating costs must be made available, for otherwise the merits of proposals for acquisitions of fixed assets could hardly be soundly evaluated. It is said, indeed, that *every* proposed addition to fixed assets that will require the expenditure of more than a modest sum of money must be shown to be necessary to maintain or expand a firm's profitability. Such a demonstration cannot be made solely in terms of projected sales. Without related cost estimates, sales projections must obviously be of little value. Attention must surely be given to the fixed costs that the very acquisitions and uses of new fixed assets will entail—that is, depreciation, maintenance and repairs, property taxes, and insurance. But deserving equal attention are the economies that the new facilities are expected to make possible, such as reduced need of labor and reduced spoilage of materials.

Contents of Long-Term Capital Budgets

For a large number of firms, plans for expenditures found in long-term capital budgets are quite closely, if not exclusively, confined to replacements of existing fixed assets. If a firm's sales volume has not been expanding, and is not expected to expand, it probably is not planning to buy additional facilities. The principal problem of capital budgeting for such firms is, therefore, one of estimating the useful lives of present facilities—a problem quite closely related, obviously, to the depreciation question. Regardless of depreciation policy, however, the possibility of extraordinary obsolescence often deserves special emphasis. In other words, due weight must be given to the possibility that the useful lives of fixed assets will be substantially shorter than the Internal Revenue Service allows for in its regulations on allowable depreciation. And always, of course, there is the additional problem of the wisdom of replacing facilities at all—the problem of purchase versus rental, which was considered in Chapter 10.

The long-term capital budgets of business enterprises that anticipate continued growth in sales must include estimated expenditures both for replacement and for the addition of facilities. As mentioned, their problems of forecasting expenditures for replacement are necessarily much the same as those for firms that do not expect to expand. As for additions to facilities, the content of budgets depends on the expected direction and rate of growth. Firms that expect simply to expand the output of their existing lines need ordinarily plan only for buying facilities of the kinds they already have. Their officers should already be thoroughly familiar with the capacities of such facilities, their costs, both present and prospective, and the competence and dependability of the various suppliers. However, firms that expect their growth to come chiefly from new product lines are likely to have their estimates of expenditures clouded somewhat by uncertainties about what kinds of new facilities should be selected, what combinations would be most efficient, and what would be the best timing for the acquisitions.

Because completion of expansion programs often requires lengthy periods, long-term capital budgets must be as accurate as possible in indicating the pace at which, month by month, payments must be made from start to completion. A capital budget would be of little value if a figure such as $5 million were entered for a given year as the estimated total cost of a building program to be started in that year, and if expectations were that completion of the program would require two or three years. Nor would the spreading of the proposed expenditure evenly on a monthly basis over the whole construction period be of much help, since payments for construction are generally contracted for, not according to any plan of even spacing, but according to the various stages of completion.

Long-term capital budgets must also include estimates of cash proceeds or trade-in values of facilities to be disposed of during the forecast period. The sale of unused present facilities in the secondhand market, or their sale as scrap, may be expected to produce a cash inflow during the forecast period that will offset in part contemplated expenditures for new facilities—perhaps only in a moderate way, but still significantly. And, of course, allowances for trade-ins in connection with the purchase of new facilities also reduce the net outlays that will be required.

Finally, long-term capital budgets (and annual ones, as well) do not include estimated expenditures for the maintenance and repair of fixed assets, and for small tools and other kinds of short-lived equipment. Although difficulties in distinguishing between repairs and maintenance, on the one hand, and betterments or improvements, on the other, are numerous (as was pointed out in Chapter 10), it is always advisable that the distinction be drawn as closely as possible, so that expenditures that can reasonably be classed as betterments can be included in the capital budget, while those for repairs and maintenance can be relegated to the ordinary annual expense budgets. In the matter of short-lived equipment such as small tools, the fixed asset designation may be given to the inventory of the quantity on hand as carried in the balance sheet, but the usual practice is to treat, much the same as any other operating expense, the cost of such equipment used up in a year or other short period. Hence, the estimated costs of replenishing short-lived equipment are customarily carried in the regular expense budgets.

Significance of Long-Term Capital Budgets

Financial managers realize that without long-range capital budgets financial planning can fall into serious error. If proposals for fixed asset expenditure are taken up one by one, and only for the year ahead, with approvals and rejections determined on the merits of each proposal standing by itself, financing capacity may be exhausted before the most important proposals—to be reached only in later years—come up for consideration. On the other hand, all the preliminary studies and analyses that are necessary for deciding what is to go into a long-term capital budget almost guarantee that each spending proposal will be evaluated, not simply on its own merits, but in relation to the merits of all others. In the purchase of fixed assets, as in so many other phases of its activities, a business enterprise does not have sufficient access to cash to do all the things that it would like to do, and even though every proposal may promise significant benefits the enterprise must often limit its choices—presumably to the proposals that promise the greatest benefits.

Long-term budgeting of fixed asset acquisitions makes possible proper timing of whatever preliminary steps must be taken to get projects under way, as well as timing of actual commencement of the projects. A new factory building requires a desirable site, architectural plans, and the working out of arrangements with building contractors. The design and manufacture of new machines often, too, require much time, so that it is highly advantageous to be able to order them well before the day when they will be needed. Delays in taking actions of these kinds can result in substantial increases in financial burdens, including higher costs for the facilities themselves, higher interest rates on money borrowed, and the loss of potential sales because of temporary inadequacies in productive capacity due to delayed construction or delivery of new facilities.

Long-term capital budgeting can also eliminate repeated heavy costs of arranging and rearranging factory, store, and office layouts.

Year to year plans confined to machinery acquisitions of the following year, for example, can result in poor placement of the successive acquisitions. Each year's additions might not seem to justify a rearrangement of factory layout, but fitting them into the existing layout could mean a considerable loss of efficiency, and a continued process of fitting in might result in general disorganization after a few years. On the other hand, should the layout be adjusted in the first year to gain the most efficient use of that year's acquisitions, costly additional adjustments might have to be made in each of the following years in aiming at the goal of maximum efficiency. But if all the acquisitions to take place over a period of, say, five years were planned for originally in a long-term budget, a single rearrangement of layout could probably also be planned at once, allowing space for the successive additions. The financial managers might decide, indeed, that it would be cheaper to immediately acquire many of the facilities expected to be needed over a five-year period than to obtain them annually, portion by portion—cheaper in precluding repeated serious disruptions in production for installation.

Finally deserving mention among the advantages of long-term capital budgeting is the possibility of concentrating expenditures in periods when the prices of such assets are relatively low. The heavy demand for productive facilities in periods of high prosperity tends to drive up their prices and to result in delays in deliveries. Hence, it would appear to be wise for the individual firm to try to concentrate its spending for fixed assets to periods of general business contraction when prices tend to fall and building contractors, machinery manufacturers, and others have idle capacity. It requires courage to go ahead with expansion projects at times when the firm itself has idle capacity, but if its managers have confidence in their own long-range sales forecast—and therefore in their long-range projections of fixed asset needs—they have good reason to accelerate spending for such assets. Not least among the merits of such a procedure is the contribution that it is likely to make to social welfare. By reducing demand for productive facilities in times of prosperity and increasing it in times of business slump, the individual firm makes a contribution toward stability in the whole economy.

THE PROBLEM OF CHOICE

One of the most important problems faced by many corporate managements in capital budgeting is that of judging among several proposed or prospective expansion projects in order to choose those likely to be most profitable. In many instances, a need to choose arises because several proposals must be considered simultaneously. In others, it is a matter of choosing today whether to go ahead with a single project when there are anticipations that other expansion opportunities—perhaps with much better profit possibilities—will turn up in the near future. For example, the managers of a manufacturing corporation may be convinced that it could expand sales and profits by taking on any one or any combination of several new product lines, but they know that sufficient cash cannot be made available to simultaneously finance all the ventures that appear to be promising. For the manufacture of each new product, cash would be needed for new machinery and, perhaps, for additional factory space for its installation, and still more would be required for investment in expanded inventories and accounts receivable. Yet, beyond a certain limit cash would be unobtainable.

In trying to make the best possible choice or choices, the managers would surely make forecasts of:

1. The anticipated annual volume of sales of each proposed new product.
2. How long the product would remain popular and the sales would continue.
3. What the additional costs of manufacturing and selling would be in raw materials, labor, factory overhead, and selling and administrative expenses.
4. What would be the resulting annual additions to profits before and after income taxes.

Among the overhead expenses, they would surely include depreciation on the machinery and other fixed facilities to be acquired. This would require an investigation into the prospective costs of the facilities and their installation, and estimates of the useful lives of these facilities (presumably limited to the number of years anticipated for product sales) and their ultimate salvage, scrap, or trade-in values, if any. The managers would also want to know the total amount of cash to be available, where they would get it, how much it would cost them, and when, if at all, it would have to be repaid.

To illustrate all this, let us assume that the managers of the Speedwell Corporation are considering the addition of four different items to its array of products, and that they have assembled price quotations and forecast data about the prospective costs and earnings related to each of these as set out in Table 13–1. The first two lines of the table indicate that varying amounts of investment in machinery and other fixed facilities will be required for the manufacture of the four products—projects A, B, C, and D, respectively—and these fixed facilities are expected to have varying useful lives. No figures are entered for salvage, scrap, or trade-in values, since it is anticipated that none of the facilities will have such values at the expiration of their useful lives. The balance of the table indicates the annual dollar profit prospects for each of the products, with forecast figures for sales and ad-

TABLE 13–1
Proposed Investment Projects of Speedwell Corporation

	Proposed Projects			
	A	*B*	*C*	*D*
Cost of fixed facilities	$100,000	$200,000	$300,000	$500,000
Useful life	5 years	5 years	10 years	20 years
Increased annual sales	$ 48,000	$100,000	$120,000	$190,000
Increased expenses:				
Materials, labor, etc.	18,000	30,000	36,000	73,000
Depreciation	20,000	40,000	30,000	25,000
Total	$ 38,000	$ 70,000	$ 66,000	$ 98,000
Increased before-tax profit	$ 10,000	$ 30,000	$ 54,000	$ 92,000
Less: Income taxes at 50%	5,000	15,000	27,000	46,000
Increased after-tax profit	$ 5,000	$ 15,000	$ 27,000	$ 46,000
Add cash throw-off from depreciation	20,000	40,000	30,000	25,000
Increased Net Cash Inflow	$ 25,000	$ 55,000	$ 57,000	$ 71,000

ditional operating costs to be incurred by each in producing, selling, and administration.[1]

In addition to out-of-pocket operating costs, allowance is made for the cost of using up the fixed facilities, and it is assumed that the depreciation charges for this will be spread evenly over the periods of useful lives—that is, on a straight-line basis. It is also assumed that the net profit to be expected annually from the sale of each new product will be reduced by federal and state income taxes totaling 50 percent. Finally, an assumption that does not appear in the table is that the total amount of money that can be made available for investment in new machinery and other fixed assets is limited to $500,000, although additional cash will also be available for whatever increases in current assets will be needed in relation to expanded volumes of operations.

The data in Table 13–1 reveal that, in the judgment of the managers of the Speedwell Corporation, each of the proposed new-product projects would be profitable, and they might be inclined to adopt all four. But they are constrained by the limited availability of cash. They could choose project D solely, and it would appear to be the best choice, since it promises additional profits after taxes of $46,000 each year for 20 years—more than the anticipated combined profits on any two of the other three projects. But 20 years is a long forecast

[1]It is assumed that the data for operating costs do not include charges for interest that may be incurred on money borrowed to finance the projects, and that the figures for income taxes ignore the effects of interest charges as a deductible expense. The role of interest and its income tax effects is examined later in this chapter and in Chapter 14. See pp. 312–14, 325–27.

period, and the managers would doubtless have less confidence in their sales and cost forecasts for project D than in the forecasts for the shorter periods of A, B, and C. Perhaps, therefore, the combination of B and C should be adopted. Or perhaps the decision should go to only one of these, or to one of these in combination with A, with some investment capacity retained in the expectation that different, more attractive expansion opportunities will turn up in the near future.

Several analytical procedures are available to business managers who have such problems of choice. None of these procedures gives final answers in the sense that choice is inevitably directed to given expansion projects, but they are expected to be quite useful in making choices. Indeed, they can often be helpful toward decision making when only single projects are being considered at a given time—especially when, as indicated earlier, the merits of the single project must be weighed against possibilities that better expansion opportunities will shortly develop. Let us consider the four most popular kinds of procedures.

Payback Periods

Technique. The simplest of the analytical procedures is the computation of payback periods—the number of years required for the recovery of money to be invested in new projects. The recovery each year will be equal to the added after-tax net profit of the year derived from a project, plus the cash throw-off from the depreciation charge on the facilities acquired for the project (provided, as always, that this charge in addition to all other increased operating costs is covered by sales proceeds). When the added after-tax net profit is expected to be uniform from year to year, depreciation is to be charged on a straight-line basis, and no salvage value is assigned to the facilities acquired, the formula for the payback period is this.

$$\text{Payback period} = \frac{\text{Original investment}}{\text{Annual cash throw-offs from profit and depreciation}}.$$

For the Speedwell Corporation, the payback period for project A would thus be $100,000/$25,000 or four years, and for each of the other three projects it would be determined as follows.

Project B: $200,000/$55,000 = 3.6 years.
Project C: $300,000/$57,000 = 5.3 years.
Project D: $500,000/$71,000 = 7.0 years.

Businessmen's Attitudes. Many business managers confess that they are always anxious to get their money out of new investment projects as quickly as possible, and their attitude is, accordingly, the shorter the payback period the better. Surveys among businessmen almost invariably reveal that for judgments about the desirability of individual projects and for choices among projects the shortness of the payback period is a much more popular criterion than the other analytical criteria to be discussed in the remainder of this chapter. Some of these surveys disclose, indeed, that a surprising number of businesses set arbitrary payback period cutoffs, such as three, four, or five years, beyond which they will not go in making investments in new facilities. Were the managers of the Speedwell Corporation to have a cutoff at four years, for example, they would give no further attention to projects C and D after determining their payback periods at 5.3 years and 7 years, respectively.

Merits. Nevertheless, the merits of the payback period device are slight. It can be useful, and even controlling, if money for projects must be borrowed and if lenders are unwilling to lend for lengthy periods. In such circumstances, projects that promise quick paybacks may have to be selected in preference to longer-term projects that, as indicated by other more realistic tests, have much greater promise. Emphasis on quick paybacks may also have some justification when the interest rates that would have to be paid on borrowings are extraordinarily high and when rates are expected to fall in the near future. Moreover, we must concede that because short-term forecasting is likely to be much more accurate than longer-term forecasting there is some justification for businessmen's enhanced feelings of safety when they can anticipate quick paybacks.

Shortcomings. A major drawback of the payback period method of assigning priorities to investment projects is its utter lack of realism in favoring short-term investments. If it alone were used in this capacity, very few long-term projects would ever be chosen, even though the history of numerous enterprises has clearly proved that long-term projects are often much more profitable than short-term ones, and that, indeed, quite a few of the most profitable kinds of projects require several years to get off the ground toward high levels of return. In the case of the Speedwell Corporation, project B and then project A would be adopted, and projects C and D would be voted down for lack of money, but our further analysis of Speedwell's affairs will indicate that this would be a poor decision for its managers to make.

Another shortcoming of the payback device is that it places no emphasis on profitability and is especially weak in giving no weight at all to profits to be earned after the payback period. Yet, the Speedwell decision just referred to would mean a choosing of $20,000 of profits a year for 5 years in preference to $27,000 for 10 years, or $46,000 for 20 years, or possibly $42,000 for 5 years and $27,000 for an additional 5 years (the combination of projects B and C).

A further weakness of the payback period criterion is that it fails to give weight to the timing of net cash inflows from profits and depreciation throw-offs. It ignores the *time value of money*—that is, the inequality in the value of identical sums of money payable or receivable at different times, an inequality that always exists because of the interest that can be earned or that must be paid. Anybody would surely prefer to receive $25,000 at the end of each year for 4 years than to receive $15,000 at the end of the first year, $20,000 at the end of the second, $30,000 at the end of the third, and $35,000 at the end of the fourth. In many instances, nevertheless, the payback period method would rate the $15,000–$35,000 sequence of cash inflows as being as good as the annual $25,000 sequence. In either case, the total 4-year inflow would be $100,000, and as applied to Speedwell's project A each sequence would give a payback period of 4 years.

Accounting Rate of Profit

Because the overriding goal of investment in new fixed assets is to augment profits (or at least to maintain an existing level of profits), analytical procedures that measure the expected profitability of proposed projects must surely be superior to the payback period procedure of ranking their desirability. However, determining the *amount* of profits expected to be derived from year to year on different projects is not likely to be very meaningful, since the respective projects will require differing amounts of investment in fixed assets and additional current assets, the fixed assets will have differing lives, and the sales results as well as the effects on operating costs will also differ. Accordingly, it is to the anticipated *rate* of profit that principal attention must be directed. The anticipated rate of profit is all the more important because it can be highly advantageous to have a magnitude that can be directly compared with the percentage cost of the money to be invested in the additional facilities—that is, the cost of capital to be discussed in Chapter 14.

Technique. There are several procedures for determining anticipated rates of profit on investment in additional facilities; the simplest is generally called the accounting method, since it is based on the kinds of figures reported in the principal accounting statements—the balance sheet and the income statement. There are, in turn, several ways of computing the accounting rate of profit, but only two of these are widely employed: determination on the basis of *original* investment in relation to anticipated annual net profit after deductions for depreciation and taxes, and determination on the basis of *average* investment in relation to anticipated annual net profit after these deductions.

To find the accounting rate of profit on the basis of original investment, one simply divides the expected average annual amount of profit after depreciation and taxes by the cost of the new facilities, so that the formula is:

$$\text{Rate of profit} = \frac{\text{Average annual net profit}}{\text{Original investment}} .$$

For determining the accounting rate of return on the basis of average investment, the investment in new facilities originally and as reduced from year to year on account of depreciation is averaged, and this average is divided into the expected average annual amount of profit after depreciation and taxes. When depreciation is to be taken on a straight-line basis and no salvage value is assumed, as in our Speedwell Corporation illustrations, the average investment is always equal to one half of the original investment, and the resulting rate of profit is always twice the rate determined on the basis of original investment. The formula is:[2]

$$\text{Rate of profit} = \frac{\text{Average annual net profit}}{\text{Original investment} \div 2} .$$

In both these procedures, of course, deduction of the depreciation charge in determining net profit automatically takes care of the pay-back or recovery of the amount originally invested. For the four projects of the Speedwell Corporation, computation of the rates of profit by the two varieties of the accounting method would be as follows.

---

[2]For Speedwell's project A, the original investment is \$100,000; the investment at the beginning of the second year, as reduced by the depreciation charge of \$20,000, is \$80,000; at the beginning of the third year, \$60,000; at the beginning of the fourth year, \$40,000; at the beginning of the fifth year, \$20,000; and at the end of the fifth year, 0. The sum of the 6 investment figures from \$100,000 to 0 is \$300,000, and division by 6 gives us an average investment of \$50,000—a result more quickly reached by simply dividing the original investment of \$100,000 by 2. The simpler procedure applies the mathematical formula for the average of an arithmetic progression (a series of figures in which there is a difference of equal amount between each figure and the figure that precedes or follows it):

$$\text{Average} = \frac{a + l}{2} ,$$

where a is the first figure of the progression and l is the last. For project A, the substitution is simply

$$\frac{\$100{,}000 + 0}{2}$$

or \$50,000. Were Speedwell to anticipate a salvage value of \$5,000 for the fixed facilities of project A, the annual straight-line depreciation charge would be \$19,000, and the successive investment values would be \$100,000, \$81,000, \$62,000, \$43,000, \$24,000, and \$5,000. The average of these would be \$52,500, equal to the result obtainable by the use of the equation:

$$\frac{\$100{,}000 + \$5{,}000}{2} .$$

	Accounting Rate of Profit	
	On Original Investment	*On Average Investment*
Project A	$\frac{\$5,000}{\$100,000} = 5\%$	$\frac{\$5,000}{\$50,000} = 10\%$
Project B	$\frac{\$15,000}{\$200,000} = 7.5\%$	$\frac{\$15,000}{\$100,000} = 15\%$
Project C	$\frac{\$27,000}{\$300,000} = 9\%$	$\frac{\$27,000}{\$150,000} = 18\%$
Project D	$\frac{\$46,000}{\$500,000} = 9.2\%$	$\frac{\$46,000}{\$250,000} = 18.4\%$

Evaluation. Unlike the payback period method, each of the two variants of the accounting method makes possible direct comparisons among proposed projects of varying lives without a built-in prejudice in favor of short-term ventures. For Speedwell, indeed, it is clearly demonstrated that the 10-year and 20-year projects (C and D) are substantially more desirable than the two 5-year projects (A and B).

Nevertheless, the accounting procedures have weaknesses of their own. The most serious weakness is that the time value of money is ignored. The profit of $5,000 and the cash throw-off from depreciation of $20,000 expected to be derived in the fifth year on project A are given equal weight with the profit and the depreciation throw-off of the same amounts anticipated for the first year, but this is most illogical. As long as money can be invested with perfect safety at given rates of interest, as in Treasury securities, an amount of money on hand is always worth more than an equal amount to be received in the future, and a sum of money to be received in one year is worth more than an equal amount to be received in five years. Obviously, therefore, this weakness of the accounting procedures becomes all the greater when on given projects profits are expected to be rather small in the first few years and much larger in the later years, since the *average* amounts may indicate quite attractive profit rates.

In fact, serious errors can occur if corporate managers accept projects whose accounting rates are equal to or above some arbitrarily selected cut-off rate, and they reject projects whose accounting rates fall short of the cut-off rate. Should Speedwell's managers, for example, set a cut-off rate of 10 percent on original investment, thinking of this as an *accurate* rate to base judgments on, they would reject all four projects. Yet, more sophisticated methods of rate of profit analysis that allow for the time value of money (to be described shortly) would indicate that only project A should be rejected if Speedwell's managers would be satisfied with an accurate rate of profit of at least 10 percent.

Between the two variants of the accounting method, that based on average investment is generally regarded as more logical than the variant based on original investment. Investments in depreciable fixed assets are unquestionably reduced over time by wear and tear and the action of the elements, so that realism would seem to require a recognition of the continuing decrease in the valuation on which a rate of profit should be expected. A minor criticism of the original value procedure is that it ignores the salvage value of the fixed assets should there be such a value.

Discounted Cash Flow

Theory. From the standpoint of both mathematical theory and realism in business management, the discounted cash flow method (or time-adjusted method) is generally regarded as the best means of determining rates of profit to be earned on investments in new facilities, and therefore the best means of ranking projects in the order of desirability. It is based on the proposition that the dollar amount of any investment being made is the *discounted* value of all future net cash inflows to be derived from the investment, and that the rate of profit is precisely the *discount rate* that must be applied to the inflows in order to equate them to the dollar amount of the investment.

If $1 invested today will yield a single cash inflow of $1.06 at the end of 1 year, the rate of profit is obviously 6 percent. But 6 percent is also the discount rate and that will equate $1.06 due in 1 year to the $1 present value of the investment. The formula for determining present values as discounted future amounts is:

$$P = A \frac{1}{(1+i)^n},$$

where P is the present value, A is the future cash inflow, i is the rate of discount, and n is the number of periods for which discount is to be taken. Substituting, we get

$$P = \$1.06 \frac{1}{1.06}$$

or $1. In a similar way, $1 invested today at a profit rate of 6 percent compounded annually[3] for a 2-year period will yield $1.1236; and $1.1236 due at the end of 2 years is worth $1 today if it is discounted at 6 percent compounded annually:

$$\$1.00 = \$1.1236 \frac{1}{(1.06)^2}.$$

[3]The compounding of interest means, of course, that interest earned in the first period is added on to the original principal at the end of that period and itself earns interest in subsequent periods, that interest earned in the second period is likewise added on and earns interest in the third and subsequent periods, and so on. If interest is compounded annually, the interest is added on at the end of each year; if semiannually, at the end of each period of six months, and so on.

TABLE 13–2
Present Value of $1 Discounted at Rate *i* for *n* Periods

n/*i*	1%	2%	3%	4%	5%	6%	7%	8%	9%	10%	11%	12%	13%	14%
1	.9901	.9804	.9701	.9615	.9524	.9434	.9346	.9259	.9174	.9091	.9009	.8929	.8850	.8772
2	.9803	.9612	.9426	.9246	.9070	.8900	.8734	.8573	.8417	.8265	.8116	.7972	.7832	.7695
3	.9706	.9423	.9151	.8890	.8638	.8396	.8163	.7938	.7722	.7513	.7312	.7118	.6931	.6750
4	.9610	.9239	.8885	.8548	.8227	.7921	.7629	.7350	.7084	.6830	.6587	.6355	.6133	.5921
5	.9515	.9057	.8626	.8219	.7835	.7473	.7130	.6806	.6499	.6209	.5935	.5674	.5428	.5194
6	.9420	.8880	.8375	.7903	.7462	.7050	.6663	.6302	.5963	.5645	.5346	.5066	.4803	.4556
7	.9327	.8706	.8131	.7599	.7107	.6651	.6228	.5835	.5470	.5132	.4817	.4524	.4251	.3996
8	.9235	.8535	.7894	.7307	.6768	.6274	.5820	.5403	.5019	.4665	.4339	.4039	.3762	.3506
9	.9143	.8368	.7664	.7026	.6446	.5919	.5439	.5003	.4604	.4241	.3909	.3606	.3329	.3075
10	.9053	.8204	.7441	.6756	.6139	.5584	.5084	.4632	.4224	.3855	.3522	.3220	.2946	.2697
11	.8963	.8043	.7224	.6496	.5847	.5268	.4751	.4289	.3875	.3505	.3173	.2875	.2607	.2366
12	.8875	.7885	.7014	.6246	.5568	.4970	.4440	.3971	.3555	.3186	.2858	.2567	.2307	.2076
13	.8787	.7730	.6810	.6006	.5303	.4688	.4150	.3677	.3262	.2897	.2575	.2292	.2042	.1821
14	.8700	.7579	.6611	.5775	.5051	.4423	.3878	.3405	.2993	.2633	.2320	.2046	.1807	.1597
15	.8614	.7430	.6419	.5553	.4810	.4173	.3625	.3152	.2745	.2394	.2090	.1827	.1599	.1401
16	.8528	.7285	.6232	.5339	.4581	.3937	.3387	.2919	.2519	.2176	.1883	.1631	.1415	.1229
17	.8444	.7142	.6050	.5134	.4363	.3714	.3166	.2703	.2311	.1978	.1696	.1456	.1252	.1078
18	.8360	.7002	.5874	.4936	.4155	.3503	.2959	.2503	.2120	.1799	.1528	.1300	.1108	.0946
19	.8277	.6864	.5703	.4746	.3957	.3305	.2765	.2317	.1945	.1635	.1377	.1161	.0981	.0830
20	.8195	.6730	.5537	.4564	.3769	.3118	.2584	.2146	.1784	.1486	.1240	.1037	.0868	.0728
21	.8114	.6598	.5376	.4388	.3589	.2942	.2415	.1987	.1637	.1351	.1117	.0926	.0768	.0638
22	.8034	.6468	.5219	.4220	.3419	.2775	.2257	.1839	.1502	.1229	.1007	.0826	.0680	.0560
23	.7954	.6342	.5067	.4057	.3256	.2618	.2110	.1703	.1378	.1117	.0907	.0738	.0601	.0491
24	.7876	.6217	.4919	.3901	.3101	.2470	.1972	.1577	.1264	.1015	.0817	.0659	.0532	.0431
25	.7798	.6095	.4776	.3751	.2953	.2330	.1843	.1460	.1160	.0923	.0736	.0588	.0471	.0378

TABLE 13–2 (Continued)
Present Value of $1 Discounted at Rate *i* for *n* Periods

n/i	15%	16%	17%	18%	19%	20%	21%	22%	23%	24%	25%	30%	35%	40%
1	.8696	.8621	.8547	.8475	.8403	.8333	.8265	.8197	.8130	.8065	.8000	.7692	.7407	.7143
2	.7561	.7432	.7305	.7182	.7062	.6944	.6830	.6719	.6610	.6504	.6400	.5917	.5487	.5102
3	.6575	.6407	.6244	.6086	.5934	.5787	.5645	.5507	.5374	.5245	.5120	.4552	.4064	.3644
4	.5718	.5523	.5337	.5158	.4987	.4823	.4665	.4514	.4369	.4230	.4096	.3501	.3011	.2603
5	.4972	.4761	.4561	.4371	.4191	.4019	.3855	.3700	.3552	.3411	.3277	.2693	.2230	.1859
6	.4323	.4104	.3898	.3704	.3521	.3349	.3186	.3033	.2888	.2751	.2621	.2072	.1652	.1328
7	.3759	.3538	.3332	.3139	.2959	.2791	.2633	.2486	.2348	.2218	.2097	.1594	.1224	.0949
8	.3269	.3050	.2848	.2660	.2487	.2326	.2176	.2038	.1909	.1789	.1678	.1226	.0906	.0678
9	.2843	.2630	.2434	.2255	.2090	.1938	.1799	.1670	.1552	.1443	.1342	.0943	.0671	.0484
10	.2472	.2267	.2080	.1911	.1756	.1615	.1486	.1369	.1262	.1164	.1074	.0725	.0497	.0346
11	.2149	.1954	.1778	.1619	.1476	.1346	.1229	.1122	.1026	.0938	.0859	.0558	.0368	.0247
12	.1869	.1685	.1520	.1372	.1240	.1122	.1015	.0920	.0834	.0757	.0687	.0429	.0273	.0176
13	.1625	.1452	.1299	.1163	.1042	.0935	.0839	.0754	.0678	.0610	.0550	.0330	.0202	.0126
14	.1413	.1252	.1110	.0986	.0878	.0779	.0693	.0618	.0551	.0492	.0440	.0254	.0150	.0090
15	.1229	.1079	.0949	.0835	.0736	.0649	.0573	.0507	.0448	.0397	.0352	.0195	.0111	.0064
16	.1069	.0930	.0811	.0708	.0618	.0541	.0474	.0415	.0364	.0320	.0282	.0150	.0082	.0046
17	.0929	.0802	.0693	.0600	.0520	.0451	.0391	.0340	.0296	.0258	.0225	.0116	.0061	.0033
18	.0808	.0691	.0593	.0508	.0437	.0376	.0324	.0279	.0241	.0208	.0180	.0089	.0045	.0023
19	.0703	.0596	.0506	.0431	.0367	.0313	.0267	.0229	.0196	.0168	.0144	.0068	.0033	.0017
20	.0611	.0514	.0433	.0365	.0308	.0261	.0221	.0187	.0159	.0135	.0115	.0053	.0025	.0012
21	.0531	.0443	.0370	.0309	.0259	.0217	.0183	.0154	.0129	.0109	.0092	.0041	.0018	.0009
22	.0462	.0382	.0316	.0262	.0218	.0181	.0151	.0126	.0105	.0088	.0074	.0031	.0014	.0006
23	.0402	.0329	.0270	.0222	.0183	.0151	.0125	.0103	.0086	.0071	.0059	.0024	.0010	.0004
24	.0349	.0284	.0231	.0188	.0154	.0126	.0103	.0085	.0070	.0057	.0047	.0018	.0007	.0003
25	.0304	.0245	.0197	.0160	.0129	.0105	.0085	.0069	.0057	.0046	.0038	.0014	.0006	.0002

One thus sees that the more remote cash inflow of \$1.1236 at the end of 2 years has exactly the same present value as the less remote cash inflow of \$1.06 at the end of 1 year, even though the more remote is larger in absolute amount than the less remote. It is this kind of precise mathematical weighting of inflows according to their degrees of remoteness—this emphasis on the time value of money—that justifies the claims for the superiority of the discounted cash flow method over the accounting method.

Technique. But finding a rate of profit by the discounted cash flow method is not nearly so easy as finding an accounting rate of profit. To understand the source of difficulty, let us refer to project A of the Speedwell Corporation. Its managers know that the project will require an investment of \$100,000 in fixed assets, and they have reasonable confidence, we may assume, in their estimates of annual cash inflow of \$25,000 to continue for 5 years. But their problem is to *equate* the total inflows of \$125,000 with a present value of \$100,000. What *single* rate of discount, compounded annually, must be applied to the successive inflows to give \$100,000 as their combined present value? This is the profit rate they are looking for. Mathematically, their problem is to solve the following formula to find i.

$$\$100{,}000 = \$25{,}000\,\frac{1}{(1+i)} + \$25{,}000\,\frac{1}{(1+i)^2} + \$25{,}000\,\frac{1}{(1+i)^3} + \$25{,}000\,\frac{1}{(1+i)^4} + \$25{,}000\,\frac{1}{(1+i)^5}\,.$$

For business analysts, a preferred method of solving such an equation is to consult tables of present values of \$1 at various rates of discount and for various time periods, such as Table 13–2. Here one finds, for example, that the present value of \$1 due at the end of 5 years discounted at 10 percent compounded annually is \$0.6209 (found where the 5-period line intersects with the 10 percent column), and one knows, therefore, that \$10,000 so discounted would be \$6,209 today. For project A, however, the rate column to be used is unknown, so that a start must be made with a reasonable approximation. Since the accounting rate of profit on project A was found to be 5 percent on the basis of original investment and 10 percent on the basis of average investment, we may well expect the discounted cash flow rate to fall between these two levels, possibly about midway. Let us therefore see what rates of profit of 7 percent and 8 percent will give us. From the table, we find that the present value of \$1 for 1 period (year) at 7 percent discount is \$0.9346 (found where the 1-period line intersects with the 7 percent column), and at 8 percent discount it is \$0.9-259. With present values of \$1 for 2 to 5 periods similarly selected from Table 13–2, we can tabulate the results as in Table 13–3.

TABLE 13–3
Present Values Related to Project A

Year	Present Values at 7% $1	Present Values at 7% $25,000	Present Values at 8% $1	Present Values at 8% $25,000
1	$0.9346	$ 23,365	$0.9259	$23,148
2	.8734	21,835	.8573	21,433
3	.8163	20,408	.7938	19,845
4	.7629	19,073	.7350	18,375
5	.7130	17,825	.6806	17,015
Total	$4.1002	$102,506	$3.9926	$99,816

The sum of the present values at 7 percent, amounting to $102,506, indicates that the rate of profit would be substantially in excess of 7 percent, while the sum of the present values at 8 percent, amounting to $99,816 (only $184 less than the $100,000 investment actually being considered), indicates that the rate of profit would be very slightly below 8 percent. Indeed, a conclusion that a rate of profit of about 8 percent could be expected on project A would be quite sufficient for its evaluation and comparison with the profit rates on the other three projects. Since the annual return of $25,000 is itself based on estimates running 5 years into the future, further degrees of mathematical precision in computing the expected rate of profit is hardly likely to be advantageous.

If, however, such precision is wanted, it can be achieved by processes of interpolation and trial and error, which we may examine. For project A, the difference in present value on a 7 percent basis and on an 8 percent basis is $102,506 – $99,816, or $2,690, and the difference between present value on an 8 percent basis and present value on the basis of the unknown rate we are seeking is $100,000 – $99,816, or $184. Accordingly, the unknown rate must be quite close to

$$.08 - \left(\frac{184}{2,690} \times .01\right),$$

or, alternatively, to

$$.07 + \left(\frac{2,506}{2,690} \times .01\right),$$

or 7.932 percent. By a further process of trial and error—a process of shading this rate slightly upward and downward—the exact rate would be found to be 7.9309 percent.

For a demonstration of the logic and mathematical accuracy of the discounted cash flow method, it should be advantageous to set out in tabular form (Table 13–4) the outcome of the investment of $100,000 in project A, assuming the results turn out as forecast and applying the rate of return of 7.9309 percent as just computed. Since the investment declines from year to year, one should particularly notice that the amount of net profit goes down from year to year (though the rate

TABLE 13–4
Outcome of Investment in Project A

Year	*Investment Beginning of Year*	*Cash Inflow*	*Profit at 7.9309%*	*Recovered on Investment (Inflow − Profit)*
1	$100,000	$25,000	$7,931	$ 17,069
2	82,931	25,000	6,577	18,423
3	64,508	25,000	5,116	19,884
4	44,624	25,000	3,539	21,461
5	23,163	25,000	1,837	23,163
Total				$100,000

of profit remains the same), while the amount of the investment recovered from year to year goes up. Speedwell would earn its 7.9309 percent profit each year on the declining balances of its investment, and by the end of the fifth year it would have recovered the amount of its investment of $100,000, as indicated by the sum of the amounts in the last column of the table.

Discounted Annuities. For the determination of discount rates as rates of profit, a procedure somewhat simpler than that just described is available when the net cash inflow is expected to be uniform from year to year, as for Speedwell's four proposed projects. Such a uniform periodic flow is described as an *annuity*, whose present value formula is:

$$P = R\,\frac{1 - \dfrac{1}{(1+i)^n}}{i},$$

where P is the present value, R is the periodic net inflow, i is the rate of discount (profit), n is the number of years or other periods, and the whole expression[4]

$$\frac{1 - \dfrac{1}{(1+i)^n}}{i}$$

[4]As students of mathematics will know, the expression may also be written:

$$\frac{1 - (1+i)^{-n}}{i}.$$

In mathematical shorthand, moreover, the expression is often abbreviated to $a_{\overline{n|}\,i}$, with a standing for 1 unit, such as $1, so that the full formula for present value is written:

$$P = Ra_{\overline{n|}\,i}$$

is the present value of $1 receivable or payable at the end of *each* period for n periods at i rate of discount.

On finding this value for a given number of periods at a given rate of discount, one has only to multiply by the value of R ($25,000 for project A) to find the total present value of the periodic flows—that is, the present value of the annuity. To determine discount rates as rates of profit, one can consult tables of present values of $1 per period, such as Table 13–5, to get approximate rates, and then, if desired, one can further refine these rates by interpolation and trial-and-error procedures. In Table 13–5, we find that the present value of $1 per period for 5 periods at a discount rate of 7 percent is $4.1002 and at a discount rate of 8 percent is $3.9927.[5] By multiplying each of these figures by $25,000, we find that at 7 percent the present value of the 5 annual net inflows is $102,505, and that at 8 percent it is $99,818—the same values (except for a slight difference due to rounding errors) that were previously derived by the somewhat more tedious procedure described above.

Using the annuity table in a similar way for Speedwell's projects B, C, and D, we can find an approximate rate of anticipated profit for each, and by interpolation we can refine these rates of profit for greater exactness. With the results already obtained for project A included for comparison, these profit rates are as follows.

	Proposed Projects			
	A	*B*	*C*	*D*
Approximate rate (from table)	8%	12%	14%	13%
Refined rate (by interpolation)	7.9309%*	11.654%	13.776%	12.961%

*Additionally refined by trial-and-error procedures.

Judgment. On the basis of the rates of profit to be expected, therefore, project C is clearly revealed to be the most attractive, even though it was ranked as substantially less attractive than projects A and B by the payback method and as slightly less attractive than D by the accounting method. Likewise, project D is revealed as being second in attractiveness, although it was ranked as least attractive by the payback method; project B is revealed as being third in attractiveness, even though it got the best rating by the payback method; and project A is revealed as least attractive, although it was second in rank on the basis of the payback method. Accordingly, Speedwell's managers would surely have reason for confidence in tentatively deciding to go ahead with projects B and C in combination or with project D by itself. Such a decision would be tentative because the managers would also want to know what cost rate should be assigned

[5]It will be noted that these sums of present values of $1 per period for five periods were already determined in Table 13–3 on page 301 (with a slight difference at 8 per cent on account of a rounding error).

TABLE 13–5

Present Value of $1 Per Period Discounted at Rate *i* for *n* Periods

n/i	1%	2%	3%	4%	5%	6%	7%	8%	9%	10%	11%	12%	13%	14%
1.....	.9901	.9804	.9709	.9615	.9524	.9434	.9346	.9259	.9174	.9091	.9009	.8929	.8850	.8772
2.....	1.9704	1.9416	1.9135	1.8861	1.8594	1.8334	1.8080	1.7833	1.7591	1.7355	1.7125	1.6901	1.6681	1.6467
3.....	2.9410	2.8839	2.8286	2.7751	2.7232	2.6730	2.6243	2.5771	2.5313	2.4868	2.4437	2.4018	2.3612	2.3216
4.....	3.9020	3.8077	3.7171	3.6299	3.5459	3.4651	3.3872	3.3121	3.2397	3.1699	3.1024	3.0373	2.9745	2.9137
5.....	4.8535	4.7134	4.5797	4.4518	4.3295	4.2123	4.1002	3.9927	3.8896	3.7908	3.6959	3.6048	3.5172	3.4331
6.....	5.7955	5.6014	5.4172	5.2421	5.0757	4.9173	4.7665	4.6229	4.4859	4.3553	4.2305	4.1114	3.9976	3.8887
7.....	6.7282	6.4720	6.2302	6.0020	5.7863	5.5824	5.3893	5.2064	5.0329	4.8684	4.7122	4.5638	4.4226	4.2883
8.....	7.6517	7.3254	7.0196	6.7327	6.4632	6.2098	5.9713	5.7466	5.5348	5.3349	5.1461	4.9676	4.7988	4.6389
9.....	8.5661	8.1622	7.7861	7.4353	7.1078	6.8017	6.5152	6.2469	5.9852	5.7590	5.5370	5.3282	5.1317	4.9464
10.....	9.4714	8.9825	8.5302	8.1109	7.7217	7.3601	7.0236	6.7101	6.4176	6.1446	5.8892	5.6502	5.4262	5.2161
11.....	10.3677	9.7868	9.2526	8.7604	8.3064	7.8868	7.4987	7.1389	6.8052	6.4951	6.2065	5.9377	5.6869	5.4527
12.....	11.2552	10.5753	9.9539	9.3850	8.8632	8.3838	7.9427	7.5361	7.1607	6.8137	6.4924	6.1944	5.9176	5.6603
13.....	12.1338	11.3483	10.6349	9.9856	9.3935	8.8527	8.3576	7.9038	7.4869	7.1034	6.7499	6.4235	6.1218	5.8424
14.....	13.0038	12.1062	11.2960	10.5631	9.8986	9.2950	8.7454	8.2442	7.7861	7.3667	6.9819	6.6282	6.3025	6.0021
15.....	13.8651	12.8492	11.9379	11.1183	10.3796	9.7122	9.1079	8.5595	8.0607	7.6061	7.1909	6.8109	6.4624	6.1422
16.....	14.7180	13.5777	12.5610	11.6522	10.8377	10.1059	9.4466	8.8514	8.3125	7.8237	7.3792	6.9740	6.6039	6.2651
17.....	15.5624	14.2918	13.1660	12.1656	11.2740	10.4772	9.7632	9.1216	8.5436	8.0215	7.5488	7.1196	6.7291	6.3729
18.....	16.3984	14.9920	13.7534	12.6592	11.6895	10.8276	10.0591	9.3719	8.7556	8.2014	7.7016	7.2497	6.8399	6.4674
19.....	17.2261	15.6784	14.3237	13.1339	12.0853	11.1581	10.3356	9.6036	8.9501	8.3649	7.8393	7.3658	6.9380	6.5504
20.....	18.0457	16.3514	14.8774	13.5903	12.4622	11.4699	10.5940	9.8181	9.1285	8.5136	7.9633	7.4694	7.0248	6.6231
21.....	18.8571	17.0111	15.4149	14.0291	12.8211	11.7640	10.8355	10.0168	9.2922	8.6487	8.0751	7.5620	7.1016	6.6870
22.....	19.6605	17.6580	15.9368	14.4511	13.1630	12.0416	11.0612	10.2007	9.4424	8.7715	8.1757	7.6446	7.1695	6.7429
23.....	20.4559	18.2921	16.4435	14.8568	13.4885	12.3033	11.2722	10.3710	9.5802	8.8832	8.2664	7.7184	7.2297	6.7921
24.....	21.2435	18.9139	16.9355	15.2469	13.7986	12.5503	11.4693	10.5287	9.7066	8.9847	8.3481	7.7843	7.2829	6.8351
25.....	22.0233	19.5234	17.4131	15.6220	14.0939	12.7833	11.6536	10.6748	9.8226	9.0770	8.4217	7.8431	7.3300	6.8729

Table 13-5 (Continued)
Present Value of $1 Per Period Discounted at Rate *i* for *n* Periods

n/i	15%	16%	17%	18%	19%	20%	21%	22%	23%	24%	25%	30%	35%	40%
1.....	.8696	.8621	.8547	.8475	.8403	.8333	.8264	.8197	.8130	.8065	.8000	.7692	.7407	.7143
2.....	1.6257	1.6052	1.5852	1.5656	1.5465	1.5278	1.5095	1.4915	1.4740	1.4568	1.4400	1.3609	1.2894	1.2245
3.....	2.2832	2.2459	2.2096	2.1743	2.1399	2.1065	2.0739	2.0422	2.0114	1.9813	1.9520	1.8161	1.6959	1.5889
4.....	2.8550	2.7982	2.7432	2.6901	2.6386	2.5887	2.5404	2.4936	2.4483	2.4043	2.3616	2.1662	1.9969	1.8492
5.....	3.3522	3.2743	3.1993	3.1272	3.0576	2.9906	2.9260	2.8636	2.8035	2.7454	2.6893	2.4356	2.2200	2.9352
6.....	3.7845	3.6847	3.5892	3.4976	3.4098	3.3255	3.2446	3.1669	3.0923	3.0205	2.9514	2.6427	2.3852	2.1680
7.....	4.1604	4.0386	3.9224	3.8115	3.7057	3.6046	3.5079	3.4155	3.3270	3.2423	3.1611	2.8021	2.5075	2.2628
8.....	4.4873	4.3436	4.2072	4.0776	3.9544	3.8372	3.7256	3.6193	3.5179	3.4212	3.3289	2.9247	2.5982	2.3306
9.....	4.7716	4.6065	4.4506	4.3030	4.1633	4.0310	3.9054	3.7863	3.6731	3.5655	3.4631	3.0190	2.6653	2.3790
10.....	5.0188	4.8332	4.6586	4.4941	4.3389	4.1925	4.0541	3.9232	3.7993	3.6819	3.5705	3.0915	2.7150	2.4136
11.....	5.2337	5.0286	4.8364	4.6560	4.4865	4.3271	4.1769	4.0354	3.9018	3.7757	3.6564	3.1473	2.7519	2.4383
12.....	5.4206	5.1971	4.9884	4.7932	4.6105	4.4392	4.2785	4.1274	3.9852	3.8514	3.7251	3.1903	2.7792	2.4559
13.....	5.5831	5.3423	5.1183	4.9095	4.7147	4.5327	4.3624	4.2028	4.0530	3.9124	3.7801	3.2233	2.7994	2.4685
14.....	5.7245	5.4675	5.2293	5.0081	4.8023	4.6106	4.4317	4.2646	4.1082	3.9616	3.8241	3.2487	2.8144	2.4775
15.....	5.8474	5.5755	5.3242	5.0916	4.8759	4.6755	4.4890	4.3152	4.1530	4.0013	3.8593	3.2682	2.8255	2.4839
16.....	5.9542	5.6685	5.4053	5.1624	4.9377	4.7296	4.5364	4.3567	4.1894	4.0333	3.8874	3.2832	2.8337	2.4885
17.....	6.0472	5.7487	5.4746	5.2223	4.9897	4.7746	4.5755	4.3908	4.2190	4.0591	3.9099	3.2948	2.8398	2.4918
18.....	6.1280	5.8178	5.5339	5.2732	5.0333	4.8122	4.6079	4.4187	4.2431	4.0799	3.9279	3.3037	2.8443	2.4941
19.....	6.1982	5.8775	5.5845	5.3162	5.0700	4.8435	4.6346	4.4415	4.2627	4.0967	3.9424	3.3105	2.8476	2.4958
20.....	6.2593	5.9288	5.6278	5.3527	5.1009	4.8696	4.6567	4.4603	4.2786	4.1103	3.9539	3.3158	2.8501	2.4970
21.....	6.3125	5.9731	5.6648	5.3837	5.1268	4.8913	4.6750	4.4756	4.2916	4.1212	3.9631	3.3198	2.8519	2.4979
22.....	6.3587	6.0113	5.6964	5.4099	5.1486	4.9094	4.6900	4.4882	4.3021	4.1300	3.9705	3.3230	2.8533	2.4985
23.....	6.3988	6.0442	5.7234	5.4321	5.1668	4.9245	4.7025	4.4985	4.3106	4.1371	3.9764	3.3254	2.8543	2.4989
24.....	6.4338	6.0726	5.7465	5.4509	5.1822	4.9371	4.7128	4.5070	4.3176	4.1428	3.9811	3.3272	2.8550	2.4992
25.....	6.4641	6.0971	5.7662	5.4669	5.1951	4.9476	4.7213	4.5139	4.3232	4.1474	3.9849	3.3286	2.8556	2.4994

to the money (capital) to be invested in the various projects. If on the basis of cost-of-capital analysis (to be described in Chapter 14) they decided that 12 percent should be the cutoff rate for approvals and rejections of proposed projects, then project B as well as project A would be labeled undesirable, but if the cutoff rate were set at 11 percent project B would join C and D in continuing to be attractive. Even with reference to a cost-of-capital cutoff rate, moreover, the decision would still have a tentative aspect, since decisions ought not be made mechanically on a basis solely of profit rates determined by the discounted cash flow method, regardless of its logic and precision, and of cost-of-capital rates, regardless of the care exercised in their determination. Even more important is confidence in the reliability of facility cost estimates, increased sales revenues, and increased costs of output, and in the stability of income tax rates, as well as some qualitative weighing—that is, some exercise of judgment going beyond the dollars-and-cents and percentage figures. For example, a recognition of greater uncertainty in the forecast for D's 20-year period than in the forecasts for the shorter periods of projects B and C may persuade Speedwell's managers to give their choice to the B–C combination.

Present Value Method with Profitability Index

Use of Cutoff Rate. Some business managers who are rather fearful of the mathematics of the discounted cash flow method—though they have great respect for the soundness of the method—employ a modification they judge to be adequate for their needs. They set a cutoff rate of profit below which they would not be willing to go in approving investment projects. They then consult the present value tables to find the present value of net cash inflows of $1 at the cutoff rate and multiply by the respective dollar amounts of the net cash inflows expected. If the resulting product or sum of products is less than the dollar amount of the investment required for a project, they conclude that the rate of profit would be less than the cutoff rate and that the project should be rejected. If the product or sum of products is greater than the proposed investment outlay, they conclude that the rate of profit would be higher than the cutoff rate and that the project should be acceptable.

For Speedwell, assume that the cutoff rate of profit is set at 10 percent. Table 13–5 reveals that the present value of $1 per year for 5 years at 10 percent is $3.7908, so that the present value of the 5 net cash inflows of its project A would be $25,000 × $3.7908, or $94,770. Since $100,000 would have to be invested to get a cash flow whose present value is thus determined to be $94,770, project A should unquestionably be rejected. For project B, also a 5-year project, the present value of its anticipated inflow of $55,000 a year would be

\$208,494 (\$55,000 × \$3.7908), and since this would exceed the \$200,000 to be invested the project would—tentatively—deserve approval. In a similar way, the anticipated cash flows of project C discounted at 10 percent would be found to have a present value of \$350,242, and those of project D, \$604,466. Since the cash investments in these two projects would be \$300,000 and \$500,000, respectively, they would clearly be shown to be attractive.

Index Determination. But the use of cutoff rates in the manner just described gives no direct basis for choosing among a variety of proposed projects—for ranking projects according to degrees of attractiveness when, for example, money available for investment is limited. Is a present value of \$350,242 in relation to an investment of \$300,000 better or worse than a present value of \$604,466 in relation to an investment of \$500,000? The very pairing of figures in this question suggests a solution to the problem of ranking—the computation of a *profitability index* for each project. Such a profitability index is usually determined by the following formula.

$$\text{Profitability index} = \frac{\text{Present value of cash inflows at cutoff rate}}{\text{Original investment}}$$

For the four projects of the Speedwell Corporation, application of the formula would give the following results.

	Proposed Projects			
	A	*B*	*C*	*D*
Profitability index............	$\frac{\$94,770}{\$100,000}$ = 94.8%	$\frac{\$208,494}{\$200,000}$ = 104.2%	$\frac{\$350,242}{\$300,000}$ = 116.7%	$\frac{\$604,466}{\$500,000}$ = 120.9%

That the profitability index for project A falls below 100 percent indicates that it should be rejected if Speedwell's managers insist on a rate of profit of at least 10 percent. At the same time, the indexes for the other three projects indicate that they are all acceptable; project D ranks as most attractive, project C is second, and project B is third.

But the discounted cash flow method gave the top position to project C and second place to D. Since the discounted cash flow method was described above as the most accurate method for determining profitability, one must conclude that the profitability index device is defective. A defect does, indeed, result from the reintroduction of original investment as a divisor. We had occasion to criticize one of the variants of the accounting method for its use of original investment as a divisor, and we must conclude that such a use equally detracts from the reliability of profitability indexes. Nevertheless, business managers may still conclude that since many elements in their forecasts are subject to considerable uncertainty, profitability indexes are sufficiently accurate for reasonable judgments.

Further Considerations

Some of the assumptions adopted in the foregoing illustrations were purposely simplified so that, as far as possible, attention could be concentrated on the project evaluation procedures themselves without undue distraction by mathematical complexities. It therefore remains to emphasize that the procedures are generally adaptable to projects whose prospects involve greater degrees of complexity, as can be shown by a further development of the illustrations with a sampling of the more common kinds of variations in prospects that one is likely to encounter. Let us consider modifications in the analytical procedures to take into account:

1. Additional investments to be made in current assets to handle forecast increases in volumes of sales.
2. Expectations that the fixed assets in which investments are proposed would have salvage values (scrap, secondhand, or trade-in values) at the expiration of their useful lives.
3. Expectations that the depreciation of new fixed assets would be charged on bases other than the straight-line basis.
4. Allowances for interest on the money to be invested in additional facilities.

Investments in Current Assets. When a firm forecasts that an increased volume of sales will result from a proposed investment in new fixed assets, it will surely expect to have an increased need of cash for investment in current assets, especially in added inventories and accounts receivable. Moreover, it must normally expect that the increased investment in current assets will be needed during the entire period anticipated for the expanded volume of sales. In other words, it can hardly expect to recover from year to year a portion of its investment in additional current assets as it can expect to recover portions of its investment in fixed assets by annual cash throwoffs from depreciation. But at the end of the useful lives of the fixed assets, the current assets as expanded originally will still be there, and the firm can logically regard them as being recoverable at that time. If sales are expected at that time to fall back to the preexpansion level, it would be reasonable to anticipate that the added current assets would no longer be needed.

To apply these ideas to project B of the Speedwell Corporation, let us assume that $50,000 would be needed for expanded inventories and accounts receivable in addition to the $200,000 to be invested in fixed assets, and let us further assume that all other facts remain as originally given. On the basis of any sound evaluation procedure, one should obviously conclude that project B would be much less attractive than before; indeed, this is indicated by all four of the analytical methods we have been studying. The payback period would be increased from 3.6 years to 4.55 years. Of the total investment of

$250,000, only $220,000 would be recovered in the first 4 years from the annual cash throwoffs from profits and depreciation of $55,000 annually, so that a little more than an additional half year would be needed for the recovery of the final $30,000. On the basis of original investment, the accounting rate of return would be reduced from 7.5 percent to 6 percent (annual profit of $15,000 divided by $250,000), and on the basis of average investment it would fall from 15 percent to 10 percent. (The average investment would be the sum of $250,000, $210,000, $170,000, $130,000, $90,000, and $50,000—the last figure is of course, the leftover current assets—divided by 6.)

To determine the rate of profit by the discounted cash flow method, one would have to find the single rate of discount that would equate the total original investment of $250,000 with the discounted annual cash inflows of $55,000, *plus* the discounted value of $50,000 of current assets to be recovered at the end of the fifth year. By consulting the present value tables and making the appropriate multiplications, one would find that at a discount rate of 8 percent the discounted value of the $55,000 5-year annuity would be $219,599, and that the discounted value of $50,000 receivable at the end of 5 years would be $34,030, for a total of $253,629. At a discount rate of 9 percent, these values would be, respectively, $213,928 and $32,497 for a total of $246,425. Accordingly, Speedwell's managers would probably be satisfied to say that the rate of profit would be approximately 8.5 percent. Finally, if Speedwell maintained its present value cutoff rate at 10 percent, the present values at 10 percent would be $208,494 and $31,045, respectively, for a total of $239,539, and the productivity index would be 95.8 percent ($239,539/$250,000), so that project B would deserve rejection.

Salvage Values. Standing by itself, an expectation that fixed assets will have substantial salvage values at the expiration of their useful lives should make proposed investments in such assets more attractive than they would be were the expectation zero or negative.[6] In Speedwell's case, its managers would surely think better of project B were they to come up with a revised estimate of $20,000 for its salvage value in contrast with their original estimate of 0. However, the revised estimate would require revisions elsewhere in the performance forecast for project B. On a straight-line basis, depreciation would be reduced from $40,000 to $36,000 a year, and annual taxable profits would be increased from $30,000 to $34,000. With tax rates assumed to be at 50 percent, annual income taxes would rise from $15,000 to $17,000, and after-tax profit would also be $17,000, while annual cash throw-offs from profits and depreciation combined would fall from $55,000 to $53,000.

[6]A negative salvage value would mean removal costs exceeding whatever might be recovered from the fixed assets at the expiration of their useful lives.

Although the salvage value revision would increase project B's 5-year profit prospects from $75,000 to $85,000, the payback period method of evaluation would fail to reflect this improvement. The payback period would rise from 3.6 years to 3.8 years because of the decline in annual cash throw-offs—because of the very deferment of the salvage value recovery to the end of the useful lives of the fixed assets.

But the other analytical methods would, more realistically, reveal a greater attractiveness for project B. On the basis of original investment, the accounting method rate of profit would rise from 7.5 percent to 8.5 percent ($17,000/$200,000), and on the basis of average investment of $110,000 $\left(\frac{\$200{,}000 + \$20{,}000}{2}\right)$, the profit rate would go from 15 percent to 15.5 percent. For the discounted cash flow method, application of a discount rate of 12 percent to the 5-year annuity of $53,000 would give a present value of $191,054, and its application to the salvage value of $20,000 recoverable at the end of 5 years would give a present value of $11,348, for a total discounted value of $202,-402. Application of a 13 percent discount rate to these two sources of cash inflow would give present values of $186,412 and $10,856, respectively, for a total of $197,268. Accordingly, the anticipated rate of profit would be approximately 12.5 percent—a rate significantly better than the 11.654 percent rate originally determined (by interpolation) on the assumption of a salvage value of 0.

Finally, in the application of the present value method the cutoff discount rate of 10 percent would give present values of $200,912 for the 5-year annuity and $12,418 for the salvage value for a total of $213,330. This total divided by the original investment of $200,000 would give a productivity index of 106.7 percent, by contrast with the index of 104.2 percent originally computed for project B on the assumption of a salvage value of 0.

Accelerated Depreciation. Many business firms prefer to charge off depreciation on their depreciable fixed assets on bases other than the straight-line basis that has been used so far in our illustrations. This preference runs almost always in the direction of accelerated depreciation—a concentration of depreciation charges as heavily as possible in the early years of asset lives. Since the deferment of income tax obligations is an outstanding reason for this preference, what is possible in accelerating depreciation charges usually turns out to be what is permissible under the federal Internal Revenue Code and the related decisions of the Treasury. Our emphasis on the time value of money—on the logic of discounting cash inflows according to their degrees of remoteness—should indicate why business managers welcome opportunities to defer tax payments. A tax of a given amount payable in five years is not equally so burdensome as a tax of equal amount payable today, since the tax money can be invested and can earn a return before payment must finally be made.[7]

If tax deferment is generally recognized to be advantageous, analytical methods employed to evaluate proposed investment projects should clearly reflect this advantage. Let us see whether or not this is done by the four analytical methods we have been studying. For this judgment, let us assume that for their project B, Speedwell's managers anticipate charging depreciation by the sum of the years' digits method, which is one of the methods of accelerated depreciation approved by the Treasury. With an assumption of no salvage value, this method would call for charging off 5/15 of the proposed $200,000 investment in project B at the end of the first year, 4/15 at the end of the second year, 3/15 at the end of the third, and so on. The more rapid charge-offs would, of course, change profit expectations from those originally forecast on the basis of straight-line depreciation, and, as already indicated, would change the timing of tax payments. The new forecast for the five-year life of project B would, therefore, be as presented in Table 13–6.

TABLE 13–6
Forecast for Project B with Sum of the Years' Digits Depreciation

	Year				
	1	*2*	*3*	*4*	*5*
Increased annual sales	$100,000	$100,000	$100,000	$100,000	$100,000
Increased expenses:					
Materials, labor, etc.	30,000	30,000	30,000	30,000	30,000
Depreciation	66,667	53,333	40,000	26,667	13,333
Total	$ 96,667	$ 83,333	$ 70,000	$ 56,667	$ 43,333
Increased before-tax profit	$ 3,333	$ 16,667	$ 30,000	$ 43,333	$ 56,667
Less: Income taxes at 50%	1,667	8,333	15,000	21,667	28,333
Increased after-tax profit	$ 1,666	$ 8,334	$ 15,000	$ 21,666	$ 28,334
Add: Cash throw-off from depreciation	66,667	53,333	40,000	26,667	13,333
Increased net cash inflow	$ 68,333	$ 61,667	$ 55,000	$ 48,333	$ 41,667

The payback period method would show the advantage of accelerating depreciation with the resulting tax deferment, since the payback period for project B would now be 3.31 years, whereas it was 3.6

[7]However, as we saw in Chapter 10, deferment of taxes is not the only reason for preferences for accelerated depreciation. See pp. 217–18.

years with straight-line depreciation. The cash throw-offs from depreciation and profits would amount to $185,000 in the first 3 years, so that approximately one third of the fourth year would be required to recover the remaining $15,000 of the $200,000 investment.

However, the accounting method for determining the rate of profit would show mixed results. On the basis of original investment, no advantage would be indicated, but on the basis of average investment the advantage of accelerating depreciation would be clearly revealed. The original investment would still be $200,000, and the average annual profit, though profits would now be concentrated in the later years, would still be $15,000, so that the profit rate would remain at 7.5 percent. On the other hand, the average investment would decline from $100,000 to $77,778, and the lower figure divided into the average annual profit of $15,000 would give a rate of profit of 19.3 percent. (The average investment would be the sum of $200,000, $133,333, $80,000, $40,000, $13,333, and 0 divided by 6.)

In its turn, the discounted cash flow method would show a significant improvement in rate of profit prospects. At a 12 percent discount rate, the present value of $68,333 receivable at the end of the first year, plus the present value of $61,667 receivable at the end of the second year, plus the separate present values of the amounts receivable at the end of the other 3 years would amount to $203,683. At a discount rate of 13 percent, the sum of present values would be $199,154, so that the rate of profit would be only slightly below 13 percent. By interpolation, this rate could be refined to 12.81 percent—substantially better than the rate of 11.654 percent found when depreciation is charged on the straight-line basis.

Finally, the present value method would also reveal the advantage of accelerated depreciation and tax deferment, with the profitability index rising from 104.2 percent to 106.6 percent. At a cutoff discount rate of 10 percent, the sum of the present values of $68,333 at the end of the first year, $61,667 at the end of the second, and so on, would be $213,294. This figure divided by the original investment of $200,000 would give a new profitability index of 106.6 percent.

Allowance for Cost of Capital. A major reason theorists generally hold the accounting, discounted cash flow, and present value methods to be superior to the payback period method is that the preferred methods yield prospective *rates of profit* that can be directly compared with the interest rates or other cost of capital rates to be incurred on the money to be invested in proposed projects. But such a comparison would tend to become somewhat confused were interest costs or other costs of capital to be included among the expanded operating costs forecast in relation to the projects. Accordingly, costs of these kinds, though necessarily to be anticipated, are usually excluded from projected operating costs, as we have ignored them up to this point in our study.

Since, however, the payback period method does not reveal rates of profit for comparison with interest or other cost of capital rates, such costs should surely be included in forecasts of operating expenses to enhance the usefulness of the method. Payback periods will unquestionably be lengthened on account of interest or other cost of capital payments, as can be seen by illustration if we adjust our data for Speedwell's project B to include an interest cost. With all other facts about project B as originally given, let us assume that $200,000 would have to be borrowed to finance the project, that Speedwell's managers would expect to be charged 8 percent a year on the loan, and that they decide to include the interest cost among the projected expanded operating costs. However, Speedwell's managers would surely expect to use the cash throw-off from depreciation of $40,000 a year to pay down the loan from year to year, so that the interest cost, starting off at $16,000 for the first year, would be expected to fall by $3,200 each year in the 4 years following. At the same time, they would surely allow for the deductibility of the interest costs for income tax purposes, recognizing that at an assumed tax rate of 50 percent the cash throw-off from profits would be reduced from year to year by only half the amount of the interest charges. For the five-year life of project B, therefore, the revised projection would be as shown in Table 13–7.

TABLE 13–7

Forecast for Project B Allowing for Interest Cost at 8 Per Cent

	Year				
	1	*2*	*3*	*4*	*5*
Increased annual sales	$100,000	$100,000	$100,000	$100,000	$100,000
Increased expenses:					
Materials, labor, etc.	30,000	30,000	30,000	30,000	30,000
Interest	16,000	12,800	9,600	6,400	3,200
Depreciation	40,000	40,000	40,000	40,000	40,000
Total	$ 86,000	$ 82,800	$ 79,600	$ 76,400	$ 73,200
Increased before-tax profit	$ 14,000	$ 17,200	$ 20,400	$ 23,600	$ 26,800
Less: Income taxes at 50%	7,000	8,600	10,200	11,800	13,400
Increased after-tax profit	$ 7,000	$ 8,600	$ 10,200	$ 11,800	$ 13,400
Add: Cash throw-off from depreciation	40,000	40,000	40,000	40,000	40,000
Increased net cash inflow	$ 47,000	$ 48,600	$ 50,200	$ 51,800	$ 53,400

Thus, the payback period would be slightly over 4 years, whereas it was found to be 3.6 years without the allowance for interest costs—a lengthening of the payback period hardly sufficient to change the judgment of Speedwell's managers about the desirability of the project, but a differential surely worthy of their consideration.

QUESTIONS

1. What kinds of expenditures are planned for in capital budgeting? Explain whether or not capital budgets include forecasts of income and other financing sources.

2. Why do some firms have both long-term and annual capital budgets? For most business firms, which kind is more important? Why?

3. What is the relationship between the long-range forecasting of sales and operating costs and the long-range budgeting of fixed asset acquisitions?

4. To what extent does capital budgeting include the planning of expenditures for the repair and maintenance of fixed facilities? Explain.

5. Explain the several reasons why it may be possible to gain substantial economies in expenditures for fixed assets by efficient long-range capital budgeting.

6. What is the problem of choice in capital budgeting that is so greatly emphasized in this chapter?

7. What is the payback period for a proposed investment project? How is it determined mathematically? For choosing among competing investment projects, what merits does the payback period method have? What shortcomings?

8. What is the mathematical procedure for determining the rate of profit on a proposed investment project by the accounting method based on original investment? Based on average investment?

9. On what grounds is the accounting method adversely criticized as a means of judging the desirability of given investment projects?

10. What is the time value of money that is emphasized so strongly in support of the discounted cash flow method of project evaluation? Is this emphasis sufficiently well grounded to prove the superiority of the discounted cash flow method over the other methods of evaluation? Discuss.

11. Explain the mathematics of the present value method of project evaluation. In what important respects does it differ from the discounted cash flow method?

12. Why is it said that a defect is introduced into the present value method through the use of profitability indexes?

13. In judging the desirability of additional investments in fixed assets, is there any reason to give consideration to the additional investment in current assets that would also be needed? Discuss.

14. Explain the effects on payback periods of (*a*) estimates of salvage values, and (*b*) differences in methods of charging depreciation.

15. Explain the effects on discounted cash flow rates of profit of the two factors mentioned in question 14.

16. In use of the payback period, accounting, discounted cash flow,

and present value methods of evaluating investment projects, what is the best way to treat the interest to be paid on money to be borrowed to finance the projects? Explain.

PROBLEMS

1. For the development of competence in using the present value table on pp. 298–99, find the present value of $20,000 to be received at the end of:

a) 20 years, discounted at 6 percent per year — Ans. $ 6,236
b) 16 years, discounted at 12 percent per year — Ans. $ 3,262
c) 6 years, discounted at 3 percent per year — Ans. $16,750
d) 18 years, discounted at 20 percent per year — Ans. $ 752

2. For the development of competence in using the annuity present value table on pp. 304–5, find the present value of $5,000 to be received at the end of each year for:

a) 5 years, discounted at 8 percent per year — Ans. $19,963.50
b) 10 years, discounted at 4 percent per year — Ans. $40,554.50
c) 25 years, discounted at 5 percent per year — Ans. $70,469.50
d) 8 years, discounted at 10 percent per year — Ans. $26,674.50

3. For the development of competence in interpolating in the present value tables, find the discount rate that would give a present value of:

a) $12,000, for $16,000 to be received at the end of 9 years — Ans. 3.26%
b) $50,000, for $200,000 to be received at the end of 6 years — Ans. 32.08%
c) $60,000, for $8,000 to be received annually for 8 years — Ans. 1.46%
d) $90,000, for $10,000 to be received annually for 20 years — Ans. 9.21%
e) $45,000, for $6,000 to be received annually for 16 years — Ans. 10.73%

4. The following data have been assembled by the officers of the Rayborn Company, Inc., regarding three fixed asset investment projects they are considering.

	Project A	*Project B*	*Project C*
Cost of facilities	$220,000	$340,000	$550,000
Useful life	5 years	8 years	10 years
Anticipated increase in annual sales	$130,000	$165,000	$240,000
Anticipated increase in annual operating costs before depreciation, interest, and income taxes	$ 47,000	$ 78,000	$145,000

Assuming that for each project the salvage value is estimated at zero, that depreciation would be charged on a straight-line basis, and that combined federal and state income taxes are estimated at 50 percent, find for each:

a) The payback period.
b) The accounting rate of return based on original investment.

c) The accounting rate of return based on average investment.
d) The discounted cash flow rate of return.
e) A profitability index based on a cutoff rate of 8 percent.
f) A profitability index based on a cutoff rate of 12 percent.

5. Corporations X, Y, and Z are each considering the taking on of a new product line, and their officers have assembled the following data on amounts to be invested and results to be anticipated.

	X	*Y*	*Z*
Cost of additional fixed assets	$115,000	$250,000	$300,000
Useful life	5 years	5 years	6 years
Salvage value	$10,000	None	$20,000
Depreciation method to be used	Years' digits	Declining balance at 40%	Years' digits
Additional current assets needed	$40,000	$75,000	$110,000
Anticipated increase in annual operating profit before deduction of depreciation, interest, and income taxes	$58,000	$102,000	$130,000
Anticipated combined rate of federal and state income taxes	50%	50%	50%
Rate of interest to be paid on money to be invested in both fixed and current assets (to be taken into consideration only for the payback period method)	8%	7%	9%

For each of these projects, determine:
a) The payback period.
b) The accounting rate of return based on original investment.
c) The accounting rate of return based on average investment.
d) The discounted cash flow rate of return.
e) A profitability index based on a cutoff rate of 9 percent.
f) A profitability index based on a cutoff rate of 12 percent.

chapter 14

THE COST OF CAPITAL

It would be pointless for business managers to make rather elaborate computations of estimated rates of profit on proposed investment projects if they did not also have reasonably accurate estimates of the costs of getting the money to be invested—the *cost of capital*, as it is usually called. Even with assurances from lenders that money would be advanced at given rates of interest, they would surely want to consider whether it would be realistic to regard these rates as the appropriate costs. At the least, they would want to give proper weight to the deductibility of interest as an expense in income tax determination. If they expected to be able to use cash throw-offs from profits for financing proposed projects, they would surely want to consider what cost they ought to attribute to the use of such funds or whether, perhaps, they ought to regard these funds as costless. In any case, they could hardly escape a need to have reasonable cost of funds estimates should they aim at setting a cutoff rate of anticipated after-tax profit below which they would refuse to go in approving expansion projects.

COST OF CAPITAL SUPPLIED BY COMMON STOCKHOLDERS

Because the proprietors' investment is an essential element among every business enterprise's sources of funds, it is well to begin an analysis of costs of capital with this source. Proprietors' investment is generally the first source of funds for launching enterprises and the last to be withdrawn when they discontinue operations. In a large proportion of business enterprises, it is the most important continuing source of funds, and in virtually all others it remains an important, if not the most important, source. It is generally *essential* in the sense that without a substantial investment of the proprietors the business enterprise would find it impossible to obtain loans and credits from banks, trade suppliers, bond buyers, and other potential fund contributors.

In business corporations, the proprietors' investment is made chiefly by purchases of common stock and by contributions of corporate profits—that is, by corporate retention of profits that if paid out would go to the common stockholders as dividends. Accordingly, the question we face is this: What is the cost to a corporation of cash acquired from common stockholders through these two channels? The answer to this question is by no means certain. It has been answered in various ways by distinguished scholars, and allowing for differences in points of view, several answers appear to have much merit. Nevertheless, we should find it most advantageous to limit attention to the one answer that appears to be most widely accepted—one that, in any event, appears to be entirely realistic.

Investment in Common Stock

New-Issue Basis. According to this answer, the cost of capital supplied by stockholder investment in common stock is the minimum rate of after-tax profit that would have to be earned on the proceeds of a new issue of common stock to avoid a fall from the rate that would be earned without the new issue. Alternatively stated, it is the minimum rate of after-tax profit that would have to be earned on new projects to ensure that earnings per share of common stock would remain at least equal to the amount the stockholders would earn per share without the new projects. From this standpoint, therefore, the par or stated value of common stock, the size of surplus accounts, the amounts and rates of profits being earned currently and earned in the past are all irrelevant in the determination of the cost of capital derived from common-stock investment. Such a determination, it is claimed, must be forward-looking. It is future profits that people are interested in when they buy common stock in the market, and they are willing to pay a certain price for a given stock because they believe that their acquired claim to participation in the stream of future profits is worth that price. For existing stockholders as well, what is important is not what they paid for a stock years ago or what additional contributions to equity they have made over the years by way of earnings retention, but what the prospects for future profits are and what investors are willing to pay in the market to share in these prospects.

Therefore, when corporate managers ponder whether or not they should adopt proposed investment projects to be financed by funds supplied by common stockholders they must first forecast what the annual after-tax rate of profit probably would be without the projects. It is this rate that they want at least to sustain; a proposed project that promises a lower rate must surely be rejected. Forecasting the *amount* of future profits should not be especially difficult, since it is a normal aspect of budgeting, but to get a *rate*, the amount of forecast annual after-tax profits would have to be divided by an estimated present value of the stockholders' equity.

Some say that such a present value is the number of shares already outstanding multiplied by the current market price per share, while others hold that it is the number of outstanding shares multiplied by the price at which additional shares could be sold. The second choice is probably the better one; it is the only proper choice when project financing by new common stock sales is specifically contemplated. It recognizes that it would normally be impossible to sell additional shares at the current market price, since deductions from this price must be made for commissions to investment bankers who undertake to do the selling, for such underpricing as the offering of new stock to existing stockholders at a bargain level,[1] and for other expenses of selling. Further supporting this choice is the proposition that even without a sale of new common stock, concerted selling of their holdings by existing common stockholders would surely tend to drive down the market price.

Illustration. To illustrate all this, let us assume that the managers of the Speedwell Corporation, whose four proposed investment projects were analyzed in detail in Chapter 13, decide that the adoption of any of the projects would require sales of additional common shares as the means of financing. Let us also assume that the corporation already has 100,000 shares of $10 par value outstanding, that the current market price is $25 a share, and that the net proceeds of sales of additional shares are estimated at $20 a share. After-tax profits are currently being earned at around $290,000 and it is expected that normal growth of operations, without the adoption of projects A, B, or D, will raise average annual after-tax profits to $320,000 in the future.

On the basis of the criteria described above, the cost of capital by way of common stock financing would be determined by the formula:

$$\begin{array}{c}\text{Cost of capital from}\\ \text{common stock}\\ \text{financing}\end{array} = \frac{\begin{array}{c}\text{Forecast annual after-tax profits}\\ \text{without new projects}\end{array}}{\begin{array}{c}\text{Number of common}\\ \text{shares outstanding}\end{array} \times \begin{array}{c}\text{Estimated proceeds}\\ \text{of new common share}\end{array}}.$$

Applying this formula, we get:

$$\frac{\$320,000}{100,000 \text{ shares} \times \$20} = 16\%.$$

---

[1]For a discussion of the bargain pricing of common stock tendered in rights offerings to existing stockholders, see pp. 466–68.

Accordingly, projects A, B, and D should be rejected. Since their projected rates of profit were determined by the discounted cash flow method to be 7.9309 percent, 11.654 percent, and 12.961 percent, respectively, the adoption of any one or any combination of them would cause the corporation's overall rate of profit to fall below 16 percent.[2] The cost of capital would exceed the estimated rate of return to be earned on its investment.

For project B, for example, the estimated after-tax profit per year would be \$335,000 (\$320,000 expected without it, plus \$15,000 estimated to be added by it), and 10,000 shares of stock would have to be sold to raise the \$200,000 needed to finance it. By the formula, therefore, the rate of profit after the addition of B would be lower than without it.

$$\frac{\$335{,}000}{110{,}000 \text{ shares} \times \$20} = 15.2\%.$$

Likewise, earnings per share of stock would fall from the \$3.20 expected without project B (\$320,000/100,000 shares) to \$3.05 (\$335,000/110,000 shares).

Let us assume, however, that project C's rejection would seriously weaken Speedwell's capacity to compete with other firms in its industry, so that future annual after-tax profits would be expected to drop to \$250,000. Without project C, Speedwell would get neither the expansion in profits to \$320,000 on account of normal growth nor the \$27,000 of additional after-tax profits assumed for it in Chapter 13. Such an important element of necessity in project C would greatly influence its acceptability, and, most significantly, this new evaluation would come from a revised estimate of the cost of common stock capital and not from a revised estimate of project C's expected profitability (or at least not directly from this source). The revised cost of capital estimate would be:

$$\frac{\$250{,}000}{100{,}000 \text{ shares} \times \$20}$$

[2]In Chapter 13, these rates of profit were determined on the assumption that the amount of investment in the projects would be reduced during the periods of their useful lives by a gradual withdrawal of investment made possible by cash throw-offs from depreciation. But when financing of projects through sales of additional common stock is contemplated, it would be most unusual to plan for the gradual retirement of the new common stock to be issued. Moveover, the future profits estimated in the cost of capital formula for common stock financing are expected to continue indefinitely. Accordingly, in comparing discounted cash flow rates of profit as determined in Chapter 13 with the cost of common stock capital as analyzed in the present chapter, it must be assumed that cash throw-offs from depreciation on each project would be immediately reinvestable elsewhere in the corporation at the discounted cash flow rate for that project.

or 12.5 percent, and since the discounted cash flow rate of profit determined for project C in Chapter 13 was 13.776 percent, it would now become fully acceptable. Without project C, earnings per share would be expected to be $2.50 ($250,000/100,000 shares); with it, after the sale of 15,000 additional shares to raise the $300,000 needed, the earnings per share would be $3.02 ($347,000/115,000 shares). Such rather sharply contrasting results should clearly indicate why, in analyses of this type, emphasis must be placed on projected future profits rather than on current or past profits.

Retained Earnings

In decision making about disposal of after-tax profits, the directors of a corporation have the choice of paying them out to common stockholders as dividends or retaining them for investment in expansion projects. Customarily, the directors of most corporations decide to pay out portions of their profits as dividends and retain the rest. But how much of the profits are they justified in retaining, or are they justified in retaining any? In what circumstances are they justified in substituting their decisions about what the stockholders should do with their money for the decisions that the stockholders themselves might make? The answer would seem to be that retention is justified to the extent that retained profits can be invested by the corporation to yield a rate of after-tax profit not less than the rate that stockholders could earn by investing elsewhere. Such a minimum rate of after-tax profit should, accordingly, be regarded as the cost of capital to be attributed to retained earnings.

Market Price Basis. It would appear reasonable for the directors to conclude that the rate of after-tax profit that the stockholders could earn elsewhere would be equal to the rate that investors are expecting to earn by investment in the common stock of the directors' own corporation. If investors are willing to pay $25 a share for the outstanding common stock of the Speedwell Corporation on the basis of after-tax profit anticipations of $3.20 per share each year, and assuming a brokerage fee of 2 percent on stock transactions, then they must be satisfied with a profit rate of 12.55 percent ($3.20/-$25.50). If investors thought that they could earn a higher rate by investing $25 in the stocks of other corporations, they would not offer that much for Speedwell's common, and its market price would surely fall. Accordingly, Speedwell's directors might well decide that they could justifiably retain profits as long as they could be invested in expansion projects promising rates of after-tax profit (most desirably estimated by the discounted cash flow method) of not less than 12.55 percent. With anticipated profits at or above that level, the directors could feel that the substitution of their judgment for the stockholders' investment judgment would do the stockholders no disservice. Their conclusion about the cost of retained earnings as a source of investment funds could be set out in formula form as follows.

(Formula 1)

$$\text{Cost of capital from retained earnings} = \frac{\text{Anticipated annual after-tax profits per share (without new projects)}}{(1 + \text{brokerage rate}) \times \text{market price per share}}.$$

Some theorists argue, however, that use of this formula results in an overstatement of the cost of retained profits. They argue that if the profits were paid out as dividends the stockholders' capacity to invest elsewhere would generally be much less than the amount of their dividend income. They would have to pay income taxes on the dividends—a cost to them likely to be much greater than the brokerage fees payable on investing the amounts left after the tax payments.

Suppose, for example, that a stockholder of the Speedwell Corporation receives dividends of $5,000 and that he must pay income taxes on these dividends at a rate of 40 percent (the marginal rate in the tax bracket to which the dividends must be allocated as additions to taxable income from all other sources). If he invests the remaining $3,000 elsewhere to earn a return of 12.55 percent,[3] his annual income on this investment will be $376.50. Accordingly, this stockholder ought to be just as well satisfied to have Speedwell retain the $5,000 and to earn on it an after-tax rate of profit of 7.53 percent, since this would also give him an annual return of $376.50 in the form of an increased ownership interest in the corporation. On the basis of this kind of evaluation of stockholders' positions, then, the formula given above would be modified as follows.

(Formula 2)

$$\text{Cost of capital from retained earnings} = \frac{\dfrac{\text{Anticipated annual after-tax profits per share (without new projects)}}{(1 + \text{brokerage rate}) \times \text{market price per share}}}{1 - \text{income tax rate applicable to dividends}}.$$

With assumptions of an income tax rate of 40 percent and brokerage fees at 2 percent, the formula for the individual stockholder illustrated would work out as follows.

$$\frac{\dfrac{\$3.20}{1.02 \times \$25}}{.60} = 7.53\%.$$

[3]The stockholder's investment would actually be less than $3,000 because of the brokerage fees he would pay, but these fees (assumed to amount to 2 percent) were already allowed for in the desired profit rate of 12.55 percent as computed by formula 1.

It is argued, therefore, that in deciding about profits retention corporate directors would generally be justified in bypassing formula 1 and choosing to base their decisions toward a more liberal retention policy primarily on formula 2 as filled in with estimates of average rates at which dividends would be taxed and average rates for the brokerage fees stockholders would have to pay on investment of their after-tax dividend income.

Problem of Taxes on Dividends. A major difficulty with estimates that try to assess the fate of stockholders who receive dividends is that the stockholders of the typical corporation whose stock is widely held are not a homogeneous group. The assumed average tax rate that the stockholders would have to pay on their dividends is especially likely to be unrealistic, no matter how much time is spent on estimating this average. Some stockholders may, indeed, be subject to a tax rate of 40 percent on the dividends they receive, but others, such as nonprofit institutions, are likely to have no taxes at all to pay on their allotments of dividends. Other stockholders may be in the lowest brackets of the income tax structure, while still others may be in the highest.

In reference to the Speedwell illustration, the nonprofit institutions and the low-bracket stockholders would suffer disadvantages were Speedwell to retain earnings to invest in projects promising rates of after-tax profit not much above 7.53 percent. On the other hand, the high-bracket people would suffer comparable harm were Speedwell to set a cutoff rate of 12.55 percent for retaining and investing profits—were it, in other words, to decide to pay out all after-tax profits as dividends unless expansion projects promising rates of profit at least equal to 12.55 percent were available. Even the assumption of brokerage fees at a set rate (in formula 1 as well as in formula 2) could affect some stockholders advantageously and others disadvantageously, since they would not all necessarily pay the same rate on investing dividend income. However, because brokerage rates are so much less than income tax rates (on stockholders who must pay income taxes) the minor inequities that an estimated average rate may occasion can generally be safely ignored.

Matter of Judgment. In view of the wide divergence among income tax rates that stockholders must pay on dividends received, decisions that corporate managers should reach on the cost of capital derived from retained earnings must be a matter of more or less arbitrary judgment. In almost all instances, they will surely be justified in deciding that the cost of retained profits is substantially less than the cost of capital derived from sales of additional common shares, as indicated by formula 1. In setting cutoff rates for new projects to be financed with retained profits, they would probably feel justified in going a reasonable distance below the rate determined by formula 1, but not so far as the rate determined by formula 2, and surely not below it. Perhaps a reasonable distance would be about half the way between—say 10 percent for Speedwell. Perhaps. In any event, mathematical analysis can give no answer.

Cash Throw-offs from Depreciation

An important source of cash for the typical corporation that already has a substantial quantity of depreciable fixed assets is the cash throw-offs from the periodical depreciation charges. If the corporation is able to cover these charges for wear and tear plus all other operating expenses in its sales to and cash collections from customers, the charges are obviously matched by cash inflows. For many corporations, indeed, cash throw-offs from depreciation are the most important source of funds available for new investment. Thus, there arises the question of the cost that should be attributed to cash so derived.

The most widely accepted answer appears to be that for cost of capital estimates, cash throw-offs from depreciation should be treated much the same as retained cash throw-offs from profits. Corporate directors have the choice of distributing the depreciation throw-offs to stockholders as dividends or using them for expansion projects, and a fair rule for this choice would presumably be that they ought not to use them for expansion projects unless they expect to earn a rate of after-tax profit at least equal to the amount the stockholders could earn through reinvestment of their net dividend income. With income taxes on the dividend income disregarded, but with the assumption that the stockholders would have to pay brokerage fees on reinvestment, this minimum rate of anticipated profit—and, therefore, the cost of capital to be attributed to depreciation throw-offs—would be as determined by formula 1.

But aside from stockholding nonprofit institutions, the stockholders would normally be required to pay income taxes on dividends received. Even though the dividends may appear to be a repayment to the stockholders of a portion of their investment in the corporation's common stock—so-called liquidating dividends—the usual rule of the taxing authorities is that if a corporation has sufficient earned surplus available its dividend payments will be regarded as distributions of accumulated earnings and therefore as taxable. Thus, the corporate directors might estimate the average rate of income tax that stockholders would have to pay and use this estimate, with one for average brokerage charges, to derive a cost of capital from formula 2. Realizing, however, that the range of tax rates imposed on dividends received by stockholders probably would vary widely, despite the estimated average rate, they might well decide that, as for retained profits, the attributed cost of capital should be placed somewhere between the results of the two formulas.

COST OF CAPITAL DERIVED FROM DEBT AND PREFERRED STOCK

Long-Term Debt as Source

Interest Costs and Tax Saving. The cost of capital directly attributable to borrowing can usually be determined quite simply. If a corporation sells at the par value of $100 a 25-year bond issue bearing interest at 6 percent a year payable annually,[4] the interest cost will be 6 percent. This may appear to be obvious, but actually it is not. The rate of the interest cost to the corporation is not necessarily the rate promised to the bondholders, since all the annual interest payments of $6 per $100 principal will be deferred for varying periods of time, and the principal itself will not have to be paid until the end of 25 years. And, as we saw in Chapter 13, allowance should always be made for the time value of money. The sum of $6 payable in 1 year or 5 years is worth less than $6 today, and $100 payable in 25 years is worth much less than $100 on hand today. Accordingly, the interest-cost rate should surely be found by the discounted cash flow method. In this instance, nevertheless, it will still turn out to be 6 percent per year.

Using the present value tables presented in Chapter 13, the student will find that the present value of a $6 annuity for 25 periods discounted at 6 percent per period is $76.70, and that the present value of $100 principal to be received at the end of 25 periods discounted at 6 percent per period is $23.30, for a total of $100. However, if the corporation were to sell the bonds at $95 per $100 of face amount the interest cost would be above 6 percent, since a discount rate in excess of 6 percent (approximately 6.4 percent) would have to be applied to the $6 annuity payable annually and to the $100 principal payable at maturity in order to arrive at a combined present value of $95. Similarly, the interest cost would be less than 6 percent (about 5.6 percent) if the bonds were sold at, say, $105 per $100 of face amount.

But the interest rate as found by the discounted cash flow method is not to be taken as the cost of capital if it is to be compared with rates of after-tax profit anticipated on expansion projects. Since interest costs are treated as deductible expenses in income tax determination, they must also be taken on an after-tax basis for a comparison of this kind. If, then, the corporation of the foregoing illustration sells its 6 percent bonds at $100 and if it is subject to an income tax

---

[4]Although interest on corporate bonds is almost always made payable semianually, annual payment is assumed here to avoid complexities that could be a source of misunderstanding.

rate of 50 percent, its cost of capital derived from its long-term borrowing is 3 percent.

Equity Element. One might conclude, therefore, that the managers of this corporation could mark as acceptable all investment projects promising rates of after-tax profits in excess of 3 percent, provided only that financing of the projects would come from the proceeds of the bond issue. For the managers, however, such a conclusion probably would be quite erroneous! They ought to realize that a corporation's borrowing capacity is dependent in a very important way on the quantity and quality of the equity contributed by the common stockholders. Prospective lenders generally demand a cushion of protection supplied by the common stockholders. They want to be protected by claims on the earning power and value of assets contributed by the common stockholders in addition to claims on the earning power and value of the assets that they themselves contribute. Thus, it is reasonable to hold that an *equity element* must be attributed to virtually all kinds and amounts of debt financing by business corporations.

What this element should or will be for the individual corporation depends on such factors as the competence of its directors and officers, the stability of its earnings record, the general prospects of the industry of which it is a part, and the customary patterns of financing in this industry. If, for example, prospective investors in the 6 percent bonds referred to earlier were to demand that the corporation have a dollar of common stock equity for every dollar of long-term debt, its cost of capital derived from the bond issue would seem to be clearly the weighted average of the cost of the bond financing (3 percent) and the cost of equity financing. Assuming the estimated cost of equity to be 12 percent, such a weighted average would be found as follows.

	Cost of Capital	*Weights**	*Cost × Weights*
Bond financing...........	.03	50	1.50
Common stock equity.....	.12	50	6.00
Total..............		100	7.50
Weighted average: 7.50 ÷ 100 = .075 or 7.5%			

*Percentages of combined bond and common stock sources.

In a similar way, were the prospective investors in bonds to demand the protection of $1.50 of common stock equity for each dollar of long-term debt (a 60–40 ratio), the weighted average would be computed as follows.

	Cost of Capital	*Weights*	*Cost × Weights*
Bond financing...........	.03	40	1.20
Common stock equity.....	.12	60	7.20
Total..............		100	8.40
Weighted average: 8.40 ÷ 100 = .084 or 8.4%			

Thus, one would conclude that the corporation's managers ought to reject all expansion projects expected to yield rates of after-tax profit of less than 7.5 percent in the first instance and less than 8.4 percent in the second, despite that the immediate source of financing would be the bond issue, which has a recognized cost of only 3 percent.

Special Circumstances. While the validity of the procedure of weighting the cost of financing with an attributed cost of equity, as just described, can hardly be questioned in its general aspects, one can think of exceptional circumstances that would justify approval of projects with expected rates of profit that fall short of the weighted averages. Assume, for example, that our illustrative corporation knows it can borrow long term on a 50–50 basis but it has no long-term debt now outstanding. It would be able to borrow at a cost of 3 percent up to the amount of its existing common stock equity, and it would not need to add a single dollar to that equity to effect this borrowing. In borrowing, it would be moving toward its optimum position at 50–50, and until this point was reached—until the time when further long-term borrowing would require additional common stock equity—the common stockholders would surely gain advantages through the acceptance of projects promising rates of after-tax profits as low as, say, 4 or 5 percent. Decisions in this direction, however, would depend on considerations such as the duration of the low-rate projects and the possibilities that better profit opportunities would turn up in the near future. And this, in turn, would mean that reasonable judgments would still have to be made—that the results of analytical mathematical techniques would need, as always, careful interpretation and wise application.

Preferred Stock as Source

Because the holders of a corporation's preferred stock have ownership interests rather than claims as creditors, one may have expected an analysis of the cost of capital derived from preferred stock to immediately follow the discussion of the cost of capital contributed by common stockholders. However, for business corporations collectively, preferred stock is much less important than long-term debt as a source of funds, and for many corporations it is not a source at all, since they do not issue it.

Unlike common stocks, almost all preferred stocks promise dividends at specified annual rates, and unlike bonds, preferred stocks have no maturity dates. In the matter of income tax treatment, dividends on preferred stock, unlike interest on bonds, are not generally deductible in tax computations, so there is no tax saving. For a 7 percent preferred stock salable to investors at the par value of, say, $100, the cost of the derived capital would appear to be 7 percent. This is the discount rate that would give $100 as the present value of an annuity of annual $7 dividend payments of unlimited duration (a perpetuity). But because buyers of preferred stocks, like bond buyers, demand a cushion of protection in the form of common stock equity, corporate managers must generally allow for a *common stock equity element* in determining the cost of capital derived from preferred stock. Assume, for example, that a corporation's managers decide that the optimum ratio for preferred stock to the common stock equity is 1 to 3, and that they estimate the cost of capital from common stock equity at 12 percent. They are now selling at par value an issue of 7 percent preferred stock, and they therefore decide that the cost of the capital thus being acquired is a weighted average derived as follows.

	Cost of Capital	*Weights**	*Cost × Weights*
Preferred stock financing...	.07	1	.07
Common stock equity.....	.12	3	.36
Total.................		4	.43
Weighted average: .43 ÷ 4 = .1075 or 10.75%			

*Proportions of preferred stock and common stock equity to total stock sources.

Short-Term Borrowing as Source

Because cost of capital estimates are chiefly made for judgments about the feasibility and desirability of acquiring additional fixed assets that will have lengthy useful lives, they are usually confined to the probable costs of long-term funds. Investments in new fixed assets are customarily financed from long-term sources. Nevertheless, the costs of short-term borrowing cannot be wholly ignored. Short-term borrowing is often depended on to finance early or preliminary outlays required for the acquisition of given types and quantities of fixed assets, often with expectations that this borrowing will be repaid from the proceeds of the later bond or stock issues that will be the principal and ultimate source of financing. Not infrequently, too, intermediate-term projects are financed throughout their lives by funds borrowed on short-term bases with lenders' understandings that the loans will be renewed annually for, say, four or five years. Much more important, however, is the fact, as recognized in Chapter 13, that expanded operations to be made possible by fixed asset acquisitions usually demand expansions in current assets as well. And anticipations may well be that short-term borrowing will be depended on to finance in whole or in part the necessary additional current assets.

However, to admit that the costs of short-term funds must be considered does not necessarily mean that they must be included in some sort of weighted average with the costs of retained earnings, long-term borrowing, and so on. In most instances, indeed, it will be found to be most advantageous not to include them in this way, but rather to allow for their influence in what may be called a supplementary way. For example, a fixed asset acquisition proposal might be found to be quite attractive on the basis of forecasts of the annual rate of after-tax profit it would yield and estimates of the cost of long-term funds to be invested, but this attractiveness might be reduced or even eliminated because of high rates of interest that would have to be paid on the short-term borrowing needed for additions to current assets. Or, on the other hand, the fixed asset acquisition might be made all the more attractive because of the availability of short-term funds on quite favorable terms.

Whatever may be the procedure for considering the prospective costs of short-term funds, they must surely be estimated as accurately as possible. If, for example, a bank agrees to grant a 1-year loan of $100,000 on a 6 percent discount basis, the borrowing corporation should recognize that the interest cost to it will be 6.383 percent. (As it would be paying $6,000 in interest on an advance of $94,000, the interest cost would be $6,000/$94,000.) Likewise, it should recognize that the interest cost would be materially higher, stated as a rate, should the bank require it to maintain a minimum balance in its deposit account equal to a certain proportion of the loan while it was outstanding. Were the minimum-balance requirement 20 percent of the face amount of the loan, the interest cost would amount to a rate of 8.11 percent ($6,000/$74,000).

Moreover, it is usually advisable to allow for an equity element in the cost of short-term borrowing, since an important determinant of short-term borrowing capacity, as of long term, is the cushion of protection provided by the stockholders' investment in the corporation. And, on the other hand, when the costs of borrowed short-term funds are to be compared with rates of after-tax profit expected to be earned from their investment, they should be reduced for the tax saving to be expected on account of their deductibility as expenses in income tax determination.

COMPOSITE COST OF CAPITAL

Assuming the accuracy of forecasts of project costs, salvage values, sales, costs of sales, and income taxes, it should ordinarily be possible for business managers to make accurate decisions on the profitability of proposed expansion projects by direct reference to the source or sources of the funds to be invested and to their costs as determined by the procedures discussed in this chapter. This means, of course, that they would make allowances for equity elements in both short- and long-term borrowing, for a common stock equity element in preferred stock financing, and for brokerage fees and individual income taxes that stockholders would have to pay on earnings and cash throw-offs from depreciation paid out as dividends rather than retained. But for long-term investment in fixed assets especially, business managers are likely to find particularly helpful in their decision making a composite rate for the costs of their long-term funds collectively. This proposition is not really a new one, since it simply says that the managers will surely find it advantageous to have a cutoff rate, as referred to repeatedly in Chapter 13—a composite rate that prompts them to give little attention to proposed projects that promise rates of after-tax profits short of this cost rate and to concentrate attention on those that promise rates of after-tax profits above it.

Such a composite rate should not be difficult to compute, since it must simply be an average of the rates of cost of all sources of long-term financing, with the cost rate of each source weighted by the quantitative position of that source in the corporation's capital structure. As always, it must be forward-looking. The rates of cost must be those that would be incurred on *new* issues of common stock, preferred stock, and bonds, and those that could reasonably be attributed to cash throw-offs from profits and depreciation *now* to be reinvested within the corporation rather than to be paid out as dividends. Likewise, *expected* after-tax profits must be the criterion for determining ratios of profits to the current market prices of the corporation's securities and to prospective interest and dividend rates, as it has been the criterion throughout this chapter. Moreover, the quantitative position of each long-term source of funds should be, not necessarily what the corporation has for this source at the moment, but what it wants that position to be in an optimum capital structure.

To illustrate, assume that the managers of a certain corporation decide that long-term sources of funds should be tapped in the following proportions for an optimum structure: common stock, 20 percent; retained earnings and accumulated allowances for depreciation, 15 percent each; preferred stock, 10 percent; and long-term debt, 40 percent. And let us further assume that estimated costs of capital attributed to these sources—as determined specifically by mathematical formulas or as attributed on the basis of judgments that modify formula results—are as follows: common stock, 16 percent; retained earnings and accumulated allowances for depreciation, 10 percent; preferred stock, 7 percent; and long-term borrowing, 3 percent. The composite cost of capital would then be determined as follows.

	Cost of Capital	*Weights**	*Cost × Weights*
Common stock	.16	20	3.20
Retained earnings	.10	15	1.50
Accumulated depreciation allowances	.10	15	1.50
Preferred stock	.07	10	.70
Long-term debt	.03	40	1.20
Total		100	8.10

Composite cost of long-term capital: 8.10 ÷ 100 = .081 or 8.1%

*Percentages of individual sources to total long-term sources.

QUESTIONS

1. In the estimation of costs of capital to business corporations, why is so much emphasis given to the cost of their common stockholders' investment?

2. For estimates of the cost of funds to be derived from sales of common stock, what weight should be given to past profits? Current profits? Expected future profits without allowance for additions from new projects? Expected future profits with such additions?

3. For estimates of the cost of funds to be derived from sales of common stock, what weight should be given to the market price of common shares already outstanding? The probable price at which additional common shares could be sold? Is there likely to be any difference between these two prices? Why or why not?

4. For estimates of the cost of funds to be derived from sales of common stock, what weight should be given to the number of shares already outstanding? To the number of shares that would have to be issued to finance proposed projects?

5. What role should be assigned to earnings per share of common stock in decision making about the acceptability of new projects to be financed by sales of additional common shares?

6. For the determination of profit rates needed on new projects to justify investing retained earnings in them, what weight should be assigned to anticipated after-tax profits per share without the new projects? With the new projects? To the market price of outstanding common shares? To the price at which new common shares could be sold? To brokerage fees? To the income tax rates that common stockholders would have to pay on dividends?

7. For the determination of earnings rates needed on new projects to justify investing retained earnings in them, why is it especially difficult to make allowance for the income tax rates that common stockholders would have to pay on dividends?

8. Why is it said that assignment of a cost of capital rate to retained earnings is a matter of judgment? Does this mean that conclusions reached by way of mathematical formulas are of no consequence? Explain.

9. What justification is there for concluding that cash throw-offs from depreciation should be treated like retained earnings in cost of capital estimation? Do you agree? Discuss.

10. Why is it said that the cost of capital derived from the sale of a long-term bond issue is not necessarily the interest rate promised to the bond buyers? What bearing do income taxes have in the assignment of a cost of capital rate to financing by bond issues?

11. What is meant by the allocation of an equity element to the cost of capital derived from bond issues? How is this allocation supposed to be made?

12. Why are preferred stock issues as a source of funds treated so differently from common stock equity in cost of capital estimation?

13. For considerations about the prospective profitability of long-term investment projects, why is the cost of short-term loan funds often important? What bearing does each of the following have on the cost of short-term loan funds: the discount procedure in bank lending, minimum balance requirements, equity element, and tax saving?

14. What objective is served by computing a composite cost of capital rate for a corporation's sources of long-term funds? How is such a composite rate determined? In what sense, if any, is it an optimum rate?

PROBLEMS

1. Zeller & Best, Inc. has outstanding 250,000 shares of common stock with a par value of $5 and a current market value of $42 a share. For the past 3 years, the corporation's average after-tax earnings per share have amounted to $6.30, and it is anticipated that for the current year they will rise to $6.50.

On the basis of the formulas presented and analyzed in this chapter, what cost of capital rate should Zeller & Best's financial officers attribute to common stock equity funds, assuming:

a) That expansion projects would have to be financed by sales of additional shares of common stock, that up to 150,000 shares could be sold at $36 a share, and that without investment in expansion projects annual after-tax earnings per share would be expected to stabilize at around $6.80 in the near future?

b) That expansion projects would have to be financed by sales of additional common shares and that up to 150,000 shares could be sold at $36 a share, but that without investment in a certain project that would cost $3,600,000 annual after-tax earnings per share would drop to about $5.50?

What cost of capital rate should the financial officers attribute to retained earnings on the assumption:

c) That the stockholders would have to pay average brokerage fees of 2 percent on the reinvestment of whatever dividends they might receive from the corporation?

d) That the stockholders would have to pay income taxes at an estimated average rate of 30 percent on dividends received from the corporation, together with average brokerage fees of 2 percent on the investment of their after-tax dividend income?

What cost of capital rate should they assign to cash throw-offs from depreciation on the basis of the assumptions stated in (*d*)?

2. On the basis of the conclusions reached in this chapter, including conclusions about equity elements, and assuming that the income tax rate where applicable is 50 percent, what would be the cost of capital rate on funds derived:

a) From a 20-year, 7 percent bond issue sold at par value, with the additional assumptions that bond buyers demand $1.50 of common stockholders' equity for each dollar of bonds, and that the corporation's estimated cost of capital rate for equity funds is 12.5 percent?

b) From an issue of preferred stock that has a dividend rate of 8 percent, with the additional assumptions that buyers of the preferred stock demand $3 of common stockholders' equity for each dollar of their investment, and that the corporation attributes to its common stock equity a cost rate of 12.5 percent?

c) From short-term, 1-year bank loans discounted at 6 percent in advance and subject to a minimum balance rule of 15 percent of the face amount, and with the additional assumptions that the lending bank demands a cushion of protection of $2 of common stock equity for each dollar of loan proceeds, and that the corporation attributes to its common stock equity a cost rate of 14 percent?

3. For the consideration of expansion projects that promise varying rates of after-tax profit, what cutoff rate would be appropriate for a corporation whose directors and officers conclude that the optimum proportions of long-term funds to be derived from the several usual sources and the cost of capital rates to be attributed to these sources are as follows.

	Proportion as Percentage of Total	*Percentage Cost Rate*
Common stock	10	17
Retained earnings	30	13
Accumulated depreciation allowances	20	13
Long-term debt	30	4
Preferred stock	10	7

Part V

FINANCIAL STRUCTURE

chapter 15

SIMPLE COMMON STOCK STRUCTURES

Financial management is as much concerned with the control of liabilities and stockholders' equity as with the control of assets. Since liabilities and stockholders' equity are sources of assets, these two aspects of financial management are inextricably interrelated. Decisions must be made about the kinds and amounts of assets that must be acquired and maintained, but such decisions require complementary ones about the sources from which the assets will be sought. Success in management requires not only a judicious selection and administration of assets; it requires a judicious selection of sources. A corporation that appears to have the right kinds and amounts of assets may run, nevertheless, into serious financial difficulties in periods of general business contraction, because it has depended too heavily on creditors to supply the assets. It may find itself top-heavy with debt. On the other hand, a corporation that has made serious errors in the acquisition and administration of assets may be saved from bankruptcy if its liability management has been wise. A corporation may suffer losses year after year because of poor asset management and yet survive long enough for the correction of its mistakes if creditors' claims have been held to a manageable minimum and if, therefore, most of the assets have been supplied by stockholders. For stockholders, as a rule, are much more willing than are creditors to await the correction of mistakes.

The liabilities and stockholders' equity of a business corporation, as the sources of its assets, constitute its financial structure or capital structure. Accordingly, the management of liabilities and stockholders' equity is the building of financial or capital structures. The objective of sound liability and equity management is to erect and maintain forms of financial structure—various combinations of amounts and types of liabilities and equity items—best suited to the circumstances of individual corporations. In working toward this objective, decisions are required, in the first place, on what proportion of the assets can appropriately be sought from creditors and what remaining proportion, therefore, must be obtained from stockholders. For assets to be sought from creditors, further decisions are necessary on the proportions that should be sought for short, intermediate, and long terms, respectively, and on the classes of creditors (trade suppliers, commercial banks, other kinds of lenders, and so on) to whom requests should go. Other decisions are required on whether owners' contributions to assets—the *equity* contributions—are to be sought from stockholders of only one class or of two or more classes, as buyers of common stock and buyers of preferred stock. And, finally, decisions are needed about the extent to which equity contributions by way of accumulation of profits can or should be depended on.

Another way of looking at liability and equity management is to say that it is concerned with "financing"—a term that was defined in Chapter 4.[1] When decisions have been made about the sources from which assets will be sought, financing comes into the picture as the actual procedure whereby the sources are reached and tapped. Some selected sources may turn out to be sterile, so that if financing is to be carried through successfully it must go off in a different direction. At any rate, decisions about sources, whether first choices or alternatives, and the actual tapping of these sources in financing determine the shape of financial structures. If less desirable sources must be reached because more desirable ones are not fruitful, the presumption is that the resulting financial structures, at least in the minds of the financial managers, are not so good as the more desirable choices would have made them.

In first taking up the matter of liability and equity management, we need a general view of the principles that govern the building of sound financial structures. A survey of principles is, therefore, the primary objective of this chapter and Chapter 16. Having a general knowledge of principles, we can then proceed safely, beginning with Chapter 17, to discuss in detail how common stock, preferred stock, accumulated profits, bonds, and other instruments are fitted into, arranged, and rearranged in financial structures—how, in other words, these are used as means of financing. An immediate examination of numerous details concerning instruments of finance and their uses, without a set of unifying principles for guidance, may appear to be quite aimless. That is a kind of danger we hope to avoid.

SCOPE OF SIMPLE COMMON STOCK STRUCTURES

The form of financial structure most favored by the managers of American business corporations is the simple common stock structure.

---

[1]See p. 69.

Such a preference is evidenced by the very large proportion of corporations that have this type of structure, including (as of early 1968) American Motors, Freeport Sulphur, Johns-Manville, Libbey-Owens-Ford, Minnesota Mining & Manufacturing, Stewart-Warner, and Zenith Radio. Its popularity is further indicated by its frequent description as the ideal form for industrial corporations, the broad class that includes all those in manufacturing, mining and quarrying, construction, wholesale and retail trade, and the service industries. However, the proposition is undoubtedly somewhat exaggerated, since what is ideal for the individual corporation depends most importantly on its peculiar circumstances. The exaggeration is clearly demonstrated by the experience of many highly successful industrial corporations that have from time to time, or apparently permanently, departed from this form of structure. Nevertheless, high esteem for the simple common stock structure can scarcely be denied.

Nature of Simple Common Stock Structures

A corporation is said to have a simple common stock structure when all its assets, other than those supplied by short-term creditors, have been contributed by its common stockholders. In a negative sense, it may be said that such a corporation does not use as means of financing preferred stock, bonds, intermediate- or long-term bank loans, or other forms of intermediate- or long-term debt.

The contribution of the common stockholders to assets can be made by various routes, and not simply in the original purchase of stock. The aggregate of their contributions will ordinarily be indicated in the balance sheet, therefore, by one or more surplus accounts in addition to the common stock account itself. But let us look at this matter in some detail.

Contributions of the Common Stockholders

For most corporations, the contributions of common stockholders to assets go at least moderately beyond the par or stated value of the stock they have acquired, as indicated by the amounts that appear on their books or in their balance sheets as capital stock or common stock. For many, indeed, the contributions far exceed the par or stated value.

Premiums and Donations. For one thing, at the time of its original issue by the corporation, buyers of common stock may pay more for it than the par or stated value. They may pay an amount equal to a substantial multiple of the par or stated value, as indicated in Table 15–1, which lists some early 1968 offerings of common stock to the general public. Note particularly the frequency of extremely wide spreads between par values and offering prices. The excess payments by investors in common stocks may be carried in surplus accounts called premium on common stock or, more popularly, in accounts labeled capital surplus. But regardless of the label, it is obvious that the account represents an additional contribution to assets by the common stock buyers.

TABLE 15–1
Some Public Offerings of Common Stock, January-July, 1968

Corporation	*Month*	*Number of Shares*	*Par Value*	*Offering Price*
Microwave Associates, Inc.	January	121,872	$ 1.00	$36.50
Seaway Food Town, Inc.	February	145,000	No par	18.25
Puget Sound Power & Light Company	February	360,000	10.00	34.00
Nationwide Industries, Inc.	March	200,000	.10	13.75
R.F. Communications, Inc.	March	100,000	.05	36.75
The Southland Corporation	April	833,623	.01	24.50
United Dollar Stores, Inc.	May	259,144	1.00	18.00
Ventron Corporation	June	268,063	5.00	68.50
Budget Industries, Inc.	July	180,000	.50	15.75

SOURCE: *The Wall Street Journal.*

Again, common stockholders may donate cash or other property to their corporations. Such action by stockholders is by no means uncommon. It is likely to be encountered especially in family corporations where, for example, a man may make a contribution with full assurance that it can benefit only himself, his wife, and his children because they are the only stockholders. The value of the property donated may be shown on the books and in the balance sheet as donated surplus, or, like the premium mentioned above, it may be included in capital surplus. Whatever it is called, however, it obviously represents a stockholder contribution to assets.

Accumulated Profits. However, by far, the greatest contribution made to assets by the generality of common stockholders beyond the par or stated value of their stock comes from the accumulation of profits. In the years since the close of World War II, as is indicated in Table 15–2, American corporations collectively have distributed cash dividends to their stockholders equal to only about 44 percent of their profits after taxes; thus, profits plowed under have been an enormous source of additional net assets to these corporations.[2]

Although it is sometimes said that corporate profits, whether distributed or not, belong to the stockholders, the fact is that the expanded net assets that retained profits represent, like all corporate assets, belong to the corporations themselves as distinct entities.

[2]The term *net assets* means the difference between total assets and the total of obligations to creditors. Accordingly, net assets are always increased through the retention of profits, whether the profits are the means of actually acquiring additional assets or the means of paying off debts.

Nevertheless, retained profits most certainly give the stockholders an additional claim against the assets—a claim over and above that measured by the par of stated value of their stock. Any claim to assets is simultaneously a source of assets; accordingly, the stockholders are unquestionably the contributors of the additional net assets acquired by way of retained profits.

TABLE 15–2
Corporate Profits and Dividends, 1946–67
(Dollar amounts in billions)

Year	*Profits after Income Taxes**	*Dividends*	*Retained Profits*	*Percentage Retained*
1946	$ 15.5	$ 5.6	$ 9.9	63.9
1947	20.2	6.3	13.9	68.8
1948	22.7	7.0	15.6	68.7
1949	18.5	7.2	11.3	61.1
1950	24.9	8.8	16.0	64.3
1951	21.6	8.6	13.0	60.2
1952	19.6	8.6	11.0	56.1
1953	20.4	8.9	11.5	56.4
1954	20.6	9.3	11.3	54.9
1955	27.0	10.5	16.5	61.1
1956	27.2	11.3	15.9	58.5
1957	26.0	11.7	14.2	54.6
1958	22.3	11.6	10.8	48.4
1959	28.5	12.6	15.9	55.8
1960	26.7	13.4	13.2	49.4
1961	27.2	13.8	13.5	49.6
1962	31.2	15.2	16.0	51.3
1963	33.1	16.5	16.6	50.2
1964	38.4	17.8	20.6	53.6
1965	45.2	19.8	25.4	56.2
1966	49.3	21.5	27.8	56.4
1967	47.5	22.8	24.7	52.0
Total	$613.6	$268.8	$344.6	56.2

*In some instances, dividends and retained profits do not add exactly to profits after income taxes because of rounding.

SOURCES: U.S. Department of Commerce, Office of Business Economics, *The National Product Accounts of the United States 1929–1965* (Washington, D.C.: U.S. Government Printing Office, 1966), p. 15; and *Federal Reserve Bulletin*, June, 1968, p. A–47. (Percentages and totals supplied by the author.)

In their books and balance sheets, corporations customarily show stockholders' claims on account of accumulated retained profits as earned surplus or simply as surplus. The simple designation *surplus* is often used especially when there are no other surplus accounts, the implication being that surplus necessarily means accumulated profits unless there is a designation to the contrary. However, many corporations use the designation *earned surplus* even when there are no other surplus accounts.

Surplus Reserves. Sometimes, accumulated retained profits are disguised under titles such as "reserve for working capital," "reserve for contingencies," and "reserve for plant expansion." A transfer is made from the earned surplus account to one or more of these surplus reserves, as they are called, but the transfer obviously has no effect on the actual amount of accumulated profits. It likewise has no effect on the stockholders' claims on assets, or, to put the same idea in different words, the contribution to assets that they have actually made.

The principal reason for the setting up of surplus reserves is to indicate to stockholders that the directors have no intention of using these portions of accumulated profits as a basis for dividend payments. In ordering a transfer from earned surplus to a reserve for working capital, for example, the directors say, in effect: we cannot pay dividends of this amount because cash must be retained for current operations. Equally, a transfer to a reserve for plant expansion is intended to mean: we cannot pay dividends of this amount because we must use some of our available cash for further investment in facilities.

Size of Surplus Accounts. In summary, then, a corporation that is described as having a simple common stock structure may have one or many accounts to indicate that the common stockholders have made contributions to assets slightly, moderately, or vastly in excess of the contribution shown in the common stock account itself. It is remarkable, indeed, that American business corporations collectively have much larger totals in their surplus accounts than in their common stock accounts. Thus, on federal income tax returns for fiscal years ending between July 1, 1964, and June 30, 1965, $503,405 million of total stockholders' equity was reported by 1,373,517 active corporations in all areas of business activity. Of this, $158,120 million was recorded in capital stock accounts and the balance of $345,285 million in surplus accounts. The surplus figure comprised $95,536 million of paid-in or capital surplus, $18,689 million of surplus reserves, and $231,060 million of earned surplus.[3] Accordingly, capital stock (common and preferred are not separately reported by the Internal Revenue Service) amounted to 31.4 percent of total stockholders' equity, paid-in or capital surplus amounted to 19 percent, surplus reserves to 3.7 percent, and earned surplus to 45.9 percent, for a total surplus proportion of 68.6 percent. It should be of further interest to mention that for the corporations referred to, total liabilities and equity amounted to $1,585,619 million, so that as a source of funds stockholders' equity amounted to 31.7 percent of total sources.

Although surplus balances are rightly regarded by a great majority of corporations as measuring asset contributions of their common stockholders, it should be mentioned that in some instances preferred

---

[3]U.S. Treasury Department, Internal Revenue Service, *Statistics of Income, 1964—U.S. Business Tax Returns* (Washington, D.C.: U.S. Government Printing Office, 1967), p. 107.

stockholders also make such contributions, such as by buying their stock at premium prices or by making donations. It is reasonable to hold, also, that such contributions are made by preferred stockholders when corporations have sufficient profits to pay prescribed dividends on their preferred stocks but choose to defer their payment for periods of varying lengths. However, contributions to assets by preferred stockholders as measured by balances in surplus accounts do not necessarily give them claims against assets of equal amount. For example, the original sale of preferred stock at a premium does not, of itself, entitle the preferred stockholder to a premium if the stock is subsequently called for redemption. That depends on the terms of the contracts between corporations and their preferred stockholders.[4]

Short-Term Debts

Although a corporation that maintains a simple common stock structure has as its only long-term source of assets the contributions made by its common stockholders—whatever avenues these may take—it may depend rather heavily on outside sources of short-term financing. It is likely to welcome opportunities to buy goods and services on account, and it would hardly pay its employees from day to day, so that it will ordinarily have a continuous liability for accrued payroll. It will surely refrain from paying taxes until approximately their due dates, so that it will usually be carrying a liability for accrued taxes, and it may depend on commercial banks or other financial institutions for short-term working capital loans, especially if its operations are subject to rather substantial seasonal fluctuations. If such a corporation has little or nothing in the way of fixed assets, the owners of its common stock may be the suppliers of hardly more than half of the total (current) assets. They would hardly provide much less than half, in view of the devotion of trade suppliers, bankers, and other short-term creditors to the 2 to 1 standard for working capital, as discussed in Chapter 14. On the other hand, if such a corporation has a large volume of fixed assets, a proportion of total assets much greater than 50 percent will necessarily have been contributed by the common stockholders—all the fixed assets plus, it is to be expected, at least half of the amount of the current assets.

ADVANTAGES OF SIMPLE COMMON STOCK STRUCTURES

The advantages and disadvantages of simple common stock structures (as well as of other forms of financial structure to be discussed in Chapter 16) may best be considered from the standpoint of the welfare of existing common stockholders. The boards of directors and

[4]The scope of preferred stockholders' claims against corporate assets is discussed below, pp. 576–78.

executive officers of most business corporations are often said to be common stock-minded, by which is meant they seek in every possible way to advance the interests of the common stockholders. This does not mean that the welfare of employees, customers, creditors, and others is neglected, for neglect of this kind could be expected in most circumstances to work out to the quite serious disadvantage of the common stockholders. What is meant, therefore, is that where a choice among alternative policies can be made, those that promise rather clear advantages for the common stockholders will almost invariably be selected in preference to those whose prospective advantages to the common stockholders are less significant or less certain. Since common stockholders usually have the exclusive or predominant voice in the election of directors, and since the directors, in turn, choose the executive officers, concern for the welfare of common stockholders is not difficult to understand.

From the standpoint of the welfare of common stockholders, then, a simple common stock structure promises advantages of the following kinds: (1) protection of the corporation's solvency, (2) maintenance of a good credit standing, (3) reservation of financing capacity for times of pressing need, and (4) avoidance of restrictions on managerial discretion. Although these advantages tend to overlap somewhat, we should find it enlightening to examine them individually.

Protection of Solvency

However strong the profit motives of corporations may be, they can never wisely be permitted to take precedence over safety. Safety means solvency—the capacity of the corporation to meet its obligations as they come due. Tens of thousands of corporations launched with enthusiasm, many with great promise, have failed because their managers neglected to protect their solvency.

Solvency is promoted by simple common stock structures, because common stockholders themselves ordinarily have no legal rights to demand cash payments from their corporations. The corporation has no obligation to pay cash dividends, nor does it have, at any time, an obligation to redeem the stock at its par or stated value. Thus, all the assets that common stockholders contribute to their corporations are held without offsetting claims that must be paid in cash at stipulated times. If cash is in short supply, therefore, it can be conserved to pay current operating expenses and to meet current liabilities.

This advantage is especially important in times of severe contractions in general business activity when the inflow of cash from operations tends to be seriously reduced. Corporations that have cumulative preferred stock issues in their financial structures often decide, despite financial strain, to continue the payment of current dividends, but they thereby weaken their capacity later to pay interest and principal on their debts. And corporations that have bond issues or other forms of intermediate- or long-term debt (fixed liabilities) *must* pay interest and maturing installments of the principal in bad times as well as in good if they are to remain safely in operation.

The consequences of nonpayment of debts are usually disastrous for common stockholders. By legal processes, all the assets may be seized and sold by creditors for the satisfaction of their claims, and because the sale takes place in demoralized markets often nothing at all is left for the common stockholders. Frequently, indeed, the sale yields much less than is necessary to satisfy the creditors' claims. Or nonpayment may lead to an expensive, time-consuming procedure of reorganization, in the course of which the claims of the common stockholders are likely to be drastically cut down or even entirely eliminated.

Nevertheless, simple common stock structures do not guarantee solvency. Many corporations with financial structures of this kind have failed. Current liabilities must still be paid. But it is clear that the chances of survival must be much greater for corporations whose assets have been supplied preponderantly by common stockholders to whom no current payments need be made than for corporations in like operating circumstances that have depended on long-term creditors for much of their assets—creditors to whom interest and principal payments must continue.

Maintenance of a Good Credit Standing

As a rule, corporations that have simple common stock structures have higher credit ratings than do those of comparable size, scope of operations, and managerial competence that have preferred stock or bonds or other forms of fixed liabilities in their financial structures. Trade suppliers, bankers approached for short-term loans, and other prospective short-term creditors expect their corporate debtors to conserve cash in difficult times by suspending the payment of dividends on common stock, but they know that interest payments and contractual payments on the principal of intermediate- and long-term debt cannot be suspended without grave danger to their own claims. They may suspect, moreover, that corporations with preferred stocks in their structures will try to maintain dividend payments on these, thereby using cash that might better be conserved for meeting their claims. Directors might feel that nonpayment of preferred dividends would reflect unfavorably on the credit standing of their corporations, since it would be a confession of cash shortage; yet, the payment, as indicated, might offend creditors and prospective creditors. Thus, some weakening of credit standing apparently results from the very existence of preferred stock in financial structures, whether or not dividends are currently being paid on it.

Even in good times, the credit standing of corporations with preferred stocks or fixed debts or both in their financial structures is likely to be somewhat inferior to that of corporations of comparable position that have simple common stock structures. Although both classes of corporations may meet their obligations to short-term creditors with ease in good times, prospective creditors can be expected to keep in mind what might happen to their claims should business conditions deteriorate suddenly. Such a consideration must generally lead them to prefer the corporations with the simpler structures.

Reservation of Financing Capacity

Corporations that maintain simple common stock structures are ordinarily in a much better position to tap additional sources of assets than are those of comparable circumstances that have already tapped several sources. Sometimes, therefore, the first may be able to take advantage of expansion opportunities not readily accessible to the second. For one thing, additional sales of common stock at good prices should be somewhat easier for the corporations with the simple structures. In times of prosperity, when investor interest in almost all kinds of common stocks is high, the common stocks of these corporations are likely to be more attractive than those of corporations that have more complex structures. Prospective buyers are well aware of the prior claims of long-term debt and preferred stocks to interest and dividend payments, as well as to principal payments—that is, their prior claims to assets.

Even in times of contractions in general business activity, the corporation that has a simple common stock structure is likely to find itself favorably situated to undertake further financing, should it want to do so. In such a period, it might want to take advantage of reduced costs of construction and relatively low prices of machinery and equipment. The market for additional common stock at a good price might, indeed, be quite poor, but its prospects for selling a new issue of preferred stock on favorable terms would surely be much better than for corporations that already have preferred stock or bonds or both outstanding. And its prospects for selling a bond issue on attractive terms would likely be far superior to those of corporations of comparable size, scope of operations, and managerial competence that already have preferred stock or bonds or both in their financial structures.

The reservation of financing capacity is sometimes said to be a retention of the best security for later issue. In this sense, the best security is understood to be the one that will continue to be attractive to investors even in bad times. In periods of depression, investor interest in common stocks, and in most new issues of preferred stock as well, is almost surely at a low ebb. But unless the financial markets are completely demoralized, as in depressions of greatest severity, it is likely to be sustained in bonds for whose safety ample assurances can be given. Although using a bond issue to finance expansion would ordinarily be looked on as anything but the best for a corporation whose management is devoted to a simple common stock structure, such financing might still be acceptable on a temporary basis. The corporate managers might anticipate a sale of common stock later, when buoyancy had been restored to the market, the proceeds of the sale to be used to retire the bond issue. Or they might make the bonds convertible into common stock at the option of the holder in the expectation that when good levels of common stock prices had been restored in the market, wholesale conversions would take place.

Avoidance of Restrictions on Managerial Discretion

When corporations issue preferred stocks or incur long-term debts, as by selling bonds or borrowing directly from banks and other lenders, they must generally agree to some limitations on their freedom of action. These limitations come into force through various kinds of protective provisions that buyers of security issues and lenders require to be included in their contracts. Typical of such protective provisions are limits placed on dividend payments to common stockholders, payment of salaries and bonuses to executive officers, sales of fixed assets, additional borrowing, pledging (or further pledging) of assets, merging or consolidating with other corporations, retirement of preferred stock (as for the specific protection of bondholders), and purchase by the corporations of shares of their own outstanding common stock. Other stipulations are that working capital ratios will not be permitted to fall below stated levels, that properties will be kept in proper repair, that adequate insurance coverages will be provided, and that taxes will be paid at the proper times.

Many such limitations, it is true, are not grievously burdensome. They may require nothing more than sound financial policy would seem to demand, even in the absence of preferred stock issues or long-term debt. It is true, too, that if the management of a corporation wants to do something that is subject to contractual restrictions, it can ask for a waiver of the restrictions by a vote of preferred stockholders or by the specific consent of direct lenders or, in the case of bond issues, of indenture trustees. Nevertheless, corporations with simple common stock structures generally avoid all or most restrictions of the kinds described, since it is not customary for short-term creditors to insist on comparable contractual provisions. Accordingly, they are free to adopt policies on their merits, without fear that the results might be interpreted as violative of contractual restrictions, nor need they seek the permission of somebody else for actions they propose to undertake. By contrast, the managers of corporations subject to contractual limitations may at times forgo attractive courses of action because of apparent conflicts with the limitations. They may request waivers, only to have their pleas rejected, or because they fear rejections they may decide not to seek concessions.

DISADVANTAGES OF SIMPLE COMMON STOCK STRUCTURES

While the advantages of simple common stock structures from the standpoint to the welfare of existing common stockholders are rather definite, the disadvantages tend to be possibilities only. Much depends on the situation of the individual corporation. What may be a clearcut disadvantage for some corporations may have elements of advantage to others, or, what is more likely, one or more of the disadvantages that could be suffered by some corporations may be easily avoidable by others. But we may best look at these cross-currents as we consider each of the possible sources of disadvantage.

With this proviso in mind, then, we may list these possible sources as follows:

1. Neglect of opportunities to trade on the equity—to obtain assets on a basis of relatively cheap interest or dividend payments.
2. Greater expense of common stock flotations by comparison with sales of preferred stock and the negotiation of long-term debt.
3. Danger of loss of control.
4. Danger of dilution of the claims of existing common stockholders to future profits.
5. Danger of dilution of their claims to assets.

Neglect of Opportunities to Trade on the Equity

As a rule, a successful corporation can sell preferred stock on the promise of a rate of dividends substantially less than its current or expected rate of profits on the investment of its common stockholders. Ordinarily, too, it can obtain funds by way of bond issues or other means of long-term borrowing at rates of interest somewhat below the dividend rate it would have to promise on a preferred stock issue. The cheapness of borrowed money is enhanced, moreover, by the deductibility of interest payments as an expense in income tax computations. Dividend payments on preferred and common stocks are not thus deductible.[5] Accordingly, the use of cheap funds can give a

[5]An exception to this rule is the deductibility of a percentage of dividends paid on the preferred stocks of certain classes of public utilities. The percentage deduction is determined by a formula in the Internal Revenue Code based on the tax rates currently in effect. If the tax rates are changed, therefore, the percentage also changes. As determined in relation to the basic corporate tax rates in effect

common stock *leverage*—they can act as a fulcrum to raise the profit rate on common stock to a level higher than could be reached without their use. It follows, therefore, that dependence on relatively expensive common stock funds as the sole long-term source of assets *may* represent an unreasonably conservative and unimaginative financial policy.

A corporation that includes fixed debt in its financial structure is said to trade on the equity. The investment of the common stockholders provides protection for the creditors. As the common stockholders' claim on assets is a residual one, unpaid creditors can seize all assets—those contributed by the stockholders as well as those contributed by themselves—to satisfy their claims. Thus, in seeking to attract funds from creditors the corporation trades on the protection given by the common stockholders, and it expects to get the creditors' funds more cheaply than it gets common stock funds precisely because of the cushion of protection provided to the creditors by the common stockholders.

The concept of trading on the equity is also applicable to issues of preferred stock. Many authorities, however, hesitate to apply the term to arrangements whereby cheaper preferred stock funds are employed to augment the rate of profit on common stock. The reason for this hesitation is that contributions to assets by preferred stockholders, no less than those of common stockholders, are *equity* contributions. The preferred stockholders of a corporation are owners and not creditors; hence, it is confusing to say that a corporation is trading on the equity when it issues preferred stock. However, when preferred stock is given a claim on assets superior to that of common stock, as is customary, the contributions of common stockholders to assets unquestionably provide a cushion of protection for preferred stockholders. The protective aspect should encourage investment in preferred stock; yet, buyers of preferred ought not to expect a rate of return as high as on common stock, which has the greater risks.

Use of Bonds. For illustration, let us assume that two corporations, A and B, are identical in their circumstances except that A has common stock and surplus as its only long-term sources of assets, whereas B has a bond issue in addition to common stock and surplus. Each corporation, let us say, has assets valued at $10 million and current liabilities of $2 million. B's bond issue amounts to $3 million; it bears interest at the rate of 5 percent. Accordingly, B's common

---

in the year 1968 (22 percent on the first $25,000 of taxable income and 48 percent on taxable income exceeding $25,000), the proportion of preferred dividends that were deductible in computing taxable income was 29.166 percent; however, the deduction could not exceed 29.166 percent of taxable income itself (as computed before any dividends-paid deduction). Some additional exceptions to the general rule of the nonductibility of dividends are provided for personal holding companies and certain classes of financial institutions, but these deductions have no bearing on the discussion in this chapter.

stock and surplus amount to $5 million, while the equity of the common stockholders of A amounts to $8 million. Now, let us assume that in a certain year each corporation has a profit of $2.4 million before the deduction of federal income taxes, and, for B, before the deduction of bond interest. It may also be assumed that there are no state net income taxes. With these assumptions, the results of operations of the two corporations can be compared as follows.

	Corporation A	*Corporation B*
Profits as indicated	$2,400,000	$2,400,000
Less: Bond interest		150,000
		$2,250,000
Less: Federal income tax[6]	1,145,500	1,073,500
Net profit to surplus	$1,254,500	$1,176,500
Rate of profit on common stockholders' equity	15.68%	23.53%

Thus, the cheapness of bondholders' funds to B, because of both the relative lowness of the rate of interest and the deductibility of the interest as an expense, enables it to earn a much higher rate of profit on the contribution of its common stockholders than is earned by A.

Use of Preferred Stock. Were B to have outstanding a preferred stock issue of $3 million rather than a bond issue of that size, and were the dividend rate on the preferred stock 6 percent, the results of its operations would be comparable with those of A as follows.

	Corporation A	*Corporation B*
Profits as indicated	$2,400,000	$2,400,000
Less: Federal income tax	1,145,500	1,145,500
	$1,254,500	$1,254,500
Less: Preferred dividends		180,000
Net profit to surplus	$1,254,500	$1,074,500
Rate of profit on common stockholders' equity	15.68%	21.49%

B's common stockholders would still have a substantial advantage over A's, although not so great as by the inclusion of the bond issue in its financial structure. The reduction in the margin of their advantage would result, of course, from both the higher rate of return on the preferred stock and the nondeductibility of the preferred dividends as an expense for income tax determination.

Adverse Aspects of Trading on the Equity. But all is not neces-

[6]In this and subsequent illustrations, the federal income tax is computed at the basic rates in effect in the year 1968—that is, at 22 percent on the first $25,000 of taxable income and 48 percent on income in excess of that figure. Thus, the surcharge of 10 percent added by legislation adopted in June of 1968, but scheduled to expire midway in 1969, is disregarded.

sarily sweetness and light in the matter of trading on the equity. The practice can turn out to be a very unhappy one for the common stockholders, as it certainly is in periods of losses or low profits. Referring to the first illustration above, suppose that in a certain year of depressed business activity the profits of Corporations A and B (with financial structures as previously described) amounted to only $200,000. Their positions would then be comparable as follows.

	Corporation A	*Corporation B*
Profits as indicated	$200,000	$200,000
Less: Bond interest		150,000
		$ 50,000
Less: Federal income tax	89,500	17,500
Net profit to surplus	$110,500	$ 32,500
Rate of profit on common stockholders' equity	1.38%	.65%

While a rate of return of only 1.38 percent would not give the common stockholders of A anything to be particularly happy about, at least they could have the satisfaction of knowing that it was more than twice that of B.

Were B to have outstanding $3 million of 6 percent preferred stock, as in the second illustration above, the margin of advantage to A's common stockholders would be even greater. In that situation, B's income tax liability would be equal to A's at $89,500, leaving it with an after-tax profit of $110,500. If, then, it decided to pay the preferred dividend of $180,000, it would have to charge $69,500 against surplus accumulated from past periods, leaving its common stockholders with a *negative* rate of profit of 1.39 percent.

It is even more discouraging—and dangerous—when the profit of a corporation that trades on the equity is less than the amount of bond interest or when it has losses before allowing for bond interest. Assume, for example, that in a certain year of depression profits for A and B before income tax deductions (and before the interest deduction for B) amount to $20,000. The comparison would work out as follows.

	Corporation A	*Corporation B*
Profits as indicated	$20,000	$ 20,000
Less: Bond interest		150,000
		−$130,000
Less: Federal income tax	4,400	
Net profit or loss (−) to surplus	$15,600	−$130,000
Rate of profit or loss (−) on common stockholders' equity	.195%	−2.60%

Under the Internal Revenue Code, however, B would be permitted to carry back its loss of $130,000 and write it off against its taxable profits of the three preceding years, or if the profits of those years were insufficient to absorb it, to carry the unabsorbed portion forward as a write-off against the profits of the following five years. If it had had a taxable profit of, say, $500,000 in the third preceding year, the effect of the carry-back would be to reduce the taxable profit of that year to $370,000, so that it would have a refund claim equal to the amount of tax it had paid on the $130,000. Actually, of course, the refund would not reduce B's loss or rate of loss in the current year. For tax purposes only, the loss would simply be transferred to another year.

However that may be, B's tax refund would undoubtedly be a most welcome means for replenishment of its working capital, drained through the payment of bond interest. But if for several years running B's profits were substantially less than the bond interest, or if it incurred losses before the deduction of that interest, it might soon exhaust its capacity to claim tax refunds. There would then be no replenishments of working capital from this source, even partial ones, and B might be pushed closer and closer to a default on its bond interest obligations. All the greater would the danger of default be if B were under contractual obligation to allocate cash each year to pay off some of the principal of the bonds, as would be likely.

Such dangers of default in times of losses and low profits explain why many corporate managements are satisfied to forgo the apparent advantages of trading on the equity. If they forgo the possibilities of raising the rate of profit on common stockholders' equity through leverage, they also avoid the dangers of default in times of business depression. For them, forgone possibilities of enhanced rates of profit are not too great a price to pay for assurances of solvency, better credit ratings, and the other advantages of the simple common stock structure.

Greater Cost of Common Stock Flotations

In addition to moderate interest and dividend rates and the deductibility of interest in determining taxable income as sources of cheapness in financing with preferred stock and bonds, the lower costs of floating issues of preferred stocks and bonds as compared with the costs of selling common stock issues are generally a further source of economy. As a rule, the expenses of selling absorb a greater proportion of the gross proceeds of common stock issues than of preferred stock issues. In turn, a greater proportion of the gross proceeds of preferred stock issues is thus absorbed than of bonds. The principal item of selling expense is the compensation paid to investment bankers for their services in finding buyers for corporate securities. Difficulty in finding buyers generally increases with the riskiness of securities.

Moreover, if the investment bankers *underwrite* securities issues—that is, guarantee their sale at specific prices—their own risk increases with the riskiness of the issues. On either or both of these counts, therefore, they expect their compensation to be graduated accordingly. Other expenses of selling include state issuance taxes,[7] attorneys' and accountants' fees, registration fees, and the costs of printing and engraving.

Thus, a manufacturing corporation might expect to incur expenses of about $480,000 in selling a common stock issue of gross proceeds of $7.5 million, about $300,000 in selling a preferred stock issue of the same gross proceeds, and about $260,000 in selling a bond issue of equal gross amount. Such figures are suggested the by costs of the securities flotations registered with the Securities and Exchange Commission in the years 1951, 1953, and 1955, as reproduced in Table 15–3. The average levels of cost indicated in the table were those of registered securities publicly offered through investment bankers—that is, offered broadside to many investors—and did not include those privately placed—that is, sold in bulk to one or a few investors, such as life insurance companies. The costs of private placements are usually considerably less than those of public offerings. Because, however, only a relatively few common stock issues are privately placed, whereas many bond issues are so sold, selling cost differentials unfavorable to common stock are accentuated.

It is clear, therefore, that high flotation costs for common stock might prompt some corporate managements to abandon their simple common stock structures. Were they to anticipate repeated trips to the market to obtain new money, they might decide that economies in flotation costs together with the benefits of trading on the equity would justify a switch to preferred stock or bonds. On the other hand, flotation-cost levels and differentials are of little or no significance to corporations able to finance expansion, moderate or extensive, with the cash throw-offs from retained profits nor to those that have only a few stockholders both willing and financially able to buy whatever additional issues of common stock are deemed necessary.

Danger of Loss of Control

The simple common stock form of financial structure could hardly look very attractive to an individual stockholder or closely knit group in control of a corporation if its continuance threatened to undermine that position of control. Control in this sense means, of course, the capacity to choose all or a majority of the board of directors, and thus to determine all operating policies, distributions of dividends,

---

[7]These are chiefly of the kinds described in Chapter 2. See p. 29, but see also pp. 528–30.

allocations of executive offices, and scales of compensation for those offices. For many persons and groups in control of corporations, the possible consequences of loss of control are truly horrible to contemplate—the rejection of operating policies that may have been developed carefully and lovingly over the years, the withholding of badly needed dividends, and the loss of the presidency, vice presidencies, and other high offices with their emoluments.

Accordingly, controlling stockholders whose margin of control is

TABLE 15–3

Cost of Flotation of Publicly Offered Security Issues Registered with the SEC and Sold through Investment Bankers, 1951, 1953, and 1955*

(As percentages of proceeds of public sale)

Size of Issue (Millions of dollars)	Industry of Issuer					
	Manufacturing	Electric, Gas, and Water	Communication	Mining	Other	All Industries
Bonds:						
Under 0.5	.....	.....	.....	.....	.....	.....
0.5– 0.9	12.12	.....	.....	.....	10.54	11.49
1.0– 1.9	9.03	5.00	4.70	.....	6.94	8.17
2.0– 4.9	6.16	2.23	.....	.....	6.26	3.78
5.0– 9.9	3.47	1.52	.....	4.40	3.35	1.83
10.0–19.9	2.34	1.28	1.25	2.64	1.97	1.52
20.0–49.9	1.71	1.20	1.04	.....	1.74	1.33
50.0 and over	1.30	1.15	1.03	.....	1.15	1.19
Total†	2.67	1.33	1.01	3.52	1.80	1.49
Preferred Stock:						
Under 0.5	.....	.....	.....	.....	.....	.....
0.5– 0.9	18.38	10.67	7.44	.....	11.57	12.63
1.0– 1.9	11.15	6.13	6.41	.....	12.68	8.07
2.0– 4.9	5.11	3.76	5.43	.....	7.34	4.88
5.0– 9.9	3.97	3.42	4.92	.....	3.63	3.72
10.0–19.9	2.62	2.84	4.15	.....	2.78	2.92
20.0–49.9	3.65	3.10	.....	.....	.....	3.20
50.0 and over	2.51	.....	.....	.....	.....	2.51
Total†	5.22	3.12	6.54	.....	6.80	4.34
Common Stock:						
Under 0.5	19.69	.....	.....	33.42	14.76	27.15
0.5– 0.9	13.68	12.23	8.19	32.96	21.43	21.76
1.0– 1.9	12.84	6.52	5.98	22.18	11.53	13.58
2.0– 4.9	8.61	5.42	5.76	17.71	12.88	9.97
5.0– 9.9	6.38	4.53	6.68	12.33	14.28	6.17
10.0–19.9	4.88	2.95	5.08	11.50	6.60	4.66
20.0–49.9	5.48	4.20	.....	15.63	.....	5.37
50.0 and over	.....	.....	.....	.....	.....	.....
Total†	10.06	4.55	6.07	20.00	12.26	10.28

*Including 265 issues of bonds with gross proceeds of $5.9 billion, 120 issues of preferred stock amounting to $850 million, and 230 issues of common stock with proceeds of almost $1 billion. The median size of issues was $15 million for bonds, $4 million for preferred stock, and $2 million for common stock. Issues ranged in size from $100,000 to $300 million.

†Median percentages.

SOURCE: Securities and Exchange Commission, *Cost of Flotation of Corporate Securities, 1951–1955* (Washington, D.C.: U.S. Government Printing Office, 1957), pp. 9, 38–40.

small will almost certainly vote to abandon the simple common stock structure if retained profits are insufficient to finance needed expansion and if they lack the means to buy additional common stock in proportion to their present holdings. A controlling group that had 51 percent of the common stock of a corporation and faced the bitter opposition of another group that held the remaining 49 percent would unquestionably consider it suicidal to vote for an additional issue unless it were in a position to subscribe to at least 51 percent of it. However, a controlling group that held, say, 80 percent of the outstanding common stock of a corporation might vote an additional issue to be sold to the minority or to outsiders as long as the sale would not reduce their own proportion of ownership below 51 percent.

Moreover, holding 20 or 30 percent of the common stock of a corporation, or even a smaller percentage, may be sufficient to give a group of stockholders control, provided that the remainder of the stock is quite widely distributed among hundreds or thousands of owners. Such a group having, say, 30 percent of the outstanding common stock might, therefore, vote an additional issue in the expectation that though it itself would not subscribe, its reduced percentage of ownership of, say, 20 percent would still be ample to ensure control. Nevertheless, the danger of loss of control would obviously be present here. In not a few situations of this kind, opposition groups have quietly bought up a sufficient amount of the scattered stock, and have just as quietly persuaded a sufficient number of the corporation's small stockholders to vote with them, to enable them to oust groups that had previously felt quite secure in their positions of control.

In some very large corporations, all of whose stock is very widely distributed, the boards of directors have come to occupy positions usually described as self-perpetuating. Only gross mismanagement or other developments of a most extraordinary character would be likely to cause the scattered stockholders to unite to oust such a board. The members of these boards often own but little stock in the corporations they control. In considering proposals for new issues, therefore, they are likely to be quite unconcerned about their own wish or financial capacity to subscribe. Indeed, it is not unreasonable for them to conclude that additional issues, by promoting an even wider distribution of the stock, will further entrench them in their positions of control.

Dilution of Claims to Future Profits

Selling additional common stock to raise money for expansion may be objectionable to the existing common stockholders of a corporation because they fear a dilution of their claims to future profits. Additional assets may be needed to enable the corporation to hold its competitive position; yet, these stockholders may expect the rate of earnings on the additions to be less than that already being earned. Their expectation would be that should additional shares be sold and should they themselves not subscribe, earning power would be transferred from them to the buyers of the new issues. The matter of control, as discussed above, might be of no consequence to these stockholders, but they would still have reason to object to financing by further common stock sales.

For illustration, let us suppose that a corporation has outstanding 100,000 shares of common stock of $40 par value and that it has surplus accounts representing accumulated profits of $3 million. Its profits after income taxes have averaged 14 percent of the common stockholders' investment. Several directors now propose the sale of 50,000 additional shares at a price equal to the book value per share of the old stock—that is, $70[8]—and they claim that a return of 20 percent could be earned on the additional assets the sale would provide. But most of the present stockholders, not expecting to subscribe to any of the additional stock, object to the proposed issue on the grounds that the rate of return on the new assets would not be more than 8 percent. They expect the outcome to be as follows.

Assumed continued profit on the old investment of $7,000,000 at 14%	$ 980,000
Assumed profit on the new investment of $3,500,000[9] at 8%	280,000
Total expected profit	$1,260,000
Expected new rate of profit, $1,260,000 ÷ $10,500,000	12%

Since each share of old stock would have rights to dividends no better than each share of the new, the present stockholders anticipate that the rate of profit attributable to their investment would be reduced from 14 percent to 12 percent. Or to state their expectation in an alternative way, they fear that the new stockholders would be very generously treated by being accorded a rate of profit of 12 percent even though their investment would earn only 8 percent.

Dilution of Claims Against Assets

If it is proposed that additional common stock be issued at a price below the book value of existing stock, and if present common stockholders are unable or unwilling to subscribe, they have an additional reason to worry about the possibilities of dilution—in this instance, dilution of their claims against the assets of the corporation. A new share of common stock, regardless of what is paid for it, has a claim

[8]In a simple common stock structure, the book value is the sum of the par or stated value of the stock and all the surplus accounts divided by the number of shares outstanding.

[9]For the sake of avoiding complexities at this point, the probable substantial costs of selling the additional stock are ignored.

against assets equal to that of an old share.[10] Therefore, a sale of new stock at a price below the book value of the old results in a transfer of claims against assets from the old to the new.

To see how this works, let us assume the same facts as those in the foregoing illustration, except that the proposal calls for the sale of the 50,000 shares of additional stock at a price of $58 a share. The existing stockholders might find the proposal seriously disadvantageous to them in a manner demonstrable as follows.

Book value of old stock:	
Common stock (par or stated value)	$4,000,000
Surplus	3,000,000
Total	$7,000,000
Book value per share, $7,000,000 ÷ 100,000 shares	$70
Book value after sale of new stock:	
Common stock	$6,000,000
Earned surplus	3,000,000
Capital (or paid-in) surplus	900,000
Total	$9,900,000
Book value per share, $9,900,000 ÷ 150,000 shares	$66

The stockholders might object to the proposed issue on the grounds that for each share held they would be losing a claim against assets of $4. And they might argue the unfairness of contributing a claim of $8 to each share of new stock, since it would immediately have a book value of $66 though only $58 would be paid for it.

Proponents of additional issues, as in the foregoing case, might argue that the book value of common stock as a measure of the claims of stockholders against assets is really not very significant and that, therefore, dilution is nothing to worry about. They might argue that common stockholders' claims against assets are likely to be asserted only in the event of dissolution, that dissolution is rarely voted by the stockholders of successful corporations, and that the dissolution of unsuccessful ones usually occurs when there is little left against which their stockholders can assert claims. Nevertheless, dilution can be hurtful. Two possibilities may be mentioned.[11] A corporation, though successful, may have reason to curtail the scope of its operations. It would then presumably have the means to pay dividends in partial liquidation to the stockholders, and these would be a settlement of claims as evidenced by the stock and surplus accounts. Again, after a corporation has completed a sale of additional stock, such as that proposed in the illustration, it may have the opportunity to sell

[10] A possible exception occurs if the new stock is sold at a discount. For a discussion of this matter, see pp. 421–22.

[11] Further attention is given to this matter in Chapter 17. See pp. 400–404.

out at a handsome price to another corporation. But the benefits of the attractive price would be shared pro rata by the former's stockholders, old and new, regardless of differences between the former book value of old stock and the selling price of new.

FEASIBILITY OF SIMPLE COMMON STOCK STRUCTURES

Decisions for or against simple common stock structures cannot always be reached solely by weighing apparent advantages and disadvantages, no matter how carefully the weighing may be done. In some situations, this kind of financial structure is forced on corporations; in others, it is departures from the simple common stock form that are forced. In a word, the feasibility of the simple structure is by no means identical with its desirability.

Two important determinants of feasibility were indicated in the foregoing discussion of the possible disadvantages of simple structures: (1) size of profits, and (2) the interests of present common stockholders in control. It is obvious that if the profits that a corporation can earn and retain are sufficient to finance all desirable expansion, its problems of maintaining the simple form of structure are minimized. Controlling interests are not disturbed; there are no high differential costs of common stock sales to be concerned about; and the stockholders need have no fears about the dilution of their claims to assets and future profits. It is likewise clear than an important obstacle to the simple form of structure is removed if the positions of control of given groups of stockholders or directors would not be threatened through additional common stock sales, because they would subscribe pro rata for additional shares, because they could afford a drop in their percentage of ownership, or because a very wide distribution of stock ownership is already the source of their power.

Other important determinants of feasibility are age, expansion requirements, stability of profits, government regulation of rates and security issues, and market conditions. These deserve analysis.

Newly Established Corporations

Youth is a most significant circumstance making for simple common stock structures. Most corporations start as small business organizations, the personal ventures, one may say, of single individuals or small groups. Until they have established a record of several years of successful operations, outsiders are strongly disinclined to be interested in them as investors—either buyers of such securities as they may want to issue or grantors of intermediate- or long-term loans. Hence, the predominant source of assets for a new corporation at its commencement and for the first few years of its operation must generally be the organizers themselves—the money they can put up originally or subsequently for its common stock and the profits, if any, they can retain for operations.

Even a new corporation, however, is not likely to be cut off completely from outside sources of assets, but such sources almost surely are short term in character. Limited amounts of raw materials or finished goods may be obtainable on account from trade suppliers; labor can ordinarily be hired on the basis of some deferment of wage payments, as a week or two weeks; certain kinds of services may be forthcoming on a deferred-payment basis; and in some cases, indeed, commercial bankers who have confidence in the managerial abilities of the organizers may be prevailed on to grant moderate amounts of short-term loans for working capital purposes. Nevertheless, longer-term sources of assets, aside from the organizers' own investment, are likely to be unavailable.

Expansion Requirements

Necessary and Optional Expansion. For corporations that survive their periods of infancy, expansion requirements are outstandingly important in determining the feasibility of continuing with simple common stock structures. Here we may distinguish between what may be called *necessary* expansion, on the one hand, and *optional* expansion, on the other. A corporation may have survived the trying years of infancy, but its situation as a maturing enterprise may be quite weak from the standpoint of profitability. Because of inadequacies in its facilities, it may be able only to break even or to garner nominal profits. The correction of these inadequacies could be said, therefore, to be *necessary* for its continued existence. But the addition of facilities to correct the inadequacies obviously could not be financed out of profits, and the poor profits record might likewise preclude further sales of common stock. Should the corporation have an opportunity to borrow on a long-term basis, it could be expected, accordingly, to depart from the simple common stock structure without much hesitation.

Another corporation may enjoy a wide range of expansion choices. It may be carrying on operations quite profitably at a given level, but its managers may believe that profits could be increased substantially through investment in additional assets. Nevertheless, they would be under no compulsion to expand. If convinced of the superiority of the simple common stock structure, they might decide to enlarge the scale of operations only to the extent that the expansion could be financed through the retention of profits and additional sales of common stock.

Rate of Expansion. Whether or not simple common stock structures can be maintained depends not only on the amount of money needed for given expansion programs but also on the time it is needed—that is, on the speed with which the expansion must be effected. A corporation that envisages substantial growth, but at a slow, steady pace over a long period of years, may have no difficulty in meeting outlays for expansion out of retained profits and the proceeds of occasional sales of additional amounts of common stock, while one that must spend large amounts of money within a short period of time may find these means of financing quite insufficient.

A corporation may find itself in the short kind of position because its competitors are adding many new facilities, perhaps to take advantage of technological developments that promise a substantial lowering of costs of production, or perhaps to make possible the manufacture of complementary products to improve service to their customers. If the corporation is to remain strong, therefore, it must quickly follow the competitors' lead. Although it may have been financing moderate growth by means of retained profits, it would be likely to find this means inadequate to finance the new requirements for rapid expansion. If, at the same time, the market for additional issues of common stock were not favorable, it might promptly decide that the better part of valor would be to give up the advantages of a simple common stock structure and issue preferred stock or contract long-term debt.

Rising Prices. The amount of money needed for expansion tends to rise, of course, with rising prices. A corporation that is planning to double its facilities over a period of years must make allowance for the possibility or probability that the costs of the additions will be rising as the expansion takes place. If on the basis of present prices the cost of the additional facilities is estimated at $5 million, but if it is anticipated that due to rising prices actual outlays will average, say, 15 percent above present prices, then obviously an additional means of financing in the amount of $750,000 must be planned for. It is conceivable that the corporation's financial managers might conclude that though $5 million could be provided out of retained profits and sales of common stock, the further requirement of $750,000 could not be so financed. They might, therefore, plan to tap the preferred stock or bond market for this additional amount.

Even corporations that are not planning expansion in the sense of adding to the volume of their assets face a problem of expansion in periods of rising prices. Simply to carry unchanged quantities of goods in their inventories and to carry the same volume of accounts receivable (in the sense of *quantity* of goods sold on account) they must expand the amount of their investment, and likewise if they must replace fixed assets when prices have risen. Thus, difficulty in maintaining simple common stock structures may ensue. Although profits tend to expand as rapidly as prices—and, for many corporations, more rapidly—stockholders may expect higher rates of dividends in view of the decline in the purchasing power of the dividend dollar. Moreover, any increase in capacity to use retained profits as a means of financing may be more than offset by inability to materially increase the amount of assets short-term creditors are willing to supply. Periods of rising prices are often periods of tight money in which short-term creditors are under great pressure to increase restrictions on credit extensions and terms.

Stability of Profits

As a rule, records of stable profits through the upswings and downswings of the business cycle weaken the attractions of simple common stock structures; in other words, they make the advantages of trading on the equity all the more attractive. Corporations well established as producers or sellers of products of stable demand, such as many kinds of processed foodstuffs, petroleum products, tobacco, and electric power, need to be much less hesitant about departing from the simple common stock structure than are those whose products are subject to erratic demand, such as most kinds of heavy goods, including automobiles, other transportation equipment, factory machinery and equipment, and farm machinery. Industries with erratic demand are much more likely than those with stable demand to place great emphasis on the dangers of trading on the equity.

Suppose, for example, that two corporations of comparable size, A and B, have profit records over an eight-year period as set down below (with negative figures indicating losses), and that these records are typical of their business cycle experience.[12] We may assume that both corporations have had simple common stock structures, and that the respective amounts of their stockholders' investments have

Year	*Corporation A*	*Corporation B*
1	$ 500,000	$ 800,000
2	520,000	900,000
3	550,000	1,000,000
4	570,000	1,200,000
5	520,000	900,000
6	470,000	−100,000
7	430,000	−400,000
8	440,000	−300,000
Total	$4,000,000	$4,000,000
Average	$ 500,000	$ 500,000

been just about identical. Accordingly, the *average* rate of return for the two groups of stockholders in the eight-year period has also been

[12]This is not meant to imply that eight years is the ordinary duration of cycles in general business activity, whether measured from peak to peak or from trough to trough. While business cycle authorities do estimate that major cycles in the United States have averaged between 8 and 9 years, they also point out that actual cycles have varied in duration from but little more than one year to as much as 11 years.

approximately equal. Such an equality in the average rate of return might suggest that trading on the equity should be no more dangerous for B than for A. Were B to have a bond issue outstanding, why could it not set aside cash in the good years to ensure its capacity to meet its obligations in the lean years?

To ask such a question is to suggest where lie the dangers of trading on the equity. The extraordinary profits of the good years may prompt the directors of B to be overgenerous in their dividend declarations, especially so if dividends had been suspended in a preceding period of losses. But an even greater danger is that the cash throw-off from profits in the good years would be used in large part immediately for the expansion of inventories, accounts receivable, and fixed facilities, so that this drain, plus that for dividends—even if dividends were held to moderate levels—would in the poor years lead to severe cash shortages of a kind to threaten solvency. Once again, the lack of a direct relationship between the size of the cash account and the size of surplus accounts must be stressed. Many corporations with comparatively large surplus accounts have defaulted on their obligations in times of business depressions. Using only the figures presented above and assuming that B paid dividends of only $300,000 each year for the first 5 years, it would reach the first loss year (the sixth year of the table) with a surplus of $3.3 million. But if it had spent for noncash assets the cash throw-offs from the accumulated profits its financial position in the last three years of the eight-year period could be dangerously weak. By contrast, A would continue to have substantial cash throw-offs from its profits of the sixth, seventh, and eighth years. Were it, therefore, to have bonds or other forms of long-term debt in its financial structure, they should offer no serious threats to its solvency.

Government Regulation of Rates and Security Issues

Rate Regulation. In one important area of business enterprise—public utility corporations—government regulation of the rates that may be charged for services to the public militates against maintenance of simple common stock structures. Rate regulation is made applicable principally to electric power, gas, and water companies; to railroads, airlines, bus lines, and other enterprises in the field of transportation; and to telephone and telegraph companies. It is imposed by both the federal and state governments, depending on the area served by the individual utility: by the federal government through the Federal Power Commission, the Interstate Commerce Commission, the Civil Aeronautics Board, and the Federal Communications Commission; by the state governments through agencies of various titles but generally known collectively as the public service commissions.

The principal objective of public utility rate regulation is to ensure a level of rates that will be fair both to the public and to the utilities themselves. Fairness is expected to be achieved by permitting service rates that will enable the utility, with good management, to earn a reasonable rate of return on the value of the assets it employs in providing its services. Problems of extraordinary complexity are involved in determining what assets are to be included in the rate base, and especially in determining what valuations are appropriate for these assets. For the moment, however, it is sufficient to note that whatever may be the final judgments about includable assets and their values, the reasonable rate of return itself is usually fixed within a range from 5 to 8 percent.

If, therefore, all or almost all of the assets of a public utility corporation are supplied by the common stockholders, if it is allowed to charge service rates designed to give it a rate of return on these assets of, say, 6 percent, and if it actually succeeds in earning this rate of return, the profit rate on the stockholders' investment is likewise limited to 6 percent. But such a profit rate may be insufficient to attract common stock funds, as profit rates in unregulated industries may actually be, or may have good prospects of being, substantially higher than that. Accordingly, to be in a position to compete effectively for common stock funds, the utility must arrange its financial structure to be able to hold out good prospects of a rate of return higher than 6 percent. In a word, it finds it highly important to give its common stock leverage by trading on the equity. If it earns 6 percent on its assets, but acquires a substantial proportion of them by selling preferred stock that carries a dividend rate of, say, 5 percent or bonds that bear interest at a rate of, say, 4 percent, or by selling both preferred stock and bonds, then it succeeds in boosting the rate of return on its common stock.

Nevertheless, public utility corporations, no less than those engaged in other areas of enterprise, may overdo trading on the equity. Many have done so, especially in the field of transportation, as has been evidenced by repeated waves of railroad bankruptcies and by the chronic difficulties of many street railway, interurban railway, and bus line systems. Service rate regulation aimed at allowing a reasonable rate of return on assets does not guarantee that the utility will actually earn that rate. Many transportation corporations have fallen far short, with difficulties in meeting obligations on bonds and other forms of long-term debt ensuing. With the railroads and electric railways, especially, excessive trading on the equity had been developed long before rate regulation had become effective, so that regulation could hardly be blamed for their difficulties in meeting obligations. Moreover, allowing railroads, electric railways, and bus lines to increase their charges to the public has often resulted simply in driving traffic to competing means of transportation. A recognition of the more circumscribed role that changing economic and technological conditions were forcing on them led many railroad managements to use much of the cash throw-offs from their extraordinary profits of the period of World War II to reduce their long-term debt. In this way, they evidenced a lessened devotion to trading on the equity as a financial policy.

Regulation of Security Issues. In most instances, federal and state agencies that are empowered to regulate the rates that public utilities may charge for their services also have the authority to approve or disapprove the issuance of additional securities by the utilities as means of financing. A utility may be steered in the direction of greater simplicity in its financial structure by official disapprovals of its proposals to issue preferred stock or to contract additional amounts of long-term debt. It is not that the regulatory agencies frown on trading on the equity, or that they are inclined to insist on a decisive movement in the direction of simple common stock structures. They recognize the importance of giving common stock leverage so that it will be attractive to investors. But they insist on a reasonable relationship between the investment of common stockholders and those of preferred stockholders and long-term creditors, while emphasizing also that such reasonable relationships are different for different kinds of utilities, depending largely on their present and prospective earnings capacities. For example, when codifying its standards for the issuance of bonds and preferred stocks by the public utility systems registered with it under the Public Utility Holding Company Act, the Securities and Exchange Commission explained its attitude on bonds as follows.

> That the achievement and preservation of sound capitalization ratios are essential to the financial health of the public utility industry has been recognized not only by the Commission and some other regulatory bodies, but also by informed writers on the subject. Most of these authorities are generally agreed on the necessity for an adequate "cushion" of common stock equity to withstand the shock of a severe decline in earnings, and for not too excessive an amount of debt, notwithstanding the apparent cheapness of bond money versus common stock money and the deductibility for tax purposes of interest expense. Quite a number urge that a company should not use up all of its bonding credit, but rather should reserve a substantial portion of it for such time when it may become difficult to sell common stock.[13]

At times, accordingly, regulatory commissions reject proposals for bond issues on the grounds that market conditions are favorable for sales of additional common stock, and reject proposals for the retire-

---

[13]Securities and Exchange Commission, *Annual Report,* 1956, p. 161.

ment of preferred stock on the grounds that the money can be better used for the retirement of long-term debt. Simplification in financial structures has also been advanced by insistence by many regulatory commissions that the individual utility limit the varieties of its security issues. The utility is told that it will be permitted to issue only one kind of preferred stock and only one kind of bonds (in addition to one kind of common stock, of course), and that, accordingly, it must plan its long-range financing on such a basis. Or if the utility already has a badly splintered financial structure, it is advised to draw its long-term financing plans with the objective of consolidating its many varieties of preferred stocks and bonds into one or two new issues of uniform character.

Market Conditions

Sometimes the market for common stock is so highly favorable that corporate managements decide on additional issues almost as a matter of course. If money is needed for expansion, taking advantage of the high prices at which common stock can be sold appears unquestionably to be the best way of getting it. This may be so even though in other circumstances the attractions of trading on the equity would be quite compelling. Thus, by force of circumstances, one may say, corporations may continue with simple common stock structures without any strong convictions on the part of their managements about the superiority of this form.

At other times, the market for common stock is so depressed that corporate managements quickly conclude that it would be a very poor source of needed funds. The sale of additional common stock at low prices, it is decided, would most unreasonably dilute the interests of present stockholders, especially, as we have seen, their claims against assets, their rights to vote, and their claims on future profits. But the markets for preferred stock or bonds or both are not necessarily depressed simultaneously with that for common stock. When they are not depressed, therefore, decisions in many cases to tap them rather than to sell common stock are surely to be expected.

At all times, the availability of funds in the hands of different classes of investors is an important determinant of the amounts that business corporations can succeed in drawing from given markets. A favorable common stock market most surely does not mean that any one corporation can sell an unlimited amount of additional common stock at a good price or, indeed, at any price. How much it can sell depends on the amount of investment funds held by individuals and institutions that are ordinarily interested in buying common stock, as well as on the amount of such funds that other corporations are seeking to draw from the market. Especially significant in this regard are provisions of law and stipulations in contracts that forbid or closely limit investment in common stocks by many of our most important classes of financial institutions. Commercial banks are generally forbidden to invest in common stocks other than the stocks of certain classes of subsidiaries, and in most states investment in common stocks by life insurance companies and mutual savings banks is subject to strict standards and limits. In a similar way, trust agreements and wills sometimes restrict investment in common stocks by trustees of personal estates and pension and endowment funds, and sometimes such restrictions are imposed by law and court decrees. Hence, it is entirely possible for financial institutions to have an abundance of funds available for investment in bonds while, simultaneously, the money holdings of investors interested in common stock issues are quite limited. Accordingly, the managements of given business corporations may decide that though the common stock market is favorable for a limited amount of money their great needs require that they go elsewhere to reach the much larger supply of funds in the hands of individuals and financial institutions that are not buying common stocks.

QUESTIONS

1. What is the composition of a corporation's financial structure? How important is care in the management of a financial structure by comparison with care in the management of assets?

2. In simple common stock structures, what place is there, if any, for surplus? Short-term debt? Long-term debt?

3. In simple common stock structures, what is the minimum proportion of total assets likely to be contributed by the common stockholders? Explain.

4. How do simple common stock structures contribute to corporations' solvency? To their good credit standing?

5. What is meant by trading on the equity? Explain why it can be both advantageous and dangerous for common stockholders.

6. Compare the advantages and disadvantages of trading on the equity with bonds with those of so trading with preferred stock.

7. To what extent, if at all, are the dangers of trading on the equity reduced by provisions of the Internal Revenue Code that permit the carry-back and carry-over of net operating losses?

8. Compare the costs of selling new issues of common stock with the costs of selling preferred stocks and bonds. What are the principal kinds of costs incurred in selling new securities issues of all kinds?

9. Explain how sales of additional common stock by a corporation may dilute the claims of its existing common stockholders (*a*) to future profits, and (*b*) against assets.

10. In what ways is the financial structure of a corporation likely to be influenced by the wish of its existing common stockholders to retain their control?

11. In what directions is the financial structure of a corporation likely to be influenced by the size of its profits? The stability of its profits?

12. What influences on the financial structures of corporations is exerted by their age? The rapidity of their growth?

13. What kinds of effects on corporate financial structures tend to result from government regulation of (*a*) corporations as issuers of securities, and (*b*) financial institutions as investors in securities?

14. What kinds of influences on corporate financial structures tend to result from changing conditions in the securities markets?

PROBLEMS

1. With flotation costs assumed to be at the levels shown in Table 15–3 on page 354, what would be the amount of these costs to a manufacturing corporation in selling a bond issue at a public offering price of $3,500,000? A preferred stock issue of the same size? A common stock issue of this size?

2. With the same assumption as that in Problem 1, what would be the respective flotation costs to an electric power company of the three kinds of securities issues if the public offering price were $12 million for each?

3. In a certain year, the Morton Corporation had a net profit of $4.3 million before the deduction of federal income taxes and any dividends or interest.

a) Assume, in the first place, that the corporation had no preferred stock or bonds in its financial structure and, therefore, no preferred dividends or bond interest to pay, that the common stockholders' equity amounted to $20 million, and that federal income tax rates were 22 percent on the first $25,000 of income and 48 percent on taxable income over $25,000. What rate of profit did it earn on the common stockholders' equity?

b) Now assume that the equity of Morton's common stockholders amounted to $15 million and that it had outstanding $5 million of 7 percent preferred stock on which the dividend of $350,000 was paid during the year. What rate of profit did the corporation earn on the common stockholders' equity?

c) Assume, finally, that the equity of Morton's common stockholders amounted to $15 million and that it had outstanding $5 million of 7 percent bonds on which the interest obligation of $350,000 was paid during the year. What rate of profit did the corporation earn on the common stockholders' equity?

4. With the assumption that the Morton Corporation's net profit before income taxes (and before deduction for preferred dividends or bond interest, where applicable) amounted to only $210,000, and with all other facts as stated in parts (*a*), (*b*), and (*c*) of Problem 3 unchanged, what would have been the rate of profit on the common stockholders' equity in each instance?

5. Dravo & Sons, Inc. has had outstanding 800,000 shares of common stock of $10 par value, and its surplus amounts to $3 million. Its after-tax profit in recent years has averaged $1,325,000. It now sells to outsiders

400,000 additional shares of common stock at $16 a share, and as a result of expanded operations financed by the stock sale its average after-tax profit rises to $1,960,000.

a) To what extent, if at all, was the claim of the old stockholders to corporate earnings improved or diluted by the sale of the new stock?

b) How was their per-share claim to assets affected?

c) Considering the effects determined in (*a*) and (*b*), was the sale of the new stock advantageous or disadvantageous to the old stockholders?

chapter 16

FINANCIAL STRUCTURES WITH PREFERRED STOCK AND LONG-TERM DEBT

The analysis in Chapter 15 indicates that corporate managements are impelled to add preferred stocks or long-term debt or both to their financial structures for a variety of reasons. Many are unquestionably persuaded to move in that direction by the attractions of trading on the equity—by convictions that good prospects for enhanced rates of profit on the investment of common stockholders more than offset mild increases in the danger of insolvency, moderate weakening of credit standing and access to funds in time of pressing need, and the acceptance of some restrictions on managerial discretion. All the more is this kind of decision likely to be made by corporations that have records of and prospects for stable profits, and still more surely by utility corporations because of rate regulation, especially when they, too, enjoy a reasonable degree of stability in their profit-making capacities.

Fear of loss of control such as would or could result from additional common stock sales is undoubtedly another very common reason for decisions to add preferred stocks[1] or fixed debt or both to financial structures. Also important is the unavailability of sufficient common stock funds to finance needed expansion, either because of the youth of corporations or because of temporary disdain of the investing public for new common stock issues, regardless of the ages and financial prestige of the issuers. Much less important, on the other hand, are

[1]Control through the ownership of common stock is not ordinarily endangered in any immediate way by the sale of preferred stock. Preferred stock can usually be made nonvoting except on proposals that would weaken the priority of its claims and in certain contingencies, such as nonpayment of dividends for a year or more. See pp. 578–81.

fears of dilution in the claim of common stockholders to future profits and assets. And, finally, a combination of reasons often accounts for corporate decisions to depart from the simple common stock form of financial structure.

PREFERRED STOCK, LONG-TERM DEBT, AND OTHER SOURCES OF ASSETS

Preferred Stock

The dollar amounts of preferred stock offered for cash sale in each year since 1946, as reported by the Securities and Exchange Commission, are set out in Table 16–1, with the figures for common stock offerings for the same period also shown for comparison. The total of preferred stock offered for cash sale for the entire period from 1946 through 1967 amounted to $13,145 million, while the total for common stock was $34,731 million. Such totals, however, do not mean that there were additions of equal amounts to net corporate assets

TABLE 16–1
New Issues of Preferred and Common Stock Offered for Cash, 1946–67*
(In millions of dollars)

Year	*Preferred Stock*	*Common Stock*
1946	$ 1,126	$ 891
1947	761	778
1948	492	614
1949	425	736
1950	631	811
1951	838	1,212
1952	564	1,369
1953	489	1,326
1954	816	1,213
1955	635	2,185
1956	636	2,301
1957	411	2,516
1958	571	1,334
1959	531	2,027
1960	409	1,664
1961	450	3,294
1962	422	1,314
1963	342	1,022
1964	412	2,679
1965	725	1,547
1966	574	1,939
1967	885	1,959
Total	$13,145	$34,731

*Gross proceeds of both registered and unregistered issues offered publicly or by private placement for cash sale but excluding issues of $100,000 or less, intercorporate transactions, issues of investment companies, and issues to be sold over an extended period of time, such as offerings under employee-purchase plans.

SOURCE: Securities and Exchange Commission, *Annual Reports* and *Statistical Bulletin*, various issues.

financed by the two stock sources, since substantial amounts of stock are retired every year. Unfortunately, the available statistics do not show how much of each kind of stock is retired from year to year. However, for a coverage somewhat different from that of the table, SEC figures show that retirements of the two kinds of stock combined in the period 1946–67 amounted to approximately 43.2 percent of the combined amount of new issues in the same period.[2]

Bonds

Statistics of new corporate bond issues, retirements of old ones, and the resulting net changes in amounts outstanding, as compiled by the SEC for the period 1946–67, are presented in Table 16–2. The enormous total of $191,430 million of new bond financing in the 22-years covered by the table might lead one to suspect that, in a collective sense, American corporations generally have been largely neglecting stock as a source of assets in favor of a heavy dependence on bonds. But bonds are debts that must be paid off periodically or at their maturity dates. Thus, when large amounts of bonds have been issued in past years, every current year must witness substantial retirements of the earlier issues as long as corporations remain solvent. Many new issues of bonds, therefore, are refunding issues, all or most of their proceeds are earmarked to pay off maturing earlier issues. Nevertheless, the net increase in bonds outstanding of $119,350 million in the 22-year period, by comparison with the net increase in stock issues in the same period, has been truly remarkable, as was the jump of over $27 billion in the years 1966 and 1967 alone. Evidently, therefore, corporate managements have been much impressed with the advantages of bond financing, as indicated in Chapter 15 and as further developed later in this chapter.

All Sources of Assets

The statistics of changes in the amount of bonds outstanding do not give a complete picture of the volume of year-by-year financing on the basis of long-term debt, since other forms of long-term corporate debt, especially mortgage loans are granted by commercial banks and other classes of financial institutions. Likewise, figures for changes in the amount of outstanding stock do not give us a complete account of year-to-year contributions to corporate assets by stockholders, for, as we saw in Chapter 15, retained earnings represent a most important additional contribution made by them. What is more, changes in the relative positions of stockholders and long-term creditors as sources

[2]Computed from data published by the Securities and Exchange Commission in "Net Change in Corporate Securities Outstanding," mimeographed, November, 1966; and in *Statistical Bulletin*, March, 1968, p. 21.

TABLE 16–2
Corporate Bond Financing, 1946–67*
(In millions of dollars)

Year	*New Issues*	*Retirements*	*Net Increase*†
1946	$ 4,702	$ 3,588	$ 1,114
1947	5,008	2,003	3,005
1948	5,936	1,212	4,725
1949	4,867	1,582	3,285
1950	4,804	2,800	2,004
1951	5,682	2,099	3,583
1952	7,344	2,402	4,942
1953	6,651	1,894	4,757
1954	7,832	4,033	3,799
1955	7,571	3,383	4,188
1956	7,814	3,203	4,611
1957	9,611	2,584	7,026
1958	9,661	3,811	5,850
1959	7,122	3,049	4,073
1960	8,072	3,078	4,994
1961	9,194	4,024	5,170
1962	8,613	3,749	4,864
1963	10,556	4,979	5,577
1964	10,715	4,077	6,637
1965	12,747	4,649	8,098
1966	15,629	4,542	11,088
1967	21,299	5,340	15,960
Total	$191,430	$72,081	$119,350

*The SEC explains that these data are not exactly comparable with those of stock sales as presented in Table 16–1 because of adjustments described as follows: "The figures on total new issues of securities are based on the corporate offering series [as are the data of Table 16–1] with certain adjustments. For instance, sales of stock to employees are included, whereas such sales are not covered in the corporate offering series, and a deduction is made from the original data for foreign issues sold in the United States. Also an adjustment is made to deduct from the total offerings the amount of issues which, although they were offered for sale, were not actually sold. The series on retirements covers the same types of issues as in the offerings series, and includes issues retired with internal funds as well as with proceeds from new issues sold for refunding purposes."

†Because of rounding, net increase in some instances is not the exact difference between new issues and retirements.

SOURCE: Securities and Exchange Commission, "Net Change in Corporate Securities Outstanding," mimeographed, November, 1966; and *Statistical Bulletin*, March, 1968, p. 21.

of corporate assets are still not clearly seen unless the roles of short-term creditors and cash throw-offs from depreciation as sources of funds are introduced for comparison. Fortunately, therefore, we are able to refer to a comprehensive accounting for all sources of corporate funds for the period 1946–67, published by the Board of Governors of the Federal Reserve System and reproduced (and rearranged) in Table 16–3.[3] The details for each year and the totals are net figures—

[3]The Board of Governors reports yearly discrepancies ranging from $100 million to $5.5 billion between the total estimated sources of funds as presented in Table 16–3 and the total estimated uses of funds—that is, net asset acquisitions. Although such discrepancies need not unduly disturb us, considering the complexity of the data and their overall size, they do remind us that the figures for sources of funds are not claimed to be exact.

TABLE 16–3
Sources of Funds for Nonfarm Nonfinancial Business Corporations, 1946–67
(In billions of dollars)

Year	Stockholders			Depreciation	Long-Term Creditors			Short-Term Sources					Grand Total†
	Stock Sales	Retained Earnings	Total		Bond Sales	Mortgage Loans	Total	Bank Loans*	Trade Payables	Federal Income Tax Liabilities	Other	Total	
1946	$ 1.1	$ 3.3	$ 4.4	$ 4.6	$ 1.0	$ .6	$ 1.6	$ 2.9	$ 3.4	$−2.0	$ 2.1	$ 6.4	$ 16.9
1947	1.2	6.9	8.1	5.7	2.8	.8	3.6	2.3	3.9	2.5	1.2	9.9	27.2
1948	1.0	11.8	12.8	6.8	4.3	.4	4.7	.5	1.1	.9	.3	2.8	27.2
1949	1.3	11.3	12.6	7.8	2.9	.5	3.4	−1.6	−1.8	−2.4	.6	−5.2	18.7
1950	1.4	9.3	10.7	8.6	1.6	.6	2.2	2.8	8.7	7.5	1.0	20.0	41.5
1951	1.9	9.9	11.8	10.0	3.3	.2	3.5	3.8	3.3	4.7	1.6	13.4	38.7
1952	2.3	10.0	12.3	11.2	4.7	.4	5.1	1.5	2.2	−3.3	2.5	2.9	31.6
1953	1.8	8.3	10.1	12.9	3.4	.3	3.7	− .4	.7	.6	2.0	2.9	29.4
1954	1.6	8.7	10.3	14.6	3.5	.7	4.2	− .9	2.2	−3.3	2.0	....	29.1
1955	1.9	12.2	14.1	17.0	2.8	.7	3.5	3.2	8.7	4.1	3.0	19.0	53.7
1956	2.3	10.5	12.8	18.4	3.6	.4	4.0	4.4	5.7	−2.0	3.9	12.0	47.2
1957	2.4	10.3	12.7	20.3	6.3	.4	6.7	1.1	.5	−2.1	2.9	2.4	42.0
1958	2.1	8.1	10.2	21.4	5.7	1.2	6.9	− .6	4.3	−2.6	2.6	3.7	42.2
1959	2.2	12.1	14.3	22.9	3.0	1.2	4.2	3.0	4.9	2.4	3.9	14.2	55.5
1960	1.6	10.2	11.8	24.2	3.5	.7	4.2	1.3	3.1	−2.2	5.0	7.2	47.3
1961	2.5	10.1	12.6	25.4	4.6	1.8	6.4	.1	6.6	1.2	2.2	10.1	54.7
1962	.6	12.6	13.2	29.2	4.6	2.9	7.5	2.5	4.5	1.1	5.4	13.5	63.3
1963	− .3	13.1	12.8	30.8	3.9	3.5	7.4	2.9	6.0	1.5	4.5	14.9	65.9
1964	1.4	17.8	19.2	32.8	4.0	3.3	7.3	3.6	4.0	.7	4.6	12.9	72.1
1965	‡	20.5	20.5	35.3	5.4	3.1	8.5	9.2	7.4	1.9	5.6	24.1	88.4
1966	1.2	22.6	23.8	37.7	10.2	2.6	12.8	6.9	7.8	.2	9.1	24.0	98.3
1967	1.6	19.7	21.3	40.0	15.0	4.0	19.0	5.1	3.9	−4.4	6.8	11.4	91.6
Total	$33.1	$259.3	$292.4	$437.6	$100.1	$30.3	$130.4	$53.6	$91.1	$ 5.0	$72.8	$222.5	$1,082.5
Percentage of grand total	3.1	23.9	27.0	40.4	9.2	2.8	12.0	5.0	8.4	.5	6.7	20.6	100.0

*Predominantly short term, but including intermediate- and long-term loans not secured by mortgages.
†In some instances, items do not add exactly to horizontal subtotals and grand totals because of rounding.
‡Less than $50 million.
SOURCE: Board of Governors of the Federal Reserve System, *Flow of Funds Accounts 1945–1967* (Washington, D.C. 1968), pp. 35–36.

not, for example, total sales of bonds but total sales less retirements, and not total short-term borrowing from banks but new loans less repayment of others. Thus, a negative figure indicates repayments or retirements greater than new amounts acquired from a given source—its reduction as a source of assets by means of funds derived from other sources.

Especially notable among the disclosures in Table 16–3 is the standout performance of depreciation throw-offs as a source of corporate funds in the postwar years—not only its total but also its tremendous rate of expansion in this period.[4] The role of stockholders as contributors to assets is seen to be much more important than is indicated when the respective volumes of stock and bond issues are simply compared. The contribution of stockholders in the 22-year period through stock-buying and the retention of earnings combined equaled

27 percent of total sources of funds, while that of bondholders and other long-term creditors amounted to substantially less than half that amount—12 percent. Nevertheless, the smaller figure remains quite impressive, though still far less than the combined total of all short-term sources of funds—20.6 percent.

CHOICE OF PREFERRED STOCK

From the standpoint of the interests of the common stockholders of a business corporation, the advantages of raising funds by means of preferred stock issues rather than by contracting long-term debt are closely comparable to the advantages of the simple common stock structure itself, as discussed in Chapter 15. Such a parallel is to be expected, since preferred stock is an equity security. Although its ownership rights are usually made to differ in various ways from those of common stock, the preferred stockholders nevertheless participate as owners of the corporation. Since preferred stock represents ownership, therefore, its issuance by a corporation is not so radical a departure from the simple common stock structure as is the incurring of long-term debt. All the more is this true because the preferred stock issues of corporations are generally held to amounts far less than the amounts of their outstanding common stock issues. Among leading corporations that had both common and preferred stocks outstanding in early 1968, had insignificant amounts of long-term debt, if any, and had par or stated values of preferreds that were much less than the assigned values of the common stocks were E. I. Du Pont de Nemours & Co., Eli Lilly & Company, the General Motors Corporation, and the United Fruit Company.

Reasons for choices in favor of preferred stock, accordingly, may

[4]How depreciation charges serve as a source of funds was explained earlier. See pp. 118–19.

be discussed under heads similar to those in Chapter 15 in the analysis of the advantages of simple common stock structures: (1) protection of solvency, (2) maintenance of credit standing, (3) reservation of further financing capacity, and (4) avoidance of restrictions on managerial discretion. The disadvantages of choosing preferred stock, on the other hand, hardly require specific detailed treatment, because they should be sufficiently indicated in the discussion of the disadvantages of simple common stock structures in Chapter 15 as well as in the discussion of the advantages of long-term debt financing presented later in this chapter.

Solvency

The solvency of business corporations is endangered much less by the issuance of preferred stock than by the contraction of long-term debt. As with common stock, dividends on preferred are payable at the discretion of boards of directors. Directors may decide, for a year or two or for a long series of years, that available cash must be conserved for current operations and for the payment of debts rather than be used for dividend payments. The nonpayment of dividends gives preferred stockholders no legal right of action, as by seeking judgments and seizing assets to satisfy them, or by initiating bankruptcy proceedings. Also, preferred stock has no maturity date when the principal (par or stated value) becomes due and payable.

Nevertheless, the presence of preferred stock in financial structures often has some effect toward increasing the danger of insolvency. The danger does not originate in bad times when the supply of cash may be short and liabilities pressing, for in such periods boards of directors will surely not hesitate to decide against the payment of preferred dividends, as well as against retirements of the preferred stock itself. Rather, the danger is likely to originate when business activity is falling off but before serious strains are felt. Boards of directors may be inclined to continue dividends on the preferred to preserve its attractiveness to investors, but subsequent events may prove that the cash so used would have been better conserved for other purposes. In their preferred stock contracts, moreover, many corporations agree to use cash equal to stipulated percentages of their profits for the retirement of the stock. Cash drains in this direction, added to all the others to which corporations are subject, may leave all too little to enable them to weather periods of business adversity without serious strain.

Credit Standing

Because the claims of preferred stockholders against the assets of a corporation are inferior to those of all classes of creditors, the presence of preferred stock in a financial structure has a tendency to enhance the corporation's credit standing. The assets contributed by preferred stockholders, no less than those contributed by common stockholders, provide a cushion of protection for creditors. This means, of course, that all such assets, in addition to what they themselves have contributed, may be seized by the creditors by legal action if their claims are not met according to contractual terms in the normal course of business.

The creditors, however, have reason to be all the more pleased when additional assets that might have been contributed by buyers of preferred stock are contributed, instead, by common stockholders. This is the basis for the conclusion stated in Chapter 15 that, other things being equal, the credit standing of a corporation with a simple common stock structure is likely to be superior to that of a comparable one with both common and preferred stocks outstanding. Creditors are likely to anticipate that in periods of declining business activity preferred dividends will be continued after dividends on common have been suspended. Moreover, they are likely to give weight to the possibility that the use of cash by corporations for the retirement of preferred stock may leave them somewhat short when their own claims come due.

Further Financing Capacity

Although the credit standing of a corporation that has issued preferred stock will probably be somewhat inferior to that of another that in like circumstances maintains a simple common stock structure, the degree of inferiority is not likely to be great. Certainly, its credit standing will tend to be substantially superior to that of a comparable corporation that has already included long-term debt in its financial structure. This kind of difference in credit position probably is especially significant at times when markets for common and preferred stocks are unfavorable. At such times, prospective lenders are reluctant to advance funds to corporations that are already saddled with debt. Though such a corporation may be in a position to give them claims against assets equal, dollar for dollar, with the claims of existing creditors, this may be insufficient inducement. And if the corporation can give them only claims subordinate to those of present creditors, all the greater will their reluctance probably be. On the other hand, a corporation with preferred stock but without long-term debt can offer prospective creditors a superior claimants' position. It is likely to be in a position, indeed, to give them priority over existing short-term creditors, as by arranging for them a mortgage lien on its properties.

However, one possible element of weakness in the position of the corporation with preferred stock but without existing long-term debt must be mentioned. This is the provision found in many preferred stock contracts requiring the consent of the owners of a substantial proportion of the preferred stock, such as two thirds or three fourths, for any long-term financing that would give rise to claims that have priority over their own. A corporation might be unable to get this consent, even though it had found investors willing to lend funds on a long-term basis.

Avoidance of Restrictions on Management

Of the kinds of restrictions on managerial discretion mentioned in Chapter 15, those contained in preferred stock contracts generally circumscribe freedom of action much less than do those of contracts on whose basis long-term debt is incurred. Buyers of preferred stock know that, by its very nature, it must be less safe than are or would be the bonds of the same issuer, and they realize that no list of restrictions on management, however long, could have the effect of giving it a degree of safety equal to that of bonds. They insist on restrictions, it is true, but because they are promised a rate of return higher than the rate that is or would be promised to bondholders, or because they are given other attractive features that bondholders do not or would not get, they are willing to be moderate in limiting managerial discretion.

Also favoring preferred stock in this regard is the fact that waivers of contractual restrictions can usually be more easily obtained from preferred stockholders than from bondholders. A corporation knows who its preferred stockholders are and where they can be reached. It can call them together for a meeting, explain as persuasively as possible the reasons for the request for a waiver, and ask for approval as a vote of confidence. On the other hand, it is not likely to know all the holders of its bonds, although it may know some of them. It may be able to reach all of them through various kinds of public notices, but considerable difficulty is involved.

CHOICE OF LONG-TERM DEBT

Impressive though the foregoing list of advantages of preferred stock issues may be, there is much to be said for the attractiveness of long-term borrowing as an alternative. The attractiveness of long-term debt appears to have been amply proved by American corporations that have resorted to it in the postwar period, as shown in the figures of sources of corporate funds presented earlier in Table 16–3. It appears to be proved by the great number of leading corporations that have substantial volumes of long-term debt but no preferred stock in their financial structures, including (in early 1968): American Telephone and Telegraph, Bethlehem Steel, Boeing, Ford Motor,

General Dynamics, General Electric, Gulf Oil, International Business Machines, McDonnell Douglas, Standard Oil (of Indiana and New Jersey), and United States Steel.

Three advantages of long-term borrowing, by contrast with the sale of preferred stock, are concerned with comparative costs: (1) lower rates payable for the use of investors' or lenders' funds, (2) lower costs in acquiring the funds, and (3) the deductibility of interest in computing income tax liabilities. Two other advantages are also worthy of consideration: (4) avoidance of sharing of control, and (5) avoidance of dilution in the common stockholders' claims to assets.

Lower Rates for the Use of Funds

When corporations choose to abandon the simple common stock form of financial structure and find, at the same time, that they have reasonable access to both the preferred stock and long-term debt markets, they are likely to be impressed by the fact that, as a rule, they can borrow at a rate of interest at least moderately below the dividend rate they would have to promise on preferred stock. If they expect levels of profits to be high enough and stable enough to justify trading on the equity, they may see no particular threat to solvency or credit standing in long-term borrowing. Accordingly, they may decide to reach for the maximum advantage of trading on the equity—that is, by financing at the lower long-term debt rate rather than at the preferred stock rate.

The size of the differentials between interest rates on long-term debt and dividend rates on preferred stock will generally vary at any time according to the investment rating—essentially, the credit standing—of the individual corporation, and from time to time on account of shifts in investor interests and the amounts of their available funds in relation to overall demand. Indeed, it is often difficult to state categorically what the differential is at any given time for a given corporation or class of corporations, because attractive terms of preferred stock contracts *other than the dividend rates* may be accepted by investors in lieu of some or all of the rate differentials that would otherwise obtain. Nevertheless, it is probably safe to say that in the absence of specially attractive features in preferred stocks not directly related to dividends the differential will normally tend to amount to at least one half of a percentage point for the typical corporation.

While a differential of about one half of a percentage point in favor of bond issues may appear to be insufficient inducement to give up the advantages of preferred stock issues as discussed above, it must be emphasized that in long-term financing the differential is multiplied over and over again. A corporation that puts out a preferred stock issue of $20 million that has a dividend rate of 6½ percent will have *each year* a financial cost $100,000 in excess of that of another corporation that puts out a bond issue of the same face amount with an interest rate of 6 percent.

Lower Costs in Acquiring Funds

Corporations that are in a position to sell either long-term debt instruments or preferred stocks generally find that the flotation costs favor long-term debt by a substantial margin. Long-term borrowing, therefore, has a cost advantage in addition to that measured by the spread between dividend and interest rates, as just described.

Some expenses of flotation of preferred stock issues tend to be less than those incurred in the flotation of bond issues of comparable size and of comparable issuers. These include transfer agency fees (as against trustees' fees for bond issues), printing and engraving expenses, and legal fees. But most of the other kinds of expenses of preferred stock issues are close to or higher than those for debt issues. Differentials unfavorable to preferred stock are especially pronounced in the compensation paid to investment bankers—by far the most sizable item of expense in flotations for which their services are employed. The size of these differentials is indicated in Table 18–2, page 433, and their effects on total flotation costs were already indicated in Table 15–3, page 354. Investment bankers ordinarily demand a higher rate of compensation on preferred stock transactions than on bond transactions because they anticipate greater difficulties in selling the preferred stock. If they *underwrite* (which is, to repeat, a guaranteeing of sale at a specific price), they demand a higher reward as compensation for the greater risks of not being able to unload preferred stocks at the prices guaranteed.

Income Tax Treatment of Bond Interest

Strong is the belief that the deductibility of interest paid for borrowed money in determining federal income tax liabilities, as against the nondeductibility of dividend payments on common and preferred stock, has been an extremely important reason for the heavy volume of long-term corporate debt financing in the period since the close of World War II, by comparison with the volume of stock financing.

The illustrations presented in Chapter 15 in the discussion of trading on the equity indicated the nature of the deductibility advantage. Nevertheless, a further illustration at this point should be useful. For this purpose, let us assume that to raise $10 million of additional funds a corporation has the choice of putting out a bond issue or a preferred stock issue. Since our objective is to see the tax advantage of the bond issue, we may ignore differences in probable flotation costs, and we may further assume that regardless of the corporation's choice the rate of return it would have to promise investors is 5 percent. A final assumption is that the corporation expects to earn an average annual profit of $2 million before the deduction of bond interest or preferred dividends, as the case may be, and before the deduction of the federal income tax. Accordingly, the tax advantage of the bond issue would be demonstrable as follows.

	Bond Alternative	*Preferred Stock Alternative*
Profit as indicated	$2,000,000	$2,000,000
Less: Bond interest	500,000	....
Taxable profit	$1,500,000	$2,000,000
Less: Federal income tax[5]	713,500	953,500
	$ 786,500	$1,046,500
Less: Preferred stock dividends	....	500,000
Profit available for dividends on common stock or retention	$ 786,500	$ 546,500

The bond route would thus be expected to result in a tax saving of $240,000. A pleasant aspect of this would be, of course, that such a tax saving would be expected year after year as long as the full amount of the bonds was outstanding. The managers of the corporation would surely feel that since the annual tax saving would amount to 2.4 percent of the face amount of the bonds, the cost of the funds supplied by the bondholders would actually be not 5 percent but only 2.6 percent. They might expect to say, as is so often said, that Uncle Sam would be bearing approximately half the interest cost on the bonds. On the other hand, they would realize that should their choice go to preferred stock the cost of the funds acquired would stand at 5 percent; Uncle Sam has no part in this.

Avoidance of Sharing of Control

Long-term lenders to corporations are creditors; as such, they get no rights to participate in management, as that expression is generally understood. They may demand that certain kinds of restrictions on managerial discretion be placed in their contracts, but they do not ask for the privilege of participating in decision making outside the scope of the restrictions. They do not vote in the annual election of directors nor on questions that corporations are required by law to submit to their stockholders.

By contrast, preferred stockholders participate directly in management in various ways. Hence, groups of common stockholders that have narrow margins of control in given corporations may vote against preferred issues and in favor of debt issues for fear that the preferred might seriously weaken their positions. Under the laws of

[5]At 22 percent on first $25,000 and 48 percent on balance—the basic rates in effect in 1968 before the addition in June of that year of a surcharge of 10 percent.

two states, Illinois and Mississippi, preferred stockholders have equal voting power, share for share, with the common stockholders. In either of these states, therefore, a group that had 51 percent of the outstanding common stock of a corporation would be most unlikely to approve a preferred stock issue if they expected that purchases by an opposing group would give it more than 50 percent of the combined total of the existing common and the new preferred. In other states, the general rule is that preferred stock may be deprived of the ordinary power to vote for directors and on questions that the law requires be submitted to the stockholders; nevertheless, certain contingent and veto voting powers are usually retained by the preferred stockholders. This reservation of limited voting powers is customarily insisted on by investment bankers as a means of making preferred stocks attractive to investors, as well as by institutional investors if they undertake to buy whole issues or large parts of issues for their own portfolios. Illustrative of contingent voting powers is a provision that preferred stockholders shall have the right to vote in the election of directors if dividends on the preferred have not been paid for a designated period of time such as a year. An example of veto powers—one mentioned earlier—is a provision requiring the approval of two thirds or three fourths or some other proportion of the preferred stock for subsequent issues of bonds.[6] Thus, a controlling group of common stockholders may shy away from a nonvoting preferred stock for fear that, at some future time, their control may be lost through the ballots of preferred stockholders in exercising contingent voting powers because of, say, nonpayment of dividends.

Avoidance of Dilution of Common Stockholders' Claims to Assets

In the matter of payments, bondholders and other long-term creditors of a corporation are likely to be quite satisfied if it pays interest periodically at the stipulated rate and the principal or face amount of the obligations at maturity. Should the corporation want to retire debt before maturity, as by calling bonds for redemption, it may be required to pay a bonus or premium over and above the face amount plus whatever interest may have accumulated. But the bonus or premium usually amounts to not more than 2 or 3 percent of the principal—sometimes it goes as high as 6 percent, but rarely beyond that—and it is likely to be considered by the debtor corporation simply as an additional interest cost. It may be so treated for federal income tax purposes, so that deductible expenses are increased and tax liabilities are reduced if such a premium is paid.

Buyers of preferred stock, on the other hand, are inclined to be

[6]The treatment here is not intended to be complete. The voting rights of preferred stockholders are analyzed at greater length in Chapter 23. See pp. 578–81.

much more generous to themselves in stipulating what redemption prices for their stockholdings they will agree to. Investment bankers and institutional investors often demand that such prices be fixed at premiums of 6 or 7 percent of the par or stated value of the stock, and sometimes at even higher percentages. Insistence by investors on such premiums is justified on the grounds that corporations are likely to decide on redemption when their financial positions are of the strongest—at the very time, therefore, when preferred stockholders are likely to be most anxious to retain their holdings. Along the same line, it is argued that when the outlook is poor, corporations can hardly be expected to be sufficiently well fixed financially to retire preferred stock; but that would be precisely the time when redemption would be most enthusiastically welcomed by preferred stockholders.

Because in considering further financing common stockholders and their representatives on a board of directors often anticipate that the good fortunes of the corporation will make possible the retirement of whatever new securities are to be issued, they may tend to veer away from preferred stock because of redemption premium demands. They may conclude that the claim of the common stockholders to assets would be threatened with unfair dilution were a generous redemption price to be included in the preferred stock contract. For illustration, assume that a corporation has outstanding 100,000 shares of common stock of $100 par value, and that it has accumulated a surplus of $4 million. The common stockholders' claim to assets is, therefore, $140 a share. Now comes a proposal that the corporation issue 20,000 shares of preferred stock. An investment banker is willing to buy this stock at the par value of, say, $100 a share, but he insists that the redemption price be placed at $115. Were the financing to be carried through on this basis, the buyers of the preferred stock could be said to have a claim against assets at the level of the redemption price. Although the claim, as originally established, would not be enforceable at any specific date, it would become so should the corporation at some time decide to redeem. The premium claim of the preferred stockholders of $15 a share, or $300,000 in total, would be granted at the expense of the common stockholders, for their claims against assets would be reduced from $140 to $137 per share.

Although dilution of common stockholders' claims to assets, as illustrated, is not likely to be considered a grave disadvantage of preferred stock issues—certainly not so great a disadvantage as the nondeductibility of preferred dividends for income tax purposes—it can at times be a strong argument against preferred stock financing. Should a corporation anticipate, for example, that it might want to retire a preferred stock issue as early as five years after the date of issuance, and should a prospective purchaser of the issue, such as an investment banker, demand a redemption premium of 15 percent, the corporation might decide that preferred stock financing would be much too expensive. Were the dividend rate to be, say, 5 percent, the corporate managers would not be unreasonable in fearing that the annual cost of preferred stock funds would actually prove to be much closer to 8 percent.

INCLUSION OF BOTH PREFERRED STOCK AND LONG-TERM DEBT

Many corporations as a matter of continuing policy include both preferred stock and long-term debt in their financial structures. The policy is especially prominent among public utilities, but it is by no means uncommon in many other areas of business enterprise. In only a few areas, indeed, is it impossible to find at least a few corporations that have adopted such a policy. Among leading corporations that have (as of early 1968) financial structures with both preferred stock and long-term debt, each of substantial amount, are Continental Can, Duquesne Light, Georgia-Pacific, International Paper, Liggett and Myers, the Mead Corporation, Reynolds Metals, Southern California Edison, Union Oil, United States Gypsum, and Westinghouse Electric.

In some cases, the inclusion of both preferred stock and long-term debt in financial structures is the result of deliberate choice on the part of corporate managements; in others, it is the result of investor attitudes and conditions in the markets for long-term funds. Managements that have decided to depart from simple common stock structures may find that they have access to sufficient additional funds either by way of preferred stock sales or long-term borrowing, but a consideration of relative advantages and disadvantages may prompt them to choose a combination of these sources. On the other hand, managements may have strong preferences for one means of financing or the other, but they may find that by the exclusive use of the means of their choice they cannot acquire on reasonable terms as much money as they want. In a word, investors will not buy as much preferred stock as they would like to issue, or long-term lenders will not advance as much money as they would like to borrow.

Managerial Choices

A corporate management may decide that though all needed funds could be raised without difficulty by means of preferred stock issues, exclusive dependence on this means of financing would not be wise. Fears that issues of preferred stock beyond a certain level would endanger its own position of control might be a reason for such a decision; a danger might be seen in the contingent voting powers that would have to be given to the preferred stockholders. Or it may be felt that too great a dilution of the common stockholders' claim to assets could result from exclusive dependence on preferred stock in the new financing. Some dilution on account of high redemption prices may be tolerable, but the management may decide to limit it by limiting the amount of the preferred stock issue itself. Even more importantly, relatively high dividend rates and the nondeductibility of dividends for tax purposes are often of great weight in decisions not to depend solely on preferred stock issues as sources of additional funds.

Moreover, the managers of a corporation that could borrow sufficient long-term funds to meet its expansion requirements fully may decide against relying exclusively on this source. They may conclude that though solvency would not be endangered by partial financing with long-term debt they would be taking undue risks were they to use only this source. Or they may conclude that exclusive dependence on long-term debt for present financing would leave the corporation with no borrowing capacity in the future—in times of emergency, in particular, when the markets for common and preferred stocks probably would be quite unfavorable. For such reasons, then, come managers' decisions to include preferred stock, as well as long-term debt, in financial structures.

Investor Attitudes and Market Conditions

Availability of Investors' Funds. An important reason that corporations cannot sell as much preferred stock as they may want to sell is that the demand for preferred at most times is much weaker than is demand for common stocks and bonds. In periods of depression, new issues of preferred stocks are often unsalable at anything close to fair prices, and even in times of prosperity the preferred stock market generally does not become so buoyant as the markets for common stock and bonds. The simple fact is that investors collectively are much less interested in investing in preferred stocks than in the other two major classes of securities. Individual investors who are willing to take risks are inclined to accept the greater risks of common stock in the hope of deriving greater rewards than can be expected from investment in preferred stocks. If they seek safety, they are inclined to want a full measure of it, as in debt instruments, rather than an in-between position, as in preferred stocks. Moreover, some of our most important classes of institutional investors are strictly limited by legal regulations in the amount of their preferred stock investment. Commercial banks are generally precluded entirely from preferred stock investment, and life insurance companies, mutual savings banks, and trustees who manage certain kinds of trusts must keep preferred stock holdings to small proportions of their total portfolios.

Investors' interest in bonds and other forms of long-term debt, on the other hand, tends to be perennial. Except in times of severest depression, substantial amounts of funds available for investment in long-term debt instruments are likely to be found in the hands of investors. In life insurance companies, for example, collections of premiums and income earned on existing investments often exceed payments on policies and operating expenses even in times of serious business setbacks, and the excess receipts must be promptly invested to provide the further income needed to fulfill accumulating policy obligations. Yet, in times of high prosperity when the market for common stock is booming and the preferred market is quite favorable, the interests of life insurance companies in further investment in bonds do not wane, since they are legally limited in their investment in stock.

Earnings Standards. The availability of large sums of money in the hands of individual and institutional investors never means that the individual corporation can get as much as it wants, whether by the issuance of preferred stock or the issuance of bonds. In deciding whether or not to buy new offerings of securities, investors judge quality and therefore attractiveness by applying various kinds of tests. Among the most important of these tests are earnings standards. Potential investors in a preferred stock want to know how much earnings the corporation will have available for dividends. They are especially concerned with what future earnings will be, but very often they must judge this by what earnings have been in the recent past. Thus, a popular test for preferred stock investment is that average earnings after the deduction of income taxes in a short period of years immediately preceding the year of the proposed issue—preferably including years both of depression and prosperity—should have been equal to two or three times the amount of annual dividends promised.

In their analysis of the investment qualities of proposed issues of bonds, individual and institutional investors generally place even greater emphasis on earnings available for bond interest in the past few years. Since, however, interest on bonds is a deductible expense for income tax purposes, bond buyers stress the ratio of average earnings *before* income taxes to the amount of bond interest to be paid, but they insist on a much higher earnings-to-interest ratio than is expected for the earnings-to-dividends ratio by buyers of preferred stock. Therefore, while preferred stock buyers may insist on average earnings *after* income taxes equal to two or three times preferred dividends, prospective long-term creditors usually demand average earnings *before* income taxes equal to three to seven times bond interest requirements.

To see how earnings standards function as determinants of the amounts of preferred stock and bonds corporations may be able to sell on reasonable terms, let us assume that a certain corporation wants to raise about $20 million, and that it is pondering the question whether it should offer preferred stock or bonds or both. It would have to set a dividend rate of 6 percent on whatever amount of preferred stock it might decide to offer, and an interest rate of 5 percent on bonds. Its average annual profit before the deduction of income taxes has been $3 million, and after this deduction, at combined federal and state tax rates of 50 percent, let us say, $1.5 million. It recognizes that earnings tests that investors are applying to proposed issues of preferred stock and bonds of the quality it would issue are, respectively, two times and six times.[7] Apparently, therefore, the corporation ought to be able to offer successfully either approximately $12.5 million of 6 percent preferred stock ($1,500,000 ÷ .12) or $10 million of 5 percent bonds ($3,000,000 ÷ .30). Apparently, too, the corporation could not raise the $20 million by sole dependence on either preferred stock or bonds. Strange though it might seem, however, both of the earnings tests could be met were the corporation to offer $10 million of bonds and an equal amount of preferred stock. This conclusion can be demonstrated as follows.

Average earnings available for bond interest (equal to 6 times annual bond interest of $500,000 on $10 million of bonds)	$3,000,000
Deduct bond interest	500,000
	$2,500,000
Deduct income taxes at 50%	1,250,000
Average earnings available for preferred dividends (equal to approximately twice annual dividend requirements of $600,000 on $10 million of preferred stock)	$1,250,000

The foregoing illustration may suggest that investors in preferred stocks and bonds are unreasonably cautious. Perhaps they are. But in planning new issues of securities corporate managers must make allowance for investors' caution, whether or not they think it unreasonable. It would be useless for them to argue that the new financing should substantially expand the corporation's earning capacity and that, therefore, earnings tests of two or three times preferred dividends or six or seven times bond interest based on *past* earnings demand too great a margin of protection. If this is the degree of protection that investors look for, they can hardly be expected to buy

[7]Such recognition is not likely to be subject to any wide margin of error. As soon as a corporation begins to negotiate with investment bankers or other prospective buyers of its securities, it is told that the preferred stock contract or the bond indenture *must* contain limitations on total issues in terms of standards of earnings and of relationships of assets to liabilities and net worth such as are discussed here and in subsequent paragraphs of the text. These limitations in preferred stock contracts and bond indentures are generally known as protective provisions. As found in preferred stock contracts, they are discussed below, pp. 582–87, and in bond indentures, pp. 725–27.

corporate offerings of preferred stocks and bonds that fall short of their standards.

Standards for Relationships of Assets to Liabilities and Equity. Even meeting investors' earnings tests, conservative though they may seem to be, does not necessarily give a corporation clear sailing in offering new issues of preferred stock or bonds. Prospective investors can be expected to apply other kinds of tests, especially tests involving relationships of assets to liabilities and stockholders' equity in total or the equity of the common stockholders in particular—relationships as they would be *after* the proposed financing had been completed. Investors want to be sure that the individual corporation will not be depending too heavily on the kind of security they buy as a source of its assets.

Standards applied by investors in preferred stocks are generally not so uniform as are those applied by buyers of bonds. For issues of industrial corporations, for example, some groups of investors are likely to be satisfied if the amount of preferred stock to be outstanding will not exceed the amount of common stock and surplus. Others are inclined to be more restrictive in their demands, as in asking that the amount of preferred stock plus all debt, current and fixed, not exceed 50 percent of the total assets.

Preferred

The various classes of investors in bonds are usually quite consistent in fixing limits beyond which, in their opinion, corporations in the different fields of business should not go in incurring debt. Their quality standards relate *total* debt, on the one hand, to current assets, total assets, or total tangible assets,[8] on the other, as well as total debt to the total equities of the stockholders. The investors often expect both of these types of standards to be satisfied simultaneously.

For the bonds of industrial corporations, for example, a widely accepted standard is that total long-term debt should not exceed the amount of working capital, and another is that total debt of all kinds should not exceed the amount of the stockholders' equity. To see how these standards would be applied both separately and simultaneously, let us assume that a corporation, if successful in proposed financing whatever direction it might take, would have assets and current liabilities as follows.

BOND

Assets		*Liabilities and Equity*	
Current assets.....	$6,000,000	Current liabilities......	$2,500,000
Fixed assets.......	7,000,000	Bonds.................	To be determined
		Common and preferred stock and surplus....	Amount needed to balance

Application of the working capital test—the amount of long-term

[8]That is, total assets less intangibles such as goodwill and stockholdings in subsidiaries.

debt should not exceed working capital—would mean a limitation of the bond issue to $3.5 million. With a bond issue at that level, stockholders' equity would have to amount to $7 million to provide the total complement of assets of $13 million. Thus, the second test—total debt of all kinds should not exceed equity—would be easily satisfied.

Suppose, however, that the corporation's assets and current liability position after the financing were expected to be as follows.

Assets		*Liabilities and Equity*	
Current assets	$7,000,000	Current liabilities	$2,500,000
Fixed assets	6,000,000	Bonds	To be determined
		Common and preferred stock and surplus	Amount needed to balance

Now the working capital standard would permit a bond issue of $4.5 million, but this amount would be excessive by the equity standard. With total assets of $13 million and a bond issue of $4.5 million, total stockholders' equity would be only $6 million, and this would be less than the total amount of debt. Accordingly, investors in bonds whose judgment was based on a simultaneous application of the two standards would probably be unwilling to buy unless the bond issue were limited to $4 million and equity increased, as by a new preferred or common stock issue, to $6.5 million.

QUESTIONS

1. How has the post-World War II volume of financing with common and preferred stocks compared with the volume of bond financing? How has the volume of stock retirements compared with the volume of bond retirements?

2. In relation to one another, how has each of the following ranked in recent years as sources of corporate funds: stockholders' investment, depreciation, long-term debt, and short-term debt?

3. Since depreciation is an operating expense, is it not unreasonable to classify it as a source of corporate funds? Explain.

4. Does any danger to solvency result from including preferred stock in corporate financial structures? Explain.

5. How is the addition of preferred stock to a corporation's financial structure likely to affect its credit standing? Its further access to long-term funds?

6. For what reason do income tax considerations often influence corporate managements toward bond financing rather than financing with preferred stocks to raise long-term funds?

7. Aside from income tax considerations, why does bond financing tend to be cheaper than preferred stock financing?

8. How do bond contracts compare with preferred stock contracts in imposing restrictions on corporate managements?

9. How is fear of loss of control likely to affect corporate choices between bonds and preferred stocks for long-term financing?

10. For choices between bonds and preferred stocks for long-term financing, what weight is likely to be given to the size of premiums to be paid on redemption?

11. For what reasons do corporate managements often decide to include both preferred stock and bonds in their financial structures?

12. Explain how investors' attitudes influence corporate decisions about issuing bonds, preferred stock, or both for long-term financing.

13. What is the nature of the earnings standards that investors commonly apply in evaluating the merits of corporate securities? How are these standards applied in judging preferred stock and bond issues?

PROBLEMS

1. The Yancey-Pike Corporation has 900,000 shares of common stock outstanding, and in the past 4 years it has had average annual earnings of $3.6 million before the deduction of federal and state income taxes, which jointly amount to 50 percent. Its management estimates that annual earnings before income taxes could be increased by $600,000 were the corporation to spend $2 million for additional facilities. The money could be raised by selling an issue of preferred stock with a dividend rate of 7 percent or a bond issue with an interest rate of 6½ percent. Assuming that the profit expectation of Yancey-Pike's management would be exactly realized, and disregarding the costs of selling the securities, what would be its after-tax profit per share of common stock if the financing were done by means of (*a*) the preferred stock issue, and (*b*) the bond issue?

2. In the past three years, the average net profit of Wells & Baxter, Inc. has been $4,680,000 before the deduction of federal and state income taxes jointly amounting to 50 percent. To finance a program of expansion, it wants to raise the largest sum of money it can lay its hands on, whether by a bond issue, a preferred stock issue, or some combination of the two. Its investment bankers are of the opinion that it would have to designate a 6 percent interest rate on a bond issue and a 6½ percent dividend rate on a preferred stock issue. The bankers say that such rates would attract many investors provided that the corporation did not attempt to market excessive issues—excessive in the sense of failing to satisfy the investors' earnings standards.

a) Assuming that investors in the corporation's bonds would expect its recent before-tax earnings to be equal to three times the interest requirement, what is the maximum amount of bonds for which it would be likely to find a ready market?

b) Assuming that investors in the corporation's preferred stock would expect its recent after-tax earnings to be equal to two times the dividend requirement, what is the maximum dollar amount of preferred shares for which it would be likely to find buyers?

c) Assuming investors' standards to be as stated in (*a*) and (*b*), what are the maximum amounts of bonds and preferred stock in combination for which the corporation would be likely to find buyers?

Part VI

FINANCING WITH COMMON STOCK

chapter 17

COMMON STOCK AS A SOURCE OF ASSETS

Common stock is of outstanding importance as a source of corporate assets. For the thousands of new business corporations that are formed every year, it tends to be almost an exclusive original source of assets; and for most of these corporations that survive, its predominant role is maintained for many years. Only with the development of good earnings capacities—usually a slow process—it is possible for retained profits as shown in surplus accounts to rival, and then perhaps to outrank, common stock as a source of assets; and only with the building of good credit reputations—usually a slow process, also—is it possible for debt as a source of assets to compete with common stock. For some corporations, common stock always remains as the most important source of assets, regardless of the duration of their lives.

As a source of assets, indeed, the role of common stock can hardly be thought of as being measured only by the amount of cash or the value of other assets turned into corporations in exchange for it. It is not unreasonable to regard it also as the source of assets acquired by way of retained profits. In consideration of the risks they assume, the owners of common stock are claimants against all corporate profits that remain after income taxes and responsibilities to preferred stockholders have been met. To the extent, therefore, that common stockholders receive dividends that fall short of these profits, they make further contributions to corporate assets.

Why are millions of investors willing to make asset contributions to corporations through the purchase and ownership of common stock? To put the question in alternative form, why do corporations find common stock a financing instrument of extraordinary usefulness? The objective of the present chapter is to provide an answer to these questions. The answer must focus on the rights or privileges that corporations afford to their common stockholders. These rights are attractive, although the degree of attractiveness differs from corporation to corporation. The rights *must* be attractive; otherwise, we have no explanation why people give huge sums of money, great aggregations of assets of other kinds, and innumerable hours of service in exchange for common stock.

COMMON STOCK AS A CONTRACT

In Chapter 2, stock was described as shares of ownership in a corporation, but it may also be defined as a contract between a corporation and its stockholders. The stockholders of a corporation are truly its owners, but ownership does not make them identical with it, as in a partnership. The corporation remains apart from its stockholders as a distinct legal entity. As a separate personality, it has the capacity to enter into contracts with people who want to become its stockholders. It does enter such contracts when it issues stock.

Nature of the Contract

To be binding, a contract must have consideration—that is, mutual promises or obligations of the parties to do or not to do something that legally can be done. With corporate stock, consideration is provided by the corporation in giving the stockholder a bundle of rights, which it promises to respect at all times, and is provided by the stockholder in his promise to pay the agreed-on price for the stock. It is, of course, the bundle of rights that attracts buyers of stock, and it is the buyers' promises to pay that are sources of corporate assets.

The terms and conditions of stock as a contract are ordinarily not found in any one place. They are determined, in the first place, by the provisions of the laws of the state in which the corporation is chartered. Such laws stipulate what rights *must* be given to the stockholders, what rights *may* be given, and how certain rights may be limited. Thus, the stockholders obtain the rights conferred by law, whether or not the corporation's articles of incorporation and bylaws have anything to say about them. Second, the corporation's articles of incorporation contain other details of the contract—granting rights of some kinds and withholding others as may be permitted by the state laws. In the third place, the corporation's bylaws may contain other provisions concerning stockholders' rights, ordinarily not granting any not contained in the state laws or in the articles, and certainly not contradicting the laws and articles in modifying rights granted in those places, but setting details about how the rights are to be exercised—for example, how the stockholders are to choose the directors at annual meetings and how they may have their stock transferred should they want to sell all or part of it. And, finally, further features of the contract are likely to be found in resolutions adopted by the corporation's board of directors, particularly designations about the price prospective stockholders must pay for the stock, whether in cash, other property, or services.

Common and Preferred Stock

Establishing that stock is a contract does not contradict the definition of stock as shares of ownership; it simply gives a legal complexion to the definition. In buying stock of a corporation, a person becomes one of its owners, but his rights as an owner are not necessarily the same as the rights he enjoys in the ownership of a house or an automobile; they depend on the terms of his contract with the corporation. The rights of stockholders of a given class sometimes differ from state to state on account of dissimilar provisions of state laws, and even within a single state they may differ among corporations as they apply in different ways permissive provisions of the state laws. Within the single corporation, furthermore, very important differences in ownership rights may be provided for contractually with stockholders of distinct classes.

It is a basic principle of corporation law, nevertheless, that every business corporation must issue and have outstanding at all times a kind of stock that carries the full rights of ownership, as those full rights are recognized in the law of the state and in the decisions of its courts. Whatever this stock may be called by the individual corporation, it is known definitively as *common* stock. The corporation may or may not have one or more additional classes of stock in which the rights of ownership are limited in various ways—generally known as *preferred* stock—but, in any event, it cannot dispense with common stock. We readily conclude, therefore, that if a corporation has only one kind of stock outstanding, such stock must be common stock. This being true, it necessarily follows that common stock is the first stock a corporation issues and the last it retires.

In passing, we may note that many corporations that have only one kind of stock outstanding refer to it simply as capital stock. Since any single issue of stock must be common stock, these corporations take it for granted that everybody must know that their capital stock is truly common stock. Sometimes, too, corporations use the word *capital* in the designation of two or more classes of stock, as common capital stock and preferred capital stock. Although such terminology is justifiable, since the words *stock* and *capital stock* may best be regarded as synonyms, the simpler designations "common stock" and "preferred stock" are more popular.

Classification of Common Stockholders' Rights

From the standpoint of the attractiveness of common stock to investors—and therefore of its usefulness to corporations as a means of financing—the full rights of common stockholders may be classified in two groups: (1) those rights, three in number, in which attractiveness chiefly resides; and (2) those rights, five in number, whose principal function, one may say, is to protect the rights of the first group.

The rights of the first group are: (1) to share in such dividends as may be distributed, (2) to have a claim against assets, and (3) to participate in management. Those of the second group are: (1) to have a stock certificate as evidence of ownership, (2) to sell or otherwise dispose of the stock, (3) to subscribe to additional issues of stock in proportion to existing holdings, (4) to inspect the books of the corporation, and (5) to take action in the courts to put a stop to or to prevent corporate activities alleged to be illegal, or *ultra vires*, or mismanagerial.

RIGHTS TO DIVIDENDS, ASSETS, AND MANAGEMENT

A large majority of investors in common stock, both individual and institutional, are undoubtedly motivated primarily by expectations of receiving dividends at a rate in excess of the rate of return expected from investment in preferred stock or bonds, or, indeed, from any other use of their money. But their motivation tends always to be a mixed one. Investors in common stock know that it is a policy of most corporations to retain substantial proportions of their net profits to finance expansion. They know also that a retention of profits adds to their claims against assets, and they expect these added claims to be reflected in increases in the market value of the common shares they hold. To put the matter in another way, they expect retained profits to add to corporate profit-making capacities—a development that should enhance the attractiveness of the common stock in the market. They buy, therefore, both for dividend income and for appreciation in market value.

For other investors, the feature of common stock that is primarily attractive is the right it accords to the stockholder to participate in management. These investors want to gain or retain control in the corporations whose common stock they buy; they regard the advantages of exercising control of greater importance than rights to share in dividends and to have claims against assets. It is not that such investors have no interests in dividends and claims against assets but, rather, that their interests in these directions are clearly subordinate to their interests in control.

Interrelationship of Rights to Dividends and Assets

The proposition that rights to share in dividends and claims to assets are intermingled as attractions to investors in common stock may be further developed by means of an illustration. Let us suppose that a certain corporation has outstanding 100,000 shares of common stock of $50 par value on which it is able to earn an annual profit of 10 percent after the deduction of income taxes. We may assume that the market value of the stock is also $50. Up to the present time, the corporation has not accumulated a surplus, because it has been paying out dividends equal to the full amount of its net profits. Now, however, it decides to cut its dividend rate to 5 percent and to use the balance of its annual net profit to finance a program of expansion. It expects to be able to earn 10 percent after taxes on the retained profits. If, then, this expectation were fulfilled, the results of its new policy in a five-year period would be as follows (with the net profit for the sixth year entered for later reference).

Year	*Net Profit after Income Taxes*	*Dividends*	*Retained Profit*	*Surplus Accumulation*
1......	$500,000	$250,000	$250,000	$ 250,000
2......	525,000	250,000	275,000	525,000
3......	552,500	250,000	302,500	827,500
4......	582,750	250,000	332,750	1,160,250
5......	616,025	250,000	366,025	1,526,275
6......	652,628			

In the five-year period, the reduced level of dividends would result in an increase in the book value of the common stock—its claim against assets per share—from $50 to $65.26. If, moreover, the expansion program had been completed by the end of the fifth year, and if, accordingly, a decision were made to distribute dividends equal to all the profits of the sixth year, the dividend rate would be 13.05 percent of the par value of the stock ($652,628 ÷ $5,000,000). Had the market value of the stock been $50 when dividends were being paid at a rate of 10 percent, prospects for future dividends at 13.05 percent of par value, evaluated jointly with the higher level of the claims of the common stock against assets, would surely tend to push the market value well above $50. Considering all the forces that play on the stock market and all its vagaries, we can hardly say what the new market price would be, but we can say that considering the affairs of our corporation solely, it ought to be in the vicinity of $65.

The illustration clearly indicates why, for many investors in common stock, possibilities of appreciation strongly rival in attractiveness the prospects of dividend payments at given levels—why such investors are not repulsed because of corporate policies of retaining substantial proportions of current profits. Had the corporation of the illustration forgone its expansion program and continued to pay dividends during the 5-year period at 10 percent of par value, they would have amounted in total to $25 a share. With the expansion program in effect, the dividends would be cut to a 5-year total of $12.50, but were it possible to sell the stock at $65 a share at the end of the fifth year, a person who had bought it at $50 at the beginning of the 5-year period would have additional income of $15 for a total of $27.50. The difference of $2.50 in stockholder income as between the two alternatives would be due to the compounding of earnings on the retained profits; this would appear to be a distinct advantage of the second route.[1] But likely to be much more important for large stockholders with high levels of income is that the $15 profit on the sale of the stock would be treated as a long-term capital gain in federal income tax determination. As a long-term capital gain, it would be subject to the relatively low tax rate applicable to such gains rather than to the steeply progressive rates of the individual income tax to which dividends are subject.[2]

Right to Share in Dividends

Although the foregoing demonstration indicates the difficulty of putting the attractiveness of the common stockholder's right to share in dividends and the attractiveness of his claim against assets in separate compartments, it is still desirable to separately treat certain aspects of these two rights.

At the very least, it is to be observed that for many small investors dividend prospects represent the principal criterion for or against buying given common stocks. Market appreciation leading to capital gains will surely be welcomed by such investors, but rarely will they consider it a reasonable substitute for dividends at a good level. Income tax rates in the higher brackets do not bother them, and matters of management and control are likely to be of slight interest. Accordingly, a corporation that has been rather niggardly in its dividend policy would probably be unsuccessful should it try to sell additional common stock to such small investors.

Directors' Discretion in Paying Dividends. Although of outstanding importance in making common stock attractive to investors, the right of common stockholders to share in dividends is a limited one. Regardless of the size of a corporation's current profit and its accumulation of profits in past periods, actual distributions of dividends depend on decisions of its board of directors. Corporation laws are quite clear in giving the directors the power to decide how profits can be best used to promote corporate objectives—whether they should be retained in whole or in part for corporate purposes or be used as the basis for dividend distributions.

---

[1]If, however, the stockholder were able to reinvest at 10 percent compounded annually half of the amount of dividends received by way of the first alternative, his total income per share for the 5-year period would likewise be $27.50.

[2]For the pertinent rules on the taxation of capital gains, see footnote 14, page 40. The advantage of the capital gains rate by comparison with the rates applicable to dividends as ordinary income is moderately offset by the provision of the law that no tax need be paid on the first $100 of dividends. However, this concession is likely to be of slight significance to taxpayers in the higher income tax brackets.

A decision of a corporation's directors to distribute dividends to the common stockholders is formalized by the adoption of a resolution stating the amount to be paid, the date of payment, and the date on which a list of the stockholders who are to receive the dividends will be taken from the stock records. If no such resolution is adopted, the stockholders ought not to expect to receive dividends. Dividend payments require formal action, whereas the payment of interest on bonds, like the payment of any other kind of expense, is a matter of routine operations. Even a handful of stockholders in a close family corporation cannot legally help themselves to cash, whether or not in some uniform percentage of their stockholdings. If they want to withdraw cash beyond whatever salaries they allow themselves, they must declare a dividend by formal resolution, taking this action in their capacity as members of the board of directors to which doubtless they will have elected themselves.

Stockholders' Actions to Force Dividends. If the stockholders are dissatisfied with the proportion of profits the board of directors is willing to allocate for dividends, their normal recourse is to elect a different, more generous group of directors. Like many remedies for injustices, however, this one may actually be of little applicability. If all the directors are chosen by a small group of stockholders who own a narrow majority of the common stock, and if this group much prefers appreciation in book and market values to dividends-in-hand, it does not help the minority much to be told that they ought to elect a different array of directors.

Occasionally, however, on appeal by unhappy stockholders of a corporation a court of equity will order the directors to make a dividend distribution. Courts of equity are most reluctant to substitute their judgment for that of boards of directors; they are inclined to believe that the directors, being on the firing line, are in a better position to know how the long-range interests of their corporations can best be promoted. Nevertheless, such a court can sometimes be convinced that directors have ulterior motives for their refusal to distribute dividends. The appealing stockholders may be able to convince the court, for example, that nonpayment of dividends over a lengthy period of years has been designed to freeze them out—to force them to sell their stock at sacrifice prices, so that it could be bought up by the directors themselves or by controlling stockholders who might not be directors. A court thus persuaded would probably issue an order to the directors to make a substantial distribution. Failure of the directors to heed such an order would make them subject to punishment for contempt of court.

The most celebrated case of this kind originated in 1916, when John and Horace Dodge brought proceedings against the Ford Motor Company to force more liberal dividend payments. Henry Ford had announced that annual dividends would be limited to 60 percent of the par value of the company's outstanding stock. But the par value of its stock at that time amounted to only $2 million, while its surplus had grown to $112 million, its profit for 1916 was expected to amount to almost $60 million, and it had over $52 million of cash on hand. A business corporation, the court said, "is organized and carried on primarily for the profit of the stockholders. The powers of the directors are to be employed for that end . . ."; and it decreed that the company should distribute an additional dividend of $19 million, at the same time enjoining it from unreasonably withholding dividends in the future.[3]

Dividends as Pro Rata Distributions. Another matter worthy of mention at this time[4] is that dividends on common stock are always pro rata distributions. The right of each common stockholder to receive dividends as declared by a corporation's board of directors is equal, share for share, with that of every other common stockholder. Were a corporation to sell an original issue of common stock of a par value of $20 at, say, $40 a share and a later issue at, say, $25 or $75, the two batches would be indistinguishable in their right to dividends. On a share for which he paid the corporation only $25, a stockholder would get a dividend, if declared, equal to that payable on a share for which another stockholder paid $40. The same would hold between shares for which the selling prices may have been $40 and $75, respectively.

In a similar way, changes in the prices at which stock transactions take place among investors in the market have no effect on rights to dividends. A and B may have originally bought their stock from a corporation at $50 a share, but A subsequently sells his holdings to C at $125 a share. C's right to dividends for each share is exactly the same as B's.

Claim against Assets

Considered by itself, rather than in combination with the right to share in dividends, the common stockholder's claim against assets may not appear to be worth much. Such an inference appears especially to be supported when the claim against assets is described, as it often is, as a claim in dissolution. The managements of successful corporations rarely set target dates for dissolution, and the dissolution of unsuccessful ones ordinarily occurs in such circumstances that little is left for the satisfaction of the claims of common stockholders, as those claims are measured in the stock and surplus accounts.

---

[3] *Dodge* v. *Ford Motor Company*, 204 Michigan 459 (1919). For an interesting account of the background, development, and aftermath of this case, including the subsequent action of Ford in buying up all outstanding minority stock of the company, see Keith Sward, *The Legend of Henry Ford* (New York: Rinehart & Co., Inc., 1948), pp. 66–74.

[4] Dividends and dividend policies are further discussed at length in Chapters 25 and 26. See especially pp. 639–43, 650–57.

Nevertheless, dissolution ought not to be emphasized. The claim of the common stockholders against assets is a continuous one, and often of much greater significance during the lives of corporations than at the time of their deaths. It is true that common stock has no date of maturity when it will be retired at book value in the ordinary course of operations, and it is not redeemable at any time or at specified times at the option of the stockholder. It is equally true that the claim of the common stockholder against assets is a residual one in the sense that it ranks last in the scale of priorities—in the sense that if all claims are to be settled as far as assets will permit, those of creditors and (usually) preferred stockholders must be satisfied in full, and only what is left can be allocated to the claims of common stockholders. Despite these shortcomings, however, the attractiveness of common stock to investors is undoubtedly greatly enhanced by its claim to assets. Let us consider why this is so.

Accumulation of Wealth in Corporations. For wealthy and well-to-do common stockholders, in particular, the build-up of corporate assets through the retention of profits is a highly popular means of amassing further wealth, just as would be the expansion of the assets of proprietorships and partnerships of which they might be owners. If their stock ownership gives them control, they have good reason to feel that the corporate assets are always at their disposal, that their wealth as stored up in the corporations can be withdrawn at any time should they want to use it elsewhere. The declaration of dividends equal to the total of accumulated surplus could be the means of withdrawing a substantial proportion of the assets. Were that not enough, they could sell their stock if it were possible to get a price close to its remaining book value, or if prices offered were not satisfactory they could vote to dissolve. It is well to keep in mind that a large majority of corporations are small and medium in size and are controlled by one or a few stockholders. Such corporations, therefore, can serve ideally as storehouses of wealth.

Even larger corporations in which the wealthy or well-to-do common stockholder does not have control, and does not expect to gain it through further stock buying, can be most attractive as storehouses of accumulating wealth. As long as the market value of his common stock goes up in some reasonable relationship to the amount of profits retained, such a stockholder can feel that his claim to assets can be cashed at any time by a sale of the stock in the market. On the other hand, he would surely allow for the probability that in times of general business slump weakness in the common stock market as a whole would temporarily make disadvantageous the cashing of his claim to assets.

Actually, many wealthy and well-to-do investors store wealth through common stock investment with no thought of withdrawing it or cashing it during their lifetimes. Having plenty of income to maintain high planes of living, they look on their accumulating claims against corporate assets as a good means of providing estates to be left at the time of death to their spouses, children, or other heirs. The workings of the federal personal income tax laws tend to encourage this kind of estate planning. As was indicated earlier in this chapter, the taxpayer may choose to have net profits derived from sales of common stock held for more than six months taxed as capital gains, rather than as ordinary income at the steeply progressive rates applicable thereto. But if the stock is not sold at all during one's lifetime, whatever appreciation in its market value may have taken place between the date of purchase and the date of one's death is not taxed *as income* at all. The value of the stock at the date of death (or its value one year thereafter, at the option of the executor or administrator) is subject to the federal estate tax, but this does not gainsay the nontaxability of the appreciation as income.

Mergers and Consolidations. Another way that the claims of common stockholders against the assets of their corporations can be cashed without liquidating assets and paying off all creditors and other prior claimants is by the transfer of these assets, and the assumption of the corporate debts, by other corporations. When such a wholesale transfer is made to another corporation, which thereafter remains in operation, the transaction is known as a *merger*. When two or more corporations make such a transfer to a newly formed corporation, it is described as a *consolidation*. Hundreds of mergers and consolidations occur every year in the United States, more abundantly, of course, in periods of high-level business activity but in sizable numbers also in periods of recession and depression. The chances are good, therefore, that the typical successful corporation will be approached from time to time by other corporations with what are thought to be attractive propositions to combine.

In working out the details of a proposal of merger or consolidation, provision is usually made for paying off current liabilities of the corporation to be absorbed, for the assumption of its long-term debts by the absorbing corporation—that is, the transfer of liability for these debts—and for an exchange of its stock at a given ratio for that of the absorbing corporation. The common stockholders of the corporation to be absorbed are not likely to vote in favor of the merger or consolidation if they think the proposed exchange ratio is unfavorable to them. If they vote in favor in the thought that the exchange offer is reasonably generous, they may plan to sell the stock to be received from the absorbing corporation, thereby cashing their existing claims against corporate assets. Of course, they may plan to hold the exchange stock as a way to continue to store wealth.

A proposal of merger or consolidation can be especially attractive to the stockholders of a closely held corporation who have already been rather anxious to cash their claims against its assets. That the stock had been closely held would probably mean that no market interest in it had been established; thus, selling to the general run of stock buyers at a reasonable price would be difficult if not impossible. If, then, the stock offered in a merger proposal had a broad, active market, the stockholders' claim against assets could be quickly cashed as soon as the exchange of stocks had taken place.

When mergers and consolidations are effected according to the procedures of state laws for statutory fusions, as they often are, the corporations whose assets have been absorbed and whose liabilities have been assumed by other corporations are dissolved by the very operation of the laws. But dissolution by this route, as has been amply indicated in the foregoing discussion, does not mean a settlement of the claims of common stockholders on a residual basis. The market value of the stock of the absorbing corporation received by the common stockholders of the absorbed corporations may be much greater than the existing book and market values of the stock given up. Hence, they may have their claims satisfied generously, while the bondholders of the absorbed corporation simply get claims of unchanged amounts as assumed creditors of the absorbing corporation. It is entirely possible for an absorbing corporation, running into financial troubles subsequent to a merger or consolidation, to default on the bonds of an absorbed corporation it has assumed. The ultimate fate of the bond owners could therefore turn out to be a rather sad one, whereas that of the common stockholders of the absorbed corporation, long since paid off, as it were, by an exchange of stock, could have been most pleasant. Such happenings have been common in the history of American corporate enterprise.

Holding Company Absorptions. A realization by common stockholders of their claim against the assets of their corporation may occur by a combination arrangement even simpler than the merger or consolidation. One corporation may want to obtain control of the assets of a second corporation, but with the expectation of keeping it in operation as a separate legal entity. In other words, it plans to occupy a position as parent or holding company to the acquired corporation. (The usual distinction is that a parent company carries on its own productive operations while holding controlling stock interests in one or more subsidiaries, and a holding company is nonoperating in the sense of turning out products, functioning simply as owner and controller of subsidiaries.)

A common procedure is for the holding company (let us call it that) to go to the stockholders of the corporation it wants to acquire and offer them some of its own stock in exchange for their holdings. As with mergers and consolidations, the offer must be reasonably generous to assure sufficient acceptance to give the holding company the control it seeks. The stockholders who accept the offer may thus be enabled, through an immediate sale of the exchange stock, to cash on a favorable basis their claim against assets. The creditors of the corporation being acquired have no such opportunity. As this corporation remains in existence as an entity distinct from the holding company, it continues to be responsible for its debts according to their original terms. It could run into difficulties and default upon its obligations. In such circumstances, the holding company might suffer the loss of its investment in the subsidiary, but the subsidiary's original common stockholders would be in the clear, assuming that they had sold their allotments of holding company stock while its market price was still good.

Partial Liquidating Dividends. Finally to be mentioned as a way that common stockholders' claims against assets may be realized without corporate dissolution is the distribution of dividends in partial liquidation. Sometimes, corporations find it advisable to curtail the scope of their operations but without going out of business. They may find, for example, that some of their lines are unprofitable while others are highly profitable, and they may decide, accordingly, to discontinue the unprofitable and concentrate on the profitable. But the change in scope of operations may mean that their assets are far beyond their need now. Hence, they sell the superfluous assets and distribute the proceeds to the common stockholders as liquidating dividends. Dividends of this kind are usually classed as liquidating dividends, even though there may be sufficient balances in the surplus accounts against which they can be charged. The designation is an appropriate one, since the dividends are obviously not distributions in the ordinary course of business. At any rate, they do constitute a realization by common stockholders on their claims against assets without dissolution.

It is of interest to point out, moreover, that liquidating dividends may ordinarily be charged against the common stock account if sufficient surplus is not available. This could be done by reducing the par or stated value of the outstanding stock, or by having the common stockholders surrender equal proportional amounts of their holdings. Actions such as these normally require amendment to the articles of incorporation, but, as we saw in Chapter 3, amendment is neither a difficult nor an expensive procedure. However, charges against the common stock account for liquidating dividends must not be carried to a point where existing creditors would be endangered. A common legal rule is that both directors and stockholders are personally liable to creditors (the directors totally, the stockholders pro rata) for assets distributed as liquidating dividends that should have been retained to meet obligations to them.

Right to Participate in Management

As indicated in Chapter 3 in connection with the discussion of managerial powers and responsibilities of boards of directors, the right of stockholders to participate in management extends in three directions: (1) to elect the board of directors; (2) to adopt, amend, and repeal bylaws; and (3) to pass directly on matters of great importance to their welfare, such as proposals for merger or consolidation with other corporations, the sale of entire assets, and dissolution. For preferred stockholders, managerial powers of these kinds may ordinarily be restricted in various ways, but never for the common stockholders. Some corporations, it is true, have outstanding two or more classes of what they call common stock; in all but one of these the voting powers of the stockholders may be restricted. Of a given corporation, for example, the Class A Common may have few or no voting powers, while the Class B Common will have such powers in full. In all such instances, therefore, the Class B Common is the true common stock, while the Class A Common is really of the nature of a preferred stock—it is most likely to be a *weak* preferred, as is often said.

For buyers of common stock who are interested in the control of corporations, the capacity to choose all, or at least a majority, of the members of the boards of directors is the matter of outstanding importance. In some instances, control may be sought to assure the approval of proposals for merger, consolidation, or sales of entire assets. Thus, a group that has large minority holdings of the common stock of a corporation may want to buy up additional shares to get the decisive voice in voting on a proposed merger it strongly favors. In rarer instances, control may be sought so that liquidation and dissolution can be voted. Some financiers—promoters in reverse, they may be called—are constantly on the lookout for corporations that are worth more dead than alive. The market price of a corporation's stock may be very low because it has been piling up losses year after year, yet the corporation may own quite valuable assets. The promoters in reverse, therefore, plan to gain control at limited cost by quietly buying up small parcels of stock here and there, perhaps over an extended period of time, then to vote dissolution, and to win, it is expected, handsome liquidating dividends after the sale of the high-quality assets. But we need say no more about procedures such as this; since our interest is in common stock as a financing device, we must concentrate on the attractiveness of new issues rather than on motives for buying stock already outstanding. Finally in regard to common stockholders' managerial powers, capacity to adopt, amend, and repeal bylaws standing by itself can be dismissed as a most unlikely objective for common stock purchases for control.

When people buy common stock primarily to gain or ensure their capacity to choose all or a majority of corporate directors rather than because of the attractions of rights to dividends and claims against assets, their objectives may be of many kinds. Among these, the following appear to be especially worthy of brief analysis: (1) the gaining of executive positions, (2) capacity to throw business to other enterprises, and (3) capacity to determine operating policies. Once control of a corporation has been gained by a given group of common stockholders, such objectives are presumably achievable whether they elect themselves to the board of directors or choose dummies who can be relied on to do their bidding.

Gaining Executive Positions. In corporations of small and medium sizes, it would seem that the chief plums to be striven for, in most instances, are the executive offices and the salaries that go with them, and not rights to dividends and claims against assets. Most corporations, it is worth repeating, are of these sizes. In such a corporation, the stockholders are generally few in number, they elect themselves to the board of directors, and as directors they appoint themselves as officers. To avoid the federal corporation income tax, they are likely to establish salary scales for themselves at levels designed to drain off virtually all the earnings left after the payment of operating expenses—certainly at the maximum level that the Commissioner of Internal Revenue is likely to permit; hence, they need have no great interest in dividends. Nor are they likely to be thinking about realizing claims to assets through dissolution, mergers with other corporations, and exchanges of stock with holding companies, for any such move could be expected to deprive them of their executive offices with the precuniary rewards thereof.

Capacity to Throw Business. Not necessarily overshadowing interests in dividends and assets, but of great importance in its own right as an attraction of common stock ownership, is the possibility of influencing corporate buying and selling policies to the personal benefit of the stockholder. The ownership of controlling interests, of course, ensures a capacity to determine buying and selling policies; but often, also, the ownership of sizable blocks of common stock by minority stockholders serve to make them quite influential. To keep such a minority stockholder on its side, the controlling group, especially if its margin of control is a narrow one, may be quite willing to throw business in directions that will make him happy.

Vast amounts of corporate business flow in peculiar directions as determined by the personal interests of directors and influential stockholders. Corporation A buys large quantities of raw materials from Corporation B rather than from any of a dozen other potential suppliers, because two directors of A have large stockholdings in B. Corporation B, in turn, buys much of its raw materials from Corporation C, because a third director of A is the principal stockholder in C. Corporation C ships its products by Railroad X rather than by Railroad Y, because three other directors of Corporation A are stockholders and directors of Railroad X. And Railroad X turns over some of its legal business to the law firm of M, N, O & O, because the two O's are, respectively, a son and a grandson of still another director of Corporation A. Such an illustration is by no means farfetched; indeed, considering the bewildering ramifications of vested interests that actually prevail in American business society, it is a highly simplified version.

All this does not mean that, typically, directors deliberately reject their responsibilities to the general run of stockholders of the corporations they manage in order to advance their own personal interests, the interests of a few influential stockholders, or those of relatives, friends, and business associates elsewhere. Some do. But it is often possible to throw business in one direction or another without disadvantage to the corporation whose business it is. In terms of the illustration, Corporation B's product may be as good as that of the other potential suppliers, and its price no higher than theirs, so that Corporation A's action in making B the exclusive supplier would apparently work no harm to A's stockholders.

Capacity to Determine Operating Policies. Although buying and selling policies designed to throw business here and there are operating policies, the objective of controlling operating policies as a reason for common stock buying is often of quite different character from that of serving the personal interests of influential people, whoever they may be. For example, minority holders of common stock and outsiders often become convinced that the existing managements of certain corporations are woefully incompetent—that expansion opportunities of most promising kinds are being ignored, that costs of operations, especially administrative expenses, have become unconscionable, and so on. They conclude, therefore, that if they could gain control and put their quite different policies into effect, the welfare of the corporations and all their stockholders would be immeasurably enhanced.

Such persons may be avid buyers of whatever new issues of common stock the criticized corporations offer for sale, provided that their purchases would give them control or, at least, move them much closer to it. Toward the same objective, of course, substantial purchases of common stock already outstanding may be made in the market. Often, however, people who want to challenge the position and competence of an existing management, do not expect to be personally able to get enough of the stock to ensure control, but they hope that their substantial voting power will be augmented by the votes of thousands of small stockholders whom they expect to persuade to join with them in their move to replace the management. Such expectations and the efforts to fulfill them sometimes lead to proxy fights of great intensity and widespread interest. The management and the challengers exert every effort to line up the general run of stockholders on their respective sides, and sometimes the outcome is not known until the votes are actually counted at the stockholders' meeting. The Securities and Exchange Commission reported that during its fiscal year ending June 30, 1966, there were "proxy contests" (obviously a more genteel descriptive term) involving the election of directors in 37 corporations subject to its proxy rules under the Securities Exchange Act. It said that 24 of the contests involved control of boards of directers and 13 were concerned with representation on boards. It further reported that 10 of the control cases were won by management, 6 were won by nonmanagement persons, 2 were settled by negotiation, and 6 were pending at the end of the year. Management retained all board positions in six of the representation cases, opposition candidates won places in six cases, and one was settled by negotiation.[5]

PROTECTIVE RIGHTS

The rights of common stockholders in business corporations included in the second grouping presented on page 396 were described as protective rights. They have little capacity in themselves to attract the funds of investors; nevertheless, they are of great importance in assuring investors that their rights to dividends, to assets, and to voting power will be safeguarded at all times.

Right to Have a Stock Certificate

At the very minimum, the individual common stockholder must be in a position to be able to prove his ownership of common shares—to prove his entitlement to all other rights. It is not enough for him to be told that the corporation will have a record of his ownership. Errors can occur in record-keeping, and the fraudulent manipulation of records is by no means impossible or unheard of. Accordingly, corporation laws invariably stipulate that the common stockholder (and the preferred stockholder, too) must be given a certificate as evidence of his ownership.

In quality, common stock certificates vary from elaborately engraved forms, specially prepared for the sole use of the given corporation, to cheap printed ones that can be bought from legal stationers and in which the name of the corporation as well as other pertinent

---

[5]Securities and Exchange Commission, *Annual Report*, 1966, pp. 52–53.

details can be typed or written in. In content, they all tend toward a uniform simplicity (see Figure 17–1). The items include:

1. The name of the corporation.
2. The state of incorporation.
3. The total authorized issue of common stock.
4. The par or stated value, if any, or a designation that the stock has no par value.
5. A serial number.
6. The name of the stockholder to whom the certificate is being issued.
7. The number of shares it represents.
8. The fact that these are common shares.
9. The date of issue.
10. The signatures of the president and treasurer or secretary (or of certain other officials who may sign alternatively).
11. The corporate seal.

A corporation must, of course, keep a record of the stock certificates it issues. It must know the names and addresses of, and the number of shares held by, each of its common stockholders, so that dividend checks, notices of annual and special meetings, proxy forms for voting at meetings, and other official communications will reach the right people. For this purpose, a *stockholders' ledger* or *stock transfer book* is used. In this record, each stockholder has an account in which he is credited with all shares he acquires and is debited for all shares he transfers to others. Most corporations find it convenient to record transfers of stock as a routine function in the treasurer's office, but larger ones that have thousands of stockholders and numerous daily transfers usually prefer to turn over the job of record-keeping to trust companies and the trust departments of commercial banks, which, among other things, offer specialized services as *transfer agents*. Many large corporations employ these institutions also as *registrars* for their stock. The function of a registrar is to see that no error is made in issuing stock—that the total of shares represented by certificates does not exceed the authorized issue, that the individual certificate is for the correct number of shares, that it bears the correct name of the stockholder, and so on. Because of the registrar's verification function, corporations that hire out both the transfer and registry functions invariably select as a registrar a trust company or trust department different from that selected as transfer agent. As the transfer agent can be counted on for a high level of accuracy, the independent check of a second institution as registrar makes for great certainty that errors will be avoided in the issuance of certificates. Transfer agents and registrars countersign the certificates they process, and these countersignatures carry strong assurances to the individual stockholder that his certificate is genuine and was properly issued.

FIGURE 17–1
Common Stock Certificate

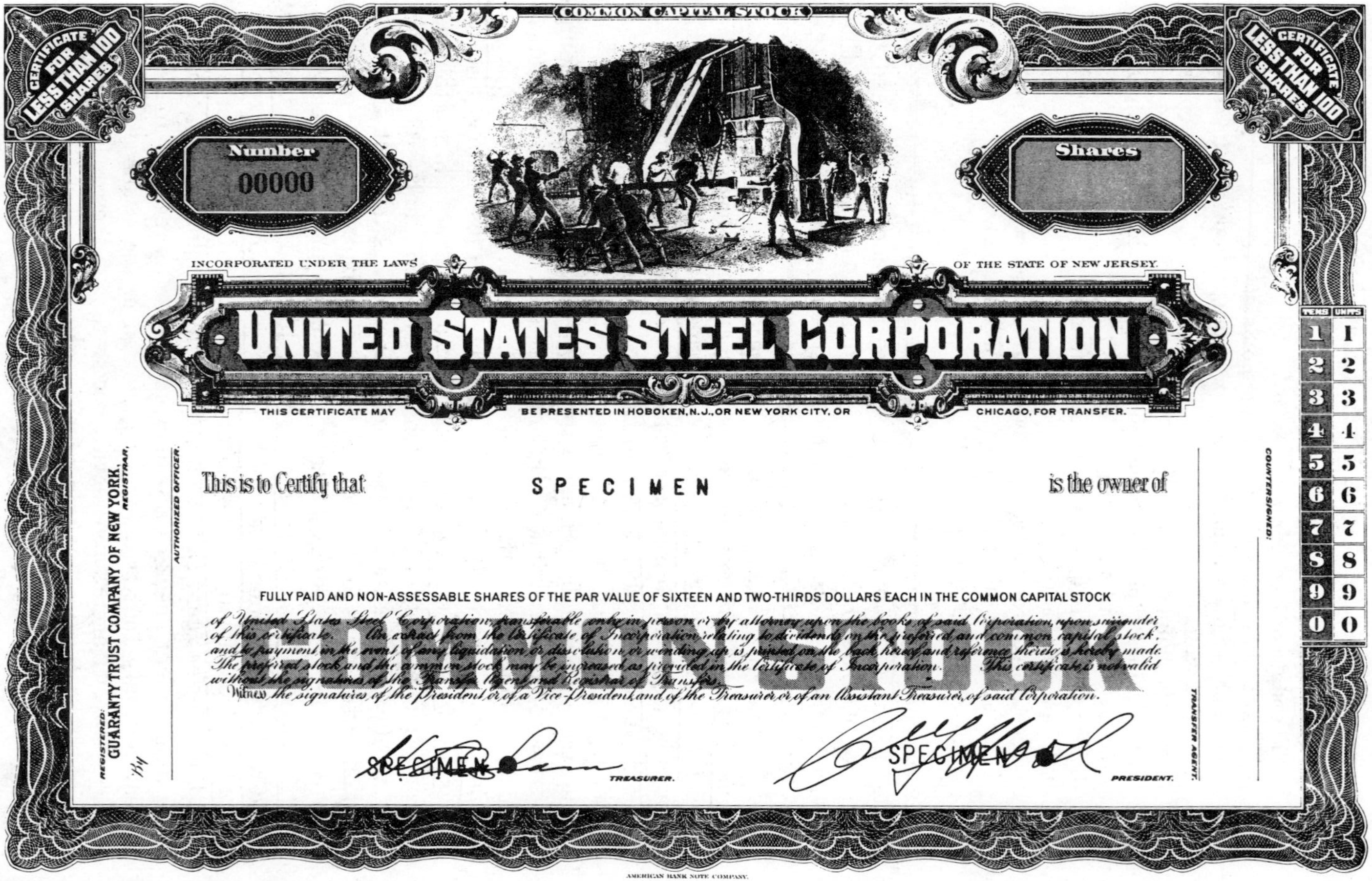

COMMON CAPITAL STOCK

CERTIFICATE FOR LESS THAN 100 SHARES

Number 00000

Shares

INCORPORATED UNDER THE LAWS OF THE STATE OF NEW JERSEY

UNITED STATES STEEL CORPORATION

THIS CERTIFICATE MAY BE PRESENTED IN HOBOKEN, N.J., OR NEW YORK CITY, OR CHICAGO, FOR TRANSFER.

This is to Certify that SPECIMEN is the owner of

FULLY PAID AND NON-ASSESSABLE SHARES OF THE PAR VALUE OF SIXTEEN AND TWO-THIRDS DOLLARS EACH IN THE COMMON CAPITAL STOCK

COMMON STOCK

of United States Steel Corporation transferable only in person or by attorney upon the books of said Corporation upon surrender of this certificate. An extract from the Certificate of Incorporation relating to dividends on the preferred and common capital stock, and to payment in the event of any liquidation or dissolution or winding up is printed on the back hereof and reference thereto is hereby made. The preferred stock and the common stock may be increased as provided in the Certificate of Incorporation. This certificate is not valid without the signatures of the Transfer Agent and Registrar of Transfers.

Witness the signatures of the President or of a Vice-President and of the Treasurer or of an Assistant Treasurer of said Corporation.

SPECIMEN TREASURER.

SPECIMEN PRESIDENT.

COUNTERSIGNED:

TRANSFER AGENT.

REGISTERED: GUARANTY TRUST COMPANY OF NEW YORK, REGISTRAR.

AUTHORIZED OFFICER.

TENS	UNITS
1	1
2	2
3	3
4	4
5	5
6	6
7	7
8	8
9	9
0	0

AMERICAN BANK NOTE COMPANY.

Right to Transfer the Stock

Were the prospective investor in common stock to be given no assurances that he could sell it or otherwise dispose of it whenever he might so choose, he probably would decide against buying it. Rights to dividends and assets and voting rights may look attractive at a given time, but the intelligent investor always wants to be able to get out should his judgment about the future prospects of the corporation become adverse. Many people are willing to buy common stock in the thought that it is, for them, a short-term investment, to be disposed of, accordingly, in a few weeks or months, so that their funds can be used elsewhere. Thus, the right to transfer is universally recognized as a basic protective provision for the common stockholder. It includes the right to sell the stock, to give it away, to bequeath it to one's heirs, and to pledge it, say, as collateral for loans.

Nevertheless, restrictions on transferability are not uncommon. They occur most often in close corporations. The handful of stockholders in such a corporation may want to exclude outsiders from stock ownership more or less permanently. In the articles of incorporation or bylaws, therefore, they may include a provision that any stockholder who wants to dispose of his holdings must first offer them to the corporation. The price at which the offer is to be made may be stipulated, or some other means of arriving at a reasonable price may be indicated. Such a restriction on transfer is probably enforceable, especially if a statement of the restriction is placed on the stock certificates. Even more assurance of enforceability can apparently be had if the stockholders merely agree among themselves that should any want to sell they would first offer their stock to the corporation or, perhaps, to the remaining stockholders, as on a pro rata basis. It is to be expected that courts would recognize the mutual promises as sufficient consideration for a binding contract.

Mechanics of Transfer. The typical corporation, however, places no obstacles in the way of stock transfers. Indeed, the process of transfer is eased in every way. On the reverse side of most stock certificates a convenient assignment form is provided (see Figure 17–2). To sell his stock, therefore, the owner need only fill in this form, designating who is the buyer and who is given the seller's power of attorney to have the stock transferred on the books of the corporation. If he so wishes, in fact, the seller can simply sign the assignment form in blank, leaving the buyer or a subsequent holder to fill in the other details. Likewise, an assignment form separate from the stock certificate may be used, filled in fully or signed in blank. This is known as a stock power. At any rate, the buyer or his agent, such as a broker, sends the endorsed stock certificate, or the stock certificate with the stock power, to the corporation or its transfer agent if it employs one.

FIGURE 17–2
Transfer Form on Back of Stock Certificate

UNITED STATES STEEL CORPORATION

EXTRACT FROM CERTIFICATE OF INCORPORATION TO WHICH REFERENCE IS MADE ON THE FACE HEREOF.

The holders of the preferred stock shall be entitled to receive when and as declared, from the surplus or net profits of the corporation, yearly dividends at the rate of seven per centum per annum, and no more, payable quarterly on dates to be fixed by the by-laws. The dividends on the preferred stock shall be cumulative, and shall be payable before any dividend on the common stock shall be paid or set apart: so that, if in any year dividends amounting to seven per cent. shall not have been paid thereon, the deficiency shall be payable before any dividends shall be paid upon or set apart for the common stock.

Whenever all cumulative dividends on the preferred stock for all previous years shall have been declared and shall have become payable, and the accrued quarterly installments for the current year shall have been declared, and the company shall have paid such cumulative dividends for previous years and such accrued quarterly installments, or shall have set aside from its surplus or net profits a sum sufficient for the payment thereof, the Board of Directors may declare dividends on the common stock, payable then or thereafter, out of any remaining surplus or net profits.

In the event of any liquidation or dissolution or winding up (whether voluntary or involuntary) of the corporation, the holders of the preferred stock shall be entitled to be paid in full both the par amount of their shares, and the unpaid dividends accrued thereon before any amount shall be paid to the holders of the common stock; and after the payment to the holders of the preferred stock of its par value, and the unpaid accrued dividends thereon, the remaining assets and funds shall be divided and paid to the holders of the common stock according to their respective shares.

For value Received ____ *hereby sell, assign and transfer unto*

____

PLEASE PRINT OR TYPEWRITE NAME AND ADDRESS OF ASSIGNEE

____

____

____________________________________ *Shares*

of the Capital Stock represented by the within Certificate, and do hereby irrevocably constitute and appoint

____________________________________ *Attorney*

to transfer the said stock on the Books of the within named Corporation with full power of substitution in the premises.

Dated ________________ *19* ____

____

In Presence of

____

NOTICE: THE SIGNATURE TO THIS ASSIGNMENT MUST CORRESPOND WITH THE NAME AS WRITTEN UPON THE FACE OF THE CERTIFICATE, IN EVERY PARTICULAR, WITHOUT ALTERATION OR ENLARGEMENT, OR ANY CHANGE WHATEVER.

THIS SPACE MUST NOT BE COVERED IN ANY WAY

The certificate is canceled, and a new one is issued in the name of the buyer. At the same time, of course, the transaction is recorded in the stock transfer book, so that the change in ownership will be a matter of record.

If a stockholder wants to sell only a portion of the shares represented by a certificate, he indicates that on the assignment form, and the certificate and form are sent to the corporation or its transfer agent. The certificate is canceled, but in this instance two new ones are issued—one to the buyer for the number of shares bought and the other to the seller for the number of shares retained.

Stock Certificates as Negotiable Instruments. Contributing to the ease of stock transfers is the fact that all our states and the District of Columbia have adopted legislation to make stock certificates negotiable instruments. Giving stock certificates the quality of negotiability means that, as the lawyers say, innocent purchasers for value ordinarily get good title to the stock represented by certificates, even though the original owners or subsequent holders did not have good title. Suppose that a stock certificate made out in the name of A and endorsed by him in blank is stolen by B and sold by B to C. C gets good title, assuming that he had no knowledge of the theft, and regardless that B, the thief, had no title at all. C is innocent in his lack of knowledge of the theft, and he is a purchaser for value in that he paid cash to B. If C were to know of the theft or were he to receive the stock certificate as a gift from B, he would not get good title, but were he, in turn, to transfer the certificate to D, who could qualify as an innocent purchaser for value, D would get good title. On the other hand, were B to steal an unendorsed stock certificate made out in the name of A and then forge A's signature on the assignment form, neither C in the first instance nor D in the second would get good title. The innocent purchaser for value is not protected against forgery.

The negotiability of stock certificates makes it possible for them to pass from hand to hand without worries on the part of purchasers for value about the goodness of title of sellers and other earlier holders. As long as the purchaser for value is satisfied about the genuineness of the endorsement of the person whose name appears on the face of the stock certificate, he need have no fears about the goodness of his own title. Accordingly, a given stock certificate that has the endorsement of the original owner in blank can be sold over and over again until some buyer decides to send it in to the corporation or its transfer agent to be exchanged for a new certificate in his own name.

Difficulties for Brokerage Firms. While the mechanics of transferring stock certificates are simple for the individual investor, they can be loaded with difficulties for the brokerage firms that have many thousands of certificates to receive and deliver daily to complete the buying and selling orders of their customers. In times of booming markets, the paper work of making transfers can become overwhelming, as it did in the early months of 1968 when, indeed, the New York and American stock exchanges curtailed their trading hours to enable the people in the back rooms of the brokerage firms to try to catch up, when some firms were ordered not to take on new customers until they had caught up, and when there were numerous reports of stock buyers who waited weeks and even months for their stock certificates. As a result, much thought was being directed to the possibilities of substituting for traditional stock certificates some kind of card that could be handled by high-speed electronic equipment.

Right to Subscribe to Additional Issues of Stock

The common stockholder's rights to dividends, assets, and voting power can be weakened or diluted if his corporation sells additional common stock to other investors. A person who owns 1,000 shares of the common stock of a corporation that has a total of 10,000 shares outstanding and no preferred stock gets a 10th of all dividends that are declared, has a 10th of the total voting power, and has a claim against assets equal to a 10th of total stockholder claims. But should his corporation sell 5,000 additional shares to other buyers, these rights would be reduced to a 15th. Hence comes the doctrine of the common stockholder's preemptive right, as it is called: before additional common stock is offered to anybody else, he should have the privilege of subscribing in the proportion of his present holdings to the total already outstanding. In terms of the illustration, were the holder of 1,000 shares privileged to buy one tenth of the additional issue, or 500 shares, he would be enabled to protect and maintain his one 10th interest. The logic of the preemptive right requires that when stock is offered to existing stockholders at a given price, and they do not buy, it will not be offered to others at a lower price; if the price is to be lowered, it must first be reoffered to the stockholders at the reduced price.

The logic of the preemptive right also requires that present common stockholders be given the first opportunity to subscribe on a pro rata basis to issues of preferred stocks and bonds that are convertible into common stock or that have attached to them warrants that empower their holders to buy common stock at stipulated prices. The dilution of the common stockholder's claims through the exercise of convertibility rights or warrants given to outsiders could be as serious as dilution resulting from outside sales of common stock itself. Since, indeed, preferred stock is usually given claims to earnings and assets that have a priority over those of common stock, it is not unreasonable to argue that the common stockholder should have the preemptive right to subscribe pro rata to new issues of preferred, whether or not it is convertible into common. All the stronger is this argument if the preferred stock carries voting power.

Present Status of the Preemptive Right. The foregoing description of the preemptive right has been set down in tentative terms—in terms of logic, of arguments, and of what could or should be—rather than in positive statements because, speaking broadly, the preemptive right is the weakest of the rights of common stockholders. Long recognized in its full scope in the common law—that is, the body of legal rules and principles built up over the centuries in the decisions of judges in Anglo-Saxon countries—it has been whittled away in recent decades by many state legislatures. The corporation laws of a few states now stipulate that the common stocks of corporations they charter do not have the preemptive right unless it is specifically provided for in the individual corporation's articles or bylaws, and a larger number provide that though the right is given in the first instance it can be removed or limited by provisions in articles or bylaws. In extensively revising its corporation code in 1967, Delaware—always important among incorporating states—provided that stockholders of corporations it chartered after the date of enactment of the revision would not have the preemptive right unless it was specifically given to them in articles of incorporation, and that for other corporations the preemptive right could be removed by simple majority vote of the stockholders. As if in response to this move, the stockholders of several prominent corporations, including the Boeing Company and the National Cash Register Company, voted to give up their preemptive rights.

At the present time, therefore, whether or not a common stock has the preemptive right—and how extensive it is—depends variously on the provisions of the state laws and each corporation's own articles and bylaws. Where it continues in effect, it usually extends to new issues of securities convertible into common stock or those with warrants attached for the purchase of common stock, as well as to additional direct issues of common itself. It usually extends, also, to new offerings of preferred stock that has voting power, although there is a tendency to make it inapplicable to new issues of nonvoting preferreds. (For a description of the preemptive rights of a few leading corporations' common stocks selected at random, see Table 17–1.)

Common stockholders are often in a position to demand the benefits of the preemptive right even though denied it in the articles or bylaws. The holders of a majority of the common shares of a corporation can, of course, put through an amendment to the articles or bylaws if only that is necessary. But probably more significant is that additional issues of stock usually require amendment to the articles—a step that must have the approval of the stockholders. In proposing additional issues, therefore, the directors may feel compelled to give

TABLE 17–1
Preemptive Rights of the Common Stocks of a Few Leading Corporations

Corporation	*Preemptive Rights Provided*
Allied Chemical Corporation	Full
Aluminum Company of America	None
American Telephone and Telegraph Company	Full, but with exceptions recognized in New York law
American Tobacco Company	Only such as are provided for in New Jersey law
Anaconda Company	Full
Borden Company	None
Chesapeake & Ohio Railway Company	Full, except when waived by 2/3 vote
Detroit Edison Company	To the extent provided for in New York law
General Electric Company	Full
Great Atlantic & Pacific Tea Company	Full
Liggett & Myers Tobacco Company	Only such as are provided for in New Jersey law
National Dairy Products Corporation	Full except for stock reserved for sale to employees
J. C. Penney Company	None
Reynolds Metals Company	None
Southern California Edison Company	None

SOURCE: Moody's Investors Service, *Manuals*.

the present stockholders the first opportunity to buy, fearing a rejection of their proposals should they attempt to ignore stockholder preferences in this matter.

Exemptions from the Preemptive Right. Even where the preemptive right continues in effect, three kinds of stock transactions are generally held to be exempt from it: (1) continuing sales of original issues, (2) direct exchanges of stock for assets other than cash, and (3) sales of treasury stock.

The first of these exemptions means that a buyer of stock does not get an immediate right to subscribe to a pro rata share of the remaining portion of the original issues. Assume that a newly formed corporation proposes to issue 100,000 shares of common stock to complete its organization and the acquisition of operating assets. When, say, 60,000 shares have been sold, an original buyer of 6,000 shares cannot assert a right to have the first opportunity to buy a 10th of the remaining 40,000 shares slated for sale.

The second exception allows for the possibility that corporations may be able to acquire desirable parcels of property in direct exchanges for common stock, even though sales of the stock at fair prices to raise cash to buy the property might be impossible. The owners of the desired properties could be quite willing to part with them in exchange for stock, while other investors, including existing stockholders, might have little interest in acquiring additional shares. The opportunity to acquire the properties might be lost if the stock had first to be offered to the present stockholders. The delay might be fatal, or refusal of the stockholders to buy might lead the property owners to change their minds about the attractiveness of the stock.

Treasury stock is a corporation's own stock, once issued and fully paid for, but subsequently reacquired by the corporation, as by gift or by purchase in the market. Resales of treasury stock are exempt from the preemptive right, because the right pertains to the first offering of *new* stock. If the right obtains, it will have been applied when the stock, now reacquired, was first sold.

Right to Inspect the Corporation's Books

The right of the common stockholder to inspect the books of his corporation, though important for his protection, is subject to rather strict limitations. It is designed essentially for two purposes: (1) to enable him to know who are his fellow stockholders and (2) to enable him to check on the performance of the corporation's management.

Access to Fellow Stockholders. Since the individual common stockholder shares his ownership jointly with all other common stockholders, he should have a means of finding out who these people are, how many shares they own, and what their addresses are. He may want to communicate with his fellow owners in order to line up votes for a slate of candidates he plans to nominate for directorships, to persuade them to join him in supporting or opposing some proposed amendment to the articles or bylaws, or for some other reason quite in keeping with his interests as an owner. He might think the present management of the corporation incompetent, but his efforts toward replacing it would be seriously impeded could he not easily reach his fellow stockholders. The criticized management could hardly be expected to help him, but at least it could not conceal information as to stockholdings. Thus, the corporation laws generally provide that the stockholders' ledger or stock transfer book must be open for inspection by stockholders at the office of the corporation or its transfer agent, usually for at least two or three hours during each business day.

In the usual circumstances, personal inspection of the stock records by individual stockholders is avoided by a willingness of the corporation, on proper request, to supply lists of stockholders, their addresses, and the number of their shares. If, however, the stockholder has reason to feel that a list is inaccurate, he may insist on actual inspection of the records. If the privilege of inspection is denied him, he may appeal to the courts for a writ directing the corporation to open the records to him. On the other hand, corporations not infrequently deny access to the stock records and refuse to supply lists of stockholders on the grounds that the stockholder has no good reason *as a stockholder* for wanting this information. They may claim, for example, that the stockholder plans to use or sell the list of his fellow stockholders as a sucker list for promotions of other enterprises or for appeals of charities of dubious reputation. If satisfied with such allegations, a court would doubtless turn down the stockholder's appeal for a writ.

Checking on Performance of Management. To check on the performance of a corporation's management, the common stockholder needs to know many details about the corporation's income, expenses, assets, and liabilities. But many details of this kind could be used to the detriment of the corporation. Accordingly, a distinction must somehow be made between what the stockholder is entitled to know to protect his interests and what he could use, or pass on to others to use, in ways harmful to the corporation. The typical corporation management is likely to feel, therefore, that the kinds of information contained in balance sheets, income statements, and statements of surplus, as supplied in annual and other reports to stockholders, is about as much as can be safely revealed. They will probably give the stockholder access to the accounting records for interim information of the same kinds included in the published reports, but rarely will they be willing to go beyond this limit. For example, managements will generally admit that the stockholder has a right to know what are the amounts of accounts receivable and payable, how much has been borrowed from banks, what is the book value of the different kinds of fixed assets, what total sales, total expenses, and net profits before and after taxes amount to, and so on. But they are likely to deny his right to know the names, addresses, and current balances of specific customers and suppliers, the names of the banks from which money has been borrowed, the unit costs of manufacture of individual products, and so on. They are likely to hold that information of the kind denied could be of inestimable advantage to competitors.

If, then, the stockholder demands detailed information different from the kinds usually included in published statements, it is likely to be refused him without hesitation. His only redress would be to appeal to the courts for an order directing the corporation to give him the desired information or access to the records where it could be found. But the court would give the management an opportunity to explain its stand. It would then be up to the court to weigh the merits of the stockholder's demands as against the reasons advanced by the management for its refusal to accede.

Right to Prevent Wrongful Corporate Actions

As losses resulting from the wrongful actions of a corporation injure its stockholders individually as well as collectively, each has standing in the courts to bring proceedings to prevent such actions as well as to secure redress if losses have already been caused. Wrongful actions include those that are illegal and *ultra vires*, all modes of conduct classified broadly as mismanagement, and acts designed unfairly to advance the interests of given groups of common stockholders at the expense of other groups. Actually, of course, the term *mismanagement* pretty well covers all the kinds of injurious actions against which the stockholder has the right to protect himself by appeal to the courts.

Agreements aimed at illegal ends are, of course, unenforceable. Also expressly forbidden by law are certain corporate acts, such as making contributions to political parties. Thus, if a corporation spends money for an illegal purpose, it stands to lose all such funds, together with whatever fines may be imposed on it.

Acts *ultra vires* are chiefly contracts outside the scope of the powers of a corporation as provided for in the state law and in its articles of incorporation. Courts have sometimes held such contracts to be unenforceable by the corporation, but enforceable by other parties. On contracts that are favorable to it, the corporation may have difficulty getting the other parties to fulfill their obligations, but on those that are to its disadvantage it may be compelled to perform. But stockholder suits to prevent *ultra vires* actions or to secure redress for losses due to them are rare. So broadly are articles of incorporation drawn nowadays in their statements of corporate purposes that courts are unlikely to find any course of (legal) action outside their scope.

Considered as a separate category, mismanagement includes gross negligence on the part of the directors in fulfilling their responsibilities, their delegation of extraordinary powers to executive officers without proper safeguards, and their authorization or permission to spend corporate funds lavishly for purposes not clearly beneficial to the corporation. As to the last-named item, even contributions to charitable and educational institutions may be condemned as a misuse of corporate funds. However, many states have amended their corporation laws to specifically authorize contributions of these kinds.[6]

Finally, actions designed to promote the interests of given groups of stockholders at the expense of other groups usually originate in efforts of majorities to take advantage of minorities. An example of

---

[6]For example, see item 9 in the list of general powers of Delaware corporations, page 57.

this kind of action would be the sale of some of the choicest assets of one corporation at a ridiculously low price to a second, because the controlling stockholders of the first are the sole stockholders of the second.

Although the individual stockholder may be convinced that his corporation is being mismanaged, he is likely to be slow in seeking legal remedies. If he is successful in taking legal action, the court is to be expected to assess the corporation for his expenses in bringing the suit, but if he is unsuccessful he must generally meet the expenses of litigation out of his own pocket. Meanwhile, in defending it or themselves the managers of the corporation can freely use its funds in hiring expensive legal talent and in meeting other costs. Usually, indeed, they are not personally assessed for the costs of the litigation, even when decisions go against them. Moreover, in bringing suit the individual stockholder does so on behalf of all the stockholders and not solely for his own benefit. Other stockholders may applaud his action, but they tend to display little enthusiasm in offering to share the expenses and other burdens of his suit.

Stockholders' suits against directors for damages alleged to have been already incurred through mismanagement are much more common than suits to prevent wrongful actions. It should be easier to prove mismanagement after severe losses have occurred than to prove that certain policies or procedures will lead to such losses. After the fact, losses are evidence in support of the stockholder's claim, but before it, he has no comparable factual support. What is more, fellow stockholders are much more likely to give aid to efforts to secure damages than they are to support mere allegations that serious losses threaten because of alleged mismanagement. Not to be disregarded, too, is that some suits against directors for damages are brought by stockholders for their nuisance value. The suing stockholders do not expect the suits to reach the trial stage. They hope to be bought off. And directors, though quite confident about the adequacy of their defense, may be strongly tempted to buy off the suing stockholders. The cost of this means of settlement may appear quite small in comparison with the expenses, the time lost, the unfavorable publicity, and other frustrations of extended litigation.

OBLIGATIONS OF THE COMMON STOCKHOLDER

In buying common stock from a corporation—in acquiring all the rights described in the preceding pages—the investor generally incurs only one obligation—to pay the price agreed on. If he subscribes at \$100 a share and pays in \$40, he remains under obligation to pay in the remaining \$60 according to the terms of the subscription contract. If he fails to pay, under the rule in most states his stock is offered at auction for whatever it will bring. If this is more than \$60, the excess up to $40 is ordinarily returnable to him, and if less he can be sued for the deficiency.

However, it is possible for the obligation of the subscriber to common stock to amount to more than the agreed-on price. This is usually so when a stock that has a par value is sold for less than that value. In a few states, moreover, even though the stockholders have paid the agreed-on price or the par value, as the case may be, they may still be obligated to make additional pro rata payments if needed (as in the event of insolvency) to meet unpaid liabilities for wages.

Discount Rule

The par value of a common stock is simply an arbitrary price tag placed on it in the articles of incorporation or, if the state law so permits, in the bylaws or resolutions of the board of directors. The organizers of corporations (or, subsequently, the directors where permitted) can choose whatever par value or price tag they want, or they may choose not to use an absolute price tag at all; then the stock is said to be no-par stock. Thus, if a par value is to be used by a given corporation for a total issue of, say, $100,000, the state is generally quite unconcerned whether this is to be made up of 100 shares of $1,000 par value or 100,000 shares of $1 par value or some other combination of number and value.

Once a par value has been selected, however, it becomes a matter of considerable importance to the corporation and the stockholder. The general rule is that if a par-value stock is sold at a price below the par the subscribing stockholder remains liable to creditors of the corporation for the difference between the price actually paid and the par value—that is, for the amount of the discount. The law assumes that trade suppliers, banks, and others who extend credit to corporations do so in the belief that their claims are protected by assets contributed by the common stockholders in an amount at least equal to the par value of the outstanding stock. In effect, then, they are held to be deceived if the contribution of the common stockholders has actually been less than this, unless they are specifically informed about the true state of affairs before their credits are granted. Hence also comes the rule that directors make themselves liable to creditors to the extent that they deliberately cause impairments of the common stock—that is, cause its book value to fall below its par value.[7] Such an action could be, for example, the payment of cash dividends in excess of the amount of accumulated profits.

It is to be emphasized that the liability of the common stockholder who buys stock at a discount is only a contingent obligation—and

[7]This rule does not apply, however, when the impairment is simply a matter of bookkeeping, as when directors decide that asset values are overstated and order their write-down on the books.

an obligation not to the corporation but to its creditors. So long as the stockholder has paid the price agreed on, the corporation has no further claim on him. If, accordingly, the corporation remains solvent at all times, the discount rule remains of little importance. The liability of the stockholder because of the discount may thus be said to materialize only when the corporation defaults on its obligations to creditors.

As a practical matter, moreover, the discount rule tends to be limited in its applicability only to sales of stock for cash. The corporation laws provide that the judgment of boards of directors about the value of property and services received in exchange for common stock is conclusive unless fraud can be proved. For example, it would be difficult for creditors to prove that a factory building for which common stock of a par value of $75,000 had been given was really worth only about $50,000.

Likewise, commissions paid to investment bankers and other expenses incurred in selling common stock for cash are commonly held to be outside the scope of the discount rule. If an issue of common stock of $1 million is offered to the public at par value, but the corporation realizes only $850,000 because commissions and other flotation costs amount to $150,000, the individual buyer, as a rule, escapes discount liability. He actually pays the par value, even though the corporation realizes only 85 percent of that value.

No-Par Stock

Although the respective merits of par-value and no-par stock may best be reserved for examination in a subsequent chapter,[8] the general inapplicability of the discount rule to no-par stock may be briefly treated here. The prime reason for the early popularity of no-par stock, once it had been authorized by the states, was precisely because it served as a means of escaping the discount rule.

Even no-par stock, of course, must have a price tag when the time comes for its sale. Generally, however, corporate directors are empowered to decide how much of the proceeds of sale is to be carried to the common stock account and how much is to be treated as paid-in surplus. Moreover, they can vary these proportions in successive sales. One corporation may sell an issue of no-par common at $40 a share and carry the whole proceeds to its common stock account. Another selling at the same price may carry $25 to the common stock account and $15 to a paid-in or capital surplus account. Later, the first corporation may sell a second batch at $55, carrying $30 to the stock account and $25 to a surplus account. The second corporation on selling its second batch at $30 may allocate $20 to the stock

[8]See pp. 526–30.

account and $10 to a surplus account. In none of these transactions, obviously, would there be a basis for claims that the stock was being sold at a discount.

It is a widely held rule, however, that once a given portion of the proceeds of the sale of no-par stock is allocated to the common stock account it then becomes stated capital, on which creditors are justified in relying for protection. Though beyond the scope of the discount rule, stated capital is subject, therefore, to the rule on impairments. Accordingly, corporate directors become liable to creditors to the extent that stated capital is deliberately impaired by actions voted by them, as by the payment of cash dividends in excess of the amount of available surplus.

Subsequent Holders of Common Stock

When people buy common stock from other holders, rather than direct from the corporation, they become entitled to all the rights of common stockholders as soon as the transfer has been recorded in the stock records of the corporation. Their obligation to pay is one in favor of the seller and not in favor of the corporation or its creditors. If the seller endorses a stock certificate made out in his name and transfers it to the buyer before receiving payment, he has a right of action against the buyer to force payment, but this does not affect the corporation. As soon as the buyer effects the transfer of ownership in its records, it recognizes his rights as a stockholder, regardless of his unpaid obligation to the seller or litigation to enforce that obligation. Likewise, the price agreed on between buyer and seller is entirely outside the scope of the discount rule. If the stock was fully paid for at the time of original issue, the discount rule has no further application to it. In subsequent transactions, it can be sold at only a minor fraction of the original price, or, indeed, it can be given away without question of contingent liability to creditors of the corporation.

Suppose, however, that a par-value stock is originally sold at a discount, that the original buyer resells to somebody else, and that the corporation later becomes insolvent. Who is liable to the creditors for the amount of the discount? Because of the diversity of laws and court decisions, the answer cannot be a simple one, but some general observations can be expressed. A few states, such as Indiana, specifically permit the sale of stock at a discount even when the sale is made for cash; in these jurisdictions, therefore, the discount rule is not applicable to either original or subsequent buyers. Elsewhere the rule appears to be that a subsequent holder of stock (that is, anybody other than an original buyer from the corporation) escapes liability for the discount if he buys the stock in good faith and without knowledge that it was originally sold at a discount. Under this rule, and on the basis of the doctrine of implied warranty, the original buyer from the corporation appears to continue to be liable for the amount of the discount. Some states provide that if stock is sold at a discount the stock certificates must clearly indicate the amount by which it is subject to assessment. Since such a notation on a stock certificate would certainly be sufficient notice to subsequent holders, it would have the effect of relieving the original owner from liability. Many states stipulate that stock certificates must not be issued unless the stock is "full paid and nonassessable," and stock certificates issued by corporations chartered in these states almost invariably bear a notation that the stock is, indeed, full paid and nonassessable. Such a notation apparently suffices to relieve subsequent holders of liability even if at the time of purchase they actually know that full payment had not been made for the stock when the certificates were originally issued. Presumably, also, it relieves original buyers from liability once they resell the stock. But directors who approve the issuance of certificates bearing the full paid and nonassessable notation apparently continue to be liable to corporate creditors indefinitely if, in fact, full payment was not received. Some states, however, put a time limit on the applicability of the discount rule. As an example, Delaware stipulates that all liabilities for discounts expire six years from the date of issuance of certificates or from the date of stock subscriptions, as the case may be. Within such a period of time, it appears, creditors are expected to be able to discover whether or not stock was fully paid for at the time of its original sale.

Risks of Common Stockownership

Although we thus give much attention to the legal obligation of the common stock buyer to pay the full agreed-on price, as well as to the applicability of the discount rule, we ought not to neglect certain economic aspects of the common stockholder's obligation. From the economic standpoint, the obligation of the common stockholder is to bear the risks of corporate enterprise—risks as measured by the full amount of his investment, both original investment and subsequent additions to it accumulated through the retention of profits. As a reward for this risk-bearing, the stockholder enjoys the rights described in this chapter.

In the abstract, the rights of common stockholders look most attractive, but in the concrete, as they apply to the affairs of individual corporations, they may turn out to be of much less value than was anticipated, or even quite valueless. In providing useful services or in turning out useful products, a corporation may be quite successful from the social point of view, but its stock may decline to negligible value because operating costs year after year absorb all its income. This is risk-bearing. Or the stockholder may be entirely dispossessed, having all his high-sounding rights taken from him, if the corporation defaults on its obligations to creditors, and if the seizure and sale of its assets yield not more than enough to satisfy their claims. This, too, is risk-bearing.

Rights attract and risks repel investors. For the individual corporation, therefore, success in using common stock as a means of acquiring assets must depend on the respective weights investors place on the attractiveness of the rights of ownership, on the one hand, and on the risks of ownership, on the other.

QUESTIONS

1. Is it possible to reconcile the description of stock as shares of ownership in a corporation with its description as a contract between the corporation and the stockholders? Explain.

2. What consideration is there to make stock a binding contract between a corporation and its stockholder? Where are the terms and conditions of the contract found?

3. What is capital stock? Preferred stock? Treasury stock?

4. Why are the common stockholder's claims to dividends and assets said to be closely interrelated?

5. With what degree of certainty can the common stockholder of a highly profitable corporation expect to receive dividends? Explain. If the amount of dividends is not to his liking, what can he do to improve the situation?

6. Why is the common stockholder's claim to assets of particular interest to wealthy investors? How is taxation related to this interest?

7. What is meant by the description of the common stockholder's claim to assets as a residual one? In what circumstances can it turn out to be not residual?

8. What is the scope of the common stockholder's right to participate in management? Why to some investors is this right much more important than the right to share in dividends and assets?

9. Is the ownership of a stock certificate really the ownership of stock? Explain. What is meant by the negotiability of stock certificates? Of what importance is it?

10. The common stockholder's right to sell his stock cannot be restricted in any way. Is this proposition true or false? Explain.

11. What is the common stockholder's preemptive right? To what kinds of stock transactions is it ordinarily inapplicable? Allowing for these exceptions, how strong is the right?

12. For what reasons may the managers of a corporation deny access to its books to certain stockholders?

13. What are the wrongful kinds of acts of corporate managements against which the common stockholder can protect himself by legal action?

14. In return for the bundle of rights given by a corporation to the common stockholder, what is his legal obligation to it? Does he have any kind of obligation of a nonlegal kind? Discuss.

15. When a par-value common stock is sold at a discount, what is the liability to creditors, if any, of the original buyer? Subsequent transferees? The corporation's directors?

16. To what extent, if at all, does the discount rule apply to no-par stock? The impairment rule? Explain.

PROBLEM

The articles of incorporation of Slocum and Seagrave, Inc. provide for its issuance of 600,000 shares of common stock of $10 par value, but the articles and bylaws say nothing further about this stock. In this circumstance:

a) To escape the application of the discount rule (assumed here to be the general rule of most of the states), what is the minimum price at which each share of the common stock can be sold to the public?

b) If the corporation's directors issue 40,000 shares of the stock to pay for a warehouse that changed hands 3 years ago at a cash price of $300,000, are these shares being sold at a discount? Explain.

c) If the corporation sells some of the common stock to investment bankers at $9.50 a share and the bankers resell to the public at $10 a share, is liability for discount incurred by the bankers, the public buyers, neither, or both?

d) If an investor subscribes to some common shares at a price of $18 a share, can he fulfill his contract by paying in only $10 a share on the grounds that the corporation must sell at the value stated in its articles, neither more nor less.

e) Assuming that the corporation has outstanding a 6 percent preferred stock, what minimum annual rate of cash dividends must it pay on the common stock?

f) What minimum proportion of the corporation's annual after-tax profit would the directors be required by law to pay out as cash dividends to the common stockholders?

g) Does the common stockholder have voting power in the election of directors? In passing on proposed changes in the corporation's articles of incorporation?

h) Would the common stockholder be required to give up his stock if the corporation wanted to call it for redemption?

chapter 18

SALES OF COMMON STOCK TO THE GENERAL PUBLIC

In using common stock as a means of acquiring assets, a business corporation may choose among several routes. These routes may be classified as follows.

1. Public offering for cash:
   a) Offering to the general public.
   b) Offering limited, in the first instance, to the corporation's existing common stockholders.
2. Private placement for cash.
3. Direct exchange for property other than cash or for services.
4. Offering for cash to specified classes of investors other than common stockholders, such as promoters, officers, employees, preferred stockholders, and bondholders.
5. Offering in exchange for the corporation's own preferred stock or bonds.
6. Miscellaneous procedures.

A very large proportion of the common stock sold annually for cash by American business corporations is disposed of by public offerings, a method of selling that includes offerings to the general public, to the corporations' existing security holders (except for close corporations whose security holders are few in number), and to other special groups such as their employees. Offerings of common stock to existing security holders are almost entirely tenders to the people who are already their common stockholders. In some years, immediate offerings for cash—as distinguished from sales over lengthy periods, as when options to buy stock are given to corporate officers—to the general public exceed offerings to existing security holders (common stockholders), and in other years these positions are reversed, with no clear trend in one direction or the other. In all years, at any rate, both of these categories far exceed offerings to other special groups. For the year ended June 30, 1966, for example, out of a total of $2,158 million of common stock registered with the SEC for immediate offering for cash $933 million was slated to be tendered to the public, $1,187 million to existing security holders, and only $38 million to other special groups. For the year ended June 30, 1967, with offerings totaling $1,484 million, those to the public were slated at $793 million, to security holders at $674 million, and to other special groups at only $17 million.[1]

In seeking to sell a new issue of common stock to the general public or to its existing common stockholders, a corporation may undertake to do the selling job entirely on its own, thereby making a direct offering, or it may employ the services of investment bankers who are specialists in merchandising securities. Direct offerings of common stock are much more popular in sales to existing stockholders than in sales to the general public, as is shown in Table 18–1. The 1959–61 data of the table were derived from a special study of the securities markets published by the SEC in 1963. Although the SEC's report did not account for direct offerings and investment banker offerings of preferred stocks and common stocks separately, other SEC figures indicate that sales of common stock amounted to 91.4 percent of the combined total of $8,914 million of registered issues offered for cash in the 3-year period.[2]

The private placement of a security issue is its sale in bulk to one or a small group of individual or institutional investors, such as individual capitalists, life insurance companies, pension and retirement funds, and religious, educational, and charitable organizations for their endowment funds. But while private placements, especially with life insurance companies, are of outstanding importance in sales of bonds, they are of quite limited significance in the sale of common stock.

Much common stock is given in direct exchange for property other than cash and for services. In the incorporation of businesses formerly carried on as proprietorships and partnerships, for example, the usual procedure is for the newly established corporations to buy out the former proprietary interests by giving common stock in exchange. In this way, assets of many kinds and values (probably including, in the typical case, some cash) are acquired by direct exchange. Similarly, mergers and consolidations are frequently completed by exchanges

---

[1]Securities and Exchange Commission, *Annual Report*, 1966, p. 156; and 1967, p. 154.

[2]Derived from Securities and Exchange Commission, *Report of Special Study of the Securities Markets* (House Doc. No. 95, Pt. 1, 88th Cong., 1st sess. [Washington, D.C.: U.S. Government Printing Office, 1963]), p. 600.

of the common stocks of the surviving or new corporations for those of the corporations being absorbed. In this way, all the net assets of the absorbed corporations are in effect financed by means of the common stocks given by the surviving or new corporations. Common stock is often exchanged for the services of promoters who establish new corporations and arrange mergers and consolidations, to investment bankers who raise funds, and to corporate officers, whose cash salaries it supplements.

Corporations often make standing offers to certain persons or groups of persons, entitling them to buy at designated prices stipulated numbers of shares at given times or from time to time. A right to buy on the basis of such a standing offer is described as a *stock option*. Options are frequently given to promoters, investment bankers, and corporate officers and other employees. Similar rights to buy are sometimes attached to preferred stocks and bonds as a means of improving their attractiveness. Often, these are described as stock-purchase warrants rather than as options.

TABLE 18–1
Selling Channels for Stock Issues Registered with the SEC, 1959–61*
(Amounts in millions of dollars)

	1959	*1960*	*1961*	*Total* *Amount*	*Total* *Percent*
Offered to stockholders:					
Through investment bankers	$ 457	$ 158	$ 319	$ 934	10.5
Direct	81	224	1,143	1,448	16.2
Total	$ 539	$ 381	$1,461	$2,381	26.7
Offered to others:†					
Through investment bankers	$2,212	$1,636	$2,408	$6,256	70.2
Direct	83	121	74	277	3.1
Total	$2,295	$1,757	$2,482	$6,533	73.3
Grand Total	$2,833	$2,138	$3,943	$8,914	100.0

*Issues of both common and preferred stocks offered for cash sale, excluding issues of investment companies and offerings under employee stock-purchase plans. In some instances, items do not add exactly to totals because of rounding. Horizontal totals and percentages supplied by the author.

†Chiefly, of course, the general public.

SOURCE: Securities and Exchange Commission, *Report of Special Study of the Securities Markets* (House Doc. No. 95, Pt. 1, 88th Cong., 1st sess. [Washington, D.C.: U.S. Government Printing Office, 1963]), p. 604.

Offerings of common stock made by corporations in exchange for their own preferred stocks or bonds are usually made at the time these securities are issued. From the beginning, the preferred stocks or bonds are convertible into common stock at stipulated ratios at the option of their holders. By this arrangement, assets are acquired in the first instance through the sale of the preferred stocks or bonds, but if conversion is later effected, common stock is substituted as the source of assets, much as if the assets had been acquired in the first place by the sale of common stock.

Finally, in miscellaneous areas, common stock is very popularly used for dividends and is quite rarely distributed as bonus stock to buyers of preferred stock and bonds.

We shall find it convenient to devote the remainder of the present chapter to the procedure of selling common stock for cash to the general public. Chapter 19 will be devoted to offerings to existing common stockholders, and Chapter 20 to the remaining uses of common stock, as indicated in the foregoing outline and discussion. The final two chapters on the use of common stock as a financing instrument, Chapters 21 and 22, will take up the major problems that arise in the management of common stock issues.

THE ROLE OF INVESTMENT BANKERS

As the data of Table 18–1 reveal, business corporations customarily employ the services of investment bankers when they decide to sell common stock for cash to the general public. The managers of the typical corporation doubtless feel that though investment bankers' commissions will take a substantial slice of the proceeds of their common stock issue their own efforts to sell direct would be even more costly. The managers of a manufacturing corporation, for example, may be thoroughly competent in technical matters pertaining to the fabrication and sale of their products, but they may know very little about the state of the securities markets and the names, finances, and interests of likely buyers of common stock. On the other hand, the investment bankers, as specialists in buying and selling securities, can be expected to know when and where and how it is best to bring out new common stock issues, as well as who among their customers probably are most interested in subscribing to them.

It must be recognized, nevertheless, that hundreds of individual issues of common stock not accounted for in the statistics of the Securities and Exchange Commission because of their small size or because they need not be registered with it are sold annually in the United States direct by promoters of new corporations and by small corporations already in operation. But the people reached in such direct selling usually constitute extremely small segments of the general public—apparently relatives, friends, business associates or acquaintances, and well-to-do fellow townspeople of the promoters or the managers of operating corporations. However, little can be said about the doorbell ringing, the buttonholing, and the sometimes tearful pleading and other procedures that go with the direct selling of small common stock issues. Accordingly, we may confine our attention to the more formal procedures of selling with the assistance of investment bankers. To be kept in mind, however, is that legal regulations pertaining to common stock sales, as discussed later, are as applicable to direct sales as to sales through investment bankers.

Nature of Investment Banking

Investment bankers are essentially merchants in securities. They buy entire issues of new securities and retail them in smaller lots to their customers. They undertake to guarantee the success of offerings of new issues of securities by corporations to their existing stockholders. They serve as agents of issuers in seeking institutional investors who may be willing to buy entire issues or large portions of them. As agents, too, they agree to exert their best efforts to help corporations dispose of security issues to the public. They effect what are called secondary distributions of securities by buying large blocks already held by individual and institutional investors and retailing them among their customers. On orders of their customers, they act as brokers in buying and selling already outstanding securities through the facilities of the stock exchanges. And in the over-the-counter market—that is, all market facilities for trading in securities other than the stock exchanges—they also buy and sell already outstanding securities, either as brokers on a commission basis or as dealers buying and selling in their own names in the expectation of making profits through differences in buying and selling prices.

In all these kinds of operations, the investment bankers function as *middlemen*, channeling funds from those who are willing to put their money into long-term securities to those who have such securities to dispose of.[3]

Underwriting

From the standpoint of corporations that want to obtain long-term funds, the first two functions of investment bankers as stated in the foregoing list are of paramount importance. If a corporation can get reputable investment bankers to agree to buy an entire issue of its securities, or to guarantee the success of an offering of new securities to its present common stockholders, it is assured of receiving cash in the amount agreed on in its contract with them. There is no such assurance when investment bankers simply agree to serve as agents or finders in looking for institutional investors that may be willing to buy or, as agents, to exert their best efforts in trying to sell to the general public.

---

[3]The student is probably familiar with the names of prominent investment banking houses, such as Merrill Lynch, Pierce, Fenner & Smith, Inc.; Equitable Securities Corporation; Allen & Company; Bache & Company; Eastman Dillon, Union Securities & Company; Francis I du Pont & Co.; Lehman Brothers; Blyth & Company, Inc.; First Boston Corporation; Morgan Stanley & Company; Halsey, Stuart & Company, Inc.; and Wertheim & Company.

Thus, it may be said that corporations are best served by the investment bankers when the bankers are willing to act as underwriters. As the term is used in investment banking, underwriting is a guaranteeing of the sale of a security issue within a specified period of time at a stipulated price. If 100,000 shares of a corporation's common stock is underwritten by investment bankers "at 85," they guarantee that the corporation will receive by a stated date, after deduction of the bankers' compensation but before deduction of other selling expenses, $8.5 million. If the stock is to be offered to the general public, the investment bankers make good on their guaranty *by actually buying* the stock in bulk "at 85," expecting to resell it among their customers in small parcels at a higher public offering price. If the stock is being offered to the corporation's existing stockholders, the investment bankers stand by with an *obligation to buy* at the agreed on price whatever portion of the issue the corporation does not succeed in selling to the stockholders or to others to whom the stockholders may assign their subscription rights.

Since underwriting is risky, investment bankers are cautious in coming to decisions on whether or not to make underwriting commitments. An obvious risk is that the bankers may have to resell at a price lower than that guaranteed to the corporation or, possibly, at a price not sufficiently higher than the guaranteed price to cover their own costs of handling the security issue. While the issuer of underwritten securities must bear all the expenses directly incurred in preparing them for the market, the bankers still must meet their own ordinary operating expenses, including, most importantly, the salaries of their staffs. Another kind of risk exists because investment bankers usually undertake to make a market for securities they have underwritten. This means that after the securities have been sold to investors, the bankers continue to quote prices at which they are willing to buy them back. Should many investors in an issue change their minds about its investment merits and decide to quickly unload their purchases, the bankers would find their inventories of reacquired securities mounting dangerously. A third kind of risk is that the investment bankers always stand in danger of losing the confidence and goodwill of their customers when securities they have underwritten and sold to these customers turn out to be disappointing in performance.

Cost of Underwriting

As a risk bearer, the investment banker expects to be suitably compensated. Difficulties in finding buyers of securities, dangers of sudden unfavorable turns in market conditions while securities are being offered, and the possibilities of subsequent poor performance all tend to vary in direct relation to the type of security. Thus, as indicated in Table 18–2, the compensation paid to investment bankers—known

TABLE 18–2
Underwriting Commissions on Publicly Offered Security Issues Registered with the SEC and Sold through Investment Bankers, 1951, 1953, and 1955*
(As percentages of proceeds of public sale)

Size of Issue (Millions of dollars)	*Industry of Issuer*					*All Industries*
	Manufacturing	*Electric, Gas, and Water*	*Communication*	*Mining*	*Other*	
Bonds:						
Under 0.5	.....	....	....	.....	.....	.....
0.5– 0.9	7.42	....	....	.....	7.69	7.53
1.0– 1.9	6.50	3.00	2.50	.....	5.25	5.80
2.0– 4.9	4.61	1.04	....	.....	4.34	2.37
5.0– 9.9	2.58	.73	....	3.04	2.50	1.01
10.0–19.9	1.70	.62	.72	1.88	1.44	.88
20.0–49.9	1.30	.68	.57	.....	1.34	.85
50.0 and over	1.02	.64	.66	.....	.91	.88
Total†	1.73	.66	.61	2.46	1.25	.80
Preferred Stock:						
Under 0.5	.....	....	....	.....	.....	.....
0.5– 0.9	11.70	8.00	5.17	.....	8.32	8.67
1.0– 1.9	8.69	4.46	4.44	.....	10.00	5.98
2.0– 4.9	4.06	2.67	4.31	.....	6.43	3.83
5.0– 9.9	3.28	2.57	4.40	.....	2.71	2.93
10.0–19.9	2.20	2.28	3.56	.....	2.23	2.40
20.0–49.9	3.23	2.76	....	.....	.....	2.84
50.0 and over	2.12	....	....	.....	.....	2.12
Total†	4.05	2.25	4.85	.....	5.80	3.34
Common Stock:						
Under 0.5	15.70	....	....	25.50	11.76	20.99
0.5– 0.9	10.63	7.96	5.95	26.52	16.32	17.12
1.0– 1.9	10.57	5.08	4.95	18.96	9.20	11.27
2.0– 4.9	7.29	4.32	4.90	15.23	11.16	8.47
5.0– 9.9	5.61	3.84	5.81	10.38	11.76	5.31
10.0–19.9	4.40	2.52	4.52	11.11	6.15	4.20
20.0–49.9	5.08	3.85	....	15.00	.....	4.98
50.0 and over	.....	....	....	.....	.....	.....
Total†	8.00	3.78	5.00	16.67	9.82	8.75

*Including 265 issues of bonds with gross proceeds of $5.9 billion, 120 issues of preferred stock amounting to $850 million, and 230 issues of common stock with proceeds of almost $1 billion. The median size of issues was $15 million for bonds, $4 million for preferred stock, and $2 million for common stock. Issues ranged in size from $100,000 to $300 million.

†Median percentages.

SOURCE: Securities and Exchange Commission, *Cost of Flotation of Corporate Securities, 1951–1955* (Washington, D.C.: U.S. Government Printing Office, 1957), pp. 9, 38–40.

variously as commission, discount, and spread—is generally much higher for underwritings of common stock than for underwritings of preferred stock and bonds.[4]

The risks incurred by investment bankers also tend to vary in re-

[4]See also Table 15–3, page 354, for a comparison for the same years of total costs for flotation of bonds, preferred stock, and common stock.

lation to the size of issues, the size of the issuing corporations, the industries they are engaged in, their profit and dividend records, their credit reputations, the state of the market from time to time, and other factors. It is impossible to say precisely, or even approximately, what weight is given to each of these factors in the determination of the bankers' commission in given underwritings. The data of Table 18–2 clearly show that commissions as percentages are generally much higher for small issues. In considering issuers' industries, it is noteworthy that bankers' compensation for public utility issues runs substantially lower in all but one of the size groupings than does compensation for issues of manufacturing corporations, and commissions for issues of mining companies run far higher than for any other industrial class.

Some of the findings of the SEC in a later study of cash commissions paid to investment bankers for their services in marketing common stock issues are presented in Table 18–3. A comparison of the

TABLE 18–3
Investment Bankers' Cash Compensation on Publicly Offered Common Stock Issues, 1949, 1953, 1960, and 1961*
(As percentages of gross proceeds†)

Size of Issue (Thousands of dollars)	*1949*	*1953*	*1960*	*1961*
300 and under	10.9	11.6	15.0	15.2
Over 300	6.4	5.8	9.4	9.6
301 to 499	11.3	14.3	15.4	11.8
500 to 999	8.4	10.9	11.5	11.8
1,000 to 2,999	9.4	8.5	9.1	9.2
3,000 to 4,999	6.4	6.4	6.6	7.2
5,000 to 9,999	6.5	3.6	6.2	5.7
10,000 and over	4.6	4.2	4.4	3.2

*Issues registered with the SEC and publicly offered issues exempt from registration under its Regulation A (see pp. 451–52) offered for cash sale through investment bankers, including offerings to issuing corporations' existing stockholders.

†Median percentages in the broad classes of the first two lines of the table; all other items as unweighted averages.

SOURCE: Securities and Exchange Commission, *Report of Special Study of the Securities Markets* (House Doc. No. 95, Pt. 1, 88th Cong., 1st sess. [Washington, D.C.: U.S. Government Printing Office, 1963]), p. 616.

commission rates of 1960–61 with those of 1949 and 1953 reveals sharp increases in the price of the bankers' services for both the issues of $300,000 and under and the issues of more than $300,000. Although the nature of the figures makes it somewhat difficult to pinpoint where among the larger issues the weight of the increased commissions chiefly fell, it is clear that the percentage increase in commission rates on the larger issues collectively was greater than on the issues of $300,000 and less. One of the most remarkable revelations of the SEC's later study, moreover, was that the bankers in 1960 and 1961 received noncash compensation in addition to cash commissions on a much larger proportion of common stock flotations than in 1949 and

1953. For flotations of over $300,000, supplementary noncash compensation was given to the bankers in only 1 percent of the offerings in 1949 and in only 11.8 percent in 1953, but in 34.7 percent in 1960 and in 41.6 percent in 1961. For flotations of $300,000 and under, the respective percentages for the 4 years were 13.1, 21.4, 46.0, and 70.8.[5] The noncash compensation consisted of cheap stock and options giving the bankers the right to buy given numbers of shares at set prices. The "cheap stock" designation was given by the SEC to shares, additional to shares in public offerings, sold to bankers at prices below the prices at which the public offerings were being made. The SEC made no attempt to put a dollar value on the noncash compensation, but it did observe that cash commission rates were generally higher for flotations in which additional noncash compensation was provided than for flotations without additional compensation. This is brought out in Table 18–4, which also provides a comparison among cash

TABLE 18–4
Investment Bankers' Cash Compensation on Publicly Offered Common Stock Issues, by Industry of Issuer and Type of Compensation Arrangement, 1949, 1953, 1960, and 1961*
(As median percentages of gross proceeds†)

	1949		*1953*		*1960*		*1961*	
	Cash Only	*Cash Plus*	*Cash Only*	*Cash Plus*	*Cash Only*	*Cash Plus*	*Cash Only*	*Cash Plus*
Issues of $300,000 and under:								
Manufacturing	4.7	16.5	6.7	20.0	11.2	19.0	10.2	16.2
Extractive	18.0	27.0	20.0	32.0	11.5	....	32.7	....
Public utilities	3.9	....	7.0	23.4	8.2	....	10.8	....
Other	12.9	42.5	11.6	....	12.8	18.0	15.1	16.6
All industries	7.8	25.5	10.0	30.0	12.4	18.3	11.6	16.4
Issues of over $300,000:								
Manufacturing	6.5	....	8.0	21.3	7.7	12.3	8.2	11.7
Extractive	14.0	28.0	10.8	18.2	17.0	7.8	14.6	15.0
Public utilities	6.0	....	2.8	....	4.0	....	3.7	15.0
Other	7.5	....	9.3	11.1	8.4	13.6	8.5	12.6
All industries	6.2	28.0	4.8	15.8	7.9	12.7	8.0	12.3

*Issues registered with the SEC and publicly offered issues exempt from registration under its Regulation A offered for cash sale through investment bankers, including offerings to issuing corporations' existing stockholders.

†Items in "cash only" column are percentage cash commissions to investment bankers in flotations for which they received no other compensation; items in "cash plus" column are percentage *cash* commissions in flotations for which the bankers received additional noncash compensation.

SOURCE: Securities and Exchange Commission, *Report of Special Study of the Securities Markets* (House Doc. No. 95, Pt. 1, 88th Cong., 1st sess. [Washington, D.C.: U.S. Government Printing Office, 1963]), p. 618.

[5]Securities and Exchange Commission, *Report of Special Study, op. cit.*, p. 619.

commission rates as paid by corporate issuers of common stock classified by industry.

Availability of Underwriting Services

The statistics of investment bankers' commissions and noncash compensation for underwriting common stock issues indicate a risk evaluation by the bankers unfavorable to small corporations. This may be due as much to a lack of competition for small issues among the bankers as to weaknesses in the issues themselves. The larger investment banking houses are inclined to have but little interest in small issues. They often have lower limits, such as $1 million, below which they are unwilling to go except in unusual circumstances. At the same time, the thousands of smaller firms of securities dealers scattered throughout the country generally look on underwriting as a minor phase of their operations. They derive most of their income as brokers and dealers in buying and selling securities already outstanding. While many of them are likely to be interested in attractive underwriting propositions, they are inclined to proceed cautiously and only on assurances of rather generous compensation. For them, therefore, underwriting tends to be an occasional operation rather than a matter of strong, sustained interest.

Accordingly, most small corporations and many of intermediate sizes have reasons to fear disappointment in seeking underwriting for new common stock issues. New corporations, smaller corporations that have been unable to establish good records of earnings, and others that, though moderately successful, have relatively weak growth prospects are all likely to arouse little interest among reputable investment bankers.[6] Hundreds of common stock underwriting proposals that come to them are rejected by the bankers. In many other cases, the managers of small corporations are told frankly that the underwriting commission would have to be set at a level so high as to

---

[6]All of this does not gainsay the fact that in a booming market small corporations are likely to find many new investment banking houses that are eager to take on their proposed issues. See Securities and Exchange Commission, *Report of Special Study, op. cit.*, pp. 15–19, 261–68, 493–94. The SEC found: "To a large extent, broker-dealers who managed the underwriting of unseasoned issues of common stock in 1961 were relative newcomers to the field. More than half (271) of these underwriters had been organized less than 6 years before the offering, while over one-fourth (146) were formed in either the year preceding or the year in which the offering was made. . . . Yet many of the new underwriters were managed by individuals who themselves were new to the securities industry. In only about 25 percent of the 271 new broker-dealer firms did a majority of the principals (i.e., partners, officers, or directors) have 5 or more years' experience. When the very new firms that were formed in 1960 or 1961 are considered as a separate group, the lack of background in the securities field becomes even more striking. . . . The more recently created underwriters operated with only modest amounts of capital. Ninety-five (or 35 percent) of the 271 new firms had net capital of less than $10,000 in 1961, and only 1 percent ranked among the rela-

make common stock financing by offering to the general public a poor means of acquiring funds. In many instances, too, requests for underwriting are withdrawn by corporation managers when they learn how high the flotation costs, especially the underwriting commissions, would be. However, requests for underwriting that would ordinarily be rejected or withdrawn at one time may be accepted on relatively favorable terms at other times. Changes in investor attitudes toward particular industries account for switches in the attitudes of the bankers. Witness the successive flurries in recent years of common stock flotations, including many small offerings, in uranium mining and prospecting, electronics and electrical equipment, solid fuels and other aerospace research and development, vending machines, scientific instruments, printing and publishing, and boats and other sporting goods.

A conclusion that the smaller corporations may find it difficult or impossible to get new issues of their common stock underwritten does not necessarily imply that large corporations have clear sailing when they seek underwriting services. At least, however, large corporations can generally expect the bankers to give their proposals most careful consideration. The larger underwriting houses want to avoid rejecting meritorious proposals, since they depend on underwriting spreads for a substantial share of their total income. Underwriting is for them a major operating area, and opportunities to underwrite attractive issues are zealously sought.

Best-Efforts Selling

Sometimes, investment banking houses though unwilling to underwrite certain issues of common stock are willing to serve as agents in seeking buyers for them. The agency arrangement is known as best-efforts selling. The bankers ask for a commission only on whatever shares they succeed in selling. However, because their very refusal to underwrite indicates expectations of extraordinary difficulties in selling, the commission rate is usually higher than for underwritten offerings. In its studies of public offerings of common stock in 1961, the SEC found the median commission rate for best-efforts selling to be 15.0 percent on issues of more than $300,000 and 12.9 percent on

---

tively big underwriters with net capital of $500,000 or more. This tendency toward smallness is even more manifest among the 146 new firms formed in 1960 or 1961. Sixty-six of these firms (or 45 percent) had net capital of less than $10,000 and none was in the large-sized category." At an earlier place in its report, the SEC noted: "Another group of specialists are those who do not purport to be financial planners but who concentrate on the sale to the public of stock of promotional or unseasoned companies. The merchandise they offer and the selling methods they use preclude concern on their part for the interests of their individual customers. Despite the intricate and specialized nature of their merchandise, they apply to the sale of securities the merchandising methods more suitable for selling vacuum cleaners or used cars."

issues of $300,000 and under on contracts without additional noncash compensation. The comparable rates for underwritten issues were 8.0 percent and 11.2 percent, respectively. For contracts with additional noncash compensation, the median cash commission rates for best-efforts selling were 15.0 percent on issues over $300,000 and 17.5 percent on issues of $300,000 and under, compared with cash commission rates on underwritten flotations of 11.6 percent and 13.3 percent, respectively.[7] Because, indeed, bankers generally fear that poorly performing securities sold on a best-efforts basis will reflect on them as unfavorably as poorly performing underwritten issues, the larger, stronger houses are generally content to leave best-efforts selling to the smaller houses.

Although best-efforts arrangements for common stock issues may be the best deals that given corporations, especially smaller ones, can get, they may not be good enough; the corporate managements may decide that they must try other alternatives for needed financing. A principal drawback is the incurring of all the expenses of preparing an issue for sale without any assurances of sale; if the flotation is unsuccessful, the venture may leave the corporation with less cash than it had at the start. Because any security issue is usually designed to produce cash needed for a specific purpose, the possibility that sales may fall short even moderately, as by one third or one fourth of the issue, tends to cast doubt on the feasibility of the best-efforts arrangement. What is more, some state securities laws—the blue-sky laws to be discussed a little later—provide that the proceeds of best-efforts sales are to be put in escrow and returned to investors, less the selling commission, unless all or almost all the issue is sold.

UNDERWRITING PROCEDURE

The first step in the procedure of underwriting a common stock issue is ordinarily the presentation of a proposal by the financial officers of a corporation to the investment banking house of their choice.[8] Sometimes, the procedure is reversed. Alert investment banking houses are constantly on the lookout for attractive financing opportunities, and they often take the initiative in suggesting to corporate managements how their financial structures could be better ordered by the replacement of existing classes of liabilities or stock issues by new issues of stocks or bonds, or in suggesting to close cor-

---

[7]Securities and Exchange Commission, *Report of Special Study, op. cit.*, p. 618.

[8]An alternative procedure is to make a public announcement of the details of the issue and invite investment bankers and anybody else who may be interested to submit bids for it. Railroads and certain classes of public utilities are required by government regulation to offer most kinds of their securities for competitive bidding. However, because many more bond issues than stock issues have been offered by the competitive bidding route a discussion of the matter is deferred to Chapter 30, where procedures in the sale of bonds are analyzed. See pp. 775–81.

porations that the time has arrived for them to go public. A corporation goes public when, for the first time, it makes an offering to the general public of a new issue of its own securities, ordinarily common stock, or its principal stockholders make such an offering of some of their holdings.[9]

When the proposal comes from a corporation, the bankers subject it, so to say, to a preliminary investigation. If this turns out favorably, they launch a much more extensive investigation. And if this, too, is favorable, they are prepared to push ahead with all the other steps that are necessary to bring the financing to completion. These steps are discussed in detail in the following pages.

To be kept in mind in the course of this discussion is that the procedures of underwriting common stock issues are closely paralleled by those in the underwriting of preferred stocks and bonds. Thus, the description of procedures in the present chapter should make unnecessary further extended treatment in later chapters, where financing with preferred stock and bonds is taken up.

Preliminary Investigation

On taking a common stock financing proposal to an investment banking house, the principal financial officer of a corporation can expect to be accorded red-carpet service. Cordial relations presumably exist already if the house has in the past successfully handled financing for the corporation, but the financial officer's reception is likely to be no less cordial if he is approaching the house for the first time.

If the contract is a first approach, the bankers will ask about the corporation's history, products, and activities, and especially about the nature and scope of the plans for financing. The financial officer will be asked to supply recent financial statements and other compilations of data, but in general only materials already available or collectible at no great expense. The bankers want such information only for purposes of a preliminary analysis, whose results will indicate whether or not a more time-consuming and costly detailed investigation would be justifiable. With assurances from the financial officer that the data called for will be quickly supplied, the bankers, in turn, are able to give him assurances that the preliminary investigation will be carried through promptly, and that a decision on whether or not they are willing to proceed further in the direction of underwriting will be quickly forthcoming.

---

[9]For a description of some kinds of efforts of investment bankers to drum up business in the period 1959–61, see Securities and Exchange Commission, *Report of Special Study*, *op. cit.*, pp. 495–500. The author advises the student to continue his reading in the SEC's report, especially pages 512–16, to see that the underwriting procedure is not always quite so thorough and orderly as described in the following pages of this textbook.

The preliminary investigation is carried on by the *buying department* of the investment banking house. For its study, it has the information supplied by the financial officer during his interview and the additional data supplied by him subsequently in documentary form, together with such further information about the corporation and its affairs that the bankers' *research department* is able to assemble from published sources.

On the basis of the earlier discussion of the risks of investment banking, one may readily conclude that many proposals for security flotations do not survive the preliminary investigation. But for those that do survive, detailed investigations become the next order of business.

Detailed Investigation

Although no contract, written or oral, is entered into before investment bankers launch detailed investigations of proposed security issues, there are certain understandings between bankers and prospective issuers that are generally recognized and observed. The corporation is expected throughout the period of investigation to give it unstinted cooperation in supplying a mass of information about itself—including, probably, some of a secret character that it would be most unwilling to disclose to anybody else—in having experts of various kinds prepare special reports, and in patiently bearing the expenses of these operations. It is also understood that the corporation will not take its proposal to any other investment banking house while the investigation is under way, and that it will not deny the investigating house the role of originator of the security issue should it be willing to go ahead with the underwriting.

Reports of experts include, at the minimum, financial statements certified by public accountants and opinions of attorneys on the corporation's legal status, the scope of its corporate powers, its capacity to issue additional common stock, and the nature of current or pending litigation, if any, in which it may be involved. Other kinds of reports that may be called for, depending on circumstances are:

1. Those of management engineers, analyzing the corporation's administrative setup, its factory facilities and their layout, the nature and composition of its products, its sources of raw materials and other supplies, and its labor relations.
2. Those of appraisers, establishing current values of its physical plant.
3. Those of market analysts on the corporation's product distribution facilities and channels, its relationships with wholesalers, jobbers, and others, and its advertising policies.

Having reports prepared by experts is costly for the corporation, as is also the time its own officers and employees must give in providing information both to the bankers and to the experts and in cooperating in other ways. Moreover, the corporation is billed for expenses specially incurred by the investment bankers in connection with the investigation, although not for the bankers' regular operating expenses, as for the wages and salaries of its staff members. But the corporation's managers are likely to conclude philosophically that most of the materials assembled will be needed anyway for the preparation of a registration statement and prospectus—documents to be discussed later. They also know that the collected data will be useful in presenting the underwriting proposition to other investment banking houses should the house that makes the investigation decide against underwriting.

Underwriting Decision

If the investment banking house finds that the results of its detailed investigation are favorable to its corporate client, and if it continues to be satisfied with the market situation in general, it is ready to commit itself to serve as the originator and as a principal underwriter of the proposed common stock issue. Such a commitment is ordinarily made in a letter from the bankers to the corporation, following a negotiation conference where the bankers and the corporate officials agree on all the details of the proposed issue and of their own relationship that can be definitely established by that time. The letter sets forth all these details as constituting the understanding between the bankers and the corporation. While the corporate officers will have been given some assurances about the probable gross proceeds of the issue, the letter is most unlikely to contain any statement about the price at which the bankers will eventually underwrite it. As further time-consuming steps must be taken before the offering is actually made to the public, and as drastic changes could take place in the market situation in the interim, it would be much too risky for the bankers to make a firm price commitment at this stage of the proceedings. On the other hand, they may be willing to come to an immediate agreement on the underwriting commission and to include this as a specific detail in their letter.

Investment bankers often recommend means of financing other than the means proposed to them. For a given corporation, they may be willing to underwrite one kind of security issue—perhaps bonds—but not another kind—say common stock. When corporate managements have strong convictions about the form their financing should take, no agreement may be possible if these convictions conflict with the judgments of the investment bankers and if the corporate officers are unwilling to switch their plans. Often, however, financial officers of corporations go to investment bankers with no strong choices on the means of financing to be used. They expect the bankers, on the basis of their expert knowledge of sources of funds and market conditions, to advise them how best to proceed. Not infrequently, too, as detailed investigations proceed both the bankers and their corporate clients come to a conclusion that financing plans different from those tentatively agreed on earlier should be substituted as having greater promise of success.

Preparation by the Corporation

A corporation whose common stock financing proposal has been accepted by an investment banking house has certain functions to perform in getting its new issue prepared for the public offering. Most obviously, it must have unissued stock available for the offering. As it would be unlikely to have such a quantity already authorized, it must have its articles of incorporation amended to provide for the additional shares. This action requires an approving vote of the existing common stockholders. Moreover, should the existing stock have the preemptive right, the stockholders must be asked to waive that right with respect to the new issue, or, alternatively, to approve a further amendment to the articles of incorporation to rescind the right as it would apply to the proposed issue as well as to future ones.

Investment bankers sometimes stipulate that they will underwrite only if certain features of authorized common stock—already outstanding and to be issued—are changed. Such changes almost invariably require the approval of the existing common stockholders. Thus, a change from an established par value to no par or one in the opposite direction may be prescribed. Or a change from a high to a low par value may be requested. This move normally is effected, with respect to shares already outstanding, by the issuance of two or more shares of the lower par value for one share of the existing higher par—for example, 5 $20 shares for 1 of $100. The investment bankers ask for such changes in the expectation that the stock will thus be made more attractive to the classes of investors to whom it is to be offered.

Further preparatory work is required of the corporation, in close cooperation with the investment bankers, in drawing up a registration statement and prospectus to qualify the common stock issue for public sale in accordance with the requirements of the federal Securities Act, as well as in taking steps to qualify the issue for sale in various states according to the provisions of their blue-sky laws.

Registration under the Federal Securities Act

The objective of the federal Securities Act is to protect investors in new security issues offered for sale in interstate commerce from misrepresentation, deceit, and other fraud, and for every issue so offered to provide them with all material facts presumably necessary for intelligent investment decisions. Use of the mails and other instrumentalities of interstate commerce is denied to issuers of securities unless (1) they file registration statements with the Securities and Exchange

Commission, (2) the registration statements are permitted by that agency to become effective, and (3) approved prospectuses are made available for the people to whom the securities are offered for sale. Use of the mails and other instrumentalities of interstate commerce in ways contrary to the prescribed procedures is a criminal offense, punishable by fine, imprisonment, or both, and it also gives rise to certain kinds of civil liabilities.

Securities and Exchange Commission. Responsibility for the enforcement of the Securities Act as adopted in 1933 was entrusted by Congress to the Federal Trade Commission, but in 1934 it was transferred to the Securities and Exchange Commission, a new agency established by the Securities Exchange Act adopted in that year. Under the 1934 legislation, as its title implies, SEC was given authority to regulate the activities of national securities exchanges, the conduct of members of these exchanges, and certain kinds of financial activities of corporations whose securities are traded on the exchanges, in addition to the powers respecting new security issues as transferred from the Federal Trade Commission. Later legislation has given the SEC much additional authority, including powers to regulate the structure and financing activities of public utility holding company systems, the operations of securities dealers and brokers in the over-the-counter market, and the activities of investment companies and investment advisers, as well as certain advisory powers related to proceedings in bankruptcy.

The SEC is composed of five members who are appointed by the President with the advice and consent of the Senate. The term of office is five years, but members may be reappointed. To contribute to continuity of policy, the terms of members are staggered, one member's term expiring each year. Not more than three members may be of the same political party.

The SEC's headquarters are in Washington. However, to speed up its work as well as to provide convenient facilities for people who have business with it, the SEC operates nine regional offices and seven branch offices in various parts of the country.

Registration Statements. Registration statements required under the federal Securities Act are generally long and complex documents. Such a statement must be signed by the corporation, its principal executive officers, including its principal financial and accounting officers, and a majority of its board of directors. All these signers are subject to criminal and civil penalties for willful omissions and misstatements of material facts, and such liability extends also to the nonsigning directors, experts who participated in preparing the registration statement, and all underwriting investment bankers. Although all these persons, except the corporation itself, can probably escape liability by demonstrating that they were reasonably prudent in their contributions (or in certain other ways), they are likely to feel that the best way to escape liability is to be clear and honest in the first place—to state clearly what are obviously material facts and to avoid concealment of details that may later be adjudged to be material facts. Hence, they are inclined to err in the direction of excessive description and to include facts of no great consequence.

The SEC itself describes the content of a registration statement as follows:

> In general, the registration statement of an issuer other than a foreign government must disclose such matters as the names of persons who participate in the management or control of the issuer's business; the security holdings and remuneration of such persons; the general character of the business, its capital structure, past history and earnings; underwriters' commissions; payments to promoters made within 2 years or intended to be made; the interest of directors, officers and principal stockholders in material transactions with the issuer; pending legal proceedings; and the purposes to which the proceeds of the offering are to be applied, and must include financial statements certified by independent accountants.[10]

In some respects, however, the SEC might be said to err on the side of brevity in this description, for registration statements have traditionally required much documentation, including copies of articles of incorporation, bylaws, contracts with underwriters, and material contracts not negotiated in the ordinary course of business, as well as various supplementary schedules to support and explain the principal financial statements. On the other hand, the SEC deserves praise for its constant efforts toward easing the burdens on registrants in preparing registration statements and prospectuses. Especially notable in this direction was its adoption in late November, 1967, of a new rule to authorize corporations "having long records of earnings and stability of management and business"—corporations to be recognized on the basis of certain standards included in the rule—to omit from their registration statements and prospectuses many of the documents, schedules, and details traditionally required. The new rule was adopted on an experimental basis, and, of course, the shortened registration statements and prospectuses were expected to still contain all necessary information for "informed judgments as to the merits" of the securities being offered.

At the time of filing a registration statement, the registering corporation must pay a fee equal to .02 percent of the "maximum aggregate price at which the securities are proposed to be offered" or a fee of $100, whichever amount is greater. For an issue of, say, 300,000 shares of common stock whose price to the public is expected to be not more than $30 a share, the fee would be $1,800—an additional

[10]Securities and Exchange Commission, *Annual Report*, 1966, p. 22.

item of expense, but surely one of the least burdensome of flotation costs.

The Securities Act provides for a waiting period of 20 days from the date of filing of a registration statement until it becomes effective—that is, until the securities may be sold. The waiting period gives the SEC's staff time to examine the registration statement to determine if, indeed, it does appear to be a straightforward disclosure of all material facts, if copies of all prescribed documents have been included, and if the prospectus is an adequate summary. The SEC has authority to permit registration statements to become effective after waiting periods of less than 20 days. It has been especially liberal in advancing effective dates when it has appeared that early offerings would materially enhance selling prospects. In every such case, of course, the SEC must be satisfied about the completeness of the registration statement, either as originally filed or as amended in accordance with its instructions.

Prospectuses. A prospectus is a part of a registration statement and, at the same time, a comprehensive summary of it. It is expected to cover all the material facts contained in the main body of the registration statement, but in briefer form. Financial statements included in the prospectus must be as complete as in the principal registration statement presentation, although supporting schedules may generally be abbreviated or omitted. Even before the adoption of the SEC's new experimental rule in late 1967 (referred to above), prospectuses generally omitted documents such as articles of incorporation, although excerpts might be included if apparently necessary to clarify something thought to be of material significance. Nevertheless, they have tended to considerable length, commonly running to 20, 30, or more large printed pages. (For an illustrative cover page of a prospectus, see Figure 18–1.)

The reason prospectuses are required is that few prospective investors in securities are expected to examine the registration statements themselves. After filing, the complete registration statements are available for examination in the reading rooms of the SEC, and photostatic copies can be obtained at a moderate cost. But if a new security issue is to be offered to thousands of investors, it is hardly to be expected that more than a handful will want to see the full registration statement. The more convenient prospectus can be mailed or handed to the prospective investor when he is asked to buy. Indeed, it *must* be tendered to people who are asked to buy. Thus, one will notice in newspaper advertising of new security issues subject to the registration requirements of the Securities Act, illustrated in Figure 18–2, a statement identical with or similar to the following: "This announcement is not an offer to sell or a solicitation of an offer to buy these securities. The offering is made only by the Prospectus."

FIGURE 18–1
Cover Page of a Prospectus

PROSPECTUS

150,000 Shares

DUCOMMUN METALS & SUPPLY CO.

COMMON STOCK

Par Value $2 Per Share

THESE SECURITIES HAVE NOT BEEN APPROVED OR DISAPPROVED BY THE SECURITIES AND EXCHANGE COMMISSION NOR HAS THE COMMISSION PASSED UPON THE ACCURACY OR ADEQUACY OF THIS PROSPECTUS. ANY REPRESENTATION TO THE CONTRARY IS A CRIMINAL OFFENSE.

From January 1, 1958 to March 9, 1959 inclusive the Common Stock was quoted in the Los Angeles over-the-counter market at prices ranging from a low of 13⅝ bid, 14⅛ asked, to a high of 22¾ bid, 23¾ asked. These prices are adjusted for the 50% stock dividend paid on February 19, 1959. The closing quotation on March 9, 1959 was 22½ bid, 23½ asked.

	Price to Public	Underwriting Discounts and Commissions(1)	Proceeds to Company(2)
Per Share	$23.00	$1.61	$21.39
Total	$3,450,000	$241,500	$3,208,500

(1) The Company has agreed to indemnify the Underwriters against certain civil liabilities, including liabilities under the Securities Act of 1933.

(2) Before deducting expenses payable by the Company estimated at $39,000.

IN CONNECTION WITH THIS OFFERING, THE UNDERWRITERS MAY OVERALLOT OR EFFECT TRANSACTIONS WHICH STABILIZE OR MAINTAIN THE MARKET PRICE OF THE COMMON STOCK OF THE COMPANY AT A LEVEL ABOVE THAT WHICH MIGHT OTHERWISE PREVAIL IN THE OPEN MARKET. SUCH STABILIZING, IF COMMENCED, MAY BE DISCONTINUED AT ANY TIME.

Among the Underwriters named herein is:

BLYTH & CO., INC.

The date of this Prospectus is March 10, 1959.

Proceedings for Injunctions. The SEC can be expected to appeal to the federal courts for an injunction to put a stop to the violations if a corporation and its investment bankers:

1. Attempt to sell a new issue of securities in interstate commerce without registering it with the SEC.
2. Register an issue but attempt to sell before the registration statement has become effective.
3. Offer an issue for sale after the effective date without making copies of the prospectus available to prospective buyers.

FIGURE 18-2
Newspaper Advertisement of a New Common Stock Issue

This is not an offer of these securities for sale. The offer is made only by the Prospectus.

NEW ISSUE

100,000 Shares

Polarad Electronics Corporation

Common Stock

($1 Par Value)

5,000 of the Shares are initially being offered to employees upon the terms set forth in the Prospectus.

Price $19 per Share

Copies of the Prospectus may be obtained from only such of the underwriters, including the undersigned, as may lawfully offer these securities in this State.

Kidder, Peabody & Co.

Paine, Webber, Jackson & Curtis **Dean Witter & Co.**

Clark, Dodge & Co. **Dominick & Dominick** **W. C. Langley & Co.**

Carl M. Loeb, Rhoades & Co. **Model, Roland & Stone** **R. W. Pressprich & Co.**

Shearson, Hammill & Co. **Shields & Company** **Tucker, Anthony & R. L. Day**

June 18, 1959.

4. Make false and misleading statements about the securities in letters, newspaper advertising, or other advertising media.

The continuance of a violation after issuance of an injunction is punishable as being in contempt of court. In addition, the SEC will be likely to certify its charges of violations of the Securities Act to the Department of Justice for action in accordance with the criminal provisions of the legislation.

Apart from making themselves subject to criminal penalties, corporations and investment bankers found guilty of selling securities in violation of the Securities Act may incur civil penalties. The legislation gives the buyer a right of action (within certain time limits) to recover the purchase price or, if he has resold at a loss, to recover the amount of the loss.

Stop-Order Proceedings. After a registration statement has been filed with it, rather than seek an injunction the SEC may issue a stop order to bring to a halt actions deemed to be in violation of the Securities Act. A stop order results in an indefinite suspension of the effectiveness of the registration statement, whether or not the effective date has been reached or passed. The SEC gives wide publicity to its stop orders to warn investors of the likelihood of fraud in the security offerings involved. To continue to sell a security issue when a stop order is in force against it is a criminal violation of the Securities Act, and rights of investors to recover the purchase price or to sue for losses are fully available.

The stop-order procedure is also used by the SEC when its staff comes to the conclusion that registrants have deliberately omitted material facts in registration statements or have tried to garble some of those included. Such strong evidence of intentions to deceive or misrepresent is regarded as justifying—indeed, demanding—a warning to the investing public.

An example should be of interest. With respect to the affairs of the Clinton Engines Corporation, the SEC explained its stop-order action of September, 1964, in this way.

> Here a registration statement that had become effective in 1960 was found seriously deficient because: (1) The unaudited financial material therein was materially deceptive by reason of a substantial inventory overstatement which led to material overstatements of earnings and assets, distorted the historical operating record, and "had the effect of presenting the financially straitened registrant in a wholly illusory picture of incipient prosperity"; (2) the discussion of the causes of registrant's low profit margins concealed significant adverse factors; and (3) a suggestion that significant improvements in efficiency could be effected by a program to be financed out of the registrant's future earnings was highly misleading since the prospectus failed to point out that such improvements would have required a massive program of capital investment that had not even been formulated and could not be financed without the sale of long-term debt or equity securities as to the successful flotation of which there was no assurance.[11]

Letter of Comment Procedure. In most instances, however, corporations and their investment bankers are quite conscientious in wanting to fulfill all the requirements of the Securities Act. Accordingly, they try to make their registration statements and related prospectuses as foolproof as possible at the time of original filing.

Even in this circumstance, however, the staff of the SEC may find some minor defects—unclear statements, inadequate cross-references, and the like—that ought to be corrected before the effective dates.

---

[11]Securities and Exchange Commission, *Annual Report*, 1965, p. 32.

But minor defects do not require drastic action. The SEC's customary procedure is simply to send the registrant a letter of comment, noting the deficiencies and prescribing that they be corrected by means of amendments. In themselves, corrective amendments to a registration statement do not cause a postponement of its effective date; hence, the SEC asks the registrant to file immediately an amendment to defer the effective date. This does not mean that the effective date actually will be deferred, but the SEC wants to be in a position to defer should the corrective amendments not be filed within a reasonable time. Were the corporation to refuse to file an amendment to defer the effective date, or were it to indicate in some other way its intention not to amend the registration statement as advised in the letter of comment, the SEC probably would issue a stop order.

One kind of amendment that the SEC ordinarily accepts as a matter of routine without deferring effective dates is the so-called price amendment. By such an amendment, the registrant inserts the selling price of the registered securities to the underwriting investment bankers and the price at which the bankers will reoffer them to the public. Because changes in market conditions from day to day can materially affect the prospects of a successful sale *at a predetermined price*, the SEC recognizes that prices can best be set just before the public offering is to be made. At the time of the original filing, therefore, registrants omit the price data from their registration statements and customarily add the price amendment the day preceding the effective date.

SEC's Responsibility. The SEC does not guarantee the completeness or accuracy of the registration statements that it permits to become effective. In view of the experience and competence of the SEC's staff, however, there is reasonable assurance for both the issuer and the investor that a registration statement that has become effective is complete and accurate. Nevertheless, as will be explained below, security buyers can still avail themselves of civil remedies on the grounds of omissions or misstatements of material facts in the registration statement or prospectus. Moreover, criminal prosecution is still possible after effective dates on the basis of allegations that material omissions or misstatements, though they slipped by the SEC, were willful.

In no circumstance does the SEC pass on the investment merits of the security issues registered with it. In permitting a registration statement to become effective, *it does not approve the securities;* it simply indicates that, as far as it can judge, the disclosure requirements and other applicable provisions of the Securities Act have been satisfied. Thus, the SEC has no duty—indeed, it has no power—to prevent registration statements covering highly speculative securities from becoming effective so long as it is convinced that the requirements of the legislation and its own rules have been met. The spirit of the regulatory legislation is that if people are willing to invest in ventures to prospect for gold in the Middle West or to attempt to convert carbon into uranium they should be permitted to do so, provided that the disclosures of registration statements and prospectuses for these ventures enable them to know what they are doing. In keeping with this principle, the SEC requires that every prospectus carry on its first page in boldface type not smaller than a stipulated size the following statement: "These securities have not been approved or disapproved by the Securities and Exchange Commission nor has the Commission passed upon the accuracy or adequacy of this prospectus. Any representation to the contrary is a criminal offense." In Figure 18–1, one may note the prominent position given to this statement near the top.

Civil Remedies. When Congress passed the Securities Act in 1933, it relied on the alertness of investors, as well as on the efficiency of the SEC,[12] to root out fraudulent practices in interstate sales of new issues of securities. It did this by giving investors rights to sue issuers, underwriters, and other responsible parties for violations of the legislation. But this feature of the legislation has not been of great significance. Relatively few suits against issuers and underwriters have been brought by investors, and in the suits that have been brought, judgments for the plaintiffs have been less common than judgments for the defendants.

Earlier in this chapter, it was mentioned that the original buyer of a security may sue the issuer and underwriters for the return of the purchase price or for the recovery of losses (should he have resold the security) if the issuer fails to file a registration statement, if the security was sold before the effective date of the registration statement or without the tendering of a prospectus, or if false or misleading statements about material facts were made in advertising the security. A similar remedy is available to the original buyer on grounds of misstatements or omissions of material facts in the prospectus, even though it was filed with a registration statement that was permitted to become effective.

Both the original buyer and subsequent holders of a security are authorized to sue the issuer, underwriters, signers of the registration statement, nonsigning directors, and experts on grounds of omissions or misstatements of material facts in the registration statement. Here the suit is for the recovery of losses as measured by the difference between the purchase price and the value of the security at the time of bringing suit or at the time of resale, as the case may be. However,

[12]Originally, of course, the Federal Trade Commission.

the issuer and other defendants can escape liability to the extent that they are able to prove that the decline in value resulted from causes not related to the omissions or misstatements of material facts. Moreover, all defendants except the issuer can escape liability if able to prove that after reasonable investigation they had reasonable grounds for believing there were no omissions or misstatements of material facts in the registration statement or, specifically, in those portions for which they were individually responsible. Still further, if the issuer has published an income statement for a period of at least a year beginning after the effective date of the registration statement the plaintiff cannot recover unless he can prove that in buying the security he *relied on* incomplete or misleading statements in the registration statement. And finally in this regard, it is to be mentioned that in all suits in which omissions or misstatements of material facts are alleged—registration statements, prospectuses, letters, or other advertising material—defendants can escape liability if able to prove that the plaintiff had knowledge of the omissions or misstatements at the time he bought.

Such limitations on security buyers' rights of recovery undoubtedly explain, in large measure, the scarcity of their lawsuits within the scope of the Securities Act. Supplementing these limitations, indeed, are others restricting the time periods within which suits may be brought. Without getting into minute technicalities, we may observe that, generally, suits must be brought within one year of the discovery of omissions, misstatements, or violations, and in any event not after three years from the date of public offering or sale.

Exemptions under Regulation A. To reduce the costs of security flotations for small enterprises, Congress permits the SEC to exempt individual issuer's flotations aggregating in any year not more than $300,000. The SEC provides for such exemptions in its Regulation A.

The general rule of Regulation A is that any corporation or other issuer that proposes to sell securities of not more than $300,000 aggregate value in any year need not file a comprehensive registration statement if it files a notification with the SEC, giving basic information about itself and the proposed issue. The notification must include certain exhibits, such as copies of agreements with underwriters and financial statements (which, however, need not be certified), and an offering circular, containing "what may be called 'bare bones' facts concerning the company and the securities to be offered."[13] Even the offering circular may be dispensed with for issues of less than $50,000, except for newly established enterprises and those that have. not had a net profit in at least one of their two preceding fiscal years.

---

[13]Securities and Exchange Commission, *Annual Report*, 1956, p. 30.

The waiting period for offerings under Regulation A is only 10 days, and this period may be further shortened at the SEC's discretion.

In view of its interests in protecting the investing public from fraud, the SEC does not grant exemptions under Regulation A as a matter of routine. It has expressed its attitude as follows:

> Regulation A is designed to assist legitimate small business and new ventures in bringing to market a small issue of securities. Regulation A was not designed as a shield for the perpetration of fraud on the investing public. One problem in this area is to detect as quickly as possible those filings which are schemes to obtain "front money" to line the pockets of the promoters rather than to obtain funds for the conduct of bona fide business. Another problem is to detect those offerings under the regulation which are sold without use of the required offering circular, but rather are sold by false and misleading sales talk by high pressure salesmen often operating out of "boiler-rooms."[14]

Other Exemptions. Other exemptions from registration requirements are provided for in the Securities Act. A blanket exemption is given to all issues of our federal, state, and local governments, although not to those of foreign governments. Securities issued by organizations that are supervised and regulated by government agencies other than the SEC are generally exempt. These include issues of national and state banks, federal and state savings and loan associations, life insurance companies, and railroads. Also exempt are securities issued by enterprises in receivership or bankruptcy, such as receivers' and trustees' certificates, and by enterprises in the process of reorganization, provided that the issues are authorized by courts or other governmental agencies. Securities of nonprofit organizations and issues of promissory notes that have maturities of not more than nine months are also given exemptions.

Since the jurisdiction of the federal government in the regulation of security transactions presumably extends only to those in interstate and foreign commerce, a further exemption is given to issues sold entirely within the borders of the individual states by enterprises incorporated or established and doing business therein. Public protection is not needed when whole security issues are sold in bulk to one or a very few investors, such as life insurance companies, as it is assumed that these buyers will have sufficient expertness in investment to protect themselves. Hence, an exemption is also provided for private placements of this character. Still another exemption is given for exchanges of securities between corporations and their own existing security holders, provided that no commission or other payment is made directly or indirectly in soliciting exchanges. This exemption applies, for example, when holders of a corporation's convertible bonds surrender them in exchange for shares of its common stock.

---

[14]*Ibid.*, p. 57.

Finally, the provisions of the Securities Act are not intended to apply to resales of securities by investors, except, of course, by underwriters and dealers. An investor who buys 100 shares of a new issue of stock for his own portfolio and later sells the stock to another investor remains entirely outside the reach of the Securities Act. However, the provisions of the legislation do apply when the controlling stockholder of a corporation seeks through underwriters to dispose of his holdings. Such a secondary distribution must be registered with the SEC in the same way as new issues.

Qualification under State Blue-Sky Laws

In addition to the federal government, all but a handful of states have enacted laws to regulate sales of securities within their respective borders. In fact, the state legislation generally antedated that of the federal government by many years, beginning with that of Kansas in 1911. The state protective laws are commonly known as blue-sky laws. The origins of this colorful designation are somewhat obscure, but its meaning was well expressed by the Supreme Court in a 1917 case, when it said that the laws were aimed at "speculative schemes which have no more basis than so many feet of blue sky."[15] Though the states were early on the scene with the regulation of security selling, their laws tended to be ineffective. It was especially difficult, and often impossible, for the state regulatory authorities to prevent or proceed against frauds attempted or perpetrated in interstate transactions, hence the need of federal regulation.

The adoption of the federal Securities Act, however, did not make the state blue-sky laws inoperative. Thus, whether or not registration with the SEC is necessary, security issues must generally be qualified with the securities commissions of the states in which they are to be offered for sale. A few states do exempt from their registration requirements issues registered with the SEC, and these and other states provide exemptions for certain reasons of other kinds. Registration, moreover, is not required in the few states, including New York, that have so-called fraud laws. In these states, not registration but injunctive and punitive proceedings initiated by the attorneys general are depended on to curb fraudulent security offerings.

Despite the exceptions, however, an offering of new securities will ordinarily require registration in a substantial number of states, assuming that underwriting bankers plan to seek buyers over a wide area. Such registration entails additional expenses, not only in filing fees but also in terms of the services of officers, attorneys, and others in preparing the necessary forms.

It is entirely possible for one or more of the state securities com-

---

[15] *Hall* v. *Geiger-Jones Co.*, 242 U.S. 539 (1917).

missions to refuse consent for the sale of a new security issue, even though the SEC permits its registration statement under the federal Securities Act to become effective. In many states, indeed, the protective function of the securities commission is broader than that of the SEC. Many commissions may deny permission for the sale of securities they consider too speculative or unfair to prospective buyers in their terms of sale. A state commission's refusal of permission to sell applies, of course, only to the state where it has jurisdiction.

Formation of Underwriting Syndicate

Investment banking houses that serve corporations as originators of their new issues of common stock or other securities are willing to take sole responsibility for the underwriting only when the issues are relatively small. Taking sole responsibility for underwriting a large issue would be much too hazardous for the typical originator. The limited proprietary interests of its partners or stockholders could be gravely impaired or even wiped out by losses should an unfavorable turn in the market make it necessary for it to cut the public offering price to a level well below the price guaranteed to the issuing corporation. For a large issue, therefore, the originator invites other investment banking firms to join with it in an underwriting syndicate or purchase group. They agree to share the underwriting commission with the bankers who accept their invitation, but they willingly pay this price because the accepting bankers also share in the risks of underwriting. What is more, a house that invites other houses to join the syndicates it forms expects to receive invitations when the others, in turn, take the lead in setting up syndicates.

It is the work of the *syndicate department* of an investment banking house serving as the originator of an issue to line up other houses as additional underwriters. While the registration statement is being prepared, the syndicate department decides how many other houses to invite, which houses these should be, and what portion of the issue should be offered to each. The location of the banking houses, their financial capacities, their prestige, their selling facilities, and other factors are considered in deciding on the makeup of the syndicate. For the flotation of very large security issues, the syndicates also tend to be extraordinarily large, including as many as 200 or 300 investment banking firms and, in a few instances in recent years, going even beyond 300.

Customarily, on the day preceding the filing of the registration statement with the SEC the originator wires or telephones its invitations. It gives a description of the proposed security issue and its estimate of what the public offering price and the price to the bankers will be, and it states the number of shares the invited house is being asked to underwrite. Following the registration statement filing, a copy of the statement or of the prospectus is sent to each invited house, together with copies of proposed contracts to cover the underwriting. The contracts include one to govern the operations of the syndicate, a purchase contract to be entered into with the corporation issuing the securities, and a selling group contract or agreement. They are understood to be subject to later amendment. Each invited house is expected, within a day or two, to notify the originator of its acceptance or rejection of the invitation. Although no contract among the acceptors is signed at this time, any accepting house that later withdrew for anything but a grave reason would suffer serious damage to its reputation.

The originator of a security issue is not likely to offer any other prospective underwriter an allotment in excess of the amount that it itself is willing to underwrite. For an issue of 300,000 shares of common stock, for example, it might decide to take responsibility as underwriter for 30,000 shares, and it might offer a block or blocks of the same size to another large house or two. Most of the invited houses, however, would be offered smaller allotments, but in any case a sufficient number of invitations would be sent out to give strong assurances that the full issue of 300,000 shares would be subscribed. This would probably mean an offer to other underwriters of more than 270,000 shares (exclusive of the originator's own allotment) to allow for the possibility that some would not accept the number of shares offered or even none at all. If, then, acceptances should amount to more than 270,000 shares, the originator would have the right to scale these down.

Formation of Selling Group

Investment banking houses that join an underwriting syndicate usually expect to sell direct to their customers a portion of the securities they underwrite, but because they are anxious to dispose of the issue as quickly as possible after the effective date of its registration statement they generally depend on other securities dealers to help them with the selling job. For this purpose, it is customary for the originating house to assemble a selling group of selected dealers. In consultation with the other houses that have accepted invitations to join the syndicate, the syndicate department of the originating house decides what dealer firms are to be invited to join the selling group. It is also the privilege of the originating house, as manager of the underwriting syndicate, to decide what portion of the issue will be reserved for offering to the selling group. The originator is also privileged to reserve a portion of the issue for offering to institutional investors, although this reservation is likely to be quite small or nil for common stock issues. The portion of the issue that is not reserved for the selling group (and possibly for institutional investors) will then be taken down by the underwriters for their own direct selling.

When issuing invitations to the selected dealers, the syndicate department of the originator provides them with copies of a red-herring prospectus so that they may know what they are being offered. Except for details on price, such a prospectus usually contains all the information that the final prospectus will have—information corrected to remedy deficiencies found by the staff of the SEC—but it bears a notice in red ink along the margin of the cover page that it is not an offer to sell or the solicitation of an offer to buy any security, that it is not a final prospectus, that the registration statement has not become effective, and that no offer to sell can be made or offer to buy accepted until the effective date. The red ink explains the popular designation for the red-herring prospectus; somewhat more elegant is its official designation as a preliminary prospectus. The originator also supplies each dealer with a copy of the proposed selling agreement, whose signing later will bind him to buy whatever number of shares he then agrees to accept.

The inducement to dealers to join a selling group is a price concession allowed by the underwriters. This means that the dealers are offered the security at a price below the public offering price, so that when they resell to their customers at the public price the differential is their (gross) profit.

Final Arrangements

Shortly before the effective date of the registration statement, the issuing corporation comes to a final agreement with the originator on the price at which its new issue of securities will be sold to the underwriters and the price at which they will be reoffered to the public. The originator then notifies the other prospective underwriters of these terms, and (assuming the terms are acceptable) all sign in person or by proxy the agreement among underwriters. Following this signing, the originator, for itself and as representative of the other underwriters, signs the purchase contract with the corporation. It is then necessary to file the price amendment to the registration statement and to dispatch numerous copies of the final prospectus—now including, of course, the price data—to the other underwriters and to the selected dealers to be available for delivery to prospective investors on and after the effective date.

On the effective date, the originator as manager of the syndicate makes its definitive offer by telegram to the prospective members of the selling group—that is, the selected dealers. It may simply ask them to offer subscriptions for whatever amounts of the security issue they want to take, or it may offer designated amounts, asking them to accept. The price of these offerings is, of course, the public offering price less the price concession. When a dealer is offered a definite amount of a security, he is usually privileged to offer to subscribe to an additional amount, with the understanding that the added subscription may be accepted in whole or in part or fully rejected at the discretion of the originator.

The dealer is expected to promptly wire his subscription or a notice of his intention not to subscribe—ordinarily by noon on the effective date. If he subscribes, he confirms the subscription by signing the selling agreement and sending it to the originator.

All is thus cleared for a concerted effort by all the underwriters and selected dealers to sell the security issue beginning at the time designated by the originator for the public offering. In most instances, the time set is the opening of business on the day following the effective date. The originator offers its takedown to its own customers and other portions of the issue to institutional investors, if some have been reserved for them. The other underwriters try to market their respective takedowns with their own customers, and the members of the selling group approach theirs. In all these offerings, it is to be presumed that, in keeping with the requirements of the Securities Act, copies of the final prospectus are tendered to all individual and institutional investors contacted.

Purchase Contract

Since a purchase contract, as referred to previously, establishes the rights and obligations of the corporate issuer of securities and those of the investment bankers who serve as underwriters, it deserves a brief description.

Of particular significance among the provisions of the typical purchase contract are the following items:

1. A description of the securities involved in the transaction.
2. Various warranties of the issuer, such as that the registration statement and prospectus at the effective date will contain no omissions or misstatements of material fact, and that it will use the proceeds of the issue fully for the purpose indicated in the registration statement.
3. The specific agreement of the issuer to sell the issue to the bankers at the designated price.
4. The closing date when the securities are to be delivered to the bankers and payment made by them.
5. The commitment of the bankers to actually make a public offering at the public offering price within a designated period.
6. The right of the bankers to sell at a price concession to the selected dealers.
7. Provisions about the issuer's responsibility for flotation expenses.
8. The issuer's obligation to make available sufficient quantities of the preliminary and final prospectuses.

9. The obligation of the issuer to indemnify the bankers for liabilities they may incur because of omissions or misstatements in the registration statement and prospectus for which the issuer was responsible, and the obligation of the bankers similarly to indemnify the issuer for liabilities arising from omissions or misstatements for which they were responsible.

The typical purchase contract also contains certain market-out provisos. They permit the bankers to cancel their commitment to underwrite should there occur before the date of the public offering—or even, in some circumstances, before the closing date—certain kinds of events, such as serious adverse changes in the financial condition of the issuer or in the market situation, the filing of certain kinds of lawsuits against the issuer, the outbreak of war, and the suspension of stock market or bank operations. The inclusion of market-out clauses in the purchase contract may appear to rob the security issuer of even minimum assurances of getting for his issue the price agreed on or, indeed, any other price—may seem to make underwriting anything but a guaranty of sale. Actually, however, investment bankers have taken advantage of market-out escape hatches in only a few instances. They doubtless realize that a frequent invoking of these clauses would gravely impair the attractiveness of their services. Accordingly, issuers who sign purchase contracts can still generally feel that the bankers' commitments are firm in every respect.

Closing Date

As set in the purchase contract, the closing date is the day on which settlement is to be made between the security issuer and the underwriters. Most commonly, it occurs from 7 to 10 days after the date of the public offering. Each underwriting house delivers to the originator, as manager of the syndicate, its check for the portion of the issue it was allotted, and the originating house delivers to the issuer all checks thus received together with its own. The issuer, in turn, delivers to the originator the securities themselves. It is then the task of the originator to parcel out the securities among the underwriters, the selected dealers of the selling group, and institutional investors according to their respective commitments. Needless to say, the underwriters must make payment for their individual allotments whether or not the securities have as yet been resold to investors or payment has been received, since this responsibility is the very essence of underwriting.

Financial Outcome

In the foregoing lengthy description of the procedure for underwriting new issues of securities to be sold in interstate commerce, many references have been made to public offering prices, prices to the investment bankers, underwriting commissions, the sharing of commissions between originators and other underwriters, and price concessions made to the selected dealers of selling groups. An illustration will clarify the relationships among these price items. Such an illustration should show, indeed, how financial considerations lead issuing corporations, originators, other underwriters, and dealers to pool their talents for the success of given security flotations.

Let us suppose that a certain manufacturing corporation is having 300,000 shares of new common stock underwritten by a syndicate of investment bankers at a price of $26.40 a share. It is agreed that the public offering price will be $28, so that the contemplated underwriting commission is $1.60 a share. The bankers therefore undertake to pay the corporation on the closing date $7,920,000, and we may assume that they do succeed in reselling the stock directly and through selected dealers for total proceeds of $8,400,000. The total commission of $480,000 would be, accordingly, the major cost of the flotation to the corporation. In addition, expenses in getting the issue ready for the public offering, including fees for lawyers, accountants, engineers, other experts, and the stock transfer agent, state capital stock taxes, printing and engraving, and the SEC registry fee, would probably run in the vicinity of $70,000 or $80,000, further reducing the proceeds to the corporation (using the smaller of these estimates) to $7,850,000. Also to be considered would be the value of the time the corporation's officers and other employees had to devote to their work with the originator in preparing the registration statement and prospectus and in taking care of the numerous other preparatory tasks. However, we need not attempt to put this value in terms of dollars, since that would largely be a matter of guessing.

As for distribution of the commission, the agreement among underwriters would probably allocate to the originator about 10 percent, or $48,000 (that is, 16 cents a share), as compensation for all its work of preparation and as manager of the syndicate and selling group, and to the underwriters about 30 percent for their risk-bearing service. The underwriters' allocation would mean a risk-bearing compensation of 48 cents a share, less a moderate deduction for the expenses of the syndicate. Were the originating house to be underwriting, say, 30,000 shares, it would have additional compensation (before the expense deduction) of $14,400. All this would leave 60 percent of the commission, or 96 cents a share, as the price concession to the selected dealers of the selling group. Out of this, they would have to meet their own selling expenses. As the originator would be likely to sell some of its block of 30,000 shares direct to its own customers, it would have still further compensation from this source. Were its takedown 16,000 shares, for example, this additional compensation would amount to $15,360, giving it a total gross profit of $77,760 in its threefold capacity as originator, underwriter, and retailer. Similarly, an underwriter of 20,000 shares with a takedown of 12,000 shares would have combined compensation of $21,120 ($9,600 plus $11,520), while the gross profit of a selected dealer taking 2,000 shares at $27.04 and reselling them to his customers at $28 would be $1,920.

A Final Observation

It might occur to the student that many corporate managements would be frightened away from efforts to sell new security issues by public offerings in interstate commerce, considering all the complexities of the procedures and of the regulatory legislation as described in the foregoing pages. It is true that before 1933 a public offering in interstate commerce was a much simpler matter, and that after adoption of the Securities Act in that year both corporations and investment bankers proceeded warily. By now, however, the provisions of the legislation are well understood, and those who set out in good faith to meet its requirements have no reason to anticipate great difficulties in procedure or the incurring of quite unexpected statutory penalties or civil liabilities. Much work has to be done in preparing registration statements and prospectuses, in qualifying under blue-sky laws, and in the formation of underwriting syndicates and selling groups, but all this is largely a matter of routine to the investment bankers. Moreover, firms of lawyers that specialize in the legal aspects of security selling can be consulted by the bankers when they run into special problems.

Accordingly, the big question for corporate managements is not whether their financing projects will survive the complexities of the laws and procedures, but whether they can find investment bankers willing to underwrite on reasonable terms. Complex procedures add to the costs of flotation, but it is the whole list of costs rather than the procedures themselves that are likely to constitute a stumbling block.

QUESTIONS

1. Distinguish between public offerings and direct offerings of new security issues and between public offerings and private placements. Which of these are important in the sale of common stock?

2. Why is it said that corporations are best served by investment bankers when the bankers are willing to act as underwriters?

3. What kinds of risks are incurred by investment bankers when they underwrite security issues?

4. What kinds of conditions determine the size of investment bankers' cash commissions for underwriting new security issues? How high do these

commissions run? How frequently do the bankers also get noncash compensation? Of what does it consist?

5. What are the respective objectives of investment bankers' preliminary and detailed investigations of proposed security issues? What is included in a detailed investigation?

6. What are the important steps that a corporation must take in getting a new common stock issue ready for an offering to the general public?

7. What are the objectives of the federal Securities Act of 1933? How are these objectives furthered by requirements for registration statements and prospectuses?

8. What kind of information must a corporation supply in its registration statement for a new security issue? What is the relationship between a registration statement and a prospectus?

9. To what use *must* prospectuses be put in the selling of securities registered effectively with the Securities and Exchange Commission? Why does the law contain this requirement?

10. For what reasons does the SEC seek injunctions? Issue stop orders? Issue letters of comment?

11. What responsibility does the SEC have to prevent the sale of fraudulent securities? Highly speculative securities?

12. What remedies does an investor have if he feels that he has been defrauded through violations of the federal Securities Act?

13. Under the federal Securities Act, what special treatment is provided for security issues of not more than $300,000? Is the SEC required to give this special treatment to all such issues? Explain.

14. What is a blue-sky law? Why were such laws not very effective in protecting investors before 1933? Are they effective today? Explain.

15. How and for what reason does the originator of a large security issue form an underwriting syndicate? A selling group?

16. What inducements do investment banking houses have for joining underwriting syndicates and selling groups?

PROBLEM

A syndicate of investment bankers has agreed to underwrite the sale of 400,000 shares of a corporation's common stock at a price of $38 a share and to reoffer it to the public at $41 a share. Among themselves, the bankers agree that the originating house will be allowed 30 cents a share for its work in preparing the issue for the market and for managing the syndicate and selling group, that 70 cents a share will be the compensation for the underwriting risk, and that the price concession to the selected dealers of the selling group will be $2 a share.

a) Leaving out of consideration flotation expenses chargeable to the issuing corporation, what total payment would it receive from the bankers if they succeeded in selling all shares at $41 each? If they had to cut the public offering price to $40 to sell all shares? If they had to drastically cut this price to $36 to unload the full issue?

b) Assuming a successful sale of all shares at $41, what would be the total compensation earned by the originating house if it underwrote 60,000 shares and took down 25,000 shares for retail sales to its own customers? What would be the total compensation earned by another underwriting firm if it underwrote 30,000 shares and took down 16,000 shares for its own retail selling?

chapter 19

SALES OF COMMON STOCK TO EXISTING STOCKHOLDERS

For many corporations, sales of common stock to their own common stockholders are much more important as a means of acquiring cash than are sales to the general public, but for many others, sales to the general public predominate. Regardless of this mixed situation, however, sales to the general public were given priority of treatment in Chapter 18 because the basic pattern of investment banking procedures and government regulation of selling could be most conveniently explained in relation to such sales. With the basic pattern in mind, therefore, it will be necessary in the present and succeeding chapters to take note only of variations in procedure and regulation.

The strong preference of many corporate managements for offerings of additional common stock to their existing common stockholders grows out of a conviction that these people constitute the best market. The very fact that certain investors have already bought and continue to hold the common stock of a given corporation indicates that they are likely to be more interested in buying additional shares than are the wide range of investors who, to date, have not been sufficiently interested to buy, or at any rate to buy and hold.

SCOPE AND PROCEDURES OF RIGHTS OFFERINGS

A corporation's offering of common stock to people who are already its common stockholders is known as a rights offering, and the stockholders are said to obtain the stock by privileged subscriptions. Having a sufficient amount of unissued stock available for the purpose,[1] the board of directors of the corporation adopts a resolution to set out the terms and conditions of the offering. The resolution states the number of shares to be offered, the price per share at which the offer

[1]Although an offering of treasury stock could be make, this rarely happens.

is made, the record date at the close of business on which the names of the stockholders entitled to buy will be determined, the date and hour at which the subscription books will be closed—the expiration date—and the manner in which payment is to be made for shares subscribed. Immediately after the record date, the corporation or its stock transfer agent, if it employs one, fills in and sends a *subscription warrant* to each stockholder whose name appeared in the stock records at the close of business on that day. (See Figure 19–1 for a reproduction of the warrant used by the Florida Power Corporation in one of

FIGURE 19–1
Face and Back of a Subscription Warrant

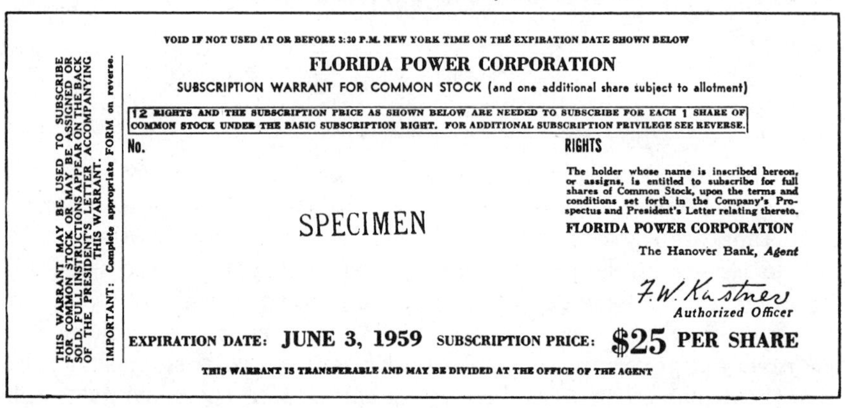
VOID IF NOT USED AT OR BEFORE 3:30 P.M. NEW YORK TIME ON THE EXPIRATION DATE SHOWN BELOW

FLORIDA POWER CORPORATION

SUBSCRIPTION WARRANT FOR COMMON STOCK (and one additional share subject to allotment)

THIS WARRANT MAY BE USED TO SUBSCRIBE FOR COMMON STOCK OR MAY BE ASSIGNED OR SOLD. FULL INSTRUCTIONS APPEAR ON THE BACK OF THE PRESIDENT'S LETTER ACCOMPANYING THIS WARRANT.

IMPORTANT: Complete appropriate FORM on reverse.

12 RIGHTS AND THE SUBSCRIPTION PRICE AS SHOWN BELOW ARE NEEDED TO SUBSCRIBE FOR EACH 1 SHARE OF COMMON STOCK UNDER THE BASIC SUBSCRIPTION RIGHT. FOR ADDITIONAL SUBSCRIPTION PRIVILEGE SEE REVERSE.

No. RIGHTS

The holder whose name is inscribed hereon, or assigns, is entitled to subscribe for full shares of Common Stock, upon the terms and conditions set forth in the Company's Prospectus and President's Letter relating thereto.

SPECIMEN

FLORIDA POWER CORPORATION
The Hanover Bank, *Agent*

F. W. Kastner
Authorized Officer

EXPIRATION DATE: **JUNE 3, 1959** SUBSCRIPTION PRICE: **$25 PER SHARE**

THIS WARRANT IS TRANSFERABLE AND MAY BE DIVIDED AT THE OFFICE OF THE AGENT

THE HANOVER BANK, *Agent*
Stock Transfer Department
70 Broadway, New York 15, N. Y.

This Warrant is transferable with the same effect as in the case of a negotiable instrument payable to a specified person, upon due execution of the Assignment Form.

FORM 1—SUBSCRIPTION: The undersigned hereby irrevocably subscribes for full shares of Common Stock as indicated below, on the terms specified in the Prospectus relating thereto, receipt of which is hereby acknowledged.

Total Rights Surrendered Herewith .... Rights

(A) BASIC SUBSCRIPTION RIGHT:
Shares Subscribed for .... Full Shares $ .... Cost
(Number of shares times subscription price)

(B) ADDITIONAL SUBSCRIPTION PRIVILEGE FOR ONE SHARE ONLY
(Subject to Allotment): $ .... Cost
(One share times subscription price)

FUNDS MUST BE ENCLOSED FOR TOTAL COST OF ALL SUBSCRIPTIONS $ ....

BEFORE SIGNING READ INSTRUCTIONS ....
(Subscriber's Signature)

DELIVERY INSTRUCTIONS: Fill out ONLY if delivery is to be made to address other than that shown on the face of Warrant or in Form 2 below.

....
(Print name and address)
....

(If Rights are sold or transferred, or if the shares are to be issued in a name other than that shown on Warrant, Form 2 must be completed.)

FORM 2—ASSIGNMENT: For value received, this Warrant and the Rights represented thereby are hereby assigned to:

....
(Print full name of Assignee)
....
(Print full address)
....

Signature ....
Signature must correspond with name as shown on face of Warrant.
Signature guaranteed by: (See Instructions in President's Letter)

its several rights offerings of recent years.) The stockholder than has the period up to the time set for the closing of the subscription books to decide whether or not he wants to subscribe. If his decision is affirmative, he endorses the subscription warrant to that effect and sends it, together with the requisite cash payment, to the corporation or its subscription agent. On the other hand, if he does not want to subscribe he is ordinarily permitted to sell or give away his subscription privilege by endorsing the subscription warrant to somebody else. (The endorsement forms are also illustrated in Figure 19-1.) The buyer may then subscribe by sending in the warrant with cash. Whether it is the existing common stockholders or the transferees of their warrants who subscribe, the final step is simply for the corporation or its stock transfer agent to fill in and deliver the new stock certificates.

The procedure of common stock financing as just outlined is described as a rights offering because, in the terminology of the securities markets, the stockholder is said to get rights to subscribe to the new stock. He gets as many rights as the number of shares already held, and in the usual circumstances a new share costs, say, a certain number of rights plus cash in the amount of the offering price. Suppose, for example, that a corporation that has 200,000 shares of common stock outstanding is making a rights offering of 40,000 shares at a price of $60 a share. Its subscription warrants would represent, therefore, 200,000 rights, so that 5 rights plus $60 would be required for the purchase of 1 new share. A stockholder who held 100 shares would receive a subscription warrant for 100 rights, entitling him to buy 20 new shares at a total cost of $1,200.

Number of Shares to Be Offered

In deciding how large a rights offering can be, the board of directors of a corporation must proceed cautiously. As a rule, the wider the distribution of existing stockholdings, the larger the amount of stock that can be sold in a rights offering. But even with a wide distribution of existing stockholders, the directors can all to easily fall into the error of making the offering too large in relation to the amount of stock already outstanding. They are going to make an abrupt demand on each of their stockholders to increase his investment in the corporation, and they must realize that the offering of large amounts of stock may make this demand unconscionable. In any event, they want to avoid the acute embarrassment of making a rights offering only to have it rejected by most of the stockholders.

Distribution of Existing Stockholdings. Given two corporations of equal size, a narrow distribution of the stock of one would mean that the average holdings of its stockholders must be large, and a broad distribution of the stock of the other would mean small average holdings. If, then, each corporation were putting up an identical amount of additional stock in a rights offering, the large stockholders of the first would be asked to make a quite large additional investment by comparison with that asked of the stockholders of the second. To illustrate, let us say that A and B each have 100,000 shares of common stock outstanding and that each plans to make a rights offering of 20,000 shares at $60 a share. A has 40 stockholders with average holdings, therefore, of 2,500 shares, while B has 1,000 stockholders whose average holdings amount to 100 shares. On the average, then, each stockholder of A is asked to buy 500 additional shares at a total cost of $30,000, whereas each of B's stockholders is offered only 20 shares at a total cost of $1,200. The chances ought to be good that the typical stockholder of B would have a balance of $1,200 or more in a savings account or other savings medium—a balance he might be willing to use to buy stock. But would the chances be as good that the typical stockholder of A would have $30,000 of readily available cash or, if available, that he would be willing to use it to buy the offered stock? It is often argued that large stockholders are much more likely to have their investment programs well planned than are small stockholders—to be much more reluctant, therefore, to make switches in their portfolios simply because corporations in which they are common stockholders decide to make rights offerings.

Size in Relation to Existing Shares. With other conditions favorable, the probabilities of success for a rights offering are likely to be greater the smaller its size. If the corporations of the illustration given above were offering only 10,000 shares at $60 to 40 and 1,000 stock holders, respectively, the small stockholders of Corporation B would surely be all the more able to find and all the more willing to invest $600, and even the large stockholders of Corporation A might be willing to change their investment plans to the extent of $15,000, though reluctant to do so to the extent of $30,000. On the other hand, were the offerings 40,000 new shares, many of the small stockholders of B might be caught with savings balances considerably less than $2,400, and the large stockholders of A, if expected to balk when asked for $30,000, would surely balk all the more on being requested to add $60,000 to their common stock investment.

So clear is the relationship between the size of rights offerings and the probabilities of their success that corporate financial managers often spread out their demands on the stockholders. Having decided that additional common stock is the appropriate medium for raising large sums of money—large in relation to the book and market values of common stock already outstanding—they plan a series of rights offerings, perhaps on an annual basis, rather than attempt a single large offering. Again in terms of the illustration, the small stockholder would surely be more able and willing to add $600 to his investment in each of 4 years than to invest $2,400 at one shot, and with the large stockholder the chances ought to be much better to persuade him to add $15,000 annually than to persuade him to invest $60,000 at any one time.

Offering Price

The price at which new common stock is tendered to the existing stockholders in a rights offering is almost invariably set substantially below the market price of shares already outstanding. In its studies of the costs of corporate security flotations in the year 1955, for example, the SEC found that the offering prices in 80 percent of the 57 common stock rights offerings registered with it were more than 5 percent below the respective market prices, and in 50 percent of the issues more than 10 percent below the market prices.[2]

It might appear that a corporation's common stockholders should want to buy their pro rata allotments of additional common shares even should they have to pay at the level of the existing market price. This willingness should be prompted, as it were, by anxiety to protect from dilution their claims to voting power and to corporate assets and earnings. As the consequences of dilution were discussed in Chapters 15 and 16, and the importance of the claims to voting power and to corporate assets and earnings was further discussed in Chapter 17, we need no further emphasis on the matter of dilution at this time. Suffice it to recall that, as an example, a stockholder who owns 5,000 shares out of a total of 100,000 has his ownership interests or claims reduced from 5 percent to 4 percent if the corporation issues 25,000 additional shares and he buys none of these.

Nevertheless, the financial managers of a corporation whose stock is widely held and continually traded in the market can hardly hope for success in a rights offering unless they offer the new stock to their existing stockholders at what appears to be a bargain—that is, at a price materially below the prevailing market price. Were they to offer the new stock at the market price, the typical stockholder, even if keenly concerned about maintaining his proportional ownership interests, would be likely to feel no great compulsion to buy direct from the corporation. He could buy as readily in the market. Moreover, he could time his market purchases to suit his own convenience rather than buy precisely within the subscription period set arbitrarily by the corporation. Even were the offering price and the market price identical at the time of the directors' resolution, moreover, the identity would not necessarily be preserved to the end of the subscription perod. Indeed, the rights offering itself, by its promise of adding to the supply of stock, would tend to cause the market price to fall. If it did fall, therefore, the stockholder could buy more cheaply in the market than direct from the corporation![3] A further reason for setting the offering price below the market price is to induce nonsubscribing stockholders to sell their subscription rights to other investors who will subscribe. But these stockholders will have no sig-

---

[2]Securities and Exchange Commission, *Cost of Flotation of Corporate Securities, 1951–1955* (Washington, D.C.: U.S. Government Printing Office, 1957), p. 23.

[3]In all such price comparisons, however, one must remember that the typical investor must pay a brokerage commission when buying in the market, whereas he pays no commission when buying direct from the corporation.

nificant inducement to transfer their subscription rights unless the rights have a market value—a market value that, as a rule, can exist only if the offering price of the new stock is less than its market value.

Stockholders' Attitudes. A rights offering can be successful, generally speaking, only if a large proportion of the new stock is actually subscribed by existing stockholders. This conclusion was implied in the earlier discussion of the breadth of the distribution of stock already outstanding and the relationship between its quantity and the size of the new issue. The corporate managers hope, indeed, that outsiders will participate in the buying through the exercise of rights sold by nonsubscribing stockholders, but they know that the market for both stock and rights will react most unfavorably and doom the offering should a large percentage of the stockholders try to sell their rights. Much depends, therefore, on the loyalty of the existing stockholders.

In view of what was said in Chapters 15 to 17 about the claims of common stockholders to voting power, it is reasonable to say that loyalty is forced on stockholders who have narrow margins of control as well as on those who seek to wrest control from intrenched groups. Indeed, groups that have narrow margins of control can surely be expected to vote against additional issues of voting stock unless they are in a position to buy their pro rata allotments, while strong minority groups that are contending for control will surely feel strong compulsion to subscribe to additional issues alloted to them, for a failure to subscribe would be tantamount to giving up the fight.

In most large corporations, and in many smaller ones as well, a very large majority of the stockholders have virtually no interest in control. Yet, great numbers of these stockholders are often enthusiastic about buying additional common stock offered by their corporations. Their loyalty to a given corporation is not forced in any way: they have been pleased with its policies. If earnings have been good and dividends liberal, the opportunity to make additional investments would seem to be, indeed, a highly appreciated privilege. These stockholders expect earnings to expand at least in proportion to their increased investment, and the going dividend rate, or even a higher one, to be maintained on the combined stock, old and new. To such stockholders, it would be unconscionable for the corporate management to offer new stock for sale without giving them the first crack at it. Perhaps these stockholders have been watching for a drop of a few points in the market price of the stock, expecting to buy additional shares should the drop take place but being disappointed repeatedly as the buying of other investors has kept the market price up. Now comes the corporation itself with an offer of shares at a price materially below the market price—truly a remarkable opportunity!

Rights offerings can be just about as attractive in corporations whose dividend policies have been relatively niggardly, provided that their earnings have been good, prospects for future earnings are likewise, and the market has behaved accordingly. Many well-to-do stockholders are quite satisfied to take small dividends, or to forgo them entirely, as long as the market price of the stock—except, of course, for temporary fluctuations—rises in reasonable relationship to the amount of retained profits. These stockholders are quite happy to accumulate wealth in the form of corporate assets, while avoiding the high federal income taxes they would have to pay on current dividends, and possibly anticipating cashing their earnings later on as capital gains subject to a limited rate of tax.

An incidental advantage of modest significance in buying stock by privileged subscriptions is that brokerage commissions are avoided—commissions that must be paid by the buyer when already issued stock is bought from other investors in the market.

Market Behavior of Stock and Rights. An explanation is appropriate for the proposition, stated above, that should a large percentage of the stockholders of a corporation try to sell their rights, the market for both stock and rights would react unfavorably. The principal determinant of the market value of rights, as will be explained below, is the difference between the market price at a given time of stock already outstanding and the offering price of the new shares. Since the market values of stock and the rights are thus tied together, any change in one of these values in a given direction will be accompanied or followed by a commensurate change in the other in the same direction.

If, therefore, many stockholders offer their rights for sale, their action will tend to cause the market price of rights to fall, and this, in turn, will exert a depressive force on the market price of the stock itself. Outsiders who are interested in buying in the market either stock or rights will hold off their purchases, expecting to be able to buy at lower prices later on. By narrowing the bargain aspect of the rights offering, an initial decline in the market prices of stock and rights may prompt the sale of rights by other stockholders who had planned to enter their privileged subscriptions. These and still other stockholders, worried by the price decline in the stock or the prospects of dilution, may decide to sell their existing stockholdings as well as the rights. Speculators would see in the declining prices favorable opportunities to sell short both stock and rights, expecting to be able to cover their short positions later by buying at still lower prices, and their sales would add to the market supplies. The cumulative effects of continued transactions of these kinds, then, might well be to depress the market price of the stock to the level of the offering price. At that level, the rights would be virtually valueless,[4] and neither present

[4]The rights might still have a slight value because brokerage commissions must be paid on stock bought in the market but not on that bought direct from

(Continued on next page.)

stockholders nor outsiders would have much inducement to enter subscriptions to the new shares.

Assignability of Rights. It would thus be most hazardous for the financial managers of a corporation to make a rights offering without strong faith in their stockholders' loyalty—strong expectations, one may say, that a large proportion of the stockholders will enter subscriptions.[5] Nevertheless, managers of corporations that have thousands of stockholders can hardly expect to get unanimous acceptance of their offers. A goodly number of stockholders in such a corporation may not have sufficient cash available to buy their allotments, and they may be unwilling to borrow or sell other assets. Stockholders who have what they think are well-balanced investment portfolios may decide that the additional stock would not fit in. A not inconsiderable number of others, probably small stockholders in particular, may think of the rights as a kind of dividend, giving little or no thought to subscribing. And at least a small percentage could be expected to toss their subscription warrants into the wastebasket—the depositary of all kinds of communications from the corporation except for dividend checks.

But in making a rights offering, as in the adoption of any other kind of financing program, the hope of the financial managers is that all or almost all of the securities offered will be sold. The offering is expected to yield cash of a given amount for a purpose such as the acquisition of additional fixed assets, so that spending plans will be frustrated if most of the rights that are not exercised by the stockholders are not exercised by somebody else. Hence come the ideas of making the rights assignable and of promoting assignment by giving them a market value. A market value is given them, as we already know, by setting the offering price of the new stock substantially below the market price of the outstanding stock. This action, therefore, contributes simultaneously to the goal of attracting stockholders' subscriptions and that of encouraging nonsubscribing stockholders to sell their rights so that other investors will subscribe.

Value of Rights. To the stockholder who is eager, or at least willing, to subscribe to his allotment of new stock—as well as to the wastebasket tosser—the market value of rights presumably has relatively little significance. But it is a matter of great importance to the stockholder who looks on his rights as a dividend, as well as to any of his

the corporation. On the other hand, commissions must also be paid on the buying and selling of rights. If, moreover, the stock were listed on a stock exchange, brokerage commissions would have no influence on the transactions of members of the exchange for their own accounts, since they pay no commissions on these transactions; yet, some of these members might be leading speculators in the stock and rights.

[5]Without prospects of strong stockholder support for the offering, investment bankers would not be likely to consent to underwrite. Thus, the hazard could not be shifted to them. Banker participation in rights offerings is discussed later in this chapter. See pp. 479–83.

fellows who decide that they cannot or must not subscribe. It is likewise of great importance to corporate financial managers who hope, as we have seen, that rights not exercised by stockholders will be sold by them so that other investors will exercise them.

But what should a right be worth in the market? Obviously, its value should be related to the size of the bargain being offered by the corporation. But if two or more rights are required to buy one new share, only a portion of the bargain is attributable to each right. What is more, the time element must be taken into consideration. In the period between the announcement of the rights offering and the record date, the bargain itself is not the difference between the market price of old stock and the offering price of new. The reason is that in this period—the rights-on period, it is called—the market price of a share of stock *includes the value of the right that still attaches to that share.* Anybody who buys a share of stock in time to get his name on the corporation's books by the record date really buys both a share and a right; hence, the value of the share alone must be what he pays minus the value of the attached right. All this is indicated in the following formula for the determination of the value of a right in the rights-on period:

$$\frac{(M - v) - O}{n} = v$$

where M is the market value of a share of the existing stock, O is the offering price for a new share, n is the number of rights required for the purchase of a new share, and v is the value of a right. The formula can be simplified as follows:

multiplying by n,	$M - v - O = vn$
transposing,	$M - O = vn + v$
factoring,	$M - O = v(n + 1)$
dividing by $(n + 1)$,	$\frac{M - O}{n + 1} = v$

For illustration, let us assume that a corporation that has outstanding 100,000 shares of common stock of \$50 par value is making a rights offering of 20,000 additional shares at an offering price of \$60 a share. It therefore issues 100,000 rights, and 5 rights and \$60 are required for the purchase of 1 new share. At a time in the rights-on period when the market value of old stock is, say, \$69 a share, the value of a right, as determined by substitution in the formula, would be as follows:

$$\frac{\$69 - \$60}{5 + 1} = \$1.50$$

When it is too late for the buyer of old shares to get his name on the corporation's books by the record date, no part of what he pays can be attributed to the value of rights, since he gets no rights. He buys ex rights. The bargain being offered by the corporation is measurable in the ex-rights period, therefore, by the exact difference between the market price of old stock and the offering price of new. The value of a right is this difference divided by the number of rights required to buy one new share. Thus, the formula for the determination of the value of a right in the ex-rights period is simply the following (the symbols have the same meaning as in the formula given previously):

$$\frac{M - O}{n} = v$$

But if a buyer gets both a share and a right in the rights-on period, and only the share itself in the ex-rights period, he ought not be willing to pay as much for the share as for the share plus right. On the basis of the nature of the transaction itself, leaving out of consideration all other kinds of influences on his decision to buy, the price he should be willing to pay in the ex-rights period is precisely the price acceptable in the rights-on period reduced by the value of the right that he does not get. Thus, we say that, abstracting from all other influences that affect price, the market price of a share should fall by the value of a right at the time that a stock goes ex rights. In terms of the illustration just given, the value of a right would still be $1.50 after the stock had gone ex rights were the market price of the stock to fall as expected from $69 to $67.50. This result can be demonstrated by substituting in the formula for the ex-rights period as follows:

$$\frac{\$67.50 - \$60}{5} = \$1.50$$

Fluctuations in Market Prices. The foregoing illustrations and related discussion are not meant to imply that the value of a right remains unchanged during the whole period from the date of the directors' resolution setting up a rights offering to the closing date of the subscription books, that the market price of stock always falls by exactly the value of a right when the old stock goes ex rights, or that the market prices at which rights are actually bought and sold are precisely what the formulas indicate they should be.

The market price of a stock is affected through the period of a rights offering not only by the special influences of the offering itself but also by all the other influences that normally play on the market—by all the forces, one may say, that affect investors' attitudes toward the corporation specifically and toward common stocks in general.

Ordinarily, therefore, the market price will be subject to at least as many fluctuations during the period of the rights offering as would be likely to occur in a period of equal length in which no rights offering was being made. All that the formulas indicate, therefore, is the approximate price at which rights ought to be selling on a given day or during a given hour if the market price of the stock and the offering price of new shares are thus and so. If the market price of the old stock fluctuates from hour to hour, then the market price of rights should do the same. For example, in the rights offering of the Florida Power Corporation, referred to previously, the market price of the stock on one of the days of the ex-rights period ranged from 27 3/4 to 28 3/8 a share, while the market price of a right varied from 7/32 to 1/4.

Moreover, while there is a normal expectation that the market price of old stock will fall by approximately the value of a right when it goes ex rights, other influences quite unrelated to the rights offering may counterbalance this tendency to fall. Indeed, they may be powerful enough to force the price up, or they may work in such manner as to extend the scope of the fall.

Finally, the prices at which rights are actually sold at given times may be somewhat different from what the formulas indicate they should be. Given the market price at which old stock is sold at a certain hour on a certain day, the appropriate formula may indicate that the value of a right is, say, $1.50, but we may learn that some rights were actually sold at that hour at 1 3/8 or 1 9/16. The market is imperfect, and buyers and sellers do not always know all that is going on around them. But speculators especially will quickly notice out-of-line relationships between the market prices of old stock and rights, and will buy or sell to take advantage of the situation. Their transactions—a kind of arbitrage, as it is called—should have corrective effects on the discrepancy in the market prices.

Selling Rights. With the foregoing discussion of the technical aspects of rights values in mind, we should be able to understand more clearly the hope of corporate managers that nonsubscribing stockholders will sell their rights to other investors. In terms of the illustrations, why should not the owner of 100 shares who does not want to subscribe sell his rights for $150 or thereabouts? The alternative is to see the rights vanish into thin air at the expiration of the subscription period. He may hold, of course, till close to the end of the subscription period in hope that the value of the stock—and, therefore, the value of the rights—will rise, but if he is wise he will not permit the rights to expire without selling. The opportunity to sell explains why some stockholders look on rights as a kind of dividend.

In this regard, one should notice the strong element of compulsion that is implicit in a rights offering. Although the existing common stockholder is said to be privileged to buy a certain number of additional shares, he is forced, in effect, to do one of two things: increase his investment in the corporation, or sell a part of his ownership interests by selling the rights. Regardless of what he does, the sale of the new stock will dilute the claims of each existing share to voting power and to corporate assets and earning. If he sells the rights allotted to him, he should know that he thereby parts with a portion of his ownership interests. And should he want to maintain the present proportion of his claims, he should know that he *must* subscribe to the shares allotted to him or, alternatively, buy an equal number in the market. The third possible alternative—to do nothing—is not a reasonable one at all. If the stockholder does nothing with the rights, his existing holdings are diluted anyway; hence, he suffers this dilution without the compensation he could get by selling the rights. Thus, we can readily conclude that the wastebasket tosser is not very smart in the ways of investment.

That a sale of rights is a sale of ownership interests is given recognition in the federal income tax regulations. The full proceeds of such a sale are not taxable as income; in fact, it is possible that no part of the proceeds will be taxable. The regulations provide that the original cost of the stock held by the stockholder is to be allocated between the stock and the rights in proportion to their respective market values at the time of the sale of the rights, and that only the difference between the selling price of the rights and the cost allocated to them is to be reported as taxable income. To illustrate, assume that a stockholder owns 5 shares which he bought some years ago at $40 a share, that he receives 5 rights, entitling him to buy 1 new share, and that he sells the 5 rights for $7.50 at a time in the ex-rights period when the market price of the stock is $67.50. The cost basis of the rights is found by the following formula:

$$\frac{\text{Market value of rights}}{\text{Combined market value of stock and rights}} \times \text{Cost of stock} = \text{Cost basis for rights}$$

Substituting, we get:

$$\frac{\$7.50}{\$337.50 + \$7.50} \times \$200 = \$4.35$$

Accordingly, only the difference between $7.50 and $4.35, or $3.15, is recognized as taxable income. In a subsequent sale of stock, its cost basis would be $195.65—that is, the original cost of $200 reduced by the cost basis of $4.35 attributed to the rights.

Buying Rights. But the existence of a market value for rights requires buyers as well as sellers. If there is obvious inducement to stockholders to sell their rights should they not want to subscribe, what inducement is there for buyers? Continuing with the illustrative figures we have been using, we may put the question this way: To acquire a share of stock, why would anyone be willing to buy 5 rights at $1.50 each and to pay the corporation $60, for a total cost of $67.50, when he could buy in the market at the same total cost per share?

One reason for buying was indicated at an earlier point in our discussion—namely, from time to time during the subscription period the market value of rights may fall somewhat short of the values computed by the formulas. Although market forces are constantly tending to correct discrepancies between rights values and stock values, the adjustment is not automatic; hence, bargains for outsiders—as distinct from the bargains for stockholders, to which frequent reference has been made—may turn up. They would presumably hurry to buy if rights were selling at 1¼ or 1⅜ at a time when, as a formula computation would show, the market value ought to be $1.50 or $1.60.

But even when the rights value in the market is equal to, or even slightly above, the formula value, there are reasons for a demand for rights. One is a saving in commissions. Were he to buy a share of stock in the market at $67.50, the investor would have to pay his broker a commission on the full amount, but were he to buy 5 rights at $1.50 each, he would pay a commission on only the total price of $7.50. In using the rights to get a share from the corporation, he would pay no commission on the $60 purchase price payable to it. Another saving is in stock transfer taxes. These would be fully assessed on the market purchase of stock, but not in the purchase of rights nor in the buying of stock direct from the issuing corporation.

Often of much more importance than these reasons for buying rights are the profit expectations of speculators. As percentages of amounts invested, profits from speculation in rights can be much higher than profits from speculation in stock. In terms of the rights offering we have been using for illustration, a rise in the market value of an outstanding share from $67.50 to $70 in the ex-rights period should be accompanied by a rise in the market value of a right from $1.50 to $2. Thus, a speculation in 5 rights at $7.50 would give the same (gross) profit of $2.50 as a speculation in a share of stock at $67.50. But a profit of $2.50 on an investment of $7.50 represents a rate of return of 33⅓ percent, while an equal profit on an investment of $67.50 amounts to a rate of return of only about 3.7 percent. Although corporations generally prefer to see their stock, old and new, go into the hands of long-term investors, they have no compelling reason to be unhappy about the temporary support that speculators give to their rights offerings. When speculators buy rights and exercise them for a quick profit, the corporation does succeed in getting its money, and the people who, in turn, buy from the speculators may be long-term investors.

Setting the Offering Price. Although the financial managers of a corporation are likely to be fully aware of the reasons why the offering price in a rights offering should be set materially below the market value of outstanding stock, this awareness does not give them a means of deciding exactly what the offering price should be. They want the offering price to remain well below the market price throughout the period of the offering, and they know that the offering itself, as a source of new supply of stock, will tend to depress the market price. However, they must also consider the possibility that the market price of outstanding stock will rise during the period of the rights offering. If the corporation appears to have good prospects for expanding its profits handsomely through an expansion of facilities, the very announcement of the rights offering as a means of financing the expansion may be so well received by the stockholders and other investors as to lead to spirited buying of both stock and rights.

The kind of dilemma faced by corporate managers in fixing an offering price may be illustrated. Suppose that a certain corporation wants to raise by a rights offering a net amount of approximately $4 million. It is anticipated that the flotation costs will be about 5 percent of the gross proceeds. The present market price of outstanding stock is $80, and the financial managers ponder the question whether they should offer 60,000 new shares at $70 a share or 56,000 shares at $75. They themselves may contemplate not buying any of the additional stock; hence they want to limit dilution of their present ownership interests. Or, regardless of their own position, they may want to limit dilution to protect the interests of all nonsubscribing stockholders. In either case, a wish to limit dilution would support a decision in favor of the smaller number of shares at the higher price. Also supporting such a decision would be the usual expectation of stockholders that the dividend rate in effect before the rights offering *will not be reduced* after completion of the financing. With approximately the same amount of money to be made available by either route, it should obviously be easier to maintain a given dividend rate on 56,000 additional shares than on 60,000. On the other hand, it would be clear that should the financing tend to move unfavorably, a drop in the market price from $80 to $75 would be much more likely to occur than a drop from $80 to $70. There is, of course, no single correct answer to a problem of this kind. Even success in the financing does not prove that the offering price selected was the best of all that could have been selected. Perhaps a higher price, giving the corporation more funds for the number of shares issued, would have been no less successful.

Rights Offerings versus Underwritten Offerings to the Public. The foregoing illustration of the financial managers' dilemma gives us the opportunity to make a rather significant comparison of the *financial* attractiveness of a rights offering with that of an offering to the general public underwritten by investment bankers, as discussed in Chapter 18.

For an offering to the general public, the corporate managers would expect to incur flotation costs higher than those for the rights offering—equal, let us say, to 8 percent of the gross proceeds. But they would expect the bankers to agree to a price for the public sale quite close to the prevailing market price. If, therefore, 54,000 shares were taken by the bankers for public sale at $80 a share, the net proceeds to the corporation, despite the higher level of flotation costs, would be approximately the same as in a rights offering of 60,000 shares at $70 or one of 56,000 shares at $75. The higher flotation costs of the offering to the general public—representing preponderantly, of course, compensation to the bankers—would thus not, of itself, make this procedure of sale unattractive. This is so because the excess costs of flotation would be less than the loss of proceeds in a rights offering on account of the lower selling price.

Such a conclusion, however, does not gainsay our earlier one that for the new issues of common stock of many corporations their existing common stockholders constitute the best market. Nor does it call into question directors' decisions that existing stockholders should be enabled to protect their ownership interests through rights offerings, even though that means of selling, in given cases and for given numbers of shares, may yield smaller net proceeds than would offerings to the general public.

Other Features of Rights Offerings

Record Date. The record date for a rights offering is customarily set from 10 days to 2 weeks from the date when the directors adopt their resolution to make the offering. People who have bought stock without having it transferred to their names on the corporation's books are thus given time to make this transfer, so that they will get the subscription warrants they are entitled to. Likewise, as we have seen, people who buy outstanding stock after the date of the resolution are able to know whether or not they can get their names on the books in time to get subscription warrants—to know, in other words, whether they are buying rights on or ex rights.

For a stock traded on a stock exchange, the governing record date is usually *not* the date set by the corporate directors. The New York Stock Exchange, for example, provides that stock sold through its facilities must be delivered on or before the fifth full business day after the date of sale. According to its rules, therefore, a listed stock for which rights have been declared goes ex rights at the close of business on the fifth full business day *before* the record date set by the corporate directors. Were the corporation's record date Friday, August 12, the stock would sell on the exchange on a rights-on basis on Friday, August 5, but on an ex-rights basis on Monday, August 8.

Subscription Warrants. After the record date, the corporation or its stock transfer agent sends a subscription warrant to each stockholder whose name appeared on the stock records at the close of business on that day. Such a warrant is a formal certificate, stating that the person named in it is entitled to buy a given number of shares of common stock at the designated offering price. It also states how many rights the certificate represents and the number required for the purchase of a new share, the time limit for subscriptions, the place or places where warrants are to be surrendered and payment made, and the means of payment that will be accepted. If installment payment is permitted, that provision will also necessarily be included. On either the front or back of the subscription warrant, two forms are ordinarily provided: the subscription form itself, to be filled in by the stockholder or buyer of rights if he wants to buy some or all the shares allotted; and an assignment form, to be filled in or endorsed in blank before transfer if he chooses to sell the rights.

The filling in and sending out of subscription warrants, together with copies of the prospectus and a covering letter, is a voluminous—and expensive—operation for large corporations that have thousands of stockholders. Such a corporation customarily hires a trust company or the trust department of a commercial bank to do this work. In addition, the same trust company or department, and perhaps one or two others, is hired to serve as subscription agent to handle incoming warrants and payments.

Closing Subscription Books. The date for closing the subscription books is usually set not less than two weeks beyond the record date—often at three or four weeks and sometimes as long as eight weeks. It is the common practice for the directors, in their resolution and in the subscription warrants themselves, to state precisely the hour beyond which subscriptions will not be accepted, such as 3 P.M., Eastern Standard Time. Warrants not received by the corporation or its subscription agents by this time are void, and the rights they represent are worthless.

Manner of Payment. Because of the abrupt way in which corporations by rights offerings ask their stockholders to buy additional stock, the directors sometimes permit payment in installments. Installment arrangements usually call for a down payment of a stipulated proportion of the offering price, to be made when the warrants are sent in, with the balance to be paid in quarterly or semiannual installments over a period of not more than a year.

Rights Offerings and the Preemptive Right

A final point to be made in this division of the chapter is that despite the prominence of the word *right* there is no necessary connection between rights offerings and the preemptive right of common stockholders to buy new common stock issues, as discussed in Chapter 17. If the preemptive right obtains—it is rather a weak one, as we have seen[6]—it exists continuously, whereas the rights of a rights offering are short-lived. The preemptive right may never be applied if a corporation has no occasion to put out additional amounts of common stock, or it may be waived by the stockholders for given issues. If it is applied, the stockholders do, indeed, get rights according to the procedure described in this chapter, but they may also get such rights even though the preemptive right is not in force, because the directors of their corporation decide that they are the best market for new offerings.

The idea here is that many new issues of common stock are offered to existing stockholders because directors think they are more likely than other people to buy whether or not the preemptive right is applicable. When directors are convinced that the stockholders are not likely to want to subscribe, they can be expected to ask the stockholders to approve the offering of new issues elsewhere, as to the general public, whether or not this requires a waiver of the preemptive right.

REGULATION OF RIGHTS OFFERINGS

Under the federal Securities Act, rights offerings to stockholders are public offerings and are fully subject to registration requirements, unless they qualify for one of the exemptions provided for in the legislation.[7] As a rule, then, all the work of preparing registration statements and the related prospectuses must be undertaken, and copies of the prospectuses must be made available to all stockholders and others to whom the new stock is offered for sale. Indeed, the directors of a corporation may not make a rights offering to its stockholders until the registration statement for it has become effective. Thus, adoption of the directors' resolution, to which frequent reference has been made in this chapter, takes place after the registration statement and prospectus have been filed with the SEC and the prescribed waiting period—possibly shortened by the SEC—has expired.

Although the state blue-sky laws are generally more liberal than the federal Securities Act in providing exemptions for rights offerings, such an offering by a large corporation to many stockholders ordinarily requires qualification in at least a few states. This, then, is another kind of preparatory work that must be taken care of.

BANKER PARTICIPATION IN RIGHTS OFFERINGS

How the work of preparing registration statements and prospectuses for rights offerings and of qualifying them under state blue-sky

---

[6]See pp. 415–17.

[7]For the scope of these exemptions, see pp. 451–52.

laws is shared, if it is to be shared, depends on whether or not issuing corporations call on investment bankers to assist in the flotations. If called on, the investment bankers aid in the preparatory work in much the same manner as described in Chapter 18 for offerings to the general public. If they are not called on, all the work of preparation remains, of course, with the corporation.

But a much more important consideration in deciding whether or not to seek the aid of investment bankers is the outlook for success in the flotation. If a corporate management has great confidence that the stockholders will respond most favorably to a rights offering, it may decide to bypass the bankers, but if it is somewhat worried about the outcome it will probably ask them to help out. For rights offerings of both common and preferred stocks (but very largely common stock) registered with the SEC for immediate cash sale to stockholders in the years 1959–61, the dollar proportion that had participations of investment bankers amounted to 39.2 percent. Data for offerings exempt from registration requirements under the SEC's Regulation A in the same three-year period indicate that the bankers participate in a substantially smaller proportion of small offerings to stockholders.[8]

When called on to assist with a rights offering, the investment bankers may also be more or less confident about the outcome. If confident, they are likely to underwrite the flotation on what is called a standby basis, but if they lack confidence they may participate only as selling agents in a so-called dealer-manager arrangement. Also, of course, they may choose not to participate at all, rejecting a plea for assistance even as they reject many proposals for underwriting security offerings to the general public.

The response of investment bankers to a request for their participation depends, of course, on what they find in an investigation of the corporation's affairs. If a preliminary investigation indicates the probability that underwriting would be feasible, it is followed by a detailed investigation like that for prospective underwritings of offerings to the general public. If, on the other hand, there is early agreement on a dealer-management arrangement, further investigation by the bankers is likely to be much less extensive.

Standby Contracts

In a standby contract for a rights offering, the investment bankers as underwriters guarantee its success. They guarantee that the corporation will receive, at the minimum, an amount equal to the number of shares being offered times the offering price, minus the com-

[8]Securities and Exchange Commission, *Report of Special Study of the Securities Markets* (House Doc. No. 95, Pt. 1, 88th Cong., 1st sess. [(Washington, D.C.: U.S. Government Printing Office, 1963]), p. 604.

mission allowed them. In so guaranteeing, they obligate themselves to take off the hands of the corporation the shares not subscribed by stockholders or by rights buyers.

Compensation for the Bankers. In the typical underwritten rights offering, the principal service supplied by the investment bankers is that of risk-bearing. In agreeing to underwrite, they have an expectation that most of the offering will be taken by stockholders and rights buyers, but it is always possible for things to turn out badly—hence the risk. On account of differences in timing, in fact, the risk in underwriting a rights offering tends to be greater than that in underwriting an offering to the general public. In the public offering, the bankers begin to sell immediately after the registration statement has become effective, but in a rights offering they have an additional waiting period to the end of the subscription period. On the other hand, if most of the stock of a rights offering is taken by stockholders and buyers of rights, as the bankers expect, their selling job will be light. On the basis of considerations of these kinds, therefore, the compensation to be paid to the bankers is generally fixed at a flat rate on the total amount of the issue. This fee is essentially a reward for risk-bearing, and there is a provision for additional compensation per share for whatever shares remain unsold at the end of the subscription period.

An illustration should help. Suppose that on an offering to stockholders at 70 the bankers are allowed a commission of 1 percent on the entire issue and an additional commission of 3 percent on shares taken over at the end of the subscription period. The bankers would get 70 cents for each share subscribed by stockholders and rights buyers, so that the proceeds to the corporation on these shares, disregarding other expenses of flotation, would be $69.30 each. Unsubscribed shares would then be taken over by the bankers at $67.20 ($70 reduced by the total commission of 4 percent allowed on these shares). But their earning of $2.80 on each of these shares would still depend on their finding buyers at 70 or better. If they had to sell at prices less than 70, they would obviously be giving up some of the 4 percent commission. Indeed, if they had to sell at prices below 67.2 they would be taking a loss, comparable with the losses that are always possible in other underwriting procedures.

In some standby contracts, the bankers are allowed the additional commission not only on shares taken over at the end of the subscription period but also for shares to which they subscribe through the exercise of rights. They are thus encouraged to buy rights during the subscription period, thereby adding a source of demand that tends to support their market value. In some contracts, too, additional compensation of a different kind is allowed the bankers for contacting stockholders, encouraging them to subscribe, and handling their subscriptions. However, all items of compensation in connection with a given rights offering ordinarily add up to a total substantially below what would be the underwriting commission were the same issue to be offered to the general public.

Many underwriting contracts for rights offerings provide that if the bankers are able to sell the leftover shares at a markup in excess of the commission rate designated in the contract, a refund of all or a portion of the excess is due the corporation. If the unsubscribed shares of the foregoing illustration taken over by the bankers at 67.2 were resold to the public at 73, the excess would obviously be $3 a share. Depending on the terms of the standby contract, then, some portion or all of the $3 would be payable to the corporation. It is for this reason that the bankers' guaranty was described above as a "minimum" one. Refunds of excess proceeds, however, are likely to occur only when the number of shares taken over by the bankers is quite small. A large number would mean that many stockholders must have decided not to subscribe and that relatively few investors must have bought rights in order to subscribe. Accordingly, the value of rights must have been driven down to zero or close thereto, and the market price of the stock itself must have fallen close to the corporation's offering price or even below. In such circumstances, the bankers would doubtless consider themselves lucky if able to sell at the offering price the shares taken over.

Illustration. In the rights offering of the Florida Power Corporation, to which several references have been made in this chapter, the underwriters were allowed 15 cents a share on the entire issue. They were to receive an additional 48 cents a share for unsubscribed shares taken over at the end of the subscription period as well as for shares subscribed by them through their own purchase and exercise of rights, provided that all shares thus acquired amounted to more than 15 percent of the total offering.

As it turned out, however, the provision for additional compensation remained inoperative because purchases by the underwriters through the exercise of rights amounted to only 10,800 shares, and those of unsubscribed shares to 15,528, the total of these two items amounting to only about 3.7 percent of the total offering of 703,485 shares. The underwriters resold the 10,800 shares at 28⅜ a share, and reoffered the 15,528 shares at 27⅜, in both instances allowing a price concession of 45 cents a share to the members of a selling group. The contract obligated the bankers to pay the corporation 50 percent of the excess of their selling price of unsubscribed shares, as reduced by the price concession, over the subscription price.

Syndicates and Selling Groups. For large rights offerings, as for large offerings to the public, originating investment banking houses invariably invite other houses to join underwriting syndicates. The originating house regards the risk as being too great for it to bear alone; it is therefore willing to share the underwriting commission with invited houses that agree to share the risk. For large offerings, too, the originator usually lines up a selling group to retail some portion of the take-over of unsubscribed shares and the shares it may buy through the exercise of rights. In many cases, however—such as the Florida Power Corporation—the members of the selling group may have very little to do.

Dealer-Manager Arrangements

In a dealer-manager arrangement for a rights offering, the investment banking house that agrees to serve as manager helps the corporation to prepare its issue for the market and then to sell it. These functions include assistance in preparation of the registration statement and prospectus and in qualifying the stock issue under applicable blue-sky laws, and formation of a group of dealers to solicit subscriptions by stockholders and assignees of their warrants. The dealer group is comparable to a selling group formed for the underwriting of an offering to the general public, but since the dealers act as agents, as does the manager, they make no commitments to buy some of the stock as would the members of a selling group.

A dealer-manager agreement specifies what compensation the manager is to receive for his advisory, preparatory, and managerial services, and the rate per share to be paid to him and the dealers for the subscriptions they obtain.

QUESTIONS

1. What is the nature of a rights offering of common stock to a corporation's existing stockholders? What, if anything, is its relationship to the stockholders' preemptive right?

2. In relation to a rights offering, what is a privileged subscription? A subscription warrant?

3. In relation to the number of shares of common stock a corporation already has outstanding, how many rights does it issue in making a rights offering? How many rights are required for the purchase of a new share?

4. Of what influence on the success of a rights offering is the distribution of common shares already outstanding? The number of new shares being offered?

5. Of what character is the loyalty of existing stockholders that is said to be of great importance for the success of rights offerings?

6. In making a rights offering, why does the corporation usually set the offering price at a level substantially below the stock's current market price?

7. Explain the mathematical procedures for computing rights values in the rights-on and ex-rights periods. Why do the formulas for the two

periods differ? Should one expect the market value of a right to be always equal to the formula value? Explain.

8. Why is there said to be a strong element of compulsion in a rights offering?

9. Why do outsiders buy rights in the market when they can as conveniently buy the stock itself?

10. Explain the nature of the problem faced by corporate managers in deciding at what level to set the offering price of a rights offering.

11. In a rights offering, what is the significance of the record date? The expiration date? If the outstanding stock is listed on a stock exchange, what bearing does this have on the record date?

12. Discuss this proposition: Because the common stockholders of a corporation should already know a great deal about it, registration of a rights offering under the federal Securities Act ought not be required.

13. In a standby contract for a rights offering, what responsibility do investment bankers accept? Do they have anything to do before the expiration date? Explain. How is their compensation determined?

14. What do investment bankers undertake to do in a dealer-manager arrangement for a rights offering?

PROBLEMS

1. For the rights offerings of common stock of Corporations A, B, and C, details of which are given in the following table, find the probable market price of a right in each case at a time in the rights-on period when the market price of the stock was at the level also indicated in the table.

	A	*B*	*C*
Shares already outstanding	600,000	150,000	2,000,000
Shares being offered	100,000	30,000	200,000
Offering price	$50	$28	$42
Market price	$55	$31	$43

2. Assuming that the market price of stock in each of the foregoing instances prevailed at a certain time in the ex-rights period, what was the probable market value of a right at that time in each instance.

3. From what level to what level did the market price of the outstanding stock of Corporation A in Problem 1 probably move in the rights-on period as the market price of a right rose from ⅝ to ⅞?

4. From what level to what level did the market price of the outstanding stock of Corporation B in Problem 1 probably move in the ex-rights period as the market price of a right fell from ½ to ¼?

5. Several years ago, John Jones bought 600 shares of the common stock of a certain corporation at a price of $55 a share. This year, the corporation gave him 600 rights, entitling him to buy 60 additional shares at a price of $70 a share. Instead of buying, however, he sold the rights for $300 at a time when the corporation's outstanding stock was selling in the market at 75½. Under federal tax regulations, what taxable income, if any, did Jones derive on the sale of rights?

chapter 20

OTHER PROCEDURES FOR COMMON STOCK FINANCING

Reserved for discussion in this chapter are all significant means for the acquisition of corporate assets through the issuance of common stock other than sales to the general public and sales to existing stockholders. As was indicated in Chapter 18, these additional means include:

1. Direct exchanges of common stock for property other than cash and for services.
2. Offerings for cash to specified classes of investors other than existing common stockholders and the general public.
3. Private placements for cash.
4. Offerings in exchange for outstanding preferred stock and to cancel outstanding bonds.
5. Procedures best classified simply as "miscellaneous."

DIRECT EXCHANGES FOR PROPERTY

Quite large amounts of land, buildings, machinery and equipment, inventories, accounts receivable, and other assets are acquired annually by business corporations in the United States in direct exchanges for shares of their common stock. In many instances, the acquisition of assets by direct exchanges is a matter of form only, as in the incorporation of businesses formerly conducted as proprietorships and partnerships. In many others, direct exchanges for property are an outstanding means of growth for individual corporate entities. This is often so in mergers and consolidations and in the acquisition of subsidiaries by holding companies. In rarer instances, they are the means whereby corporations, large and small, come into possession of individual parcels of property.

Incorporation of Proprietorships and Partnerships

The acquisition of all the operating assets of a proprietorship or partnership by a newly formed corporation in exchange for some or all of its authorized common stock is describable as a matter of form only, since the character and scope of the enterprise, except in its legal complexion, is unlikely to be changed by the transaction in any material way. The legal form is changed, the corporation as an entity now owns the assets, and the former proprietor or partners now as stockholder or stockholders own the corporation and not the assets. But policies, procedures, the owners' attitudes, and their participation in management are likely to be much the same as before.

Basically, therefore, the means of financing the corporate assets continues to be the cash invested in the proprietorship or partnership by the owners, whether derived from their original resources, accumulated through the retention of profits, or borrowed. Nevertheless, from the standpoint of *corporate* financing, it is technically true to say that the means used in acquiring assets is the direct exchange of common stock for them.

Mergers, Consolidations, and Holding Company Acquisitions

The acquisition by given corporations of all or substantially all of the operating assets of other corporations has long been a favored method of corporate growth. A corporation that wants to expand the scope of its existing kinds of operations or to diversify its lines has the choice of building or buying new facilities or of trying to acquire those held by other enterprises. The acquisition procedure has much to recommend it. It makes possible what may be called instantaneous growth, whereas the building or buying of new facilities is a slower process. It limits competition, since new productive facilities are not added to existing ones. It also eliminates uncertainities about the cost of facilities and their capacities to do particular kinds of jobs.

Exchanges of Common Stocks. Especially significant from the standpoint of finance is that the acquisition of the operating assets of other enterprises can often be arranged by simple exchanges of common stocks. "The most widely used method of financing acquisitions," says the Federal Trade Commission, "is that of exchanging the stock of the acquiring firm for the stock of the acquired firm or firms."[1] In a merger proposition, Corporation A offers a certain number of shares of its common stock in exchange for the common stock of Corporation B. If the stockholders of B accept the offer, the stock of A is distributed to them in the ratio agreed on, the assets of B become the property

[1]Federal Trade Commission, *Report on Corporate Mergers and Acquisitions* (Washington, D.C.: U.S. Government Printing Office, 1955), p. 9.

of A, and B is dissolved. In a proposal for consolidation, the newly formed Corporation C offers some of its common stock in exchange for that of A, and another block of shares in exchange for that of B. If the stockholders of A and B accept the offer, they receive C's stock in the agreed-on ratios, the assets of their corporations are transferred to C, and their corporations are dissolved. In the holding company arrangement, Corporation A offers some of its common stock in exchange for some or all of that of Corporation B (presumably for at least enough to give it control). If the offer is accepted, the exchange is made, and A then holds the stock in B, continuing it in existence as its subsidiary.

In each of these transactions, it is clear that common stock is the financing medium—the acquiring corporation becomes the owner of aggregations of assets (or the holding company gets control) by simply giving some of its common stock in direct exchange.

Advantages of Exchanges of Common Stock. But would it not be as feasible for Corporation A (whether the surviving corporation of a merger, the new corporation of a consolidation, or a holding company) to sell a new issue of its common stock to the general public or to its existing stockholders, and then go to Corporation B or to B's stockholders with an offer to buy it or them out for cash? Many combinations are, indeed, effected as cash transactions; nevertheless, the use of cash can be much less attractive then direct exchange offers. If B were a large corporation, the large amount of new common stock that A would have to sell to raise the cash necessary for a buying-out transaction might not be salable at a reasonable price. An attempt to sell this amount might cause a sharp drop in the market price of A's stock already outstanding, while an offer of the same amount in exchange for B's stock would be unlikely to produce such a market reaction. Indeed, the prospects of a combination favorable to A, to be effected by an exchange of stock, might result in a rise in the market value of its outstanding shares. Moreover, A might expect to be able to carry through the exchange transaction without having it underwritten by investment bankers; therefore, it would anticipate the avoidance of an underwriting commission such as it would expect to pay were the stock to be offered in a public sale. It might plan to hire investment bankers to solicit the stockholders of B to accept the exchange offer, but it would expect the cost of this service to be much less than an underwriting commission. Still another advantage to A would be the avoidance of upward pressure on the market price of B's stock. Were A to proceed to quietly buy up B's stock in the market, its very buying would tend to drive up the market price, making successive purchases more and more costly. Were it to go to B's stockholders individually with cash offers, the word of its activities would soon get around, and it could expect many to hold out for fancy prices.

A final advantage to A would be that many, and perhaps most, of B's stockholders would be likely to prefer stock to cash. The prospect of becoming stockholders in the merged or consolidated enterprise or in the holding company, as the case might be, could be much more attractive to them than the prospect of getting cash for which they would have to find new investment outlets. Strongly contributing to such a preference is the fact that direct exchanges of common stock can generally be arranged on a tax-free basis under the terms of the federal income tax regulations. Thus, if A were to pay cash for B's assets in an amount in excess of their book values (or other cost bases, as prescribed in the tax regulations), the excess would be taxable income to it. On B's distribution of this cash to its stockholders as a liquidating dividend, moreover, the stockholders would be individually subject to a capital gains tax on the amount by which the dividend exceeded the price they originally paid for their stock. But a direct exchange arranged on a tax-free basis would result in no immediate tax liability either to Corporation B or to its stockholders.

Treatment of Debt and Preferred Stocks. All this does not mean that mergers, consolidations, and holding company acquisitions can usually be carried through without some outlay of cash. Although it is a common practice for acquiring corporations to assume the debts of acquired corporations (or simply to let them stand, as in holding company acquisitions of new subsidiaries), there may be good reasons to pay off some of these debts, particularly some or all of the current liabilities and perhaps small bond issues. If an acquired corporation has preferred stock outstanding, it must be separately taken care of. If callable, it may be paid off in cash at its redemption value, or callable or not, preferred stock in the acquiring corporation, or even some of its common stock, may be offered in exchange for it.

In exchange offers, however, individual preferred stockholders have the right to refuse what is offered and to demand redemption of their stock in cash at a fair value—a value to be determined by negotiation, by an appropriate court to which an appeal is made, or by appraisers appointed by such a court. The right of the individual preferred stockholder to demand payment of the fair value in cash can be exerted, even though a very large proportion of his fellow preferred stockholders approve an exchange offer. Indeed, common stockholders have a similar right of dissent—a right to demand cash, even though a large majority of other common stockholders assent to an exchange offer. Thus, cash must be provided to pay off dissenting stockholders, preferred or common.

The fact is that many proposals for mergers, consolidations, and holding company acquisitions fall through simply because there are too many dissenters, for the managers of the acquiring corporations see that much of the advantage of direct exchange will be lost. In making exchange offers, therefore, financial managers of acquiring corporations often stipulate that the offers will be binding only if accepted by holders of 85 or 90 percent or some other high percentage of the outstanding common stock of the corporations to be acquired. Sometimes, indeed, such stipulations for high percentages of acceptances are extended to preferred stock as well. Stipulations of the kinds described are often made even though the state law may provide that the merger or other combination requires the approval of holders of only a simple majority or two thirds of the stock entitled to vote on the proposal.

Recent Developments. The number of mergers, consolidations, and holding company acquisitions in the period since the close of World War II has been phenomenal. Records accumulated by the Federal Trade Commission disclose that such acquisitions reached their highest all-time level in 1967. The heaviest concentration by far was in the areas of manufacturing and mining, in which 1,496 firms were taken over by other firms compared with acquisitions of 995 firms in 1966. Especially concerned about absorptions of large manufacturing and mining firms—firms with assets individually of $10 million or more—the FTC reports that in the period from 1948 through 1967 a total of 1,067 of these firms, with assets of approximately $39 billion, were absorbed, and that in the year 1967 alone large manufacturing and mining firms absorbed numbered 155, with assets totaling about $8 billion—an asset total about double that of the 98 such firms absorbed in 1966.[2]

Moreover, the FTC's concern, and the concern of many other organizations and individuals, has been increasingly directed to the recent extremely rapid growth of conglomerates—huge corporations that result from numerous acquisitions of other enterprises of widely diverse products, policies, and markets, chiefly in manufacturing but in many instances spreading over into finance, communications, and other service areas. The student must surely be familiar with the names of some of these conglomerates: Litton Industries, Inc.; Ling-Temco-Vought, Inc.; the International Telephone and Telegraph Corporation; Gulf & Western Industries, Inc.; Ogden Corporation; Glen Alden Corporation; and Teledyne Inc. For example, Gulf & Western started out as a producer and distributor of auto parts, and within about five years its operations had reached into areas such as motion pictures, television, sugar, cigars, metalworking machinery, tools, bearings, paper, consumer finance, and insurance. The International Telephone and Telegraph Corporation, whose corporate name indicates its original area of operations, rapidly extended its interests into such fields as pulp and paper, glass, bakery products,

---

[2]Federal Trade Commission, *Annual Report,* 1967, pp. 45–46; and *The New York Times,* March 19, 1968, p. 61.

hotels, homebuilding, car rentals, publishing, and insurance once the idea of wide diversification had taken hold on its management. Deserving emphasis here, at any rate, is the probability that many of the absorptions referred to, including the extraordinarily rapid build-up of many of the conglomerates, would not have occurred had not the common stockholders of absorbed corporations been willing to give up their stock in exchange for common stock in the absorbing corporations.

Individual Parcels of Property

In direct common stock exchanges for incorporations of proprietorships and partnerships and in mergers, consolidations, and holding company acquisitions, corporations generally obtain arrays of assets of many kinds and values. Occasionally, however, corporations are able to obtain individual parcels of desirable property by giving some shares of their common stock in exchange. The owners of a factory site or a store building, for example, may be willing to part with it for stock, or perhaps partially for stock and partially for cash. Where it is possible to qualify such a transaction as a tax-free exchange in accordance with the federal income tax regulations, the inducement to sell for stock can, indeed, be much stronger than one to sell for cash.

Temptation toward Generosity

When a corporation buys assets with cash, the amount of cash available for other purposes is immediately reduced, and because the conservation of cash is an ever-present objective of sound financial management the corporate managers are likely to bargain closely. When, however, it buys by giving common stock in exchange, the temptation is strong to be relatively liberal in the amount of stock offered. The amount of stock that can be issued is without limit, for the articles of incorporation can be readily amended to provide for additional amounts if the quantity already authorized but unissued is insufficient for the offer. The only costs involved are the state capital stock taxes and minor printing and clerical expenses. In propositions for mergers, consolidations and holding company acquisitions, moreover, generous offers should ensure close to unanimous acceptance, thus reducing the amount of cash needed to pay off dissenters.

Getting something of value for pieces of paper (stock certificates) that a corporation can issue in unlimited amounts may appear to justify generosity of a very great degree; nevertheless, corporate managers have every reason to be just about as cautious in their bargaining when offering common stock as when offering cash. Too-generous exchanges of common stock for property will seriously dilute the ownership interests of existing stockholders, and may give rise to great difficulties in future financing.

Dilution of Ownership Interests. How a dilution of the ownership interests of existing stockholders may occur as a result of a too-liberal issue of common stock may be illustrated in terms of a merger. Let us look simply at possibilities of dilution in stockholder claims on earnings. Suppose that Corporation A has outstanding 500,000 shares of common stock of a book value of $50 a share, on which it has been earning a return after taxes of 12 percent—that is, $3 million in total, or $6 a share. It wants to acquire the operating assets of Corporation B. B has outstanding 100,000 shares of common stock with a book value of $25 a share, and it has been earning a return after taxes of 20 percent—that is, $500,000 in total, or $5 a share. In their anxiety to acquire the high earning power of B and in the expectation that through various economies of integration, the earnings of the merged companies will be substantially greater than the sum of their separate earnings, the managers of A offer one share of its stock in exchange for each share of B's. The offer is accepted unanimously by B's stockholders, and the stock of A issued to them is entered on its books at $50 a share. This means, of course, that the value of the assets taken over from B is written up on A's books by the amount of $2.5 million. Accordingly A now has outstanding 600,000 shares with a book value of $50 a share.

Now suppose that the expectations of A's managers are fulfilled. The earnings of A, the surviving corporation of the merger, rise to $4.2 million. This amounts to $7 a share, so that all stockholders of A—the original ones and those who were formerly stockholders of B—are benefited. All presumably would praise A's managers for their wisdom in having pushed the merger. But suppose that the earnings of A amount to only $3.5 million, an amount equal to the sum of the formerly separate profits of A and B. This amounts to $5.83⅓ a share. The result is favorable to the former stockholders of B, since their earnings per share rise from $5 to $5.83⅓, but this occurs at the expense of the original stockholders of A, for their earnings per share fall from $6 to $5.83⅓.

Difficulties in Future Financing. The proposition that too-generous exchanges of common stock for property may set the stage for difficulties in future financing can be illustrated in terms of the incorporation of a partnership. Since such an incorporation is likely to involve only a few people, it may appear inconsequential how much stock they decide to have their corporation issue to themselves in exchange for the partnership assets. Not so, however, should the corporation have occasion later to go to the market to raise additional funds. Let us assume that the net value of the assets of the partnership have been carried on its books at $300,000, but that the partners decide to carry them over to the corporation's books at a value of $500,000. The corporation issues them 50,000 shares of common stock of $10 par value. As it turns out, the profits of the corporation after taxes average $30,000 annually. Needing more cash, the corporate managers investigate the possibilities of selling some additional common stock to outside investors. But investment bankers and other potential investors are not likely to be interested. The rate of the corporation's earnings is only 6 percent on the book value of its common stock investment, and that is hardly high enough to induce outsiders to part with their money. An offer of the additional common stock at a price substantially below $10 a share would promise a rate of return substantially higher than 6 percent, but investors could be expected to still refuse to come in on consideration of the contingent liabilities incident to buying a par-value stock at a discount.[3]

It is probable, too, that an attempt to sell preferred stock would also fail. People interested in such investment would fear that profits would be unduly drained to maintain dividends at a given rate on the excessive amount of common stock, leaving insufficient cash and surplus for the continuance of preferred dividends in bad times. Similar fears of excessive cash drain by way of dividend payments on the common stock probably would repel prospective investors in any bond issue that the corporation might try to sell. In any case, prospective investors in either preferred stock or bonds would undoubtedly be quite suspicious of the integrity and competence of a corporation's managers (the former partners, we may assume) who had deliberately watered the common stock at the time of original issuance—that is, given it a value far in excess of the reasonable value of the assets received in exchange for it.

Justification for Some Generosity. The foregoing illustrations do not necessarily lead to the conclusion that the market value of common stock offered in direct exchanges for assets should never exceed what would be the prices of the assets in cash transactions. A more realistic conclusion is that there must be a material advantage to justify what may appear to be an excessive offer of common stock. Suppose, for example, that the owners of a store building that is outstandingly attractive to a certain corporation are willing to sell it for $1.9 million. This is recognized by the corporate managers as a fair price, but in the course of negotiations they learn that the owners would be willing to give the building in exchange for an amount of the corporation's common stock with a value of $2 million as measured by the current market price of outstanding shares. They estimate that the flotation costs of selling that much stock in a public offering would amount to around $200,000; hence, they come quickly to the conclusion that getting the building for stock worth $2 million would be a much better buy than getting it for $1.9 million in cash.

---

[3]See pp. 421–22.

Registration and Qualification

Transactions in which common stock is given for isolated parcels of property and in connection with the incorporation of proprietorships and partnerships are generally classified as private. As such, they are exempted from the registration requirements of the federal Securities Act and the qualification requirements of the state blue-sky laws. Exemption is also the rule for common stock offers related to proposed mergers, consolidations, and holding company acquisitions when there are only a few stockholders in the corporation that is to be acquired. However, when many stockholders of other corporations are approached with exchange offers, the offers become public, and are, accordingly, subject to the registration requirements of the Securities Act and in some states to the qualification provisions of the blue-sky laws.

In the Securities Act, the distinction between a "few" and a "large number" of persons to whom an offering of any kind of security is made is not clearly drawn. In close decisions, indeed, the test for a public offering tends to be more qualitative than quantitative. The investment community has generally accepted as a rule of thumb the proposition that an offering to fewer than 25 persons is private and an offering to 25 or more is public. Yet, it is also a widely accepted proposition that what is public and private depends greatly on the knowledge and investment acumen of the people to whom the offers are made. It may be expected, therefore, that an offering to 35 or 40 persons who know a great deal about the offering corporation's affairs will get by as a private transaction, but an offering to 15 or 20 persons who know little about the offeror and investment in general may be judged by the SEC to be public.

DIRECT EXCHANGES FOR SERVICES

Common stock is often given as full or partial compensation for services received by business corporations. Especially notable in this regard is the payment of common stock to promoters for their services in organizing new corporations or in arranging combinations among existing ones, to investment bankers for their services in floating new security issues, and to executive officers for their services as managers.

Compensation for Promoters

A promoter is a person who discovers what he thinks to be a favorable opportunity for a new business enterprise or for a combination of existing enterprises, and who to exploit the discovery takes steps to assemble and organize facilities, materials, men, and money. In the sense of this definition, most promoters obviously are individuals who set out to establish single businesses, which they expect to manage indefinitely as sole owners or, in combination with others as partners or as corporate stockholder-managers. But there are also outside promoters who are interested in establishing new businesses not in the expectation of remaining with them long as owners or managers but in the expectation of profiting from their very work of assembling and organizing facilities, materials, men, and money. These outsiders include professional promoters who constantly seek opportunities for new enterprises and combinations and take care of the developmental tasks of bringing them into being, as well as others who engage only occasionally in promotional activities. The occasional promoters include, in turn, individual capitalists, investment bankers, officers of existing corporations, commercial bankers, engineers, and lawyers.

What amounts of common stock are taken by promoters who expect to indefinitely run the business corporations they establish is a matter that need not detain us. The considerations are much the same as those in the incorporation of partnerships, discussed above. Especially must such promoters keep in mind the possible difficulties in future financing should they give themselves common stock of a book value far in excess of the reasonable value of the specific assets they invest—an excess presumably to compensate themselves for their promotional services.

In a different category, the outside promoter has every reason to expect fair compensation for his services. He spends a considerable amount of his own money in seeking investors willing to supply funds to the proposed enterprise, looking for and interviewing prospective managerial and technical personnel, working out tentative contracts with suppliers, perhaps taking options on factory or store sites or buildings, and so on. At the least, therefore, he expects reimbursement for such outlays, but in addition he demands a substantial reward for his intangible contribution in setting the stage for a going concern. But the big problem is to determine what this contribution is worth. Should the enterprise turn out to be eminently successful, a high value of the contribution would be proved, but should it fail after a short term of operations, the promoter's contribution would be proved worthless. The outcome can be known only with the passing years, but the promoter's compensation must be fixed at once if the enterprise is to be launched at all.

What the promoter gets, therefore, is likely to depend very largely on how effective he is in persuading prospective investors and prospective managerial personnel of the soundness and the good profit-making potential of the projected enterprise. If these people are anxious to go ahead, they will surely be inclined to reward him generously, but if only lukewarm they may feel that all he deserves is reimbursement for his out-of-pocket expenses. In any event, the more willing he is to take common stock as compensation, the more generously is he likely to be treated. New enterprises usually have great difficulties in raising enough cash for all their spending requirements; accordingly, opportunities to gain the benefits of promoters' services in direct exchange for common stock are likely to be much appreciated.

Compensation for Investment Bankers

Sometimes, investment bankers are willing to take common stock as partial compensation for their services in underwriting securities issues or in selling them on best-efforts terms, especially when the issues themselves are common stocks. Such an arrangement is rare in flotations handled by the larger investment banking houses, but is frequently met in underwritings by smaller houses. Thus, it tends to be limited to flotations handled for corporations of small and medium sizes.

In a transaction of this kind, the cash commission is still likely to be substantial as a percentage of the gross proceeds, but the banker demands a portion of the common stock issue as additional compensation. Even though corporate managers may feel that these demands are exorbitant, they may acquiesce if a lack of adequate cash threatens the very survival of their enterprise, and if they do not have access to alternative sources of supply. The banker, in turn, may sell his allotment along with the balance of the issue, thus immediately realizing the additional compensation in cash, or may hold it for his own account as a continuing investment.

In its special study of the securities markets, published in 1963, the SEC found that, in addition to cash compensation, stock or options to buy stock were given to investment bankers in 34.7 percent of the common stock issues of more than $300,000 registered in 1960 for cash sale through bankers. In 1961, the percentage was 41.6 of those registered for cash sale through bankers. For issues of $300,000 or less offered for cash sale through bankers, the percentages were 46 in 1960 and 70.8 in 1961. The SEC noted that income tax considerations often prompt investment bankers to make some payment for stock or options in order to try to qualify their acquisitions as investments rather than as compensation. It also pointed out that, in some instances, the investment bankers got stock or options in connection with interim financing that preceded the making of public offerings. Referring to stock acquired by underwriters in some of the 22 common stock offerings for cash in the 1959–61 period selected for intensive study, it said:

> It is not unusual for an underwriting firm to purchase a substantial block of stock from the issuer or the selling stockholders prior to or simultaneous with the offering, at prices significantly below the offering price. In connection with the Arco offering of 170,000 shares at a price of $5 per share, Kletz, who managed the underwriting, purchased 10,000 additional shares

at 50 cents per share. In the Gremar offering of 100,000 shares at $4.25 a share, Blauner, the managing underwriter, purchased 7,500 shares for [*sic*—read "from"] the president and sole stockholder at a price of $1 per share. In 4 others of the 22 new issues, the managing underwriters purchased cheap stock, which was placed either in account of the firm or principals of the firm and their associates. In all six cases in which cheap stock was purchased, the purchase price was less than 50 percent of the offering price and in two cases it was less than 10 percent.

On the other hand, the SEC noted the stated policy of some investment banking houses not to accept cheap stock or options as compensation for their services, and added: "By and large, these were the larger and older firms, which had comparatively rigorous standards as to the kind of issues which they would handle."[4]

Compensation for Managerial Services

Shares of common stock have often been given in generous quantities as supplemental compensation or bonuses to the top executives of many of our larger corporations. However, the practice has become much less common than it was. By reason of tax-saving possibilities, it has been largely supplanted by the giving of stock options to executives. But such companies as General Motors, Du Pont, General Electric, Federated Department Stores, and Container Corporation still have provisions for stock bonuses in addition to stock option plans.

Competition among corporations for executive talent of high quality always tends to be extremely keen, for, as is often said, such talent is all too rare. It is not surprising, therefore, that bidding for top-quality executives often gets quickly into high figures. Such heady bidding convinces most boards of directors that they must be satisfied with somewhat less talented executives, but some hope to remain in the running by offering common stock or stock options in addition to cash. The board of a given corporation may decide that a cash salary of $300,000 for a most desirable president would put too great a strain on the corporation's cash resources, but that a salary of $200,000 in cash plus common stock worth $100,000 could be safely managed.

As in direct exchanges of common stock for noncash property, corporations are subject to temptations toward generosity when they find it possible to use common stock to buy high-quality executive services. There is a temptation to think of the issuance of common stock as costless, except for issuance taxes and a few other minor expenses. Certainly it is from the standpoint of cash drain, but certainly it is not from the standpoint of the interests of existing stockholders

---

[4]Securities and Exchange Commission, *Report of Special Study of the Securities Markets* (House Doc. No. 95, Pt. 1, 88th Cong., 1st sess. [Washington, D.C.: U.S. Government Printing Office, 1963]), pp. 506–8, 510–11, 619.

and the possibilities of success in future financing. Insufficient weight may be given to the dilution of other stockholders' ownership interests by the issuance of common stock to executives, and also to the probability that the threat of continued dilution will weaken the attractiveness of the common stock in future public offerings.

All this does not mean that it is bad policy to pay executives partially in common stock. Whether the policy is good or bad depends on the circumstances of the individual corporation. If a man is really worth a given amount of cash plus a given array of claims to voting power, dividends, and assets, as represented by a certain amount of common stock—determined, let us say, by competition for him in the market—that is what he should get. But corporations often do a poor job in defending human valuations of this kind when they explain to other stockholders, labor leaders, congressional committees, and the public at large that stock is given to executives to induce them to exert their best efforts for the corporations. They thereby imply that the executives are worth only the cash portion of their salaries, but that this portion would be insufficient to induce them to exert their best efforts. Moreover, generous cash-and-stock salary and bonus payments—or, for that matter, generous salaries in cash exclusively—always justify suspicions of bad policy when they are determined by the very executives who receive them, such as when they constitute a majority of the board of directors and when the board, because of a wide scattering of stockholdings, is self-perpetuating.

Registration and Qualification

The giving of common stock for the services of promoters and executives is ordinarily a private transaction not subject to the registration requirements of the federal Securities Act or to the qualification requirements of the state blue-sky laws. On the other hand, if common stock given to investment bankers is to be reoffered by them in interstate commerce to many buyers, registration according to the terms of the Securities Act is required, and the qualification provisions of the blue-sky laws generally apply. When, however, the common stock received by investment bankers as compensation is simply a portion of an issue for which they are making a public offering, the registration and qualification of the whole issue automatically take care of the portion allotted to them.

OFFERINGS BY OPTIONS

As a means of providing partial or supplemental compensation to investment bankers and executive personnel, the issuance of *stock options* is much more popular than the giving of common stock itself. Promoters, too, are often rewarded with options in lieu of common stock or in addition to it; and options often make possible arrangements of greatest convenience with individual capitalists and institutional investors that are willing to advance substantial amounts of money on what is essentially an equity basis.

Nature of Options

A stock option is a contract in which a corporation agrees to sell a specified number of shares of its common stock to a designated person or institution at a stated price. Usually the contract stipulates a time period, such as 2, 5, or 10 years, within which the option must be exercised. It states that at the end of the indicated time period the option becomes void. Options are usually nontransferable, so that only the person or institution named in the contract can exercise the right to buy.

Disadvantageous Aspects of Options

Stock options are an uncertain means of financing. If the market price of a stock rises to and continues at levels above the price designated in the options, the option holders will surely buy, but just when they will buy—how long they will hold out for still better market prices—is problematical. Corporations that are growing rapidly and that, accordingly, tend to suffer a chronic shortage of cash welcome the additional amounts that flow in through the exercise of options; but those whose cash resources are already adequate may be able to use the inflowing cash only uneconomically. If, for example, a corporation with sufficient cash retires bonds with cash received through the exercise of options, it loses the advantages of trading on the equity. If the existing stock had been earning a return of, say, 12 percent, and the bonds carried an interest rate of 5 percent, issuance of the new stock would mean a dilution of the earning power of the old. There is also uncertainty in the possibility that the market price of outstanding stock may never rise above the option price, so that the options prove to be no source of cash at all.

Diution of the ownership interests of existing stockholders always stands as a probable disadvantage of the use of stock options, not only in the sense of using cash uneconomically as illustrated above, but in the more general sense of weakening claims to voting power, assets, and earnings. For illustration, assume that the option price of a stock is $50 a share and that the market price goes to $80. The market evaluates the claims attaching to each share at $80, and the existing stockholder has reason to feel that his ownership interests per share are worth that much. But along come the option holders with their privilege of buying equal shares in ownership interests for only $50, and sales to them obviously reduce the per-share interests of the other stockholders—a reduction that, if not offset by other market forces, should be matched by a decline in the market value of the stock.

The issuance of stock options may also have unfavorable repercussions on common stock financing through other channels. A corporation that has been generous in issuing options is likely to find its existing stockholders and the investing public as a whole much less interested in buying new offerings than they might otherwise be. As many of these people understand the theory of dilution, they can be expected to make their investment decisions accordingly. Why, they may ask themselves, should they buy new stock at $70 or $80 a share when sizable sales to option holders at $50 and resales by them will exert significant downward pressures on the market price? That investors should know about the danger of dilution through the exercise of options is indicated in the requirements of the federal Securities Act. Registration statements and prospectuses filed in accordance with that legislation must state what options the corporation has already issued or is to issue in connection with the security for which the registration is made, their terms, and the names and addresses of all persons who have received or are to receive more than 10 percent of the total.

Popularity of Options

Considering the potential disadvantages to corporations in the use of options, one may wonder why they have been so popular. A reason applicable in some cases is undoubtedly the idea that the giving of options is a costless procedure, but the earlier discussion about the giving of stock itself for services has indicated how erroneous this notion can be. Another reason is compulsion of a sort. Corporate managements find themselves in weak bargaining positions, and they give options to get what they want though they would much prefer not to do so. This must be true in many instances where options are given to promoters and investment bankers. Still another reason, apparent in at least a small minority of situations, is self-serving, as when corporate officers who are directors with de facto independence of the stockholders authorize the issuance of options to themselves ostensibly as partial compensation for their services. But surely the most important reason must be a conviction of corporate managements that they are getting full value for the options—that the disadvantages of options are fairly balanced by the worth of the money and services acquired.

Options as Compensation

Compensation for Promoters and Bankers. Sometimes stock options are the sole reward received by promoters for their services in developing new enterprises and combinations. More commonly, they are received in addition to cash—cash in an amount at least sufficient to reimburse the promoters for their out-of-pocket expenses—or in addition to some shares of the common stock itself, or in addition to both cash and some common stock. When stock options are given to investment bankers for their services in connection with the flotation of securities, almost invariably they are supplemental to cash commissions. In some cases, the bargaining position of promoters and bankers is so strong that they demand and get stock options sufficient to enable them to buy control in the corporations involved. If the ventures turn out successfully, they can exercise the options and get control; if the ventures are failures, they simply allow the options to expire.

In the statistics of noncash compensation reported by the SEC in its special study of the securities markets, published in 1963, no distinction was made between the sale of cheap stock to investment bankers and their taking of options. However, for the 22 issues of common stock offered for cash sale in the period 1959–61 that the SEC selected for intensive study it found that "the managing underwriter or persons connected with it" obtained options in 10. In only 1 of these 10 instances, however, were the options exercisable at a price below the public offering price. The SEC described this case as follows.

> This was the Custom Components offering of 165,000 shares at an offering price of $3. In this instance, the principal stockholder of the issuer granted to the managing underwriter, Manufacturers Securities Corp., warrants to purchase up to 16,500 shares at a price of $1 per share. The grant of the warrants was conditioned upon a successful offering, 1,000 warrants being granted for every 10,000 shares sold by the underwriter. For these warrants, the underwriter paid 1 mill each, or a total of $16.50.

The report of the SEC then continued as follows.

> Although there was only one example among the 22 issues, the granting of warrants to the underwriter exercisable below the offering price was not at all uncommon during 1959–61. For example, in the offering of 150,000 shares of the common stock of Admiral Plastics Corp. on January 11, 1960, at $4, the managing underwriters received options to purchase 10,000 shares at 75 cents per share. Similarly, the managing underwriter of Astrex, Inc., which offered 100,000 shares to the public on September 20, 1960, at $4, received warrants to purchase 12,500 shares at a price of $2.25 per share. The study of underwriters' compensation conducted by the New York Stock Exchange revealed that out of 186 issues in 1960 that were reviewed, 36 (or 19.5 percent) involved warrants exercisable below the offering price, and of the 342 offerings in 1961, 61 (or 17.8 percent) involved warrants of this type. The percentage for the first quarter of 1962 dropped steeply to 1.7 percent.[5]

Compensation for Executives. The granting of stock options to corporate executives as supplements to their cash salaries has had

---

[5] *Ibid,* p. 507.

enormous popularity in most of the post-World War II period. Thousands of corporations have set up programs for the awarding of option privileges to their officers and other key employees. There was some cooling of enthusiasm after adoption of the Revenue Act of 1964 because of its reduction in the tax-saving potential of options, but no widespread reversal of attitude. Continued popularity is surely indicated by the size of option figures reported by leading corporations. As of the end of 1967, for example, General Electric reported that it had executive options outstanding for the purchase of 767,207 shares, with 915,656 additional shares available for further option grants. United States Steel reported these two categories at 1,006,700 and 558,775 shares, respectively, and Scott Paper reported outstanding executive options for the purchase of 1,034,878 shares.[6] Although for the individual corporation the shares offered for purchase on option typically amount to only a very small fraction of total shares outstanding, generosity in granting options to executives sometimes seems to get out of hand, so that dangers of dilution are multiplied. The SEC has cited two instances, as follows.

> . . .Seventeen of the 22 issuers instituted stock-option plans shortly before or at the time of their public offerings. A comparison of the number of shares of outstanding stock of some of the issuers with the number of shares subject to option reflects the importance of the stock-option plans. For example, Geophysics' stock-option plans covered 143,209 shares, or over 35 percent of its outstanding stock, and Universal Electronics Laboratories Corp's. stock-option plan covered 60,000 shares, or 31 percent of its outstanding stock.[7]

Given the idea that stock bonuses, options, or something else must be used as supplements to cash salaries in the fierce competition for executives of top quality, it is not difficult to understand why options have generally been preferred. The reason has been clear: the relatively gentle treatment in federal income tax regulations of profits from the sale of stock obtained under option—a gentleness that largely remains despite the tightening of the Revenue Act of 1964. If options satisfy the conditions for qualified options under the Internal Revenue Code, the executive has no income to report on receiving them, and, much more important, he can limit to the relatively low long-term capital gains rate the federal tax he must pay on whatever profits he earns on the sale of stock obtained under options, provided that he holds the stock for at least three years. By contrast, if he receives shares of common stock itself as supplementary compensation, he must report them as taxable income at their fair

---

[6]Annual reports: General Electric, p. 35; United States Steel, p. 26; and Scott Paper, p. 27.

[7]Securities and Exchange Commission, *Report of Special Study*, *op. cit.*, p. 492.

market value—income taxable at the steeply progressive rates applicable to ordinary income.

Illustration. Suppose, for example, that Jones, a man of great executive abilities, has the pleasant task of deciding which of two liberal offers for his services would be most rewarding in the long run. Corporation A offers him a cash salary of $200,000 and shares of common stock that have a fair market value of $100,000. Corporation B offers a cash salary of the same amount plus options to buy 8,000 shares of its common stock at $38 a share, its current fair market value. At the moment, then, the additional compensation that B is offering appears to be valueless. But prospects are excellent that within a few years the market value of B's stock will rise to at least $48. Jones would thus have good reasons to anticipate being able to derive a long-term capital gain of $80,000 by buying 8,000 shares at $38 for a total of $304,000 through the exercise of the options, holding the stock for at least 3 years, and then selling it at $48 for a total of $384,000. Should Jones, therefore, be confident in the gain prospect, he would surely strongly favor B's offer. Assuming that he is married, has 3 dependent children, has no income from other sources, and has deductible expenses of $20,000, his individual income tax (computed at the rates in effect in 1968[8]) on a salary of $200,000 together with shares of stock with a market value of $100,000 would be $164,880, leaving him with after-tax income of $135,120. In relation to B's offer, the tax on the $200,000 salary would be $95,310, leaving him with after-tax income of $104,690. But if he later derived a profit of $80,000, the tax on it at the long-term capital gains rate would be only $20,000, leaving him with after-tax income of $60,000 to be added to the $95,310 cleared earlier.

Conditions for Qualified Options. For a corporation to be in a position to make its offer attractive, and for the executive to be certain that his gains will be taxable only as long-term capital gains, both the corporation and the executive must be careful that all option transactions satisfy the rules set for qualified options in the Internal Revenue Code. These rules are chiefly as follows.

1. The options must be granted under a plan approved by the stockholders within 12 months before or after its adoption.
2. The plan must be limited to not more than 10 years and must state the classes of employees eligible to receive options.
3. Each employee who receives an option must actually be employed by the corporation, its parent corporation, or a subsidiary at the time he receives it and *continuously* thereafter up to at least three months before exercising it.

---

[8]Both here and in the remainder of the illustration, however, the special surcharge of 10 percent enacted in June, 1968, and applicable to both the individual tax rates and the capital gains rate, is ignored.

4. The option must provide that it is to be exercised within five years after being granted, that it is nontransferable except on account of death, and that, subject to some exceptions, it may not be exercisable while the employee has unused prior options to buy at higher prices.
5. The option price must be at least equal to the fair market value of the stock at the time the option is granted.
6. At the time the option is granted, the combined ownership interests of the employee, his spouse, and certain other designated relatives must not exceed 5 percent of the value or voting power of the corporation's stock.

For the sixth rule, ownership interests include options to buy stock. This rule further provides that if the new option would cause the ownership interests to go above 5 percent, the option may still be qualified for stock purchases within the 5 percent limit. On the other hand, a limit to ownership interests of 10 percent is set for corporations with total stockholders' equity of $1 million or less, and proportionately between 5 and 10 percent for those with stockholders' equity between $1 million and $2 million.

Evaluation of Granting Options to Executives. What was said earlier on the appropriateness of corporate policies of giving common stock as partial compensation to executives is clearly applicable to the giving of stock options. The possibilities of dilution and of difficulties in future common stock financing should surely be carefully weighed by boards of directors in considering the grant of options. But if access at a cost to claims to voting power, dividends, and assets, in addition to cash compensation, is not beyond the worth of the services of particular executives, there certainly is every justification for giving it. Nevertheless, justification is hardly proved by claims that stock options will prod executives to exert their best efforts in order to cause the market price of the stock to rise and thus to increase the value of the options.

Options for Individual and Institutional Investors

Newly established corporations, operating corporations of small and medium sizes, and others that have little or no access to the general markets for outside equity funds are sometimes able to acquire such funds direct from individual and institutional investors through arrangements in which stock options play a significant role. The individual and institutional investors include wealthy capitalists, partners and members of investment banking houses, officers of corporations other than those actually seeking the funds, trustees of family estates, pension funds, investment companies, so-called venture capital firms, investment banking houses that may be interested in investing for their own accounts rather than for resale as in normal underwriting procedures, and nonfinancial business corporations that hold cash in excess of their need for their own customary operations. The list of investors is rather long, but the total amounts of money they are willing and able to make available on an equity basis are quite small in relation to the volume of requests they are likely to get from the classes of corporations mentioned—hence the much-heard plaint of a chronic shortage of outside equity funds for small business.

When individual and institutional investors advance equity funds, they seek every possible tax saving. The investor wants his rewards to be taxable chiefly as long-term capital gains rather than as ordinary income. His advances to a corporation, therefore, might be made entirely in the form of loans, but he would receive from the corporation not only its notes or bonds as evidence of its obligation to pay but also options for the purchase of common stock. Because he would probably want to be in a position to take control of the corporation to protect his investment, he would be likely to demand options for sufficient shares to give control, and at a total price not exceeding the amount of the loans. Then, should things go badly he could demand repayment of the loans and take as much on them as the corporation would be able to pay, thereby minimizing his losses. Should he think the prospects good, but not with the existing management, he could simultaneously call the loans and exercise the options, paying for the stock with the loan repayments, and then substitute his own management. Should all go well, he could exercise the options, with or without calling the loans, hold the stock for more than six months, and then sell for a profit that would be taxable as a long-term capital gain.[9]

One might inquire why the investor would not, in the first place, take a sufficient amount of common stock to give him control—why, when advancing what would really be equity funds despite the loan technique, he would not take an equity security. The fact is that in making advances of equity funds to the classes of corporations we are considering individual and institutional investors often do take common stock, or preferred stock plus common stock options, or preferred stock convertible at the investors' option into common stock. As a rule, the capital gains goal can be thus achieved as well as in the manner described. But the loan and stock option procedure has at least two advantages over the immediate taking of equity securities. One of these advantages is obvious. Should the investor want to pull out because things are going badly, his claim for loan repayment would rank ahead of the claims of stockholders—that is, the original owners of the corporation to which he granted the loans. The other

[9]An alternative procedure would be for the investor to have the corporation issue him bonds convertible into common stock at his option. This would give him about the same degree of flexibility as the stock option arrangement.

is that interest paid to him by the corporation on his loans—which, incidentally, would probably be charged at a moderate rate, such as 5 or 6 percent—would be deductible by the corporation as an expense in its income tax return, whereas dividends paid on stock that he might have taken would not be deductible.

OFFERINGS BY STOCK PURCHASE WARRANTS

Quite similar to stock options in character, but differing in use, are stock purchase warrants. Like an option, a stock purchase warrant is a contract in which a corporation agrees to sell a designated number of its common stock shares at a stipulated price to the person or institution that the warrant is issued to, and sometimes to anybody else to whom the original holder may assign it. Thus, three kinds of contracts for the delivery of common stock at stated prices are recognized: (1) subscription warrants whereby existing stockholders are privileged to buy on a pro rata basis, as analyzed in Chapter 19; (2) stock options, as discussed in the preceding division of this chapter; and (3) stock purchase warrants, to be discussed in this division. In practice, the three designations are sometimes used interchangeably; nevertheless, restricting the use of each term to a specific class of transactions, as indicated above, should doubtless aid understanding.

Warrants for Preferred Stockholders and Bondholders

Sometimes corporations attach stock purchase warrants to their issues of preferred stock or bonds or both to enhance the salability of these kinds of securities. Weaknesses in a corporation's credit standing or earnings record may preclude a sale of preferred stock or bonds on what it would consider satisfactory terms; accordingly, it casts about to find a sweetener or two to add to its proposed issue. Stock purchase warrants serve as such a sweetener. The prospective buyer of preferred stock is offered not only a dividend at a given rate and the other ordinary rights of preferred stockholders but also the right to buy at a stated price a certain number of shares of common stock. Or a similar right to buy is offered to the prospective buyer of bonds in addition to a promise of interest at a designated rate and the repayment of principal at a specific time. Stock purchase warrants are said to give the preferred stockholder or bondholder a speculative interest in the progress of a corporation over and above his ordinary interests; thus, it is thought that many investors who would not buy for the ordinary interests alone may be persuaded to buy the package of combined interests.

The price at which common stock is offered in stock purchase warrants is usually well above the market price prevailing at the time the warrants are issued. If a corporation is unable to sell preferred stock or bonds without adding sweeteners, the market price of its common stock almost surely is much lower than the level where the corporation thinks it ought to be, and it would not want to sell common at that level. Whether or not, therefore, it will ever sell any common through the exercise of the stock purchase warrants depends on the subsequent behavior of the market price of the stock. There is some danger that because it faces difficulty in selling the preferred stock or bonds it will be overgenerous in the terms of its stock purchase warrants, so that if the market price of the common does rise substantially and the warrants are exercised, the ownership of other common stockholders will be unreasonably diluted. To provide some protection on this score, warrants often set a scale of rising prices at which, from period to period, the common stock can be bought—for example, at one level during the first five years from the date of the issuance of the preferred stock or bonds, at a higher level during the next five years, and so on. On the other side, however, it can be argued that if a corporation is enabled to carry on in a difficult situation by means of money supplied by buyers of preferred stock or bonds, and if it is quite successful in carrying on, these selfsame buyers deserve to be amply rewarded.[10]

Other Uses of Warrants

Speculative Interests of Other Investors. Since corporations often succeed in adding to the attractiveness of their preferred stock and bond issues by attaching stock purchase warrants, one might expect that warrants would also be helpful toward persuading investors to supply funds through other channels. Indeed, this is so. Especially popular in recent years has been the corporation issuance of stock purchase warrants to institutional investors, especially life insurance companies, as partial compensation for long-term loans privately arranged. In such transactions, the institutional investors get regular claims to interest and principal as creditors, plus the frosting of speculative interests in the market performance of the borrowers' common stocks.

More peculiar have been some other uses to which warrants have recently been put by a few imaginative corporations, especially in the rather hectic 1966–68 scramble for long-term funds. Such uses are: selling units, consisting of a share of common stock and a warrant to buy an additional share or fraction; offering warrants with cash, other securities, or both as packages in exchange for outstanding securities of other corporations sought for merger; and even selling warrants directly for cash (or pretending to do so) by offering units of bonds

---

[10]For a further discussion of the use of stock purchase warrants in connection with preferred stock issues, see pp. 597–98; in connection with bond issues, see pp. 769–70.

and warrants, with each separately priced although not separately purchasable.

Warrants as Dividends. Peculiar, too, are the occasional instances in which corporations distribute warrants as dividends—peculiar because they hardly qualify as dividends in any real sense of the word.[11] It is rather difficult to say what a corporation accomplishes by such a distribution, although one can see possibilities of some benefit to the stockholder. If the corporation really wants to sell additional stock to its existing stockholders, it can do so at any time by making a rights offering. But dividends in warrants may contribute to stockholder happiness at the expense of speculators. If speculators bid up the price of warrants in the market, if the stockholders sell their warrants, and if the warrants are never exercised because the stock price does not go high enough to make this advantageous, the stockholders succeed in getting some of the speculators' cash "for free." But if the warrants are exercised by the speculators, what the stockholders got in selling them turns out to be compensation for the dilution in ownership interests that they suffer.

Warrants in Reorganizations. As the term is used in finance, a corporate *reorganization* is a comprehensive recasting of the financial structure of a corporation, necessitated by actual or threatened insolvency, and designed to rehabilitate it so that it can continue operating. In a reorganization, creditors and stockholders are subject to strong pressure to yield some of their rights, for the alternative is the liquidation of assets and the paying off of claims in order of priority. Most reorganizations of corporations that have more than a few creditors and stockholders are reorganizations in bankruptcy effected in accordance with the provisions of the federal bankruptcy statutes. The general rule in reorganizations in bankruptcy is that acceptance of a plan of reorganization by the holders of two thirds of the claims of any class of creditors makes it binding on all the creditors of that class, provided that the plan is also approved by the court that has jurisdiction. Also, with similar court approval, acceptance of a plan by holders of one half of the shares of any class of stock makes it binding on all the stockholders of that class. Accordingly, some creditors and stockholders who may prefer liquidation may be compelled by law to go the other way and yield some of their rights.

In a reorganization, then, the goal is to reshuffle the claims of creditors and stockholders in such a way that the rehabilitated corporation will be able to continue operations without further imminent danger of insolvency and, indeed, with a fair credit standing. Important to this goal is the scaling down or elimination of creditors' and

[11] At any rate, the author finds no justification for including such distributions in his classification of dividends in a later chapter. See pp. 639–41.

stockholders' claims to periodic payments of interest and dividends, as well as claims to the principal of obligations by short-term creditors and bondholders, or to unpaid accumulated dividends by preferred stockholders. Accordingly, plans of reorganization call for such adjustments as reduction of the interest rate on bonds, making some or all of this interest contingent on earnings, reducing the principal of one or more classes of debts, getting creditors of one or more classes to take preferred or common stock in exchange for their claims, having preferred stockholders give up their claims to unpaid accumulated dividends, having them give up their cumulative preferred for noncumulative preferred or common, and requiring common stockholders to give up their holdings for a much smaller number of shares.

The strongest claimants, such as mortgage bondholders and other secured creditors, are called on to make the least sacrifice, if any, and the residual claimants—the common stockholders—make the greatest sacrifice. Indeed, such a treatment of claims may be said to be required by the absolute priority rule, which has, in effect, been established for corporate reorganizations by the Supreme Court. By this rule, the respective classes of stockholders, as junior claimants, can be permitted to participate in a reorganized corporation only if the rights of the senior claimants, in the order of their priority, are fully taken care of.

All of this leads up to the use of stock purchase warrants. Warrants are occasionally given in corporate reorganizations to fully or partially replace claims that must be given up. These claims may appear to be worthless on the basis of the present liquidating values of the assets, but not necessarily on the basis of the value the assets might prove to have should the reorganization be successful with the earning power of the corporation restored. By means of stock purchase warrants, a stake in this potentiality of restored earning power can be given. If earnings are restored, and the market price of the common stock rises accordingly, the holders of warrants can buy in on favorable terms. If these developments do not take place, the worthlessness of the holders' original claims is definitely established.

Decisions about the classes of claimants who are to get warrants, if any, depend on the severity of the situation facing the corporation that seeks to reorganize. In a less severe case, unsecured creditors may get preferred stock, the preferred stockholders may get common stock, and the common stockholders may have to be satisfied with warrants. In a more severe one, the unsecured creditors may get common stock, and both the preferred and common stockholders may only receive warrants, with the preferred getting a more generous allotment than the common. In situations of even greater severity, it should be added, the common stockholders, or both the preferred and common stockholders, may receive nothing. In some reorganizations, warrants have been given in partial satisfaction of claims. For example, preferred stockholders have received some common stock plus warrants to buy some additional shares of common.

EMPLOYEE STOCK-OWNERSHIP PROGRAMS

Apart from the stock given to corporate executives as bonuses and the very large amounts offered to them on the basis of restricted options, substantial volumes of common stock are sold direct to employees outside the executive classes, as well as indirectly for the benefit of both executives and the rank and file of employees.

Direct offerings of common stock are made by many corporations in stock purchase plans and savings plans to the general run of their employees or to particular classes, such as salaried workers or employees not covered by collective bargaining contracts with labor unions. In both kinds of plans, officers and other key employees are included in many instances, and in others they are excluded. If excluded, the principal reason is the availability of executive stock options to these people. In a stock purchase plan, the corporation's stock is generally offered to employees at a price below the current market value, and the corporation absorbs all costs of administering the plan. In a savings plan, the corporation usually *contributes* shares of its common stock (or cash to buy shares), often in relation to the amount of its profits, in addition to picking up the tab for administrative expenses.

Indirect sales of stock for the benefit of employees occur in pension plans. While some of the savings plans just referred to are really pension plans in that they provide for distributions of accumulations to each participating employee on an annuity basis after his retirement, the great mass of corporation pension plans are not of this profit-sharing variety but instead call for regular corporate contributions regardless of the amount of profits, and invariably provide for distribution on an annuity basis following the employee's retirement. The point here is that corporate contributions to pension funds not of the profit-sharing kind are often invested largely or partially in the corporations' own common stocks. According to SEC data, the book value of corporations' own common stock held by their pension funds at the end of 1966 (including pension funds of the profit-sharing variety) amounted to $1,957 million out of a total book value of common stock holdings of $26,693 million, with the respective market values at $3,340 million and $35,556 million.[12]

---

[12]This refers to assets held by "trusteed" pension funds as distinct from "insured" funds. For insured funds, corporate cash contributions are turned over to and invested by life insurance companies which contract to pay the pensions much as they pay benefits on other kinds of insurance and annuity contracts. For the report on trusteed funds, see Securities and Exchange Commission, *Statistical Bulletin*, August, 1967, pp. 24–29.

Although some of the common stock sold to employees in stock purchase plans and acquired for pension funds is bought in the open market, much of it is previously unissued stock, and, of course, the sale of unissued stock is a means of corporate financing as well as a means of providing fringe benefits to employees.

The terms on which common stock is offered in employee stock purchase plans are generally tailored to make the offerings qualified stock options, so that the tax concessions of the Internal Revenue Code, as described earlier in this chapter, can be gained. Likewise, the pension programs are patterned to make them qualified plans eligible for other kinds of tax concessions under the Code.

Development of Stock Purchase and Savings Plans

Although the beginnings of employee stock-ownership plans are dated from the plan set up in 1901 by the newly formed United States Steel Corporation, the most enthusiastic early development came in the 1920's, particularly in the later years of that decade, in line with the stock market boom of that period. Employee plans were widely hailed as the dawning of a new day in labor–management relationships. The employee was to become a capitalist, to be sympathetic toward the problems of management, and, presumably, to tone down his demands as a laborer. It should have been apparent, however, that ownership of one or two or three thousand dollars' worth of stock, paying dividends of, perhaps, 6 percent, could hardly cause many employees to neglect their interests as workers in favor of their interests as capitalists. At any rate, the stock market crash of 1929 put an end to many of the more grandiose expectations of the plans, as well as to many of the plans themselves.

Beginning about 1950, however, a renewed interest in employee stock-ownership plans developed, strongly encouraged no doubt, as in the 1920's, by the sustained upward push in stock prices. While most of the plans established in the 1950's and early 1960's, like those that mushroomed in the 1920's, have been straight employee-purchase plans, a substantial shift in preference toward plans of the savings or thrift variety was apparent in the late 1950's and the early 1960's. In a study made in 1961, the New York Stock Exchange found that 114 of its listed corporations had purchase plans in which 530,000 employees were participating, 80 firms had savings plans with participation by 753,000 employees, and 39 corporations had profit-sharing plans in which 260,000 employees were participating. In all, about one fifth of the listed corporations had an employee-ownership plan of one of these three types, and by industry the leaders were public utility corporations and producers of petroleum and natural gas.[13] In a study published in 1967, the Bankers Trust Company

[13]New York Stock Exchange, *The Exchange*, September, 1961, pp. 17–18.

of New York reported that one out of nine of the corporations listed on the New York Stock Exchange had savings plans in operation, a large majority having been established within the preceding 10 years.[14]

Features of Employee Stock-Ownership Plans

Stock Purchase Plans. Taking a crosscut view, the principal features of employee stock purchase plans are the following.

1. From time to time, perhaps annually, the corporation makes an offering of a specific number of shares to its employees.

2. The employee must have some minimum period of service to the corporation, such as six months or a year, to be eligible to subscribe.

3. Each employee is limited in the number of shares of each offering to which he may subscribe; the limitations is based on criteria such as wage and salary levels, years of employment, and type of work done, or a combination of criteria. In many plans, subscriptions may not exceed 10 percent of the employee's annual salary or wages. Often, the eligible employee may not subscribe to a new offering if he has not completed payments on an earlier subscription.

4. The price at which the stock is offered is not less than 85 percent of the market price at the time of offering *or* at the time of purchase, so that the tax concessions of the Internal Revenue Code will not be lost.[15]

5. Payment is normally to be made in installments by payroll deductions. In some plans, the employee may add cash payments from other sources.

6. The payment is to be completed within a period generally varying between six months and two years.

7. While the employee's payment is being accumulated, the corporation normally pays interest on the balances in his account.

8. The employee may cancel his purchase commitment at any

---

[14] *1967 Study of Employee Savings Plans* (New York: Bankers Trust Company, 1967), p. 3. This excellent report presents a comprehensive analysis of the plans in general as well as specific details about 132 plans.

[15] It was indicated previously that for qualified stock options granted to officers and key employees the offering price must be not less than the market value of the stock at the time options are granted in order to have profits on subsequent sales of stock obtained by option treated as long-term capital gains. But offerings of stock to employees in stock purchase plans (including offerings to officers if included in the plans) can satisfy the conditions for qualified stock options if the offering price is not less than 85 percent of the market price when the stock is offered or when it is bought by the employee. To the extent, however, that profits on subsequent resales of the optioned stock represent differences between the option price paid by the employee and the market price at the time the stock was offered him, they are treated as ordinary income, and only profits in excess of these amounts are treated as capital gains. It should be mentioned, also, that the holding period for stock bought in employee stock-ownership plans for long-term capital gains qualification is six months from the time of purchase *and* two years from the time the buying privilege was granted.

time. He is entitled to the balance in his account, including interest as credited, and he may take this in cash or use it to buy outright the smaller number of shares it will cover. A cancellation of the commitment and the settlement are usually handled in the same way for an employee who quits or is fired.

9. Stock certificates are delivered to the employee only when he has paid his subscription in full.

Savings Plans. The features of savings plans differ in important details from those of stock purchase plans because of some differences in goals but especially because the corporations make substantial contributions to the accumulations of the savings plans. Again, let us have a cross-section view, as follows.

1. The corporation announces that for the year it will accept employee contributions to the savings fund up to a stated total amount, and that it itself will add to the fund amounts equal to 20, 25, or 50 percent or some other percentage of the employee contributions. Proposed employee contributions are scaled down if they exceed the total stipulated by the corporation.

2. To be eligible, the employee must have some minimum period of service with the corporation.

3. How much the individual employee may contribute is governed by criteria similar to the criteria of stock purchase plans. A common rule is that an employee's participation may not exceed 6 percent of his annual wage or salary.

4. The employee's contribution is made only by payroll deductions.

5. All the employee contributions are invested immediately in U.S. savings bonds or other Treasury obligations, the corporation's common stock, or a combination of Treasury obligations and the corporation's stock, such as 50-50, or in some instances in a variety of stocks or bonds. In many plans, the employee is privileged to choose proportions to be invested in Treasury obligations and the corporation's stock, and in some he may choose among two, three, or four different portfolios. Because of the immediate investment of the payroll deductions, the question of the corporation's paying interest on balances in employee accounts does not arise. On the other hand, the employee is entitled to interest and dividends received on the securities held for his account.

6. The corporation's contribution is made in shares of its own common stock or in cash for the purchase of shares of its stock.

7. Employees who wish to withdraw from the savings plan or who sever their employment, voluntarily or involuntarily, take out of the fund whatever securities their own contributions have bought, usually with no sharing or reduced sharing in the corporation's contribution.

8. For those who stay, there is a holding period of several years. At its expiration, a distribution of the securities acquired, including

the stock contributed by the corporation, is made. Thus, the securities acquired five years ago may be distributed at the end of this year, those acquired four years ago, at the end of next year, and so on.

Evaluation from the Corporate Standpoint

Motives for the installation and continuation of employee stock purchase and savings plans appear to be mixed between financial and labor–management relationship goals. In most plans, employee contributions do serve as a source of cash by way of common stock sales, but the typical corporation could obtain an equal amount of cash more quickly by selling common stock to its stockholders or to the public. Thus, the only purely financial advantage of sales to employees are the avoidance of underwriting costs and the gaining of a somewhat wider diversification in ownership. But labor relations objectives also have financial aspects. It is claimed that the employee-stockholder is likely to be more efficient and more reluctant to quit his job than is the worker who is not a stockholder. Increased efficiency and a reduction in labor turnover mean a reduction in costs—obviously a financial advantage. In addition, employee stock purchase and savings plans are said to encourage thrift, which, in turn, makes for labor stability and satisfaction.

From the corporate standpoint, a disadvantage alleged for the savings plans is that employees' virtues cannot be measured by their capacities to save. The benefits of the corporations' contributions are denied to employees who are unable to save because of extraordinary personal financial burdens, even though they may be good or even outstanding performers on the job. For both kinds of plans, to the extent that they involve spending employees' money for common stock, a possible major disadvantage is that the stock will not do well in earnings, dividends, and market price, with a resulting blow to morale. Disgruntled employee-stockholders would doubtless suffer a loss of efficiency, perhaps feel impelled to look for jobs elsewhere, and surely conclude that their thrift had been directed into wrong channels. In this regard, the claim is sometimes made that it is fundamentally unfair for a corporation to encourage its employees to invest in its own stock, since both their jobs and what is likely to be a substantial portion of their savings depend on the fortunes of the single enterprise. The very business conditions that may force a corporation to lay off workers are likely to cause a sharp drop in the market price of its stock. At the very time, therefore, that the worker needs to draw on his savings, he finds that they are evaporating.

Registration and Qualification

An offering of common stock in an employee stock purchase or savings plan to a large number of employees located in two or more states is a public offering within the meaning of the federal Securities

Act. Accordingly, it requires the formal process of preparing and filing a registration statement, the making of such amendments as the SEC prescribes, waiting for the effective date, and providing prospectuses to the employees to whom the offering is made. In some states, moreover, offerings to substantial numbers of employees require qualification under the blue-sky laws.

Probably exempt from the prescriptions of both federal and state laws, on the other hand, are small offerings (except for the notification requirement of the SEC's Regulation A) and offerings by corporations that have only a few employees.

PRIVATE PLACEMENTS OF COMMON STOCK

As defined in Chapter 18, a private placement of a security issue is its sale in bulk to one or a small group of institutional or individual investors. Of the total amount of common stock issued annually by business corporations in the United States, only a small percentage is sold by private placement. For the year 1967, for example, figures published by the SEC indicate that of total common stock issues of $1,959 million and preferred stock issues of $885 million offered for cash sale for the account of the issuers (excluding issues of investment companies and stock offered under employee-ownership plans), only $218 million of common and preferred combined took the private placement route.[16] However, because the SEC data cover only issues of more than $100,000, it is reasonable to assume that a goodly additional volume of stocks in issues of $100,000 or less was privately placed in that year. Nevertheless, it is appropriate to keep our discussion of private placement quite brief at this point, since its principal application is in the sale of bonds.[17]

Occasions for Private Placements of Common Stock

Corporations of substantial size that have established good records of profits and that have good growth prospects occasionally find wealthy individual capitalists, trustees of family estates or of pension funds, or other individual or institutional investors who offer to buy the entire amount of new issues of stock. Such corporations could doubtless sell the stock to their existing stockholders or to the general public without difficulty, but sometimes they accept the offers of bulk purchases because they feel that they can get a better price that way or—what comes to the same thing—that the expenses of flotation will be much less.

More commonly, however, private placements of common stock are made by newly established corporations, small ones that have been

[16]Securities and Exchange Commission, *Statistical Bulletin,* April, 1968, pp. 11, 12.

[17]See pp. 785–90.

in operation for some years, and others that have little or no access to alternative sources of equity funds. These private placements represent, therefore, simply a variant in arrangements between corporations and individual and institutional investors, as discussed earlier in this chapter in relation to the use of stock options. In that discussion, it was pointed out that, while some such investors advance equity funds ostensibly on a loan basis and take stock options, others are content to take common stock at once in exchange for their funds. The immediate taking of common stock, then, is a private placement.

Direct Placement and Finders

The financial managers of a corporation that wants to sell an issue of common stock in bulk to one or a few individual or institutional investors may themselves set out to look for such investors, or they may employ the services of middlemen who are expected to know where equity funds can be found. The middlemen, who are called finders, include investment bankers, lawyers, management consultants, and tax accountants. For their services, they expect to receive a finder's fee. Corporate managers may themselves seek investors in the hope of avoiding the finder's fee, or they may be quite willing to pay a finder's fee in the expectation that the finder will be able to obtain equity funds more readily and on better terms than they could. Corporations that have access to alternative markets for funds can generally expect to be more successful in reaching willing investors without the assistance of finders than can those whose access to alternative sources is severely limited or nonexistent.

In a study of securities flotations in the years 1951, 1953, and 1955, the SEC found that 70.3 percent of the number and 75 percent of the amount of both common and preferred stock issues privately placed were sold with the assistance of finders, and that finders' fees on these issues (average fees in various groupings) ranged from .62 percent to 4.15 percent, the size of the fees as percentages generally running inversely to the size of the issues.[18] It is a reasonable presumption that for issues of a given size and quality of issuer, finders' fees on common stock issues would run substantially higher than on preferred stock issues, and that those on common stock issues of small corporations that were not included in the SEC's survey would run substantially higher than on the included issues. Thus, the Federal Reserve System received reports of finders' fees running from 5 to 10 percent of the proceeds of equity advances of a common stock character.[19]

---

[18]Securities and Exchange Commission, *Cost of Flotation of Corporate Securities, 1951–1955* (Washington, D.C.: U.S. Government Printing Office, 1957), pp. 63, 64.

[19]*Financing Small Business: Report to the Committees on Banking and Currency and the Select Committees on Small Business by the Federal Reserve System*, (Pts. 1 and 2, 88th Cong., 2nd sess. [Washington, D.C.: U.S. Government Printing Office, 1958]), p. 530.

Exemption from Registration

Since the individual and institutional investors who buy common stock by way of private placements are presumed to be sufficiently knowledgeable and intelligent to make careful investigations of the affairs of corporations seeking their funds, private placements are exempt from the registration requirements of the federal securities legislation. Once in a while, however, the question arises of when a private placement becomes, in effect, a public offering. The applicability of the Securities Act is supposed to be determined by the number of prospective investors to whom a security is *offered*, not by the number who actually *buy*. An issue of a corporation's common stock may be offered in bulk by its officers or by a finder to many wealthy individuals or institutions one after another as, one after another, they reject the offer. Sometimes, too, investors form groups to advance funds to given corporations, each agreeing to contribute a specific amount or percentage of the total to be advanced.

But, as was indicated earlier in this chapter, the law and regulations draw no sharp lines between public offerings and private placements in terms of the number of people to whom securities are offered, whether simultaneously or successively. Moreover, it is well to recall that for determining the public or private character of transactions knowledge of offerers' affairs and investment acumen are tests at least as important as the number of persons involved.

EXCHANGES FOR PREFERRED STOCK AND DEBT

Common stock often serves as a means of financing in an indirect fashion: it is substituted, on a voluntary basis, for preferred stock or bonds that corporations had previously issued or for other debts they had previously contracted. Preferred stockholders, bondholders, or other creditors may be willing to give up their existing claims for claims as common stockholders. If they do consent to the exchange, the preferred stock or debt, though the original source of given quantities of assets, is replaced in this function by common stock. A recasting of the financial structure of a corporation by voluntary exchanges of this kind is described as a *recapitalization*, in contrast with a reorganization in which, as was pointed out earlier in this chapter, a strong element of compulsion is present.

Exchange offers of common stock for preferred stock or debt are most commonly made at the time the preferred stock is issued or the debt is contracted. From the moment of its issuance, a preferred stock or a bond may be convertible. The preferred stock or bond contract stipulates that the holder may at any time or within a designated period of time exchange his shares of preferred or his bond for a specific number of shares of common stock. A share of preferred stock, for example, may be exchangeable for two or three or five shares of common stock, and a bond of $1,000 par value may be exchangeable for common stock at a price of $25 a share, which would mean, of course, for 40 shares of common. But there is nothing to prevent a corporation from going to its preferred stockholders, bondholders, or other creditors and making a common stock exchange offer, even though it did not contract for convertibility in the first place. Such latter-day offers occur in goodly numbers, although not nearly so frequently as do offers from the beginning.

Convertible Preferred Stocks and Bonds

When at the time of issuance a corporation makes a preferred stock or bond issue convertible into common stock, it does so either because it thinks that the convertibility feature will enhance salability or because it actually wants the conversion to take place. The two motives may be mixed, but in the individual case the one or the other tends by far to predominate.

Addition of the convertibility feature to enhance the salability of a preferred stock or bond issue is to give it a sweetener. Beyond the ordinary rights of preferred stock or bonds, the prospective buyer is offered a speculative interest that, like any speculation, may or may not turn out to be valuable, much as he is offered a speculative interest when stock purchase warrants are attached to preferred stock or bonds. If the corporation's earnings advance markedly and the dividends on its common stock are generous, the buyer may switch his limited-return preferred stock or bonds to enjoy the higher return being paid on the common stock. If earnings so advance but dividends on common are continued at a modest level, although its market price advances materially in keeping with the high level of retained earnings, he may make the conversion with the intention of selling the common stock for a capital gain. If neither of these developments takes place, he may continue to hold the preferred shares or bonds with their superior claims on earnings and assets. Here, as in the use of stock purchase warrants in similar circumstances, issuing corporations may, in their anxiety to sell, err in the direction of generosity in setting the terms for conversion.

Many of the corporations that make their preferred stock and bond issues convertible to improve their appeal to prospective buyers are weak enterprises, but those that add the convertibility feature in the hope and expectation that conversion will take place are likely to be quite strong. In most cases, those that want conversion would prefer to issue common stock in the first place, but in view of temporary weaknesses in the common stock market they choose not to sell common at a price that would unreasonably dilute the ownership interests of existing stockholders. If they need money at once, and if the market for preferred stock or bonds of the quality they can issue continues favorable, they offer one or the other with the conversion feature. They are confident that when strength returns to the common stock market conversion will take place; hence, they are likely to look on the preferred stock or bonds simply as a means of interim financing.[20]

Later Offers of Conversion

When a corporation makes an offer of common stock in exchange for its outstanding preferred stock or bonds that did not originally include the conversion feature, it may be in a position to redeem the securities whether or not their holders accept the exchange offer, or it may be faced with financial difficulties of considerable severity.

Although exchange offers of this kind by corporations in strong positions are rather rare, they can be advantageous. Suppose that a corporation intends to retire its outstanding preferred stock or bonds, having the right to do this by simply calling the securities for redemption. Its managers know that it can make a public offering of common stock on favorable terms and use the proceeds for the redemption. But, to reduce flotation costs, especially underwriting commissions, they decide to go direct to the preferred stockholders or bondholders with an exchange offer. In so doing, they inform the security holders that securities not offered for exchange are to be presented for redemption on or before a designated day. To the extent, then, that the offer is accepted, the common stock flotation for cash can be reduced.

Small corporations in financial difficulties are much more likely than large ones in similar straits to go to bondholders and other creditors with proposals for exchanges of common stock in whole or in part for their claims as creditors. Such a proposal may be made to only one or two of the larger creditors in the expectation that should they accept, the remainder of the debt could be met without difficulty. Large creditors of small corporations may accept offers of this kind in the hope of realizing a larger proportion of their claims in the long run as common stockholders than what could be realized by immediate legal proceedings to enforce payment. Such an acceptance would be all the more likely should the amount of stock offered to the large creditor or creditors be a substantial proportion of the total to be outstanding, or should they be otherwise assured of a substantial voice in management. A large corporation, on the other hand, would probably have to approach a goodly number of creditors to reach a sufficient aggregate of claims to make its effort worthwhile. If it had already defaulted on some or all these claims, or had to confess the probability of default, it would have reason to fear that one or more of the creditors would file a petition for its reorganization or dissolution in bankruptcy.

---

[20] Convertibility as a feature of preferred stock issues is further discussed on pp. 590–97, and as a feature of bond issues on pp. 763–69.

In the making of latter-day offers of common stock in exchange for preferred stock, large corporations have generally played a more prominent role than have small ones; but this may be only because more publicity has been given to the offers of the large firms. At any rate, offers of this kind are most commonly made when unpaid dividends on cumulative preferred stock have reached substantial levels. For example, a corporation that for 6 years has not paid its prescribed dividend of, say, 5 percent a year on its preferred stock may hope to work out an adjustment with the preferred stockholders. Unless it is willing to go through a lengthy and expensive process of reorganization, the only ways it can get rid of the arrearages is by paying them in cash or by *getting the preferred stockholders to consent* to waive their accumulated dividend claims in whole or in part. Accordingly, it may offer a certain number of shares of common stock in full settlement of the arrearages, or it may offer a certain amount of cash plus shares of common stock. It may, indeed, go further than this in the hope of getting rid of some or all of the preferred stock itself, as by offering a larger number of shares of common stock in exchange for all the rights of the preferred stockholders—that is, for the preferred stock itself along with the claims to unpaid dividends.[21]

STOCK DIVIDENDS AND BONUS STOCK

Two further uses of common stock deserve only brief treatment in this chapter: its use for stock dividends and its use as bonus stock. Stock dividends can be treated briefly because a more lengthy discussion can best be reserved for Chapter 26, where dividend policies are examined in detail. Bonus stock is of little importance.

Stock Dividends

Although the typical common stockholder is primarily interested in the amount of cash dividends he receives or can expect to receive, boards of directors are frequently convinced that the interests of the common stockholders can be better served if all or very large proportions of the cash throw-offs from profits are retained to finance expansion or for other corporate purposes. But many boards feel that the common stockholder should get something currently as a reward for his investment, despite an apparent need to retain all or a large percentage of profits. Hence, the device of the stock dividend[22]—the something that the stockholder gets is simply some additional shares of common stock, and of course, like any dividend, he gets this on a pro rata basis. If, indeed, the stockholder needs or wants cash, he can

[21]A further discussion of procedures aimed at adjusting the claims of preferred stockholders will be found on pp. 621–25.

[22]This is not to imply that the only reason for the distribution of stock dividends is to give common stockholders a reward in lieu of cash dividends in whole or in part. Other reasons for stock dividends are discussed on pp. 662–66.

sell the shares he receives as a dividend. Although he would thereby reduce his ownership in the corporation, as when he sells stock rights,[23] that may not worry him much.

Common stock that is distributed as a dividend appears not to be a source of assets, and one could argue that it ought not to be classified as a means of financing. There is much truth in the contention, for the assets acquired through retained profits are there whether or not stock dividends are distributed. In at least one significant sense, however, common stock distributed as dividends may justifiably be called a means of financing. That is, stock dividends can reasonably be said to be the source of the amount of cash that boards of directors would have to pay out as cash dividends (or as additional cash dividends) to satisfy the clamor of stockholders were they not distributing the stock dividends. In other words, to the extent that stockholders are content with stock dividends, cash that otherwise would be paid out to them can be retained.

Bonus Stock

In earlier days, a practice of some popularity was the offering of shares of common stock as a bonus to buyers of preferred stock and bonds, particularly preferred stock. Bonus stock was used as a sweetener to improve the attractiveness of issues of preferred stock and bonds of relatively poor investment qualities. However, when the bonus stock had a par value there was always danger that the recipient would be held liable to corporate creditors for this value. Since it was apparently given free, the creditors could argue that it had actually been sold at a discount of 100 percent. To clear the way for the use of bonus stock without this danger was, indeed, an important reason for the advocacy of state legislation to permit the issuance of common stock without par value.

The giving of speculative interests to preferred stockholders and bondholders by convertibility provisions and by the attachment of stock purchase warrants has displaced, except in rare instances, the use of common stock itself as bonus stock.

QUESTIONS

1. For acquisitions of corporate properties in mergers and consolidations, why are direct exchanges of common stock for common stock often expecially favored by the acquiring corporations? By the stockholders of corporations being acquired?

2. How extensive has the merger movement been in recent years? Why has the Federal Trade Commission been especially concerned about large mergers? What are conglomerates? Do they pose any threat to competition? Discuss.

---

[23]See pp. 470–72.

3. Why are there said to be temptations toward generosity when common stock is offered in exchange for noncash assets? Can such generosity harm anybody? Whom? Is there justification for it? Explain.

4. In what circumstances does an offering of common stock in exchange for noncash assets, as in a merger proposal, become a public offering that requires registration?

5. What are the functions of promoters of business enterprises? What logic is there in giving them common stock as compensation for their services?

6. Why are stock options much more popular than stock bonuses as means of supplementing the cash salaries of corporate officers?

7. Under federal income tax regulations, how are stock bonuses treated? Profits on the sale of stock bought according to the terms of executive stock options?

8. Why are stock options described as an uncertain means of financing?

9. Describe the loan and option procedure sometimes arranged with wealthy investors for the acquisition of what are essentially equity funds? What are the advantages of this procedure to such investors?

10. What are stock purchase warrants? For what purposes do corporations issue them?

11. How do employee stock purchase plans differ from employee savings plans? How can one account for the recent shift in popularity toward the savings plans?

12. On what grounds are employee stock purchase and savings programs sometimes adversely criticized? Is there justification for such criticism? Discuss.

13. In comparison with public offerings of common stock, how important are private placements? What is the function of finders in private placements? What compensation do they get?

14. Why do some corporations make their new issues of preferred stocks and bonds convertible into common stock? Do the same reasons apply when corporations make later offers of conversion? Explain.

PROBLEMS

1. The directors and officers of the Hartley Corporation are quite anxious to absorb the Pennant Corporation, and they have made several offers that have been rejected as inadequate. Hartley's after-tax profits have been averaging around $4 a share on the 2 million common shares of $10 par value it has outstanding. Pennant's after-tax profits have been close to $8 a share on its 250,000 shares of $1 par value. After some further haggling, Hartley makes a final offer of 2½ shares of its common stock in exchange for each share of Pennant's, and the offer is unanimously accepted by Pennant's stockholders.

To what extent, if at all, does each group of stockholders benefit or suffer harm from the merger, assuming that subsequently the after-tax profits of Hartley as the surviving corporation aveage (*a*) $9 million, (*b*) $10 million, and (*c*) $11 million?

2. In seeking the services of William White as financial vice president, the directors of the Quincy Corporation offer him the choice of a straight cash salary of $120,000 a year or a cash salary of $90,000 plus qualified options to buy 4,000 shares of the corporation's common stock at the current market price of $50 a share. Mr. White is married and has three children, so that his exemptions for federal income tax purposes total $3,000. He normally has about $15,000 of expenses deductible for tax purposes, and he would expect to have no other sources of income should he take the appointment with Quincy.

a) Assuming that White is willing to give his services to Quincy, which of its two offers would he be likely to find most acceptable? Portions of the federal income tax rate schedule applicable to married taxpayers filing joint returns (at 1968 levels, but ignoring the surcharge of 10 percent added in that year) are as follows. (1) If the amount of taxable income is over $64,000 but not over $76,000, the tax is $24,420 plus 55 percent of the excess over $64,000. (2) If the amount of taxable income is over $100,000 but not over $120,000, the tax is $45,180 plus 62 percent of the excess over $100,000.

b) Remembering that for federal income tax purposes a corporation is allowed no expense deduction in connection with stock options granted for employee services (unless the employee has gains taxable as ordinary income on a subsequent sale of the stock, as in a sale before expiration of the three-year holding period), which offer is more generous from the standpoint of Quincy's common stockholders?

NOTE: The questions posed in both parts of this problem should be regarded as discussion questions, since they can have no categorical answers.

chapter 21

SOME PROBLEMS OF COMMON STOCK MANAGEMENT

Although many of the important problems of common stock management were analyzed in the three preceding chapters, a few remain for study in this chapter and Chapter 22. Some of these were implied in the earlier discussion, but they deserve more detailed treatment. In the present chapter, then, the following topics will be examined: determination of appropriate amounts of authorized common stock, original selection of pars and no pars, reasons for subsequent changes in pars and no pars, and the role of treasury stock. This will leave for study in the Chapter 22 the pros and cons of listing common stock on the stock exchanges.

AUTHORIZED ISSUES OF COMMON STOCK

In Chapter 3, the point was made that corporations can easily increase their authorized issues of stock, whether common or preferred, by a simple procedure of filing amendments to their articles of incorporation. It was also said that authorizations of stock far beyond what a corporation is likely to issue within a few years is unnecessarily expensive, because many state organization taxes and some annual capital stock taxes are levied on amounts authorized, regardless of the number of shares actually sold or otherwise disposed of.

But shortages in the supply of authorized but unissued stock can be a source of difficulties. Such a shortage can obviously cause acute embarrassment if it makes it quite difficult or impossible for a corporation to fulfill contracts to deliver stock, and it can prevent a board of directors from making advantageous exchanges of stock for assets or services. Liberal authorized issues and liberal waivers of preemptive rights can be provided for quite simply by the few organizers of a corporation, while getting approvals of the requisite majorities of stockholders when a corporation has grown large and its stockholders quite numerous may be both difficult and expensive. In some cases, of course, it is impossible to get a sufficient number of stockholders to approve increased authorizations, or if this approval is obtained, to get also a waiver of the stockholders' preemptive right to the added shares. Getting approvals is expensive if special meetings of the stockholders must be called, and special literature must be prepared to set out the merits of the proposals.

Contract Requirements

Corporations with excess cash sometimes buy shares of their common stock in the market to be held for future delivery against options given to executives or for resale in employee stock purchase programs. But for most corporations, such a procedure would eliminate a major advantage of offers by options and offers to employees in stock purchase plans—the advantage of using these as means of financing, of raising new money. For these corporations, it would be equally unrealistic to issue stock options to promoters and investment bankers, to attach stock purchase warrants to preferred stocks or bonds, to make such securities convertible into common stock, and to give stock purchase warrants to institutional investors in connection with long-term borrowing without having authorized but unissued stock available for delivery if and when called for by the contract holders.

None of the possible alternatives to holding unissued stock for this purpose would make much sense. Stockholders might be expected to approve amendments to articles of incorporation in order to increase authorized issues to meet stock delivery demands when made by contract holders, but the stockholders would be under no legal compulsion to give this approval. Shares could be bought in the market immediately to be held against future stock delivery demands, but this would make the contracts (except for convertible preferred stocks and bonds) sources of cash drain rather than means of financing. For the convertible securities, the cash received in their sale would be largely used up in the purchase of shares to take care of possible conversions. Finally, even more serious cash drains could result if the plan were to buy shares in the market only when contract holders called for delivery. If, for example, a corporation had to buy shares in the market at a price of $30 a share to meet the demand of a holder of a $1,000 bond convertible into 40 shares, it would, in effect, be paying $1,200 to settle a debt of $1,000.

Authorized Stock at Directors' Disposal

When the stockholders of a corporation have a high degree of confidence in the acumen of its board of directors and its devotion to their welfare—when, in other words, they are confident that the board will not fritter away their ownership rights through excessive dilution—

they have good reason to put at its disposal a rather generous amount of authorized common stock and to free this stock from the preemptive right. The directors will have elbow room to take quick advantage of opportunities to acquire assets and services in direct exchanges for stock. Often it happens that given parcels of property, all the assets of smaller concerns, or the services of especially desirable executives can be acquired on highly favorable terms only if offers can be made promptly and without question about the acquiring corporation's capacity to deliver. Offers of common stock for the assets of another corporation or of stock or stock options as supplements to the proposed cash salary of a man of high executive qualities "provided our stockholders agree to the issue" may not be enough. Even when owners of desirable properties and great executive skills appear to be willing to wait to see what the stockholders will do, the delay may prove fatal. During the waiting period, the owners of the properties and skills may have a change of heart, or, what is more probable, they may receive more favorable offers from other quarters.

Another reason for placing unissued stock at the unhampered disposal of the directors is to enable them to declare and distribute stock dividends. Because most stockholders are extremely pleased to get stock dividends, they can generally be counted on to vote approval for new authorizations for this purpose. But as dividend policies are at the discretion of the directors, presumably this discretion should extend to distributions of dividend stock without a need of repeated referral of the matter to the stockholders for their vote.

That common stockholders are by no means averse to putting large amounts of unissued common stock at the disposal of boards of directors is indicated by the authorized issues in relation to shares outstanding of several well-known corporations listed in Table 21–1. One will notice that the unissued shares of the Scott Paper Company exceeded the number outstanding.

TABLE 21–1
Authorized and Outstanding Common Stock of a Sample of Corporations, December 31, 1967

Corporation	*Shares Authorized*	*Shares Outstanding*
American Cyanamid Co.	60,000,000	44,690,608
Burlington Industries, Inc.	40,000,000	25,312,110
El Paso Electric Co.	7,500,000	6,389,340
General Electric Co.	105,000,000	91,306,551
Owens-Illinois, Inc.	24,000,000	14,819,625
Pacific Lighting Corporation	22,000,000	16,192,683
Scott Paper Co.	80,000,000	33,862,032
United States Steel Corporation	90,000,000	54,143,937
Virginia Electric and Power Co.	30,000,000	23,366,126
Youngstown Sheet & Tube Co.	15,000,000	10,679,946

SOURCE: Annual reports of corporations cited.

THE QUESTION OF PAR AND NO-PAR VALUES

In the second and third decades of the present century, a controversy raged in American financial circles about the merits and demerits of provisions of state corporation codes that required the stock of business corporations to have par values. In the early part of this period, the par value of the stock of the great majority of corporations was $100, and some of the state codes stipulated that par value could not be less than this figure. Critics of the par-value requirements emphasized the difficulties they engendered in corporate financing, and demanded the enactment of amendments to the laws to permit the issuance of no-par stock. Their campaigns were extraordinarily successful, for, beginning with New York in 1912, all the states except Nebraska adopted legislation to permit no-par issues.

But the sale of no-par stock at a wide range of prices generally below $100 tended to take away from that figure any remaining glory it may have had for par-value issues. States that enacted no-par provisions saw no reason to continue to require values of not less than $100 for par stocks, if they had previously had such stipulations. They amended their laws to permit lower par values; some set the minimum at a figure such as $1, and some set no minimum at all. Corporations that continued to prefer par values increasingly experimented with pars of $1, $5, $10, and other figures much below $100, whether or not they had previously been restricted by law. In fact, with the passing of time and especially in the period since the 1930's, many corporate managements have become convinced that setting low par values for stocks is a means of getting all the advantages claimed for the no-par device together with the additional advantage of avoiding some of the tax discriminations to which no-par stock is sometimes subject. In the past two decades, accordingly, a strong trend from high pars and no pars toward low pars has been apparent, just as, in the 1920's especially, a strong movement from par-value stocks to no-par issues developed. Illustrative of these two trends was the action of the General Electric Company in changing from a par value of $100 to no par in 1926, and then switching from no par to a par of $5 in 1954. The Eastman Kodak Company changed from $100 to no par in 1922, and from no par to a par of $10 in 1947; Crucible Steel Company went from $100 to no par in 1940, and then to a par of $25 in 1951.

Typical of present-day low pars are those of Textron, Inc., at 25 cents; the Aluminum Company of America and Lockheed Aircraft Corporation, at $1; Sears, Roebuck, $1.50; General Motors, $1.66 2/3; Ford Motor, $2.50; the Borden Company, $3.75; National Dairy Products, International Business Machines, National Lead, and Cities Service, all at $5; Mobil Oil, $7.50; Armco Steel, $10; and

Texaco, Inc., $12.50. However, many corporations continue with no-par common stocks, including Inland Steel, Montgomery Ward, and American Hospital Supply among industrials, and Philadelphia Electric and Gulf States Utilities among many public utility corporations with which no-par designations continue to be especially popular.

At the present time, therefore, the organizers of new corporations will almost invariably decide on low pars and no pars for the common stocks they plan to have authorized. Why this is so can be best discussed in terms of the advantages and disadvantages attributed to no-par stock. This discussion will be followed by an examination of the more recent claims for the superiority of low par values over no pars.

Advantages of No-Par Stock

Ease in Further Financing. The principal advantage claimed for no-par stock is that it makes for ease in further common stock financing, even though the market price of stock already outstanding has fallen. If a corporation originally sold an issue of common stock at its par value of $50 a share, and if the market price of this stock is now $40, it cannot sell an additional issue at $50. Nobody will pay that price to the corporation when he can buy in the market at $40, nor can investors safely buy the new issue at $40, for the discount rule would apply. The investors, as well as directors who did not have their dissents entered in the minutes, would be contingently liable to creditors for the amount of the discount. Were the stock no par, however, the second issue could readily be offered at $40—or at a lower price as in a direct offering to existing stockholders—without question about further liability.

Source of Paid-in Surplus. Closely related to the foregoing is the contention that the sale of no-par stock enables corporations to begin business with paid-in surpluses. The no-par provisions of state statutes generally permit the corporate directors to decide what portion of the proceeds of stock sales is to be carried to the capital stock account as stated capital and what portion is to be designated paid-in surplus. Many new corporations, it is said, must expect to incur net losses in the first few years of operations—until, that is, they get firmly established—and it is most desirable to have surpluses against which the losses can be charged. If surplus is not available to absorb losses, they result in impairments of the capital stock itself—the appearance of *deficits* on the books and in the financial statements—which is hardly helpful in buying on credit, getting bank loans, or making further sales of securities. With a par-value stock, on the other hand, the very designation of a permanent price tag or par value, especially if a high one, may militate against sales of the stock at prices in excess of par, making the acquisition of a paid-in surplus at the start much less probable than in the use of no-par stock.

Avoidance of Subterfuges. Also related to the principal advantage claimed for no-par stock is the avoidance of subterfuges that were commonly employed in connection with par-value issues to try to avoid contingent liabilities for discount. In the incorporation of partnerships, for example, it was a common practice to issue stock of a total par value substantially in excess of the reasonable value of assets taken over. In the individual case, the former partners would agree among themselves to donate back to the corporation a goodly proportion of the stock thus received for the partnership assets. To raise cash, then, this donated stock could be sold at whatever price it would bring, supposedly without making directors and buyers liable to creditors for the amount of any discount.

But discount liabilities could not be removed with certainty by transactions of this kind, for creditors might sue on the grounds that the partnership assets plus the cash received in the sale of the donated stock still did not constitute full payment for the stock at its par value—that a fraud had been worked on them. With no-par stock, on the other hand, there need be no occasion for worries about discounts: the partners can take as many shares for their assets as they think reasonable, decide what value to put on these for entry in the capital stock and paid-in surplus accounts, and then sell additional shares at whatever price can be obtained for them.

Promoting Investor Understanding. A fourth advantage claimed for no-par designations is that they minimize misunderstandings on the part of investors. Poorly informed investors may be misled by par values, thinking that shares must truly be worth the price tags placed on them. Being offered a share at $50 when it is designated in a corporation's articles of incorporation to be worth that much is not the same as being offered at $50 a share to which no specific value is ascribed in the articles. In the second circumstance, the would-be investor, even if poorly informed, would surely ask himself whether the share was really worth the offering price, and take steps to find out by analyzing the corporation's position and prospects. That, at any rate, is the nature of the claim made for no-par stock. If the claim is valid, the advantage *to the corporation* is clear, for it wants to have loyal, satisfied stockholders—stockholders who will be inclined to buy its products and to invest in more of its securities and to advise others to do the same.

Disadvantages of No-Par Stock

Discriminatory Taxation. The most obvious disadvantage in the use of no-par stock is found in discriminatory tax burdens that it must sometimes bear. Although not of great weight, differentials in tax liabilities unfavorable to no-par shares can still be of material significance. Such differentials obtain in some of the state organization and entrance taxes and in a few of the state annual capital stock or franchise taxes.

In New York, the rate of the organization tax on corporations with par-value stock is .05 percent, and on those with no-par stock it is 5 cents a share. Accordingly, a newly organized corporation with authorized common stock of 100,000 shares of $50 par value would pay an organization tax of $2,500, while the comparable tax bill for a corporation with 100,000 authorized shares of no-par stock destined to be sold at $20 a share would be $5,000. If the same corporations were organized in New Jersey where the tax rate is 20 cents per $1,000 of par-value stock and 1 cent a share on no-par stock, each would pay an organization tax of $1,000, even though the par-value stock of the one might be sold for $5 million or more and the no-par stock of the other for only $2 million. Again, were they chartered in Maine the corporation with par-value stock would pay an annual franchise tax of $300, while the corporation with no-par stock would pay $550. In their organization taxes, some states discriminate against no-par stock by basing the taxes on the dollar amounts of authorized stock while assigning an arbitrary value such as $10, $50, or $100 to each no-par share authorized, regardless of the price at which it may be sold.

Dangers of Dilution. A second disadvantage attributed to no-par stock is the possibility of serious dilution of the ownership interests of existing stockholders through successive issues of the stock. Boards of directors, it is said, are likely to be more liberal in giving no-par shares for services, for specific parcels of property, and for all the operating assets of other firms, as in mergers, than when giving par-value shares. If, for example, directors want to acquire property reasonably worth $100,000 in exchange for stock that has a par value of $50, they are unlikely to offer much more than 2,000 shares. But no price tag stands in the way of a more liberal offer of no-par shares. Although already outstanding no-par shares might have a book or market value of $50, that would not preclude the offering of, say, 2,500 such shares for the property. It would be as easy to enter 2,500 shares on the books at a stated value of $40 as to enter 2,000 shares with a stated value of $50.

Attractiveness of Low Par Values

The reason for the recent strong trend toward using low par values for common stocks can be readily adduced from the foregoing discussion of the advantages and disadvantages of no-par stocks. It appears that all the advantages claimed for no pars can be claimed also for low pars, while the low pars also avoid the kinds of tax discriminations that sometimes burden no pars.

If a corporation sets the par value of its common stock at $1 and sells the original issue at $20 a share, and if the market value falls below this level, it can offer further issues at $16, $12, $8, and at still lower prices down to $1 without worry about the discount rule. The sale of the original issue, furthermore, would provide a paid-in surplus equal to $19 a share—a surplus against which such losses as might occur in the first few years of operation could be charged. No subterfuge, such as the donated stock procedure, would be needed to get these results. Moreover, the prospective investor, on being offered $1 shares at $20, would have just about as much reason to make a careful investigation as when offered no-par shares. Finally, the shares of low par value, depending on the state of incorporation, might turn up favorable tax discrimination. In New York, a corporation authorized to issue 100,000 shares of stock of $1 par value would pay an organization tax of $50, whereas one with the same number of no-par shares, as indicated earlier, would pay $5,000, even though each stock might be sold at, say, $20 a share. In Maryland, where the tax law assigns a value of $20 to no-par stock, the corporation with 100,000 shares of $1 par value would pay an organization tax of $20, while the no-par corporation with an equal number of shares would pay $300. In New Hampshire, where an arbitrary value of $50 is assigned to no-par stock, the respective bills for organization taxes would be $150 and $2,750.

CHANGES IN PAR, NO-PAR, AND STATED VALUES

That a corporation starts out with a specific par or no-par designation for its common stock does not mean that it must hold to this designation for the whole of its operating life. This provision of its articles of incorporation, like so many others, can be changed by subsequent amendment provided that the amendment has the approval of whatever proportion of stockholdings the state law or the articles themselves prescribe.

Effecting changes in par and no-par designations is an extremely common procedure. When brought about by the voluntary approval of stockholders of solvent corporations, such changes come under the head "recapitalizations"; when forced on stockholders as in bankruptcy proceedings, they come within the scope of "reorganizations." The changes may be said to be of two classes: (1) those in which the designations are changed without simultaneous changes in the number of shares, and (2) those in which the designations and number of shares are changed at the same time. Reasons for the selection of one procedure rather than the other will be brought out in the following discussion of the scope of the two kinds of changes. However, the discussion will be limited to recapitalizations, since the fate of common stock in reorganizations was sufficiently indicated in Chapter 20.

Changes without Variations in Number of Shares

The managements of corporations, with the approval of their stockholders, often decide to reduce the par value of their common stock from high to low figures, to switch from pars to no pars, and to switch from no pars to low pars without, at the same time, changing the number of shares to be outstanding. The objective sought may be one or a combination of the following: (1) to gain the advantages of no pars and low pars as discussed earlier in this chapter, (2) to eliminate deficits already on the books or expected to occur, and (3) to make possible write-downs or write-offs of asset values.

Gaining Advantages of No Pars and Low Pars. The most obvious reason for changes in pars and no pars is to enable corporations to gain the advantages of no pars and low pars already discussed. A great number of corporations have made switches precisely for this reason—so much so that the trends to no pars and low pars, referred to earlier, have been even more significant because of switches by long-established corporations than because of the selection of no pars and low pars by new ones.

Suppose, for example, that a corporation's financial position is as indicated in the following condensed balance sheet.

Assets	$10,000,000	Liabilities	$4,000,000
		Common stock	5,000,000
		Earned surplus	1,000,000

The common stock consists of 100,000 shares of $50 par value, and its book value is obviously $60 a share. The corporation's earnings after taxes have been averaging around $200,000, or $2 a common share. The corporation wants to sell some additional stock to take advantage of highly favorable opportunities for expansion, but the market value of its stock, in view of its limited earning power, is now only $30. Clearly, new stock cannot be sold at $50, nor can the corporation, because of the discount rule, expect to find many buyers at a price in the vicinity of $30. Accordingly, a decision is made to reduce the par value from $50 to $5 a share—an action reflected in a revised balance sheet as follows.

Assets	$10,000,000	Liabilities	$4,000,000
		Common stock	500,000
		Capital surplus	4,500,000
		Earned surplus	1,000,000

As the action does not change the book value or the earnings record per share, it should have no immediate material effects on the market value of the stock. Now, however, the corporation is in a position to offer the additional stock at a price around $30 a share—at or any price down to $5—without worry about the discount rule.

In a similar way, a corporation in the position of the one just described may decide to switch from its par value of $50 to the no-par designation, perhaps feeling that tax discriminations against no-par stock are of no importance, considering its location and the states in which it does business. Such a switch, in truth, would allow for somewhat more flexibility than in the illustrated switch from a par of $50 to one of $5. In changing to no par, the corporation could leave its common stock account undisturbed, allowing the shares already outstanding to remain temporarily at a stated value of $50 a share. Or it could reduce the stated value to $25, carrying $2.5 million to capital surplus, or to $15 with $3.5 million going to capital surplus, or to some other level. If it then sold new stock at, say $28, the directors would be in a position to decide what percentage of this amount should go to the capital stock account as stated capital and what percentage to a paid-in or capital surplus account. Likewise, if it appeared to be necessary for it later to accept a price even below $5 a share for another issue of common stock, it could go ahead with the financing without hesitation, whereas to effect the same kind of transaction the corporation of the preceding paragraph would find it necessary again to amend its articles. (It should be noted that the sale of additional no-par stock at $28 would necessarily reduce the stated value of the original shares, assuming it to have been left temporarily at $50. If, to illustrate, 50,000 shares were sold at $28 and the directors decided to allocate $20 of the proceeds to the capital stock account, that account would amount to $6 million—the original $5 million plus the $1 million thus allocated. Since old stock of a given class is indistinguishable from new in the rights it accords to stockholders, the stated value of each share, old and new, would now be $40, that is, $6,000,000 ÷ 150,000 shares outstanding.)

Almost needless to add is that many corporations have made and are continuing to make switches from no pars to pars, especially low ones, specifically to gain the tax advantages indicated in our earlier discussion. Decisions on whether the selected pars should be equal to or less than the stated values of no pars replaced vary according to the levels of these stated values and the outlook of the corporations individually. A corporation that switches from a no par with stated value of $25 is likely to choose a much lower par value, and one switching from a no par with a stated value of $5 may be quite satisfied to continue with the same figure as its par value.

Elimination of Deficits. The elimination of deficits, whether already incurred or in prospect, has been an important reason for the scaling down of par and stated values of corporate common stocks. A deficit is a debit or red balance in the earned surplus account. Unless it is offset by credit balances in one or more capital surplus accounts, it signifies that the capital stock has been impaired. When shown in the balance sheet in the manner generally preferred by reputable accountants, the impairment is indicated by the deduction of the deficit from the stock accounts on the liability side. Operating losses in excess of earned surplus earlier accumulated are the principal source of deficits, but they may also occur because of embezzlements, destruction of property by storms, floods, and other acts of God, and losses on sales of obsolete fixed assets carried on the books at substantial values.

Corporate managements do not like to show deficits in their balance sheets. It is not good for credit standing and for sales of additional securities. Nor is it good for one's reputation with employees, customers, and the public generally. Hence, anxiety to get rid of deficits as quickly as possible is quite understandable. The most pleasant way to do this is to have earnings mount up rapidly, but this solution is not easy to come by, since it must depend on many circumstances beyond the control of the managers. Were it not so, the deficits would not have appeared in the first place. Accordingly, adjusting the par or stated value of the common stock often suggests itself as the next best procedure, even though it is well understood that eliminating deficits by adjustments does not change the fact that losses have occurred and that they remain in the corporations' records.

For illustration, let us assume that the financial position of a certain corporation is as indicated in the following condensed balance sheet.

Assets	$9,000,000	Liabilities		$4,000,000
		Common stock	$6,000,000	
		Less: Deficit	1,000,000	5,000,000

It may be assumed that the common stock account represents 150,000 shares of $40 par value. For the elimination of the deficit, a reduction in the par value to $33.33 1/3 a share would clearly suffice, but the corporation's managers would probably want to have some additional capital surplus to absorb further losses should they occur. Thus, the par value might be reduced to, say, $30, thereby making possible both the elimination of the deficit and the provision of a capital surplus of $500,000. In view of the trend toward low par values, however, the managers would be even more likely to recommend to the stockholders for their approval a reduction of the par value to some low figure such as $1 or $5.

The setting up of a balance in a capital surplus account in the way illustrated would not justify the payment of dividends chargeable against that account. Such a dividend payment would constitute a deliberate impairment of the capital stock; it would be potentially a means of defrauding existing creditors. Any competent court could be expected to hold that the dividend was being charged against the capital stock account, despite the initial transfer from the capital stock account to the capital surplus account. In most jurisdictions, on the other hand, a transfer from the capital stock account to surplus accounts to eliminate a deficit, in the manner illustrated, would enable the corporation to pay dividends either on common or preferred stock or on both in an amount not exceeding current and future net profits. For example, if the corporation of the foregoing illustration were to have in the present year a net profit of $100,000, it could not pay any cash dividends whatsoever, according to the rule in most states, had it not reduced the par value of its common stock to eliminate the deficit. The profit would simply reduce the deficit to $900,000, and a dividend payment would add to this deficit, thus further impairing the stock. But had it eliminated the deficit by reducing the par value of its stock, cash dividends not exceeding $100,000 could be paid, as it would have an earned surplus of that amount against which the dividends could be legitimately charged.

A recapitalization of the kind described here was effected by the J. I. Case Company in April, 1962, when its stockholders approved a write-down from $12.50 to $1 in the par value of its 2,863,193 shares of outstanding common stock. The total write-down amounted, therefore, to $32,926,720. Of this, $26,814,519 was credited to the earned surplus account to eliminate an accumulated deficit of that amount, and the balance of $6,112,201 was credited to capital surplus.

Adjustments in par and stated values to eliminate deficits can be made ahead of time, so that the deficits will never appear on the books and in balance sheets. Assume that a corporation has outstanding 200,000 shares of no-par common stock of a stated value of $20. It has an earned surplus of $75,000, but it expects to incur a loss of $300,000 in the current year. Accordingly, it takes action immediately to reduce the stated value of its no-par stock to, say, $5 a share, thus providing a capital surplus of $3 million. Should, then, a loss of $300,000 actually take place, $75,000 could be charged against earned surplus, and the remainder against the capital surplus, so that no deficit would appear.

Write-downs and Write-offs of Asset Values. Corporate managements often recognize that some of their assets are carried on the books at valuations unreasonably high in relation to the contribution to earnings made by these assets. But write-downs and write-offs of asset values by realistic amounts, they know, would result in deficits because of the meagerness of the surplus accounts to which the reductions would have to be charged. Overvaluations are most commonly recognized in fixed assets, both tangible and intangible, but sometimes in inventories and even in other current assets as well. A corporation may have spent a lot of money in buying a patent covering a particular product or in developing a product for which it succeeds in getting a patent, only to find that high costs of production would require a selling price that would put the product beyond the reach of most potential buyers. Or it may have bought out a competing concern for an amount much more than the fair value of its net tangible assets, the excess payment representing compensation for goodwill—that is, for the superior earning capacity of the purchased concern as derived from a large body of loyal customers. It carries the excess payment as goodwill on its books but—alas!—it has not succeeded in bringing over many of the purchased concern's customers. Or, again, it may be carrying plant and equipment on the books at what are known to be unrealistic valuations, because of consistent undercharging of depreciation over the years.

Overvaluations of the kinds described usually mean that earnings records show up poorly. The earnings of a corporation that has overvalued assets may be satisfactory in relation to a *reasonable* valuation of its assets, but they are poor when measured in terms of the book value of assets, the par or stated value of the capital stock, and the book amount of the total equity accounts. Yet, these are criteria by which credit grantors decide whether or not to grant loans or other credits, and security buyers decide whether or not to buy a corporation's stocks and bonds. Overvaluations, in a word, tend to weaken a corporation's credit standing and its access to the securities markets for long-term funds.

But there is a remedy. An immediate improvement in a corporation's appearance to prospective creditors and security buyers and to the public in general can usually be gained by write-downs and write-offs of asset values to be charged against surplus—surplus provided, in part at least, by reductions in the par or stated value of outstanding common stock. To see how an adjustment of this kind can be made to work out, let us consider the situation of a corporation whose financial position is indicated by the following condensed balance sheet.

Current assets		$4,500,000	Liabilities	$3,750,000
Fixed assets:			Common stock	6,000,000
Plant and equipment	$3,500,000		Earned surplus	250,000
Patents	800,000			
Goodwill	1,200,000	5,500,000		

We may assume that the corporation's common stock consists of 200,000 shares of a par value of $30 a share, and that its net profits have been averaging around $300,000 annually. Thus, the profits have amounted to a return of 3 percent on total assets, 5 percent on the stock itself, and 4.8 percent on the total equity accounts as shown in the balance sheet; all these are rather weak rates of return. But the managers of the corporation recognize that the patents and goodwill are valueless and that plant and equipment, because of inadequate depreciation charges in past years, are overvalued by $1 million. With the approval of the stockholders, a decision is made to write off the patents and goodwill and to reduce the book value of plant and equipment to $2.5 million, as well as to reduce the par value of the stock from $30 to $15 a share in order to provide sufficient surplus to absorb the reductions in asset values. Since the write-offs and write-down amount to $3 million, this amount is exactly balanced by the transfer to be made from the common stock to the capital surplus account. Nevertheless, it is decided that the surplus of $250,000 that remains will be carried as capital surplus rather than as earned surplus. Since the underdepreciation of plant and equipment and the overvaluation of patents have resulted in overstatements of profits in preceding years, earned surplus is also overstated, and the recognition of past errors in accounting must result in its elimination. Accordingly, the corporation's balance sheet, after all changes have been entered on its books, would appear as follows.

Current assets	$4,500,000	Liabilities	$3,750,000
Plant and equipment	2,500,000	Common stock	3,000,000
		Capital surplus	250,000

Immediately, therefore, the corporation's record is made to look better. On the basis of the figures of the revised balance sheet, its average earnings of $300,000 a year have amounted to 4.29 percent on its assets, 10 percent on its common stock, and 9.23 percent on its total equity accounts. Moreover, the changes effected might bring about an improvement in future earnings figures. The amortization of patents would be eliminated as an annual charge, although book charges for depreciation, in view of the undercharging of depreciation in prior years, probably would be higher. If, then, the elimination of patent amortization should exceed the increased charges for depreciation, and if the corporation should maintain the same scale of operations and the same selling prices for its products, it would have a larger margin of profit. Or with lowered costs, the corporation might reduce its selling prices to capture a larger share of the market, thereby seeking a larger profit by way of a larger volume of sales.

Changes with Variations in Number of Shares

Changes in the par or stated values of common stock with simultaneous changes in the number of shares to be outstanding usually take the form of what are called *split-ups* and *reverse splits*. A corporation that has outstanding 200,000 shares of $100 par value may decide on a 5-for-1 split-up, substituting 1 million shares of $20 par value. Or one that has outstanding 2 million no-par shares of a stated value of $1 may effect a 1-for-10 reverse split, substituting 200,000 no-par shares of a stated value of $10. These examples illustrate what may be labeled simple split-ups and reverse splits, whereby the number of shares is changed in inverse proportion to the change in par or stated value, but no switch is made from par to no par or vice versa, no change is made in the total dollar amount of the common stock account, and no surplus account is affected. Not infrequently, however, corporations provide simultaneously for switches between par and no-par values when effecting split-ups and reverse splits. For example, a corporation with 200,000 common shares of $50 par value may in a 4-for-1 split-up, substitute 800,000 no-par shares of a stated value of $12.50 each. Much more rarely, split-ups and reverse splits are accompanied by other adjustments in the common stock account to provide a capital surplus—for example, the split-up of 200,000 shares of stock of $50 par value for 1 million shares of $8 par value, with a capital surplus of $2 million resulting. In the following discussion of split-ups and reverse splits, however, only the simple variety will be considered, because the reasons for the other kinds of adjustments that may be used in combination have already been analyzed at length.

Split-ups to Promote Wide Distribution. The most important reason for split-ups is to lower the market value of outstanding common stock—a reason indicated by the concentration of a large majority of split-ups in periods of stock market boom. The rise in the market price of a corporation's stock in such a period may put it, in the judgment of the corporation's managers, beyond the reach of the great mass of potential investors. It is generally taken for granted that the typical investor would much rather buy, say, 5 shares of a given stock at $30 a share than 1 share at $150, even though 1 share at $150 would give him the same proportional ownership rights as would 5 shares at $30. The typical investor has the conviction, it is claimed, that the $30 share is more likely to rise to, say, $40 in market value than is the $150 share to rise in an equal proportion—that is, to go to $200. Studies of the market behavior of stocks after split-ups tend to support this kind of expectation, although the evidence, considering the complex of forces always bearing on the stock market, is by no means conclusive. At any rate, the decision of a corporation to split up 5 for 1 its common stock selling at $150 would be in harmony with prevailing thinking. Such harmony in thinking has been amply demonstrated by the very large number of split-ups that have been effected in the long period of advancing stock prices since the end of World War II—a period in which pauses and setbacks in the price advances have been of relatively short duration. By way of illustration, a few of the many split-ups of the early months of 1968 may be cited: 2 for 1 by Houdaille Industries, Melville Shoe, Raytheon, and Todd Shipyards; 3 for 1 by Texas Gulf Sulphur; 3 for 2 by B. F. Goodrich, House of Fabrics, and the Zale Corporation; 4 for 3 by the Soss Manufacturing Company; 5 for 2 by Bell Electronics; and 7 for 4 by the DWG Corporation.

But the occurrence of a great number of split-ups raises the question why many corporate managements are anxious to bring down the market prices of their stocks within a range presumably favored by the great mass of investors. Widespread ownership—"wide distribution" is the popular term—is apparently desired. Why? One reason is the enhancement of prospects for success in further offerings of common stock to existing stockholders. In Chapter 18, it was indicated that small stockholders are likely to be more willing to buy their allotted shares in new offerings than are large ones. Likewise, widespread ownership should mean general investor interest in any securities the corporation might want to offer and by whatever means—offerings of common stock through investment bankers to the general public, as well as offerings of preferred stocks and bonds. For corporations that produce consumer goods, in particular, widespread ownership of the stock is usually thought to be highly desirable. Consumers should surely be inclined to favor the products of the corporations in which they own stock. Especially if, in their minds, the choice between these products and those of competing concerns is a narrow one, the fact of their stockholding should weigh their buying decisions in the right direction. Finally, a reason for favoring wide distribution is fear of loss of control by corporate managements in shaky positions. A minority faction seeking to gain control might be expected to have much greater difficulty in trying to buy sufficient shares from numerous owners of small holdings, or to line up their votes, than it would have were it necessary only to approach a few large stockholders.

Split-ups Preparatory to New Offerings. Split-ups are often useful not only to promote general investor interest in corporations' securities, as indicated above, but also as steps immediately aimed at easing the sale of new offerings. Suppose, for example, that $150 is the market price of the stock of a corporation that is planning a new offering to its stockholders. The corporation's managers are reasonably confident that the contemplated flotation would be successful at an offering price of, say, $135, but for the kinds of reasons already stated they would be all the more confident were it possible to make the offering at a price in the vicinity of $25. A split-up of 5 for 1, therefore, would pave the way for the second choice. The split-up would be expected to bring the market price down to approximately $30. Accordingly, an offering of 5 times as many shares as originally contemplated at a price of, say, $27 could be made in the expectation that, if successful, it would yield the same gross proceeds as expected of the offering originally planned.

Split-ups for Secondary Distributions. Sometimes, split-ups are preliminary steps to sales of all or substantial portions of the holdings of large stockholders—a kind of operation described as a secondary distribution. For illustration, let us say that a large stockholder wants to sell out his holdings of a stock quoted in the market at 200. In view of the limited number of investors interested in high-priced stocks, he fears that his attempt to unload will sharply force down the market price. To reach a much larger number of potential investors, therefore, he persuades the corporation—his vote alone may be sufficient—to effect a 10-for-1 split. He is then able to offer the stock at a price around 20—surely with much less danger of a sharp drop in market value. In such a secondary distribution, the corporation itself receives no money; nevertheless, because wider distribution is promoted, this can be beneficial for its own financing or for other reasons.

A rather spectacular split-up of this kind was effected in December, 1958, by the Great Atlantic & Pacific Tea Company to prepare the way for the disposal of some of the stock interests of members of the Hartford family. The existing common was split 10 for 1, an additional nonvoting common was replaced by voting common also on a basis of 10 for 1, and the existing preferred was exchanged for voting common—3 shares of common for each share of preferred. Later, in March, 1959, Hartford interests offered for sale to the public 1.8 million shares of the voting common (the sole remaining class of stock).

Split-ups in Planning Combinations. Corporations not infrequently split up their common stock to make it more attractive to the stockholders of other corporations they hope to absorb. Split-ups can be most helpful in advancing merger proposals and holding company acquisitions. Corporation A wants to absorb Corporation B in a merger or to gain control of it and continue it in operation as a subsidiary. In keeping with the usual attitude, it hopes that the combination can be effected very largely on the basis of an exchange of some of its stock for that of B. Careful studies of B's asset values, and especially of its earnings record and prospects, lead A's managers to the conclusion that they could afford to offer one share of its stock for six shares of B's. But immediately it is felt that the very exchange ratio mentioned might make the proposal *sound* unattractive to B's stockholders. A 1-for-1 exchange would surely sound much better, and it could be easily managed. Let A simply split up its stock on a 6-for-1 basis and then make its offer at 1 for 1—a more pleasant offer, presumably, although not essentially different from the one originally contemplated.

Split-ups and Bargaining Position. A final reason for split-ups is to make earnings records look much poorer than they actually are or have been. This may seem a strange objective in view of the emphasis placed by credit grantors, investors, and security analysts on earnings per share of common and earnings on stockholders' investment. But employees, labor union officials, tax assessors, potential competitors, and customers may also be inclined to give much attention to these measures of profitability. While, therefore, a corporation wants to look quite affluent to people of the first group mentioned, it probably prefers to be looked on by those of the second group as having a tough struggle. Too much affluence is all too likely to lead to demands for higher wages, higher assessments for property taxes, greater reluctance of income tax agents to allow deductions in tax computations for disputed items of expense, dissatisfaction on the part of customers who may feel that high profit rates must mean that the prices of the corporation's products are unreasonable, and incursions into the corporation's field of operations by other firms.

Sometimes, of course, the stand taken by employees, tax collectors, customers, and others is fully or partially justified, but at other times it is clearly built on false premises, often related to some simple measure of profitability such as earnings per share of common, with other financial facts ignored. To the untutored or the careless investigator, a corporation that has earnings per share of common of $20 may appear to be 10 times as profitable as one whose earnings per share of common amount to only $2, whereas the fact may be that the second is much more profitable than the first in percentage rates of return on total assets or on total stockholders' investment. At any rate, split-ups can be used as a means of defense against attacks based on isolated measures of profitability such as earnings per share of common. Obviously, earnings per share of common can readily be reduced from $20 to $2 by simply splitting up the common on a 10-for-1 basis.

Reverse Splits. Reverse splits—or *split-downs*, as they are sometimes called—are much less common than split-ups. As one would expect, they are chiefly a phenomenon of periods of business depression and depressed stock market prices.

If a high price for a share of stock, such as $150 or $200, tends to take the stock out of the investment range of the great mass of investors, an extremely low price, such as 50 or 75 cents, or even a dollar or two, tends to do exactly the same. The stock gets into the company of cats and dogs or penny stocks, where it has attractions only for the wilder groups of speculators and those who lack investment acumen. Witness the flood of new uranium stocks offered in recent years at 1 cent, 5 cents, and 10 cents a share. Moreover, the cats-and-dogs area is the happy hunting ground of fraudulent promoters who defy the securities laws to try to make a quick dollar. Accordingly, reverse splits effected by reputable corporations are chiefly designed to get their stocks out of association with the motley array of cats and dogs and up to a more dignified level. Indeed, it is now the policy of the American Stock Exchange to proceed toward the delisting of corporations whose stocks fall in price to the cats-and-dogs level and remain there unduly long, unless the corporations effect reverse splits within a reasonable time. For this reason, among others, four of its listed corporations were dropped in June, 1968, with the approval of the SEC. To avoid a similar fate, the directors of the Siboney Corporation proposed a 1-for-5 reverse split, but its stockholders found the proposal distasteful and voted it down.[1]

A reverse split has the secondary effect of raising the level of profits per share, assuming that the corporation is not operating in the red. In time of business slump, this is likely to be regarded by corporate managers as desirable for its own sake. Like increases in market price, it should be good for credit standing and investor interest. A report of earnings at $1 a share of common stock after a 1-for-10 reverse split is likely to sound much better than would one of 10 cents a share without the reverse split.

TRANSACTIONS IN TREASURY STOCK

Treasury stock, as we know, is a corporation's own common stock originally issued as full paid and nonassessable and reacquired by the corporation by gift or purchase or in some other way.[2] We have already seen that corporations sometimes buy their own common stock in the market for resale to employees under the terms of their employee stock-purchase plans as well as for making deliveries to executives on the surrender of stock options. We have also considered donations of common stock for resale made by stockholders to whom entire original issues have been given, as in exchanges for partnership assets—a practice much more common in earlier days of high par values than now. But a few aspects of treasury stock remain for examination: certain legal and accounting considerations and the scope of certain kinds of transactions other than those already discussed. For the transactions, we shall find it convenient to classify some as legitimate and others as questionable.

Legal and Accounting Aspects of Treasury Stock

Legal Rules. In their corporation laws, all states permit the corporations they charter to acquire treasury stock by purchase, gift, or in other ways, and to sell it, pledge it, or otherwise dispose of it. But it is not required that treasury stock be held for subsequent disposal. It can be canceled by means of an amendment to the articles of incorporation, reducing the authorized issue by the amount of the treasury stock. A cancellation might be decided on to reduce the burden of annual capital stock or franchise taxes.

Subject to some exceptions to be mentioned later, the principal limitation found in state laws is that a corporation's expenditures in

---

[1] *The Wall Street Journal*, Midwest Edition, June 5, 1968, p. 12; June 19, 1968, p. 12; and June 21, 1968, p. 9.

[2] Corporations may, of course, reacquire some of their own preferred stock that was fully paid and made nonassessable at the time of issuance. Such reacquired stock could reasonably be called "preferred treasury stock" or "treasury preferred stock." Ordinarily, however, when the term *treasury stock* is used without modification it is understood to be common stock. A reason for this is that corporations generally cancel reacquired preferred stock, whereas they often have no intention to cancel when reacquiring common stock.

acquiring treasury stock must not exceed the amount of its earned surplus. The corporation's directors have the power to declare and distribute cash dividends in an amount equal to the earned surplus; hence, they presumably do no injury to creditors if they choose to use cash to buy treasury stock, paying not more than the balance in earned surplus after cash dividends, if any, have been deducted.

Other general rules found in the state laws and in court decisions include the following: treasury stock cannot be voted by the directors or by anybody else, it does not share in dividends, it may be disposed of by the directors without the consent of the stockholders unless the articles of incorporation require this consent, and it is not subject to the stockholders' preemptive right.

Accounting Treatment. In the accounting aspects of treasury stock, two rules are most emphasized by reputable accountants: treasury stock should be carried as a deduction from the common stock account rather than as an asset, and gain recognized *on the acquisition of the stock* should be carried as capital surplus or, even better, as a surplus account specifically titled to show its source. Suppose, for example, that the financial position of a certain corporation is as indicated in the following condensed balance sheet.

Assets	$10,000,000	Liabilities	$4,000,000
		Common stock	5,000,000
		Earned surplus	1,000,000

The common stock, let us say, consists of 100,000 shares of $50 par value. Now assume that 10,000 shares of the corporation's stock are donated to it by one or more of its stockholders. The preferred way of showing the effects of this transaction would be as follows.

Assets	$10,000,000	Liabilities		$4,000,000
		Common stock	$5,000,000	
		Less: Treasury stock	500,000	4,500,000
		Earned surplus		1,000,000
		Donated surplus (or surplus from donation of treasury stock)		500,000

Or assume that the corporation, instead of receiving a donation of stock, buys 10,000 shares in the market at $40 a share. Preferably, the result would be shown as follows.

Assets	$9,600,000	Liabilities		$4,000,000
		Common stock	$5,000,000	
		Less: Treasury stock	500,000	4,500,000
		Earned surplus		1,000,000
		Surplus from purchase of treasury stock		100,000

The last illustration demonstrates the reason for the rule limiting purchases of treasury stock to the amount of earned surplus. On the basis of the balance in its earned surplus account, the corporation before buying the treasury stock was in a position to pay cash dividends of $1 million, but after spending $400,000 in the treasury stock purchase, further purchases or the distribution of cash dividends for any amount in excess of $600,000 would unfairly threaten the safety of creditors. In fact, many accountants would insist that the balance sheet clearly show the reduction in the corporation's capacities to pay dividends and to buy treasury stock. This would be accomplished by reducing the earned surplus account to $600,000 and showing the $400,000 removed from it in a separate account with a descriptive title such as "surplus appropriated for treasury stock purchase." It may be observed, too, that by no stretch of the imagination could the surplus from purchase of treasury stock of $100,000 be said to add anything to the corporation's dividend-paying capacity.

Legitimate Transactions in Treasury Stock

Certain kinds of transactions in treasury stock are described here as legitimate in the sense that they clearly benefit corporations and their stockholders and, at the same time, do not weaken in any significant way the position of creditors.

For Options and Employee Stock Purchase Plans. Purchases of outstanding stock to make delivery on stock options held by executives and for the purposes of employee stock purchase plans generally fall in the category of legitimate transactions. New money is not raised when treasury stock is so used, except to the extent that selling prices to executives and employees exceed the prices at which treasury stock is bought. For at least a few corporations, however, acquiring additional cash is not an important objective of stock option arrangements and employee purchase plans. When, therefore, a corporation does not need additional money, a delivery of unissued stock would seem to be less desirable than a purchase and delivery of treasury stock.

For Merger Transactions. Much the same can be said for the use of treasury stock in acquisitions of enterprises in mergers and other forms of combination. In the drive for diversification that has been pronounced in recent years, many corporations have accumulated large amounts of cash earmarked for absorbing other firms. Often, however, the stockholders and managements of firms singled out for absorption refuse to sell for cash because of the tax liabilities on the capital gains that would result. They would much prefer to sell out on a basis of exchanges of common stocks, since such exchanges can usually be worked out as tax-free arrangements. Therefore, if the acquiring firm already has cash to pay for an acquisition it may prefer to buy up its own common stock in the market to make the exchange rather than to offer unissued stock. Indeed, many corporations have bought up some of their own common stock ahead of time, simply to have it available for exchanges should attractive merger opportunities turn up. In November, 1962, for example, the Standard Pressed Steel Company revealed that it had recently bought 25,400 shares of its common stock in the market and that it planned to continue to buy "for use in possible future acquisitions"; and in August, 1963, the Skelly Oil Company invited its common stockholders to tender to it up to 300,000 shares at prices not exceeding $70, the stock to be held "for use in acquisitions and its management stock-option plan."[3]

Donations. Also within the category of legitimacy are many transactions in which corporations' own common stock is donated to them. A corporation may be sorely in need of working capital at a time when the possibilities of selling new securities or borrowing direct from financial institutions are quite slim. Accordingly, one or a few of its stockholders, or perhaps all the stockholders on a pro rata basis, may donate a portion of their shares to the corporation in the belief that the corporation, and the remaining portion of their investment in it, can be saved by resale of these shares. Donations for this purpose are most likely to occur in family corporations, but they have sometimes been made even to large corporations that have wide common stock distributions. Donations of common stock may also be a means of eliminating deficits from corporate books, as an alternative to reductions in par or stated values of all such stock outstanding. On receiving a donation of some of its common stock, a corporation is justified in carrying a credit to a surplus account equal to the par or stated value of the donated stock. If, then, the earned surplus account has a debit balance, this can be directly offset by the credit for donated stock.

Settlement of Claims. Sometimes, corporations receive their own stock in settlement of obligations due them. A debtor who is unable to pay in cash may offer his holdings of the stock of the creditor corporation. Or having pledged his stock for the satisfaction of his obligation, the debtor may forfeit it on default. Again, on a debtor's default a corporation may sue and obtain judgment, thereafter seizing the debtor's holdings of its own stock in satisfaction of the judgment. Acquisitions of treasury stock in these ways appear to be quite legitimate; indeed, the state laws generally indicate specific approval by exempting such acquisitions from the rule limiting total acquisitions to the amount of earned surplus.

Use by Close Corporations. Another type of transaction that

[3]*Ibid.*, November 9, 1962, p. 19; and August 9, 1963, p. 12.

leads to acquisitions of treasury stock on what appears to be a legitimate basis is the buying back by close corporations of shares held by stockholders who want to sever their connections. The few stockholders of such a corporation may agree that their *esprit de corps* and, with that, the corporation's profitability would be ruined by the admission of outsiders as stockholders. In keeping with this conviction, they may enter into a contract among themselves to give the corporation the first chance to buy their stockholdings should they want to depart. A departure, therefore, would be the occasion for a treasury stock acquisition by the corporation.

Questionable Transactions in Treasury Stock

Certain kinds of treasury stock transactions are described in these pages as questionable because they can prove to be harmful to corporations and all their stockholders, to particular groups of stockholders, or to their creditors.

Purchases for Retirement. A most interesting question of legitimacy arises when corporate boards of directors decide to use excess cash to buy up outstanding common stock for retirement. It is a question for which, in truth, there is no clear-cut answer, but some of the pros and cons may be mentioned.

A corporation may have curtailed the scope of its operations, and prospects for reexpansion may be nil. At the same time, the directors may want to avoid the distribution of redundant cash by way of extraordinary dividends because substantial amounts of these dividends would be subject to income taxes when received by the stockholders. The buying up of stock in the market may thus appear to be an easy solution to the problem. The directors could argue that stockholders who offer their shares in the market are the very ones who want to give up their ownership interests—that, accordingly, buying up these shares would be preferable to reducing the interests of all stockholders indiscriminately, as by the distribution of dividends in partial liquidation. If the shares could be bought in the market at less than their book value, the directors could also argue that the corporation's purchases would give the remaining stockholders increased per-share claims against assets. On the other hand, if more than book value had to be paid for the treasury stock, the remaining stockholders would seem to have a good reason to complain about the resulting reduction in the book value of their own shares. Even more gravely would they be injured if, subsequent to the purchase and retirement of the treasury stock, the affairs of the corporation were to go badly and operating losses make serious inroads on the assets. The board of directors could be condemned as having given preferential treatment of an extreme kind to the stockholders from whom the treasury stock had been bought.

Doubts about the legitimacy of purchases by corporations of their own common stocks for retirement can always be resolved, of course, by submitting the question to the stockholders themselves. This was done by the Richmond, Fredericksburg & Potomac Railroad Company when, in August, 1962, it asked its stockholders to tender to it their common or preferred shares so that it could use up $3 million of cash for which it had "no need." The secretary-treasurer said that investment of the money in short-term securities would yield a lower rate of return than the dividend rates the company was paying on its stocks, so that it would "save money" by buying back stock.[4]

Slack Season Investment. More clearly worthy of adverse criticism is a use of excess cash for dealings in treasury stock on a temporary basis. In the off-season of a corporation whose pattern of operations is highly seasonal, the directors might decide that the best way to invest excess cash until needed for the active season would be to buy some of the corporation's own common stock available in the market. The intention clearly would not be to retire the stock but to resell it at or before the time cash would be needed for operations. The directors might try to justify the treasury stock transactions on the grounds that the dividends saved on the stock while held in the treasury would be much greater than the interest that could be earned by temporary investment in, say, short-term government securities. Moreover, the directors might be inclined to feel that, by astutely playing the market they would be able to sell at a net gain. It is clear, at any rate, that a temporary investment of excess cash in treasury stock could hardly be other than speculative. Even if the possibility of capital gains were given no great weight in the directors' decision, it is obvious that the net saving as between dividend and interest rates could be more than offset by losses on resale. Stockholders, therefore, would have a sound basis for arguing that the risks of stock market speculation ought not to be added to the unavoidable risks of day-to-day operations.

Supporting Market Prices. Most questionable of all, in the realm of treasury stock transaction, are purchases made to arrest declines in the market values of stocks. To justify actions of this kind, corporate managements have advanced the argument that sharp and rapid declines in the market prices of stock are injurious to credit standing and prospects for future financing, and some have even claimed that corporations have a duty to see that their stockholders get a reasonable value for their stock if they want to sell; but such arguments are quite unconvincing. Corporations have no duty to selling stockholders to take extraordinary measures in order to protect the market value of their shares, and their buying has generally

[4]*Ibid.*, August 8, 1962, p. 4.

been of little help in saving credit standing and prospects for future financing when prices have been under the pressure of floods of selling orders. In fact, the very use of cash for stock purchases to stem price declines is likely to be much more injurious to credit standing and future prospects of all kinds, including survival, than are the price declines themselves.

In the second quarter of 1962 when a very sharp drop in stock prices in all markets took place, many corporations bought up extraordinary amounts of their common stock. According to a report of the New York Stock Exchange, these corporations included McCrory Corporation, which bought 195,100 shares during the quarter; Allied Supermarkets, Inc., 247,200 shares; Schering Corporation, 50,000 shares; Consolidation Coal Company, 140,857 shares; Gulf Oil Corporation, 225,000 shares; and Skelly Oil Company, 152,375 shares. In all instances, however, it was denied that purchases had been made to support market prices. Instead, the general attitude was that the period was a very favorable time to acquire treasury stock for possible future acquisitions and for delivery against stock options. For McCrory, raising earnings per share of the stock that remained outstanding was given as a reason for buying.[5]

QUESTIONS

1. If a corporation lacks sufficient unissued common stock to make deliveries on stock options, stock purchase warrants, and convertible securities, what other means could it employ to fulfill such contractual obligations? Why would these other means be likely to be disadvantageous to it?

2. In what kinds of transactions might it be advantageous for a corporation's stockholders to supply its directors with an ample quantity of unissued shares?

3. What disadvantages might a corporation and its stockholders suffer on account of having large amounts of authorized but unissued stock?

4. How can one account for the campaign in the early part of the present century for state laws permitting issuance of no-par stock, as well as for the more recent swing of popularity toward stocks of low pars?

5. To what extent is there discrimination in taxation as between no-par stocks and stocks of low pars? What kinds of taxes are involved?

6. How do stocks of low par values compare with no-par stocks in enabling corporations to avoid the discount rule? To allocate substantial proportions of the proceeds of stock sales to paid-in surplus accounts?

7. Corporations can offset operating losses by simply writing down the par or stated values of their common stocks. Is this proposition true or false? Explain.

8. What effect, if any, does a write-down in the par or stated value of a corporation's stock have on its dividend-paying capacity? Explain.

---

[5] *Ibid.*, July 20, 1962, p. 2.

9. In what circumstances would it be advantageous to a corporation to write down the value of its assets with an accompanying write-down in the par or stated value of its common stock?

10. What relationship is there, if any, between split-ups of corporate stock and the wide distribution of this stock? Why is wide distribution desired? By whom?

11. Why might it be advisable for a corporation to split up its common stock preparatory to negotiations for the absorption of other enterprises by merger?

12. Distinguish between unissued stock and treasury stock. Is it proper for corporations to treat as profits any gains made on treasury stock transactions? Discuss.

13. What kinds of legal restrictions apply to corporations' acquisitions of their own outstanding common stocks?

14. Discuss the reasonableness of a corporation's buying its own common stock in the market (*a*) to make delivery on stock options, (*b*) to be held for offering in merger proposals, (*c*) to use up excess cash with the intention of retiring the purchased stock, (*d*) to invest cash temporarily in excess supply on account of seasonal factors, and (*e*) to try to check a decline in the market value of the stock.

PROBLEMS

1. Eager to absorb the Linton Manufacturing Corporation in a merger by means of an exchange of common stocks, the directors of the Able Manufacturing Company want to make their offer as attractive as possible to Linton's stockholders, while avoiding dangers of dilution to the ownership interests of their own stockholders. Some of the directors think the offer should be one share of Able's stock for three shares of Linton's, because recent annual after-tax profits on Able's stock have been averaging around $6 a share, but only $2 on Linton's. A second group are of the opinion that the offer should be 1 to 4, because the current market price of Able's stock is $83, while Linton's is $22. And a third group think that neither of these offers would *sound* attractive to Linton's stockholders—that there ought to be some way the offer could be made on a 1-for-1 basis.

a) While protecting Able's stockholders from dilution dangers, how could its directors make arrangements for a 1-to-1 offer in conformity with the ratio suggested by the first group? The ratio recommended by the second group?

b) For discussion: Should the offer be made in conformity with the ratio suggested by the first group of directors or with that proposed by the second group?

2. At the end of the year 19xx, the financial position of the Meany Products Company was as indicated in the following condensed balance sheet.

Current assets	$ 4,800,000	Current liabilities	$ 2,300,000
Land	300,000	Bonds payable	3,000,000
Buildings	1,800,000	Common stock	7,000,000
Machinery and equipment	3,800,000	Deficit	−1,000,000
Patents	600,000		
	$11,300,000		$11,300,000

The common stock consists of 1.4 million shares of $5 par value. In recent years, Meany has suffered annual net losses averaging $180,000. Its average profit before deductions for depreciation and amortization has been $240,000, but its depreciation charge has been $270,000 a year and its charge for patent amortization $150,000. As it has been suffering a steady deterioration in credit standing, its directors propose to the stockholders that the value of the tangible fixed assets be written down by 40 percent and that the value of the patents be written off completely. They further recommend that the par value of the stock be reduced to $1 to absorb the write-downs, to eliminate the deficit already accumulated, and to provide a balance in capital surplus. The stockholders approve these recommendations, and the books are adjusted accordingly.

a) Prepare a revised balance sheet to show the effects of the adjustments.

b) Assume that in the following year the corporation's profit after the deduction of depreciation charges (reduced to $162,000) amounts to $78,000, and that it has no income taxes to pay on this profit, since it is allowed to deduct for tax purposes depreciation and amortization charges at the former levels. What rate of return would it now be earning on (1) total assets, (2) the stockholders' total equity, and (3) each share of common stock? How would these rates compare with the preadjustment rates of return?

3. A corporation has outstanding 250,000 shares of common stock of $20 par value. It has incurred operating losses for several years and now has an accumulated deficit of $4 million in its earned surplus account. It has no paid-in or capital surplus.

a) How could it manipulate its equity accounts to eliminate the deficit and give it, at the same time, a surplus credit balance of about, say, $500,000?

b) Could the directors legally declare cash dividends on the basis of the surplus balance established in (*a*)? Explain.

c) If the corporation had an operating profit of $400,000 after the manipulation, could cash dividends up to this amount be legally paid? Explain.

d) Would the manipulation require the approval of the stockholders? Amendment of the corporation's articles of incorporation?

chapter 22

THE LISTING OF COMMON STOCK ON STOCK EXCHANGES

The listing of a common stock or other security may be defined as the supplying of facilities by a stock exchange to its members, on the basis of an agreement with the issuer, for trading in the security. A corporation that wants to have its common stock listed makes application to the stock exchange of its choice, as well as to the Securities and Exchange Commission if the exchange is registered as a national securities exchange, as are all but three of our exchanges. Both the exchange and the SEC investigate the affairs of the applying corporation, the exchange with particular attention to the prospective trading interests of its members, and the SEC with special concern for the protection of the investing public. If both the exchange and the SEC approve the application, the common stock becomes listed. The exchange then designates a post on its floor where its members can meet to effect buying and selling transactions in the stock.

Whether or not to list common stock on one or more of our stock exchanges is a problem that faces the managements of only a small minority of American business corporations. On the basis of the exchanges' own admission standards, most corporations do not qualify for the listing of their common stocks, and a goodly number of those that could qualify find one or more reasons for not making applications for listing. As of December 31, 1966, according to a report of the SEC, only 3,106 issues of common stock in total were listed on all exchanges (avoiding duplications on account of dual listings of given common stocks on two or more exchanges).[1]

That a corporation does not have its common stock and other securities issues listed on a stock exchange does not mean there is no

[1]Securities and Exchange Commission, *Annual Report*, 1967, p. 58.

market for them. In almost all instances, the holder of an unlisted security who wants to sell can find one or more dealers who will either buy the security from him or undertake to find a buyer. Such transactions are said to take place in the over-the-counter market, located principally in the hundreds of offices of securities dealers throughout the country, rather than at a single site, as is a stock exchange. Indeed, the volume of transactions in the over-the-counter market in many unlisted securities far exceeds the volume on the stock exchanges in inactive and less active listed securities. Moreover, the over-the-counter market accounts for a substantial volume of transactions in listed securities, especially transactions in which large institutional investors are buyers or sellers. To buy large blocks of given stocks, institutional investors often find the total cost lower in the over-the-counter market than would be the price plus commissions they would have to pay if buying through stock exchange members. To sell large blocks, they often find better offers in the over-the-counter market than would be the price less commissions for stock exchange transactions.

Nevertheless, the question of listing is important, as it must be considered at one time or another by most of the larger corporations of the country. Somewhere along the line, the management of a corporation that is reaching substantial size is likely to come to a realization that it could qualify for listing—and this brings up the question whether or not listing would be advantageous. Accordingly, the principal aim of the present chapter is to analyze the pros and cons of listing, as they are likely to be seen from the standpoint of corporate managements. First, however, it is desirable to survey some general aspects of the listing question.

GENERAL ASPECTS OF LISTING

Business corporations do not raise new money for their operations by the sale of common stock (or other securities) through the facilities of the stock exchanges. They do not deliver batches of new common stock to an exchange and expect its members to sell it to their customers. If they want to use common stock as a means of financing, they offer it to the public direct or through investment bankers, offer it to their existing stockholders with or without the aid of investment bankers, or use one or more of the additional selling procedures described in Chapter 20.

Only after a common stock has been rather widely distributed by one or more of these means, as well as by subsequent transactions among holders, is an exchange likely to consider accepting it for listing. Most members of an exchange—that is, the owners of seats who alone have the privilege of buying and selling through its facilities—make a large part of their income from commissions derived in handling buying and selling orders for their customers. Hence, in general, they want the exchange to list for trading only securities that are distributed widely enough to promise numerous transactions.

In having its common stock listed on an exchange, therefore, a corporation obtains market facilities, not for its own selling, but for selling by its stockholders and for buying by those who want to become stockholders. Through investment bankers, a corporation may have sold its common stock to A, B, C, and thousands of other investors. But now that the stock has been listed, A may hire a member of the exchange to sell his shares through its facilities, C may hire another member to buy some additional shares, and later C may resell to D, D to E, and so on.

The Exchanges

Although 16 stock exchanges, listed in Table 22–1, are currently in operation in the United States,[2] stock exchange transactions are

TABLE 22–1
Sales of Stock on Stock Exchanges in 1967
(All amounts in thousands)

	Market Value	*Number of Shares*
Registered exchanges:		
American Stock Exchange	$ 23,111,274	1,290,205
Boston Stock Exchange	1,086,315	20,084
Chicago Board of Trade	0	0
Cincinnati Stock Exchange	62,234	1,185
Detroit Stock Exchange	715,625	15,269
Midwest Stock Exchange	4,995,648	109,226
National Stock Exchange	22,214	3,032
New York Stock Exchange	125,329,105	2,885,748
Pacific Coast Stock Exchange	4,530,208	113,001
Philadelphia-Baltimore-Washington Stock Exchange	1,830,742	38,464
Pittsburgh Stock Exchange	51,964	1,151
Salt Lake Stock Exchange	8,265	12,439
San Francisco Mining Exchange*	860	4,187
Spokane Stock Exchange	8,010	10,167
Total	$161,752,464	4,504,157†
Exempted exchanges:		
Colorado Springs Stock Exchange	$ 0	0
Honolulu Stock Exchange	16,716	1,024
Richmond Stock Exchange	1,789	48
Total	$ 18,505	1,072

*By order of the SEC, this exchange discontinued operations and dissolved in August, 1967.
†Items do not add exactly to this total because of rounding.
SOURCE: Securities and Exchange Commission, *Statistical Bulletin*, March, 1968, p. 11.

[2]Although 17 exchanges are listed in the table, it will be noticed that the San Francisco Mining Exchange discontinued operations in August, 1967. It is also noteworthy that the Chicago Board of Trade and the Colorado Springs Stock Exchange reported no stock transactions in 1967.

heavily concentrated on the New York and American exchanges. Percentages computed from the data presented in Table 22–1 reveal that transactions on the New York Stock Exchange in the year 1967 amounted to 64.1 percent of the number of shares of stock, common and preferred, sold on all exchanges, and to 77.5 percent of the total market value of shares sold on all exchanges. Of the 3,106 issues of stocks traded on all exchanges on December 31, 1966, 1,665 were listed on the Big Board. On the same date, the American Stock Exchange, also located in New York City, had 1,038 stocks posted for trading. In 1967, it accounted for 28.6 percent of the number and 14.3 percent of the market value of shares sold on all exchanges, leaving for all the remaining exchanges only 7.3 percent of the number and 8.2 percent of the market values of shares traded. At the end of 1966, stocks traded exclusively on exchanges other than the New York and American exchanges numbered 403.[3]

Stocks listed on the New York and American exchanges are generally of nationwide and often international interest, while many of those listed solely on the other exchanges are of interest especially to the people living in the respective regions they serve. However, quite a few important corporations of nationwide interest are listed on the regional exchanges—especially on the Midwest Stock Exchange of Chicago and the Pacific Coast Stock Exchange, which maintains trading facilities in both Los Angeles and San Francisco. These are sometimes sole listings—a given stock not being traded on any other exchange—and more often dual listings, with the stock also listed on one or more additional exchanges—most likely the New York or the American. For some examples of single and dual listings, see Table 22–2.

Listings with the New York and American exchanges are likely to be sought especially by large corporations that have wide distributions of their common stocks, recurring needs of additional funds to be sought from many sources scattered over a wide area, and market outlets for their products throughout the country and perhaps abroad, assuming that they want to list at all. Such corporations are likely to have a decided preference for the New York Stock Exchange in view of its unequaled prestige. They sometimes also seek dual listing with one or more of the regional exchanges. However, corporations whose operating facilities, markets, and prospective sources of long-term equity funds are largely confined to given areas of the country may be quite satisfied to have their common stocks listed solely on one of the regional exchanges—again, if there is a wish to list at all.

In the matter of pros and cons, therefore, the managers of a corpora-

---

[3]Data on number of stocks posted for trading from Securities and Exchange Commission, *Annual Report*, 1967, p. 58.

tion whose interest are largely concentrated regionally are likely to feel that all the advantages of listing can be had by listing on an exchange that specifically serves its region—that, indeed, the disadvantages of listing on the New York or American exchange or on another outside its region would tend to outweigh the advantages. But the managers of a corporation that has broad, national interests

TABLE 22–2
A Sample of Stock Exchange Listings and Admissions to Unlisted Trading of Common Stocks as of December 31, 1967*

Corporation	*Listed on*	*Unlisted Trading on*
Briggs Manufacturing Co.	Detroit	
Crown Zellerbach Corporation	New York Pacific	Philadelphia
Firestone Tire & Rubber Company	Boston New York	Cincinnati Detroit Midwest Pacific
General Motors Corporation	Detroit Midwest New York Pacific Philadelphia	Boston Cincinnati Pittsburgh
Holly Oil Company	Pacific	
Kaiser Industries Corporation	American Pacific	Boston Philadelphia Pittsburgh
McDonnell-Douglas Corporation	New York	Detroit Philadelphia
Northeast Airlines, Inc.	American	
Northern Indiana Public Service Company	Midwest New York	Boston
Reynolds Metals Company	New York	Cincinnati Detroit Midwest Pacific Philadelphia
Todd Shipyards Corporation	American	

*The Philadelphia-Baltimore-Washington Stock Exchange is entered as "Philadelphia," and the Pacific Coast Stock Exchange as "Pacific."
SOURCE: Moody's Investors Service, *Manuals*.

are likely to decide that the maximum advantages of listing can be had only by listing with the New York Stock Exchange or possibly, as a second choice, with the American, and that, accordingly, disadvantages would tend to outweigh advantages if only one of the regional exchanges were available as a third choice.

Government Regulation

Regulation of Exchanges and Their Members. The federal Securities and Exchange Act denies the use of the mails and other instrumentalities of interstate commerce to stock exchanges unless they register with the SEC or unless that agency exempts them from registration. Of our 16 exchanges, 13 are registered with the SEC as "national securities exchanges,"[4] and the other 3 have been exempted from registration.[5] Registered exchanges *and their members* must abide by many rules set down in the Securities and Exchange Act and by many regulations of the SEC issued under authority of that legislation—rules and regulations specifically designed to protect investors.

Regulation of Listed Corporations. But the Securities Exchange Act and the rules of the SEC do not stop with regulation of the practices of the exchanges and their members; they reach out to the corporations whose securities are listed on the national securities exchanges. A corporation that wants to have its common stock (or other security) listed must file with the exchange and the SEC an application containing an extensive array of information about its history, its properties, the scope of its operations, its management, its financial structure, and other material facts—information of the kinds presumably necessary, as in registration statements under the Securities Act, for intelligent investment decisions. Indeed, the contents of applications for listing and those of registration statements for new securities issues are closely comparable—to be expected, of course, since both have been prescribed by the SEC for the identical purpose of investor protection. Listed corporations must also file with the exchange and the SEC annual and semiannual financial reports to bring up to date the financial data originally filed in the application, and monthly reports if certain extraordinary developments occur, such as changes in controlling interests, material changes in the volume of outstanding stocks and bonds, important acquisitions and dispositions of assets, and the initiation or termination of important legal proceedings. Furthermore, directors and officers of corporations that have stocks listed on registered exchanges, as well as owners of more than 10 percent of any class of a listed stock, must file statements of their holdings with the SEC and keep these up-to-date by making further reports in any months when changes in holdings take place. All the information supplied in applications, annual and semiannual financial reports, special reports, and reports of stockholdings becomes public property. The documents can be examined at the respective exchanges or in the offices of the SEC, and, of course, many significant items are published by newspapers and other purveyors of financial information.The prospective investor can readily pick up much more extensive details about the affairs of the typical listed corporation than about those of the typical unlisted one.

Of the additional rules imposed on listed corporations for investor

---

[4]One must not be misled by the word *national*. The registered exchanges are national for purposes of the legislation and regulations, but as brought out in the foregoing discussion, most of them are regional in the scope of their listings.

[5]As indicated in Table 22–1, the exempted exchanges are the Colorado Springs, Honolulu, and Richmond exchanges.

protection, only three need be mentioned here. One is concerned with the solicitation of stockholders' proxies for voting at annual and special meetings. Whether a solicitation is being made by a corporate management or by somebody else, such as a group seeking to oust the existing management, the proxy form must be drawn in accordance with SEC prescriptions, and when sent to the stockholders it must be accompanied by a proxy statement declaring who is making the solicitation and who is bearing the cost, giving details about the issues to be raised at the meeting, and supplying certain facts of other kinds as prescribed by the SEC's rules. When the solicitors know in advance that certain proposals are to be presented at a meeting, they must design the proxy form in such manner that the stockholder can indicate his vote for or against the proposals. Copies of proposed proxy forms and statements must be filed with the SEC at least 10 days before distribution to the stockholders. If the SEC finds them defective under its rules, it notifies the solicitors so that corrections can be made before distribution.

A second rule is that the directors and officers of a corporation whose stock is listed on a registered exchange, as well as stockholders who own directly or indirectly more than 10 percent of any class of its stock, are forbidden to sell the stock short.

A third rule is that a listed corporation, by lawsuit brought by itself or by any stockholder, may recover from its directors and officers and from owners of more than 10 percent of any class of its stock any profits made by them in transactions in its stock held for periods of less than 6 months.

SEC Action. Indicative of the SEC's role in protecting investors was its action in May, 1964, in suspending the registration of the Precision Microwave Corporation on the American Stock Exchange—an action it explained as follows.

> . . . the Commission found that a Securities Act registration statement, incorporated by reference in the issuer's application for registration of its common stock on the American Stock Exchange, contained false and misleading financial information, including a material understatement of liability for sales commissions, a material overstatement of work-in-process, and distorted comparative sales and earnings figures. It further found that the accountant's certificate was false and misleading because he did not follow generally accepted auditing procedures and was not in fact independent, having employed the office manager and accountant of the issuer's major subsidiary, who was responsible for maintenance of books and records reviewed during the audit, to assist him in the audit. . . .[6]

Listing Standards

For admission of its common stock to a stock exchange, a corporation must generally be able to offer something more than proof of a

[6]Securities and Exchange Commission, *Annual Report*, 1964, p. 52.

reasonably wide distribution of the stock and a willingness to abide by the rules and regulations of the SEC and of the exchange itself. The exchanges do not want to list corporations that are obviously being mismanaged, those whose financial structures are so complex that it is difficult to know what are the respective rights of the various classes of security holders, or those that consistently operate in the red so that they are obviously moving fast toward bankruptcy. The listing of the common stocks of such corporations could only detract from the prestige of an exchange, and exchanges are most anxious to preserve their good names, considering that even when they conduct their affairs in a most careful way they are often subjected to unfair criticism by the uninformed.

More positively, the exchanges want the listings of well-managed corporations that have established solid places for themselves in their respective industries, that have good records of earnings, and that have good promise of continued growth and prosperity. In this regard, the New York Stock Exchange describes its standards of eligibility as follows:

> . . .it must be a going concern with substantial assets and demonstrated earning power. The Exchange places emphasis on such considerations as degree of national interest in the company, the character of the market for its product, relative stability and position in its industry. The stock should have a sufficiently wide distribution to offer reasonable assurance that an adequate auction market in its securities will exist.[7]

From time to time in recent years, the New York Stock Exchange, like some of the other exchanges, has upgraded its standards for listing; the latest such revision was adopted in May, 1968. For the listing of its stock according to the provisions of this revision, a corporation is expected to have:

1. A before-tax profit of not less than $2.5 million in its most recent fiscal year, and an average of not less than $2 million in the preceding two years.
2. At least 1 million shares of the stock outstanding with a market value of not less than $14 million.
3. At least 800,000 of its shares publicly held by not fewer than 2,000 stockholders, of whom at least 1,800 should be round-lot owners—that is, owners of 100 shares or more.
4. Net tangible assets of at least $14 million—a qualification apparently given less weight than a market value of that amount for the outstanding stock, as already mentioned.

Under the latest revision, likewise, it is the policy of the exchange to consider the advisability of dropping common stocks from its list when the qualifications of the issuing corporations and their stocks

[7]New York Stock Exchange, *Understanding the New York Stock Exchange*, 1967, p. 22.

fall to levels in the vicinity of 50 percent of the listing standards: when the number of shares publicly owned has fallen to 400,000 or less, the number of stockholders has fallen to 1,000 or fewer, the number of round-lot owners has shrunk to 900 or fewer, or—not exactly conforming to the 50 percent rule—when earnings have averaged as low as $600,000 or less for three years *and* the market value of the stock *or* the value of net tangible assets has fallen to less than $7 million.[8]

To have its common stock listed on the American Stock Exchange, a corporation must have, as a rule, net tangible assets of at least $3 million, annual before-tax earnings of at least $500,000 and annual after-tax earnings of at least $300,000, and outstanding publicly held shares numbering not less than 300,000 with a market value of not less than $2 million. In addition, the stock must have already been selling in the market "for a reasonable period of time" at a price of not less than $5. In February, 1968, the American adopted tougher standards for dropping stocks from its list. Under these standards, it considers the advisability of delisting a stock if the corporation's net tangible assets fall below $1 million and if it had net losses in its two most recent fiscal years, or if its net tangible assets fall below $3 million and if it had net losses in three of its four most recent fiscal years; if the number of publicly held shares falls below 150,000, or the number of stockholders below 450, or the number of holders of 100 shares or more below 300; or if the total value of publicly held shares falls under $750,000.[9] As was pointed out in Chapter 21, the American also has a prejudice against low-priced stocks evidenced by its action in June, 1968, in dropping four whose issuers had not been sufficiently prompt in inaugurating moves toward reverse splits.[10]

Unlisted Trading

Under the Securities Exchange Act, the SEC may permit exchanges to admit for unlisted trading securities that are formally listed on other exchanges, and it has reported that as of June 30, 1967, there were 1,824 such admissions of both common and preferred stocks in effect—the total not adjusted for duplications.[11] Unlisted admissions were illustrated earlier in this chapter in Table 22-2, in which were named the exchanges where the stocks of the cited corporations are traded on an unlisted basis. An exchange's acceptance of a stock for trading on an unlisted basis does not, of course, relieve the issuing corporation of regulation, since it is already subject to the SEC's

[8]New York Stock Exchange, *The Exchange*, July, 1968, pp. 24-25.
[9]*The Wall Street Journal*, Midwest Edition, February 20, 1968, p. 10.
[10]See p. 540.
[11]Securities and Exchange Commission, *Annual Report*, 1967, p. 63.

regulations because of its formal listing on one or more other exchanges, as well as to whatever additional rules these exchanges may have in effect. However, any admission on an unlisted basis gives it an additional market without added burdens.

ADVANTAGES OF LISTING

From the standpoint of corporate welfare, the advantages of having common stocks listed on the stock exchanges are likely to be thought of as including chiefly the following: (1) wider distribution of the stock, (2) aid in selling additional issues of the stock, (3) aid in selling other securities, (4) improved credit standing, and (5) advertising of products. Such a classification undoubtedly overlaps, for, as was pointed out in Chapter 21, wide distribution is not so much an advantage in itself as it is a source of other advantages, such as aid in selling additional stock or other securities and the promotion of product sales. To be kept in mind, moreover, is the idea that the advantages of listing are importantly influenced and conditioned by the scope of operations of the particular exchange on which a stock is or is to be listed, national or regional.

Wider Distribution of the Stock

It may seem strange to say that exchanges are not interested in listing common stocks unless they are widely distributed, but that an advantage of listing is to get wider distribution. But there is no conflict in the two propositions: a common stock, already widely held, tends to get even more widely scattered as a result of transactions in it effected through the market machinery of a stock exchange. Some investors refuse to buy unlisted stocks; many are much more reluctant to buy these than listed ones.

Regardless of intentions to hold stocks for long periods, virtually all investors want market facilities that ensure quick sale at fair prices. Changing conditions, they know, may make changes in investment plans imperative. Exchanges provide good market facilities. Buying and selling orders pour in to members from all parts of the country, or from all parts of a given region, and prices determined by these concentrated forces of supply and demand are likely to be fairer than those negotiated in random transactions in dealers' offices. Factors that tend to enhance the attractiveness of listed stocks include the following.

1. Members of exchanges must obey an extensive body of rules promulgated by the exchanges themselves and by the SEC for the protection of their customers.
2. The scales of their commission rates are widely publicized.
3. The prices at which transactions actually take place are quickly reported and widely disseminated.

4. Some members provide special facilities for odd-lot transactions—that is, purchases and sales of fewer than 100 shares.
5. Listed securities are usually more acceptable as collateral for loans than are comparable unlisted ones.

Aid in Selling Additional Common Stock

The belief of corporate managements that listing aids the sale of common stock is indicated by the fact that in advertising new issues of such stock, as yet unlisted, they sometimes promise that an application for listing will be made to this or that exchange. Once a stock has been listed, moreover, additional shares, when sold, are included in the listing as a matter of course; thus, prospective buyers have this assurance of the availability of market facilities.

Because the market prices of listed stocks result from numerous buying and selling orders coming in from all directions, they tend to be highly reliable as guides to corporations and investment bankers in fixing the prices at which additional issues are to be offered—much more so than are price quotations given by dealers for stocks traded in the over-the-counter market. Indeed, since listing appears to increase demand by attracting investors who would not otherwise buy, the price of a stock as listed should be somewhat higher than it would be were it unlisted. It is likely, therefore, that the price at which additional shares of a listed stock are offered can be somewhat higher than it could be if the stock were unlisted. Moreover, investment bankers may pare their underwriting commissions in favor of flotations of additional shares of listed stocks, anticipating less selling effort than would be required if the already outstanding stock were unlisted. Either or both these factors may thus mean greater net proceeds to the issuing corporation.

Of even more direct aid to corporations in selling additional shares of listed stocks is the practice of the exchanges, for offerings to existing stockholders, of providing facilities for the buying and selling of rights. The stockholder who does not want to subscribe knows that he can sell his rights just about as readily as he could sell his shares themselves, and the publicity given to rights values through market transactions gives him a constant reminder to sell before the end of the subscription period. Likewise, the ready availability of rights on the exchange at well-publicized prices tends to attract buyers of rights —both those who want to subscribe and those who choose to speculate.

Aid in Selling Other Securities

All the publicity given to listed common stocks in daily newspapers, financial journals, investment newsletters, and the publications of investment information services tends to be helpful to the sale not only of additional issues of the common stocks of listed corporations but also their issues of preferred stocks and bonds. Whether or not the corporations promise to apply for the listing of the preferred stocks and bonds, investor interest in these kinds of issues is ready-made. Although published information about the finances of listed corporations usually emphasizes the position of their common stocks, the same information is obviously useful to prospective investors in judging the investment qualities of their offerings of other types of securities.

In view of the ready-made interest of investors in the preferred stock and bond issues of listed corporations, investment bankers, in underwriting these issues, may expect a relatively easy selling job, and may accordingly demand somewhat lower commissions than they would ask of unlisted corporations. Facilities provided by the exchanges for trading in rights may also contribute to ease in selling new issues of preferred stocks and bonds of listed corporations. When such securities are made convertible into common stock, very often existing common stockholders are given the first opportunity to subscribe; hence, subscription rights become available for trading in the same manner as for new offerings of common stock by this route.

Improved Credit Standing

Aside from improving prospects of attracting buyers of bonds, by having its common stock listed a corporation tends to enhance its credit standing with other prospective creditors, especially if the exchange on which the stock is listed itself has prestige. A wide distribution of a corporation's common stock and developed investor interest in other classes of its securities, as promoted by listing, should give prospective short- and intermediate-term creditors some confidence that obligations to them could be liquidated, if necessary, by flotation of equity securities or long-term bonds. Contributing additionally to creditor confidence should be the management standards that exchanges expect listed corporations to maintain. Also, creditors may have more confidence in financial data filed with the exchanges and the SEC—considering the penalties for omissions and misstatements—than they would have in credit data supplied by the corporations direct to them.

Advertising of Products

The point was made in Chapter 21 that corporations, especially those producing consumer goods, favor wide distributions of their common stocks in the belief that stockholders will be inclined to prefer their products to those of competitors. But listing also appears to have some value in advertising products to people who do not become stockholders. Many people look at stock market quotations even though they have little interest in buying stocks, but the names of listed corporations thereby become familiar to them. Familiarity with the names of listed corporations is also promoted by the many news items that are published concerning them—a frequency of publication promoted, in turn, by constant disclosures of new information required by federal reporting requirements. In shopping, therefore, people who are not stockholders may be strongly inclined to buy products of corporations whose names are familiar to them rather than the products of unknown enterprises.

DISADVANTAGES OF LISTING

Effects of 1964 Amendments

For most of the unlisted corporations that would be eligible for listing on the basis of the standards of the stock exchanges, certain disadvantages of listing, as these corporations might have seen them, were eliminated by amendments to the Securities Exchange Act adopted in August, 1964. These amendments require unlisted corporations that have individually $1 million or more of assets and 500 or more stockholders to comply with almost all of the regulations that apply to listed corporations registered with the SEC—to file registration statements, to issue periodic financial reports, to have changes in the stockholdings of insiders reported, to observe the SEC's proxy rules, and so on.

Up to the time these rules were made applicable to unlisted corporations of the size indicated, it was generally thought that among the principal reasons for their choosing to remain unlisted were avoidance of all the disclosure requirements and costs of registration, and avoidance of restrictions on transactions by insiders. For many of these corporations, there was undoubtedly great reluctance to make public a lot of information that they preferred to withhold as being confidential—details such as sales, operating expenses, and profits, officers' salaries, bonuses, and options, and the stockholdings of directors and officers and their buying and selling of stock. And surely at least a few expected their insiders to be able to make killings from time to time if certain kinds of decisions could be adopted and put into action without obligations to promptly inform the public about them.

Remaining Disadvantages

With disclosure requirements, restrictions on insiders, and costs of registration out of the way as possible disadvantages of listing, there appear to remain three significant reasons that corporations, though eligible for listing on the basis of size of assets, number of stockholders, and so on, may regard listing as disadvantageous: (1) fear of excessive speculation in their stocks, with resulting extreme market price fluctuations; (2) desire to avoid certain restrictions on freedom of action; and (3) wish to escape additional expense burdens.

Possibilities of Excessive Speculation. The fear of excessive speculation in their stocks was recognized for generations as a principal reason commercial banks—though including some of the largest corporations in the country—showed little inclination to have their stocks listed on stock exchanges. But in recent years, the listing of the stocks of some of our leading banks indicates that the fear is much less than it used to be. Moreover, steady improvement in the facilities of the over-the-counter market in which unlisted stocks are traded have tended to make many of these stocks subject to the same kinds of speculative interests and forces that were formerly thought to be largely limited to listed securities.

Nevertheless, many unlisted corporations probably remain justified in thinking that after being accorded but little attention in the over-the-counter market for years their stocks could readily become the focus of speculative interests after being listed. The directors and officers of such a corporation might anticipate a poor market performance for its stock, especially in periods of business recession and stock market slumps with or without business recessions. They might anticipate that though the corporation might continue to operate at a comfortable percentage of capacity, and though its prospects for the future might be good, the market price of its stock would be driven down as a result of widespread weaknesses in buying interests and the unloading of shares by poorly informed stockholders. If such a development actually took place, the corporation's managers might wish that much less publicity were given to the market quotations on its shares, as might have been so had they remained unlisted. Such a wish would be all the stronger, of course, were the corporation contemplating a new issue of securities, whether stocks or bonds. In any case, there would be reason to worry about the reactions of the corporation's present and prospective creditors, such as trade suppliers and short-term lenders, to the unfavorable market price performance.

Even in periods of prosperity, moreover, the typical listed stock probably stands a much better chance of becoming the object of speculative raids than does the typical unlisted one. Professional speculators may buy the stock of a given corporation in expectation of a substantial improvement in its earnings. Their buying causes the price to rise. Then the lambs—less well-informed or even ignorant speculators—come in, and their buying causes the price to rise to unreasonable heights. The professionals then sell to cash their profits, and the resulting fall in price alarms the lambs and prompts them to sell also. The professionals may add price-depressing weight on the supply side by selling short. The result is that the price falls to a level far below what is reasonable in relation to the corporation's earnings prospects, and it is then time for the professionals to buy both to cover their short sales and to take a long position for an expected rise. The procedure may be repeated over and over again, and the stock itself may come to be regarded as highly speculative—not very helpful for additional sales of securities or for credit standing.

Another basis for a fear of excessive speculative interests is that the corporation's directors and officers themselves may be led to give too much attention to the market price performance of its stock, with a resulting neglect of its long-term goals. They may deliberately adopt policies expected to have favorable market effects, and zealously avoid others expected to bring unfavorable market reactions. Such a choice of policies may be prompted by hopes of personal gain on the managers' own speculative stock transactions (to be completed in periods longer than six months), or by expectations of improved marketability of new flotations or of better credit standing. But, as indicated, the choice may be contrary to the long-run interests of the corporation. Thus, a write-down in the book values of outmoded fixed assets or slow-moving inventories, or the ommission of dividends when cash is in short supply, may be highly desirable from the standpoint of a corporation's continued good health, but not desirable if the primary goal is to prevent even temporary declines in the market value of its stock.

Restrictions on Freedom of Action. A corporation may decide against having its stock listed because the stock exchange that it would choose for listing has certain kinds of restrictions on financial policy that the corporation's managers do not like—restrictions quite apart from the kinds that are imposed by government regulation. An outstanding example is the dislike of the New York Stock Exchange for nonvoting common stocks—a dislike that it itself expresses as follows.

> The Exchange feels strongly that the right to vote is a fundamental of our corporate democracy, and has refused, since 1926, to list novoting common stock. The Exchange will not list the common voting shares of a company which also has nonvoting common shares outstanding. Moreover, it will consider delisting the common voting shares of a company which creates a nonvoting common stock. The Exchange expects, too, that the owner of common stock in a listed company shall have the right to vote in reasonable proportion to the ownership interest represented by his stock.[12]

Accordingly, a corporation would hardly apply to the New York Stock Exchange for listing if, though otherwise qualified for admission,

---

[12]New York Stock Exchange, *Understanding the New York Stock Exchange*, 1967, p. 23.

it did not want to give votes to an outstanding Class A common stock now nonvoting, or to give five votes per share to its one-vote Class A common to match the five votes already possessed by its Class B common, or if it contemplated later having outstanding paired common stocks with such voting disparities.

Additional Expense Burdens. Aside from the costs of preparing registration statements, financial reports, proxy statements, and the like, as required by SEC regulation—costs no longer avoided by unlisted corporations that were made subject to regulation by the 1964 amendments—listed corporations have a few additional sources of expense that unlisted corporations, at least in a few instances, may want to avoid. These are chiefly listing fees payable to the exchanges and certain expenses related to stock certificates.

Illustrative of exchange fees are the listing fees charged by the New York and American exchanges. For stocks listed on the New York Stock Exchange, an initial fee must be paid at the rate of 1 cent a share on the first 1 million shares, ½ cent a share on the next million, ¼ cent a share on the next million, and ⅛ cent a share on all shares over 3 million, together with an annual fee of $100 per 100,000 shares for the first 2 million shares, and $50 per 100,000 shares in excess of 2 million. The minimum initial fee is $2,000, and the minimum annual fee, $1,000. The annual fee is paid for only 15 years, provided, of course, that the stock remains listed that long. For its initial fee, the American Stock Exchange charges 1 cent a share on the first 250,000 shares and ¼ cent a share for shares in excess of 250,000, with a maximum charge of $5,000. Its annual fee is $250.

As for expenses related to stock certificates, the exchanges generally insist on high-quality engraving for certificates to reduce the dangers of counterfeiting, ample supplies of certificates so that transfers will not be delayed, and convenient transfer facilities. The last-named requirement usually necessitates the hiring of separate banks or trust companies to serve respectively as stock transfer agents and registrars.

QUESTIONS

1. Why might a given stock exchange be described simultaneously as a national securities exchange and as a regional exchange?

2. What is meant by the listing of a stock on a stock exchange? A dual listing? Unlisted trading?

3. What facilities are available for buying and selling securities not traded on stock exchanges? Where are they located? How do they operate?

4. Explain whether or not all transactions in a listed stock must be executed on the floor of the exchange where listed.

5. Explain the proposition that corporations do not raise new money by the sale of securities through the stock exchanges. Is it reasonable to claim that listing aids in the raising of new money? Why or why not?

6. In discussions about stock exchanges, why are the operations of the New York and American exchanges almost always emphasized? To get its stock listed on either of these exchanges, what must a corporation do?

7. Why should the regulation of stock exchanges by the federal government have the effect of promoting a wide distribution of listed stocks?

8. What kinds of regulations must be observed by corporations that have their common stocks listed on stock exchanges registered with the SEC?

9. Can a stock exchange delist a corporation's common stock against the corporation's wishes? Explain.

10. Why should the listing of a corporation's common stock be helpful toward the sale of its preferred stock and bonds?

11. How is the credit standing of a corporation likely to be affected by having its common stock listed on a stock exchange?

12. Explain the scope and purpose of the 1964 amendments to the Securities Exchange Act. How did this legislation affect the attractiveness of listing for unlisted corporations?

13. In what ways are the activities of insiders of listed corporations restricted by federal law? Who are classified as insiders?

14. As possible disadvantages of listing, how important are (*a*) dangers of excessive speculative interests, (*b*) loss of freedom of action, and (*c*) additional expenses?

PROBLEMS

1. What initial fee would a corporation have to pay the New York Stock Exchange for listing its 4.5 million shares of common stock of $10 par value? Of $5.00 par value? Of no par value? What annual fee would it have to pay in each instance? For how long?

2. What initial fee would the corporation of the foregoing problem have to pay to have its common stock listed on the American Stock Exchange? What annual fee would it have to pay?

Part VII

FINANCING WITH PREFERRED STOCK

chapter 23

CHARACTERISTICS OF PREFERRED STOCK

The recommendations of boards of directors to common stockholders for the approval of preferred stock issues presumably follow exhaustive studies of the pros and cons of further financing with common stock and financing with long-term debt—pros and cons of the kinds discussed in Chapters 15 and 16. Financing with preferred stock is selected because it appears to offer greater net advantages than are offered by each of the two principal alternatives. There may be danger of loss of control to existing controlling groups in further issues of common stock, the market for common stock may be poor while that for preferred issues is good, the issuance of bonds may too seriously endanger solvency in view of unstable earnings records, there may be a need of preserving future financing capacity—these kinds of considerations lead to decisions for preferred stock financing.

While decisions in favor of preferred stock depend in part on the pros and cons of alternative means of financing, they also depend on the kinds of features that must be included in preferred stock contracts. If buyers of preferred stock demand no great concessions, then that means of financing is made all the more attractive, but if prospective buyers demand quite extensive concessions, preliminary choices for preferred on the part of corporate managements may be judged to be poor ones after all. As corporate boards of directors are generally common-stock minded—and as they need, in any event, the approval of common stockholders for preferred issues—they are doubtless inclined to pare the rights of preferred stockholders to the greatest possible extent. But investment bankers and other important buyers of preferred stock, usually being astute also, are unwilling to advance their funds unless the features of preferred stock contracts are to their liking. Thus, what goes in and what is kept out of preferred stock contracts are arrived at through a process of bargaining.

In the great majority of cases, certain minimum features will be demanded by prospective buyers: that the stock have preferences to dividends and assets, that the preference to dividends be cumulative, and that special kinds of protective provisions be included. Likewise, certain minimum features will be insisted on by the issuing corporations: that the stock be nonparticipating, that it be callable for redemption, that its voting powers be limited, and that it be deprived of preemptive rights. Such a combination of features demanded and conceded is often described as conventional—a combination, in other words, that one would expect to find in most preferred stocks outstanding at the present time. Other features depend more directly on the bargaining process—on, therefore, the financial position and prospects of the individual corporation, as well as on the investment enthusiasm of prospective buyers. A strong corporation is unlikely to find it necessary to make many additional concessions, whereas a weak one may have to be quite generous in its efforts to attract buyers. Again, any corporation is likely to be asked to make fewer concessions in periods of prosperity and buoyant security markets than would be demanded of it in periods of business and financial strain.

The hows and whys of the various kinds of features that get into preferred stock contracts may be conveniently treated under four heads: (1) modifications in the seven basic rights of stockholders as owners, as discussed in Chapter 17 (2) additional protective provisions for the benefit of the preferred stockholders; (3) special rights reserved to the corporation; and (4) special features to enhance attractiveness.

MODIFICATIONS IN BASIC OWNERSHIP RIGHTS

Like common stock, preferred stock is a contract between its owners and the issuing corporation. The corporation gives the buyers of preferred stock certain rights in dividends, assets, and management and in other matters, and the buyers, in turn, obligate themselves to pay the price agreed on, whether in cash, other assets, or services. It is a generally accepted legal doctrine that the rights of preferred stockholders *are exactly the same as those of common stockholders* unless the preferred stock contract specifically provides to the contrary. Thus, the description of an authorized issue of stock simply as "preferred" in a corporation's articles of incorporation, *without any designation of a dividend rate,* does not make it differ from the same corporation's common stock, unless the law, or the articles in keeping with the law, permits the board of directors to set the terms of the preferred contract, or unless the law itself has certain stipulations of its own differentiating preferred stock from common. (In the last regard, it is always to be remembered that the terms of stock contracts necessarily include whatever stipulations the state law prescribes, whether or not these stipulations are repeated in the articles, corporate bylaws, or directors' resolutions.)

TABLE 23–1

Dividend and Asset Preference Features of Sample of Preferred Stocks

Corporation	*Shares Outstanding End of 1967*	*Par Value*	*Dividend Rate*	*Cumulative Feature*	*Participating Feature*	*Preference to Assets in Dissolution**	
						Voluntary	*Involuntary*
E. I. Du Pont de Nemours & Company							
$4.50 series	1,688,850	No par	$4.50	Yes	No	$115	$100
$3.50 series	700,000	No par	$3.50	Yes	No	$107	$100
El Paso Electric Company	400,000	No par	$4.56	Yes	No	RCP†	$100
General Motors Corporation							
$5.00 series	1,835,644	No par	$5.00	Yes	No	$100	$100
$3.75 series	1,000,000	No par	$3.75	Yes	No	$100	$100
International Paper Company	118,940	No par	$4.00	Yes	No	RCP	$100
Liggett & Myers, Inc.	142,021	$100	7%	Yes	No	$100	$100
New England Power Company	100,000	$100	4.56%	Yes	No	RCP	$100
Owens-Illinois, Inc.	511,294	$100	4%	Yes	No	RCP	$100

*Including accumulated unpaid dividends in all instances.

†RCP stands for "redemption call prices"—the prices at which the corporation is authorized to call the stock for redemption, and usually exceeding the par or stated value.

SOURCE: Moody's Investors Service, *Manuals*.

In general, then, preferred stockholders have the seven basic rights of stock ownership described in Chapter 17, unless they are modified in the preferred stock contract. Accordingly, it is important that we analyze the kinds of modifications commonly introduced. (In connection with the following discussion of preferences to dividends and assets, some attention should be given to Table 23–1, in which the dividend and asset preference features of a few preferred issues of prominent corporations are set out.)

Preference to Dividends

Almost all preferred stock offered in the ordinary course of business for cash or in exchange for other assets or services is given a preference to dividends at a designated rate. This preference is ordinarily the strong selling point for preferred issues; fundamentally, it is the feature that makes such stock *preferred.* The preference means that dividends at the designated rate must be paid before any dividends whatsoever may be paid on the common stock, unless, of course, the preferred stockholders are willing to waive their prior claim. So strong is the tradition of the preference to dividends that a stock simply described in a corporation's articles as, say, a "5% preferred stock of $100 par value," with nothing else said about it except the number of shares authorized, would universally be recognized as having a preference to dividends of $5 a share annually. In disputes, the courts could be counted on so to hold.

If a corporation has only sufficient profits to pay dividends on its preferred stock and does pay them, why the stock is preferred may clearly be seen: the preferred stockholders get their dividends and the common stockholders get none. But one may wonder about the "preferred" designation in a corporation that has lavish earnings and pays dividends on its common stock at a level per share several times that of the preferred dividends. Nevertheless, the preferred stock of the second corporation would be much more attractive to investors than that of the first. The slim earnings of the first might be further reduced, necessitating a suspension of payment of preferred dividends, whereas the great volume of earnings of the second would give strong assurance of the continuance of its preferred dividends.

Dividend Rates and Frequencies. The rate of dividends on a no-par preferred stock is always stated as a certain number of dollars or cents a share annually, while that on a par-value preferred may be stated either in this way or in terms of a percentage. Thus, we may encounter a $2 dividend par or no-par preferred or a 5 percent preferred. The dollar amount indicates that the dividend is to be $2 a share each year, whatever the par or stated value may be, and the percentage indicates that the annual amount of dividends is to be equal to 5 percent of the par value, whatever it may be.

Almost invariably, corporations make their preferred dividends payable quarterly. Accordingly, the holder of a $2 dividend preferred expects to receive 50 cents a share quarterly, while the holder of a 5 percent preferred that has a par value of $100 expects to get $1.25 a share quarterly. It follows that a corporation that is up-to-date in the payment of quarterly dividends on its preferred stock may immediately pay dividends on its common stock. It is under no obligation to hold up dividends on the common until it has paid the full-year rate or amount on the preferred.

Cumulative Feature. In all but a few instances, the preferred stockholder's preference to dividends is made *cumulative*. This means that if the preferred dividends at the designated rate are not paid at the time specified, they must be paid subsequently before any dividends may be paid on the common stock, unless, again, the preferred stockholders are willing to waive their prior claims. Without a waiver, a corporation that fails in a given year to pay its designated preferred dividend of, say, $5 a share cannot pay any dividends on its common stock until it has made up this arrearage of $5 a share on its preferred stock, together with the additional preferred dividend requirements as they continue to accumulate, presumably quarterly. If the quarterly dates for the payment of preferred dividends are March 1, June 1, and so on, the corporation could make up the arrearage, say, in the middle of January, and immediately pay dividends on its common stock. But if it should make no distribution till March 1 or shortly thereafter, it would have to pay $6.25 a share on the preferred stock before making a payment on the common, and if on or after June 1 but before September 1, $7.50 a share on the preferred before any payment on the common, and so on. Similarly, missing dividends on the preferred for 2 years would require a payment to the preferred stockholders of $10 a share plus current quarterly dividends of the third year before any dividend distributions on the common stock could be made.

Like the preference to dividends feature itself, the cumulative feature is universally recognized as an attribute of preferred stock unless it is specifically removed by contract. Were a corporation to call a stock issue "preferred" and give it a specific dividend rate without saying anything about cumulation, the courts, if called on to decide, would surely hold it to be cumulative.

Noncumulative Preferred. A limited number of noncumulative preferred stock issues are outstanding in the United States at the present time, and some of them have high investment rating on account of the excellent records of earnings of their issuers and the scrupulous payment of dividends. The noncumulative feature means that dividends on the preferred missed in any year or series of years need not be made up in subsequent years before the payment of dividends on common stock. Even if profits are sufficient to pay preferred dividends, the preferred stockholders get no holdover claim if the directors decide in good faith that expansion requirements or other legitimate corporate objectives demand that the profits be retained. Such is the doctrine that was established by the Supreme Court in the celebrated *Wabash Railway* case of 1930.[1]

Therefore, unless a noncumulative preferred has stood the test of time it is likely to have very little investment appeal. That being so, corporations that bring out *new* issues of preferred stock are hardly likely to try to make them noncumulative. Most noncumulative preferreds have originated and continue to originate in reorganizations of corporations that have fallen into severe financial difficulties—in reorganizations where, in effect, they have been or are forced on security holders of weak bargaining positions.

Noncumulative preferreds originating in reorganizations have been especially prominent in the railroad industry. Railroads that have such preferreds outstanding at the present time include the Atchison, Topeka, and Santa Fe, the Milwaukee, the Southern, and the Union Pacific. The Santa Fe's 5 percent noncumulative preferred paid dividends regularly from 1900 through 1932, 4 percent in 1933, 5.8 percent in 1934,[2] 5 percent in 1935 through 1937, 2½ percent in 1938, and 3½ percent in 1939. From 1940 to the present time, it has paid the dividend regularly. The Union Pacific's 4 percent issue of $10 par value originated in its reorganization of 1897. It paid dividends of 1½ percent in 1898 and 3½ percent in 1899. Since then, its dividends have been met regularly.

Participation in Further Dividends. Some preferred stocks are described as "participating"; their contracts provide for some sharing in dividend distributions beyond the designated rate to which they are basically entitled. However, the general rule is that unless the contract specifically provides for participation the preferred stockholders have no claim to dividends beyond the designated rate, no matter how great a corporation's profits may be, and no matter how generous the dividends paid on its common stock.

Corporations whose proposed issues of preferred stock are likely to have no great investment appeal sometimes add a participation feature as a sweetener. Accordingly, further consideration of this feature may best be deferred to the last division of this chapter, where the matter of adding attractions to preferred issues is taken up.

Dividend Position of Preferred Stockholders. The holders of a corporation's preferred stock get their dividends only if declared by its board of directors. The corporation has no obligation to pay dividends, as it has obligations to pay its debts. The dividend commitment is not

[1] *Wabash Railway Co.* v. *Barclay*, 280 U.S. 197 (1930).

[2] The dividend in excess of 5 percent was accounted for by a difference between the railroad's fiscal year and the calendar year.

a debt; it becomes a debt only after the act of declaration. In fact, the corporation cannot legally pay prescribed dividends on its preferred stock if the surplus available for dividend distributions, as determined in accordance with the rules of the state law, is insufficient to cover them. The directors would make themselves contingently liable to creditors for the amount by which the dividends exceeded the available surplus.

Still more important is that the directors of a corporation are under no obligation to declare and pay preferred dividends even if sufficient surplus is available. Dividend distributions to preferred stockholders, as to common stockholders, are at the discretion of the directors. They may decide that the payment of a preferred dividend is practically impossible because of a shortage of cash, though legally permissible because of the existence of a sufficient balance in the surplus accounts. Or with liberal mounts of cash available, they may decide that the welfare of the corporation—and presumably, therefore, of all its stockholders, both common and preferred—would be better served by using the cash to finance expansion projects rather than to distribute it as dividends. Or they may decide simply to hold the cash for contingencies, as when the business outlook is cloudy. Only in relatively rare circumstances can preferred stockholders get the assistance of courts to force the payment of dividends. They can probably get such assistance if able to prove to the satisfaction of the court that the withholding of dividends is tainted with fraud—designed, for example, to force them to sell their stockholdings at sacrifice prices.

Accordingly, one should notice that descriptions of the dividend preference and dividend cumulation features of preferred stocks always include, if complete, two provisos: that dividends are payable *before any dividends may be paid on the common stock,* and that they are payable *unless the preferred stockholders waive their rights to them.* These provisos indicate that the preferred stockholders may not get all the dividends they expected to get or in the form expected. Indeed, they may get none indefinitely, especially if the corporation whose preferred stock they own operates at a loss year after year or if its earnings are of negligible amounts. The first proviso does not say categorically that preferred dividends *must* be paid; it only indicates a condition that must be satisfied before common dividends may be paid. However, preferred stockholders who do not receive dividends year after year are not likely to find much consolation in the fact that common stockholders also are not getting dividends. The second proviso indicates a possibility that preferred stockholders may give up their rights to unpaid dividends. They have often done so, especially when dividends have not been paid for several years and the accumulated arrearages have amounted to substantial sums. In some cases, they accept corporate managements' offers of additional shares of preferred, some shares of common, or something else in exchange for their dividend claims. In some cases, they are, in effect, forced to agree to some such exchange, as in procedures of corporate reorganization.

Much of the foregoing discussion of the preferred stockholder's claims to dividends indicates that they are quite weak, but this point must not be overemphasized. A great number of corporations make quarterly dividend payments on their preferred stocks without fail, and many additional ones, though they may pass one or more quarterly payments now and then, make these up subsequently without hesitation. Even when faced with arrearages equal to 30, 40, or 50 percent or more of the par or stated value of their preferred stocks, a goodly number, with improvements in earnings and cash positions, have set to work to clear them up by cash payment, and many have succeeded. Most corporate managements, it is reasonable to think, feel duty-bound to respect the dividend rights of their preferred stockholders and to meet them if at all feasible. But a conscientious attitude of this kind is not the only reason for faithfulness in dividend payments. As unpaid preferred dividends stand in the way of dividends on the common, they can hardly be appealing to boards of directors that are common-stock minded. Probably even more important is that possibilities of additional flotations of either common or preferred on fair terms are greatly reduced as long as there are arrearages on the existing preferred. And probably most important of all is the blow to a corporation's credit standing that comes with nonpayment of preferred dividends. Though prospective buyers of its bonds, bank lenders, trade creditors, and others know that nonpayment of preferred dividends does not mean insolvency, their attention is strongly directed to the weaknesses in the corporation's earnings or cash position or both that must have occasioned the nonpayment.

Preference to Assets

A large majority of preferred stock contracts give the preferred stockholders a priority over common stockholders in claims on corporate assets in the event of dissolution. The basic priority or preference is stated as a specific dollar amount per share. A stock of $100 par value is likely to have a basic preference to assets of $100; a stock of $5 par value originally sold at $100, a preference also of $100; and a no-par stock originally sold at $10, a preference of $10. Often the preference is larger in voluntary dissolutions than in involuntary ones. For example, in considering the $4.50 preferred of Du Pont, listed in Table 23-1, it will be noticed that if the corporation were to dissolve involuntarily, as for insolvency, the claim per preferred share would be $100, but if the dissolution were voluntary, the claim per share would be $115. In this way the preferred stockholder is to be given a premium if the corporation dissolves but not under pressure.

In addition to the basic preference just described, preferred stock contracts usually give preferred stockholders an additional prior claim for unpaid cumulative dividends of earlier years as well as for dividends accrued in the current year up to the time of approval of the dissolution move. All the preferred stocks listed in Table 23–1, it will be noticed, have this additional claim. This is a significant claim, since it is not determinable on the basis of earnings that may be or may have been available for the payment of preferred dividends. To illustrate, assume that a corporation paid no dividends on its 5 percent preferred stock of $100 par value for 6 years prior to dissolution because it operated at a loss in each of those years. It is dissolving voluntarily—not yet having become insolvent—and its contract gives the preferred stock a basic preference in case of voluntary dissolution of $110 a share as well as the additional claim to unpaid cumulative dividends. Accordingly, the preferred stockholders would be entitled to receive a total of $140 a share before any payment in liquidation could be made to the common stockholders.

Legal Aspects. The common-law rule is that in the event of dissolution common and preferred stocks have equal claims to assets, share for share. This rule could work a grave hardship on a corporation's preferred stock if, for example, it had originally been sold for $100 a share and its common stock at $10 a share. Or the hardship could be shifted the other way were these original selling prices reversed. But, as was indicated in the preceding paragraphs, a prior claim for the preferred stock is usually contracted for. At any rate, it is important to emphasize that the preferred gets only such prior claims as are provided for in state laws or as specifically stated in the contract; otherwise, the common-law rule applies. On the other hand, when a prior claim is given the preferred stock it is usually interpreted legally as *limiting* the preferred stockholder's right of recovery. When the prior claim has been satisfied, he has no further right to share in assets, regardless of the amount that the common stockholders may receive.

In the absence of contractual provisions, the only prior claim in dissolution that preferred stockholders may succeed in asserting is one for unpaid dividends to the extent that earned surplus is available. Even this claim, however, is a doubtful one in the light of the Wabash Railway decision. Accordingly, an attempt to enforce it would doubtless require a lawsuit.

Practical Aspects. The preferred stockholder's prior claim to assets, as contractually provided for, may appear to be of little value, because wealthy corporations rarely dissolve and poor ones that do dissolve have little or nothing left for any class of stockholders after settlement of creditors' claims. Though preferred stockholders usually have claims prior to those of common stockholders, they still rank as claimants behind all classes of creditors, and all too often the liquidation of assets of dissolving corporations brings in much less than is needed to meet creditors' claims.

However that may be, the preference to assets held by preferred stockholders, as for the residual claims of common stockholders, is often important when danger of dissolution on account of financial difficulties is exceedingly remote. When a corporation is approached with a proposition of merger or consolidation, considerable weight is likely to be given to its preferred stock's claims against assets. Promoters of combinations of these kinds usually seek to carry them through as far as possible on the basis of simple exchanges of securities. They want to avoid a need to pay off in cash a large number of dissenting stockholders. Thus, an asset preference feature, among others, is likely to give the preferred stockholders of the approached corporation a strong position to demand generous treatment. They know they can dissent and demand payment in cash, because they expect that in deciding how much they ought to be paid a court or an appraisal committee appointed by a court will likewise give considerable weight to the asset preference feature. Indeed, if they do dissent and are paid the full amount of their claims, these claims are immediately satisfied, but the claims of the prior-ranking bondholders may be simply assumed by the surviving or new corporation without the bondholders' consent.

Voting Powers

The common-law rule is that preferred stock is indistinguishable from common stock in the scope of its voting powers. For the election of directors and on all questions requiring stockholder approval, it has one vote per share, the same as common stock. However, all states except Illinois and Mississippi permit the corporations they charter to modify these basic voting powers in various ways.

Even when preferred stocks have ordinary or regular rights to vote in the election of directors and in passing on matters subject to stockholder approval, they are often given certain special voting powers in addition. In almost all instances, these special voting powers are given to preferred stocks that are denied the ordinary voting rights. The special powers are generally called "vetoing" and "contingent" voting rights.

Ordinary Voting Power. Despite permissive laws, many corporations make no attempt to limit the ordinary voting power of their preferred stocks in the choice of directors and in other corporate decisions that require stockholder ratification. In voting capacity, their common and preferred stocks are identical in having one vote per share. On the other hand, some preferred stocks issued many decades ago and still outstanding give their preferred stocks more voting strength than their common stocks, and many of the more recent issues of preferred have no ordinary voting power but only the special kinds of voting capacities mentioned above and described below. Examples of older preferred stocks with strong voting capacities are those of the American Can Company, with six votes per share, and of Liggett & Myers, Inc., with eight votes per share, standing side by side with common stocks that have only one vote per share.

For the typical corporation that has preferred stock in its financial structure, the number of its preferred shares is much less than the number of its common shares, so that giving ordinary voting power—or even multiple votes, as in some of the older issues—need not be a matter of much concern to the common stockholders. The controlling interests may have such a large percentage of the common stock that there is little danger of loss of control, even should all preferred shares be voted in opposition. Or both the common and preferred stocks may be so widely distributed that control does not depend in any essential way on stock ownership.

Vetoing Voting Power. The approval of the holders of two thirds or three fourths of preferred shares is often required for mergers, consolidations, sales of entire assets, and voluntary dissolution. On proposals aimed in these directions, the preferred *votes as a class*—in other words, the holders of a little more than one third or one fourth of the preferred shares may *veto* proposals, even though only a majority vote of the common stock may be necessary to approve them and even though the common stockholders may vote very heavily in favor. Frequently, however, the preferred stock has such a veto power only if it *would be adversely affected* by the merger or other proposed action.

Aside from questions of merger, consolidation, sale of entire assets, and dissolution, many preferred stocks are given power to veto corporate actions that would materially affect their prior claims to dividends and assets. In virtually all preferreds, approval of the holders of two thirds or three fourths of the preferred shares is required to change the stock's par or stated value, to change from par to no par or vice versa, to change the dividend rate, and, indeed, to alter other terms of the contract. Without a reservation of voting power in this area, preferred stock would hardly be salable. But the veto power is often extended to include proposals for:

1. Further issues of the same kind of preferred.
2. Issues of any other class of preferred that would have equal ranking in claims to dividends and assets.
3. Issues of any other class that would have claims to dividends or assets or both prior to those of the existing preferred—often called a prior-preference preferred.
4. Issues of bonds.

5. The mortgaging of corporate properties, whether or not in connection with bond issues.

As examples we may cite the two issues of preferred stock of General Motors, listed in Table 23–1, which have been long outstanding, and the $1 cumulative convertible preferred, which was issued in 1968 by Chris Craft Industries, Inc. to the former stockholders of Montrose Chemical Co., Inc. in a merger transaction that, of course, Chris Craft survived. In the General Motors issues, the approval of holders of 75 percent of the preferreds is required for mortgaging the corporation's properties and for all amendments to its articles of incorporation that would affect their rights and security. The Chris Craft provisions are more detailed in requiring an approval vote of two thirds of the preferred shares for increases in the authorized issue of the preferred itself, for the issuance of other preferreds that would have prior or equal ranking, for voluntary dissolution of the corporation or its partial liquidation, for split-ups, for the sale or lease of all or substantially all of its assets, for mergers and consolidations, and for any changes in the terms of the preferred that would affect it adversely.

On the other hand, no vetoing power is ordinarily given to preferred stock pertaining to further issues of common stock or to issues of preferreds, often called second preferreds, whose claims to dividends and assets would be inferior to its own claims. Such issues, it is thought, tend to strengthen rather than weaken the claims of the existing preferred.

Contingent Voting Power. In the great majority of instances, the contingency to which the contingent voting powers of preferred stocks are related is the nonpayment of dividends. Whether or not they share with common stocks ordinary voting powers in the election of directors, many preferreds give their holders special rights in the choice of directors if a certain number of *quarterly* dividends on the stock—usually two to six—have not been paid. The preferred, voting as a class separately from the common, is privileged to elect some number of directors or some proportion of the total board—usually a minority of the members but not infrequently a majority, especially in the preferreds of public utility corporations. For example, holders of the 4½ percent cumulative preferred stock of the Celanese Corporation get the right to choose one fourth of the directors but not fewer than two if four quarterly dividends are in arrears. Holders of the 4.5 percent cumulative second preferred of the Carrier Corporation, while having ordinary voting power, also have the right to choose two additional directors if six quarterly dividends are in arrears. The Crown Cork and Seal Company, Inc., provides in the contract for its $2 dividend no-par preferred that the holders shall be privileged to choose one half of the board members if six quarterly dividends have not been paid.

The theory of contingent voting powers is that the preferred stockholders must have specific representation on the board of directors to look after their interests. The implication is that the nonpayment of dividends may indicate some neglect of those interests by board members who have been too common-stock minded. Logically, therefore, the special powers of the preferred stockholders to choose directors customarily expire if and when the arrearages in dividends have been cleared up.

In some contracts, contingent voting powers in the choice of directors, comparable to those just described, are available to the preferred stockholders should the corporations fail to meet prescribed redemption fund contributions or violate other contract terms, as designated.

Preemptive Rights

Already the weakest of the seven basic rights of ownership as they pertain to common stock, the preemptive right is even weaker in preferred stocks. In most preferred stock contracts, it is taken away completely. As most preferreds have no claims on earnings beyond the established dividend rates, no claims on assets beyond the amounts fixed in the contracts, and for the election of directors only contingent voting powers, it is commonly held that they need no preemptive rights for protection. Indeed, it is often argued that to give preferred stockholders subscription rights to new issues of common stock would work an injustice on the existing common stockholders. Were the preferred stockholders to exercise subscription rights to common, they would get some ordinary voting power whereas before they had none, and new and different claims to earnings and assets—all at the expense of the common stockholders. Were they to sell their subscription rights, the proceeds would be, in effect, an unmerited cash contribution to them made possible by dilution of the common stockholders' interests. On the other hand, a good case can be made for giving preemptive rights to preferred with respect to common if the preferred has ordinary voting rights, if it participates in dividend distributions beyond its stipulated rate, or if it has claims on assets in dissolution beyond a fixed amount or no preference to assets at all. Sometimes, the preemptive right is given for reasons such as these, but more often it is not.

As for new issues of preferred of the same class or of prior-preference preferreds, the usual justification for denying the preemptive right to the existing preferred is its possession of the vetoing power. If the holders of an existing preferred conclude that a proposed new issue would weaken their voting powers (if they have these) and their claims to dividends and assets, they can simply vote down the proposal. Or they can approve on condition that the new stock be first offered to them; then, they could be said to have the preemptive right *de facto*, although not by the terms of their contract with the corporation.

Other Basic Rights

In designing their preferred stock issues, corporations usually have no reason to disturb the four remaining basic rights of stockownership, discussed in Chapter 17 in connection with common stock. They recognize that the preferred stockholder should have a stock certificate, illustrated in Figure 23–1, in order to prove his ownership. They willingly accord him the same privileges of inspection of books and records as they grant to the common stockholders. They certainly would not want to suggest any limitation on his right to go to court to protect the corporation and his own interests from actions alleged to be illegal, *ultra vires*, or mismanagerial. Once in a while, a preferred stock contract includes some kind of limitation on resale, or the preferred stockholders themselves agree to limit resale, but such restrictions do not differ essentially from the similar ones sometimes found in connection with common stocks.[3]

PROTECTIVE PROVISIONS FOR PREFERRED STOCK

Investors in preferred stocks, including investment bankers who expect to hold only temporarily as underwriters, want all reasonable assurances that their preferences to dividends and assets will be continuously protected. They realize that as participants in the ownership of corporations they cannot get absolute assurances, but they often want some protection beyond vetoing and contingent voting powers and the right to inspect corporate books and records. They want more than the right of appeal to the courts to stop activities claimed to be illegal, *ultra vires*, or mismanagerial, as well as to try to force payment of dividends alleged to be unjustly withheld. They often demand that the contracts include one or more additional provisions for their protection.

Additional protective provisions are generally of three kinds: (1) restrictions on the payment of dividends on common stock, (2) limitations on further issues of the same class of preferred stock, and (3) requirements for the gradual retirement of the preferred stock itself. Some preferred stock contracts contain no protective provisions of these additional kinds; some contain only one or two of the three varieties; and some contain all three.

Restrictions on Dividends on Common Stock

Protective provisions that impose restrictions on the payment of dividends on common stock are designed to preserve the capacity of

---

[3]See p. 411.

FIGURE 23–1 Preferred Stock Certificate

corporations to continue uninterrupted dividends on the preferred at the prescribed rates. If in prosperous years a corporation, after having taken care of its preferred dividend requirements, distributes common dividends equal to most of the remaining profits, it may in lean years have insufficient cash or earned surplus or both to continue dividends on the preferred.

Restrictions on common stock dividends are of several kinds, and two or more are sometimes included in the individual preferred stock contract. Two examples may be cited. In the contract covering the 4 percent cumulative preferred stock of Owens-Illinois, Inc., it is provided that cash dividends may not be paid on the common stock if total common and preferred dividends paid after October 4, 1956, would exceed $53 million plus net earnings after December 31, 1956. As of the end of 1967, Owens-Illinois reported that slightly over $234 million was unavailable for dividends on account of restrictions in its long-term debt contracts, indicating that this large amount superseded the "less restrictive" provision on unavailability in its preferred stock contract.[4] For the cumulative first preferred of the Ethyl Corporation, the provision is simply that dividends on junior stock—that is, common stock and any preferreds that have claims to earnings inferior to the claims of this preferred—must not exceed 75 percent of net earnings after December 31, 1964, plus $5 million, but with net earnings reduced by both dividend and sinking fund payments on this preferred.

Limitations on Further Issues

We have seen that preferred stockholders are usually given the power to approve or disapprove further issues of the same class of stock and issues that would have prior preferences. Often, however, corporations expect to put out additional quantities of preferred stocks of a given class from time to time over the years. This is especially true of certain classes of public utility corporations for which permanent preferred stock financing is considered normal and justifiable. A corporation with such expectations does not want to have its financial planning clouded by possibilities of vetoes of existing preferred stockholders. If it starts out with 100,000 preferred shares, expecting eventually to have 500,000 or more outstanding, vetoes could seriously cripple its expansion program. In its preferred stock contract, accordingly, it will reserve the right to sell additional preferred shares of the same class from time to time without having to get the approval of the existing preferred stockholders.

But investors in preferred stock will not accept such a reservation without appropriate protective provisions. These are generally of two kinds: limitations of total preferred issues in relation to assets or

---

[4] *Annual Report*, 1967, p. 33.

common stock or both, and limitations in relation to profits. Both kinds of limitations are ordinarily employed simultaneously. For example, the contract for the 4.28 percent cumulative preferred stock of the Southwestern Electric Power Company permits the corporation to issue additional shares of preferred that has equal ranking with the existing preferred without the consent of that existing, provided that (1) its net income for 12 months within the preceding 15 months was at least 1½ times the sum of annual interest on debt and annual preferred dividend requirements on all preferred and all stocks of equal or prior ranking to be outstanding, and (2) the common stock equity is not less than the value in involuntary liquidation of all preferred and all stocks of equal or prior ranking to be outstanding.

Requirements for Gradual Retirement

Especially in industrial corporations, preferred stock financing is often looked on as a temporary expedient, to be used, for example, when the common stock market is depressed and the market for preferred stocks is still favorable. This view is in line with the doctrine that the simple common stock structure is the ideal one for industrials. To the extent, therefore, that the doctrine is accepted by corporate managements and by the investment community, it is appropriate to include in contracts for preferred stock provisions for its gradual retirement. Many industrial corporations do include such provisions, and some public utility corporations also accept them, although many do not.

Protective Aspect of Retirement. Such provisions are looked on as protective for preferred stockholders, since the position of remaining stockholders is presumably enhanced as more and more shares are retired. If a corporation has been able to pay dividends on an original issue of 10,000 shares, it should be all the more able to pay when the number of outstanding shares has been reduced to, say, 6,000. Moreover, the very action of the corporation in periodically acquiring shares for redemption tends to support the market value of unredeemed shares.

Redemption Funds. Retirement provisions usually prescribe the setting up of a redemption fund or sinking fund by periodic contributions of cash equal to a stipulated proportion of current profits, or current profits after the deduction of dividends on the preferred. If there are no profits, no contributions need be made, although often there is a supplementary requirement for some minimum contribution in fixed dollar amount or equal to the call price of a fixed percentage of the outstanding preferred shares. Fairly often, indeed, the prescribed contribution is set at such a fixed dollar amount or percentage rather than as a percentage of current profits. Two examples may be cited. The contract of the H. K. Porter Co., Inc., covering its 5½ percent cumulative sinking fund preference stock, requires allocations to the redemption fund of 10 percent of annual net earnings after tax deductions. However, this percentage requirement is reduced proportionally if the outstanding preferred is less than the total authorized issue. Owens-Illinois, Inc. is required to set aside $2 million on May 1 of each year for the retirement of its 4 percent cumulative preferred, but the money need not be so used if the corporation is unable to buy in shares at the par value of $100 plus costs of acquisition. If not spent for redemption on this basis within a year, the money or any remaining portion of it is freed for ordinary corporate purposes.

Retirement Procedures. Preferred stock contracts generally require corporations to use at once the money set aside in their redemption or sinking funds. The money is to be be paid out in actually redeeming preferred shares at a price not in excess of the call price—that is, the redemption price as set in the contract. The favored way is to buy up shares in the market, since the sellers obviously want to give up their ownership. If stock can be bought in the market at prices below the call price, so much the better. But the corporation's very buying tends to drive up the market price. Moreover, that a preferred stock is callable for redemption at a specified price tends to have some influence in sustaining its market price. Many state laws forbid corporations to pay in the market prices higher than the call price, and many preferred stock contracts also so provide. If sufficient stock is not available in the market to exhaust the redemption or sinking fund, or if the market price exceeds the call price, the corporation may use either of two rights it almost always reserves—a right to draw lots to determine whose shares shall be called for redemption and a right to make pro rata calls on all shareholders. Sometimes, corporations invite tenders by notifying all preferred stockholders that money is available for redemption and asking them to signify their willingness to sell and the price they would be willing to take. The tenders (offers) are accepted beginning with the lowest price stipulated and continuing up the line until the available funds have been used up. Tenders at prices in excess of the call price are summarily rejected.

Legal Limitations on Retirement. An interesting legal question arises when a corporation has a contractual obligation to provide retirement of a fixed dollar amount or a fixed percentage of outstanding preferred stock and yet has no earned surplus. In our discussion of common stock, we saw that money spent to acquire treasury stock is legally limited to the amount of earned surplus. Does the same rule apply to the retirement of preferred stock? In some states, such as California, it does. In such states, the law must be obeyed; the contractual provisions fail because there can be no binding obligation to do something that is illegal. In many states, however, the laws are much more generous toward the retirement of preferred stock than toward the purchase of common treasury stock. The statutes of these states permit the direct reduction of the preferred stock account itself by amounts equal to the par or stated value of redeemed preferred stock, provided that the value of remaining assets is at least equal to outside liabilities and remaining stated capital. To retire preferred stock in these states, therefore, corporations need only sufficient earned surplus for charging off retirement premiums. Indeed, they need no earned surplus at all if they can acquire the stock for retirement at prices no greater than par or stated value.

SPECIAL RIGHTS RESERVED TO THE CORPORATION

In issuing preferred stock, almost all corporations reserve the right to call it in for redemption, and some also reserve the right to issue additional shares of a given class without having to get the consent of the existing shareholders of that class. These two special rights were introduced in the forgoing discussion of preferred stock protective provisions, but they deserve further brief treatment.

Right to Call for Redemption

Corporations' reservation of the right to call their preferred stocks for redemption is a special privilege because, by nature, preferred stock is a permanent kind of security. Rights of ownership generally have no maturity; hence, preferred stockholders, as owners, give up something of great significance when they accord their corporations the power to cause their ownership to cease—the power to set a maturity, as is done when a call for redemption is made.

Scope of Call Privileges. Corporations that obligate themselves unconditionally to redeem certain portions of their preferred stocks annually must of necessity reserve the call privilege. Almost invariably, however, they reserve the right to call all the stock for redemption whenever they so choose, and not simply the amount needed to use up the cash allocated to their redemption funds. The broader call privilege may never be used, but the corporations want to be free to use it should circumstances so warrant.

The broader privilege is wanted, indeed, by almost all corporations, whether or not they have redemption fund provisions in their contracts. Thus callability can be said to be a conventional feature of present-day issues of preferred stocks. In corporations without redemption fund provisions, the expectation ordinarily is that the call privilege will be exercised, if at all, only when a decision has been made to call all shares for redemption simultaneously. A corporation may issue preferred stock as a temporary substitute for common stock financing, and from the beginning it may expect to retire the preferred from the proceeds of common stock sales when the market for common has improved. Or the accumulation of retained earnings may make possible the retirement of whole issues of preferred originally designed as temporary means of financing. Or again, the retirement of whole preferred stock issues may be decided on to get rid of unduly oppressive protective provisions that had to be accepted at the time of original sale. Funds for some such retirements may, indeed, be supplied from sales of new preferred stocks that have protective provisions of a much less restrictive character. Nevertheless, corporations that expect to call their entire preferred stock issues at one stroke, if they call at all, do not lose sight of the fact that partial redemptions may turn out to be advantageous. Hence, they reserve the right to make partial calls, both by lot and on a pro rata basis, as well as to buy in the market and to invite tenders.

Call Prices. Call prices are usually set at par value (or at stated value for no-par preferreds) and accrued dividends for calls in connection with redemption fund provisions, and they are frequently set at premium levels for calls beyond the scope of such provisions. The theory appears to be that because redemption fund calls are for the protection of the preferred stockholder he has no fair claim to a bonus on redemption, but because calls not related to redemption fund operations are for the particular benefit of the corporation, in rearranging its financial structure, the preferred stockholder should receive some compensation for being forcibly deprived of his investment. For example, the H. K. Porter preferred, referred to earlier, is callable for its redemption fund at the par value of $100, but otherwise at $103. Call prices outside the scope of redemption funds are sometimes set at figures such as H. K. Porter's $103, and sometimes they are scaled downward with the passing years. The scaled arrangement is exemplified in the preferred stock of the New England Power Company, listed in Table 23–1, for which the call price is $105.90 to the end of 1972, then $104.99 to the end of 1977, and thereafter $104.08, the lowest level to which it falls.

Issuance of Additional Shares

Corporations that plan to continue to expand their preferred stock issues want to avoid having to obtain the consent of the holders of two thirds or three fourths or some other relatively high percentage of the already outstanding preferred shares every time new shares are to be offered for sale. The protective provisions they must add to their contracts to compensate for this privilege, they are likely to feel, will tie their hands less tightly than would an obligation to obtain repeated consents. If they did not have the privilege, if permission to put out additional shares of the same class of preferred stock were refused by the existing preferred stockholders, and if they wanted, nevertheless, to employ preferred stock financing, all they could do would be to issue a second preferred whose claims to dividends and assets would necessarily be inferior to those of the existing preferred and whose attractiveness to investors would accordingly be much weaker.

When the privilege is reserved, it can be used to greatest advantage if the board of directors is empowered to set varying contractual terms for the successive issues, such as different dividend rates, claims to assets on dissolution, and call prices. In this way, advantage can be taken of growing strength in the preferred stock market generally or in the investment appeal of the corporation's preferred specifically. If, for example, the original issue of a preferred stock of $100 par value carried a dividend rate of 5 percent and a call price and claim to assets in voluntary dissolution of $105, a second issue might be salable later with a dividend rate of 4½ percent and a call price and claim to assets of $103. Likewise, preferred stock financing can be continued even if

TABLE 23–2
Preferred Stock of Northern States Power Company (Minnesota) Issued in Series

Year Issued	*No. of Shares*	*Annual Dividend per Share*	*Call Prices in Effect, July 31, 1968**
1946	275,000	$3.60	$103.75
1950	175,000	$4.10	$102.50
1954 (April)	150,000	$4.08	to 12/31/69, $103 thereafter, $102
1954 (August)	200,000	$4.11	$103.732
1956	100,000	$4.16	to 12/31/71, $104.75 thereafter, $103.75
1964	150,000	$4.56	to 12/31/69, $105.89 to 12/31/74, $104.75 to 12/31/79, $103.61 thereafter, $102.47
1968	200,000	$6.80	to 12/31/73, $108.29 to 12/31/78, $106.59 to 12/31/83, $104.89 thereafter, $103.19

*The prevailing call price in any period is simultaneously the liquidation value in the event of voluntary dissolution. A succession of dates indicates a succession of periods in each of which the call price is below that of the preceding period, and "thereafter" means at any time following the date immediately preceding.
SOURCE: Moody's Investors Service, *Manuals.*

the market situation deteriorates. In terms of the foregoing illustration, a third issue might be put out with a dividend rate of 5½ percent and a call price and claim to assets in voluntary dissolution of $108.

The three separate issues illustrated would be said to rank *pari passu* in their claims to dividends and assets; that is, they would have equal *priority* of claims, although obviously not equal amounts of claims. Thus, the corporation would pay a quarterly dividend of $1.25 a share on the first issue, $1.125 on the second, and $1.375 on the third, or it might omit all three simultaneously. On the basis of its contract, it could not pay one of these dividends and not the other two, or any two but not the third. To indicate equal priority but unequal claims of successive issues of preferred stock, corporations often designate them as Series A, Series B, and so on, or as the 4.75 percent series, the 5.25 percent series, and so on.

Illustrating differences in the terms of the separate series of a given authorized issue of preferred stock are the flotations of the Northern States Power Company of Minnesota, ranging from 1946 to 1968, as set out in Table 23–2. Its total authorized issue is 2 million shares, all of $100 par value. One may well note the extraordinarily high dividend rate and call prices of the 1968 flotation.

SPECIAL FEATURES TO ENHANCE ATTRACTIVENESS

In the discussion of miscellaneous methods of common stock financing in Chapter 20, it was pointed out that common stock is sometimes issued in exchange for preferred stock, as when holders of the preferred exercise the privilege of conversion granted to them in preferred stock contracts. It was also explained that common stock is sometimes sold through the exercise of stock purchase warrants attached to preferred stocks. Both the conversion privilege and the attachment of stock purchase warrants are generally recognized as strengthening the sales or swap appeal of preferred stocks. Another means of trying to promote sales—but one very rarely used—is to add so-called participation features to preferred stocks.

In the matter of the *swap* appeal of preferred stocks, one must surely mention the great burst in the popularity of convertible preferreds during the hectic merger activity of recent years, especially of the period beginning with 1966. For reasons to be mentioned in the subsequent discussion, many corporations that want to acquire others in mergers have been finding that their new issues of convertible preferred are, or can be tailored to be, much more acceptable than their common stocks in exchange offers for the common stocks of corporations to be acquired.

Convertibility

In making their preferred stocks convertible into common stock, some corporations thus signify that they would much rather be issuing common stock. Money is needed quickly, or certain other properties (corporations) look most attractive as potential acquisitions by merger, but temporary weaknesses in the common stock market or in the attractiveness of their own common stock make new offers of common inadvisable or unacceptable. Accordingly, convertible preferred is offered for cash or exchange with expectations that it will be much more attractive, and with confidence that in the not-too-distant future the holders of this preferred will find it to their material advantage to make the conversion and will actually make it.

Suppose, for example, that a corporation wants to raise approximately $3 million. It would like to sell additional common stock, but its common is now selling in the market at only $33. Investment bankers are willing to underwrite a new issue at $30, so that it would be necessary to issue 100,000 shares to produce the sum of money wanted. But the bankers are also willing to underwrite a preferred issue at $49 a share. Indeed, the bankers indicate that if the preferred shares were made convertible into common on a 1-for-1 basis, they would boost the underwriting price to $50—they anticipate that investors would be willing to pay approximately $1 for the added conversion privilege. As giving the conversion privilege is entirely in line with the corporation's goal of ultimate common stock financing, it readily agrees to offer 60,000 shares of convertible preferred. Subsequently, the market price of the corporation's common rises to $60, and by the time that level has been reached all the preferred stockholders have converted. Thus, the corporation succeeds, in effect, in selling 60,000 shares of common at $50 a share,[5] whereas the sale price would have been only $30 had the corporation sold common originally.

Justification for offering convertible preferred stock in place of common in merger negotiations at times when the market situation of the common is unfavorable was very nicely expressed by J. R. Fluor, president of the Fluor Corporation, quoted in *The Wall Street Journal:*

> At the time we started talking, the price of our stock was around $28 a share. We had a good idea that our fiscal-year earnings would be about $3.80 a share, and we thought at that price–earnings ratio we wouldn't be doing our stockholders any favor by paying out common.[6]

Another reason for the substitution of offers of convertible preferreds for common shares in merger deals is the poor cash dividend records of the common stocks of the offerors. Some of these corporations, including some of the conglomerates described in Chapter 20, have been so anxious to proceed rapidly with acquisitions that they have devoted most of their cash throw-offs from profits in that direction rather than for dividends. As a result, however, their common stocks do not look very appetizing to the stockholders of desirable corporations who have been getting cash dividends at good levels on

---

[5]Leaving out of consideration the difference between actual preferred dividends and what the dividends on common might have been up to the time of conversion.

[6]Midwest Edition, December 27, 1966, p. 10.

their stocks. But convertible preferreds can fill the bill. They can promise cumulative preferred dividends at rates at least equal to the rates on the common stocks for which the exchange offers are made, and at the same time the conversion feature can offer owners of these stocks speculative interests in the market performance of the common stocks of the would-be acquiring corporations probably more exciting than the interests of this kind that they have had in the stock they are being asked to give up.

In some cases, it must be added, corporations provide for convertibility because they have good reasons to feel that they could not sell preferred stocks that lack this feature, unless, perhaps, they were to set unrealistically high dividend rates. These corporations may have only scant anticipations that the market prices of their common stocks will ever rise to levels to promote conversions. They may not want to issue additional common stock by the conversion route or otherwise. But they are extremely anxious to sell preferred stock, and they hope that the conversion privilege will be a sufficient sweetener to attract buyers, as it may truly be in periods of high speculative fever among securities buyers.

Conversion Terms. The terms of conversion are set in such a way that the immediate surrender of preferred stock in exchange for common is out of the question. In the foregoing illustration, had the corporation made each share of its preferred stock convertible into 1⅔ shares of common, it might just as well have issued the common right away and been done with it. Thus, what the preferred stockholder gets in the conversion privilege is a speculative interest in the corporation's earnings and dividend policies and in the market behavior of its common stock.

The essential element in the conversion terms is, of course, the *conversion ratio* or *price*, by which is indicated how many shares of common may be obtained for one share of preferred. Examples of conversion ratios have already been given: 1 for 1, and 1 for 1⅔. Others may be found in Table 23–3, in which the conversion features of a sample of recently issued convertible preferreds are described. Ratios are necessarily used when no-par stocks are involved, although they are often used also for stocks that have par values. When a conversion price is used, it indicates how much of the par value of a preferred share must be spent to buy a common share. For the Detroit Edison Company, as an example, a preferred share of $100 par value will exchange for 3⅓ shares of common, since the conversion price of a common share is set at $30.

Devices to Force Conversion. From the standpoint of corporations that want conversion to take place, a difficulty of the conversion feature is that owners of convertible preferred may be quite satisfied to hold it indefinitely, even though conversion *and sale* would be profitable, and perhaps highly profitable. Accordingly, such corporations usually modify the conversion privilege in such manner that with favorable market conditions conversion can be forced. Suppose that each share of a corporation's preferred is convertible into two shares of its common. The preferred was issued at $50 a share at a time when the common was selling at $18. Although the corporation has been quite profitable since issuing the preferred, it has been retaining most of its profits for expansion, so that dividends on common per share have been just about half the per-share level on preferred. Thus, the preferred stockholder has had no reason to convert to common to get larger dividends. However, the corporation's good earnings record and its excellent prospects have pushed the market price of its common stock to $40. But even this development gives the preferred stockholder no reason to convert unless he wants to take his capital gain and cease to be a stockholder. He can continue his speculative ride by simply holding the preferred stock, for its market price should have risen and should continue to behave in close relationship with the market price of the common. If the market price of the common is $40, and if 1 share of preferred is convertible into 2 shares of common, then the market price of preferred should be in the vicinity of $80; and if the common should go to 50, the preferred should go to 100.[7]

One device for forcing conversion is simply to limit the duration of the conversion privilege, as in the Murphy Oil Corporation's preferred, listed in Table 23–3. This stock was tendered to Murphy Oil's common stockholders in a rights offering in late July, 1967, so that the conversion period was limited to a little less than 15 years. Lim-

[7]Some discrepancy in the relationship of the market price of a preferred stock to that of the common stock into which it is convertible is possible on account of commissions payable on stock transactions and stock transfer taxes. But underpricings of the preferred by amounts larger than accounted for by commissions and taxes tend to be quickly eliminated as a result of transactions described as arbitrage. Arbitrage is a simultaneous buying and selling of some thing or things to earn a profit made possible by price discrepancies. Leaving commissions and taxes out of consideration, a price of 78 for the preferred stock of the illustration at a time when the common was selling at 40 would cause arbitragers to rush to buy preferred and to sell common. Each share of preferred bought would be converted into two shares of common for delivery on the sales contracts, and the profit on the simultaneous transactions would obviously be $2 per share of preferred. But the rush of buying orders for preferred would drive up its price, perhaps to 79; and the rush of selling orders would drive down the price of common, perhaps to 39½. If this were the outcome, further arbitraging would not be profitable.

In relation to discrepancies on account of commissions and stock transfer taxes, it should be mentioned that members of a given stock exchange pay no commissions on transactions that they themselves put through on its floor. Thus, the size of market price discrepancies that will occasion arbitrage is considerably narrowed when the convertible preferred and the related common are listed on an exchange whose members are constantly on the lookout for opportunities for arbitrage, as they can certainly be expected to be.

TABLE 23–3
Conversion Features of a Sample of Preferred Stocks

Corporation	*Description of Stock*	*Par Value*	*Expiration of Conversion Period*	*Conversion Price or Ratio*
Avco Corporation	\$3.20 cumulative convertible preferred stock	No par	No limit	2 shares of common
Baltimore Gas and Electric Company	Convertible cumulative preference stock, 6½% series	\$100	No limit	\$32
Blue Bell, Inc.	4¾% cumulative convertible preferred stock	\$100	No limit	\$53
Detroit Edison Company	Convertible cumulative preferred stock, 5½% series	\$100	No limit	\$30
Dresser Industries, Inc.	\$2 convertible preferred, series B	No par	No limit	.909 share of common
Emerson Electric Company	\$1.80 cumulative convertible preferred	\$5.00	No limit	.7 share of common
Long Island Lighting Company	Convertible preferred stock, 5¾%, series I	\$100	No limit	\$28
Murphy Oil Corporation	Cumulative preference stock, 5.20% series	\$100	6/1/82	2.5 shares of common
Occidental Petroleum Company	\$4 cumulative convertible preferred	\$1.00	No limit	3 shares of common

SOURCE: Moody's Investors Service, *Manuals*.

itations of 5 or 10 years have also been popular, although the fact that all other entries in Table 23–3 set no limits to their conversion periods indicates some trend away from restrictions of this kind, since all these stocks were issued in 1967 and 1968. At any rate, if the conversion period for a preferred stock is about to expire, and if conversion would be financially advantageous to the holder, then obviously he must either convert or lose the financial advantages. If the common stock of the forgoing illustration is selling at 40 and the preferred at 80, and if the conversion privilege is just about to expire, the preferred stockholder must act quickly to protect the benefits that have accumulated for him. He knows that the market price of the preferred will fall back to the vicinity of 50 on expiration of the conversion privilege. He may convert and hold the common stock in expectation of further market appreciation; he may convert and sell the common stock to take his capital gain; or he may take his capital gain by selling the preferred stock itself. If he sells the preferred stock, the buyer will surely convert it. Regardless of who actually effects the conversion, therefore, the corporation's goal is achieved.

Another forcing device is the setting of a scale of conversion prices or ratios that with the passing of time will be less and less favorable to the preferred stockholder. The longer he holds his preferred shares, the fewer the common shares he will get when and if he does convert. It may be provided, for example, that within the first five years after issue each share of preferred is convertible into three shares of common, within the next five years into two and one half shares, and thereafter into two shares. Where stipulations of this kind obtain, there is often a rush for conversion near the end of each successive period. Whether or not this will happen continues to depend, nevertheless, on the amount of dividends being paid on the common and the behavior of its market price.

A third device for forcing conversions, assuming market conditions to be favorable, is to call convertible preferreds for redemption. As was indicated earlier in this chapter, corporations almost always reserve the right to call their preferreds for redemption at any time in whole or in part. In contracts for convertible preferreds, however, they provide that should the stock be called for redemption, the holder may elect to surrender his shares *for conversion* rather than for redemption up to the date set for redemption or up to a time shortly before this date. If, then, the market price of the convertible preferred of the illustration is 80 and the call price is 55, a call for redemption will surely result in a flood of conversions. In a large proportion of recent issues of convertible preferreds, there is a provision that the corporation may not call its issue for redemption within the first several years—usually five—or within this period if the interest cost on money to be used for redemption would be less than the dividend rate on the preferred. Such a provision assures the holder that the conversion privilege is not likely to be taken away shortly after he buys the preferred or accepts it in a merger transaction, although, on the other hand, it has the complexion of a limitation on the conversion period, having at least a family relationship with limitations of the kind described in the second preceding paragraph.

Antidilution Provisions. The conversion privilege would be of little or no value to investors were it possible for corporations to weaken or virtually annihilate it by split-ups of their common stock or by the distribution of stock dividends to their common stockholders. If, therefore, the conversion feature is to be made attractive to prospective investors in preferred stock, it must generally be buttressed with appropriate antidilution provisions.

Assume, for example, that a corporation's preferred stock is convertible into common at a ratio of 1 for 2. The market price of the preferred is 100, and that of the common is 44. But the price of the common has been advancing rapidly, and prospects are that it will go well beyond 50. The preferred stockholders, therefore, have reason to begin to anticipate speculative profits, but at this very time a decision is made to split up the common stock on a 2-for-1 basis. An effect of the split-up would be a drop in the market price of common to a level around 22, and the preferred stockholders would have to give up their pleasant anticipations of profits were they not protected by an appropriate antidilution provision—one that, in this instance, would automatically cause a conversion ratio of 1 for 4 to supersede the original one of 1 for 2.

Since stock dividends given to common stockholders have effects similar to the effects of split-ups, investors in convertible preferred generally insist on protection against dilution from this source. Suppose that a corporation has outstanding 400,000 shares of common stock of $20 par value, that it has an earned surplus of $7 million, and that its preferred stock is convertible into common at the ratio of 1 share of preferred for 2 of common. The corporation declares and distributes a 50 percent stock dividend on the common, and each common stockholder gets, of course, 1 additional share for each 2 shares held. Whereas the corporation formerly had 400,000 shares of common outstanding with a book value of $37.50 a share, it now has 600,000 shares with a book value of $25 each. Moreover, the market value of common should decline in like proportion, since the arbitrary change in the number of common shares outstanding does not increase the corporation's earning power. But the holders of convertible preferred ought not to be penalized by the stock dividend; accordingly, the workings of a proper antidilution clause would cause the automatic substitution of a new conversion ratio of 1 for 3.

Illustrative of how an antidilution provision works, and also illustrative of limitations on conversion periods and less favorable conversion prices or ratios in successive periods, was the Schenley Industries, Inc. announcement to holders of its cumulative preference stock in March, 1968, following a 3-for-2 split-up of its common stock. The announcement stated that for the period from March 22 through December 31, 1968, the conversion price would be $46.66⅔ per share of common instead of the former $70, and that for the period January 1, 1969, through December 31, 1969, the conversion price would be $53.33⅓ rather than the former $80. It also called attention to the fact that the conversion privilege would expire "after the close of business" on December 31, 1969.

Use of Stock Purchase Warrants

By attaching to their preferred stocks warrants to buy common stock, corporations generally expect results quite similar to those they seek when they add the convertibility feature. Corporations that would prefer to sell common stock in the first place but do not do so because of unfavorable market conditions may anticipate calling the preferred stock for redemption when the funds to make this possible are obtained from later sales of common stock through the exercise of warrants. In some instances, corporations stipulate that their preferred stocks are receivable at par or stated value in payment for common stock purchased with warrants, thereby largely wiping out the distinction between the stock purchase and convertibility devices. On the other hand, corporations of relatively weak position that are inclined to think of warrants and convertibility purely as promotional features for the sale of preferred are likely to conclude that either of these devices can be made about as attractive as the other.

It appears that equality of attractiveness can easily be provided for. If the market price of a corporation's common stock is 18, it would not seem to matter whether it issues at 50 a preferred share that is made convertible into two shares of common, or at the same price a preferred share that has attached warrants to buy two shares of common at 25. Should the market price of the common go to, say, $40, the convertible preferred share could be exchanged for two shares of common and the common sold at a profit of $30. In the case of the attached warrants, two common shares could be bought at $50 and resold for $80, also at a profit of $30.

But there is a difference. The investor in convertible preferred, on converting and selling the common stock received in exchange, gets his profit but ceases to be a stockholder. The investor in preferred with warrants continues to be a preferred stockholder after exercising the warrants and selling the common stock thus obtained. Any investor may anticipate a desire to stay as a preferred stockholder; hence, at the time of the original offer of a preferred stock he may be more attracted by warrants than by a convertibility privilege. Another apparent advantage of warrants is that they are usually made detachable. This means that the preferred stockholder can sell them without in any way disturbing his position as such a stockholder. If common stock is purchasable by warrants at 25 at a time when its market price is 40, then the market price of a warrant for 1 share should be close to 15. Thus, it should be possible for the preferred stockholder to take his speculative profit without first having to put up the money to buy the common stock from the corporation.

On the other side of the picture, however, warrants may promise poorer prospects for sharing in generous dividends on common stock than does convertibility. Suppose, for example, that the dividend rate on the preferred stock referred to in the illustration above is 5 percent, or $2.50 a share annually. With improvement in earnings, the corporation later establishes regular dividend payments at 8 percent on the stated value of its common stock of $25, that is, $2 a share annually. The holder of a convertible preferred share may exchange it for 2 shares of common, on which he would earn $4 a year, equal to 8 percent on his original investment of $50. But the holder of a preferred share with warrants, after buying 2 shares of common at $25, would have an investment of $100 in the corporation, on which he would get $2.50 in preferred dividends and $4 in common dividends, equal to an average return of only 6.5 percent.

Wherever the weight of advantage to preferred stockholders may appear to lie, corporations themselves cast their vote in favor of convertibility. The convertibility feature is employed much more commonly than the warrant feature.

Little need be said about the terms for the exercise of stock purchase warrants, since they closely parallel in purpose and effect the terms provided for in connection with convertibility. The number of common shares that the preferred stockholders may buy for each preferred share held and the price to be paid for the common must of necessity be clearly established. Especially in corporations that are anxious to sell common stock, the period in which the warrants may be exercised is usually limited, such as 5 or 10 years, in order to force exercise of the warrants. For the same reason, a scale of successively higher prices of the common is often designated for subperiods within the longer period. Also, the privilege of buying with warrants must normally be protected by antidilution clauses.

Participation Rights

Arrangements for Participation. A preferred stock is said to be participating if it has rights established by contract to share in dividend distributions beyond the amount of its stated preferential dividend rate. Participation arrangements of three types are recognized—full participation, immediate participation, and special participation.

In full participation, the preferred shares equally with the common in all distributions after the preferred has been allotted its regular dividend and the common a dividend of the same rate or dollar amount. In immediate participation, the preferred begins to share in additional distributions as soon as it has been allotted its preferential rate. And special participation comprises all kinds of arrangements other than full and immediate participation. In the most common special arrangement, the preferred is limited to not more than one, two, or three percentage points beyond its preferential rate.

The more generous participation arrangements—full, immediate, and generous varieties of the special class—are rather well confined to family and other closely held corporations. A father who sets up his son in an incorporated business may take preferred stock for his investment and be satisfied to let the son have the common stock. But it may be agreed that the son will take most of his compensation as a salary, and that most of the profits, if and when distributed, will go to the father. Thus, the preferred stock could be given a very liberal participation feature.

For corporations that offer their preferred stock widely to many investors, however, the usual participation feature, if one is included at all, is the allotment of not more than two or three extra percentage points to the preferred. A limited participation right is more likely to appeal to the mass of investors than is a more generous one. They know that the boards of directors of most corporations are common-stock minded—that while directors may not hesitate unduly before paying dividends equal to 7 percent of the par value of preferreds when the preferential rate is, say, 5 percent, they are likely to be most unwilling to pay dividends on preferreds equal to 10, 12, or 15 percent of their par values. In other words, investors expect corporations to call preferred stocks for redemption to get rid of generous participation features when earnings are high and high rates of dividends *could* be paid.

As a device for enhancing the salability of preferred stocks, even special participation features of the limited variety are much less popular than convertibility and warrant features. Relatively strong corporations tend to shy away from participation arrangements. Their managers are likely to take the position that if the preferred stockholder is to share in extraordinary earnings he should do so by becoming a common stockholder, either by way of conversion or by the exercise of stock purchase warrants, rather than to enjoy this sharing while maintaining his preferential standing as a preferred stockholder. And weaker corporations, accordingly, have reason to fear that the very inclusion of participating features will unduly call attention to their weakness.

Some Outstanding Participating Preferreds. Some details about the feature of a few outstanding participating preferreds and their recent dividend records through 1967 should be of interest.

The participation feature has been very valuable to the holders of the 6 and 7 percent "guaranteed" stocks of the Richmond, Fredericksburg & Potomac Railroad Company, both of $25 par value. These stocks have preference over the common stock to dividends at the "guaranteed" rates, but they get dividends per share equal to the per-share distributions on the common stock if these distributions exceed dividends at the "guaranteed" rates. The dividend record of the period 1958–67 indicates the value of the participation. In this period, the annual dividends on the two preferred stocks averaged $5.825, equal to a rate of 23.3 percent on the par value.

Not nearly so valuable but still advantageous to the preferred stockholders is the participation feature of the $3 divided no-par preferred of Arden-Mayfair, Inc. It is preferred over common for its dividend of $3 a share, and it gets additional dividends equal to 25 percent of any dividends declared on the common, with a participation limit of $1 a share. In the period 1944–67, its participation ranged between 20 and 25 cents a year.

The 5 percent preferred stock of $100 par value of the Chicago, Milwaukee, St. Paul and Pacific Railroad Company is peculiar, not only in having a right of participation but also in its cumulation feature. Although this preferred is basically noncumulative, no dividends may be paid on the company's common stock unless dividends for the current and two preceding years on the preferred have been paid or provided for. As for participation, it shares dividends equally with the common stock up to $1 after the common has received a dividend of $3.50. The Milwaukee's preferred paid dividends of $5 in 1946, $7.50 in 1947, $4 in 1948 and 1949, $7 in 1950, and $5 regularly from 1951 through 1967.

The participation feature of the 5 percent convertible preferred of $100 par value of the Chicago and North Western Railway Company is offset by a provision making preferred dividends cumulative only to the extent that they are covered by earnings. Beyond dividends at its 5 percent rate, this stock is entitled to participate equally with common in additional dividends up to $1 after the common has received $5 a share. But the recent record of this participating preferred has not been pleasant for the preferred stockholders. It paid regular dividends of $5 a year in the period 1945–48; nothing in 1949; $5.15 in 1950; nothing in 1951; $2.55, $3.25, and $3.30, respectively, in the years 1952–54; nothing in the whole period 1955–63; and $5 annually in the period 1964–67.

QUESTIONS

1. In the absence of specific contractual provisions, in what ways does a corporation's preferred stock differ from its common stock in (*a*) preference to dividends, (*b*) preference to assets in the event of dissolution, and (*c*) voting capacities?

2. From the investor's standpoint, is any corporation's preferred stock always *better* than its common stock? Discuss.

3. What is meant when a preferred stock is described as being cumulative? On what basis or by what procedure does a preferred stock get the cumulative status?

4. Does a corporation really have an *obligation* to pay dividends on its preferred stock at the rate stated in its contract? Does it have an *obligation* to pay subsequently cumulative preferred dividends not paid in the current year? Explain.

5. Why are corporate boards of directors generally inclined to declare and pay dividends on their corporations' preferred stocks regularly at the times prescribed, even though they are usually described as being common-stock minded?

6. What is the scope of the preference to assets usually given to preferred stockholders? Explain the significance of this preference.

7. What kinds of corporate actions are often made subject to vetoing voting powers held by preferred stockholders? What is the logic of giving such voting powers to these stockholders?

8. What is the reason for giving preferred stockholders contingent voting powers? What is the scope of these powers?

9. If a corporation is up-to-date in its payment of dividends to its preferred stockholders, why would they have any reason for objecting to the amount paid as dividends to the common stockholders? Would not such an objection indicate a selfish attitude on the part of the preferred stockholders?

10. When a corporation reserves the right to sell additional preferred shares of a given class, how is it likely to be limited, nevertheless, in the number it may issue? Must it give the additional shares the same terms, such as the dividend rate, as were given to the original issue? Explain.

11. What circumstances might make redemption of a corporation's preferred stock illegal, even though required by its contract?

12. Explain what is indicated by each of the following designations for preferred stocks: prior-preference preferred, second preferred, Series B preferred.

13. When a corporation is required by contract to set up a redemption fund for its preferred stock, how and when is the money actually used for redemption?

14. Explain why convertible preferred stocks have recently been very popular for exchange purposes in merger transactions. Do convertible preferreds have any other significant uses? Explain.

15. What means are often available to corporations to force the conversion of their convertible preferred stocks? Why would they want to force conversion?

16. What is the purpose of antidilution provisions found in almost all contracts for convertible preferred stocks? Explain how and in what circumstances they are effective.

17. What is distinctive about a so-called participating preferred stock? Why is a moderate participation feature likely to be more attractive to investors than a liberal one?

PROBLEMS

1. The Burns Steel Company is authorized by its charter to issue 50,000 shares of 6 percent preferred stock of $100 par value, but nothing further is said about this preferred stock in the charter or in the corporation's bylaws or the resolutions of its board of directors. According to the weight of legal opinion as it applies in most states:

a) Does the preferred stock have a preference to dividends?
b) If it does have such a preference, is it cumulative?
c) Does it have a preference to assets in the event of voluntary dissolution? Involuntary dissolution?
d) Does it have power to vote in elections of directors? On proposed amendments to the articles of incorporation?
e) Does it have the right to participate in distributions of profits beyond its 6 percent rate?
f) Is it callable for redemption by the corporation? If so, what is the call price?
g) Is it convertible into common stock of the corporation at the option of the stockholder? If so, what is the conversion price or ratio?

2. The preferred stock contract of Best and Burns, Inc. provides for the payment of quarterly dividends on March 1, June 1, September 1, and December 1 on a cumulative basis at the annual rate of 6 percent. Up to the year 19xx, it regularly paid the quarterly dividends, but in 19xx it paid only 2 percent on June 1 and 1 percent on December 1.

a) In the following year 19yy, what rate of dividends would it have to pay on the preferred stock on June 1 to be free to pay dividends on its common stock on that day or shortly thereafter?
b) If it paid no preferred dividends till December 1, 19yy, what rate would it have to pay on that day to be free to pay dividends on its common stock?
c) If it paid no preferred dividends till September 1, 19zz, what rate would it have to pay on that day to be free to pay dividends on the common stock?

3. The outstanding Series A preferred stock of the Cort Manufacturing Company consists of 100,000 shares of $100 par value with a dividend rate of 5 percent, and its outstanding Series B preferred stock amounts to 80,000 shares of $100 par value with a dividend rate of 5½ percent. The corporation's contract with the preferred stockholders authorizes it to issue additional preferred shares of equal ranking without their consent,

provided that it satisfies these two conditions: (1) average earnings available for preferred dividends in the preceding two years must have been equal to two times the dividend requirement on all preferred to be outstanding; and (2) total outstanding preferred plus long-term debt must not exceed 50 percent of the corporation's assets (including any assets to be acquired by issuing preferred stock) as reduced by the amount of its current liabilities.

Cort Manufacturing would like to issue as many shares of Class C preferred stock as the foregoing limitations would permit. Such stock would have a par value of $100 and a dividend rate of 6 percent, and the proceeds of its sale would be expected to be equal to the par value.

Determine how many shares the corporation could issue, assuming that its average earnings available for preferred dividends in the preceding two years have been $3.2 million, and that its most recent balance sheet was, in summary form, as follows.

Current assets	$45,000,000	Current liabilities	$20,000,000
Fixed assets	50,000,000	Bonds payable	12,000,000
		Preferred stock	18,000,000
		Common stock	30,000,000
		Earned surplus	15,000,000
	$95,000,000		$95,000,000

4. At the time of issue, each share of the preferred stock of Meyer, Inc. was made convertible into two and one half shares of its common stock within a first five-year period, and into two shares of common within a second five-year period. The contract for the preferred contains the usual kinds of antidilution provisions. Within the first 5-year period, Meyer effected a 3-for-1 split-up of its common stock, and later in the same period it distributed a 40 percent stock dividend on the common stock.

On the basis of the contract's antidilution provisions, what would be the new conversion ratios for the two five-year periods (*a*) as a result of the common stock split-up, and (*b*) as a result of the subsequent stock dividend? (*c*) What were the original conversion *prices*? (*d*) What would the conversion prices be after the split-up and the stock dividend distribution, respectively?

chapter 24

ISSUE AND MANAGEMENT OF PREFERRED STOCKS

DISTRIBUTION CHANNELS

Principal Channels

Registered Issues. The statistical compilations of registered securities issues published by the Securities and Exchange Commission for the past few years indicate consistently that the principal channels for the distribution of registered issues of new preferred stocks are offerings to the general public, offerings to security holders, and exchanges for the stock of other corporations acquired in mergers and consolidations and by holding companies. For the year ending June 30, 1967, out of total registrations "for account of issuer" of $756.4 million, the amount of preferred stock issues registered by corporations for offering to the general public amounted to $408.9 million, and for offering to security holders, $63.2 million. The amount registered for the "account of issuer for other than cash sale"—surely preponderantly for exchange in merger transactions—was $198 million.[1]

Offerings to security holders largely comprise tenders of convertible preferred stocks to common stockholders, although occasionally corporations offer additional preferred to their existing preferred stockholders, especially preferreds that do not have the convertibility feature. It is safe to assume that most of the preferred stock registered with the SEC for the account of the issuer "for other than cash sale" is stock destined for distribution to stockholders in corporations absorbed or to be tempted toward absorption in merger transactions and proposals. For preferred stocks, the SEC's category *for other than cash sale* comprises "exchange transactions" almost entirely,

[1]Securities and Exchange Commission, *Annual Report*, 1967, p. 154.

and in consideration of ordinary business practices one knows there is little of significance to exchange for *registered* preferred stocks except the stocks of other corporations desired as acquisitions. It is true that individual corporations not infrequently make offers to their preferred stockholders—and even, in rare instances, to their common stockholders—to exchange new preferred stocks for those they already have, and that, briefly discussed later, it is sometimes exchange in reorganization proceedings, but such exchange transactions are generally exempt from registration with the SEC. However, in view of the emphasis given in Chapter 23 to the exchange of convertible preferred stocks of absorbing corporations for the common stocks of absorbed corporations in merger deals, it should be added here that preferred stocks of absorbing corporations are also often given to the preferred stockholders of corporations being absorbed—the preferred stock offered usually has exactly the same features of the preferred stock to be surrendered, whether or not the convertibility feature is included.

Private Placements. In addition to preferred stocks registered with the SEC, we must allow for what are substantial amounts of private placements from year to year, and sales and exchanges made entirely within the borders of individual states. None of these classes of transactions is subject to registration with the SEC. There is no accurate keeping of records of these transactions, but the volume of private placements of issues of more than $100,000 individually offered for immediate cash sale can be at least roughly estimated from SEC figures. For the calendar year 1967, for example, it reported preferred issues of more than $100,000 offered for immediate cash sale by issuers at $884.6 million, and registered offerings for immediate cash sale for the account of issuers at $794.2 million,[2] so that the difference of $90.4 million is at least a rough estimate of private placements on this basis. But one must keep in mind that every year there are also noncash private placements, such as exchanges in merger transactions that do not require securities registration with the SEC. At any rate, private placements surely deserve to be ranked among the principal channels of preferred stock distribution.

Limited Importance of Other Distribution Channels

On the other hand, most of the remaining distribution channels surveyed in Chapter 20 in connection with common stock financing are generally of slight importance for the disposition of preferred

[2]Securities and Exchange Commission, *Statistical Bulletin*, March, 1968, pp. 16, 25. The estimate mentioned subsequently is necessarily rough for such reasons as the frequent differences in dates on which registration statements become effective and the dates on which offerings are actually made, the fact that preferred stocks registered for immediate cash sale may not actually be offered because of issuers' changes in plans, and the exclusion from registered securities data of issues up to $300,000, exempt under the SEC's Regulation A.

stocks. Of some importance among these miscellaneous channels as they pertain to preferred stock is its occasional use in exchanges for the claims of certain classes of creditors in final settlements in corporate reorganizations. Holders of second and subsequent mortgages, debenture bondholders, and unsecured short-term creditors may realize that only a small percentage of their claims against bankrupt corporations would be satisfied were their assets to be sold, and they may be persuaded, however reluctantly, that the corporations as reorganized could hardly survive for very long should their claims be simply postponed. Accordingly, they may agree to give up their claims as creditors in whole or in part and to take preferred stock in exchange. Although the reorganized corporations do not acquire assets by such issues of preferred stock, the issues surely enable them to retain assets already acquired.

In the incorporation of businesses formerly conducted as proprietorships and partnerships, preferred stock is sometimes given in part for proprietary interests. A limited partner, for example, may be willing to go along with the incorporation only if he is given preferred rather than common stock. Sometimes, too, holders of specific parcels of property, such as store and factory buildings, are willing to part with them in exchange for preferred stock, or perhaps for a combination of preferred and common.

But rare are the transactions in which preferred stock is given for the services of promoters, investment bankers, and corporate executives, and even more rarely are they given options to buy preferred. Sometimes, it has been used in employee stock-ownership plans, particularly by public utility corporations, but emphasis in the general run of such plans has been on common stock. While preferred stock is frequently convertible into common stock, and sometimes has warrants attached for the purchase of common stock, it is most unusual for another kind of security, such as bonds, to be convertible into preferred or to have warrants attached for the purchase of preferred. Finally, the distribution of preferred as dividends or as bonuses in connection with the sale of other types of securities is a rarity.

In the subsequent discussion of the use of preferred stock in financing, therefore, we will be justified in confining our attention to three of the four channels of distribution as indicated by the statistics cited, omitting at this time further discussion of its use in merger transactions because of the discussion in Chapter 23. Moreover, for the three channels remaining for discussion here—offerings to the general public, offerings to security holders, and private placements—no useful purpose would be served in repeating the mass of details about preparation for sale and the actual selling, covered in Chapters 18–20 in the analysis of common stock flotations. The preparation of preferred stock issues for sale and the procedures of selling them in the three channels follow quite closely the patterns of common stock financing. Our interest, therefore, should be largely directed to an analysis of the differing significance of each of the three channels as between preferred stock and common stock flotations. Nevertheless, the student should not forget that public offerings of preferred stock in interstate commerce require all the detailed work incident to complying with the provisions of the federal Securities Act on registration statements and prospectuses, except, of course, that offerings of not more than $300,000 in any year may get by with the much less rigorous notification requirements. Also to be kept in mind are the additional government regulations embodied in the state blue-sky laws—regulations that are generally applicable to new offerings of preferred stock whether or not sold in interstate commerce. Finally to be kept in mind is that employing the services of investment bankers also requires a great deal of preparatory work on the part of both the issuing corporations and the bankers themselves.

Offerings to the General Public and to Security Holders

Differences in Investor Interests. A much larger proportion of preferred stock issues are sold by offerings to the general public than to existing security holders because of the very nature of the investment interests of these two classes of potential buyers. By no means are all investors included in the "general public" classification interested in preferred stock investment, but except in times of severe depression there is usually a sufficient number to enable worthy corporations to successfully float preferred issues. Therefore, when corporate managers—and investment bankers as their advisers—conclude that interest in preferred issues is much stronger in the open market than with existing security holders, it is more reasonable for them to choose to make offerings to the general public. Especially when they are planning to offer preferred stocks that lack the convertibility feature, they are likely to conclude that successful flotation is much more probable in offerings to the public than to existing security holders.

Interests of Common Stockholders. As just indicated, a corporation's common stockholders are unlikely to have much interest in its proposed flotations of nonconvertible preferred stock. The very fact that they are already common stockholders indicates that they are willing to take risks; accordingly, they may find little attraction in the relative safety of preferred stock. But more than this, they may not want to buy the preferred because they see in it no threat to their ownership interests as common stockholders. If the proposed preferred is to have voting power, they may not be interested in control; if it is to be nonvoting, and they do have an interest in control, they may not be worried about its contingent voting rights. Similarly, the preferred's preference to dividends may not bother them; by reason of the corporation's satisfactory earnings record, they do not expect defaults in dividend payments to occur. And they may pay little attention to its preference to assets, because they think of this privilege as so many people do, in terms of a dissolution whose possibilities they consider to be exceedingly remote. If, therefore, they have the preemptive right to preferred issues, they may readily waive it so that an offering to the general public may be made.

But adding the convertibility feature to proposed issues of preferred stock (or, much more rarely in actual practice, adding stock purchase warrants) can certainly be expected, in many instances, to perk up the buying interests of corporations' existing common stockholders. For some, buying may seem to be imperative for the protection of their ownership interests, but for many who have been well satisfied with the performance of the corporation's common stock the proposed preferred may simply appeal to them as a good investment, not only for its own qualities to be immediately effective but also as a means of eventually getting additional common shares on terms they expect to become quite favorable.

Thus, of the convertible preferreds listed in Table 23–3, page 594, the issues of Baltimore Gas and Electric, Detroit Edison, Long Island Lighting, and Murphy Oil were all tendered in rights offerings to their common stockholders. (The Avco, Dresser, Emerson Electric, and Occidental Petroleum preferreds were exchanged for stocks in other corporations acquired in mergers, and the Blue Bell issue was offered to the general public.) Purchases of new issues of preferred stock by common stockholders are also strongly promoted when it is given voting power—or when such power *must* be given by law, as in Illinois, or by provisions in corporate articles—if there is much anxiety about control. All the more is this desirable, of course, the greater the actual jockeying among factions to gain or retain control. Finally to be mentioned is that giving participation rights to preferred stock, especially generous ones, should surely promote sales among common stockholders, although, as was indicated in Chapter 23, this is a matter of very little practical importance.

Interests of Other Security Holders. In the SEC's statistical reports, moreover, the existing security holders to whom new issues of preferred stock are offered are not distinguished by classes. While the security holders to whom new issues of common stock and of convertible preferreds are offered are almost invariably the existing common stockholders, it is not necessarily they to whom new issues of nonconvertible preferred are offered. A corporation's existing preferred stockholders may be enthusiastic about buying additional preferred shares. Although probably not having the preemptive right, they may still be the most likely class of investors; and the offering can be made to them if the common stockholders also do not have the preemptive right or are willing to waive it. On the other hand, corporations can hardly expect many of their bondholders or creditors of other classes to be much interested in buying new issues of their preferred stocks. Rarely, therefore, are offerings made to creditor groups.

Private Placements of Preferred Stock

An important reason that private placements of preferred stock are much more numerous than private placements of common stock is that the laws and regulations of many states permit certain classes of financial institutions—notably, life insurance companies and trust institutions in their management of nondiscretionary trust estates—to invest more liberally in preferred stocks than in common stocks. In many instances, moreover, such institutional investors much prefer to buy in bulk by the private placement route rather than by piecemeal acquisitions in the open market. By direct negotiation with the issuing corporations, they can have terms and features of the preferred stock contracts tailored specifically for them instead of taking those already designed to appeal to the tastes of many different kinds of investors. Often, indeed, they are able to arrange for dividend rates slightly higher than they would get on preferred stocks available in the open market.

As the principal class of long-term institutional lenders to business enterprises, the life insurance companies are especially likely to be interested in buying convertible preferred stocks by way of private placement. Indeed, they may *require* corporations that apply for long-term loans to sell them convertible preferreds (or to give or sell them stock purchase warrants) as a condition for the approval of the loan applications. They thus display a hope for rewards beyond the interest to be paid on the loans—a hope for capital gains to be derived from market appreciation in the borrowers' common stocks.

Another channel for the private placement of convertible preferred stocks was referred to in Chapter 20, where it was pointed out that such issues are sometimes taken by individual capitalists who are willing to advance substantial amounts of equity funds to small and medium-sized corporations. Such capitalists, it was said, generally want to take their income from these ventures as capital gains rather than as ordinary income. Thus, they may be satisfied with moderate dividends on preferred stocks, expecting to convert to common stock or to exercise the options to buy it should they want to take control or, on the successful outcome of the ventures, to sell the common to realize their capital gains.

PROBLEMS OF PREFERRED STOCK MANAGEMENT

Most of the problems encountered in the management of preferred stock issues closely parallel those of common stock management, as discussed in Chapters 21 and 22. Such a parallel is to be expected, since both kinds of securities represent ownership or equity interests. Decisions must be made whether the directors should have at their disposal authorized but unissued preferred and how much; whether preferred should have a par value and, if so, at what level, or whether it should be no par; whether the corporation should deal in its own preferred stock in the market; and whether it should have the preferred listed on one or more of the stock exchanges. Generally, however, problems of these kinds as they pertain to preferred stocks are much more easily solved than when they pertain to common stocks. For preferred stocks, solutions tend to fall into the category of customary procedures, which is to say, they tend to be uniform from corporation to corporation.

Certain problems encountered in common stock management are rarely found in the control of preferred stock issues—questions of changing from par to no par, from no par to par, and from high pars to low pars, write-downs in par or stated values, split-ups, and reverse splits. As a rule, original decisions on pars and number of shares stand as long as given preferred stock issues are outstanding. For example, the holders of preferred stocks—except in closely held corporations where almost anything can happen—can rarely be expected to consent to write-downs in the par or stated values of their stocks to eliminate deficits or to permit write-downs in asset values. As long as corporations are solvent, they expect the common stockholders to bear such burdens.

On the other hand, because preferred stock is not the same as common stock it has certain management problems peculiarly its own. Two kinds stand out: the elimination or replacement of preferred issues themselves, and the elimination of dividend arrearages.

In the remainder of the present chapter, therefore, we shall look briefly at what may be called the routine problems of preferred stock management closely resembling the comparable problems of common stock management, and then at greater length at the two special kinds of problems just mentioned.

ROUTINE PROBLEMS

Authorized Issues

The possibility that the common stockholders of a corporation will refuse to approve from time to time new issues of preferred is rarely a good reason for placing at the disposal of the directors substantial amounts of authorized but unissued preferred.[3] If a proposed issue of preferred is to have voting power or if it is to be convertible or to have stock purchase warrants attached, the common stockholders

[3]For an analysis of the considerations involving common stock in this regard, see pp. 524–25.

may insist that it first be offered to them, or they may make no such demand should they feel that the preferred will not significantly affect their own ownership interests. In either case, however, they are likely to approve the proposed issue without much delay. A deferral of requests for approval until such time that preferred is actually to be issued means, therefore, that state taxes on authorized but unissued stock can be avoided.

But requirements for the approval of existing *preferred* stockholders for additional issues of preferred may change the outlook. Sound financial programming may be hamstrung if further offerings of preferred of the kind already outstanding or of kinds that would have prior preferences must have the consent of the holders of a substantial majority of the existing preferred. In the absence of such a consent, further financing with preferred would require replacement of the entire existing issue, which could be quite costly in flotation expenses. Therefore, if a corporation plans to put out additional preferred from time to time over a period of years, its plans should presumably be matched with an original authorization to take care of these successive issues. At any time, accordingly, the existing preferred stockholders would not have the power to veto further sales from the authorized issue; their veto power would reach only issues going beyond the original authorization.

However, when additional issues of preferred are not subject to the veto power of existing preferred stockholders but only depend on the satisfaction of protective provisions in the existing contract, such as those in terms of earnings, the ratio of preferred to assets, and its ratio to common, no need for authorized but unissued preferred stock obtains. If the protective provisions can be satisfied, consent of the common stockholders for the additional issues, when needed, will presumably be readily forthcoming. Here, of course, it is generally important to give the directors standing authority to serialize the successive issues, so that different dividend rates, call prices, and preferences to assets in dollars per share can be set in accordance with changing conditions in the preferred stock market.

Par and No Par

Although preferred stocks have generally shared with common stocks the earlier trend from par values to no pars and the later trend from high pars and no pars to low pars—and for the same reasons that have applied to common[4]—this movement in the new directions has been slower than has that of common. Many preferred stocks of $100 par value remain outstanding, and a goodly number of new issues with pars at that figure come to the market each year. A reason is

---

[4]See pp. 526–30.

that corporations, when devising preferred stock issues for a receptive market, have no difficulty in selling them at or above a par value such as $100. If the dividend rate and other terms as originally decided on are found on investigation to preclude sale at par value, an increase in the proposed dividend rate and perhaps improvements in other terms can generally be expected to remedy the situation. Likewise, corporate managements do not ordinarily envisage pricing difficulties in selling successive issues of given preferreds. If an outstanding preferred is selling at 95 whereas its par value is 100, a second issue, Series B, can be given a better dividend rate and perhaps better terms of other kinds to ensure its sale at 100 or better.

Preferred Treasury Stock

While many corporations never deal in their common stocks once they have been issued, most of those that issue preferreds typically regard it as highly probable that they will have occasion to buy back all or portions of their preferred issues. Such an expectation goes hand in hand with contractual agreements to set up redemption or sinking funds for retirement, but it is also strongly indicated by the customary reservation of rights to call preferred for redemption, regardless of redemption fund provisions.

Usually, however, the status of reacquired preferred stock as "treasury stock" is short-lived. Investors in a preferred stock would see little protection in a redemption fund requirement if the corporation could reissue at will preferred shares acquired in fulfillment of the requirement; hence, they generally insist on a provision that reacquired stock must be promptly canceled. Even in the absence of redemption fund provisions, moreover, corporations do not ordinarily plan to resell when they buy up their preferred stocks in the market or call them for redemption. Their intention is to move toward the simple common stock form of financial structure or to replace the existing preferreds with new preferreds that have materially different features or with long-term debt. Accordingly, immediate steps to cancel the reacquired preferred are usually taken as a matter of course.

In rare circumstances, it is true, corporations do reacquire their preferred stocks with the intention of reselling them. The most probable occassion for this is the disposal of preferred shares donated to provide working capital—much more likely in family and other closely held corporations than in those of wide stock distributions.

As was pointed out in Chapter 23, state laws are generally more liberal in permitting reacquisitions of preferred stocks than common stocks. The general rule is that the cost of common treasury stock must not exceed the amount of earned surplus, whereas the cost of reacquired preferred stock may ordinarily be charged against the preferred stock account itself as long as this charge does not exceed par or stated value. Such a difference in legal stipulations gives corporation managements a comparatively wide degree of freedom in buying and calling preferred for cancellation and, indeed, in acquiring for resale, should that kind of transaction be favored.

Listing

The question of listing a preferred stock on one or more of the stock exchanges seldom arises independently of the question of listing common stock of the same corporation. Rare is the corporation that would want to list its preferred but not its common, both being widely distributed. And rare, too, is the corporation whose common stock is closely held but whose preferred shares would nevertheless qualify for listing on the basis of their number and wide distribution.

Corporations that have their common stocks listed on a given exchange ordinarily apply to the same exchange to have their preferreds listed. If advantages are gained by the listing of common, presumably advantages of the same kinds, although probably of less significance, can be had by the addition of preferreds to the list. The exchanges themselves encourage the listing of preferreds by making listing requirements in terms of number of shares and distribution much milder for preferreds than for common stocks.

CHANGES IN TERMS AND REPLACEMENT OF PREFERRED STOCK

Changing circumstances in the economic system or in the affairs of individual corporations often lead corporate managements to decide to eliminate preferred stocks from their financial structures, or to decide that the terms and features of their outstanding preferreds are unsatisfactory and must, if possible, be altered. The preferred stocks may have been issued when the corporations were under considerable financial pressure of some kind, were not well known, had limited earning capacity, or were subject to other unfavorable conditions. Or they may have been issued in periods of tight money, when interest and dividend rates were high and when investors were in a position to impose restrictive provisions that would not have been acceptable at other times. With the changing circumstances, at any rate, moves toward elimination of the preferreds themselves or toward alteration in terms and features seem to be in order.

Decisions aimed at the elimination of preferred stocks usually occur because corporate managements see great merit in the simple common stock form of financial structure. Much more likely, however, they expect to gain quite substantial advantages from substituting bonds for their preferred stocks—chiefly in the deductibility of bond interest in the determination of taxable income, but possibly also in having interest rates on bond issues below the dividend rates they have been paying on their preferred stocks. But for most corporations, the problem of elimination has not been a difficult one: they have simply sold additional shares of common stock or floated bond issues and used the proceeds to redeem the no longer desirable preferred stocks. A very large number of refinancing operations of this kind have been effected in recent years—especially the substitution of new bond issues for preferred stocks. In any event, the question of elimination hardly needs further discussion in this chapter, since any such discussion would necessarily be repetitious of materials covered elsewhere. The advantages and disadvantages of common stock structures and of preferred stock financing as against bond financing were discussed in Chapters 15 and 16, the procedures of common stock financing in Chapters 18 to 20, and the procedures of bond financing will be discussed in Chapter 30.

Our immediate attention, then, may best be confined to situations in which corporate managements are quite satisfied to have preferred stocks in their financial structures but are unhappy about the status of their existing preferreds. Dividend rates considered to be excessive are an outstanding source of dissatisfaction. A corporation that put out its preferred in relatively unfavorable circumstances may have had to designate a cumulative dividend rate of, say, 6 or 7 percent. But now, with improvements in its financial position and increased demand for preferred stocks among investors generally, its managers are confident that a dividend rate of 4½ or 5 percent would suffice to attract buyers of a new preferred issue. What to do?

Managerial dissatisfaction with the terms of existing preferred stock issues may have for its source terms of the contracts other than dividend rates. A corporation may want to issue additional preferred of the same class as that already outstanding, but its proposals to do so may have been vetoed by the existing preferred stockholders, or it may have found that additional issues are precluded by what it considers to be unduly oppressive protective provisions in its existing contract. Another corporation, originally planning to work toward a simple common stock structure, may now be quite satisfied to have preferred stock permanently in its financial structure; accordingly, it finds the redemption fund provisions of its existing contract distasteful. Another decides that restrictions on common stock dividends in the existing contract are unreasonable. Another concludes that managerial discretion is seriously hampered by requirements in the existing contract about the maintenance of certain balance sheet ratios. Another wants to get rid of a participation feature. And in another, intense jockeying for control makes the present management, holding on by a narrow margin, extremely anxious to eliminate the conversion feature in the outstanding preferred. What to do?

Sale of New Preferred Stock

An obvious way for a corporation to eliminate sources of dissatisfaction of the kinds mentioned is to issue a new preferred stock and to use the proceeds of its sale to retire the outstanding issue that has the obnoxious features. With the existing issue still outstanding, restrictive provisions in its contract may preclude the new issue, or its owners may be expected to vote against the new issue. But obstacles of this kind can easily be overcome. Assuming the outstanding stock to be callable—as, of course, it would be likely to be—the corporation could call it for redemption, borrow money from a bank to redeem it, and then use the proceeds of the new issue to repay the bank loan. With the old preferred eliminated, only the approval of the common stockholders would be required for the new offering of preferred. For an example, we may refer to a year when interest and dividend rates on new issues of securities were much lower than they have been more recently—to 1963, say, when the Northwest Natural Gas Company arranged the sale of 60,000 shares of 4.68 percent preferred stock of $100 par value to 16 institutional investors, and shortly thereafter called for redemption at $107 a share the 60,000 shares of its outstanding 5.72 percent preferred also of $100 par value.

Replacement to Reduce the Dividend Rate. When the objective in issuing a new preferred is to get the advantage of a lower dividend rate, a corporate management must be quite careful in estimating the costs of flotation, the cost of retirement in terms of the call-price premium, and the interest to be paid on the interim financing with bank loans. If it is not careful, it may find that it has gone to a great deal of trouble to no material advantage; in truth, the net result may be disadvantageous. That a new preferred can be sold on the basis of a dividend rate of 5 percent, whereas the dividend rate on the existing preferred is 6 percent, does not mean that the corporation will have its annual bill for dividends cut by an amount equal to 1 percent of the par or stated value of the existing issue.

For illustration, assume that a certain corporation has outstanding 100,000 shares of 6 percent cumulative preferred of $50 par value. The stock is callable at $56, so that a total of $5,600,000 would be needed to pay off the stockholders. In addition, it would be necessary to borrow to effect the retirement pending sale of the new stock, and it is estimated that the loan funds would be needed for two months. A bank is willing to lend $5,600,000 for that period at an interest rate of 4½ percent per annum, or for a total interest charge of $42,000. However, the interest charge would be deductible against ordinary income in the determination of the corporation's income tax liability. Assuming that the corporation's income is taxable at 48 percent within the range affected, the charge would be offset by a tax saving of $20,-160. This means that the corporation could use $20,160 of the cash throw-off from its earnings for preferred stock redemption or bank loan repayment, thus decreasing the amount needed from the new preferred stock issue for these purposes. Accordingly, the net amount needed to retire the preferred stock and to repay the bank loan would be $5,600,000 + $42,000 − $20,160 or $5,621,840. How much of the new preferred stock would have to be sold to provide cash in the amount of $5,621,840 would depend on the deal that could be made with investment bankers. The bankers assure the corporate management that they could sell approximately 120,000 shares of 5 percent preferred at $50 a share, the proposed par value of the new issue. They estimate that flotation costs, including expenses of registration and their own underwriting commission, at 4 percent of the gross proceeds of the issue. The refinancing should thus require the issuance of new preferred amounting to $5,621,840 ÷ .96 or (rounded) $5,856,-000. Dividends on the old stock amounted to $300,000 a year, and on the new they would amount to $292,800. Thus, what would appear to be a reduction in dividend requirements of $50,000 a year, were one simply to apply the two dividend rates to the par value of the old stock, would turn out to be a true reduction of only $7,200.

Obviously, the corporation of the illustration would fare badly were it required to offer in the new preferred a dividend rate of 5¼ or 5½ percent; its dividend requirements would be increased as a result of the refinancing. Even with the new rate at 5 percent, as given in the illustration, the small annual saving in dividends of $7,200 could hardly be attractive to a common-stock minded board of directors. Were the contract for the new preferred to set down substantial call-price premiums and were there some likelihood that it would sooner or later be called for redemption, the saving would appear to be a mere pittance. In terms of par value, moreover, the prospect of having $5,856,000 of new preferred to redeem, in place of $5,000,000 of old, would further reduce the significance of the saving. Even should the directors be planning to keep the new preferred outstanding permanently, the fact that the refinancing would add $856,-000 to the preferred stockholders' claims to assets in the event of merger, reorganization, or dissolution could hardly be palatable.

Replacement to Eliminate Unsatisfactory Features. When corporate managements plan new issues of preferred stocks to get rid of undesirable features in existing issues, they must estimate the costs of elimination as carefully as when estimating the probable level of savings through dividend-rate reductions. Assuming that no change is to take place in the dividend rate, these costs are clearly as indicated previously: premiums paid in calling the old preferred, flotation expenses of the new, interest payments for interim financing less the related tax saving, and the *annual* dividend differential on the increased amount of preferred stock to be outstanding. In the illustration, the first three of these items totaled $856,000, and the annual dividend differential would be $51,360 (that is, dividends at 6 percent on $5,856,000 of stock by comparison with dividends at the same rate on the existing $5,000,000 of preferred stock). Would this be too much to pay for the elimination of severe restrictions on additional issues under an existing contract, redemption fund requirements, the convertibility feature, or some other obnoxious feature or combination of features? It might or might not be in given circumstances, but nobody would deny that the cost should be known before action is taken.

The costs of eliminating unsatisfactory provisions in preferred stock contracts may be reduced, of course, by some adjustment downward in the dividend rate in the new issue, perhaps by something less than the full percentage point of the illustration. However, no such downward adjustment may be possible; in fact, the costs of eliminating unsatisfactory provisions may be increased by an upward adjustment in the dividend rate. What the corporation wants in its new preferred is to have weaker or fewer protective provisions than in the old, or it wants to take away such attractive features as ordinary voting power, convertibility, or participation. Though, therefore, its financial position and the market situation may have improved since the old preferred was issued, this improvement as an influence on dividend rates may be offset or more than offset by weaknesses for the investor in the new contract as compared with the old.

Changes by Vote of the Preferred Stockholders

A second way to reduce dividend rates or remove objectionable features of existing preferreds is simply to get the preferred stockholders to approve the change. The state laws provide that the holders of a majority, two thirds, three fourths, or some other proportion of the outstanding preferred shares (most commonly, two thirds) may approve changes in the terms of preferred stock contracts, including dividend rates. The general rule is that when holders of the prescribed proportion of shares approve, the changes are binding on all the preferred shareholders. By this procedure, therefore, the same preferred stock remains outstanding with the voted changes in effect but with all other features unchanged.

But a corporation is unlikely to get the approval of its preferred stockholders for a lower dividend rate or other contractual changes unfavorable to them unless it is willing to simultaneously offer material concessions elsewhere in the contract. At a stockholders' meeting in April, 1963, for example, the holders of the prior preferred stock of the Curtis Publishing Company rejected a proposal to eliminate a contractual provision requiring approval of two thirds of this stock for mortgaging the corporation's property or adding to its long-term debt. The preferred stockholders objected that they would be giving up some of their rights while getting nothing in return.

However, the corporation may be inclined to offer no concessions. Its managers may be confident that a new preferred with the features wanted, and without new kinds of concessions, could easily be sold in the market. Hence, their position may be that the preferred stockholders should also be sufficiently aware of market conditions to accept the proposed change without demur. Nevertheless, the preferred stockholders would know that redemption of the preferred would be the alternative to their vote of approval. Without attractive concessions, therefore, they would surely be inclined to vote negatively, to take the redemption price with its premium (as would probably have been provided for), and then to decide whether or not to reinvest in whatever security the corporation might bring out as a replacement. Indeed, the corporation would have some basis for making concessions, since an approval vote by the stockholders would save it the premiums on redemption, flotation costs of a new security, and interest costs (after the tax saving) for any necessary interim financing. Concessions to avoid these costs would appear to be especially advisable, of course, if the corporation were not contemplating expanding the amount of its preferred stock. If, however, the very changes proposed were designed to set the stage for much larger issues of such stock, the long-run burden of concessions needed to get an approval vote might be regarded as prohibitive.

Exchanges of New Preferred for Old

When the managers of a corporation come to the conclusion that they would have to offer concessions of certain kinds to preferred stockholders to get their approval for changes in the preferred stock contract, they may decide that the better procedure would be simply to devise a new issue and offer it in exchange for the present one. Apart from the proposed changes and the concessions to be offered, there may be many minor points in the existing contract that have been ambiguous, difficult to apply, or otherwise awkward. The opportunity to start from scratch in writing a new contract may be quite appealing. Moreover, the expenses involved in an exchange procedure, if successful, may turn out to be not much more than would be incurred in taking a vote. An advantage of the exchange procedure—but applicable also to approvals of changes by vote—is that the filing of a registration statement with the SEC is not required, provided that "no commission or other remuneration is paid or given directly or indirectly for soliciting such exchange."[5] Usually, qualification under

[5]Sec. 3(a)(9) of the federal Securities Act.

state blue-sky laws also is unnecessary. A disadvantage is that, except in extraordinary cases, some of the preferred stockholders can be expected to refuse to make the exchange. Accordingly, the corporation must have cash available or means to acquire it to redeem the stock of these holdouts at the call price.

ELIMINATION OF DIVIDEND ARREARAGES

General Aspects of the Problem

If corporate managements are sometimes unhappy because dividend rates in their preferred stock contracts are higher than they would have to set in new issues, or because other contractual provisions seem to be unreasonably burdensome, they have all the more cause for unhappiness when they contemplate dividend arrearages on their preferreds. Arrearages equal to 5 or 10 percent of the par or stated value of outstanding preferred stock may not be particularly worrisome, especially if general business conditions and the affairs of the individual corporation are showing marked improvement. But arrearages of 20, 25, or 30 percent and of higher percentages are definitely a source of much corporate unhappiness, even when business conditions and the operating results of the individual corporation are improving.

Consequences of Large Arrearages. Although large dividend arrearages never in themselves threaten insolvency, they are quite burdensome. Access to new funds is sharply restricted. The possibility of selling new common or preferred stock at anything close to reasonable terms, as those terms are judged by the corporate managements, is exceedingly remote. Potential investors in bonds, too, are likely to shy away. Though they would have claims prior to those of the preferred stockholders, the very arrearages call attention to the corporation's poor earnings record, its weak cash position, or both. For the same reason, short-term lenders and trade suppliers may be niggardly in extending credit. All potential creditors may fear that, when cash does become available to the corporation in fair amounts, too much of it will be drained in efforts to clean up the arrearages.

Payment in Cash. Thus, corporations have good reason to try to avoid arrearages in the first place, and to try to get clear of them once they have accumulated. The hard route is to pay off the arrearages in cash. It has been taken valiantly by numerous corporations, some of them meeting in this way arrearages as high as 30, 40, and 50 percent, and in some instances much greater arrearages. Outstanding records of arrearage clear-ups by the cash route have been made in recent years by the Alleghany Corporation and the Maine Central Railroad. In 1958, Alleghany paid $149.87½ a share on its 5½ percent preferred to clear up a 27-year accumulation of arrearages. The Maine Central in many of the years of the 1950's and early 1960's paid dividends in excess of the regular rate of $5 to clear up an arrearage accumulation that amounted to $90 at the end of 1949, finally becoming current by the end of 1965. However, Maine Central's problem was greatly reduced in burden when most of its preferred stockholders accepted an offer it made in 1959 of $5 in cash and $150 of 50-year 5½ percent debenture bonds in exchange for each share of the preferred and its claim to arrearages as they stood at that time.

But the cash payment route is, indeed, difficult principally because it can ordinarily be expected to require a considerable period of time, even though current earnings may be good. The greater the arrearages, the longer, of course, the period of time. During this period, the corporation's access to new funds and its credit standing, though steadily improving, may continue to suffer to an extent as to seriously circumscribe its activities. Prospective creditors, as was said previously, may be concerned about the very drain of cash in settling the arrearages.

The cash payment route must surely impress the common stockholders as being a hard one. Already without dividends for at least the period of years during which the arrearages were accumulating, they must contemplate a further dreary series of dividendless years while the arrearages are being made up. Not only have they been starved for dividends and can expect further starvation of this kind, but also they have seen the market price of their stock fall to low levels, where they can expect it to remain for a considerable stretch into the future. How nice it would be, therefore, if all the arrearages could be wiped out at one stroke by means of some kind of deal with the preferred stockholders!

Possibility of Settlement Deals. Because corporate managements are vitally concerned with access to funds and credit standing, and because, be it repeated, they are usually common-stock minded, possibilities of working out deals with preferred stockholders to eliminate dividend arrearages have strong appeal. Over the years, hundreds of deals have been devised and offered and many of them have been accepted. In offering deals, corporate managements tend to have a strong bargaining position, since the preferred stockholders, too, have been starved for dividends, they, too, have probably seen the market value of their stock sink well below par or stated value, and they know that boards of directors can continue the policy of nonpayment even if earnings are good. This does not mean, however, that deals always or usually work to the disadvantage of the preferred stockholders. Some do have such results, but in many instances preferred stockholders who agree to adjustments gain more in the long run than do dissenters who eventually receive their back dividends in full.

Position of Dissenters. In the matter of dissenters, only a minority of states stipulate that the acceptance of deals for the settlement of claims to dividend arrearages by some designated proportion of preferred stockholders shall be binding on all. While, therefore, the dividend rate, the call price, and other terms of preferred stock contracts can generally be changed for all preferred stockholders by a vote of holders to two thirds, three fourths, or some other proportion of the preferred stock, the most common rule that applies to arrearage deals is that only the preferred stockholders who vote in favor are bound to the settlement thus agreed on.

In any of the minority states, therefore, the managers of a corporation know that if they can get a favorable vote of the holders of the prescribed majority of the preferred stock, their offer of a settlement deal will be completely successful. In making the offer, they would be likely to stipulate that unless an approval vote of the prescribed size is obtained the offer will not be binding on the corporation itself. Completion of a deal with the holders of a minority or even a small majority of the outstanding preferred shares could hardly be regarded by them as a sound solution to their problem. They would continue to face the question of what to do with the arrearage claims of the large number of stockholders who refused to vote approval.

In a state wherein the dissenting preferred stockholder is not bound by the approval vote of fellow stockholders, a corporation that wants to offer a settlement deal has equal reason to avoid binding itself unless a large percentage of the shares are voted in favor of the offer. Were the corporation not to stipulate what favorable vote is necessary to make its offer effective, the acceptance of the offer by holders of 30 or 40 per cent of the shares would be binding both on these stockholders and on itself, but this would leave 60 or 70 percent of the dividend arrearages unaffected, and that could hardly be hailed as a reasonable solution to the corporation's difficulties. Usually, indeed, corporations stipulate that their offers will not be effective unless quite high percentages of the shares are voted in favor—85 or 90 percent or more.

Attitude of Common Stockholders. As a group, common stockholders, too, have a right of dissent: proposed deals may fail to get the support of the holders of requisite majorities of the common shares. Most kinds of deals offered for the settlement of arrearages require amendments to the articles of incorporation, and this requires the consent of the common stockholders. Usually, however, favorable action by the common stockholders can be counted on, since a basic objective of settlement deals is to clear the way for early resumption of dividends on the common stock. Only when proposed offers to the preferred, as devised by corporate managements, are thought by the common stockholders to be much more generous than necessary to secure acceptance are they likely to vote them down.

Replacement of Preferred Stock and Its Arrearages

Offers of Prior-Preference Stock. A popular method of clearing up large arrearages of preferred stock dividends is to offer new prior-preference preferreds in exchange for existing preferreds together with the claims for back dividends accumulated thereon. Suppose, for example, that arrearages on an existing preferred amount to 40 percent of its par value. The corporation might ask its preferred stockholders to take 1.4 shares of the new prior-preference preferred in exchange for each share of their present holdings, including the accumulated dividend claims. The new stock would have the prior-preference designation or a similar one because the corporation would want to give it claims to dividends and assets that had priority over those of the existing preferred. To issue such a new preferred, the corporation would doubtless need the approval of the holders of two thirds or some other proportion of the existing preferred shares, but if holders of this proportion were to find the exchange offer attractive they would surely also vote in favor of the new issue. Thus, the corporation would expect to get simultaneous acceptance of the exchange offer and approval of the new issue.

In making offers of prior-preference preferreds in exchange for existing preferreds with their arrearages, corporate managements often stress the point that current earnings are large enough to enable them to begin payment of dividends on the new stock at once. At the same time, they confess great uncertainty about when it will be feasible to make an attack on the arrearages on the existing stock should it not be exchanged. The implied threat not to resume dividends on the existing stock, coupled with what almost amounts to a promise to pay dividends immediately on the proposed prior-preference stock, is usually all that is needed to convince the divided-starved preferred stockholders that they should make the exchange. Indeed, the implied threat and promise appear to be potent enough sometimes to enable corporations to designate dividend rates in the prior-preference preferreds lower than the rates of the existing issues.

Joint Offers of Prior-Preference and Common Stocks. Sometimes corporations offer prior-preference stock in exchange for existing preferred shares on a share-for-share basis, adding offers of common shares to take care of the dividend arrearages. In some proposed deals of this kind, cash to meet a limited amount of the arrearages, with common shares for the balance, is offered. Obviously, a wide range of proposals of this variety is possible in terms of the number of common shares solely or in terms of common shares plus cash.

Exclusive Offers of Common Stock. In a few instances, corporations offer common shares exclusively in exchange for the preferred and its arrearages. To get acceptance for such an offer, however, a corporation may have to give the preferred stockholders so many shares of common that the existing common stockholders would be displaced in their position of control. The arrangement, then, tends to be a drastic one, by which the common stockholders, since they must vote approval, acknowledge that their stock must be of little value from the standpoint of earnings and dividend prospects as long as the preferred stock remains outstanding. It must appear to them that they could hardly expect a dividend for themselves even were the preferred stockholders to give up all claims to the arrearages and simply demand current dividends.

Offers of Bonds. In some instances, offers of bonds are made as full or partial settlement for the claims of preferred stockholders, including their claims to dividends in arrears. Replacement of preferred stocks with their contingent claims to earnings and assets by bonds with fixed claims to interest and principal would hardly appear to be a good way to improve access to markets for new funds and to strengthen credit standing, but so-called income bonds may serve rather conveniently as a replacement security. A distinctive feature of income bonds is that the interest is payable only to the extent that it is covered by earnings; it is not a fixed charge as for ordinary bonds. Hence, failure to pay interest because earnings are not available, like failure to pay dividends on preferred stock, does not mean that the corporation can be declared insolvent. A strong point favoring the replacement of preferred stocks with income bonds is that interest paid on the bonds is deductible for income tax purposes, but as we know, preferred dividends are not deductible.[6]

Compensation for Arrearages Only

Corporations sometimes ask their preferred stockholders to give up their rights to dividend arrearages for something offered in exchange without offering or requesting any other change in the stockholders' position. They are satisfied to let the preferred stock stand as is, provided only that a settlement for the arrearages can be worked out. The preferred stockholders may be told that dividends at the contractural rate can be resumed immediately if only the arrearages can be cleared out, but that if they are not cleared out it is difficult to see when cash payments to meet them can be made. To dividend-starved preferred stockholders, such a declaration, as indicated above, tends to have compelling force.

Offers of Additional Shares of the Same Stock. Often offered as compensation are preferred shares of exactly the same kind as those on which the arrearages have accumulated. The amount of the offer in terms of par or stated value is related to, although not necessarily identical with, the amount of the arrearages. If, for example, arrearages amount to 40 percent of the par value of the preferred, the offer may be three, four, or five tenths of an additional share for each share held. The acceptance of such a proposal might appear to promise

[6]For a discussion of the distinctive features of income bonds, see pp. 701–4.

little help toward a solution of the corporation's problem, since its bill for dividends would be increased. But such proposals are ordinarily made only after earnings have improved and when they are continuing to improve, so that the corporate managements expect to be able to pay dividends on a larger amount of preferred stock if they do not have to drain earnings in making up the arrearages.

To illustrate, assume that the par value of a corporation's 5 percent preferred stock is $5 million, that arrearages amount to 40 percent of this value, and that current earnings available for dividends amount to $650,000. If the corporation undertook to pay off the arrearages, and if earnings continued to amount to $650,000 annually, 5 years would be required for it to become current in its preferred dividend payments—that is, to pay off the arrearages as well as to meet the additional dividend requirements of that period. During much of this five-year period, access of the corporation to new funds and its credit standing, though doubtless improving, would continue to be clouded, and the common stockholders, of course, could not hope for dividends. But if, on the other hand, the preferred stockholders accepted additional preferred—four tenths of a share for each share held, let us say—as compensation for surrendered rights to the arrearages, the outlook for the corporation and for both the common and preferred stockholders would immediately brighten. The annual dividend requirements on total preferred would rise from $250,000 to $350,000, but the remaining $300,000 of current earnings would be available annually for dividends on the common. Not that the board of directors would necessarily distribute this entire amount as common dividends, but its very availability should greatly improve the investment status of the common stock. Thus, the market value of the common should recover sharply, and the credit position of the corporation should look much stronger.

Offers of Common Stock. In some instances, the compensation offered for the surrender of claims to dividends in arrears is a stipulated number of shares of common stock. If a corporation is currently earning reasonable profits, its managers can say to the preferred stockholders that elimination of the arrearages will clear the way for an immediate resumption of dividends on both preferred and common. The foregoing illustration demonstrates why such a claim or prediction could be an honest one. At any rate, the preferred stockholders might accept the offer of common in the expectation of receiving dividends on it in addition to restored dividends on the preferred at the designated contractual rate.

Other Types of Offers. Sometimes prior-preference preferred stock is offered for the arrearages only, rather than for both the existing stock and its arrearages.

In some cases, changes in existing preferred stock contracts favorable to the preferred stockholders are offered as compensation for a yielding of claims to arrearages. A corporation may make an offer to increase the preferred dividend rate, to make the stock convertible, to give it a participation feature or warrants for the purchase of common stock, or to introduce provisions for a redemption fund. Contractual changes are offered sometimes as sole compensation for the yielding of claims to back dividends, and sometimes as inducements in addition to some cash or shares of the same preferred, a prior-preference preferred, or common. For example, the preferred stockholders of the foregoing illustration might not ask for additional shares were they to be offered an increase from 5 to 7 percent in the dividend rate on their existing holdings. The amount of their prospective dividends would thus be made the same as by the stock for compensation route of the illustration. At the same time, avoidance of the additional issue of stock could be of material advantage to the corporation in future financing.

Cash is frequently used as a supplemental means of persuading preferred stockholders to give up their claims to back dividends. Cash may be offered to clear arrearages of, perhaps, one year, with the balance of the arrearages to be compensated for by additional stock or contract changes or both.

Troubles of the Curtis Publishing Company

The several kinds of difficulties that corporations may encounter in the management of their outstanding preferred stocks, as well as the various kinds of action they may take to try to clear up these difficulties, have been quite well encompassed in the single case of the Curtis Publishing Company. Its troubles with preferred stock began in the 1930's, when it accumulated arrearages on its then outstanding 7 percent issue. In July, 1940, when the arrearages amounted to $19.375 a share for a total of approximately $14 million, Curtis asked its preferred stockholders to take in exchange for each share of their stock and its arrearage claims $10 of debenture bonds, 1 share of a new prior-preferred stock, and 2½ shares of common stock. Most of the 7 percent preferred was turned in for exchange on this basis, even though the new prior-preferred had a peculiarity in providing for a $1 dividend contingent on the amount of earnings available in addition to a regular cumulative dividend of $3 a share.

But Curtis became dissatisfied with the presence of this stock in its financial structure, chiefly, no doubt, because of the nondeductibility of dividends, whether regular or contingent, as an expense in income tax determination. In 1956, accordingly, it made a new exchange offer, tendering for each share of the $3–$4 dividend stock $40 in 6 percent debenture bonds and a share of a new prior-preferred stock with the same kind of regular-contingent dividend arrangement at 60 cents and $1.60. It thus envisaged paying a minimum of 60 cents in dividends plus $2.40 in interest, or a maximum of $1.60 in dividends plus $2.40 of interest in place of straight dividends of $3 or $4 on the older preferred stock. In either case, it would get the deductibility of the interest payment for tax purposes.

Although many of the preferred stockholders accepted the 1956 exchange offer, a larger proportion did not, and on both issues Curtis began to run into arrearages in the early 1960's. In 1967, with the arrearages continuing to mount, it decided to try to rid itself utterly of both issues. It made an offer in October of that year of 2.6 shares of common stock and $28.50 of 6½ percent debenture bonds (with warrants attached for the purchase of 1.425 shares of common stock) for each share of the $3–$4 preferred, and .9 share of common stock and $10 of the debenture bonds (with warrants for ½ share of common stock) for each share of the $.60–$1.60 preferred. However, when the response of the preferred stockholders turned out to be less than lukewarm, Curtis sweetened its offer by hiking the interest rate on the proposed debenture bonds to 7 percent, adding to the amount of common stock to be purchasable by warrants, and cutting the warrant price for common stock purchases, at the same time extending the period for stockholder acceptances. But the preferred stockholders seemed to remain unimpressed.

It should be of interest to add that Curtis might have been able to tackle its financial problems of the 1960's more effectively if it had had greater capacity for long-term borrowing. But it needed the approval of holders of two thirds of the shares of its two preferred stock issues to mortgage its properties or to add to its long-term debt. It asked the preferred stockholders in 1963 for the deletion of this contractual restriction, but they voted in the negative on the grounds, widely expressed at that time, that they would be giving up some of their rights while getting nothing in return.

QUESTIONS

1. For immediate offerings of new issues of preferred stock for cash, how do the selling procedures compare with those for new issues of common stock?

2. In merger transactions, to what classes of security holders in corporations to be acquired is the absorbing corporation likely to offer preferred stock? Explain.

3. To what extent, if at all, are offerings of new issues of preferred stock to the public for cash subject to regulation under the federal Securities Act? Offerings for cash to existing security holders? Exchange offers in merger transactions?

4. Why are private placements for preferred stock issues more popular than for new issues of common stock?

5. Why is the choice between par and no-par values for preferred stock issues of much less importance than for common stock issues?

6. What costs are likely to be incurred in replacing an outstanding preferred stock issue through the sale of a new preferred to get a lower dividend rate? What weight are these costs likely to have in replacement decisions about preferred stocks with undesirable features other than high dividend rates?

7. From the legal standpoint, what terms of preferred stock contracts can be changed by consent of the preferred stockholders? What are the rights of dissenters? In what circumstances are a corporation's preferred stockholders likely to consent to changes?

8. In what circumstances, if any, can a corporation force its preferred stockholders to accept a new preferred stock in exchange for their existing holdings? Explain.

9. Why is it generally advisable for corporations to try to avoid arrearages in preferred dividends and to clear up as quickly as possible arrearages that have accumulated?

10. When offering deals to preferred stockholders to clear up preferred dividend arrearages, why are corporations likely to be in rather strong bargaining positions?

11. What are the rights of dissenting preferred stockholders who refuse to agree to deals for the settlement of preferred dividend arrearages?

12. Why may offers of prior-preference preferred stock be especially attractive to preferred stockholders as a means of persuading them to give up claims to dividends in arrears?

13. In what ways is common stock sometimes used in offers to preferred stockholders for the settlement of preferred dividend arrearages?

PROBLEMS

1. In April, 1968, the stockholders of P. Lorillard Company, the well-known tobacco manufacturing concern, voted approval of a directors' proposal to offer $140 principal amount of 25-year, 6⅝ percent debenture bonds in exchange for each of the 98,000 shares of its outstanding 7 percent preferred stock of $100 par value. P. Lorillard had a New Jersey charter, but the bonds were to be issued by a newly established Lorillard Corporation chartered by Delaware, into which P. Lorillard was to be immediately merged. The proposed shift of securities between the two corporations was simply an aspect of the way that P. Lorillard chose to change its state of incorporation, but with respect to the offer to the preferred stockholders it was seeking to substitute long-term debt of a face amount of $13,720,000 for the preferred stock that had total par value of only $9,800,000. And perhaps more significantly, it was displaying a willingness to replace a dividend *commitment* to the preferred stockholders of $686,000 a year with an interest *obligation* on the bonds of $908,950 a year.

a) What advantages and disadvantages do you see in Lorillard's swap offer of bonds for preferred for (1) its common stockholders, and (2) the preferred stockholders?

b) Had you been a Lorillard common stockholder, would you have voted in favor of the corporation's making the offer? Why or why not?

c) Had you been a Lorillard preferred stockholder, would you have accepted the bonds in exchange for your stock? Why or why not?

2. The directors of the Batten Products Company are pondering the question whether they should undertake to replace its outstanding 7 percent preferred stock by calling it for redemption with the proceeds, in effect, of a new issue of preferred, which, in the opinion of its investment bankers, would need a dividend rate of only 5½ percent to be salable to the public at its par value. There are 200,000 shares of the 7 percent stock outstanding, its par value is $100, and its call price is $108. The new preferred would also have a par value of $100, and the size of the issue would be whatever number of shares would be required for the replacement. The bankers estimate that the flotation costs, including their commission, would amount to about $500,000. An additional source of expense would be a bank loan that would be needed for about a month to take care of the redemption of the old stock, and that would be repaid from the proceeds of the sale of the new stock. Interest on this loan would be charged at a rate of 6 percent per annum.

Batten's directors ask you to advise them on the wisdom of the proposed substitution of preferred stocks, with as much support for this advice in figures as you can reasonably produce. (For any income tax considerations you may want to take into account, assume that the corporation's taxable income is subject to combined federal and state rates totaling 50 percent.)

Part VIII

FINANCING WITH RETAINED EARNINGS

chapter 25

THE NATURE OF EARNINGS AND DIVIDENDS

IMPORTANCE OF EARNINGS AS A SOURCE OF ASSETS

For a very great number of American business corporations, retained earnings or profits constitute the most important source of assets. For almost all business corporations that are profitable, they represent a significant source of assets, if not the most important.

Corporations of small and middle sizes often have little or no access to outside sources of long-term funds, and their stockholders have but small amounts of free cash for buying additional stock. To finance expansion, therefore, though these corporations may be able to get fair amounts of short-term credits they must depend chiefly on the retention of earnings. The managements of many corporations, small and large, choose not to tap outside sources of long-term funds even when readily available. They choose the simple common stock form of financial structure, decide that they do not want to offer additional common stock to outsiders, and expect, therefore, to be quite liberal in retaining earnings as a means of financing growth. And the managements of most others, though they may tap many financial markets in their search for funds, generally decide that these sources must be substantially supplemented with generous amounts of retained earnings.

Data introduced in earlier chapters of this textbook indicate the great dependence of business corporations collectively on retained earnings as a means of financing. Table 15–2, page 341, shows the large amounts and proportions of earnings retained in relation to total earnings available after the payment of income taxes throughout the entire post-World War II period. It is especially noteworthy that in this period from 1946 through 1967 retained earnings exceeded dividends in all but three years, that even in these three exceptional years retained earnings fell only slightly short of dividends, and that for the whole period earnings retained amounted to $344.6 billion, equal to 56.2 percent of total after-tax profits of $613.6 billion. The importance of retained earnings by comparison with all other sources of corporate funds in the postwar period is indicated in Table 16–3, page 373, where it is shown that they comprised 23.9 percent of all funds acquired by nonfarm nonfinancial corporations, while net sales of stock supplied only 3.1 percent of new funds, net bond sales 9.2 percent, and net short-term sources 20.6 percent.

PROBLEMS OF EARNINGS AND THEIR ALLOCATION

From the standpoint of the typical corporate management, the most important problem relating to earnings is that of finding ways of expanding them. Rare is the management that is thoroughly satisfied with the level of earnings that has been achieved. On the contrary, most managements are constantly on the lookout for ways to expand sales and to cut costs so as to increase the margin of profits. Various aspects of this striving for increased earnings were discussed in the chapters on the management of assets—Chapters 7–10—as well as in the discussion of the pros and cons of the different kinds of financial structures in Chapters 15–16, and certain further considerations pertaining to corporate expansion will be examined briefly in Chapter 26. But the problem of boosting earnings impinges on every phase of business management, so that its treatment in a textbook in corporate financial management must necessarily leave many things unsaid.

Clearly a financing question is that of determining what earnings amount to. If a corporation borrows money, the sum involved is known precisely, but there is no such precision in accounting for earnings. One of the major responsibilities of corporate boards of directors is to decide what is to be done with earnings, but to fulfill this responsibility they must know, at least approximately, what results of transactions can be properly treated as earnings and what results should be excluded. Moreover, they must surely know that there is no precise relationship between the amount of earnings reported *for specific periods* and the availability of additional cash *at specific times*. When one speaks of the allocation of earnings, one is inclined to think of allocations of cash, but these two concepts are by no means identical. Boards of directors have responsibility to decide what portion of the earnings will serve as a basis for dividend distributions, but they must know that such decisions are not entirely free ones. They must abide by legal prescriptions and limitations. These, then, are the topics for discussion in the remainder of the present chapter. With knowledge of the nature of earnings, their relationship to cash, and legal provisions on dividend payments, the boards of directors are in a position to tackle the problem of the actual allocation of earnings—a problem to which Chapter 26 will be devoted.

THE NATURE AND DETERMINATION OF EARNINGS

The question "*What are earnings?*" may appear to be a witless one. One has only to look at corporate income statements to see what earnings are. In such a statement, the various sources of income—sales, commissions, interest, dividends, and so on—are listed by name and amount. The various kinds of expenses—cost of goods, wages and salaries, cost of supplies, property taxes, depreciation, and so on—are similarly listed. The net difference between the sums of income and expense items, respectively, is set out as net income before income taxes or net earnings before income taxes or net profit before income taxes, and then income taxes are deducted to give a final figure for net income or net earnings or net profit. Some income statements, it is true, are more elaborate than others; some differentiate between operating and nonoperating income and expenses, and some add still a third classification, such as nonrecurring income and expenses. Some show a further deduction from net earnings for dividends paid, so that the final figure is for net earnings retained or net earnings reinvested in the business. But, elaborate or not, every income statement seems to show much the same kind of thing, and there appears to be nothing mysterious about the result.

Earnings as Estimates

In every income statement, nevertheless, there is much uncertainty, if not mystery, even though the statement has been prepared by highly competent accountants who observe generally accepted accounting principles. The final figure for net earnings is always an estimate; whether or not it is a true or close one will ordinarily be determinable only in subsequent years.

For corporations that sell on account, the figure for sales income is really only an estimate; its accuracy depends on the charge for bad debts. More important for the typical corporation is that the cost of goods sold is an estimate, its accuracy depending on the skill with which inventories are valued. The depreciation charge—a very important expense item for many corporations—depends for its accuracy on the wisdom with which useful lives and scrap values are judged, but even more on what the tax authorities will allow as a deduction in income tax computations. Having similar degrees of uncertainty are depletion charges against wasting assets and amortization charges against intangibles. More modest variations in net earnings can also result from differing valuations of supplies inventories.

Also contributing to a lack of precision in determining what net earnings amount to are differences in the treatment of certain kinds of expenditures. A corporation spends considerable sums of money in renovating its factory buildings, and it regards these expenditures as a cost of repairs and charges them currently as an expense. Another making similar expenditures classifies the results as improvements or betterments, and adds the outlays to the asset account. By comparison with the second corporation, the first overstates its expenses in the current year but will understate them in subsequent years as it will have no depreciation charges against the outlays, but by comparison with the first corporation the second is in error for the opposite reasons.

Earnings Excluded from Income Statements

Sometimes there is uncertainty about the amount of corporate net earnings, because certain items are not shown in income statements. Accountants differ in their opinions on how certain kinds of extraordinary transactions should be treated. Although the weight of opinion favors showing as much as possible in income statements, almost all accountants make some allowance for direct credits to and charges against surplus accounts.

Examples of earnings that are often credited directly to surplus accounts are profits derived in the sale of treasury stock and discounts in the retirement of outstanding securities. A corporation that makes such direct credits to surplus is likely also to make direct charges against surplus accounts for losses on treasury stock transactions and for premiums paid in the retirement of its own securities. Such transactions are sometimes said to involve capital rather than income —hence the argument that they should not be shown in income statements. But if a corporation sells donated stock, it acquires new funds equal to the proceeds no less than when it derives funds through what are called ordinary earnings. Similarly, a corporation derives new funds if it resells treasury stock at a higher price than its buying price, or suffers a loss of funds if it resells at a lower price. Much the same can be said for discounts and premiums in the retirement of its own outstanding securities. An opportunity to retire a $1,000 bond by buying it in the market at $95 would seem to be equally advantageous with an opportunity to earn a profit of $50 in an ordinary sales transaction.

Some additional kinds of income and expense items, though shown in income statements by most accountants, are handled by others as direct credits and charges against surplus accounts. These include profits and losses on the sale of tangible assets not currently used in operations, as land that has been held as a possible future factory or store building site, and profits and losses on the sale of investment securities when the investment was not made in the ordinary course of business.

Position of the Directors

When, therefore, boards of directors take up the matter of deciding what portion of earnings should be retained and what portion distributed as dividends, their viewpoint must not be too closely circumscribed by figures that appear in income statements. While they may have great confidence in their accountants, they must realize that the statement figures are tentative and may be incomplete. Indeed, a realization that figures for net earnings are estimates is likely to prompt the typical board to be somewhat cautious in dividend declarations. Even when inclined not to retain any portion of current earnings for corporate purposes, a board might nevertheless decide to retain some simply to be able to offset revisions downward in the earnings estimate should such revisions later appear to be advisable. In this way, earned surplus would be available to absorb write-downs in inventory values, charge-offs of accounts receivable in amounts exceeding the existing reserve for bad debts, losses on the disposal of fixed assets on which adequate depreciation had not been charged, and so on.

That a substantial amount of earnings had been carried directly to surplus accounts, on the other hand, might prompt a corporate board of directors to be much more liberal in dividend distributions than the earnings figure in the current income statement might seem to warrant. In a given case, for example, most of the funds currently needed for expansion might have been supplied by large profits derived in the sale of holdings of extraneous investment securities. Accordingly, the directors might decide on a much larger dividend distribution than would have been advisable in the absence of such a special source of funds.

RELATIONSHIP OF NET EARNINGS TO CASH

When one hears or reads of decisions about the distribution of net earnings made by the directors of corporations, one may be inclined to think of the net earnings as a sum of cash that can be retained or paid out in the form of dividends. The corporations report their net earnings as excesses of income over expenses, and income may be thought of as being received in cash and expenses as being paid in cash—hence the temptation to regard net earnings as a net increase in cash balances. A relationship does, indeed, exist between the amount of earnings and changes in cash holdings, but it is not necessarily a close one. This fact must ever be kept in mind by corporate directors. Their decisions about the distribution of net earnings must always be made with an eye on the cash account as well as on the figures for current net earnings and for accumulated earnings carried in the surplus accounts.

Accrual System of Accounting

An important reason that earnings at a given level are not necessarily accompanied by an increase in cash of the same amount is that most corporations maintain their accounting systems on what is called the accrual basis. This means, in brief, that income is taken up in the period in which it is earned, whether or not it is realized in cash in that period, and that expenses are charged to the period they belong to, whether or not they are met by cash payments in that period.

How the accrual system works—why it does not match cash inflows and outflows with income credits and expense charges—was demonstrated in the discussion and illustrations of cash flows presented in Chapters 5 and 6. At this time, therefore, we need not review these matters in detail. Reference to a few aspects of the workings of the accrual system should suffice. Within a given period, some goods may be bought and then resold at a profit, but though income is taken up as having resulted from these transactions, cash is actually reduced if payment has been made to the suppliers before payment from the corporation's customers has been received. Or cash is increased by an amount exceeding the income taken up if payment has been received from the customers before payment to the suppliers has been made. Wages and salaries earned by employees in the last few days of an accounting period are entered as an expense of the period, but cash is not spent immediately if the payday for these days of service comes in the following period. Substantial amounts of goods and supplies may be bought and paid for in a given period, but if they are still on hand at the end of the period they are not chargeable as expenses in the income statement of the period. Similarly, services may be paid for in advance, as in the immediate payment of the full premiums on three-year and five-year insurance policies. Likewise, cash may be received in one period for goods to be delivered or services to be performed in a later period, so that the cash balance is augmented though there is no matching item of income in the income statement.

Effect of Book Charges

An additional aspect of the accrual system of accounting is that the depreciation, depletion, and amortization of fixed assets are universally recognized as expenses and are entered as such in income statements, though there are no current matching outlays of cash. Cash is spent when the fixed assets are acquired, but expense is recognized only as they are used up, and this may take place over a long period of years. Thus, the original cash outlays are not shown in income statements, but so shown are the annual charges for depreciation, depletion, and amortization, though no related cash disbursements are being made.

The relationship between charges of these kinds and cash flows was indicated in Chapters 5 and 6, in the discussion of the influence of depreciation charges specifically.[1] Again, therefore, it should not be necessary to review the matter at length. But two facts should be kept in mind. One is that charges for depreciation, depletion, and amortization (particularly depreciation charges for the great mass of corporations) are usually quite substantial as sources of differences between reported net earnings and changes in cash balances. The other is that depreciation, depletion, and amortization charges, regarded by themselves, have the effect of causing reported net earnings to be less than net cash inflows. This point, of course, simply recalls to mind the proposition of Chapter 6 that there is a cash throw-off approximating these charges, provided that they and all other expenses are covered in the selling prices of goods or services. In addition, it gives us the opportunity to lay renewed emphasis on depreciation charges, in particular, as an enormously important source of corporate funds in the postwar period, as shown in Table 16–3, page 373.

Direct Charges and Credits to Surplus

The earlier discussion in this chapter of direct charges and credits to surplus accounts was introduced to show that the net earnings as determined in a corporation's income statement may not allow for all its gains and losses in a given period. In the present analysis of the relationship of net earnings to cash, therefore, it is necessary only to point out that net inflows of cash may be more than reported net earnings on account of cash receipts credited directly to surplus accounts, and to note that they may be less on account of cash payments charged directly to these accounts.

Timing of Cash Flows and the Recognition of Net Earnings

Relationship of Earnings to Changes in Cash Balances. Probably the most important thing that can be said about the relationship of net earnings and cash is that no matter how closely the amount of net cash inflows matches the amount of net earnings, the timing of increases in cash balances *on account of earnings* is rarely the timing of the recognition of earnings. Cash collected by a corporation from its customers in March can be said to be in part profit and in part a return on the costs of the goods sold and the overhead expenses of selling, but how much is the one or the other cannot be known until after the books have been closed at the end of the following December! The cash balance goes up in March, but it can go down again—per-

[1]See pp. 95, 117–21.

haps far down—long before the end of December, and not necessarily according to any pattern of relationship with the net earnings or losses to be reported for the year in an income statement.

In the course of a year, therefore, a corporation may have available to it a net new supply of cash approximately equal to the net earnings as determined at the end of the year plus the cash throw-offs resulting from charges for depreciation, depletion, and amortization. But, as indicated, it does not follow that the cash balance *at the end of the year* must be greater than the balance at the beginning of the year by the amount of this net new supply. It is entirely possible that the net new supply, and perhaps more, will have been spent in the course of the year for additional fixed assets or inventories or for the redemption of preferred stock or bonds; thus, the closing balance may be no greater, or perhaps it will be less, than the opening balance. Were the directors of the corporation, therefore, to make a decision about the payment of cash dividends solely on the basis of reported net earnings, they could be gravely misled. They could be misled even though making proper allowance for the possibility of error in estimating earnings, as well as for direct charges and credits to surplus accounts. Solvency might be endangered by a drain of cash for dividends capping other drains that had taken place in the course of the year. In a word, earnings may be available for dividends, but cash may not be!

Earnings Allocation Decisions and Budgets. All this suggests that in the well-managed corporation decisions about the retention and distribution of earnings are likely to be made well ahead of the beginning of the year in which they are expected to be derived. In our examination of budgetary principles and procedures in Chapters 11 and 12, we saw the need of cash budgets in which, so to say, all the varied activities of enterprises in buying, selling, paying wages and salaries, meeting other expenses, and so on, are translated into cash inflows and outflows. We saw that income from sales may be reflected in increases in accounts receivable rather than in expanded cash balances, and that though earnings are being derived, cash balances may not rise because inventories are being expanded or the net amount of accounts payable is being reduced. We saw, too, that estimated monthly cash balances are a basis for decision making about borrowing and the repayment of debt, the sale and retirement of securities, expenditure for new fixed assets, and the payment of cash dividends.

Thus it is that in the workings of a budgetary system, and particularly in the use of cash budgets, decisions about the distribution of earnings are a matter of forecasting and not of looking back after the results of operations are known. In effect, the financial managers say that at such and such time they expect to have a given amount of cash, and that they will do thus and so with it. All the demands for cash will be simultaneously evaluated, and decisions will be made on how much cash should be absorbed in increased receivables and expanded inventories, how much spent in reducing accounts payable, how much borrowed and when and how repaid, how much spent for new facilities, and how much distributed as cash dividends. Cash expected to be derived from earnings must be lumped with that expected to come in from other sources in determining what the corporation can and cannot do in its overall financial planning. Actual developments may turn out to be different from those forecast, and budgets may have to be revised as the year progresses. But changes in spending plans on account of such developments must still be based on a simultaneous reconsideration of all cash sources and demands if decisions are to be sound.

Borrowing to Pay Dividends. Sometimes, the question is raised whether it is sound policy for corporations to borrow money to pay cash dividends to their stockholders. But if dividend payment is a matter of financial planning—a matter of simultaneous decision making, just discussed—the question tends to be pointless. The financial managers of a corporation may anticipate that earnings in the coming year will justify the payment of quarterly dividends at a given rate, but the cash budget may indicate that at one or more of the quarterly dates sufficient cash will not be available. Accordingly, they may plan to borrow. But it would be pointless to say that they were going to borrow in order to pay dividends. Since the anticipated shortage of cash would be expected to result from all kinds of spending, it would be more appropriate to say that the borrowing would partially finance the whole combination of outlays, rather than dividends specifically. Were this not so, any corporation that paid cash dividends while it had liabilities for borrowed money on its books could be said to be paying the dividends with borrowed money, for, obviously, an alternative use of the dividend moneys would be repayment of the loans.

THE NATURE AND LEGALITY OF DIVIDENDS

Chiefly for the protection of creditors, our states place limitations on the payment of dividends by the corporations they charter. Having granted the stockholders of these corporations the privilege of limited liability for corporate debts, they take the reasonable position that distributions of corporate assets by the dividend route must be limited so that debt-paying capacity will be preserved. In some states, protection is extended to preferred stockholders, such as by provisions that dividends must not reduce assets below the amount of outside liabilities, the par or stated value of the common stock, and the total *preference to assets* of the preferred stock.

Nature of Dividends

A dividend is a pro rata distribution of cash, other assets, promises to pay, or additional stock to the stockholders of a corporation chargeable against its surplus accounts or (for certain liquidating dividends only) against its capital stock accounts. To say that a dividend is a pro rata distribution means that all shares of outstanding stock, or all shares of a given class, participate equally in whatever is distributed.

Kinds of Dividends. By far the majority of corporate dividends are cash distributions, and they accordingly garner most attention of boards of directors, stockholders, other investors, lenders, and the rule-making authorities of state governments.

Once in a while, corporations have reason to distribute some asset other than cash. Such *asset* or *property dividends,* as they care called, have most commonly consisted of stocks or bonds held by the dividend-paying corporations in other corporations. Distributions of this kind have been made, for example, in the process of simplifying holding company structures under the terms of the federal Public Utility Holding Company Act, and also when as a result of antitrust proceedings corporations have been ordered to divest themselves of interests in other corporations. A rather spectacular illustration of antitrust proceedings was the Supreme Court decision of 1961 which found that an illegal combination in restraint of trade resulted from the ownership by the E. I. Du Pont de Nemours & Co. of approximately 63 million shares of the General Motors Corporation. On the basis of the decision, the federal district court ordered Du Pont to dispose of the General Motors stock, starting not later than July 30, 1962, and completing the disposal not later than February 28, 1965. Du Pont decided to pass the stock on to its own stockholders as dividends. Each share of Du Pont stock got a half share of General Motors stock in July, 1962, 36/100 of a share in January, 1964, and a half share in a final distribution in January, 1965.

Even in the absence of legal compulsion, however, directors of parent corporations sometimes decide to spin off stockholdings in subsidiaries by distributing them in whole or in part as dividends to the parents' stockholders. A complete distribution is likely to occur when a parent's directors decide that a subsidiary's field of operations has moved too far from the area of the parent's major interests. A partial distribution is likely to be aimed at establishing a wide market for the subsidiary's stock, so that the parent's remaining shares will likewise have enhanced marketability and probably greatly increased potential market value.

In relatively rare instances, corporations distribute dividends in the form of promissory notes. These promises to pay or *scrip dividends* are simply a means of deferring the actual distributions of cash; when the notes mature, the cash is distributed.

In the area of rather frequent occurrence and high popularity are *stock dividends,* which, indeed, are next to cash dividends in the order of frequency. As the term is used in finance, a stock dividend is *always* a distribution of additional shares of a corporation's own stock to its existing stockholders. Accordingly, the term must be carefully distinguished from the term *dividend on stock,* which can be used broadly to describe distributions of cash or anything else. By definition, a stock dividend could consist of common shares given to either common or preferred stockholders, or preferred shares given to either of these two classes of stockholders, but, in fact, stock dividends almost always consist of common shares given to common stockholders.

What Is Distributed? It must be strongly emphasized that dividends are not distributions of profits or surplus. These things cannot be distributed. Surplus is only a book account, designed to show the claims of stockholders against corporate assets over and above the par or stated value of their stock. The very presence of a credit balance in surplus indicates that the stockholders already have this claim against assets; thus, it is meaningless to say that a dividend represents a distribution of surplus—of the claim—to them. The claim can be reduced by distributions of dividends in cash or other assets; it can be changed in character by dividends in promises to pay; or it can be changed in form only by distributions of stock dividends. But it is the cash, other assets, scrip, or additional shares of stock that are distributed, and not the surplus. Thus, it can be said that a dividend is chargeable against surplus or earnings or profits, or that it is based on surplus or earnings or profits. However, one need not raise an outcry against people who say that this or that corporation distributed $50,000 of its surplus as a dividend, or that another paid a dividend of $75,000 out of its earnings. One has only to understand that what these people mean is that cash dividends of these amounts, chargeable against surplus, were paid.

Dividends as Liabilities. When the board of directors of a solvent corporation declares a cash dividend, the amount declared becomes an obligation to pay. It is proper, therefore, to debit the surplus account at once and to include the dividend among the current liabilities, assuming the usual practice of setting the payment date not more than a few weeks beyond the declaration date. Were the directors to try to rescind the dividend, the stockholders would have a right of action to force payment—the same as other creditors to whom payments due might be refused. However, the decision to rescind would probably be upheld if the directors were able to prove that the dividend payment would violate restrictive provisions of the state law of the kinds to be discussed shortly. There can be no legal compulsion to do something that is illegal. The same rule would appear to apply to asset and scrip dividends.

The weight of legal opinion for stock dividends, on the other hand, is that the directors are free to rescind them at any time before the actual distribution is made. Accounting for this difference in viewpoint is the fact that distribution of a stock dividend causes no changes in total or individual stockholder claims against earnings and assets or to voting power; so it is argued that nondistribution works no hardship on them.

Basic Legal Rules

The states have adopted three kinds of basic rules to govern dividend distributions. (1) The surplus rule: dividends may be paid only to the extent that surplus is available. (2) The impairment rule: dividends may not be paid if the capital has been impaired or if the payment would cause an impairment. (3) The insolvency rule: dividends may not be paid if the corporation is insolvent or if the payment would cause it to be insolvent. Some states have only one of these rules, some have two, and some have elements of all three.

The surplus and impairment rules are quite similar in scope and effect. "Capital" for the impairment rule is usually understood to be the par or stated value of the corporation's stock, whether common only or common and preferred. To say, therefore, that a dividend may not impair the capital is much the same as saying that a surplus must be available. In some cases, however, courts have interpreted "capital" to mean amounts actually received in the sale of stock, whether more or less than par or stated value. With such an interpretation, a dividend charged against premiums received in the sale of stock (or paid-in surplus) would appear to be illegal in a state that has the impairment rule but legal in one that has the surplus rule.

Even the insolvency rule, though it sounds quite different from the other two, may not differ significantly from them in application. The insolvency rule is usually applied in the equity sense—that is, in terms of ability to pay debts.[2] A dividend may not be paid if the corporation is unable to pay its debts as they come due or if the dividend would put it in that position. But in a state where the surplus rule applies, were a corporation to pay a dividend in an amount not exceeding its surplus and then be unable to pay its maturing debts, the courts might well hold that the dividend was an illegal one. Courts are not bound by surplus figures entered on corporations' books or shown in their balance sheets. They can take the nonpayment of debts as proof that assets are overvalued and that the surplus figures are therefore fictitious. In a state that has the impairment rule, decisions of courts may follow the same line of reasoning. Though a dividend may appear *on the books* not to impair capital because of the avail-

[2]In the bankruptcy sense, by contrast, insolvency is understood to mean that the reasonable value of the assets of an enterprise is less than the total amount of its obligations to creditors.

ability of balances in surplus accounts, a court may look on the inability to pay debts as proof that an impairment had, indeed, taken place—that, again, assets must be overvalued and a genuine surplus nonexistent.

Legal Actions

Tendencies toward uniformity of results in the application of the three kinds of basic dividend rules should be expected because of their identical objective of protecting creditors. If on nonpayment of obligations due them the creditors of a corporation take legal action to prevent the distribution of a dividend that has been declared, the court will surely issue an injunction to stop the dividend payment, regardless of what the basic dividend rule of the state may be. The court would doubtless look on the proposed dividend as being of a fraudulent character. Similarly, were a corporation to default on maturing obligations shortly after having distributed a cash dividend to its stockholders, lawsuits brought by the creditors for the recovery of the dividend could be expected to be successful for the same reason. The court might hold that the corporation's surplus was fictitious or that the dividend did, indeed, impair the corporation's capital, but basically its attitude would probably be that the dividend was fraudulent because of proved insolvency. On the other hand, if a corporation pays its debts when due, no creditor is likely to contest dividend declarations and payments on any grounds, whether lack of surplus, impairment of capital, or insolvency.

Thus it is that the applicability of basic dividend rules, as for other kinds of legal prescriptions, depends primarily on court interpretations of the law and evaluations of the individual corporation's situation in the course of legal actions brought by persons who feel that their rights are being injured. The rules protect the creditors, but this protection demands action by them to safeguard their rights. The directors of a well-managed corporation are unlikely to adopt any dividend policy that would endanger its solvency, regardless of the state's rule and the likelihood of action on the part of creditors. But a likelihood of action by the creditors would probably be the controlling consideration to be weighed by the directors of another corporation who are anxious to pay a dividend despite doubts about its legality.

The actions that creditors can take are of two kinds: proceedings in equity for injunctions to prevent the distribution of declared dividends alleged to be illegal, and lawsuits for the recovery of cash or other assets allegedly distributed illegally. Preventive actions in equity are likely to be more helpful to creditors than are lawsuits to recover assets already distributed. If a corporation can be barred from paying a cash dividend, the money remains available for the settlement of creditors' claims, but if the cash has already been distributed as a dividend, getting it back can be a difficult matter. As for recovery, the general rule is that directors are liable to creditors for the amount of dividends illegally distributed. In some states, they are also subject to criminal penalties. However, a dissenting director can ordinarily escape all responsibility, civil and criminal, if he has his negative vote entered in the minutes. In some states, indeed, even the directors who voted what is later determined to have been an illegal dividend can escape liability if able to prove that they acted in good faith, as by relying on profits or surplus figures contained in statements certified by reputable accountants. The legal principle for stockholders appears to be that they can be forced to return illegal dividends if the distribution has caused the corporation to be insolvent. But the right of creditors to recover from stockholders tends to be even less certain than the right to recover from directors. Some states provide, for example, that illegal dividends cannot be recovered from stockholders who have received them in good faith. At any rate, even if directors, or directors and stockholders, are not provided with ready-made defenses, recovery can be expensive in attorneys' fees, court costs, and delays. And even when judgments are obtained, the directors or stockholders may have no assets that can be seized for their satisfaction.

Dividends Based on Capital Surplus

Looking at the matter broadly, one can say that, as a rule, any kind of surplus that a corporation has on its books can serve as a basis for cash dividends. Under the surplus rule, surplus obviously exists. Under the capital impairment rule, distributions chargeable against any surplus account do not appear to impair capital. Under the insolvency rule, a dividend is not illegal, regardless of the account against which it is charged, if the corporation is not insolvent at the time of its declaration or is not made insolvent by its payment. Ordinarily, therefore, surplus arising from such varied sources as the following can serve as the basis for dividends: premiums received in the sale of par-value stocks, portions of the proceeds of no-par stocks allocated by the directors to paid-in or capital surplus accounts, receipts from the sale of donated stock, profits on dealings in treasury stock, profits on the sale of nonoperating assets that may have been credited to capital surplus, write-ups in asset values, and write-downs in the par or stated value of outstanding stock.

Dividends from Asset Write-ups. Always a doubtful basis for dividend payments, nevertheless, is surplus created by simply writing up the book values of assets. The directors of a corporation may claim that the assets have been undervalued (and earnings and surplus, therefore, understated) through the overcharging of depreciation and bad debts, the undervaluing of inventories, and earlier write-offs of assets that still have recognizable values. The substantiation of such a claim would appear to justify the write-up and therefore the payment of a dividend based on it. But if the write-up is defended on the grounds that rising replacement costs justify it, or that the value of assets held in combination by a going concern is greater than the sum of the values of the separate items of property regarded individually, a dividend based on it would surely be subject to criticism. Such criticism would be in line with the generally accepted accounting doctrine that gains should be recognized only when realized through actual transactions.

Dividends from Write-downs of Stock Values. Under both the surplus and impairment rules, it appears that dividends paid on the basis of surplus created through write-downs in the par or stated value of outstanding stock could be legal or illegal, depending on circumstances. Existing creditors could certainly claim that an impairment results from such a dividend even if not from the write-down itself, and under the surplus rule they could claim the surplus to be fictitious. People who became creditors after the write-down, however, would have no standing to make similar claims, even if they became creditors before payment of the dividend. The formal action of the corporation in amending its articles to provide for the write-down would be notice to them that its capital had been reduced.

When corporations write down the par or stated values of their stock to eliminate deficits and then pay dividends chargeable against subsequent earnings, there ordinarily need be no misgivings about legality. Under the impairment rule, impairments that result from operating losses give rise to no liability on the part of directors or stockholders; these are not deliberate impairments. But dividends may not be paid so long as the impairment stands; hence, subsequent earnings must be used first to correct the impairment, and then, if there is an excess, dividends may be paid. However, if a corporation, through a write-down in par or stated value, shows to all the world that its capital has been reduced as a result of losses, it clears the way for the payment of legal dividends chargeable against any subsequent earnings. Under the surplus rule, likewise, a corporation may not pay a dividend unless there is a sufficient net credit balance in one or more of its surplus accounts; hence a net debit balance—a deficit—must be more than cleared up by subsequent earnings before dividend-paying capacity is revived. But if the corporation eliminates the debit balance by a write-down in par or stated value—by an acknowledgment, once again, that its capital has been impaired by losses—any subsequent earnings would seem to establish a proper credit balance against which dividends could legally be charged.

Prescriptions of State Laws. Some states have in their laws specific provisions on the payment of dividends from sources other than earnings. Maine and Indiana, for example, authorize dividends chargeable against paid-in surplus and surplus created by reductions in the par or stated value of outstanding stock. But most of the prescriptions are restrictive. Illinois provides that paid-in surplus and surplus originating from donations of stock may be used only for dividends on preferred stock, and it prescribes that the preferred stockholders must be told of these sources when so used. Illinois also stipulates that surplus created through write-ups in asset values may be used only for stock dividends. Other states, including California, Pennsylvania, Michigan, and Ohio, have comparable restrictions. Several states in addition to Illinois require notification to the stockholders when dividends are paid from sources other than earnings. Notification of this sort is always strongly advisable, whether or not required by state law. Lawsuits for damages have been brought by stockholders against directors on the grounds that the directors' misrepresentations of earnings led them to pay excessive prices for stock—misrepresentations in that dividends from sources other than earnings were not so described by the directors.

Dividends Chargeable against Current Profits

A few states permit the payment of dividends "out of net profits or surplus"—a stipulation understood to mean that dividends may be paid on the basis of current profits, even though they are insufficient to eliminate deficits standing in the surplus accounts. Delaware, for example, provides that dividends may be paid out of profits of the current and the preceding year, even though capital has been impaired through earlier losses; however, such dividends must not reduce the value of net assets (that is, assets less outside liabilities) below the total preference to assets of outstanding preferred stock. Thus, a Delaware corporation could pay dividends chargeable against the profits of the current and preceding years, though losses had reduced the book value of common stock to a negligible amount. Comparable provisions are found in the laws of California, Minnesota, and New Jersey.

Liquidating Dividends

The legal rules on dividend payments already discussed have to do with distributions in the "ordinary course of business." In addition, however, corporations are permitted to make distributions of cash or other assets to their stockholders, chargeable against the capital stock accounts themselves, when these assets are no longer needed for corporate purposes. Such distributions are said to be made in partial or complete liquidation.

A complete liquidation generally requires a formal process of dissolution, whose steps are prescribed in detail in the state laws. The directors adopt a resolution, which must be approved by the holders of such share majorities as the laws stipulate. Usually, an approving vote of a simple majority of the shares suffices if the dissolving corporation is insolvent, while larger majorities are required if it is solvent. On approval, formal articles of dissolution are prepared and submitted to the secretary of state. Thereupon, the assets are distributed as the law prescribes—always with safeguards to ensure that the creditors are paid in full before any distribution is made to the stockholders. After the creditors have been satisfied, dividends may be distributed from time to time to the stockholders as portions of the assets are successively turned into cash.

Sometimes, however, corporations curtail their activities without intending to go out of business. Such curtailments will ordinarily result in excesses of assets; yet, the corporations may have no balances in surplus accounts against which ordinary dividends could be charged. Accordingly, dividends in partial liquidation chargeable against the stock accounts themselves are permitted, always with the proviso that distributions to the stockholders do not endanger the claims of creditors. Strictly speaking, the retirement of preferred stock is a kind of partial liquidation, although, as we have seen, it may not presage any significant curtailment of operations. But cash paid to preferred stockholders for their holdings is rarely described as a liquidating dividend.

Restrictions on Dividends in Contracts

Provisions of contracts, as well as state laws, often restrict corporate dividend-paying capacities. Contractual stipulations have a legal complexion, of course, since courts can be called on to enforce the terms of valid contracts and to assess damages for their violation.

In Chapter 23, we saw that restrictions on the payment of dividends on common stock are a popular kind of protective provision in preferred stock contracts. Similar restrictions are customarily placed in bond contracts or indentures. Sometimes, indeed, such contracts require that portions of earnings be specifically set aside and labeled not available for dividends, as in sinking fund reserves. Restrictions on dividend payments are often prescribed also in contracts covering term loans granted by commercial banks and other financial institutions—that is, loans that have original maturities of more than one year. Lenders want to be sure that cash needed for working capital and eventually for the repayment of the loans is not too generously drained by dividend payments.

QUESTIONS

1. In the post-World War II period, how have cash dividends paid by corporations collectively compared with their retained after-tax profits?

2. As a source of corporate assets in the postwar years, how have re-

tained earnings compared with net stock sales, net bond sales, and the net expansion of short-term debt?

3. Is it reasonable to say that retained earnings are only a temporary source of corporate assets? Explain.

4. As reported by business corporations, "net earnings" are only estimates. Is this proposition true or false? Explain.

5. Why is the amount of net earnings reported by the typical corporation for a year unlikely to have any close relationship with its cash holdings at a given time, such as the end of the year?

6. What effects do depreciation charges have on corporations' net earnings? On their cash balances?

7. What is the relationship between a corporation's net earnings and its capacity to distribute dividends? To distribute *cash* dividends?

8. What is a dividend? Distinguish between a dividend on stock and a stock dividend. What is a liquidating dividend?

9. In what circumstances would it seem to be proper for corporations to borrow in order to be able to pay cash dividends to their stockholders?

10. May a board of directors legally revoke a dividend that it has declared? Explain.

11. Distinguish among the surplus, impairment, and insolvency rules that pertain to the legality of corporate dividends. Is it realistic to hold that the three rules tend to be much the same in application? Explain.

12. For their own protection, how can creditors take action to prevent the distribution of alleged illegal dividends? To recover the amounts of alleged illegal dividends already distributed? What is the liability of directors who distribute illegal dividends and of the stockholders who receive them?

13. Disregarding restrictions peculiar to a few states, to what extent, if at all, may corporations legally pay cash dividends chargeable against each of the following sources: (*a*) premiums received on stock sales, (*b*) portions of the proceeds of no-par stock credited to paid-in surplus accounts, (*c*) profits on the sale of treasury stock, (*d*) current profits that are insufficient to eliminate earlier deficits, (*e*) write-ups in asset values, and (*f*) write-downs in the par or stated value of outstanding stock?

14. In any of our states, is it ever permissible for a corporation to distribute cash dividends even though it has a net deficit in its surplus accounts collectively? Explain.

PROBLEM

Several corporations have only negligible balances in their earned surplus accounts accumulated from profits on ordinary operations, but the directors of all these corporations would like to pay dividends much in excess of these balances on the basis of surplus derived from other sources. They ask your advice on the legality of the proposed distributions.

a) Corporation A sold its original issue of 100,000 shares of common stock of $25 par value at $30 a share, so that it has a $500,000 balance in a paid-in surplus account against which its dividend would be charged.

b) Corporation B sold its original issue of 100,000 shares of no-par common stock at $25 a share, and the directors at the time of sale adopted a resolution to credit $100,000 to the capital stock account and $2.4 million to a paid-in surplus account. The proposed dividend would be charged against this paid-in surplus.

c) Some years ago, the president of Corporation C donated to it 10,000 shares of its common stock of $30 par value, and the dividend would be charged against the $300,000 donated surplus placed on the books at that time. The 10,000 shares are still held as treasury stock.

d) The directors of Corporation D last year ordered the book values of some of its fixed assets to be written up by $450,000 on the grounds that depreciation charges had been excessive. At the same time, a credit of $450,000 was entered on the books as surplus from asset revaluation. The proposed dividend would be charged against this surplus balance.

e) Corporation E's proposed dividend would be charged against a capital surplus balance entered on the books last year, when the par value of its common stock was reduced from $25 to $5 a share. There were 200,000 shares outstanding at the time of this action, so that the surplus credit amounts to $4 million.

f) Several years ago, Corporation F bought 20,000 shares of its outstanding stock at $15 a share. The stock had originally been sold at its par value of $20, so that at the time of repurchase the directors instructed the accountants to credit surplus from treasury stock for $100,000. The proposed dividend would be charged against this balance.

g) Several years ago, Corporation G bought 40,000 shares of its outstanding stock from the estate of a deceased stockholder at the par value of $10 a share. This year, it sold 25,000 of these shares at $18 a share, crediting $200,000 to capital surplus. Its proposed dividend would be charged against this account.

chapter 26

EARNINGS RETENTION AND DIVIDEND POLICIES

CRITERIA FOR POLICY

In decision making by boards of directors on the retention of earnings and their use as the basis of dividend distributions, three important factors are involved: (1) liquidity needs, (2) cash requirements for growth, and (3) the position of the stockholders. Let us consider these in the order indicated.

Liquidity Needs

A fundamental proposition that few will dispute is that a corporation must not endanger its solvency through the distribution of cash dividends to its stockholders, whether preferred or common. Regardless of the size of its surplus accounts and the amount of its current earnings as reported in the income statement, if holdings of cash and short-term, high-quality securities have been seriously depleted through expansion of inventories and receivables, purchase of fixed assets, payment of debt, or for any other reason, the corporation's directors would obviously be unwise to drain these holdings further by paying cash dividends.

It is true that, in some cases, directors may decide that depletions of cash and other liquid resources are only temporary—that normal inflows will soon restore the liquid resources to a safe position for dividend payment; hence, they may see justification for short-term borrowing as a means of financing immediate dividend distribution. Even here, however, there is danger, for expectations of normal inflows may not be fulfilled. General business conditions, or conditions in the industrial areas where a corporation's customers operate, may deteriorate rather abruptly, with the result that inventories become slow-moving and some of the receivables difficult to collect.

In part, at least, liquidity needs explain why many corporations discontinue the payment of cash dividends in periods of business recessions and depressions, particularly prolonged ones. Although balances in surplus accounts may be substantial, they may largely represent investments in fixed assets, inventories, and receivables or reduced volumes of outside liabilities; if so, they are not matched by holdings of liquid assets. Holdings of cash and other liquid resources may not be unduly weak, but managers may decide to preserve them against possible drains through operating losses or to meet liabilities coming to maturity, and even to add to them the cash throw-off from current earnings, if there are any, and from depreciation charges, if these are being covered in whole or in part by current sales.

Cash Requirements for Growth

Multiplicity of Growth Opportunities. It is probably safe to say that a large majority of corporate managers more or less constantly see important prospects for profit enhancement through expansions of facilities and scopes of operations.

1. Sales can be expanded by larger expenditures for advertising, the hiring of more salesmen, the invasion of broader territories, the setting up of branch warehouses and display rooms, the opening of retail outlets.
2. Sales can be stabilized by adding new product lines.
3. Costs can be cut by the acquisition of more suitable quarters, changes in location, the installation of laborsaving devices, large-scale purchasing of materials and supplies, the hiring of more specialized technical personnel.
4. Many things can be done at a stroke through the absorption of other enterprises in mergers or consolidations or as subsidiaries.
5. Many things can be done eventually if not immediately through greater expenditures for research.

The list tends to be endless. Adoption of given programs suggests other steps that ought to be taken to get the full benefits, and successful completion of given projects often opens new avenues for development not previously thought of.

A constant procession of what appear to be favorable opportunities to expand sales and cut costs must strongly tempt corporate managements to be very generous in their earnings retention policies or, looking at the matter from the other side, to be quite illiberal in the distribution of cash dividends. Money is needed to take advantage of the opportunities, money is provided by earnings, and decisions to use this money for expansion rather than to look elsewhere for financing may appear to be thoroughly sound. Cash obtainable elsewhere is costly, in the sense both of flotation expenses and of periodic outlays in the form of interest and dividends, whereas money provided by earnings retention, already in hand, may seem to be costless. To distribute generous amounts of cash as dividends and then try to get an equal amount back by the sale of new securities may seem to some corporate managers not only a costly procedure but a needless one. If all the earnings can be profitably used to finance expansion projects, why not devote them to this purpose and forgo dividends as long as may be necessary?

Growth in Relation to Stockholder Interests. It immediately becomes apparent, however, that an affirmative answer to this question would mean, for many corporations, no prospects for dividends indefinitely. If new opportunities for expanding sales and cutting costs constantly open up, there must be no limit to the amount of earnings that could be profitably retained and reinvested. Then comes the question: Why does a corporation expand its facilities in order to increase its earning power? And the answer seems to be that it does this for the benefit of its stockholders. But benefits for stockholders are subject to various kinds of evaluations, and corporate managers surely have some responsibility to avoid narrow evaluations entirely their own. It is surely their duty to distinguish their personal interests in expansion—possibly their desire for increased power and prestige and for higher levels of compensation—from those of the stockholders.

The principal benefit of stockownership that millions of stockholders look to is periodic cash income in the form of dividends. They may justly feel that to be denied cash dividends or to be allowed only niggardly ones when earnings are good, is a policy contrary to their best interest. They may be compelled to cut their expenditures for consumption if they do not get the cash dividends their corporations are apparently able to pay, considering the level of their earnings, and this is a sacrifice they may not want to make. Or they may feel that they should have the right to choose how income earned on their stock investments should be reinvested rather than to have boards of directors make this decision for them.

As we shall see in the subsequent discussion of the position of stockholders, directors' policies of no dividends or niggardly ones are sometimes thoroughly in accord with the wishes of stockholders, but much more frequently such policies are quite out of line with stockholders' evaluations of their own interests. At any rate, it is surely clear that the power of directors to determine policies on earnings retention and distribution is by no means easy to exercise justly. It is, indeed, most difficult to weigh, with maximum justice to the stockholders themselves, their short-run interests to be served by cash dividends as against their long-run interests to be promoted by earnings retention. That the boards of directors of many of our leading corporations—generally recognized, of course, to be people of high competence—are inclined to give at least as much attention to stockholders' short-term interests as to their long-term ones is indicated by the maintenance of regular cash dividend payments over the years, regardless of the pressures of expansion requirements; their overall distributions of 50 or 60 percent or more of the earnings despite the same pressures; and their extreme reluctance to suspend cash dividend payments in periods of general business contraction during which the stockholders will probably have all the more need of cash income.

Liberality of Dividends and Future Financing. Aside from the question of justice to the short-run interests of stockholders, corporate managements generally realize that policies of relatively liberal cash dividends—where earnings justify them of course—are likely to be a fine advertisement for further financing ventures. The common stocks of corporations that pay relatively generous dividends usually sell at substantially higher prices than those of corporations whose earnings are comparable but whose dividend policies are illiberal. Thus, if it is able to get premium prices for additional shares it sells, a corporation that has a liberal policy recoups in effect some of the dividends it has paid. In other words, it would need to sell fewer shares to bring in a given sum of money than would a comparable corporation whose dividend policy had been illiberal. Likewise, investors in preferred stocks are easily attracted to a corporation that has a long record of dividend payments on its common stock. If the corporation has been able to pay dividends on the common year after year, a reasonable expectation is that it should have no difficulty in paying dividends on a stock that has a prior claim to earnings. Even buyers of bonds and other classes of lenders are inclined to look with great favor on corporations with good dividend-paying records. The periodic draining of cash for dividends may appear to be an unfavorable factor, but a regular payment of dividends indicates a continued availability of cash—cash that could be diverted to payment of interest and principal on debt, should the need arise. On the other hand, a policy of not paying dividends tends to give rise to fears of the unavailability of cash for debt service—fears that too much cash will be tied up in buildings, machinery, and other illiquid assets.

Position of the Stockholders

The problem of what to do with earnings is eased for many corporations' boards of directors because they are the sole stockholders; what they decide as directors is necessarily in full accord with their interests as stockholders. The problem is more difficult when stockholders are widely scattered and the directors' holdings amount to only a minor fraction of total shares outstanding. The problem tends to be most difficult when directors own controlling interests but the remainder of the stock is widely scattered.

Corporations Closely Held by Wealthy Stockholders. A few wealthy persons who are the sole stockholders in a highly profitable corporation, whatever its size, would be likely to regard with considerable loathing the prospect of receiving sizable cash dividends. Already perched in the higher brackets of the federal individual income tax on account of income derived from other sources, and having the means of meeting their consumption expenditures amply assured, they could hardly want further amounts of income that would be taxable at the regular rates. For them, therefore, a policy of a generous or complete retention of the corporation's earnings would be uniquely attractive. They would expect expansion, financed with retained earnings, to result in increases in the value of their stock. If, then, they wanted later to realize the rewards of their corporation's profitability, they could do so by selling some or all of the stock and have the increment in value taxed as a capital gain at the relatively moderate rate of 25 percent. In fact, they might contemplate holding on to the stock with its increment until the time of their deaths, so that their shares in corporate profits would never be taxed *as income* to them or to their heirs.

For such a corporation, then, the major problem in the disposal of earnings probably is not deciding what proportion should be distributed as dividends but finding opportunities for the investment of retained earnings reasonably related to corporate purposes in order that the special federal surtax on unreasonable accumulations of surplus can be avoided.[1]

Corporations Closely Held by Others. Tens of thousands of corporations are closely held by individuals whose livelihood depends largely or exclusively on what income they can draw from these corporations. After withdrawals to take care of the stockholders' consumption needs have been allowed for, the problem of what to do with the remaining earnings is usually a slight one; the remainder, if it amounts to anything at all, is negligible. Indeed, corporations of this description are not likely to report much in the way of profits. If the stockholders hold positions as officers, as is probable, money needed for their livelihoods will be withdrawn as salaries to the extent likely to be deemed reasonable by the Internal Revenue Service. In this way, corporate income taxes are avoided. But the point is that whether withdrawals are salaries or dividends, not much is left after living expenses have been provided for.

Corporations with Wide Distributions of Stock. In a corporation whose stock is so widely distributed that no holder or closely knit group of holders has a controlling interest, the board of directors tends to be self-perpetuating. Although the directors themselves may own but little stock, they control the voting machinery, and they can

[1]See p. 40.

ordinarily be confident that the stockholders will not band together to oust them unless large numbers become convinced that their interests are being gravely neglected.

In corporate situations of this kind, the personal interests of the directors often conflict, in part at least, with those of the stockholders. Expansion promises greater prestige and power and, for the directors who are also officers, a means of justifying larger salaries as well as bonus and stock-option arrangements. Accordingly, a policy of liberal retention of earnings to finance expansion is likely to be quite attractive.

But the directors do not want to lose their jobs, and they have reason to fear that a niggardly dividend policy is the very kind of thing that will convince many stockholders of the grave neglect of their interests. Thus, a subordination of the directors' personal interests to the stockholders' interests may seem to make good sense. Moreover, the directors have responsibility to serve the stockholders' interests rather than their own, and justice in caring for the stockholders' interests would seem to require a relatively liberal cash dividend policy. A wide scattering of stockholdings means numerous small owners whose short-run interests in dividends are likely to outrank by far their long-run interests in appreciation.

Beyond this, a relatively liberal dividend policy appears to be in order—always assuming a good level of earnings—if the directors anticipate that expansion requirements will demand funds in excess of earnings, even if all should be retained. The consequence of a liberal policy, as explained previously, should be relative ease in floating new security issues, whether common stock, preferred stock, or bonds. Even should the directors anticipate that total expansion could be financed by the retention of all earnings for a limited period of, say, five or six years, they would have to give due weight to the possibilities that actual requirements would prove to be much greater than anticipated. After the limited period of earnings retention, therefore, they might have to go to the market in relatively unfavorable circumstances, and especially so if they wanted to sell additional common stock.

Corporations with Mixed Stockholder Situations. Probably the most difficult problem of what to do with earnings is faced by the directors of corporations that are controlled by small groups of wealthy stockholders and have the remainder of their stock widely distributed in the hands of small investors. The wide distribution of the noncontrolling stock would indicate a past policy of rather generous dividend distributions; otherwise, the small investors would not have bought. But a board of directors can change from a generous dividend policy, even though it has been in effect for many years. Would it be justified in doing so?

It can hardly be denied that, in a situation of this kind a serious conflict exists between the interests of the controlling stockholders and the interests of the small stockholders. The conflict cannot be shrugged off, nor can it be easily resolved by appeals to justice. The controlling stockholders can claim the justice of their wish to avoid high tax rates on dividends they do not need; the small stockholders can demand justice in the treatment of their need of current income. Probably, one can say only that a golden mean should be sought. It would be easy, on one hand, to condemn a policy of nonpayment or one of very low payment as being utterly selfish on the part of the controlling interests. On the other hand, dissatisfaction with distributions that fall short of very large proportions of earnings would reflect an extremely selfish stand of the small stockholders. Perhaps the golden mean would be distributions materially less generous than those of corporations whose stock is all widely held.

Here, again, prospective needs of further security flotations could be an important consideration in dividend policy determination. Should financing beyond the amount of retained earnings be anticipated—allowing for the possibility of retaining all earnings—and should the controlling interests not want to provide the additional funds expected to be needed, a more generous dividend policy would appear to be advisable. The corporation would want to have a receptive public for its new security offerings, and it could work toward this goal in no better way than by cultivating its existing public—its small stockholders.

Conclusions

In deciding whether to retain earnings or distribute dividends, boards of directors must simultaneously study the three factors we have examined individually. Their decisions are not always sound. Not infrequently, the decisions are selfish in the sense of unreasonably favoring the directors' own interests or those of controlling groups of stockholders. But this does not mean that illiberal dividend policies are necessarily selfish ones. Quite different policies can be both wise and unselfish for different corporations, even though, at first glance at least, their dividend-paying capacities appear to be much the same.

Thus, one corporation that has earnings at a given level may be quite generous in paying cash dividends because it is in a declining industry and earnings retention to finance growth is out of the question. Another with the same level of earnings may distribute quite modest cash dividends because it is in a rapidly growing industry and because its access to the market for funds, for reasons of its immaturity, is not strong. In a period of depression, one corporation, despite current losses, may dip into its surplus to pay dividends because its cash position is strong, and another, though it has a large surplus, may quickly suspend dividend payments because its cash holdings are scanty. One corporation may diligently search for new avenues along which to expand so that earnings can be withheld from its stockholders, all of whom are wealthy, while another may cancel certain expansion projects because its directors feel that the thousands of its small stockholders need dividends as current income.

REGULARITY OF CASH DIVIDENDS

It is one thing for the board of directors of a corporation to decide on the distribution of cash dividends equal to 40, 50, or 60 percent or some other percentage of earnings as a continuing policy; it is another for them to decide on the timing of the distributions. If it is decided that the distribution pattern shall closely match that of current earnings, a high degree of irregularity in dividend payments can result. This would be necessarily so in corporations with highly unstable earnings—the "prince and pauper industries," including most of the so-called heavy-goods industries. But it would be at least moderately so additionally in many industries whose earnings are usually said to be stable, such as producers of processed foods, tobacco, and electric power. Even industries such as these often have substantial cyclical fluctuations in earnings.

It may be decided, however, that the rate of dividends shall be uniform or regular from year to year, regardless of the irregularity of the earnings pattern. In good years, an extraordinary amount of earnings can be retained to serve as the basis for dividends at an unchanged rate in poor years. Suppose, for illustration, that a certain corporation with 100,000 shares of common stock outstanding has earnings after taxes in an 8-year period as indicated in Table 26–1. It is the directors' policy to distribute dividends equal to 60 percent of earnings. If the distribution were matched annually to current earnings, the rate of dividends per share (earnings pattern policy) would be as shown in the third data column of the table. But if at the beginning of the period the directors were to anticipate earnings of the amounts shown, and were to decide on a uniform rate of dividends throughout the eight-year period, the result would be as shown in the last two columns (regular policy).

Advantages of Regularity

For the welfare of business corporations themselves, a policy of regularity in the payment of cash dividends to common stockholders tends to be highly beneficial. Stockholder loyalty is developed. Investors who are interested in income buy the stock and hold it for long periods, while speculators who are interested in short-run trading profits are not so likely to be attracted. Investors appreciate not only the steady income but also the relatively stable market prices that dividend regularity promotes. They have less reason to fear extraordinary sacrifices should they find it necessary to sell in periods of low or negative corporate earnings. But the very tendencies toward stability in market price tend to preclude extraordinary short-run gains for speculators. In terms of the illustration, the market price of the stock would tend to fluctuate over a broad range, as do the earnings and dividends, were the earnings pattern policy to be in effect. With the regular policy in effect, the depressive force of the deteriorating earnings situation through the fifth year would tend to be strongly counteracted by the uninterrupted payment of dividends at the established rate. Indeed, chances would be good that stockholder loyalty would be much greater with a regular dividend rate of,

TABLE 26–1
Illustration of Dividend Payment Patterns

Year	Earnings after Taxes	Earnings Allocated to Dividends	Earnings Pattern Policy, Dividends per Share	Regular Policy: Earnings Retained for Future Dividends (Cumulative)	Regular Policy: Dividends per Share
1	$1,500,000	$ 900,000	$ 9.00	$ 600,000	$ 3.00
2	1,200,000	720,000	7.20	1,020,000	3.00
3	600,000	360,000	3.60	1,080,000	3.00
4	200,000	120,000	1.20	900,000	3.00
5	−300,000	0	0	600,000	3.00
6	−150,000	0	0	300,000	3.00
7	250,000*	0*	0	0	3.00
8	700,000†	300,000†	3.00	0	3.00
Total	$4,000,000	$2,400,000	$24.00		$24.00
Annual average	$ 500,000	$ 300,000	$ 3.00		$ 3.00

*No allocation to dividends because of application of earnings against deficits of years 5 and 6.
†Remaining deficits of years 5 and 6 of $200,000 reduce allocable earnings of year 8 to $500,000, of which 60 per cent, as allocated to dividends, is $300,000.

say, $2.50 a share than with earnings pattern dividends averaging out, as in the illustration, at $3.

Stockholder loyalty means wide interest among the stockholders in buying such additional issues of common stock and securities convertible into common stock as a corporation may decide to issue. Offerings by the rights procedure are likely to go extremely well. Loyal stockholders are likely to carry their message of satisfaction to other investors, urging or encouraging them to buy. Moreover, loyal stockholders are surely inclined to buy the corporation's products, and to urge others to buy if within the range of their usual kinds of purchases.

A policy of regular cash dividends on common stock, especially if long maintained, attracts investors other than the present holders of a corporation's securities. Much publicity is given by brokers and dealers and by the stock exchanges to long unbroken records of dividend payments, exemplified at the extreme by the records of the Washington Gas Light Company running back to 1852, the Singer Company to 1863, the American News Company to 1864, Pullman Incorported to 1867, the American Telephone and Telegraph Company to 1882, the New England Telephone and Telegraph Company to 1886, the Commonwealth Edison Company to 1890, the Boston Edison Company and the Consolidated Edison Company to 1892, and the Wickes Corporation to 1895. Although few corporations qualify for the 100-year club, substantially larger numbers are eligible for the 50-year club, and ever larger numbers qualify for the clubs at 40-, 30-, and 20-year levels. Even a 10-year record of regular dividend payments will hardly be ignored as a selling point by brokers and dealers in negotiations with their customers.

At any rate, all the favorable publicity that goes with good dividend records generates investor interest not only in the common stocks of the record-making corporations but also in their preferred stocks and bonds. Wise investors pride themselves on making investment decisions based primarily on forecasts of what is going to happen, but they can hardly avoid being influenced by what has already happened. The very fact that a corporation has been able to pay regular dividends on its common stock for a considerable period of years may seem to be a good basis for a judgment that it ought to have little difficulty in paying dividends on a new preferred stock, and even less in meeting interest and principal obligations on bonds.

Disadvantage of Regularity

A disadvantage of a policy of regular cash dividends on common stock is the danger that it will be overdone. The rate selected for dividends may be too high. Though earnings for a considerable period of years may be forecast, such an estimate, because it is long range, may prove to be much too optimistic. If, therefore, the board of directors originally fixes the dividend rate in the expectation of devoting, say, 60 percent of average earnings to dividends, they may find with the passing years that continuance of this *amount* of dividends requires the paying out of 70 or 80 percent or a still higher percentage of average earnings. The high payout percentage may not embarrass the corporation for lack of cash, but earnings as a means of financing expansion become much less important than had been anticipated. Because the original anticipations of the directors come thus to be frustrated, the temptation must be strong to cut the regular dividend rate. But this would not be a happy solution. It would surely be a blow to the stockholders' loyalty as their income was reduced and the market price of their stock fell, and it would give rise to uncertainties about future policy, thus weakening the market for new securities of whatever kind the corporation might want to offer.

A greater danger than selection of a rate too high for regular dividends is that a policy of regular dividends will be continued long after it should have been abandoned. Reluctance to depart from the 50-year club or the 20-year club may lead directors to continue cash dividends that definitely threaten solvency. Changing conditions in an industry may have brought earnings to a low level, with little prospect of their substantial revival; yet, the decision is that the dividend record must be maintained. Or in a period of depression, though the surplus account of a corporation may be large, its cash balance may be small; yet, a decision is made that cash must be further drained to maintain the record.

Extra and Special Dividends

The boards of directors of many corporations reduce the danger of setting a rate too high for regular dividends by choosing quite conservative rates when they first adopt a policy of regularity. If forecasts indicate that the distribution of a given percentage of earnings over a period of years would make possible a regular dividend rate on par or stated value of 6 percent, perhaps a start will be made with a rate of 4 percent. Should earnings fall short of expectations by as much as one third, the regular dividends could be continued at 4 percent without difficulty; but should they be as high as or higher than forecast, additional distributions could be made from time to time, specifically labeled extra dividends and so reported, as in Figure 26–1.

Although the payment of extra dividends introduces an element of irregularity in a program of regular payments, it is a highly popular device for experimentation in dividend-paying capacity. In declaring an extra dividend, the directors of a corporation inform its stockholders, in effect, that there is present justification for paying a dividend in excess of the regular one, but that there is no assurance that the higher level of payment can be or will be continued. If, then, earnings available for dividends continue to run well above the regular requirement, and if, accordingly, extra dividends have been distributed over a series of years, the directors may think it safe to step up the regular rate. They would then discontinue extra dividends until such time that excess earnings again suggested a need of experimenting toward a still higher regular rate. If, on the other hand, earnings continued only sporadically to be enough for extra dividends, a policy of sporadic extra dividends, without thought of raising the regular rate, could be continued indefinitely. And if but small amounts of excess earnings should become available after one or two extra dividends had been paid, the nonpayment of further extras would

FIGURE 26–1
Report of Dividends Declared from *The Wall Street Journal*

Dividends Reported November 20

Company	Period	Amt.	Payable date	Record date
Allied Thermal Corp	Q	.37½	12–16–68	12– 6
Anchor Capital Fund		h.05	12–24–68	12– 2
Am Distilling Co	Q	.35	1– 2–69	12–18
Am Distilling Co	Yr-End	.10	1– 2–69	12–18
Am District Tele	Q	.10	12–20–68	11–29
Am Home Assurance	Q	.25	12–27–68	12–16
Am Home Assurance	Stk	20%	12–13–68	12– 2
Am Ship Bldg Co	Q	.15	12–31–68	12– 2
Am Tel & Tel	Q	.60	1– 2–69	11–29
Assoc Mortgage Cos	Stk	3%	12–13–68	11–29
Atlantic Steel Co		(Omitted common dividend)		
Atlas Corp 5% pf		p.25	12–16–68	12– 2
p-On arrears.				
Atlas Press Co	Q	.20	12–20–68	12– 2
Automatic Fire Alarm	S	.35	12– 9–68	11–27
Axe-Houghton Stk Fd	Yr-End	j.46	12–27–68	11–25
Axe-Houghton Stk Fd		h.04	12–27–68	11–25
Becton Dickinson & Co	Q	.07½	12–27–68	12– 6
Becton Dickinson & Co	E	.07½	12–27–68	12– 6
Becton Dickinson & Co		(k)	..	..
(k)- 3 for 2 stock split subject to stockholders approval Feb. 4.				
Book-of-Month Club new	Q	.32	11– 2–69	12–16
Burroughs Corp	Q	.25	1–20–69	12–20
Century Shares Trust		h.12	12–23–68	12– 2
Chemway Corp	Q	.05	12–16–68	12– 2
Chesapeake Utilities	Q	.17½	1– 6–69	12–16
Chesebrough-Pond's Inc	Q	c.23	12–16–68	12– 2
Chris-Craft Indus	Q	.25	12–31–68	12– 3
Cohu Electronics Inc	A	.15	1–10–69	12– 5
Cont'l Oil Co	Q	c.75	12–13–68	12– 2
Cont'l Oil Co	Stk	n100%	..	..
n-Subject to stockholders approval Feb. 18.				
Conwood Corp	Q	.40	1– 2–69	12–10
Dexter Corp	Q	.07½	1–10–69	12–16
Diversified Growth Stk		h.06½	12–24–68	12– 2
Elizabethtown Gas Co	Q	.45	12–15–68	11–27
Explorer Fund	A	h.48	12–13–68	11–29
Factor Max & Co cl A	Q	c.21	12–30–68	12– 9
Factor Max & Co cl A	Stk	2%	12–30–68	12– 9
Federated Growth Fd		h.12	12–20–68	11–20
Federated Growth Fd		j.93	12–20–68	11–20
Fiduciary Trust NY	Q	.55	12–19–68	12– 5
Fiduciary Trust NY	E	.25	12–19–68	12– 5
First Westchester Nat'l	Q	.25	12– 9–68	11–22
Forest City Enterprises	S	.12½	12–16–68	12– 2
Franklin Elec Co	Stk	3%	12–31–68	12–13
Fundamental Investors		h.07	12–24–68	12– 2
Gen'l Cable Corp	Q	.30	1– 2–69	12–13
Gen'l Employment Enterp	Q	c.06	12–20–68	12– 5
Giant Yellowknife Mines	Q	.10	12–27–68	12– 6
Grain Belt Breweries	Q	.15	12–16–68	12– 2
Grain Belt Breweries	E	.20	12–16–68	12– 2
Greyhound Computer	A	.20	12–20–68	12– 2
Grinnell Corp	Q	.50	12–20–68	11–29
Grinnell Corp	E	.50	12–20–68	11–29
Grinnell Corp	Stk	5%	12–20–68	11–29
Grocery Stores Prod	Q	c.35	12–13–68	12– 2
Grocery Stores Prod	E	.25	12–13–68	12– 2
Hart-Carter Co	Q	.20	12–31–68	12–13
Int'l Salt Co	Q	.60	12–27–68	12– 4
Investment Co Amer		.14	12–27–68	12– 2
Jergens Andrew	Q	.22½	1–31–69	1–10
Johns-Manville Corp	Q	.55	12–10–68	11–29
Johnson Service Co	Q	.40	12–31–68	12–13
Kencorp		(y)	12–15–68	11–29
(y)-Kencorp said it was making a pro rata distribution to its stockholders on a share for share basis of the capital stock of its wholly owned subsidiary SMB Corp.				
Litton Ind $2pfB	Q	.50	1– 1–69	12–11
Lorillard Corp		v.63	12–20–68	11–29
v-Lorillard said the declared .63 cents dividend payments would cease afetr Nov. 29 if the proposed merger into Loew's Theatres Inc. is approved by shareholders of both companies.				
LTV Aerospace Corp	Q	.20	1– 6–69	12–13
Maul Bros Inc	..	(w)	1–16–69	12–20
(w)-2-for-1 stock split.				
Maul Bros Inc new	S	c.10	3–28–69	3–14
Mesta Machine Co	Q	.50	1– 2–69	12–16
Mickelberry's Food Prod	Q	.25	12–14–68	11–30
Michelberry's Food Prod	E	.25	12–14–68	11–30
Mid-Continent Tele	Q	c.21	1– 3–69	12–12
Morse Shoe Inc	Q	c.15	1– 6–69	12–13
Nat'l Cash Register	Q	.30	1–15–69	12–12
Nat'l Steel Corp	Q	.62½	12–11–68	11–29
Nestle-LeMur Co	Q	.05	12–19–68	12– 5
North Am Sug Ind	Q	.20	1– 2–69	12– 9
Northrop Corp	Q	.25	12–16–68	11–29
Northrop $1.45pf	Q	.36¼	1– 8–69	12–20
Parker-Hannifin Corp	Q	.35	12–20–68	12– 6
Penn-Dixie Cement	Q	.15	12–13–68	11–29
PepsiCo Inc	Q	.22½	12–31–68	12–10
Phoenix Steel Corp	Stk	3%	2–14–69	1–10
Pioneer Fund		h.12	12–16–68	11–29
Pioneer Fund		j.80	12–16–68	11–29
Pittsburgh Forgings Co	Q	.20	12–18–68	12– 6
Pittway Corp	Q	.15	12–17–68	12– 2
Pittway Corp	Stk	2%	12–27–68	12– 2
Planning Reserch Corp	Stk	100%	1–10–69	12– 6
Raybestos-Manhattan	Q	.75	1– 2–69	12– 4
Reeves Brothers Inc	Stk	10%	12–23–68	12– 2
Reeves Brothers Inc	Q	.37½	12–11–68	12– 2
Robbins & Myers Inc	Q	.30	12–16–68	12– 5
Robertshaw Controls Co	Q	.30	12–20–68	12– 6
Scott O M & Sons		.10	12–20–68	12– 2
St. Joseph L&P Co	Q	c.26	12–18–68	12– 3
Tecumseh Products Co	E	.60	12–10–68	11–29
Tenneco $1.60 2nd pf	Q	.40	1–18–69	12– 6
Tobin Packing Co	Q	.25	1– 2–69	12–16
Tropical Gas Co	Q	c.27½	12–15–68	12– 2
US Tobacco Co	Q	.25	12–16–68	12– 2
US Tobacco 7% pf	Q	.43¾	12–16–68	12– 2
United Utilities Inc	Q	.21	12–20–68	12– 2
United Utilities pf	Q	.22½	12–20–68	12– 2
Utah P&L	Q	c.43	1– 1–69	12– 1
Valley Natl Bank Ariz	Q	c.14	12–16–68	12– 2
Westminster Fund		h.06	12–24–68	12– 2
Wheelabrator Corp	Q	.15	1– 1–69	12– 3
Wheelabrator Corp	E	.10	1– 1–69	12– 3
Wheelabrator $1.50pf	Q	.37½	1– 1–69	12– 3
Wiley John & Sons	S	.15	12–18–68	11–25
Wiley John & Sons	Stk	5%	12–18–68	11–25
Wolverine Industries	Q	.07½	12–30–68	12– 2
Woods Corp	Q	.12	12–16–68	12– 2
Woodward Corp	Q	.40	12–10–68	11–30
Zero Mfg		(x)	12–13–68	11–22
(x) 3-for-2 split voted by holders.				

c-Increased dividend. d-Reduced dividend. h-From income. j-From capital gains.

A, annual; Ac, accumulation; E, extra; F, final; G, interim; In, initial; Liq, liquidation; M, monthly; Q, quarterly; R, resumed; S, semi-annual; Sp, special.

require no apology, since no basis was given to the stockholders to expect their continuance.

Because, however, stockholders may have some temptation to look on extra dividends as paving the way for higher regular rates, corporate directors sometimes label as "special dividends," rather than as extras any distributions that are not likely to be repeated. Such a distinction in terminology appears to be particularly desirable when the distribution is based on profits not derived in the ordinary course of operations. For example, a profit gained on a sale of stock held by a corporation in a subsidiary might serve as the basis of a "special" dividend as distinguished from an "extra" one.

STOCK DIVIDENDS

Stock dividends are a strange breed. They are second in popularity to cash dividends from the standpoint of both the frequency of their distribution by corporations and the satisfaction with which they are received by stockholders; yet, they appear to give the stockholder nothing. For illustration, assume that a certain corporation has outstanding 100,000 shares of common stock of $50 par value, that it has no preferred stock, and that it has an accumulated earned surplus balance of $3 million. A stockholder who owns 10,000 shares has one tenth of the total voting power, one tenth of the total claims to earnings, and one tenth of total ownership claims to assets as measured by the total book value of his holdings of $800,000. Now assume that the corporation distributes a stock dividend of 20 percent or 20,000 shares, and that the stockholder referred to gets 2,000 of these shares. A transfer of $1 million is made from the earned surplus account to the common stock account. The stockholder now has 12,000 shares of a total of 120,000, and, accordingly, he still has one tenth of the total voting power and one tenth of total ownership claims to earnings and assets. Moreover, his claim to assets remains at $800,000 (12,000 shares at $50 par value plus a one tenth interest in the remaining surplus of $2 million).

What, then, is accomplished by a transaction of this kind? The answer depends on its objectives, chiefly two: (1) to reduce the market value of the stock or the earnings and dividends per share, and (2) to substitute for or supplement cash dividends. As these two objectives are quite distinct in character, they merit separate examination. In relation to this examination, the data of stock and cash dividends distributed on the common stocks of several corporations in the period 1963–67 as presented in Table 26–2 should prove instructive, and the following discussion should enable one to recognize which of the two objectives, if either, the included corporations were pursuing in their declarations of stock dividends. The expression "if either" in the foregoing sentence indicates the possibility of a third objective, such as that attributed to the Northern Pacific Railway Company in 1958 when it distributed a stock dividend of 20 percent. The thought was that Northern Pacific wanted to bring the level of its outstanding shares closer to that of the Great Northern Railway Company, with which a merger was being discussed—a discussion, one might add, that was still in progress in the summer of 1968, with the Interstate Commerce Commission approving and the Department of Justice indicating its disapproval.

TABLE 26–2
Dividend Records of a Sample of Common Stocks, 1963–67
(Cash dividends in dollars and dollar fractions; stock dividends in percentages)

			Dividends				
Corporation	*Par Value*	*Class*	*1963*	*1964*	*1965*	*1966*	*1967*
American Electric Power Co., Inc.	$6.50	Cash	1.10	1.18	1.26	1.35	1.56
		Stock		3			2.5
Carnation Company	$2.00	Cash	2.00	2.30	1.775*	1.70	1.80
		Stock	3	3			2
Collins Radio Company	$1.00	Cash	.20	.40	.525	.55	.70
Ingersoll-Rand Company	$2.00	Cash	4.00	3.00†	2.00	2.00	2.00
Interstate Bakeries Corporation	$1.00	Cash	1.60	1.60	1.60	1.60	1.25‡
		Stock					100
International Business Machines Corporation	$5.00	Cash	4.25	5.00	6.00	4.80§	4.40
		Stock					2.5
Jantzen, Inc.	$1.00	Cash	.80	.80	.80	.80	.80
		Stock	4	5		5	
Republic Steel Corporation	$10	Cash	2.00	2.00	2.00	2.125	2.50
St. Regis Paper Company	$5.00	Cash	1.40	1.40	1.40	1.40	1.40
		Stock	2	2	2	2	2
Sangamo Electric Company	$5.00	Cash	.25	nil	.20	.40	.40
		Stock					50
Sun Oil Company	No Par	Cash	1.00	1.00	1.00	1.00‖	1.00
		Stock	6	5	6	6	5
Union Pacific Railway Company	$10	Cash	1.70	1.80	1.80	2.00¶	2.00¶

*Before 2-for-1 split on April 15, 1965, 55 cents; after, $1.225.
†Dividend cut from $1 per quarter to 50 cents per quarter after 2-for-1 split effective June 16, 1964.
‡Quarterly dividend cut from 40 cents to 22.5 cents following distribution of 100 percent stock dividend.
§Quarterly dividend reduced from $1.50 to $1.10 after 3-for-2 split effective May 18, 1966. IBM also had a split of 5 for 4 effective May 15, 1964, without any change in its quarterly cash dividend rate.
‖No change in quarterly dividend rate of 25 cents despite 4-for-3 split effective June 19, 1966.
¶Twenty cents labeled "extra."
SOURCE: Moody's Investors Service, *Manuals.*

Adjustments in Market Value or Per-Share Earnings and Dividends

Comparison with Split-ups. Because stock dividends aimed at effects on the market price of stock or earnings and dividends per share are closely comparable to split-ups discussed at length in Chapter 21, they require only brief treatment. With respect to adjustments in market value, one will recall that action to get the market price of a stock down from a very high level to a level more attractive to most classes of investors is undertaken to: promote wide distribution; prepare for new offerings of additional stock for cash; prepare for offerings of stock to the stockholders of other corporations in connection with proposed mergers, consolidations, and holding company acquisitions; and aid large stockholders to dispose of some or all of their holdings. If the market price of a stock is $150, a stock dividend of 200 percent should have about the same effect as a 3-for-1 split-up in bringing the price down to the vicinity of $50.

With respect to adjustments in per-share earnings and dividends, one will remember the fears of corporate managements that high ratios will invite competition, lead to unreasonable wage and salary demands by labor unions, result in unfair treatment by tax assessors, and engender customer dissatisfaction because of suspicions that the high ratios result from exorbitant selling prices. If a certain corporation's earnings per share have been $25 and its dividends per share $15, these can be reduced to $5 and $3, respectively (assuming no changes in the levels of earnings and dividends), by either the distribution of a stock dividend of 400 percent or a split-up of 5 for 1. Needless to say, a given stock dividend may have for its objectives reductions in market value, per-share earnings, and per-share dividends, all three.

Infrequency of Stock Dividends for Adjustment. Stock dividends designed for the class of objectives discussed here are usually quite large—50 percent, 100 percent, 200 percent, and so on. The very nature of the objective requires that they be quite large. Because of their size, however, the individual corporation rarely has occasion to repeat such a dividend in any short period of years. Once the market price of a stock or the per-share figures related to it have been substantially reduced, a considerable period of years usually elapses before a further adjustment of the same kind becomes advisable. This period may be shortened, of course, for corporations with profit prospects that build up most extraordinarily year after year, but it may stretch out indefinitely for corporations whose profit potentials decline after one or two such adjustments have been made.

The performance of two corporations may be cited as illustrating what has just been said. The United Engineering & Foundry Company distributed a stock dividend of 100 percent in 1911, one of 50 percent in 1923, and one of 200 percent in 1952, and none since 1952. The Island Creek Coal Company, after distributing a 400 percent stock dividend in 1927, made no further distributions of stock dividends except for one of 2½ percent in 1955 and one of 2 percent in 1967, before its absorption by the Occidental Petroleum Corporation in a merger in January, 1968. On the other hand, one can almost always find exceptions. In this instance, for example, the White Motor Corporation distributed 100 percent stock dividends in both 1958 and 1963, as well as 5 percent stock dividends in 1959 and 1960, and one of 10 percent in 1967.

Relation to Cash Dividends. Large dividends to reduce market prices and per-share earnings and dividends are rarely distributed in lieu of cash dividends. The likely situation is that cash dividends have already been quite large—the very thing that has caused the market price of the stock to soar to a level out of the investment range of large numbers of investors. The surplus on which the large stock dividend is based will have been accumulated in spite of the payment of handsome cash dividends. In the minds of the directors, it will already represent additional permanent investment by the stockholders; hence, they would have no expectation of its use as a basis for cash dividends. By the same token, they would hardly object to the proposition that the stockholders should have additional shares, to be provided by the stock dividend, as evidence of this additional permanent investment.

When a corporation distributes a large stock dividend for adjustment purposes, it usually reduces the cash dividend rate, so that total cash dividends will be no greater than before, or not much greater. If, for example, it has been paying cash dividends at 15 percent on a par-value stock, it may reduce the rate to 5 or 6 percent should it distribute a 200 percent stock dividend. If it has been paying, say, $3 a share on a no-par stock, it may, in the same circumstances, reduce the rate to $1 or $1.25 a share. As the accumulated surplus on which the stock dividend is based has already been contributing to earnings, its mere transfer in part to the common stock account incident to the stock dividend adds nothing to earning power. If, therefore, the cash dividend *rate* already in effect was reasonable, all circumstances considered, the stock dividend gives no basis for a sharp increase in the *amount* of cash distributions. In this regard, one should notice in Table 26–2 that the distribution of a 100 percent stock dividend by the Interstate Bakeries Corporation was followed by a sharp reduction in the rate of its quarterly cash dividends, although, to be sure, by a little less than a full 50 percent.

Relation to Surplus. While stock dividends and split-ups can be used with equal effectiveness for adjustment objectives, the results are different in effects on surplus. A stock dividend of 200 percent, as we have seen, tends to have the same effects on market price and earnings and dividends per share as a 3-for-1 split-up. But the stock dividend requires a transfer equal to the par or stated value of the dividend from the surplus account or accounts to the common stock account, whereas the split-up requires no such transfer. Thus, a corporation that has been extremely liberal in paying cash dividends, so that it has little remaining surplus, is necessarily limited to the split-up device, whereas one that has accumulated a large surplus has a choice between the two devices.

Substituting for and Supplementing Cash Dividends

Size and Frequency. The use of stock dividends for objectives of the second type is ordinarily easy to recognize because the dividend rate is so much smaller than when the objectives are of the adjustment kind. The directors of a corporation might decide that earnings would justify a cash dividend equal to 6 percent of par or stated value, but because of a concurrent decision that all earnings must be retained for corporate purposes they might substitute a stock dividend of 6 percent. Or they might decide that cash equal to only 3 percent of par or stated value could be spared for dividend purposes, and they might therefore add a stock dividend also of 3 percent.

Moreover, stock dividends of the second type, unlike those of the first, are often repeated periodically, sometimes for lengthy periods of years. In some instances, indeed, they come to be looked on as regular. A corporation's directors, having decided in one year that a stock dividend must be substituted for a cash dividend, are likely to make the same kind of substitution in subsequent years if they continue to decide that cash cannot be paid.

Directors' and Stockholders' Attitudes. Stock dividends of the second class, therefore, are generally voted by corporate directors to give the stockholders something as a current reward for their investment when earnings justify a reward but pressing needs to retain cash for corporate purposes obtain. In some cases, directors might prefer not to distribute dividends of any kind, but decide on stock dividends so that records of long-continued dividends of one kind or another will not be broken. However, a more likely reason for declaring stock dividends when directors would prefer to distribute nothing is the belief that stock dividends will prevent stockholder clamor for cash distributions, or for larger cash distributions if modest ones are already being made. The thought is that stockholders—even widely scattered ones—will be quite critical of management if they see in corporate reports pleasant figures for profits and if they then must wait in vain for something as their share in these profits.

The fact is that great numbers of stockholders are often quite content to receive stock dividends in full or partial substitution for the cash dividends that corporate earnings would seem to justify. They are content provided that the directors of their corporations do not overdo the stock dividend policy, such as by trying to continue it indefinitely. The typical stockholder in a large corporation whose stock is widely distributed is not much interested in voting power and in his claim, as owner, to corporate assets. He is interested in current income, and this he can get in cash by simply selling the shares he receives as dividends. The amount of cash he gets may vary from year to year as the market price of the stock fluctuates, but as long as the market price prevails at good levels he may feel that he has no reason to complain. His proportionate claim to future earnings is diluted by the sale of the dividend stock, but this ought not to disturb him if the *rate* of dividends, as paid in stock or in stock and cash, is not reduced. Nor should the rate be reduced. According to generally accepted doctrine, the distribution of stock dividends in lieu of cash does not justify reducing the dividend rate, even though maintaining the rate means a continued increase in dividend requirements as more and more dividend stock is issued. That earnings must be retained for corporate purposes is the justification for distributions of stock dividends in lieu of cash, but the retention, in turn, can be justified in most cases only if it expands earning capacity. The expansion in earning capacity, accordingly, should enable the corporation to meet the higher dividend requirements without difficulty.

Another reason for stockholder satisfaction with stock dividends is applicable chiefly to people who have large incomes and extensive stockholdings. This reason is that, as a rule, profits from the sale of stock received as dividends can be reported as capital gains rather than as ordinary income. The maximum capital gains rate on stock or other property held for more than 6 months is a straight 50 percent, whereas the tax rates on ordinary individual income are graduated to a high of 70 percent.[2] Thus, a stockholder whose income from sources other than dividends gets into brackets taxable at rates well over 50 percent has reason to welcome stock dividends in lieu of cash dividends, and obviously, the greater the rate applicable to the top bracket of his income, the greater the reason for this welcome. (A modest offsetting factor is that with cash dividends the first $100 of dividends is excluded from taxable income, but this factor is surely of little importance to people with large incomes.)

Tax Treatment of Stock Dividends

On the basis of decisions of the Supreme Court dating from 1920, stock dividends that did not change the stockholders' ownership interests were recognized as not constituting taxable income. Common

[2]It will be recalled that only 50 percent of the amount of net long-term capital gains is counted as taxable income, so that the maximum tax rate on the full gain is only 25 percent (.50 × .50). If the taxpayer chooses to have his net long-term capital gains taxed as ordinary income, he likewise, of course, includes only 50 percent of the amount of these gains. (One should note that these statements about tax rates ignore the additional surcharge of 10 percent applicable to both the long-term capital gains rate and the rates on ordinary income adopted in June, 1968, supposedly on a temporary basis.)

shares given to common stockholders as dividends were declared to be nontaxable as income, whereas preferred shares given as dividends to common stockholders were held to be taxable. However, the Internal Revenue Code of 1954 extended the exemption of stock dividends by making all kinds or classes nontaxable as income when received, with two exceptions. The exceptions are unusual kinds of distributions: (1) when preferred stockholders are given stock in lieu of cash dividends for the current or preceding year, and (2) when the stockholder takes stock though he has the choice of taking cash or some other kind of property—such a distribution is known as an optional dividend.

Most stock dividends consist of common shares given to common stockholders. Under the present regulations, these are clearly nontaxable as income when received, but subsequent sales of such shares generally result in taxable capital gains or deductible capital losses. Assume that a stockholder owns 1,000 common shares that he bought some years ago at $40 a share. This year he receives a stock dividend of 50 shares. He now has 1,050 shares that cost him $40,000; therefore, $38.10 ($40,000 ÷ 1,050) is the basis price for the determination of capital gains or losses on sales of any of the shares. Should he sell the dividend stock at $50 a share, he would have a gain of $595 that would be taxable at the most at 25 percent. If in the following year he received a further stock dividend of 60 shares, the new basis price would be computed as follows: $40,000 less $1,905 (the portion of the original cost attributed to the 50 shares sold earlier) divided by 1,060 (the number of shares now held). The new basis price would thus be $35.94.

ENTITLEMENT TO DIVIDENDS

Who is entitled to a dividend that a board of directors has declared? More specifically, the question may be put this way: If a stockholder sells his stock between the date on which a dividend is declared and the date on which it is payable, does he or the buyer get the dividend?

Rights of Buyers and Sellers

The answer depends on the details of the directors' resolution declaring the dividend and, if the stock is listed on a stock exchange, the rules of the exchange. In their resolution declaring a dividend, it is customary for directors to set a record date a week or two beyond the date of the resolution, and a payment date another week or two beyond the record date. Stockholders whose names are on the books at the close of business on the record date are entitled to receive the dividend. Thus, anybody who has bought the stock and has not had it transferred to his own name must effect the transfer by the record date if he is to get the dividend allotted to his shares. It is clear, likewise, that anybody who buys the stock after the date of declaration but in time to get his name on the stockholders' ledger or stock transfer book by the record date will also participate in the dividend, but he will not participate if his purchase is made without enough time for the recording of the transfer by the record date. Sellers and buyers may agree among themselves, of course, on who is to receive a dividend, regardless of the date of sale, but the general rule is that a corporation discharges its responsibility by making the distribution to the stockholders of record on the designated date without having to give attention to such private agreements. If in declaring a dividend the directors do not set a record date, the rule is that the date of declaration is itself the record date.

Stock Exchange Rules

The stock exchanges have their own rules on the entitlement to dividends of buyers and sellers of stocks sold through their facilities. The settlement policy of the New York Stock Exchange, for example, is that each transaction must be settled by the delivery of securities and cash by the fifth full business day following the day of the transaction. Hence, its rule on entitlement to dividends is that the buyer gets the dividend if he buys at any time up to the close of business on the fifth full business day preceding the record date, but the seller gets it if the transaction takes place thereafter. If Friday, August 22, is the record date, the buyer gets the dividend if he buys on Friday, August 15, since the stock will be delivered by the seller's broker on the following Friday, and the transfer can be recorded on that day. But he does not get the dividend if he buys on Monday, August 18, since delivery will not be made until Monday, August 25. When the buyer is entitled to the dividend, the stock is said to sell *dividend-on* or *cum-dividend*—the price he pays covers both the share and the dividend that has been declared on it. When the buyer does not get entitlement to the dividend, the stock is described as selling *ex-dividend*—the price covers the value of the share only. If not affected by immediate influences other than the dividend, the price of the stock at the opening of trading on the fourth full business day preceding the record date—when it goes ex-dividend—can be expected to be lower than the closing price of the preceding day by the amount of the dividend.

Payment Procedure

The secretary of the corporation makes up a list of the stockholders as of the close of business on the record date, their respective shareholdings, and the amount of dividend to which each is entitled. This list is turned over to the treasurer, who makes out and mails the dividend checks. Usually, the checks are mailed ahead of the payment date so that they will reach the stockholders on that date. When corporations employ stock transfer agents, the work both of compiling the list of stockholders and of preparing and mailing the dividend checks is customarily turned over to them.

QUESTIONS

1. Corporations that have large amounts of liabilities shortly coming due should not pay cash dividends to their stockholders. Is this proposition true or false? Discuss.

2. For the typical corporation whose stock is widely held, why is there likely to be some conflict between the corporation's need of cash for expansion and the stockholders' wish to receive cash dividends? How can the conflict be resolved, if at all?

3. In what circumstances may a corporation's policy of paying liberal cash dividends to its stockholders ease its problem of financing expansion?

4. Is it possible for corporations with widely fluctuating annual profits to maintain a policy of regularity in the payment of cash dividends? Explain.

5. What influence should a policy of regular cash dividends on common stock be expected to have on sales of additional common? Sales of preferred stocks? Sales of bonds?

6. Describe the possible dangers of a policy of regularity in the payment of cash dividends.

7. What is implied when the directors of a corporation label a cash dividend as an "extra" dividend? As a "special" dividend?

8. Why are stock dividends described as a strange breed? Why are they, nevertheless, quite popular with most stockholders?

9. How do the objectives of boards of directors usually differ when they declare large stock dividends of, say, 50 or 100 percent, and small stock dividends of, say, 3 or 4 percent?

10. What justification is there for reducing the regular rate of cash dividends following the distribution of a large stock dividend? A small stock dividend? Explain.

11. In their effects, how do large stock dividends resemble and differ from split-ups?

12. In relation to federal income taxation, why may wealthy investors prefer to receive stock dividends in lieu of cash dividends?

13. If a stockholder sells his stock between the date of a dividend declaration and the date of its payment, who, if anybody, is entitled to receive the dividend? Explain.

PROBLEMS

1. At the beginning of the year 19xx, the Dalton Corporation had outstanding 5 million shares of common stock of $5 par value and a balance in its earned surplus account of $20 million. Early in the year, it effected a 5-for-1 split-up of its common stock, reducing the par value to $1, and later in the year it distributed a 40 percent stock dividend.

a) What effect did the split-up have on the number of common shares outstanding and on the corporation's earned surplus?

b) What effect did the stock dividend have on the number of common shares outstanding, the par value of these shares, and the corporation's earned surplus?

2. At the beginning of the year 19xx, Hans Doe owned 1,000 shares of the common stock of the Dalton Corporation referred to in problem 1. He had bought these shares in the preceding year at $84 a share, and in 19xx, several months after he received his stock dividend of 2,000 shares, he sold the dividend shares at $23 a share.

a) Under federal tax regulations, what was Doe's taxable income on receiving 4,000 additional shares on account of the split-up? On receiving the 2,000 shares as a stock dividend? On selling the 2,000 dividend shares?

b) Assuming that in the following year, 19yy, Doe received an additional 300 shares of Dalton stock as a dividend and later sold 200 of these shares at $35 a share, what was his taxable income on receiving the 300-share dividend? On the sale of the 200 shares?

Part IX

FINANCING WITH BONDS

chapter 27

THE NATURE OF BONDS

BONDS AND NOTES

A corporate bond may be described as an unconditional promise of a corporation in writing under seal to pay a specific sum of money to the bearer or to the registered holder at a designated time. Technically, it is the seal that distinguishes corporate bonds from other kinds of corporate promises to pay. Under the common law, a seal made a contract binding on the person who used it with his signature, whether or not other parties to the contract could prove that they had provided consideration. But state statutes have generally demoted seals to a position of insignificance, so that at the present time the person who signs under seal can, as a rule, deny his obligations on the grounds that the party or parties to whom the promise was made gave or promised nothing of value in return.

Practically, therefore, bonds are distinguished from other kinds of corporate promises to pay chiefly by reason of the following features.

1. They are long-term obligations.
2. They are simultaneously promises to pay the face amount, or principal, at a designated date of maturity and to pay interest at a specified rate periodically.
3. They are units of a large number of instruments of identical terms (except, sometimes, the maturity) issued simultaneously.
4. They are issued according to the provisions of a separate comprehensive contract, called an *indenture*, to which reference is made in the bond itself.
5. The separate comprehensive contract is entered into between the corporation and a third party, the *trustee*, to whom reference is also made in the bond.
6. A certification by the trustee appears on the bond to indicate that it is one of the units covered by the indenture.

Bond Certificates

Simply by inspection, a bond or bond certificate, illustrated in Figure 27–1, is readily distinguishable from any other form of corporate promise to pay. For one thing, a bond is usually labeled as such in its heading. For another, it is usually carefully engraved on paper of special quality to discourage attempts at counterfeiting. Again, it usually contains a goodly amount of detail following the specific promise to pay.

1. A statement that it is one of a group issued according to the terms of an indenture entered into on a stated date between the corporation and such-and-such bank or trust company as trustee.
2. A declaration that the bond is issued only in registered form or only in coupon form, or that the bondholder has the right to have the bond in either form and to switch from one to the other.
3. A statement of the corporation's right to call the bond for redemption.
4. A description of the corporation's obligation, if any, to provide for bond retirement through sinking fund contributions.
5. A statement of any special privileges the bondholder may have, such as to convert the bond into common stock.
6. A statement to the effect that provisions of the indenture, except as to the payment of interest and principal, may be modified with the approval of the holders of a stipulated proportion of the bonds (usually 66⅔ or 75 percent).
7. A denial of personal liability of the stockholders, directors, and officers of the corporation for its obligation represented by the bond.
8. A statement that the bond is not valid unless it bears a certification or authentication by the trustee.

Finally, the seal of the corporation continues to be an identifying feature, despite its slight legal importance in most jurisdictions.

By contrast, short-term promissory notes, for example, are often quite simple documents, containing nothing more than the bare recital of the promise to pay with the corporation's signature and those of one or two of its officers. Even when note forms are complex, as are judgment notes and so-called collateral notes such as one signs when borrowing money for stock market transactions, the details included are generally quite different from those of bond certificates, and there is no reference to an indenture or a trustee.

Corporate Issues of Long-Term Notes

Often, corporations put out what appear to be bond issues, but the separate certificates are labeled "notes" rather than "bonds." A newspaper advertisement of a public offering of one corporation's issue of 20-year bonds may appear in close proximity to a notice of the sale of another corporation's issue of 20-year notes. Almost always, however, one will observe that the designation *notes* is reserved for sales of long-

FIGURE 27–1 Bond Certificate

1000 1000

STANDARD OIL COMPANY

(AN INDIANA CORPORATION)

Nº M 00000

THIRTY YEAR 3 1/8% DEBENTURE, DUE OCTOBER 1, 1982

(CONVERTIBLE ON OR BEFORE OCTOBER 1, 1962 UNLESS PREVIOUSLY REDEEMED)

Nº M 00000

Standard Oil Company, a corporation duly organized and existing under the laws of the State of Indiana (hereinafter called the "Company"), for value received, hereby promises to pay to bearer ... the principal sum of

ONE THOUSAND DOLLARS $1000,

[illegible]

Dated October 1, 1952

Standard Oil Company

By Robert E. Wilson SPECIMEN
CHAIRMAN OF THE BOARD

SPECIMEN
PRESIDENT

SPECIMEN
ASST. TREASURER

TRUSTEE'S CERTIFICATE OF AUTHENTICATION

This is one of the Debentures described in the within mentioned Indenture.

CONTINENTAL ILLINOIS NATIONAL BANK AND TRUST COMPANY OF CHICAGO,
AS TRUSTEE

By

AUTHORIZED OFFICER

term debt issues in bulk to one or a few institutional investors—in other words, for private placements.

A reason for the popularity of the designation *notes* for private placements is that, very often, the separate certificates or instruments are, indeed, rather simple note forms rather than elaborately engraved certificates. Another reason is that, sometimes, no trustees are employed in long-term debt transactions via the private placement route. But these are differences in form rather than in substance. For long-term note issues sold to institutional investors, it is customary to draw up long and detailed contracts governing all the terms of the issuing corporations' obligations, whether or not they are called indentures, and whether or not trustees are appointed. Thus, a corporation's obligations on notes sold to institutional investors will generally be much the same as its obligations on bonds sold to the general public. It is to be kept in mind, therefore, that virtually all that is said in these pages about bonds, indentures, pledges of assets, sinking funds, protective provisions, and so on applies as well to notes sold to institutional investors as to bonds sold to the public.

Another Matter of Terminology: Debentures

One may notice that long-term debt instruments offered publicly are often described as "debentures" rather than as "bonds." In August, 1968, for example, a syndicate of investment bankers advertised a public offering of $50 million of 36-year, 6¼ percent debentures of the Wisconsin Telephone Company. In the reports of government agencies, too, one may notice that long-term corporate debt instruments are often described as "bonds, notes, and debentures."

Really, however, the term *debenture* is simply a short form of the more formal term *debenture bond.* As we shall see, debenture bonds are distinguished from other classes of bonds by the fact that the issuing corporations pledge no assets for their safety. For this reason, some people reserve the term *bond* for issues that specify pledges of assets, and use the unadorned term *debenture* for those that lack pledges. But debentures or debenture bonds that are publicly offered are issued according to the terms of detailed contracts or indentures entered into with trustees, so that aside from the matter of pledged assets there is no essential difference between them and instruments that are invariably called bonds. Again, it should be said, therefore, that descriptive materials in these pages pertaining to bonds apply fully to so-called debentures, save where distinctions are clearly indicated.

THE INDENTURE AND THE TRUSTEE

The Indenture

The whole array of terms and conditions on the basis of which bonds are issued is contained in the indenture. Some of these terms and conditions are set out completely in the bond certificates themselves, but most are mentioned only briefly there, if at all, with reference to the indebture for the full statement. The certificate may state, for example, that the bond is secured by a pledge of property, but the description of the property pledged is to be found in the indebture, where, in truth, it may require many pages, such as for a large corporation that pledges widely scattered plant properties of diverse kinds. In the indenture covering the 3⅛ percent first-mortgage bonds of the National Steel Corporation due in 1982, the description of the property pledged requires 49 large printed pages!

The indenture is ordinarily the complete contract. Should there be discrepancies between what is said in the bond certificates and what is said in the indenture, a court might have to be called on to decide which statement should be binding. Customarily, however, greatest care is exercised to ensure that there will be no discrepancies. Nor is there likely to be any question about which indenture applies to which bond issue, as when a corporation has two or more bond issues outstanding simultaneously. Cross-references between certificates and indentures are precise in terms of descriptive titles of the bonds, dates of the indentures, and who are the trustees (the trustee of one bond issue will not ordinarily serve as trustee for another of the same corporation to be outstanding simultaneously). What is more, each indenture contains the complete form of the bond certificates to be issued under it (and the form of the coupons for interest payments, if they are provided for). The wordings of the forms as contained in the indenture are followed with scrupulous accuracy when the certificates (and coupons) are actually engraved and printed.

Indentures are lengthy documents, often running to a hundred or more printed pages. Descriptions of pledged property, as was indicated previously, may require many pages, but even when no property is pledged a great mass of detail must be covered. The objective is to have everything stated so clearly that there will be no occasion for subsequent disputes and litigation over the nature of the rights and privileges of and limitations on the bondholders, the rights and obligations of the corporation, and the duties and powers of the trustee. Because an indenture is a long-term contract, the objective is to anticipate how the corporation and its obligations and the trustee and its relationship to the corporation may be affected by many different kinds of events, and to incorporate provisions for adjustment to these events, such as: how the bonded debt is to be treated should the corporation be involved in a merger or consolidation; how the conversion privilege, if it is given, is to be modified should the corporation effect a split-up in its stock; how supplemental indentures may be used for further issues of bonds of the same kind; how a successor trustee is to be appointed if the original one becomes disqualified or wants to resign; and so on.

No attempt need be made here to outline in detail the contents of typical bond indentures. Without an immediate explanation of the items, a mere listing would be of little value. We can pick up the contents of indentures as we go along, for all features of bonds as discussed in this and subsequent chapters necessarily constitute the substance of indentures.

But a concluding remark: One should know that, in practice, indentures for bond issues are given several names, especially bond indentures, mortgage indentures, trust indentures, trust agreements, and deeds of trust. The names are not fully interchangeable. For example, the contract for a bond issue that contains no pledge of property would not be called a mortgage indenture or a deed of trust; nevertheless, it could be called, with equal propriety, a bond indenture, a trust indenture, or a trust agreement.

The Trustee

On issuing bonds, a corporation becomes indebted to the people who buy them, but its obligation is governed by the indenture—a contract entered into by the corporation with a trustee. Because the bondholders are likely to be widely scattered, and because, in any case, they are likely to hold individually only small portions of the total debt, the trustee is appointed to safeguard their interests, as well as to represent them collectively in any necessary dealings with the corporation. Accordingly, the bondholders are said to be the beneficiaries of the relationship between the corporation and the trustee.

Because trust companies and the trust departments of commercial banks, particularly those of the larger cities, have long specialized in serving as indenture trustees, corporations that issue bonds are inclined to turn to them as a matter of course. Sometimes, investment bankers who are to underwrite a bond issue have something to say about who the trustee shall be, but usually there is not much room for dispute, since the fees and capabilities of the larger trust companies and departments are close to uniformity. Individuals may be selected as trustees, but if they are appointed their role is ordinarily that of cotrustees with trust companies or departments, to which most of the work is delegated.

For indentures that must be qualified under the federal Trust Indenture Act of 1939 (to be further discussed later), appointment of a bank or trust company as trustee is required, although it is permissible to have one or more individuals as cotrustees. The bank or trust company appointed—described as a corporate trustee—must have capital stock and surplus of not less than $150,000 and be subject to supervision by federal or state authorities.

While the role of an indenture trustee as a protector of the bondholders is always stressed, that its services are of great convenience to the corporation ought not to be overlooked. It should be helpful to look separately at these two aspects of its work.

Convenience

If property is pledged for the security of the bondholders, it is easy to make the pledge to the trustee as a single entity; it would be most difficult to try to make pledges individually to hundreds or thousands of bondholders. After a pledge has been made to the trustee, the corporation may want from time to time to sell parcels of the pledged property that have lost their usefulness and to substitute new parcels. Although such a substitution should be advantageous for the bondholders, it would be most difficult to effect were it necessary for the corporation to reach and get the consent of every one of the bondholders. A much more convenient procedure is to provide in the indenture that the trustee shall have the right to approve substitutions. In issuing bonds, many corporations agree to make periodical contributions of cash to sinking funds to be used for retirement of the bonds. It is easy to make these contributions in lump sum to a trustee who then has the responsibility to use the money as the indenture stipulates. Were the corporation not to use the services of the trustee in this connection, disgruntled bondholders might constantly accuse it of improper or unfair management of its sinking fund.

Also for convenience, the corporation can arrange with the trustee for various kinds of useful services of a routine character, thereby relieving itself of clerical burdens, although, of course, for a fee. It may pay interest on an entire bond issue by writing a single check payable to the trustee, and depend on the trustee to make the piecemeal distribution to the bondholders. In a similar way, it may proceed to retire a portion of its bond issue by turning over to the trustee funds equal to the total call price of all bonds called for redemption, and let it parcel these out as the bonds are actually surrendered.

Protection of the Bondholders

The devotion of trustees to their duty of protecting the interests of bondholders is always expected to take precedence over serving the convenience of corporations. That is why they are trustees rather than agents, for trusteeship always implies a high degree of responsibility for the welfare of beneficiaries.

Authentication. A primary protective duty is to see that the bond buyers get genuine bonds of the form provided for in the indenture, and that the corporation does not put out more bonds than the number authorized. Before the delivery of bonds to investment bankers or other buyers, therefore, they are dispatched to the trustee for its certification or authentication. The trustee checks the wording of the bond, the interest coupons (if coupons are being used), and the authentication form to be sure that they are in exact conformity with the wording of these instruments as set out in the indenture itself. The trustee also checks all bond serial numbers to be sure that they are in proper sequence and that there are no duplications. If coupons are being used, the trustee determines that the proper number with the correct interest payment dates are attached to each bond. When these items have been checked to its satisfaction, the trustee signs the authentication form, which appears on the face of the bond certificate. The form is ordinarily a simple statement such as the following.

Trustee's Certificate

This is one of the Bonds described in the within-mentioned Indenture.

FIRST NATIONAL BANK AND TRUST CO.,
As Trustee

By______________________________
Authorized Officer

Checking Compliance with Obligations. Like authentication, some of the other protective duties of the trustee are relatively easy to fulfill. If property is pledged, it is pledged to the trustee; hence, it is readily apparent when and if this obligation is met. Whether or not property is pledged, the corporation agrees to provide adequate insurance coverages on its properties, for the interests of the bondholders would be seriously endangered were they to be destroyed without insurance compensation. But the trustee can easily check on insurance coverages. The corporation agrees to pay all its taxes promptly, since taxing authorities can be expected to obtain tax liens against properties for the amount of unpaid taxes and penalties—liens that generally have a priority of claim over bonds and other ordinary debt. However, checking to see whether or not the corporation is paying its taxes currently is not a difficult task for the trustee. The corporation agrees to keep its properties in good operating condition. Checking for compliance may be a little more difficult here, but surely much less difficult for a single trustee than it would be for hundreds or thousands of scattered bondholders if, individually, they had to check on fulfillment of this covenant.

Problem of More Positive Protective Action. But protection of bondholders surely requires much more than simple checking procedures of the kinds mentioned. Suppose, indeed, that the trustee does find that the corporation is not providing adequate insurance, that it is not paying its taxes when due, and that it is not keeping its properties in a proper state of repair. These are defaults[1]—violations of the corporation's obligations or, to use the term just introduced, its covenants. The defaults may be even more serious, such as nonpayment of stipulated sinking fund contributions or nonpayment of interest. To protect his interests following such defaults, the holder of a $1,000 bond could hardly do much; were he to institute legal actions on his own, the value of his bond would soon be exhausted by the expenses involved. Hence, the idea is that he should be able to look to the trustee for appropriate action, since the trustee's major role is that of protector.

In times past, nevertheless, trustees were often not very enthusiastic about taking action after defaults. In accepting appointments as trustees, they anticipated no vigorous protective action; they indicated this by insisting on the inclusion of exculpatory clauses in indentures. The purpose of these clauses was specifically to relieve them of liability to their beneficiaries—that is, the bondholders—for failure to take protective actions. In fairness to them, it must be said that their fees as trustees were moderate and that they generally had no assurances of reimbursement for money spent in taking protective actions. Accordingly, they were usually satisfied to wait till bondholders banded together to request action, at which time they could demand assurances that whatever expenses might be involved would be reimbursed.

In these circumstances, bondholders simply were not getting the protection that the trustee arrangement was theoretically supposed to give them. On the basis of its own investigations and those of the SEC in the 1930's, Congress took steps to remedy the situation by the adoption of the Trust Indenture Act of 1939. The legislation applies to bond issues for which registration statements must be filed under the Securities Act of 1933, and to those issued in interstate commerce in exchange for other securities of the issuers in recapitalizations—reshufflings of financial structures—and reorganizations (such exchanges in many instances not requiring registration under the Securities Act).

Provisions of the Trust Indenture Act. The Trust Indenture Act outlaws exculpatory clauses, requires the inclusion in every indenture of certain kinds of protective provisions, and imposes on trustees a positive protective role. If there is danger that a trustee may neglect the interests of bondholders because it has other interests in or con-

---

[1]Technically, such violations become "events of default" when a written notice has been given to the corporation, calling attention to them and demanding their correction, and the corporation has failed to make the correction within the period stipulated in the indenture, usually 90 days. The written notice may be given by the trustee or by holders of not less than a stipulated proportion of the bonds, usually 25 percent.

nections with the corporation or the underwriters of the bonds—if, in other words, there is a conflict of interests—it must resign as trustee, eliminate the conflict, or notify the bondholders of the conflict so that they may exercise their powers to terminate the trusteeship. The first step, and probably the third, would lead to the naming of a new or successor trustee. The corporation is required to provide various kinds of information to the trustee, and the trustee, in turn, must make an annual report to the bondholders, accounting for any advances it may have made to the corporation, whatever corporate moneys it may hold, substitutions in pledged property it may have allowed, and whatever amounts of additional bonds it may have authenticated for issue. The trustee is also required to make lists of the bondholders available to individual bondholders on request—a requirement designed to enable bondholders to get in touch with others should they want to propose some kind of concerted action.

However, the most important prod to prositive protective action contained in the Trust Indenture Act is the proviso that on the occurrence of defaults the trustee must exercise its powers with the degree of care and skill that a prudent man would exercise in a similar situation. The prudent man rule is vague—perhaps necessarily so, since it is designed to be applicable in a great variety of circumstances. Nevertheless, it appears to be a great advance beyond exculpatory clauses. At the least, the trustee is on notice that a do-nothing policy after defaults may result in lawsuits brought by bondholders, charging it with negligence and demanding damages for losses incurred on account of the alleged negligence. A court might decide, for example, that a trustee was prudent in letting ride a corporate default in tax payments when prospects were good that the default would be corrected within a few months. But it might decide that another trustee, by letting ride a default in required sinking fund contributions, imprudently permitted an incompetent management to continue to dissipate corporate assets. Even in the matter of the defaulted tax payments, the first trustee could hardly expect to be adjudged prudent were it not to notify the bondholders of the default. In fact, a specific provision of the Trust Indenture Act is that the trustee must give bondholders notice of any default within 90 days of its occurrence.

DETERMINATION OF BOND FEATURES

As soon as a corporate management begins to plan a bond issue, it initiates, in effect, a process of bargaining. For a time, the bargaining may be entirely internal as the members of the management team discuss what they can afford to give and what they hope to get as features of the proposed bond issue. They will expect, as a matter of course, to make certain kinds of concessions and to gain certain ones—

these are the standard features of bond indentures. They may readily admit that certain additional concessions will have to be made because of weaknesses in the corporation's financial position or the state of the securities markets, but, in general, they will want to give as little as possible and to gain as much as possible. But prospective buyers, such as investment bankers and institutional investors, are likely to be astute; they will have an attitude of much the same kind. When, therefore, an approach is made to the prospective buyers, the bargaining will quickly become a serious matter of give and take, with ground yielded or a concession made here to gain an advantage there. Sometimes, managements are thoroughly disillusioned at the outset in finding that prospective investors demand much greater concessions than had been anticipated. In many such cases, plans for bond financing are dropped. At other times, the surprise is the other way around. Management finds that prospective investors are avid for new bond issues and are willing, therefore, to buy on terms quite favorable to the issuers. In the great majority of successful offerings, at any rate, a considerable amount of horse trading will have occurred during the bargaining.

For an analysis of the features of bond issues about which bargaining revolves, we may keep in mind the following classification.

1. The form that the bonds are to have, the unit amounts of their principal, their interest rate, and their maturity.
2. The security to be provided by pledges of assets, if any.
3. Any guaranties the bonds are to have.
4. Protective provisions for the bondholders.
5. Privileges wanted by the corporation.
6. Special inducements to be offered by the corporation.

Unfortunately, however, an examination of these features cannot be made to follow the classification in any precise way. The reason for this is that all the features are closely interrelated. The pledging of a corporation's operating properties may have a significant influence on the interest rate, and even on the maturity of the bond issue. At the same time, the pledge is obviously a protective provision for the bondholders; yet, it could also be considered a special selling feature offered by the corporation. And when a corporation pledges operating property, it is sure to demand certain privileges of possession and use of that property.

Although the overlap can thus be seen to be pervasive, it should be convenient to keep as close to the classification outline as possible. The remainder of the present chapter, therefore, will concentrate on form, principal, interest, and maturity. In Chapter 28, the main focus of attention will be security and guaranties, and in Chapter 29 what is left of items 4, 5, and 6 will be taken up for study.

FORM AND PRINCIPAL

Bond Forms: Registered and Coupon Bonds

Until the middle 1960's, the great mass of new bonds issued year after year by American corporations were coupon bonds, although many issuers were willing to give bond buyers registered bonds should they specifically ask for that form. Beginning in 1963, however, a revolution in the use of the two bond forms took place—a revolution because the switch to registered bonds as the preferred form was so swift that it was virtually complete by the fall of 1967. At the present time, the great majority of new corporate bonds are made available only in registered form, although some corporations, more or less reluctantly, still make the coupon form available to investors who do not like the registered form.

Coupon Bonds. Coupon bonds are so called because there is attached to the bond certificate itself a sheet of coupons, one for each interest payment to be made from the date of issue to the date of maturity. The bond certificate is a promise to pay the principal of the bond to the bearer at maturity, and each coupon, illustrated in Figure 27–2, is of the nature of a promissory note for the interest due on the date inscribed on it payable also the the bearer. As it is customary practice among corporations to make their bond interest payable semiannually, a typical 20-year bond will have 40 coupons attached at the time it is issued.

Despite the revolution, there are great numbers of coupon bonds still outstanding, mostly of older issues, of course, but including portions of some current issues when bond buyers have chosen the coupon form on being given a choice. Accordingly, the merry activity of coupon clipping still goes on, and it will go on for many years, although doubtless in steadily decreasing volume as older coupon bonds mature. As each interest-payment date approaches, the bondholder clips the proper coupon so that it can be sent in as a means of claiming the interest due. In the usual procedure, he turns the coupon over to a commercial bank for collection, depending on it to take care of the clerical chores of picking up the payment. The bank, in turn, sends the coupon direct to the corporation or its designated paying agent, or indirectly through a metropolitan bank serving as correspondent. Most likely, the corporation will have issued to the trustee as its paying agent a single check for the total amount of interest on all coupons coming due at the time, and the trustee then parcels out this money when it makes payment on the coupons as they come in from all directions.

Registered Bonds. In the days when coupon bonds predominated some of the corporations that were willing to provide alternative registered bonds designated that these bonds could be registered

FIGURE 27–2 Bond Coupons

"as to principal" only, while the rest were willing to have their bonds "fully registered"—that is, registered as to both principal and interest. But the revolution of the 1960's, referred to previously, has been almost entirely a movement toward fully registered issues.

A registered bond, whether fully registered or registered only as to principal, bears the name of the owner on its face, for it is "to the order of" this named owner that the corporation promises to make its payment of principal at maturity (or earlier, should the bond be called for redemption before maturity). In the case of fully registered bonds, likewise, it is "to the order of" the named owner that the corporation promises to make its semiannual interest payments by check direct or through a paying agent. For either type of registration, in any event, the corporation or the trustee keeps a record of the owners of the registered bonds, and the record must be changed, as for stock certificates, when a sale or other transfer takes place. The original owner endorses the bond certificate in blank or to the order of the buyer or other transferee, and the buyer sends it in for cancellation, getting a new registered bond payable to his order or, possibly, a coupon bond if he has that choice and exercises it.

If a bond is registered as to principal only, coupons in bearer form for all interest-payment dates are attached, and as each date approaches the proper coupon is clipped and sent in for payment as with regular coupon bonds.

Advantages of Registered Bonds. Most of the advantages claimed for registered bonds appear to be quite valid, as one would expect in trying to account for the extraordinary speed with which the preference for them developed. For all classes of investors, large and small, individual and institutional, a principal claimed advantage is

safety. Since a corporation has no complete record of the owners of its coupon bonds, it is often difficult if not impossible for owners of such bonds that have been lost, stolen, or destroyed as by fire to prove ownership and to get replacements. Moreover, because bonds and coupons are negotiable instruments, even proof of (previous) ownership is of no avail toward gaining repossession of lost or stolen coupon bonds and coupons that get into the hands of people who qualify as innocent third parties—"innocent holders for value," in legal terms.[2]

On the other hand, a person can get good title to a registered bond only if the original owner endorses it. If a registered bond is stolen, destroyed, or lost, the registered owner can usually get a replacement from the corporation with little difficulty and only slight cost.[3]

---

[2]For an earlier brief treatment of the quality of negotiability, introduced in the discussion of stock certificates, see p. 413.

[3]The corporation is likely to require an indemnity bond to protect itself should the bond alleged to have been stolen, lost, or destroyed turn up properly endorsed in legitimate hands. But insurance companies supply indemnity bonds at moderate cost to people who have good reputations.

Another advantage claimed for registered bonds, especially from the standpoint of small investors, is that the corporation or trustee can notify them by letter should their bonds be called for redemption or should a privilege of convertibility be about to expire. Holders of coupon bonds, on the other hand, may lose interest income by retaining them beyond their redemption dates, or much more in potential capital gains by retaining them beyond the expiration dates for conversion rights because they failed to see newspaper advertisements announcing the redemption or the approaching expiration of convertibility.

For institutional investors that hold large volumes of bonds in their investment portfolios, and for banks and trust companies that hold large volumes for the investment and safekeeping accounts of their customers, additional advantages claimed for registered bonds are principally economies in the time required to clip and handle coupons, and economies in the storage space needed for the bonds. In 1963, when the revolution in bond forms was just starting, the United States Trust Company of New York reported its estimate that 300 million coupons were being clipped annually at a labor cost of 113,200 man-days worth $1.8 million—a cost that did not cover all the additional work of counting, processing, and burning coupons after they had been turned in. It also reported that it had a mile and a half of shelves for the storage of its customers' bonds.[4] It is pointed out, in regard to storage, that coupons make bonds bulky and that registered bonds can be issued quite conveniently in large denominations, as, for example, a single registered bond for $1 million in place of 1,000 coupon bonds of $1,000 denomination, or 200 of $5,000 denomination.

The principal advantages to the corporate issuer of bonds claimed for fully registered issues are elimination of the costs of engraving and printing coupons, reduction of the cost of printing bond certificates, avoidance of the substantial expense of newspaper advertising of calls for redemption and expirations of conversion rights, and, especially, its knowledge at all times of who its bondholders are, thereby giving it the means to reach them direct should it have any problems to take up with them, such as proposals to amend the indenture.

Defense of Coupon Bonds. However, some classes and groups of investors have been displeased with the sweeping substitution of registered bonds for coupon bonds in most of the recent and current issues. These investors do not object to the issuance of registered bonds to buyers who prefer that form, but it is their position that investors who want the coupon form, including themselves, should be able to get it, too. Their preference for the coupon form is based

---

[4] *The Wall Street Journal,* Midwest Edition, July 9, 1963, p. 6.

chiefly on ease of transfer. Because a coupon bond is payable to bearer, it is transferable by mere delivery, but transfer of a registered bond requires its cancellation, the issuance of a new bond to the transferee, and the making of appropriate entries in the record books. These investors claim, therefore, that the marketability of registered bonds is reduced somewhat by the very process of registration, that this lessened marketability results in lower selling prices for holders who want to sell, and that it is even possible for investors to suffer interest losses because of delays in registration. They also claim that delays in registration and lessened marketability often result when investors want to sell registered bonds that they have placed with custodians for safekeeping—that the custodians must be supplied with bond powers (powers of attorney) to effect transfers, whereas with coupon bonds they could be simply instructed to make delivery. And, further, the claim is made that large investors may want to keep secret the fact that they are selling large blocks of given bond issues from their portfolios. This is possible with bearer instruments but not with registered instruments.[5]

Principal

When bond issues consisted chiefly or entirely of coupon bonds, there was not much question about the principal or face amount of each bond, as $1,000 was the standard denomination. If you were simply offered "a bond" or if you said you had "a bond" to sell, the implication was always that the face amount of the instrument was $1,000. Some corporations also made bonds available in $5,000 denominations, and a few went higher, while a few went in the opposite direction from $1,000, providing for baby bonds in denominations of $500 or $100 or both, and occasionally even smaller denominations.

On the other hand, a much wider range of registered bond denominations especially in the upward direction is usually available, although $1,000 is still the basic unit. A small proportion of issuing corporations also make provisions for registered bonds with denominations of less than $1,000. A feature of the revolutionary switch of recent years from coupon bonds to registered bonds is that the owner of registered bonds is usually privileged to have their denominations changed without charge, as by surrendering a $5,000 bond for 5 of $1,000 denomination, whereas before the switch a service charge of $2 per bond was usually levied to have a bond registered and to change denominations among registered bonds.

---

[5]The mutual savings bankers, in particular, have been critical of corporate bond issues of the all-registered kind. For a description of the report on this matter by a committee on portfolio management of the National Association of Mutual Savings Banks, see *Savings Bank Journal,* May, 1968, pp. 22–23.

Bond Price Quotations

While the standard unit for corporation bonds remains at $1,000, bond prices are quoted in terms of $100 of face value. If a corporation sells a bond issue to investment bankers "at 98," it received $980 for each $1,000 of the issue; similarly, if a person buys a bond of $1,000 denomination at a price of 103, he pays $1,030.

Bonds are usually sold at a designated price "plus accrued interest." If the interest payment dates on a $1,000 bond quoted at 103 are January 1 and July 1, and if the buyer buys on January 16, he pays $1,030 plus interest for 15 days on the principal of $1,000 at the rate designated in the bond itself. But on July 1 he receives interest for a full six-month period, so that his net interest income represents, as it should, earnings for the actual period of ownership from January 16 to July 1. Similarly, for bonds originally issued on January 16, with January 1 and July 1 designated as interest payment dates, a corporation receives the selling price and accrued interest for 15 days; but on July 1 it has a full 6-month interest payment to make.

When a corporation has failed to meet its interest obligation on any due date, or when it has announced that it cannot meet an approaching interest obligation, market prices for its bonds will ordinarily be quoted "flat." This means that buyers pay the prices at which bonds are offered without any additions for accrued interest. Because of uncertainty about the size of interest payments, if any, to be expected on income bonds, discussed in the next section of this chapter, they are usually also bought and sold in the market on a flat basis.

INTEREST RATES AND YIELDS

Interest is the price paid for the use of loanable funds. When a corporation borrows by selling a bond issue, it contracts to pay this price periodically at a designated rate over a long period of time. Whether it can afford to pay the price demanded by prospective buyers depends, as we saw in Chapter 13, on the rate of profit it expects to earn from use of the proceeds in its productive operations, and as we saw in Chapter 14, on how the interest rate is to be weighted to make it a realistic cost of capital. Surely the best method for estimating the anticipated rate of profit to be earned on money borrowed by means of a bond issue is the discounted cash flow method, since it exactly parallels the preferred method for determining the interest cost of such borrowing—determination on the basis of the *discounted* cash flows *outward* for interest and principal payments. In weighting the interest rate to derive a realistic cost of capital, one will recall from the discussion in Chapter 14 that: (1) allowance must be made for the deductibility of interest in the determination of taxable income; (2) the interest rate to be paid on borrowings must generally be weighted with a higher rate "equity element" because of bond buyers' insistence on a cushion of protection provided by stockholders; and (3) on the other hand, an existing debt-equity ratio much below the corporation's optimum ratio (as judged by its management) justifies giving reduced weight to the equity element.

If, then, the corporation's anticipated rate of profit to be derived from the investment of money to be derived from a bond issue is significantly higher than the interest rate *as converted to a cost-of-capital rate,* and if other aspects, such as dangers of insolvency and the kinds of restrictive covenants to be included in the indenture, are favorable, it will surely want to go ahead with the bond flotation. But if these elements are adverse, proceeding with the bond issue would surely appear to be a foolish venture.

Determinants of Interest Rates

All the bargaining in connection with proposed bond issues tends to focus on the interest rate; it is not something to be considered as if it were an independent feature. If the corporation is willing to grant certain kinds of special concessions to the bond buyers, it will expect to be able to shade the interest rate downward (or, perhaps, to *move* it downward by as much as a percentage point or two if the concession is a quite attractive one, such as convertibility into common stock offered at a time of stock market boom). But if it wants to reserve certain special rights to itself, the corporation may have to pay for them through an upward shading of the interest rate. Thus, many of the major features of the indenture will directly influence the level of the interest rate as finally agreed on—if, indeed, agreement is reached.

But the shading or moving of an interest rate upward or downward requires a starting point. The bargaining does not wander over a wide range of possible interest rates. With allowance for special concessions and reservations of rights, bargaining tends to be quickly confined to a narrow range based on two considerations: the state of the market for long-term obligations, and the credit standing of the corporation that proposes to put out a new bond issue.

State of the Market. An analysis of the state of the market usually begins by reference to the current yields on the long-term obligations of the U.S. Treasury. If these are relatively high, the market is tight—that is, the supply of funds investors are willing to commit to long-term debt instruments is moderate in relation to the demand for such funds. Accordingly, any corporation, regardless of its credit standing, must expect to set a relatively high interest rate on any new bond issue it proposes to sell. If, however, the current yields on long-term Treasury obligations are relatively low, the supply of funds available for long-term investment in bonds and other obligations is plentiful in relation to demand, and the market is therefore easy. Regardless of its credit standing, a corporation planning to put out a new bond issue will expect to obtain its funds at a rate of interest substantially less than it would have to name in a tight situation.

The state of the market for long-term Treasury obligations is determinable at all times, and not simply at times when the Treasury is offering new long-term issues. This is the significance of yields. The yield of a bond is the *true* or *effective* rate of interest that the buyer will earn from the time of purchase till maturity if he buys at a given price. It is determined by the price, the rate of interest that the issuer of the bond has promised to pay (the *nominal* rate), and the time to maturity. It changes with every change in market price. If a Treasury obligation due in 10 years and bearing interest at 4 percent can be bought at par, the yield is also 4 percent—the nominal and effective rates are identical. But if the 10-year, 4 percent bond is selling in the market at 85⅛, investors are obviously demanding a rate of return higher than 4 percent. They want $20 as interest each 6 months on an investment of $850.125, and they also want $1,000 at maturity, even though they invest only $850.125 now. Actually, as one may see in the sample portions of bond tables presented in Table 27–1, the investor would be earning 6 percent on his investment of $850.125—6 percent would be the effective rate or yield. The market would be much tighter than it was when the bond sold at par. (The effective rate or yield of 6 percent is found in the 4 percent bond table by running down the 10-year maturity column until the price 85.12 is found, then horizontally leftward to the yield column where the [percentage] yield of 6.00 is found. Needless to add that the table price of 85.12 is so close to the hypothetical market price of 85⅛ that they are virtually identical.)

Similarly, if the investor were willing to pay 118 for the bond he would be accepting a yield of only 2 percent, and the market would be extremely easy by comparison with its state when the yield was 4 percent. (Again, the yield is found by running down the 10-year maturity column, but in this instance stopping at the first price entry of 118.05, and then going horizontally leftward to the 2.00 in the yield column.) If the bond had 15 years to run until maturity, a market price of 118 would give a yield of approximately 2.5 percent, and a market price of 85⅛ would give a yield of approximately 5.5 per cent—yields that the student should check by consulting Table 27–1.

Digression on the Use of Bond Tables. Aside from their usefulness for the determination of yields when the nominal interest rate, the market price, and the maturity of bonds are known, bond tables are useful when the investor wants to know what price he should pay

TABLE 27–1
Sample Portions of Bond Tables

	Years to maturity											
Yield	¼	½	*1*	*2*	*3*	*5*	*10*	*15*	*20*	*25*	*30*	*40*
	4% bond, with interest payable semiannually											
2.00	100.49	100.99	101.97	103.90	105.80	109.47	118.05	125.81	132.83	139.20	144.96	154.89
2.50	100.37	100.74	101.47	102.91	104.31	107.01	113.20	118.67	123.50	127.76	131.53	137.79
3.00	100.24	100.49	100.98	101.93	102.85	104.61	108.58	112.01	114.96	117.50	119.69	123.20
3.25	100.18	100.37	100.73	101.44	102.13	103.44	106.36	108.85	110.97	112.77	114.30	116.72
3.50	100.12	100.25	100.49	100.96	101.41	102.28	104.19	105.80	107.15	108.29	109.24	110.72
3.75	100.05	100.12	100.24	100.48	100.70	101.13	102.07	102.85	103.50	104.03	104.48	105.16
4.00	99.99	100.00	100.00	100.00	100.00	100.00	100.00	100.00	100.00	100.00	100.00	100.00
4.25	99.93	99.88	99.76	99.53	99.30	98.88	97.98	97.25	96.65	96.17	95.78	95.21
4.50	99.87	99.76	99.52	99.05	98.61	97.78	96.01	94.59	93.45	92.54	91.81	90.76
4.75	99.80	99.63	99.28	98.59	97.93	96.70	94.08	92.02	90.39	89.09	88.07	86.63
5.00	99.74	99.51	99.04	98.12	97.25	95.62	92.21	89.53	87.45	85.82	84.55	82.77
5.50	99.62	99.27	98.56	97.20	95.90	93.52	88.58	84.81	81.94	79.75	78.08	75.84
6.00	90.49	99.03	98.09	96.28	94.58	91.47	85.12	80.40	76.89	74.27	72.32	69.80
	5% bond, with interest payable semiannually											
3.00	100.49	100.99	101.96	103.85	105.70	109.22	117.17	124.02	129.92	135.00	139.38	146.41
3.50	100.36	100.74	101.46	102.87	104.24	106.83	112.56	117.39	121.45	124.86	127.72	132.16
4.00	100.24	100.49	100.97	101.90	102.80	104.49	108.18	111.20	113.68	115.71	117.38	119.87
4.25	100.17	100.37	100.73	101.42	102.09	103.35	106.06	108.26	110.04	111.48	112.65	114.37
4.50	100.11	100.24	100.48	100.95	101.39	102.22	103.99	105.41	106.55	107.46	108.19	109.24
4.75	100.05	100.12	100.24	100.47	100.69	101.10	101.97	102.66	103.20	103.64	103.98	104.46

TABLE 27–1 *Continued*
Sample Portions of Bond Tables

					Years to maturity							
Yield	*¼*	*½*	*1*	*2*	*3*	*5*	*10*	*15*	*20*	*25*	*30*	*40*
5.00	99.98	100.00	100.00	100.00	100.00	100.00	100.00	100.00	100.00	100.00	100.00	100.00
5.25	99.92	99.88	99.76	99.53	99.31	98.91	98.07	97.43	96.93	96.54	96.24	95.84
5.50	99.86	99.76	99.52	99.07	98.63	97.84	96.19	94.94	93.98	93.25	92.69	91.95
5.75	99.80	99.64	99.28	98.60	97.96	96.78	94.36	92.53	91.15	90.12	89.34	88.31
6.00	99.74	99.51	99.04	98.14	97.29	95.73	92.56	90.20	88.44	87.14	86.16	84.90
6.50	99.61	99.27	98.57	97.23	95.97	93.68	89.10	85.76	83.34	81.59	80.31	78.71
7.00	99.49	99.03	98.10	96.33	94.67	91.68	85.79	81.61	78.64	76.54	75.06	73.25
					6% bond, with interest payable semiannually							
4.00	100.48	100.98	101.94	103.81	105.60	108.98	116.35	122.40	127.36	131.42	134.76	139.74
4.50	100.35	100.73	101.45	102.84	104.17	106.65	111.97	116.23	119.65	122.38	124.56	127.71
5.00	100.23	100.49	100.96	101.88	102.75	104.38	107.79	110.47	112.55	114.18	115.45	117.23
5.25	100.17	100.37	100.72	101.41	102.06	103.26	105.78	107.72	109.22	110.38	111.27	112.49
5.50	100.10	100.24	100.48	100.93	101.37	102.16	103.81	105.06	106.02	106.75	107.31	108.05
5.75	100.04	100.12	100.24	100.47	100.68	101.07	101.88	102.49	102.95	103.29	103.55	103.90
6.00	99.98	100.00	100.00	100.00	100.00	100.00	100.00	100.00	100.00	100.00	100.00	100.00
6.25	99.92	99.88	99.76	99.54	99.33	98.94	98.16	97.59	97.17	96.86	96.63	96.34
6.50	99.85	99.76	99.52	99.08	98.66	97.89	96.37	95.25	94.45	93.86	93.44	92.90
7.00	99.73	99.52	99.05	98.16	97.34	95.84	92.89	90.80	89.32	88.27	87.53	86.63

for a bond if he wants to earn a specific yield. If, for example, he wants to earn at least 5¾ percent on a bond bearing interest at 5 percent and having 25 years to run to maturity, the 5 percent table shows him that he should pay not more than 90⅛ for it (really 90.12 as found where the 5.75 percent yield line intersects with the 25-year column). If he would be satisfied to earn 5¼ percent on a 6 percent bond that had 20 years to run to maturity, the 6 percent table would show him that he should pay about 109¼ for it (indicated by the price 109.22 at the intersection of the 5.25 percent yield line with the 20-year column). Knowing the yield, the market price, and the maturity of a bond, the investor or the student could also use bond tables to determine the interest rate carried by the bond. Knowing the yield, interest rate, and market price, he could determine the maturity from bond tables; but so much publicity is given to interest rates on and maturities of outstanding bond issues and new issues to be marketed that bond tables are rarely used to answer these two kinds of questions.

Even though exact yields and exact market prices cannot be found in a given bond table, they can be readily approximated from the entries there. The student was introduced to the procedure of interpolation in Chapter 13 in connection with the use of present-value tables (if he did not know about it already) so that the explanation here can surely be brief. Suppose, for example, that a 20-year bond bearing interest at 5 percent is selling in the market at 92. The 5 percent bond table reveals that at a price of 93.98 the yield would be 5.5 percent, and that at a price of 91.15 the yield would be 5.75 percent, so that a difference in price of $2.83 accounts for a difference in yield of .25 percent. Relating the market price of 92 to the two table prices in the process of interpolation, we could then say that the yield at 92 must be approximately 5.5 plus $\frac{198}{283} \times .25$, or that it is 5.75 minus $\frac{85}{283} \times .25$. In either case, the result is 5.67 percent. Similarly, if one wants a yield of 4.75 percent on a 6 percent bond that has 15 years to run to maturity, he finds that he should be willing to pay 116.23 for a 4.50 percent yield, and 110.47 for a 5 percent yield. Since the desired yield is midway between the 4.5 percent and 5 percent yields, the price to give this yield should be approximately midway also—that is, 116.23 minus 5.76/2 or 110.47 plus 5.76/2, resulting in either case in a price of 113.35.

Finally for this digression, it should be instructive to point out that the price entries in the bond tables are simply sums of present values of the kinds that were treated at length in Chapter 13. The market price of a bond at any time is the present value of its principal amount to be paid at maturity, discounted at the yield rate per period for the number of interest periods to maturity, *plus* the present value of an annuity of the semiannual interest payments to be received, discounted also at the yield rate per period for the number of interest periods to maturity. For example, Table 27–1 shows that the market price of a 4 percent bond that has 5 years to run to maturity is 109.47 to yield 2 percent per year, and that it is 91.47 to yield 6 percent. But Table 13–2, page 298, reveals that the present value of $1 discounted for 10 periods at 1 percent per period (that is, the yield for each 6-month period) is .9053, and Table 13–5, page 304, reveals that the present value of an annuity of $1 of 20 (semiannual) periods discounted at 1 percent per period amounts to 9.4714. Accordingly, the present discounted value of $100 face amount of bonds is $100 × .9053, or $90.53, and the present discounted value of the annuity of semiannual interest payments of $2 to be received on the bond is $2.00 × 9.4714 or $18.94, for a total of $109.47, which is the entry in the bond table. Likewise, Table 13–1 reveals that the present value of $1 discounted for 10 years at 3 percent per period of 6 months is .7441, and Table 13–2 reveals that the present value of an annuity of $1 for 20 periods discounted at 3 percent per period amounts to 8.5302, so that the combined present values for $100 face amount of bonds amount to $100 × .7441, or $74.41, plus $2.00 × 8.5302, or $17.06, for a total of $91.47, which, again, is equal to the entry in the bond table.

Credit Standing of the Issuer. Besides indicating degrees of ease and tightness in the market for long-term funds, current yields on long-term Treasury obligations are useful as guides to the specific levels at which interest rates on new bond issues should be set for given corporations in view of their very different credit standings. The yields on Treasury obligations are basic because of their risklessness in the credit sense. No investor doubts that the Treasury will meet its interest and principal obligations on time and in full. The federal government has broad taxing powers with which it can *compel* people to pay into the Treasury a sufficient amount of money to enable it to meet all its obligations, and should its finances really get into a chaotic state it could use its sovereign money-creating powers and simply print new money to pay interest and principal on its obligations.

No corporation can claim risklessness of this degree. But some can claim a very high degree of risklessness when bargaining with investment bankers or other prospective buyers of proposed new bond issues. Their credit standings, as judged by their financial structures, their records of meeting obligations in the past, their earnings and dividend records, their prospective future earnings, investor evaluations of the competence of their managements, and other factors, are extremely good. These corporations can argue, therefore, that interest rates to be set on their new issues of bonds need not be much higher than the yields on Treasury obligations of comparable maturities, that differentials of one fourth, one half, or three fourths of a percentage point ought to suffice to attract buyers. The managements of other corporations of somewhat weaker credit positions may concede at the outset of bargaining negotiations that the differential could hardly be less than 1 or 1½ percentage points; and the managers of still weaker corporations may readily agree that the differential could hardly be less than 2 or even 3 percentage points. Bargaining at a time of ease in the market for long-term funds when the yield on 20-year Treasury bonds is, say, 3 percent, a strong corporation may expect to sell a 20-year issue at an interest rate of 3¼ or 3⅜ percent. But if the market is tight and the yield on the Treasury bonds is 5¼ percent, bargaining on the corporation's issue may start in the vicinity of 5¾ percent. Similarly, rate discussions concerning a proposed bond issue of a corporation that has material credit weaknesses may start at 5 or 5½ percent in a period of ease and at 6½ or 7 percent in a period of tightness.

When a corporation negotiates with investment bankers to have its bond issue underwritten, it must expect its true interest cost to be somewhat higher than the yield that the ultimate investor is willing to accept. Its flotation costs, including most importantly the bankers' commission, increase the price it must pay for borrowed money. A bond issue bearing interest at 5 percent to be offered to the public at par will obviously cost the corporation more than 5 percent annually if it is underwritten by the investment bankers "at 98." Moreover, a tentative agreement about the interest rate and the price to the bankers reached early in the negotiations remains subject to adjustment until shortly before the effective date of the registration statement required by the federal Securities Act.[6]

Other Aspects of Interest Rates

As a rule, any corporation must expect to pay a higher rate of interest on a bond issue than would be asked of it on short-term bank loans or on other forms of short-term borrowing. For lengthy periods before the early 1930's, short-term rates for given classes of borrowers were higher than long-term rates for the same classes; during these periods, therefore, a rate advantage could be enjoyed in long-term borrowing. But since the early 1930's, long-term rates for specific classes of borrowers have persisted at higher levels than comparable short-term rates. Except for brief intervals, as the year 1966 and the first quarter of 1967, the yield curve, as we say, has been continually upsweeping.

An upsweeping yield curve indicates that corporations and other

[6]This timing of the final agreement was mentioned in Chapter 18 in connection with the pricing of underwritten stock issues. See p. 456.

borrowers can economize in interest payments by borrowing for short terms, even though the money is to be used for long-term purposes. If money is needed for 20 years, why not borrow for one year at the lower rate, borrow elsewhere for another year at the end of the first to repay the original loan, and so continue throughout the 20-year period? But corporate managements do not see it this way. For one thing, short-term borrowing for long-term purposes would weaken their working capital ratios, probably endangering their access to trade credit, inventory loans, and the like. Another consideration is the danger of insolvency—the danger of not being able to refinance the loans on schedule annually, as in periods of tight money. Finally, there is the possibility that the whole schedule of interest rates will rise. Though the yield curve might still be upsweeping after two or three years, the short-term rate for a given borrower at that time might be higher than the rate for a bond issue would have been originally.

An upsweeping yield curve or pattern of interest rates means that for given classes of borrowers higher and higher rates must be designated the longer the maturities of their obligations. A corporation of a certain credit ranking can expect to pay a higher interest rate on a 10-year bond issue than on one for 5 years, a higher rate on a 20-year issue than on one for 15 years, and so on. This suggests a means of economizing more practical than annual borrowings and repayments. Corporations can save interest expenses from year to year while given bond issues are outstanding by not overestimating the periods for which long-term funds will be needed. Often, corporations have put out bond issues running for 20 years and longer only to find that they could devote a sufficient amount of the cash throw-offs from depreciation and earnings to retire the bonds in much shorter periods. Had they made the maturities of the bond issues 10, 12, or 15 years in the first place, therefore, their annual interest charges while the bonds were outstanding would have been less.

The practical aspect of this for the generality of corporations was indicated by a strong trend toward shorter maturities for many years up to the early 1950's, followed by a moderate movement in the opposite direction. In the early years of the present century, maturities of 40 and 50 years and longer were common, but nowadays new bond issues with maturities beyond 30 years are exceptional. Often, indeed, corporations put out bond issues of 15- and 20-year maturities even when the proceeds are to be used to acquire assets expected to have lives much longer than 15 or 20 years. The individual corporation expects to pay off a portion of such an issue during the initial period, and then to float a new issue to obtain funds to pay off the balance at its maturity—that is, as we say, to refund the balance.

When yield curves are upsweeping, a further means of economizing in interest payments is to issue bonds that have staggered maturities. Such serial bonds, as they are called, will be examined later in the discussion of bond maturities.

Importance of Timing

Because a bond interest rate, once set, must be paid during the entire life of the bonds, regardless of what may happen to market rates of interest during that period, and because the whole schedule of market rates fluctuates upward and downward with changes in the overall demand for and supply of long-term funds, care in timing bond issues is important. Suppose, for example, that a corporation puts out a 20-year bond issue bearing an interest rate of 5 percent, and that within a year or two the market rate for bonds of similar quality goes to 6 percent and stays in that vicinity for a lengthy period. The corporation's managers would have good reason to be pleased with their timing. The corporation would continue to pay 5 percent on its outstanding bonds, while other corporations of comparable credit standing would have to pay 6 percent on theirs were they to be borrowing in the later period. The differential of 1 percentage point could represent quite a handsome saving; for example, it would amount to $200,000 a year if the corporation's bond issue amounted to $20 million. On the other hand, the corporation's managers would have reason to regret their poor timing were they to put out the bond issue at 5 percent and then find market rates for bonds of the same quality and maturity falling to 4½ percent within a period of a few months. Better forecasting, they might conclude, should have indicated the desirability of a deferment of the financing or, perhaps, the desirability of short-term interim financing to be repaid out of the proceeds of a deferred bond issue.

A difficulty of timing is that long-term interest rates—and, in truth, the whole schedule of interest rates—tend to be relatively low in periods of business recession and depression, and relatively high in periods of prosperity and boom. In the periods of recession and depression, however, expansion projects are neither pressing nor attractive for most businesses, and, of course, their very lack of demand for funds is a principal reason that interest rates fall. Thus, advantage of the low rates cannot be gained by most corporations. Some, however, borrow new money for expansion projects despite the cloudy outlook, and a larger number sell refunding issues—borrow at the low rates and use the proceeds to retire earlier issues bearing higher interest rates. In periods of business expansion, the renewed attractiveness of projects for the acquisition of facilities prompts corporations to hurry into the market to get long-term funds, but their very demand causes interest rates to rise. Probably most managements take the attitude that though they missed the opportunity to borrow at the lowest rates they had better go ahead with the financing before rates move to still higher levels. Some, however, decide that a rise in rates is temporary. At such times, as in the fall of 1967 and the spring of 1968, we hear that the financing of this or that corporation has been postponed. In many cases, too, a rise in rates brings them to a level above anticipated rates of profit on expansion projects, so that common sense demands that the projects be postponed or abandoned.

Interest Rates and Bond Prices

From what was said earlier about nominal and effective rates of interest on bond issues, one should see that a corporation can agree to pay a certain effective rate without actually naming this rate in its bond certificates and indenture. On a 15-year issue, for example, it could set a 5 percent rate but by selling the bonds at 94.94 actually provide the investor a yield of 5½ percent. Other combinations of prices and nominal rates could similarly be chosen to give an effective rate of 5½ percent on a 15-year issue, such as a nominal rate of 4½ percent and a price of 89.88, a rate of 5¼ percent and a price of 97.47, a rate of 5¾ percent and a price of 102.53, and a rate of 6 percent and a price of 105.06.

All this suggests that careful pricing may give some advantage in selling, even though it is not designed to alter the effective rate and has no such result. Offering bonds at prices below par, in particular, tends to enhance their attractiveness to certain classes of investors. Small investors sometimes feel they are getting a bargain in being able to buy at a discount. But more important is that within certain limits large investors who report their income for tax purposes on a cash basis may report as a long-term capital gain, rather than as ordinary income, the difference between the price paid and the price at which a bond is redeemed (provided that it has been held by the taxpayer for more than six months). Nevertheless, most issues of bonds are offered to ultimate investors at their par value of $100.

Income Bonds

Outstanding at the present time are a few issues of bonds on which the interest obligation need not be met currently if earnings are insufficient to cover it. These issues are known as income bonds, although the word *income* does not necessarily appear in their titles. For example, the 4 percent "adjustment" bonds of the Atchison, Topeka & Santa Fe Railway Company, due in 1995, are of the income variety.

Features of Income Bonds. Since interest is payable currently on income bonds only if earned, a failure to pay for lack of earnings is not a default; it does not give the bondholders and their trustee the right to take action to force payment, such as by seeking judgment or forcing a reorganization in bankruptcy. As a rule, last year's earnings determine how much interest is to be paid this year. The indentures for income bonds set down in considerable detail the rules for determining what amounts of earnings are available for bond interest. Whatever earnings are determined to be available by application of these rules *must* be used in meeting the interest obligation up to the full amount of the coupon rate. If the earnings are sufficient to meet only a part of the obligation, they must be so used. Some indentures provide, however, that interest need be paid only in round amounts, such as even ¼ or ½ percentage points or multiples thereof.

In some indentures, interest unpaid for lack of earnings cumulates fully and must be paid when earnings become available or, if the insufficiency of earnings continues, at maturity when the principal comes due. But a corporation that, for lack of earnings, has a big accumulation of interest to pay at maturity may find it impossible to pay either the accumulation or the principal. In other indentures, interest accumulates for only three years or thereabouts. If, therefore, earnings still do not materialize, the interest payment obligation goes into suspension, although the three-year accumulation or whatever it may be is still added to the principal as an absolute obligation at maturity.

It is stipulated in some indentures that interest may be paid on the bonds at the discretion of corporate directors, even though sufficient earnings are not available. In some, it is provided that certain events will make the interest obligation a fixed one, as in other classes of bonds, or that the corporate directors may simply make a decision to fix the interest obligation.

Finally, income bonds, like other bonds, have fixed dates of maturity. The obligation of a corporation to pay principal (and unpaid cumulative interest) at that time is not subject to deferment, regardless of the state of earnings.

Reasons for Use. Prominent among the reasons for use of income bonds has been to speed the process of corporate reorganizations, particularly of railroad companies. Several of the issues now outstanding originated in the railroad reorganizations of the 1890's and the 1930's. In a reorganization, a major objective is to cut down substantially on the fixed charges to which the rehabilitated enterprise will be subject. It presumably got into difficulties because of the disproportion between its debt burdens and its earning capacity; hence, it would benefit little if it emerged from reorganization with the same debt burdens. One way to cut down on these burdens is to make what was formerly a fixed-interest obligation a contingent one. Thus, income bonds have been forced on bondholders and other creditors who have had weak claims—holders of the bankrupt enterprises' junior obligations.

More recently, some interest in income bonds has developed among the managers of solvent corporations because of their important possibilities as substitutes for preferred stock. Several corporations have offered income bonds to their preferred stockholders in exchange for their shares, and a few have sold issues of income bonds and used the proceeds to retire their outstanding preferred stock or to pay off debts. For example, Armour & Company put out a very large issue of income bonds in 1954 in exchange for its outstanding $6 cumulative preferred stock. In 1956, the Curtis Publishing Company likewise offered income bonds as partial payment for the surrender of preferred stock. Trans World Airways sold an issue of well over $100 million in 1961, and used the proceeds to pay off interim notes that had been issued to institutional investors for borrowings to buy aircraft. The Armour issue has had a clear record of regular interest payments. The Curtis Publishing Company failed to pay any interest in 1965 and again the payment due on April 1, 1968, so that it then had an arrearage of 9 percent. Trans World Airways missed interest payments in 1962 and 1963, but made them up in 1964 and has since made regular payments. In view of their not unfavorable experience with income bonds in reorganizations, railroads have shown considerable interest in using income issues in less trying circumstances, especially for the replacement of preferred stocks. Recent issues of railroad income bonds—all turned out in the late 1950's—include those of the Gulf, Mobile & Ohio, the Missouri-Kansas-Texas, the Monon, the St. Louis-San Francisco, and the Virginian. The Gulf, Mobile & Ohio offer of income bonds in exchange for its preferred stock, originally made in 1957, has been left open on a continuing basis to the present time. Outside the railroad industry, however, no strong move in the direction of income bonds is apparent.

Income Bonds and Preferred Stocks. The big argument in support of the replacement of preferred stocks with income bonds, or the issuance of income bonds in the first place in lieu of preferred stocks, is the deductibility of bond interest for income tax purposes. Whenever a corporation meets its interest payments on income bonds, whether currently or after a delay, its interest costs are cut approximately in half by the tax saving; it gains no such benefit when it pays dividends on preferred stock. At the same time, its solvency is not endangered by the nonpayment of interest currently, just as it is not endangered by the nonpayment of dividends on preferred stock. And it is argued that people who are willing to invest in preferred stocks should be all the more willing to invest in income bonds, especially if in the bonds the interest is fully cumulative. Their claim to interest is stronger than would be their claim to dividends as preferred stockholders. The interest must be paid if earned, whereas preferred dividends need not be paid, regardless of the size of earnings.

Unpaid interest must be paid at maturity if not before, but the corporation has no obligation to pay preferred dividends at any time. Finally, the principal of income bonds comes due at a fixed maturity, but preferred stock has no maturity.

An equally big argument against solvent corporations' new financing with income bonds is simply lack of investor appreciation of their alleged merits. People buy income bonds that have stood the test of time, but they appear to have little enthusiasm for new issues. If corporations of unimpeachable credit standing were to decide in large numbers to put out income bonds, doubtless investor interest would increase enormously. But if such corporations want bonds in their financial structures to gain tax advantages or for other reasons, they are not likely to hesitate to put out bonds with the time-honored fixed obligation to pay interest every six months. As long, therefore, as corporations of this description avoid income bonds, there is a suspicion that corporations that do issue such bonds must have serious misgivings about their capacity to pay interest regularly.

MATURITY

Single Maturities

In the typical corporate bond issue sold at a given time, all the bonds have a single maturity date. Such an arrangement is reasonable for corporations that plan to trade on the equity indefinitely, expecting to put out new issues to raise money to pay off old ones as the old ones come to maturity. This has been the traditional policy of public utility and railroad companies, although a recent trend in the policy of some of these enterprises is to plan for at least partial retirement during the life of their issues. The policy of partial retirement has been adopted voluntarily in some instances, and in others as a result of the prodding of government regulatory commissions. Most industrial corporations, on the other hand, plan for a continuous procedure of retiring their bonded debt so that all but minor fractions will have been redeemed by final maturity dates. They agree to include in their indentures sinking fund provisions that call for periodical contributions aimed at this objective. A common sinking fund arrangement, for example, requires annual or semiannual allocations of cash for bond redemption such that equal portions of the issue will be retired in each of these periods and all by the final maturity. Thus, the sinking fund provisions for a 20-year issue would require an annual cash allocation sufficient to retire 5 percent of the whole issue, or a semiannual allocation sufficient to retire 2½ percent of the whole issue. The fulfillment of such a sinking fund requirement would mean, therefore, that only 5 percent or 2½ percent would still be unredeemed at the maturity date.

A policy of gradual redemption of a bond issue during the period of its life is in keeping with the doctrine that the simple common stock form of financial structure is the most desirable one for industrial corporations. According to this point of view, long-term borrowing is a substitute for financing with common stock or earnings, necessitated by unfavorable conditions in the market for common stocks or by temporary weaknesses in corporate earnings positions. Thus it follows that a program of substantial periodic reductions in the debt is appropriate. The fact that facilities acquired with the proceeds of bond issues depreciate supports this view, especially from the standpoint of investors. As the assets wear out through use and the action of the elements, the argument runs, the debt through which they were acquired should be continually reduced.

For single-maturity bond issues registered with the SEC for public offering in the period 1950–61, the most popular maturity was 30 years. As shown in a study published by the Federal Reserve Bank of Philadelphia, this maturity accounted for 26.4 percent of the dollar volume of such registrations. Second in popularity was 25 years, accounting for 19.7 percent of the registrations; followed by 20 years, 17.5 percent; 15 years, 7.2 percent; 12 years, 6 percent; and 35 years, 3.2 percent. Issues with maturities exceeding 25 years were largely those of public utility corporations supplying electric, gas, and sanitary services.[7]

Serial Maturities

If a corporation plans to retire equal portions of a bond issue annually or semiannually during its life, so that only a small fraction of the total, such as 5 percent, will be left for redemption at maturity, why does it not set different maturity dates for different portions of the issue? For a 20-year issue, why not give 5 percent of the bonds a 1-year maturity, another 5 percent a 2-year maturity, and so on up to a final 5 percent with a 20-year maturity? As mentioned earlier in this chapter, bonds that have their maturities arranged like this are known as serial bonds.

Advantages of Serial Issues. It was also stated earlier that in periods of upsweeping yield curves an advantage of serial issues is a reduction in interest expense. With all the bonds of a 20-year issue dated to mature in 20 years, all must be given a relatively high long-term rate, but with some dated to mature in one year, some in two years, and so on, a graduated scale of rates up to the top long-term rate could be provided.

Another advantage would appear to be a widening of the investment attractiveness of the bonds. Many investors do not want 20-year bonds. Some want only short-term outlets for their funds, some want

[7]Federal Reserve Bank of Philadelphia, *Business Review*, February, 1963, pp. 14–17.

intermediate-term outlets up to 5 years, some are satisfied to go to 10 years, and others to 15 years. Bonds with serial maturities, then, could appeal to each of these groups of investors.

A third advantage is that premiums need not be paid on the redemption of serial bonds, whereas the payment of premiums is not uncommon in the periodic redemption of most bonds in single-maturity issues. If an investor really wants a long-term outlet for his funds, he may hesitate to buy a *callable* 20-year bond, since the call feature indicates that he may be able to retain the bond only for a much shorter period. Hence comes the idea that the corporation may be able to overcome this hesitation by promising to pay a premium on redemption before maturity to compensate the investor for the trouble of having to find a new outlet for his funds. But if a person buys a serial bond coming due in two years, that must be precisely when he wants the principal returned to him; so he deserves no special compensation when it is returned at that time.

Use of Serial Issues. To gain these advantages, many corporations do put out serial issues, although the practice is not nearly so widespread as one may expect. Virtually all the issues of railroad companies to finance the acquisition of locomotives and cars (issues called equipment trust certificates for special reasons to be examined in Chapter 28) are serial issues, and a large number of the issues of notes sold by industrial companies by private placement also have serial maturities. But the use of serial issues elsewhere in corporate financing is slight, although they are of outstanding importance in the financing of state and local governments.

Patterns of maturities for serial bonds often vary from issue to issue. While railroads usually set semiannual or annual maturities for equal portions of their issues, beginning six months or a year after the date of issue, maturity patterns of the privately placed serial issues of industrial corporations are subject to wide variations. Sometimes, the earliest maturities are set two or three years after the date of issue, and sometimes unequal amounts are scheduled to mature on the different dates, with the larger amounts scheduled for later years. Illustrating a pattern of uniform maturities are the certificates issued under the "First Equipment Trust of 1968" of the Great Northern Railway, which amounted to $4,695,000 in total and were offered in February, 1968. The contract called for equal annual redemptions of $313,000 of certificates, and the certificates were offered to the public at various prices to give yields as follows.

Maturity	*Yield*
March 1, 1969	5.60
March 1, 1970	5.80
March 1, 1971	5.90
March 1, 1972	5.95
March 1, 1973–83	6.00

Disadvantages of Serial Issues. The principal reason that business corporations, particularly industrials, have not made greater use of serial maturities in their publicly offered bonds, despite their obvious advantages, appears to be the fear of defaults. A default on any maturity of a serial issue is a grave occurrence. If not corrected quickly, it is likely to require the slow and costly procedure of reorganization in bankruptcy, with a complete or partial loss of ownership interests by the stockholders. But a corporation's failure to make a sinking fund payment as prescribed in an indenture for a single-maturity bond issue, while also a serious default, is not likely to have such dire consequences—at least, not so quickly. Bondholders and their trustees are inclined to look rather tolerantly on sinking fund defaults, and tend to be generous in allowing time for their correction.

Another reason for the limited use of serial issues, especially by industrial corporations, is custom. Traditionally, bond issues have been long-term obligations, not a mixture of short-, intermediate-, and long-term obligations. This tradition was long buttressed by the fact that before the 1930's long-term interest rates were often below short-term rates for lengthy periods of time, so that the use of the serial device would have meant increased interest costs, rather than reduced ones as in periods of upsweeping yield curves.

Difficulties in quoting prices and in effecting transactions in serial bonds subsequent to their issue constitute a further disadvantage of serial issues. It is customary to give an entire serial issue a single nominal rate of interest (6 percent in the Great Northern issue just cited), but to vary the selling prices of the several maturities to give varying effective rates according to the pattern of prevailing yield curves. If the prevailing yield curves are upsweeping, the earliest maturity will be given the highest price, the final maturity the lowest price, and the intervening maturities will have prices scaled downward between these extremes. Throughout the life of the issue, therefore, each maturity will ordinarily continue to require price quotations different from those of all other maturities. Moreover, buyers and sellers of serial bonds do not simply want to buy and sell bonds of the Blank Corporation; a given buyer wants to acquire an 8-year maturity, and a given seller has a 12-year maturity to offer for sale. For this reason, the market for certain maturities may be quite thin, even though overall supply and demand may be substantial. This makes for difficulty in bringing buyers and sellers together at prices they regard as reasonable. Because of quotation and transactions difficulties of these kinds, some stock exchanges, including the New York Stock Exchange, refuse to list serial bonds.

QUESTIONS

1. What is a bond? A bond indenture? In general terms, state what goes into a bond indenture.

2. What kinds of details are stated in bond certificates? In scope, how do these details compare with those stated in the indenture?

3. In what ways does the trustee of a bond issue protect the interests of the bondholders? How is this protective role treated in the federal Trust Indenture Act?

4. In addition to its protective role for bondholders, the trustee of a bond issue ordinarily provides what services to the corporate issuer of the bonds?

5. How does a bondholder collect interest on a bond registered as to principal? On a bond fully registered? What is the procedure for transferring ownership of bonds in these two registered classes?

6. What is a coupon bond? How does the bondholder collect interest on such a bond? What is the procedure of transfer should he want to sell the bond?

7. How can one account for the revolutionary shift in preference from coupon bonds to registered bonds that occured in the past few years? Why are some investors unhappy about the shift?

8. When bonds are bought and sold between interest-payment dates, how does interest enter the transactions, if at all?

9. As a determinant of the rates of interest corporations must pay on new bond issues, how is the state of the market measured or evaluated?

10. How is it possible to determine the market rate on long-term Treasury obligations when the Treasury is not offering any new long-term issues for sale?

11. Aside from general conditions of supply and demand for long-term funds, what are the principal determinants of the rates of interest corporations must pay on new bond issues?

12. In periods of upsweeping yield curves, would it not be advantageous for corporations to borrow on a short-term basis even for long-term purposes? Discuss. Would not serial bond issues be helpful in holding down the total cost of borrowing? Explain.

13. If a corporation sells a 6 percent bond issue to investment bankers at 97, why would its cost of borrowing really be more than 6 percent? At this selling price, would the cost rate be higher for a 20-year issue than for a 25-year issue or vice versa? Explain.

14. How do the interest-payment provisions of income bonds differ from these provisions in bonds not so described? To what two uses have income bonds been chiefly put? Why have they not been more popular?

15. What advantages are claimed for serial bonds? To what extent are they used in corporate financing? Why are they not used more extensively?

PROBLEMS

1. From Table 27–1, find the yield on:

a) a 4 percent bond maturing in 20 years priced at 123½ Ans. 2.5%
b) a 4 percent bond maturing in 3 years priced at 97¼ Ans. 5%
c) a 5 percent bond maturing in 25 years priced at 93¼ Ans. 5.5%
d) a 5 percent bond maturing in 40 years priced at 73¼ Ans. 7%

e) a 6 percent bond maturing in 15 years priced at 95¼ Ans. 6.5%
f) a 6 percent bond maturing in 25 years priced at 106¾ Ans. 5.5%

2. From Table 27–1, find the price at which a bond should sell to give a yield of 4.5 percent if the bond bears interest at:
a) 4 percent and matures in 5 years Ans. 97.78
b) 4 percent and matures in 20 years Ans. 93.45
c) 5 percent and matures in 6 months Ans. 100.24
d) 5 percent and matures in 10 years Ans. 103.99
e) 6 percent and matures in 3 months Ans. 100.35
f) 6 percent and matures in 40 years Ans. 127.71

3. From Table 27–1, find the price at which a bond should sell to give a yield of 5.5 percent if the bond bears interest at:
a) 4 percent and matures in 3 months Ans. 99.62
b) 4 percent and matures in 3 years Ans. 95.90
c) 5 percent and matures in 1 year Ans. 99.52
d) 5 percent and matures in 30 years Ans. 92.69
e) 6 percent and matures in 2 years Ans. 100.93
f) 6 percent and matures in 25 years Ans. 106.75

4. By interpolation in Table 27–1, find the yield on:
a) a 4 percent bond maturing in 5 years and selling at 97 Ans. 4.68%
b) a 4 percent bond maturing in 15 years and selling at 115 Ans. 2.78%
c) a 5 percent bond maturing in 10 years and selling at 107½ Ans. 4.08%
d) a 5 percent bond maturing in 15 years and selling at 84¾ Ans. 6.62%
e) a 6 percent bond maturing in 2 years and selling at 99¼ Ans. 6.41%
f) a 6 percent bond maturing in 25 years and selling at 112¾ Ans. 5.09%

5. By interpolation in Table 27–1, find the price at which a bond should sell to give a yield of 5⅜ percent if the bond bears interest at:
a) 4 percent and matures in 3 years Ans. 96.23
b) 4 percent and matures in 10 years Ans. 89.49
c) 5 percent and matures in 5 years Ans. 98.375
d) 5 percent and matures in 20 years Ans. 95.455
e) 6 percent and matures in 6 months Ans. 100.305
f) 6 percent and matures in 20 years Ans. 107.62

6. By interpolation in Table 27–1, find the price at which a bond should sell to give a yield of 4⅛ percent if the bond bears interest at:
a) 4 percent and matures in 10 years Ans. 98.99
b) 4 percent and matures in 40 years Ans. 97.605
c) 5 percent and matures in 5 years Ans. 103.92
d) 5 percent and matures in 25 years Ans. 113.595
e) 6 percent and matures in 20 years Ans. 125.43
f) 6 percent and matures in 30 years Ans. 132.21

7. By use of the present-value tables, pages 298 and 304, check the accuracy of the price entries in Table 27–1 for:
a) a 5 percent bond maturing in 5 years to yield 4 percent
b) a 6 percent bond maturing in 10 years to yield 4 percent
c) a 6 percent bond maturing in 3 years to yield 6 percent
d) a 4 percent bond maturing in 2 years to yield 6 percent

chapter 28

SECURED BONDS AND DEBENTURE BONDS

In bargaining between corporations that want to issue bonds and investment bankers, institutional investors, and other prospective buyers of the bonds, the question of security is a matter of great importance. A corporation provides security for a bond issue by pledging some of its assets, very carefully designated, for the safety of the bondholders. All classes of bonds for which there are pledges of assets of one kind or another are known collectively as *secured bonds*, while those that lack pledges are described as *debenture bonds*.

Title to the assets pledged on secured bonds may be transferred to the trustee, or the trustee may simply be given a lien on them. Whatever the procedure, the theory of security is that should the corporation default on its obligations to the bondholders, the trustee may sell (or seize and sell) the pledged assets and use the proceeds to pay off the bondholders' claims to interest and principal. Only after the bondholders' claims have been fully satisfied can these proceeds be used to meet the claims of other creditors. It is possible, however, for certain claims against the corporation to rank ahead of those of holders of bonds for which security has been provided—claims given preference in federal and state bankruptcy laws and state insolvency laws, such as those for unpaid taxes and wages and for the expenses of administration during the period of bankruptcy. On the other hand, the seizure and sale of pledged assets, if insufficient to meet the bondholders' full claims, does not relieve the corporation of liability for the unsatisfied portion. It had promised to pay full principal and interest, and not simply the amount recoverable through the sale of pledged assets.

GENERAL ASPECTS OF SECURITY

Influence on Indenture Terms and Provisions

Whether or not security is provided for a bond issue usually has important influence on many of the terms and conditions set forth in the indenture. Often, the provision of security means that bond buyers will be willing to take a rate of interest lower than they would otherwise demand. Sometimes, in fact, they would not buy the bonds, whatever the rate of interest, were security not provided. In many cases, too, the question of security has important bearings on what the maturity of the bonds will be. Security or the lack of it significantly influences the kinds of protective provisions an indenture will have, the rights that a corporation will want to reserve to itself, and the special inducements it may offer to promote sales. As mentioned in Chapter 28, security is itself a protective provision, and it may also be regarded as a special kind of feature to promote sale. But the influence of security on indenture provisions is so pervasive that it hardly lends itself to treatment simply as a protective provision or as a selling feature—hence the separate, detailed treatment planned for this chapter.

But a word of caution: the influence of security must not be exaggerated. Bond buyers want payment of interest and principal in the regular course of business by solvent corporations. In deciding whether or not to buy, therefore, they are likely to give much more attention to a corporation's present and prospective working capital position and to its earning power than to the character and value of assets pledged. They realize that the terms *safety* and *security* do not necessarily mean the same thing—that the debenture bonds of a corporation in a strong financial position and with excellent earning capacity are likely to be much safer than the secured bonds of another whose financial position and earning capacity are considerably weaker. They know, too, that after default there are likely to be long and troublesome delays in realizing on pledged assets, even though ultimately their claims may be fully satisfied. And they also recognize the possibility that after long and troublesome delays they may incur losses because the cash realized in liquidating pledged assets may prove to be much less than the value of the assets as originally pledged or as reduced by ordinary depreciation.

An illustration of the point that the influence of security must not be exaggerated was the experience of the Ohio Power Company in selling on a single day in August, 1967, a $50 million first-mortgage bond issue bearing interest at 6½ percent and a $20 million debenture issue bearing interest at 6⅝ percent. The ⅛ point differential in nominal interest rates measured almost exactly the comparative evaluations of the two syndicates of investment bankers that bought the issues separately on a competitive bidding basis. The first syndicate reoffered the first-mortgage bonds to the public at a price to yield 6.33 percent per annum, and the second syndicate made its public offering at a price to yield 6.45 percent. It should be of interest to add that Ohio Power's dual offering had originally been scheduled for April but had been deferred on three occasions because of "market conditions"—expectations or hopes, no doubt, that market rates of interest would be falling.

Attitudes of Corporate Managements

In bargaining about a bond issue, the typical corporate management would doubtless prefer to avoid a pledge of assets. But that managerial reluctance, of whatever degree, is not insuperable is proved by the existence of hundreds of secured bond issues in the United States at the present time. Corporate managements are surely inclined to yield when salability of issues is found finally to depend on their willingness to pledge assets, and they are often persuaded to pledge assets as a means of obtaining concessions, such as lower interest rates or less oppressive sinking fund requirements. Custom, too, is an important factor in determining whether or not given kinds of bond issues, as well as the varying kinds sold in given industries, will be secured. Railroads of the highest credit standing provide security for their equipment-financing issues no less than do those of much weaker credit positions. Also, a tradition of providing security is much stronger in the railroad and public utility industries than, for example, among manufacturing and mercantile corporations. Secured bond issues of public utility corporations have been especially numerous in recent years.

At any rate, competent corporate managements can hardly be expected to pledge assets without a careful weighing of the pros and cons. Any pledge restricts freedom of action. Certain kinds of actions with respect to pledged property may be forbidden in the indenture, and permission of the trustee may be required for others. Restrictions on further issues of secured bonds may be accepted as entirely reasonable at the time an indenture is drawn up, only to prove quite unrealistic with changing circumstances in later years. A pledge of assets, too, tends to weaken further debt-incurring capacity. Prospective unsecured creditors, such as commercial banks, trade suppliers, and investors in debenture bonds, are likely to conclude that to satisfy their own claims in case of default little would be available from assets pledged to secured bondholders; hence, they are likely to be less liberal in extending loans or credits and more rigorous in setting terms and conditions for their advances than they would be were there no pledges.

WHAT IS PLEDGED

Mortgages on Real Property

Land, buildings, machinery and equipment, and other things more or less inseparably attached to land and buildings (in the sense of not ordinarily being movable) are the kinds of property most commonly pledged as security for bond issues. Property of this description is known at law as *real property* or *realty*, and it is pledged by means of *real mortgages*. In popular usage, however, issues secured by real property are designated simply as *mortgage bonds* rather than as real mortgage bonds.

Priority of Mortgage Claims. A corporation may pledge all or almost all of its real property as security for a single bond issue, or separate parcels for separate bond issues. Moreover, it may pledge a portion of its properties for a bond issue and other portions as security for loans negotiated with banks or other financial institutions. When the property pledged on a bond issue has not already been pledged to secure other obligations, the bondholders are said to have a first mortgage or a first lien—terms that simply indicate that there is no prior mortgage claim.

However, it is possible for a corporation to pledge the same property successively on two or more bond issues or loan contracts, so that lenders on a second pledge would be said to have a second mortgage or lien, those on a third pledge of the same property a third mortgage or lien, and so on. In the event of a sale of pledged property after a default, the proceeds are used first to meet the full claims of the holders of the first mortgage and then, to the extent possible, to meet the full claims of the holders of the second mortgage, and so on. If the proceeds are only enough or are less than enough to meet the full claims of the holders of the first mortgage, the security of the second and subsequent mortgages is proved worthless. If a corporation that has, say, three successive mortgages on the same property pays off the obligation for which the first was given, the mortgage previously in the second position becomes a first mortgage, and that previously in the third position becomes a second mortgage.

First mortgages are often described as senior or underlying liens, and second and subsequent mortgages as junior or overlying liens. The "underlying" and "overlying" designations are used especially in reference to the financing of railroads.

Value of Property Pledged. Prospective investors in mortgage bonds (and in other classes of secured bonds, as well) can generally be expected to insist that the value of property pledged be substantially in excess of the face amount of the bonds to be issued. These investors know that prices obtainable in the market for property seized and offered for sale to satisfy debts are likely to be much less than the going-concern values of the same property as carried on the books. Indeed, defaults are most likely to occur in periods of general business depression when markets will probably be weak. On the other hand, allowance is usually made for the adaptability of the pledged property for alternative uses. When highly specialized property is pledged, bond buyers may insist that the bond issue be limited in amount to 50 percent of the value of the property, but when the property is highly adaptable they may be willing to agree to an issue equal to 75 or 80 percent of its value. The most common limits to the size of bond issues in relation to the value of pledged property appear to be 60 and 66⅔ percent.

Such limits apply also, of course, when the same property is pledged successively for two or more bond issues. Were a corporation, for example, to pledge property worth $20 million for a bond issue of $5 million, it might not have much difficulty in selling a second-mortgage issue of $4 million, and even an additional third-mortgage issue of $3 million. But were the first-mortgage issue $12 million, it is likely that repledging the same property for a subsequent issue would add little to its attractiveness. This would not mean that the second issue could not be sold, but that investors would be likely to regard a proposed second-mortgage issue as hardly better than a debenture issue.

How Pledges Are Made. In pledging real property for the security of a bond issue, a corporation may transfer its title to the trustee or simply give the trustee a lien on it, depending on the law of the state in which the mortgage is executed. In the title-theory states, a corporate mortgage, like any other mortgage, is a conveyance of title, and it reads much as if it were a deed. However, it contains a *defeasance* or *defeating clause* that says, in effect, that the transfer of title shall be void if the corporation fulfills its obligations as set out in the indenture. In a title-theory state, it might seem that on default the trustee, having title, could immediately sell the pledged properties for the benefit of the bondholders. Nevertheless, the title-theory states prescribe certain kinds of *foreclosure* proceedings that the trustee (or other mortgagee) must take to make the transfer of title absolute. In the lien-theory states, the giving of a mortgage by a corporation places in the hands of the trustee a prior claim to the property for the satisfaction of the bondholders' claims, but title remains with the corporation. In the event of default, to get title the trustee must likewise follow through with a foreclosure procedure. Accordingly, the requirements for foreclosure in both classes of states, as well as defeasance clauses in mortgages in the title-theory states, tend to give mortgages much the same complexion regardless of the individual state's theory.

Possession and Use. Although the term *mortgage* means literally a "dead pledge," real property mortgaged in a bond indenture actually remains very much alive. Indenture provisions invariably stipulate that the corporation shall have possession and use of the pledged property so long as it does not default on its obligations. Even after default, possession and use continue until foreclosure actions have been completed if, indeed, the trustee chooses to take such actions. It is important for the bondholders that the corporation's earning power be not impeded by restrictions on the regular productive use of the mortgaged property, so that making the property a dead pledge would clearly be contrary to their own interests.

However, possession and use do not require freedom to sell pledged properties piecemeal or in bulk or to combine them with those of other corporations, as in mergers and consolidations. Hence, restrictions on actions of these kinds are commonly found in indentures. Piecemeal sales are usually permitted so that a corporation can get rid of items of property that are no longer useful to it. But permission of the trustee is normally required, and there is usually a stipulation that property purchased in replacement will be pledged under the existing indenture or that the cash proceeds of piecemeal sales will be used for bond retirement if replacement is not contemplated. Bulk sales of all or most of the mortgaged property and combinations by way of mergers and consolidations are sometimes forbidden, but much more often the indenture simply provides that such transactions can be effected only if the buying or successor corporation accepts responsibility for all the indenture obligations of the corporation that issued the bonds.

Pledges of Personal Property

At law, all kinds of movable property, tangible and intangible, are classified as *personal property* or *personalty*. The classification includes many kinds of (movable) factory, store, and office equipment; rolling stock, such as locomotives, cars, trucks, busses, and airplanes; and inventories, accounts receivable, cash, stocks, and bonds. Any such property may be pledged as security for bond issues by means of *chattel mortgages*. The term *chattel* is simply a synonym for the term *personal property*.

Actually, however, personal property ordinarily classified in business practice as "current assets," such as inventories and accounts receivable, is rarely pledged for bond issues. These kinds of personal property are too volatile to serve conveniently as pledges for long-term obligations, although they are frequently pledged as security for short-term loans obtained from commercial banks and other lenders. When movable factory, store, and office equipment is pledged, it is generally included with real property in issues of ordinary mortgage bonds, although, to be sure, separate parcels are often pledged individually for specific loans, ordinarily intermediate in term.

Thus, we have left rolling stock and stocks and bonds as kinds of personal property that appear to be independently available for pledge purposes in connection with bond issues. The fact is that these two kinds of personal property do serve as security for almost all secured bond issues that lack pledges of real property. Accordingly, we may give our attention specifically to what in the case of rolling stock are called *equipment obligations*, and in the case of pledged stocks and bonds are called *collateral trust bonds*.

Equipment Obligations. Some railroads and other transportation companies, especially airlines, obtain part of the purchase price of their rolling stock by selling bond issues for which this equipment is pledged by means of chattel mortgages. Such mortgages are customarily called equipment mortgages to distinguish them from mortgages by which real property is pledged.

For the acquisition of rolling stock by railroads, however, the most common arrangement by far is the issuance of equipment trust certificates. The arrangement is known as the Philadelphia Plan. Let us assume that a railroad wants to buy a group of locomotives, which will cost $6 million. It gives its specifications to the manufacturing company. When the locomotives have been built, they are delivered to the railroad, but title to them goes to the trust department of a commercial bank or to a trust company chosen to serve in the capacity of trustee. The railroad enters into a *lease* contract with the trustee, agreeing to rent the equipment and to pay an advance rental and periodical rents sufficient in total to meet principal and interest requirements on the equipment trust certificates that are to be issued. The advance rental, or down payment, usually ranges from 10 to 25 percent of the cost of the equipment; for example, let us say that it is 20 percent or $1.2 million. Accordingly, an issue of equipment trust certificates is sold to raise the balance of the purchase price, $4.8 million. The proceeds of the sale of the certificates and the advance rental payment of the railroad are used, of course, to pay off the manufacturing company.

The equipment trust certificates are obligations neither of the railroad nor of the trustee; rather, they represent participations in the ownership of the locomotives. They thus resemble stock. Indeed, the return on such instruments is often described as a dividend rather than as interest. But, unlike stock, they have maturity dates. As in the Great Northern Railway issue referred to in Chapter 27, the invariable procedure is to provide serial maturities, ordinarily with equal amounts to be retired semiannually or annually over a period that most commonly ranges between 10 and 15 years. For our illustrative issue, semiannual maturities of $160,000 would be set were semiannual redemption over a 15-year period decided on. Unlike most stocks, too, equipment trust certificates have guaranties. Our railroad would endorse the certificates with a guaranty of the payment of interest (dividends) periodically and the face amounts at their respective maturities. This kind of endorsement, coupled with the obligations under the lease, justifies the classification of equipment trust certificates as bonds rather than as stocks. Railroad corporations include them among their long-term debt, and investors think of them essentially as debt instruments rather than as participations in ownership.

When our railroad company had made its rental payments faithfully over the 15-year period of the lease, the trustee would transfer to it the title to the locomotives. It would then have paid for them in full. Were it to default along the way, the trustee, as holder of the title to the locomotives, could seize them and sell or rent them to another line. No time-consuming foreclosure procedures, as for pledged property, would be necessary. Moreover, the trustee should have no difficulty in finding a buyer or renter whose payments would be sufficient to take care of the certificates still outstanding. As 20 years or more is the expected useful life of locomotives, the rapid pace of certificate retirement by comparison with the pace of depreciation, together with the railroad's advance rental or down payment, generally assures an ample margin between the declining book (and market) value of the equipment and the volume of certificates still outstanding. In terms of the illustration, the book value at the time of issuance of the certificates was $6 million—the cost of the locomotives—but the debt was only $4.8 million; thus a margin of safety of $1.2 million was provided by the advance rental. Allowing for depreciation on a 20-year straight-line basis, the book value at the end of one year would be $5.7 million, but the debt after retirement of the first two maturities would be down to $4.48 million. Five years after issue, the book value would be $4.5 million, but the debt would have been reduced to $3.2 million. Ten years after issue, while the book value of the locomotives would be $3 million, the remaining debt would be only $1.6 million. It appears, therefore, that the margin of protection should be ample throughout the life of the certificates.

The principal reason that railroads have favored financing with equipment trust certificates rather than with equipment mortgages has been the presence of after-acquired property clauses in existing indentures for outstanding mortgage bonds. As we shall see in a later discussion, such a clause automatically extends the lien of an existing mortgage to newly acquired property. In using the Philadelphia Plan, however, the railroad does not take title to new locomotives and cars until they have been fully paid for; therefore, during the period of payment—the period of the lease—the equipment is held, as it were, out of the reach of the after-acquired property clause. The buyers of equipment trust certificates can be given the protection of what amounts to a first lien, whereas the lien could be no better than a second or a subsequent one were the railroad to take title immediately and issue equipment mortgage bonds. A weak railroad already mortgaged to the hilt would probably not be able to sell equipment mortgage bonds at all, or only on terms severely unfavorable to itself, but its equipment trust certificates may well be grabbed up by investors of the most conservative classes, precisely because of the first-lien feature and the other protective aspects that have been described.

Collateral Trust Bonds. Collateral trust bonds, secured by pledges of stocks or bonds or both, once were an extremely important kind of financing instrument, especially in the public utility and railroad fields. Among other things, they served as most useful building blocks in the erection of massive, many-tiered holding company empires in these two fields. Would-be empire builders might start out by establishing Corporation A to fill the role of a pure public utility holding company. They would have it sell nonvoting preferred stock and probably a minority portion of its common stock to the public, keeping a majority of the common shares for themselves. With the proceeds of sales of stock, Corporation A would buy up a controlling common stock interest in Corporation B, an operating public utility company. Then A would put out an issue of collateral trust bonds, with the stock of B as the collateral, and use the proceeds to buy a controlling common stock interest in Corporation C, another operating company. Then C's stock could be put up as security for a second collateral trust issue, the proceeds to be used to buy up common stock of another operating company. About this time, the promoters of A—the empire builders—might decide to set up a second-degree holding company, let us say, Corporation X. They would have X sell an issue of nonvoting preferred stock and some of its common stock to the public, but the majority portion of X's common stock they would issue to themselves in exchange for their holdings of A's common stock. In this way, X would have cash from the sales of its own stock to be spent in buying up controlling interests in other companies—perhaps, like A, first-degree holding companies. And, of course, it would have A's stock available as collateral for an issue of collateral trust bonds to raise additional cash for the same purpose.

This kind of thing could go on and on. In the 1920's, it did go on and on—not necessarily precisely according to the pattern just outlined but certainly according to patterns not far different. In the old Associated Gas & Electric Company empire, for example, there were 12 layers or tiers of holding companies! But many of these pyramids got into financial difficulties in the depression of the 1930's, and some even earlier than that, discrediting their builders as well as their means of financing, including collateral trust bonds. Opportunities for further pyramid building or rebuilding, regardless of the methods of financing, appear to have vanished forever because of the strict regulation of railroad holding companies by the Interstate Commerce Commission, under the Emergency Transportation Act of 1933, and of public utility holding companies by the Securities and Exchange Commission, under the Public Utility Holding Company Act of 1935, and because of the strict disclosure requirements of the Securities Act of 1933.

All this does not deny that there have been and are less spectacular uses of collateral trust bonds. Some corporations do own controlling common stock interests in other corporations. If they want to borrow by means of bond issues and must provide security, they have every reason to offer to pledge these common stock interests. Other corporations own stocks and bonds but do not have controlling interests in the securities' issuers, and they, too, may legitimately pledge these as collateral for their own issues. Some corporations have financed the operations of their subsidiaries by buying the subsidiaries' mortgage bond issues and using these as security for their own collateral trust issues. This device is useful when single large issues of collateral trust bonds are able to gain better terms than would have been available to the subsidiaries were their small issues of mortgage bonds to be offered individually to the public. Some corporations have financed their own operations by putting out collateral trust bonds with some of their own mortgage bonds pledged as security—when the trust bonds could be sold on better terms or on a basis more attractive to investors than could the mortgage bonds. Moreover, stocks and bonds are not infrequently pledged in given indentures as important additions to pledged real property—indicated by bond issues called first-mortgage and collateral trust bonds—such as recent issues of the Potomac Edison Company and the Delmarva Power & Light Company. Nevertheless, as a distinct type of debt instrument, collateral trust bonds have been relegated to a minor role in corporate financing.

General or Blanket Mortgages

Particularly common in railroad and public utility financing is the practice of pledging in single indentures everything in sight except current assets. For a given bond issue, the corporation may pledge all its real property, all its movable equipment including rolling stock, its patents and franchises, and its holdings of stocks and bonds (except short-term government obligations in which cash is temporarily invested when in surplus supply). Though bond issues of this description have real mortgage, equipment mortgage, and collateral trust features simultaneously, they are usually classified simply as mortgage bonds, for the good reason that the value of pledged realty usually far exceeds the value of pledged personal property. In popular parlance, however, such bonds are often said to be secured by general or blanket mortgages to distinguish them from issues that have simple real or chattel mortgages.

But one must not read too much meaning into a word such as *general*, especially if one is looking at the titles of older railroad issues. A goodly number of these continue to be outstanding, although many railroads have made great progress in the last three decades in simplifying their debt structures. At any rate, a bond issue of a public utility described as a general mortgage is very likely to have a first lien on all its operating properties and intangibles, as mentioned in the preceding paragraph, but an older railroad issue so described could have quite a different kind of standing.

In the heyday of railroad finance, fancy titles for bond issues were selected unconscionably, and, as a rule, it was *de rigueur* to somehow get in the word *first* so that unwary investors would have visions of a first lien. Thus, a "first general mortgage" might actually represent quite inferior liens. A railroad might have pledged Parcel A of its properties on two successive divisional bond issues, Parcel B on three, and Parcel C on two. Yet, its management would feel free to call a later bond issue, for which all three parcels were pledged, a "first general mortgage," because this would be the first time the properties "in general" had been pledged on a single issue. Obviously, therefore, the word *first* modified "general" and not "mortgage," for the new bonds would have only third liens on Parcels A and C, and a fourth lien on Parcel B. Similarly, Railroad X might have pledged all its properties on two successive bond issues, and Railroad Y also on two. The two railroads having been subsequently merged, a new bond issue might be planned. Would it be called a "third-mortgage" issue? Decidedly not. Much better sounding would be a title such as *first consolidated mortgage*. But we need not look at all such attractive titles. Two more examples should suffice. The title *first refunding mortgage* indicated that at least part of the proceeds of the bond issue was to be used to retire one or more earlier issues, but the investor could have been in serious error were he to conclude that as a result of the retirement he would have a first lien on the railroad's property. In the title *first and general mortgage*, the "first and" indicated that a first lien on some part of the railroad's property was being given to the buyers of the bond issue. But this parcel might be of minor importance and value, while the "general" portion of the mortgage might represent second, third, or subsequent liens on the rest of the railroad's property.

SIGNIFICANCE OF SECURITY

In the course of the preceding discussion, repeated references were made to the sale of pledged property for the satisfaction of bondholders' claims, but the point was also made that, except for equipment trust certificates, long and troublesome delays are likely to occur in connection with the enforcement of these claims. The delays are chiefly occasioned by efforts of defaulting corporations to work out means of settlement that will preclude the seizure and sale of their assets, the most significant means of settlement being the procedures of reorganization according to the terms of the federal bankruptcy laws.

To understand the significance of security for bondholders, therefore, it is desirable to consider, first, how bondholders' claims of various priorities are met if assets are actually liquidated, and, secondly, what influence these priorities have in procedures for reorganization.

Satisfaction of Claims by Liquidation

The extent to which bondholders are protected by security when the assets of an insolvent corporation are actually sold to satisfy creditors' claims may best be seen in a series of illustrations. For this purpose, let us assume that at the time of its default a certain corporation had current assets valued on its books at $20 million and fixed assets valued at $25 million, and that, at the time of final settlement, its debts were as follows.

Current liabilities	$12,000,000
First-mortgage bonds	10,000,000
Second-mortgage bonds	5,000,000
Debenture bonds	4,000,000

For the sake of simplicity, we may assume that none of the current liabilities have preferences in liquidation as provided for in the bankruptcy laws and that none have been secured by pledges of assets—that all, therefore, have equal standing as unsecured claims. For convenience, also, let us assume that the amount shown for each of the four classes of liabilities includes all unpaid interest to the date of settlement. In this regard, it is to be remembered that interest claims rank with claims to principal; both are equally secured or unsecured, as the case may be. Finally, let us assume that all the fixed assets were pledged for the security of the first-mortgage bonds, and then repledged under the indenture for the second-mortgage bonds.

First Illustration. For a first illustration, let us say that the current assets realize in liquidation $18 million, and the fixed assets $7 million. The $7 million would be devoted to meeting the claims of the first-mortgage bondholders, and their unsatisfied claims of $3 million would be added as an unsecured claim against the balance of the assets. (The corporation promised to pay these bondholders $10 million. It did not promise to pay them only what could be realized out of the pledged assets; hence, the unsatisfied portion of their claims remains as a corporate obligation.) The holders of the second-mortgage bonds would get nothing out of the proceeds of the sale of the pledged assets, so that their entire claims of $5 million would simply be added to all others against the unpledged assets. Accordingly, the total claims against the $18 million realized from the liquidation of the current assets would amount to $24 million (first-mortgage bonds, $3 million; second-mortgage bonds, $5 million; debenture bonds, $4 million; and current debts, $12 million). Thus, all classes of creditors except the first-mortgage bondholders would receive 75 cents on each dollar of their claims. For each dollar of first-mortgage claims, the bondholder would receive 70 cents from liquidation of the pledged assets plus 75 percent of his remaining claim of 30 cents, or 22.5 cents, for a total of 92.5 cents.

Second Illustration. For a second illustration, let us say that the current assets are liquidated for $15 million, and the fixed assets for $13 million. Out of the $13 million, the claims of the first-mortgage bondholders could be completely satisfied, so that they would receive 100 cents on the dollar. In addition, $3 million of the claims of the second-mortgage bondholders could be met out of the sales proceeds of the pledged assets, leaving them with unsecured claims of $2 million against the balance of the assets. Thus, there would be total claims of $18 million against the cash realized from the liquidation of the current assets, so that a settlement at 83⅓ cents on the dollar could be made. For each dollar of his claims, a second-mortgage bondholder would receive 60 cents from the liquidation of the pledged assets and 33⅓ cents on the balance of his claim of 40 cents. Thus, recovery per dollar of claims would be as follows: first-mortgage bondholders, 100 cents; second-mortgage bondholders, 93⅓ cents; and other creditors, 83⅓ cents.

Third Illustration. To make our concluding illustration extreme—but still realistic in terms of what could happen in a period of severe depression—let us assume that the current assets realize only $9 million, and the fixed assets only $4 million. The $4 million would go entirely to the first-mortgage bondholders, leaving them with unsatisfied claims of $6 million to be added to those of the other creditors. The claims of the holders of the second-mortgage bonds would shift entirely to the general or unsecured classification, bringing the total to $27 million. Accordingly, the $9 million realized from the liquidation of current assets would permit a settlement at the rate of 33⅓ cents on the dollar. So the recovery of the first-mortgage bondholders, per dollar of claims, would amount to almost twice that of the creditors of all other classes. It would be 60 cents on the dollar—40 cents from the pledged assets plus 20 cent from the unpledged ones.

Conclusions. Certain general conclusions about how bond owners fare in liquidations can be drawn from the foregoing illustrations. (1) Except when pledged assets are absolutely worthless, holders of first-mortgage bonds always get a better settlement than do other classes of creditors (disregarding creditors whose claims are preferred in the bankruptcy statutes, as well as those to whom other assets may have been pledged, such as short-term lenders who have liens on inventories). (2) Nevertheless, first-mortgage bondholders may suffer severe losses, as in the third example—security does not give complete assurance against loss. (3) Depending on the liquidating values of pledged assets, holders of bonds with second and subsequent liens may or may not benefit from these liens. (4) Holders of debenture bonds have claims no stronger than those of other unsecured creditors.

Claims in Reorganizations

For the reason that many corporations that default on their obligations take quick steps to prevent the seizure and sale of their properties by creditors and their trustees, the consideration just given to the satisfaction of claims in liquidation may appear to be of theoretical interest only. Not so, however. It is true that corporations that get into severe financial difficulties are inclined to hurry to the federal courts in order to start proceedings for reorganization in bankruptcy, and that creditors and their trustees are held off from seizure and sale to give the courts time to study proposed plans of reorganization. It is true, too, that other corporations that find themselves in financial trouble, especially smaller ones, try to work out informal arrangements with their creditors for postponing settlement and even for the scaling down of their obligations—often with the implied threat also to petition for reorganization in bankruptcy should the creditors be reluctant to bargain.

But the federal courts can hardly be expected to approve plans of reorganization unless these plans treat fairly all classes of creditors according to the priority of their respective claims. In judging fair treatment, the courts are likely to give considerable weight to the liquidation value of assets—to what each class of creditors would receive were the corporation to be dissolved rather than reorganized. These conclusions appear to follow from the decision of the Supreme Court in *Case* v. *Los Angeles Lumber Products Co.*,[1] in which it established what is called the absolute priority doctrine for reorganizations. In an approved plan of reorganization, therefore, because of their prior claim to pledged assets first-mortgage bonds may remain undisturbed—that is, they have claims of the same scope in the reorganized corporation as they had previously. But in view of the relative weakness of their claims, other creditors may be less generously treated. The holders of second-mortgage bonds may be offered debenture bonds in the reorganized corporation, or possibly such bonds for part of their claims, and preferred or common stock for the

[1] 308 U.S. 106 (1939).

balance. The holders of debenture bonds and other unsecured creditors may be offered some combination of new bonds and preferred or common stock, or possibly preferred or common stock solely. If new bonds are given to second-mortgage bondholders and to debenture bondholders and other unsecured creditors, some or all of them may be of the income variety, with interest to be payable for a period of years or indefinitely only if earned. In this way, therefore, what each class of creditors gets in a reorganization by comparison with what other classes get is likely to match rather closely the proportion of cash it would probably get were the corporation to be liquidated and dissolved.

In reorganization proceedings, the liquidation value of assets and the respective priorities of creditor classes are important for another reason. Although such proceedings temporarily hold off creditors and their trustees from the seizure and sale of assets, the court must be satisfied that the adoption of a proposed plan of reorganization will restore the corporation to good financial health and enable it to stay well (solvent) for a lengthy period. In numerous instances, this is not the finding of the court, so that proceedings for reorganization are switched to proceedings for liquidation and dissolution, whereby, in effect, seizure and sale actually do take place.

Moreover, liquidation values of assets and rankings of creditors' claims are immediately of controlling importance in many business failures. Often, the financial difficulties of corporations, especially those of small and medium sizes, are so grave that no effort is made to reorganize. Liquidation and dissolution, whether in bankruptcy or by way of less formal procedures, are decided on at the outset.

OPEN-END AND CLOSED INDENTURES

When they first borrow by means of secured bond issues, many corporations have only moderate amounts of assets available for pledging and need only moderate amounts of funds, but they anticipate further needs of long-term funds as they grow and acquire additional properties. Sometimes, they pledge the original assets for bond issues of small size and then, with each major addition to assets, have new indentures drawn up, pledging the new properties for separate bond issues. Each such indenture is a *closed* one: all the bonds that it authorizes are immediately sold, so that later issues are necessarily outside its scope. But the procedure of using successive closed indentures soon results in a complex financial structure. There is a separate trustee for each indenture, and the individual indentures, being agreed on at different times and in varying circumstances, are likely to differ from one another in restrictions, concessions, and other provisions. The procedure tends to be unduly expensive, and compliance with many different indenture conditions is quite burdensome.

A better procedure would appear to be an original indenture that permitted the issuance of additional bonds from time to time, subject to strict limitations. Such an indenture may be an *open-end* one wherein no specific dollar amount is stated as the authorized bond issue, or it may be a *limited open-end* one wherein a maximum dollar amount is stated, but the amount is much greater than that of the original issue. Under an open-end indenture of either variety, the successive issues of bonds have equal rank; all the assets as successively pledged secure all the bonds equally, regardless of when they may have been issued. A first group of bondholders has no greater claim on the assets first pledged than have buyers of bonds issued later under the open-end indenture, nor do buyers of later issues have greater claims on assets pledged after the original pledge than has the first group. However, a limited open-end indenture becomes closed when the maximum stipulated amount of bonds has been issued.

But investors in bonds issued under open-end indentures demand safeguards. Early buyers of bonds, knowing that investors in subsequent issues will have equal rank with them, fear excessive total issues. The safety of their bonds could be dissipated by the corporation's lack of restraint in selling further quantities. Although, therefore, they may agree to no dollar limit or to a high dollar limit in the indenture, they will surely insist that limits be set in other ways. On the other hand, they are ordinarily willing to concede that differences in circumstances at the time various issues of bonds are sold may justify differences in interest rates, maturities, and call prices.

Earnings Limitations

Many open-end indentures contain restrictions on further issues of bonds in terms of earnings available for bond interest. The most common kind of earnings limitation provides that additional bonds may be issued only to the extent that earnings actually available for bond interest in some past period equaled some multiple of the interest requirement on the total amount of bonds *to be outstanding* after the new issue. The multiple generally ranges from 2 to 4, and the test period is usually a rather short one immediately proceeding the date of the proposed new issue. For example, the indenture covering the many issues of mortgage bonds of the Commonwealth Edison Company stipulates that earnings available for bond interest in 12 of the preceding 15 months must have equaled 2½ times the interest requirement on all such bonds to be outstanding. Sometimes, alternative test periods are designated. For example, it may be stipulated that the corporation may issue additional bonds if earnings available for bond interest in 10 of the preceding 12 months *or* on the average in the preceding 3 years were equal to 3 times the interest requirement.

Property Limitations

Further issues of bonds under open-end indentures are often restricted, not only in relation to earnings available for bond interest, but also in terms of the value of property pledged. The most popular kind of restriction on pledged property simply stipulates that additional issues of bonds under the indenture must not exceed some percentage, such as 60 or 70 percent, of the cost or fair value of additional property pledged, whichever of these measures of value is less. For example, a corporation whose indenture has a 70 percent restriction may put out an original bond issue of $7 million on pledging assets worth $10 million. If, later, it wanted to buy additional facilities at a cost of $4 million, it could meet part of the purchase price by issuing bonds of a face value of $2.8 million. The total pledged assets of $14 million would then protect total outstanding bonds of $9.8 million. The older bonds would have equal ranking with the later issue in claims against the new assets, and the later issue would have equal ranking with the original one in claims against the assets originally pledged.

Property limitations sometimes take other forms, of which the following are examples: (1) The total of outstanding bonds shall not exceed working capital or some percentage of it. (2) The total shall not exceed the par or stated value of outstanding stock, both common and preferred, or some percentage or multiple of this figure. (3) The total shall not exceed the book value of stock and surplus, or some percentage or multiple. (4) *Total debt* shall not exceed 33⅓ percent, 40 percent, or some other percentage of total tangible assets. As an example, the indenture of the Louisville & Nashville Railroad, covering its first and refunding mortgage bonds, provides that the total amount of bonds "and prior liens" shall not exceed three times the amount of its capital stock. In some indentures, these kinds of restrictions—one or more—are used in addition to the kind of property limitation described in the preceding paragraph; in others, they are used in lieu of it. It will be noticed that a restriction of the fourth type, as listed here, has the effect of limiting the amount of debt of all kinds and maturities, and not simply the amount of secured bonds.

Separate Application of Earnings and Property Limitations

Where indentures contain both earnings and property limitations on further issues, as in the common practice, the usual rule is that the stricter standard governs. To see how this works, let us return to the illustration in which the application of a 70 percent property limitation was demonstrated. Let us assume that the indenture also provides that additional bonds may be issued only if earnings available for bond interest in a designated test period were equal to three times the interest requirement on total bonds to be outstanding. Assume that the original bonds bear interest at 5 percent, that the same rate would be paid on the additional bonds the corporation proposes to issue, and that test period earnings available for bond interest amounted to $1.35 million. Although, therefore, the property restriction would permit the issuance of $2.8 million of bonds, as we have already seen, the application of the earnings restriction would cut this figure to $2 million. Three times the interest requirement of $350,000 on the bonds already outstanding is $1.05 million. This amount subtracted from $1.35 million leaves $300,000 which is 3 times the amount of interest the corporation is permitted to pay on additional bonds. The actual amount of interest permitted would be $100,000, and at a rate of 5 percent this would allow for only $2 million of bonds ($100,000 ÷ .05).

Variations in Terms

Original investors in bonds to be issued under an open-end indenture are likely to be quite willing to give the corporation latitude in fixing for later issues interest rates, maturities, and call prices for redemption that are different from those of the original issue. The very authorization of further issues argues that the corporation should be empowered to tailor its successive offerings in keeping with changing conditions in the market for long-term funds.

Under a single open-end indenture, accordingly, a corporation might sell a first issue that had an interest rate of 4½ percent, a 20-year maturity, and call prices ranging downward from 103; a second issue with an interest rate of 4 percent, a 15-year maturity, and call prices graduated downward from 102; and a third issue with an interest rate of 5 percent, a 25-year maturity, and call prices ranging downward from 105. For separate issues with varying terms under a single indenture, a corporation is likely to use series labels. Thus, the 4½ percent bonds would be labeled Series A, the 4 percent issue Series B, and so on. For example, the Virginia Electric and Power Company reported that at the end of 1967 it had outstanding $541.2 million of "first and refunding" mortgage bonds from Series E through Series V, with interest rates ranging from 2¾ percent to 6 7/8 percent, and with maturities ranging from March 1, 1975, to December 1, 1997.[2]

Restrictions in Closed Indentures

Except for priorities of claims such as taxes and wages, allowed for in the bankruptcy statutes, buyers of bonds issued under a closed indenture have no reason to fear that other creditors will get claims on the pledged property prior or equal to their own. Without their consent, the corporation cannot give such prior or equal claims. Nor are they asked to permit variations in the terms of later issues, since by definition there are to be no later issues under a closed indenture. Nevertheless, the owners of a corporation's closed indenture bonds

[2]*Annual Report*, 1967, p. 26.

have reason to be concerned about the total amount and kinds of debts that it may contract. The corporation's default on subsequently issued debenture bonds or on bank loans or, in truth, on its obligations to trade creditors would be anything but pleasant for the secured bondholders. Despite the priority of their position, they could anticipate a long period of reorganization or liquidation during which interest would not be paid on their bonds and in which both the accumulated interest and the principal would be in jeopardy.

To reduce the dangers of default in any direction, therefore, prospective buyers of secured bonds issued under closed indentures do not hesitate to demand indenture restrictions on the total debt or the total long-term debt that the corporate issuers may contract. Such restrictions are commonly in the form of one or more of the broad types of property limitations referred to previously—that is, limitations of total debt or of total long-term debt in relation to working capital, total tangible assets, capital stock, or capital stock and surplus.

AFTER-ACQUIRED PROPERTY CLAUSES

A danger that buyers of mortgage bonds want to guard against is the possibility that debtor corporations will shift the bulk of their operations to new properties and will pledge these new properties for bond issues under separate indentures. A corporation that has been operating in the North, for example, may build new facilities in the South, and rapidly concentrate more and more of its operations at the new location, perhaps eventually discontinuing production in the North. Such a shift would not reduce in any way the corporation's obligations under the original mortgage indenture, but *in case of insolvency* the lien on the original properties would be likely to be of little value. Thus, the position of the bondholders for whose safety these properties had been pledged could hardly be much better than that of unsecured creditors.

Accordingly, investors in mortgage bonds usually insist that "after-acquired property" clauses be included in indentures. Such a clause obligates the corporation to pledge under the indenture all property "hereafter acquired" of a character identical with or similar to that already pledged. To fail to pledge newly acquired property of this description would be a violation of a covenant no less than the nonpayment of interest or principal. On such an occurrence, the trustee could take legal action to safeguard the bondholders' position.

Application in Open-End Indentures

After-acquired property clauses, one might say, go hand in hand with open-end indentures (including limited open-end ones in which the maximum dollar figure is set quite high). As the use of an open-end indenture envisages the sale from time to time of additional bonds to finance property acquisitions, and as its property limitation is likely to stipulate what amount of bonds in relation to the value of added pledged property may be issued, it probably is not a hardship *to be required* to pledge the newly acquired property. Such a requirement could be a hardship, however, if the earnings and property restrictions in the existing indenture were unduly severe.

Application in Closed Indentures

Not infrequently, after-acquired property clauses find their way into closed indentures, although their presence there may appear to be quite illogical. Newly acquired property must be pledged under the existing indenture, but additional bonds that have the same rank as the existing ones cannot be issued. If the new property is pledged for a separate bond issue, only a second lien can be given.

Sometimes, corporate managements, particularly those of manufacturing enterprises, accept after-acquired property clauses for their closed indentures because they have few prospects of acquiring additional properties of a value that would justify further bond sales. Sometimes, they accept such clauses because they look on the bond financing as a temporary departure from the simple common stock form of financial structure, which they plan to restore as quickly as possible. They expect to have the bonds retired before occasions arise for substantial additional acquisitions of property. In some cases, no doubt, the after-acquired property clause is forced on corporations in weak bargaining positions, and even though their managements anticipate that it will be the source of difficulties in future financing. And it appears that in at least a few cases the after-acquired property clause is inadvertently accepted by corporate managements—without their realizing its consequences for future financing.

Avoidance of After-Acquired Property Clauses

Many writers on corporation finance give much attention to ways by which corporations can acquire property, or its use, without making it subject to the liens of existing indentures that contain after-acquired property clauses. But investment bankers, institutional investors, and other bond buyers know of these means of avoidance no less than do corporate managements and their attorneys. Therefore, when prospective investors anticipate that specific means of avoidance, if employed, would be harmful to them, they insist that the indentures contain covenants expressly precluding their use. But when, on the other hand, no harm is expected to result from the employment of certain means of avoidance, the investors may be willing specifically to allow them by indenture provisions, or they may be satisfied to consent by silence—to have the indentures say nothing about them.

One means of avoidance is to lease property rather than to buy it outright, as in the Philadelphia Plan for acquiring railroad rolling stock. Another is to establish subsidiaries and have them acquire the new property. Another is to give to the sellers of newly acquired property purchase-money mortgages for the noncash part of the purchase price. The liens of such mortgage obligations are held by the courts to have priority over the liens of bonds whose indentures have after-acquired property clauses. A fourth means is for the corporation to have its properties absorbed by another in a merger or consolidation, for the general rule is that after-acquired property clauses in indentures of absorbed corporations cease to operate. A final and quite obvious way is to call for redemption the bonds that have an after-acquired property clause that is proving to be obnoxious.

For protection against methods of avoidance that could prove harmful to their interests, bond buyers often insist on indenture prohibitions or restrictions on mergers, consolidations, establishment and operations of subsidiaries, and certain kinds of leasing arrangements. For example, a corporation may be required to stipulate in its indenture that it will not allow itself to be absorbed by another in a merger or consolidation unless the absorbing corporation will specifically agree to make subsequently acquired property (and perhaps even its existing property) subject to the lien of the existing indenture. On the other hand, bond buyers are usually willing to permit, or at least to have the indentures remain silent about, the leasing of equipment according to the Philadelphia Plan and the use of purchase-money mortgages. Acquiescence in the equipment leasing arrangement is prompted by the very need of the corporation—say, a railroad—to have ready access to an adequate supply of locomotives and cars, the relative cheapness of financing by the equipment trust procedure, and the fact that the existing bonds will get a first lien on the equipment when the corporation pays off the equipment trust certificates and takes title to it. It is prompted in acquisitions involving purchase-money mortgages because the existing bonds immediately get a second lien on the property so acquired—property that the corporation otherwise might not want to acquire at all.

DEBENTURE BONDS

Considering all that has been written in the foregoing pages about security for bond issues, one might be tempted to give but brief attention to debenture bonds—to treat them as simply occupying the other side of the picture. By definition, debenture bonds are unsecured, and so are lacking in the kinds of security features that have been discussed. But debenture bonds are now so outstandingly important as instruments of corporate financing that they hardly deserve analysis simply on the basis of what they lack.

The great present-day popularity of debenture bonds with both issuers and investors can be largely explained on the basis of the proposition, stated earlier in this chapter, that safety and security do not necessarily mean the same thing. In the liquidation of a corporation after a default, the holders of its debenture bonds can hardly expect to realize as much on their claims as the holders of its mortgage bonds and other secured creditors, and in a reorganization the debenture bondholders must ordinarily expect to make greater sacrifices than the secured bondholders and other secured creditors. In these respects, the secured bonds *of a given corporation* can almost always be said to be safer than the debenture bonds *of the same corporation.* But the capacity of corporations to avoid defaults—after all, the final criterion of safety—obviously does not depend on whether or not their bonds are secured. It depends on their financial position in general and on their earning power. Thus, the debenture bonds of corporations with strong financial position and high earning capacity almost invariably rank higher from the standpoint of safety than do the secured bonds of corporations of weaker financial position and more limited earning power. Moreover, the holders of debenture bonds are not without claims to assets. Like any other class of creditors, they have legal rights to take action to seize assets for the satisfaction of their claims if unpaid when due. For this reason, the debenture bondholders of a corporation that has no obligations for which it has pledged assets generally have every reason to believe that their claim to assets is almost as strong as it would be were their bonds to have a mortgage lien—*almost* as strong, because other unsecured creditors would have equal pro rata claims. But even the "almost" deserves little emphasis when the amount of other unsecured claims is quite small in comparison with the amount of the debenture bonds.

Revolution in Debenture Financing

The steady post-World War II growth in the use of the debenture bond as a principal instrument of corporate financing has been truly phenomenal. We have had another revolution in the field of finance, much less speedy in its development than the revolutionary switch from coupon to registered bonds, described in Chapter 27, but much more important to the attitudes and interests of both corporations and investors. Among new issues of securities of all classes and subclasses, as measured by dollar amounts, debenture bonds now hold the leading position by a wide margin. Moreover, the revolution continues, for the powerful movement toward the substitution of debenture bonds for secured issues and the substitution of convertible debentures for common stock issues, especially notable in the long period of business expansion and extraordinarily high levels of corporate financing beginning in 1961, shows no signs of abatement. One cannot but be impressed by the virtual flood of new issues of debentures reported almost on a daily basis in the financial press, including the many recent issues that because of our balance-of-payments difficulties have been offered exclusively to foreigners.

The revolutionary aspect of the post-World War II growth in the use of debenture bonds stands out all the more clearly because debentures as a class did not have a very good reputation in the prewar period. Not much can be said in this regard about the depressed decade of the 1930's, during which financing for growth was minimal. But in the decade of the 1920's when corporate borrowing reached unprecedented levels, the mortgage bond was the premier instrument, while collateral trust bonds also occupied an important position. A goodly number of corporations were successful in financing with debenture bonds, but investors' suspicions about their lack of security was generally evidenced by the substantially higher interest rates that many carried by comparison with the rates set on secured bond issues.

Issuers of Debentures

So high is the esteem in which some corporations are held by the investment community that they are able to issue debenture bonds on terms as favorable to themselves as would be obtainable on secured bonds. For such corporations, the issuance of debenture bonds rather than secured bonds is a mark of distinction. Though these corporations may have vast aggregations of pledgeable assets, they are quite pleased to take the debenture route and thus avoid all the complexities that secured issues involve.

At the other extreme are corporations that in order to borrow on a long-term basis have no choice but to sell debenture issues; they have no assets that could be conveniently used for pledge purposes. Such is often the situation with mercantile corporations that rent all or most of their operating facilities.

In between are large numbers of corporations that may be able to get better terms with secured issues than with debenture issues but that, nevertheless, prefer debentures. This kind of choice is made by many manufacturing corporations. In many instances, it is made almost as a matter of course because the better terms that could be had on secured issues—in view of the revolutionary change in investors' attitudes toward debentures—are so slight as to merit little serious consideration. Aside from this, however, the managements of many manufacturing corporations are often convinced that their access to short-term credit would be too greatly restricted should they pledge their fixed assets on bond issues. They want to avoid such a restriction because they are accustomed to depending heavily on trade suppliers and banks as sources of current assets. Public utility corporations frequently put out debenture issues because of decisions that their existing mortgage debt is as large as it should be. Although they may have additional pledgeable assets, and although their open-end indentures would permit new series of mortgage bonds, they decide that proposed long-term borrowing, though justifiable in existing circumstances, does not fit in with their long-range standards for trading on the equity. Hence, they choose debenture issues as a kind of temporary financing, quite often setting the stage to eliminate them painlessly by making them convertible at the holders' option into common stock. Even with public utilities, however, attitudes have been changing, so that many now look on debenture bonds as the much preferred means of debt financing and not simply as a supplement to financing with mortgage bonds. Among the leading exemplars of this new attitude toward debenture financing have been the American Telephone and Telegraph Company and its Bell System subsidiaries, a very large proportion of whose many billions of dollars of debt financing in recent years has taken the debenture route, and the Columbia Gas System, Inc., which reported that at the end of the year 1967 it had outstanding approximately $723 million of debentures in 24 series and *no* mortgage obligations.[3]

Protective Provisions for Debentures

Theoretically, a corporation can issue as many debenture bonds as people are willing to buy. If an original indenture is closed, a whole succession of additional indentures can be drawn up for further issues, and because nothing is pledged, the buyer of a bond anywhere along the line has claims of equal standing with those of any other buyer, even those who may have bought many years earlier. But original buyers of debenture bonds know of this possibility, and they are usually wise enough to insist on indenture restrictions on further indebtedness closely comparable with those contained in indentures for secured issues.

One danger that buyers of debenture bonds want especially to guard against is a weakening of their claims against corporate assets by pledges of these assets to *other* creditors after the debenture bonds have been sold. Accordingly, indentures for debenture issues commonly provide that if secured bonds are subsequently issued the existing debentures will be secured equally and ratably. A corporation that first issues, say, $10 million of debenture bonds and later sells $20 million of mortgage bonds would really have a total issue of $30 million of mortgage bonds and no longer any debentures, although the debentures would probably still be alluded to by that designation. Often, too, indentures for debenture issues contain restrictions on any other pledging of property, its leasing to other concerns, and sale-and-leaseback arrangements, although usually with an exception allowing

[3]*Annual Report*, 1967, p. 16.

for pledges on bank loans and other short-term advances not exceeding in maturity some limited period, such as one year.

In many instances, too, investors in debenture bonds demand protection against the dangers of excessive piling up of unsecured debts by the issuing corporations—debts that would have equal pro rata claims with their own in the event of financial difficulties. The most popular way of getting this protection is to insist on indenture restrictions limiting further issues of all classes of long-term obligations. Sometimes, the restrictions are extended to further short-term as well as to long-term indebtedness, and sometimes earnings limitations are inserted as means of holding in check the further incurring of debt. For example, the indenture covering the 4½ percent debentures of the Caterpillar Tractor Company, maturing in 1977, provides that it may incur no further long-term debt unless, afterward, its tangible assets less current liabilities are equal to at least 2½ times the total long-term debt. The indenture for the Phillip Morris 4⅞ percent debentures, maturing in 1979, has an identical provision with a 2-times instead of a 2½-times limit. The indenture covering the 3⅞ percent debentures of the Seaboard-Atlantic Coast Line Railroad, due in 1977, provides that no long-term debt may be added unless available earnings in 12 of the preceding 15 calendar months were equal to at least 3 times the annual fixed charges on all long-term debt to be outstanding.

Subordinated Debentures

Subordinated debenture bonds are so called because in the indentures on whose basis they are issued their claims against assets in corporate dissolution or reorganization are made inferior to those of designated kinds of senior debt. Whereas an ordinary debenture bond has claims inferior to those of a mortgage bond of the same corporation because of the pledge of assets given to the mortgage bond, the inferiority in the position of the subordinated debenture comes about because *it is specifically provided for in its own indenture.* The senior debt to which the claims of debenture holders are made inferior usually comprises all liabilities for borrowed money, whether short term or long term, and whether already contracted or contracted after the subordinated debentures have been issued. It therefore consists of bonds of other classes, including ordinary debentures, and secured or unsecured bank loans, but not accounts payable to trade creditors, accrued expenses, and dividends payable.

Although bonds with subordinated claims had sometimes been issued in corporate reorganizations long before the late 1930's it was not until then that the use of subordinated debentures as ordinary financing instruments began its development. They were introduced as such by sales finance and consumer finance companies—organizations whose principal function is to grant loans to individuals for consumption purposes. In the post-World War II years, the finance companies have expanded their use of subordinated debentures, but their issues have been swamped in a great flood that has come from industrial corporations, augmented by smaller flows from public utilities and airlines and even from railroads. In sum, the revolution in debenture financing, which has been emphasized in the foregoing pages, has been a development in two directions—one encompassing ordinary debentures and the other encompassing subordinated debentures.

Reasons for Use. For issuing corporations, the principal reason that subordinated debentures have grown so rapidly in popularity is that they serve excellently as a substitute for common and preferred stocks in providing protection for creditors. Their sale provides cash directly but also sets the stage for additional borrowing. This is so because subordination of the claims of subordinated debentures extends not only to senior debt existing at the time of their sale *but also to that contracted thereafter*. Like a sale of stock, therefore, a sale of subordinated debentures, by expanding a corporation's assets and presumably its earning power, should encourage other lenders to supply funds to the corporation. Like investors in stock, the buyers of subordinated debentures supply assets that serve as a cushion of protection for other classes of lenders, and they contribute earning power to which they give these lenders claims superior to their own.

An illustration will clarify the protective role of subordinated debentures for holders of corporate obligations designated "senior." Assume that the assets of a failed corporation are liquidated for $8.55 million and that creditor claims at the time of final settlement are as follows (including interest when allowable and disregarding the possibility of preferred claims under the bankruptcy statutes).

Debenture bonds	$ 4,000,000
Subordinated debenture bonds	2,400,000
Unsecured short-term bank loans	2,000,000
Other unsecured short-term obligations	3,000,000
Total	$11,400,000

Both the debenture bonds and the short-term bank loans qualify as senior debt as that category is defined in the indenture for the subordinated debentures. The cash realized in liquidation is sufficient to pay 75 cents on each dollar of all classes of claims, but most of the $1.8 million first tentatively allocated to the subordinated debenture bondholders does not stay with them. At 75 cents on the dollar, the debenture bonds have an unsatisfied claim of $1 million, and the bank lenders an unsatisfied claim of $500,000. Accordingly, to satisfy these claimants, in whose favor the claims of the subordinated debentures have been waived, a transfer of $1.5 million is made to them from the $1.8 million first assigned to the subordinated debentures.

As a result, the ordinary debenture bonds and the bank loans are paid off in full; the holders of the subordinated debentures receive only $300,000 in settlement of their total claims of $2.4 million, or 12.5 cents on the dollar, and the other short-term creditors receive an unadjusted 75 cents on the dollar for a total of $2.25 million.

In issuing subordinated debentures, many corporations indicate their expectation that the debentures will serve only temporarily as a substitute for common stock financing. They indicate this expectation by making the debentures convertible into common stock at the option of the holders, and by setting conversion prices not very far above the current market prices of their common stocks. Why, then, does not a corporation sell common stock in the first place and be done with it? The answer in part is that in making conversions later it really gets a better price for the common stock than it would have got had it sold common at the time of offering the debentures. Another facet of the answer is that flotation costs on the issue of subordinated debentures are likely to be considerably less than would be those of a common stock flotation. As long as the debentures remain outstanding, moreover, the interest rate paid on them may be less than the dividend rate being paid on the common stock; hence, like any debt issue they provide the advantages—and give rise to the dangers—of trading on the equity. Whatever the relationship between the interest rate and the dividend rate, indeed, there is always the consideration that interest is deductible for income tax purposes while dividends are not.

Appeal to Investors. But a security cannot be sold simply because it has features to the liking of many potential issuers; investors, too, must find it to their liking. It might seem strange that individuals and institutions would be willing to buy a *bond* that is expressly given an inferior status in its claims to principal and interest in the event of reorganization or dissolution. Why do they buy? The answer must be primarily that the interest rate or some other feature, most likely convertibility into common stock, is attractive and that the buyers do not expect the issuers' reorganization or dissolution.

If relatively conservative investors would be willing to buy a corporation's preferred stock issue, all the more should they feel safe in buying its subordinated debentures. They would buy the preferred stock in the expectation that the corporation would be able to meet all its maturing debts, that dividends at the prescribed rate, though payable at the discretion of the board of directors, would actually be earned and paid, and that any redemption fund provisions for the retirement of the stock would be fulfilled. In buying subordinated debentures, similarly, investors expect the corporation to have no difficulties in meeting its obligations on them as well as on all debts designated as "senior." The corporation's obligation to pay interest and principal is absolute; as long as it is able to pay, the inferiority of the bondholder's position is not at all apparent. Moreover, the indenture of a subordinated issue, like that for any other kind of bonds, will surely have various kinds of safeguards for the bondholders.

As for the interest rate, it is likely to be somewhat higher than the corporation would have to pay were it selling an issue of ordinary debentures, but not so high as the probable dividend rate were it selling preferred stock. Thus, the investor is allowed some compensation for the additional risks he accepts, but not so much as he could doubtless demand were he to accept the greater risks of ownership by becoming a preferred stockholder.

Making subordinated debentures convertible into common stock has been a very popular alternative to giving them a relatively high interest rate. Indeed, it appears that the typical corporation of fairly good financial position and earning power can borrow at most times on convertible subordinated debentures at a significantly lower rate than it would have to pay on nonconvertible ordinary debentures. Financing with convertible issues that carry relatively low rates of interest is especially likely to be successful when they are offered to corporations' existing common stockholders, as has been the practice with a large proportion of these issues in recent years. If satisfied with a corporation's earnings record, dividends, and prospects, its common stockholders are likely to be most interested in acquiring additional shares and willing to buy bonds as an indirect way of getting access to them. They could go into the market to buy additional shares at once, but they may be somewhat cautious about extending their common stock commitments. By buying the debentures, they can hold the relatively safe position of bondholders until the market price of the stock has risen well above the conversion price—or indefinitely should it never reach that level, or, indeed, should it fall. At any rate, accustomed as common stockholders are to their risky position as residual claimants against assets, they may give little thought to the inferior position of subordinated debentures. Nevertheless, many corporations find that investors other than their existing common stockholders can be attracted as buyers of their relatively low-rate subordinated debentures by the addition of the convertibility feature, so that offerings of such issues to the general public have also been quite numerous.

GUARANTEED BONDS

A bond is said to be guaranteed when one or more corporations or individuals other than the issuer accept contractual responsibility for the payment of interest or principal or both interest and principal. Most guaranties extend simultaneously to both interest and principal. According to accepted terminology, a corporation never guarantees its own bonds. It has the unquestioned obligation to pay interest and principal, but this is not described as a guaranty. Even for equipment trust certificates, which bear the guaranty of the railroad in whose behalf they are issued, the issuer, we have seen, is the trustee rather than the railroad.

Some guaranties for bond issues are made at the time of the original sale of the bonds, and others come into being only after the bond issues have been outstanding for some time. We may proceed to examine the whys and hows that explain this difference in timing.

Guaranties from the Beginning

When one or more individuals or corporations other than the issuer guarantee the payment of interest and principal on a bond issue at the time of its origin, the objective is almost always to make the bonds more attractive to investors than they otherwise would be. The credit position of the issuer is likely to be relatively weak, and without the guaranty the bonds may not be salable at anything close to what the issuer and guarantor regard as fair terms, if salable at all. Therefore, the guaranty is expected to be of decisive importance in toning up the investment appeal of the bonds.

Guaranties for Subsidiaries' Bonds Offered to Foreigners. By a very wide margin, the most prominent use of guaranties for bond issues at the present time originates in borrowing by American industrial corporation subsidiaries from foreign investors—a use dating chiefly from the fall of 1967 but reaching flood proportions in the spring of 1968. This use has been attributable almost entirely to our balance-of-payments difficulties, which have led to a variety of governmental measures to curb the outflow of American funds for investment in foreign plants, machinery and equipment, and securities—measures that were largely enforced by persuasion before 1968 but became mostly compulsory by decree of the Johnson Administration at the beginning of that year. As a result, our corporations have found it increasingly necessary to borrow from foreigners when they want to finance operating facilities located outside the United States—whether to provide new facilities or to expand facilities already held. To do this, they have had subsidiary corporations that were already in operation in the overseas areas, or subsidiaries newly established as purely financing entities, offer new bond issues exclusively to foreign investors, with the parent corporations adding their guaranties to make the bonds attractive to these investors.

As for attractiveness, the advantage of guaranties in making bonds salable though carrying interest rates at moderate levels has been proved beyond question. The guaranteeing parent corporations generally have credit standings of high international repute, whereas their subsidiaries have not been well known or, if newly established for the sole purpose of foreign borrowing, have had no credit reputations at all.

Almost all the guaranteed issues offered to foreigners have been debenture bonds, and almost all have been offered for Eurodollars and not for foreign currencies. (Eurodollars are U.S. dollars owned by foreigners and generally held as deposits with foreign banks or with foreign branches of American banks, and therefore not subject to our restrictive balance-of-payments regulations. Despite the descriptive title given to these dollars, many are owned by foreigners who live outside Europe.) A large proportion of the issues have been given the privilege of conversion into the common stock of the guaranteeing *parent* corporation—a privilege apparently worth as much as two percentage points in the interest rates carried by the bonds. And, finally, despite our domestic revolution in registered as opposed to coupon bonds, virtually all the guaranteed issues offered to foreigners have been in coupon form. Foreign investors seem to be unanimously of the opinion that they ought to keep their ownership secret—especially from tax-gatherers, one presumes.

By way of illustration, several guaranteed issues of the spring of 1968 may be cited.

1. A $25 million issue of "6¾% Guaranteed Debentures Due 1983" of Amoco International Finance Corporation, with payment "of principal, premium, if any, interest and sinking fund unconditionally guaranteed" by the Standard Oil Company (of Indiana).
2. A $60 million issue of "4¾% Guaranteed Convertible Sinking Fund Debentures Due 1988" of the Chrysler Overseas Capital Corporation "convertible on and after December 15, 1968 into Common Stock of and Unconditionally Guaranteed" by Chrysler Corporation.
3. A $15 million issue of "5.5% Guaranteed (Subordinated) Debentures Due 1988" of Genesco World Apparel, Ltd., convertible into the stock of and guaranteed "on a subordinated basis" by Genesco Inc.
4. A $70 million issue of "4½% Convertible Guaranteed Debentures Due 1988" of Eastman Kodak International Capital Company, Inc., convertible into the common stock of and unconditionally guaranteed by Eastman Kodak Company.

Guaranties by Individuals. Bond issues guaranteed by individuals are almost always of small size. They are generally the issues of small, closely held corporations, and the guarantors are usually one or more of the principal stockholders. Such bond issues, moreover, are much more often sold by private placement with institutional investors than by public offerings. The high flotation costs of public offerings and the lack of interest of investment bankers in small issues tend to preclude public offerings.

Suppose, for example, that the president of a relatively small corporation goes to a life insurance company looking for funds. His corporation needs approximately $250,000, and he proposes that the insurance company buy a new bond issue of that face amount. But the insurance company learns that the president owns 85 percent of the stock of the corporation and that he is quite wealthy. As any loan to the corporation will principally benefit this man, the insurance company is likely to stipulate that it will buy the bonds, if at all, only if he will guarantee them.

Guaranties for Domestic Subsidiaries. Corporations sometimes guarantee the payment of interest and principal on the bonds of their domestic subsidiaries. If a subsidiary's proposed bond issue is being offered to institutional investors, they are likely to have exactly the same attitude as that in the foregoing case—the financing of the subsidiary must be for the benefit of the parent corporation principally or exclusively (depending on what proportion of the subsidiary's stock it owns), and therefore the parent should be willing to stand behind the subsidiary's bonds. If, on the other hand, the bonds are to be offered to the public, the parent, without any pressure from investment bankers or anybody else, may add its guaranty as a means of getting a lower interest cost. Should its credit rating be higher than that of its subsidiary and its affairs better known to the investment community, as would be likely, the interest rate differential between guaranteed and nonguaranteed bonds could be substantial. Any saving of interest expense to the subsidiary would be of direct benefit to itself. A recent example of a public offering of this type was the $10 million issue of 5¼ percent subordinated debentures of Pueblo Supermarkets of New York, Inc., which were guaranteed as to both principal and interest by its parent, Pueblo Supermarkets, Inc., and also made convertible into the parent's common stock.

Joint Guaranties in the Railroad Industry. Many guaranteed bond issues have originated in the railroad industry in connection with the building of bridges, terminal properties, and beltline facilities for the interchange of cars in and around our larger cities. The distinctive feature of these issues is that they have simultaneously the joint and several guaranties of two or more railroads. Assume, for example, that three railroads decide that they should have a new union station in a given city. They establish a new corporation to construct and operate the station, apportioning its stock among themselves. However, they want to obtain most of the money for construction from a bond issue to be sold by the joint subsidiary—the terminal corporation. But they know that the newly established terminal corporation can hardly have much of an investment rating, and that mortgaging the union station can hardly add much to the attractiveness of the proposed bonds—what could the bondholders do with the station if they had to foreclose on it? To make the bonds salable on reasonable terms, therefore, they add their guaranties. At the same time, they enter into contracts with the terminal subsidiary to use its facilities on a rental basis. Each railroad agrees to pay an annual rental in proportion to its prospective use of the facilities, and the rents in total are set at a level to cover interest and sinking fund requirements on the bonds and to meet maintenance expenses.

On bonds for which there are two or more guarantors—they are usually called joint bonds—the standard practice is for each guarantor to accept liability for the full principal and interest. This is what is meant by the "several" of a joint-and-several guaranty. After a default, therefore, the bondholders or their trustee could bring suit against any one of the guarantors for full payment. On payment, this guarantor would then have a right of action against the other guarantors according to the proportions of their joint obligations. A joint bond issue guaranteed by a strong railroad and by two weak ones, therefore, would have its investment appeal primarily in the guaranty of the strong road.

Illustrative of the position of joint guaranties in the railroad industry was the notation in the 1967 annual report of the Penn Central Company that in addition to the liabilities shown in its balance sheet it had contingent liabilities of approximately $265 million on December 31 "in respect to the principal of obligations issued by affiliated companies," and that approximately $246 million of these contingent obligations "have been entered into jointly or jointly and severally with other companies."[4]

Later Guaranties

The guaranteeing of bond issues after they have been outstanding for some time has been a practice very largely confined to the railroad industry, and even in that industry it is now a matter chiefly of historical importance. In the discussion of leases in Chapter 10, it was pointed out that many of our large railroad systems, particularly those of the East, were largely built up by leasing the entire operating properties of many smaller companies. When approached with propositions for the leasing of their facilities, the smaller companies, as a rule, had bonds outstanding, so that acceptance of responsibility for these issues by the system companies became a normal feature of the lease contracts. Whether or not formal guaranties were expressly given by the system companies, they obligated themselves to pay annual rentals sufficient to take care of the interest and principal requirements of the lessors' bonds, as well as to pay dividends at stipulated rates on their outstanding stock.

---

[4]*Annual Report,* 1967, p. 32. The figures cited "gave effect to" the subsequent absorption of the New York Central Railroad by the Pennsylvania in a merger that became effective on February 1, 1968.

QUESTIONS

1. If a corporation has outstanding both a mortgage bond issue and a debenture bond issue, are the mortgage bonds necessarily safer than the debenture bonds? Discuss.

2. Is the secured bond issue of any corporation necessarily safer than the debenture bond issue of any other corporation? Explain.

3. With respect to priority of claims, what is indicated by bond designations such as first mortgage, second mortgage, first general mortgage, and first and refunding mortgage?

4. Explain the procedure for issuing equipment trust certificates according to the Philadelphia Plan. Are such certificates debt instruments or equity instruments? Explain.

5. Why are collateral trust bonds so called? Could a single issue of bonds be simultaneously a mortgage and a collateral trust issue? Why or why not?

6. When defaulting corporations seek to reorganize in bankruptcy, of what value to the owners of secured bonds is the security previously provided for these bonds?

7. What is the distinction between open-end and closed indentures? How, if at all, are they related to after-acquired-property clauses?

8. Explain how earnings and property limitations are applied to restrict the volume of bonds that may be issued under open-end indentures.

9. To what extent is it permissible for corporations to vary the terms and features of successive issues of bonds covered by a single open-end indenture?

10. How important are debenture bonds as an instrument of corporate financing? For what reasons have they grown enormously in popularity in recent years?

11. On the basis of indenture provisions, how is it possible for debenture bonds, in certain circumstances, to become secured bonds?

12. What is the nature of the subordination of subordinated debenture bonds? What effect does it have on the capacity of the issuing corporations to incur debt? Explain.

13. To what extent is the popularity of debenture bonds and subordinated debenture bonds attributable to convertibility into common stock?

14. What are Eurodollar bonds? Who issues them? What influence do guaranties and convertibility have on their successful flotation? On the interest rates they carry?

15. How important are guaranties as a feature of bond issues other than Eurodollar bonds?

PROBLEMS

1. The open-end mortgage indenture of the Valley Power Corporation permits it to issue additional bonds from time to time, provided that such issues do not exceed 66⅔ percent of the value of additional property

pledged, and provided that average earnings available for bond interest in the 3 preceding years have been equal to 2½ times the interest requirement on the total amount of bonds to be outstanding. The corporation's outstanding mortgage bonds consist of a Series A issue of $10 million, bearing interest at 5 percent, and a Series B issue of $20 million, bearing interest at 5½ percent. It now wants to put out a Series C issue for the largest permissible amount to finance the acquisition of land and generating facilities, which will cost $24 million and which will be pledged under the indenture. Investment bankers advise the corporation that to find a market the new bonds must bear interest at 6½ percent. On the basis of this rate, and assuming that average annual earnings available for bond interest in the past 3 years have been $6,800,000, determine the maximum amount of Series C bonds that the corporation may issue while keeping within the limits of the indenture restrictions.

2. Claims against the Benedict Manufacturing Company as it reaches the final stages of dissolution in bankruptcy are as follows.

First-mortgage bonds	$ 9,000,000
Debenture bonds	2,500,000
Citizens State Bank (short-term loans)	4,500,000
Other short-term creditors	3,800,000
Preferred stock (at par value)	5,000,000
Common stock (at par value)	15,000,000

There are dividend arrearages of $2,400,000 on the preferred stock, and its contract gives it a preference to assets at its par value in the event of involuntary dissolution as in bankruptcy. The common stock was originally sold at a premium of 20 percent. No dividends have been paid on it for 16 years, although for 10 years before that regular dividends were paid upon it at the rate of 8 percent per annum.

The fixed assets pledged as security for the first-mortgage bonds were sold for $7,500,000; the inventories pledged as security for the short-term loans from the Citizens State Bank were sold for $4,200,000; and $4,860,000 was realized from the liquidation of other current assets and some unpledged fixed assets.

Of these amounts received in the liquidation of the corporation's assets, determine (*a*) how much in total would be distributed to each class of claimants, and (*b*) what percentage of its claims each class would recover.

3. The Good Hope Corporation is being liquidated in bankruptcy, and its assets realize $11,640,000. This money is to be distributed among the corporation's creditors, whose claims at the time of final settlement are as follows.

Short-term bank loans	$5,200,000
Other current liabilities	6,900,000
Debenture bonds	9,000,000
Subordinated debenture bonds	8,000,000

None of the corporation's assets had been pledged as security for any of its debts, but the indenture for the subordinated debenture bonds makes the claim of these bonds subordinate to senior debt, which is so described as to include the short-term bank loans and the ordinary debenture bonds.

Determine what portion of the $11,640,000 would be paid to each of the four classes of creditors, and what percentage of its claims each class would recover.

chapter 29

OTHER FEATURES OF BOND ISSUES

FURTHER PROTECTIVE PROVISIONS

As creditors, investors in bonds demand many kinds of safeguards to protect their claims to interest and principal. In Chapters 27 and 28, many of these safeguards were examined. We saw that corporate issuers of bonds must include in their indentures various promises, such as their covenants to keep their properties in good operating condition, to provide adequate insurance coverage, and to pay all taxes when due, and they must appoint trustees whose principal function it is to look after the interests of the bondholders. We saw that they agree to limit further issues of bonds and, quite often, the incurring of additional debt of all kinds. Many corporations, we saw also, provide pledges of assets for the protection of bondholders, and some obtain for their issues guaranties of other corporations or individuals. It was disclosed, too, that corporations often protect their bondholders by agreeing to pledge for their safety not only existing properties but after-acquired property as well. For debentures, it was brought out that corporations agree not to issue secured bonds unless the debentures are given equal security.

In Chapter 27, mention was made of the protective aspect of sinking funds set up by corporate debtors for the retirement of their single-maturity bonds. But this is a topic that deserves further examination. Three additional kinds of indenture provisions for the protection of bondholders await analysis: (1) limitations on divided payments while bonds are outstanding, (2) other restrictions on cash payments, and (3) authorizations for legal actions on default.

Sinking Funds

The typical buyer of corporate bonds thinks that the issuers should be making provisions to pay them off during the course of their lives, and should not cast about for means of paying them only as they approach maturity. Especially when the proceeds of bond issues are invested in assets subject to depreciation, depletion, or amortization does it seem reasonable that periodical reductions in the bonded debt should take place as the assets decline in value. The safety of the bondholders would seem to be progressively undermined were such a decline in asset values to take place while the full amount of original issues of bonds continued to be outstanding.

A mandatory periodical allocation of cash to a sinking fund for the redemption of portions of a bond issue obviously gives absolute and final protection to those bondholders whose bonds are thus redeemed, but it also strengthens the position of the remaining bondholders. When sinking fund requirements are placed in indentures, it is anticipated that payments into the sinking fund will be made possible by the cash throw-offs from depreciation, depletion, and amortization charges and from earnings. If, therefore, such throw-offs have enabled a corporation to retire in 10 years 40 percent of a 25-year bond issue, it should be all the more able to meet its remaining sinking fund obligations, as well as its interest obligations, on the greatly reduced and steadily declining amount of bonds in the remaining 15 years. Moreover, the remaining bondholders should have the advantage of a steady demand for bonds for sinking fund redemption. This demand for bonds should support their market price, so that possibilities of loss on sale, should the bondholder want to sell, ought to be greatly reduced.

Objectives. The objective of most mandatory sinking fund arrangements is to protect the bondholder by steady substantial reductions in the volume of outstanding bonds. In many cases, the protection demanded and given is provision for the elimination of almost the entire bond issue by sinking fund payments during its life, so that only a small fraction of the original amount is expected to remain to be redeemed at the final maturity. In the Armco Steel Corporation indenture for its $75 million of 4.35 percent debentures to mature in 1984, this is obviously the goal of the mandatory provision that requires sinking fund contributions of $1,875,000 per year from 1963 through 1966, and of $3,750,000 from 1967 through 1983. Protection of this degree is very commonly provided for in the indentures of industrial corporations. This is in keeping with the idea that long-term borrowing by such corporations should be regarded as only temporary departures from financial structures of the simple common stock form. But some managers of industrial corporations, especially those of stable earning power, think otherwise when they are bargaining over sinking fund provisions, and their attitude is generally shared by managers of public utilities and railroads. This attitude is that sinking fund payments should be designed to extinguish only part of a given bond issue during its life, with the balance to be paid off at its maturity out of the proceeds of a new flotation at that time. As such managers look with favor on a policy of continuous trading on the equity, they can see no grounds for unseemly haste in trying to eliminate long-term debt. Why, they may ask, should a corporation try to retire by periodic payments in 20 years the whole of a bond issue whose proceeds have been invested in assets expected to have useful lives of 40 or 50 years?

Some sinking fund arrangements have a second kind of objective for providing bondholder protection: to preserve the values of pledged properties so that the margin of security for the outstanding bonds is maintained, even though relatively few are redeemed until the final maturity. Such arrangements are found almost exclusively in the indentures covering secured bonds of public utility corporations. They provide that at the discretion of the corporation, cash contributed to its sinking fund as prescribed in the indenture may be spent for improvements and additions to fixed facilities rather than for bond retirement. Whether or not the indenture has the after-acquired property clause—as it is likely to have—the improvements and additions must be pledged. Moreover, no additional bonds may be sold in relation to the value of these improvements and additions, as may otherwise be permitted in an open-end indenture. Because a sinking fund is designed to sink or eliminate a debt, it is sometimes suggested that the term *improvement fund* would be a better title for a fund set up on the basis described. Nevertheless, the usual requirement is that if prescribed cash allocations are not spent for improvements they must be spent for bond redemption as for any ordinary sinking fund. Some public utilities, indeed, provide for some sinking of the debt as a contractual obligation, even though a substantial proportion of the sinking fund contributions may be spent for improvements. In the indentures of such utilities, it is typically provided that the periodical contribution to the sinking fund shall be thus-and-so, that this contribution shall be used for bond retirement unless spent for improvements and additions, but that, in any case, not less than a stipulated moderate portion will be used for retirement.

Contributions. A popular type of mandatory sinking fund provision is that the corporation will allocate annually or semiannually for bond retirement an amount of cash sufficient to redeem equal face amounts or equal percentages of the total quantity of bonds issued or of the total quantity outstanding at a given time. An example is the indenture for the 4½ percent debenture bonds of the Standard Oil Company (of Indiana), originally amounting to $200 million and maturing in 1983, which require annual sinking fund contributions of $6.5 million. Another is the indenture for the 4¼ percent convertible subordinated debentures of the Phillips Petroleum Company, originally amounting to approximately $171 million and maturing in

1987, which requires annual contributions from 1968 through 1977 equal to 3 percent of the amount of bonds outstanding on February 15, 1967 (when the convertibility privilege became exercisable), and equal to 7 percent of this amount annually from 1978 through 1986. A percentage stipulation is especially convenient for convertible issues, as in the Phillips Petroleum bonds. At the time that sinking fund payments are scheduled to begin, the volume of outstanding bonds may have already been substantially reduced through conversions, so that an adjustment in the *amount* of the mandatory requirement is reasonable.

Another popular arrangement for mandatory sinking fund contributions is to have them increase from year to year or at one time or several times during the lives of bond issues, as typified in the Armco Steel and Phillips Petroleum indentures. In support of this arrangement is the argument that the corporation ought to be given a period of years to develop the income potential of the facilities acquired with the proceeds of the bond issue before having to make substantial outlays for its retirement. The same argument supports a delay of a few years before the start of mandatory sinking fund contributions—a very common feature of recent indentures.

Sometimes, it is argued that sinking fund contributions should be large in the early years and smaller in later years because expenditures for repairs and maintenance almost surely will vary in the opposite direction. With sinking fund contributions arranged in this way, annual outlays for redemptions and for repairs and maintenance in combination should tend to be equalized. However, there must be some weakness in this argument, as the pattern of contributions suggested is rarely encountered.

In a goodly number of indentures, the size of the required sinking fund contribution is related to the amount of net profit after the deduction of income taxes. Sometimes, in such indentures minimum and maximum limits are placed on the contributions. It may be provided, for example, that the annual sinking fund contribution shall be an amount sufficient to retire bonds of $100,000 par value plus an amount equal to 10 percent of net profit in excess of $500,000, but in no case shall it exceed an amount sufficient to retire bonds of $300,000 par value. Annual redemption of $100,000 of bonds would, therefore, be the minimum requirement and the redemption of $300,000 the maximum, the actual level, whether at one of these extremes or in between, depending on the amount of profit in excess of $500,000. Sometimes, it is provided that when actual contributions fall below the maximum, the deficiency must be made up in later years if the margin of profits so permits. *From the standpoint of the bondholders' welfare* relating sinking fund contributions to the size of profits may prove to be a better procedure than setting fixed contributions to be met in fair weather and foul. Fixed requirements can straitjacket a corporation to the detriment of the bondholders; in other words, demands of bondholders for protection by way of sinking funds can be overdone. If operating losses drain a corporation's working capital, its bondholders may be imperiled when a further sizable drain from working capital to a sinking fund must be made. An illustration of the kind of sinking fund arrangement described here is that found in the Seaboard-Atlantic Coast Line indenture for its Series B first-mortgage bonds maturing in 1980, which stipulates that each year's contribution is to be the amount needed to retire 1 percent of the total amount of bonds issued under the indenture and to make up deficiencies in the contributions of prior years, provided that this amount is available from the income of the preceding year.

A final point on mandatory sinking fund contributions is that indentures for convertible bonds usually provide for a reduction in any year's contribution by the amount of bonds that have been surrendered in exchange for common stock in that year up to the time the sinking fund contribution is due. The convertibility feature of bond issues will be discussed later in this chapter, so it suffices here to observe that actual conversion serves the same purpose that sinking funds are designed to serve—elimination of bonded debt. Accordingly, the greater the number of bonds that take the conversion route, the less necessary is dependence on the operations of sinking funds.

Use of Sinking Fund Cash. In times past, it was a common practice of corporations to invest their cash contributions to sinking funds in government bonds and in corporate bonds other than their own. The interest earned on such investments was used to buy additional bonds of the same description, the idea being that when the whole accumulation of investment securities was sold at the maturity of the bond issue for which the sinking fund was established, the sale would provide sufficient cash for its redemption. Often, however, the proceeds of sale were found to fall far short of amounts needed to retire maturing bonds. Interest had not been earned on the sinking fund investments at the rate anticipated, or the market for the sinking fund investments turned out to be poor when the time for sale arrived. Even high-quality bonds might be down in market value simply because market rates of interest had risen since the time of their purchase. In many instances, the bonds selected for sinking fund investment simply proved not to be of the high quality that trustees had judged them to be.

The multiplication of difficulties of these kinds led to a recasting of sinking fund management. Why not invest sinking fund contributions in the bonds whose redemption was being provided for? A corporation could hardly go wrong in buying back its own obligations in preference to those of other issuers whose market performance might turn out to be bad. For a time, however, the older idea of accumulation continued to prevail. When a corporation or its trustee invested sinking fund cash in the corporation's own bonds, these were held alive in the sinking fund, and the corporation continued to pay interest on them. The interest payments supplemented the regular sinking fund contributions as means to buy back additional bonds. But the payment of interest into a sinking fund was obviously nothing more than a stepping up of the cash contribution, and it was clear that the same result could be obtained more simply by setting the periodical sinking fund requirement at a higher level in the first place. Hence, the idea of accumulation has likewise become outmoded, although once in a while one still hears of sinking funds in which bonds are held alive.

The general rule at the present time, therefore, is that money allocated by corporations to sinking funds is used directly to redeem the bonds for which the sinking funds are established, that it is used *immediately* for this purpose, and that once reacquired bonds get into the hands of the trustee they are immediately canceled.

The corporation itself is usually privileged to proceed direct in redeeming its bonds, using for this purpose cash that it would otherwise have to turn over to the trustee. As a rule, sinking fund contributions may be made in cash or in the very bonds scheduled for retirement. If the market prices of a corporation's bonds fall below the call price from time to time during the year, the corporation can buy up enough to satisfy the sinking fund requirement. Indeed, if it has plenty of cash available and the market price is well below the call price it may buy up enough bonds to take care of its sinking fund obligations for two or more years. At the time that its sinking fund contribution is due, then, it simply turns bonds over to the trustee rather than cash. The corporation also may make a partial contribution in bonds, as, for example, $125,000 in bonds and a sum of cash sufficient to retire another $75,000 face amount when the indenture requirement is for the annual redemption of a face amount of $200,000. Sometimes, as in Figure 29–1, corporations publish notices to bondholders that they have cash available for bond retirement, and invite those who want to sell to submit tenders at the prices they are willing to take. If a bond is selling in the market at 98, a corporation's buying will tend to drive up the price; but if all bondholders are simultaneously approached for tenders many may be influenced by the market quotation of 98 to offer to sell at that price or at other prices not much higher.

Sinking Fund Calls. In most indentures of recent origin, sinking fund calls are prescribed somewhat as follows. Some 40 or 50 days before the sinking fund payment date, the corporation notifies the trustee how much of its obligation will be met in cash and how much in bonds that it has bought or perhaps got back through conversion.

If the obligation is to be be met wholly or partially in cash, the trustee immediately draws lots to determine whose bonds are to be called for redemption—a sufficient number, of course, to exhaust the cash contribution. Holders of called registered bonds are notified by mail individually, and advertisements listing the serial numbers of called coupon bonds, as in Figure 29–2, are published in newspapers. All holders of called bonds are thus informed of the time and place of redemption. The time usually is the day following that on which the

FIGURE 29–1

Invitation for Tenders

Notice Requesting Tenders

To the Holders of

Westinghouse Electric Corporation

3½% Thirty Year Debentures Due December 15, 1981

NOTICE IS HEREBY GIVEN that the undersigned desires to purchase not more than $15,000,000 principal amount of its 3½% Thirty Year Debentures, due December 15, 1981, and that, in accordance with the provisions of Section 4.02 of the Indenture dated December 15, 1951 pursuant to which said Debentures were issued, the undersigned hereby requests tenders of said Debentures, for purchase by it, at prices up to but not exceeding the principal amount of the Debentures plus accrued interest to October 2, 1967. To the extent required by said Indenture, tendered Debentures will be purchased first from registered holders of said Debentures at the principal amount thereof plus accrued interest, regardless of the price at which such Debentures shall be tendered.

Tenders of said Debentures will be received on behalf of the undersigned by **Chemical Bank New York Trust Company at its Corporate Trust Department, 20 Pine Street, New York, N.Y. 10015,** up to the close of business on September 11, 1967, and notice of acceptance or rejection of tenders will be mailed as promptly as practicable thereafter. Holders of Debentures whose tenders shall be accepted, in whole or in part, will be required to deliver the Debentures accepted to Chemical Bank New York Trust Company for the account of the undersigned not later than October 2, 1967, on and after which date interest on said Debentures will cease to accrue.

Copies of the form of tender may be obtained from Chemical Bank New York Trust Company, Corporate Trust Department, 20 Pine Street, New York, N.Y. 10015, and at the offices of the undersigned in Pittsburgh, Pa., or New York, N.Y. All tenders must be made on such form.

WESTINGHOUSE ELECTRIC CORPORATION

By R. B. READ, *Vice President and Treasurer*

Dated: August 7, 1967.

corporation is obligated to make its sinking fund payment, as November 1 when the sinking fund payment date is October 31. By this procedure, therefore, the trustee does not buy in the market or invite tenders, regardless of how low the market price may be. Its function in redemption is simply to draw lots, to make the call, and then to pay off the called bonds at the call price with the money supplied by the corporation.

(In older indentures, the trustee was often given a choice of drawing lots, buying bonds in the market, or itself inviting tenders, or it could be directed by the corporation to take one of these routes. As

FIGURE 29-2

Sinking Fund Call Advertisement

To the Holders of

Alabama Gas Corporation

First Mortgage Bonds, 5⅛ % Series E
Due 1984, Due August 1, 1984

Notice is hereby given that, pursuant to the provisions of Section 5 of Article II of the Fifteenth Supplemental Indenture dated as of August 1, 1959, supplemental to First Mortgage and Deed of Trust dated as of April 1, 1941, as supplemented, amended and restated in a Ninth Supplemental Indenture dated as of April 1, 1949, between Alabama Gas Corporation and Chemical Bank & Trust Company (now Chemical Bank New York Trust Company), as Trustee, the undersigned, as Trustee, has drawn by lot, for redemption on September 15, 1963, out of moneys in the Sinking Fund applicable to such redemption $100,000 principal amount of the above-described Bonds bearing the following numbers:

Coupon bonds of $1,000 principal amount each bearing the distinguishing prefix "M":

4	286	756	2148	2630	3089	3480
21	343	806	2185	2678	3152	3524
50	363	855	2253	2717	3180	3559
70	397	1786	2302	2775	3221	3602
104	425	1818	2353	2796	3255	3616
141	466	1868	2402	2836	3284	3657
163	516	1933	2440	2859	3321	3709
166	561	1972	2474	2883	3378	3760
190	618	2018	2492	2925	3391	3849
219	686	2059	2543	3002	3421	
264	750	2102	2570	3052	3452	

Portions of registered bonds as follows:

Number	Portion being redeemed
RE 2	$ 3,000
RE 5	1,000
RE 27	20,000
RE 28	1,000

On September 15, 1963, there will become and be due and payable upon each coupon bond, and upon the portions of the registered bonds, so designated for redemption, the principal amount thereof, together with accrued interest thereon to said date, and a premium of 0.97% of such principal amount (being the price at which such Bonds are redeemable for the Sinking Fund on said date) upon presentation and surrender thereof at the Corporate Trust Department of the Trustee, 20 Pine Street, New York 15, N. Y.

From and after September 15, 1963, interest will cease to accrue on the coupon bonds and the portions of the registered bonds so designated for redemption.

CHEMICAL BANK NEW YORK TRUST COMPANY, *as Trustee.*

Dated: August 16, 1963.

many of the older indentures are still in effect, one may occasionally see invitations for tenders published in the names of trustees.)

Holders of bonds that are called for redemption are hardly in a position to resist the call. No matter how much an investor may cherish the investment qualities of a called bond, he knows that he can never get more for it than the call price plus interest to the redemption date. In the redemption notice, he will have been told that no interest will accrue after that date. He can hold on to the bond if he wants to, and the trustee will continue to hold for him the cash allocated for its retirement, but holding would surely be a witless act since he would no longer earn interest. Only in exceptional circumstances, on the other hand, are people likely to inadvertently continue to hold called coupon bonds—not having seen or been told of the newspaper advertisements of the redemption call. Such a bondholder, in sending in to the trustee the interest coupon for the six months ending with the redemption date, would receive a return notice from the trustee that he should have sent in the bond itself with the interest coupon still attached.

Call Prices. Although bondholders as a class usually demand protection through the periodic scaling down of corporate bonded debt by the operation of sinking funds, they are not likely to be individually enthusiastic at the prospect of having their holdings called for redemption. An investor who wants a long-term outlet for his funds has reasons to be displeased if his bondholdings are called well before the final maturity, and the earlier in the life of an issue that his holdings are called, the greater is his dissatisfaction likely to be.

Even more important from the standpoint of corporations that are anxious to obtain long-term funds by the sale of bond issues is the possibility that people who are interested in long-term investment simply will not buy because of their expectation that redemption calls will deprive them of their purchases long before they want to give them up. How, then, can a corporation give the protection of a sinking fund and yet garner the funds of prospective investors who fear early calls for redemption?

In times past, the answer to this question was generally that the bondholder should be given a premium to compensate him for his disappointment in having his bond called early in its life, and that the earlier the call, the larger the premium should be. During the first 5 years of the life of a 25-year bond issue, the call price may be, say, 106, for the next 5 years 104.5, for the next 5 years 103, for the next 5 years 101.5, and for the final 5-year span 100—that is, the par value. However, the recent trend has been strongly in the direction of making the call price for mandatory sinking fund redemptions 100, although a moderate number of new indentures continue to have an array of call prices scaled downward, as in the illustration. For the large proportion of new indentures that set the call price at 100, the problem of investor disappointment with early calls and investor reluctance to buy for fear of early calls is tackled by provisions for *call protection*—stipulations deferring the start of sinking fund calls, most commonly for 5 or 10 years from the date of issue.

Restrictions on the Payment of Cash Dividends

Basis of Restrictions. Always of concern to investors in bonds is the possibility that the corporate issuers of the bonds, if not restrained in some way, will be too generous in the payment of cash dividends to their common stockholders. The danger envisaged is not so much that the draining of cash for dividend payments will leave too little for bond interest and sinking fund requirements as that the double drain for dividends and bond servicing will leave too little cash for ordinary operations—that, in other words, operations will be crippled by inadequacies in working capital. As a rule, therefore, bond buyers insist that certain restrictions on dividend payments be included in indentures. Quite often, the restrictions are so stated that, given certain circumstances, dividends on preferred stock as well as on common will be precluded.

Restrictions in Terms of Surplus and Working Capital. A popular kind of restriction is that while the bonds are outstanding, dividends shall not be paid "out of" surplus accumulated before a stated date. This means, of course, that the dividends shall not be so large as to reduce surplus below the balance obtaining at the stipulated date. This date is usually that of the bond issue or one within the preceding year or two. An alternative way of putting this restriction is to stipulate that the amount of dividends shall not exceed profits derived since the stated date. Rather often, however, a portion of the earned surplus extant at the stated date, specified as a dollar amount, is made available for cash dividends. For example, it may be provided that dividends may not exceed the sum of net earnings after a given date and $10 million. Sometimes, the restriction is that dividends must not reduce earned surplus below a stated dollar amount or, alternatively, that they must not reduce net tangible assets (defined as total tangible assets less all debt including the bonds) below a given figure.

Restrictions in terms of working capital are also popular—for example, the amount of working capital or the working capital ratio must not be reduced below a stated level through the payment of dividends. Another working capital provision commonly found in indentures is that dividend payments must not cause the amount of bonds outstanding to exceed the amount of working capital or some percentage of it.

Restrictions in effect at the end of 1967 as reported by two corporations may be cited to illustrate limitations on cash dividend payments. The Youngstown Sheet and Tube Company reported that of its total earned surplus of approximately $504 million, $138.8 million was "free of restrictions under the First Mortgage on the payment of cash dividends." The American Bakeries Company reported that of its retained earnings of approximately $34 million, a little more than $29 million was not available for cash dividends under the agreement covering its outstanding long-term notes. American Bakeries also noted that the agreement requires it to maintain net working capital of not less than $10 million.[1]

Other Restrictions on Cash Payments

In the absence of indenture restrictions, boards of directors could undermine the position of bondholders by draining corporate assets in reacquiring outstanding stock issues. The directors of a corporation may decide to call a preferred stock issue for redemption or to buy in common shares to be held as treasury stock, only to find, perhaps not long after, that the corporation lacks sufficient cash to meet its mandatory sinking fund payments as provided for in its bond indenture. In this way, the former owners of the stock redeemed or reacquired as treasury stock, instead of being kept in their customary position as inferior claimants to corporate assets, would actually have been treated as if their claims had priority over those of the bondholders. But prospective buyers of bonds know of such possibilities and often insist on indenture restrictions on drains of cash for stock retirement.

Sometimes, there is an absolute prohibition on the purchase by the corporation of shares of its outstanding common and preferred stock, and on calls of the preferred stock for redemption. When, however, an outstanding preferred stock has a provision for a redemption fund, calls of the stock for redemption in accordance with this provision are permitted. It is usual, also, to provide that if new stock issues are sold after the date of the bond issue an amount equal to the proceeds of the stock sales may be used subsequently for stock retirement, even while the bonds remain outstanding. Quite frequently—as, indeed, in the American Bakeries case cited above—restrictions on dividend payments and on stock retirements are telescoped to give the directors a choice: cash may be used for stock retirement to the extent that actual dividends fall short of amounts permitted by the indentures.

Some indentures place limits on corporate investment in subsidiaries set up to operate in foreign countries. The danger aimed at is that assets of foreign subsidiaries may be beyond the reach of the bondholders should the corporations default, because their availability depends on the laws and attitudes of the foreign governments—that, indeed, the seizure of the assets by governments turned hostile could be the cause of defaults.

In indentures covering bond issues sold in bulk to institutional

---

[1]Youngstown, *Annual Report*, 1967, pp. 13, 14; American Bakeries, *Annual Report*, 1967, pp. 7, 10.

investors, additional kinds of restrictions on cash payments are often found. Quite common are limitations on the payment of salaries and bonuses to executive officers. Often, too, permission of the institutional investor must be obtained for expenditures for new fixed assets beyond certain moderate limits, for the repayment before maturity of indebtedness other than the bonds, and for investment in subsidiaries, whether domestic or foreign.

Legal Remedies

Although bondholders as creditors, and trustees in their role as protectors of bondholders' interests, would have full power to take legal actions to enforce their rights in the absence of permissive provisions in indentures, the fact is that indentures usually specifically authorize various kinds of legal actions. They define what are events of default, and then go on to say what the trustees and bondholders may do for the bondholders' protection on the occurrence of such events.

Events of Default. The typical indenture designates as an event of default the nonpayment of any mandatory sinking fund contribution at the time due, the nonpayment of any principal obligation at the due date, and the nonpayment of interest after the elapse of a certain number of days of grace from the due date. The number of days of grace allowed before a nonpayment of interest becomes an event of default is usually 30, 60, or 90. No days of grace are ordinarily allowed for defaulted sinking fund and principal payments. For principal payments, courts have held that allowing days of grace destroys the negotiability of bonds.

Other failures of a corporation to fulfill its covenants become events of default when the corporation has been notified of such failures, has been asked to correct them, and has not corrected them within a stipulated period, usually 60 or 90 days. The notice of failure to fulfill covenants and the demand for correction may be given by the trustee or by the owners of a stipulated proportion of the outstanding bonds, usually 25 percent. If, therefore, the corporation fails to pay its taxes when due or to keep its properties in a good state of repair, the matter may be called to its attention by the trustee or by the requisite proportion of the bondholders, with demand that the payment be made or the repairs effected.

If the corporation gets involved in certain kinds of legal processes and does not extricate itself from these within a short period, such as 60, 75, or 90 days, the result is also an event of default. Such involvements include:

1. Filing a petition in a federal court for reorganization or dissolution in bankruptcy.
2. Confessing in writing that it is unable to pay its debts as they mature.

3. Asking that a receiver be appointed.
4. Making an assignment of assets for the benefit of some or all of its creditors.
5. Consenting to creditors' filing of a petition for the appointment of a receiver or for reorganization or dissolution in bankruptcy.

They include also court orders or decrees finding the corporation to be insolvent, appointing a receiver, and approving as properly filed a petition for reorganization or dissolution in bankruptcy.

Finally, the typical indenture provides that an event of default occurs if the corporation fails to meet some debt other than the bonds covered by the indenture, if the maturity of this debt is accelerated because of this failure, and if the matter is not cleared up within, say, 10 days after written demand for its correction has been made by the trustee or by holders of at least 25 percent of the outstanding bonds. Suppose, for example, that a corporation has outstanding a mortgage bond issue and a debenture bond issue, and the indenture for each has the provision just described. If, then, the corporation suffers an event of default on the debenture issue, if as a result the maturity of the debenture issue is accelerated, and if the corporation, after notice, fails to pay off the debenture bonds or have the acceleration rescinded within the allowed period of grace, the result is *an event of default on the mortgage issue.* (Acceleration is explained below.)

Remedies Available to the Trustee. The typical bond indenture contains a sweeping authorization of legal action on the part of the trustee such as the following.

> In case of an event of default hereunder, the Trustee may in its discretion proceed to protect and enforce the rights vested in it by this Indenture by such appropriate judicial proceedings as the Trustee shall deem most effectual to protect and enforce any of such rights, either by suit in equity or by action at law or by proceeding in bankruptcy or otherwise, whether for the specific enforcement of any covenant or agreement contained in this Indenture or in aid of the exercise of any power granted in this Indenture, or to enforce any other legal or equitable right vested in the Trustee by this Indenture or by law.

If an event of default seriously threatens the interests of the bondholders, and if it is one that the corporation is unlikely to be able to clear up within a reasonable time, the trustee may decide to accelerate the maturity of the bond issue as a preliminary to further legal action. The acceleration clause of the indenture will authorize the trustee to declare the entire principal amount of the bond issue "immediately due and payable." Assume, for example, that a corporation defaults upon an interest payment upon its 20-year bond issue at the end of the fifth year. At the same time, the corporation is failing to meet maturing obligations owing to other creditors, and these creditors are hastening to the courts with suits to obtain judgment against it. In these circumstances, the trustee would be in a ridiculous position if it could sue only for the defaulted interest. The other creditors, if successful in their judgment suits, would be able to seize the corporation's best assets (if not pledged for the bond issue, of course) leaving little to meet the corporation's future obligations upon the bonds. Indentures, therefore, not only provide for acceleration, but also set forth as an additional covenant the corporation's obligation to pay the full principal upon acceleration. Nonpayment thus becomes an additional event of default—one that, since it concerns the payment of principal, permits no days of grace.

After acceleration, the trustee may sue the corporation for the payment of the full principal and accumulated interest; if property has been pledged for the bond issue, it may institute proceedings for the foreclosure of this property and its public sale, the proceeds to be used as far as possible to pay off the bondholders' claims. However, the trustee may decide that the bondholders would fare better if the corporation's properties were kept intact and a plan of reorganization worked out. If so, it would be likely to file with the federal district court a petition for the corporation's reorganization in bankruptcy. An advantage of this move would be its effect of holding in abeyance legal actions of other creditors to seize the corporation's assets.

For less serious defaults, the trustee may show forbearance. Should extreme tightness in the corporation's cash position prevent its paying some of its taxes on their due dates, though permitting it to meet all the rest of its obligations under the indenture and to other creditors, the trustee might let the default "ride" in the expectation that later cash inflows would suffice to clear up the delinquencies. In a period of business slump, it would be likely to ignore inadequacies in the corporation's expenditures for the maintenance of its plant and equipment. On the other hand, should the corporation have sufficient cash to meet all its obligations and simply be negligent in doing so, the trustee might take proceedings in equity asking for a writ directed to the corporation commanding it to fulfill these obligations.

Remedies Available to the Bondholders. In the typical bond indenture, the bondholders are not bereft of rights to take action to protect their interests even though this is supposed to be principally the job of the trustee. For one thing, they are usually privileged to accelerate the maturity of the bond issue when defaults have occurred. This action can be taken by written notice to both the corporation and the trustee, provided, usually, that holders of at least 25 percent of the outstanding bonds concur.

As a rule, bondholders may take direct legal action against the corporation to enforce their claims if the trustee fails to take such action after a proper request. The trustee must have been notified in writing of an event of default by one or more of the bondholders.

Holders of some proportion of the outstanding bonds—usually 25 percent—must have submitted a written request for action with an offer to indemnify the trustee for expenses to be incurred; and the trustee must have neglected to take action for some period of time—usually 60 days—after receiving the written request. The typical indenture stipulates that when a group of bondholders take direct action they must do so for the benefit of all the bondholders, and not simply for themselves. Nevertheless, an exception is made for the right of the individual bondholder to sue in his own name and for his own benefit to recover defaulted interest and principal payments.

In the typical indenture, too, it is stipulated that holders of a majority of the outstanding bonds may direct the time, method, and place of actions to be taken by the trustee. However, this provision is usually weakened by the further stipulation that the trustee may decline to act as directed if, in good faith, it feels that the action would be contrary to the interests of bondholders who are not taking part in the move.

RIGHTS RESERVED BY CORPORATIONS

When corporations pledge their operating properties as security for bond issues, they demand the right to retain possession of the properties and to use them in the ordinary course of business. They reserve the right to sell pledged property no longer useful to them, but agree to substitute other properties of at least equal value or to turn the cash proceeds of sale over to the trustee for bond retirement. They often reserve the right to issue additional bonds according to the terms of existing indentures and to set varying interest rates, call prices, and maturities for these additional bonds, but they subject themselves to limitations in terms of earnings and property in the exercise of this privilege. These matters we examined in Chapter 28. In the foregoing division of this chapter, we saw that corporations usually ask for days of grace for the correction of certain kinds of defaults before trustees may take action of a decisive character to protect the bondholders.

What other kinds of rights do corporations insist on reserving to themselves in their indentures? Two kinds deserve analysis: (1) the right to call bonds for redemption, and (2) the right to have the terms of indentures modified, provided that holders of certain proportions of the outstanding bonds consent.

Callability

The right of corporations to call their bonds for redemption goes hand in hand with the present-day theory of sinking fund management. As we have seen, this theory is that cash contributed to sinking funds should be used at once to retire the bonds for which the sinking funds are set up. It is envisaged that bonds may not be available in the market at reasonable prices to use up the sinking fund contributions. Thus, the right of the corporation to force surrender at predetermined call prices appears to be entirely logical. Hence comes the indenture provision for the drawing of lots by the trustee to determine whose bonds shall be called and the stipulation that interest on called bonds that are not surrendered will not accrue after the call date.

Most corporate issuers of bonds, however, demand and get call privileges much broader than those directly related to sinking fund requirements. Their financial managers hope that good fortune will enable them to retire bonds more rapidly than the sinking fund provisions require. They surely think it possible that long-term interest rates may fall during the lives of their bond issues, so that their replacement with new bonds bearing lower rates of interest would be advantageous. Fearing that certain terms of indentures will turn out to be too restrictive, they may want to be in a position to remove these restrictions by calling all outstanding bonds. If they are issuing bonds reluctantly in the first place because of devotion to the simple common stock form of financial structure, they may hope to be able to replace all the bonds by common stock sales when the market situation for common stock improves.

Call privileges beyond what are needed in connection with mandatory sinking fund contributions are generally of two kinds: (1) those related to *optional* sinking fund payments, and (2) those related to redemption outside the scope of sinking fund operations. The sinking fund provisions of many indentures state that the corporation shall make an annual or semiannual contribution sufficient to retire a given face amount of bonds, and that it may, at its option, make an additional contribution on any sinking fund payment date. It is usually stipulated, as in the Armco Steel indenture cited earlier in this chapter, that the optional contribution may not exceed the mandatory one, and that the right to make optional contributions does not cumulate—that optional contributions missed cannot be made up by later ones that exceed the stipulated limit. (The reason for such limitations is that, as noted later, call prices for sinking fund redemptions are almost always less than for those outside the scope of sinking fund operations.) Obviously, however, the combination of mandatory and optional sinking fund calls still envisages only gradual retirement; it does not permit the complete elimination of large amounts of remaining bonds at one stroke. Hence, the typical corporation asks for and gets the additional privilege of making calls for redemption unrelated to its mandatory and optional sinking fund contributions. The additional privilege is usually stated sweepingly as the right to call any quantity of bonds for redemption at any time, but one or more provisos that tone down the scope of this right often follow its broad declaration. Even corporations that have no sinking fund provisions in their indentures, or whose indentures permit the spending or sinking fund money for improvements, generally demand a broad call privilege of this kind.

Any limitation on the broad call privilege is usually designed to assure investors that they will not be quickly deprived of their bondholdings. It is often provided, for example, that the privilege may not be used within the first 5 or 10 years from the date of issuance of the bonds. A variation of this proviso, found in many recent indentures, is that money borrowed at a rate of interest lower than the rate carried by the bond issue may not be used in the exercise of the broad call privilege within the first five years or thereabouts. This variation is designed to preclude for the stated period of years calls prompted solely by the corporation's desire to reduce its interest costs.

The trend toward making the par value of bonds—that is, $100—their call price for all mandatory sinking fund calls regardless of their timing has not carried over to nonsinking fund calls. Accordingly, the typical corporation incurs a penalty for redeeming by means of nonsinking fund calls. The idea seems to be that because sinking fund redemptions are demanded by bondholders for their own protection, they deserve no bonus or premium when their bonds are actually called through sinking fund operations. But because nonsinking fund redemptions are undertaken purely to serve the corporation's own financial objectives, the bondholder should be compensated for the part that he is called on to play, however unwittingly. Note, however, that optional sinking fund contributions almost always get by with the same call prices as the mandatory ones, even though they, too, appear to serve the corporation's objectives much more closely than those of the bondholders.

Modification of Indenture Terms

As was pointed out previously, the financial managers of a corporation may want to reserve a broad call privilege as a means of eliminating a bond issue should its indenture terms prove to be too restrictive. It would let them call for redemption all the bonds with the obnoxious features and put out a new issue with terms more to their liking. But complete replacement or refunding is likely to be expensive, especially in underwriting commissions and costs of preparing a registration statement and prospectus. Moreover, the obnoxious features may prove to be most burdensome at a time when market conditions are quite unfavorable for new bond flotations. Accordingly, an alternative way for getting rid of unduly burdensome features of an indenture is usually provided for in the indenture itself.

The alternative way is to get the bondholders to consent to the desired change in indenture terms or features. The typical indenture provides that any of its terms and conditions, *except the interest rate, the principal obligation, and the due dates of interest and principal*, can be modified with the consent of holders of 66⅔ percent, 75 percent, or some other large proportion of the outstanding bonds.[2]

Since the exceptions specifically provide that the corporation's principal and interest obligations are not to be reduced or deferred by any modifications agreed on, courts generally hold that consent of the proportion stipulated makes a change binding on all bondholders—on those who dissent as well as on those who approve. With the hope of getting a sufficient number of bondholders to approve, therefore, a corporation may propose that:

1. Its sinking fund obligations be reduced or rearranged.
2. It be permitted to issue new bonds that have a prior lien over the existing ones or to incur debt beyond the limits set in the indenture.
3. Requirements in the indenture for maintaining a given amount of working capital or a given working capital ratio be modified.
4. Restrictions on dividend payments be relaxed.
5. For a debenture issue, it be permitted to sell an issue of mortgage bonds without giving the debentures equal security.

Necessarily, of course, the financial managers must explain clearly to the bondholders why the change is desired—how it will benefit the corporation and, perhaps, strengthen the bondholders' own position, or at least not weaken it. On the other hand, should it be clear that the bondholders' interests would be affected adversely, the corporation may have to offer them something in compensation, such as a moderate increase in the interest rate. If sufficient assents are obtained, the corporation gets rid of the obnoxious feature or gets permission rather painlessly for what it wants to do. If not, it may decide on a new issue whose proceeds are to be used to retire the existing one, or it may decide, in view of the costs of refunding, to try to go along with the existing indenture with all its burdens.

Although indentures exclude principal and interest obligations from the matters subject to modification with the consent of given proportions of bondholders, a corporation can still go to its bondholders with proposals that affect these obligations. Corporations in financial difficulties often propose to their bondholders the reduction or deferment of interest payments, the extension of maturities, and even reductions in the principal amounts of their obligations. But seeking the help of bondholders in these directions pertains to the management

[2]Another exception is that the proportion of bondholders' assents required for modifications cannot itself be modified. Thus, holders of, say, 66⅔ percent of outstanding bonds cannot approve an indenture amendment making the consent of holders of only 51 percent of the bonds sufficient for further adjustments in terms.

of outstanding bond issues, to be considered in Chapter 31,[3] rather than to the reservation of rights in indentures, as discussed here.

SPECIAL FEATURES TO PROMOTE SALE

Just as convertibility and warrant features are added to some issues of preferred stock to increase their attractiveness to investors, so also are such features given to some bond issues for the same objective. As with preferred stocks, too, common stock is almost always the security for which convertible bonds may be exchanged or for which warrants attached to bonds may be exercised. Occasionally, bond issues are made convertible into preferred stock and short-term issues into longer-term ones, but these occasional departures from the general rule only emphasize the preeminent role of common stock as the thing offered. As indicated in the discussion of debenture bonds and subordinated debentures in Chapter 28, making bonds convertible into common stock has been highly popular in recent years. There has also been a considerable increase in the number of new issues of bonds with warrants attached for the purchase of common stock, although the attachment of warrants continues to be much less significant than the grant of conversion privileges.

Convertibility

Although promotion of sale is the objective of convertibility features in bond issues, circumstances differ among corporations on why such a promotional device is needed. Corporations of weak credit standing can hardly expect to attract the more conservative classes of bond buyers, regardless of what they offer, but they may hope to successfully reach less conservative classes that may be impressed by the speculative interest that convertibility provides. They may or may not want conversion to take place, but they are extremely anxious to borrow, and they can offer convertibility without apparent immediate cost. They may have little or nothing to pledge as security for their bond issues, and the only alternative may be the offering of an extremely high interest rate, something that may threaten solvency.

But many corporations of strong financial position also offer convertible bonds. Some do so when the supply of long-term loan funds in the market is tight while the common stock market is booming. The tightness in the bond market means that long-term interest rates are high, but by offering the conversion privilege these corporations expect to be able to trim their rates by as much as two percentage points and still have a rush of investors anxious to get access to new stock issues, even by the roundabout conversion machinery. These

---

[3] See pp. 809–18.

corporations do not want to issue additional common stock, so that their offer of conversion privileges is made in the expectation that a break in the stock market will occur before their exercise becomes advantageous to the bond buyers.

On the other hand, many convertible issues of strong corporations are offered at times when the supply of funds in the bond market is relatively large but stock prices are not nearly so buoyant as the corporate managements think they should be. The managers decide that projects for which they need long-term funds cannot conveniently be postponed, and they would prefer to sell additional shares of common stock to raise these funds; yet, they conclude that sales at current prices would unreasonably dilute the ownership interests of existing stockholders. Confident that the market prices of their common stocks will soon begin a spirited advance, they now sell convertible bonds, setting the conversion terms at levels to ensure conversion when this advance has taken place.

Assume, for example, that a corporation finds it possible to sell a $60 million issue of convertible debenture bonds at their par value. At the time of sale, the market price of the corporation's common stock is 45, but the conversion price of the bonds is set at 50. If, then, the market price of the common stock subsequently advances to levels beyond 50, as anticipated, and if all the bonds, sooner or later, are converted, the result is much as if the corporation had originally sold 1.2 million shares at $50 for the total of $60 million, whereas if it had originally offered that number of shares it would have received not more than $54 million. Moreover, its margin of advantage by way of the convertible bond issue probably would have exceeded $6 million because the bond issue's flotation costs would be lower than would have been payable on a stock sale, and especially should it have planned rights offerings to its common stockholders of either the bonds or the stock. The usual procedure in rights offerings is to offer convertible bonds to stockholders at par, but to offer additional shares of common stock, as we saw in Chapter 19, at a bargain price. Even the interst rate paid on the convertible bonds before their conversion might have been less than the corporation's dividend rate on common stock; at any rate, its making the bonds convertible should have enabled it, as we saw above, to get by with an interest rate materially lower than the rate it would have had to designate on a nonconvertible issue.

Conversion Provisions. In setting conversion terms, some corporations use *ratios* and others use *prices*. The distinction is of no great importance, as either kind of designation can be readily translated into the other. For example, a stipulation that $100 of bonds is convertible into two shares of common stock means that the conversion price is $50 a share. A stipulation that the conversion price is $33⅓ a share means that the conversion ratio is 3—that 3 shares of stock will be given for $100 of bonds.

In most instances, the conversion price, stated or translated from a stated ratio, is set well above the common stock's market price prevailing at the time the bonds are sold. Such an arrangement is logical for the corporation that does not want conversion to take place—one that offers convertibility purely as a sales attraction. But it is also logical for the corporation that has every wish to replace the bond issue with common stock. Since such a corporation issues bonds only because the common stock market is temporarily unfavorable, it would be defeating its purpose were it to set the conversion price close to the existing market price of the common stock.

A second common practice is to establish scales of conversion prices graduated upward for successive time periods (or, alternatively, scales of conversion ratios graduated downward). Again, such a provision appears to be logical whatever the long-range financing objectives of corporations may be. The corporation that wants to have its bonds remain outstanding hardly expects the market price of its common stock to reach the level of the first conversion price in the first period, and all the less to the levels of the higher conversion prices of the later periods. On the other hand, the corporation that favors conversion expects it to be *forced* near the end of the first period or, if not then, near the end of a subsequent period. Although this practice appears to be somewhat less popular in new issues of convertible bonds than it used to be, there remain outstanding many convertibles with two or more conversion prices or ratios for successive periods according to the pattern mentioned. As an example, the convertible subordinated debentures of the American Machine & Foundry Company, bearing interest at 4¼ percent and maturing in 1981, have a conversion price of $59.63 to March 1, 1971, and one of $64.56 thereafter till the maturity date. Accordingly, the conversion of a $1,000 bond before March 1, 1971, would bring about 16.8 shares of common stock, but only about 15.5 shares were conversion delayed to a later date.

Another feature quite common in convertible bonds is a limitation on the duration of the conversion period, typified by the 4 percent convertible subordinated debentures of the Consolidated Electronics Industries Corporation, which were offered to stockholders in the total amount of approximately $32 million in May, 1967, and which were made convertible at $58 a share "on or prior to June 1, 1982," although not scheduled to mature till 10 years later. Also illustrative is the approximate $120 million of 4½ percent convertible subordinated debentures of the United Aircraft Corporation, offered to stockholders in September, 1967, and made convertible at $100 a share "on or before October 1, 1977," although not scheduled to mature until October 1, 1992. Such a limitation appears advisable for a corporation that adds the convertibility feature as a sales attraction but does not want conversion to take place; however, it can obviously err by making the conversion period too brief, thus losing the force of the sales attraction. A limitation of this kind also appears to be advisable for a corporation that hopes for conversion, provided that it is fully confident that the market price of its common stock will rise well above the conversion price during the limited period. While a rising scale of conversion prices tends to force conversion before the ends of successive periods, some bondholders may hold off more or less indefinitely, but nobody who is wise in the ways of investment will fail to convert if it would be profitable to do so and if the conversion privilege is just about to expire.

Indentures for convertible bonds almost invariably provide that if the bonds are called for redemption their owners may still convert to common stock up to the date of redemption or up to a date a few days earlier. Much of the attractiveness of the privilege of converting would be lost if it were possible for corporations to nullify it by calls for redemption. Issuing calls for redemption is, indeed, a third important means of forcing conversion—in addition, that is, to rising scales of conversion prices and time limits on the conversion privilege. If a corporation's common stock is selling in the market at a price at least moderately above the conversion price, almost all the bondholders, on receiving a redemption call, can be expected to convert rather than to permit their bonds simply to be paid off at the call price. Corporations usually try to give wide publicity to the pending expiration of conversion privileges because of calls for redemption, illustrated in the newspaper notice reproduced as Figure 29–3, and all the more so if the value of the common stock into which a bond is convertible is much greater than the call price. Once in a while, however, a mixup occurs, as in the spring of 1966 when the Boeing Company was strongly condemned by irate holders of about 5 percent of its convertible 4½ percent debentures who failed to convert and who claimed that the company had neglected to give sufficient publicity to the approaching end of the conversion privilege on account of its call for redemption. Whether or not their accusation was justified, their irritation was understandable, since the call price was 103.25 per $100 of bonds, but that amount of bonds could have been turned in for 2 shares of common stock worth $160 a share in the market at that time!

Finally, indenture provisions concerning the convertibility feature usually include antidilution clauses for investor protection. Like the similar provisions found in the contracts for convertible preferred stocks, these clauses require that adjustments be made in conversion prices and ratios when corporations effect split-ups in their common stocks or distribute stock dividends to their common stockholders. The operation of antidilution clauses is illustrated by the March Supermarkets, Inc. announcement in August, 1968, that the conversion price per share of common stock as provided for in its 5 percent convertible subordinated debentures would shift from $20.62 to $10.31 effective August 15 because of a 2-for-1 common stock split-up, distributable to stockholders of record on August 14.

FIGURE 29–3
Notice of Redemption of Convertible Bonds

THE FLYING TIGER LINE INC.

Notice of Redemption and Termination of Conversion Privilege

To the Holders of The Flying Tiger Line Inc.
5½% Debentures Due 1967 (Subordinate) due July 1, 1967

NOTICE IS HEREBY GIVEN that, pursuant to the provisions of the Indenture dated as of July 1, 1952, between The Flying Tiger Line Inc. and Bankers Trust Company, Trustee, the Company has elected to redeem on July 1, 1959 all of its then outstanding 5½% Debentures Due 1967 (Subordinate) due July 1, 1967 at the redemption price of 102% of the principal amount thereof together with interest accrued thereon to the redemption date.

Accordingly, on or after July 1, 1959, unless the Debentures are previously converted into shares of Common Stock of the Company, the redemption price of such Debentures will become due and payable and will be paid at the office of BankersTrust Company, Corporate Trust Division, 16 Wall Street, New York 15, New York, upon presentation and surrender of such Debentures, accompanied by all coupons appertaining thereto maturing on and after January 1, 1960. Coupons maturing on July 1, 1959 should be detached by the holders of Debentures to be redeemed and presented for payment in the usual manner. Interest on the Debentures will cease to accrue on and after July 1, 1959.

The Debentures are presently convertible into shares of Common Stock of the Company at the conversion price of $8.50 principal amount of Debentures for each share of Common Stock. The Indenture provides, however, that such right to convert shall terminate and expire at the close of business on the third full business day prior to the date fixed for redemption. Accordingly, the right to convert Debentures into Common Stock will terminate at the close of business on June 26, 1959.

Debentures to be converted accompanied by all coupons appertaining thereto maturing on or after July 1, 1959 should be surrendered, on or before June 26, 1959, at the office of Bankers Trust Company, Corporate Trust Division, 16 Wall Street, New York 15, New York, accompanied by a written notice of election to convert such Debentures.

THE FLYING TIGER LINE INC.

May 29, 1959. *By* BANKERS TRUST COMPANY, *Trustee*

Attractiveness of Convertibility. The reason that the privilege of conversion is attractive to bond buyers is that it gives them possibilities of substantial gains while detracting not at all from the relative safety of their positions as creditors.

If during the life of a bond issue the market price of the corporation's common stock never goes appreciably above the conversion price, the bondholders may still be fairly well satisfied, since they collect interest semiannually and the principal as the bonds are called or paid off at the final maturity. They may feel, however, that they have lost something—not only the substantial gains that failed to show up but also a differential in interest income if they accepted a lower rate of interest than they would have demanded had the bonds not been convertible. But even with the market price of common remaining at or below the conversion price, gains may be possible. Should the interest rate on the bonds be 4 percent and should the corporation pay dividends of 5 percent on its common stock, the bondholders might convert to get the advantage of the higher rate of return. They might wait two or three years to be sure that the common dividend rate had become regular, and they would surely weigh the prospects of its continuance, but their judgment of the corporation's outlook might lead them to give up the relative safety of their position as bondholders for the more speculative one as stockholders.

If, moreover, the market price of a common stock goes well above the conversion price, the bondholder finds himself under no immediate pressure to convert. He may be satisfied to continue to earn interest at the established rate in his relatively safe position as a creditor, while expecting to supplement the interest by a handsome capital gain by selling the bonds some months or years later.

Suppose, for example, that a corporation's dividend rate on its common stock is the same as the interest rate on its convertible bonds, but that its prospects are so good that many people are buying the common stock, thereby driving up its price. Assume that the conversion price is $50 and the market price of the common stock goes to $80. This should cause the market price of the bonds to go to approximately $160. Thus, the bondholder may plan to sell out when satisfied that the price of the common stock is unlikely to rise further, or when, indeed, he expects it to fall. Or he may plan to sell before an increase in the subscription price occurs, as scheduled by a provision in the indenture, described earlier. At any rate, he would be unlikely to see any advantage in converting and thereby assuming the risks of common stockownership without getting any increase in the rate of return. Nor would he have to convert to get his capital gain, as by obtaining the common stock and immediately selling it, since, as indicated, he could get it by selling the bond directly. If, on the other hand, the corporation were to step up its dividend rate to, say, 6 percent, he might convert to take advantage of the higher rate of return. In surrendering his bond, he would be in the pleasant position of being able to buy at $50 a share while other investors would be paying $80 in the market.

But a word of caution: The bondholder may be extremely disappointed, not only because the conversion privilege may prove to be of no value but also because the corporation defaults on interest or principal payments somewhere along the way. A convertibility feature does not guarantee a corporation's continued solvency. When, indeed, convertibility is offered by corporations of weaker financial positions to attract investors who would not otherwise be attracted, the investors must realize that incurring dangers of defaults is the price they pay for the added privilege.

Use of Stock Purchase Warrants

As a rule, a corporation can make an offer of stock purchase warrants about as attractive to bond buyers as an offer of convertibility. If a conversion ratio of 20 shares of common stock for a $1,000 bond would be attractive in a given instance, the attachment of warrants to buy 20 shares of common at $50 a share should have about equal investment appeal. Should the market price of the common go to $80, and should the warrants be *nondetachable* (exercisable, therefore, only by the bondholder himself), the market price of the bond should go to approximately $160. At this level the bondholder might sell the bond with attached warrants to take his capital gain; he might hold for a bigger gain expected to result from a further rise in the stock price; or he might surrender the warrants with $1,000 in cash to buy the 20 shares he is entitled to. Should he take the last-named step, he would have further choices: to take the capital gain by selling the stock, or to hold it for a further rise. And, of course, he would have to make an additional decision whether to keep the bond, now bereft of its speculative feature, or to sell it. Should the warrants be *detachable*—as they are often made to be—they themselves should have a market value close to $600, so that the bondholder could sell them for his capital gain, and keep the bond as a continuing investment or sell it, too, should he want to pull out completely.

Nevertheless, corporations look with much less favor on the warrant device than on convertibility. It has advantages for those corporations that expect to have a continual need of additional funds and are content to draw them from whatever sources may be available. They get the proceeds of their bond issues in lump sum and then additional cash inflows if and when the warrants are exercised. But most corporations that put out bond issues want to raise specific sums of money for specific projects. They are not interested in setting the stage for further inflows that may occur within a relatively short period of time, that may be delayed for many years, or that may not take place at all—inflows that may occur in driblets or in great spurts, all depending on the uncertain time when, if at all, bondholders (or the buyers of detachable warrants) will decide that the common stock is a good buy at the warrant price. Through the exercise of warrants, new money might flow in when it could not be used economically. This would mean a dilution in the claims to earnings of the existing common stock. In a word, issuance of stock purchase warrants attached to bonds tends to introduce an important element of uncertainty in long-range financial planning.

Indenture provisions governing the use of warrants parallel those pertaining to convertibility.

1. Subscription prices are almost always set well above the market prices of common stock at the time the bonds are issued.
2. There is sometimes a rising scale of subscription prices for successive periods.
3. Often, the period in which warrants may be exercised is limited.
4. The protection of antidilution clauses is provided.

In March, 1968, for example, in an offering to the public the AMK Corporation sold a $30 million issue of 6¾ percent debentures with warrants attached for the purchase of 300,000 shares of its common stock at $69 a share. This meant, of course, that the buyer of a $1,000 bond gained the privilege of buying 10 shares of common at the price mentioned. The warrants could be detached on or after May 15, 1968, and they were made exercisable until March 1, 1978.

QUESTIONS

1. Do not investors in long-term bonds act against their own interests when they insist that the issuing corporations provide sinking funds for *early* redemption? Discuss.

2. In what way does the attitude of industrial corporations toward sinking funds for bond redemption generally differ from that of public utilities? Why is this so?

3. What support is there for the proposition that the size of sinking fund contributions should increase from time to time during the life of a bond issue? That it should fall?

4. What merit is there in basing the size of sinking fund contributions on the amount of the corporation's profits?

5. Distinguish between the older and the modern theories of sinking fund management.

6. What choices does the typical corporation have in disposing of the cash that it is required by its indenture to allocate to a sinking fund?

7. Why are corporations moving away from the older practice of setting sinking fund call prices at levels above par value? Are they substituting anything for the premiums formerly paid? Explain.

8. What kinds of restrictions on payments of cash dividends are commonly found in bond indentures? On other kinds of cash payments?

9. What are the varieties of "events of default" on account of which trustees and bondholders can take action to protect the bondholders' interests? What are days of grace? What connection is there between events of default and days of grace?

10. What kinds of actions can trustees take to protect bondholders' interests following events of default? What can the bondholders themselves do?

11. What is acceleration? What bearing does it have on the protection of bondholders' interests?

12. Why do corporations generally want rights to call bonds for redemption beyond what are needed for sinking fund calls? What is the usual scope of such additional call privileges?

13. If the holders of a large proportion of a corporation's bonds, such as 75 percent, approve changes in the indenture, are nonvoting and dissenting bondholders bound by these changes? Explain.

14. Why can both strong and weak corporations benefit from adding convertibility features and stock purchase warrants in their bond issues?

15. In what circumstances can holders of convertible bonds be forced to exercise their conversion privileges? Why may a corporation want to exert force in this direction?

PROBLEMS

1. The bond issues of five corporations, designated by the letters A to E, are convertible into their respective common stocks at the ratios and prices indicated in the following table. All the common stocks are affected by split-ups or distributions of stock dividends as described in the table, so that in accordance with antidilution provisions in the bond indentures the conversion prices and ratios must be changed proportionally. What would be the levels of the new conversion ratios or prices for the five bond issues?

Corporation	*Conversion Price*	*Conversion Ratio*	*Changes in Common Stock*
A	$65		2 percent stock dividend
B	42		4-for-3 split-up
C		2.5 shares	5 percent stock dividend
D		3 shares	3-for-2 split-up
E	18		50 percent stock dividend

2. A corporation's outstanding stock purchase warrants have been exercisable at $45 a share, but on two occasions the corporation announces that on account of the requirements of antidilution clauses the price has been reduced, first to $30 a share and later to $22.50 a share. What must have happened to the corporation's common stock on these separate occasions to require the price cuts?

3. The bonds of a certain corporation are convertible into its common stock at a conversion price of $40. What, if anything, would be indicated about the probable level of the market price of the common stock if the bonds were selling in the market at each of the following prices: 93, 100, 106, 180, and 250?

chapter 30

THE SALE OF BOND ISSUES

Offerings to the general public, offerings to existing security holders, and sales in bulk to institutional investors (private placements) are the three principal channels for the selling of bond issues. Offerings to existing security holders are, for the most part, the tendering of new issues of convertible bonds; however, bondholders are occasionally offered new bonds in exchange for their present holdings. How offerings to the public and to security holders in combination compare with private placements is indicated in Table 30–1, where SEC data on bond sales for the period 1946–67 are presented. One will note, however, that the comparison reveals very little about patterns and trends. While it is apparent that the race between public offerings and private placements has been close to a dead heat in a good proportion of the years since 1946, the rather wide gyrations of the percentages in other years cannot be easily explained. For the most recent years, specifically the period 1964–67, at any rate, the sharp decline in the proportion of private placements, with its percentage falling in 1967 to its lowest level in the whole postwar period, is surely impressive.

Related to sales of bonds in some respects is the assumption of bond issues in mergers and consolidations. It is a common practice for the surviving corporation in a merger or the new corporation in a consolidation to take full responsibility for the outstanding bond issues of the corporation or corporations it is absorbing, and to carry them thereafter as its own liabilities. While this is not a sale of new bonds, it is an important means by which corporations gain the ownership of operating assets—often great volumes of assets of large values. Accordingly, the assumption of bond issues should be discussed in this chapter as a means of financing with bonds.

SALES TO THE GENERAL PUBLIC

In offering new bond issues to the general public, corporations in almost all instances use the services of investment bankers—a fact indicated by SEC data of registered corporate securities flotations in the year 1967. Of a total of $14,425 million of bonds registered for immediate offering for cash for the accounts of the issuing corporations, $14,301 million was underwritten by investment bankers, about $11.5 million was handled by the bankers on an agency basis, and only about $112.5 million was sold by the corporations without banker participation. While these registrations included offerings to existing security holders and to "other special groups," most of the bond issues handled by the investment bankers had to be offerings to the public, since the SEC also reports that for the year 1967 total offerings of *both* stocks and bonds to security holders and special groups amounted to only about $2,008 million.[1]

TABLE 30-1
Corporate Bonds Publicly Offered and Privately Placed, 1946-67*
(Estimated gross proceeds in millions of dollars)

Year	*Publicly Offered*	*Privately Placed*	*Private Placements as Percentage of Total*
1946	$ 3,019	$1,863	38.2
1947	2,889	2,147	42.6
1948	2,965	3,008	50.4
1949	2,437	2,453	50.2
1950	2,360	2,560	52.0
1951	2,364	3,326	58.4
1952	3,645	3,957	52.1
1953	3,856	3,228	45.6
1954	4,003	3,484	46.5
1955	4,119	3,301	44.5
1956	4,225	3,777	47.2
1957	6,118	3,839	38.6
1958	6,332	3,320	34.4
1959	3,557	3,632	50.5
1960	4,806	3,275	40.5
1961	4,700	4,720	50.1
1962	4,440	4,529	50.5
1963	4,714	6,158	56.6
1964	3,623	7,243	66.7
1965	5,570	8,150	59.4
1966	8,018	7,542	48.5
1967	14,990	6,964	31.7

*Substantially all new issues of corporate bonds offered for cash sale in the United States in amounts over $100,000 and with terms to maturity of more than 1 year.

SOURCE: Securities and Exchange Commission, *Annual Report*, 1964, p. 179; and *Statistical Bulletin*, March, 1967, p. 15, and March, 1968, p. 16. (Percentages for 1964-67 supplied by the author.)

When corporations want to have the assistance of investment bankers in floating bond issues, they make their approach to the bankers in either of two ways: (1) by direct negotiation with single houses, or

[1]SEC, *Statistical Bulletin*, March, 1968, p. 25.

(2) by broadside invitations to many banking houses to submit bids for the issues. The procedure of direct negotiation was described at length in Chapter 17 in the discussion of common stock flotations; as the procedure is much the same for bond flotations, little need be added here. On the other hand, because competitive bidding was passed over earlier it deserves a more extended examination at this time.

Direct Negotiation

The typical corporate management prefers to take its proposition for a bond flotation to the single investment banking house of its choice, just as it so chooses when planning to bring out additional issues of common or preferred stock. If it is turned down by the first house approached, it may go to a second and then to a third—but always to each house individually, without attempting to offer its bonds broadside to many houses simultaneously. This preference is surely indicated by the fact that the procedure of competitive bidding is little used outside the areas wherein it has been promoted by government regulation. It is also demonstrated by the fact that public utility and railroad corporations subject to competitive bidding rules often use the direct negotiation approach when possible because of exceptions to or special exemptions from the competitive bidding rules. However, offers of bond issues for competitive bids are often made by utilities that are not subject to competitive bidding requirements imposed by government regulation.

In direct negotiation with the single investment banking house of its choice, a corporation usually seeks an underwriting commitment. The bankers make a preliminary investigation and, if things look promising, follow up with a detailed investigation. If that, too, comes out satisfactorily, they are likely to agree to make the underwriting commitment. They then help the corporation to prepare the registration statement and the related prospectus for filing with the SEC, as well as documents necessary for qualifying the bonds for sale in various states according to the terms of their blue-sky laws. This kind of preparatory work is more complex for a bond issue than for a stock issue, made so by the necessity of drawing up the bond indenture which is itself, as we have noted, a long and complex document. A trustee must be selected, and the details of the indenture worked out in meticulous detail. If the bonds are to be offered in interstate commerce, the indenture must meet the requirements of the federal Trust Indenture Act,[2] and copies must be filed with the registration statement. Further work falls to the originating investment banking house when it decides to form an underwriting syndicate with other houses

---

[2]See above, pp. 683–84.

and a selling group of securities dealers—as it is most likely to decide for any issue of substantial size.

In some instances, investment bankers refuse to underwrite but agree to assist with the sale of bond issues on a best-efforts basis. As a rule, however, best-efforts selling is much less common in the flotation of bond issues than in the flotation of stock issues. Most investment bankers doubtless conclude that if underwritten bonds would be difficult to sell, the bonds must be so unsafe or otherwise lacking in investment qualities as to make it unwise for them, on any basis, to urge their customers to buy. Because stocks are by nature speculative, they are likely to have fewer qualms in offering on a best-efforts basis those issues thought to be too risky for underwriting.

Competitive Bidding

Although competitive bidding rules imposed by governmental agencies are applicable to the stock issues as well as to the bond issues of regulated corporations, competitive bidding for bond issues has been much more significant than for stock issues. For one thing, the regulated corporations have issued much greater volumes of bonds than of stocks since the rules were imposed; for another, exemptions from the rules have been and are granted much more often for stock issues than for bond issues. Accordingly, except for a footnote, the matter of competitive bidding was ignored in the earlier discussion of stock selling and deferred to this chapter, where it most importantly applies.

Scope of Competitive Bidding. Although governmental bodies had long offered some or all their debt issues for competitive bids, it was not until 1926 that a significant requirement in this direction was imposed on business corporations. This was the rule of the Interstate Commerce Commission, requiring railroads subject to its jurisdiction to offer their equipment trust certificates on a competitive bidding basis. The next important step in the same direction was taken by the SEC by virtue of its powers under the Public Utility Holding Company Act of 1935. It prescribed, effective May 7, 1941, that registered public utility holding companies and their operating subsidiaries use the competitive bidding procedure for most of their new issues, as well as for sales of securities from the portfolios of the holding companies. Next came, in 1944, a broadening of the rule of the Interstate Commerce Commission, making it applicable to all issues of securities of interstate railroads with proceeds of more than $1 million. This was followed up in 1950 by the imposition of a competitive bidding rule by the Federal Power Commission, applicable to public utilities operating in interstate commerce but not subject to the jurisdiction of the SEC. Meanwhile, some of the state public service commissions, by exercising powers already held or on the basis of new grants of power by the legislatures, imposed competitive bidding rules on utilities and railroads that came under their regulatory jurisdiction.

The competitive bidding rules are generally subject to certain exceptions set forth in the laws or regulations. For issues under the SEC's jurisdiction, for example, exceptions are granted for those with proceeds of less than $1 million, for private borrowings from financial institutions with maturities of 10 years or less, and for nonunderwritten rights offerings to existing security holders. Moreover, the regulatory agencies are empowered to grant specific exemptions for given flotations, as when they are persuaded that better prices can be obtained by direct negotiation. In some instances, regulated corporations offer issues for competitive bids only to receive none, and then receive permission to proceed with direct negotiation.

The extent to which competitive bidding requirements are applicable, as well as the significance of exemptions, is indicated by the record of offerings of public utility holding companies and subsidiaries that are subject to the supervisory authority of the SEC. In the period from May 7, 1941, through June 30, 1967, these companies sold by the competitive bidding route 969 issues of securities, chiefly bonds, with an aggregate sales value of $14,930 million, while 238 issues with a total sales value of $2,636 million were sold by other procedures allowed as exceptions to the SEC's competitive bidding rules.[3]

Competitive bidding procedures are available, of course, to any corporation, even though it is not required by government regulation to take that route. As was stated earlier, many public utility corporations do offer their securities for competitive bids, even when not required to do so. On the other hand, the offering of securities by the competitive bidding route has made very little progress among the mass of industrial corporations.

Procedure. A corporation that plans to offer a bond issue for competitive bids must largely go it alone in preparing the issue for the market. It may ask an investment banking house for advice, but it can hardly expect to get a great amount of detailed assistance from it, as in direct negotiation procedures. No matter how great might be its desire to underwrite the issue, the investment banking house would hardly want to go to much expense in helping, knowing that its bid might prove not to be the best one. The corporation might ask the bankers for help by promising them a fee for their services, but under the rules of the regulatory commissions the acceptance of a fee in this connection generally precludes the submission of a bid. Thus, bankers willing to provide help for a fee would have to have no interest in submitting a bid.

With preparations completed and, if applicable, legal requirements

---

[3]SEC, *Annual Report*, 1967, pp. 125–26.

of registration satisfied, the corporation publishes a notice in which it invites bids for the whole issue, as in Figure 30–1. In this notice, the bonds are described briefly, the place where all documents can be examined is named, how copies of the prospectus and the statement setting forth the rules for the bidding can be obtained is indicated, and the day and hour by which bids must be submitted are stated. Usually, also, the notice sets a time and place for a meeting at which corporation officials will be on hand to explain whatever details of the proposed issue prospective bidders want to inquire about. The meeting is usually set for a time several days before the day the bids are to be submitted.

FIGURE 30–1
Advertisement for Competitive Bids for a Bond Issue

BROCKTON EDISON COMPANY

Public Invitation for Bids for the Purchase of $5,000,000 Principal Amount of First Mortgage and Collateral Trust Bonds, ...% Series due 1989

BROCKTON EDISON COMPANY hereby invites bids for the purchase from it of $5,000,000 principal amount of First Mortgage and Collateral Trust Bonds, ...% Series due 1989. Such bids will be received by the Company at 49 Federal Street (8th Floor), Boston, Massachusetts, up to 11:00 A. M., Boston Time, on Tuesday, June 23, 1959, or such later date as may be fixed by the Company as provided in the Terms and Conditions for Bids for the Purchase of such Bonds dated June 16, 1959. Copies of such Terms and Conditions for Bids, the Registration Statement and Prospectus and other related documents are available and may be examined at 49 Federal Street (8th Floor), Boston, Massachusetts, or 90 Broad Street (21st Floor), New York, N. Y. Bids need be considered only from persons who shall have furnished to the Company certain information on the questionnaire referred to in said Terms and Conditions for Bids before 11:00 A. M., Boston Time, on Friday, June 19, 1959, and who have received copies of such Prospectus, and only if made in accordance with and subject to the Terms and Conditions for Bids.

Officers and representatives of the Company, counsel for the Company, representatives of Messrs. Patterson, Teele & Dennis, independent public accountants, and Messrs. Ropes, Gray, Best, Coolidge & Rugg, counsel for the prospective Purchasers of the above-mentioned securities, will be available at 49 Federal Street (8th Floor), Boston, Massachusetts, on Friday, June 19, 1959 at 11:00 A. M., Boston Time, to meet with prospective bidders for the purpose of reviewing with them the information with respect to the Company contained in the Registration Statement and Prospectus and for the purpose of considering matters referred to in the Terms and Conditions for Bids. All prospective bidders are invited to be present at such meeting.

BROCKTON EDISON COMPANY
By PAUL E. MILSTEAD, *President.*

June 16, 1959.

Several prominent investment banking houses that often serve as originators of new security issues may be interested in submitting bids for the proposed bond issue. Such a house will tentatively line up other houses for an underwriting syndicate. Conferences will be held with the representatives of these houses, with particular attention to the level of the bid to be submitted, but usually the final decision is deferred until a meeting on the morning of the day the bids are to be submitted. When a bid has been accepted, the originator signs the underwriting agreement with the corporation, the syndicate agreement is signed by all the underwriting houses, and arrangements are completed for setting up a selling group if one has been decided on, as is most likely.

It is possible, of course, that no investment banking house will be sufficiently interested in a proposed bond issue to submit a bid for itself or for itself and the other houses of a tentative syndicate. A moderate number of invitations for bids meet such negative responses. Moreover, the offering corporations invariably reserve the right to reject all bids, so that offerings may fail, at least on the first round, because all bids are thought to be too low.

Bids. In offering a bond issue for competitive bids, the corporation usually names neither the price at which it will sell the bonds nor the interest rate that the bonds will carry. It is left to the bidders to name both price and interest rate. For a 20-year bond issue, one group of houses may offer 102.61 for the bonds, stipulating that the interest rate shall be 4¾ percent; another may offer 100.66, stipulating that the interest rate shall be fixed at 4½ percent. The corporation will accept the better bid, unless it chooses to reject both. But which of these is the better bid? The first will give the corporation $1,026.10 for each $1,000 bond of its issue, it will have to pay back only $1,000 at maturity, and in the meantime it will be paying interest at 4¾ percent on only the par value. The second bid will give the corporation only $1,006.60 for each $1,000 bond, it will have to pay back $1,000 at maturity, but in the meantime it will get by with a slightly lower rate of interest on the par value. The answer to the question, therefore, must be in terms of *effective* rates of interest. Bond tables reveal that the effective rate on a 20-year, 4¾ percent bond sold at 102.61 is 4.55 percent, and on a 20-year, 4½ percent bond sold at 100.66 it is 4.45 percent. The bid at 100.66 with a 4½ percent interest rate proves to be the more favorable one.

To illustrate how the bidding goes, the offering of $20 million of 30-year first-mortgage bonds of the Louisville Gas & Electric Company in June, 1968, may be cited. The winning bid of 100.159 with the interest rate designated at 6¾ percent was submitted by a group of investment bankers headed by the First Boston Corporation. Four other bids, all with designations of the interest rate at 6⅞ percent, were received from the prospective managers of other underwriting syndicates as follows.

Kidder, Peabody & Co., and Goldman, Sachs & Co., jointly....	101.479
Eastman Dillon, Union Securities & Co., and White, Weld & Co., jointly....	101.43
Lehman Brothers, Blyth & Co., Merrill Lynch, Pierce, Fenner & Smith, Inc., and Salomon Brothers & Hutzler, jointly......	101.369
Hasley, Stuart & Co., Inc....	101.05

In setting a price in its bid, an investment banking house, needless to say, expects that it, the other underwriters, and the dealers of the selling group will be able to resell to their customers at a higher price. And, of course, the bankers must agree among themselves how the expected margin between buying and selling prices is to be shared among the manager of the syndicate, the syndicate members, and the members of the selling group.

Pros and Cons of Competitive Bidding. There has been a long debate about the merits and drawbacks of competitive bidding. With some exceptions, the investment bankers have been critical, but the government regulatory agencies appear to be satisfied with the results of their competitive bidding rules. The corporations subject to these rules seem, too, to be generally satisfied, but it is noteworthy that most unregulated corporations, especially industrials, do not take the competitive bidding route although free to do so.

Since the development of competitive bidding has been largely the result of government regulation, most of the arguments in favor have been focused on the promotion of the general welfare rather than on the advancement of the interests of particular groups, whether corporations, bankers, or investors. From this standpoint, it is argued that competitive bidding enables corporations to get long-term funds more cheaply; that the bankers will have relatively little influence on the policies of corporations whose securities they underwrite; and that a few large houses will be prevented from getting the lion's share of underwritings.

The gist of the first of these arguments is that lower costs of funds to public utilities and railroads should enable them to supply their services to the public at lower rates. The second argument is predicated on the propositions that investment bankers have often tried to dominate the affairs of corporations whose securities they have underwritten on a direct negotiation basis, and especially that such domination, if effective simultaneously over many corporations, leads to many kinds of restraints of trade. The third argument grows out of allegations that in a system of direct negotiation, large corporations, in particular, limit their proposals of security flotations to a handful of large investment banking houses of national reputation, and that these houses, in forming syndicates, repeatedly invite given groups of houses and repeatedly ignore many others than could function just as effectively. The argument is, therefore, that underwriting by direct negotiation leads toward monopoly in the investment banking industry itself. Obviously, the three arguments are closely related. If a small group of large houses dominate the affairs of many corporations, the corporations will undoubtedly go to this group with their flotations, and, at the same time, the dominating bankers will surely dictate the allocation of handsome underwriting commissions to themselves.

The opponents of competitive bidding—chiefly the investment

bankers, although not all are opponents—have some difficulty in advancing their position on the grounds of general welfare. They are more inclined to argue that direct negotiation is beneficial for corporate issuers of securities and for investors, although they often carry their arguments further to say that benefits to corporations and investors also contribute to the general welfare. In the first place, the bankers find it imperative to deny that they try to dominate the corporations whose securities they underwrite by direct negotiation. They often admit that attempts at domination were common in the past, but they claim that this aspect of finance capitalism is now obsolete. Corporate managements, they say, welcome them to their boards of directors to gain the benefits of their broad knowledge of financial markets and security management, just as they welcome outside directors from other walks of life to get the benefits of knowledge and experience of other kinds. An investment banking house to which a corporation always takes its long-term financing will have a continuing interest in its welfare—all the more so if a member of the house sits on the corporation's board of directors where he can keep an eye on developments. In times of difficulty, investment bankers in this position can be expected to do everything possible to aid the corporation, which should be of benefit to all its employees, to all the people who own its securities, and probably to its customers as well. It is argued that such devotion can hardly be expected of bankers who win a corporation's security issue by a low bid. Such bankers know that future business with the corporation will depend, not on what help they may thereafter give to it but simply on how the bids turn out the next time it offers a security issue.

In answer to the argument that competitive bidding enables corporations to obtain long-term funds more cheaply—evidenced by the fact that underwriting commissions on competitive bidding deals are generally substantially less than on negotiated deals—the opponents of competitive bidding argue that the corporations pay less because they get fewer services. The competitive bidder, it is argued, incurs no expense in helping the corporation to prepare its security issue for the market; it does not even offer advice on the character and terms of the issue; and it accepts no responsibility for continued interest in the corporation and its securities in the future. Services that the corporation does not pay for and does not get are likely to be the very ones that would be of most benefit to the investing public. An investment banking house that bids for a security issue thereby signifies its willingness to take it as the corporation designed it, but if it had worked out the details on a negotiated basis it might have insisted on a much stronger array of protective provisions in the interests of its customers, the security buyers.

It is more difficult for the opponents of competitive bidding to explain away the fact that underwriting commissions for all issuers, both those that sell by direct negotiation and those that sell by the competitive bidding route, are nowadays generally much less than they used to be. Because this is true, it can hardly be explained away. But to preclude giving to competitive bidding too much credit for this development, opponents of that practice often argue that the rapid growth of private placements has been the more important reason for the decline in the size of underwriting commissions. Such an argument, however, only indicates that there may be more than one reason investment bankers are now willing to work harder for a given reward.

SALES TO EXISTING SECURITY HOLDERS

The sale of bonds by corporations to their existing security holders is very largely the sale of convertible issues to common stockholders. Whether or not the preemptive right obtains, such offerings are made chiefly because of convictions of corporate managers that the common stockholders are the most likely buyers, not for reason of their interests in bond investment as such, but for reason of their interests in eventually getting additional common shares by the conversion route. In some instances, corporations offer new bonds to existing bondholders in exchange for their holdings, but a discussion of this kind of operation can best be deferred to Chapter 31, which is devoted to the management of outstanding bond issues.

Corporations that offer convertible bonds to their common stockholders are generally of the class that would prefer to be issuing common stock in the first place. They want conversion to take place, and they anticipate that the common stockholders will actually convert when the market prices of their common stocks improve. In other words, these corporations issue convertible bonds because the market for bonds is generally favorable, while that for their common stocks is not so strong as they think it should be. Their managers may fear that the depressive effect on the market prices of their stocks would be too great were they to offer at once the same number of shares as the amount into which the bonds are made convertible. But their expectation is that, when the market for their stocks has gained strength, the bonds will flow back for conversion, perhaps gradually or perhaps in bulk, especially near the times when the conversion prices are scheduled to rise.

Well-known corporations that have made recent offerings of convertible bonds to their stockholders include: the National Cash Register Company, approximately $89 million; the United Aircraft Corporation, about $120 million; R. H. Macy & Co., Inc., about $22 million; Twentieth Century-Fox Film Corporation, approximately $28 million; American Broadcasting Companies, Inc., $50 million;

United Air Lines, Inc., about $141 million; the Kerr-McGee Corporation, about $95 million; and Hart Schaffner & Marx, about $19 million. In all these instances, the offerings were subordinated debenture bonds, and the offering price was 100. The privilege of subscribing to $100 of bonds was accorded to each 7 shares of Kerr-McGee stock; to each 10 shares for American Broadcasting, National Cash Register, and United Aircraft; to each 13 shares for United Air Lines; to each 20 shares for Macy; and to each 25 shares for Hart Schaffner & Marx and Twentieth Century-Fox. The bonds offered by United Air Lines had a peculiar convertibility feature in their provision that 1½ shares of its common stock would be obtainable for $100 principal amount of bonds *and $26 in cash.*

Procedure

The procedure of making a rights offering of convertible bonds is much the same as that for additional issues of common stock, described at length in Chapter 19. The directors adopt a resolution, setting forth the terms of the offering, establishing a record date when the names of the stockholders to whom the offering will be made are to be determined, and setting a later date and hour when the subscription books will be closed. As soon as possible after the record date, the secretary of the corporation or the stock transfer agent sends a subscription warrant to each stockholder whose name appeared on the books at the close of business on that day. The stockholder may then subscribe by filling in the warrant and submitting it to the corporation or its subscription agent with his payment (or with the first installment of his payment, if payment in installments has been authorized); he may endorse the warrant and sell it to somebody else or give it away; or, of course, he may do nothing.

A rights offering for convertible bonds, like one for additional common stock, is made on a pro rata basis. Each stockholder is given the right to subscribe in the proportion of the number of his shares to the total outstanding. Suppose, for example, that a corporation that has 500,000 shares of common stock outstanding is making a rights offering of $5 million of convertible bonds. The subscription warrants that it issues represent 500,000 rights, and 100 rights and cash equal to the subscription price are required for the purchase of a $1,000 bond. The owner of 400 shares gets 400 rights, and with the requisite amount of cash he may buy bonds of a par value of $4,000.

Transactions in Rights

As in a rights offering for new common stock, a corporation that offers bonds by the rights procedure expects most of its stockholders to subscribe, but, if there are hundreds or thousands of stockholders it hardly anticipates a perfect response. Because it wants to sell all the bonds offered, it hopes, therefore, that nonsubscribing stockholders will pass on their warrants to other investors who will enter subscriptions. It does more than hope for this; it strongly encourages it by offering the bonds at a price somewhat below what it would expect to set were it making an offering to the general public. As the subscription price in rights offerings of convertible bonds is set at 100 in a great majority of cases, the interest rate designated for the bonds is set slightly higher than would be needed for a sale to the public at 100. If the corporation's estimation proves to be reasonably accurate, the rights will have a market value determined by the difference between the offering price and what investors think the bonds will be worth when they have been issued. With a rights value established, stockholders who do not want to exercise their rights will surely have every reason to sell them.

Let us assume that the corporation of the foregoing illustration offers its bonds to the stockholders at the customary subscription price of 100. This is a bargain price—the corporate managers intend it to be that—but outsiders also recognize it as such. The outsiders accordingly begin to bid prices higher than 100 for bonds to be delivered to them "when issued." They want to enter into contracts at once at, say, 101 or 102 for future delivery, for they expect to be able to resell at, say, 103 or 104 when delivery is made after the end of the subscription period. They hope to make a nice profit on a speculation of quite short term. But their spirited bidding may drive up the when-issued price of bonds to, say, 103. Stockholders who do not want to buy and hold the new bonds to which they are entitled should be quite willing to enter into contracts for future sales at 103. They have the pleasant prospect of buying from the corporation at 100 and then quickly selling at 103. Speculators who do not think the market price will reach 103 may sell short for future delivery, expecting to make a profit equal to the difference between that selling price and the lower price at which they hope they can buy later to make delivery. At any rate, bids and offers from sources such as these establish a market value for the not-yet-issued bonds, and if this value is in excess of the subscription price, the stockholders' rights to subscribe also acquire a market value. In terms of the illustration, a when-issued market price of 103 should give each right a market value of close to 30 cents, as determined by the following formula.

$$\frac{\text{Market value of bond} - \text{Subscription price}}{\text{Number of rights required to buy one bond}} = \text{Value of a right}$$

Substituting, we get:

$$\frac{\$1{,}030 - \$1{,}000}{100} = 30 \text{ cents.}$$

Thus, the stockholder who does not want to buy and hold bonds may sell for future delivery as many bonds as he is entitled to buy from the corporation, with assurances of a gain of $30 on each, or for a gain of equal amount he may simply sell each 100 of his rights. In either transaction, the corporation's objective, to dispose of the bond issue, is served. In the first alternative, the stockholder actually subscribes for his allotment of the bonds, although he does not hold them for long. In the second, whoever buys his rights in the market or, anyway, whoever holds them near the end of the subscription period will presumably subscribe.

In the American Broadcasting Companies' rights offering of $50 million of its 5 percent convertible subordinated debentures in July, 1968, referred to previously, the bonds sold on a when-issued basis throughout the subscription period at prices ranging from 105 to 115¼, and rights reached a high of 1 7/16—about $1.44.

Question of Dilution

The gain derived by a stockholder who sells his rights to subscribe to convertible bonds, or who subscribes and then immediately sells the bonds, is not necessarily all frosting on the cake. It will prove so to be if no subsequent conversion of bonds into common stock takes place; in that circumstance, the stockholder suffers no dilution in his rights to earnings, assets, and voting power. The amount of common stock outstanding remains the same, and his proportionate interests are as before. But if subsequent conversions do take place, dilution results, so that the gain turns out to be, in part at least, the proceeds of the sale of some of the stockholder's ownership interests.

Stockholders' Attitudes

As in the disposal of rights to subscribe directly to additional shares of common stock, the stockholders' attitudes toward subscriptions to convertible bonds differ. All who are interested in control will be strongly inclined to exercise their rights to subscribe. Hardly less attracted will be the stockholders who choose to accumulate wealth in the form of corporate assets, as well as those who are loyal to the corporation in appreciation of its dividend policies. Some may subscribe to bonds, though they would not subscribe direct for additional stock, because they want to balance their investment portfolios. But many, particularly smaller stockholders, are likely to look on the rights as a dividend and sell them in the market. Nor may we fail to mention those who deposit their subscription warrants in the wastebasket because they do not understand what the rights offering is all about.

Registration and the Bankers

When rights to subscribe to convertible bonds are to be offered in interstate commerce to many stockholders, registration with the SEC is required no less than when rights offerings of common stock are made. For such offerings, too, the bond indentures must satisfy the requirements of the federal Trust Indenture Act. Also applicable are the qualification requirements of many of the state blue-sky laws.

In making rights offerings of bonds to their stockholders, most corporations that have many stockholders call on investment bankers for assistance, and because they want assurances of the success of their flotations they generally ask the bankers for underwriting commitments. As in the underwriting of rights offerings of common stock,[4] this means that the bankers, on the basis of stand-by contracts, undertake to buy from the issuing corporations whatever bonds are not sold to the stockholders and transferees of rights. Occasionally, the bankers help out on the basis of best-efforts dealer-management agreements, but this procedure is much less popular for bond offerings than for rights offerings of stock.

PRIVATE PLACEMENTS

Although the private placement of common and preferred stocks was briefly treated in Chapters 20 and 24, this procedure of selling occurs much more frequently in the sale of bond issues. The importance of the private placement of bond issues in the period since 1946 was indicated earlier in this chapter in Table 30–1. Presumably, the private placement of bond issues would have accounted for an even larger proportion of total bond sales in recent years were it not for the competitive bidding rules applicable to most public utility and railroad issues. The institutional investors that buy bonds by private placement rarely submit bids for bonds or other securities offered for competitive bids. Although as free to submit bids as are other classes of investors, they choose to buy bonds in bulk on a more certain basis than the hit-or-miss basis of competitive bidding. For this reason, bonds sold by competitive bidding are almost always public offerings, and very rarely do they become private placements.

Private Buyers

Institutional investors buy bonds for their own long-term investment; unlike investment bankers, they do not buy for resale. But what classes of institutions have so much money that they can, at a stroke, buy entire bond issues of $10, $20, or $30 million? It should be interesting to approach an answer to this question indirectly by analyzing some overall estimates of corporate bonds outstanding and corporate bond ownership at the end of 1967 as published by the Board of Governors of the Federal Reserve System. According to the Federal Reserve figures, there were outstanding $152 billion of

[4]See pp. 480–83.

corporate bonds at market value. Of this total, issues of nonfinancial business corporations amounted to $123 billion, finance companies $17.5 billion, and commercial banks $2 billion, while the balance of $9.5 billion consisted of bonds of foreign corporations held by American owners.[5] In its ownership data, however, the Federal Reserve does not distinguish among these different classes of issuers, so that the ownership of the $152 billion of corporate bonds of all issuers without this distinction is accounted for by the array presented in Table 30–2. The enormous total of the holdings of life insurance companies, amounting to about 44 percent of all corporate bonds estimated to be outstanding, immediately suggests that they must be the most important buyers by the private placement route. They

TABLE 30–2
Ownership of Corporation Bonds,
December 31, 1967
(In billions of dollars at market value)

Owning Class	*Amount*
Life insurance companies	$ 67.1
State and local governments	36.0
Private noninsured pension funds	25.6
Households*	6.8
Mutual savings banks	5.2
Other insurance companies	3.9
Open-end investment companies	3.0
Rest of the world†	2.8
Commercial banks‡	1.6
Total	$152.0

*Including personal trust accounts, colleges and universities, charitable organizations, and other nonprofit institutions.

†Ownership by foreigners of bonds issued by American corporations.

‡Owned as their own investments, and not as investments for others as in their trust departments.

SOURCE: Board of Governors of the Federal Reserve System, *Flow of Funds Accounts 1945–1967* (Washington, D.C., 1968), pp. 171A, 174A.

could hardly accumulate such a huge portfolio by buying in the market a few thousand dollars' worth of this and that; they would have to buy in large chunks. Indeed, we know from many sources of information that they are by far the most important class of buyers by private placement. The huge holdings of state and local governments in corporate bonds at $36 billion are accounted for very largely by acquisitions for the pension funds for the employees of these governments. The great size of these accumulations suggests that the managers of many of these funds, including the trust institutions that serve as trustees for some, may well be interested in buying entire bond issues or large portions by the procedure of private place-

[5]Board of Governors of the Federal Reserve System, *Flow of Funds Accounts 1945–1967* (Washington, D.C., 1968), p. 174A.

ment, and we know this to be so. The holdings of private noninsured pension funds in the huge total of $25.6 billion are almost entirely in the hands of the trust institutions, so that these institutions show up again as important potential buyers of bonds privately placed. Even the bond ownership of "households," as the term is used by the Federal Reserve in the flow-of-funds accounts, is substantially in the hands of trust institutions in their roles as trustees of personal trusts, guardians, executors of wills, and so on.

On the basis of the ownership figures, as well as knowledge of the hows and whys of institutional procedures and policies derived from other sources, we can say that the principal buyers of bonds by private placement are the life insurance companies, and that the runner-up position is unquestionably held by trust institutions—trust companies and the trust departments of commercial banks—in buying and holding for pension funds of state and local governments, private noninsured pension funds, and personal trust accounts of various classes. For the other classes of institutional investors listed in Table 30–2, we can also say that a few of the larger institutions of each class will doubtless be interested in buying by private placement from time to time, but that a big majority of the institutions of each class will hardly be interested for lack of sufficient buying capacity individually.

While there is good reason to emphasize the far-in-the-lead position of life insurance companies as buyers of bond issues by private placement, one must still concede to them plenty of room for buying in the open market. The smaller companies surely acquire all or most of their investment portfolios by such buying, and even with the larger companies buying by private placement is heavily concentrated in acquisitions of industrial and miscellaneous bonds, for which competitive bidding rules do not apply. Since, however, industrial and miscellaneous bonds dominate the corporate bond portfolios of the life companies collectively, as Table 30–3 shows, and since about 85 percent of these bonds are acquired by private placement,[6] the importance of this procedure is clearly revealed.

Cost Factors in Private Placements

At first glance, one might conclude that any corporation planning to sell a bond issue should first offer it to life insurance companies, trust institutions, or other institutional investors. The flotation costs ought to be much less in a private placement than for a public offering. Some of the economies come readily to mind: no underwriting commissions to investment bankers; no expenses for preparation of a registration statement and prospectus and for qualifying under blue-

---

[6]Estimate of the Institute of Life Insurance for holdings at the end of 1966. See its *1967 Life Insurance Fact Book,* p. 77.

sky laws; no need, probably, to hire a trustee; and no expense for engraving bond certificates should the institutional investor be willing to accept simple note forms. Even further, the legal staff of the institutional investor ought to be willing to bear most of the burdens of preparing the indenture. Since the institution would want to have a hand in working out all details of the indenture, it would probably be happy to have its own people take major responsibility for preparation of the document.

TABLE 30–3
Corporate Bondholdings of Life Insurance Companies, Selected Years, 1917–67
(In millions of dollars)

Year	*Railroad*	*Public Utility*	*Industrial and Miscellaneous*	*Total*
1917	$1,813	$ 113	$ 49	$ 1,975
1920	1,775	125	49	1,949
1925	2,238	687	97	3,022
1930	2,931	1,631	367	4,929
1935	2,625	2,114	575	5,314
1940	2,830	4,273	1,542	8,645
1945	2,948	5,212	1,900	10,060
1950	3,187	10,587	9,526	23,300
1955	3,912	13,968	18,179	36,059
1960	3,668	16,719	26,728	47,115
1965	3,314	17,046	38,338	58,698
1966	3,389	16,686	41,203	61,278
1967	3,433	17,081	44,621	65,135

SOURCE: Institute of Life Insurance, *Life Insurance Fact Book*, 1968, p. 64.

All such economies—or many of them, in the individual case—are quite real in private placements.[7] But this does not necessarily mean that the *total cost of borrowing* to the corporation—flotation costs plus interest burdens during the life of an issue—will be less in a private placement than in a public offering. The investment officers of life insurance companies and other institutional investors are shrewd bargainers. Fully aware of the economies of private placements, they will surely insist that their institutions share in these benefits, and demand interest rates somewhat higher than would be designated were the bonds being offered publicly. Especially will they want an upward adjustment of interest rates to compensate for expenses incurred by their institutions in the acquisition of bonds on a private placement basis, as when their legal staffs do most of the work of pre-

[7]Rarely are estimates published on differences in costs, but the Brooklyn Union Gas Company gave us one in 1963. It estimated that it saved $36,000 in expenses in selling a $19.2 million issue of first-mortgage bonds by private placement rather than by competitive bidding. *The Wall Street Journal*, Midwest Edition, April 26, 1963, p. 21.

paring the indentures. Another adverse cost factor may arise in the retirement of the indebtedness. Privately placed bonds are always redeemable at the full contract price, whereas corporations that sell bonds by public offerings may at times be able to buy them in the market for retirement at prices substantially below the call prices.

Other Pros and Cons of Private Placements

Closely related to economies is the typical institutional investor's willingness to buy corporations' bond issues in installments over periods of months or years. The institutional investor's takedowns can be scheduled to match each corporation's spending plans. If a corporation is launching a three-year building program, for example, it can arrange to have portions of the bonds taken from time to time as money is needed to pay the building contractor, and it begins to incur interest obligations on the bonds only when they have been thus taken by the institutional investor. On the other hand, successive public offerings of groups of bonds in a relatively short period such as three years would multiply flotation costs, while a single public offering of the full issue at the beginning of the construction period would require the temporary investment of much of the proceeds pending their eventual spending for the building program. In the second alternative, because of the high degree of safety that would doubtless be wanted the rate of interest earned on the temporary investments would surely be less than that being paid on the bonds themselves.

Another comparable advantage of private placements is gained when institutional investors make commitments to take bonds to be issued at some time in the future. The financial managers of a corporation may know that their expansion program will require a very large outlay of cash in 10 to 12 months, and they may want to finance this with a bond issue. Investment bankers would hardly be willing to make an immediate underwriting commitment for a public offering subject to such a lengthy delay, but institutional investors often find that advance commitments tie in most conveniently with their own financial planning. The institutional investor may have already chosen investment outlets for currently inflowing funds, but as it expects the inflow to continue indefinitely it finds imperative a constant lining up of outlets for future inflows.

If a corporation that has sold a bond issue to an institutional investor by private placement gets into financial difficulties, it has, so far as the bonds go, only one creditor to deal with. This could be advantageous. To arrange deferments of obligations to pay interest or principal, temporary reductions in the interest rate, or other modifications of the corporation's obligations should be an easier task than getting the approval of a large majority of hundreds or thousands of individual bondholders. Moreover, the institutional investor may be willing to advance additional funds to save the corporation from a perilous situation, whereas widely scattered individual bondholders would doubtless be unwilling to pay in assessments for a purpose of this sort.[8] Likewise, when indenture terms prove to be too restrictive, getting the consent of a single institutional investor to modifications should be much easier than getting the approval of the scattered holders of two thirds or three fourths of bonds sold by a public offering.

But having only one bondholding creditor to deal with can be a source of disadvantages. It is often claimed to be so. Indentures drawn for private placements often contain more restrictive provisions and tighter ones than do those for public offerings. The institutional investor may not want to rigorously enforce all the restrictive provisions, but at least it must be consulted by the corporate managers should they want permission to do something that the indenture forbids or limits. In short, the institutional investor expects to have a much more decisive influence on the financial policies of the corporation whose bonds it buys in bulk than is expected or wanted by the trustee of a publicly offered bond issue.

Investment Bankers as Finders

Although corporations that place their bonds privately with institutional investors need no underwriting by investment bankers, they often employ the bankers as finders. They are willing to pay the bankers a finder's fee in the belief that the bankers will be able to find institutional buyers, even though they themselves could not, or that the bankers will be able to get for them better terms than they themselves could hope to get by a direct approach. To call attention to their services as finders, investment bankers often insert advertisements of successful placements in prominent newspapers and financial publications. Such an advertisement is reproduced in Figure 30–2.

THE ASSUMPTION OF BOND ISSUES

In numerous instances, corporations use bonds for financing asset acquisitions in what may be called an indirect fashion. This is the procedure of assuming the bond liabilities of other corporations, a common practice in mergers and consolidations. Corporation A sells a bond issue by a public offering or a private placement and uses the proceeds to acquire a given array of assets. Then along comes Corporation B with a merger proposition that the stockholders of A find irresistible. The merger is effected, and B now owns the assets that A had acquired with its bond issue; but at the same time B becomes fully responsible for meeting all the obligations and covenants of

[8] What corporations can try to do to meet difficulties in fulfilling their obligations on bond issues is discussed further in Chapter 31. See pp. 809–18.

A's bond indenture. It alone remains with this responsibility, for A ceases to exist as a separate entity if the merger is carried through as a statutory fusion in the manner provided for in state corporation laws, which is most likely.

FIGURE 30–2
Newspaper Notice of a Private Placement

The undersigned represented the Company in negotiating an agreement for the purchase of these Notes by certain institutions.

$15,000,000

United Artists Corporation

6% Participating Promissory Notes

An agreement has been executed which permits the Company to sell $10,000,000 of the above amount on or before July 2, 1959, and the balance on or before July 1, 1961.

F. EBERSTADT & CO.

May 7, 1959

Choice of the Surviving Corporation

Now it is clear that the surviving corporation of a merger or the new corporation of a consolidation could choose to sell its own bond issue in order to raise cash for retirement of the outstanding bonds of the corporation to be absorbed. The merger agreement could provide that the cash be paid over so that the bonds of the corporation to be absorbed could be called for redemption before the effective date of the merger. The surviving corporation would then acquire the assets of the other without any need of assumption.

However, the prime movers in many mergers and consolidations want to carry them through with minimum outlays of cash. Common stockholders of the corporation to be absorbed are offered common stock of the surviving corporation. Similarly, if the corporation to be absorbed has preferred stock outstanding, an exchange offering of preferred stock in the surviving corporation is ordinarily made. If, then, it is also possible to take over the bonds (and other liabilities) of the corporation to be absorbed just as they stand, a very important further economy in the use of cash results. Indeed, very little cash may be needed if most of the stockholders agree to accept the exchange offers and if all, or almost all, the liabilities are assumed—very little cash for the acquisition of assets of many kinds and substantial values.

Position of the Bondholders

A curious thing about assumptions of bond issues is that the owners of the bonds themselves ordinarily having nothing to say about the matter. The corporation that issued the bonds passes out of existence, as Corporation A in the illustration, and its bondholders simply become creditors of the surviving corporation. The bondholders or their trustee, it is true, can take legal proceedings to stop a proposed merger on the grounds that its results would be fraudulent, but if fraud is not intended, the promoters of the merger can usually satisfy the court that the safety of the bondholders' position would not be impaired. Sometimes, moreover, indentures have restrictions on mergers and consolidations—outright prohibitions in some instances, and in others requirements for consent of the holders of two thirds or three fourths of the outstanding bonds. Nevertheless, the more common practice is for indentures to reserve to the corporation the right to merge or consolidate with others, provided only that should it be absorbed, the successor corporation will accept full liability for the bonds.

Such an acceptance of liability—the specific assumption of the bonds—is usually set forth in a supplementary indenture entered into between the surviving corporation and the original trustee or a successor trustee. The supplementary indenture, needless to say, cannot change the interest rate, maturity, sinking fund requirements, or any of the other terms of the original indenture. Nor can it disturb any of the liens held by the bonds being assumed. If, however, the original indenture was an open-end one, the supplementary indenture may close the issue should the surviving corporation so wish. Likewise, it is generally understood that an after-acquired property clause in the assumed bonds no longer will have effect, unless the original indenture specifically prescribed how it should continue to apply after merger or consolidation. Finally, a supplementary indenture must usually provide adjusted conversion prices or ratios for assumed bonds whose conversion rights are to continue after the merger or consolidation.

Even if agreements for merger or consolidation say nothing about the disposition of outstanding bonds and other debts of corporations being absorbed, and even if supplementary indentures binding the surviving corporations are not drawn up, there is no question as to their liability for these debts. It is a well-settled principle of law that if no provision is made in a merger settlement for the paying off of such debts, the surviving corporation necessarily accepts responsibility for them. Provisions in the state corporation codes are generally quite clear and unequivocal on this score. For example, the Delaware law puts it this way:

> . . . but all rights of creditors and all liens upon any property of any of said constituent corporations shall be preserved unimpaired, and all debts, liabilities and duties of the respective constituent corporations shall thenceforth attach to said resulting or surviving corporation, and may be enforced against it to the same extent as if said debts, liabilities and duties had been incurred or contracted by it.[9]

QUESTIONS

1. In the period since 1946, how has the proportion of bonds offered to the public and to security holders compared with the proportion sold by private placement? Have these proportions had a consistent pattern from year to year? Explain.

2. To what extent, if at all, do the registration requirements of the federal Securities Act apply to sales of bonds (*a*) to the general public, (*b*) to corporations' own common stockholders, and (*c*) to institutional investors as private placements?

3. To what extent, if at all, are the services of investment bankers employed when bonds are sold in each of the three channels mentioned in question 2? Distinguish between the services of the bankers as underwriters and as finders.

4. Describe the steps in selling a bond issue by the competitive bidding procedure.

5. What classes of corporations are required to offer their bond issues for competitive bids? Why are they so required?

6. For what reasons are investment bankers generally critical of the competitive bidding procedure for selling new bond issues?

7. What is the significance of the fact that investment bankers name both a price and an interest rate when submitting competitive bids for a new bond issue?

8. In what circumstances is an offering of convertible bonds to a corporation's existing common stockholders likely to be successful?

9. Do stockholders' rights to subscribe to new issues of convertible bonds always have a market value? Why or why not?

10. Why is it said that a stockholder's ownership interests may or may not be diluted if he fails to subscribe to his allotment of convertible bonds offered by the rights procedure?

11. Why is the private placement of bonds much more voluminous than the private placement of common and preferred stocks?

---

[9] State of Delaware, *General Corporation Law*, sec. 259(a).

12. In view of the economies of private placements, why do not all corporations dispose of their bond issues in this way?

13. What are the principal institutional buyers of privately placed bonds? Why do these institutions strongly favor buying by private placement?

14. What is meant by the assumption of a bond issue? In what kinds of transactions are assumptions quite common? Why is this procedure favored by assuming corporations?

15. Is there risk to the owner of assumed bonds that the assuming corporation may repudiate its apparent obligations on the grounds that it was not the issuer? Explain.

PROBLEMS

1. From the bond tables on pages 694–95, determine which bid in each of the following pairs is the better one from the standpoint of a corporation that is offering a 25-year bond issue.

   a) 98.35 with a 4 percent interest rate or 111.48 with a 5 percent rate.
   b) 103.29 with a 6 percent interest rate or 90.05 with a 5 percent rate.
   c) 107.46 with a 5 percent interest rate or 123.38 with a 6 percent rate.

2. The Leading Manufacturing Company has outstanding 800,000 shares of common stock of $20 par value, and its earned surplus amounts to $18 million. It is now making a rights offering of $10 million of convertible debenture bonds to its common stockholders. The bonds are to bear interest at $5\frac{1}{4}$ percent and are to be convertible into common stock at $42 a share. The offering price is 100.

   a) How many rights does the owner of 1,200 shares get?
   b) What amount of bonds is he privileged to buy with these rights (plus cash)?
   c) For how much should he be able to sell his rights at a time when the bonds are selling in the market on a when-issued basis at $106\frac{1}{2}$?
   d) What would probably be the market price of the bonds on a when-issued basis if rights were selling at $1\frac{1}{8}$?

chapter 31

THE MANAGEMENT OF OUTSTANDING BOND ISSUES

Once a corporation has sold or assumed a bond issue, its principal problems related to the management of the issue are those of fulfilling the obligations it has undertaken. It must find the means to pay interest at the designated rate as the semiannual payment dates come around, to make such sinking fund contributions annually or semiannually as the indenture prescribes, and to pay off the principal of whatever bonds remain at the final maturity date. (For a serial issue, of course, the sinking fund requirement is generally absent, but in its place is the even more pressing requirement for the direct retirement of portions of the issue as they mature periodically.) In addition, the corporation must be ever on guard to fulfill the other convenants of the indenture—those concerned with prompt payment of its taxes, keeping its properties in a good state of repair, providing adequate insurance protection, and so on. The corporation's financial managers can hardly afford to lose sight of the probable grave consequences of defaults that are not or cannot be quickly corrected.

For many bond-issuing corporations, nevertheless, problems of management of the kinds mentioned are not at all difficult to cope with. They remain comfortably solvent throughout the lives of their bond issues, in good times and bad, and rarely is there question about their capacity to do all the things promised in their indentures. Such a corporation, however, faces certain managerial problems of a different kind. Two are considered in this chapter: whether bond retirement should be pushed at a pace beyond that prescribed by the mandatory sinking fund provisions of the indenture, and whether somewhere along the way the whole issue, or what remains of it, should be replaced by a new one. The answer to the first question will generally depend on the original attitude of the corporation toward bond financing, while the answer to the second will generally be based on a variety of circumstances.

But a goodly number of corporations encounter much more pressing problems in the management of their bond issues. They do not remain comfortably solvent during the lives of these issues; sooner or later, they come to the rather scary realization that they face a default. It may be that cash is not available, and cannot be made available, to meet an interest or sinking fund payment. It may be that though the corporation scrapes together enough cash to meet current interest and sinking fund obligations it is unable to get enough in addition to pay some of its maturing taxes or to repair its operating properties. It may be that all goes well until the approach of the final maturity, when comes the realization that cash cannot possibly be supplied for the redemption of the bonds still outstanding. In circumstances such as these, what can the corporate managers do?

SOLVENT CORPORATIONS—THEIR PROBLEM OF SPEED OF RETIREMENT

A corporation whose bond issue was a second or third choice in the order of its financing preferences probably wants to eliminate it from its financial structure as quickly as possible. If it wanted to issue common or preferred stock but chose bonds because the bond market was buoyant while that for stocks was in the doldrums, a rapid retirement of the bonds would appear to be in order. On the other hand, a corporation that issues or assumes bonds because it wants to trade on the equity will probably want to slow down the process of retirement as far as possible.

Corporations That Choose Rapid Retirement

A corporation that puts out a bond issue reluctantly because it prefers stock financing may change its attitude, of course, while the bonds are outstanding. Because of unstable earnings, it managers may have feared the dangers of trading on the equity, but they encounter no difficulty in making interest and sinking fund payments, and they are most pleased to see the rate of earnings on the common stock expand as a result of the bond financing. Perhaps earnings prove to be less unstable than they had been, or perhaps it is found to be much less difficult than expected to manage the cash account in such manner that a sufficiency is available for bond requirements even in years when earnings are small or negative.

Assuming, however, that there is no such change in attitude, what can the corporation do to speed bond retirement? In the indenture itself, it will surely have set the stage for speedy retirement. First, it will probably have trimmed the maturity as closely as safety would seem to permit, making it, for example, 15 years, even though investors would have been as willing to buy, say, 20- or 25-year maturities. Second, it will probably have obligated itself to make sinking fund contributions sufficient to retire the entire issue by approximately equal installments during its life. Third, it will surely have reserved the right to call any amount of bonds for redemption beyond the amounts required for the sinking fund. And, finally, it may have made the bonds convertible into common stock at the option of the holder, while limiting the duration of the conversion privilege or setting a scale of rising conversion prices for successive periods to exert pressure toward early conversion.

If, then, the cash throw-off from depreciation and profits after taxes is only sufficient to meet the stipulated sinking fund requirements, after allowance for the replacement of depreciating assets, for expansion, and for the payment of reasonable dividends, the corporation must be satisfied with a pace of retirement no greater than that envisaged in the skinking fund provisions, unless, perhaps, conversion becomes advantageous for the bondholders, so that bonds are retired by that route. If, however, the cash throw-off is well in excess of what is needed for the sinking fund, dividends, replacement of assets, and expansion, the corporation will be able to use the excess for further retirements by buying up bonds in the market or by exercising the call privilege. Moreover, substantial increases in the market price of the corporation's common stock probably go hand in hand with the development of excess cash throw-offs, so that conversion is likely to proceed rapidly.

In either of the situations just described, the corporation is not likely to have any problems of special difficulty at the time the bond issue matures. If redemption has taken place only at the sinking fund pace, the final installment to be retired will be no greater or not much greater than earlier ones, and if these earlier installment have been met without strain the final one should likewise be no great burden. If additional redemptions have taken place by calls beyond sinking fund requirements and by conversions, it may be that very few or none of the bonds will still be outstanding at the final maturity.

Corporations That Choose to Continue Trading on the Equity

Corporations that issue bonds with the intention of keeping bonded debt in their financial structures indefinitely in order to gain the advantages of trading on the equity may also have a change in attitude while the bonds are outstanding. Perhaps earnings that had been stable begin to develop a pattern of considerable instability, or perhaps the margin of earnings available for bond interest falls considerably below the level anticipated, even though it has a pattern of stability at the lower level.

Indenture Provisions. But again assuming no such change in attitude, what can a corporation do to slow the pace of bond retirement—to continue, as far as feasible, the program of trading on the equity? In its indenture, it would probably have given the bonds a remote date of maturity; nevertheless, it may not have been able to go beyond 25 or 30 years for lack of investor interest in still longer maturities. Moreover, were it issuing bonds at a time of upsweeping yield curves, it would have had economy in interest charges as a strong incentive for keeping the life of the issue down to a moderate length. It might have wanted to avoid mandatory sinking fund provisions, but here again, investors would probably have insisted on some provision for periodic retirement. At least, they would have been likely to demand sinking fund contributions to keep pace with the depreciation of the assets to be acquired with the proceeds of the bond issue. However, they might have been satisfied to permit the corporation to use much of the sinking fund contributions for additions and improvements to operating properties. Accordingly, the corporation could slow down the pace of bond retirement by scheduling expenditures for expansion in such manner as to use up the skinking fund contributions to the extent permitted. The corporation would surely not have made the bonds convertible into common stock, but on the other hand, it would probably have reserved the right to call bonds for redemption beyond the amounts provided for in the sinking fund stipulations. This call power it would hardly expect to use, but it would be convenient to have it available should there be a change of attitude while the bonds were outstanding.

Additional Issues. A corporation that wants to continue to trade on the equity can reach that goal, of course, not only by slowing the pace of redemption of existing bonds but also by putting out additional bonds from time to time. It will surely have had the foresight to make its indenture an open-end one, so that additional bonds subject to its terms can be issued as additional properties are acquired, provided, of course, that earnings limitations and other protective restrictions in the indenture on total bonds to be outstanding are not violated. Thus, as some of the bonds of earlier series are retired by sinking fund operations, they may be more than replaced by new series.

Meeting Maturities. But bonds have maturity dates. No matter how reluctant a corporation may have been during the life of a bond issue in providing for some periodic retirement, and no matter how gladly it may have used sinking fund cash for improvements rather than for retirements, it must definitely do something about the bonds at their maturity. By the very circumstances of its management, most of the bonds will be outstanding as the maturity date approaches, and by the circumstances of its objectives it will have anticipated all along putting out a refunding issue to take the place of the maturing one. But it may run into difficulties. The bonds may mature at a time of tight money, and the tightness may be especially severe in the market for long-term funds. That would mean that interest rates for new long-term borrowing would be quite high, perhaps much higher than the rate on the maturing bonds.

Suppose, for example, that a corporation's 25-year bond issue, bearing interest at the rate of 4 percent, is coming due at a time when the rate on new borrowings for almost any maturity is 5½ percent (the yield curve is, we would say, flat or horizontal). Were the corporation to refund with a new 25-year issue, it would have the unpleasant prospect of having to pay the much higher rate for that lengthy period—certainly a change in the cost situation that would cloud the advantages of trading on the equity.[1] What to do? Had the corporation's managers forseen the coming of the tight money situation and taken prompt action in keeping with that foresight, they might have had an ideal solution to their problem. Assume that 2 years before the maturity date the corporation could have put out a new 25-year bond issue at a rate of 4½ percent. It might have looked strange to be issuing 4½ percent bonds and using the proceeds to retire 4 percent bonds, but the wisdom of the action would be proved if, as assumed above, the rate actually did go to 5½ percent 2 years later. The payment of an extra 0.5 percent in each of the 2 years would seem to be a small price to pay for a saving of 1 percent annually for 23 years.

In the absence of a fortunate anticipation and action of this kind, a possible solution would be retirement of the maturing bonds out of the proceeds of bank loans. This, too, would be an anticipatory procedure, taken in the expectation of a fall in long-term interest rates in a short period of years. For example, it might be possible to borrow from commercial banks on the basis of a one-year loan, renewable for two additional years at the option of the corporation. Even if the interest rate on the bank loan were somewhat higher than 5½ percent, it would prove to be cheap should the long-term rate actually fall to a level around 4 or 4½ percent within the 3-year period.

Needless to emphasize is the possibility that a bond maturity can also come at a highly favorable time. If the corporation of the illustration found it possible, at the maturity of its original bonds, to put out a 25-year refunding issue at, say, 3½ percent, the advantages of trading on the equity would doubtless appear to be all the more glamorous.

---

[1]It might be anticipated that long before expiration of the 25 years, it would be possible to effect another refunding at a lower rate of interest. But refundings in themselves are expensive in flotation costs and call-price premiums on bonds to be replaced.

Exchange Offers. When corporations put out refunding bond issues, they sometimes offer them on a direct exchange basis to the holders of the older issues that are slated for replacement. The holder of a maturing bond thus may take cash or a bond of the new issue. If the original bonds were sold by private placement to institutional investors and if these institutions want to take the new issue, the exchange takes place at one stroke. But even when the existing bonds were originally sold by public offering and are widely held, exchange offers are usually advantageous for the corporations making them. With respect to public offerings especially, an advantage of the exchange procedure is that it cuts down flotation costs. This is so even though investment bankers are usually called on to underwrite exchange offers—to agree to buy at a designated price whatever bonds of the refunding issue are not exchanged. But they fix a moderate commission for the entire issue, and a higher margin only for the bonds that they have to take over. Thus, the more bonds that are exchanged, the less proportionately the total underwriting cost will be. (The amount paid by the bankers for bonds taken over is the means, of course, whereby the corporation can pay off in cash the maturing bonds not offered for exchange.)

But whether or not existing bondholders will accept exchange offers is another question; that depends on what advantage, if any, they see for themselves in such offers. In terms of the illustration, many holders of the 4 percent bonds would presumably have been highly pleased to have received 2 years before maturity an exchange offer of 4½ percent bonds. Were the corporation of the illustration actually to decide on a 5½ percent issue at the time of maturity of the original bonds, it would probably also count on many exchanges. But were it able to offer a refunding issue at only 3½ percent because of easy conditions in the market for long-term funds, exchanges would probably be much fewer.

Arranging exchanges tends to be relatively easy when the exchange proposals are made to institutional investors by strong corporations or by corporations that have grown in strength from the time of earlier, still outstanding borrowings. An illustration is the announcement of the Reynolds Metals Company, in the summer of 1964, that it had arranged deferments of the maturities of approximately $90 million of first-mortgage bonds previously sold to institutional investors, and that it had also arranged for additional long-term loans from them of $74.5 million on further issues of the first-mortgage bonds. An illustration of an exchange transaction in this direction by a corporation that had grown greatly in strength is the arrangement announced by Trans World Airlines in December, 1967. Trans World had not been able to borrow long-term money on a nonmortgage basis since 1947, and in 1960, in obtaining $375.6 million from a group of institutional investors on equipment mortgage notes, it had to agree to extremely tight restrictions on its further financing ventures. But its finances and financial outlook were so much better in 1967 that the institutional lenders were willing to accept unsecured notes in exchange for the mortgage equipment notes with no increase in interest rates—an important concession, since the general level of interest rates in 1967 was much higher than it had been in 1960—and to provide an additional $178.1 million of long-term loans, also on unsecured notes.

SOLVENT CORPORATIONS—REFUNDING ALONG THE WAY

Reasons for Early Refundings

Often, corporations that are able to maintain sound financial positions decide on switches in their bonded debt long before the maturities of bonds already outstanding. The objectives of this kind of action vary; most commonly they are the following: (1) to get rid of obnoxious indenture restrictions, (2) to consolidate several existing issues, (3) to effect a substantial lengthening of maturity, and (4) to reduce the costs of carrying long-term debt.

Getting Rid of Indenture Restrictions. The most direct way to get rid of obnoxious restrictions in a bond indenture is to get rid of the indenture itself. This can be done by calllng and paying off all the bonds issued under the indenture. When this has been done, the indenture no longer has any binding force; it is a completed contract.

Very often corporations take steps to get rid of indenture restrictions in connection with plans for new financing. Let us assume that a corporation has outstanding a closed-mortgage bond issue of $8 million. It wants to borrow an additional $5 million, but its financial managers realize that to find buyers they will have to offer a mortgage lien. With the closed-mortgage issue outstanding, they can only offer a second mortgage. Accordingly, they decide to make the new issue $13 million, and they are able to give it a first-lien status by using a sufficient amount of the proceeds to retire the existing bonds. Again, the existing issue may be an open-end one, but with property and earnings limitations so severely drawn that the corporation's additional issue must be limited to $3 million. Thus, drawing up a new indenture with property and earnings limitations designed to permit an initial new issue of $13 million of bonds would seem to meet the corporation's problem. In each of these instances, of course, the new issue would be only partially a refunding one.

Sometimes, however, corporations find indenture restrictions so burdensome that they are willing to go to the bother and expense of refunding without at the same time trying to raise new money. If they can find investors who are willing to buy new issues under indentures that do not have the obnoxious features, they may decide to go ahead. An original indenture may have provided for sinking fund contributions at a level designed to retire the whole bond issue by equal installments during the period of its life. But the corporation finds that these contributions are gravely draining its working capital, thereby endangering its solvency. At the same time, the financial managers have every reason to believe that the corporation would have no difficulty refunding a substantial part of the debt if it were left at maturity. Hence, they may decide to refund at once to slow down the rate of sinking fund retirements.

Consolidation of Two or More Issues. Refunding to consolidate existing bond issues most commonly occurs after corporate mergers and consolidations, and usually the raising of new money is a goal in addition to the bond consolidation itself. Suppose that Corporation A has absorbed Corporations B and C in a merger. At the time of the merger, each of the three corporations had a bond issue outstanding. In the merger agreement, A assumed the bond issues of B and C. Therefore, it has three bond issues now outstanding, doubtless with different interest rates, maturities, sinking fund requirements, restrictive provisions, and so on. This might not be too difficult to handle, but now A wants to do some additional long-term borrowing. Will it add a fourth issue to which probably it can give a standing only inferior to that of the existing three? It would seem much better to make the new issue large enough to supply not only the new money desired but also the means to call and pay off the three existing bond issues. This would make for simplicity in the corporation's financial structure—almost always desirable in itself—as well as for ease in complying with contractual obligations. Even more than this, the consolidated issue might be salable with an interest rate lower than the rates of the existing issues. If the merger has been successful in the sense of making A's earning power greater than the former separate earning capacities of itself, B, and C, its bonds ought to be more attractive to investors than had been those of the formerly separate corporations—hence the probability of a lower interest rate.

Extending Maturities. At times when the bond market is buoyant, corporations may have inducement to refund existing issues to lengthen their long-term debt, even though the existing issues still have many years to run. There could be such an inducement even though the interest rates to be paid on the refunding issues were no lower, or even slightly higher, than those carried on the issues to be replaced. Suppose, for example, that a corporation 8 years ago put out a 15-year bond issue, bearing interest at the rate of 5 percent. It strongly favors trading on the equity; it did not favor the 15-year maturity of its present issue, but that was the longest term it was able to get at the time of its flotation. Now, however, the corporate managers are convinced that they could sell a 30-year issue with an interest rate of 5 percent. To financial managers strongly wedded to a policy of trading on the equity, the immediate replacement of an issue due to mature in 7 years by one to mature in 30 years could appear to be highly advantageous.

Reducing the Costs of Long-Term Debt. By far, however, refundings that are effected long before the scheduled maturities of the issues replaced are chiefly attributable to strivings toward reduced interest costs. A corporation may have had to designate a quite high rate of interest on its bond issue because at the time of its sale its financial position was weak; without the high rate, the bonds would not have been salable at all. But the corporation has been highly successful, and its credit rating is now quite strong. Yet, its high-rate bonds have still many years to run to maturity. It could now sell a bond issue of equal size—or of a much larger size, if it so wanted—at a much lower rate of interest. Should it do so? Or, again, a blue-chip corporation during a period of tight money may have been hard pressed for cash to complete an expansion program, and it may have put out a bond issue at that time to raise the money. Because of the dearth of loan funds, and despite its blue-chip status, it may have had to set a relatively high interest rate. But now, a few years later, a plentiful supply of long-term funds is available, and corporations comparable to it in prestige are borrowing at rates much lower than it is paying. Should it proceed with a refunding operation?

To this twice-raised question, most corporation managements answer with a hearty yes—*after analyses of all the costs involved in refunding* have clearly shown that it would result in substantial savings over the years. They know that a simple comparison of interest rates is not an adequate analysis. For example, a corporation surely will not save $100,000 annually if it now has outstanding a bond issue of $10 million, bearing interest at 5 percent, and if it could sell an issue of equal amount with an interest rate of 4 percent. Beyond a comparison of interest rates, consideration must be given to the premiums to be paid on retirement of the outstanding bonds, flotation costs of the new issue, sinking fund and call-price provisions in both old and new indentures, possibilities that the new bonds would be retired more rapidly than the sinking fund provisions in the new indenture would require, and the income tax effects of the refunding.

Cost Factors—Illustration

For illustration, let us assume that a certain corporation 5 years ago put out a $12.5 million issue of 25-year bonds, bearing an interest rate of 5 percent. In conversations with investment bankers near the end of the fifth year, the managers of the corporation learn that they could sell new bonds to the public at par at a rate of 4 percent. As this sounds like a favorable opportunity for refunding, they decide to explore the matter further. The existing bond indenture has a sinking fund provision requiring the retirement of $500,000 face amount of the bonds annually; the sinking fund call price is par value. So far, then, $2 million of the bonds have been retired, and the fifth year's sinking fund payment will bring this figure up to $2.5 million. The prospective new issue, therefore, would presumably be in the vicinity of $10 million. But not exactly $10 million. For calls outside the scope of the sinking fund, the old bonds have a call price of 103. Thus, it would appear that the corporation would need a new issue of $10.3 million to retire the old bonds. Moreover, the investment bankers estimate that flotation costs of a new issue of between $10 million and $11 million would be about $260,000, so that this would seem to bring the cash needed for refunding to $10,560,000.

But the corporate managers realize that tax savings would become available in connection with the refunding. The premium of $300,000 to be paid on retirement of the old bonds could be deducted in the fifth year as an expense for income tax purposes, as could any unamortized costs of flotation on the old bonds till standing on the books. We may assume that total costs of selling the old bonds amounted to $312,500 and that this has been subject to a straight-line charge-off to expenses annually. After the regular charge of the fifth year, therefore, $250,000 would remain unamortized, but, should the refunding be effected, this amount could likewise be taken at once in lump sum as an income tax deduction. Thus, the total charge-offs incident to the refunding would be $550,000, and assuming that the corporation always has income high in the 48 percent bracket of the federal corporation income tax, the tax saving would be 48 percent of $550,000, or $264,000. Since the corporation's tax liabilities would be reduced by $264,000, this sum could presumably be diverted from operations to be used for retirement of the old bonds, reducing the needed amount of the refunding issue from $10,560,000 to $10,296,000.

In order to estimate the dollar advantage or disadvantage of refunding as closely as possible, we may assume that the new bonds would closely parallel the old in terms and conditions—that they would have a 20-year maturity (equal, therefore, to the remaining life of the old bonds), that 5 percent of the face amount would be retirable annually by mandatory sinking fund requirements, and that the sinking fund call price, as in the old bonds, would be the par value. With these assumptions in mind, then, would it be advantageous for the corporation to issue $10,296,000 of new 4 percent, 20-year bonds to take the place of the existing bonds? The existence of an advantage and its size could be demonstrated as follows.

Net Cost of Carrying Old Bonds to Maturity		*Net Cost if Refunding Is Effected*	
Interest at 5 percent for 20 years on average amount of bonds to be outstanding—that is, $5,250,000[2]	$5,250,000	Interest at 4 percent for 20 years on average amount of bonds to be outstanding—that is, $5,405,400[3]	$4,324,320
Remaining flotation costs to be amortized	250,000	Flotation costs of new bonds	260,000
	$5,500,000		$4,584,320
Less tax saving at 48 percent[4]	2,640,000	Less tax saving at 48 percent	2,200,474
			$2,383,846
		Add additional debt to be amortized[5]	296,000
Net cost	$2,860,000	Net cost	$2,679,846

It would appear, therefore, that the refunding would be quite advantageous. Over the period of 20 years, the net saving would be the difference between the net cost of $2,860,000 for carrying the old bonds and that of $2,679,846 for carrying the new, or $180,154. While this would be much less than a saving of $100,000 a year that a simple application of a 4 percent rate as against a 5 percent rate on $10 million of bonds would produce, it would surely be well worth the taking.

Would the refunding be advantageous if, all other terms and con-

---

[2]Found by adding the amount of bonds to be outstanding at the beginning of the 20-year period and the amount to be outstanding in the 20th year and dividing by 2. Bonds of a total of $10 million will be outstanding at the beginning of the 20-year period (the 6th year of the original 25-year period, of course) and of $500,000 in the 20th year. Hence:

$$\frac{\$10,000,000 + \$500,000}{2} = \$5,250,000.$$

[3]See the preceding footnote. Here, the result works out as follows:

$$\frac{\$10,296,000 + \$514,800}{2} = \$5,405,400.$$

[4]As long as interest and amortizable flotation costs can be taken as income tax deductions against income taxable at 48 percent, the net cost to the corporation is really only the remaining 52 percent. We assumed that the corporation of the illustration always has income well into the 48 percent tax bracket. The computation indicates, of course, that the corporation expects to continue to have income at that level and that it anticipates no change in the tax rate in the 20-year period. Either expectation could prove to be faulty, as, indeed, the 10 percent surcharge added to the federal income tax rates in 1968 demonstrated. Needless to add that the surcharge was ignored in the illustration and that it is again ignored in the subsequent determination of a break-even rate for the refunding.

[5]The payment of the additional debt would not represent a deductible expense; hence, no tax saving is entered with respect to it.

ditions being as described, the rate of interest to be offered on the new bonds had to be 4¼ percent or 4½ percent? The best way to answer a question of this kind is to compute a break-even rate for the new bonds—one above which there would be some advantage in refunding, however small, and below which refunding would be clearly disadvantageous. Obviously, the break-even rate is one that would make the cost of carrying the new bonds exactly the same as that of carrying the old—that is, \$2,860,000. Letting x stand for the rate we are seeking, our formula, based on the analysis presented in the table above, would be as follows.[6]

$$\begin{aligned} .52\ [(5{,}405{,}400 \times 20x) + 260{,}000] + 296{,}000 &= 2{,}860{,}000 \\ 56{,}216{,}160x + 135{,}200 + 296{,}000 &= 2{,}860{,}000 \\ 56{,}216{,}160x &= 2{,}428{,}800 \\ x &= 4.32\% \end{aligned}$$

It is thus clear that the corporation would still be ahead were the new bonds to bear interest at 4¼ percent, but that the refunding would increase its costs were the rate to be 4½ percent.

Cost Considerations

When the question of refunding is entirely one of seeking lower overall costs of carrying bonded indebtedness, an analysis such as the foregoing should suffice for a sound decision. However, factors ignored in the illustration or different from those of the illustration could complicate the estimation of savings. If, for example, the sinking fund call prices, instead of being par for both old and new issues as in the illustration, were to be higher in the new indenture than in the old, the prospective saving would be somewhat reduced. Likewise, the refunding would appear to be less attractive—perhaps materially so—should there be strong probability that within a few years the corporation would want to reduce its bonded debt by substantial calls beyond sinking fund requirements. Again, the maturity of the new issue might be different from the remaining life of the old. Were the corporate managers to be told by the bankers that the new issue could not carry a maturity of more than 15 years, the attractiveness of the refunding would be materially diminished. It would be necessary to amortize the added debt of \$296,000 and to prorate the flotation costs of the new bonds over the shorter period. On the other hand, were the corporate managers to be told that the new issue could be a 25-year one, the refunding project would look all the better, because the annual prorations would be smaller than in the illustration.

[6]The multiplier .52 is, of course, the net cost to the corporation of its interest and flotation expenses after allowing for the tax saving of 48 percent.

Even when the primary interest in refunding is one of eliminating restrictive indenture terms, consolidation of several existing issues, or extending the maturity of bonded debt, cost factors are not likely to be ignored. As was indicated earlier, refunding for these purposes is often combined with projects for raising new funds by the bond route. Thus, the corporation with mortgage bonds already outstanding under a closed indenture might decide to go ahead with a second-mortgage issue were its estimates of the total costs of carrying the two issues less than for a large new issue whose proceeds would be used in part to pay off the closed-mortgage bonds. In a similar way, the surviving corporation in a merger, in consideration of the costs involved in refunding, might decide against the consolidation of bond issues assumed in the merger process. When, however, the elimination of objectionable features in existing indentures seems to corporate managers to be extremely important and additional financing, if considered at all, to be of secondary importance, cost comparisons tend to break down. The objective becomes primarily qualitative, and though a dollar value can be put on it when the costs of refunding are considered, this value can be set at almost any level, depending on the intensity of the managers' dissatisfaction with the existing indenture.

Refundings in Relation to Interest-Rate Levels

In the past few years, refundings of bond issues well in advance of their maturities have become relatively rare events. Because the principal reason for refunding along the way is to cut the cost of long-term money, the steadily advancing levels of long-term interest rates dating from 1963 have simply eliminated favorable opportunities for this kind of financial transaction—an elimination that became especially apparent in 1967 and 1968, when long-term rates reached their highest levels since the 1920's and, in some months and weeks, levels not experienced since the period immediately following the Civil War. But if refundings have recently been rare, one can surely say that the huge volume of recent new bond financing has set the stage for huge volumes of refundings in coming years. That is when and if long-term rates fall appreciably below the extraordinarily high rates that were set on most of the recent issues, especially those of 1967–68 and especially on the nonconvertibles, and provided that the lower rates prevail after the periods of call protection of the recent high-rate issues have expired. Meanwhile, to find good examples of refundings related to interest cost economies, one must generally go back a few years, and for illustration here we may cite two 1963 transactions of this kind.

A long-term saving in interest costs was specifically stated to be the reason for the Brooklyn Union Gas Company sale of $19.2 million of 25-year debenture bonds to a group of institutional investors in April, 1963. The proceeds, with a small amount of additional cash, were used to redeem $19.6 million of 25-year debentures sold only two years earlier on the basis of competitive bids. The interest rate on the new bonds was 4⅜ percent, while the rate on the called bonds had been 5⅛ percent.

In May, 1963, the American Telephone and Telegraph Company sold a $250 million issue of 4⅜ percent debenture bonds due in 1999 and used the proceeds in calling for redemption a $250 million issue of 5 percent debentures issued in 1957 and maturing in 1983. Although the 5 percent coupon of 1957 had been A.T. & T.'s costliest financing since 1930, investment bankers expressed surprise that the refunding was undertaken on such a narrow margin between the two interest rates—a narrowness emphasized by the fact that while a price of 100.171 was received from the underwriting syndicate for the new bonds, the call price of the 5 percent bonds was 106.461. Accordingly, the A.T. & T. was probably less interested in the differential in interest rates than in the 16-year extension in maturity that it achieved by the refunding.

CORPORATIONS IN FINANCIAL DIFFICULTIES

Difficulties in meeting indenture obligations may be encountered by corporations at any time during the lives of their bond issues, or they may come to the fore only as the bonds approach the final maturity dates. The nature of the difficulties tends to vary somewhat according to the timing of their appearance, although, obviously, temporary solutions for difficulties encountered along the way may only intensify those faced at maturity.

Difficulties along the Way

Nature of Difficulties. It is patent that the inability of a corporation to fulfill the covenants of its indenture in the payment of interest, the making of sinking fund contributions, the payment of taxes, the keeping of properties in a state of proper repair, and so on, results from a shortage of working capital and, specifically, of cash. In most instances, this shortage is due, in turn, to operating losses. Such losses drain working capital. If the drain is heavy or if, though moderate, continued long enough, the capacity of the corporation to maintain normal operations and at the same time to meet all kinds of obligations coming due must be diminished. If the cash throw-offs from depreciation charges are covered in part, they may be sufficient to save the corporation from embarrassment for a while, or even indefinitely. But it may be that for the continuance of normal operations they must be promptly spent for the replacement of fixed assets. And, of course, there may be no cash throw-offs from this source, because the operating losses exceed the amount of the depreciation charges.

The corporate managers face a dilemma. The cash balance and inflowing cash are insufficient to meet all the outlays necessary to keep the corporation operating *and solvent.* If they use cash to fulfill all the covenants of the indenture, they will not have enough left both to meet the claims of creditors other than the bondholders and to carry on operations. If they decide that they must remain solvent at any cost by meeting the claims of other creditors, in addition to those of the bondholders, they probably will succeed only in deferring the day of insolvency. For they would have to cut back on inventories, credit extensions to customers, and outlays for day-to-day operating expenses, and this policy could hardly result other than in greater operating losses. If they choose to maintain operations by using for that purpose cash that would otherwise be earmarked for the non-bondholding creditors, default occurs at once, and default on obligations to trade creditors, to banks on their short-term loans, and so on, can have consequences as dire as defaults on bond obligations. Of course, the choice could be to default on one or more of the indenture obligations.

Clearing the Way for Short-Term Borrowing. Possibly the corporation can save itself if it is able to get the bondholders to agree to relax some of the restrictive provisions of the indenture. It may have agreed to maintain a working capital ratio of 2½ or 3 to 1, or to limit its total indebtedness to what now appears to be a much too small percentage of its net tangible assets. Banks and other lenders may be quite willing to grant new short-term loans, but not so long as these restrictions stand. Hence, an obvious remedy for the corporation's problem would be to seek the bondholders' consent to a relaxation of these restrictions in order to permit the additional borrowing. The corporation will surely have provided in the indenture that the holders of some large proportion of the outstanding bonds, such as 66⅔ or 75 percent, could approve indenture modifications *binding on all the bondholders.* Such a provision, therefore, would seem to open the door for an attempt to apply this remedy.

Clearing the Way for Additional Bonds. Getting bondholders to consent to modifications in the terms of existing indentures may enable corporations to correct working capital deficiencies through new long-term borrowing. For many corporations, this apparently would be an even better solution to financial difficulties than having indentures modified to permit new short-term borrowing. Investors may be willing to buy new bonds—expecially, of course, those of corporations whose difficulties are not extreme—if only the corporations can clear the way for their issuance. It is even possible that a corporation could find buyers for a new issue of bonds that have claims inferior to those of the existing bonds—a new debenture issue when the existing one is a mortgage issue, or a new issue of subordinated debentures when the existing one is an ordinary debenture issue—if only it can get the existing bondholders to relax indenture provisions limiting total indebtedness in relation to working capital or to capital stock and surplus. Or it might be able to find buyers of bonds of the same ranking as those already outstanding, whether mortgage bonds or debenture bonds, if it could get the existing bondholders to open a closed indenture or to relax the property, earnings, and other restrictions of an open-end indenture.

Should its difficulties be of a greater degree of severity, however, it might be able to find buyers for new bonds only if it is in a position to give them ranking prior to the existing bonds. Hence, its solution would be to ask the holders of mortgage bonds to yield the priority of their liens to the new issue, or to ask the holders of debenture bonds to permit a new issue of mortgage bonds without securing the debentures equally and ratably. For all such kinds of consents on the part of bondholders, the typical indenture provides, once again, that approval by the holders of 66⅔ percent of 75 percent of the outstanding bonds makes the modifications agreed on binding on all the bondholders.

Although not in financial difficulties in the sense of facing insolvency, several corporations in recent years have sought and obtained the consent of bondholders to changes in indenture terms to obviate difficulties in borrowing, financing foreign subsidiaries, and meeting other financial problems. In the summer of 1958, the then Atlas Plywood Corporation was successful in getting holders of sufficient percentages of its two 5 percent debenture issues to permit a relaxation in indenture requirements for the maintenance of certain ratios between current assets and current liabilities, and between current assets and funded debt, as well as a relaxation in restrictions on the payment of cash dividends. To get sufficient assents, Atlas offered an increase in the interest rate of one fourth of a percentage point. In March, 1963, the Allied Chemical Corporation announced that holders of more than 66⅔ percent of its debenture bonds had approved amendments to the indenture: (1) modifying restrictions applicable to its foreign subsidiaries in mortgaging properties, incurring and guaranteeing debt, selling additional stock, and effecting mergers: (2) expanding the borrowing capacity of its domestic subsidiaries; and (3) authorizing the creation and assumption of certain liens in connection with its oil and gas production. And in October, 1965, Foremost Dairies, Inc. (as it then was) got approval of holders of an issue of debenture bonds for the rewording of certain restrictions in their indenture on its borrowing capacity—restrictions so ambiguously stated that it was uncertain whether a certain stock acquisition was to be treated as an asset or as a liability!

Cutting Expenditures for Maintenance. Should the corporation, however, have no prospective suppliers of additional working capital, the relaxation of indenture terms concerned with total indebtedness or working capital ratios would be of no help. Another remedy would have to be sought. Should the shortage of working capital be not especially severe, a decision might be made to remedy it by cutting to the bone expenditures for the repair and maintenance of the corporation's properties. Consent might be asked of the bondholders for this departure from the obligations of the indenture—the covenant to keep the properties in a proper state of repair—but the cutback might be effected without the bondholders' consent in the expectation that neither the trustee nor the bondholders would be likely to get excited about it.

Seeking Relaxation of Sinking Fund Requirements. Should the shortage of working capital be of greater severity, a more likely point of attack would be the sinking fund provisions of the indenture. On an outstanding bond issue of $10 million, bearing interest at 5 percent, the corporation's interest cost for the year would be $500,000, but its sinking fund obligation might be an equal amount. Its financial managers might realize that they could meet one of these obligations together with all other necessary outlays not related to the bond issue, but not both. They would be much more likely to attack the sinking fund provisions than the interest obligation. They would know that holders of, say, 66⅔ percent of the bonds could authorize a change in the sinking fund requirements that would be binding not only on themselves but also on dissenting bondholders. On the other hand, their indenture would surely provide that the right of the *individual* bondholder to interest at the prescribed rate could not be affected without his specific consent. An effort to get the bondholders' consent to a modification of sinking fund requirements could be couched in moderate terms. The bondholders might be asked to waive the whole requirement for only a year or two, to cut the requirement in half for two or three years, or perhaps to cut the mandatory requirement to a modest figure, making the rest depend on the size of earnings.

Seeking Relaxation in Interest Obligations. But the sinking fund requirements might already be moderate, or getting the bondholders to consent to their reduction might not be enough to repair the corporation's working capital position. After meeting operating expenses and liabilities unrelated to the bond issue, it still would not have enough money to pay the prescribed interest on the bonds. In this situation, an attack on the interest obligations themselves would appear to be in order. The financial managers of the corporation might simply ask the bondholders to consent to an extension in the time of payment. Such a request would be appropriate should they expect that an early improvement in operating results would enable the corporation to make up the amount deferred as well as to meet further accruals. Were they not so optimistic, however, they might ask that the fixed rate be cut down substantially, the balance of the prescribed rate to be made contingent on earnings. Or they might ask for such a cut coupled with a deferment of even the reduced rate for one or two or more periods. Knowing that no bondholder would be bound by other bondholders' assenting votes, no matter how large the proportion of assents might be, the corporate managers might look around for something to offer as compensation for votes of approval. Being already in distress, they would hardly seem to be in a position to offer something attractive, but an effort in that direction could be made—perhaps a new convertibility feature, a more generous sinking fund arrangement *contingent upon earnings*, or even a more generous rate of interest. Were the fixed rate of interest to be cut from, say, 5 percent to 2 percent, according to the corporation's proposal, the offer might be an additional 4 percent if earned.

Seeking Exchanges for Other Securities. In some circumstances, the managers of corporations in financial difficulties along the way may be able to persuade bondholders that their long-run interest would be best served by giving up their existing absolute claims to principal and interest—possibly including interest already defaulted—for some type of security with contingent claims. In exchange for bonds that had standard features, for example, they might offer income bonds, subordinated debentures, preferred stock, common stock, or some combination of these. Their ambitions in this direction would be all the stronger should they be able to assure the bondholders that new sources of outside financing would be immediately available when the bondholders' fixed claims were yielded.

In the summer of 1967, the Associated Oil & Gas Company asked holders of 2 issues of its 6 percent convertible debenture bonds to tender them in exchange for shares of its common stock—a move apparently aimed at reducing the amount of its existing debt in order to improve its capacity to incur new debt as a source of badly needed working capital. It had earlier reported that "limited budget available" had necessitated cuts in the staff of its oil and gas division and a curtailment of exploration activities. Although the two debenture issues were already convertible, the inducement for their immediate exchange for common stock was a substantial increase in the number of common shares offered for each $1,000 of bonds. Even so, the offer did not appear to be particularly generous, considering the market price of the common at that time. Nevertheless, tenders of approximately $8.5 million of the bonds were received, though the corporation had set a maximum of $4 million for the amount of tenders to be accepted. It may be added that subsequent advances in the market price of the corporation's common stock proved the wisdom of those who took advantage of the corporation's exchange offer. It should be of interest to add, too, that some of the bonds included in the tender transaction of 1967 had been issued in 1963 in exchange for outstandings bonds of a 6½ percent convertible issue. In that deal, the inducement for the sacrifice of one half of a percentage point in the interest rate had been a reduction in the range of conversion prices and an extension of maturity.

Possibility of Reorganization in Bankruptcy. Another remedy that the corporation could select would be to file a petition for its reorganization in bankruptcy. But that could result in such a sweeping change in the corporation's position, including possibly the wiping out of all the interests of the common stockholders, that it probably would be chosen voluntarily only if all other kinds of adjustment proposals proved to be fruitless. This possibility, then, we may ignore beyond its mention, since out interest here is in what corporate managements can do to try to weather difficulties in meeting indenture obligations, not what successors to management, such as trustees in bankruptcy, have powers to do under the laws.[7]

Difficulties at Maturity

Nature of Difficulties. The use of one or more of the remedies just described to meet financial difficulties in managing outstanding bond issues along the way may simply postpone the evil day. If, for example, a corporation gets its bondholders to consent to a substantial cutback in periodic sinking fund contributions, it will have all the more of its bonds remaining to be paid off at the final maturity. If substantial redemption periodically was found to be financially impossible, all the more difficult will be a need to redeem a very large proportion of the bond issue at one stroke. On the other hand, difficulties in meeting obligations under bond indentures often originate only as the maturity date approaches. Until close to maturity, a corporation may have been able to pay interest, to meet sinking fund payments, and to fulfill all the other covenants of its indenture with relative ease. But the sinking fund provisions may have been designed for only partial redemption, as the corporation, wishing to continue to trade on the equity, planned for a substantial refunding at maturity. But maturity may come at a time when the corporation is operating deep in the red, so that it cannot hope to find buyers for a refunding issue. Nor can it arrange short-term bank loans to pay off the bond issue as a stopgap

---

[7]Some discussion on the fate of bonds in corporation reorganizations was presented in Chapters 20 and 28. See pp. 507–8 and 723–24.

measure, because the bankers quite reasonably decide that lending to it would be much too risky.

Possible Remedies. Short of filing a petition for reorganization in bankruptcy, or of taking even more drastic steps toward liquidation and dissolution, a corporation that found itself unable to pay off the principal of its bonds at maturity would be most likely to propose to the bondholders an extension of the maturity for a period of years, possibly 5 or 10. Of course, it would agree to pay interest during the additional period, as well as to fulfill other indenture obligations. In fact, to induce acceptances of its proposal it might offer a higher rate of interest for the additional period. Alternatively, or in addition, it might offer some other inducement, such as to make the bonds convertible into common stock or to give them a mortgage lien when before they had none. All the more could it hope for the success of its proposal for an extension, whether or not offering a higher interest rate or some other inducement, were it able to effect a partial redemption. For example, bondholders would be more likely to go along with the extension were they offered cash equal to, say, 40 percent of the principal of their bonds, so that the extension would involve only the remaining 60 percent of their claims. In deciding what to offer and how to go about making the offer, the corporate managers would have to keep in mind the right of nonassenting bondholders to be paid off in full. This right of the individual bondholder could not be disturbed by fellow bondholders, no matter how large their vote to accept the corporation's proposal for an extension. Thus, acceptance of an offer by holders of, say, 65 percent of the maturing bonds might still not save the corporation from reorganization in bankruptcy if it still could not provide the cash to pay off the holders of the remaining 35 percent. A recent move by the Erie Lackawanna Railroad Company may be cited to illustrate actions of the kinds described. In the summer of 1964, it was able to get the approval of holders of more than 80 percent of its 3¼ percent first consolidated mortgage bonds for an extension of their maturity from October 1, 1964, to October 1, 1969. The inducement for approvals was an increase in the interest rate to 6 percent!

As many things are possible, the corporation could offer the holders of its maturing bonds preferred or common stock in full or partial settlement of its principal obligations. Typically, however, bondholders would not be interested in such an offer unless they were owners individually of large blocks of the bonds and the offer was extremely generous, probably to the extent of giving them a large measure of control.

Small corporations in particular are sometimes able to get by with partial payment of the principal of their bond issues at maturity as final settlement. Such a scaling down in the total obligation would probably be a composition settlement. The corporate managers would tell the bondholders that the corporation could pay, say, 60 cents per dollar of principal claims, and ask them to accept this and to discharge the corporation from all further liability. Acceptance of the offer by two or more bondholders would make it binding on them, unless, as would be likely, the corporate managers stipulated that the settlement would be effective only if approved by holders of, perhaps, 80 or 90 percent or more of the bonds, in which case it would not be binding on any assenting bondholder until assents had been received from the prescribed proportion. Such a stipulation would be virtually indispensable, since nonassenting bondholders would still have to be paid off in full. A sufficient number of assents might be obtained if most of the bondholders were convinced that an extension would not help—that the corporation would have difficulty in paying the interest during the extension period and the principal at its end—and that a forced liquidation of the corporation's assets would give them less than 60 cents on the dollar. To the corporation, in turn, the settlement would be expected to be advantageous in permitting it to survive and in letting the stockholders retain their ownership interests, though sadly depleted. The offer would presumably permit the corporation to retain some assets to carry on with; indeed, it might have access to new equity or loan funds once the bonds had been eliminated.

Application of Remedies

The manner in which and the extent to which remedies for difficulties in the management of outstanding bond issues can be applied depend very importantly on who the bondholders are. If they are few in number and are relatives, close friends, or business associates of the managers of the corporations that experience difficulties, as is entirely possible in small corporations, various remedies may be accepted unanimously without much delay, although possibly with a goodly show of anger. The bondholders may readily agree to deferments of interest, sinking fund, and principal payments, or to the scaling down of one or more of these types of payments. Even in relatively large corporations, if the bondholders are chiefly stockholders who bought and hold the bonds because they are convertible, ready acceptance of adjustments to the corporations' obligations on the bonds can ordinarily be expected. Such owners are unlikely to want the seizure and sale of the corporation's properties for the satisfaction of their claims as bondholders, or to demand reorganization in bankruptcy, since the result would tend to be disastrous to their position as stockholders.

Even when bond issues are large and amounts held by stockholders are inconsequential, who the bondholders are remains important. The application of remedies, if possible at all, necessarily follows different courses if, on the one hand, the bonds are held in bulk by institutional investors or if, on the other, they are widely scattered in the hands of hundreds or thousands of individual investors.

Issues Held by Institutional Investors. The position of a corporation that faces default on a bond issue sold in bulk to, say, a life insurance company may appear to be not unduly alarming. So far as the bonds go, it has only one creditor to deal with. Moreover, that one creditor is likely to have a lot of money available for helping the corporation to solve its financial problems, if only it chooses to use some of it for this purpose. Much the same can be said if the entire issue was split up between two or three institutional investors. Dealing with two or three creditors should not be particularly difficult, and possibilities of direct financial aid should be no less promising.

It is true that an institutional investor hardly will rush to seize assets to satisfy its claims or to institute legal proceedings for the reorganization or liquidation of a debtor corporation. And it is true that it may advance additional funds to the corporation so that it can pay off the claims of other creditors who might be more inclined to take legal actions that would be crippling to the corporation. Beyond this, it may be willing to advance funds for working capital, so that the debtor corporation can continue normal operations. But there is a price for such forebearance and assistance. The usual price is the surrender of some or many of the ordinary prerogatives of management. As a condition for its forebearance and assistance, the institutional investor may demand that some of the corporation's operating policies be changed. It may, in effect, order the adoption of certain kinds of new policies. Usually, it will demand that all new policies, and especially all proposals for sizable expenditures, be made subject to its veto. It may go further than this: it may demand a comprehensive change in managerial personnel—the resignations of present directors and officers, or some of them, and their replacement by people in whom it has more confidence.

If measures of the kinds just described prove successful in enabling the corporation to make up its defaulted payments of interest and principal and to cure other defaults that may have occurred, the institutional investor may be quite satisfied to revert to its former position simply as a creditor, retaining only such rights as were accorded to it as such in the indenture. If the measures prove unsuccessful, or if the corporation refuses to accept its dictates in the first place, it can ordinarily be expected to take legal steps to enforce its claims. In effect, it may ask for either reorganization or liquidation, although the final decision on which of these procedures will be adopted would be that of the court rather than its own decision.

Bonds Widely Held. The fact that a large bond issue is said to be widely held does not mean that the entire issue is owned in driblets.

In almost all cases, there will be at least a few individual and institutional investors who hold blocks of substantial size, perhaps bought in the course of the original flotation or accumulated by purchases from time to time in the market. The combined holdings of the 8 or 10 largest investors in a given issue might not amount to more than 15 or 20 percent of the total outstanding, yet an indenture modification proposal would surely be off to a good start if approval of all or most of these large investors were assured. Hence, a corporate management that is in difficulties in meeting indenture obligations will typically sound out such investors first. If it gets their assent to a given proposal, it can use this fact as a bit of advertising when it takes the proposal to the smaller bondholders. If it does not gain their approval, it may be able to change its proposal in such manner as to get the large investors to switch their negative votes to affirmative ones. The large investors, in turn, may suggest modifications in proposals that would make them acceptable or, indeed, recommend quite different approaches to the problem that the corporate management would find not unreasonable. The large investors, at any rate, are much less likely to demand comprehensive changes in managerial policies or in the management itself than an institutional investor or two or three who own the entire issue.

If the corporation's situation is really grave and prospects are that it will continue to deteriorate, the large bondholders may be satisfied with nothing short of reorganization in bankruptcy; they may show interest in no proposal other than this. Should this be their attitude, the corporate managers are unlikely to take their proposal to the mass of small bondholders. With the threat of a negative vote of 15 or 20 percent of the bonds hanging over, the prospect of getting the approval of 66⅔ or 75 percent for indenture modifications not involving principal or interest, or of 80 or 90 percent for adjustments to claims to principal or interest, would obviously be slim.

But if all or most of the large investors in a corporation's bond issue are willing to go along with a proposed adjustment in indenture terms, the prospects are good that a sufficient number of the smaller bondholders will find the proposal reasonable enough to deserve their approval also. In presenting the proposal to the smaller bondholders, the corporate management must set forth its case as clearly as possible, showing the source and nature of the difficulties, trying to demonstrate how helpful the proposed modifications in indenture terms will be toward clearing up the difficulties, and emphasizing that the bondholders' interests will be better protected through adoption of the proposal than they could be in any other way. The usual procedure is to ask the bondholders to deposit their bonds with a designated bank or trust company as an evidence of their assent. However, the bondholder is ordinarily privileged to withdraw his bond at will if he wants to sell it or if he changes his mind and wants to cancel his assent. Thus, there may be considerable uncertainty from day to day about how many of the bonds placed on deposit will be left there for final tabulation. At any rate, if the aggregate of bonds deposited and left reaches the level necessary to put the corporation's proposal into effect, a supplemental indenture is entered into between the corporation and the trustee, in which the modifications of the original indenture's terms are stated. If the modifications include changes in the corporation's interest or principal obligations, notation of these changes is stamped on each bond before it is returned to the assenting bondholder. For modifications that do not involve adjustments in interest or principal, however, stamping is ordinarily unnecessary.

QUESTIONS

1. What kinds of indenture provisions should be helpful to corporations that want to speed up the retirement of their bond issues?

2. How can indenture provisions be written to enable corporations to slow down reductions in the volume of their outstanding bonds?

3. In what circumstances would it be advisable for corporations to refund their outstanding bond issues a year or two before maturity, even though required to set higher rates of interest on the new issues than the rates carried on the old?

4. In what circumstances might corporations be wise to meet maturities of bond issues out of the proceeds of short-term bank loans, even though they want to continue to trade on the equity with long-term debt?

5. What advantages are there for corporations in persuading holders of maturing bonds to exchange them for new bonds instead of selling the new bonds and using the proceeds to pay off the maturing issues?

6. For what reasons do corporations sometimes float new bond issues and use the proceeds to retire outstanding bonds long before their maturities?

7. When corporate managements are tempted to refund outstanding bond issues to gain the advantage of lower rates of interest, what kinds of costs should they consider before finally deciding?

8. For decisions about refunding outstanding bond issues, why are income taxes an important factor?

9. With regard to favorable opportunities for the refunding of bond issues, what has been peculiar about the period since 1963? What influence on future refundings are the developments of this period likely to have?

10. For corporations that are in financial difficulties, what kinds of indenture modifications might clear the way for new short-term borrowing? For new bond issues?

11. To what extent are indenture modifications agreed to by given proportions of bondholders binding on those who do not give their consent?

12. Why are corporations in financial difficulties more likely to seek

bondholders' consents to modifications of indenture requirements on sinking fund obligations than on interest obligations?

13. For the corporation that is unable to pay off its bonds at maturity, what remedies short of reorganization in bankruptcy might be sought? Would not the bondholders, in the typical case, be hurting their own interests were they to consent to such remedies?

14. If a corporation is unable to pay off its bonds at maturity, are its chances of survival likely to be better if the bonds are held in bulk by institutional investors or in small amounts by many investors? Discuss.

PROBLEM

Sophocles Brothers, Inc. has outstanding $24 million of 25-year, 6 percent bonds. The original issue, which was sold 5 years ago, amounted to $30 million, but $6 million of the bonds have been retired by sinking fund calls amounting to $1.2 million a year. The sinking fund call price is the par value, and the call price for calls outside the scope of the sinking fund is 104. Flotation costs of the bond issue amounted to $380,000, and this outlay is being charged off on a straight-line basis of $15,200 a year.

As a means of reducing interest costs, the directors of Sophocles Brothers are considering the refunding of the outstanding bonds. They are assured by investment bankers that they would have no difficulty in selling at par a new 20-year issue of 5 percent bonds in an amount around $24 million. The bankers estimate that the flotation costs would amount to about $300,000, and they say that the new bonds, like the old, would have to provide for equal annual sinking fund contributions, beginning within a year, designed to retire all bonds by the final maturity date. They say that a sinking fund call price of 100 would be satisfactory.

Assuming that the corporation's income is subject to tax at combined federal and state rates of 50 percent, determine what net increase or decrease in costs in the whole 20-year period would result from the refunding.

Part X

FINANCING WITHOUT SECURITIES

chapter 32

CURRENT LIABILITIES AS SOURCES OF ASSETS

Because of their very great importance as means of acquiring assets, stocks and bonds deserve the many chapters devoted to them in this textbook. Nevertheless, for many corporations, securities flotations and the management of outstanding securities issues typically require much less of the time and attention of corporate financial managers than the search for and the administration of asset sources not related to securities issues. Many corporations have only one security flotation during their lifetimes—the common stock issue at the time of their establishment—and this is true even of some corporations that are long-lived. Many never issue preferred stock. Many never sell bonds. And even when corporations frequently add to their outstanding securities issues, the frequency for the individual corporation is not likely to be oftener than every few years, unless something routine is done, such as giving the common stockholders a stock dividend every quarter or every six months, or selling according to the terms of an employee stock-purchase plan. For many corporations, too, the management of outstanding securities issues requires relatively little of the time and attention of its financial officers. As long as it remains solvent and reasonably profitable, decisions about its securities issues are required only occasionally. These decisions include: whether to pay the quarterly dividend on the preferred, how much to pay on the common, how much must be turned into the redemption fund for the preferred, whether the common should be split up, what optional contribution, if any, should be made to the bond sinking fund, whether cash should be used to redeem bonds outside the scope of sinking fund operations, and so on.

NATURE AND IMPORTANCE OF DEBT UNRELATED TO SECURITIES

The asset sources not related to securities are of two kinds: (1)

earnings, and (2) debt incurred with trade suppliers, banks and other lenders, employees, sellers of equipment, taxing authorities, and others. Since earnings as a source of assets were analyzed at length in Chapters 25 and 26, we shall confine our attention in the present chapter and the two following to the asset sources of the second kind.

The main reason why obligations to creditors such as trade suppliers and banks, as asset sources, require much time and attention of financial managers is that they are chiefly short term. A trade supplier may allow 30 days for payment, but he may permit a discount if payment is made within 10 days; therefore, if advantage is to be taken of the discount offer not much delay in finding a means of payment is possible. The corporation may obtain a loan from a bank repayable in 60 days; so it hardly gets the money before it must be thinking about paying it back—a situation quite different from a sale of common stock, whose proceeds never have to be paid back. Even when liabilities of the kinds considered here are intermediate or long term, close and continuous attention to their management is generally necessary. For the most part, such debts are repayable in monthly, quarterly, or semiannual installments—quite unlike a bond issue for which the required sinking fund contribution may be payable only annually, and the total contributions over the life of the issue may be designed to retire only a portion of it. Thus, if a corporation signs an equipment purchase contract, obligating itself to make payments in equal quarterly installments over a three-year period, the debt it incurs is one third short term and only the remaining two thirds is intermediate term.

A second reason that liabilities owing to trade suppliers, banks, and other creditors of this class require much time and attention is the turnover among credit grantors. Negotiations with prospective new credit grantors are frequently necessary. The turnover may be the result of deliberate choices of the corporation, or it may be required by the attitudes and policies of the credit grantors. Though a given supplier of certain raw materials may be able and willing to sell on credit all that the corporation needs, it may choose to buy from many suppliers to promote competition for its business among them as well as to avoid becoming dependent on the one. Some suppliers may give poor service or deliver goods not of the quality contracted for, so that others must be substituted. Substitution may also be necessary if given suppliers pass out of the picture through failure. A bank may be unwilling to grant the amount of short-term loans for which the corporation thinks its financial position qualifies it, so it must seek a substitute lender or, at least, other lenders that will supply funds over and above what the bank will advance.

A basic fact about debts unrelated to securities issues is that virtually all corporations, regardless of area of operations, size, and other characteristics, make substantial use of them. By definition, corporations that have simple common stock structures depend on such liabilities as the only source of assets beyond the common stock and retained earnings sources themselves. But substantial dependence on these sources generally features also the policy of other corporations even though they may also depend quite heavily on preferred stocks or bonds or both as other sources of assets.

The liabilities unrelated to securities, as indicated above, are chiefly short term in nature, but some are intermediate and long term. In this chapter and Chapter 33, we shall limit our attention to the short-term liabilities, whose recent statistics are presented in Table 32–1. Here we have a compilation of the current liabilities of corporations as found in the balance sheets filed with their federal income tax returns for fiscal years ending between July 1, 1964, and June 30, 1965. All the important industrial areas in which corporations operate are included, except for the fields of financial institutions and real estate operations, which are excluded because of their peculiar asset and liability structures, and because, in any case, they are ordinarily outside the purview of corporate financial management as our field of study.

On the basis of the data in Table 32–1, and with the knowledge that the 1964–65 experience was not significantly out of line with the continuing situation, we conclude that corporations of the included industrial groups obtain collectively between one fourth and one fifth of their total assets by contracting short-term liabilities unrelated to securities—truly a proportion of no mean importance. The very great dependence of contract construction and wholesale trade corporations on these short-term sources is especially noteworthy, but not too far off is their importance for corporations in retail trade and in the service industries. It is often said that transportation, electric, gas, communications, and other public utility corporations, because of the preponderance of their investment in fixed assets, are much less dependent on short-term debt than are corporations in other industrial fields, and, of course, the figures of the table bear this out. Nevertheless, the dependence of these corporations on short-term debt is obviously not inconsequential. Certainly, the use of short-term sources by the public utilities as a group in the amount of more than $18.4 billion could hardly be dismissed as inconsequential.

The bottom line of Table 32–1 indicates that among the short-term liabilities that serve as sources of corporate assets those made available by trade suppliers—accounts payable—are by far the most important. The other two sources are shown to be of close to equal weight; "other current liabilities," including chiefly accrued expenses, have a moderate edge over "bonds, notes, and mortgages." The item "bonds, notes, and mortgages"—even with the footnote addition, "maturity of less than one year"—is somewhat disturbing. At this stage of our discussion, we are not especially interested in bonds nor, indeed, in mortgage loans, which generally are of long term. What the designation means is that the short-term liability for borrowed money includes the principal of bonds and mortgage obligations

TABLE 32–1
Current Liabilities of Business Corporations, 1964–65*
(Dollar amounts in millions)

Industry	*Number of Tax Returns*	*Accounts Payable*	*Bonds, Notes, and Mortgages*†	*Other Current Liabilities*	*Total*‡	*Percent of Total Assets*
Agriculture, forestry, fisheries	25,933	$ 537	$ 892	$ 199	$ 1,628	25.2
Mining	14,487	1,349	828	1,116	3,293	18.6
Contract construction	104,134	5,627	2,783	2,458	10,868	46.6
Manufacturing	184,961	33,748	15,102	24,352	73,202	21.8
Public utilities	56,338	4,650	3,608	10,183	18,441	10.5
Wholesale trade	142,603	12,298	6,249	2,673	21,221	42.0
Retail trade	272,166	10,240	6,110	4,164	20,514	33.7
Services	176,902	3,135	3,578	1,863	8,576	28.6
Total	977,524	$71,584	$39,150	$47,008	$157,743	22.6
Percent of total current liabilities		45.4	24.8	29.8	100.0	

*Corporations filing federal income tax returns for fiscal years ending between July 1, 1964, and June 30, 1965, excluding: corporations engaged in trade not allocated to wholesale or retail; in finance, insurance, and real estate; and in miscellaneous operations not classified by industry.

†Maturity of less than one year.

‡In some instances, items do not add exactly to horizontal totals because of rounding.

SOURCE: U.S. Treasury Department, Internal Revenue Service, *Statistics of Income, 1964—U.S. Business Tax Returns* (Washington, D.C.: U.S. Government Printing Office, 1967), pp. 107–13. (Percentages supplied by the author.)

coming due within one year—whether partial payments due on continuing obligations or payments due because maturities come within the year—as well as installment payments on intermediate- and long-term loans not evidenced by bonds or secured by mortgages. But we must be satisfied with the kinds of statistics that are available. In any event, it is reasonable to assume that a very large part of the liability of $39,150 million for bonds, notes, and mortgages consists of short-term loans—loans with original maturities of not more than one year—the kinds in which we are particularly interested at this juncture. Such an assumption is strongly and consistently supported by the quarterly reports on the finances of manufacturing corporations published jointly by the Federal Trade Commission and the Securities and Exchange Commission.

For the discussion of the three kinds of short-term liabilities, as classified in the table, attention will be given in the present chapter to accounts payable and other current liabilities, leaving for Chapter

33 an examination of the sources of short-term loans. Before getting into this discussion, however, we should find it advantageous to consider the principles of financing by means of short-term debt as they relate to business corporations.

PRINCIPLES OF FINANCING WITH SHORT-TERM DEBT

The principles that should serve as guides to corporate managements in the use of short-term liabilities as sources of assets are the following.

1. For greatest safety, short-term debt financing should be avoided.
2. There is generally justification for short-term debt financing to provide for seasonal expansion of current assets.
3. If trading on the equity is an appropriate financial policy, either long-term or short-term debt financing of current assets is acceptable.
4. Special circumstances at times justify temporary short-term debt financing beyond what would otherwise be appropriate.

Avoidance of Short-Term Debt

Debt is always a source of danger to solvency, and corporations that avoid it are relieved of many anxieties. They may be unsuccessful, with operating losses consuming their assets, but they can decide to quit business, to liquidate their remaining assets gradually and carefully, and thus conserve something for the stockholders. On the other hand, unsuccessful corporations that have many debts may be forced by unpaid creditors to reorganize or liquidate at the very times when the stockholders' claims would be most adversely affected. Corporations without debt can often weather severe financial reverses—to make up their losses after coming through periods of difficulties—but unpaid creditors are often unwilling to wait to see whether debtor corporations can overcome adversities.

As a rule, short-term debt is more dangerous than long-term debt. It is true that when short-term debt is contracted the financial managers of a corporation have only to look a short distance into the future in judging its capacity to make payment, whereas capacity to repay long-term debt is clouded by all the uncertainties about what may happen in a lengthy period of years. But should an optimistic short-term forecast turn out to be a bad one—should cash inflows suddenly fall off sharply because of an unforseen recession in business activity—the corporation might be very quickly in trouble if it has many short-term obligations. This would hardly be true were its debts chiefly long term.

Suppose, for example, that Corporation A has $8 million of current assets, no fixed assets, $4 million of current liabilities, and $4 million of stockholders' equity, and that Corporation B has an identical asset situation, $4 million of bonds, and $4 million of stockholders' equity. Corporation B's bonds have a sinking fund provision, requiring the retirement of 5 percent of the issue annually. Should, then, a business setback occur and cash inflows be greatly reduced for the two corporations, surely Corporation A would have much greater difficulty in paying off $4 million of obligations, all maturing within a short period of time, than would Corporation B in meeting its sinking fund requirement of $200,000.

A policy of avoiding short-term debt in the interests of greatest safety can hardly mean, however, an absolute avoidance of such debt. A corporation that had such a policy would hardly pay its payroll daily, pay its accruing taxes and other expenses—light, power, water, and so on—before their due dates, and insist on cash payment to trade suppliers who customarily allow, say, 30 days for payment. What the policy means, then, is that the corporation would hold cash or high-quality short-term investments over and above its other requirements to take care of these *unavoidable* short-term debts, as they may be called. Assume that it needs $6 million of current assets for the usual scope of its operations, and that unavoidable short-term debts usually run around $1.5 million. Accordingly, it should have $7.5 million of current assets, the additional $1.5 million made up of cash or short-term high-quality investments. Essentially, therefore, it would be financing its normal current asset requirements of $6 million without debt or, at least, without current debt.

Short-Term Debt Financing for Seasonal Expansion

A policy of avoiding short-term debt can be quite expensive for corporations whose scale of operations fluctuates substantially according to seasonal patterns. The greater the size of the fluctuations, the greater the cost probably would be. If short-term debt is avoided, current assets must be supplied from long-term sources, either from the contributions of stockholders or from the proceeds of long-term borrowing. But such assets, once supplied from long-term sources, remain continuously on hand (although, of course, changing in composition more or less constantly). If, then, substantial amounts of these assets are needed only for peak periods, they must remain out of operation for the remainder of the year. It would appear to be quite uneconomical to have stockholders supply on a full-time basis assets subject to only part-time use, or to pay interest to bondholders for 12 months for the use of assets for periods of, perhaps, 3 or 4 months.

Accordingly, incurring short-term debt for seasonal current asset requirements is generally regarded in the business community as strongly justified. Although many corporate managers are wedded to the doctrine that debt should generally be avoided as dangerous to solvency, they are often willing to make an exception for incurring short-term debt for seasonal purposes. Their defense for the exception is: if orders or market prospects justify peak-period operations, debt contracted to finance this expansion ought not be difficult to pay off—should not, therefore, be a serious source of danger. Many commercial bankers, too, emphasize seasonal lending, as when they say that most of their working capital loans to business are or should be confined to financing the expanded requirements of peak seasons.

To illustrate the theory of short-term debt financing for peak-season requirements, we may expand on the example given previously. For its normal operations outside the peak season, the corporation needs $6 million of current assets, but because it has unavoidable current liabilities of $1.5 million, it customarily carries an additional $1.5 million in short-term investments. Let us say, therefore, that its ordinary working capital position is somewhat as follows.

Current Assets		*Current Liabilities*	
Cash and short-term investments	$2,500,000	Accounts payable, accrued wages, etc.	$1,500,000
Accounts receivable	2,200,000		
Inventories	2,800,000		

For its peak period, the corporation must carry accounts receivable of $4 million and it needs inventories of $6 million; hence, it must expand these two assets by a total of $5 million. Its managers would probably decide that if incurring short-term debt is justified for seasonal expansion, all the more reasonable would be the use for this purpose of the $1.5 million of short-term investments. That would leave only $3.5 million of the expansion in receivables and inventories to be financed with debt, and the result would show up as follows.

Current Assets		*Current Liabilities*	
Cash	$1,000,000	Accounts payable, accrued wages, bank loans, etc.	$5,000,000
Accounts receivable	4,000,000		
Inventories	6,000,000		

Were the trade creditors and the lending bank or banks to insist on the maintenance of a working capital ratio of, say, 2 to 1, the corporation obviously would easily qualify.

Trading on the Equity

As was just indicated, financing peak-season additions to current assets by way of short-term debt is a means of avoiding the cost of idle assets, whether supplied by stockholders or bondholders. Another way of putting this is to say that it is a means of trading on the equity—of using debt as a lever to raise the rate of earnings on the common stockholders' investment. If short-term loans can be obtained from commercial banks at a rate of interest of 5 percent per annum, and if the banks' advances can be employed to yield a return of 10 percent, the rate of net earnings for the common stockholders is obviously increased. Thus, short-term debt, no less than bonds and other forms of long-term debt, can be employed to give common stock leverage.

It is obvious, too, that nothing in the nature of short-term debt necessarily limits its use to peak-season requirements. Corporations that have no pronounced seasonal patterns in their operations often depend rather heavily on short-term debt as a source of current assets. Their managers deliberately accept the risks of trading on the equity—of insolvency—in striving toward a higher rate of earnings for the common stock. In many instances, they doubtless conclude that these risks are not great because of the stability of their operations. In any case, they do not expect to go to extremes in incurring short-term obligations. Even if they should be so inclined, they would surely be held in restraint by limits imposed by creditors and prospective creditors—limits in terms of working capital ratios and relationships of total debt to equity. Nevertheless, the statistics of business failures always remind us that many corporations do go much too far in incurring short-term debt, and that, accordingly, creditors are not sufficiently careful in setting their limits.

In certain respects, the use of short-term debt for trading on the equity has advantages over the use of long-term debt for this purpose. Interest always has to be paid on bonds, but there appears to be no charge of this kind on trade debts and on accrued wages, taxes, and other expense items. Also, interest rates on short-term loans are often lower for the given borrower than on bonds, as is generally true in periods of upsweeping yield curves. In short-term debt financing, there are no flotation costs comparable to those on bond issues. And, finally, short-term creditors are generally much less inclined to impose restrictions on managerial discretion than are bond buyers, as by protective provisions in indentures.

But a price is paid for these advantages—if it is true that short-term debt is a greater danger to solvency than is long-term debt. The comparison of the positions of Corporations A and B on pages 827–28 showed why there usually is greater danger in short maturities. Thus, corporate managers may well decide that the weight of advantage is on the side of long-term debt. They may decide that having chosen to go after the advantages of trading on the equity they had better do this by concentrating rather heavily on long maturities.

That this is the decision of many corporate managers is indicated, at least roughly, by recent statistics of new financing. As shown in Table 32–2, a substantial proportion of the new money raised in recent years through the cash sale of corporate securities was earmarked for working capital—very clearly a use of long-term funds for the acquisition of short-term assets.[1] Especially interesting among the disclosures of Table 32–2 are the sharp drop in security issues to raise working capital in 1966 and the huge rebound in 1967. Many corporate managements decided that long-term borrowing for working capital was out of the question in 1966 because of the high long-

TABLE 32–2
Securities Issues to Raise Working Capital, 1946–67*
(Dollar amounts in millions)

Year	*Total Issues for New Money*	*Issues to Raise Working Capital*	*Percent of Working Capital Issues to Total*
1946	$ 3,279	$1,164	35.5
1947	4,591	1,182	25.7
1948	5,929	1,708	28.8
1949	4,606	882	19.1
1950	4,006	1,041	26.0
1951	6,531	1,421	21.8
1952	8,180	1,868	22.8
1953	7,960	2,313	29.1
1954	6,780	1,670	24.6
1955	7,957	2,624	32.9
1956	9,663	2,954	30.6
1957	11,784	2,744	23.3
1958	9,907	2,115	21.4
1959	8,578	2,494	29.0
1960	8,758	3,097	35.4
1961	10,715	3,303	30.8
1962	8,240	2,588	31.4
1963	8,993	3,588	39.9
1964	11,233	4,230	37.7
1965	13,063	5,352	41.0
1966	15,806	3,376	21.4
1967	22,230	6,076	27.3

*Substantially all new issues of securities offered for cash sale in the United States in amounts over $100,000 and with terms to maturity of more than one year, but excluding intercorporate transactions and issues of investment companies.

SOURCE: Securities and Exchange Commission, *Annual Reports* and *Statistical Bulletin*, February, 1967, p. 18, and February, 1968, p. 19. (Percentages supplied by the author.)

term rates then prevailing. But many soon had reasons to regret these decisions as they observed the rapid rise in the rates for alternative short-term loans and, much more startling, the rapid development of a situation of extreme tightness in the availability of short-term funds—a situation that has been widely described as a "credit crunch." Accordingly, many of the financial managers who were inclined to seek working capital by way of security issues concluded that it was imperative to go ahead with these issues in 1967, even

[1]By definition, new money is earmarked for the expansion of plant and equipment or for working capital, and not, for example, for the redemption of existing debt.

though long-term rates were then still higher than they had been in 1966. They did not want to be caught in another crunch in the short-term market.

Also significant are the data in Table 32–3 that show that in the years 1965–67 combined—a combination that tends to smooth out the distortion of 1966—corporations of all industrial groups except public utilities routed to working capital quite large proportions of the new money raised through securities issues offered for cash sale.

TABLE 32–3
Securities Issues to Raise Working Capital, by Industry, 1965–67 Combined*
(Dollar amounts in millions)

Industry	*Total Issues for New Money*	*Issues to Raise Working Capital*	*Percent of Working Capital Issues to Total*
Manufacturing	$20,000	$ 6,407	32.0
Mining	1,051	429	40.8
Electric, gas, and water	10,620	44	.4
Railroad	878	17	1.9
Other transportation	3,635	97	2.7
Communication	4,698	66	1.4
Financial and real estate	7,120	5,932	83.3
Commercial and other	3,097	1,811	58.5
Total	$51,099	$14,803	29.0

*Substantially all new issues of securities offered for cash sale in the United States in amounts over $100,000 and with terms to maturity of more than one year, but excluding intercorporate transactions and issues of investment companies.

SOURCE: Derived from Securities and Exchange Commission, *Statistical Bulletin*, February, 1968, p. 19.

These indications are rough because the reports of the SEC from which the data of the two tables were taken do not distinguish between stock and bond issues as sources of the new money, and because we do not know to what extent the corporations that issued securities were simultaneously expanding their short-term debt. On the first of these points, however, we do know from other SEC statistics that the volume of nonrefunding bond issues offered for cash sales in the respective periods covered in the two tables far exceeded the volume of stock issues similarly offered.

Special Circumstances for Short-Term Debt Financing

One instance of a special circumstance that might justify extraordinary short-term borrowing was mentioned in Chapter 31: the maturing of bond issues in times of tight money and high interest rates, and the temporary use of short-term loans pending later bond issues. Other occasions for such interim financing sometimes arise. As an example, a corporation may use short-term loan funds to meet the early costs of constructing a new factory building, and plan a later bond issue both to repay these loans and to meet the remainder of the construction costs.

Usually, there is danger in expanding short-term debt on the grounds that it is justified by special circumstances—not simply the ordinary danger of short maturities but, additionally, the temptation to regard too many kinds of circumstances as special. Thus, incurring extraordinary amounts of short-term debts to finance the introduction of new lines of goods or to carry through extraordinary advertising campaigns might be justified by the expectation that cash returns from greatly expanded sales will easily take care of the additional debt. But the new lines of merchandise may flop and the advertising campaigns miscarry, leaving the corporations with very serious problems of meeting their short maturities. On the other hand, it may be possible to avoid even the ordinary danger of short-term debt. If, for example, short-term borrowing is undertaken in anticipation of a later bond issue, and if the corporation has a commitment from a reputable life insurance company to buy the issue at the later date, the interim financing would seem to be an entirely safe procedure.

ACCOUNTS PAYABLE

Scope of Accounts Payable

In Table 32–1, we saw that accounts payable represent by far the most important short-term source of assets for American business corporations collectively. According to corporate balance sheets filed with federal tax returns for 1964–65 (excluding some classes of corporations as noted in the table), they amounted to 45.4 percent of the total of short-term sources. But the significance of trade payables differs from industry to industry, as is revealed by the additional data from the same source, presented in Table 32–4. From these data, we conclude that trade payables are least significant for manufacturing corporations and most significant in the contract construction, wholesale trade, and service industries.

A further observation is that in almost all fields of enterprise trade payables as a source of assets tend to be much more important for small corporations than for large ones. Often, large corporations are able to get special price concessions on the goods they buy by agreeing to pay cash on delivery or, indeed, by making advance payments to help their suppliers to meet their costs of production. Small corporations are rarely in a position to bargain in this way. When, moreover, trade suppliers allow discounts for payment within a few days, the large corporations are much more likely to have cash to take advantage of these discount offers than are small ones. Suppose, for example, that a given corporation buys on terms of 2/10 n/30, and that it gets a shipment of goods every 10 days billed at $20,000. If it pays on the 10th day to take advantage of the discount, the average amount of its accounts payable is $20,000, but if it ignores the discount offer and waits till the 30th day to make payment, the average amount of its trade payables is $60,000.

TABLE 32-4
Accounts Payable in Relation to Total Current Assets, by Industry, 1964-65*
(Dollar amounts in millions)

Industry	*Accounts Payable*	*Current Assets*	*Percent of Accounts Payable to Current Assets*
Agriculture, forestry, fisheries....	$ 537	$ 2,043	26.3
Mining........................	1,349	5,984	22.5
Contract construction..........	5,627	15,856	35.5
Manufacturing................	33,748	172,329	19.6
Public utilities................	4,650	23,239	20.0
Wholesale trade...............	12,298	38,041	32.3
Retail trade..................	10,240	41,402	24.7
Services......................	3,135	10,333	30.3
Total...................	$71,584	$309,227	23.1

*For corporations filing federal income tax returns for fiscal years ending between July 1, 1964, and June 30, 1965, excluding corporations in trade not allocated to wholesale or retail.

SOURCE: U.S. Treasury Department, Internal Revenue Service, *Statistics of Income, 1964–U.S. Business Tax Returns* (Washington, D.C.: U.S. Government Printing Office, 1967), pp. 107–13. (Percentages supplied by the author.)

Significance of Accounts Payable

In view of earlier discussions in this textbook, little need be added here about the significance of accounts payable as a source of assets. In Chapter 6, it was explained that accounts payable constitute a *permanent* source of assets equal to the minimum level to which they fall over the years, and that they constitute a temporary source in amounts by which they rise above this minimum. It was also pointed out that when trade creditors sell goods on account, and await payment for some days or weeks after their business customers have resold the goods for cash, they, in effect, supply the customers with cash for general operations.

All of Chapter 9 was devoted to the management of accounts receivable. But in interbusiness transactions, the accounts receivable of some firms are simply the accounts payable of others. Hence, an attempt to treat accounts payable at length here would require a repetition of most of what was said in that chapter, although, to be sure, with a switch in viewpoint. A few observations, therefore, should suffice.

While retail and service establishments usually have a choice to sell on account or only for cash, the general rule for sales transactions among businesses is that credit will be made available to the buyer *if he qualifies.* Manufacturers are generally willing to sell on account to other manufacturers and to wholesalers and jobbers, and the wholesalers and jobbers, in turn, to sell on account to retailers. But the business buyer must qualify. He must satisfy the seller concerning his character, capacity, and capital, with the seller's judgment based on an analysis of credit information gathered from the sources described in Chapter 9. Although, therefore, the availability of trade credit may be said to be the rule, it may be denied to given firms because of serious weakness in character, capacity, or capital. Nevertheless, trade suppliers are generally more liberal in granting credit to weak firms than are financial institutions in granting loans. It is not unusual for trade suppliers to sell on account to firms already in a bad way, to lengthen the allowed credit period, and to grant other concessions precisely to try to rescue them from their difficulties. Wanting to preserve outlets for their goods in given cities or regions, these trade suppliers are sometimes ready to accept quite serious risks.

Cost of Trade Credit

Sometimes, it is said that trade credit is expensive. In the selling price of his goods, if the seller-on-account is at least to break even he must cover interest on the cash absorbed in the goods he sells, the expenses of credit administration, and his bad-debt losses. Hence, the buyer who always pays within the allowed credit period, it is said, shares these costs, no less than the delinquent buyer whose very delinquency gives rise to a goodly portion of the costs. But if the seller has only one price at which he will sell either on account or for immediate cash payment, the buyer is hardly in a position to avoid his share of the costs of credit selling. Were he to insist on making immediate or early cash payment without getting a price concession or a discount, he would simply be adding to his costs; he would have an interest cost in supplying cash before being obliged to do so. Accordingly, buyers usually accept sellers' extensions of credit without a lot of worry about the costs involved.

However, when sellers allow liberal discounts for early payment the buyers are given the opportunity to avoid all or most of the costs of trade credit. If all buyers from a given seller take the discounts, the seller's costs of credit administration must be quite substantially reduced, so that any buyer's remaining share in these costs must be quite small. If only some of the buyers take the discounts, they presumably shift most of the seller's credit costs to the buyers who do not. Thus, the expensiveness of trade credit should be especially apparent to buyers unable to take advantage of discount allowances. The illustration in Chapter 8 showed that a buyer of goods could, in effect, earn interest for 20 days at the rate of 30.7 percent per annum by borrowing money at 6 percent to take advantage of a 2 percent discount allowed for payment within 10 days, the net being due in 30 days.[2] Surely, a reduction in the cost of goods of this proportion—$167.33 on a bill of $10,000 in the illustration—would go a long way toward offsetting whatever costs of credit had been included in the seller's original invoice.

OTHER CURRENT LIABILITIES

Corporate short-term liabilities other than trade payables and liabilities for borrowed money also make an appreciable contribution to assets. For the corporations surveyed in Table 32–1, this contribution amounted to 29.8 percent of the total current liability contribution. In relation to the current assets of these corporations, as indicated in Table 32–4, it amounted to 15.2 percent.

In compiling the statistics of corporate income and expenses and financial positions, from which the data in Table 32–1 were drawn, the Treasury includes in "other current liabilities" all kinds of accrued expenses payable within a year, such as: accruals for wages, taxes, rent, and interest; certain additional liabilities related to payrolls; dividends payable; and other items "not arising from the purchase of goods and services and not evidenced by bonds, notes, or mortgages."[3] For the typical corporation, however, accrued expenses far exceed in size and importance all other items of "other" current liabilities.

Accrued Expenses

Accrued expenses, or at least substantial proportions of them, may be said to be volunteer sources of assets. They are, in large part, unavoidable even for corporations that have plenty of current assets supplied from long-term sources. It is accepted practice to pay payrolls every week or every two weeks or, in some cases, monthly; hence, any corporation that continues to operate will have some liability for accrued wages. It will have its assets augmented by the contribution of service made by the employees, and it is hardly likely to insist on paying wages daily, even if it is already well heeled in its cash balance. It is accepted practice for taxing authorities to set tax payment dates beyond the dates of tax accruals, and corporate managers in their right minds can hardly be expected to insist on advance payments. Thus, their corporations temporarily retain assets equal to the amount of accruing taxes. It is accepted practice for public utilities to supply their power, gas, water, and telephone services on a daily basis but to bill for these services only monthly. Therefore,

---

[2]See pp. 173–74.

[3]U.S. Treasury Department, Internal Revenue Service, *Statistics of Income, 1964–U.S. Business Tax Returns* (Washington, D.C.: U.S. Government Printing Office, 1967), p. 138.

they contribute to corporate assets as their services are used—a contribution measured, at any time, by the amount of accrued expenses for such services.

Corporations that have no need to engage in short-term debt financing are generally pleased to accept contributions to assets by way of accruing expenses. It is a matter of convenience; it would be quite burdensome to them to try to pay their payrolls or their bills for electric power from day to day. But corporations in general doubtless accept such contributions with enthusiasm because they can conserve cash. They are thereby relieved of the necessity of relying more heavily on other sources of assets—sources that for many in relatively weak financial positions may be difficult to tap. As was explained in Chapter 6, a corporation whose accrued expenses never fall below a certain level has in these accruals a permanent source of assets of that amount, and a temporary source of fluctuating amounts as the accruals rise above the minimum level.

An interesting aspect of accrued expenses is that though largely a volunteer source of assets, they are subject to some management. Corporations that are hard pressed financially may be able to ease their difficulties somewhat by increasing their dependence on this source. Any deferment of the payment of accrued expenses would be helpful. If the payroll period is now one week, it may be made two weeks; or if salaries are now paid twice a month, they may be made payable only monthly. A mild degree of slowness in paying utility bills may be tolerated, at least for a time, by the utility companies. Even the nonpayment of taxes on their due dates may be a remedy for short-run financial difficulties—the penalties for delinquencies may not be too great a price to pay for a breathing spell.

Other Payroll Obligations

For the typical corporation, other payroll obligations are similar to accrued wages in consisting of temporarily unpaid compensation for labor service. Specifically, they are accumulated obligations to make payments into pension funds, union welfare funds, and the like, whether required by collective-bargained contracts or voluntarily provided by corporations to make employment more attractive. While obligations of this kind are accruing in the course of the year, the corporation is able to retain and use in ordinary operations assets of equivalent amount, so that the accruals, entered as liabilities, are recognized as the temporary source of these assets.

Dividends Payable

When cash dividends are declared by the directors of solvent corporations, they become, as we know, obligations to pay; as such, they are carried as current liabilities in corporation balance sheets. Between the date of declaration and the date of payment, however, the corporation continues to have the use of assets equivalent to the amount of the dividends, so that the dividend liability can be said to be the source of these assets. The dividend liability can also be described as a contribution of the stockholders, since dividends are chargeable against the surplus accounts, and these accounts constitute a part of the stockholders' equity.

Deferred Items

Many corporations receive cash as income before it is earned. The cash obviously adds to their assets, and it is available for general corporate use, but that goods must be delivered or service provided against the cash already received is indicated by the inclusion of "deferred credits" or "deferred credits to income" among current liabilities in balance sheets.

Transportation companies incur liabilities for services when they sell tickets in advance of voyages, flights, and trips scheduled for later dates, as do theater corporations in selling tickets for later performances—sometimes, performances scheduled months ahead for hits. In a similar way, retail store corporations that sell gift certificates obligate themselves to deliver goods as selected by the holders of these certificates, as do restaurant corporations that sell meal tickets.

Manufacturing companies that produce machinery and equipment according to the specifications of buyers sometimes require the buyers to make advance payments. Large buyers sometimes make advance payments to small suppliers on a voluntary basis to help the suppliers meet costs of production. In buying military equipment and supplies, the federal government has been especially generous in making advance payments to producers. Its advances were especially large during the period of World War II, when it supplied numerous firms with the means to produce war materials, but its policy of making advances has been continued—although, of course, on a reduced scale—in the postwar period. As of the end of the first quarter of 1968, for example, outstanding advances and prepayments of the federal government to business corporations were reported at $6.1 billion.[4]

Corporations that own facilities that they rent out often receive advance rental payments that are included as deferred credits among their current liabilities. Similarly, royalty payments by patent licensees are sometimes made in advance.

---

[4]Excluding banks, savings and loan associations, and insurance companies. Securities and Exchange Commission, *Statistical Bulletin*, July, 1968, p. 22.

QUESTIONS

1. Why is the management of debt unrelated to security issues usually much more time-consuming than the management of security issues? Is it more complex? Discuss.

2. What is the importance of current liabilities as sources of corporate assets? How does this importance differ from industry to industry? Among current liabilities, what is the relative importance of accounts payable?

3. Why is it proper to speak of some current liabilities as being unavoidable? How can the presence of such liabilities be reconciled with the proposition that, for greatest safety, short-term debt financing should be avoided?

4. Why is it said that avoiding short-term debt can be quite expensive for firms whose operations are subject to wide seasonal fluctuations?

5. Is there any danger to a corporation's solvency if it confines short-term financing very largely to seasonal requirements? Explain.

6. Aside from seasonal financing, what justification is there for the use of short-term debt financing as a means of trading on the equity?

7. What justification is there for corporate long-term financing to acquire working capital? What was peculiar about this kind of financing in 1966 and 1967?

8. Why is it said that, as a rule, trade payables are a relatively more important source of assets for small corporations than for large ones?

9. Compare the availability of trade credit for business firms with the availability of credit for consumers.

10. Would it not be economical for business firms to pay cash for what they buy in order to avoid the costs of trade credit? Discuss.

11. What justification is there for saying that accrued wages, accrued taxes, and other accrued expenses are sources of assets?

12. To what extent are accrued expenses as a source of assets subject to management by the individual corporation?

13. Explain how deferred credits function as sources of assets.

PROBLEM

At the end of the year 19xx, the financial position of the Rex Corporation stood as indicated in the following abbreviated balance sheet.

Assets		*Liabilities and Net Worth*	
Current assets	$18,000,000	Current liabilities	$ 7,000,000
Fixed assets	6,000,000	Common stock	12,000,000
		Earned surplus	5,000,000
	$24,000,000		$24,000,000

The corporation's operations are quite stable throughout the year and are not seriously affected by cyclical fluctuations in general business activity. Nevertheless, the corporation has long had a policy of avoiding debt except for the unavoidable kinds. Normally, the corporation has been carrying about $7 million of this kind of debt, but because of the large excess of its current assets in relation to this debt it has made no special provision to meet it, such as by holding short-term high-quality securities. The corporation is subject to federal and state income taxes at a combined rate of 50 percent, and its after-tax earnings have been averaging 12 percent of assets.

The financial managers of the Rex Corporation are now questioning the wisdom of the policy of debt avoidance. The question has come up because the corporation needs $5.5 million for fixed asset expansion and $2.5 million for additional current assets. They expect that earnings after taxes on the additional assets will likewise be close to 12 percent. The problem, then, is whether the needed amount of $8 million should be acquired by the sale of common stock or by borrowing.

a) What is the current rate of earnings on the stockholders' equity?

b) What would this rate be if the $8 million were raised (1) by the sale of additional common stock, or (2) by borrowing, assuming that the interest cost would be 6 percent? (For both possibilities, costs of security flotation and the like should be disregarded. For (2), the interest cost would be an offset against the expected rate of return of 12 percent on assets, but at the same time, consideration should be given to the tax saving on account of the deductibility of interest.)

c) If the borrowing route were decided on, would short-term or long-term borrowing be the more advisable, assuming that the interest rate on short-term loans would be 5½ percent, and on long-term loans 6½ percent?

chapter 33

SHORT-TERM LOANS

Corporations that want to borrow for short-term purposes may seek loans from one or more of several sources. Most corporations, however, go first to the commercial banks; these are the predominant short-term lenders to business. Some borrow from the commercial banks indirectly, through the use of letters of credit and bankers' acceptances. Some, though usually depending in part on commercial bank direct loans, go to the open market and have their promissory notes offered broadside to investors. Others find commercial finance companies especially responsive to their requests for loans on pledges of accounts receivable. And sellers of durable goods on installment contracts find several classes of institutions willing to grant inventory loans in order to get assignments of the installment contracts themselves. For the present chapter, then, the objective is an examination of these varied sources of short-term loans.

SHORT-TERM LOANS OF COMMERCIAL BANKS

For most business corporations, the commercial bank is the logical place to turn to if there is a need of current assets over and above what can be supplied from long-term sources and on the basis of trade payables, accrued expenses, and other current liabilities. As was pointed out in Chapter 7, commercial banks are distinguished from all other classes of financial institutions in that they receive deposits of the public subject to the obligation to repay on demand on the written order of the depositor. Any bank that provides checking accounts to the public, is therefore, a commercial bank.

Short-term loans may be sought from commercial banks when:

1. Businesses must pay cash for the goods they buy.
2. Cash is needed to make early payments to trade suppliers in order to take advantage of discounts.
3. There are seasonal periods of expansion.

4. There is a shortage of cash in paying payrolls and in meeting operating expenses for other than seasonal reasons.
5. It is desirable to make preliminary payments on fixed asset acquisitions pending later bond or stock issues.
6. Tax bills come due without sufficient cash to meet them.
7. Rising prices make extraordinary drains on cash.

Commercial banks are readily accessible to business enterprises. Granting loans is their principal source of profits, so that they welcome business borrowers and, indeed, borrowers of many other classes. What is more, large numbers of these institutions are scattered throughout the country, so that every city, town, and village, except for the very smallest, is served by one or more or, at least, by a branch of an institution whose principal office is located elsewhere. At the end of 1967, 13,721 commercial banks were in operation in the United States, and some of these were maintaining branches to the total number of 17,931.[1] Commercial banks vary in size from California's Bank of America, with $22,357 million total assets at the end of June, 1968, to quite small village and hamlet institutions with assets individually of much less than $500,000.

From the standpoint of total assets, the commercial banks are our most important class of financial institutions. Their total assets at the end of 1967 amounted to $451 billion, far in excess of the $177 billion total assets at that time reported by life insurance companies, which are second in total resources among our financial institutions.[2]

Volume of Short-Term Loans

General Reports. Although commercial banks are the principal short-term lenders to business, it is impossible at most times to discover what their outstanding volume of these loans amounts to. Statistics of their total outstanding commercial and industrial loans are published semiannually by the Board of Governors of the Federal Reserve System and the Federal Deposit Insurance Corporation, but these statistics do not differentiate between short-term loans and so-called term loans—that is, those with original maturities of more than one year. In their reports of commercial and industrial loans, moreover, the two bank supervisory agencies do not include loans to businesses secured by real estate mortgages, although, to be sure, most real estate loans to business firms are of the term variety. It is probable, too, that a moderate amount of reported consumer loans is actually used for business purposes. However, the figures for commercial and industrial loans remain of great importance in indicating the predominant position of the commercial banks as lenders to busi-

[1]Federal Deposit Insurance Corporation, *Annual Report*, 1967, p. 160.
[2]*Federal Reserve Bulletin*, August, 1968, pp. A–19, A–36.

ness. Even without a breakdown for short-term and term loans, the data of commercial and industrial loans of all insured commercial banks, presented on an annual basis for the period 1946–67 in Table 33–1, must impress one with the outstanding role of the commercial banks as suppliers of assets to business enterprises. The absolute level of their loans in each year of this period is impressive, but even more so, of course, is the record of expansion, especially the increase of about $43 billion in the short period from the end of 1961 to the end of 1967.

TABLE 33–1
Outstanding Commercial and Industrial Loans of Insured Commercial Banks, 1946–67*
(In millions of dollars)

End of Year	*Amount*	*End of Year*	*Amount*
1946	$14,019	1957	$40,546
1947	18,015	1958	40,457
1948	18,765	1959	40,195
1949	16,939	1960	43,132
1950	21,808	1961	45,157
1951	25,788	1962	48,668
1952	27,816	1963	52,984
1953	27,158	1964	60,040
1954	26,823	1965	71,235
1955	33,210	1966	80,408
1956	38,707	1967	88,258

*Beginning in 1959, loans by commercial banks to other financial institutions that had previously been included very largely in commercial and industrial loans were placed in a separate category. For June 10, 1959, this change in classification resulted in a reduction in reported commercial and industrial loans of $4,447 million. But the year-end data for 1958 and earlier years, as shown in this table, were not adjusted to conform to the change in classification. Accordingly, the amounts of commercial and industrial loans reported for the period 1959–67 are not closely comparable with the amounts reported for 1946–58.

SOURCE: Federal Deposit Insurance Corporation, *Annual Reports.*

Data on Large Commercial Banks. In addition to their semi-annual reports on the commercial and industrial loans of all commercial banks, the Federal Reserve authorities publish weekly reports giving many details about the commercial and industrial loans of about 160 large commercial banks located in all parts of the country, and monthly reports giving further details on these loans. Because these banks are estimated to hold about 70 percent of the total volume of the commercial and industrial loans of all commercial banks, what they do in business lending, as revealed in the reports, undoubtedly reflects quite closely what all commercial banks collectively are doing in this area of lending. The weekly reports are especially useful in revealing week-to-week changes in business lending and in disclosing what industries are expanding and contracting their bank borrowings. The monthly reports are additionally instructive in presenting separate figures for term loans, also with subgroups of borrowers classified by industry.

Illustrative of the kinds of information the Federal Reserve authorities supply in their weekly and monthly reports on commercial and industrial loans of large banks are the data in Table 33–2. Here we see that the total of the outstanding commercial and industrial loans of these banks at the end of July, 1968, amounted to $61,969 million,[3] of which $33,285 million, or 53.7 percent, were short-term and the balance of $28,684 million, or 46.3 percent, were term loans. The table reveals that firms engaged in manufacturing are by far the most important class of borrowers from commercial banks, on both short-

TABLE 33–2
Commercial and Industrial Loans of Large Commercial Banks
Outstanding July 31, 1968*
(Dollar amounts in millions)

Business of Borrower	*Total Loans*	*Short-Term Loans*	*Percent of Total*	*Term Loans*	*Percent of Total*
Durable goods manufacturing....	$12,760	$ 6,218	48.7	$ 6,542	51.3
Nondurable goods manufacturing..	10,020	4,801	47.9	5,219	52.1
Mining, including crude petroleum and natural gas..............	4,688	646	13.8	4,042	86.2
Wholesale trade................	4,239	3,516	82.9	723	17.1
Retail trade....................	3,776	2,624	69.5	1,152	30.5
Transportation................	4,972	1,284	25.8	3,688	74.2
Communication................	1,012	559	55.2	453	44.8
Other public utilities...........	2,370	1,442	60.8	928	39.2
Construction...................	2,775	1,996	71.9	779	28.1
Services........................	5,507	3,183	57.8	2,324	42.2
All other domestic loans.........	7,293	6,351	87.1	942	12.9
Foreign........................	2,557	665	26.0	1,892	74.0
Total....................	$61,969	$33,285	53.7	$28,684	46.3

*As reported by about 160 large commercial banks located in leading financial centers. It is estimated that these banks hold approximately 70 percent of the total commercial and industrial loans of all commercial banks.

SOURCE: Derived from *Federal Reserve Bulletin*, August, 1968, p. A–30.

term and term bases, but that all industrial areas are well represented among borrowers, as indicated by the total amounts entered for the separate classes. For the present chapter, the figures on short-term loans and their percentages are especially significant. Also noteworthy are the revelations that short-term borrowing is much more important than term borrowing for firms engaged in wholesale and retail trade and in the construction industry; that it is apparently much less favored than term borrowing by mining, transportation, and foreign enterprises; that it has a moderate edge for the service establishments

[3]The large banks were reported as having an additional $6,367 million of unclassified commercial and industrial loans and $845 million in holdings of bankers' acceptances, for a grand total of $69,181 million. The author subtracted the figure for bankers' acceptances to allow for their separate treatment later in this chapter.

and for the public utilities other than those in transportation; and that it has close to equal ranking with term borrowing for the manufacturing industry.

Lines of Credit

When corporations have repeated occasions to borrow from the commercial banks, they generally seek to clear the way for this borrowing in advance by asking for "lines of credit," and banks are usually quite willing to regularize their relationships with their customers by establishing lines of credit for them. A line of credit is a commitment of a bank to grant loans to a given customer up to a specified amount within a given period of time, usually one year. If a corporation has a line-of-credit commitment of $50,000, it can expect to have its requests for loans for any sum up to that total honored without delay. In its financial planning for the year ahead, therefore, it can proceed with confidence that the bank funds will be available when needed.

Features of Lines of Credit. When a line of credit is arranged for, a bank and its business customer usually agree on the maturity of the loans to be granted, whether or not they are to be secured by pledges of property, the kind and value of the property to be pledged, if any, and perhaps the interest rate to be charged. Sometimes, however, the interest rate is set only on a contingent basis, to be actually determined, when the loans are granted, in relation to the bank's prime rate at that time (to be discussed later), the discount rate of the Federal Reserve bank of the district, or some open-market rate. For example, it may be stipulated that the rate of interest will be 2 percentage points above the Federal Reserve discount rate in effect at the time the loans are granted. As a rule, lines of credit are revolving, so that if early loans during the designated period are repaid, further loans to the full amount of the credit line may be readily obtained. If a corporation with a $50,000 credit line borrows $30,000 and then repays $15,000 of this loan, it has further borrowing rights of $35,000.

Sometimes, the individual bank receives requests from well-qualified corporations for lines of credit too large, in its judgment, to be granted entirely on its own. In such instances, it is likely to ask other banks in the same city or in other cities to participate with it in providing the line. In October, 1967, for example, the B. F. Goodrich Company announced that it had arranged for a $150 million revolving line of credit with 21 banks, headed by the First National City Bank of New York. On the same day, Delta Air Lines disclosed that it had arranged for a similar line amounting to $175 million with 25 banks, headed by the Citizens & Southern National Bank of Atlanta.[4]

---

[4]*The Wall Street Journal*, Midwest Edition, October 5, 1967, p. 19.

As lines of credit are usually opened for one year, annual negotiations with banks for continuation of the lines are generally necessary. This is convenient for the customer in further financial planning. If, for example, he wants to have his line increased, the annual conference with the bank's lending officer is the time to arrange for it. It is also convenient for the bank in planning its own lending and investing policies for the year ahead. Should a situation of tight money be developing, for example, it may find it necessary to scale down all or most of its advance loan commitments.

Qualifications for Lines of Credit. To obtain a line of credit and have it kept open, a corporation must play ball with the bank. First, a well-managed bank will surely ask for copies of the corporation's articles of incorporation and bylaws in order to determine whether or not these contain any limitations on its capacities to incur debt and to pledge assets. Second, it will ask for a resolution of the corporation's board of directors, specifically stating that the designated officers with whom the bank is to deal are authorized to borrow in its behalf and to pledge its property if the loans are to be secured. Third, the bank will demand financial statements and other credit information. Indeed, the line of credit will be opened, if at all, only after these data, as well as credit information drawn from other sources, have been thoroughly analyzed to yield a judgment on character, capacity, and capital. Finally, the corporation will be expected to continue to supply the bank with information relevant to continuing credit analysis: copies of financial statements, possibly monthly or quarterly, and details about its borrowings from other banks or other lenders; important changes contemplated in its operating policies; new litigation in which it may be involved; and so on. As was pointed out in an earlier chapter, cash budgets are often highly useful in negotiations for bank loans.[5]

Firm Commitments. The ordinary line of credit, as just described is often said to be a moral commitment of the bank. It has no contractual obligation to grant the loans as agreed on, but if it is a competently managed institution it will surely make every effort to honor requests for loans from those that have credit lines. Its reputation would suffer severe damage were it to take its moral commitments lightly. Only if there is serious deterioration in the financial affairs of corporations and other firms that have credit lines—between the times the lines are opened and the loans are requested—are banks held to be justified in refusing credit-line loans.

Sometimes, however, corporations want absolute assurances that loans requested up to given amounts will be granted within designated periods of time, regardless of banks' judgments about their

---

[5]See p. 258.

financial positions at the time the loans are requested. They therefore ask for firm commitments. In making such a commitment, a bank obligates itself contractually to grant the loans under the credit line when requested to. However, it usually asks for compensation for thus binding itself. In ordinary credit-line borrowing, the corporation pays interest only on loans actually taken, but for a firm commitment it must pay a low-rate fee, perhaps 0.5 or 0.75 percent per annum, on the whole line for its full duration, whether or not it is used. For a firm-commitment line of $100,000 for a year and actual borrowings of $80,000 for an 8-month period within the year, a corporation would pay the commitment fee on $100,000 for the full year and an additional regular interest charge on $80,000 for the 8 months.

Multiple Lines of Credit. Many larger corporations seek and obtain lines of credit at several banking institutions simultaneously. An important reason for this is that banking laws limit the amount that a bank can lend to the individual borrower. In the federal law applicable to national banks, for example, the general rule is that loans to the individual borrower cannot exceed an amount equal to 10 percent of the bank's capital stock and surplus.[6] Exceptions are made for certain kinds of secured and guaranteed (endorsed) loans, but not for loans secured by real estate and equipment or by stocks and bonds other than securities of the federal government itself.

A second reason that corporations obtain multiple lines of credit is to avoid too close dependence on single lending institutions. A corporation that can qualify for total short-term loans of $500,000 may prefer to borrow $100,000 from each of five banks rather than the entire amount from one, even though the one would not be hampered by loan limits in the banking laws. With its credit reputation established at the five banks, the corporation would presumably have no difficulty in getting its lines at three or four of the banks increased should one or two get into tight situations, necessitating a curtailment of their lines.

Still another reason for multiple lines is the desire of corporations to continue short-term borrowing the year around. Many banks insist that the individual borrower clean up his short-term loans at some time within the year and remain out of debt to them for, say, a month. Short-term loans are supposed to be chiefly for short-term purposes, as for seasonal expansion, so that repayment should be forthcoming when the short-term objective has been accomplished. Banks are pleased to lend to good customers, but they want to have assurance that the customers remain good in the sense of having the capacity

---

[6]Banks, of course, do not lend their capital stock and surplus, since these are simply book accounts, representing the equity of their stockholders. Capital stock and surplus, therefore, are referred to only as a measuring device in the application of the 10 percent rule as well as other rules for limiting bank loans.

to repay. The annual cleanup therefore gives them this assurance. But some corporations do not go along with this idea; they want to have short-term bank loans as a continuing source of current assets. By having two or more credit lines they can keep each bank happy, cleaning up their loans with it by simply using the lines of credit established elsewhere.

Other Short-Term Lending

The foregoing discussion is not meant to imply that commercial banks lend only to corporations and other businesses that have arranged for lines of credit. Many short-term loans are granted on the basis of immediate negotiations as funds are needed. Some corporations borrow only sporadically; they prefer to wait until shortly before the time funds will be needed to open negotiations. In anticipation of their sporadic borrowings, however, they may be quite willing to submit statements and other credit information to the bank in advance, and to continue to supply data on current developments, so that delays for credit analysis will be avoided when the time for borrowing arrives. Even, indeed, should they be negligent in this matter, the banks in their respective communities would be likely to build up credit files concerning them, from information picked up here and there, so as to be ready for them should they come around to borrow.

Size Relationships in Short-Term Lending

As a rule, large corporations gravitate toward large banks for loans, both short term and longer term, and small corporations toward smaller banks. Small corporations located in big cities will generally be well received by the lending officers of the big banks of these cities, but since most small corporations are located in small towns and cities they are likely to turn first to local institutions. On the other hand, large corporations located in small towns and cities, knowing the loan limits that apply to the banks of these communities, often go direct to the banks of the big cities. The loan limits apply to these banks, too, but because of their large capital stock and surplus balances, they can grant much larger loans to individual borrowers than can banks of the smaller cities and towns.

Sometimes, nevertheless, relatively large corporations are able to make quite satisfactory arrangements for loans with banks in the smaller communities. Although such banks may not be able to lend as much as their corporate customers might want and can qualify for, the banks themselves may go to the big city banks—their correspondent banks—and get them to advance whatever amounts they themselves cannot advance. Such participations by big city banks in loans arranged by out-of-town banks are quite common.

But sometimes even a big city bank cannot provide as much as a giant corporation wants and can qualify for, or it may not want to make the full loan requested, even if not precluded by legal loan limits, for reasons of avoiding too great a concentration of risk. In such circumstances, banks often call on other banks in the same cities and in other cities to join them in lending syndicates. The bank that issues the invitation and the banks that accept it split up the loan among themselves in agreed-on proportions.

Promissory Notes

The promissory note may be said to be the standard instrument for short-term bank loans. The vast majority of borrowing corporation sign promissory notes as evidence of their obligations to repay. For unsecured loans especially, quite simple note forms are often used, containing only the date of the instrument, the promise to pay to the order of the bank, the time of payment—"on demand" or "60 days after date"—and the signature of the corporation as attested by the signature of its treasurer or other authorized officer or officers. Oftentimes, more elaborate note forms are used with a great number of if's, and's, and whereas's, and some have so many provisos that they resemble bonds in complexity. Of considerable complexity, for example, is the collateral note, which is generally used when assets are pledged for the security of a loan. Nevertheless, the essential feature of any promissory note is the unconditional promise to pay, on demand or at the designated time in the future, a sum certain in money.

In relatively rare instances, corporations obtain short-term bank loans by discounting other obligors' promissory notes and accepted drafts. In some lines of business—a very few—buyers on time are required to give the sellers promissory notes, promising payment at the expiration of the allowed credit period. Sometimes, too, sellers draw drafts or orders to pay on buyers; when these have been accepted by the buyers they become their promises to pay. In borrowing at a bank, then, a corporation that has such notes and accepted drafts in its possession may ask the bank to discount them in lieu of signing its own promissory note for the amount of the loan. In discounting such instruments, the bank deducts from their maturity value its interest charge for the loan, and the remainder thus is the net amount or proceeds of the loan. The signers of the promissory notes and the drawees (acceptors) of the drafts are primarily liable on their instruments, but the borrowing corporation, as endorser of the notes and as drawer of the drafts, is secondarily liable. The bank is much more interested in the corporation's secondary liability than in the primary liability of the signers and drawees about whose credit standing it may know nothing. Hence, it consents to the discount transaction only when, on the basis of the usual kind of credit analysis, it has confidence in the corporation's capacity to make good on the instruments should the signers and acceptors default.

Interest Rates on Short-Term Bank Loans

Spreads in Interest Rates. Interest rates on short-term bank loans being granted at any time vary rather widely, depending on the size of the loans, the size and location of lending banks, the intensity of competition among them and with other classes of lenders, the size and, particularly, the credit standing of the borrowers, and the purposes of the loans. They also vary from time to time depending on changes in the lending capacities of the banks and in total demands for short-term funds. Some of these influences are clearly reflected in the data in Table 33–3 on rates set by a sample of about 125 large

TABLE 33–3
Interest Rates on Short-Term Business Loans, First Quarter, 1968*

Interest Rate (percent per annum)	*All Loans*	*Size of Loans (thousands of dollars)*				
		1–9	*10–99*	*100–499*	*500–999*	*1,000 and over*
		Percentage distribution of dollar amounts†				
Less than 6.00	3.2	1.3	1.3	1.7	2.2	5.2
6.00	34.6	10.0	13.1	20.8	32.4	48.7
6.01–6.49	26.8	20.9	16.7	26.4	35.3	27.3
6.50	7.8	8.2	12.9	10.8	7.8	4.9
6.51–6.99	10.5	12.6	19.4	15.2	8.8	6.2
7.00	6.1	13.6	11.5	8.8	5.0	3.3
7.01–7.49	3.8	14.8	10.0	5.1	3.5	1.3
7.50	3.1	4.8	4.7	4.0	1.7	2.6
7.51–7.99	1.1	5.2	3.0	1.5	0.9	0.1
8.00	1.1	3.9	2.8	1.7	0.7	0.3
Over 8.00	1.8	4.6	4.4	3.9	1.7	0.3
Total	100.0	100.0	100.0	100.0	100.0	100.0

*Rates charged on new short-term loans and on short-term renewals of maturing loans in the first half of February, 1968, as reported by about 125 large commercial banks located in 35 leading financial centers throughout the country.

†In some instances, items do not add exactly to totals because of rounding.

SOURCE: *Federal Reserve Bulletin*, May, 1968, p. A–30, and August, 1968, p. A–31.

commercial banks in 35 leading financial centers in the first half of February, 1968, on new short-term loans and short-term renewals of maturing loans. This was a time of tight money—of limited lending capacity on the part of the banks and huge demands for short-term funds on the part of bank customers—so that the whole array of rates for loans of all sizes was much higher than, say, in 1964, when the rates in comparable Federal Reserve reports were less than 6 percent for loans of all sizes.[7] The rates of Table 33–3 were being charged by large banks that were generally subject to intense compe-

[7]*Federal Reserve Bulletin*, March, 1965, p. 453.

tition in early February, 1968, and the probability is that smaller banks in small cities and towns were charging somewhat higher rates, although, to be sure, chiefly on smaller loans because of their limited capacities to meet the needs of large borrowers.

Since large loans go chiefly to large enterprises and small loans to small enterprises, one may reasonably conclude from the evidence of Table 33–3 that small business firms must generally pay higher interest charges for short-term money than do large enterprises. While 81.2 percent of loans of $1 million or more and 69.9 percent of loans of $500,000 to $999,000 were being granted at rates of less than 6.5 percent, only 32.2 percent of the $1,000–$9,000 loans and 31.1 percent of the $10,000–$99,000 loans were getting rates below 6.5 percent. And at the other end of the scale, while 33.3 percent of the $1,000–$9,000 loans and 24.9 percent of the $10,000–$99,000 loans were being charged interest at rates exceeding 7 percent, only 8.5 percent of the $500,000–$999,000 loans and 4.6 percent of the loans of $1 million and over were as costly as that.

A final point to emphasize about the data in Table 33–3 is that most of the loan funds of the large banks were obviously going to large borrowers, as indicated by the fact that 64.6 percent of the dollar amount of all loans had interest charges of less than 6.5 percent—a result necessarily caused by the weighing of the loans in the two largest size classes.

Prime Rates. The commercial banks of our large cities have in effect at all times a rate of interest for business loans that they describe as the "prime rate." It is the rate at which they are willing to lend to prime business firms, which are generally understood to be chiefly large corporations of high credit standings. However, smaller enterprises of strong financial positions are often able to borrow at the prime rate also, as indicated by the lower rates for some of the smaller loans reported in Table 33–3. In early February, 1968, the prime rate was 6 percent, and Table 33–3 shows that moderate proportions of the dollar amounts of loans in the two smallest size groups were being granted at that rate (and minor proportions at even lower rates). It is noteworthy that for the large prime corporations 48.7 percent of the dollar amount of loans of $1 million or more were being granted at the prime rate and 5.2 percent at rates even below the prime rate.

The prime rate is usually uniform among metropolitan commercial banks throughout the country, since they all compete as lenders in the national short-term market (and, for many, in an international market). But the prime rate is subject to change as conditions in the short-term market get tighter or easier. A change upward or downward usually becomes effective quickly following an announcement of a single leading bank; other banks in the same city and then in other cities come out promptly with identical announcements. On November 20, 1967, for example, the prime rate was boosted from 5½ to 6 percent, and on April 19, 1968, it was further raised to 6½ percent. Once in a while, however, a bank that announces a change in the prime rate finds that it has no followers, and it hastily retreats to where it had been.

Discount Procedure. For most of their short-term loans to business enterprises, commercial banks use the discount procedure in charging interest. On its face, the borrower's promissory note is non-interest-bearing, and the bank advances the face amount as reduced by its interest charge. This, once again, is the proceeds of the loan. Thus, on a loan of $10,000 for 60 days with an interest charge of 6 percent per annum the borrower would receive $9,900, and would have the obligation to pay back $10,000 in 60 days. Actually, then, the effective rate of interest would be slightly more than 6 percent. Interest of $100 on an advance of $9,900 for 60 days means a rate of approximately 6.383 percent per annum. Should this borrower want exactly $10,000 as the proceeds of his loan, he would have to make the face amount of the note $10,101.01—if the bank insisted on the last penny.

Security for Short-Term Loans

Reasons for Security. The principal reason that banks require borrowers to pledge assets is to compensate for weaknesses in the borrowers' capacity or capital or both. If a bank has misgivings about the managerial competence of a loan applicant, or if the applicant wants a larger loan than the bank thinks justified in consideration of his own equity in his business, it is likely to grant the loan only if it itself is protected by a pledge of acceptable assets. To a given applicant, for example, a bank might be willing to lend up to $10,000 on an unsecured basis, but, should he want to borrow $15,000 it would be likely to want security *for the entire amount.* According to typical bank practice, this would mean that the value of the assets pledged would have to be substantially in excess of $15,000. If the bank decided, on the other hand, that the loan applicant was lacking in character—in integrity—it would probably conclude that no amount of security would compensate for this deficiency. Most banks avoid loans to people of shady reputations if for no other reason than that dealings with such people reflect unfavorably on their own reputations.

A second reason for pledging assets as security for business loans is to enable the banks to grant larger loans than they otherwise would be legally permitted to grant. It was mentioned earlier that the banking laws set limits to the amounts banks may lend to the individual borrower, and specifically cited was the national bank rule restricting loans to the individual borrower to an amount not exceeding 10 percent of the lending bank's capital stock and surplus. But the banking laws make exceptions for certain kinds of secured loans. In some cases, the exceptions permit loans of unlimited amount on certain kinds of security; in others, they merely raise the loan limit. For example, a national bank may lend to a single borrower an amount up to 50 percent of its capital stock and surplus if the loan is secured by warehouse receipts covering readily marketable nonperishable staple commodities, provided that the market value of the pledged commodities exceeds the amount of the loan by certain stipulated percentages.

A third reason for secured loans is the unwillingness of loan applicants to reveal as much information about themselves as the banks consider necessary for adequate credit judgments. If the banks are satisfied about the character of these applicants, they may decide that ample collateral will be accepted as compensating for their own lack of information.

In some areas, assets are pledged for the safety of business loans because, one may say, it is a matter of custom. But it is a custom largely confined to financial institutions. Thus, when commercial banks themselves borrow from other commercial banks, they almost invariably pledge assets.

Kinds of Assets Pledged. Probably the most common reason that business enterprises obtain short-term loans from commercial banks is to buy raw materials for manufacturing operations and finished goods for resale. Hence, it is no surprise to find that inventories are the assets most commonly pledged on short-term business loans. If it is possible to store goods in warehouses under the control of licensed and bonded warehousemen, a bank that takes a pledge of these goods is assured that the borrower will not be able to sell them and use the proceeds without its knowledge and consent. It will demand warehouse receipts issued by the warehouseman, thus gaining control of the goods. The warehouseman will release the stored goods only on instructions from the bank as the holder of the receipts. If the loan matures and remains unpaid, and if the bank expects no payment in the ordinary course of business, even should it give the borrower more time, it can itself obtain the goods from the warehouseman, sell them, and thus reimburse itself. Loans on warehoused goods, it may be mentioned, are made whether the goods are stored in warehouses owned by licensed warehousemen or owned by the borrowers but placed under the control of such warehousemen. Warehouses owned by storers of goods but controlled by licensed warehousemen are known as field warehouses.

Goods that borrowers must keep in their possession can be pledged by means of other kinds of instruments sanctioned by law. Raw materials to be used in production by manufacturers can be pledged by chattel mortgages, and finished goods held for display and sale by chattel mortgages or trust receipts. A chattel mortgage represents a lien on pledged goods, while a trust receipt acknowledges that title to the goods is in the lending bank and that the borrower serves as trustee for the bank in handling and selling the goods. Trust receipts are most commonly used when goods pledged are readily distinguishable from other goods, as when they bear serial numbers or other identifying marks. Thus, they are convenient in obtaining loans for carrying automobiles, electrical appliances, typewriters, other kinds of office machines, and similar goods. Should a borrower sell goods held under trust receipts without accounting to the bank for the proceeds, he might be charged not only with breach of contract but also with the crime of fraudulent conversion (embezzlement).

Second in importance among types of assets pledged for short-term business loans are stocks and bonds. Stocks and bonds are easily used for pledge purposes. In putting them up as collateral, the borrower authorizes the lending bank to sell them to reimburse itself should there be a default. If he fulfills his obligations, it is a simple matter for the bank to return the pledged securities to him. Corporations not infrequently pledge stocks and bonds owned in subsidiaries and, sometimes, securities held in unrelated corporations. As a rule, however, the pledging of stocks and bonds on short-term loans is a more likely procedure for proprietorships and partnerships than for corporations. A proprietor may own securities for investment purposes in addition to the assets of his business, and he may pledge some of these if he wants to borrow to expand the assets of his business. But the typical nonfinancial corporation has no stocks and bonds of subsidiaries because it has no subsidiaries, and if it holds other securities as a means of temporarily putting idle funds to work it is much more likely to sell them when it needs cash rather than pledge them as security for loans.

Although accounts receivable outrank inventories among the current assets of nonfinancial business corporations collectively, and by wide margins in many areas of business, they are used much more rarely than inventories as security for short-term bank loans. Until late in the 1930's, most commercial banks showed little interest in accounts receivable financing. Since then, many have developed interests in and facilities for this kind of financing, but the major role in lending on accounts receivable is held by commercial finance companies. Accordingly, an examination of the procedures of accounts receivable financing may be deferred to a later point in this chapter, where the work of the commercial finance companies is discussed.

In some cases, chattel mortgages on equipment and mortgages on real property are provided by borrowers as security for short-term business loans. However, many advances so secured probably have only the appearance of short-term loans; in other words, banks may grant them originally on a short-term basis with the understanding that they will be renewed, perhaps repeatedly, for a longer period. Certainly, the mortgaging of real property, which itself is a rather complicated operation, appears to be a cumbersome short-term lending procedure. Even so, if banks insist on security, and business firms desperately need money, they are unlikely to hesitate long in giving pledges of equipment and real property.

Endorsements and Other Guaranties

When commercial banks are unwilling to grant short-term loans on an unsecured basis, they may be satisfied to go ahead without pledges of assets, provided that the would-be borrowers can get endorsements or other guaranties for their notes from third parties whose credit reputations are impressive. A third party who is willing to accept responsibility for the repayment of a borrower's loan can so signify by cosigning the borrower's promissory note, by endorsing it, or by signing a letter of guaranty, addressed to the lending bank. The legal significance of these three procedures is much the same, since the bank is usually accorded the right to proceed directly and immediately against the guarantor to collect payment if the borrower defaults. Naturally, therefore, banks accept guaranties in lieu of pledges of assets only if confident of the guarantors' ability to pay. The very acceptance of a guaranty indicates, indeed, greater confidence in the guarantor than in the borrower.

In corporate financing, officers and especially principal stockholders of small, close corporations most commonly provide guaranties on loans to these corporations, and parent companies guarantee loans to their subsidiaries. To the principal stockholder of a close corporation, a bank may be willing to lend very large sums, but because he has invested only a small part of his wealth in the corporation it is unwilling to lend to it without special protection. If the corporation does not want to pledge its assets, or if it has no assets that would be acceptable for pledge purposes, a guaranty by the principal stockholder is the logical alternative. In a similar way, a subsidiary of a strong parent corporation may have a weak credit standing, or no credit standing at all, as in the case of a newly established foreign subsidiary; yet, because of its status as a distinct legal entity it alone would be responsible for the repayment of any loans it might obtain. But it would quickly become an attractive customer for loans were banks assured by the parent that it would guarantee all advances to it.

Bankers' Acceptances

A peculiar means whereby business concerns obtain short-term bank loans to buy goods for inventory is in the use of commercial letters of credit and bankers' acceptances. The means is peculiar because the banks that advance the funds have no negotiations with the borrowers, and usually, indeed, do not even know who they are or what their credit standing is.

As commercial letters of credit and bankers' acceptances are chiefly used for transactions in international trade, we may take an import transaction to illustrate their use. Suppose that an American firm is negotiating with a British manufacturer for the purchase of a shipment of dinnerware valued at $20,000. The British manufacturer is willing to sell on a 60-day deferred-payment basis but is unwilling to rely on the unsupported promise to pay of the American firm. He stipulates, therefore, that he will ship the goods if the American firm will get from its bank a commercial letter of credit authorizing him to draw a 60-day draft on the bank itself. On applying to its bank for the letter of credit, the American firm would be subjected to a credit investigation much as if it were applying for a direct loan, unless, of course, the bank already had a complete credit file on the firm, kept up-to-date with its cooperation. Since the bank is being asked to authorize the drawing of a draft that, on acceptance, will become its own promise to pay, it wants to be sure that the applying firm will be able to provide it with the means to fulfill this promise.

If the bank is satisfied with the credit standing of the importing firm, the importer must sign a contract promising to pay the bank at or shortly before the maturity of the draft (acceptance) an amount of money sufficient to meet it, plus a commission for the bank's services. The bank then issues the letter of credit—it is, indeed, in the form of a letter—addressed to the British manufacturer specifically authorizing him within a given period of time to draw one or more drafts payable in 60 days up to the total of $20,000. In the letter, certain conditions are set out to be satisfied by the manufacturer—stipulations about the kinds and qualities of the merchandise, the method of shipment, insurance on the shipment, and so on. The manufacturer's failure to fulfill these conditions would release the bank from its obligation to accept the draft or drafts to be drawn.

With assurances of getting the American bank's promise to pay, the manufacturer ships the goods, draws the draft on the American bank, and sells it to his own (British) bank for British money—that is, sterling. Since the draft is non-interest-bearing, and since the British bank will not be able to collect the full amount of the draft until its maturity, it pays the manufacturer less than its face value—that is to say, it discounts it. Now the owner of the draft, the British bank, sends it to its correspondent bank in the United States, and this bank, in turn, presents it to the bank that issued the letter of credit. If the issuer is satisfied that the conditions of its letter have been satisfied, it writes its acceptance on the face of the draft, thus making it specifically its promise to pay. The instrument, now a *banker's acceptance*, is then returned to the correspondent bank.

If the British bank, as owner, decides to have the correspondent bank as its agent hold the acceptance to maturity, enabling it to earn the full amount of the discount charged the manufacturer, it thereby, in effect, grants a loan to the American importer whom it presumably does not know. The importing firm gets its goods and has approximately 60 days to pay, and the British exporter got his money when he sold the draft. It is the British bank, therefore, that is providing the financing. But if the British bank decides that it wants dollars at once instead of waiting until the maturity of the acceptance, it orders its correspondent to sell the acceptance to a dealer in such instruments. Like the British bank itself, the dealer buys on a discount basis, expecting to make a profit by reselling the acceptance at a lower rate of discount (which means, of course, a higher price). He offers the acceptance, with others, to customers who are interested in investing in such instruments. Such customers are chiefly our metropolitan banks. Thus, the buying bank substitutes itself for the British bank as the lender to the American importing firm—again, we may assume, knowing little or nothing about it.

The British bank would be willing to buy the draft in reliance on the obligation to pay of the American bank that issued the letter of credit, as would the acceptance dealer and his customer in buying the acceptance. Thus, the American bank, though not lending money to the importing firm, would be "lending its good name," as is often said. For this loan of its good name, as mentioned above, it would charge a commission, not interest.

As a rule, the issuance of commercial letters of credit and the acceptance of drafts drawn under them is quite closely confined to the large banks of our principal cities. However, almost every commercial bank in the country has correspondent relationships with one or more of these institutions, so that through them it can arrange financing by means of bankers' acceptances for its business customers. According to a Federal Reserve report, the outstanding dollar acceptances of American banks amounted to $4,286 at the end of June, 1968.[8]

THE SALE OF COMMERCIAL PAPER

Just as a corporation may sell a bond issue in bulk to a syndicate of investment bankers, depending on them to peddle the bonds among their customers, so may it also sell to a commercial-paper dealer a batch of short-term promissory notes, expecting the dealer to resell these notes to his customers. However, financing by selling open-

---

[8] *Federal Reserve Bulletin*, August, 1968, p. A–35.

market commercial paper, or simply commercial paper, as the notes are called, is much less popular than financing with bond issues. The number of firms borrowing in the commercial-paper market at any given time probably does not exceed 400.[9] But one must allow for increased interest in this market as a source of short-term funds, as evidenced by a doubling of the volume of commercial paper outstanding in the brief period from the beginning of 1966 to the middle of 1968.

The principal borrowers in the commercial-paper market are sales and consumer finance companies, manufacturing and mercantile companies in many areas of operation, and, of late, a moderate number of public utilities. The larger finance companies peddle their own notes. They depend on the market so heavily and so continuously that they save considerable sums on commission and interest charges by bypassing the dealers. Indeed, their volume of direct paper far exceeds that of dealer paper sold through dealers by virtually all other issuers, including smaller finance companies. At the end of June, 1968, for example, outstanding commercial paper sold direct by finance companies was estimated at $12,976 million, and that marketed through dealers at $5,822 million.[10]

When a corporation approaches a commercial-paper dealer for the first time, it is subjected to a rigorous credit investigation. Because the dealers buy issues of notes outright, and because they want to resell quickly, they want to be sure that the notes are of such good quality that their customers will readily buy. For the same reasons, corporations that have sold many issues of notes to the dealers must continue to maintain high credit standings to qualify for still further sales. Defaults on open-market commercial paper have been exceedingly rare.

Open-market promissory notes sold through dealers are usually made out for round amounts, such as $5,000, $10,000, and $25,000, and sometimes for amounts up to $100,000. As the issuing corporation does not know who the ultimate payees of the notes will be, it makes them payable to the order of itself and then endorses them, so they can then pass from hand to hand without further endorsements. The dealer himself does not endorse the notes, nor are they secured by pledges of assets. Accordingly, open-market buyers depend entirely on the unsupported promises to pay of the issuing corporations. The maturity is usually 90, 120, or 180 days, although in some cases it is as long as 270 days.

Open-market commercial paper sold through dealers usually does not bear any interest rate on its face. The dealer buys the notes on a

---

[9]For some recent figures on this, see Federal Reserve Bank of San Francisco, *Monthly Review*, July, 1968, pp. 138–39.

[10]*Federal Reserve Bulletin*, August, 1968, p. A–35.

discount basis, charging a rate of discount that varies with the degrees of tightness or ease in the whole market for short-term funds. He ordinarily expects to earn a return by reselling the notes to his customers at a lower rate of discount; nevertheless, the principal source of his profit is a commission charged to the issuing corporation. Commissions usually range between 0.125 and 0.25 percent of the face amount of total note issues.

On buying issues of short-term notes, the dealer quickly offers them to his customers, often selling on an option basis. On this basis, the customer is allowed 10 days, or in some instances 14 days, to make his own investigation of the issuing corporations and return the notes to the dealer if not satisfied with the results of this investigation. The buyers of commercial paper, both that offered direct by finance companies and that sold through dealers, are chiefly nonfinancial business corporations and smaller commercial banks. As we saw in Chapter 7, corporate treasurers often buy commercial paper as a means of investing cash that is temporarily in excess supply.[11] By buying, they make this idle cash available to the finance companies and other issuers. Among commercial banks, institutions located in smaller cities and towns are most prominent among buyers. Regardless of the size and location of the buyers, however, a situation results comparable to that found in the use of bankers' acceptances. The corporations and banks that buy commercial paper are grantors of short-term loans to the issuers of the paper, but the loans are made indirectly and impersonally, since obviously the issuers make no applications for loans to the buyers.

LOANS OF COMMERCIAL FINANCE COMPANIES

Burden of Carrying Receivables

For many manufacturing and mercantile enterprises, a principal problem of short-term financing is that of carrying large volumes of accounts receivable. All or almost all sales may be made on account, and credit periods, due to custom or sharp competition, may be relatively long. Many buyers on account may be slow pay—desirable customers because they ultimately pay, but they stretch out the credit period by allowing their accounts to go delinquent. The volume of accounts receivable may constitute a very large proportion of total current assets, probably exceeding the value of inventories—perhaps, indeed, by a wide margin—or at least not falling far short of that value. Such enterprises may be in a position to borrow limited amounts from the commercial banks on an unsecured basis or by the pledge of inventories, or they may not qualify to borrow on an unsecured basis or

[11]See p. 150.

their inventories may be of a kind not readily adaptable for pledge purposes. For one reason or another, at any rate, they cannot obtain from the commercial banks as much in short-term advances as they need. As security for loans that would be commensurate with their needs, the best they have to offer are the very accounts receivable that give rise to their problem, but the commercial banks with which they deal may have no enthusiasm for loans on accounts receivable. Where can they go?

Role of Commercial Finance Companies

One answer is that such enterprises can turn to the specialized lenders on accounts receivable, known as commercial finance companies and sometimes as commercial receivables companies. Commercial finance companies differ from sales finance companies in that they are specialists in lending on *interbusiness* accounts receivable, while the sales finance companies are principally buyers of contracts evidencing *consumers'* obligations to pay. Commercial finance companies differ from factors in that factors buy interbusiness accounts receivable outright, whereas commercial finance companies, as indicated, simply grant loans on the security of such accounts. In Chapter 9, it was pointed out that business enterprises can economize in their investment in accounts receivable by using the services of factors. In using the aid offered by commercial finance companies, on the other hand, they enjoy no such economy; they must still carry their own accounts receivable, but they are helped in doing so.[12]

As indicated, then, the commercial finance companies are interested in granting loans on accounts owned by business concerns but representing the obligations of other business concerns. Such accounts receivable originate, of course, when manufacturers sell on account to other manufacturers and wholesalers, and when wholesalers sell to retailers. It is in these areas that the commercial finance companies concentrate their work: they stand ready to lend to the manufacturers and wholesalers on pledged receivables, provided, as always, that the borrowers can qualify on the basis of character, capacity, and capital.

Loan Procedures and Terms

After a manufacturer or wholesaler has satisfied a commercial finance company on its creditworthiness, it usually proceeds to borrow on a day-to-day basis. As sales are made, it turns copies of the invoices over to the finance company. The finance company immedi-

---

[12]Although a distinction is thus made among the *functions* of commercial finance companies, sales finance companies, and factors, a few large sales finance companies have divisions or subsidiaries providing commercial finance and factoring services; some commercial finance companies also provide factoring services; and some factors have facilities for lending on business accounts receivable.

ately grants loans equal to an agreed-on percentage of the amount of these invoices, at the same time, of course, getting a lien on the obligation of the buyers of the invoiced goods. The buyers are not notified of the assignment of their accounts to the finance company; hence, they make payment to the manufacturer or wholesaler in the regular way. But the borrower is under contractual obligation to turn all such payments over to the finance company. To the extent that these payments exceed the finance company's loans and charges, they are returned to the borrowing manufacturer or wholesaler. In this way, the amount of a finance company's loans to a given customer changes from day to day, being increased as new invoices are assigned, and being reduced as payments are received from the enterprises whose accounts had previously been assigned.

Depending on manufacturers' and wholesalers' financial positions, the volume of their credit sales, the quality of the accounts assigned, the size of invoices, and other circumstances, commercial finance companies vary the amount of their loans between 70 and 90 percent of the face amount of the assigned accounts, but occasionally going as high as 95 percent. Advances at 80 percent are probably most common. The finance company takes no responsibility for bad-debt losses, as does a factor. If accounts turn out to be uncollectible, the borrower must substitute good accounts or repay the loan out of his portion of collections from good accounts or from other sources.

Because the loan balance of each customer of the commercial finance companies is likely to fluctuate quite frequently—for many, indeed, from day to day—they customarily charge interest on the basis of per diem rates. The customer's monthly bill for interest is determined by multiplying the sum of the daily loan balances by the agreed-on per diem rate. Thus, a charge of 0.0329 percent a day would amount to an annual effective rate of approximately 12 percent on the fluctuating amounts borrowed. Per annum rates, as thus translated, appear to range most commonly between 9.5 and 18.5 percent. For this reason, receivables financing is often said to be an expensive way to borrow. However, the commercial finance companies defend their charges on the grounds that their administrative costs in taking care of the numerous details of receivables financing are high; that they take greater risks than do, say, the commercial banks in the size of their loans in relation to borrowers' equities and in lending to less creditworthy applicants; and that borrowers pay the charges only on money actually used and precisely for the number of days that it is used.

Other Functions

Although the commercial finance companies do not absorb bad-debt losses on accounts assigned to them, they customarily work closely with the manufacturers and wholesalers that use their services in evaluating the creditworthiness of the borrowers' customers, as well as in advising on other matters of financial management. In any case, they find it expedient to keep rather careful watch on borrowers, chiefly by means of frequent audits of their books. Since the obligors on assigned accounts make their payments to the borrowing firm, it is in a position to defraud the finance company by using these payments for purposes other than meeting its obligations to it. Since this supervisory and advisory work is expensive, it accounts for a goodly part of the administrative costs referred to above.

Manufacturers and wholesalers that borrow from the commercial finance companies on assigned accounts receivable are sometimes granted additional loans for extraordinary purposes, as to expand the scope of operations or to take advantage of opportunities to buy large quantities of raw materials or finished goods at favorable prices. These additional loans are almost always secured, usually by pledges of inventories, but occasionally by pledges of other kinds of assets, including even real estate.

LOANS FOR INVENTORY TO INSTALLMENT SELLERS

In Chapter 9, we saw that the sale or assignment of installment contracts by dealers in certain kinds of goods to institutions such as sales finance companies enables the dealers to economize their investment in accounts receivable. Installment buyers of automobiles, electrical appliances for the home, other consumer durable goods, farm machinery, machine tools and other manufacturing equipment, and heavy construction equipment sign contracts—usually conditional sales contracts—in which they obligate themselves to make payments monthly or at other intervals over a period of two or three or more years. If, then, the seller of such durable goods is in need of cash, he may sell these installment contracts to a sales finance company, a commercial finance company, or a commercial bank.

Often, however, the need of dealers for cash precedes the time of sale; they need cash to acquire the goods to be sold. They want inventory loans, and they expect the subsequent sale of their customers' installment contracts to provide the funds with which these loans can be repaid. Because, indeed, the purchase of installment contracts is highly profitable to the financial institutions, the dealers are often in a strong position to demand inventory financing. They agree to sell their customers' installment contracts to a given financial institution only if it will supply them with funds for the acquisition of inventory.

Commercial finance companies grant inventory loans to dealers in manufacturing, construction, and farm machinery and equipment. Sales finance companies supply dealers especially in automobiles and other consumer durable goods, but also some of them supply dealers in industrial and farm equipment. Commercial banks grant inventory loans to dealers in most lines, but especially to those in consumer durables. Inventory loans for the acquisition of consumer durables are often called floorplan loans; others of the kinds described are variously referred to as wholesale financing, industrial financing, and equipment financing.

As a rule, the financial institutions are not at all enthusiastic about granting inventory loans to dealers. Competition is so keen among the different classes of institutions and among those of each class that interest rates are kept at quite moderate levels, and most of the institutions complain that they make no profit on this phase of their business. Supervision is expensive, and in some instances its costs may even exceed interest earnings. Although the loans are usually secured by pledges of the inventories themselves, much policing is necessary to be sure that the dealers properly account for all sales of the pledged goods. It is all too easy for dealers to defraud the lenders if they have a mind to. In the absence of constant surveillance, a dishonest dealer can pledge the same goods to two or more lenders, sell the goods for cash without accounting for the proceeds, sell on installment contracts but assign the contracts to a lender other than the lender on inventory, strip pledged goods, selling parts thereof and leaving only shells for the lender's security, and so on. Of course, lenders try to avoid unscrupulous dealers; nevertheless, in their competition for installment contracts they are inclined to be less strict in selecting the dealers to whom they will lend than in other phases of their lending operations.

QUESTIONS

1. How are commercial banks distinguished from other classes of financial institutions? How important are they as short-term lenders to business enterprises?

2. What is a line of credit as provided by a commercial bank? Why do business firms find it convenient to have lines of credit? Can any business firm get a line of credit if it wants it? Explain.

3. How does a firm commitment of a commercial bank differ from a line of credit?

4. Defend or attack this proposition: Most commercial banks charge about 6 percent a year on their short-term loans to all classes of business borrowers.

5. In short-term lending by commercial banks to business firms, what use is made of each of the following: promissory notes, trust receipts, warehouse receipts, letters of guaranty?

6. For what reasons do commercial banks require some of their business customers to pledge assets as security for short-term loans?

7. It is said that commercial banks usually charge interest on short-term business loans by the discount procedure. What does this mean?

8. What is a commercial letter of credit as issued by a commercial bank? What is a banker's acceptance? Explain how these instruments are

used in inventory financing. Why is this kind of financing often described as being indirect or impersonal?

9. What is open-market commercial paper? What is the procedure in using it as a means of short-term borrowing? Who are the ultimate lenders?

10. What is accounts receivable financing? Explain the procedure of commercial finance companies in providing this kind of financing.

11. What rates do commercial finance companies charge for their financing services? How do they justify the relatively high levels of these rates?

12. If the institutions that grant inventory loans to installment sellers make little or no profit on these loans, as they claim, why do they not simply eliminate this kind of lending?

PROBLEMS

1. For the year 19xx, the Padwell Sales Company has a bank line of credit of $600,000 on a firm commitment basis. It is to pay a commitment fee of 0.5 percent for the full year whether or not it borrows, and interest at the rate of 6 percent on the amount of its borrowings. The commitment fee and all interest charges are to be paid at the end of the year, and interest is to be computed for the exact number of days but on a 360–day basis (for example, the time factor on a 25-day loan would be 25/360). Determine how much Padwell would owe the bank at the end of the year for the fee and interest if its borrowings and repayments were as follows.

Date	*Borrowed*	*Repaid*
February 12	$280,000	
March 15	300,000	
June 16		$220,000
September 20	180,000	
November 18		250,000
December 18		290,000

2. Bester & Co., Inc. has an arrangement with a commercial finance company for continuous borrowing on the security of pledged accounts receivable. The finance company advances 80 percent of the face amount of assigned invoices, and charges interest on these advances at the rate of 0.0411 percent per day. In the month of July, advances made to Bester and payments received from its customers and turned over to the finance company were as follows.

Date of Assignment	*Amount Advanced*	*Payoff Date*
July 6	$25,000	July 26
July 9	32,000	July 29
July 15	18,000	Unpaid
July 22	24,000	Unpaid
July 29	15,000	Unpaid

a) What would be the finance company's total charge for interest for the month of July?

b) At what effective annual rate of interest is Bester borrowing?

chapter 34

LONGER TERM LOANS AND CREDITS

In addition to short-term means of acquiring assets, such as trade credit and short-term loans, many business enterprises have access to intermediate- and long-term sources of assets other than stocks, bonds, and the accumulation of retained earnings. These additional sources include term loans of commercial banks, mortgage loans of life insurance companies, equipment credits and loans of sellers and certain classes of financial institutions, and loans of the Small Business Administration, an agency of the federal government.

TERM LOANS OF COMMERCIAL BANKS

Although the commercial banking system long had the tradition of granting to business enterprises only short-term loans for what were said to be "working capital purposes," the tradition began to break down in the decade of the 1930's. The sharp decline in loan demands of all kinds in that decade led the commercial banks to cast about for new loan outlets, and on finding sound business firms that wanted to borrow for periods longer than one year, they were generally pleased to forget their tradition and grant the loans. Even before the 1930's, loans that had the complexion of present-day term loans were often granted. The purposes for which loans were granted were often long term, as for the purchase of real property and equipment, even though the maturities were short. There were usually understandings between bankers and borrowers that the loans, though ostensibly short term as evidenced by the borrowers' promissory notes, would be renewed periodically.

Nowadays, at any rate, most commercial banks as a matter of routine operations grant business loans that have original maturities beyond one year. Some continue to camouflage some of their longer maturity loans by having borrowers sign short-term notes with understandings about renewals, but most apparently see no good reasons for such juggling of maturities.

Frequently, two or more banks participate in granting term loans to given corporations (much as they often participate in arranging large lines of credit for short-term purposes, as mentioned in Chapter 33), and sometimes banks and other classes of lenders, especially life insurance companies, join forces in providing large term loans. When banks participate with life insurance companies and other nonbank lenders, the borrower's installment repayments in the first few years of the life of the loan usually go to the banks, and the nonbank lenders wait for the later installments for their repayment. The B. F. Goodrich and Delta Air Lines line-of-credit transactions briefly described in Chapter 33 may be cited here as illustrative also of participations among financial institutions in term lending. In their separate arrangements with some 20 commercial banks, Goodrich and Delta were authorized to borrow up to $150 million and $175 million, respectively, on essentially short-term bases until the end of 1969, but the arrangements also provided that their line-of-credit loans outstanding at that time could be converted at their option into five-year term loans. Accordingly, the separate groups of banks were participating simultaneously in commitments for both short-term and term lending.

Extent of Term Lending

Although no comprehensive survey of the extent of term lending by commercial banks generally has been made since 1957, we still get a good idea of what happens in this area from the weekly and monthly statistics of the commercial and industrial loans of large banks, described in Chapter 33. Referring to Table 33–2, page 844, we see that of these (some 160) banks' total classified commercial and industrial loans of $61,969 million outstanding as of July 31, 1968, $28,684 million, or 46.3 percent, were of the term variety. We see that when loans are measured by dollar amounts, manufacturing companies have a long lead as the principal industrial class of term borrowers, although we note that their short-term borrowings do not fall much below their term borrowings. On the other hand, when term loans are measured in relation to total commercial and industrial loans we find that mining companies have the strongest preference for them. Their proportion of term loans to total loans stands at 86.2 percent, and transportation companies and foreign enterprises are not far behind with proportions of 74.2 per cent and 74.0 percent, respectively. Further in terms of proportions, we see that term loans are highly favored by firms in the communication, services, and "other" public utility industries, although not so highly favored by these firms as short-term loans. Firms engaged in wholesale and retail trade and in construction have much smaller proportions of term loans than of short-term loans in their overall bank borrowings.

Purposes of Term Loans

Probably the most common reason that corporations seek term loans from the commercial banks is to acquire equipment. Manufacturers borrow on a term basis to buy machinery and other factory equipment; merchants, to buy or have installed shelves, cabinets, showcases, warehouse equipment, and delivery trucks; hotels and restaurants buy furniture, carpet, kitchen equipment, and so on; and transportation companies buy airplanes, trucks, busses, taxicabs, and other rolling stock. The acquisition of real property is also an important reason for term borrowing. Such funds are used to buy land as sites for factory, store, and office buildings, garages, and warehouses, to purchase existing buildings, and to meet the costs of the construction of new buildings.

Not infrequently, term loans represent interim financing—a means of defraying the developmental costs of sizable expansion projects over a period of a few years, pending later issues of stocks or bonds as the long-term means of financing.

Rather often, too, term loans are granted for working capital purposes, that is, for the acquisition of inventories, the carrying of accounts receivable, and the repayment of various kinds of short-term debt. Although banks are inclined to insist that working capital loans should generally be short term, they are often willing to make exceptions to their own rules. Term loans for working capital appear to be reasonable for firms that are expanding rapidly. Such firms may acquire needed additions to fixed assets by stock and bond issues, but, as they must also expand inventories and receivables substantially and cumulatively over a period of years, they may look to the commercial banks for special help in this direction. Because of the cumulative aspect of the expansion, short-term loans would not be particularly helpful. In other instances, even when expansion is not taking place rapidly some bankers do not hesitate to provide working capital advances on what may be called a continuous basis, by term rather than by short-term loans. As long as they are confident of the solvency of borrowing firms, why, these bankers ask themselves, should they insist on annual cleanups of working capital loans? If borrowers simply go to other institutions to get funds to clean up their loans at a given bank, that bank, in effect, drives profitable business to rival lenders.

Maturities of Term Loans

Judging from Federal Reserve surveys of term lending made in the 1950's, and from current reports in the financial press of specific term-loan arrangements, such as those of Goodrich and Delta Air Lines, one concludes that a substantial majority of term loans have maturities not exceeding 5 years, and that the maturities of most of the remainder do not exceed 10 years, so that only a quite small proportion run for longer than 10 years. Although the recent evidence is rather scanty, it appears that five years is the most popular maturity.

The maturity of most term loans is simply the date on which a final installment on the loan is due. Most term loans are repayable in equal installments periodically, such as monthly, quarterly, or semiannually. Thus, a bank can consider as short-term loans one third of a three-year advance and one fifth of a five-year advance. Such a short-term element in term lending has doubtless been a major factor in encouraging banks to expand the volume of their term loans so heavily in the postwar years. It is of major importance, too, for borrowers' financial planning. If a corporation obtains a 5-year term loan repayable in equal quarterly installments, a 20th of the loan is really a 3-month loan, another 20th a 6-month loan, and so on. Of course, only a final 20th is truly a 5-year loan.

The final installment on some term loans is a balloon payment—much larger than the regular installments up to that time. For example, a corporation might obligate itself to pay off half of the amount of a five-year loan by regular semiannual installments within four and a half years and the remainder of the loan at the end of the fifth year. Such an arrangement ordinarily indicates either an understanding between the bank and the borrower that the balance of the loan will be extended at the end of the original period, or the borrower's expectation that he will be able to make the balloon payment from some special source of funds, as from the proceeds of a stock or bond issue.

Interest Rates on Term Loans

For interest rates on term loans, we get no monthly report as for short-term loans, illustrated in Table 33–3. Indeed, we must go back to the Federal Reserve surveys of 1955 and 1957 for a comprehensive picture of term-loan rates compared with short-term rates, presented in Table 34–1. Despite the rather long time span, it is reasonable to conclude that the *patterns* of rate relationships are probably much the same today as in the 1950's, although, of course, at much higher levels for all loan sizes. Certainly, we would expect rates on smaller loans of all maturities to exceed those on larger loans of the same maturities, and strange though the proposition may sound for times of upsweeping yield curves, we should not be surprised to find the over-5-years rates running in almost all instances below the 1-to-5-years rates, and in the case of some of the smaller loans, running equal to or below the 1-year-or-less rates—that is, the short-term rates. The reason the 1-to-5-years rates exceed over-5-years rates is that a large proportion of the 1-to-5-years loans are loans for equipment acquisitions, on which it is a common practice for banks to charge interest for the full loan periods on the original amounts, though requiring installment repayment. The over-5-years rates run equal to or below short-term rates on smaller loans because the short-term loans are often unsecured, whereas the longer-term loans are likely to be secured by mortgages on real property or otherwise. This additional safety factor permits the banks to shade the rates downward.

TABLE 34–1
Interest Rates on Member Bank Loans to Business, by Size of Borrower and Maturity of Loan, 1955 and 1957
(Average rates on loans made between July 1 and survey date, percent per annum)

Size of Borrower (Total assets in thousands of dollars)	*1955*			*1957*		
	1 Year or Less	*1 to 5 Years*	*Over 5 Years*	*1 Year or Less*	*1 to 5 Years*	*Over 5 Years*
Less than 50	5.5	7.9	5.2	6.1	8.7	5.8
50 to 250	5.0	6.2	5.0	5.6	7.1	5.6
250 to 1,000	4.6	5.2	4.8	5.4	6.0	5.4
1,000 to 5,000	4.1	4.6	4.3	5.1	5.7	5.1
5,000 to 25,000	3.7	3.9	4.1	4.8	4.9	4.8
25,000 to 100,000	3.4	3.9	3.6	4.6	4.6	4.3
100,000 and over	3.2	3.2	3.6	4.4	4.4	3.9
All borrowers*	4.2	4.9	4.1	5.0	5.7	4.7

*Includes a small amount of loans to borrowers whose size was not ascertained.

SOURCE: *Financing Small Business: Report to the Committees on Banking and Currency and the Select Committees on Small Business by the Federal Reserve System* (85th Cong., 2d sess.), Parts 1 and 2 (Washington, D.C.: U.S. Government Printing Office, 1958), p. 388.

For the equipment loans, it is a common practice of banks (and other lenders) to have the borrower sign a promissory note that has a face amount equal to the amount of the loan *plus* interest on this amount at the agreed-on rate for the full period of the loan, and then to require him to pay off this combined face amount in equal installments periodically. If the borrower so pays, the *effective* interest cost to him becomes approximately twice the agreed-on or quoted rate. He pays interest on the full amount of the loan for the full period to maturity, even though he is periodically reducing the principal by his installment payments. A popular formula for estimating effective rates in such installment payment arrangements is the following.

$$i = \frac{2pc}{n + 1},$$

where i is the effective rate of interest per annum, p is the number of installment payments in one year, c is the interest charge as a percentage of the principal of the loan, and n is the total number of installment payments to be made. For illustration, let us assume that a corporation borrows $10,000 to buy equipment. The nominal rate of interest is 5 percent, the term of the loan is 3 years, and the corporation is to repay in equal quarterly installments within that period. It signs a note for $11,500 (the principal plus interest at 5 percent for each of the 3 years or a total of 15 percent), and each of its installment payments will therefore amount to $958.33. Substituting in the formula and solving:

$$i = \frac{2 \times 4 \times .15}{12 + 1} = \frac{1.20}{13} = 9.23\%.$$

Security for Term Loans

Security is much more frequently provided by borrowers of term loans than by short-term borrowers. In the Federal Reserve loan survey of 1957, the proportions were found to be 44 percent of the amount of short-term business loans and over 60 percent of the amount of term loans. Nevertheless, it was also disclosed that, as in short-term lending, small borrowers are more often required to provide security on term loans than are borrowers of large amounts. For maturities of more than five years, for example, it was found that virtually every loan to borrowers that had less than $1 million of assets was secured, while only two thirds of the number and one third of the amount of such loans to larger borrowers were secured.[1]

The mortgaging of real estate is the predominant means of providing security for term loans, especially those with maturities of more than five years. Loans for the purchase or construction of real property are almost always secured by mortgages on the property itself. Quite often, however, real property is pledged, even when the proceeds of loans are to be used for the acquisition of equipment, for working capital, or for other purposes. For many borrowers, real property is the most valuable asset and the most convenient one available for pledge purposes.

Because great numbers of term loans are granted for buying and installing equipment, it is understandable that equipment constitutes the second most important kind of asset put up as security for term loans. Equipment is pledged by the use of instruments such as chattel mortgages.

As for other kinds of assets pledged for the safety of term loans, stocks and bonds are of some prominence. But, as was pointed out in Chapter 33 in the discussion of security for commercial bank short-term loans, stocks and bonds are much more likely to be pledged by

[1]*Financing Small Business: Report to the Committees on Banking and Currency and the Select Committees on Small Business by the Federal Reserve System* (85th Cong., 2d sess.), Parts 1 and 2 (Washington, D.C.: U.S. Government Printing Office, 1958), p. 384.

proprietors and members of partnerships than by corporations. Stocks and bonds held by corporations in subsidiaries may, indeed, be pledged, but the typical corporation, if it held stocks and bonds in unrelated companies simply for investment returns, would probably sell these to raise money rather than borrow and pledge them.

Term-Loan Agreements

While many term loans are granted on terms and conditions hardly more elaborately set out than for typical short-term loans, a great number are governed by the provisions of comprehensive term-loan agreements, which the borrowers sign. In content, a term-loan agreement resembles a bond indenture, although rarely is it as long and detailed. Term-loan agreements tend to be somewhat more restrictive on the borrowers' discretion in choosing financial policies than are indentures. On the other hand, no trustee is needed, since the lending bank expects to be able to police the borrower and thus look after its own interests.

As signed by a corporate borrower, a term-loan agreement, first, establishes all the features of the loan—the amount, the interest rate, a description of the property pledged, if any, and repayment obligations, such as the timing and amount of installment payments to be made. Almost always there is provision for acceleration of the maturity of the whole obligation, at the discretion of the lending bank, should terms of the agreement be violated by the borrower. In addition, there are warranties of the corporate officers who sign for the corporation, stating their authority to act in its behalf, assuring the lending bank that the loan is not precluded by any provisions of the corporation's charter or bylaws, and giving assurance, likewise, that financial statements submitted and to be submitted are and will be accurate and complete.

As indicated, the typical term-loan agreement contains various restrictions on the borrower's financial policy. Consent of the bank must be obtained for borrowing from other sources, pledging the corporation's properties for any purpose, and guaranteeing the obligations of other enterprises or individuals. Usually, there are requirements that working capital not be reduced below a stipulated level or that a given working capital ratio be maintained. Usually, too, there are limitations on the payment of cash dividends, increases in officers' salaries, and the payment of bonuses to them, as well as limitations or absolute prohibitions on the purchase of treasury stock and the retirement of preferred stock. Fixed assets may ordinarily be sold only with the consent of the lending bank. Moreover, the bank is usually privileged to require that the proceeds of such sales be used to pay down the amount of the loan (usually to be applied first to the most remote installments).

The typical term-loan agreement contains a list of additional covenants closely comparable with those contained in bond indentures: the borrower will pay all its taxes promptly, keep its properties in a good state of repair, provide for adequate insurance protection, maintain adequate accounting records, give the bank access to these records for purposes of verification, and supply financial statements to the lender at stipulated intervals.

MORTGAGE LOANS OF LIFE INSURANCE COMPANIES

As we saw in Chapter 30, life insurance companies are of outstanding importance as buyers of corporation bonds, chiefly by private placements. But these financial institutions are also of major importance as grantors of long-term loans to business borrowers without the formalities of bond issues. Smaller enterprises, in particular, find it highly convenient to be able to borrow without having to work up all the details and to incur the expenses of bond issues. Of total mortgage loans of $67,516 million held by life insurance companies at the end of 1967, more than two fifths were reported as loans on business properties and apartment developments.[2]

Purposes of Loans

The great majority of life insurance company loans to business enterprises are mortgage loans. The reason for this is that most of the loans of this majority are for the purchase of land and for the purchase and construction of buildings. In a special 1956 survey of the business loans of 67 life companies (having in total about three fourths of the assets of all life companies), the Life Insurance Association of America found that over two fifths of the mortgage loans authorized in that year were loans on retail trade properties, about one seventh on office buildings, and about one ninth on manufacturing plants. Loans on office buildings were substantially larger on the average than those on retail trade properties and manufacturing plants.[3]

Mortgage loans granted by insurance companies on manufacturing plants usually go to the enterprises that occupy and use these plants. On the other hand, most of the loans for which office buildings are pledged are granted to investors who plan to rent out space in the buildings. In between are the mortgage loans granted on retail trade properties. The Federal Reserve authorities, on the basis of interviews, estimate that about half of these loans go to investors and the other half to those that occupy and use the properties.[4] Although loans to investors in real estate are not of direct concern to us in our

[2]Institute of Life Insurance, *Life Insurance Fact Book*, 1968, p. 82.
[3]*Financing Small Business*, *op. cit.*, p. 514.
[4]*Ibid.*, p. 517.

study of corporate financial management, it is to be remembered that the leasing of fixed facilities enables corporations and other business enterprises to economize in their investment in assets—in their need of cash. Thus, in lending to real estate investors for the purchase and construction of office buildings and retail trade properties—such as in the shopping centers that have mushroomed in recent years in many suburban sections of the country—the insurance companies expand opportunities for business enterprises to economize in their asset requirements.

The life insurance companies often grant loans for the acquisition of machinery and equipment—chiefly the heavier varieties—as well as, sometimes, for the purchase of inventories and for other working capital purposes. As a rule, however, they still demand real estate mortgages as security for these loans.

Terms and Conditions

Life insurance companies are basically interested in long-term investment. Because their liabilities are predominantly long term—building up over the years as long as the people they insure survive—they like to find outlets for their investment funds that will stay put for lengthy periods. While the typical commercial bank hesitates to go beyond 10 years in term lending, the typical insurance company is inclined to think of maturities of less than 10 years as much too short. Thus, their mortgage loans to business generally run from 15 to 25 years, and sometimes as long as 30 years. But while they want long-term investment, the insurance companies also want to be reasonably sure of payment. Hence, their mortgage loan contracts with business borrowers usually call for installment repayment, with the installments most commonly payable at semiannual or annual intervals.

It is likely that the rates of interest charged by life insurance companies on mortgage loans to business borrowers run somewhat higher than the rates they earn on corporation bonds bought by private placement. Such a relationship, at any rate, was disclosed by special surveys made by the Life Insurance Association in 1955 and 1956, although the differentials were not wide and, indeed, ran in the opposite direction in some instances. As one would expect, the surveys also revealed differentials in favor of the larger mortgage loans, a relationship chiefly accounted for, doubtless, by lower relative costs of administering the larger loans as well as by the fact that the larger borrowers generally have better credit standings than the smaller ones. Again, however, the differentials appeared to be moderate.

Lending Facilities

Applications for mortgage loans are customarily accepted by life insurance companies at their head offices and at branch offices. The branches are scattered throughout the country or in various states or regions, depending on the individual company's geographical expansion. Some companies, such as the Prudential, depend heavily on their own personnel to find and promote lending opportunities, but most prefer to rely mainly on correspondents to find good mortgage outlets for their funds.

Commercial banks, mutual savings banks, and other classes of financial institutions that are themselves mortgage lenders often serve as correspondents by referring to given insurance companies applications for mortgage loans that they do not want for their own portfolios. But the principal correspondents of the life insurance companies are the individuals, partnerships, and corporations, known as mortgage bankers, that specialize in the origination and supervision of mortgage loans. Essentially, the mortgage bankers are middlemen: their very function is to find good loans to be passed on to life insurance companies and other long-term investors. They may grant some loans on their own, but even when they do they usually expect to carry the loans only temporarily. In most instances, they will have commitments from life insurance companies and other investors to take these loans off their hands in a few months or in a year or two. A second function of the mortgage bankers is to service the loans passed on. In working with a life insurance company, a mortgage banker will agree to collect interest and principal on the loans he has originated, at the same time seeing that the borrowers pay their taxes promptly, have their properties adequately insured, keep them in good repair, and so on. The mortgage bankers receive commissions both for originating loans and for servicing them after they have been taken over by the life insurance companies. Since, indeed, the servicing of loans produces annual commissions continuing for many years, whereas the origination of a given loan occurs but once, the mortgage bankers find their servicing function especially profitable.

EQUIPMENT FINANCING BY SELLERS

If it is reasonable for dealers in automobiles and other consumer durable goods to sell on contracts providing for installment payments over periods of two or three years or more, selling on such a basis would appear to be all the more reasonable for sellers of machinery and other equipment to be used by manufacturers, wholesalers, retailers, and service establishments. Whereas consumer durable goods are not sources of income to the buyers, machinery and equipment sold to businesses are expected to serve very importantly as producers of income, so that the installment buyers of such productive facilities should be all the more able to meet their installment obligations.

Many kinds of machinery and equipment are, indeed, available for purchase by business concerns on a deferred-payment basis, and much use is made of this means of financing fixed asset acquisitions. Credit granted by sellers of equipment might be regarded as a kind of trade credit, but trade credit, as we saw in Chapter 32, is regarded as essentially short term in character. Equipment credit, on the other hand, is almost always of intermediate term.

Scope of Equipment Financing

Most equipment credit originates in direct sales of machinery and other operating facilities to the ultimate business users; hence, manufacturers of the equipment are the chief suppliers of the credit. To accelerate sales, and especially to push their products competitively, manufacturers often allow liberal periods of payment. Distributors of and dealers in industrial equipment also often provide intermediate-term credit to their business customers—for example, dealers in automobiles in providing credit to taxicab and other transportation companies; dealers in refrigeration equipment for installations in hotels, restaurants, and grocery stores; and dealers in many lines of store and office equipment. The manufacturers of equipment of these kinds often extend credit to the dealers and distributors, but these extensions of credit are generally of short term. The dealers and distributors are expected to have relatively rapid turnovers; it is, therefore, the ultimate buyer who wants a longer time for payment.

In numerous instances, too, manufacturers provide their business customers with credit to acquire facilities they themselves do not produce. An outstanding example of this kind of financing is the assistance given by oil companies to service station operators in buying tanks, pumps, and other facilities. Other examples are the assistance given by grain companies to millers in acquiring grain storage facilities and that given by dairies to grocery stores to acquire dairy product refrigeration equipment.

Terms in Equipment Financing

The business enterprise that buys equipment on the installment plan is usually required to make a down payment, ranging from 20 to 33⅓ percent of the cost of the equipment. Interest at 5 or 6 percent per annum is then added to the balance of the purchase price, and the balance as thus augmented is apportioned over the credit period. If in a given transaction the balance after the down payment amounted to $20,000, the interest rate 5 percent, and the credit period 3 years, the debtor would have a total obligation of $23,000. Assuming a provision for monthly installments, each payment would be approximately $640. (Since the monthly payments would be constantly reducing the principal of the obligation, while the interest had been computed on the entire amount of the principal for the full period of

3 years, the effective rate of interest, as demonstrated earlier with different figures, would be close to 10 percent a year.) Monthly installments are usually provided for, and the credit period customarily does not exceed three years except for sales of heavy industrial machinery, for which it may be as long as five years or even longer.

The seller usually retains title to, or obtains a lien on, equipment sold on the installment plan. The buyer may sign a conditional sales contract and the seller retain the title until final payment is made, or the title may go to the buyer while the seller gets a lien by means of a chattel mortgage.

Sellers' Position in Equipment Financing

In selling equipment on the installment plan to business customers, some manufacturing companies hold the buyers' contracts to maturity. Strongly financed themselves, they have ample funds not only to carry inventories and meet current operating expenses but also to invest heavily in intermediate-term receivables. In this way, they gain the profits of both manufacturing and financing—the financing profits by earning the interest charged on their customers' installment contracts. In quite a few instances, manufacturing companies want to enjoy the profits of installment financing but prefer to separate their manufacturing and customer-financing operations. Accordingly, they establish subsidiaries to buy and hold their customers' contracts. This accounts for the operations of enterprises such as the General Electric Credit Corporation, the Westinghouse Credit Corporation, the Allis-Chalmers Credit Corporation, and the International Harvester Credit Corporation. Still other manufacturers, not so well heeled, prefer to get their money from customers' contracts at once, so they sell them to commercial finance companies or to the commercial finance subsidiaries or divisions of sales finance companies.

Unlike manufacturers, equipment distributors and dealers rarely carry the paper of customers who buy on the installment plan. They establish continuing relationships with commercial finance and sales finance companies, turning over to them the installment contracts as soon as signed by their customers.

LOANS OF THE SMALL BUSINESS ADMINISTRATION

If smaller corporations and other small business enterprises are unable to obtain adequate intermediate-term loans on reasonable terms from commercial banks and other private lending institutions, they may be able to obtain them from the Small Business Administration (SBA). This agency of the federal government was set up in 1953 precisely for the purpose of promoting the interests of small businesses. The SBA's functions include lending, assisting small enterprises to get a fair share of government procurement contracts, and helping them to solve managerial problems. In addition, the SBA is authorized to grant loans to businesses and homeowners for rehabilitation following storms, floods, and other natural disasters and to businesses in areas declared by the President or the Secretary of Agriculture to be disaster areas on account of droughts.

Qualifications for SBA Business Loans

To qualify for an SBA business loan (other than a disaster loan) a firm must be small according to the criteria established in the legislation. This means that, as a rule, it must have not more than 250 employees if a manufacturing concern, less than $5 million of annual sales if a wholesaler, and less than $1 million of annual sales if a retailer or a service establishment. Other criteria of smallness are set up for other lines of business, such as construction and transportation companies. However, the SBA is permitted to make exceptions in applying these criteria. In manufacturing, for example, firms that have more than 1,000 employees are definitely classified as large, but those that have between 250 and 1,000 employees may be designated small or large, depending on the type of manufacturing activity.

Besides qualifying on its smallness, a business firm that applies for an SBA loan must be able to show that it has made reasonable efforts to obtain loans from private sources, and that the private lenders have turned down its application or have agreed to lend only on terms regarded by it as unduly onerous.

As a third qualification for borrowers, the SBA has generally required that they be able to provide adequate collateral for the loans applied for. Although the law it operates under states that its loans "shall be of sound value or so secured as reasonably to assure payment," its policy until May, 1964, was to insist on 100 percent collateral. In that month, however, it announced new rules, conceding its willingness to accept good credit standing or good reputation at least as a partial substitute for collateral, especially on loans of the smaller size classes.

Scope of the SBA's Lending Authority

For the individual borrower, loans of the SBA for business purposes are limited to $350,000 and to maturities of not more than 10 years. Although the maturity stipulation permits short-term loans, only a few of the SBA's advances have had maturities of one year or less. The most common maturity appears to be 5 years, but a good proportion of the loans have maturities over 5 years, with a significant concentration at the maximum maturity of 10 years. A much smaller proportion have maturities of less than five years, chiefly in the range between three and five years.

The SBA's total lending capacity for ordinary business purposes (excluding lending for rehabilitation following disasters) is limited to $2 billion. This sum serves as a revolving fund in the sense that as loans are repaid, new loans up to the maximum may be granted.

Lending Procedures and Terms

Even when the SBA decides that applicants are deserving of its financial aid on the grounds both of creditworthiness and inability to obtain adequate funds on reasonable terms from private sources, it prefers to have commercial banks and other private lenders participate in granting the loans—to take responsibility for some portion of each loan, but not less than 25 percent.[5] It prefers what it calls "deferred participations" or "guaranteed loans." By this arrangement, the private lender grants the entire amount of the loan originally, but the SBA stands ready to take off its hands the portion that represents its own commitment should the borrower default. For example, an SBA deferred participation commitment of 75 percent on a $10,000 loan would mean that the private lender, on the borrower's default, could demand $7,500 from the SBA. It would therefore remain as the lender of only the balance of $2,500, but would have the full risk of nonpayment of this amount. When the SBA cannot get private lenders to agree to deferred participations, it asks them for immediate participations, by which it and they at once advance funds to borrowers according to their respective commitments. In terms of the illustration just given, the SBA would immediately advance $7,500 of the $10,000 loan, and the private lender would advance the remaining $2,500. For immediate participations, as for deferred ones, private lenders must be willing to take responsibility for at least 25 percent of the amount of each loan; in other words, the SBA's own participation does not go beyond 75 percent. If, however, the private lender is willing to take a participation of at least 50 percent of a loan for at least half of the period it is to be outstanding, the SBA is willing to give it priority in repayment. By this arrangement, the earlier installment payments of the borrower go to the private lender until it is fully paid off, so that the SBA depends on the later installments for repayment of its own participation.

The final alternative open to the SBA—and the least desirable one from the standpoint of its general policy—is to grant loans without the cooperation of commercial banks and other private lenders. On

---

[5]This proportion was set in August, 1968. The proportion had previously been 10 percent.

such direct loans, it advances all the funds, has the sole responsibility for supervision, and absorbs all losses on defaults.

On its direct loans and on its advances in participation with private lending institutions, the SBA charges interest at a uniform rate of 5½ percent per annum. However, the private institutions are permitted to charge up to 8 percent on their portions of the participation loans.

Volume of Operations

The SBA figures for its activities in business lending in 1966 may be cited to indicate the size and significance of its operations. In that year, it granted 2,504 direct loans totaling $32.9 million, had immediate participations of $88.3 million in 1,542 loans granted in cooperation with private financial institutions, and provided guaranties totaling $149.5 million (the deferred-participation arrangement) on 2,958 loans granted by private financial institutions. Of the total number of loans of these three classes (7,004), 17.6 percent amounted individually to $5,000 or less, 32.2 percent to $10,000 or less, 62.1 percent to $25,000 or less, and 91.8 percent to $100,000 or less.[6]

PROBLEM

1. How does the volume of term lending by large commercial banks compare with the volume of their short-term business lending? Among the corporations of what industries is term borrowing especially popular?
2. For what kinds of operations do business firms generally prefer bank term loans to short-term advances?
3. What kinds of participations do banks sometimes arrange when requested to grant term loans of very large amounts?
4. What is the usual range of the maturities of term loans? What requirements are there, if any, for installment repayment? What is a balloon payment? Why is such a payment provided for?
5. How do the rates of interest charged on term loans compare with rates charged on short-term business loans?
6. What is the distinction between nominal and effective rates of interest as charged on term loans? How is it possible for these two kinds of rates to differ as they apply to a given loan?
7. What is the nature of the protective provisions in favor of lending banks often contained in term-loan agreements?
8. For what purposes do life insurance companies grant mortgage loans to business firms? For what maturities? On what basis of repayment?
9. What is the function of firms such as the General Electric Credit Company and the International Harvester Credit Company?
10. What role is played by commercial finance companies in equipment financing? How are installment contracts used in financing of this kind?

---

[6]Small Business Administration, *Annual Report*, 1966, pp. 11–12.

11. What qualifications must business firms have to borrow from the Small Business Administration? For what purpose does the SBA grant loans? For what maturities?

12. How does the SBA participate with private financial institutions in granting loans on an immediate basis? On a deferred basis? Who bears the loss on defaults of participation loans?

PROBLEM

In each of the following instances, using the formula on page 869, determine what effective rate of interest the buyer would be paying for the financing of equipment purchases on an installment basis. Assume in all cases that interest at the nominal rate for the full period of financing is added to the original unpaid balance. In (*a*), for example, interest at 20 percent is to be added to the original balance of $40,000, and the total of $48,000 is then to be paid off in 16 equal quarterly installments.

	Original Balance	*Period of Financing*	*Nominal Rate of Interest*	*Timing of Payments*
a)	$40,000	4 years	5	Quarterly
b)	50,000	4 years	6	Quarterly
c)	50,000	4 years	6	Monthly
d)	20,000	7 years	4	Monthly
e)	60,000	3 years	5	Semiannually

INDEX

INDEX

B

D

F

This book has been set in 10 and 9 point Century Schoolbook, leaded 2 points. Part titles and numbers and chapter titles and numbers are 18 point Futura Demibold. The size of the type page is 27 by 46½ picas.